CW00796169

speedwaystar

WORLD SPEEDWAY YEARBOOK 2009

EDITED BY

peter OAKES
&
david ROWE
with
joshua Gudgeon

FRONT PAGE BOOKS

First published in Great Britain by

FRONT PAGE BOOKS
The Old Bakery
4 The Green
Yaxley
Peterborough
PE7 3LT
England

ISBN: 978-0-948882-37-1

CONTENTS

INTRODUCTION

WELCOME to a brand new addition to the bookshelf – the first edition of the *Speedway Star* WORLD SPEEDWAY YEARBOOK, a publication that covers the 2008 season in comprehensive detail but also has time to look at the 2009 campaign.

In recent seasons speedway has become a totally global sport with interest well, well beyond the geographical boundaries of England, Scotland and Wales.

These days the top (and that word probably covers up to 100) racers don't simply perform in one country with a weekend jaunt to Germany as they did in the past.

A typical diary will have a competitor racing in England on a Monday, Sweden on a Tuesday, maybe Denmark on a Wednesday, back to England for the Thursday or Friday, out to a fortnightly Grand Prix on a Saturday and then to Poland for a Sunday meeting.

With a stable of bikes in three countries and a pits crew in at least two, it's a high-speed, travelling life where sleep is often caught in the uncomfortable surroundings of an airport lounge and where check-in desks at Ryanair or Easyjet are as familiar as the rider's own front room.

Fans in Britain eagerly search for the latest results from Sweden's ElitSerien; supporters in Poland log on to the multitude of websites covering 'zuzel' outside their own country.

We felt this worldwide interest had to be reflected in an English language reference work and we would like to think the end result has taken the title Yearbook to a totally new level, rather in the way Ivan Mauger, Tony Rickardsson and now Nicki Pedersen lifted the bar on the track!

Naturally we have majored on what happened and is happening in our own country but we hope readers spend hours ands hours trawling through literally thousands of results and hundreds and hundreds of names to track the life of their own particular heroes.

For nearly 40 years, football has been superbly served by Jack Rollins' *Football Yearbook* (sponsored in its third year by Rothmans and now branded by Sky) and cricket's feats and deeds have been meticulously recorded in the yellow bound pages of the *Wisden Cricketers' Almanack* for the last century, but speedway has, generally, been ill-served.

In the immediate post-war era, *Stenner's Speedway Annuals* were a veritable treasure trove of information; the various editions of the *Speedway Yearbook* in the late seventies, early eighties and then early nineties, continued in that tradition and, more recently, Robert Bamford has produced a Speedway Yearbook.

When he first said that he was discontinuing the publication towards the end of last season, we decided to not only fill the gap but take it even further by extendings its coverage to beyond the domestic scene.

Our intention is to make it into an annual addition to the market but whether that happens will depend on how the prospective audience reacts.

The real intention is to ensure that speedway once again has a reference work that chronicles the minutae of a season and, hopefully, it is the first of a series of offerings from *Front Page Books*, the company that originally published a catalogue of sports' books in the early nineties and has now risen, Phoenix-like, from the ashes.

You will be able to read about some of the exciting plans elsewhere – but the intention is to produce well-written, meticulously researched volumes of interest to every English-speaking fan whether he follows Crossbone Pirates in the Swedish First Division; Torun in the Polish Ekstraliga; or Conference (or should that now be National?) League champions Weymouth!

PETER OAKES & DAVID ROWE

Editors
Speedway Star WORLD SPEEDWAY YEARBOOK

THE TEAM

PETER OAKES

is one of the best known speedway journalists and has been writing about the sport since he was a local reporter in his native Liverpool in 1960.

In a long Fleet Street career, he was an awarding-winning TV and Showbusiness columnist at The People and is a former Sports Editor of the Daily Star.

He's written nearly 30 sports books, collaborating with the likes of the late Bob Paisley, Trevor Francis and soccer star turned Hollywood hardman Vinnie Jones.

His by-line is familiar to readers of the Daily Star (he writes a weekly speedway and ice hockey column), the Daily Star on Sunday and the Sunday Express, for whom he covers football on a Saturday.

Away from journalism, he was Great Britain's team boss when they won the silver medal at the 2007 Under 21 World Cup, has managed Exeter and Coventry to the top-flight league title and, in that role, has won 17 major trophies.

DAVID ROWE

is a freelance sports journalist specialising in speedway and football.

Having been a speedway supporter as a youngster, he moved into sports media in 2002 and became Press Officer at his local club Coventry three years later, overseeing major improvements to their internet presence and also editing the Bees' programme. He is the club's commentator for their internal TV and DVD service.

He is a regular contributor to speedway coverage in the local and national press, including the Coventry Telegraph and Speedway Star, and is also a member of the British Speedway Press Office team with responsibilities for fixtures, results and the sport's official weekly media bulletin, as well as being the track announcer at Birmingham.

After several years covering football for local radio and telephone hotlines, he is also a regular member of the reporting team on national station TalkSPORT.

JOSHUA GUDGEON

is a budding sports journalist who also confesses to being a speedway nut.

He still studying at school but has already had by-lined stories in Speedway Star and SKID! and evening newspapers.

He had a regular two page feature in the 2008 Coventry match magazine *The Buzz* and will be a regular contributor to this season's Super7even programmes.

Last summer he had work experience in the media department of Championship soccer club Watford and has been invited back during this year's holidays.

He represented Peterborough United at football when he was 13 but later decided that he was never going to be good enough to become a professional and instead has plumped for a career in sports writing.

He has carried out a lot of the unsung research for this book and rarely lets a night go by without checking the latest score updates.

THE PHOTO TEAM

We would like to thank the following photographers who have contributed their work to this book.

LES AUBREY: Resident track photographer at Swindon, usually follows the Robins home and away.
Contact
Telephone: 07886 662348.
leslieaubrey22@tiscali.co.uk

STEVE BROCK: *Newcastle track photographer who has more than 30 years' experience. Covers social, corporate, Press and PR as well as speedway.*
Contact
steve@stevebrock.co.uk
www.stevebrock.co.uk
Telephone: 07932 948245.

KAREN CHAPPELL: Has been Lakeside's official photographer since 2006, the year after she launched fotoadventures. Studying at Reigate School of Art, Design and Media for the Photography HND qualification. Specialists in motor sports and ski-jumping.
Contact
enquiries@fotoadventures.co.uk
www.fotoadventures.co.uk

IAN CHARLES: *Regular at Belle Vue and also many overseas meetings.*
Contact
iancharlesphotos@googlemail.com

JEFF DAVIES: Track photographer at Coventry and has also done extensive work for individual riders – including a recent photo-book to chart the career of the retiring Billy Hamill. Especially proficient at picking up more unusual shots, Jeff's photography has been of particular benefit to us in putting the book together.
Contact:
jeff@davies170.fsnet.co.uk
Telephone: 07525 974036.

STEVE DIXON: *Has always been interested in sports photography (mainly speedway) and dabbled a little in the eighties. Returned when digital photography reduced costs and admits he was in the right place at the right time in 2005, when Scunthorpe re-opened and needed a photographer.*
Contact
dixpix05@yahooo.co.uk
www.stevedixonphotography.co.uk
Telephone: 07811965015.

TIM HELM PHOTOGRAPHY: Freelance motorsports, portrait and event photography. Has also designed websites for Redcar and Mildenhall, among others.
Contact
stressed@timhelmmedia.co.uk
www.timhelmphotography.co.uk
Telephone: 01202 488474/07809 224893.

JEFF HIGGOTT: *Freelance photographer based near Ipswich, he specialises in live music, landscapes, butterflies and moths as well as speedway and has had his photos published widely in books, magazines and journals.*
Contact
info@sequella.co.uk
www.sequella.co.uk

JOHN HIPKISS: Track photographer at Wolverhampton and also a regular at Birmingham, his work is often used in the BSPA's major events coverage and in *Speedway Star* magazine. Runs Halesowen-based John Hipkiss Photography Ltd.
Contact
hippopix@blueyonder.co.uk
22, Clyde Avenue, Hurst Green, Halesowen, B62 9PW.
Telephone: 07836 386169.

STEVE HONE: *Based in East Anglia, he is probably the only speedway photographer who really knows what it is like to be the object of a cameraman! He rode in 15 Division Two matches for Canterbury and Exeter in the eighties.*
Contact
steve.hone@o2.co.uk

MIKE MANNING: Recorded the Rebels victorious Premier League Knock Out Cup season as Somerset's official track photographer.
Contact
mike@home210.demon.co.uk

JULIE MARTIN: *From sunny Weymouth in Dorset and track photographer for Weymouth Wildcats. Also covers football matches mainly at two local clubs – Blue Square Premier League Weymouth and Blue Square South Dorchester Town.*
Contact
www.juliemartinphotography.co.uk
Telephone: 07967 221475.

MIKE PATRICK: Probably the world's best known speedway photographer, he covered his first meeting – the Wills Internationale – at Wimbledon on May 15, 1970. Since then he has become best-known for his work at Speedway Star but his award-winning photos have appeared in practically every motor sports publication as well as regularly in the national press, Grand Prix and World Final programmes.
Contact
mike@mike-patrick.com
PO Box 178, Bicester, Oxford, OX25 2GX.
Telephone: 07981 592886 (photo sales); 07710 510610 (media inquiries).

SPORTS MEDIA PARTNERSHIP: *Sports Media Partnership primarily specialise in sports, commercial photography and WEB design but also cover corporate, social events and weddings. Photographers Jan Orkisz, Ron McNeil and Jack Cupido are regulars at Armadale.*
Contact
SMP.jan@gmail.com
www.sports-media-partnership.com/speedway

DAVID VALENTINE: Based on the sunshine holiday Isle of Wight, he has been a virtual everpresent at Smallbrook Stadium since the birth of the sport there.
Contact
davidvalentineiow@tiscali.co.uk
www.davidvalentineiow.com

STEVE WALLER: *Based in Felixstowe, Suffolk, he covers Ipswich and is a full-time photographer. Responsible for stunning studio shots of the Ipswich Witches.*
Contact
www.photography4you.co.uk
Telephone: 01394 274707.

ALAN WHALE: The country's leading grass track photographer, he is a familiar figure on the centre green at all Poole's matches. All his photographs are available at the stall on the third bend at Wimborne Road on race-nights.
Contact
awhale@photo2001.ndo.co.uk

■ *Other photographs used by* ***JORDAN EARL, DARREN FLETCHER, DEREK FRY, JOSHUA GUDGEON*** *and* ***FRONT PAGE BOOKS ARCHIVE.***

If we have inadvertently omitted any photographers from either this page or by crediting them on their pictures we can only apologise and hope to put matters right in the 2010 edition of the WORLD SPEEDWAY YEARBOOK.

AVERAGES

ONE of the first decisions we had to take was to determine the ground rules for averages from a variety of leagues, many of which operate under completely different formulae.

So in the cause of uniformity we made a number of decisions, the principal of which is that all averages, unless stated otherwise, are based on four rides per meeting.

Secondly, any extra points scored from what are either known as tactical rides or Joker rides have been included in the total of points scored.

Reasoning for this is simple: those were the points a rider scored in a meeting and in years to come if they were excluded then records will appear to be incomplete with points scored by individuals not tallying with a team's total.

However, for those who prefer to exclude the extra points, we have also included the number of points scored by way of tactical rides along with the number of tactical (or tactical substitute) rides taken.

BIBLIOGRAPHY

A VARIETY of written sources have been used throughout production of the *Speedway Star* **WORLD SPEEDWAY YEARBOOK 2009**.

We acknowledge the following publications:

Annuaire FIM (various); Bahnsport Aktuell; Homes of British Speedway (Robert Bamford & John Jarvis); Jugoslovanski dirt track in speedway 1920-1991 (Franci Tomazic); Loader's International Speedway Annual (1991-92, Tony Loader); Methanol Press Speedway Yearbook 2008 (Robert Bamford); Riemann's Speedway Chronik (Dirk Riemann); Riemer's Sandbahn Chronik (Dirk Riemann); Speedway / Daily Mirror Speedway Yearbooks (1977-82, 1986, 1990-91, 1993, Peter Oakes); Speedway Sanomat; Speedway Star Almanac (Peter Oakes); Stenner's Speedway Annuals (1947-54. Tom & Jim Stenner); SVEMO Motorkalendar (various); Swiat Zuzla; Tempus Speedway Yearbook (2004-07, Robert Bamford); The Complete History of the British League; The Ultimate Speedway Guide (1999, Peter Oakes), Zuzlowe ABC (I, II, III, IV, V, VI, VII, Wieslaw Dobruszek).

CONTRIBUTORS

WE could fill several pages thanking those people who have contributed in some way to this book. They know who they are and we offer our heartfelt thanks but special mention must be made of Tony Olsson, Petteri Pohjola and Tony Skach for their individual input.

DEADLINE

THE final deadline for information in this book was Thursday, April 2, 2009. All ages quoted as of that date.

PHOTOGRAPHS

WE are indebted and appreciative of the help and assistance we have received from individual clubs for supplying 2008 team photographs.

However, we know that this book would never have been possible without the backing of a batch of photographers who willingly supplied pictures from their own files.

We have attempted to list all the photographers involved but if we have inadvertently missed anyone's name out from our list of contributors we apologise unreservedly and assure them it was by oversight rather than design.

ROLL OF HONOUR

WE have endeavoured to produce a comprehensive and accurate list of winners of major events such as the World and European Championships as well as national individual and team events.

Sadly it can never be a definitive list because in many countries there is no specific governing body record.

Even in Sweden – a country that has had a responsible governing body in SVEMO – there is some confusion.

Some reference books will credit Filbyterna as the 1948 Swedish league champions but, according to SVEMO's own records, the championship was not given official status until 1950. Similarly the 1962 competition was not officially recognised by the governing body.

Usually where no winners are listed for a season it means the championship was not staged that year.

SOURCES

UNLESS humanly impossible, we have used official records for all league statistics.

Joint Editor Peter Oakes is also the British Speedway Promoters' Association official archivist and as such receives a marked programme from the referee of every meeting.

All the statistics are based on these programmes and do, on occasions, contradict information published in good faith by the sport's weekly magazine *Speedway Star*.

For the overseas records we have relied on official sources but can only be as complete as they are and can take no responsiblity for inaccuracies.

TEAM NAMES

WHEREVER possible we have used the team name under which a club rode in any particular season.

This might lead to some confusion as the years roll by and a full list of past names will be included in a future publication currently on the drawing board.

...AND FINALLY

We have checked, double-checked and treble-checked the pages for errors but we would not be human if some haven't slipped through the net. We trust they will be minimal and as such will not spoil your reading pleasure.

And if there is anything you would like to see included in future editions then please let us know at the address on page two.

2008 GRAND PRIX

THE world belongs to Nicki Pedersen – and so does the 2008 Grand Prix World Championship.

The Danish international arguably joined the ranks of the legends with his near start to finish domination of the sometimes troubled 11 (or was it 12?) round series.

Nicki was second to Tomasz Gollob in the opener in Slovenia but that was the only time he ended a Grand Prix in any overall placing other than first.

He took over the leader's yellow race-bib in the European GP in Poland and that was, effectively, that.

There was a slight hiccup in the tenth round when he had his worst display of the year (in fact his worst for two years) but still held a defining points cushion at the top of the table.

And he did it all despite a debilitating gallstone problem and his coronation was a painful one as he was still recovering from the effects of a heavy crash in Poland.

As it happened he could actually have stayed at home – either with his parents in Denmark or his own house in Stevenage – watched the meeting on Sky TV and still been crowned World Champion for a third time!

Surprisingly he actually won only one round and had it been F1's Bernie Ecclestone in charge rather than Ole Olsen he would have spent the winter trying to introduce a new points system.

But no-one in speedway circles was doubting Nicki's right to that golden trophy yet again.

He was, simply, the best....

He had an unexpected incentive after being dropped by Eastbourne and then ignored by the rest of their Elite League rivals when they were assembling sides under the reduced points limit.

He admitted: "I was out to show myself, see if I could retain the title, and show the rest I could do it without England.

"It's my best year ever, even though I only had one Grand Prix win – I threw it away two of three times when I was leading."

But he wasn't claiming all the glory, adding: "To be a World Champion is a hell of a job, you can't do it on your own. Without having the boys behind you, you're never going to make it."

Nicki's magnaminous title speech at least helped make up for the disaster that was Gelsenkirchen – and thank the stars for that!

FINAL STANDINGS

Pos	Rider	GPPts	R1	R2	R3	R4	R5	R6	R7	R8	R9	R10	R11
1	Nicki PEDERSEN	**174**	17	16	16	20	11	22	14	18	21	6	13
2	Jason CRUMP	**152**	10	8	12	18	22	17	12	19	9	18	7
3	Tomasz GOLLOB	**148**	19	12	8	19	4	12	8	16	20	9	21
4	Greg HANCOCK	**144**	8	20	6	10	20	13	12	13	18	9	15
5	Hans ANDERSEN	**140**	14	6	8	11	9	16	20	7	11	21	17
6	Leigh ADAMS	**125**	5	20	9	8	7	10	21	9	9	12	15
7	Andreas JONSSON	**100**	12	9	8	9	8	9	6	10	8	9	12
8	Rune HOLTA	**80**	5	4	17	7	6	9	5	4	6	10	7
9	Scott NICHOLLS	**77**	7	2	7	7	12	6	4	7	10	8	7
10	Fredrik LINDGREN	**73**	7	7	22	3	2	4	7	7	0	5	9
11	Bjarne PEDERSEN	**69**	4	❍	❍	7	14	7	6	7	4	17	3
12	Niels-Kristian IVERSEN	**59**	8	10	2	6	6	7	9	1	4	6	❍
13	Chris HARRIS	**58**	6	6	5	3	10	7	3	9	5	❍	4
14	Krzysztof KASPRZAK	**57**	6	3	5	3	4	1	9	7	6	8	5
15	Lukas DRYML	**47**	9	2	3	1	1	4	5	7	3	4	8
16	Jaroslaw HAMPEL	**16**		❖16									
17	Kenneth BJERRE	**11**				❖11							
18	Wieslaw JAGUS	**9**									❖9		
19	Lubos TOMICEK	**8**		3	5			❖0					
20	Matej ZAGAR	**7**	❖7										
21	Jonas DAVIDSSON	**7**			❖7				▲				
22	Edward KENNETT	**4**					❖4						
23	Peter LJUNG	**3**							❖3				
24	Billy FORSBERG	**2**			I2								
24	Grigori LAGUTA	**2**								❖2			
24	Mattia CARPANESE	**2**										❖2	
27	Krzysztof BUCZKOWSKI	**1**		▲							I1		
28	Nicolai KLINDT	**1**				I1							
29	Maciej JANOWSKI	**1**									▲		I1
30	Izak SANTEJ	**0**	▲										
30	Denis STOJS	**0**	▲										
30	Damian BALINSKI	**0**		▲									
30	Sebastian ALDÉN	**0**			I0								
30	Patrick HOUGAARD	**0**				▲							
30	Tai WOFFINDEN	**0**					▲						
30	Simon STEAD	**0**					▲						
30	Adrian RYMEL	**0**						▲					
30	Filip SITERA	**0**						▲					
30	Thomas H. JONASSON	**0**							▲				
30	Maksim BOGDANOVS	**0**								I0			
30	Kjastas PUODZHUKS	**0**								▲			
30	Guglielmo FRANCHETTI	**0**										I0	
30	Alessandro MILANESE	**0**										I0	
30	Martin SMOLINSKI	**0**											❖0

Key: ❖ Wild Card. I Riding reserve. ▲ Non-riding reserve. ❍ Injured.

Medal winners

Rider	
Nicki PEDERSEN	9
Hans ANDERSEN	5
Jason CRUMP	5
Tomasz GOLLOB	5
Greg HANCOCK	4
Leigh ADAMS	2
Rune HOLTA	1
Fredrik LINDGREN	1
Bjarne PEDERSEN	1

2008 GP champions

Rider	
Tomasz GOLLOB	3
Leigh ADAMS	2
Jason CRUMP	2
Hans ANDERSEN	1
Greg HANCOCK	1
Rune HOLTA	1
Nicki PEDERSEN	1

Finalists

Rider	
Nicki PEDERSEN	9
Jason CRUMP	7
Hans ANDERSEN	6
Greg HANCOCK	6
Tomasz GOLLOB	5
Leigh ADAMS	4
Scott NICHOLLS	2
Jaroslaw HAMPEL	1
Rune HOLTA	1
Andreas JONSSON	1
Fredrik LINDGREN	1
Bjarne PEDERSEN	1

2008 GRAND PRIX

ROUND 1: SLOVENIAN GRAND PRIX, SATURDAY, APRIL 26

THIRTEEN years ago the first-ever Grand Prix was won by Tomasz Gollob – fast forward to 2008 and it was the Polish legend who triumphed in the 101st event of the series with victory in Krsko.

Gollob, who has only ever missed four GP meetings, timed his run to perfection on a night of changing conditions and fortunes, eventually getting the better of World Champion Nicki Pedersen in a re-started Final.

It was the 12th GP win of his career, and a result which gave him an early lead at the top of the standings although the overall scorechart in Slovenia was remarkably close with no rider able to emulate Pedersen's perfect start to 2007 .

The opening 12 races showed the Grand Prix at its very best as the competitors put on some of the finest action ever seen in the series on the wide Krsko circuit with several racing lines available.

Pedersen was on top at that stage with eight points from a possible nine, while Andreas Jonsson and Hans Andersen had recovered from problems in their first rides to record two race wins each – Andersen finally getting the better of countryman Bjarne Pedersen in an epic Heat 10 which went right to the wire.

Heavy rain during the interval then totally changed the track conditions, and gating became a matter of paramount importance with the inside route offering the fastest way around the circuit.

Gollob was arguably the main beneficiary as the luck of the draw handed him gate 1 in Heat 16 and 18

And it also meant he was not on the circuit at the time when the rain was at its heaviest.

By contrast, world number two Leigh Adams failed to score in his last two rides from outside gates, and went out with just five points, and Niels-Kristian Iversen took advantage of gate two to snatch the last semi-final place by winning Heat 20.

The points spread for the whole field was just six, with the top four riders each on 10 points and Bjarne Pedersen on four - and 13 of the 16 competitors managed at least one race win.

Iversen was eliminated in the first semi-final along with Lukas Dryml, who also made a fine return to the series despite a heavy fall in Heat 18 when he came down as Jason Crump sailed through on the inside.

Jonsson and Nicki Pedersen progressed to the Final, and were joined by Gollob and Andersen in the second semi as Crump and Greg Hancock went out.

Jonsson, off gate three, gambled on a fast start in the Final but his wheel clipped the tapes and he was excluded, leaving three men to contest the decider.

Gollob gated with Andersen initially cutting back for second place, only to be re-passed by Pedersen going into the second lap.

The Dane then put pressure on Gollob, but the leader held his line to take the flag.

Gollob said: "I'm very happy tonight, it was certainly a lucky day for me and I don't really know what to say at the moment.

"I'm really pleased with my team and I want to say a big thank you to them and my sponsors, who paid for a new engine for today's meeting.

"In the last race I had to make a quick start with Nicki next to me going into the first corner, and I'm so happy.

"It's a good start to the year for me, and I like the next track at Leszno as well so maybe that will be the same result."

With new national manager Jim Lynch in the pits he didn't see the best of the British: Scott Nicholls was a single point away from getting through to the semi finals and Chris Harris scored in all five rides but managed only one second place and the rest were thirds.

Perhaps the best individual performance came not from any of the four Grand Finalists but Dryml who returned to the GP scene and won his opening ride, finishing ahead of Harris, Andreas Jonsson and Bjarne Pedersen in the second fastest time of the night.

He stopped second time out and then baled out after Crump arrowed underneath him in Heat 18 but still had enough points to go into the first semi final where he was third behind Nicki Pedersen and Jonsson but must have been well content with his comeback.

Rune Holta was also a winner first time out: but that was as good as it got for the Norwegian as he slipped out of contention with only a further two points from his last four outings.

One familiar name was missing from the top eight this time: Leigh Adams never really looked on the pace and had three blobs from his five starts, an inauspicious beginning for the Aussie who had such high hopes of finally winning that world title he has craved for so long.

the VENUE

Track: *Stadion Matije Gubca, CKZ 130C, 8270 Krsko, Slovenia.*
Telephone: *(00386) 74925302.*
Website: *www.amd.krsko@siol.net*
Track Length: *387 metres.*
Track Record: *64.75 secs. Matej Zagar, June 10, 2006.*
First Grand Prix: *Saturday, June 22, 2002.*
Grands Prix staged: *7.*

Roll of Honour

2002 ....Ryan Sullivan
2003 ....Leigh Adams
2004 ....Tony Rickardsson
2005 ....Tony Rickardsson
2006 ....Nicki Pedersen
2007 ....Nicki Pedersen
2008 ....Tomasz Gollob

■ *All Slovenian GPs have been held at the Stadion Matije Gubca in Krsko.*

Quote...unquote

HANS ANDERSEN

It was good to have a start like this - it is really important to be consistent in the Grand Prix.

ANDREAS JONSSON

My goal this year has been to make a good start and to be a bit clever by getting two points from a race and the wins when I can.

CHRIS HARRIS

I was quite happy with what we did and I'm ready to move on to the next meeting.

JASON CRUMP

It was a frustrating night because I had three starts from the two outside gates while one and two were much better.

SCOTT NICHOLLS

I'm not going to make excuses but you neeed a bit of luck with the draw.

the RESULTS

Rider									
1 Tomasz GOLLOB	**0**	**2**	**2**	**3**	**3**	**10**	**3**	**6**	**19**
2 Nicki PEDERSEN	3	2	3	1	1	10	3	4	17
3 Hans ANDERSEN	0	3	3	2	2	10	2	2	14
4 Andreas JONSSON	1	3	3	0	3	10	2	E	12
5 Jason CRUMP	1	1	2	3	2	9	1		10
6 Lukas DRYML	3	R	2	3	FX	8	1		9
7 Greg HANCOCK	2	3	1	1	1	8	0		8
8 Niels-Kristian IVERSEN	3	2	0	R	3	8	0		8
9 Scott NICHOLLS	1	1	1	2	2	7			7
10 Fredrik LINDGREN	1	0	1	2	3	7			7
11 ❖Matej ZAGAR	2	3	0	2	F	7			7
12 Chris HARRIS	2	1	1	1	1	6			6
13 Krzysztof KASPRZAK	2	0	0	3	1	6			6
14 Leigh ADAMS	0	2	3	0	0	5			5
15 Rune HOLTA	3	1	0	1	0	5			5
16 Bjarne PEDERSEN	0	0	2	0	2	4			4
17 Izak SANTEJ [R]						*did not ride*			
17 Denis STOJS [R]						*did not ride*			

Final: Gollob, N.Pedersen, Andersen, Jonsson (excluded, tapes), 71.00 secs.
Semi Final: N.Pedersen, Jonsson, Dryml, Iversen, 71.56 secs.
Semi Final: Gollob, Andersen, Crump, Hancock, 70.68 secs.

1: Holta, Kasprzak, Nicholls, Adams, 65.18 secs.
2: Dryml, Harris, Jonsson, B.Pedersen, 65.68 secs.
3: N.Pedersen, Hancock, Lindgren, Gollob, 66.14 secs.
4: Iversen, Zagar, Crump, Andersen, 66.41 secs.
5: Zagar, Gollob, Holta, B.Pedersen, 66.53 secs.
6: Hancock, Iversen, Harris, Kasprzak, 66.95 secs.
7: Andersen, N.Pedersen, Nicholls, Dryml (r), 67.26 secs.
8: Jonsson, Adams, Crump, Lindgren, 66.96 secs.
9: N.Pedersen, Crump, Harris, Holta, 67.64 secs.
10: Andersen, B.Pedersen, Lindgren, Kasprzak, 68.30 secs.
11: Jonsson, Gollob, Nicholls, Iversen, 67.27 secs.
12: Adams, Dryml, Hancock, Zagar, 67.75 secs.
13: Dryml, Lindgren, Holta, Iversen (r), 71.61 secs.
14: Kasprzak, Zagar, N.Pedersen, Jonsson, 72.59 secs.
15: Crump, Nicholls, Hancock, B.Pedersen, 72.03 secs.
16: Gollob, Andersen, Harris, Adams, 72.38 secs.
17: Jonsson, Andersen, Hancock, Holta, 71.17 secs.
18: Gollob, Crump, Kasprzak, Dryml (fell, excluded), 71.01 secs.
19: Lindgren, Nicholls, Harris, Zagar (fell), 71.78 secs,
20: Iversen, B.Pedersen, N.Pedersen, Adams, 71.26 secs.
Fastest time: 65.18 secs, Rune Holta, Heat 1.
Referee: *Tony Steele (Great Britain).*

■ ***Tomasz Gollob****'s victory was his 12th Grand Prix success but his first outside Poland since being crowned German GP winner at Berlin on Saturday, May 5, 2001. In between he had won five rounds – the Polish GPs in 2002, 2003, 2004, 2005 and 2007.*
■ ***Bjarne Pedersen*** *made his 50th Grand Prix appearance – having made his debut as a wild card in the 2002 Scandinavian round.*
■ *All 18 riders on parade had previous Grand Prix experience although* ***Krzysztof Kasprzak*** *and* ***Fredrik Lindgren*** *were making their Slovenian round debuts.*

2008 GRAND PRIX

ROUND 2: EUROPEAN GRAND PRIX, SATURDAY, MAY 10

IF it wasn't to be Tomasz Gollob then who better to skip up onto the rostrum as the 2008 European Grand Prix champion than Leigh Adams?

After all the Australian is as close to being an adopted son of Leszno as anyone can possibly be.

He made his debut for the reigning Polish Ekstraliga champions way, way back in 1996 and has given unstinted service ever since.

No wonder then that 20,000 Poles – give or take the thousand or so visitors – rose as one to greet his popular victory.

He was the recipient of a tumultuous reception after a fantastic performance that put his World championship bid back on course after a disappointing opening round in Slovenia.

Adams won the Final ahead of another 37-year-old, American Greg Hancock, who also had three seasons with Leszno, while defending World Champion Nicki Pedersen was third, which was enough to give him a two point lead in the title pursuit.

Pedersen, second in Slovenia, qualified for the final despite crashing on the final bend of his semi final after 2006 World Champion Jason Crump had attempted to pass him on the inside.

German referee Frank Ziegler excluded Crump and awarded Pedersen second place although many claimed that this was in direct contradiction to the FIM rules and that, as the Dane did not cross the finish line and the race hadn't been stopped, Poland's Tomasz Gollob should have gone through.

That, of course, would have been a more popular decision but Ziegler did what he believed as right and fair rather than what would have gone down well on the packed terraces.

Gollob, like Hancock, had started with three race wins and looked unbeatable but the longer the night wore on the more the Polish superstar waned.

In the end he lost a golden opportunity to add a second victory after his triumph in Slovenia.

Adams, despite a third ride blip and a last place, fought back strongly and ultimately it was wild card Jaroslaw Hampel who was the only Polish rider in the final.

At least his presence gave the home fans double hope of one of their own winning: and most of them wouldn't have worried about which of the duo took the winner's laurels as long as it wasn't an outsider like Greg Hancock or Pedersen!

It turned out to be Adams, using all his vast knowledge of the track, to hold off every effort of the rejuvenated American.

Adams could hardly contain his joy, bubbling: "The 2008 World Championship starts now. We have put Krsko behind us.

"This is the one that I really wanted to win, it is my adopted home. The Leszno club did a fantastic job, the track was great, the atmosphere was terrific and I am right back in the race."

And so he was although Pedersen was already giving notice that he wouldn't lightly surrender his title.

Veteran Hancock, who dropped just one point in his five qualifying heats, showed what a class act he is, on and off the track.

Pedersen, though disappointed not to win, looked at the bigger picture and happily settled for a two point lead going into the third round in Gothenburg, Sweden.

Gollob, who was undone by three successive third places, retained second place but the omens were ominous for Jason Crump, widely expected to be hotfooting it to regain his world title.

He didn't win a race and that exclusion in the semi final ended his hopes of reaching his first Grand Final of the season.

Yet again the night didn't fall kindly for the Brits – this time Chris Harris finishing the higher although once again neither reached the final eight.

Scott Nicholls simply wasn't at the races on a track he will never rank as one of his favourites: after the 2007 World Cup Final mauling he only avoided bottom place by dint of his higher starting number over Lukas Dryml who also ended the night with a paltry two points.

Harris did a little better but couldn't win a race and was already beginning to face a struggle to book his place in the 2009 series as an automatic qualifier.

His six points was only enough for 11th place, denied a top 10 finish by virtue of Hans Andersen's Heat 10 race victory.

Leszno could be happy with their first Grand Prix although there were bound to be inquests into the one blot on their impressive staging – the track turned into a practice day dustbowl.

the VENUE

Track: *Alfred Smoczyk Stadium... Strzelecka 7, 64-100 Leszno, Poland.*
Telephone: *(0048) 655299977.*
Website: *www.unia.leszno.pl*
Track Length: *330 metres.*
Track Record: *58.4 secs, Krzysztof Kasprzak, May 3, 2007.*
First Grand Prix: *Saturday, May 10, 2008*
Grands Prix staged: *1.*
The first European GP was held at Bydgoszcz, Poland, on Saturday, September 23, 2000.

Roll of Honour

2000....................................Billy Hamill
2002 ....Nicki Pedersen
2003..........................Tony Rickardsson
2004 ....Bjarne Pedersen
2005..........................Tony Rickardsson
2006..................................Jason Crump
2007 ....Nicki Pedersen
2008 ....Leigh Adams

■ *Previous European GPs – all raced in Poland – have been held at Bydgszocz (2000), Chorzow (2002), Katowice (2003) and Wroclaw (2004, 2005, 2006 and 2007).*

Quote...unquote

TOMASZ GOLLOB

I do believe the leader's yellow race-jacket will change hands frequently this season.

NICKI PEDERSEN

It was a bit more grippy here than in other Grands Prix, and that makes everybody fast. I'd rather have it a bit slicker, then you have to race for it.

JAROSLAW HAMPEL

My intention is to ride well and to get myself noticed by people. Maybe the GP promoters will see that I am still able to win.

GREG HANCOCK

I felt awesome, everything was perfect.

the RESULTS

1 Leigh ADAMS	**2**	**3**	**0**	**3**	**3**	**11**	**3**	**6**	**20**
2 Greg HANCOCK	3	3	3	3	2	14	2	4	20
3 Nicki PEDERSEN	3	2	1	3	3	12	2	2	16
4 ❖Jaroslaw HAMPEL	2	2	3	3	3	13	3	0	16
5 Tomasz GOLLOB	3	3	3	1	1	11	1		12
6 Niels-Kristian IVERSEN	2	0	2	2	3	9	1		10
7 Andreas JONSSON	3	3	1	0	2	9	0		9
8 Jason CRUMP	0	2	2	2	2	8	X		8
9 Fredrik LINDGREN	1	1	1	2	2	7			7
10 Hans ANDERSEN	0	1	3	1	1	6			6
11 Chris HARRIS	2	1	2	1	0	6			6
12 Rune HOLTA	0	0	2	2	0	4			4
13 Lubos TOMICEK	0	2	0	0	1	3			3
14 Krzysztof KASPRZAK	1	0	1	0	1	3			3
15 Scott NICHOLLS	1	1	0	0	R	2			2
16 Lukas DRYML	1	0	0	1	0	2			2
17 Damian BALINSKI [R]									*did not ride*
17 Krzysztof BUCZKOWSKI [R]									*did not ride*

Final: Adams, Hancock, N.Pedersen, Hampel, 60.28 secs.
Semi Final: Adams, Hancock, Iversen, Jonsson. 60.73 secs.
Semi Final: Hampel, N.Pedersen, Gollob, Crump (excluded), 60.19 secs.

1: N.Pedersen, Harris, Dryml, Tomicek, 60.91secs.
2: Hancock, Hampel, Lindgren, Crump, 60.82 secs.
3: Jonsson, Adams, Kasprzak, Andersen, 60.63 secs.
4: Gollob, Iversen, Nicholls, Holta, 59.44 secs.
5: Adams, Tomicek, Lindgren, Holta, 60.62 secs.
6: Jonsson, Crump, Harris, Iversen, 59.94 secs.
7: Hancock, N.Pedersen, Nicholls, Kasprzak, 60.10 secs.
8: Gollob, Hampel, Andersen, Dryml, 60.09 secs.
9: Gollob, Crump, Kasprzak, Tomicek, 60.47secs.
10: Andersen, Harris, Lindgren, Nicholls, 60.85 secs.
11: Hampel, Iversen, N.Pedersen, Adams, 60.04 secs.
12: Hancock, Holta, Jonsson, Dryml, 60.25 secs.
13: Hancock, Iversen, Andersen, Tomicek, 60.96 secs.
14: Hampel, Holta, Harris, Kasprzak, 60.38 secs.
15: N.Pedersen, Lindgren, Gollob, Jonsson, 60.45 secs.
16: Adams, Crump, Dryml, Nicholls, 60.19 secs.
17: Hampel, Jonsson, Tomicek, Nicholls (r), 60.28 secs.
18: Adams, Hancock, Gollob, Harris, 60.38 secs.
19: N.Pedersen, Crump, Andersen, Holta, 60.67 secs,
20: Iversen, Lindgren, Kasprzak, Dryml, 61.14 secs.
Fastest time: 59.44 secs, Tomasz Gollob, Heat 4.
Referee: *Tony Steele (Great Britain).*

■ ***Bjarne Pedersen*** *withdrew because of a broken wrist and was replaced by series first reserve* ***Lubos Tomicek****.*
■ *Leszno became the 28th different venue for what was the 102nd Grand Prix – and the fourth different Polish track to hold the event.*
■ ***Leigh Adams, Jaroslaw Hampel, Krzysztof Kasprzak*** *and reserve* ***Damian Balinski*** *all claimed Leszno as their 2008 home track.*
■ ***Leigh Adams'*** *victory took his Grand Prix gold medal total to seven, in his 23rd Grand Final from 94 appearances.*
■ *The waiting goes on for reserves* ***Damian Balinski*** *and* ***Krzysztof Buczkowski*** *as they seek their GP debut.*

2008 GRAND PRIX

ROUND 3: SWEDISH GRAND PRIX, SATURDAY, MAY 24

A GRAND Prix returned to the magnificent Ullevi Stadium in Gothenburg, Sweden, after a four-year absence and a 20,000 plus crowd were witness to a truly memorable night.

The Swedish stadium has been the scene of so many remarkable sporting achievements over the years – including soccer legend Pele's introduction to the World Cup as a teenager – but this night will also remain in the memories of anyone who was there.

Rune Holta, born in Norway but now riding under the flag of Poland, duly won the FIM Sapa Swedish Grand Prix, his first victory in 50 attempts, but that doesn't begin to tell the story of a meeting than over-ran by almost an hour.

Referee Tony Steele, who has officiated at more Grands Prix than anyone, admitted that he could not remember a more incident packed event which saw two riders taken to hospital and with so many races having to be stopped and rerun.

The track, which had been perfect for Friday's practice, did cause problems to some riders but Sweden's home grown star, Freddie Lindgren, simply breezed through the qualifying stages, unbeaten in five rides.

Eventually, after also winning his semi final, passing pre-meeting favourite Leigh Adams who had won in Poland two weeks before, in the process, Lindgren was headed home in the final by Holta who made a terrific start round the outside.

Defending World Champion Nicki Pedersen was also passed by Holta, taking third spot overall.

He hadn't won any of the first three GPs but did made the rostrum in each and that was enough to keep him on top of the championship table.

Pedersen found the right words: "Consistency is the key.

"I know that if I can keep reaching finals I will be there or thereabouts but, of course, I want to win."

Holta was naturally ecstatic.

Understandably so.

For so long a journeyman Grand Prix rider, he always had the potential to be a winner and on this night he took every opportunity that came his way and made the most of it.

"Three different riders have won this year," said Holta, "and that says it all about the Grand Prix.

"Anyone can win. I have been last and now I am a winner."

The added bonus for Holta was that the FIM Sapa Swedish Grand Prix was also the first of the season's Superprix, to determine the four riders to chase a prize pot of $200,000 in what everyone believed (at that time) would be the final round of the season in Germany.

Holta not only assured himself of a place in that race but also the red, and number one, gate position.

"It is great to have done that," added Holta, "and now I can concentrate on doing well in the rest of the season."

For Lindgren, who quietly went about his business, it was an almost flawless display.

Had the track not been watered before the Grand Final, which made the inside lines difficult, he might have withstood Holta's charge round the outside.

But he was delighted with his night's work.

"Six wins and a second isn't bad is it?" he asked rhetorically.

Australia's Jason Crump, at times looking almost back to his best, came fourth in his seasonal first taste of the last race

But for many the night was not only long but also painful.

Sweden's top rider, Andreas Jonsson, was involved in a fearful looking crash after hitting the back wheel of Poland's Tomasz Gollob while both were at full speed.

Jonsson, who looked as if he might have suffered long damaging injuries, was eventually stretchered from the track and taken to hospital where, remarkably, he was found to have escaped relatively unscathed from a crash which stunned and silenced the partisan Ullevi crowd.

Niels-Kristian Iversen also went to hospital where doctors quickly diagnosed a dislocated shoulder that was to play a major part in the Dane's season.

Fellow countryman Hans Andersen was also in the wars but at least he was able to return to the fray after a heavy fall that saw him tenderly nursing his right arm and wrist.

Chris Harris, Lukas Dryml, Scott Nicholls and Lubos Tomicek (once again stepping in for the still injured Bjarne Pedersen) also took hefty, bone-jarring tumbles on the inconsistent surface.

But nothing could deny Holta his special anniversary – and didn't he just show it as he went on his victory parade as the first Norwegian-born rider to win a GP round?

the VENUE

Track: *Ullevi Stadium, Skånegatan, Gothenburg, Sweden.*
Telephone: *(0046) 313684500.*
Website: *www.ullevi.se*
Track Length: *416 metres.*
Track Record: *69.1 secs, Greg Hancock, May 24, 2008.*
First Grand Prix: *Saturday, August 31, 2002 – Scandinavian GP.*
Grands Prix staged: *4.*

Roll of Honour

1995 .... Tommy Knudsen
1996 .... Billy Hamill
1997 .... Tomasz Gollob
1998 .... Tony Rickardsson
1999 .... Mark Loram
2000 .... Jason Crump
2001 .... Jason Crump
2002 .... Tony Rickardsson
2003 .... Ryan Sullivan
2004 .... Leigh Adams
2005 .... Jason Crump
2006 .... Jason Crump
2007 .... Leigh Adams
2008 .... Rune Holta

■ *Previous Swedish GPs have been staged at Linköping (1995, 1996, 1997, 1998 and 1999); Stockholm (2000, 2001, 2002 and 2004); Avesta (2003); and Eskilstuna (2005, 2006 and 2007).*

■ *Ullevi Stadium, Gothenburg, has also hosted the Scandinavian GP in 2002, 2003 and 2004.*

Quote...unquote

FREDRIK LINDGREN

They are not normal meetings but I try to approach as if they were.

JASON CRUMP

At least tonight I was in the races. I know it's not going to come back overnight but there were positive steps.

LEIGH ADAMS

I guess the whole meeting was a bit of a downer, wasn't it?

the RESULTS

Rider						Pts	SF	F	Total
1 Rune HOLTA	**3**	**1**	**2**	**0**	**3**	**9**	**2**	**6**	**17**
2 Fredrik LINDGREN	3	3	3	3	3	15	3	4	22
3 Nicki PEDERSEN	2	1	3	3	2	11	3	2	16
4 Jason CRUMP	3	3	1	2	1	10	2	0	12
5 Leigh ADAMS	2	1	2	2	1	8	1		9
6 Tomasz GOLLOB	0	2	3	FX	3	8	0		8
7 Hans ANDERSEN	1	3	3	F	0	7	1		8
8 Andreas JONSSON	2	2	1	3	FX	8	N		8
9 ❖Jonas DAVIDSSON	R	3	1	1	2	7			7
10 Scott NICHOLLS	1	2	2	FX	2	7			7
11 Greg HANCOCK	3	0	0	3	FX	6			6
12 Krzysztof KASPRZAK	0	0	0	2	3	5			5
13 Lubos TOMICEK	0	2	0	1	2	5			5
14 Chris HARRIS	1	1	2	0	1	5			5
15 Lukas DRYML	1	0	1	1	FX	3			3
16 Niels-Kristian IVERSEN	2	FX				2			2
17 Billy FORSBERG [R]	2					2			2
18 Sebastian ALDÉN [R]	0	0				0			0

Final: Holta, Lindgren, N.Pedersen, Crump, 71.5 secs.
Semi Final: Lindgren, Holta, Adams, Jonsson (unfit to start), 71.1 secs.
Semi Final: N.Pedersen, Crump, Andersen, Gollob, 70.5 secs.

1: Crump, Jonsson, Nicholls, Kasprzak, 71.1 secs.
2: Holta, N.Pedersen, Andersen, Gollob, 69.5 secs.
3: Hancock, Iversen, Dryml, Davidsson (r), 69.1 secs.
4: Lindgren, Adams, Harris, Tomicek, 69.2 secs.
5: Crump, Tomicek, Holta, Iversen (fell, excluded), 71.1 secs.
6: Davidsson, Gollob, Harris, Kasprzak, 70.0 secs.
7: Lindgren, Jonsson, N.Pedersen, Hancock, 69.1 secs.
8: Andersen, Nicholls, Adams, Dryml, 70.0 secs.
9: Gollob, Adams, Crump, Hancock, 71.1 secs.
10: Lindgren, Holta, Dryml, Kasprzak, 70.3 secs.
11: Andersen, Harris, Jonsson, Aldén, 70.4 secs.
12: N.Pedersen, Nicholls, Davidsson, Tomicek, 71.1 secs.
13: N.Pedersen, Crump, Dryml, Harris, 71.1 secs.
14: Hancock, Kasprzak, Tomicek, Andersen (fell), 71.5 secs.
15: Jonsson, Adams, Davidsson, Holta, 71.5 secs.
16: Lindgren, Forsberg, Gollob (fell, excluded), Nicholls (fell, excluded), 72.8 secs.
17: Lindgren, Davidsson, Crump, Andersen, 72.7 secs.
18: Kasprzak, N.Pedersen, Adams, Aldén, 71.5 secs.
19: Gollob, Tomicek, Jonsson (fell, excluded), Dryml (fell, excluded), 78.8 secs,
20: Holta, Nicholls, Harris, Hancock (fell, excluded), 71.1 secs.

Fastest time: 69.1 secs, Greg Hancock, Heat 3 and Fredrik Lindgren, Heat 7.
Referee: *Tony Steele (Great Britain).*

■ ***Bjarne Pedersen*** *missed a second successive round with his broken wrist and was again replaced by Lubos Tomicek.*
■ ***Rune Holta*** *won his first Grand Prix at the 50th attempt – the longest it has taken anyone to break their duck.*
■ ***Fredrik Lindgren*** *finished five points clear of his nearest rival – but missed out on his first Grand Prix victory after losing in the Grand Final. Until then he had won all his six races.*

2008 GRAND PRIX

ROUND 4: DANISH GRAND PRIX, SATURDAY, JUNE 14

Tomasz Gollob took the win and the plaudits – but there was only one real hero.

The Pole became the first rider to win two Grand Prix rounds denying World Champion Nicki Pedersen his first ever victory in his home event.

Having to settle for another second place had its consolation for Pedersen though as he actually stretched his seasonal lead, eking out another point's advantage over Gollob, actually outscoring him 20-19 despite missing out on the gold medal.

Australian Jason Crump made a welcome return to the rostrum and was the first rider to halt Pedersen's winning run when he raced inside the Dane on a dash to the chequered flag in Heat 14.

Until then Pedersen had looked invincible on a magnificently prepared track that produced outstanding racing for a full house of 29,000 at PARKEN.

Pedersen won his final qualifying race but was then passed by Gollob in a superb semi final that meant he had third choice of gate for the Final.

Crump won semi final two and had first pick, taking the favoured gate two and looked set to become a three-time winner at PARKEN.

But by now Gollob, who won the opening round of the 2008 series in Slovenia, had the bit between his teeth.

He swept majestically round the first corner and into a lead that despite the best efforts of Pedersen and Crump, they simply couldn't catch him.

Denmark's Hans Andersen was fourth and once again there were signs that he, like Crump, is within a whisker of returning to the winner's circle.

After all the drama, crashes and controversy that took place in Gothenburg three weeks earlier the second Scandinavian event was very different but a succession of top class races and countless overtaking meant it was a magnificent meeting.

Oh, and the real hero?

Well, that was wild card Kenneth Bjerre who defied logic by taking his place at PARKEN.

On Wednesday, May 21 – just over three weeks earlier – he had smashed his thigh in a crash during a Danish domestic meeting.

At first everyone had written off his season but Bjerre had other thoughts and after lengthy chats with his specialist he began to believe he could ride again.

He was actually in action within 10 days, racing in a GP qualifier and that encouraged him to tell the PARKEN organisers that if they offered him a wild card he would gratefully snap it up.

Riding with a metal rod holding the two fractured pieces of his bone together, he revelled in the slick conditions and, incredibly, had 11 points from his five qualifying rounds.

His biggest problem was when he missed the gate and his luck ran out in the semi final when he trailed in last.

But the reception he got as he made his way back into the pits for the last time could have been accorded the night's champion.

It was a remarkable show of bravery and courage.

Bjerre is just starting off on his career at World Championship level – at the other end of the scale is Greg Hancock, wearing a Grand Prix race-jacket for the 104th successive round.

Herbie also reached the semis again and was fourth in the overall rankings, still not out of contention and ready to capitalise on any possible slips from the top three.

Sweden's Andreas Jonsson, who pipped Pedersen at PARKEN a year ago, began with a blistering win and reached the semis before going out.

Gollob, rated by many as the greatest rider never to have won the World Championship, was ecstatic and sent out a warning ahead of the FIM Meridian Lifts British Grand Prix at Cardiff's Millennium Stadium.

"I like that track," he confirmed.

PARKEN suited his style but a watching Barry Briggs, himself a four-times World Champion, was full of awesome praise for the Pole.

"Tomasz is a great rider who can do unbelievable things on a bike anywhere," opined Briggo.

Crump, annoyed at losing out, said: "It is good to be competing with these boys again."

And his biggest points haul of the year (18) helped him climb into third place overall as he began to mount a genuine title challenge despite his slow start in Slovenia and Poland where he gained only 18 points over the two rounds.

It was another below par night for Leigh Adams, though, as he managed only eight points to leave him 27 points off Pedersen's supersonic pace.

the VENUE

Track: *PARKEN, Øster Allé 50, 2100 Copenhagen Ø, Denmark.*
Telephone: *(0045) 35433131.*
Website: *www.parken.dk*
Track Length: *275 metres.*
Track Record: *54.2 secs, Nicki Pedersen, June 14, 2008.*
First Grand Prix: *Saturday, June 28, 2003.*
Grands Prix staged: *6.*

Roll of Honour

1995 .... Hans Nielsen
1996 .... Billy Hamill
1997 .... Mark Loram
1998 .... Hans Nielsen
1999 .... Tony Rickardsson
2000 .... Greg Hancock
2001 .... Tony Rickardsson
2002 .... Tony Rickardsson
2003 .... Jason Crump
2004 .... Jason Crump
2005 .... Tony Rickardsson
2006 .... Hans Andersen
2007 .... Andreas Jonsson
2008 .... Tomasz Gollob

■ *The Danish GP has been staged at PARKEN since 2003. All previous Danish GPs were held at Vojens.*

Quote...unquote

CHRIS HARRIS

I need to get a Grand Prix race win under my belt again because it's just not happening for me at the moment.

LEIGH ADAMS

I've been up and down like a yo-yo this season.

KENNETH BJERRE

I want to be World Champion one day and that's what I think about.

SCOTT NICHOLLS

I'm so angry and frustrated at missing out again. I finished with seven points again but it so, so easily could have been 10.

the RESULTS

Rider									
1 Tomasz GOLLOB	**2**	**2**	**3**	**1**	**2**	**10**	**3**	**6**	**19**
2 Nicki PEDERSEN	3	3	3	2	3	14	2	4	20
3 Jason CRUMP	1	3	3	3	3	13	3	2	18
4 Hans ANDERSEN	3	1	2	3	0	9	2	0	11
5 ❖Kenneth BJERRE	2	3	0	3	3	11	0		11
6 Greg HANCOCK	2	3	1	1	2	9	1		10
7 Andreas JONSSON	3	1	2	2	0	8	1		9
8 Leigh ADAMS	3	2	0	0	3	8	0		8
9 Bjarne PEDERSEN	1	2	3	0	1	7			7
10 Rune HOLTA	1	2	1	3	0	7			7
11 Scott NICHOLLS	0	1	2	2	2	7			7
12 Niels-Kristian IVERSEN	1	0	2	2	1	6			6
13 Chris HARRIS	2	0	1	0	0	3			3
14 Krzysztof KASPRZAK	0	0	0	1	2	3			3
15 Fredrik LINDGREN	0	1	X	1	1	3			3
16 Lukas DRYML	0	0	N	0	1	1			1
17 Nicolai KLINDT [R]	*0*					*0*			*0*
18 Patrick HOUGAARD [R]						*did not ride*			

Final: Gollob, N.Pedersen, Crump, Andersen, 55.9secs.
Semi Final: Gollob, N.Pedersen, Hancock, Adams, 55.8 secs.
Semi Final: Crump, Andersen, Jonsson, Bjerre, 56.1 secs.

1: Jonsson, Hancock, B.Pedersen, Lindgren, 55.8 secs.
2: Andersen, Bjerre, Crump, Nicholls, 55.4 secs.
3: Adams, Gollob, Holta, Dryml, 55.3 secs.
4: N.Pedersen, Harris, Iversen, Kasprzak, 55.4 secs.
5: N.Pedersen, B.Pedersen, Nicholls, Dryml, 54.2 secs.
6: Hancock, Holta, Andersen, Iversen, 55.4 secs.
7: Bjerre, Adams, Lindgren, Kasprzak, 55.1 secs.
8: Crump, Gollob, Jonsson, Harris, 56.1 secs.
9: B.Pedersen, Andersen, Harris, Adams, 55.0 secs.
10: Gollob, Nicholls, Hancock, Kasprzak, 55.8 secs.
11: Crump, Iversen, Klindt, Dryml (excluded, 2 minutes), Lindgren (excluded), 55.6 secs.
12: N.Pedersen, Jonsson, Holta, Bjerre, 56.0 secs.
13: Bjerre, Iversen, Gollob, B.Pedersen, 55.1 secs.
14: Crump, N.Pedersen, Hancock, Adams, 55.8 secs.
15: Holta, Nicholls, Lindgren, Harris, 56.2 secs.
16: Andersen, Jonsson, Kasprzak, Dryml, 55.8 secs.
17: Crump, Kasprzak, B.Pedersen, Holta, 55.1 secs.
18: Bjerre, Hancock, Dryml, Harris, 55.3 secs.
19: N.Pedersen, Gollob, Lindgren, Andersen, 56.0 secs,
20: Adams, Nicholls, Iversen, Jonsson.
Fastest time: 54.2 secs, Nicki Pedersen, Heat 5.
Referee: *Tony Steele (Great Britain).*

■ ***Tomasz Gollob*** *became only the second rider to make 100 Grand Prix appearances and celebrated with his 13th Grand Prix victory.*
■ ***Tomasz Gollob*** *was the ninth different rider to win the Danish Grand Prix.*
■ ***Nikolai Klindt*** *became the 126th different rider to appear in a Grand Prix race when he replaced out of time Lukas Dryml in Heat 11.*
■ *Continuing his consistent record,* ***Nicki Pedersen*** *made it seven Grand Final appearances in his last eight appearances.*

2008 GRAND PRIX

ROUND 5: BRITISH GRAND PRIX, SATURDAY, JUNE 28

OH dear, oh dear, oh dear, oh dear, oh dear, oh dear, oh dear, oh dear, oh dear.

Jason Crump burst back into title contention but the man everyone was talking about as they mingled with the Saturday night revellers in Cardiff's Westgate Street bars was referee Marek Wojaczek.

He had an absolute shocker and was to pay the penalty when he was unceremoniously axed from the rota following a behind-closed-doors inquest.

His contentious decisions benefited World Champion Nicki Pedersen enormously and helped the Dane to reach his fifth Final out of five.

Let's study the debateable.

Heat 6: Pedersen clearly touched the tapes but Wojaczek allowed the race to progress and Nicki picked up a valuable third place point.

Heat 17: Leigh Adams, off an inside gate, and Pedersen, closest to the fence, came down in the first turn.

The easy decision (and probably the right one) would have been to order a re-run with all four starters but the erring official decided to plunge the red light exclusion button and an aggrieved Adams, who had already missed out on one doubtful photo finish, was thrown out.

Semi Final 1: While no two races can ever be exactly the same you would have needed an acutely analytical eye to discern any difference between what happened in Heat 17.

Again Pedersen was involved but this time his immediate opponent was Bjarne Pedersen rather than Adams.

This time Pedersen was excluded, but Bjarne rather than Nicki!

The crowd could scarcely believe either eyes or ears and vented their anger at the world number one as he was handed a third reprieve of the night.

He took advantage to win the semi although the toll on his body finally caught up with him as he fell in the Grand Final although, much to his sporting credit, he hauled his bike onto the synthetic carpeted centre green to avoid the stop lights having to come on again.

For the fifth time this year lucky Nicki reached a Final and he could probably argue that there have been plenty of occasions when he's suffered from similarly bizarre refereeing decisions.

And as he pointed out in his post-meeting Press briefing: "I think it [the crowd's booing] was disgraceful because I had nothing to do with them [referee's decisions].

"If that was me making the decisions then, yes, I would probably have been putting all four back but it's up to the referee to make the decisions.

"I would not have argued with an all-four decision, absolutely not, but the booing just makes me think even more about British speedway.

"If anything the booing spurred me on even more to show that I'm still going to be up there fighting and I'm still going for the Championship."

To his credit Wojaczek didn't shy away from giving his side on matters.

He said: "In my opinion the riders in red (Adams and Bjarne Pedersen) were trying to race too far to make the straight longer.

"I considered it dangerous riding because they took the front wheel of the riders on the outside. I feel both should turn earlier.

"I looked at the replays but in my opinion it was not all four back because for two riders it was nothing to do with the first bend.

"I told the riders at the briefing that because there was a crash on the first bend, it would not be all four back. I always work like this.

"I try to avoid all four back because it's not tennis with second serves."

Amid all the furure there was, for a second successive year, real home interest in the later stages.

With Chris Harris' 2007 triumph etched in the Millennium pysche, Scott Nicholls reached the final.

Sadly his bid to emulate his former Coventry teammate ended in anti-climax as he broke the tapes and was rightly excluded from the re-run.

Track conditions had become more and more difficult as the night wore on and it was the vast experience of Hancock and Crump that shone through.

Both were critical of track conditions but at the same time were eager to extol the virtues of the Millennium Stadium as the jewel in the GP crown.

But they were mindful of the plethora of crashes, one of which ended Harris' defence of his hard-won title at a time when it looked distinctly possible that he could provide another uplifting finale to a never dull British Grand Prix.

the VENUE

Track: *Millennium Stadium,, Westgate Street, Cardiff. CF10 1JA, Wales.*
Telephone: *(0044) 8700138600.*
Website: *www.millenniumstadium.co.uk*
Track Length: *275 metres.*
Track Record: *55.8 secs, Jason Crump, June 28, 2008.*
First Grand Prix: *Saturday, June 9, 2001.*
Grands Prix staged: *7.*

Roll of Honour

1995 .... Greg Hancock
1996 .... Jason Crump
1997 .... Brian Andersen
1998 .... Jason Crump
1999 .... Tony Rickardsson
2000 .... Martin Dugard
2001 .... Tony Rickardsson
2002 .... Ryan Sullivan
2003 .... Nicki Pedersen
2004 .... Greg Hancock
2005 .... Tony Rickardsson
2006 .... Jason Crump
2007 .... Chris Harris
2008 .... Jason Crump

■ *The British GP has been held at the Millennium Stadium, Cardiff, since 2001. Previous Brtish GPs were staged at Hackney (1995 and 1996), Bradford (1997) and Coventry (1998, 1999 and 2000).*

Quote...unquote

BJARNE PEDERSEN

The decision in the semi final was unbelievable – I think there are 15 other riders out there who have the same feelings as me.

HANS ANDERSEN

Not only did we have the opponents to battle with we had the state of the track as well.

KRZYSZTOF KASPRZAK

This track is terrible, this is a World Championship meeting and we must have a normal track; a track like Poole or Peterborough.

the RESULTS

Rider									
1 Jason CRUMP	**3**	**2**	**3**	**3**	**3**	**14**	**2**	**6**	**22**
2 Greg HANCOCK	3	3	3	3	1	13	3	4	20
3 Nicki PEDERSEN	2	1	2	0	3	8	3	F	11
4 Scott NICHOLLS	1	3	2	2	2	10	2	E	12
5 Bjarne PEDERSEN	2	3	3	3	3	14	X		14
6 Chris HARRIS	3	1	2	1	2	9	1		10
7 Hans ANDERSEN	0	3	1	1	3	8	1		9
8 Andreas JONSSON	1	2	1	2	2	8	0		8
9 Leigh ADAMS	2	2	1	2	X	7			7
10 Niels-Kristian IVERSEN	3	0	F	3	X	6			6
11 Rune HOLTA	2	1	3	0	X	6			6
12 Tomasz GOLLOB	0	2	2	R	0	4			4
13 ❖Edward KENNETT	1	0	0	1	2	4			4
14 Krzysztof KASPRZAK	0	1	0	2	1	4			4
15 Fredrik LINDGREN	1	0	X	FX	1	2			2
16 Lukas DRYML	0	0	0	1	0	1			1
17 Tai WOFFINDEN [R]						*did not ride*			
17 Simon STEAD [R]						*did not ride*			

Final: Crump, Hancock, Nicki Pedersen (fell), Nicholls (excluded, tapes), 57.9 secs.
Semi Final: Nicki Pedersen, Nicholls, Andersen, Bjarne Pedersen (excluded), 57.6 secs.
Semi Final: Hancock, Crump, Harris, Jonsson, 57.7 secs.
1: Iversen, Adams, Nicholls, Dryml, 56.6 secs.
2: Harris, Holta, Lindgren, Gollob, 56.0 secs.
3: Crump, N.Pedersen, Kennett, Kasprzak, 55.8 secs.
4: Hancock, B.Pedersen, Jonsson, Andersen, 56.9 secs.
5: Hancock, Adams, Harris, Kennett, 55.9 secs.
6: Andersen, Gollob, N.Pedersen, Dryml, 56.5 secs.
7: Nicholls, Jonsson, Kasprzak, Lindgren. 56.5 secs.
8: B.Pedersen, Crump, Holta, Iversen, 56.8 secs.
9: B.Pedersen, Gollob, Adams, Kasprzak, 57.4 secs.
10: Crump, Harris, Jonsson, Dryml, 56.2 secs.
11: Holta, Nicholls, Andersen, Kennett, 57.6 secs.
12: Hancock, N.Pedersen, Iversen (fell), Lindgren (excluded), 56.7 secs.
13: Crump, Adams, Andersen, Lindgren (fell, excluded), 56.2 secs.
14: Hancock, Kasprzak, Dryml, Holta, 57.2 secs.
15: B.Pedersen, Nicholls, Harris, N.Pedersen, 57.3 secs.
16: Iversen, Jonsson, Kennett, Gollob (r), 57.1 secs.
17: N.Pedersen, Jonsson, Adams (excluded), Holta (excluded), 57.1 secs.
18: B.Pedersen, Kennett, Lindgren, Dryml, 57.5 secs.
19: Crump, Nicholls, Hancock, Gollob, 57.8 secs,
20: Andersen, Harris, Kasprzak, Iversen (excluded), 57.5 secs.
Fastest time: 55.8 secs, Jason Crump, Heat 3.
Referee: *Marek Wojaczek (Poland).*

■ ***Jason Crump*** *ended a 20-round barren spell with his fourth British GP win and his 17th overall. His previous victory had been at the Italian GP on July 29, 2006.*
■ ***Scott Nicholls*** *made the Grand Final for the first time in nine British Grand Prix appearances.*
■ *Wild card* ***Edward Kennett*** *made his second Grand Prix appearance, having previously been a riding reserve in 2005 and non-riding reserve in both 2006 and 2007.*

2008 GRAND PRIX

ROUND 6: CZECH REPUBLIC GRAND PRIX, SATURDAY, AUGUST 2

NICKI Pedersen moved into the mid-summer break holding a comfortable 10 point lead.

He finally – at the sixth time of asking – claimed the round win he had been craving to reinforce his reputation as the world's top rider.

Consistency had been the key to the Dane's advantage over all his rivals and he made it six Finals out of six at Prague.

His determination to take the top step of the podium at the Marketa Stadium was clear.

Pedersen duly delivered, taking a second consecutive win at the venue – and he received a bonus from fellow countryman Hans Andersen, very strong at the end of the meeting, who relegated Jason Crump to third place in the Grand Final.

Crump remained Pedersen's closest challenger overall, but 10 points behind with five rounds to go with Greg Hancock and Tomasz Gollob losing ground on the top two .

The formbook was a good pointer to what happened in the Czech Republic with seven of the top eight riders going into the event reaching the semi finals.

The other man to make it was Rune Holta, courtesy of a trademark last-gasp win in Heat 20.

He not only reached the top eight he also passed Fredrik Lindgren on the way to confirm his status in the series top eight, reaching the cut-off point that was so important to those without a shout on a medal.

But Prague only ever belonged to Pedersen who was largely untroubled in scoring 14 points in the qualifiers.

His only defeat came against Leigh Adams in Heat 6, while Crump's two dropped points came against Pedersen and an up-and-down Chris Harris in Heat 13, the British rider making a terrific start from the outside.

Andersen endured a mid-meeting lull and had to wait until his last outing to book his semi final spot, but he moved himself right into contention by defeating Pedersen in the semi, a race which saw Andreas Jonsson and Adams make their exits.

Hancock and Crump fought out a splendid duel in the second semi, and Crump felt his defeat in that race proved costly in the final by way of his gate choice.

They progressed at the expense of Holta and Gollob, although Holta, in particular, gave Crump some anxious moments.

Andersen, off gate two, made fractionally the best start in the Final but Pedersen, from gate four, was quickly around the outside and clear, leaving Andersen to defend second place and make his own position in the top eight much more comfortable.

But it was the World Champion's night, and a delighted Pedersen said: "I keep reaching the Finals but I said to myself for this one that I didn't want to just reach the Final, I wanted to win it.

"I felt I had a little more confidence than the others and the set-up was great all night, so I'm very, very happy and the tracks coming up are all good race-tracks.

"We had a talk among the team beforehand because last year the lead was down to 11 points in the middle of the season, and we really wanted to extend it this year.

"We did it, so the plan is working!"

The switch back to a permanent track – after the trials and tribulations at both Ullevi and Cardiff – robbed the meeting of some of the unpredictable and again underlined one of the biggest beefs of the unconverted: speedway is about whoever gets out of the start wins.

This was another night of further evidence for the doubters. Certainly there was only a few foot wide strip of racing line throughout the night although it did move wider as the evening wore on.

Passing was at a premium with riders making few forced or unforced errors and 11 of the 16 starters won at least one race.

Harris, as ever, provided much of the excitement that was on display, bravely squeezing between Leigh Adams and the fence in Heat 9 although the pity was he was only racing for a point as Greg Hancock and Lukas Dryml had already built up a considerable lead!

Holta was another to buck the processional trend after storming past home favourite Dryml and with a bit more grip it would have been a true classic as Nicholls went through the subsequent hole and then spent the rest of the race virtually rubbing tyres with the Norwegian without ever summoning up the extra speed that would have taken him to the front.

The British Champion, never the sharpest at the starting gate, suffered from his own tardiness out of the tapes: the chief victim of conditions.

the VENUE

Track: *Marketa Stadium, U Vojtesky 11, 162 01, Prague, Czech Republic.*
Telephone: *(00420) 233358487.*
Website: *www.speedway-prague.cz*
Track Length: *353 metres.*
Track Record: *62.4 secs, Greg Hancock, May 17, 1997.*
First Grand Prix: *Saturday, May 17, 1997.*
Grands Prix staged: *12.*

Roll of Honour

1997 ....Greg Hancock
1998 ....Tony Rickardsson
1999 ....Tomasz Gollob
2000 ....Billy Hamill
2001 ....Billy Hamill
2002 ....Jason Crump
2003 ....Jason Crump
2004 ....Jason Crump
2005 ....Tony Rickardsson
2006 ....Hans Andersen
2007 ....Nicki Pedersen
2008 ....Nicki Pedersen

■ *All Czech Republic GPs have been held at the Marketa Stadium, Prague.*

Quote...unquote

SCOTT NICHOLLS

I felt fast enough, it was just the same old story from the starts. I had some clutch problems all night and it just unsettles you. You can't give them a head start so I need to do some work on the starts.

JASON CRUMP

I thought I was quick enough in the heats and then just made a mess of the start in the semi and paid the price by getting red in the Final. I'm probably riding the best I have for a long time.

RUNE HOLTA

I was very close to the final. Actually, I was second at one time in the semi final but in that moment I hit a big hole which sent me wide. In one moment I was taken from the middle of the track to the safety fence. I hit the fence and I was lucky to stay on the bike.

the RESULTS

Rider									
1 Nicki PEDERSEN	**3**	**2**	**3**	**3**	**3**	**14**	**2**	**6**	**22**
2 Hans ANDERSEN	2	3	1	1	2	9	3	4	16
3 Jason CRUMP	2	3	3	2	3	13	2	2	17
4 Greg HANCOCK	3	1	3	1	2	10	3	0	13
5 Tomasz GOLLOB	2	2	3	3	2	12	0		12
6 Leigh ADAMS	3	3	0	3	1	10	0		10
7 Andreas JONSSON	1	3	2	2	0	8	1		9
8 Rune HOLTA	1	2	FX	2	3	8	1		9
9 Bjarne PEDERSEN	FX	2	2	0	3	7			7
10 Niels-Kristian IVERSEN	3	0	1	2	1	7			7
11 Chris HARRIS	2	0	1	3	1	7			7
12 Scott NICHOLLS	0	1	2	1	2	6			6
13 Lukas DRYML	0	1	2	0	1	4			4
14 Fredrik LINDGREN	1	1	1	1	0	4			4
15 Krzysztof KASPRZAK	1	0	0	0	0	1			1
16 ❖Lubos TOMICEK	0	0	0	0	0	0			0
17 Adrian RYMEL [R]						*did not ride*			
17 Filip SITERA [R]						*did not ride*			

Final: N.Pedersen, Andersen, Crump, Hancock, 63.86 secs.
Semi Final: Andersen, N.Pedersen, Jonsson, Adams, 63.87 secs.
Semi Final: Hancock, Crump, Holta, Gollob, 64.81 ecs.
1: Iversen, Harris, Kasprzak, Tomicek, 63.34 secs.
2: Adams, Gollob, Holta, B.Pedersen (fell, excluded), 63.28 secs.
3: N.Pedersen, Crump, Lindgren, Dryml, 62.73 secs.
4: Hancock, Andersen, Jonsson, Nicholls, 64.98 secs.
5: Andersen, Holta, Lindgren, Harris, 63.88 secs.
6: Adams, N.Pedersen, Nicholls, Iversen, 63.15 secs.
7: Jonsson, B.Pedersen, Dryml, Kasprzak, 63.28 secs.
8: Crump, Gollob, Hancock, Tomicek, 63.06 secs.
9: Hancock, Dryml, Harris, Adams, 63.95 secs.
10: Crump, Jonsson, Iversen, Holta (fell, excluded), 63.86 secs.
11: Gollob, Nicholls, Lindgren, Kasprzak, 64.49 secs.
12: N.Pedersen, B.Pedersen, Andersen, Tomicek, 63.36 secs.
13: Harris, Crump, Nicholls, B.Pedersen, 63.99 secs.
14: Gollob, Iversen, Andersen, Dryml, 64.72 secs.
15: N.Pedersen, Holta, Hancock, Kasprzak, 63.98 secs.
16: Adams, Jonsson, Lindgren, Tomicek, 64.01 secs.
17: N.Pedersen, Gollob, Harris, Jonsson, 65.85 secs.
18: N.Pedersen, Hancock, Iversen, Lindgren, 64.24 secs.
19: Crump, Andersen, Adams, Kasprzak, 64.78 secs,
20: Holta, Nicholls, Dryml, Tomicek, 64.39 secs.
Fastest time: 62.73 secs, Nicki Pedersen, Heat 3.
Referee: *Krister Gardell (Sweden).*

■ ***Nicki Pedersen*** *made it six out of six 2008 Final appearances.*

■ ***Lubos Tomicek*** *became the season's first wild card to fail to score a point in his five qualifying rides.*

■ ***Leigh Adams*** *missed out on the top four and has never reached a Czech Republic Final despite riding in all 12 stagings.*

■ ***Filip Sitera*** *was named as reserve for the first time – but never got an outing.*

2008 GRAND PRIX

ROUND 7: SCANDINAVIAN GRAND PRIX, SATURDAY, AUGUST 16

TON-UP kid Leigh Adams celebrated his 100th Grand Prix in true winning style.

Adams, only the third rider to reach the century mark after everpresent Greg Hancock and Tomasz Gollob, had vowed to forget about the mounting points gap to series leader Nicki Pedersen and concentrate fully on the meeting.

And his reward for single-minded pursuit of his immediate goal was a second successive Grand Prix win at Målilla.

The victorious Adams said: "We're a long way adrift, but this is a stepping stone.

"We said we had to forget about the points and just try to enjoy it, and that's what we did.

"I'm still enjoying my speedway, still riding pretty well and I've got great people around me.

"With those 100 Grands Prix, it takes a dedicated team, and I have to say a big thank you to my mechanics and my family because it's been a long old haul for many years.

"We've got to finish on top of the box a few more times. A few more of these and we'll be up there!"

The Aussie veteran got the better of Hans Andersen in the Final, the Dane having appeared to be the dominant force for much of the meeting after winning five of his first six rides and being able to pick the inside gate for both his semi final and the Final.

Andersen led away but came under pressure from Adams' outside run as he initially blocked Nicki Pedersen on the inside and although Andersen seemed to just have Adams covered as they went into the second lap, he moved further across the track on the back straight than he would have wanted, lost speed and Adams took full advantage.

Pedersen's third place was another triumph of consistency on a night when he was suffering mechanical troubles, the reigning champion still reaching the Final despite breaking down at the start of his third ride.

And that ensured he extended his overall lead by two points to 17 as his nearest challenger Jason Crump was behind him in the Final, having matched Pedersen's performance in the heats and semi.

Greg Hancock looked a possible winner with 12 points from the heats, but he ran a last in the second semi final, which left him 10 points behind Crump and under threat from Andersen for a top-three position.

Tomasz Gollob dropped out of the top four – overhauled by Andersen – after going out in the same race as Hancock.

Racing was close with plenty of overtaking and several of the lower riders in the standings threatened to take big results from the meeting before fading later on.

Both Krzysztof Kasprzak and Lukas Dryml, some way adrift going into the event, took welcome race wins with Kasprzak making the first semi-final before going out at the expense of Andersen and Pedersen.

Niels-Kristian Iversen added a useful nine points to his total thanks to a semi-final appearance, and both he and Fredrik Lindgren kept in touch with Rune Holta for a top eight finish.

But it was a disastrous meeting for the British duo.

Scott Nicholls scored only four points and Chris Harris fared even worse on three.

The pair of them came together when they met in Heat 14 and it had a familiar result with Harris going down as Nicholls came through on the inside.

Harris was excluded on that occasion but Nicholls had cause to rue his misfortune in Heat 17 when he was on the receiving end of a baffling exclusion after tangling with Holta as the duo left the start-line.

He was adamant Hungarian Istvan Darago, back in control of a GP for the first time in nine years, got it wrong: "I don't think anyone could understand that decision. I was going straight so how could they exclude me?

"We didn't even get to the first corner and I couldn't understand how I could have been the one to blame.

"I could have won that race and if I had I would have been in the semi final.

"We've had some really bad refereeing decisions in a couple of meetings and they are hard to take because it's our jobs, our lives which are at stake."

Andreas Jonsson, who had become a father for the first time on the eve of the meeting, failed to provide the Swedish fans with a home win and was never in with a realistic chance of a double celebration.

He ran into the side of Nicholls in Heat 2 and was thrown out and never really recovered with an inconsistent performance which included a win, a second, a third, a last and that exclusion!

the VENUE

Track: *Målilla MK, Box 18, 57082, Målilla, Sweden.*
Telephone: *(0046) 49521248.*
Website: *www.scandinaviangp.com, www.dackarna.nu*
Track Length: *305 metres.*
Track Record: *55.9secs, Hans Andersen, August 1, 2006.*
First Grand Prix: *Saturday, August 13, 2005.*
Grands Prix staged: *4.*

Roll of Honour

2002	Leigh Adams
2003	Ryan Sullivan
2004	Hans Andersen
2005	Jason Crump
2006	Andreas Jonsson
2007	Leigh Adams
2008	Leigh Adams

■ *The Scandinavian GP has been held at Målilla, Sweden, since 2005. Previous Scandinavian GPs were staged at Ullevi Stadium, Gothenburg (2002, 2003 and 2004).*

Quote...unquote

NIELS-KRISTIAN IVERSEN

Before the meeting I would have been satisfied with reaching the semi final but it was my own mistake that stopped me getting into the Final.

GREG HANCOCK

I'm still learning every day and you have got to use every race as a learning experience.

NICKI PEDERSEN

I am not thinking about getting closer to the world title with four rounds to go. If I do that I might slip up. What is working for me is concentrating on consistency and to continue extending the lead.

the RESULTS

Rider									
1 Leigh ADAMS	**3**	**3**	**1**	**3**	**2**	**12**	**3**	**6**	**21**
2 Hans ANDERSEN	3	3	3	3	1	13	3	4	20
3 Nicki PEDERSEN	2	2	R	3	3	10	2	2	14
4 Jason CRUMP	2	1	2	3	2	10	2	0	12
5 Greg HANCOCK	3	2	3	2	2	12	0		12
6 Niels-Kristian IVERSEN	3	1	3	0	1	8	1		9
7 Krzysztof KASPRZAK	0	3	2	2	2	9	0		9
8 Tomasz GOLLOB	1	R	2	1	3	7	0		7
9 Fredrik LINDGREN	1	2	2	2	F	7			7
10 Bjarne PEDERSEN	0	2	0	1	3	6			6
11 Andreas JONSSON	X	1	3	2	0	6			6
12 Rune HOLTA	2	0	R	R	3	5			5
13 Lukas DRYML	0	3	1	1	0	5			5
14 Scott NICHOLLS	1	1	1	1	FX	4			4
15 ❖Peter LJUNG	2	0	0	0	1	3			3
16 Chris HARRIS	1	0	1	FX	1	3			3
17 Jonas DAVIDSSON [R]						*did not ride*			
17 Thomas H JONASSON [R]						*did not ride*			

Grand Final: Adams, Andersen, N.Pedersen, Crump, 59.7 secs.
Semi Final: Andersen, N.Pedersen, Iversen, Kasprzak, 59.6 secs.
Semi Final: Adams, Crump, Gollob, Hancock, 59.8 secs.
1: Andersen, Holta, Lindgren, Dryml, 57.2 secs.
2: Iversen, Crump, Nicholls, Jonsson (excluded), 56.9 secs.
3: Hancock, Ljung, Harris, B.Pedersen, 58.7 secs.
4: Adams, N.Pedersen, Gollob, Kasprzak, 59.2 secs.
5: Kasprzak, Hancock, Crump, Holta, 59.4 secs.
6: Andersen, N.Pedersen, Iversen, Ljung, 59.3 secs.
7: Adams, Lindgren, Jonsson, Harris, 59.3 secs.
8: Dryml, B.Pedersen, Nicholls, Gollob (r), 60.1 secs.
9: Iversen, Gollob, Harris, Holta (r), 59.7 secs.
10: Andersen, Crump, Adams, B.Pedersen, 59.5 secs.
11: Hancock, Lindgren, Nicholls, N.Pedersen (r), 59.8 secs.
12: Jonsson, Kasprzak, Dryml, Ljung, 59.8 secs.
13: N.Pedersen, Jonsson, B.Pedersen, Holta (r), 59.2 secs.
14: Andersen, Kasprzak, Nicholls, Harris (fell, excluded), 60.2 secs.
15: Crump, Lindgren, Gollob, Ljung, 59.9 secs.
16: Adams, Hancock, Dryml, Iversen, 60.0 secs.
17: Holta, Adams, Ljung, Nicholls (fell, excluded), 60.2 secs.
18: Gollob, Hancock, Andersen, Jonsson, 60.3 secs.
19: B.Pedersen, Kasprzak, Iversen, Lindgren (fell), 61.2 secs,
20: N.Pedersen, Crump, Harris, Dryml, 60.4 secs.
Fastest time: 56.9 secs, Niels-Kristian Iversen, Heat 2.
Referee: *Istvan Darago (Hungary).*

■ ***Leigh Adams*** *celebrated his 100th Grand Prix with victory – his ninth overall win. He made his GP debut on May 18, 1996.*

■ ***Greg Hancock's*** *miserable Scandinavian Grand Prix record continued as he missed out on the Grand Final for the seventh time in a row.*

■ ***Bjarne Pedersen*** *completed his 20th successive Grand Prix without making it into the Final four.*

2008 GRAND PRIX

ROUND 8: LATVIAN GRAND PRIX, SATURDAY, AUGUST 30

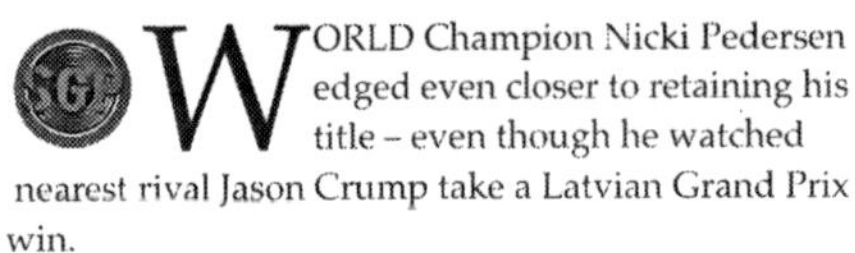

WORLD Champion Nicki Pedersen edged even closer to retaining his title – even though he watched nearest rival Jason Crump take a Latvian Grand Prix win.

Crump's second GP win of the year – his other victory came at the British round at Cardiff earlier this summer – kept the title race simmering.

But he was running out of time and had only three rounds left to overhaul Pedersen's 16 point lead at the top of the standings.

The Danish superstar kept up his remarkable run with an eighth podium in a row even though he was buffeted in the first turn by Poland's Tomasz Gollob.

But Crump pulled it out when it mattered to come from last to first on the opening lap of the Final to claim his 18th GP win, leaving him just two behind all-time record holder Tony Rickardsson.

Pedersen said: "I would have liked to win the Final but unfortunately me and Gollob fought hard in the first bend which opened the door for Jason.

"I'm happy about the result. Things fell out to Jason's advantage but I'm happy.

"I guess that's racing. I only lost one point in the championship and, for me, that's the most important thing."

The Australian was beaten by Pedersen when they clashed in the second semi final but conjured a move of true brilliance in the first half-lap of the Final to take the full six points from the race.

Tomasz Gollob also put himself in the race by vaulting over Hans Andersen into fourth spot after a third place finish in Daugavpils.

His rostrum finish left him just four adrift of Greg Hancock after beating the American in the Final.

A meeting of ever-changing fortunes saw the eventual top four on the night all score 11 points in their qualifying races.

Crump, Pedersen and Hancock all won three heats but also suffered a last place – Crump's coming when he was excluded for a second-bend fall in Heat 13 as Andersen swept through on his inside to force the referee into a decision which could have gone either way.

Pedersen ran a last in Heat 20 although his semi final qualification was never threatened, and Hancock was always at the sharp end too despite a mid-meeting blank in Heat 10.

The battle for the other semi final places was intense with no fewer than six riders tieing on seven points, Bjarne Pedersen taking the final spot on the countback system.

While Krzysztof Kasprzak and Lukas Dryml could reflect on positive performances, seven points would have been a particular disappointment for overall rostrum contender Andersen, who was left to rue a fall in Heat 11, a race which seemed likely to net him useful points.

Chris Harris lifted his slim chances of clinching a return ticket to next year's series by finishing sixth for the second time in four rounds.

The Coventry skipper closed the gap on Fredrik Lindgren, filling the last automatic qualifying slot in eighth position, to 10 points.

He claimed: "My target has been to get into the semi final every round and I did it although I would liked to have scored more points to make the gap even closer."

Fellow Brit Scott Nicholls, who has been plagued by bad luck throughout the series, again missed out on the semis – this time because he had been excluded from one race!

He started well enough with five points from two rides but a last place in Heat 12 put him back under pressure, and it was followed by a fall on turn two in Heat 14 at a stage where track conditions were tricky.

Nicholls managed a last-ditch pass on Kasprzak in Heat 19 for second place, but it still left him a point short of countryman Harris whose night ended in the first semi final although he gained a point by passing Adams on the third lap as Gollob and Hancock went through.

Pedersen and Crump took control of the second semi, which left Pedersen going from the inside gate in the Final with Crump on the outside.

Pedersen appeared to initially be in control of the Final as he forced Gollob aside, but Crump then produced a marvellous cut-back off turn two to slice between his rivals up the back straight.

It was a move out of the top drawer which secured an 18th overall Grand Prix triumph for Crump, with Gollob fending off Hancock for third place during one of the best first laps of the season so far.

Overall, though, Pedersen was still smiling with 134 points compared to Crump's 118 as the final stages of the season approached.

the VENUE

Track: Lokomotiv Stadium,, Jelgavas iela 54, Daugavpils. Latvia. LV-5404.
Telephone: (00371) 65438807.
Website: www.speedway-loko@inbox.lv
Track Length: 375 metres.
Track Record: 68.6 secs, Grigori Laguta, August 13, 2006.
First Grand Prix: Saturday, September 9. 2006.
Grands Prix staged: 3.

Roll of Honour
2006 ....Greg Hancock
2007 ....Leigh Adams
2008 ....Jason Crump

■ *All Latvian GPs have been held at the Lokomotiv Stadium, Daugavpils.*

Quote...unquote

TOMASZ GOLLOB

Nicki and I were battling on the first corner but Jason came from nowhere!

GREG HANCOCK

I've been in a few Finals now and not made it happen, so we're failing somewhere and we need to figure out where.

LEIGH ADAMS

I was never really on the pace and you kind of know when you're not.

JASON CRUMP

You'd start to go a bit crazy if you start looking at the points so I try not to do that. You bust your gut but you end up with a one point difference, it's a lot of effort for one point.

ANDREAS JONSSON

I feel I could have done a little better but the track was really strange and difficult, dangerous even in places.

the RESULTS

Rider									
1 Jason CRUMP	**3**	**2**	**3**	**FX**	**3**	**11**	**2**	**6**	**19**
2 Nicki PEDERSEN	2	3	3	3	0	11	3	4	18
3 Tomasz GOLLOB	2	2	1	3	3	11	3	2	16
4 Greg HANCOCK	3	3	0	3	2	11	2	0	13
5 Andreas JONSSON	3	1	3	2	N	9	1		10
6 Chris HARRIS	1	1	2	1	3	8	1		9
7 Leigh ADAMS	3	1	2	2	1	9	0		9
8 Bjarne PEDERSEN	0	0	2	2	3	7	0		7
9 Scott NICHOLLS	2	3	0	FX	2	7			7
10 Hans ANDERSEN	1	2	0	3	1	7			7
11 Fredrik LINDGREN	0	3	2	1	1	7			7
12 Krzysztof KASPRZAK	0	2	3	1	1	7			7
13 Lukas DRYML	2	R	1	2	2	7			7
14 Rune HOLTA	1	0	1	0	2	4			4
15 ❖Grigori LAGUTA	1	1	0	0	0	2			2
16 Niels-Kristian IVERSEN	0	0	1	FX	0	1			1
17 Maksim BOGDANOVS [R]	*0*					*0*			*0*
18 Kjastas PUODZHUKS [R]						*did not ride*			

Final: Crump, N.Pedersen, Gollob, Hancock, 70.36 secs.
Semi Final: Gollob, Hancock, Harris, Adams, 71.55 secs.
Semi Final: N.Pedersen, Crump, Jonsson, B.Pedersen, 70.74 secs.
1: Hancock, N.Pedersen, Harris, Kasprzak, 68.85 secs.
2: Adams, Gollob, Laguta, Iversen, 69.09 secs.
3: Crump, Dryml, Holta, B.Pedersen, 69.29 secs.
4: Jonsson, Nicholls, Andersen, Lindgren, 69.47 secs.
5: Nicholls, Gollob, Harris, B.Pedersen, 69.54 secs.
6: Hancock, Andersen, Laguta, Holta, 69.39 secs.
7: Lindgren, Kasprzak, Adams, Dryml (r), 70.44 secs.
8: N.Pedersen, Crump, Jonsson, Iversen, 69.77 secs.
9: Jonsson, Harris, Dryml, Laguta, 70.35 secs.
10: Crump, Lindgren, Gollob, Hancock, 69.40 secs.
11: Kasprzak, B.Pedersen, Iversen, Andersen, 70.03 secs.
12: N.Pedersen, Adams, Holta, Nicholls, 70.30 secs.
13: Andersen, Adams, Harris, Crump (fell, excluded), 69.31 secs.
14: Hancock, Dryml, Iversen (fell, excluded), Nicholls (fell, excluded), 70.07 secs.
15: Gollob, Jonsson, Kasprzak, Holta, 70.50 secs.
16: N.Pedersen, B.Pedersen, Lindgren, Laguta, 71.00 secs.
17: Harris, Holta, Lindgren, Iversen, 71.32 secs.
18: B.Pedersen, Hancock, Adams, Bogdanovs, Jonsson (excluded 2 minutes), 71.05 secs.
19: Crump, Nicholls, Kasprzak, Laguta, 70.35 secs,
20: Gollob, Dryml, Andersen, N.Pedersen, 70.71 secs.
Fastest time: 68.65 secs, Greg Hancock, Heat 1.
Referee: *Krister Gardell (Sweden).*

■ *Originally allocated referee **Marek Wojaczek** was dropped from the Grand Prix after his poor showing at Cardiff and replaced by Swede **Krister Gardell**.*

■ *All 18 riders (including the two reserves) on parade at the Lokomotiv Stadium had previous Grand Prix experience.*

■ ***Hans Andersen** made his 50th Grand Prix appearance but couldn't improve on his 14 top four finishes.*

2008 GRAND PRIX

ROUND 9: POLISH GRAND PRIX, SATURDAY, SEPTEMBER 13

HE'S been there, done that, and worn out a dozen or more t-shirts along the way.

But for everpresent Greg Hancock victory in the Polish Grand Prix will have a lasting place in his treasured memory bank.

It was his first round victory since Latvia on September 9, 2006, and ended a 20 round gold medal drought.

He'd been close – runner-up in Poland (twice), Italy, Great Britain (twice) and Sweden – so he knew he was still on the fastest pace but that win had been an elusive Holy Grail.

And when it did come it was a triumph masked in tragedy.

Greg remembered an old pal who couldn't be there to see him win his ninth Grand Prix.

The American veteran – at 38 the oldest rider in the series – dedicated his Polish GP victory to Brit Darren Boocock, a vital part of his pits crew.

Boocock, son of former Great Britain skipper Nigel Boocock, and his wife Sharon died in a road accident only nine weeks earlier.

Hancock, an everpresent in the GP series since it began in 1995 and the only rider to have ridden in all 109 rounds, had a special sticker on his pits wall since Booey's tragic death.

And as he climbed onto the rostrum after his latest win he told the packed Polonia Stadium in Bydgoszcz: "I want to dedicate this to my late friend Darren Boocock, Booey – that was for you!"

Herbie's win edged him closer to second place as Jason Crump slipped up and went out in the semi-final, leaving defending World Champion Nicki Pedersen, who was runner-up, to stretch his lead to a virtually insurmountable 28 points with only two rounds left.

Hancock said: "I'd known Booey for a long time and he and Sharon were close friends.

"I'll never forget him and I think about him a lot. I know how pleased he would have been for me to win a GP again.

"I've been struggling all year to get a win, things have been going wrong in finals and semi-finals, but I really wanted to get it right."

The brilliant Pedersen was happy to protect his second place in the Final, knowing it would extend the gap between him and his last remaining title rival.

He claimed: "I started feeling all the pressure now it's getting to the end of the season so it was a tremendous night.

"I haven't been looking at it as having one hand on the trophy but now I can – I said I wanted to finish off in the next round in Italy and now I can do it although anything can happen."

Great Britain skipper Scott Nicholls revived his hopes of a top eight finish – and a guaranteed spot in the 2009 series – with his second fourth place of the year.

He edged to within a point of the cut-off with two meetings – in Italy and Germany – to go.

But he still wasn't entirely satisfied, explaining: "I'm disappointed not to get on the rostrum but it's all going in the right direction and I'm pretty happy."

While Pedersen took the most points of any rider, Gollob undoubtedly had the most support and was so close to adding yet another Bydgoszcz victory to his CV.

In race after race he delighted his fans with surging moves from the back, showing total expertise of the circuit on his way to a 15-point maximum and a win in the semi final as well.

However, the Final was a different story as Gollob, having picked the inside starting position, missed the gate fractionally and was clamped by Pedersen.

As they disputed the lead, Hancock saw his chance to turn back on the inside, and Gollob lost further time in re-taking third place from Nicholls.

Pedersen was content to follow Hancock home and keep Gollob at bay, and Crump's score of only nine points left a fascinating duel for second place overall, Crump, Hancock and Gollob covered by a mere nine points.

Nicholls' fine showing included wins in both of his first two rides, and that helped him to move to within one point of the top eight.

The eighth position changed hands again, Rune Holta taking possession of the last automatic place in next year's series, even though he did not make the semi finals.

But the last word came from Hancock as he spoke for everyone else: "Nicki is almost like a machine but we'll keep trying to take points away from him.

"I'm going for everything I can, and we'll keep fighting all the way."

the VENUE

Track: *ZKS Polonia Stadium, ul. Sportowa 2, 85-091 Bydgoszcz, Poland.*
Telephone: *(0048) 525830030.*
Website: *www.speedway@polonia.bydgoszcz.pl*
Track Length: *348 metres.*
Track Record: *60.11 secs, Tomasz Gollob, June 20, 1999.*
First Grand Prix: *Friday, September 18, 1998.*
Grands Prix staged: *15.*

Roll of Honour

1995 .... Tomasz Gollob
1996 .... Tommy Knudsen
1997 .... Greg Hancock
1998 .... Tomasz Gollob
1999 (I) .... Tomasz Gollob
1999 (II) .... Hans Nielsen
2000 .... Tony Rickardsson
2001 .... Jason Crump
2002 .... Tomasz Gollob
2003 .... Tomasz Gollob
2004 .... Tomasz Gollob
2005 .... Tomasz Gollob
2006 .... Nicki Pedersen
2007 .... Tomasz Gollob
2008 .... Greg Hancock

■ *The Polish GP was staged at Wroclaw in 1995, 1996, 1997 and 1999. All other Polish GPs have been held at Bydgoszcz. In 1999 two Polish GPs were staged. Bydgoszcz also hosted the European GP in 2000.*

See Round 11 for re-arranged German Grand Prix.

Quote...unquote

JASON CRUMP

It wasn't the result we were looking for.

NICKI PEDERSEN

It's never over before the chequered flag but we're definitely getting there now.

SCOTT NICHOLLS

I was just over the moon to be in the Final, another two points on the board.

the RESULTS

Rider									
1 Greg HANCOCK	**2 2 1 3 2**	**10**	**2**	**6**	**18**
2 Nicki PEDERSEN	3 3 2 3 3	14	3	4	21
3 Tomasz GOLLOB	3 3 3 3 3	15	3	2	20
4 Scott NICHOLLS	3 3 1 1 0	8	2	0	10
5 Hans ANDERSEN	1 2 3 2 2	10	1		11
6 Jason CRUMP	3 1 2 0 3	9	0		9
7 Leigh ADAMS	1 3 2 1 2	9	0		9
8 ❖Wieslaw JAGUS	2 0 3 2 1	8	1		9
9 Andreas JONSSON	2 1 3 1 1	8			8
10 Rune HOLTA	0 1 0 2 3	6			6
11 Krzysztof KASPRZAK	0 R 1 3 2	6			6
12 Chris HARRIS	2 2 1 0 0	5			5
13 Niels-Kristian IVERSEN	0 2 0 1 1	4			4
14 Bjarne PEDERSEN	1 1 0 2 0	4			4
15 Lukas DRYML	0 0 2 0 1	3			3
16 Krzysztof BUCZKOWSKI [R]	*1*	*1*			*1*
17 Fredrik LINDGREN	E 0 0 R 0	0			0
18 Maciej JANOWSKI [R]					*did not ride*

Grand Final: Hancock, N.Pedersen, Gollob, Nicholls, 65.10 secs.
Semi Final: Gollob, Nicholls, Andersen, Adams, 65.97 secs.
Semi Final: N.Pedersen, Hancock, Jagus, Crump, 65.41 secs.
1: Nicholls, Jagus, Andersen, Iversen, 65.19 secs.
2: Crump, Harris, Buczkowski, Dryml, Lindgren (excluded, tapes), 64.87 secs.
3: N.Pedersen, Hancock, Adams, Kasprzak, 64.76 secs.
4: Gollob, Jonsson, B.Pedersen, Holta, 64.22 secs.
5: Gollob, Andersen, Crump, Kasprzak (r), 65.85 secs.
6: N.Pedersen, Harris, Jonsson, Jagus, 65.44 secs.
7: Adams, Iversen, B.Pedersen, Lindgren, 65.47 secs.
8: Nicholls, Hancock, Holta, Dryml, 65.00 secs.
9: Andersen, Adams, Harris, Holta, 66.99 secs.
10: Jagus, Crump, Hancock, B.Pedersen, 66.22 secs.
11: Jonsson, Dryml, Kasprzak, Iversen, 65.75 secs.
12: Hancock, N.Pedersen, Iversen (fell), Lindgren (excluded), 56.7 secs.
13: Hancock, Andersen, Jonsson, Lindgren (r), 64.59 secs.
14: Gollob, Jagus, Adams, Dryml, 64.85 secs.
15: N.Pedersen, Holta, Iversen, Crump, 64.57 secs.
16: Kasprzak, B.Pedersen, Nicholls, Harris, 64.94 secs.
17: N.Pedersen, Andersen, Dryml, B.Pedersen, 64.76 secs.
18: Holta, Kasprzak, Jagus, Lindgren, 64.38 secs.
19: Gollob, Hancock, Iversen, Harris, 64.24 secs,
20: Crump, Adams, Jonsson, Nicholls, 64.66 secs.
Fastest time: 64.22 secs, Tomasz Gollob, Heat 4.
Referee: *Istvan Darago (Hungary).*

■ *Leader* **Nicki Pedersen** *made his 75th Grand Prix appearance.*

■ *Winner* **Greg Hancock** *reached the Grand Final for the 44th occasion in 109 Grand Prix appearances.*

■ **Leigh Adams** *failed to smash his Polish Grand Prix jinx as he rmissed out on the Grand Final again in his 14th appearances. He's only ever finished in the top four once and has never figured on the rostrum.*

2008 GRAND PRIX

ROUND 10: ITALIAN GRAND PRIX, SATURDAY, SEPTEMBER 27

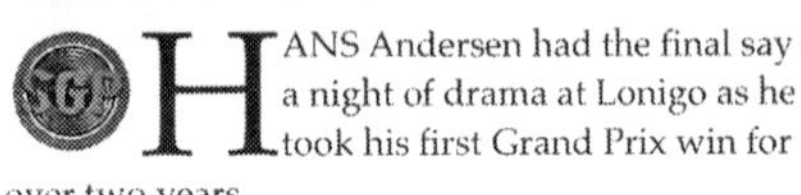

HANS Andersen had the final say on a night of drama at Lonigo as he took his first Grand Prix win for over two years.

There were tears of joy for the Danish star but you couldn't hide the hurt as Jason Crump fought back his tears to concede the world crown to rival Nicki Pedersen.

The Belle Vue star almost broke down when he saw his chances of a hat trick of titles end on a soul-destroying last bend in the Italian Grand Prix.

Crump went into the penultimate round a whopping 28 points behind defending champ Pedersen.

But he was on track to slash that margin by more than half as he led the Final after Pedersen had crashed out in the early stages.

But the Aussie ace slowed down dramatically within sight of the chequered flag and he couldn't believe it when Andersen and Bjarne Pedersen passed him.

Crump defied a suspected broken foot to carry on after a high-speed and controversial clash with the World Championship leader.

Battered and bruised, he slumped broken-hearted over his bike on the centre green as Andersen celebrated his first GP victory for two years.

And then he glumly admitted: "Twelve points was do-able – 16's not. It's all over, Nicki's lead could have been a lot less.

"I think we had an ignition problem."

Crump had been in sizzling form and sliced into Pedersen's big lead to set up a seemingly crunch showdown in the final round in Germany.

But that engine splutter cost him dearly to leave the hat trick in Pedersen's hands as he could afford to finish 15 points behind Crump in Gelsenkirchen and still keep his number one race-jacket.

But the Stevenage-based title-winner found little consolation in Crump's final demise – after crashing twice and failing to make the top four for the first time this season.

He grumbled: "It's a complete disaster for me."

The two title contenders had endured a painful evening, both finding themselves involved in two major talking points.

Pedersen was first to hit the deck, brought down on the second lap of Heat 2 by Fredrik Lindgren as the Swede became trapped between Pedersen and Andreas Jonsson as the three riders chased the same line.

With machine damage, Pedersen was limited to one point in the re-run and was then excluded from his next ride when he hit the fence on turn three after colliding with Crump's machine as his rival moved through on the inside.

That left Pedersen up against it, but Crump didn't emerge unscathed with a knock to his leg in the incident – not that it hampered his progress en route to 13 points as Pedersen eventually made his way to six, not enough to move on in the meeting.

There was more action in the first semi final when Crump and Tomasz Gollob contested the lead despite the pair being clear of Rune Holta and Leigh Adams.

Crump went down under Gollob's challenge, with the Polish rider being excluded and Adams also took a second opportunity to reach the Final.

The second semi saw Andersen and Bjarne Pedersen come through at the expense of Greg Hancock and Jonsson – and that turned out to be the one-two outcome in the Final after Crump's late setback.

Andersen said: "It's been a long time but we've been pushing hard .

"It's been a hard season, we changed to GMs halfway through and there have been other problems but the engines have been really good lately.

"My ambition from the beginning of the season was to get onto the rostrum and it seemed to have been slipping away.

"Today was a good one, it's still going to be mighty tough but I'll be there doing my best."

It was a familiar story for sorry Brits Scott Nicholls and Chris Harris in their twin attempt to reach 2009 safety.

Once again, an eight-point score was not automatically enough to qualify for the semi-finals.

Nicholls had particular cause to rue a first-race tapes exclusion, especially as the rest of his meeting included one of the rides of the season in Heat 7 when he breached Lukas Dryml's fierce defences.

The Lions' skipper missed out on the chance of climbing into the top eight but at least he had the chance of pressing his claims to a top eight finish.

Harris never even got to the starting line.

Doctors refused to let him ride after a practice crash left him nursing damaged ribs.

the VENUE

Track: *Santa Marina Stadium, Via San Marina, 65-36045 Lonigo (Vicenza), Italy.*
Telephone: *(0039) 444831884.*
Website:
Track Length: *334 metres.*
Track Record: *59.8 secs, Tony Rickaordsson, June 1, 1996.*
First Grand Prix: *Saturday, June 1, 1996.*
Grands Prix staged: *5.*

Roll of Honour
1996 ....Hans Nielsen
2005 ....Tony Rickardsson
2006 ....Jason Crump
2007 ....Nicki Pedersen
2008 ....Hans Andersen

■ *All Italian GPs have been held at Lonigo.*

Quote...unquote

SCOTT NICHOLLS

I am gutted. I was obviously up against it from that first race but it's done now. I don't regret it, these things happen.

TOMASZ GOLLOB

I really wanted to add a few points to get closer to Greg Hancock in third place. I am not giving up and will fight for the bronze medal.

BJARNE PEDERSEN

I had the luck today and it's a good feeling. Finally something turns my way. It's been a hard season.

CHRIS HARRIS

It's not very good. I tore the ligaments in my knee and pulled a muscle away from my ribs. It's a bit sore to breathe, I think it was the right decision from the doctors. I came out of the corner and it was almost as if I hit a bit of a rise and just took off.

the RESULTS

Rider									
1 Hans ANDERSEN	**3**	**2**	**3**	**2**	**2**	**12**	**3**	**6**	**21**
2 Bjarne PEDERSEN	3	0	2	3	3	11	2	4	17
3 Jason CRUMP	3	3	3	2	2	13	3	2	18
4 Leigh ADAMS	1	2	1	3	3	10	2	0	12
5 Rune HOLTA	2	3	2	1	1	9	1		10
6 Greg HANCOCK	1	3	1	3	0	8	1		9
7 Tomasz GOLLOB	2	2	1	1	3	9	X		9
8 Andreas JONSSON	2	0	3	3	1	9	0		9
9 Krzysztof KASPRZAK	2	1	2	0	3	8			8
10 Scott NICHOLLS	E	3	1	2	2	8			8
11 Nicki PEDERSEN	1	FX	3	0	2	6			6
12 Niels-Kristian IVERSEN	3	1	0	1	1	6			6
13 Fredrik LINDGREN	FX	1	2	2	0	5			5
14 Lukas DRYML	1	2	0	1	0	4			4
15 Mattia CARPANESE [R]	*0*	*1*	*0*	*0*	*1*	*2*			*2*
16 ❖Guglielmo FRANCHETTI	0	0	0	0	0	0			0
17 Alessandro MILANESE [R]	*0*					*0*			*0*
18 Chris HARRIS	*injured in practice, did not ride.*								

Grand Final: Andersen, Bjarne Pedersen, Crump, Adams, 66.71 secs.
Semi Final: Crump, Adams, Holta, Gollob (excluded), 66.28 secs.
Semi Final: Andersen, B.Pedersen, Hancock, Jonsson, 66.65 secs.
1: Iversen, Kasprzak, Hancock, Carpanese, 66.69 secs.
2: B.Pedersen, Jonsson, N.Pedersen, Lindgren (fell, excluded), 66.85 secs.
3: Crump, Gollob, Adams, Milanese, Nicholls (excluded, tapes), 66.28 secs.
4: Andersen, Holta, Dryml, Franchetti, 67.01 secs.
5: Holta, Adams, Iversen, B.Pedersen, 67.74 secs.
6: Hancock, Gollob, Lindgren, Franchetti, 68.20 secs.
7: Nicholls, Dryml, Kasprzak, Jonsson, 68.46 secs.
8: Crump, Andersen, Carpanese, N.Pedersen (fell, excluded), 67.60 secs.
9: Andersen, Lindgren, Nicholls, Iversen, 67.15 secs.
10: Crump, B.Pedersen, Hancock, Dryml, 66.70 secs.
11: N.Pedersen, Kasprzak, Adams, Franchetti, 66.97 secs.
12: Jonsson, Holta, Gollob, Carpanese, 66.97 secs.
13: Jonsson, Crump, Iversen, Franchetti, 69.77 secs.
14: Hancock, Nicholls, Holta, N.Pedersen, 68.94 secs.
15: B.Pedersen, Nicholls, Harris, N.Pedersen, 68.44 secs.
16: Adams, Lindgren, Dryml, Carpanese, 67.77 secs.
17: Gollob, N.Pedersen, Iversen, Dryml, 66.93 secs.
18: Adams, Andersen, Jonsson, Hancock, 66.63 secs.
19: Kasprzak, Crump, Holta, Lindgren, 67.13 secs,
20: B.Pedersen, Nicholls, Carpanese, Franchetti, 67.47 secs.
Fastest time: 66.28 secs, Jason Crump, Heat 3; Semi Final 2.
Referee: *Wojciech Grodzki (Poland).*

■ ***Scott Nicholls*** *set a new Grand Prix appearance record for a British rider when he rode in his 67th round – taking over from former World Champion* ***Mark Loram.***

■ ***Nicki Pedersen*** *missed out on the Final for the first time in 10 Grand Prix appearances – the all-time record.*

2008 GRAND PRIX

ROUND 11: GERMAN GRAND PRIX, SATURDAY, OCTOBER 11, CANCELLED.

THERE are bad days. There are horrible days. And there are days that you don't ever want to talk about again.

Saturday, October 11, 2008, will definitely fall into the latter category as far the history of the World Championship is concerned.

The introduction of the Grand Prix series was definitely a red-letter day for the sport – but there have been nights to forget.

Like the debacle at Gothenburg's Ullevi Stadium on August 23, 2003, when the Scandinavian GP had to be called off after only three races because of dangerous track conditions.

Everyone thought that would remain the all-time low point in the competition's history.

But not any more after the scheduled final round of 2008 had to be called off because of the weather even though it was being held indoors!

The VELTINS-Arena was lauded as a showpiece venue but the fans were stunned to hear the meeting had been cancelled a few hours before the electronic turnstiles were due to open.

The warning signs had already been there some 24 hours earlier when practice was called off because of serious problems with the temporary surface at the 60,000 capacity state-of-the-art home of German Bundesliga club Schalke.

A GP had been raced there, successfully, in 2007 and one of the major attractions of what should have been a dramatic finale to the 2008 series was the $200,000 Superprix Final.

Practice was re-arranged for ten o'clock on the Saturday morning but, once again, there were concerns about the track and after lengthy discussions it was formally announced that the meeting was being cancelled and would be re-staged a week later.

Not in Gelsenkirchen but instead across the Polish border at Bydgoszcz.

It was the first time a GP had ever been scrapped and re-run in a different country and there were deep red faces everywhere you looked.

An embarrassed GP Race Director Ole Olsen, who had been in charge of track preparation, told a shocked Press Conference: "There's nobody more disappointed than me.

"We've had very difficult conditions here, prior to the event taking place [sic] there's been heavy rain so

the dirt had absorbed a lot of moisture.

"We've had this before when we've built these one-off tracks, and we've had moisture in the dirt, which is what we need actually to put the track in properly, but the conditions at this stadium are obviously different in October and also the coldness of the stadium, and we just haven't been able to get the top surface as hard as we needed and as dry as we needed."

In other words – even though the meeting was being held in an indoor arena and the weather was fine outside the track was too wet for a meeting to go ahead.

Olsen continued: "We've tried everything, we've worked through the night, we've turned the whole thing over, we've aired it, we did everything we possibly could to make it right.

"Obviously we want to put on a race-track that the riders can go and have a go on.

"We know there's a risk in motor sport, and in speedway, but we don't want to extend that risk at all, so that's why we have decided what you've just heard.

"I can only apologise but we are working with natural material, so the risk is there."

Olsen and his team had transported nearly 4,000 tons of dirt to Gelsenkirchen and admitted that the first worrying signs had come a month earlier when it was realised the dirt was wetter than ideal.

But Olsen had encountered, and overcome, similar concerns at Denmark's PARKEN and had always managed to conquer any moisture hurdles.

He went on: "It had the same kind of moisture but not as heavy as this. And it dries better, it's in June, you have a lot of hot weather. The problem here was you came in every morning and it's quite cold and

what BSI Speedway said

"Following adverse weather conditions last week and during the construction of the track at VELTINS-Arena, Gelsenkirchen, Germany, the FIM Jury has decided it is necessary to postpone the 2008 FIM German Speedway Grand Prix due to track safety concerns. The event will now take place on 18 October 2008, at ZKS Polonia Stadium, Bydgoszcz, Poland, at 1900h.

All ticket holders will be refunded their ticket money and, as a gesture of goodwill, will be offered a free ticket to a BSI promoted Grand Prix of their choice in 2009.

In order to obtain their refund, ticket holders must contact the agency from where they purchased their ticket.

Paul Bellamy, Managing Director, BSI Speedway, commented: "We are very sorry for all the fans who have booked tickets and were looking forward to a great night of speedway. If there was any way we could have put this event on we would have, but the decision of the FIM Jury with regard to rider safety is paramount and we fully support this decision.

"We now need to focus on the event next weekend in Bydgoszcz and make sure the final Grand Prix of the season is a great event for everyone involved, in particular the fans."'

what the FIM said

"Following adverse weather conditions last week and during the construction of the track at VELTINS-Arena, Gelsenkirchen, Germany, the FIM Jury has decided it was not possible to run the 2008 FIM German Speedway Grand Prix due to track safety concerns.

The adverse weather conditions prior to the event affected the moisture levels in the dirt used in the build-up of the track, and together with the very cold conditions in the stadium the track was unable to dry out sufficiently in order to have a suitable race track.

The event will be postponed, taking place on 18 October 2008, at ZKS Polonia Stadium, Bydgoszcz, Poland, at 1900h.'

the VENUE

Track: *VELTINS-Arena, Ernst-Kuzorra-Weg 1, 45891 Gelsenkirchen, Germany.*
Telephone: *(0049) 1805/150810*
Website: *www.veltins-arena.de*
Track Length: *283 metres.*
Track Record: *56.90 secs, Greg Hancock & Andreas Jonsson, October 13, 2007.*
First Grand Prix: *Saturday, October 13, 2007.*
Grands Prix staged: *1.*

Roll of Honour

1995 ....Tommy Knudsen
1996 ....Hans Nielsen
1997 ....Hans Nielsen
1998 ....Tony Rickardsson
2001 ....Tomasz Gollob
2007 ....Andreas Jonsson

■German GPs were held at Pocking (1996, 1998), Abensberg (1995), Landshut (1997), the Ludwig Jahn Stadium in Berlin (2001) and at the VELTINS-Arena (2007).

the moisture is still in the air, so there's no dryness, and there's no wind inside at all."

Olsen claimed they had looked at getting drying machines in but their weight would have seen them sink right down to the stadium concrete floor, wrecking any chances of improving conditions.

He added: "Believe me, we tried everything possible. Why go to a stadium as fantastic as here and not do your utmost and look at every possible angle?

"We have done that, we can't do more than that."

With disappointing ticket sales – around 11,500 compared with nearly 20,000 in 1997 – there were some cynics who believed it had been a financial decision to cancel.

But that was without taking into account the money it cost for the organisers to pull out.

Not only did they still have to find rent and all other expenses but they refunded ticket monies and as a further goodwill gesture offered a free ticket to anyone wanting to attend a BSI promoted round of their choice in 2009.

The VELTINS-Arena was only in the second season of a three-year contract but it now seems unlikely they will ever return as there is no German GP on the 2009 calendar.

Rob Armstrong, IMG's Senior Vice President, Motorsports, slammed any fears about the future of indoor venues.

He said: "We've got a deal with Cardiff until 2012, a five year deal with PARKEN and we don't envisage any problems with those stadiums.

"We've had successful events there before, and we'll have successful events there in the future."

Jorgen Jensen, President of the FIM Jury, said: "This was one of the toughest decisions I've ever had to take.

"But considering the safety of the riders and the importance of the meeting, the Jury felt the only decision we could take was to cancel the meeting."

It certainly was the only decision....

2008 GRAND PRIX

ROUND 11: THE FINAL GRAND PRIX, SATURDAY, OCTOBER 18

AFTER the debacle that was Gelsenkirchen, normal service was resumed.

That meant a captivating end to the title chase and the sight of a delirious Nicki Pedersen lovingly clutching the silver trophy that confirmed him as the 2008 World Champion.

He had to put the victory champagne on ice for a week but it tasted as sweet as ever as he toasted his back-up team.

And, in particular, personal trainer Lisa Thorney who had guided him through a campaign in which he'd been beset by painful setbacks through both ill health and injury.

He paid tribute to her expertise: "I don't respect that many people but she is one of them.

"Without the energy and focus she has, I wouldn't have been in the shape and condition I'm in."

Pedersen had discovered that a finely tuned athlete has an edge over rivals who merely pay lip service to fitness.

And his regime has been rewarded with back-to-back world titles.

While there was that delay to his official coronation he didn't have to wait too long to know he was mathematically certain to be receiving that FIM gold medal again.

It took just seven heats at Bydgoszcz, swiftly brought on stream to stage the cancelled German round.

By then Nicki had six points in the bank to take his season's total to the magical 167 – with Jason Crump, the only man capable of derailing his bid, restricted to a maximum of 166 even if he won his last five rides, including both the semi and Grand Final.

It put Pedersen on level terms with two of his country's greatest-ever riders – Ole Olsen and Erik Gundersen – in terms of World Championships won and one of only nine to have successfully defended the coveted crown.

He confessed: "I hardly understand it yet. All my focus in the last three weeks has been on this last GP, and I really thought that Jason could put the pressure on me, and then after only two heats I'm the champ - that's just crazy.

"I'm so relieved and so grateful. This is what I live for."

Crump sealed second place even though Tomasz Gollob won his third GP of the season and the Pole again proved he is the true Master of Bydgsozcz.

He stopped in his opening ride but then reeled off six successive wins to again feature on the rostrum and end Hans Andersen's dream of his first individual medal.

In reality, the Dane's chances of third place disappeared once the final round was re-allocated to Gollob's birthplace.

He couldn't even overcome Greg Hancock's six point lead going into the meeting and had to be content with fifth place while Leigh Adams, Andreas Jonsson and Rune Holta sealed their places in the top eight, guaranteeing they would be back for more of the same in 2009.

It left Scott Nicholls, Fredrik Lindgren, Bjarne Pedersen, Niels-Kristian Iversen, Chris Harris, Krzysztof Kasprzak and Lukas Dryml all sweating on the wild card nomination – some were going to be happy others miserable when the final decision was made.

As it turned out only Nicholls, Lindgren and Harris got back in with the fourth permanent pick going to Russia's two-time World Under 21 Champion Emil Sajfutdinov.

2008 Superprix

The Superprix was to be contested by the individual winners of theSwedish, Danish, British and German Grands Prix.

After the German GP was abandoned the winner of the Final GP would fill the fourth slot but with Tomasz Gollob already qualifed as winner of the Danish round the fourth place went to the highest-finishing non-qualifier – in this instance World Champion Nicki Pedersen.

The purse on offer for the Superprix Final, which was the last race of the season, was a total of $200,000 (approximately £130,000) with the winner taking $120,000, second placed rider $40,000, third $25,000 and fourth $15,000.

Result:

1 Tomasz GOLLOB
2 Jason CRUMP
3 Rune HOLTA
4 Nicki PEDERSEN (E)
Time: 63.98 seconds.

the VENUE

Track: ZKS Polonia Stadium, ul. Sportowa 2, 85-091 Bydgoszcz, Poland.
Telephone: (0048) 525830030.
Website: www.speedway@polonia.bydgoszcz.pl
Track Length: 348 metres.
Track Record: 60.11 secs, Tomasz Gollob, June 20, 1999.
First Grand Prix: Friday, September 18, 1998.
Grands Prix staged: 16.

See Round 9 for full details of Bydgoszcz as a GP venue.

Quote...unquote

PAUL BELLAMY, managing director of BSI Speedway on the four 2009 wild cards

Russia's Emil Sajfutdinov is one of the sport's hottest prospects at the moment and will be an exciting addition to the Series.

At 19-years-old he will be the youngest permanent rider in the 2009 Series and already has an unprecedented two World Under-21 titles under his belt that underlines his flair and aptitude for the sport.

Sweden's Fredrik Lindgren, who at 23 was the youngest rider in this year's Series, has shown great maturity and ability in his first season as a Grand Prix rider and is also widely recognised across Europe as one of the sport's rising stars.

This year Scott Nicholls made two finals and only just finished outside the top eight.

His performances have shown he still has the commitment and drive to be World Champion.

Chris Harris knows he needs to prove he is world class next year following a disappointing 2008 campaign but we all know that he has the ability to be a great rider.

the RESULTS

Rider									
1 Tomasz GOLLOB	**R**	**3**	**3**	**3**	**3**	**12**	**3**	**6**	**21**
2 Hans ANDERSEN	2	2	2	3	1	10	3	4	17
3 Greg HANCOCK	2	3	0	3	3	11	2	2	15
4 Leigh ADAMS	3	3	3	2	2	13	2	0	15
5 Nicki PEDERSEN	3	3	1	2	3	12	1		13
6 Andreas JONSSON	3	1	3	3	2	12	X		12
7 Fredrik LINDGREN	2	1	2	1	2	8	1		9
8 Lukas DRYML	2	0	2	1	3	8	0		8
9 Jason CRUMP	3	0	2	1	1	7			7
10 Rune HOLTA	1	2	E	2	2	7			7
11 Scott NICHOLLS	1	2	1	2	1	7			7
12 Krzysztof KASPRZAK	0	2	1	1	1	5			5
13 Chris HARRIS	1	0	3	0	0	4			4
14 Bjarne PEDERSEN	1	1	1	0	0	3			3
15 Maciej JANOWSKI [R]	*0*	*1*	*0*	*0*	*0*	*1*			*1*
16 ❖Martin SMOLINSKI	0	0	0	0	0	0			0
17 Grzegorz ZENGOTA (R)	*0*					*0*			*0*
18 Niels-KRISTIAN IVERSEN						*injured, did not ride*			

Grand Final: Gollob, Andersen, Hancock, Adams, 64.00 secs.
Semi Final: Andersen, Adams, N.Pedersen, Dryml, 64.27 secs.
Semi Final: Gollob, Hancock, Lindgren, Jonsson (X), 64.25 secs.
1: Adams, Lindgren, Holta, Gollob (R), 60.44 secs.
2: N.Pedersen, Andersen, Nicholls, Kasprzak, 61.22 secs.
3: Crump, Dryml, Harris, Smolinski, 61.66 secs.
4: Jonsson, Hancock, B.Pedersen, Janowski, 61.69 secs.
5: Hancock, Andersen, Lindgren, Crump, 61.91 secs.
6: Adams, Nicholls, Jonsson, Dryml, 62.22 secs.
7: N.Pedersen, Holta, B.Pedersen, Harris, 62.25 secs.
8: Gollob, Kasprzak, Janowski, Smolinski, 62.82 secs.
9: Harris, Lindgren, Nicholls, Janowski, 63.91 secs.
10: Adams, Andersen, B.Pedersen, Smolinski, 62.68 secs.
11: Jonsson, Crump, Kasprzak, Zengota, Holta (E), 62.78 secs.
12: Gollob, Dryml, N.Pedersen, Hancock, 63.62 secs.
13: Jonsson, N.Pedersen, Lindgren, Smolinski, 62.88 secs.
14: Hancock, Adams, Kasprzak, Harris, 63.12 secs.
15: Andersen, Holta, Dryml, Janowski, 63.75 secs.
16: Gollob, Nicholls, Crump, B.Pedersen, 63.48 secs.
17: Dryml, Lindgren, Kasprzak, B.Pedersen, 64.44 secs.
18: N.Pedersen, Adams, Crump, Janowski, 63.79 secs.
19: Hancock, Holta, Nicholls, Smolinski, 63.88 secs,
20: Andersen, Harris, Kasprzak, Iversen (excluded) 57.5secs.
Fastest time: 60.44 secs, Leigh Adams, Heat 1.
Referee: *Tony Steele (Great Britain).*

■ *Niels-Kristian Iversen attended the Grand Prix but did not ride because of a dislocated shoulder. His place was taken by round reserve Maciej Janowski.*
■ *When he took his opening ride in Heat 4, Poland's Maciej Janowski became the youngest-ever Grand Prix competitor. He was 17 years, 68 days-old, beating the previous record held by the Czech Republic's Matej Kus (18 years, 17 days).*
■ *Three riders made their Grand Prix debuts – wild card Martin Smolinski and reserves Maciej Janowski and Grzegorz Zengota.*

WORLD CHAMPIONS

In the three pre-War World Finals (1936-1938) riders were awarded bonus points on their ranking based on the points they scored in five earlier rounds.

Bonus points and points scored on the night were added together to give an overall score which determined final placings.

The 1939 World Final was cancelled because of the declaration of war and was not reinstated until 1949.

Roll of Honour

1936 ....Lionel VAN PRAAG (Australia)
1937 ....Jack MILNE (United States of America)
1938 ....Arthur 'Bluey' WILKINSON (Australia)
1939-48....................Not staged
1949 ....Tommy PRICE (England)
1950 ....Freddie WILLIAMS (Wales)
1951 ....Jack YOUNG (Australia)
1952 ....Jack YOUNG (Australia)
1953 ....Freddie WILLIAMS (Wales)
1954 ....Ronnie MOORE (New Zealand)
1955 ....Peter CRAVEN (England)
1956 ....Ove FUNDIN (Sweden)
1957 ....Barry BRIGGS (New Zealand)
1958 ....Barry BRIGGS (New Zealand)
1959 ....Ronnie MOORE (New Zealand)
1960 ....Ove FUNDIN (Sweden)
1961 ....Ove FUNDIN (Sweden)
1962 ....Peter CRAVEN (England)
1963 ....Ove FUNDIN (Sweden)
1964 ....Barry BRIGGS (New Zealand)
1965 ....Björn KNUTSSON (Sweden)
1966 ....Barry BRIGGS (New Zealand)
1967 ....Ove FUNDIN (Sweden)
1968 ....Ivan MAUGER (New Zealand)
1969 ....Ivan MAUGER (New Zealand)
1970 ....Ivan MAUGER (New Zealand)
1971 ....Ole OLSEN (Denmark)
1972 ....Ivan MAUGER (New Zealand)
1973 ....Jerzy SZCZAKIEL (Poland)
1974 ....Anders MICHANEK (Sweden)
1975 ....Ole OLSEN (Denmark)
1976 ....Peter COLLINS (England)
1977 ....Ivan MAUGER (New Zealand)
1978 ....Ole OLSEN (Denmark)
1979 ....Ivan MAUGER (New Zealand)
1980 ....Michael LEE (England)
1981 ....Bruce PENHALL (United States of America)
1982 ....Bruce PENHALL (United States of Ameirca)
1983 ....Egon MÜLLER (Germany)
1984 ....Erik GUNDERSEN (Denmark)
1985 ....Erik GUNDERSEN (Denmark)
1986 ....Hans NIELSEN (Denmark)
1987 ....Hans NIELSEN (Denmark)
1988 ....Erik GUNDERSEN (Denmark)
1989 ....Hans NIELSEN (Denmark)
1990 ....Per JONSSON (Sweden)
1991 ....Jan O. PEDERSEN (Denmark)
1992 ....Gary HAVELOCK (England)
1993 ....Sam ERMOLENKO (United States of America)
1994 ....Tony RICKARDSSON (Sweden)

In 1995 the FIM introduced a Grand Prix system to decide the World Champion. Until then (with the exception of a two-day World Final at Amsterdam, Holland, in 1987) the title had always been decided by a one-off meeting.

1995 ....Hans NIELSEN (Denmark)
1996 ....Billy HAMILL (United States of America)
1997 ....Greg HANCOCK (United States of America)
1998 ....Tony RICKARDSSON (Sweden)
1999 ....Tony RICKARDSSON (Sweden)
2000 ....Mark LORAM (England)
2001 ....Tony RICKARDSSON (Sweden)
2002 ....Tony RICKARDSSON (Sweden)
2003 ....Nicki PEDERSEN (Denmark)
2004 ....Jason CRUMP (Australia)
2005 ....Tony RICKARDSSON (Sweden)
2006 ....Jason CRUMP (Australia)
2007 ....Nicki PEDERSEN (Denmark)
2008 ....Nicki PEDERSEN (Denmark)

2009 Venues and Riders

Round 1
CZECH REPUBLIC, Prague, Saturday, April 25.
Round 2
POLAND, Leszno, Saturday, May 9.
Round 3
SWEDEN, Gothenburg, Saturday, May 30.
Round 4
DENMARK, Copenhagen, Saturday, June 13.
Round 5
GREAT BRITAIN, Cardiff, Saturday, June 27
Round 6
LATVIA, Daugavpils, Saturday, August 1.
Round 7
SWEDEN, Målilla, Saturday, August 15
Round 8
DENMARK, Vojens, Saturday, August 29.
Round 9
SLOVENIA, Krsko, Saturday, September 12
Round 10
ITALY, Terenzano, Saturday, September 26
Round 11
POLAND, Bydgoszcz, Saturday, October 17.

1 Nicki PEDERSEN (Denmark)
2 Jason CRUMP (Australia)
3 Tomasz GOLLOB (Poland)
4 Greg HANCOCK (United States of America)
5 Hans ANDERSEN (Denmark)
6 Leigh ADAMS (Australia)
7 Andreas JONSSON (Sweden)
8 Rune HOLTA (Norway/Poland)
9 Scott NICHOLLS (England)
10 Fredrik LINDGREN (Sweden)
11 Chris HARRIS (England)
12 Kenneth BJERRE (Denmark)
13 Grzegorz WALASEK (Poland)
14 Sebastian ULAMEK (Poland)
15 Emil SAJFUTDINOV (Russia)
16 Wild card per meeting
Qualified reserves: Niels-Kristian **IVERSEN** (Denmark), Tomasz **JEDRZEJAK** (Poland), Ryan **SULLIVAN** (Australia), Jesper B. **MONBERG** (Denmark), Adrian **MIEDZINSKI** (Poland), Jurica **PAVLIC** (Croatia).

SPEEDWAY WORLD CUP

THE chorus of Red and White Dynamite rang around the Vojens Speedway Center again, reviving memories of the days when Denmark ruled the speedway world.

Once again the Danes were World Champions – as the competition returned to the track that their greatest ever ambassador Ole Olsen built in the wake of his determined individual successes.

Vojens hadn't hosted a World Cup Final since 2003 – and the home fans hadn't seen their own go on the victory parade since way back in 1991 when Jan O. Pedersen, Hans Nielsen, Tommy Knudsen, Gert Handberg and Brian Karger were feted as conquering home grown heroes.

Denmark had won their 15th gold medal at Reading, England, in 2006 and set about regaining the championship with a magnificent display of skill and team spirit.

They had all the pressure of being the favourites to win and there was even talk of them finishing as political runners-up in their opening round at Coventry to ensure they would be the main attractions at the Race off.

If that was the plan then it came spectacularly off the rails as they totally dominated at Brandon, filling first or second place in 24 of the 25 races.

Only their skipper Hans Andersen finished pointless throughout a night that was as glorious for the Danes as it was inglorious for a humiliated Great Britain squad, seeking a first World Cup victory since 1989.

In those intervening years, Australia, Denmark, Poland, Sweden and the United States of America have all been multiple winners.

But for GB, nothing but the consolation of silver medals in 1990, 1995, 2000 and 2004.

It has been scant pickings for a nation that was so, so dominant in the seventies and led, directly, to the sacking of team manager Jim Lynch after only one summer in charge.

It is now left to Rob Lyon – a surprise choice as successor over the far more vocal favourite Alun Rossiter – to try and end that barren spell although there are precious few signs that a gold medal is within reach.

At one stage Poland had a four point cushion after Tomasz Gollob was first over the line in Heat 17.

But that margin was immediatley slashed when Kenneth Bjerre won the following race and Grzegorz Walasek trailed in at the back.

Heat 19 saw the Poles inch a further point ahead but when Hans Andersen was first, and Rune Holta last, in Heat 20 the writing was on the pits wall.

After that Denmark weren't going to be caught and not even a bold tactical ride by Gollob in the penultimate heat could keep them in the race any more.

Sweden had made it a three-nation race for much of the Final but the hugely-fancied Australians were a collective big night disappointment.

It would be too harsh to say they flopped under the pressure because they might still have figured in the shake-up had Jason Crump not been forced to pull out after hurting his wrist in a Heat 3 pile-up.

Intermittent rain showers made conditions tricky but there's little doubt that Denmark deserved their overall success as they wrested the Ove Fundin Trophy from the holders Poland who have never been over happy at Vojens.

2009 Competition

QUALIFYING

Round 1

Terenzano, Italy, Saturday, May 2

ITALY v GERMANY v SLOVENIA v HUNGARY

Round 2

Daugavpils, Latvia, Saturday, May 2

CZECH REPUBLIC v FINLAND v LATVIA v UNITED STATES OF AMERICA

FINALS

Event 1

Vojens, Denmark, Saturday, July 11

DENMARK v SWEDEN v RUSSIA v Winners, qualifying Round 2

Event 2

Peterborough, England, Monday, July 13

GREAT BRITAIN v AUSTRALIA v POLAND v Winners, qualifying Round 1

Race Off

Leszno, Poland, Thursday, July 16

Second and third placed teams, Events 1 and 2.

FINAL

Poland, Leszno, Saturday, July 18

Winners Events 1, 2 and Race off, runners-up Race off.

SPEEDWAY WORLD CUP

EVENT 1: LESZNO, POLAND, SATURDAY, JULY 12

Qualifying Rounds

Round 1
Miskolc, Hungary, Sunday, May 25
1 HUNGARY 51+3 (Matej Ferjan 13+3, Norbert Magosi 12, Laszlo Szatmari 11, Jozsef Tabaka 7, Sandor Tihanyi 8), **2 GERMANY 51+2** (Martin Smolinski 12, Richard Speiser 7, Tobias Kroner 12+2, Kevin Wölbert 8, Christian Hefenbrock 12), **3 LATVIA 36** (Andrej Korolev, did not ride, Kjastas Puodzhuks 10, Evgeny Petukochov 5, Vyatcheslav Gerutsky 9, Leonids Paura 12), **4 UNITED STATES OF AMERICA 12** (Billy Janniro 2, Ryan Fisher 6, Shaun Harmatiuk 0, Kenny Ingalls 3, Tommy Hedden 1).

Round 2
Ljubljana, Slovenia, Sunday, June 29
1 CZECH REPUBLIC 59 (Matej Kus 12, Ales Dryml 13, Adrian Rymel 10, Lukas Dryml 13, Lubos Tomicek 11), **2 FINLAND 40** (Tomi Reima 6, Juha Hautamäki 8, Kauko Nieminen 12, Tero Aarnio 4, Kaj Laukkanen 10), **3 SLOVENIA 35** (Denis Stojs 0, Izak Santej 9, Matej Zagar 15, Maks Gregoric 10, Ales Kraljic 1), **4 ITALY 16** (Mattia Carpanese 3, Alessandro Milanese 4, Daniele Tessari 0, Marco Gregnanin 4, Andreas Maida 5).

NOT everything always goes according to the pre-ordained script – and that was certainly the case in the opening round of the 2008 Speedway World Cup.

Hungary – who joined the Czech Republic in the Finals after winning their qualifying round – weren't expected to get the better of an ever-improving German side despite their home track advantage.

And Poland were certainly the favourites to become the first nation to book their place in the World Cup Final.

Instead it was Australia who automatically went through after defeating the hosts in a run-off at the end of a thrilling tournament opener at Leszno.

The meeting's two outstanding riders – Leigh Adams and Jaroslaw Hampel – clashed after both sides had finished on 56 points and it was Adams, who had previously dropped his only point to maximum man Hampel, who emerged on top.

Hampel, after five straight wins, made the start from the inside but Adams cut back on the second bend and raced clear to leave Poland heading for Thursday's Race off.

They were joined by Russia, who put in a thoroughly entertaining showing highlighted by the performance of fast-rising star Emil Sajfutdinov, indicating that they are a nation who will only improve over the coming years.

The expected battle for top honours between Poland and Australia started with Australia in terrific form as they took 13 of the first 15 points available with Poland left on 10.

However, the consistency of Hampel, Rune Holta and Tomasz Gollob saw Poland take control during the middle stages of the meeting, leaving Australian boss Craig Boyce contemplating his tactical options.

When he did make his move in Heat 19, it turned out to be perfectly timed because not only did Adams bank a full six-pointer, but Wieslaw Jagus broke down on the first lap so their lead was wiped out in the space of one race.

Australians then won the next three races courtesy of Chris Holder, Jason Crump and Adams, and they received a bonus when Hungarian Joker rider Matej Ferjan held on to second place ahead of Jagus in Heat 21.

It left Poland with a four point gap to make up, and the final races provided more dramatic action as Sajfutdinov totally eclipsed the battle between the big two by winning Heat 23 for six points, Holta keeping the Poles in contention by taking second ahead of Ryan Sullivan.

Then Gollob showed remarkable awareness to maintain first place in Heat 24 while also ensuring that Grigory Laguta came home ahead of Davey Watt, to give Hampel a chance of completing a late comeback.

Hampel duly won Heat 25 but Holder limited the damage by going between Ferjan and Daniil Ivanov coming out of turn two, leaving Australia and Poland all-square – and it was the Aussie skipper who had the final word in the run-off.

Russia were mightily handicapped by the absence of another of their bright young things – Grigori Laguta's younger brother Artem.

He was denied entry to Poland at the last moment and their team boss Andrey Sawin claimed: "It was unfortunate that Artem had problems with his visa, had he ridden we might have got more points."

Adams said: "We'll take the week's rest ahead of the Final."

And Poland's Marek Cieslak added: "We lost to Australia by one point in the Race off last year and went on to win it – let us hope history can be repeated this time."

the VENUE

Track: *Alfred Smoczyk Stadium, Strzelecka 7, 64-100 Leszno, Poland.*
Telephone: *(0048) 655299977.*
Website: *www.unia.leszno.pl*
Track Length: *330 metres.*
Track Record: *58.4 secs, Krzysztof Kasprzak, May 3, 2007.*
Major meetings staged: *Polish GP (2008), World Cup Final (1984 and 2007), World Pairs Final (1989).*

Quote...unquote

LEIGH ADAMS (Australia)

We're expecting a lot from some pretty inexperienced guys and it was a tough meeting, as the Poles are renowned to be very good on their home turf.
Everyone rode their socks off, we had a great atmosphere.
We're delighted, all the boys put such an effort in and rose to the occasion.
We were here to come away with the win, and we'll take the week's rest ahead of the Final.

ROMAN POVAZHNY (Russia)

It was a good effort and we're happy with it. There was some good racing and we had a couple of very good heat wins.
[Denis] Gizatullin won a race well and Emil [Sajfutdinov] was our best rider on the night.
I don't know how we'll do on Thursday, but we'll try to score some good points and I think we'll be alright.

RUNE HOLTA (Poland)

The Australians came really good in the end, they had the advantage with the joker and Leigh [Adams] did the job to cash six points. But we're quite happy with the meeting. Most of the guys were going well by the end, and now we have to go to Denmark and start working again on a different track and in different conditions.
We're looking forward to Thursday. For us it might be an advantage – it's a smaller track and different to the ones in Poland so in one way it will be good for us.
We want to qualify for the Final and do a good Final as well, and I think this might give us a better chance.

the RESULTS

1 AUSTRALIA 56+3			
Jason CRUMP	3 1 2 2 3	11	
Leigh ADAMS	3 2 3 3 6^ 3	20	3
Ryan SULLIVAN	2 3 1 1 1	8	
Davey WATT	2 3 0 1	6	
Chris HOLDER	3 2 1 3 2	11	
2 POLAND 56+2			
Krzysztof KASPRZAK	1 2 3 2 2	10	
Rune HOLTA	2 3 3 3 2	13	
Tomasz GOLLOB	3 3 2 1 3	12	
Jaroslaw HAMPEL	3 3 3 3 3	15	2
Wieslaw JAGUS	1 2 2 R 1	6	
3 RUSSIA 36			
Denis GIZATULLIN	0 1 3 2 1	7	
Grigori LAGUTA	1 1 1 2	5	
Daniil IVANOV	1 1 1 1 1	5	
Renat GAFUROV	1 1 2 0 1 0	5	
Emil SAJFUTDINOV	2 2 2 2 6^	14	
4 HUNGARY 10			
Matej FERJAN	2 0 1 2 4^ R	9	
Sandor TIHANYI	E 0 0 0	0	
Jozsef TABAKA	0 0 0 1 0 0	1	
Norbert MAGOSI	0 0 0 0 0	0	
Laszlo SZATMARI	0 R 0 R	0	

Australia qualify for the Final; Poland and Russia go through to the Race off.

1: Crump, Ferjan, Kasprzak, Gizatullin, 61.10 secs.
2: Adams, Holta, Laguta, Tihanyi (E), 59.77 secs.
3: Gollob, Sullivan, Ivanov, Tabaka, 61.40 secs.
4: Hampel, Watt, Gafurov, Magosi 61.44 secs.
5: Holder, Sajfutdinov, Jagus, Szatmari, 61.63 secs.
6: Gollob, Sajfutdinov, Crump, Magosi, 60.75 secs.
7: Hampel, Adams, Gizatullin, Szatmari (R), 61.08 secs.
8: Sullivan, Jagus, Laguta, Ferjan, 61.52 secs.
9: Watt, Kasprzak, Ivanov, Tihanyi, 62.03 secs.
10: Holta, Holder, Gafurov, Tabaka, 62.15 secs.
11: Hampel, Crump, Laguta, Tabaka, 61.51 secs.
12: Adams, Jagus, Ivanov, Magosi, 61.80 secs.
13: Kasprzak, Gafurov, Sullivan, Szatmari, 62.64 secs.
14: Holta, Sajfutdinov, Ferjan, Watt, 62.43 secs.
15: Gizatullin, Gollob, Holder, Tihanyi, 62.51 secs.
16: Holta, Crump, Ivanov, Szatmari (R), 61.70 secs.
17: Adams, Ferjan, Gollob, Gafurov, 61.68 secs.
18: Hampel, Sajfutdinov, Sullivan, Tihanyi, 62.20 secs.
19: Adams (J), Gizatullin, Tabaka, Jagus (R), 62.16 secs,
20: Holder, Kasprzak, Gafurov, Magosi, 62.98 secs.
21: Crump, Ferjan (J), Jagus, Gafurov, 62.37 secs.
22: Adams, Kasprzak, Gizatullin, Tabaka, 62.23 secs.
23: Sajfutdinov (J), Holta, Sullivan, Magosi, 63.48 secs.
24: Gollob, Laguta, Watt, Tabaka, 63.44 secs.
25: Hampel, Holder, Ivanov, Ferjan (R), 62.94 secs.
Run-off: Adams, Hampel.
Fastest time: 59.77 secs, Leigh Adams, Heat 2.
Referee: *Krister Gardell (Sweden).*

SPEEDWAY WORLD CUP

EVENT 2: COVENTRY, ENGLAND, MONDAY, JULY 14

OVER the years every country has had a World Cup nightmare – but this probably ranks as Great Britain's nadir.

It leapt into the record books alongside that depressing performance in the 1986 World Pairs Final in Germany that spawned the unforgettable *Speedway Star* headline: Pocking Hell!

This time the banners weren't quite as lurid but the trade magazine pulled no punches in a strident verdict on what quickly became labelled the Brandon Debacle.

We can do no better than quote the opening half dozen paragraphs or so of their report:

'Thirteen excruciating heats gone, staring down the business end of twin barrels labelled exit and abject failure. It's life Jim, but not as you planned it.

'Instead, new Great Britain team boss Jim Lynch's first day in the office was as humiliating as they come.

'A hand stacked with a fistful of Brandon know-how simply added up to no advantage whatsoever to write home about.

'In fact it came perilously close to absolutely zilch to write home about.

'When six of those painful races have gone, you've played your joker and mustered a grand total of seven points, including a big fat zero on your double-bluff, who you gonna call?

'Ghostbusters? The Samaritans?

'Jim Lynch probably felt like the loneliest man on planet speedway at that point.

'Yep, as bad nights go, this one was right up there.'

One disgruntled fan, admittedly worse the wear for a pint or ten, summed up the feeling around the place when he leaned over the pit wall and yelled abuse at several of the riders.

His language was unforgiveable: but his sentiments were probably felt by 99% of the big Brandon crowd.

And certainly by the five GB riders and their new supremo.

Denmark and Sweden battled it out for top spot and an automatic route into the Final while the Brits were locked in a tense fight with unfancied Czech Republic to grab a possible escape route via Thursday's Race off.

Skipper Scott Nicholls had his worst-ever World Cup back at his old home track and even when he was named for double points finished last.

Then he was thrown out of his next race after being blamed for Swede Peter Ljung's crash.

Home fans had to wait until the 17th race to cheer a first British race win but by then the Scandinavians were out of sight.

Coventry skipper Chris Harris broke the duck and then figured in the first-ever World Cup dead heat as Britain staged a late rally.

Harris said: "The only consolation we have is that we are still in with a chance – but we've got to do much, much better on Thursday."

Lynch didn't try to disguise his feelings: "It was a dreadful performance to be honest, and we had to recover in the races after Heat 15 just to see off the Czech Republic – and we should never have been in that position.

"I don't really think that anybody rode particularly well, so we have to get our heads together over the next couple of days.

"We've got a couple of new riders coming in on Thursday night, and we've got to be positive and go to Denmark and try our hardest – but it's very difficult to get up and enthusiastic when we've performed like that on a track which belongs to us.

"The lads know how to ride

Nicki Pedersen sets the pattern in Heat 1

the VENUE

Track: *Coventry Stadium, Rugby Road, Brandon, Nr. Coventry, CV8 3GJ, England.*
Telephone: *(0044) [0]247 6542395.*
Website: *www.coventrymotorspeedway.com*
Track Length: *301 metres.*
Track Record: *57.8 secs, Chris Harris. May 30, 2008.*
Major meetings staged: *British Grand Prix (1998, 1999 and 2000), World Under 21 Final (1991), World Cup Final (1987, 1993, 2000, 2007).*

it but it's one of those nights and we've got to put it behind us."

All five Danish riders were in double figures, and the last place suffered by captain Hans Andersen in Heat 7 was the only time one of their team finished outside the top two in any of the 25 races.

World Champion Nicki Pedersen and a very impressive Kenneth Bjerre both dropped just one point, although the Danes did have to fight off a strong mid-meeting challenge from Sweden.

The meeting looked set to be all one-way traffic when Denmark scored 14 points from the first 15 available, but a well-timed Swedish joker saw Jonas Davidsson take a maximum six points in Heat 10.

The Swedes chipped away and consecutive race wins for Andreas Jonsson, Davidsson and Daniel Nermark in Heats 12, 13 and 14 brought them level.

But the Danes steadied the ship, winning five of the next six races as Sweden suffered a succession of third places which ended their enthusiastic challenge.

Danish manager Jan Stæchmann said: "Everyone was asking whether we wanted to go into the Race off and I said we're racers, we want to win, and the boys proved it – I was really proud of them.

"I think everyone expected Great Britain to do a lot better but the Swedes really gave us a fight, and I'm chuffed that we've gone straight to the Final.

"We'll be relaxing now until the practice and the hard work really starts then.

"The riders have it in them, they all want to win and as soon as they get the Danish flag on their chest they seem to rise to the occasion.

"Fingers crossed for Saturday night and hopefully a lot of Danes will cheer us on."

the RESULTS

1 DENMARK 63

Nicki PEDERSEN	3 3 2 3 3	14
Niels-Kristian IVERSEN	3 2 2 3 2	12
Kenneth BJERRE	3 3 3 2 3	14
Hans ANDERSEN	2 0 2 3 3	10
Bjarne PEDERSEN	3 3 2 3 2	13

2 SWEDEN 50.5

Fredrik LINDGREN	2 3 2 1.5 3	11.5
Peter LJUNG	1 2 1 1 2	7
Andreas JONSSON	1 2 3 1 2	9
Jonas DAVIDSSON	3 6^ 3 1 3	16
Daniel NERMARK	1 2 3 1 FX	7

3 GREAT BRITAIN 25.5

Scott NICHOLLS	1 0^ X 2 1	4
Chris HARRIS	2 1 1 3 1.5 0	8.5
Lee RICHARDSON	2 1 0 2 1	6
Simon STEAD	0 1 1 0	2
Oliver ALLEN	2 0 1 2 0	5

4 CZECH REPUBLIC 13

Matej KUS	0 0 1	1
Ales DRYML	0 0 0 0	0
Adrian RYMEL	0 1 3 X^ 0 2	6
Filip SITERA	1 1 0 0 0 0	2
Lubos TOMICEK	0 2 1 0 0 1	4

Denmark qualify for the Final; Sweden and Great Britain go through to the Race-off.

1: N.Pedersen, Lindgren, Nicholls, Kus, 58.6 secs.
2: Iversen, Harris, Ljung, Dryml, 59.1 secs.
3: Bjerre, Richardson, Jonsson, Rymel, 59.4 secs.
4: Davidsson, Andersen, Sitera, Stead, 58.9 secs.
5: B.Pedersen, Allen, Nermark, Tomicek, 59.9 secs.
6: Bjerre, Nermark, Sitera, Nicholls (J), 59.6 secs.
7: Lindgren, Tomicek, Harris, Andersen, 59.9 secs.
8: B.Pedersen, Ljung, Richardson, Kus, 60.0 secs.
9: N.Pedersen, Jonsson, Stead, Dryml, 59.2 secs.
10: Davidsson (J), Iversen, Rymel, Allen, 60.2 secs.
11: Rymel, Andersen, Ljung, Nicholls (X), 60.7 secs.
12: Jonsson, B.Pedersen, Harris, Sitera, 59.8 secs.
13: Davidsson, N.Pedersen, Tomicek, Richardson, 59.8 secs.
14: Nermark, Iversen, Stead, Rymel (J) (FX), secs.
15: Bjerre, Lindgren, Allen, Dryml, 60.8 secs.
16: Iversen, Nicholls, Jonsson, Tomicek, 60.1 secs.
17: Harris, Bjerre, Davidsson, Sitera, 60.3 secs.
18: Andersen, Richardson, Nermark, Dryml, 60.5 secs.
19: B.Pedersen, Harris and Lindgren (dead heat), Rymel, 60.4 secs.
20: N.Pedersen, Allen, Ljung, Sitera, 60.1 secs.
21: Davidsson, B.Pedersen, Nicholls, Tomicek, 60.0 secs.
22: N.Pedersen, Rymel, Harris, Nermark (FX), 61.0 secs.
23: Lindgren, Iversen, Richardson, Sitera, 61.0 secs.
24: Bjerre, Ljung, Tomicek, Stead, 61.2 secs.
25: Andersen, Jonsson, Kus, Allen, 61.1 secs.
Fastest time: 58.6 secs, Nicki Pedersen, Heat 1.
Referee: *Christian Froschauer (Germany).*

RACE OFF: VOJENS, DENMARK, THURSDAY, JULY 17

IN every storm you can always find a silver lining – and the rainbow that might conceivably lead you to that crock of gold....

And, in Great Britain's case, elimination from the competition threw up an unlikely hero: debutant Tai Woffinden.

GB boss Jim Lynch had already decided to blood Woffy in Denmark before the Brandon debacle and what a shrewd decision it turned out to be.

There may have been fears that the occasion would prove one step too far for the precocious teenager who had already added the British Under 21 title to his 2007 Under 18 crown.

But not a bit of it.

He didn't have long to wait for his first taste of World Cup action once the parade was over, coming out in the second heat and pushing Andreas Jonsson and Wieslaw Jagus all the way.

That was an impressive performance for openers – but what came after that was a feast fit for speedway royalty.

The youngster, barely two years since making his Conference League debut, won his second race and went on to score a superb nine points, headed in the Lions' scorecharts by only Chris Harris.

Nigel Pearson and Kelvin Tatum – the Sky commentating duo – helped turn the Race off into the Tai Woffinden show.

Superlatives came out like a sandblasting machine and amid the obvious disappointment of missing out on the Speedway World Cup Final at least there was the consolation of having unearthed a new-found star in the red, white and blue.

Lynch's bold gamble had paid off big-time and he enthused: "To score nine points in your first World Cup justified completey him being there."

But then he offered a miserable verdict on GB's current place in the world pecking order: "We now have to realise that we are the fifth best nation in the world. No disrespect to anybody else, Poland and Sweden were better teams than we were, end of story.

"I think we've got to go back home now and sit down and think about what we have to do.

"Stop kidding ourselves that it's something to do with next year or the year after, this has got to be a three to five year plan to get back in terms of world speedway.

"Everybody should get their heads together and move forward together. I always believe, for things to come out of the ashes, you have to go down to the absolute low."

In all honesty the Race off turned into a two nation race and the only question was who would win the private battle at the top of the leaderboard.

There were optimistic signs early on that GB had recovered from the Brandon humiliation but it turned into something of a mirage.

Three early race wins – from skipper Scott Nicholls, rookie Woffinden and Chris Harris – saw the Brits sharing the lead with defending champs Poland after Heat 8, virtually a third of the way through.

But that was as good as it got and a disastrous next four races in which Edward Kennett was rightly blamed for a crash and then Nicholls, Lee Richardson and Woffinden could do no better than third place saw Poland and Sweden stride out at the front.

Mathematically, Lynch was still in with an outside chance of making it through to the Final when he brought out the Joker card in Heat 15.

Unfortunately it didn't have the sort of reward needed as the captain trailed in behind Jonas Davidsson and Wieslaw Jagus and the game was all but up.

With Great Britain fading, attention switched to the battle for the win on the night, with Sweden hauling in early leaders Poland with their Grand Prix regulars Fredrik Lindgren and Andreas Jonsson in majestic form.

The Poles, too, were consistent and they suffered their only last place with Rune Holta's retirement in Heat 22.

That was the prelude to a dramatic Joker race in Heat 23 when Grzegorz Walasek – who rode well as a replacement for Krzysztof Kasprzak – took four points for second place but was upstaged by a fine effort from Grigory Laguta to give Russia six.

Sweden were in control after that even though Jaroslaw Hampel got the better of Jonsson in an epic Heat 24, with Peter Ljung's Heat 25 win over Tomasz Gollob ensuring a final three-point margin.

Russia were never in the hunt, at least not once they announced their line-up. Teenage star Emil Sajfutdinov was missing as he prepared for a World Under 21 round and his replacement, the experienced Sergey Darkin, never turned up.

The official line was that his ferry had been delayed but the truth was he was never going to ride.

the VENUE

Track: *Vojens Speedway Center, Tinglykke 9, DK-6500 Vojens, Denmark.*
Telephone: *(0045) 74504441 (office). (0045) 74543132 (stadium).*
Website: *www.speedway.dk*
Track Length: *300 metres.*
Track Record: *57.8 secs. Jason Crump, August 9, 2003.*
Major meetings staged: *World Final (1988 and 1994); Danish GP (1995, 1996, 1997, 1998, 1999, 2000, 2001 and 2002); World Cup Final (1983, 1986, 1991, 1998, 2003 and 2008); European Under 21 Final, 1977:*

Quote...unquote

SCOTT NICHOLLS (Great Britain)

Thursday's performance was much better than Monday, everyone was up for it but the Poles and the Swedes were that little bit ahead of us.

Sadly we're lacking a bit of experience, Tai [Woffinden] did a brilliant job for us but we needed a little more from everyone else.

Tai looked so at home and his riding style is very comfortable.

He's done fantastically well, and it's a good positive sign for the future.

TAI WOFFINDEN (Great Britain)

It can only improve my riding. It was good to get a win in my first World Cup, I just hope there's plenty more to come.

I really enjoyed it, it was a good experience and it was good to be up against these guys when I'm in the Premier League and these are the guys you want to be racing against.

FREDRIK LINDGREN (Sweden)

We are the surprise team because we haven't got so much experience.

It's pretty young, I'm young as well and yet I'm probably one of the ones with the most experience.

It's good to get this generation and see what we can do.

It's going to be super-tough, every team in the Final is strong, but it's different when it's four really good teams, anything can happen.

the RESULTS

1 SWEDEN 53

Rider	Heats	Total
Jonas DAVIDSSON	2 2 3 2 1	10
Andreas JONSSON	3 2 3 3 2	13
Peter LJUNG	1 3 0 3 3	10
Fredrik LINDGREN	3 2 3 3 3	14
Daniel NERMARK	0 0 3 0 3	6

2 POLAND 50

Rider	Heats	Total
Tomasz GOLLOB	3 1 2 2 2	10
Wieslaw JAGUS	2 2 2 3 2	11
Rune HOLTA	3 3 2 1 R	9
Grzegorz WALASEK	1 3 3 1 4^	12
Jaroslaw HAMPEL	2 1 1 1 3	8

3 GREAT BRITAIN 36

Rider	Heats	Total
Lee RICHARDSON	0 2 1 1	4
Tai WOFFINDEN	1 3 1 1 2 1	9
Chris HARRIS	2 3 2 2 2 0	11
Edward KENNETT	2 FX 1 0	3
Scott NICHOLLS	3 1 2^ 2 1	9

4 RUSSIA 17

Rider	Heats	Total
Denis GIZATULLIN	1 1 0 0 0 1	3
Sergey DARKIN		
Daniil IVANOV	0 1 0 0 0 0	1
Renat GAFUROV	X 0 0 R 1 R	1
Grigori LAGUTA	1 0 2 3 X 6^	12

Sweden and Poland qualify for the Final.

1: Gollob, Davidsson, Gizatullin, Richardson, 59.7 secs.
2: Jonsson, Jagus, Woffinden, three riders only, 59.3 secs.
3: Holta, Harris, Ljung, Ivanov, 59.0 secs.
4: Lindgren, Kennett, Walasek, Gafurov (X), 59.5 secs.
5: Nicholls, Hampel, Laguta, Nermark, 59.7 secs.
6: Walasek, Richardson, Ivanov, Nermark, 59.6 secs.
7: Woffinden, Davidsson, Hampel, Gafurov, 59.5 secs.
8: Harris, Jonsson, Gollob, Laguta, 58.8 secs.
9: Ljung, Jagus, Gizatullin, Kennett (FX), 60.0 secs.
10: Holta, Lindgren, Nicholls, Ivanov, 59.6 secs.
11: Jonsson, Holta, Richardson, Gafurov, 59.8 secs.
12: Walasek, Laguta, Woffinden, Ljung, 60.1 secs.
13: Lindgren, Harris, Hampel, Gizatullin, 60.0 secs.
14: Nermark, Gollob, Kennett, Gafurov (rel), 61.2 secs.
15: Davidsson, Jagus, Nicholls (J), Ivanov, 60.5 secs.
16: Ljung, Harris, Hampel, Gizatullin, 60.5 secs.
17: Lindgren, Gollob, Woffinden, Ivanov, 60.4 secs.
18: Jagus, Harris, Gafurov, Nermark, 60.2 secs.
19: Laguta, Davidsson, Holta, Kennett, 60.9 secs,
20: Jonsson, Nicholls, Walasek, Gizatullin, 60.0 secs.
21: Lindgren, Jagus, Richardson, Laguta (X), 61.3 secs.
22: Nermark, Woffinden, Gizatullin, Holta (R), 61.4 secs.
23: Laguta (J), Walasek (J), Davidsson, Harris, 61.1 secs.
24: Hampel, Jonsson, Woffinden, Ivanov, 60.7 secs.
25: Ljung, Gollob, Nicholls, Gafurov (R), 60.2 secs.
Fastest time: 58.8 secs, Chris Harris, Heat 8.
Referee: *Frank Ziegler (Germany).*

SPEEDWAY WORLD CUP

FINAL: VOJENS, DENMARK, SATURDAY, JULY 19

DENMARK sent a sell-out Vojens crowd home in raptures after regaining the World Cup in a highly dramatic Final.

The pre-meeting favourites had to withstand a remarkable challenge from holders Poland, but they finally secured victory in Heat 24 when Niels-Kristian Iversen headed home Tomasz Gollob, who was taking a Joker ride in the Poles' last throw of the dice.

But there had been an almost unprecedented number of twists and turns to get to that stage in a meeting which included a break for heavy rain, numerous incidents and a power cut too!

The early stages saw Denmark, Poland and Australia evenly-matched, but the latter received a serious blow in Heat 3 when Jason Crump was taken down by Peter Ljung on turn two and suffered wrist damage.

Crump re-emerged to compete in the re-run and his next ride, but was unable to go further in the meeting and Australia never seriously threatened thereafter, their night being summed up when Chris Holder stopped in Heat 24 when set for their only win of the meeting.

Sweden suffered a nightmare start with no points in the first three races, and were further hampered when the outstanding Fredrik Lindgren was excluded from Heat 6 after a fourth-bend tangle with Davey Watt.

But Lindgren recovered to take Heat 9 as a Joker, and at one stage the Swedes threatened to upset the two leaders before being forced to settle for third place.

The main battle featured Denmark and Poland, with the Poles initially seeming to adapt better to constantly changing track conditions.

Their spirit was indicated by Tomasz Gollob's sensational last-lap pass of Bjarne Pedersen in Heat 17, but Kenneth Bjerre responded in the next after being involved in a three-way second bend spill.

Poland had held a four-point lead, but the meeting swung on Heats 20 and 21. Rune Holta led away in the former, but Danish captain Hans Andersen shot to the front as Holta went into reverse and eventually retired.

Then, with Denmark one point in front, Jarek Hampel crashed out of Heat 21 when Nicki Pedersen was leading – although the damage was limited by Pedersen then being kept in third place in a thrilling battle involving Andreas Jonsson and Ryan Sullivan.

Iversen, who had not enjoyed the best of meetings, became the Danish hero to lead the double-points Gollob, and then inherit the lead when Holder stopped, the celebrations in the home camp beginning as soon as he crossed the line.

A win for Gollob could have changed everything as Greg Walasek pulled off one of the rides of the night to win Heat 25, but by that stage the majority of the supporters were awaiting the trophy presentation.

Denmark's second win in three years means that each of Saturday's four Finalists have won the Ove Fundin Trophy twice in the present World Cup era.

The other nations could take plenty of credit – Poland having never come so close away from home shale, Sweden with several riders who can improve still further, and Australia superb in Leszno, but their Final chances so badly hit by Crump's injury.

Andersen said: "We knew we were the favourites but we said before the meeting how hard it was going to be, and that all four teams could win on the night.

"There was a lot to fight against with the weather and getting all the riders clicking, but we came together and it's fantastic to win on home soil.

"We managed to get ahead after 20 heats but it wasn't easy with Poland having the chance to put in the Joker – we didn't really want to go six points up, but we managed to pull through anyway."

Less happy was Australian boss Craig Boyce who was at a loss to explain why his side collapsed so dramatically.

He savaged his riders: "It was a shocking night, I'm a bit baffled really.

"We were beaten by three much better teams on the night. They can complain and argue about no practice set-ups for the bikes but it was the same for everybody on the track.

"Jason got injured and the morale always goes down in the team when he leaves us, which I think is rubbish.

"I'm bitterly disappointed with the way all the riders rode. I don't think any of them, except for Chris Holder, were riding to their best.

"Chris had some bad luck, he's the most inexperienced but he probably put on the best show out of the Aussies.

"I can't say what I really want to say, I'm bitterly disappointed in all my riders' performances, I thought it was disgraceful.

"Nothing happened, morale in the pits was terrible and it was almost like, as soon as Jason walked out of the pits, we were defeated."

Quote...unquote

NICKI PEDERSEN (Denmark)

The pressure is always on when you're on your home track and we didn't start off too well.
I won my first three but we were struggling with set-ups and the Poles were really fired up.
We worked all the way together, we had the camp talking together about what we were going to do and in the end after the interval we got it working better.
We could have blown it with the Joker, but we got it in the end and we're really happy.
Poland have so many good riders and for them to come to Vojens and nearly beat us was tremendous, it's great for the sport."

TOMASZ GOLLOB (Poland)

The Polish team are very happy and have worked well together, there was good co-operation and the problem was in the two heats when Rune Holta stopped and Jarek Hampel crashed.
But everybody rode well and we're happy.
The Vojens track is very bumpy but it wasn't a problem for the Polish team.
I think next year the Final will be in Poland at Leszno, so maybe it will be first place for us there.

ANDREAS JONSSON (Sweden)

I think we were too far behind from the beginning – we had three points after six heats and that was the problem.
We rode pretty well towards the end, and the really strong guys were definitely Freddie Lindgren and Jonas Davidsson.
Those two were brilliant and it's a bit sad that I couldn't keep up with them, but I tried my best like the other guys and I still think we did a pretty good job.
The really positive thing is that we worked well together, and that's very good.

CHRIS HOLDER (Australia)

That was a shocker. Losing Crumpie [Jason Crump] early on killed us big time, he is our best rider and losing him was a shame.

the RESULTS

1 DENMARK 49

Nicki PEDERSEN	3 3 3 1 1	11
Bjarne PEDERSEN	2 3 1 2 3	11
Kenneth BJERRE	1 0 2 3 3	9
Niels-Kristian IVERSEN	1 0 1 2 3	7
Hans ANDERSEN	2 2 3 3 1	11

2 POLAND 46

Rune HOLTA	1 2 1 R 1	5
Wieslaw JAGUS	3 3 3 2 1	12
Tomasz GOLLOB	3 2 2 3 4^	14
Grzegorz WALASEK	0 0 1 0 3	4
Jaroslaw HAMPEL	3 3 2 3 FX	11

3 SWEDEN 39

Andreas JONSSON	0 1 2 1 3 2	9
Daniel NERMARK	0 0	0
Peter LJUNG	X 0 2 F 2	4
Fredrik LINDGREN	3 X 6^ 3 2 2	16
Jonas DAVIDSSON	0 1 3 3 2 1	10

4 AUSTRALIA 21

Leigh ADAMS	2 2 1 1 0 0^	6
Chris HOLDER	1 2 0 FX 1 R	4
Jason CRUMP	2 1	3
Ryan SULLIVAN	2 1 R 0 2	5
Davey WATT	1 1 0 0 1 0	3

1: N.Pedersen, Adams, Holta, Jonsson, 60.4 secs.
2: Jagus, B.Pedersen, Holder, Nermark, 59.6 secs.
3: Gollob, Crump, Bjerre, Ljung (X), 59.4 secs.
4: Lindgren, Sullivan, Iversen, Walasek, 59.3 secs.
5: Hampel, Andersen, Watt, Davidsson, 59.1 secs.
6: N.Pedersen, Gollob, Watt, Lindgren (X), 59.1 secs.
7: B.Pedersen, Adams, Davidsson, Walasek, 59.7 secs.
8: Hampel, Holder, Jonsson, Bjerre, 59.5 secs.
9: Lindgren (J), Holta, Crump, Iversen, 60.1 secs.
10: Jagus, Andersen, Sullivan, Ljung, 59.4 secs.
11: N.Pedersen, Ljung, Walasek, Holder, 63.2 secs.
12: Lindgren, Hampel, B.Pedersen, Holder (FX), 62.2 secs.
13: Davidsson, Bjerre, Holta, Sullivan (R), 62.3 secs.
14: Jagus, Jonsson, Iversen, Watt, 62.2 secs.
15: Andersen, Gollob, Adams, Nermark, 62.4 secs.
16: Davidsson, Jagus, N.Pedersen, Watt, 61.1 secs.
17: Gollob, B.Pedersen, Jonsson, Sullivan, 61.4 secs.
18: Bjerre, Davidsson, Watt, Walasek, 60.5 secs.
19: Hampel, Iversen, Adams, Ljung (F), 60.9 secs.
20: Andersen, Lindgren, Holder, Holta (ret), 61.3 secs,
21: Jonsson, Sullivan, N.Pedersen, Hampel (f.exc), 61.8 secs.
22: B.Pedersen, Ljung, Holta, Watt, no time .
23: Bjerre, Lindgren, Jagus, Adams, 60.3 secs.
24: Iversen, Gollob (J), Davidsson, Holder (ret), 60.1 secs.
25: Walasek, Jonsson, Andersen, Adams (J), 60.4 secs.
Fastest time: 59.1 secs, Jaroslaw Hampel, Heat 5; Nicki Pedersen, Heat 6.
Referee: *Frank Ziegler (Germany)*

Roll of Honour

1960	SWEDEN
1961	POLAND
1962	SWEDEN
1963	SWEDEN
1964	SWEDEN
1965	POLAND
1966	POLAND
1967	SWEDEN
1968	GREAT BRITAIN
1969	POLAND
1970	SWEDEN
1971	GREAT BRITAIN
1972	GREAT BRITAIN
1973	GREAT BRITAIN
1974	ENGLAND
1975	ENGLAND
1976	AUSTRALIA
1977	ENGLAND
1978	DENMARK
1979	NEW ZEALAND
1980	ENGLAND
1981	DENMARK
1982	UNITED STATES OF AMERICA
1983	DENMARK
1984	DENMARK
1985	DENMARK
1986	DENMARK
1987	DENMARK
1988	DENMARK
1989	GREAT BRITAIN
1990	UNITED STATES OF AMERICA
1991	DENMARK
1992	UNITED STATES OF AMERICA
1993	UNITED STATES OF AMERICA
1994	SWEDEN
1995	DENMARK
1996	POLAND
1997	DENMARK
1998	UNITED STATES OF AMERICA
1999	AUSTRALIA
2000	SWEDEN
2001	AUSTRALIA
2002	AUSTRALIA
2003	SWEDEN
2004	SWEDEN
2005	POLAND
2006	DENMARK
2007	POLAND
2008	DENMARK

THE FIM originally introduced the World Best Pairs as the newest addition to the international calendar in 1969.

It grew into a major competition until it was finally disbanded and merged with the flagging World Team Cup in 1994.

Each pairing raced against each other to decide the overall winners.

Even though the 1969 meeting was given official FIM status at the time and the FIM issued medals to riders from the first three nations, the World Final is no longer recognised by the world governing body.

1969

Stockholm, Sweden, Thursday, September 25

1 NEW ZEALAND 28 (Ivan Mauger 18, Bob Andrews 10:6), **2 SWEDEN 27** (Ove Fundin 14:1, Göte Nordin 13:4), 3 **ENGLAND 21** (Nigel Boocock 11, Martin Ashby 10:3), 4 DENMARK 17 (Ole Olsen 13, Bent Nørregaard Jensen 4:1), 5 CZECHO-SLOVAKIA 15 (Jan Holub 9:1,Zdenek Majstr 6:2), 6 EAST GERMANY 9 (Gerhard Uhlenbrock 8, Jochen Dinse 1), 7 BULGARIA 8 (Petr Petkov 6, Peter Iliev 2:1).

■ *Czechoslovakia's Zdenek Majstr was excluded for tape-breaking in Heat 12 and replaced by meeting reserve Leif Enecrona (Sweden) who finished third. His point did not count in final results.*

The winners of the Speedway World Cup are presented with the Ove Fundin Trophy.

The trophy is a lasting tribute to five-times World Champion Ove Fundin and was originally unveiled at the 2000 European Grand Prix.

Royal jewellers Asprey & Garrard prepared a selection of concept drawings before the final design was chosen.

The trophy is 24 inches (61 centimetres) tall and made from sterling silver and gilt.

The centrepiece of the design is a world globe mounted on a speedway style rear sprocket.

Roll of Honour

1970	NEW ZEALAND
1971	POLAND
1972	ENGLAND
1973	SWEDEN
1974	SWEDEN
1975	SWEDEN
1976	ENGLAND
1977	ENGLAND
1978	ENGLAND
1979	DENMARK
1980	ENGLAND
1981	UNITED STATES OF AMERICA
1982	UNITED STATES OF AMERICA
1983	ENGLAND
1984	ENGLAND
1985	DENMARK
1986	DENMARK
1987	DENMARK
1988	DENMARK
1989	DENMARK
1990	DENMARK
1991	DENMARK
1992	UNITED STATES OF AMERICA
1993	SWEDEN

RIDER BY RIDER – GOLD MEDALS

HANS NIELSEN (Denmark)	7
ERIK GUNDERSEN (Denmark)	5
PETER COLLINS (England)	4
ANDERS MICHANEK (Sweden)	3
MALCOLM SIMMONS (England)	3

†Not including the 1969 World Final which no longer has official recognitition. §Not including 1970 World Final.

WORLD CHAMPIONSHIPS

2009 GRAND PRIX QUALIFICATION

FINAL (GRAND PRIX CHALLENGE)
Zielona Gora, Poland, Sunday, September 14

	1	2	3	4	5	Tot	RO
1 Kenneth BJERRE	**3**	**1**	**2**	**3**	**3**	**12**	**3**
2 Grzegorz WALASEK	**3**	**2**	**2**	**3**	**2**	**12**	**2**
3 Sebastian ULAMEK	**3**	**3**	**R**	**3**	**3**	**12**	**1**
4 Niels-Kristian IVERSEN	2	3	3	1	2	11	
5 Tomasz JEDRZEJAK	2	2	2	2	3	11	
6 Ryan SULLIVAN	3	3	3	1	F	10	
7 Jesper B. MONBERG	1	1	3	2	3	10	
8 Adrian MIEDZINSKI	1	3	1	2	2	9	
9 Jurica PAVLIC	0	0	3	3	1	7	
10 Matej ZAGAR	2	2	1	0	2	7	
11 Mads KORNELIUSSEN	2	0	F	2	1	5	
12 Peter KARLSSON	0	2	1	1	0	4	
13 Lee RICHARDSON	1	R	2	R	0	3	
14 Charlie GJEDDE	0	1	R	1	1	3	
15 Matej FERJAN	0	R	1	R	1	2	
16 Peter LJUNG	1	1	F			2	
17 Ales DRYML [R]	R	0				0	

● *Jonas Davidsson and Daniel Nermark withdrew because of injury.*

Qualifying Round 1
Abensberg, Germany, Monday May 12
1 Davey WATT (Australia) 15, 2 Rafal DOBRUCKI (Poland)11+3, 3 Adrian RYMEL (Czech Republic) 11+2, 4 David HOWE (Great Britain) 11+1, 5 Edward KENNETT (Great Britain) 11+X, 6 Tobias KRONER (Germany) 10, 7 Mikael MAX (Sweden) 10, 8 Martin SMOLINSKI (Germany) 9, 9 Richard SPEISER (Germany) 8, 10 Josef FRANC (Czech Republic) 5, 11 Niklas KLINGBERG (Sweden) 5, 12 Mathias SCHULTZ (Germany) 4, 13 Manuel HAUZINGER (Austria) 4, 14 Friedrich WALLNER (Austria) 3, 15 Sébastian TRESARRIEU (France) 2, 16 Frank FACHER (Germany) 1, 17 Max DILGER (Germany) 0, Manfred BETZ (Germany) [R], did not ride.

Qualifying Round 2
Gorican, Croatia, Saturday, May 31
1 Charlie GJEDDE (Denmark) 14, 2 Jurica PAVLIC (Croatia) 13+3, 3 Matej ZAGAR (Slovenia) 13+2, 4 Tomasz JEDRZEJAK (Poland) 12, 5 Christian HEFENBROCK (Germany) 10, 6 Rory SCHLEIN (Australia) 10, 7 Kevin WÖLBERT (Germany) 9+3, 8 Kenneth BJERRE (Denmark) 9+2, 9 Lubos TOMICEK (Czech Republic) 8, 10 Renat GAFUROV (Russia) 7, 11 Izak SANTEJ (Slovenia)5, 12 Radik TIBEEV (Russia) 4, 13 Michal SZCZEPANIAK (Poland) 3, 14 Carl Johan RAUGSTAD (Norway) 2, 15 Nikola PIGAC (Croatia) 1, 16 Ivan VARGEK (Croatia) [R] 0, 17 Nikola MARTINEC (Croatia) 0.

Qualifying Round 3
Czestochowa, Poland, Sunday, June 15
1 Grzegorz WALASEK (Poland) 14, 2 Lukas DRYML (Czech Republic) 13, 3 Peter KARLSSON (Sweden) 11, 4 Lee RICHARDSON (Great Britain) 10, 5 Ales DRYML (Czech Republic) 10, 6 Sebastien ULAMEK (Poland) 10, 7 Daniel NERMARK (Sweden) 9, 8 Emil SAJFUTDINOV (Russia) 8, 9 Denis GIZATULLIN (Russia) 7, 10 Jaroslaw HAMPEL (Poland) 7, 11 Janusz KOLODZIEJ (Poland) 6, 12 Oliver ALLEN (Great Britain) 5, 13 Maksim BOGDANOVS (Latvia) 3, 14 Nicolai KLINDT (Denmark) 3, 5 Andrey KARPOV (Ukraine) 3, 16 Leonids PAURA (Latvia) 1, 17 Borys MITURSKI (Poland) [R] 0.

Qualifying Round 4
Lonigo, Italy, Saturday, June 21
1 Ryan SULLIVAN (Australia) 14+3, 2 †Matej FERJAN (Hungary) 14+2, 3 Peter LJUNG (Sweden) 12+3, 4 Mads KORNELIUSSEN (Denmark) 12+2, 5 Jesper B. MONBERG (Denmark) 10+3, 6 Daniel KING (Great Britain) 10+2, Simon STEAD (Great Britain) 10+1, 8 Mattia CARPANESE (Italy) 10+0, 9 Chris HOLDER (Australia) 5, 10 Andrea MAIDA (Italy) 5, 11 Maks GREGORIC (Slovenia) 5, 12 Hynek STICHAUER (Czech Republic) 4, 13 Kyle LEGAULT (Canada) 3, 14 Kaj LAUKKANEN (Finland) 2, 15 Marco GREGNANIN (Italy) 2, 16 Zsolt BENCZE (Hungary) 1.

Semi Final 1
Terenzano, Italy, Saturday July 5
1 Lee RICHARDSON 12+3, 2 Jesper B. MONBERG 12+2, 3 Peter LJUNG 11+3, 4 Sebastian ULAMEK 11+2, 5 Matej ZAGAR 10, 6 Charlie GJEDDE 10, 7 Ryan SULLIVAN 10, 8 Adrian MIEDZINSKI (Poland) 9+3, 9 Jurica PAVLIC 9+2, 10 Lukas DRYML 8, 11 Mikael MAX 6, 12 David HOWE 4, 13 Christian HEFENBROCK 3, 14 Kevin WÖLBERT 3, 15 Mattia CARPANESE 2, 16 Guglielmo FRANCHETTI (Italy) 0. Andreas MAIDA [R] did not ride.

Semi Final 2
Motala, Sweden, Saturday, July 5
1 Peter KARLSSON 14, 2 Jonas DAVIDSSON (Sweden) 11+3, 3 Niels-Kristian IVERSEN (Denmark) 11+2, 4 Grzegorz WALASEK 9, 5 Matej FERJAN 9, 6 Daniel NERMARK 9, 7 Kenneth BJERRE 9, 9 Tomasz JEDRZEJAK 9, 9 Mads KORNELIUSSEN 8+3, 10 Edward KENNETT 8+2, 11 Daniel KING 7, 12 Ales DRYML 7, 13 Simon STEAD 6, 14 Rory SCHLEIN 1, 15 Adrian RYMEL 1, 16 Tobias KRONER (Germany) 1.

Roll of Honour

1995	Leigh ADAMS
1996	Simon WIGG
1997	Piotr PROTASIEWICZ
1998	Leigh ADAMS
1999	Billy HAMILL
2000	Peter KARLSSON
2001	Greg HANCOCK
2002	Lee RICHARDSON
2003	Piotr PROTASIEWICZ
2004	Antonio LINDBÄCK
2006	Wieslaw JAGUS
2007	Niels-Kristian IVERSEN
2008	Kennth BJERRE

No meeting in 2005.

WORLD CHAMPIONSHIPS

UNDER 21 CHAMPIONSHIP

FINAL

Pardubice, Czech Republic, Saturday, October 4

EMIL Sajfutdinov re-wrote the record books – as the first rider to successfully defend the World Under 21 crown.

After his 2007 victory in Poland, he dropped his only point in his opening ride at Pardubice to ensure another 12 months as the title-holder.

Poole's Troy Batchelor became the first rider to beat him in two World Finals – but he recovered to win his remaining four outings.

That included the vital Heat 19 success over his nearest challenger Chris Holder who needed to finish ahead of the Russian to force a race-off.

With Eastbourne teenager Lewis Bridger also ahead of Holder over the line, the Australian ended with 12 points but clinched the silver medal with a run-off win over Swindon's Jurica Pavlic.

It means Holder has now just missed out on the title two years in a row and, unlike Sajfutdinov, who still has two seasons left at this age level, doesn't have another chance of finally winning the elusive jewel.

Bridger was top Brit but still finished a lowly tenth while Ediburgh's William Lawson got only four points and highly-rated Tai Woffinden had a nightmare debut, failing to recover from a tapes exclusion in his opening ride after a sizzling practice session the previous day.

		1	2	3	4	5	Tot	RO
1	**Emil SAJFUTDINOV**	**2**	**3**	**3**	**3**	**3**	**14**	
2	Chris HOLDER	3	3	3	2	1	12	3
3	Jurica PAVLIC	2	3	1	3	3	12	2
4	Troy BATCHELOR	3	2	1	2	3	11	
5	Martin VACULIK	2	0	3	3	1	9	
6	Matej KUS	0	3	0	2	3	8	
7	Grzegorz ZENGOTA	1	0	2	3	2	8	
8	Patrick HOUGAARD	3	2	1	0	2	8	
9	Ludvig LINDGREN	1	0	2	2	2	7	
10	Lewis BRIDGER	0	1	3	0	2	6	
11	Igor KONONOV	3	1	0	1	1	6	
12	Morten RISAGER	2	1	2	1	0	6	
13	Andrey KARPOV	1	2	0	0	1	4	
14	William LAWSON	1	1	1	1	0	4	
15	Tai WOFFINDEN	E	2	0	1	0	3	
16	Filip SITERA	0	0	2	0	0	2	
17	Simon GUSTAFSSON [R]	0					0	
18	Kamil BRZOZOWSKI [R]						did not ride	

Qualifying Round 1

Norden, Germany, Sunday, May 18

1 Robert KASPRZAK (Poland) 14, 2 Adam KAJOCH (Poland) 13+3, 3 Patrick HOUGAARD (Denmark) 13+2, 4 Hynek STICHAUER (Czech Republic) 13+1, 5 Max DILGER (Germany) 11, 6 Ricky WELLS (USA) 9, 7 Richard SPEISER (Germany) 8+3, 8 Jozsef TABAKA (Hungary) 8+2, 9 Jannick DE JONG (Holland) 8+1, 10 Adam VANDIREK (Czech Republic) 7, 11 Jade MUDGWAY (New Zealand) 4, 12 Sönke PETERSEN (Germany) 4, 13 Grant TREGONING (New Zealand) 4, 14 Denis WIENKE (Germany) 3, 15 Alex MARCUCCI (USA) 1, 16 Henry van der STEEN (Holland) 0.

Qualifying Round 2

Zielona Gora, Poland, Sunday, May 18

1 Chris HOLDER (Australia) 15, 2 Adrian GOMOLSKI (Poland) 12, 3 Mateusz SZCZEPANIAK (Poland) 11, 4 Andrey KARPOV (Ukraine) 10, 5 Grzegorz ZENGOTA (Poland) 9+3, 6 William LAWSON (Great Britain) 9+2, 6 Artem VODYAKOV (Russia) 9+R, 8 Tyron PROCTOR (Australia) 8, 9 Alexander KOSOLAPKIN (Russia) 8, 10 Frank FACHER (Germany) 7, 11 Adam ROYNON (Great Britain) 7, 12 Kevin WÖLBERT (Germany) 6, 13 Martin GAVENDA (Czech Republic) 3, 14 Aleksander CONDA (Slovenia) 3, 15 Matija DUH (Slovenia) 3, 16 Andrey KOBRIN (Ukraine) 0. Marcin JEDRZEJEWSKI (Poland) [R], Maciej JANOWSKI (Poland) [R], did not ride.

Qualifying Round 3

Zarnovica, Slovakia, Sunday, May 25

1 Emil SAJFUTDINOV (Russia) 15, 2 Lewis BRIDGER (Great Britain) 12+3, 3 Maksim BOGDANOVS (Latvia) 12+2, 4 Martin VACULIK (Slovakia) 11, 5 Filip SITERA (Czech Republic) 11, 6 Matej KUS (Czech Republic) 10+3, 7 Joshua AUTY (Great Britain) 10+2, 8 Patryk PAWLASZCZYK (Poland) 8, 9 Evgeny KARAVATSKAYA (Latvia) 7, 10 Michal MITKO (Poland) 7, 11 Nikola MARTINEC (Croatia) 6, 12 Nikola PIGAC (Croatia) 4, 13 Roland KOVACS (Hungary) 3, 14 Jan HOLUB (Czech Republic) 2, Tamas SZILAGYI (Hungary) 1, 16 Michal DUDEK (Czech Republic) 1, 17 Rastislav BANDZI (Slovakia) [R] 0.

Qualifying Round 4

Pori, Finland, Saturday, May 31

1 Linus EKLÖF (Sweden) 13, 21 Ludvig LINDGREN (Sweden) 12+3, 3 Morten RISAGER (Denmark) 12+2, 4 Simon GUSTAFSSON (Sweden) 12+1, 5 Kim NILSSON (Sweden) 12+0, 6 Nicolai KLINDT (Denmark) 10+3, 7 Leon MADSEN (Denmark) 10+R, 8 Tomas H. JONASSON (Sweden) 8, 9 Jan GRAVERSEN (Denmark) 8, 10 Peter Juul LARSEN (Denmark) 5, 11 Robin TÖRNQVIST (Sweden) 5, 12 Kalle KATAJISTO (Finland) 4, 13 Niko SILTANIEMI (Finland) [R] 3, 14 Tord SOLBERG (Norway) 2, 15 Teemu LAHTI (Finland) 1, 16 Jari MAKINEN (Finland) 1, 17 Kenneth Kruse HANSEN (Denmark) 1, 18 Aarni HEIKKILÈ (Finland) [R] 0.

Qualifying Round 5

Gustrow, Germany, Saturday, May 31

Troy BATCHELOR (Australia) 15, 2 Tobias BUSCH (Germany) 13, 3 Robert KSIEZAK (Australia) 12+3, 4 Kamil BRZOZOWSKI (Poland) 12+R, 5 Igor Kononov (Russia) 10, 6 Robert BAUMANN (Germany) 10, 7 Erik PUDEL (Germany) 7, 8 Niklas LARSSON (Sweden) 7, 9 Michael HADEK (Czech Republic) 7, 10 Ben BARKER (Great Britain) 6, 11 Andrew TULLY (Great Britain) 6, 12 Manuel NOVOTNY (Austria) 4, 13 Matic VOLDRIH (Slovenia) 4, 14 Theo DI PALMA (France) 4, 15 Maxime MAZEAU (France) 2, 16 Hans-Peter KULTERER (Austria) 1, 17 Sergej MALYSCHEW (Germany) [R] 0.

Semi Final 1

Rye House, England, Sunday, June 15

1 Troy BATCHELOR 15, 2 Tai WOFFINDEN (Great Britain) 13, 3 Chris HOLDER 12+3, 4 Morten RISAGER 12+2, 5 Grzegorz ZENGOTA 9, 6 Lewis BRIDGER 8, 7 William LAWSON 8, 8 Ludvig LINDGREN 8, 9 Simon GUSTAFSSON 7+3, 10 Mateusz SZCZEPANIAK 7+2, 11 Linus EKLÖF 7+1, 12 Ricky WELLS 6, 13 Tobias BUSCH 3, 14 Tyron PROCTOR [R] 2, 15 Max DILGER 1, 16 Robert KASPRZAK 1, 17 Joshua AUTY (Great Britain) [R] 1, 18 Kim NILSSON 0.

Semi Final 2

Gorican, Croatia, Saturday, July 19

1 Jurica PAVLIC (Croatia) 15, 2 Patrick HOUGAARD 13, 3 Matej KUS 12, 4 Emil SAJFUTDINOV 11, 5 Andrey KARPOV 9, 6 Adrian GOMOLSKI 8, 7 Igor KONONOV 7+3, 8 Filip SITERA 7+2, 9 Martin VACULIK 7+1, 10 Kamil BRZOZOWSKI 7+FX, 11 Adam KAJOCH 5, 12 Robert KSIEZAK 4, 13 Robert BAUMANN 5, 14 Nicolai KLINDT 4, 15 Hynek STICHAUER 3, 16 Maksim BOGDANOVS 2, 17 Richard SPEISER [R], did not ride.

Roll of Honour

1988 ....Peter NAHLIN (Sweden)
1989 ....Gert HANDBERG (Denmark)
1990 ....Chris LOUIS (England)
1991 ....Brian ANDERSEN (Denmark)
1992 ....Leigh ADAMS (Australia)
1993 ....Joe SCREEN (England)
1994 ....Mikael MAX[1] (Sweden)
1995 ....Jason CRUMP (Australia)
1996 ....Piotr PROTASIEWICZ (Poland)
1997 ....Jesper B. MONBERG[2] (Denmark)
1998 ....Robert DADOS (Poland)
1999 ....Lee RICHARDSON (England)
2000 ....Andreas JONSSON (Sweden)
2001 ....Dawid KUJAWA (Poland)
2002 ....Lukas DRYML (Czech Republic)
2003 ....Jaroslaw HAMPEL (Poland)
2004 ....Robert MISKOWIAK (Poland)
2005 ....Krzysztof KASPRZAK (Poland)
2006 ....Karol ZABIK (Poland)
2007 ....Emil SAJFUTDINOV (Russia)
2008 ....Emil SAJFUTDINOV (Russia)

THE forerunner of the World Under 21 Championship – first given FIM recognition in 1988 – was the European Junior Championship which was open to riders from any affiliated motor-cycling Federation. The competition was discontinued with the launch of the new World Under 21 Championship.

Roll of Honour

1977 ....Alf BUSK (Denmark)
1978 ....Finn Rune JENSEN (Denmark)
1979 ....Ron PRESTON (United States of America)
1980 ....Tommy KNUDSEN (Denmark)
1981 ....Shawn MORAN (United States of America)
1982 ....Antonin KASPER II (Czechoslovakia)
1983 ....Steve BAKER (Australia)
1984 ....Marvyn COX (England)
1985 ....Per JONSSON (Sweden)
1986 ....Igor MARKO (Russia)
1987 ....Gary HAVELOCK (England)

Mikael MAX[1] rode under the name Mikael Karlsson before 2003; Jesper B. MONBERG[2] rode under the name of Jesper B. Jensen before 2008.

Lukas Dryml became his country's first shale World Champion when he won the World Under 21 Championship in 2002

2005 World Under 21 Champion Krzysztof Kasprzak – one of four Poles to win the title in successive years between 2003 and 2006

WORLD CHAMPIONSHIPS

UNDER 21 WORLD CUP

FINAL
Holsted, Denmark, Sunday, September 21

POLAND kept hold of the Under 21 World Cup in the tightest of finishes.

Hosts Denmark gave them their toughest battle for gold since the launch of the new competition in 2005 but the Poles made it four victories in a row.

And what made their success even more remarkable is that they didn't score a single point from the first three races!

Michal Mitko finished last in the opener; Artur Mroczka fell in heat two and then skipper Grzegorz Zengota trailed behind Chris Holder, Simon Gustafsson and Peter Kildemand.

At that stage the defending champions were seven points behind Denmark, six adrift of Australia and trailed the third of their rivals, Sweden, by five points.

Maciej Janowski started the revival with race wins in the space of three important heats and such was Poland's grip of the middle stages they still won despite adding only eight points to their total in the last six heats.

Denmark suffered big-time from the competition format. When Peter Kildemand crashed out in Heat 9 he couldn't take his place in his next two rides and the Danes had to watch while three of their rivals garnered points at their expense.

Austalia missed out on the rostrum despite the brilliance of their captain Holder who was the stand-out star of the day on the 300 metre Holsted track.

He won his first five rides (including a tactical substitute outing instead of Robert Ksiezak) and the only points he dropped were in the final race when he was beaten by Ricky Kling and Daniel Pytel.

By then the Poles were already celebrating yet another gold medal and the only way the Aussies could have got onto the podium was if Holder had won and Kling finished pointless.

Great Britain, who had won silver in 2007, went out in the semi final in the Czech Republic but only just....

Injury ruled out Adam Roynon and surprise replacement Simon Lambert looked out of his depth, failing to pick up a point.

Going into the last heat only Sweden were safe from elimination with only three points splitting all four nations.

Tai Woffinden, shrewdly named at reserve by GB boss Graham Reeve, had won four out of five rides, but the Rye House man was shut out by Sweden's Thomas H. Jonasson and Czech Republic skipper Filip Sitera, playing a real captain's role.

In the other semi in Germany, Poland ran away with it – racking up a massive 63 points to end up 16 points in front of Australia who booked the fourth and final spot in the Final.

The Poles provided 16 race winners – although Robert Kasprzak, Adrian Gomolski and reserve Maciej Janowski all dropped one point to a different opponent.

Slovenia, who ended with only four points, were totally outclassed and Germany had too many weak links lower down the chain to challenge.

1 POLAND 40							
Michal MITKO	0	1	2	2	2		7
Artur MROCZKA	F	1	3	2	3		9
Grzegorz ZENGOTA	0	2	3	3	0		8
Maciej JANOWSKI	3	3	2	1	2		11
Daniel PYTEL	2	2	0	1	0		5
2 DENMARK 39							
Nicolai KLINDT	3	3	2	1	3		12
Patrick HOUGAARD	3	2	2	3	3	3	16
Peter KILDEMAND	1	R	0				1
Rene BACH	1	3	2	R	0		6
Morten RISAGER	1	2	1	0			4
3 SWEDEN 38							
Kim NILSSON	1	3	1	2	2		9
Ludvig LINDGREN	2	1	0	2	0		5
Simon GUSTAFSSON	2	1	1	3	1		8
Ricky KLING	2	1	1	1	3		8
Billy FORSBERG	3	F	1	2	2		8
4 AUSTRALIA 32							
Troy BATCHELOR	2	0	0	3	1		6
Robert KSIEZAK	1	0	1				2
Chris HOLDER	3	3	3	3	3	1	16
Tyron PROCTOR	0	2	3	0	2		7
Kozza SMITH	0	0	0	0	1		1

Qualifying Round 1
Pardubice, Czech Republic, Saturday, June 7
1 SWEDEN 41 (Tomas H. Jonasson 14, Billy Forsberg 10, Ludvig Lindgren 8, Ricky Kling 6, Simon Gustafsson 3), 2 CZECH REPUBLIC 38 (Filip Sitera 12, Hynek Stichauer 9, Matej Kus 9, Michael Hadek 5, Adam Vandirek 3), 3 GREAT BRITAIN 36 (Tai Woffinden 14, Lewis Bridger 9, William Lawson 7, Ben Barker 6, Simon Lambert 0), 4 RUSSIA 35 (Artem Laguta 14, Emil Sajfutdinov 11, Artem Vodyakov 6, Alexander Kosolapkin 3, Igor Kononov 1).

Qualifying Round 2
Didenbergen, Germany, Sunday, June 22
1 POLAND 63 (Robert Kasprzak 14, Adrian Gomolski 14, Maciej Janowski 14, Mateusz Szczepaniak 11, Grzegorz Zengota 10), 2 AUSTRALIA 47 (Chris Holder 13, Kozza Smith 13, Robert Ksiezak 9, Tyron Proctor 8, Aaron Summers 4), 3 GERMANY 36 (Richard Speiser 10, Frank Facher 10, Kevin Wölbert 8, Max Dilger 6, Erik Pudel 2), 4 SLOVENIA 4 (Aleksander Conda 1, Matija Duh 1, Aljosa Remih 1, Dalibor Bot 1, Matic Voldrih 0).

Roll of Honour

2005	POLAND
2006	POLAND
2007	POLAND
2008	POLAND

POLAND are the only country to have won the Under 21 World Cup since its launch in 2005. They have used a total of 16 different riders to win their four gold medals – with Karol Zabik having ridden in three successive finals.

WORLD CHAMPIONSHIPS

WORLD LONG TRACK CHAMPIONSHIP *final standings*

Rider					Total
1 Gerd RISS	20	18	25	16	79
2 Glen PHILLIPS	18	10	20	18	66
3 Dirk FABRIEK	12	25	14	14	65
4 Andrew APPLETON	11	13	18	20	62
5 Theo PIJPER	10	7	13	25	55
6 Matthias KRÖGER	8	16	12	12	48
7 Stephan KATT	6	14	5	13	38
8 Stéphane TRESARRIEU	–	11	16	10	37
9 Jannick de JONG	4	9	9	11	33
10 Joonas KYLMÅKORPI	13	20	–	–	33
11 Daniel BACHER	25	2	2	–	29
12 Sirg SCHÜTZBACH	14	0	8	5	27
13 Jörg TEBBE	–	6	11	9	26
14 Herbert RUOLPH	7	1	10	6	24
16 Daniel RATH	3	8	7	3	21
17 Enrico JANOSCHKA	9	12	–	–	21
18 Zdenek SCHNEIDERWIND	16	3	–	–	19
19 Jérome LESPINASSE	–	4	3	8	15
20 Pavel ONDRASIK	2	-	1	4	7
21 Erik EIJBERGEN	1	–	4	1	6
22 Toni KRÖGER	–	–	–	2	2

Scoring: 25-20-18-16-14-13-12-11-10-9-8-7-6-5-4-3-2-1-0. Top six qualify for the 2009 World Long Track Championship.

Qualifying Round 1
Artigues de Lussac, France, Saturday, May 17
1 Stéphane Tresarrieu 12, 2 Richard Hall 16, 3 Bernd Diener 14, 4 René Lehtinen 17, 5 Sébastian Tresarrieu 13, 6 Paul Cooper 13, 7 Zdenek Schneiderwind 10, 8 Philippe Ostyn 12, 9 Rodney McDonald 11, 10 Herbert Rudolph 9, 11 Jérome Lespinasse 12, 12 Pavel Ondrasik 12, 13 Christian Hülshorst 6, 14 Pascal Swart 7, 15 Sjoerd Rozenberg 4, 16 Jerome Turani 4, 17 Gabriel Dubernard 3, 18 Sébastien Brousillou 4.

Qualifying Round 2
Mulmshorn, Germany, Sunday, June 1
1 Jörg Tebbe 20, 2 Benjamin Hegener 18, 3 Richard Speiser 15, 4 Vladimir Trofimov 15, 5 Alessandro Milanese 14, 6 Erik Eijbergen 15, 7 Ilya Bondarenko 9, 8 Marius Røkeberg 11, 9 Richard Wolff 11, 10 Mark Stiekema 8, 11 Vince Kinchin 7, 12 Willy Tjessem 8, 13 Maxime Mazeau 5, 14 Theo de Palma 5, 15 Steve Leigh 5, 16 Antonin Klatovsky 6, 17 Karel Kadlec 1, 18 Berry de Vos 4.

FINAL 1
Marianske Lazne, Cech Republic, Saturday, May 24
1 Daniel Bacher 25, 2 Gerd Riss 20, 3 Glen Phillips 18, 4 Zdenek Schneiderwind 16, 5 Sirg Schützbach 14, 6 Joonas Kylmåkorpi 13, 7 Dirk Fabriek 12, 8 Andrew Appleton 11, 9 Theo Pijper 10, 10 Enrico Janoschka 9, 11 Matthias Kröger 8, 12 Herbert Rudolph 7, 13 Stephan Katt 6, 14 Richard Wolff 5, 15 Jannick de Jong 4, 16 Daniel Rath 3, 17 Pavel Ondrasik 2, 18 Erik Eijbergen 1, Jörg Tebbe, Alessandro Milanese, did not ride.

FINAL 2
St. Macaire, France, Saturday, June 28
1 Dirk Fabriek 25, 2 Joonas Kylmåkorpi 20, 3 Gerd Riss 18, 4 Matthias Kröger 16, 5 Stephan Katt 14, 6 Andrew Appleton 13, 7 Enrico Janoschka 12, 8 Stèphane Tresarrieu 11, 9 Glen Phillips 10, 10 Jannick de Jong 9, 11 Daniel Rath 8, 12 Theo Pijper 7, 13 Jörg Tebbe 6, 14 Richard Wolff 5, 16 Jérome Lespinasse 4, 16 Zdenek Schneiderwind 3, 17 Daniel Bacher 2, 18 Herbert Rudolph 1, 19 Sirg Schützbach 0.

FINAL 3
Morizes, France, Saturday, September 6
1 Gerd Riss 25, 2 Glen Phillips 20, 3 Andrew Appleton 18, 4 Stéphane Tresarrieu 16, 5 Dirk Fabriek 14, 6 Theo Pijper 13, 7 Matthias Kröger 12, 8 Jörg Tebbe 11, 9 Herbert Rudolph 10, 10 Jannick de Jong 9, 11 Sirg Schützbach 8, 12 Daniel Rath 7, 13 Richard Wolff 6, 14 Stephan Katt 5, 15 Erik Eijbergen 4, 16 Jérome Lespinasse 3, 17 Daniel Bacher 2, 18 Pavel Ondrasik 1, Gabriel Dubernard, Maxime Mazeau, did not ride.

FINAL 4
Vechta, Germany, Sunday, September 13
1 Theo Pijper 25, 2 Andrew Appleton 20, 3 Glen Phillips 18, 4 Gerd Riss 16, 5 Dirk Fabriek 14, 6 Stephan Katt 13, 7 Matthias Kröger 12, 8 Jannick de Jong 11, 9 Stéphane Tresarrieu 10, 10 Jörg Tebbe 9, 11 Jérome Lespinasse 8, 12 Richard Wolff 7, 13 Herbert Rudolph 6, 14 Sirg Scützbach 5, 15 Pavel Ondrasik 4, 16 Daniel Rath 3, 17 Toni Kröger 2, 18 Erik Eijbergen 1.

CHALLENGE

Aduard, Holland, Saturday, October 18

1 Stéphane Tresarrieu, 2 Bernt Diener, 3 Richard Hall, 4 Jörg Tebbe, 5 Alessandro Milanese, 6 Paul Cooper, 7 Richard Speiser, 8 Jannick de Jong, 9 Richard Wolff, 10 Erik Eijbergen, 11 Sébastien Tresarrieu, 12 Stephan Katt, 13 René Lehtinen, 14 Herbert Rudolph, 15 Vladimir Trofimov, 16 Daniel Bacher, 17 Pavel Ondrasik, 18 Sjoerd Rozenberg, 19 Sirg Schützbach, 20 Mark Stiekema.

Top eight finishers qualify for the 2009 World Long Track Championship.

Roll of Honour

1971 .... Ivan MAUGER
1972 .... Ivan MAUGER
1973 .... Ole OLSEN
1974 .... Egon MÜLLER
1975 .... Egon MÜLLER
1976 .... Ivan MAUGER
1977 .... Anders MICHANEK
1978 .... Egon MÜLLER
1979 .... Alois WIESBÖCK
1980 .... Karl MAIER
1981 .... Michael LEE
1982 .... Karl MAIER
1983 .... Shawn MORAN
1984 .... Erik GUNDERSEN
1985 .... Simon WIGG
1986 .... Erik GUNDERSEN
1987 .... Karl MAIER
1988 .... Karl MAIER
1989 .... Simon WIGG
1990 .... Simon WIGG
1991 .... Gerd RISS
1992 .... Marcel GERHARD
1993 .... Simon WIGG
1994 .... Simon WIGG
1995 .... Kelvin TATUM
1996 .... Gerd RISS

In 1997 the World Long Track Final was replaced by a Grand Prix series

1997 .... Tommy DUNKER
1998 .... Kelvin TATUM
1999 .... Gerd RISS
2000 .... Kelvin TATUM
2001 .... Gerd RISS
2002 .... Robert BARTH
2003 .... Robert BARTH
2004 .... Gerd RISS
2005 .... Robert BARTH
2006 .... Robert BARTH
2007 .... Gerd RISS
2008 .... Gerd RISS

THE forerunner of the World Long Track Championship – first given FIM recognition in 1971 – was the European Long Track Championship which was open to riders from any affiliated motor-cycling Federation. The competition was discontinued with the launch of the World Long Track Championship.

Roll of Honour

1957 .... Leif [Basse] HVEEM
1958 .... Josef HOFMEISTER
1959 .... Josef HOFMEISTER
1960 .... Josef HOFMEISTER
1961 .... Timo LAINE
1962 .... Bertil STRID
1963 .... Bertil STRID
1964 .... Kurt W. PETERSEN
1965 .... Björn KNUTSSON
1966 .... Manfred POSCHENRIEDER
1967 .... Manfred POSCHENRIEDER
1968 .... Manfred POSCHENRIEDER
1969 .... Don GODDEN
1970 .... Jon ÖDEGARD

EUROPEAN CHAMPIONSHIPS

THE Union Européenne de Motocyclism (UEM) was established on February 17, 1996, at a meeting in Paris attended by a total of 21 national federations.

The UEM was officially recognised in its own right by the world motorcycling governing body, the Fédération Internationale de Motocyclisme (FIM) in 1997.

The UEM unifies 42 member countries and is the largest Continental Union for motorcycling in the world and the largest partner of the FIM with almost half of its members and 80% of all activities organised world wide in the field of motorcycling.

The UEM is responsible for all motorcycle sports activities outside World Championships and is home not only for the large, traditional Motorcycle Federations but also for those which are small and need support and encouragement.

It also has a heavy non-sporting programme, promoting tourism, road safety and environmental issues.

It now organises five major speedway events – the European Championship (since 2001), the European Pairs Championship (2004), the Club Champions Cup (1998), the European Junior Championship (1998) and the European Junior Team Championship (2008) – the last two events being restricted to riders under the age of 19.

EUROPEAN CHAMPIONSHIP

FINAL

Lendava, Slovenia, Sunday, August 24

BARELY 2,000 fans saw Matej Zagar win his second European Final – even though it was held in his homeland.

The former Reading star had to wait more than 24 hours for his chance after the original staging was called off because of heavy rain.

But he certainly wasted no time: winning his first three races before he was beaten by the Czech Republic's Matej Kus.

That dropped point hardly mattered and Zagar could actually afford to have finished pointless in his fifth ride – as his nearest challengers were four marks adrift at the end of the 20th race.

And that's when the real action began with a titanic battle for the other rostrum places in a nail-biting finale.

Six riders tied for second place on 10 points each to trigger a complicated race-off schedule – a series of four extra heats before Sebastian Ulamek eventually came out on top, winning both his qualifier and the silver medal decider.

Mads Korneliussen had to go through three extra races before he could join Zagar and his former Swindon team-mate on the rostrum!

Because of the weather, the meeting also counted as the 13th staging of the Lendava Golden Helmet so there was double delight for Zagar, firmly reinforcing his position as the best-ever Slovenian rider.

	1	2	3	4	5	Tot	RO
1 Matej ZAGAR	**3**	**3**	**3**	**2**	**3**	**14**	
2 Sebastian ULAMEK	3	1	3	0	3	10	3 3
3 Mads KORNELIUSSEN	1	2	2	3	2	10	2 2 2
4 Matej KUS	2	3	0	3	2	10	1 3 N
5 Denis GIZATULLIN	2	2	2	1	3	10	3 X
6 Josef FRANC	3	2	1	3	1	10	R 1
7 Ales DRYML[2]	3	3	3	1	0	10	R R
8 Daniil IVANOV	1	1	1	3	3	9	
9 Mikael MAX	2	1	3	2	1	9	
10 Martin SMOLINSKI	1	3	0	1	2	7	
11 Adrian MIEDZINSKI	R	E	2	2	2	6	
12 Ulrich ØSTERGAARD	2	0	2	1	1	6	
13 Sergey DARKIN	0	2	1	2	0	5	
14 Filip SITERA	1	0	1	0	0	2	
15 Sandor TIHANYI	0	1	0	0	1	2	
16 Mattia CARPANESE	0	0	0	0	0	0	

■ *Qualifiers Christian Hefenbrock and Maksim Bogdanovs withdrew through injury.*

● *The original staging of the final on Saturday, August 23 was postponed and put back a day because of heavy rain.*

Qualifying Round 1

Neustadt/Donau, Germany, Sunday, April 27

1 Adrian RYMEL (Czech Republic) 13, 2 Kevin WÖLBERT (Germany) 13, 3 Daniel JELENIEWSKI (Poland) 10, 4 Patrick HOUGAARD (Denmark) 10, 5 Izak SANTEJ (Slovenia) 8, 6 Mathias SCHULTZ (Germany) 7, 7 Maks GREGORIC (Croatia) 6, 8 †Frank FACHER (Austria) 5, 9 †Ivan VARGEK (Austria) 5, 10 †Manuel NOVOTNY (Switzerland) 4, 11 †Friedrich WALLNER (France) 4, 12 †Sirg SCHÜTZBACH (Switzerland) 3, 13 Sébastien TRESSARIEU (France) 2, 14 Nikola MARTINEC (Croatia) 2, 15 Theo DI PALMA (France) 1.

Qualifying Round 2

Gyula, Hungary, Saturday, May 17

1 †Matej FERJAN (Hungary) 14, 2 Morten RISAGER (Denmark) 12+3, 3 Filip SITERA (Czech Republic) 12+2, 4 Laszlo SZATMARI (Hungary) 11, 5 Aleksey KHARCHENKO (Russia) 10, 6 Robert NAGY(Hungary) 9, 7 Zsolt BENCZE (Hungary) 9, 8 Anders ANDERSEN (Denmark) 8+3, 9 Marcin PIEKARSKI (Poland) 8+2, 10 Josef FRANC (Czech Republic) 8+1, 11 Ruslan GATYATOV (Russia) 8+R, 12 Matic VOLDRIH (Slovenia) 4, 13 Petri KOSKELA (Finland) 3, 14 Roland KOVACS (Hungary) 3, 15 Jeroen van der VEEN (Holland) 1.

Qualifying Round 3

Lviv, Ukraine, Sunday, May 18

1 Tomasz GAPINSKI (Poland) 14+3, Maksim BOGDANOV (Latvia) 14+2, 3 Roman IVANOV (Russia) 11, 4 Matej KUS (Czech Republic) 190, 5 Michael HADEK (Czech Republic) 10, 6 Evgeny KARAVATSKAYA (Latvia) 10, 7 Karol BARAN (Poland) 9, 8 Daniil IVANOV (Russia) 8+3, 9 Alexander BORODAJ (Ukraine) 8+2, 10 Jaroslav POLIUCHOVIC (Ukraine) 7, 11 Vladimir TROFIMOV (Ukraine) 6, 12 Alessandro MILANESE (Italy) 5, 13 Aleksandru TOMA (Romania) 3, 14 Ronny WEIS (Germany) 3, 15 Fanica POPA (Romania) 1, 16 Andriy

†Racing on licences other than their country of birth.

SINKOVSKY (Ukraine) 1.

Semi Final 1

Terenzano, Italy, Saturday, May 24

1 Denis GIZATULLIN (Russia) 14+3, 2 Sebastian ULAMEK (Poland) 14+2, 3 Adrian MIEDZINSKI (Poland) 12, 4 Mads KORNELIUSSEN (Denmark) 11, 5 Ales DRYML II (Czech Republic) 10, 6 Mattia CARPANESE 9+3, 7 Kevin WÖLBERT 9+2, 8 Adrian RYMEL 8, 9 Daniel JELENIEWSKI 7, 10 Izak SANTEJ 6, 11 Juha HAUTAMÄKI (Finland) 5, 12 Patrick HOUGAARD 5, 13 Tomas SUCHANEK (Czech Republic) 4, 14 Maks GREGORIC 3, 15 Marco GREGNANIN (Italy) 2, 16 Ivan VARGEK 1.

■ *Qualifiers Matthias Schultz and Manuel Hauzinger withdrew through injury.*

Semi Final 2

Herxheim, Germany, Saturday, June 21

Mikael MAX (Sweden) 14, 2 Martin SMOLINSKI (Germany) 13+3, 3 Christian HEFENBROCK (Germany) 13+2, 4 Sergey DARKIN (Russia) 12, 5 Filip SITERA 12, 6 Josef FRANC 7+3, 7 Aleksey KHARCHENKO 7+2, 8 Morten RISAGER 6, 9 Matej FERJAN 6, 10 Henk BOS (Holland) 6, 11 Ruslan GATIYATOV 6, 12 Robert NAGY 5, 13 Borys MITURSKI (Poland) 5, 14 Anders ANDERSEN 3, 15 Marcin PIEKARSKI 2, 16 Przemyslaw ZARZYCKI (Poland) 1, 17 Matic VOLDRIH [R] 1.

■ *Qualifier Laszlo Szatmari withdrew through injury.*

Semi Final 3

Debrecen, Hungary, Saturday, June 21

1 Daniil IVANOV 15, 2 Matej ZAGAR (Slovenia) 13, 3 Sandor TIHANYI (Hungary) 11, 4 Ulrich ØSTERGAARD (Denmark) 10, 5 Matej KUS 9, 6 Maksim BOGDANOVS 9, 7 Alexander BORODAJ 8, 8 Jurica PAVLIC (Croatia) 8, 9 Roman IVANOV 8, 10 Andrey KARPOV (Ukraine) 7, 11 Karol BARAN 5, 12 Peter Juul LARSEN (Denmark) 5, 13 Jozsef TABAKA (Hungary) 4, 14 Evgeny KARAVATSKAYA 4, 15 Michael HADEK 3, 16 Rastislav BANDZI (Slovakia) 1, Jaroslav POLIUCHOVIC [R], Vladimir Trofimov [R], did not ride.

■ *Qualifier Tomasz Gapinski withdrew through injury.*

Roll of Honour

2001	Bohumil BRHEL
2002	Magnus ZETTERSTRÖM
2003	Krzysztof KASPRZAK
2004	Matej ZAGAR
2005	Jesper B. MONBERG[1]
2006	Krzysztof JABLINSKI
2007	Jurica PAVLIC
2008	Matej ZAGAR

It is always difficult to determine the correct Anglicised spellings of riders whose birth names were recorded in the Cyrillic alphabet, this mainly applies to competitors from what was known as the former Eastern bloc, principally nations such as Bulgaria, Ukraine and the old Soviet Union.

There is not necessarily a universally accepted translation of many of the symbols used (there are more than 40 compared with the 26 of the English language) and we have, therefore, tried to adapt what we believe is the closest true translation although accept other sources will vary.

PAIRS CHAMPIONSHIP

FINAL

Natschbach-Loipersbach, Austria, Saturday, September 20

The lights might have gone out in Austria – but it was sunshine all the way as the Polish trio won a third European Pairs Championship in five years.

Sebastian Ulamek had been a member of the 2006 title winning line-up and was the individual star of the evening.

He was actually left out of Poland's opening ride but replaced Karol Zabik for the Heat 7 clash with eventual runners-up the Czech Reopublic.

And after teaming up with Adam Skornicki for a 5-1, he took another four rides, and ended the evening with a five ride full house.

The only points Poland dropped were in Heat 3 when Hungarian licence holder Matej Ferjan (born in Slovenia) beat both Skornicki and Zabik.

Russia lost out on the silver medal after what later appeared to be a major tacticval error.

They replaced Roman Povazhny (who had scored paid 10 from his first five rides) with Aleksey Kharchenko but he trailed in last against Latvia on a cold engine!

1 POLAND 28								
Karol ZABIK	**1**	N	N	3	3	3	10:1	
Adam SKORNICKI	2	3	3	N	N	N	8	
Sebastian ULAMEK	N	**2**	**2**	**2**	**2**	**2**	10:5	
2 CZECH REPUBLIC 21+3								
Ales DRYML[2]	0	1	**1**	N	N	N	2:1	
Lukas DRYML	3	X	2	3	3	3	14	3
Adrian RYMEL	N	N	N	1	**2**	**2**	5:2	
3 RUSSIA 21+0								
Aleksey KHARCHENKO	N	N	N	N	N	0	0	
Renat GAFUROV	3	**1**	3	R	3	3	13:1	R
Roman POVAZHNY	**2**	2	**2**	1	1	N	8:2	
4 HUNGARY 18								
Matej FERJAN	3	3	3	3	2	2	16	
Sandor TIHANYI	N	1	N	0	N	**1**	2:1	
Norbert MAGOSI	0	N	0	N	0	N	0	
5 LATVIA 15								
Leonids PAURA	X	0	**2**	0	**1**	1	4:2	
Vyatcheslav GIRUTSKY	2	2	3	2	2	0	11	
6 AUSTRIA 13								
Manuel HAUZINGER	3	3	1	1	1	3	12	
Manuel NOVOTNY	1	0	N	0	0	N	1	
Andreas BÖSSNER	N	N	0	N	N	0	0	
7 GERMANY 10								
Martin SMOLINSKI	1	2	1	2	1	1	8	
Kevin WÖLBERT	0	**1**	0	N	N	N	1:1	
Tobias BUSCH	N	N	N	**1**	0	0	1:1	

Semi Final 1

Rivno, Ukraine, Saturday, July 19

1 RUSSIA 21 (Sergey Darkin 12, Roman Ivanov 6, Semen Vlasov 3:1), 2 LATVIA 19 (Vyatcheslav Girutsky 11, Leonids Paura 8:3), 3 POLAND 17 (Karol Zabik 11, Zbigniew Czerwinski 6:2), 4 UKRAINE 16 (Alexander Borodaj 11:1, Vladimir Kolody (sen) I 5:1), 5 SLOVENIA 12 (Izak Santej 9, Maks Gregoric 3:1, Matej Zagar, did not ride), 6 UKRAINE II 5 (Michail Oneszko 3, Vladimir

Omelian 1, Vladimir Kolody (jun) 1).

Semi Final 2
Miskolc, Hungary, Saturday, September 13
1 CZECH REPUBLIC 26 (Filip Sitera 13:2, Adrian Rymel 13:1, Ales Dryml II, did not ride), 2 HUNGARY 25 (Norbert Magosi 12:2, Matej Ferjan 9:1, Laszlo Szatmari 4:1), 3 GERMANY 25 (Martin Smolinski 16:1, Richard Speiser 9:2), ●HUNGARY II 17 (Sandor Tihanyi 12:1, Jozsef Tabaka 5:1), 4 FINLAND 14 (Ari-Pekka Mustonen 8:1, Kaj Laukkanen 6:2), 5 ITALY 13 (Guglielmo Franchetti 8:1, Mattia Carpanese 4, Alessandro Milanese 1), 6 CROATIA 6 (Ivan Vargek 3, Renato Cvetko 3).
● A second Hungarian duo competed in the round but could not qualify for the European Final.

Roll of Honour

2004	CZECH REPUBLIC
2005	POLAND
2006	POLAND
2007	CZECH REPUBLIC
2008	POLAND

CLUB CHAMPIONS CUP

Nicki leads the way....

FINAL
Slany, Czech Republic, Saturday, September 6

NOT so long ago the European Club Champions Cup was looked upon as a major trophy to be won, particularly by the Continental sides.

But those days are fast going – and you only had to look at the respective line-ups to realise this has rapidly become a second-rate competition.

At least to the majority of countries although Russian side Mega Lada Togliatti took it seriously enough to use a five-rider squad that included World Champion Nicki Pedersen and World Under 21 title-holder Emil Sajfutdinov.

But just take a look at the team put out by Polish club Unia Leszno!

The reigning Extraleague champions have Grand Prix stars Jaroslaw Hampel, Krzysztof Kasprzak and Leigh Adams (who actually rode for Togliatti) on their books but didn't use any of them in the semi final.

And they never bothered to call up Jurica Pavlic or Adam Shields who would have have strengthened the team that travelled to Latvia.

Instead they used a youthful side – all of their quartet being under 21.

1 MEGA LADA TOGLIATTI 46		
Nicki PEDERSEN	3 3 3 3 3	15
Denis SAJFUTDINOV	2 N 1 N R	3
Leigh ADAMS	3 1 3 3 3	13
Emil SAJFUTDINOV	3 3 3 3 1	13
Daniil IVANOV [R]	N FX N 2	2
2 SIMON & WOLF DEBRECEN (Hungary) 31		
Maciej KUCIAPA	1 1 2 1 2	7
Jozsef TABAKA	1 2 0 3 2	8
Sandor TIHANYI	0	0
Matej FERJAN	0 3 3 2 3	11
Hynek STICHAUER [R]	N 2 1 F 2	5
3 AK SLANY (Czech Republic) 30		
Peter KARLSSON	3 2 2 2 2	11
Tomasz PISZCZ	1 1 R 1 3	6
Daniel JELENIEWSKI	2 3 FX 1 1	7
Michal SZCZEPANIAK	0 1 2 2 1	6
Martin MALEK [R]	did not ride	
4 SK LOKOMOTIV DAUGAVPILS (Latvia) 13		
Leonids PAURA	0 N 0 F N	0
Maksim BOGDANOVS	2 0 2 0 0	4
Andrej KOROLEV	2 2 1 1 0	6
Kjastas PUODZHUKS	1 0 1 N 0	2
Vyatcheslav GIRUTSKY [R]	N 0 N 0 1	1

Semi Final 1
Daugavpils, Latvia, Saturday, May 31
1 MEGA LADA TOGLIATTI (Russia) 45 (Nicki Pedersen 14, Roman Ivanov 10, Leigh Adams [R] 10, Emil Sajfutdinov 7, Daniil Ivanov 4), 2 SK LOKOMOTIV DAUGAVPILS (Latvia) 41 (Grigori Laguta 12, Pawel Mesiac [R] 12, Andrej Korolev 7, Maksim Bogdanovs 6, Kjastas Puodzhuks 4), 3 SHAKTER CHERVONOGRAD (Ukraine) 18 (Andrey Karpov 7, Alexander Borodaj 5, Ruslan Gatiyatov 5, Evgeny Karavatskaya 1), 4 UNIA LESZNO (Poland) 16 (Przemyslaw Pawlicki 5, Adam Kajoch 4, Slawomir Musielak 4, Mateusz Lukaszewski 3).

Roll of Honour

1998	BYDGOSZCZ (Poland)
1999	BYDGOSZCZ (Poland)
2000	PILA (Poland)
2001	BYDGOSZCZ (Poland)
2002	TOGLIATTI (Russia)
2003	TOGLIATTI (Russia)
2004	CZESTOCHOWA (Poland)
2005	TOGLIATTI (Russia)
2006	TARNOW (Poland)
2007	MISKOLC (Hungary)
2008	TOGLIATTI (Russia)

UNDER 19 CHAMPIONSHIP

FINAL
Stralsund, Germany, Saturday, August 30

ARTUR Mroczka cashed in on his fellow countryman Maciej Janowski's misfortune – as he became the surprise winner of the European Junior Championship Final.

The Grudziadz youngster was beaten by both Kevin Wölbert and Artem Laguta – younger brother of Grand Prix wild card Grigori – in his opening rides but kept his nerve when it really mattered.

Janowski saw his hopes all but disappear as early as Heat 6 when he was excluded.

He then went on to win his next four races – including a silver medal race-off against 17-year-old Russian Artem Vodyakov.

A blissful Mroczka said: "I was surprised. I am satisfied – very, this is the biggest progress in my career."

Only two British riders took part in the championship and

both found the going quite tough in Slovenia.

Workington's Joe Haines only just missed out on the cut – but Birmingham's Jack Roberts struggled to make any sort of impact.

It was, though, a valuable learning experience for both teenagers and Poland again illustrated their strength in depth with five riders in the Final and a one-two when it really mattered.

Three former champions have gone on to become Grand Prix regulars – Lukas Dryml, Matej Zagar and Kenneth Bjerre – which proves that the competition is certainly a hotbed for exciting young talent.

	1	2	3	4	5	Tot	RO
1 Artur MROCZKA	**2**	**2**	**3**	**3**	**3**	**13**	
2 Maciej JANOWSKI	3	R	3	3	3	12	3
3 Artem VODYAKOV	2	3	3	3	1	12	2
4 Patrick HOUGAARD	3	1	2	3	2	11	
5 Artem LAGUTA	3	3	2	2	X	10	
6 Kevin WÖLBERT	3	3	1	0	2	9	
7 Dennis ANDERSSON	2	2	2	2	1	9	
8 Linus EKLÖF	2	2	1	2	1	8	
9 Kim NILSSON	0	0	3	1	3	7	
10 Simon NIELSEN	1	1	1	1	3	7	
11 Dawid LAMPART	0	2	1	2	2	7	
12 Michael HADEK	1	1	2	1	0	5	
13 Marcel KAJZER	1	0	0	1	2	4	
14 Borys MITURSKI	0	3	0			3	
15 Denis NOSOV	0	1	0	0	1	2	
16 Peter KILDEMAND	1	X	0	0	0	1	

Semi Final 1
Balakovo, Russia, Friday, May 9
1 Artem LAGUTA (Russia) 14, 2 Artem VODYAKOV (Russia) 13+3, 3 Kevin WÖLBERT (Germany) 13+2, 4 Borys MITURSKI (Poland) 12, 5 Denis NOSOV (Russia) 10, 6 Maksim BOGDANOVS (Latvia) 9, 7 Evgeny SIDORIN (Russia) 8, 8 Andrey KUDRIASHOV (Russia) 7, 9 Jan HOLUB (Czech Republic) 7, 10 Michal LOPACZEWSKI (Poland) 7, 11 Oleg BESCHASTNYH (Russia) 6, 12 Sergey KARACHINTSEV (Russia) 5, 13 Michael DUDEK (Czech Republic) 3, 14 Maksim LOBZENKO (Russia) 2, 15 Andrey KOBRIN (Ukraine) 2, 16 Stanislav OGORODNIK (Ukraine) 1.

Semi Final 2
Fjelsted, Denmark, Friday, June 6
1 Patrick HOUGAARD (Denmark) 14, 2 Peter KILDEMAND (Denmark) 13, 3 Kim NILSSON (Sweden) 11, 4 Jonas MESSING (Sweden) 10+3, 5 Simon NIELSEN (Denmark) 10+2, 6 Linus EKLÖF (Sweden) 10+1, 7 Dennis ANDERSSON (Sweden) 10+0, 8 Peter Juul LARSEN (Denmark) 9, 9 Linus SUNDSTRÖM (Sweden) 8, 10 Nicklas LARSSON (Sweden) 7, 11 Patrick NØRGAARD (Denmark) 5, 12 Klaus JAKOBSEN (Denmark) 4, 13 Niko SILTANIEMI (Finland) 4, 14 Jari MAKINEN (Finland) 3, 15 Kalle KATAJISTO (Finland) 1, 16 Tord SOLBERG (Norway) 0. Rene BACH [R], Nicky BARRETT [R] did not ride.

Semi Final 3
Krsko, Slovenia, Saturday, July 5
1 Matej KUS (Czech Republic) 14, 2 Dawid LAMPART (Poland) 13, 3 Maciej JANOWSKI (Poland) 12, 4 Michael HADEK (Czech Republic) 11, 5 Artur MROCZKA (Poland) 10+3, 6 Marcel KAJZER (Poland) 10+2, 7 Frank FACHER (Germany) 10+1, 8 Joe HAINES (Great Britain) 9, 9 Matija DUH (Slovenia) 7, 10 Erik PUDEL (Germany) 6, 11 Aleksander CONDA (Slovenia) 5, 12 Jack ROBERTS (Great Britain) 4, 13 Max DILGER (Germany) 4, 14 Nikola PIGAC (Croatia) 3, 15 Aljosa REMIH (Slovenia) 1, 16 Dalibor BOT (Slovenia) [R]1, 17 Pavel PUCKO (Czech Republic) 0.

Roll of Honour

1998 ....Rafal OKONIEWSKI (Poland)
1999 ....Rafal OKONIEWSKI (Poland)
2000 ....Lukas DRYML (Czech Republic)
2001 ....Lukasz ROMANEK (Poland)
2002 ....Matej ZAGAR (Slovenia)
2003 ....Kenneth BJERRE (Denmark)
2004 ....Karol ZABIK (Poland)
2005 ....Karol ZABIK (Poland)
2006 ....Jurica PAVLIC (Croatia)
2007 ....Nicolai KLINDT (Denmark)
2008 ....Artur MROCZKA (Poland)

A European Junior Cup was staged in 1997 as the forerunner of the European Junior Championship.

1997 ....Bartlomiej BARDECKI (Poland)

DOUBLE CHAMPION

Karol Zabik emulated his fellow countryman Rafal Okoniewski by successfully defending the title in 2005.

UNDER 19 TEAM CHAMPIONSHIP

SWEDEN'S energetic youth policy brought its own reward – as they were crowned the first European Junior Team champions.

And they did it in Poland – a remarkable achievement for their talented teenagers.

While they only won five of the 20 heats, they packed the minor placings and the only pointless ride was when Linus Sundström crashed and was excluded from an unlucky Heat 13.

The biggest surprise was the eclipse of the home side despite Maciej Janowski – who was only 16 at the time – winning four of his six races.

But the individual performance of the championship belonged to Jurica Pavlic.

He was named as reserve by Croatia in their semi-final in Germany – and was used the maximum six times, recording an 18 point maximum, the only rider to be unbeaten in the first year of the championship.

Even then it wasn't enough to take the Croats into the final, as they could only finish third behind Germany and Denmark.

Great Britain decided against entering the competition, missing out on the golden opportunity to give youngsters like Joshua Auty and Joe Haines valuable experience of racing against their continental peers.

FINAL: RAWICZ, POLAND, THURSDAY, MAY 22

1 SWEDEN 36		
Simon GUSTAFSSON	1 3 2 1 2	9
Linus EKLÖF	3 3 1 2 2	11
Ludvig LINDGREN	2 3 2 1 2	10
Linus SUNDSTRÖM	1 1 3 FX 1	6
Niklas LARSSON [R]	did not ride	
2 GERMANY 29		
Max DILGER	2 R N N N	2
Erik PUDEL	3 1 2 1 0	7
Frank FACHER	2 2 2 2 0	8
Sönke PETERSEN	N N 0 N 0	0
Kevin WÖLBERT [R]	1 R 3 2 3 3	12
3 DENMARK 28		
Patrick HOUGAARD	1 3 3 3 2 1	13
Klaus JAKOBSEN	3 1 1 0 N	5
Peter Juul LARSEN	0 2 1 0 1	4
Patrick NØRGAARD	2 0 N N N	2
Simon NIELSEN [R]	0 3 1	4
4 POLAND 26		
Marcel KAJZER	R FX R N 2	2
Maciej JANOWSKI	3 2 3 1 3 3	15
Borys MITURSKI	0 2 0 N N	2
Michal LOPACZEWSKI	0 N N FX N	0
Dawid LAMPART [R]	1 3 0 FX 3	7

HOW THEY GOT THERE....

Semi Final 1

Güstrow, Germany, Saturday, March 22

1 GERMANY 45 (Kevin Wölbert 14, Max Dilger 12, Erik Pudel 11, Frank Facher 4, Sönke Petersen [R] 4), 2 DENMARK 38 (Patrick Hougaard 14, Klaus Jakobsen 10, Patrick Nørgaard 8, Peter Juul Larsen 4, Simon Nielsen [R] 2), 3 CROATIA 28 (Jurica Pavlic [R] 18, Nikola Pigac 4, Renato Cvetko 3, Andrej Kezman 3, Nikola Martinec, did not ride), 4 ‖FRANCE 9 (Theo De Palma 5, Maxim Mazeau 4, Benoit Lorenzon 0).

‖ *France used three riders only.*

Semi Final 2

Wiener Neustadt, Austria, Saturday, April 19

1 SWEDEN 37 (Linus Sundström 11, Ludvig Lindgren 10, Linus Eklöf 9, Simon Gustafsson 7, Kim Nilsson [R], did nit ride), 2 ‖RUSSIA 31 (Artem Laguta 15, Artem Vodyakov 8, Oleg Beschastnov 8), 3 LATVIA 28 (Maksim Bogdanovs 14, Evgeny Karavackis 6, Viatcheslav Gerutsky 4, Evgeny Petukhov 4), 4 CZECH REPUBLIC 24 (Matej Kus 13, Michal Hadek 8, Michal Dudek 1, Pavel Pucko 1, Jan Holub [R] 1).

‖ *Russia used three riders only.*

Roll of Honour

2008 .... SWEDEN

LINUS EKLÖF

top scorer for Sweden's gold medal winning squad

2009 FIXTURES

SPEEDWAY GRAND PRIX

CZECH REPUBLIC GP: Saturday, April 25, Prague.
EUROPEAN GP: Saturday, May 9, Leszno, Poland.
SWEDISH GP: Saturday, May 30, Gothenburg.
DANISH GP: Saturday, June 13, Copenhagen.
BRITISH GP: Saturday, June 27, Cardiff.
LATVIAN GP: Saturday, August 1, Daugavpils.
SCANDINAVIAN GP: Saturday, August 15, Målilla.
NORDIC GP: Saturday, August 29, Vojens.
SLOVENIAN GP: Saturday, September 12, Krsko.
ITALIAN GP: Saturday, September 26, Terenzano.
POLISH GP: Saturday, October 17, Bydgoszcz.

SPEEDWAY WORLD CUP

Qualifying Round 1: Saturday, May 2, Terenzano, Italy.
Germany, Hungary, Italy, Slovenia.
Qualiying Round 2: Saturday, May 2, Daugavpils, Latvia.
Czech Republic, Finland, Latvia, United States of America.
EVENT 1: Saturday, July 11, Vojens, Denmark.
Denmark, Russia, Sweden, winners Round 2.
EVENT 2: Monday, July 13, Peterborough, England.
Australia, Great Britain, Poland, winners Round 1.
RACE-OFF: Thursday, July 16, Leszno, Poland.
Second and third placed teams Event 1 and Event 2.
FINAL: Saturday, July 18, Leszno, Poland.
Winners Event 1 and Event 2, first two nations Race-off.

2010 GRAND PRIX qualification

Round 1: Saturday, June 6, Lonigo, Italy.
Round 2: Sunday, June 7, Divisov, Czech Republic.
Round 3: Saturday, June 27, St. Johann-im-Pongau, Austria.
Round 4: Sunday, April 12, Pocking, Germany.
Round 5: Saturday, June 27, Gorican, Croatia.
Semi Final 1: Saturday, July 4, Motala, Sweden.
Semi Final 2: Saturday, July 4, Daugavpils, Latvia.
GRAND PRIX CHALLENGE: Friday, September 18, Coventry, England.

Under 21 World Championship

Round 1: Saturday, April 26, Neustadt Donau, Germany.
Round 2: Saturday, May 16, Krsko, Slovenia.
Round 3: Sunday, May 17, Rye House, England.
Round 4: Saturday, May 16, Mseno, Czech Republic.
Round 5: Sunday, May 24, Elgane, Norway.
Semi Final 1: Saturday, June 20, Miskolc, Hungary.
Semi Final 2: Saturday, June 27, Kumla, Sweden.
FINAL: Saturday, October 3, Gorican, Croatia.

Under 21 World Cup

Round 1: Monday, June 1, Abensberg, Germany.
Australia, Germany, Great Britain, Sweden.
Round 2: Saturday, June 6, Pardubice, Czech Republic.
Czech Republic, Denmark, Finland, Russia.

FINAL: Saturday, September 5, Gorzow, Poland.
Poland, winners Round 1 and Round 2, highest scoring runners-up from Rounds 1 and 2.

World Long Track Championship

Qualifying Round 1: Saturday, May 16, Artigues de Lussac, France.
Qualifying Round 2: Sunday, June 7, Bielefeld, Germany.
FINAL 1: Saturday, June 20, Marianske Lazne, Czech Republic.
FINAL 2: Monday, July 13, Marmande, France.
FINAL 3: Sunday, August 23, Herxheim, Germany.
FINAL 4: Saturday, September 5, Morizes, France.
FINAL 5: Saturday, September 12, Vechta, Germany.
CHALLENGE (qualification for 2010): Sunday, September 27, Pfarrkirchen, Germany.

World Long Track Team Championship

FINAL: Sunday, August 16, Eenrum, Holland.
Finland, France, Germany, Great Britain, Holland, Czech Republic.

European Championship

Round 1: Friday, May 1, Mureck, Austria.
Round 2: Saturday, May 9, Stralsund, Germany.
Round 3: Saturday, May 16, Lviv, Ukraine.
Semi Final 1: Saturday, May 16, Natschbach-Loipersbach, Austria.
Semi Final 2: Sunday, July 5, Diedenbergen, Germany.
Semi Final 3: Saturday, July 25, Gorican, Croatia.
FINAL: Sunday, August 23, Togliatti, Russia.

European Pairs Championship

Semi Final: Saturday, May 23, Ljubljana, Slovenia.
Austria, Croatia, Finland, Germany, Italy, Slovenia, Ukraine.
FINAL: Saturday, September 26, Miskolc, Hungary.
Czech Republic, Hungary, Latvia, Poland, Russia and first two from semi final.

Europa Champions Cup

Semi Final: Saturday, July 18, Rivne, Ukraine.
Austria, Hungary, Latvia, Ukraine.
FINAL: Saturday, September 19, Torun, Poland.
Poland, Russia and first two from semi final.

European Under 19 Championship

Round 1: Saturday, April 4, Teterow, Germany.
Semi Final 1: Friday, May 1, Debrecen, Hungary.
Semi Final2: Saturday, May 16, Hallstavik, Sweden.
Semi Final 3: Saturday, June 13, Lendava, Slovenia.
FINAL: Saturday, July 11, Tarnow, Poland.

European Under 19 Team Championship

Semi Final 1: Saturday, July 18, Moorwinkelsdamm, Germany.
Czech Republic, Germany, Russia, Ukraine.
FINAL: Sunday, August 23, Holsted, Denmark.
Denmark, Poland, Sweden and winners of semi final.

■ ***All fixtures subject to alteration.***

2010 FIXTURES

SPEEDWAY GRAND PRIX

GRAND PRIX 1: Saturday, April 24, venue to be confirmed.
GRAND PRIX 2: Saturday, May 8, venue to be confirmed.
GRAND PRIX 3: Saturday, May 29, venue to be confirmed.
GRAND PRIX 4: Saturday, June 12, venue to be confirmed.
GRAND PRIX 5: Saturday, June 26, venue to be confirmed.
GRAND PRIX 6: Saturday, July 31, venue to be confirmed.
GRAND PRIX 7: Saturday, August 14, venue to be confirmed.
GRAND PRIX 8: Saturday, August 28, venue to be confirmed.
GRAND PRIX 9: Saturday, September 11, venue to be confirmed.
GRAND PRIX 10: Saturday, September 25, venue to be confirmed.
GRAND PRIX 11: Saturday, October 9, venue to be confirmed.

SPEEDWAY WORLD CUP

Qualifying Round 1: Monday, May 24, Abensberg, Germany.
Qualiying Round 2: Saturday, May 1, venue to be confirmed, Italy.
EVENT 1: Saturday, July 10, venue to be confirmed.
EVENT 2: Monday, July 12, venue to be confirmed.
RACE-OFF: Thursday, July 15, venue to be confirmed.
FINAL: Saturday, July 17, venue to be confirmed.

2011 GRAND PRIX qualification

Round 1: Saturday, June 5, Fjelsted, Denmark.
Round 2: Saturday, June 5, venue to be confirmed, Italy.
Round 3: Saturday, June 5, Miskolc, Hungary.
Round 4: Saturday, June 5: Balakovo, Russia.
Round 5: Saturday, June 5, Gorican, Croatia.
Race-off 1: Saturday, July 3, venue to be confirmed, Poland.
Race-off 2: Saturday, July 3, venue to be confirmed, Italy.
Race-off 3: Saturday, July 3, Diedenbergen, Germany.
GRAND PRIX CHALLENGE: Saturday, September 18, Vojens, Denmark.

Under 21 World Championship

Round 1: Monday, April 26, Neustadt Donau, Germany.
Round 2: Saturday, May 15, venue to be confirmed, Poland.
Round 3: Saturday, May 15, Gorican, Croatia.
Round 4: Saturday, May 15, Lendava, Slovenia.
Round 5: Saturday, May 15, venue to be confirmed, Denmark.
Semi Final 1: Saturday, June 26, Krsko, Slovenia.
Semi Final 2: Saturday, June 26, Landshut, Germany.
FINAL 1: Sunday, July 11, venue to be confirmed, Poland.
FINAL 2: Saturday, August 7, Daugavpils, Latvia.
FINAL 3: Saturday, September 18, Pardubice, Czech Republic.

Under 21 World Cup

Round 1: Saturday, May 29, venue to be confirmed, Czech Republic.
Round 2: Saturday, May 29, venue to be confirmed, Germany.
FINAL: Saturday, September 4, venue to be confirmed, England.

World Long Track Championship

Qualifying Round 1: Saturday, May 22, Artigues de Lussac, France.
Qualifying Round 2: Sunday, June 6, Bielefeld, Germany.
FINAL 1: Saturday, June 12, St. Macaire, France.
FINAL 2: Tuesday, July 13, Marmande, France.
FINAL 3: Monday, August 23, venue to be confirmed, Germany.
FINAL 4: Saturday, September 11, Vechta, Germany.
ROUND 5: Date to be confirmed, Marianske Lazne, Czech Republic.
CHALLENGE (qualification for 2011): Saturday, September 25, Forssa, Finland.

World Long Track Team Championship

FINAL: Saturday, September 4, Morizes, France.

FIM Youth Gold Cup (250cc)

FINAL: Saturday, July 24-Sunday, July 25, venue to be confirmed, Great Britain.

All dates and venues are subject to confirmation at the FIM Autumn Congress and subject to change.

IMPORTANT ADDRESSES

FIM

International Motorcycling Federation
Route de Suisse, 11,
1295 Mies,
Switzerland.
Telephone: 0041 022 9509500.
E-mail: info@fim-live.com
Website: www.fim-live.com

UEM

Union Européenne de Motocyclisme
Via Giulio Romano 18,
00196 Roma,
Italy.
Telephone: 0039 063226746.
E-mail: office@uem-online.org
Website: www.uem-moto.eu

British Under 15 Championship

OUTSTANDING talent Jason Garrity edged out James Sarjeant in a thrilling finale to the fifth British Under 15 Championship.

The pair went into the fourth and final round with Sheffield youngster Sarjeant knowing he had to finish ahead of his rival to have a chance of bettering his previous year's runner-up position.

With all riders being able to drop the worst of their four scores, Garrity actually held a three point lead but he had a lowest score of 14 while Sarjeant was hoping to shed just 11 points.

Mancunian Garrity – a regular at Belle Vue – made no mistake at Buxton, winning his five rides to cement his position at the top of the standings.

For the first time a complimentary 250cc championship was also held and that title went to Rhys Naylor who was either first or second in the three rounds he completed.

Ben Morley had a troublesome opening round at Stoke, missed the second ride at Northside (Workington) but then won the last two meetings at Weymouth and Buxton.

FINAL STANDINGS

500cc

	R1	*R2*	*R3*	*R4*	*Tot*
1 Jason GARRITY	**14**	**16**	**14**	**18**	**48**
2 James SARJEANT	11	18	12	16	46
3 John RESCH	18	14	11	11	43
4 Joe JACOBS	12	10	16	9	38
5 Marc OWEN	–	–	18	12	30
6 Jack HIRST	8	12	–	10	30
7 Cameron HOSKINS	9	11	8	7	28
8 Jack BUTLER	10	–	9	8	27
9 Scott DAY	6	8	10	6	24
10 Daniel GREENWOOD	16	–	–	–	16
11 Scott GIBBONS	–	9	7	–	16
12 Kyle HOWARTH	–	–	–	14	14
13 Ashley MORRIS	7	–	–	–	7

250cc

	R1	*R2*	*R3*	*R4*	*Tot*
1 Rhys NAYLOR	**–**	**18**	**16**	**16**	**50**
2 Nathan STONEMAN	18	16	12	–	46
3 Ben MORLEY	9	–	18	18	45
4 Conor DWYER	16	12	10	7	38
5 Lloyd BARRETT	14	10	9	10	34
6 Daniel I'ANSON	10	9	-	14	33
7 Jack CORNES	8	14	8	9	31
8 Daniel SIBSON	7	8	–	6	21
9 Brendon FREEMANTLE	–	–	14	12	26
10 Tyler GOVIER	–	–	7	8	15
11 Marc OWEN	12	–	–	–	12
12 Matthew ALLITT	–	–	6	–	6

Riders were awarded championship points in relation to their finishing position in each round (1 —18; 2 – 16; 3 –14; 4 –12; 5 – 11; 6 – 10; 7 – 9; 8 –8, 9 – 7; 10 – 6. Best three rounds count towards title.

Round 1
Stoke, Sunday, July 10
500cc

	1	*2*	*3*	*4*	*5*	*Tot*	*SFGF*	
1 John RESCH	**3**	**3**	**3**	**3**		**12**		
2 Daniel GREENWOOD	3	X	3	3		9		
3 Jason GARRITY	2	X	3	3		8		
4 Joe JACOBS	3	1	2	1		7		
5 James SARJEANT	1	2	2	2		7		
6 Jack BUTLER	2	1	2	1		6		
7 Cameron HOSKINS	X	2	1	0		3		
8 Jack HIRST	R	0	1	2		3		
9 Ashley MORRIS	2	X	R			2		
10 Scott DAY	F	X	0	0		0		

250cc

	1	*2*	*3*	*4*	*5*	*Tot*	*SFGF*	
1 Nathan STONEMAN	**2**	**3**	**3**	**3**		**11**		**3**
2 Conor DWYER	3	1	2	2		8		2
3 Lloyd BARRETT	1	2	2	1		6		1
4 Marc OWEN	3	3	3	3		12		R
5 Daniel I'ANSON	2	1	1	0		4		
6 Ben MORLEY	1	2	0			3		
7 Jack CORNES	0	0	1	2		3		
8 Daniel SIBSON	0	0	0			0		

Round 2
Northside, Workington, Saturday, August 16
500cc

	1	*2*	*3*	*4*	*5*	*Tot*	*SFGF*	
1 James SARJEANT	**2**	**2**	**2**	**3**		**9**		**3**
2 Jason GARRITY	3	3	3	3		12		2
3 John RESCH	3	3	X	2		8	3	1
4 Jack HIRST	1	2	2	2		7	2	0
5 Cameron HOSKINS	0	X	1	1		2	1	
6 Joe JACOBS	2	X	3	X		5	0	
7 Scott GIBBONS	1	1	0	R		2		
8 Scott DAY	R	1	1	X		2		

250cc

	1	*2*	*3*	*4*	*5*	*Tot*	*SFGF*	
1 Rhys NAYLOR	**3**	**3**	**3**	**3**		**12**		**3**
2 Nathan STONEMAN	2	X	X	3		5	3	2
3 Jack CORNES	2	2	2	1		7	2	1
4 Conor DWYER	3	3	2	R		8		F
5 Lloyd BARRETT	1	2	3	2		8	1	
6 Daniel I'ANSON	1	1	1	2		5	0	
7 Daniel SIBSON	R	1	1	1		3		

Round 3
Weymouth, Saturday, September 13

500cc	*1*	*2*	*3*	*4*	*5*	*Tot*	*SFGF*	
1 Marc OWEN	**3**	**2**	**3**	**3**		**11**		
2 Joe JACOBS	3	3	2	2		10		
3 Jason GARRITY	3	3	R	3		9		
4 James SARJEANT	3	1	2	3		9		
5 John RESCH	FX	2	3	2		7		
6 Scott DAY	2	2	FX	1		5		
7 Jack BUTLER	0	2	2	FX		4		
8 Cameron HOSKINS	1	1	1	1		4		
9 Scott GIBBONS	F	2	R	1		3		

BERST OF BRITISH
Rhys Naylor – the first-ever British Under 15 250cc Champion

250cc

	1	2	3	4	5	Tot	RO
1 Ben MORLEY	**3**	**3**	**3**	**3**		**12**	
2 Rhys NAYLOR	3	2	3	2		10	3
3 Brendon FREEMANTLE	3	3	2	2		10	2
4 Nathan STONEMAN	1	2	2	3		8	
5 Conor DWYER	2	1	1	3		7	
6 Lloyd BARRETT	2	1	3	0		6	
7 Jack CORNES	1	2	0	2		5	
8 Tyler GOVIER	FX	2	1	1		4	
9 Matthew ALLITT	1					1	

Round 4
Buxton, Sunday, October 12
500cc

	1	2	3	4	5	Tot	GF
1 Jason GARRITY	**3**	**3**	**3**	**3**		**12**	**3**
2 James SARJEANT	2	3	3	2		10	2
3 Kyle HOWARTH	3	2	3	2		10	1
4 Marc OWEN	3	2	2	F		7	
5 John RESCH	3	X	2	2		7	
6 Jack HIRST	1	3	1	1		6	
7 Joe JACOBS	2	2	X			4	
8 Jack BUTLER	2	X	1	1		4	
9 Cameron HOSKINS	1	1	1	0		3	
10 Scott DAY	1	R	1			2	

250cc

					Tot	RO
1 Ben MORLEY	**3**	**2**	**3**	**3**	**11**	
2 Rhys NAYLOR	3	R	3	2	8	3
3 Daniel I'ANSON	3	2	X	3	8	F
4 Brendon FREEMANTLE	X	2	3	2	7	
5 Lloyd BARRETT	1	3	1	2	7	
6 Jack CORNES	1	2	2	1	6	
7 Tyler GOVIER	3	0	1	1	5	
8 Conor DWYER	2	1	1	1	2	
9 Daniel SIBSON	2	0	0	0	2	

Roll of Honour

2004 .... Joshua AUTY
2005 .... Joshua AUTY
2006 .... Joe HAINES
2007 .... Daniel GREENWOOD
2008 .... Jason GARRITY
2008 [250cc] .... Rhys NAYLOR

*The 2009 British Under 15 Championship will be held over six rounds. **Round 1:** Saturday, May 2, Scunthorpe; **Round 2:** Saturday, May 23, Newport; **Round 3:** Saturday, June 13, Weymouth; **Round 4:** Saturday, July 25, Buxton; **Round 5:** Saturday, August 22, to be arranged; **Round 6:** Saturday, September 19, Northside Training Track, Workington.*

British Under 18 Final

BEST OF BRITISH
Jerran Hart (left), Tai Woffinden and Joshua Auty

Scunthorpe
Monday, October 27

THERE was only ever going to be one winner – and Tai Woffinden didn't disappoint!

Defending his title and hoping to add a second British crown to his 2008 collection, he looked the total class act.

Untroubled in his five qualifying races he stormed to victory in the Grand Final.

While Woffinden's success was all too predictable the major surprise was Jerran Hart's fighting display that won him a place on the rostrum, ahead of Joe Haines who had been the other stand-out star of the preliminaries.

The late October staging produced a freezing cold night and much of the action was lukewarm, not helped by the absence of two named starters and the lack of any reserves.

It meant Heat 4 went ahead with only two riders and there were six other races without a full complement of four starters.

But, on the bright side, there was a sparkling performance from 14-year-old Marc Owen in only his third official meeting on a 500 cc machine.

	1	2	3	4	5	Tot	SF	GF
1 Tai WOFFINDEN	**3**	**3**	**3**	**3**	**3**	**15**	**–**	**3**
2 Joshua AUTY	1	3	2	3	3	12	3	2
3 Jerran HART	2	3	2	2	2	11	2	1
4 Joe HAINES	3	3	3	2	3	14	–	0
5 Ben TAYLOR	3	2	3	1	3	12	1	
6 Ben HOPWOOD	2	2	2	2	2	10	0	
7 Marc OWEN	2	1	3	0	2	8		
8 Richard FRANKLIN	3	F	1	3	R	7		
9 Brendan JOHNSON	1	1	2	2	FX	6		
10 Paul STARKE	0	2	1	2	1	6		
11 Jaimie PICKARD	2	2	0	1	1	6		
12 Aaron BASEBY	1	0	1	1	2	5		
13 James SARJEANT	0	E	1	0	1	2		
14 Chris WIDMAN	R	1	0	1	0	2		
15 John RESCH	did not arrive							
15 Jason GARRITY	did not arrive							

Roll of Honour

2004 .... Daniel KING
2005 .... William LAWSON
2006 .... Lewis BRIDGER
2007 .... Tai WOFFINDEN
2008 .... Tai WOFFINDEN

BEST OF BRITISH
2004 Champion
Daniel King

BEST OF BRITISH
2005 Champion
William Lawson

BEST OF BRITISH
2006 Champion
Lewis Bridger

HAIL the new superstar – Tai Woffinden became the first rider to simultaneously hold national titles at both Under 21 and Under 18 level.

And the 17-year-old Scunthorpe-born, Australian-educated gilt-edged prospect did it in scintillating style.

He booked his place in the title-deciding Grand Final by topping the qualifying scorers despite dropping a point to his likeliest rival Lewis Bridger in his last race.

Bridger's win allowed him the luxury of watching the semi final to decide who would be joining him and Tai in the last race.

Sadly for Bridger, though, he was never to complete those last four laps of the night – rightly excluded by referee Paul Carrington after he'd fallen trying to regain the lead from his teenage opponent.

It was a bitter blow for the prodigiously talented Bridger who had suffered a similar fate 12 months earlier when he'd also been blamed for a crash, this time in the semi final.

Woffy accepted: "It was unfortunate Lewis went out the way he did. I was really looking forward to riding against him after he got the upper hand on me in Heat 19."

FINAL
Lakeside, Friday, April 25

	1	2	3	4	5	Tot	SF	GF
1 Tai WOFFINDEN	**3**	**3**	**3**	**3**	**2**	**14**	**–**	**3**
2 Adam ROYNON	2	2	3	3	3	13	2	2
3 Ben BARKER	3	3	2	2	1	11	3	1
4 Lewis BRIDGER	3	1	3	3	3	13	–	FX
5 William LAWSON	1	3	1	3	3	11	1	
6 Steve BOXALL	2	2	3	1	2	10	0	
7 Joe HAINES	0	3	2	1	3	9		
8 Jack ROBERTS	3	1	1	1	2	8		
9 Joshua AUTY	2	0	2	2	2	8		
10 Charles WRIGHT	1	2	2	0	0	5		
11 Sean STODDART	2	1	0	1	1	5		
12 Lee SMART	1	0	1	2	1	5		
13 Daniel HALSEY	F	2	0	0	1	3		
14 Andrew TULLY [R]	2					2		
15 Harland COOK	1	0	1	0	0	2		
16 Lee STRUDWICK	0	1	0	0	0	1		
17 Kyle HUGHES [R]	0					0		
18 Daniel BETSON	R	0	FX			0		

Qualifying Round
King's Lynn, Wednesday, April 2

	1	2	3	4	5	Tot	SF	GF
1 Joe HAINES	**2**	**3**	**3**	**3**	**3**	**14**	**–**	**3**
2 Sean STODDART	3	3	2	3	1	12	3	2
3 Charles WRIGHT	2	2	2	3	2	11	2	1
4 Andrew TULLY	3	3	3	2	3	14	–	FX
5 Byron BEKKER	3	0	1	2	3	9	F	
6 Sam MARTIN	2	3	3	3	R	11	R	
7 Jerran HART	FX	2	3	1	3	9		
8 Simon LAMBERT	3	R	2	1	2	8		
9 Adam LOWE	2	1	1	2	1	7		
10 Guy KENDREW	1	2	0	1	2	6		
11 Scott CAMPOS	R	2	2	0	R	4		
12 Keiran MORRIS	1	1	1	0	1	4		
13 Scott WHITTINGTON	FX	R	0	1	2	3		
14 Scott RICHARDSON	FX	1	0	2	FX	3		
15 Oliver RAYSON	1	0	1	0	0	2		
16 Ben HANNON	F	R	0	FX		0		
17 Richard FRANKLIN [R]	0					0		

Qualifying Round
Plymouth, Friday, April 11

	1	2	3	4	5	Tot	SF	GF
1 Harland COOK	**2**	**3**	**3**			**8**		
2 Daniel BETSON	3	3	2	3		8		
3 Jack ROBERTS	3	3	1			7		
4 Kyle HUGHES	3	2	2			7		
5 Robert MEAR	2	2	3			7		
6 Paul STARKE	3	1	2	2		6		
7 Nicki GLANZ	2	3	1			6		
8 Jamie COURTNEY	1	2	3	1		6		
9 Ben TAYLOR	0	1	3			4		
10 Jaimie PICKARD	2	2	F			4		
11 Rob SMITH	FX	F	2			2		
12 Ben READE	1	1	0			2		
13 Chris WIDMAN	0	1	1	0		2		
14 Nicky MALLETT	1	0	1			2		
15 Scott MEAKINS	1	0	F			1		
16 Daniel BLAKE	0	0	F			0		
17 Russell BARNETT [R]						did not ride		

Heavy rain forced the abandonment of the meeting after Heat 13.

The results of that race were ignored to find the

qualifiers for the British Under 21 Final with each rider's points tally after their first three races determining the three riders to go through.

Qualifying Round
Weymouth, Saturday, April 12

	1	2	3	4	5	Tot	SF	GF
1 Lee SMART	**3**	**3**	**3**	**3**	**3**	**15**	**–**	**3**
2 Daniel HALSEY	2	3	2	2	3	12	3	2
3 Lee STRUDWICK	2	1	3	3	3	12	–	1
4 Gareth ISHERWOOD	3	2	1	3	2	11	2	0
5 Barry BURCHATT	3	3	R	2	3	11	1	
6 Kyle NEWMAN	FX	3	3	3	2	11	FX	
7 Matt BATES	2	2	3	0	FX	7		
8 Tim WEBSTER	3	F	0	2	1	6		
9 Nick LAURENCE	1	1	2	0	2	6		
10 Adam CHANDLER	2	2	1	0	1	6		
11 Aaron BASEBY	0	2	2	1	0	5		
12 Andrew BRAITHWAITE	FX	1	2	1	1	5		
13 Niall STRUDWICK	1	R	1	1	1	4		
14 John MacPHAIL [R]	1	0	2			3		
15 Brendan JOHNSON [R]	2	0				2		
16 Oliver GAY	FX	Fx	F	1	FX	1		
17 Gary IRVING	FX	F				0		
17 Mark BASEBY	Fx	FX	R			0		

Roll of Honour

1969 .... Graham PLANT
1970 .... Barry THOMAS
1971 .... Ian TURNER
1972 .... Alan EMMETT
1973 .... Peter COLLINS
1974 .... Chris MORTON
1975 .... Neil MIDDLEDITCH
1976 .... Michael LEE
1977 .... Les COLLINS
1978 .... Phil COLLINS
1979 .... Kenny CARTER
1980 .... Mark COURTNEY
1981 .... Rob LIGHTFOOT
1982 .... Peter CARR
1983 .... Keith MILLARD
1984 .... Marvyn COX
1985 .... Carl BLACKBIRD
1986 .... Gary HAVELOCK
1987 .... Darren SUMNER
1988 .... Mark LORAM
1989 .... Martin DUGARD
1990 .... Joe SCREEN
1991 .... *Not staged*
1992 .... Scott SMITH
1993 .... Joe SCREEN
1994 .... Paul HURRY
1995 .... Ben HOWE
1996 .... Savalas CLOUTING
1997 .... Leigh LANHAM
1998 .... Scott NICHOLLS
1999 .... Scott NICHOLLS
2000 .... David HOWE
2001 .... Simon STEAD
2002 .... Simon STEAD
2003 .... Simon STEAD
2004 .... Ritchie HAWKINS
2005 .... Edward KENNETT
2006 .... Ben WILSON
2007 .... Edward KENNETT
2008 .... Tai WOFFINDEN

BEST OF BRITISH
Exeter's Keith Millard

BEST OF BRITISH – inaugural champion Graham Plant

BEST OF BRITISH – Neil Middleditch in 1975

SCOTT Nicholls moved to within reach of Barry Briggs' all-time British Championship record.

The New Zealand legend won six titles between 1961 and 1969 and Nicholls can join the Kiwi if he contests and wins again in 2009.

His name is now engraved five times on the trophy after his latest success at Blunsdon.

That takes him one ahead of another Australasian, six-times World Champion Ivan Mauger who won his four British crowns in the space of five seasons.

Nicholls' first victory came in 2002 and only Joe Screen (2004) and Chris Harris (2007) have prevented him the clean sweep ever since.

It was a major blow to his pride when he lost out to his British Grand Prix rival and he was a fully deserved winner at the Abbey Stadium.

After winning his first two rides he stopped while at the front third time out but wrapped up win number five with two further race victories, including the Grand Final.

Other than that machinery problem Nicholls had things his own way and surprisingly considering his reputation, he demonstrated flawless gating skills in the all important last race.

Harris, hoping to make it back-to-back victories, was trypically entertaining throughout the night as he just dropped a single point from his five qualifying rides.

However, the popular Cornishman didn't conjure a decent getaway in the final race and on a track that had become slicker as the evening wore on, he was powerless to stamp his authority on the race.

His eventual fourth place finish wasn't perhaps a fair

BEST OF BRITISH

Title-winner Scott Nicholls is flanked by third placed Tai Woffinden (left) and runner-up Edward Kennett.

HOW THEY SCORED....

	1	2	3	4	5	Tot	SF	F
1 Scott NICHOLLS	**3**	**3**	**R**	**3**	**3**	**12**	**–**	**3**
2 Edward KENNETT	3	2	2	1	1	9	3	2
3 Tai WOFFINDEN	1	3	3	1	3	11	2	1
4 Chris HARRIS	2	3	3	3	3	14	–	0
5 Simon STEAD	3	1	2	2	2	10	1	
6 James WRIGHT	0	2	3	3	3	11	0	
7 Lewis BRIDGER	2	1	F	3	2	8		
8 Leigh LANHAM	2	3	0	2	1	8		
9 Adam ROYNON	2	0	2	1	1	6		
10 Daniel KING	1	2	1	1	1	6		
11 David HOWE	3	R	2	0	0	5		
12 William LAWSON	0	1	0	2	2	5		
13 Chris NEATH	1	0	1	2	0	4		
14 Richard HALL	1	2	1	0	0	4		
15 Ricky ASHWORTH	0	0	3	0	0	3		
16 Ben BARKER	F	R	1	0	2	3		
17 Charlie SAUNDERS [R]					did not ride			

● *Lee Richardson and Oliver Allen withdrew through injury.*

reflection of his performance over the course as he was ousted from the rostrum by the new breed duo of Edward Kennett and Tai Woffinden.

Kennett, Nicholls' Eastbourne teammate, collected second place and the prized gift of the wild card at the British Grand Prix .

It had already been decided before the meeting that the highest placed finisher outside GP regulars Nicholls and Harris, would claim the number 16 race jacket at the Millennium Stadium.

For much of the meeting it looked an elusive target for the two-time British Under 21 champ as Kennett struggled through the preliminaries.

At one stage he looked like missing out on the semi final even – but scraped through as the lowest scorer, a point ahead of Lewis Bridger (foiled by an expensive fall) and Leigh Lanham who upstaged some of the young pretenders.

Kennett turned it on when it mattered, winning the semi final ahead of Woffinden, Simon Stead and James Wright who recovered from a shaky start to win three heats in a row before dropping out at the penultimate stage.

But at least he gave a healthy crowd something to cheer as the sole Swindon representative in the line-up which was denied the presence of former Robins' Lee Richardson and Oliver Allen through injury.

While Woffinden was a revelation, he wasn't the only youngster to have tongues wagging on the terraces.

Fellow teenager Adam Roynon did enough to convince watching Great Britain manager Jim Lynch that he was ready for a taste of the Speedway World Cup atmosphere although a broken leg eventually prevented the Cumbrian joining the squad in Denmark.

Woffinden was absolutely superb and had three wins and two third places in his 11 point qualifying tally.

But he reserved his best for the most important races: crossing the line second in the semi final and then blocking every one of Chris Harris' moves in the Grand Final.

Third spot was enough to provide Woffy with a ticket to the British GP – as first reserve with Stead filling the other standby role in Cardiff. And it was also the major factor in convincing Lions' chief Lynch that he was ready for his joust at the big-time in the Speedway World Cup.

Nicholls, accompanied at Blunsdon by partner Sophie Blake, adjusting to motherhood during her leave of absence from Sky's coverage of the Elite League, said: "I was really disappointed last year to lose the title so it was a big win for me to get it back.

"I wanted to prove I was top dog again, definitely. Not for one minute did I like losing it last year. It was a wake-up call, I want to be British number one."

Woffinden added: "I've shocked myself and I'm sure I've shocked everyone else as well by how far I've come on in the last two years.

"Hopefully, there's bigger and better things to come. Edward has been reserve at Cardiff for three years so he fully deserves it."

And Kennett said: "It means a lot to me – it is fantastic to get there and finally get my five rides."

Roll of Honour

1961 .... Barry BRIGGS
1962 .... Peter CRAVEN
1963 .... Peter CRAVEN
1964 .... Barry BRIGGS
1965 .... Barry BRIGGS
1966 .... Barry BRIGGS
1967 .... Barry BRIGGS
1968 .... Ivan MAUGER
1969 .... Barry BRIGGS
1970 .... Ivan MAUGER
1971 .... Ivan MAUGER
1972 .... Ivan MAUGER
1973 .... Ray WILSON
1974 .... Eric BOOCOCK
1975 .... John LOUIS
1976 .... Malcolm SIMMONS
1977 .... Michael LEE
1978 .... Michael LEE
1979 .... Peter COLLINS
1980 .... Dave JESSUP
1981 .... Steve BASTABLE
1982 .... Andy GRAHAME
1983 .... Chris MORTON
1984 .... Kenny CARTER
1985 .... Kenny CARTER
1986 .... Neil EVITTS
1987 .... Kelvin TATUM
1988 .... Simon WIGG
1989 .... Simon WIGG
1990 .... Kelvin TATUM
1991 .... Gary HAVELOCK
1992 .... Gary HAVELOCK
1993 .... Andy SMITH
1994 .... Andy SMITH
1995 .... Andy SMITH
1996 .... Joe SCREEN
1997 .... Mark LORAM
1998 .... Chris LOUIS
1999 .... Mark LORAM
2000 .... Chris LOUIS
2001 .... Mark LORAM
2002 .... Scott NICHOLLS
2003 .... Scott NICHOLLS
2004 .... Joe SCREEN
2005 .... Scott NICHOLLS
2006 .... Scott NICHOLLS
2007 .... Chris HARRIS
2008 .... Scott NICHOLLS

■ *The British Championship wasn't introduced to the domestic calender until 1961 although in 1946 a British Riders' Final was staged.*

Roll of Honour

1946 .... Tommy PRICE

Belle Vue, who operated throughout the Second World War, also staged an annual British Individual Championships, the winners of which were:

1940 .... Eric CHITTY (Canada)
1941 .... Eric CHITTY (Canada)
1942 .... Eric CHITTY (Canada)
1943 .... Ron CLARKE (England)
1944 .... Frank VAREY (England)
1945 .... Bill KITCHEN (England)

ELITE LEAGUE

2008 Elite League champions Poole: Adam Skornicki, Karol Zabik, Zbigniew Suchecki, team manager Neil Middleditch, skipper Bjarne Pedersen, Freddie Eriksson, Chris Holder, Davey Watt and promoter Matt Ford. Inset: Magnus Zetterström, Daniel Davidsson and Krzysztof Kasprzak

POOLE began the season as the firm favourites to lift their third Elite League championship in six seasons.

And they ended it splendidly, beating Grand Final play-off rivals Lakeside home and away in a convincing performance that fully justified all the pre-season predictions.

But that was about the only thing that was totally predictable about the 2008 campaign.

The Pirates recovered from shock back-to-back home defeats (against Ipswich and struggling Peterborough) in early summer but responded magnificently to their loss against the Panthers by putting together a 13-match winning run that took them to the top of the table.

At one stage it looked as if Swindon, written off by the so called experts at *Speedway Star*, could claim their first top-flight title in half a century and they led the race for a while.

But they lost their momentum in the wake of an away win at the East of England Showground and showed nothing like title winning form in the crucial months of July and August.

They managed an away win only once in their last eight league matches, including their capitulation in Essex in the play-off semi final.

Bizarrely after signing Jurica Pavlic – the find of the season – they won only three of the nine matches in which he competed!

Lakeside, still seeking their first-ever top tier trophy, were undone by cruel injuries that robbed them of Jonas Davidsson, Joonas Kylmåkorpi and, devastatingly, skipper Adam Shields, who, thankfully, made a complete winter recovery and is back on his bike in 2009.

Their season, full of such hope and optimism at one stage, disintegrated in the final weeks of the season when, simply, they ran out of steam despite late changes which saw Tomasz Jedrzejak (a success) and Krzysztof Jablonski (a failure) arrive.

Champions Coventry never recovered from a below par start to their title defence and were hamstrung by the regulations which didn't allow team changes until they'd completed six home and six away matches – in their case the beginning of August.

But perhaps the biggest surprise, other than Swindon stoutly upsetting the odds, was to see Wolverhampton and Peterborough battling it out in the newly-introduced relegation play offs.

The Panthers suffered from financial instability that eventually saw a new owner in Rick Frost, while the Parry's International Wolves had their worst season for many years and were probably thankful they didn't have to face King's Lynn to preserve their top-flight status.

ELITE LEAGUE REGULAR SEASON STANDINGS

		Home			Away					
	M	W	D	L	W	D	L	PtsF	PtsA	Pts
1 POOLE	32	14	0	2	8	0	8	1600	1321	52
2 LAKESIDE	32	15	0	1	7	1	8	1551	1375	52
3 SWINDON	32	12	2	2	5	0	11	1498	1434	41
4 IPSWICH	32	11	1	4	5	2	9	1483	1439	40
5 EASTBOURNE	32	11	0	5	4	0	12	1462	1472	34
6 COVENTRY	32	10	2	4	2	1	13	1418	1506	29
7 BELLE VUE	32	13	0	3	0	2	15	1423	1491	28
8 PETERBOROUGH	32	12	1	3	1	0	15	1371	1528	28
9 WOLVERHAMPTON	32	8	0	8	0	0	16	1341	1581	16

PLAY-OFFS

Semi Final
LAKESIDE 56 SWINDON 33
POOLE 59 IPSWICH 33

FINAL
First leg
LAKESIDE 42 **POOLE 48**
Second leg
POOLE 60 LAKESIDE 33

POOLE *win 2008 Elite Laague championship 108-75 on aggregate.*

Roll of Honour

1932 WEMBLEY
1933 BELLE VUE
1934 BELLE VUE
1935 BELLE VUE
1936 BELLE VUE
1937 WEST HAM
1938 NEW CROSS
1939 See footnote
1940-1945 No competition
1946 WEMBLEY
1947 WEMBLEY
1948 NEW CROSS
1949 WEMBLEY
1950 WEMBLEY
1951 WEMBLEY
1952 WEMBLEY
1953 WEMBLEY
1954 WIMBLEDON
1955 WIMBLEDON
1956 WIMBLEDON
1957 SWINDON
1958 WIMBLEDON
1959 WIMBLEDON
1960 WIMBLEDON
1961 WIMBLEDON
1962 SOUTHAMPTON
1963 BELLE VUE
1964 OXFORD
1965 WEST HAM
1966 HALIFAX
1967 SWINDON
1968 COVENTRY
1969 POOLE
1970 BELLE VUE
1971 BELLE VUE
1972 BELLE VUE
1973 READING
1974 EXETER
1975 IPSWICH
1976 IPSWICH
1977 WHITE CITY (London)
1978 COVENTRY
1979 COVENTRY
1980 READING
1981 CRADLEY HEATH
1982 BELLE VUE
1983 CRADLEY HEATH
1984 IPSWICH
1985 OXFORD
1986 OXFORD
1987 COVENTRY
1988 COVENTRY
1989 OXFORD
1990 READING
1991 WOLVERHAMPTON
1992 READING
1993 BELLE VUE
1994 POOLE
1995 EASTBOURNE
1996 WOLVERHAMPTON
1997 BRADFORD
1998 IPSWICH
1999 PETERBOROUGH
2000 EASTBOURNE
2001 OXFORD
2002 WOLVERHAMPTON
2003 POOLE
2004 POOLE
2005 COVENTRY
2006 PETERBOROUGH
2007 COVENTRY
2008 POOLE

Since 2002 the league championship has been determined by play-offs.

Between 1929 and 1931 there were two regional leagues operating, the Southern League and the Northern League (also known as the English League).

From 1932 onwards there has been a easily recognisable tiered league competition and the Roll of Honour above is for what was the highest level of league competition in each year.

In 1939 all racing ceased on September 3, 1939, at the declaration of the Second World War. At the time Belle Vue led the table but were never officially declared champions.

KNOCK OUT CUP

EASTBOURNE were the long-shot underdogs when they hosted the first leg of the Knock Out Cup Final at their own raceway.

And even when they ended the night with a healthy looking 22 point lead the majority of Poole fans were still quietly confident they would end the season as the double winners.

But the Eagles weren't reading the same script and when Magnus Zetterström (who was sitting behind partner Chris Holder with British Champion Scott Nicholls pegged back to third) ground to a halt in the opening Wimborne Road race the sense of belief spread around their pit bays.

And that belief was turned into genuine confidence when Lee Richardson won Heat 3.

Poole never really got going after that opening race upset and with five races left they had gnawed only minutely into Eastbourne's lead, reducing the original deficit to an insurmountable 20 points.

The Pirates' cause hadn't been helped by the first leg absence of Adam Skornicki who, as Polish Champion, had been ordered, at the threat of a ban, to compete in the previous night's Golden Helmet in his homeland.

Chris Holder's Heat 5 exclusion for unfair riding, after a coming together with Richardson, had been another blow for the favourites but over the two legs few could argue that, on this occasion, Eastbourne were the better team.

They swept any thought of an undeserved overall victory by holding onto a draw with a last race win from Nicholls, repeating his vital Heat 13 victory.

The Eagles had already shown their mighty resolve with a from-behind success against Lakeside in the less dramatic of the two semi finals.

Even though they trailed by 11 points after the first leg they eventually came out on top by four points on the back of another splendid home showing.

The real excitement, though, was in the other tie in which Coventry had to finally give up their hold on a trophy they'd held since 2006.

It looked all over for the Bees when they were held 45-45 at Brandon but, amazingly, it was exactly the same scoreline in the second leg.

And Coventry could count themselves doubly unfortunate as they were on their way to a win at Wimborne Road when Chris Harris suffered engine gremlins while leading the final race and was overtaken by a relieved Chris Holder.

Track conditions, wet and sticky, played into the visitors' hands, but Poole made no mistake in the replay, winning comfortably at home and extravagantly in the Brandon return to end Coventry's reign.

Round 1

IPSWICH 50 **WOLVERHAMPTON 42**
WOLVERHAMPTON 54 IPSWICH 38
WOLVERHAMPTON win 96-88 on aggregate.

Quarter Finals

BELLE VUE 49 **COVENTRY 44**
COVENTRY 56 BELLE VUE 37
COVENTRY win 100-86 on aggregate.

EASTBOURNE 62 WOLVERHAMPTON 30
WOLVERHAMPTON 52 **EASTBOURNE 40**
EASTBOURNE win 102-82 on aggregate.

PETERBOROUGH 39 **LAKESIDE 51**
LAKESIDE 50 PETERBOROUGH 42
LAKESIDE win 101-81 on aggregate.

POOLE 53 SWINDON 40
SWINDON 50 **POOLE 40**
POOLE win 93-90 on aggregate.

Semi Finals

LAKESIDE 52 **EASTBOURNE 41**
EASTBOURNE 54 LAKESIDE 39
EASTBOURNE win 95-91 on aggregate.

COVENTRY 45 POOLE 45
POOLE 45 COVENTRY 45
Tie drawn 90-90 on aggregate.

Semi Final Replay

POOLE 56 COVENTRY 36
COVENTRY 38 **POOLE 54**
POOLE win 110-74 on aggregate.

FINAL

EASTBOURNE 57 POOLE 35
POOLE 45 **EASTBOURNE 45**
EASTBOURNE win 102-80 on aggregate.

Roll of Honour

1961 .... SOUTHAMPTON
1962 .... WIMBLEDON
1963 .... SOUTHAMPTON
1964 .... OXFORD
1965 .... WEST HAM
1966 .... HALIFAX
1967 .... COVENTRY
1968 .... WIMBLEDON
1969 .... WIMBLEDON
1970 .... WIMBLEDON
1971 .... HACKNEY
1972 .... BELLE VUE
1973 .... BELLE VUE
1974 .... SHEFFIELD
1975 .... BELLE VUE
1976 .... IPSWICH
1977 .... KING'S LYNN
1978 .... IPSWICH
1979 .... CRADLEY HEATH
1980 .... CRADLEY HEATH
1981 .... IPSWICH
1982 .... CRADLEY HEATH
1983 .... CRADLEY HEATH
1984 .... IPSWICH
1985 .... OXFORD

1986 ....OXFORD & CRADLEY HEATH
1987 ....CRADLEY HEATH
1988 ....CRADLEY HEATH
1989 ....CRADLEY HEATH
1990 ....READING
1991 ....BRADFORD
1992 ....BRADFORD
1993 ....BRADFORD
1994 ....EASTBOURNE
1995 ....BRADFORD
1996 ....................WOLVERHAMPTON
1997 ....EASTBOURNE
1998 ....IPSWICH
1999 ....................PETERBOROUGH
2000 ....KING'S LYNN
2001 ....................PETERBOROUGH
2002 ....EASTBOURNE
2003 ....POOLE
2004 ....POOLE
2005 ....BELLE VUE
2006 ....COVENTRY
2007 ....COVENTRY
2008 ....EASTBOURNE

The National Trophy was the forerunner to the Knock Out Cup and the first truly national competition. When it was launched in 1931 teams from both the Southern League and the Northern League raced against each other, ties being decided on aggregate scores after home and away legs.

The competition was eventually discontinued on the amalgamation of the National League (First Division) and Provincial League (Second Division) in 1965.

Roll of Honour

1931 ....WEMBLEY
1932 ....WEMBLEY
1933 ....BELLE VUE
1934 ....BELLE VUE
1935 ....BELLE VUE
1936 ....BELLE VUE
1937 ....BELLE VUE
1938 ....WIMBLEDON
1939 ....See footnote
1940-1945 ....No competition
1946 ....BELLE VUE
1947 ....BELLE VUE
1948 ....WEMBLEY
1949 ....BELLE VUE
1950 ....WIMBLEDON
1951 ....WIMBLEDON
1952 ....HARRINGAY
1953 ....WIMBLEDON
1954 ....WEMBLEY
1955 ....NORWICH
1956 ....WIMBLEDON
1957 ....No competition
1958 ....BELLE VUE
1959 ....WIMBLEDON
1960 ....WIMBLEDON
1961 ....SOUTHAMPTON
1962 ....WIMBLEDON
1963 ....NORWICH
1964 ....OXFORD

In 1939 Belle Vue qualified for the Final and were awaiting the outcome of the Southampton-Wembley semi final.

2009...2009...2009...2009

MAJOR changes were made to the overall scoring system for the 2009 season – in an effort to reward teams putting up spirited yet losing performances in away meetings.

Teams can now earn up to three points for a home win and up to four points if they come out on top in their travels.

It will ensure team managers have to be on their toes – and will also keep the fans on the terraces consulting their programmes frequently as teams get close to increasing their points tally.

Points gained are as follows:

0 losing at home and losing away by seven points or more.

1 a home draw or losing by no more than six points in an away match.

2 home win by between one and six points or an away draw.

3 home win by seven points or more and an away win by between one and six points.

4 winning on the road by seven points or more.

■ The controversial tactical ride rule (in which a rider can score double points for his team) was also amended.

Teams will be allowed to use the rule TWICE in a meeting – one occasion if they are losing by 10 points or more and the other when they are 12 points or more down. But they MUST be be used in that order.

■ The tactical substitute rule (in which a rider can start off a handicap and gain double points) has been abolished.

■ In the Premier League Knock Out Cup only, a new tactical gate regulation is being trialled under which the losing team can, on two separate occasions, choose gate positions if they are six points or more behind.

■ The points limit in the 2009 Elite League is 39.90 and teams may chose two Premier League riders to share a team place as long as the rider had a 2008 Premier League average below eight.

■ The team's highest-average rider must be programmed at number one but the next four riders can occupy any position between two and five.

■ The two lowest averaged riders must be programmed at six and seven and the home team must notifiy the opposition of their line-up first, allowing the visitors to make any tactical switches in race order they so wish.

CRAVEN SHIELD

Coventry salvaged something from an instantly forgettable season by inflicting a second big occasion defeat on luckless Lakeside.

The Hammers, still suffering from the hangover of a Grand Final defeat, succumbed in front of their own fans – and it was virtually one way traffic in the second leg at Brandon, a meeting notable for Ben Barker's first senior maximum.

Southern Group

EASTBOURNE 52 **POOLE 42**
EASTBOURNE 52 SWINDON 41
POOLE 51 EASTBOURNE 43
POOLE 54 SWINDON 39
SWINDON 48 EASTBOURNE 42
SWINDON 46 **POOLE 44**

Eastern Group

IPSWICH 43 **LAKESIDE 47**
IPSWICH 61 PETERBOROUGH 31
LAKESIDE 40 IPSWICH 52
LAKESIDE 58 PETERBOROUGH 35
PETERBOROUGH 47 IPSWICH 43
PETERBOROUGH 45 **LAKESIDE 45**

Northern Group

BELLE VUE 50 **COVENTRY 42**
COVENTRY 54 BELLE VUE 39
BELLE VUE 49 WOLVERHAMPTON 41
COVENTRY 59 WOLVERHAMPTON 33
WOLVERHAMPTON 53 **COVENTRY 37**
WOLVERHAMPTON 48 BELLE VUE 44

Semi Final

POOLE 58 **COVENTRY 34**
COVENTRY 58 POOLE 32
COVENTRY win 92-90 on aggregate.

FINAL

LAKESIDE 43 **COVENTRY 47**
COVENTRY 58 LAKESIDE 35
COVENTRY win 105-78 on aggregate.

Roll of Honour

1997 .... COVENTRY
1998 .... IPSWICH
1999 .... PETERBOROUGH
2000 .... COVENTRY
2001 .... POOLE
2002 .... POOLE
2005 .... OXFORD
2006 .... POOLE
2007 .... COVENTRY
2008 .... COVENTRY

Victorious Craven Shield winners Coventry parade their silverware

Southern Group

	M	W	D	L	PtsF	PtsA	Pts
POOLE	4	2	0	2	191	180	4
Eastbourne	4	2	0	2	189	182	4
Swindon	4	2	0	2	174	192	4

Eastern Group

	M	W	D	L	PtsF	PtsA	Pts
LAKESIDE	4	2	1	0	190	175	6
Ipswich	4	2	0	2	199	165	5
Peterborough	4	1	1	2	158	207	3

Northern Group

	M	W	D	L	PtsF	PtsA	Pts
COVENTRY	4	2	0	2	192	175	4
Belle Vue	4	2	0	2	182	185	4
Wolverhampton	4	2	0	2	175	189	4

Highest points scoring group winners seeded direct to the Final. The two other group winners to meet in home and away semi final with the winners going through to the Final.

Robins' boss Alun Rossiter proudly shows off the Elite Shield

ELITE SHIELD

Swindon ordered a few extra cans of polish after starting their season with a trophy.

The Robins gained some revenge for their big-night defeats against Coventry the previous year by parading the Elite Shield.

In a one-sided contest, the Robins virtually wrapped up victory with their 22 point home win, Leigh Adams starting the new campaign with a customary Blunsdon maximum.

SWINDON 57 COVENTRY 35
COVENTRY 52 **SWINDON 41**
SWINDON win 98-87 on aggregate.

Roll of Honour

2006 .... COVENTRY
2007 .... PETERBOROUGH
2008 .... SWINDON
2009 .... EASTBOURNE

The Elite League Shield has been contested between the Elite League champions and the Knock Out Cup winners although it is not recognised as an official competition by the authorities.

In 1982 the British Speedway Promoters Association introduced the Premiership – an annual early season curtain-raiser between the previous year's league champions and Knock Out Cup (or, in some cases, League Cup) winners.

Roll of Honour

1982 .... CRADLEY HEATH
1983 .... BELLE VUE
1984 .... CRADLEY HEATH
1985 .... CRADLEY HEATH
1986 .... COVENTRY
1987 .... OXFORD
1988 .... CRADLEY HEATH
1989 .... CRADLEY HEATH
1990 .... CRADLEY HEATH
1991 .... READING
1992 .... WOLVERHAMPTON
1993 .... READING
1994 .... BRADFORD
1995 .... EASTBOURNE
1996 .... EASTBOURNE
1997 .... WOLVERHAMPTON
2001 .... EASTBOURNE

INTER LEAGUE KO CUP

Roll of Honour

1975 .... BELLE VUE
1976 .... HULL
1977 .... IPSWICH
1978 .... KING'S LYNN
1979 .... CRADLEY HEATH
1980 .... KING'S LYNN
1991 .... BRADFORD
1992 .... READING
2003 .... POOLE

FOURS CHAMPIONSHIP

Similar to the ultra successful Premier League competition, the Elite League Four Team Championship was discontinued at the end of 1997.

Roll of Honour

1991 .... IPSWICH
1992 .... BELLE VUE
1993 .... READING
1994 .... POOLE
1995 .... CRADLEY HEATH
1996 .... OXFORD
1997 .... PETERBOROUGH

LEAGUE CUP

The League Cup was introduced to the top-flight calendar in 1981 and quickly became the third most prestigious trophy – after the league and KO Cup.

Initially the16 teams were split into two regional groups, with the section winners meeting in a home and away Final.

In 1985 it was run as a parallel competition to the British League with the top four meeting in play-offs.

Roll of Honour

1981 .... COVENTRY
1982 .... CRADLEY HEATH
1983 .... BELLE VUE
1984 .... CRADLEY HEATH
1985 .... COVENTRY
1986 .... CRADLEY HEATH & OXFORD
1987 .... COVENTRY

A similar competition the Gold Cup (which had been run as a regional tournament between 1972 and 1980) was re-introduced in 1989.

Roll of Honour

1972 .... READING
1973 .... KING'S LYNN
1974 .... NEWPORT
1975 .... NEWPORT
1976 .... IPSWICH
1977 .... READING
1978 .... EXETER
1979 .... WIMBLEDON
1980 .... KING'S LYNN
1989 .... OXFORD
1990 .... BRADFORD
1991 .... BERWICK
1992 .... WOLVERHAMPTON

ELITE LEAGUE RIDERS' FINAL

BIRMINGHAM
Wednesday, October 8

JASON Crump won his fourth Elite League Riders' Championship in a meeting sadly depleted by mass withdrawals and absences.

Despite being switched to Premier League Birmingham – a neutral venue – the event continues to lose its former prestige as riders pull out with the flimsiest of excuses.

It was a bitter blow for the Super7even organisers and the Brummies who laid out the red carpet at the biggest event since their return to racing.

The first attempt to run at Perry Barr – on Wednesday, August 20 – was called off by referee Ronnie Allan 35 minutes before the parade because of heavy rain.

	1	2	3	4	5	Tot	SF	GF
1 Jason CRUMP	**3**	**2**	**1**	**3**	**3**	**12**	**2**	**3**
2 Rory SCHLEIN	3	1	1	3	2	10	3	2
3 Kenneth BJERRE	3	2	3	2	3	13	–	1
4 Leigh ADAMS	1	3	3	3	3	13	–	0
5 Chris HOLDER	2	3	3	1	2	11	1	
6 Davey WATT	2	1	2	2	3	10	0	
7 Lewis BRIDGER	2	2	3	0	1	8		
8 Niels-Kristian IVERSEN	1	0	2	2	2	7		
9 Daniel KING	F	2	2	1	2	7		
10 Fredrik LINDGREN	0	0	2	3	1	6		
11 Jonas DAVIDSSON	3	1	0	0	1	5		
12 Piotr SWIDERSKI	R	3	1	0	1	5		
13 Troy BATCHELOR	1	3	R	1	0	5		
14 Edward KENNETT	1	0	1	2	0	4		
15 Billy JANNIRO	2	0	0	R		2		
16 Charlie GJEDDE	0	1	0	1	0	2		
17 Jay HERNE [R]	0							

Roll of Honour

1965 .... Barry BRIGGS (Swindon)
1966 .... Barry BRIGGS (Swindon)
1967 .... Barry BRIGGS (Swindon)
1968 .... Barry BRIGGS (Swindon)
1969 .... Barry BRIGGS (Swindon)
1970 .... Barry BRIGGS (Swindon)
1971 .... Ivan MAUGER (Belle Vue)
1972 .... Ole OLSEN (Wolverhampton)
1973 .... Ivan MAUGER (Exeter)
1974 .... Peter COLLINS (Belle Vue)
1975 .... Peter COLLINS (Belle Vue)
1976 .... Ole OLSEN (Coventry)
1977 .... Ole OLSEN (Coventry)
1978 .... Ole OLSEN (Coventry)
1979 .... John LOUIS (Ipswich)
1980 .... Les COLLINS (Leicester)
1981 .... Kenny CARTER (Halifax)
1982 .... Kenny CARTER (Halifax)
1983 .... Erik GUNDERSEN (Cradley Heath)
1984 .... Chris MORTON (Belle Vue)
1985 .... Erik GUNDERSEN (Cradley Heath)
1986 .... Hans NIELSEN (Oxford)
1987 .... Hans NIELSEN (Oxford)
1988 .... Jan O. PEDERSEN (Cradley Heath)
1989 .... Shawn MORAN (Belle Vue)
1990 .... Hans NIELSEN (Oxford)
1991 .... Sam ERMOLENKO (Wolverhampton)
1992 .... Joe SCREEN (Belle Vue)
1993 .... Per JONSSON (Reading)
1994 .... Sam ERMOLENKO (Wolverhampton)
1995 .... Gary HAVELOCK (Bradford)
1996 .... Sam ERMOLENKO (Sheffield)
1997 .... Greg HANCOCK (Coventry)
1998 .... Tony RICKARDSSON (Ipsqwich)
1999 .... Jason CRUMP (Peterborough)
2000 .... Ryan SULLIVAN (Peterborough)
2001 .... Jason CRUMP (King's Lynn)
2002 .... Tony RICKARDSSON (Poole)
2003 .... Lee RICHARDSON (Coventry)
2004 .... Bjarne PEDERSEN (Poole)
2005 .... Nicki PEDERSEN (Eastbourne)
2006 .... Jason CRUMP (Belle Vue)
2007 .... Nicki PEDERSEN (Eastbourne)
2008 .... Jason CRUMP (Belle Vue)

Milestones

Only eight riders have competed the double by following up a World Championship victory with a win in the Riders' Championship Final: Barry Briggs (1966), Ole Olsen (1978), Erik Gundersen (1985), Hans Nielsen (1986 and 1987), Greg Hancock (1997), Tony Rickardsson (1998 and 2002), Jason Crump (2006) and Nicki Pedersen (2007).

In the first four seasons of the Riders' Final Barry Briggs was beaten only twice in 21 races – by Nigel Boocock in 1965 and his younger brother Eric in 1968!

Seven riders have taken advantage of the Riders' Final being on their home track – Ivan Mauger (Belle Vue), Peter Collins (Belle Vue, twice), Chris Morton (Belle Vue), Shawn Moran (Belle Vue), Tony Rickardsson (Poole), Lee Richardsson (Coventry) and Bjarne Pedersen (Poole).

Hans Nielsen holds the all-time appearance record – 14.

ELITE LEAGUE PAIRS

WHAT A PAIR: Coventry duo Chris Harris and Hans Andersen

SWINDON
Sunday, August 17

HANS Andersen, who had joined Coventry at the beginning of the month, provided the Bees with their first trophy of the season.

Clever teamwork in the final saw him and Chris Harris elect to allow Mads Korneliussen a free run at the front while they blocked all Leigh Adams' efforts to claim what would have been a third Pairs title in the last five years and brought Coventry their first success since 1978.

	1	2	3	4	Tot	SF	GF
1 COVENTRY							
Hans ANDERSEN	4	4	**2**	4	14	3	**2**
Chris HARRIS	FX	**3**	3	**3**	9	**2**	3
2 SWINDON							
Leigh ADAMS	4	4	4	4	16	**2**	0
Mads KORNELIUSSEN	**3**	**3**	2	2	10	3	4
3 IPSWICH							
Piotr SWIDERSKI	0	**3**	4	4	11	0	
Rory SCHLEIN	4	4	0	2	10	4	
4 BELLE VUE							
Jason CRUMP	3	4	4	4	15	4	
Charlie GJEDDE	**2**	2	**3**	**3**	10	0	
5 POOLE							
Bjarne PEDERSEN	3	**2**	3	**3**	11		
Chris HOLDER	**2**	3	0	4	9		
6 WOLVERHAMPTON							
Fredrik LINDGREN	0	R	0	2	2		
Niels-Kristian IVERSEN	3	3	3	4	13		
7 PETERBOROUGH							
Kenneth BJERRE	2	2	2	0	6		
Daniel KING	0	4	F	2	6		
8 EASTBOURNE							
Cameron WOODWARD	0	F	2	0	2		
Lee RICHARDSON	2	4	E	3	9		
9 LAKESIDE							
Adam SHIELDS	2	2	3	2	9		
Jonas DAVIDSSON	0	0	0	0	0		

Semi Final 1: Swindon 5 (Mads Korneliussen 3, Leigh Adams 2:1), Ipswich 4 (Rory Schlein 4, Piotr Swiderski 0).

Semi Final 2: Coventry 5 (Hans Andersen 3, Chris Harris 2:1), Belle Vue 4 (Jason Crump 4, Charlie Gjedde 0).

Final: Coventry 5 (Chris Harris 3, Hans Andersen 2:1), Swindon 4 (Mads Korneliussen 4, Leigh Adams 0).

Roll of Honour

1976 .... IPSWICH
1977 .... IPSWICH
1978 .... COVENTRY & CRADLEY HEATH
1984 .... BELLE VUE
1985 .... OXFORD
1986 .... OXFORD
1987 .... OXFORD
2004 .... SWINDON
2005 .... SWINDON
2006 .... BELLE VUE
2007 .... POOLE
2008 .... COVENTRY

Elite League

BELLE VUE

TRACK FILE

Track: Greyhound Stadium, Kirkmanshulme Lane, Gorton, Manchester, M18 7BA.
Telephone: 0161 223 7720 (race-days only).
Hotline: 09068 664678
Website: www.bellevuespeedway.co.uk
Track Length: 285 metres.
Track Record: 56.9 secs, Jason Crump, June 9, 2008.
Promoters: David Gordon, Chris Morton, MBE, Gordon Pairman.
Team Sponsors: one51.
Colours: Red and white with black ace of clubs.
Nickname: Aces.

HONOURS

Major honours: 43.
Division One champions (10†), 1933-34-35-36, 1963, 1970-71-72, 1982, 1993.
Division One Knock Out Cup winners (5), 1931, 1972-73, 1975, 2005.
Division One Trophy winners (9), 1933-34-35-36-37, 1946-47, 1949, 1958.
Division One League Cup winners (1), 1983.
Division One ACU Cup winners (5), 1934-35-36-37, 1946.
Division One Premiership winners (1), 1983.
Division One Four Team champions (1), 1992.
Division One British Speedway Cup winners (1), 1939.
Division One Britannia Shield winners (3), 1957-58, 1960.
Division One Pairs champions (1), 2006.
Inter League Knock Out Cup winners (1), 1975.
Division Two champions (2), 1968-69.
Division Two Knock Out Cup winners (1), 1969.
Northern League champions (2), 1930-31.
†Belle Vue were top of Division One when racing was suspended at the outbreak of the Second World War in 1939 but never officially declared champions.

2008 REVIEW

THE return of Jason Crump to Kirkmanshulme Lane ensured plenty of optimism that the Aces could banish the memories of their wooden-spoon finish in 2007.

However, despite Charlie Gjedde enjoying a strong first season with the club and supporting Crump well at the top of the order, the Aces too often found themselves struggling in their lower order.

Part of that was due to injuries, with first-choice reserve Steve Boxall crashing out at Coventry in the first month of the season and suffering shoulder damage which effectively ended his season.

A host of riders filled the reserve berths with the Aces never truly finding a solution, and they also went through the campaign without an away win - although they did draw at both Coventry and Swindon and were desperately close at Blunsdon in particular with guest Kevin Doolan suffering a last-bend engine failure to rescue the Robins.

In addition to Boxall's misfortune, second-string Pole Lukasz Jankowski was ruled out for the season in June, and veteran Joe Screen also suffered his own injury problems.

The Aces had been fallible at home in the first half of the season with defeats against Swindon, Eastbourne and Lakeside – but that June 2 loss against the Hammers proved to be their last on their own shale, and a win over Coventry in their last match ensuring that they moved above Peterborough and out of the bottom two.

Danish youngster Patrick Hougaard was introduced mid-season and made a strong impression during his 11-match spell – the Aces will see more of him, but more rebuilding was needed with Crump's shock decision to quit British speedway.

The club also staged a hugely successful 80th anniversary event at the end of July, with the Peter Craven Memorial Trophy being won by Leigh Adams.

HISTORY

First meeting: July 28, 1928, Golden Helmet individual trophy.
Leagues: Division One (1929-39, 1946-2009); Division Two (1929-31, 1939, 1968-69); Division Three (1948, 1997).
Meetings have also been held at the following Manchester venue.

● *Zoological Gardens, Hyde Road, Gorton, Manchester, M12 5PX.*
First meeting: March 23, 1929, Golden Helmet.
Leagues: Division One, 1931-39, 1946-1987. Division Two, 1929-1931, 1939, 1968-69. Open licence, 1940-45.

2008 RESULTS

Elite League

Final position..Seventh

LAKESIDE (H)
Monday, March 31,
Won 47-43
Crump 14, Forsberg 4:1, Gjedde 10:2, Jankowski 5:1, Screen 10:1, Rajkowski 1:1, Ksiezak 3.

SWINDON (A)
Thursday, April 3
Lost 43-49
Crump 13, Forsberg 2, Gjedde 15:1 (TS4), Jankowski 5:3, Screen 7:1, Rajkowski 0, Ksiezak 1.

POOLE (H) *SKY TV*
Monday, April 7
Won 50-43
Crump 13:1, Forsberg 5:1, Gjedde 14, Jankowski 4, Screen 8, Ksiezak 5:2, Rajkowski 1:1.

COVENTRY (A)
Friday, April 11
Drew 45-45
Crump 15, Forsberg 6:1, Gjedde 11, Jankowski 6:2, Screen 3, Rajkowski 1, Ksziezak 3:1.
▲ *Aces pulled back from six points down in the last five heats, Gjedde passing Chris Harris in Heat 15 to claim a point.*

PETERBOROUGH (A)
Thursday, April 17
Lost 45-47
Crump 16 (4), Forsberg 5, Gjedde 6:2, Jankowski 6:1, Screen 9:1, Rajkowski 0, Ksiezak 3:1.

EASTBOURNE (A)
Saturday, April 19
Lost 40-50
Crump 14, Forsberg 5, Gjedde 5:1, Jankowski 7:1, Screen 4, Rajkowski 3, Tomas Suchanek [G] 2:1.
▲ *Crump broke track record and was only beaten by Scott Nicholls in Heat 15.*

SQUAD
Steve Boxall, Joe Screen, Nick Simmons.
Foreign: Stanislaw Burza, Jason Crump, Billy Forsberg, Charlie Gjedde, Patrick Hougaard, Lukasz Jankowski, Robert Ksiezak, Tomasz Piszcz, Michael Rajkowski , Jonas Raun.

SWINDON (H)
Monday, April 21
Lost 42-51
Crump 17 (6), Forsberg 7:2, Gjedde 4:1, Jankowski 4, Screen 5, Rajkowski 2, Ksiezak 3:1.
▼ *Major disappointment as Aces trailed throughout. Too reliant on Crump and Forsberg, who was unbeaten after finishing last in Heat 1.*

EASTBOURNE (H)
Wednesday, May 7
Lost 42-48
Crump 13, *rider replacement for Forsberg*, Gjedde 12:1, Jankowski 0, Screen 6, Rajkowski 3, Ksiezak 5:2, Proctor 3.
▼ *Jankowksi aggravated a shoulder injury in Heat 3. Used Ty Proctor as No.8, to cover the absence of Forsberg.*

SWINDON (H)
Monday, May 12
Won 47-43
Crump 14, Tai Woffinden [G] 9:1, Gjedde 11, *rider replacement for Jankowski*, Screen 10:1, Ksiezak 1, Raun 2.
▲ *Crump's win in a last heat ended a run of four straight defeats to lift Aces off the bottom of the table.*

POOLE (A)
Wednesday, May 14
Abandoned 12-24. Rain.
Crump 4, rider replacement for Jankowski, Gjedde 0, Lewis Bridger [G] 2, Screen 4, Raun 1, Nick Simmons [G] 1.

POOLE (H),
Monday, May 19
Won 48-42
Crump 13, Jason Lyons [G] 11, Gjedde 11:1, *rider replacement for Jankowski*, Screen 10, Ksiezak 2:1, Raun 1.

IPSWICH (A)
Thursday, May 22
Lost 41-52
Crump 14 (6), *rider replacement for Jankowski*, Gjedde 7:1, Tai Woffinden [G] 8, Screen 10, Simmons 2:1, Raun 0.

WOLVERHAMPTON (A)
Monday, May 26
Lost 45-49
Crump 16 (6), Jason Lyons [G] 9:1, Gjedde 11:2, *rider replacement for Jankowski*, Screen 5, Simmons 3, Ksiezak 1.
● *Lyons guested for Forsberg, who had been reserve for the weekend's Swedish Grand Prix.*

LAKESIDE (H)
Monday, June 2
Lost 42-48
Crump 15, Forsberg 4:1, Gjedde 12, Jankowski 1, Screen 5, Simmons 4, Raun 1.
▲ *Crump's first home maximum of the season on his 200th Aces appearance.*

COVENTRY (A)
Friday, June 6
Lost 40-52
Crump 18 (4), Forsberg 2:1, Gjedde 4, Jankowski 8, Screen 6, Simmons 2, Raun 0.

EASTBOURNE (H)
Monday, June 9
Won 48-45
Crump 15, Forsberg 6:1, Gjedde 12, Jankowski 1:1, Screen 9, Simmons 3, Raun 2:1.
▲▼ *Crump shattered track record in Heat 1 and reeled off four more wins, taking a last-heat 4-2 with Gjedde to secure victory. Jankowski suffered a season-ending shoulder injury.*

IPSWICH (H) *SKY TV*
Monday, June 23
Won 52-38
Crump 15, Jason Lyons [G] 7, Gjedde 15:1, Forsberg 11:3, *rider replacement for Screen*, Simmons 0, Raun 4:2.
▼ *Crump briefly held another track record when the time, incorrectly clocked by television coverage, was given officially. The clock had stopped two seconds early!*

EASTBOURNE (A)
Saturday, June 29
Lost 37-56
Crump 15 (6), *rider replacement for Joe Screen*, Gjedde 8:3, Forsberg 4:1, Kevin Doolan [G] 8, Simmons 1, Raun 1.
▲ *Jason Crump set a new track record, lowering the time to 54.8 seconds in Heat 1.*

PETERBOROUGH (H)
Monday, June 30
Won 52-41
Crump 10:1, *rider replacement for Jankowski*, Gjedde 14, Forsberg 6:2, Screen 11:1, Ksiezak 10:3, Raun 1:1.
▲ *Ksiezak produced his best top-flight performance.*

PETERBOROUGH (A)
Thursday, July 3
Lost 42-52
Crump 18 (6), Lewis Bridger [G] 5:2 (TS2), *rider replacement for Gjedde*, Forsberg 5, Screen 9, Robert Mear [G] 1,Hougaard 4:1.
▼ *Crump ran surprise last place in Heat 1 but then reeled off five wins. Gjedde absent on paternity leave.*

LAKESIDE (A)
Friday, July 4
Lost 39-54
Crump 20 (6), Lewis Bridger [G] 5, *rider replacement for Gjedde*, Forsberg 5, Screen 6, Ksiezak 2, Hougaard 1.
▼ *Crump's only defeat at hands of Andreas Jonsson, with Screen and guest Lewis Bridger supplying the other two race wins.*

COVENTRY (H) *SKY TV*
Monday, July 7
Won 46-43
Crump 15, James Wright (G) 3:1, Gjedde 12:1, Forsberg 7:1, *rider replacement for Screen*, Simmons 2, Hougaard 7:1
▲ *Hougaard impressed on debut. Trailed by eight points with four heats to go – but 5-0 in Heat 13 and 5-1 in Heat 15, both involving Crump, generated massive turnaround.*

SWINDON (A)
Thursday, July 11
Drew 45-45
Crump 12:1, Kevin Doolan [G] 9:1, Gjedde 11:1, Forsberg 0, *rider replacement for Screen*, Simmons

Charlie Gjedde, Robert Ksiezak, Lukasz Jankowski, Michael Rajkowski, Joe Screen, Billy Forsberg, Steve Boxall, Jason Crump

PHOTO: **Ian Charles**

4:3, Hougaard 9.

▼▼ *Forsberg crashed in Heat 3 and was unable to play any further part in the meeting. Yards away from a dramatic win only for Doolan's machine to expire off the final bend of Heat 15 to hand the Robins a draw.*

PETERBOROUGH (H)
Monday, July 21
Won 53-39
Kevin Doolan [G] 5,*rider replacement for Jankowski*, Gjedde 14, Forsberg 8:3, Screen 12:1, Simmons 1:1, Hougaard 13:1.

▲ *Hougaard served full notice of his potential with three race wins as the Aces won without Crump (broken finger).*

POOLE (A)
Wednesday, July 23
Lost 33-59
Adam Shields [G] 9, *rider replacement for Jankowski*, Gjedde 4:1, Forsberg 7, Screen 5:1, Simmons 0, Hougaard 8:2.

▼ *Hougaard again provided the bright spot with two race wins – the only two occasions Aces took the flag.*

IPSWICH (H)
Monday, August 4
Won 48-42
Crump 12:2, *rider replacement for Jankowski*, Gjedde 11:1, Forsberg 7:2, Screen 6, Simmons 1, Hougaard 11:1.

▲ *Another new track record for Crump, although his team trailed in the early stages before wrapping up victory with 4-2 in Heat 14.*

IPSWICH (A)
Thursday, August 7
Lost 42-48
Crump 14, *rider replacement for Jankowski*, Gjedde 5, Forsberg 9:1, Screen 5, Simmons 2, Hougaard 7:1.

▲ *Forsberg and Hougaard both made encouraging first appearances at Foxhall.*

POOLE (A) *SKY TV*
Monday, August 18
Lost 31-50
Crump 15 (6), *rider replacement for Jankowski*, Gjedde 4, Hougaard 3, Screen 2, Burza 4:1, Forsberg 3.

●▲ *Meeting abandoned after 13 heats, rain. Result to stand. Crump reeled off four race wins.*

WOLVERHAMPTON (A)
Monday, August 25
Lost 45-48
Crump 12 (6), *rider replacement for Jankowski*, Gjedde 7, Hougaard 7, Screen 7, Craig Watson [G] 0, Forsberg 12.

▼ *Having trailed 7-17, Aces rallied and took the lead with a Hougaard/Forsberg 5-1 in Heat 14 – only for Crump and Gjedde to concede maximum points in the decider.*

WOLVERHAMPTON (H)
Wednesday, August 27
Won 60-30
Crump 11, *rider replacement for Jankowski*, **Gjedde 15**, Hougaard 10:4, Screen 7:1, Ksiezak 8, Forsberg 9:4.

▲ *Took out their frustration from two days earlier against a depleted Wolves side who saw Niels-Kristian Iversen crash out in Heat 7.*

COVENTRY (H)
Monday, September 1
Abandoned 10-14, rain.
Crump 1, *rider replacement for Jankowski*, Gjedde 0, Jason Lyons [G] 1, Screen 0, Ksiezak 3, Forsberg 5:1.

● *Abandonment may have been a stroke of fortune after Aces struggled early on, with Crump on the end of a 1-5 reverse in Heat 1.*

WOLVERHAMPTON (H)
Monday, September 8
Won 49-41
Crump 14, Kevin Doolan [G] 7:1, Gjedde 14:1, Jason Lyons [G] 8:2, *rider replacement for Screen*, Simon Lambert [G] 5, Ksiezak 1.

▲ *Patched-up side did just enough for win, with ex-Aces Kevin Doolan and Jason Lyons making solid contributions.*

LAKESIDE (A)
Friday, September 10
Lost 34-59
Crump 18 (6), *rider replacement for Jankowski*, Gjedde 7, Barrie Evans [G] 0, Screen 4, Ksiezak 0, Forsberg 5.

▼ *Could have been billed Lakeside v Crump as the Aces failed to make any impact.*

COVENTRY (H)
Monday, October 6
Won 50-40
Crump 11:1, *rider replacement for Jankowski*, Gjedde 7, Jason Lyons [G] 7:1, Screen 12, Piszcz 6:1, Forsberg 7:2.

▲ *Secured Elite League status with Screen rounding off the season in fine form with four wins and a fall. Crump was unbeaten and Gjedde finished with two wins.*

ELITE LEAGUE

	M	*W*	*D*	*L*	*PtsF*	*PtsA*	*Pts*
Poole	32	22	0	10	1600	1321	52
Lakeside	32	22	1	9	1551	1375	52
Swindon	32	17	2	13	1498	1434	41
Ipswich	32	16	3	13	1483	1439	40
Eastbourne	32	15	0	17	1462	1472	34
Coventry	32	12	3	17	1418	1506	29
BELLE VUE	**32**	**13**	**2**	**17**	**1423**	**1491**	**28**
Peterborough	32	13	1	18	1371	1528	28
Wolverhampton	32	8	0	24	1341	1581	16

2009 Squad

Jason Crump's decision to give Elite League racing a miss in 2009 left a huge gap in the Aces line-up and they've gone for strength in depth for the new season.

Krzysztof **KASPRZAK** (8.68), Charlie **GJEDDE** (7.86), Ulrich **ØSTERGAARD** (5.17), James **WRIGHT** (4.90), Billy **FORSBERG** (4.81), Henning **BAGER** (4.63), Patrick **HOUGAARD** (4.00), *Steve* ***BOXALL*** *(3.63)/Thomas H.* ***JONASSON*** *(3.66), Josh* ***GRAJCZONEK*** *(3.00).*

Knock Out Cup

First round, first leg
COVENTRY (H)
Monday, June 16
Won 49-44
Crump 15, *rider replacement for Jankowski*, Gjedde 11:1, Forsberg 7:2, Screen 10, Simmons 2, Raun 4:1.

First round, second leg
COVENTRY (A)
Friday, June 20
Lost 37-56
Piotr Swiderski [G] 15 (6), *rider replacement for Jamnkowski*, Gjedde 8, Forsberg 4:1, Screen 3:1, Simmons 5, Raun 2:2.

▲▼ *Guest Piotr Swiderski, replacing absent Crump who was racing in Polish League, won his first three rides. Screen suffered concussion in a second-bend crash with Chris Harris in Heat 6.*

Aggregate: Lost 86-100.

Crump stunner

Skipper Jason Crump shocked Belle Vue a few hours after he'd been confirmed as the world number two again by revealing that he wouldn't be racing in the 2009 Elite League.

He explained: "The simple truth is that I am doing too many meetings and the time has come to cut back.

"I can't go on like this or I'll burn myself out and that wouldn't be any good for anyone.

"I have been thinking about this for some time, it was not a spur of the moment decision."

Craven Shield

WOLVERHAMPTON (H)
Friday, March 21
Won 49-41
Crump 14, Forsberg 4:3, Gjedde 10, Jankowski 2:2, Screen 12:1, Rajkowski 2, Boxall 5.

● *Result changed from 49-44 as Wolverhampton's Nicolai Klindt was ineligible to take a tactical ride in Heat 14 (he won it) as a replacement for Christian Hefenbrock.*

WOLVERHAMPTON (A)
Monday, March 24
Lost 44-48
Crump 16 (4), Forsberg 1:1, Gjedde 9:1, Jankowski 4, Screen 4, Rajkowski 1, Boxall 9:1.

▲ *Jason Crump's only defeat came against David Howe, when he was taking a tactical ride in Heat 11.*

COVENTRY (A)
Friday, March 28
Lost 39-54
Crump 15 (6), Forsberg 2:1, Gjedde 8, Jankowski 4:1, Screen 5, Rajkowski 2, Boxall 3.

COVENTRY (H)
Monday, April 14
Won 50-42
Crump 12:2, Forsberg 9:2, Gjedde 13, Jankowski 3, Screen 7:1, Rajkowski 2:1, Ksiezak 4:1

● *Number eight Ksiezak replaces the injured Boxall.*

CRAVEN SHIELD
Northern Group

	M	W	D	L	PtsF	PtsA	Pts
Coventry	4	2	0	2	192	175	4
BELLE VUE	**4**	**2**	**0**	**2**	**182**	**185**	**4**
Wolverhampton	4	2	0	2	175	189	4

BELLE VUE

Rider	M	R	Pts	BP	TPts	Ave	F	P	TR	TPts	TS	TSPts
Jason CRUMP	35	174	504	8	512	11.77	9	1	11	32	2	4
Charlie GJEDDE	**36**	**177**	**352**	**23**	**375**	**8.47**	**1**	**0**	**0**	**0**	**2**	**2**
Joe SCREEN	33	149	234	13	247	6.63	0	0	1	0	0	0
Billy FORSBERG	**32**	**150**	**178**	**39**	**217**	**5.79**	**0**	**0**	**1**	**2**	**0**	**0**
Patrick HOUGAARD	11	64	80	12	92	5.75	0	0	0	0	0	0
Tomasz PISZCZ	**1**	**5**	**6**	**1**	**7**	**5.60**	**0**	**0**	**0**	**0**	**0**	**0**
Lukasz JANKOWSKI	15	56	60	12	72	5.14	0	0	0	0	0	0
Steve BOXALL	**3**	**14**	**17**	**1**	**18**	**5.14**	**0**	**0**	**0**	**0**	**0**	**0**
Stanislaw BURZA	1	5	4	1	5	4.00	0	0	0	0	0	0
Robert KSIEZAK	**16**	**77**	**52**	**12**	**64**	**3.32**	**0**	**0**	**0**	**0**	**0**	**0**
Nick SIMMONS	15	64	32	5	37	2.31	0	0	0	0	0	0
Jonas RAUN	**11**	**51**	**18**	**7**	**25**	**1.96**	**0**	**0**	**0**	**0**	**0**	**0**
Michal RAJKOWSKI	12	44	18	3	21	1.91	0	0	0	0	0	0
Guests	***22***	***105***	***136***	***11***	***147***	***5.60***	***0***	***0***	***1***	***3***	***1***	***1***

For Tomasz PISZCZ see Birmingham; for Stanislaw BURZA see Coventry; for Robert KSIEZAK see Glasgow; for Nick SIMMONS see Newport; for Michal RAJKOWSKI see Mildenhall.

Individual

PETER CRAVEN MEMORIAL TROPHY

Monday, July 28

PETER CRAVEN was one, if not the greatest ever English rider, the only Brit to win two world titles.

He made his racing debut for hometown club Liverpool in 1951 before moving to their Division Two rivals Fleetwood.

He moved to National League First Division Belle Vue on a permanent basis in 1953, spending his entire top-flight career at Hyde Road.

Crowned World Champion in 1956, he won his second title in 1962.

He died in Edinburgh Royal Infirmary four days after being rushed there in a coma following a crash during heat 12 of a challenge match for Belle Vue against the Monarchs at Old Meadowbank Stadium.

Craven, unbeaten in his first three rides, had been racing off a handicap and when George Hunter came off in front of him he unselfishly turned towards the fence rather than run over his fallen rival.

He suffered severe head injuries and never regained conciousness.

Born: Liverpool, June 21, 1934.

Died: Edinburgh, September 24, 1963

	1	2	3	4	5	Tot	RO
1 Leigh ADAMS	**3**	**3**	**3**	**2**	**3**	**14**	**3**
2 Scott NICHOLLS	2	3	3	3	3	14	2
3 Charlie GJEDDE	3	2	2	3	2	12	
4 Tai WOFFINDEN	3	2	0	3	3	11	
5 Jason CRUMP	X	3	3	3	2	11	
6 Joe SCREEN	3	1	3	2	1	10	
7 Kevin DOOLAN	2	3	2	2	1	10	
8 Billy FORSBERG	2	2	1	1	3	9	
9 James WRIGHT	1	0	1	2	2	6	
10 Ricky ASHWORTH	1	2	1	0	1	5	
11 Jason LYONS	1	1	2	R		4	
12 Patrick HOUGAARD	2	R	0	0	1	3	
13 Lewis BRIDGER	0	0	X	1	2	3	
14 Jurica PAVLIC	0	F	2	1	0	3	
15 Ben WILSON	1	1	0	1	0	3	
16 Nick SIMMONS	0	1	1	0	0	2	
17 Ben HOPWOOD [R]	0					0	

Roll of Honour

1967 .... Ivan MAUGER
1969 .... Ole OLSEN
1970 .... Jim AIREY
1971 .... Ole OLSEN
1974 .... Chris MORTON
1975 .... Chris MORTON
1978 .... Peter COLLINS
1980 .... Dennis SIGALOS
1985 .... Andy SMITH
1986 .... Chris MORTON
1988 .... Kelly MORAN
1989 .... Shawn MORAN
1990 .... Billy HAMILL
2007 .... Scott NICHOLLS
2008 .... Leigh ADAMS

1990 winner Billy Hamill

GREGGS NORTH WEST JUNIOR CHAMPIONSHIP

Wednesday, July 16

	1	2	3	4	5	Tot	R
1 John BRANNEY	**2**	**3**	**3**	**3**	**3**	**14**	
2 Aaron SUMMERS	3	3	3	3	1	13	
3 Daniel HALSEY	3	3	1	2	3	12	3
4 Peter Juul LARSEN	3	2	3	3	1	12	2
5 Adam McKINNA	3	2	3	2	2	12	X
7 Ben TAYLOR	2	2	2	1	3	10	
7 Byron BEKKER	R	2	2	3	2	9	
8 Benji COMPTON	2	3	2	2	0	9	
9 Gareth ISHERWOOD	FX	1	0	2	3	6	
10 Scott RICHARDSON	2	1	2	1	0	6	
11 Jade MUDGWAY	1	1	1	1	2	6	
12 Adam WRATHALL	0	0	1	0	2	3	
13 Ben HOPWOOD	1	0	1	0	1	3	
14 Gary IRVING	1	1	0	0	0	2	
15 Paul STARKE	1	F	E	1	X	2	
16 Scott MEAKINS	0	0	0	0	1	1	
17 Keiran MORRIS [R]	0					0	

Weather...

Manchester's reputation for being wet was reinforced by three Elite League postponements.

Elite League

Monday, April 28 .... COVENTRY (H)
Wednesday, May 28 .... WOLVERHAMPTON (H)
Monday, September 29 .... COVENTRY (H)

...beaten

Elite League

COVENTRY

TRACK FILE

Track: Coventry Stadium, Rugby Road, Brandon, Nr. Coventry, CV8 3GJ.
Telephone: 02476 542395.
Hotline: 09068 664677.
Website: www.coventrymotorspeedway.com
Track Length: 301 metres.
Track Record: 57.8 secs, Chris Harris, May 30, 2008.
Promoters: Allen Trump and Colin Pratt.
Team Sponsors: Buildbase.
Colours: Gold, black and white with yellow fighting Bee.
Nickname: Bees.

HISTORY

First meeting: September 29, 1928, Coventry Handicap individual trophy.
Leagues: Division One (1929-33, 1957-2009); Division Two (1949-56); Division Three (1948, 2004).

Meetings have also been held at the following Coventry venue.

- *Lythalls Lane, Foleshill, Coventry.*

First meeting: July 21, 1928,Coventry Challenge Cup.
Leagues: Open licence, 1928, 1930.

HONOURS

Major honours: 21.
Division One champions (8), 1953, 1968, 1978, 1979, 1987, 1988, 2005, 2007.
Division One Knock Out Cup winners (3), 1967, 2006, 2007.
Division One League Cup winners (3), 1981, 1985, 1987.
Division One Craven Shield winners (4), 1997, 2000, 2007, 2008.
Division One Premiership winners (1), 1986.
Division One Pairs champions (2), 1978 (shared), 2008.

2008 REVIEW

THE reigning champions were hit hard by the 38.85 points limit and had to shed three of their title-winning team – but they still felt they had the strength-in-depth to mount another strong challenge.

The reality was somewhat different as the Bees endured a troubled first half of the season with numerous points being dropped at home, while they were unable to recapture their previous away form with their top three all searching for consistency and their reserves finding things tough despite some sterling home displays from Stanislaw Burza.

Eventually, with the club looking nervously over their shoulders at a possible drop into the relegation zone, new owner Allen Trump made the bold decision to pursue the services of Grand Prix star Hans Andersen after the problems encountered by the Dane at Peterborough.

Andersen's arrival after a protracted saga with his former club signalled the departure of Rory Schlein to Ipswich, and – along with the inclusion of Czech youngster Filip Sitera – provided the catalyst for an improvement during the last two months.

The Bees edged themselves away from danger with Andersen and captain Chris Harris combining to good effect in a dramatic away win at Eastbourne, and their hold on the Knock Out Cup was only ended in a semi-final replay against Poole after the clubs had drawn 45-45 in both legs of the original tie.

But Coventry were destined to extend their run of major honours to six in four years as they successfully retained the Craven Shield, first with a remarkable semi-final win over Poole when they overturned a 24-point first leg deficit, and then by comfortably overcoming injury-hit Lakeside in the Final, number eight Ben Barker scoring a total of 26 points across the two legs.

Andersen and Harris also secured the Elite League Pairs title with victory at Swindon.

2008 RESULTS

Elite League

Final position .... Sixth

SQUAD
Oliver Allen, Ben Barker, Chris Harris, Simon Stead.
Foreign: Hans Andersen, Stanislaw Burza, Billy Janniro, Robbie Kessler, Andreas Messing, Rory Schlein, Filip Sitera.

EASTBOURNE (H) *SKY TV*
Monday, March 31
Lost 43-47.
Schlein 4:2, Allen 8, Harris 11:1, Janniro 4:2, Stead 9:1, Messing 1:1, Burza 6.

IPSWICH (H)
Friday, April 4
Won 52-37.
Schlein 5:1, Allen 12:1, Harris 5:1, Janniro 8:1, Stead 13:1, Messing 0, Burza 9:3.
▼ *Messing fell in Heat 2 and took no further part in the meeting, suffering from a whiplash injury.*

BELLE VUE (H)
Friday, April 11
Drew 45-45.
Schlein 12, Allen 7:2, Harris 8, Janniro 5:1, Stead 5:1, Messing 4, Burza 4:1.

POOLE (A)
Wednesday, April 16
Lost 39-53
Rider replacement for Schlein, Allen 1:1, Harris 13 (4), Janniro 13:2, Stead 6, Messing 2, Burza 4:1.
▼ *Allen pulled out after two rides due to concussion.*

POOLE (H)
Friday, April 18
Won 48-45
Harris 9:2, Allen 8, Schlein 8:1, Janniro 5:2, Stead 5, Burza 10:1, Messing 3:1.
▼ *Messing withdrew with a friction burn after Heat 8 clash with Karol Zabik.*

WOLVERHAMPTON (A)
Monday, May 5
Won 45-44
Schlein 4, *rider replacement for Allen*, Harris 13, Janniro 8:2, Stead 9:1, Burza 9, Messing 2:1

SWINDON (A)
Thursday, May 8
Lost 43-49
Harris 12 (4), *rider replacement for Allen*, Schlein 8:1, Janniro 5:4, Stead 9:1, Burza 0, Barker 9.
▼ *Came back from ten down to force a last-heat decider, but Harris touched the tapes and was then excluded after a clash with Troy Batchelor.*

LAKESIDE (H)
Monday, May 12
Lost 41-49.
Harris 10, *rider replacement for Allen*, Schlein 10:2, Janniro 3:2, Stead 8, Burza 9:1, Barker 1.

WOLVERHAMPTON (H)
Friday, May 30
22-14, abandoned after six heats.
Harris 6, *rider replacement for Allen*, Mads Korneliussen [G] 3:1, Janniro 3:1, Stead 3, Burza 5:1, Barker 2.
▲ *Chris Harris set new track record (57.8 seconds) in opening race.* ● *Meeting abandoned after an hour's delay following a local power cut.*

BELLE VUE (H)
Friday, June 6
Won 52-40.
Harris 13, Allen 5:1, Schlein 11:1, Janniro 5:2, Stead 8, Burza 6:1, Messing 4

PHOTO: Jeff Davies

Oliver Allen, Rory Schlein, Andreas Messing, Chris Harris, Simon Stead, Stanislaw Burza, Billy Janniro, Ben Barker

▼ *Allen did not take the re-run of Heat 10 after crashing heavily under Charlie Gjedde's challenge.*

LAKESIDE (A) *SKY TV*
Monday, June 30
Lost 29-63
Rider replacement for Harris, Allen 6:1, Schlein 12 (TR4), Janniro 0, Stead 5, Burza 1, Messing 5.
▼ *Janniro withdrew after Heat 1 fall. Sustained shoulder muscle damage. Harris missing after suffering several injuries after crash at British GP.*

POOLE (A)
Wednesday, July 2
Lost 36-54
Rider replacement for Harris, Allen 9:1, Schlein 14, Daniel King [G] 3:1, Stead 6, Burza 4:1, Messing 0.

POOLE (H)
Friday, July 4
Lost 37-56.
Rider replacement for Harris, Tai Woffinden [G] 5, Fredrik Lindgren [G] 15:2[6], Allen 4, Piotr Swiderski [G] 8, Burza 2, Messing 3:2.
▼ *Only three of the regular team available – reduced to two when Allen withdrew with a shoulder injury in a Heat 9 crash. Tai Woffinden withdrew after four rides after aggravating a shoulder injury.*

EASTBOURNE (A)
Saturday, July 5
Lost 40-50
Rider replacement for Harris, Chris Schramm [G] 4:1, Fredrik Lindgren [G] 14, Steve Johnston [G] 4:1, Henning Bager [G] 6, Burza 7, Messing 5:2.
▼ *Coventry without top five, with Schlein and Stead away on World Championship duty, Harris, Allen and Janniro all out injured. Bees were captained by a guest rider – former Coventry man Johnston stepping in.*

BELLE VUE (A) *SKY TV*
Monday, July 7
Lost 43-46
Harris 7, Barker 6:3, Stead 12:1, *rider replacement for Janniro,* Schlein 11, Burza 1:1, Messing 6:1.
▼ *Shattered by late drama at Kirkmanshulme Lane with Harris and Schlein both excluded from Heat 13 and then conceding maximum points again in Heat 15.*

IPSWICH (A)
Thursday, July 10
Lost 43-50
Harris 14:1 (6), Allen 7:2, Stead 5, *rider replacement for Janniro,* Schlein 14, Burza 1, Messing 2.
▼ *Burza suffered a back injury in what turned out to be his last Coventry meeting.*

SWINDON (H)
Friday, July 11
Won 52-41
Harris 16 (6), Janniro 5:2, Stead 7:1, Allen 6, Schlein 6:1, Barker 12:3, Messing 0.
▲ *Trailed by 12 points after five races. Chris Harris (TR) and Billy Janniro recorded 8-1 in Heat 6.*

LAKESIDE (H)
Monday, July 21
Lost 42-51
Harris 6, Allen 0, Stead 8:1, Janniro 14:2[6], Schlein 7, Messing 4, Barker 3.
▼ *Injury problems continued with both Allen (shoulder) and Harris (back) crashing out.*

WOLVERHAMPTON (H)
Friday, July 25
Won 48-45
Harris 6:3, Allen 14:1[6], Stead 13, *rider replacement for Janniro,* Schlein 8:1, Messing 1, Barker 6:1.
▲ *Another stirring home comeback having trailed 16-26 after Heat 7. Janniro in America winning the national championship at Auburn, Northern California.*

PETERBOROUGH (H) *SKY TV*
Monday, July 28
Won 48-39
Harris 9:1, Allen 8, Stead 12:1, Janniro 4:2, Schlein 8:1, Messing 0, Barker 7:1.
● *Result amended from 48-42 because of ineligibility of Peterborough's Ty Proctor (4-3:1) as replacement for Henrik Moller.*

LAKESIDE (A)
Wednesday, July 30
Lost 37-56
Harris 4:1, Allen 4, Stead 4, Janniro 1, Schlein 15 (6), Barker 9, Auty [G] 0.
▼ *Reserve Burza missing with back injury, replaced by number eight Barker. Joshua Auty drafted in for Messing, suffering from food poisoning.*

PETERBOROUGH (A)
Thursday, August 7
Lost 38-51
Harris 9:2, Allen 8, Schlein 6, Janniro 2:1, Stead 7:1, Barker 6, Messing 0.
▼ *New Coventry signing Andersen due to make his debut. Last minute confusion prevented him from doing so, with Schlein continuing.*

EASTBOURNE (H)
Friday, August 8
Won 52-41
Schlein 8:3, Allen 7:1, Harris 11, Janniro 8:2, Stead 8:1, Joe Haines [G] 2:1, Barker 8.

WOLVERHAMPTON (A)
Monday, August 18
Lost 43-47
Andersen 12:1, Allen 6:1, Harris 11, Janniro 6:2, Stead 3, Sitera 3, Kessler 2.
▼ *Stead, who damaged his thumb when brought down by Jesper B Monberg in Heat 4, had to pull out.*

SWINDON (A)
Thursday, August 21
Lost 39-51
Andersen 11, Allen 7:3, Harris 9, Janniro 1:1,

Stead 7, Sitera 4:1, Kessler 0.

PETERBOROUGH (H)
Friday, August 22
Won 59-36
Andersen 13:2, Allen 10:2, Harris 14:1, Janniro 6:1, Stead 2, Kessler 1, Barker 13:2.
▼▲ *Stead's engine seized while leading heat 7 and teammate Kessler could not avoid running into him. Both riders were taken to hospital, Stead (broken collar bone) and Kessler (arm injury). Allen recorded his first-ever Elite League maximum.*

IPSWICH (H) *SKY TV*
Monday, August 25
Drew 45-45
Andersen 13, *rider replacement for Stead,* Harris 11, Janniro 4, Allen 10, Barker 2:2, Sitera 5:2, Josh Auty [G] 0.
▲ *Barker rode for Stoke at Rye House and was whisked the 96 miles to Brandon by promoter Allen Trump in 78 minutes and arrived as the two minute warning was sounded for his first ride. Auty had been conveniently excluded for touching the tapes as he took a rider replacement ride in Heat 1.*

BELLE VUE (A)
Monday, September 1
14-10, Abandoned after four heats.
Andersen 3, *rider replacement for Stead,* Harris 2:1, Janniro 3, Allen 2, Barker 2:1, Sitera 2:1
● *Andersen and Barker raced to a Heat 1 maximum over Jason Crump but referee Jim McGregor called off meeting before start of Heat 5 because of rain with Coventry leading 14-10.*

IPSWICH (A)
Thursday, September 4
Abandoned.
Andersen 0, *rider replacement for Simon Stead,* Harris, Janniro, Shane Parker [G] 0, Sitera, Barker, Jerran Hart [G].
● *Meeting abandoned by referee Ronnie Allan because of heavy rain after the first heat had been stopped when Ipswich's Piotr Swiderski crashed through the fence, clipping Andersen's rear wheel on the way. Race never re-staged.*

PETERBOROUGH (A)
Monday, September 15
Lost 42-51
Andersen 16:1 (6), *rider replacement for Stead,* Harris 13, Janniro 0, Allen 6, Sitera 6:1, Barker 1.

WOLVERHAMPTON (H)
Thursday, September 18
Won 53-40
Andersen 7:1, *rider replacement for Stead,* Harris 12, Janniro 10:1, Allen 8, Ryan Fisher [G] 10:3, Sitera 6:2.
▼ *Allen fell in heat 11 in a first bend melee and teammate Sitera couldn't avoid him. Withdrawn from the meeting with suspected rib injuries. Club asset Ryan Fisher guested well.*

EASTBOURNE (A)
Saturday, September 20
Won 47-46
Andersen 16 (6), *rider replacement for Stead,* Harris 10:2, Shane Parker [G] 3:1, Rory Schlein [G] 9, Ryan Fisher [G] 7:1, Joe Haines [G] 2:1.
▲ *Andersen and Harris twice combined to set-up the Bees' second away win of the season, and guest Ryan Fisher's win in Heat 14 crucial.*

SWINDON (H)
Monday, September 22
Won 52-43
Andersen 12:2, Allen 10:1, Harris 16, Shane Parker [G] 6:2, *rider replacement for Stead,* Sitera 6:1, Barker 2:1.
▲ *Three successive mid-meeting 5-1s gave Bees control despite their middle order being depleted. Andersen's only dropped point was against Leigh Adams in Heat 15.*

IPSWICH (A)
Thursday, September 25
Drew 45-45
Bjarne Pedersen [G] 13:1, Allen 8:2, Harris 8:1, Janniro 9:1, *rider replacement for Stead,* Sitera 6, Joshua Auty [G] 1:1.
▲ *Secured Elite League safety with an exciting draw, fighting back from an early six-point deficit with Bjarne Pedersen guesting well for an unwell Andersen.*

BELLE VUE (A)
Monday, October 6
Lost 40-50
Andersen 3, Allen 6:1, Harris 3, Janniro 4:1, Stead 5:2 (1), Barker 5:1, Joe Haines [G] 14.
▼ *Harris withdrew on medical advice after his second ride, still suffering from the injuries he picked up when he crashed at practice for the Italian GP. Andersen came down heavily on his shoulder in Heat 11 and withdrew.*

ELITE LEAGUE

	M	*W*	*D*	*L*	*PtsF*	*PtsA*	*Pts*
Poole	32	22	0	10	1600	1321	52
Lakeside	32	22	1	9	1551	1375	52
Swindon	32	17	2	13	1498	1434	41
Ipswich	32	16	3	13	1483	1439	40
Eastbourne	32	15	0	17	1462	1472	34
COVENTRY	**32**	**12**	**3**	**17**	**1418**	**1506**	**29**
Belle Vue	32	13	2	17	1423	1491	28
Peterborough	32	13	1	18	1371	1528	28
Wolverhampton	32	8	0	24	1341	1581	16

Double joy for Olly

Oliver Allen landed an end-of-season double at Coventry's dinner.
He won the Nuneaton Speedway Supporters' Club Rider of the Year and also was presented with a trophy by Geoff Dagger as the Bees' Most Improved Rider having put more than a point a meeting on his official average.
Billy Janniro was the recipient of the Bonus Point Trophy.

Knock Out Cup

First round, first leg
BELLE VUE (A)
Monday, June 16
Lost 44-49
Harris 15 (6), Allen 1, Schlein 5:1, Janniro 0, Stead 4:1, Burza 10:2, Barker 9:1
▼ *Janniro withdrew after second ride due to leg injury. Andreas Messing was absent because of old leg injury.*

First round, second leg
BELLE VUE (H)
Friday, June 20
Won 56-37
Harris 5, Allen 12:2, Schlein 10:1, *rider replacement for Janniro*, Stead 15:2, Burza 9:2, Barker 5:1.
▲ *Harris crashed in Heat 6. Took one further ride before withdrawing with a knee injury.*
Aggregate: Won 100-86.

Semi Final, first leg
POOLE (H)
Monday, August 11
Drew 45-45
Andersen 12, Allen 3, Harris 10, Janniro 5:1, Stead 10:1, Barker 4:1, Sitera 1.
▲ *Andersen finally made debut, along with Sitera, and helped Bees to a draw after being 33-39 down.*

Semi Final, second leg
POOLE (A)
Wednesday, August 13
Drew 45-45
Andersen 11:2, Allen 5:1, Harris 10, Janniro 8:2, Stead 8:1, Robbie Kessler 2:1, Sitera 1.
▲▼ *Kessler made his Bees debut, as the tie went to a replay. Harris leading last race when he suffered a misfire, allowing Chris Holder to overtake for draw-clinching race win.*
Aggregate: Drew 90-90.

Semi Final Replay, first leg
POOLE (A)
Wednesday, September 3
Lost 36-56
Andersen 14 (4), *rider replacement for Stead*, Harris 14 (TS0), Janniro 2:1, Allen 2, Barker 4:1, Sitera 0.
▼ *Stead's absence compounded by Allen withdrawing after Heat 9 complaining of difficulty breathing due to a vrius which affected his balance. Bees were holding Poole to a 10-point margin.*

Semi Final Replay, second leg
POOLE (H)
Thursday, September 18
Lost 38-54
Andersen 10:1 (4), *rider replacement for Stead*, Harris 10, Janniro 5, Jesper B. Monberg [G] 2:1, Ryan Fisher [G] 6:1, Sitera 5:2.
▼*Allen's absence proved costly in the second half of the double-header, and Bees saw their two-year reign as Cup holders ended.*
Aggregate: Lost 74-110.

Craven Shield

WOLVERHAMPTON (A)
Monday, March 17
Lost 37-53
Schlein 7:1, Janniro 8:1 (2), Harris 9, Allen 7:1, Stead 5, Messing 1, Burza 0.

WOLVERHAMPTON (H)
Friday, March 21
Won 59-33.
Schlein 7:1, Allen 10, Harris 8:3, Janniro 12:1, **Stead 12**, Messing 4:2, Burza 6.
▲ *Stead scored his first official Coventry maximum.*

BELLE VUE (H)
Friday, March 28
Won 54-39.
Schlein 8:2, Allen 10:1, Harris 12:1, Janniro 6:1, Stead 7:1, Messing 5, Burza 6:2.

BELLE VUE (A)
Monday, April 14
Lost 42-50
Rider replacement for Schlein, Allen 3:1, Harris 9:2, Janniro 14:1 (4), Stead 9, Messing 7:1, Burza 0.
▼▲ *Schlein missing after being injured in Poland. Confirmed as group winners, but required a win on the night to book a direct place in the Final.*

CRAVEN SHIELD
Northern Group

	M	W	D	L	PtsF	PtsA	Pts
COVENTRY	**4**	**2**	**0**	**2**	**192**	**175**	**4**
Belle Vue	4	2	0	2	182	185	4
Wolverhampton	4	2	0	2	175	189	4

Semi Final, first leg
POOLE (A)
Wednesday, April 30
Lost 34-58
Schlein 5, Allen 1:1, Harris 13 (4), Janniro 5:3, Stead 5, Burza 1:1, Barker 4.

Semi Final, second leg
POOLE (H)
Friday, May 2
Won 58-32.
Harris 14:1, *rider replacement Allen*, Schlein 6, Janniro 14:3, Stead 14:1, Burza 9, Ben Barker 1.
Aggregate: Won 92-90.
▲ *Scored 5-1s in each of the last three races to complete remarkable comeback. Rider replacement for absent Allen (broken hand).*

FINAL, first leg
LAKESIDE (A)
Thursday, October 16
Won 47-43
Andersen 13, Allen 0, Harris 9, Janninro 3, Stead 4:1, Sitera 4:2, Barker 14.
▼▲ *Allen crashed in opening race and suffered a groin injury. Took second ride but pulled out midway through the race and withdrew. Terrific performance from Barker with Andersen winning four races including Heat 15.*

FINAL, second leg
LAKESIDE (H)
Friday, October 24
Won 58-35
Andersen 14:1, Allen 8:2, Harris 6:2, Janniro 7:1, Stead 6:2, Sitera 5:2, **Barker 12**.

▲ *Barker's maximum was the highlight, with Andersen also unbeaten as the Bees continued their excellent recent record in Cup Finals, taking control with three 5-1s in the first four heats.*

Aggregate: Won 105-78.

Elite Shield

SWINDON (A)
Sunday, March 23
Lost 35-57
Schlein 2:1, Allen 3, Harris 9:3, Janniro 14 (4), Stead 5, Messing 1, Burza 1:1.

SWINDON (H)
Monday, March 24
Won 52-41
Schlein 9:1, Allen 7, Harris 9, Janniro 11:2, Stead 9:1, Messing 0, Burza 7.

▼ *Allen's first race breakdown on the line virtually ended Coventry's slim hopes of overcoming the first leg deficit.*

Aggregate: Lost 87-98.

Testimonial

STEVE JOHNSTON TESTIMONIAL
Sunday, June 22
Scott Nicholls 15, Jason Crump 14, Leigh Adams 13, Rory Schlein 11, Simon Stead 10, Davey Watt 9, Jason Lyons 8, Cameron Woodward 8, Cory Gathercole 6, Steve Johnston 6, David Howe 6, Mikael Max 5, Linus Sundström 3, Carl Stonehewerr 3, Morten Risager 2, Jack Hargreaves 0.

See Ipswich for career information.

Inter League Challenge

First leg
SHEFFIELD (A)
Thursday, March 13
Won 56-37
Schlein 6:1, Janniro 11:2, Harris 9, Allen 7:2, Stead 12, Messing 4:1, Burza 7:3.

Second leg
SHEFFIELD (H)
Friday, March 14
Won 61-31
Schlein 8:1, Allen 7:1, Harris 13:1, Janniro 11:3, **Stead 12**, Messing 5:3, Burza 5:1.

Aggregate: Won 117-68

▲ *Stead marked his Coventry home debut with a four-ride maximum.*

Weather...

Two scheduled trips to Belle Vue were scrapped because of the weather.

Elite League
Monday, April 28 .... BELLE VUE (A)
Monday, May 26 .... PETERBOROUGH (A)
Monday, May 26 .... PETERBOROUGH (H)
Friday, September 5 .... SWINDON (H)
Monday, September 29 .... BELLE VUE (A)

Craven Shield
Friday, October 17 .... LAKESIDE (A)
Meeting postponed because of re-staging of Final Grand Prix.

...beaten

2009 Squad

Chris **HARRIS** (7.71), Rory **SCHLEIN** (7.24), Edward **KENNETT** (7.11), Oliver **ALLEN** (6.57), Ben **BARKER** (4.02), Ricky **WELLS** (4.00), Filip **SITERA** (4.00), *Jordan* ***FRAMPTON*** *(3.17)/Joel* ***PARSONS*** *(3.03)*, Joshua **AUTY** (3.00).

COVENTRY

Rider	*M*	*R*	*Pts*	*BP*	*TPts*	*Ave*	*F*	*P*	*TR*	*TPts*	*TS*	*TSPts*
Hans ANDERSEN	15	72	177	11	188	10.44	0	2	4	10	0	0
Chris HARRIS	**42**	**210**	**427**	**26**	**453**	**8.63**	**0**	**2**	**6**	**15**	**1**	**0**
Rory SCHLEIN	26	125	219	20	239	7.65	0	0	2	5	0	0
Simon STEAD	**36**	**157**	**275**	**23**	**298**	**7.59**	**1**	**1**	**1**	**0**	**0**	**0**
Oliver ALLEN	38	155	247	30	277	7.15	0	1	1	3	0	0
Billy JANNIRO	**37**	**161**	**219**	**49**	**268**	**6.66**	**0**	**0**	**3**	**6**	**0**	**0**
Ben BARKER	24	121	145	19	164	5.42	1	0	0	0	0	0
Stanislaw BURZA	**23**	**116**	**114**	**17**	**131**	**4.52**	**0**	**0**	**0**	**0**	**0**	**0**
Filip SITERA	13	63	52	13	65	4.13	0	0	0	0	0	0
Andreas MESSING	**21**	**83**	**57**	**10**	**67**	**3.23**	**0**	**0**	**0**	**0**	**0**	**0**
Robbie KESSLER	4	13	5	1	6	1.85	0	0	0	0	0	0
Guests	***22***	***102***	***134***	***18***	***152***	***5.96***	***0***	***0***	***2***	***3***	***0***	***0***

For Hans ANDERSEN see Peterborough; for Rory SCHLEIN see Ipswich; for Ben BARKER see Stoke; for Stanislaw BURZA see Belle Vue; for Robbie KESSLER see Mildenhall.

Elite League

EASTBOURNE

TRACK FILE

Track: Arlington Stadium, Arlington Road West, Hailsham, East Sussex, BH27 3RE.
Telephone: 01323 841642.
Hotline: 09068 664672.
Website: www.elite-eagles.com
Track Length: 275 metres.
Track Record: 54.8 secs, Jason Crump, June 29, 2008 & Chris Holder, August 23, 2008.
Promoter: Bob Dugard.
Team Sponsors: Dugard.com
Colours: Blue, yellow and black with eagle logo.
Nickname: Eagles.

HISTORY

First meeting: August 5, 1929, Arlington Trophy, individual.
Leagues: Division One, 1979-84, 1991-2009. Division Two, 1969-78, 1985-90. Division Three, 1947, 1996. Southern Area League, 1954-57, 1959. Metropolitan League, 1964.

HONOURS

Major honours: 19.
Division One champions (2), 1995, 2000.
Division One Knock Out Cup winners (4), 1994, 1997, 2002, 2008.
Division One Elite Shield winners (1), 2009.
Division Two champions (4), 1971, 1977, 1986-87.
Division Two Knock Out Cup winners (6), 1975, 1977-78, 1985-86-87).
Division Three champions (1), 1947.
Southern Area League champions (1), 1959.

2008 REVIEW

WHEN the reduced points limit caused the top two clubs of 2007 to shed riders, the new Eagles promotional duo of Bob Dugard and Martin Hagon moved quickly to take advantage.

The signings of Scott Nicholls from Coventry and Lee Richardson from Swindon into a predominantly British team had many expecting the Arlington club to mount a significant title challenge.

Things started well with Nicholls inspiring a win in the first away match back at Brandon, but success on the road dried up and inconsistency within the team caused successive home defeats against Poole and Ipswich.

The Eagles were unable to live up to their billing, often struggling at reserve with the promising Simon Gustafsson missing meetings due to European commitments, and they eventually faded to a fifth-place finish in the Elite League, showing what might have been with a late-season win at Peterborough.

But despite their failure to reach the play-offs, there was still plenty to race for as the Eagles set up a South coast battle with Poole in the Knock Out Cup Final after overcoming Wolverhampton and Lakeside in the early rounds.

The Pirates were the favourites having recently clinched the title, but the Eagles got everything together in the first leg at home and roared to a 57-35 win – and that proved to be more than enough as they adapted well to wet conditions in the return and came away from Wimborne Road with a 45-45 draw.

Richardson was voted Rider of the Year after a consistent campaign despite a mid-season wrist injury.

And there was plenty of progress from several of the younger riders – but with Hagon stepping down after the final meeting, more changes were on the cards at Arlington.

Bob Dugard resumed full control and set about trying to fill the gaps left by the departures of Nicholls, Richardson and Edward Kennett who signed off his Eagles' Elite League career with a max.

2008 RESULTS

Elite League

Final position .... Fifth

PETERBOROUGH (H)
Saturday, March 29
Won 59-35
Nicholls 10:3, Bridger 10:1, Richardson 12, Woodward 7:1, Kennett 11, Gustafsson 4:2, Brundle 5.

COVENTRY (A) *SKY TV*
Monday, March 31
Won 47-43
Nicholls 12, Bridger 3:2, Richardson 9, Woodward 9:1, Kennett 7, Gustafsson 7:1, Brundle 0.
▲ *Nicholls led charge against parent club, winning his first four rides before suffering hand injury when colliding with Chris Harris in Heat 15.*

PETERBOROUGH (A) *SKY TV*
Tuesday, April 8
Lost 42-48
Chris Harris [G] 9:1, Bridger 2, Richardson 12, Woodward 6:2, Kennett 8, Gustafsson 5:1, Brundle 0.
▼ *Led at halfway stage but just one heat win in last six races.*

WOLVERHAMPTON (H)
Saturday, April 12
Won 53-40
Bjarne Pedersen [G] 8:2, Bridger 9, Richardson 11:1, Woodward 10:2, Kennett 5:1, Gustafsson 10:2, David Mason [G] 0.

WOLVERHAMPTON (A)
Monday, April 14
Lost 39-50
Rider replacement for Nicholls, Bridger 6:1, Richardson 9, Woodward 11:2, Kennett 10, Gustafsson 2:2, Brundle 1.

SQUAD
Lewis Bridger, James Brundle, Edward Kennett, Scott Nicholls, Lee Richardson.
Foreign: Simon Gustafsson, Tomas Suchanek, Brent Werner, Cameron Woodward.

SWINDON (A) *SKY TV*
Monday, April 28
Lost 37-56
Nicholls 15 (6), Bridger 2, Richardson 5, Woodward 4:2, Kennett 5, Gustafsson 6, Andrew Bargh [G] 0.

IPSWICH (A)
Thursday, May 15
Lost 41-52
Nicholls 15:1 (6), Bridger 10:1, *rider replacement for Richardson,* Woodward 5, Kennett 7:1, Gustafsson 4:1, Nick Simmons [G] 0.

BELLE VUE (H)
Saturday, April 19
Won 50-40
Nicholls 12:1, Bridger 4:1, Richardson 11, Woodward 5:1, Kennett 10:1, Werner 2:1, Brundle 6.

POOLE (A)
Wednesday, April 23
Lost 41-52
Nicholls 14 (6), Bridger 4, Richardson 10, Woodward 3:1, Kennett 4 (TS0), Gustafsson 5:1, Brundle 1:1.

IPSWICH (A)
Thursday, April 24
Lost 39-51
Nicholls 12 (4), Bridger 1:1, Richardson 11, Woodward 2, Kennett 9:1, Gustafsson 4, Danny Betson [G] 0.

SWINDON (A)
Monday, April 28
Lost 37-56
Nicholls 15 (6), Bridger 2, Richardson 5, Woodward 4:2, Kennett 5, Gustafsson 6, Andrew Bargh [G] 0.

Co-promoter Martin Hagon, Edward Kennett, James Brundle, Lee Richardson, co-promoter Bob Dugard, Lewis Bridger, Scott Nicholls, team manager Trevor Geer. Front – Simon Gustafsson, Cameron Woodward.

SWINDON (H)
Saturday, May 3
Won 46-44
Nicholls 14, Bridger 4, Richardson 8:1, Woodward 8, Kennett 10:1, Nick Simmons [G] 2, Werner 0.

BELLE VUE (A)
Wednesday, May 7
Won 48-42
Nicholls 13, Bridger 6:1, Richardson 4, Woodward 6:1, Kennett 6:1, Gustafsson 7:1, Werner 6:1.
▲ *Eagles took first win in Manchester for four years, coming back from six down despite Richardson's mid-meeting withdrawal with hand injury.*

POOLE (H) *SKY TV*
Monday, May 12
Lost 41-48
Nicholls 13:1, Bridger 6:1, Richardson 2, Woodward 6:1, Kenneth Bjerre [G] 10, Gustafsson 2:1, Werner 2.
▼ *Stunned by Adam Skornicki's reserve contribution of 18 (paid 19) and continuing injury problems for skipper Richardson.*

IPSWICH (A)
Thursday, May 15
Lost 41-52
Nicholls 15:1 (6), Bridger 10:1, *rider replacement for Richardson*, Woodward 5, Kennett 7:1, Gustafsson 4:1, Nick Simmons [G] 0.

LAKESIDE (A)
Friday, May 16
Lost 45-48
Nicholls 15, Bridger 3, *rider replacement for Richardson*, Woodward 9:1, Kennett 13, Gustafsson 3, Nick Simmons [G] 2:1.
▼ *Built 10-point lead in early stages as Kennett won his first four rides – but ex-Eagle Joonas Kylmåkorpi led Hammers' fightback with paid 20.*

IPSWICH (H)
Saturday, May 17
Lost 42-48
Nicholls 9, Bridger 9, *rider replacement for Richardson*, Woodward 8:1, Kennett 13, Gustafsson 3, Nick Simmons [G] 0.
▼ *Nicholls fell in Heat 1; excluded for unfair riding in Heat 13 and crashed out of Heat 15 as Eagles fell to defeat.*

PETERBOROUGH (H)
Saturday, May 31
Won 46-44
Nicholls 14:1, Bridger 6:2, *rider replacement for Richardson*, Woodward 11:2, Kennett 10:1, Werner 2, Brundle 3:1.

SWINDON (H)
Saturday, June 7
Won 50-43
Nicholls 9:2, Joonas Kylmåkorpi [G] 7:2, Richardson 12, Woodward 8:4, Kennett 10, Suchanek 1, Brundle 3.

BELLE VUE (A)
Monday, June 9
Lost 45-48
Nicholls 17 (TR6), Bridger 3:1, Richardson 7:1, Woodward 6:3, Kennett 6:1, Gustafsson 5:1, Brundle 1:1.
▼ *Took 8-1 from Heat 14 to set up last-heat decider but could find no way past maximum man Jason Crump.*

SWINDON (A)
Thursday, June 12
Lost 39-53
Nicholls 10:2, Bridger 5, Richardson 14 (4), Woodward 3, Kennett 4:1, Gustafsson 1, Brundle 2.

LAKESIDE (H) *SKY TV*
Monday, June 16
Won 53-39
Nicholls 11:1, Bridger 11:2, Richardson 11, Woodward 6:1, Kennett 10, Gustafsson 4:1, Brundle 0.

BELLE VUE (H)
Saturday, June 29
Won 56-37
Nicholls 12:1, Bridger 8:3, Richardson 9, Woodward 5, Kennett 10, Gustafsson 4:2, Brundle 8:2.
▲ *Brundle enjoyed his best-ever Elite League performance and was one of six home riders to take the chequered flag first.*

COVENTRY (H)
Saturday, July 5
Won 50-40
Rider replacement for Richardson, Bridger 4:1, Bjarne Pedersen [G] 15, Woodward 9:2, Adam Shields [G] 13:1, Gustafsson 8:1, Brundle 1:1.
▲ *Eagles were missing their top three against a Bees team missing their top five. Home regulars Woodward and Gustafsson clinched the win with a 5-1 in Heat 14.*

WOLVERHAMPTON (A)
Monday, July 21
Won 48-45
Nicholls 11:1, Bridger 9:2, Richardson 7, Woodward 3:2, Kennett 9, Gustafsson 7:1, Brundle 2.
▲ *Important Heat 14 5-1 from Gustafsson and Woodward after Kenneth Hansen had been excluded.*

LAKESIDE (H)
Saturday, July 26
Won 49-44
Nicholls 13, Bridger 7:2, Richardson 9, Woodward 6, Kennett 7:1, Gustafsson 6, Brundle 1:1.

POOLE (A)
Wednesday, July 30
Lost 33-60
Nicholls 7, Bridger 3:1, Richardson 14 (6), Woodward 4:1, Kennett 4, Gustafsson 1, Brundle 0.

LAKESIDE (A) *SKY TV*
Monday, August 4
Lost 37-56
Nicholls 16 (6), Bridger 0, Richardson 8, Woodward 1, Kennett 7 (TS1), Gustafsson 5:1, Brundle 0.
▼ *Richardson won first two rides and Nicholls took three wins, but nightmare for Bridger and Woodward.*

COVENTRY (A)
Friday, August 8
Lost 41-52
Nicholls 18 (6), Bridger 5:1, Richardson 7, Woodward 4, Kennett 5, Suchanek 1:1, Brundle 1.
▼ *Nicholls could have done no more on his old home circuit, but again disappointments lower down the order.*

IPSWICH (H)
Saturday, August 16
Lost 41-49
Richardson 12, Woodward 3:2, Adam Shields [G] 11, Bridger 3:1, Kennett 6, Gustafsson 6, Brundle 0.
▼ *Fatal blow to play-off chances. Bridger's future left in doubt after pits bust-up with skipper Richardson.*

POOLE (H)
Saturday, August 23
Lost 41-52
Nicholls 5:1, Bridger 4:2, Richardson 14 (6), Woodward 5:1, Kennett 7, Gustafsson 5, Brundle 1.
▼ *Richardson left out on his own as Chris Holder (new track record and paid maximum) and Bjarne Pedersen had things almost all their own way.*

PETERBOROUGH (A)
Thursday, September 4
Won 54-39
Nicholls 7:1, Bridger 10:2, Richardson 9:2, Woodward 5:3, **Kennett 12**, Gustafsson 11:1, Brundle 0.
▲ *Another case of what might have been this season, Kennett's perfect showing being well supplemented by five of his team-mates with Gustafsson also impressive.*

COVENTRY (H)
Saturday, September 20
Lost 46-47
Nicholls 13, Bridger 7:1, Richardson 9:1, Woodward 6:1, Kennett 8, Suchanek 0, Brundle 3.
▼ *Again hampered by a tactical ride with Hans Andersen and Chris Harris taking an 8-1 in Heat 11 – and the same combination completed the comeback in the last race.*

WOLVERHAMPTON (H)
Sunday, October 19
Won 63-27
Rory Schlein [G] 12:3, Bridger 13:1, Richardson 11:1, *rider replacement for Woodward*, **Kennett 14:1**, Gustafsson 11:2, Brundle 2:1.
▲ *Guest Rory Schlein and Richardson were untroubled and Bridger was close to a full house with rampant Eagles winning 14 of the 15 races.*

ELITE LEAGUE

	M	W	D	L	PtsF	PtsA	Pts
Poole	32	22	0	10	1600	1321	52
Lakeside	32	22	1	9	1551	1375	52
Swindon	32	17	2	13	1498	1434	41
Ipswich	32	16	3	13	1483	1439	40
EASTBOURNE	**32**	**15**	**0**	**17**	**1462**	**1472**	**34**
Coventry	32	12	3	17	1418	1506	29
Belle Vue	32	13	2	17	1423	1491	28
Peterborough	32	13	1	18	1371	1528	28
Wolverhampton	32	8	0	24	1341	1581	16

Weather...

Eastbourne escaped the worst of the summer weather with only two home meetings affected.

Elite League
Wednesday, May 28 .... POOLE (A)
Saturday, September 6 .... WOLVERHAMPTON (H)
Knock Out Cup
Saturday, August 9 .... LAKESIDE (H)
Craven Shield
Saturday, March 15 .... SWINDON (H)
Individual
Saturday, October 4 .... ARLINGTON TROPHY (H)

...beaten

Happy ending

Martin Hagon ended his time as Eastbourne promoter after 24 home meetings but at least had the satisfaction of going out on a high when the Eagles overcame red-hot favourites Poole to win the Knock Out Cup.

EASTBOURNE

Rider	M	R	Pts	BP	TPts	Ave	F	P	TR	TPts	TS	TSPts
Scott NICHOLLS	35	177	426	25	451	10.19	1	1	9	24	1	3
Lee RICHARDSON	**36**	**166**	**354**	**13**	**367**	**8.84**	**1**	**3**	**3**	**8**	**0**	**0**
Edward KENNETT	40	183	337	14	351	7.67	2	0	0	0	3	2
Cameron WOODWARD	**41**	**178**	**248**	**51**	**299**	**6.72**	**0**	**0**	**0**	**0**	**0**	**0**
Lewis BRIDGER	42	178	242	39	281	6.31	0	0	0	0	0	0
Simon GUSTAFSSON	**36**	**171**	**184**	**28**	**212**	**4.96**	**0**	**0**	**0**	**0**	**0**	**0**
Brent WERNER	5	18	12	2	14	3.11	0	0	0	0	0	0
James BRUNDLE	**33**	**119**	**56**	**10**	**66**	**2.22**	**0**	**0**	**0**	**0**	**0**	**0**
Tomas SUCHANEK	3	10	2	1	3	1.20	0	0	0	0	0	0
Guests	***15***	***61***	***89***	***10***	***99***	***6.49***	***0***	***1***	***0***	***0***	***0***	***0***

For Brent WERNER see Somerset; for Tomas SUCHANEK see Reading.

Eastbourne number one SCOTT NICHOLLS had a superb first season at Arlington and his all-action style made him a firm favourite on the South Coast

Knock Out Cup

WOLVERHAMPTON (H)
Saturday, June 21
Won 62-30
Nicholls 12:3, Bridger 9, **Richardson 14:1**, Woodward 6:1, **Kennett 12**, Gustafsson 6:1, Brundle 3:1.
▲ *Hit 60-point mark for the first time this season with British trio Nicholls, Richardson and Kennett all unbeaten.*

WOLVERHAMPTON (A)
Monday, June 23
Lost 40-52
Nicholls 12 (4), Bridger 3, Richardson 5, Woodward 7:1, Kennett 6:1, Gustafsson 4:1, Brundle 3:1.
Aggregate: Won 102-82.

LAKESIDE (A)
Wednesday, August 13
Lost 41-52
Nicholls19 (6), Bridger 2, *rider replacement for Richardson*, Woodward 5:1, Kennett 11, Gustafsson 4, Brundle 0.
▲ *Nicholls won his last four rides, and Kennett also took the flag three times to keep the tie very much alive.*

LAKESIDE (H)
Saturday, August 30
Won 54-39
Rider replacement for Nicholls, Bridger 13:3, Richardson 14:1, Woodward 7:2, Kennett 10, Gustafsson 8:1, Brundle 2.
▲ *It all came right after a poor run of form. Eagles into the Final thanks to Bridger, as they coped with the absence of GP-riding Nicholls. Richardson and Bridger were the Heat 15 heroes with a 5-1.*
Aggregate: Won 95-91.

FINAL
POOLE (H)
Saturday, October 25
Won 57-35
Nicholls 6:2, Bridger 9:1, Richardson 12:1, Woodward 8:2, Kennett 12, Gustafsson 9, Brundle 1.
▲ *Elite League champions reduced to three heat wins as Eagles gave one of their best showings of the season, Kennett unbeaten save for a Heat 11 fall.*

POOLE (A)
Sunday, October 26
Drew 45-45
Nicholls 13, Bridger 4:1, Richardson 11, Woodward 4:1, Kennett 8, Gustafsson 5:1, Brundle 0.
▲ *Never in danger to ensure the season ended with silverware, Nicholls and Richardson winning three races each on their final appearances for the club.*
Aggregate: Won 102-80.

2009 Squad
Davey **WATT** (8.15), David **NORRIS** (5.91), Cameron **WOODWARD** (5.41), Lewis **BRIDGER** (5.11), Ricky **KLING** (4.90), Simon **GUSTAFSSON** (4.28), Lukas **DRYML** (5.98), Denis **GIZATULLIN** (4.00), James **HOLDER** (3.00).

Craven Shield

SWINDON (H)
Monday, March 17
Won 52-41
Nicholls 10:1, Bridger 7:1, Richardson 10:1, Woodward 9:2, Kennett 9, Gustafsson 6:1, Brundle 1.

SWINDON (A)
Thursday, March 20
Lost 42-48
Nicholls 10:1, Bridger 4, Richardson 11:1, Woodward 7:1, Kennett 5:1, Gustafsson 2, Brundle 3.
▲ *Brundle took first race win in Eagles' colours in Heat 2.*

POOLE (A)
Friday, March 21
Lost 43-51
Nicholls 16 (4), Bridger 6:1, Richardson 6, Woodward 3:1, Kennett 11 (TS4), Gustafsson 0, Brundle 1.

POOLE (H)
Friday, March 21
Won 52-42
Nicholls 11:2, Bridger 8:1, **Richardson 14:1**, Woodward 8:1, Kennett 6, Gustafsson 4, Brundle 1.
▼ *Kennett concussed in Heat 11 crash, but Eagles 16 points clear.*

CRAVEN SHIELD
Southern Group

	M	W	D	L	PtsF	PtsA	Pts
Poole	4	2	0	2	191	180	4
EASTBOURNE	**4**	**2**	**0**	**2**	**189**	**182**	**4**
Swindon	4	2	0	2	174	192	4

Inter League Challenge

ISLE OF WIGHT (H)
Saturday, April 26
Won 57-37
Richardson 8:2, Bridger 12:1, Kennett 14, Gustafsson 5:3, Woodward 11, Rodney MacDonald [G] 0, Werner 7:3.
▲ *Australian Rodney MacDonald, 32, made his debut after winning a second half competition to ride in the meeting.*

Individual

SUSSEX JUNIOR CHAMPIONSHIP
Saturday, May 24
1 Aaron Baseby 11+3, 2 John Resch 11+2, 3 Scott Campos 11+1, 4 Nick Laurence 11+0, Scott Meakins 10, Michael Bovis 10, Jon Stevens 7, Alex McLeod 7, Niall Strudwick 6, James Walker 2, Ross Buchanan 2, Jamie Dixon 1.

STEVE HEATH MEMORIAL
Saturday, August 2
1 Rob Smith 11+3+3, 2 Gary Cottham 10+3+2, 3 Trevor Heath 8+2+1, 4 Scott Campos 10+2+0, 5 John Resch 9+1, 6 Michael Bovis 8+1, 7 Matt Bates 9+0, 8 Jon Stevens 7+0, *Lewis Bridger 12*, Mark Richardson 6, Nick Laurence 6, Sam Heath 5, Niall Strudwick 5, Thomas Young 4, Kevin Howse 3, Alex McLeod 3, Chris Neame 1, Kieron Davidson 1, Mark Baldock 1, Luke Coleman 0.
● *Lewis Bridger rode in the qualifying races as a late replacement but was not eligible for the semi-finals.*

Elite League

IPSWICH

TRACK FILE

Track: Foxhall Stadium, Foxhall Road, Ipswich, Suffolk, IP4 5TL.
Telephone: 01473 623640.
Hotline: 09068 664687.
Website: www.ipswich-witches.com
Track Length: 305 metres.
Track Record: 57.5 secs, Jaroslaw Hampel, September 12, 2002.
Promoters: John Louis.
Team Sponsors: Evening Star.
Colours: Blue, white black and yellow.
Nickname: Witches.

HISTORY

First meeting: May 14, 1951, Ipswich v Great Yarmouth, challenge.
Leagues: Division One, 1957-58, 1960-62, 1972-88, 1991-2009. Division Two, 1954-56, 1969-71, 1989-90. Division Three, 1997. Southern League, 1952-53. Southern Area League, 1959. Metropolitan League, 1964.
Previous meetings were held on October 25, 1950 (Norwich practice match) and March 24, 1951, when a Norwich v Southampton challenge was abandoned.

HONOURS

Major honours: 16.
Division One champions (4), 1975-76, 1984, 1998.
Division One Knock Out Cup winners (5), 1976, 1978, 1981, 1984, 1998.
Division One Craven Shield winners (1), 1998.
Division One Four Team champions (1), 1991.
Division One Pairs champions (2), 1976-77.
Inter League Knock Out Cup winners (1), 1977.
Division Two Knock Out Cup winners (2), 1970-71.

2008 REVIEW

THE Witches signed Polish rider Piotr Swiderski on loan from Peterborough on an average of just over five – and it was his emergence into a genuine heat-leader which played a big part in a much more successful season.

With Jaroslaw Hampel returning to the Elite League after five years away, the Foxhall club had two riders who were able to make significant gains.

And that meant they were always a force to be reckoned with despite suffering some surprise home defeats.

A memorable week of away wins at Eastbourne, Wolverhampton and Poole initially took the Witches to the top of the table.

Although they couldn't keep up that rate of consistency and eventually had to settle for an away tie in the play-offs.

One early setback had been a serious injury to long-serving skipper Chris Louis, who suffered a broken upper arm in an accident when the Witches raced at home to Eastbourne.

The Witches used the rider replacement facility for the majority of the summer, waiting for the right rider to become available, and were rewarded for their patience when they signed Coventry's Rory Schlein for the final two months of the campaign.

However, there was a late-season blow when Polish fixture clashes prevented Hampel from taking his place in the team and led to him receiving a 28-day ban, effectively for withholding his services.

With Tobias Kroner, who had proved to be a potent reserve at several stages of the season, on the injured list, the Witches went into the closing weeks some way below full strength.

And this caught up with them in the play-off semi-final at Poole when they were swept aside by a 59-33 margin which did not fully reflect what a generally positive campaign they had enjoyed.

PHOTO: *Steve Waller*

Chris Schramm, Chris Louis, Steve Johnston, team manager Pete Simmons, Robert Miskowiak, Piotr Swiderski, Tobias Kroner and Jaroslaw Hampel

2008 RESULTS

Elite League

Final position .... Fourth

COVENTRY (A)
Friday, April 4
Lost 37-52
Miskowiak 4:1, Swiderski 10:1, Louis 3, Johnston 3:1 (0), Hampel 10, Kroner 6, Shaun Tacey [G] 1:1.

SWINDON (H) SKY TV
Monday, April 14
Lost 43-50
Miskowiak 7:1, Swiderski 2:1, Louis 11:1, Johnston 4:1, Hampel 10, Schramm 2, Kroner 7:1.
▼ *Unsuccessfully protested Swindon's inclusion of Joel Parsons as a guest after a shock paid-11 contribution from the Sheffield rider.*

SWINDON (A)
Thursday, April 17
Drew 45-45
Miskowiak 8, Chris Holder [G] 9:1, Louis 6, Johnston 10:2, *rider replacement for Hampel*, Kroner 9:1, Schramm 3:1.
▲▼ *Led all the way in the absence of Hampel and Swiderski (Polish meetings), but conceded 5-1 Heat 15 .*

PETERBOROUGH (A)
Monday, April 21
Lost 41-49
Miskowiak 5, Chris Holder [G] 13, Louis 6:1, Johnston 7:2, *rider replacement for Hampel*, Kroner 9:1, Schramm 1:1.

SQUAD
Chris Louis, Chris Schramm.
Foreign: Jan Graversen, Jaroslaw Hampel, Steve Johnston, Robbie Kessler, Tobias Kroner, Robert Miskowiak, Rory Schlein, Piotr Swiderski.

EASTBOURNE (H)
Thursday, April 24
Won 51-39
Miskowiak 4:2, Johnston 7, Louis 4, Swiderski 12:1, Hampel 10:2, Kroner 11:2, Schramm 3:1.
▼ *Louis fractured right arm when fetched off by the machine of the fallen Lewis Bridger in Heat 5.*

LAKESIDE (A)
Friday, May 2
Lost 42-51
Edward Kennett [G] 6:3, Johnston 14:2, Miskowiak 1, Swiderski 11, Hampel 4, Kroner 5, Schramm 1.

PETERBOROUGH (H)
Monday, May 5
Won 60-31
Rider replacement for Louis, Swiderski 11:1, Miskowiak 14:2, Johnston 11:3, Hampel 12, Kroner 9:2, Schramm 3:1.
▲ *Topped 60-point mark despite seeing riders excluded on three occasions – Swiderski dropped only points in Heat 6 crash.*

WOLVERHAMPTON (H)
Thursday, May 8
Won 53-38
Rider replacement for Louis, Swiderski 9:1, Miskowiak 12:2, Johnston 9:1, Hampel 13, Kroner 9:1, Schramm 1.

EASTBOURNE (H)
Thursday, May 15
Won 52-41
Rider replacement for Louis, Miskowiak 11, Kroner 5, Johnston 8:1, Hampel 10:1, Swiderski 10:2, Schramm 8:2.
▼ *Rider replacement for injured Louis accrued just three points, but both Hampel and Miskowiak won three races.*

EASTBOURNE (A)
Saturday, May 17
Won 48-42
Rider replacement for Kroner, Miskowiak 6:1, Fredrik Lindgren [G] 11:1, Johnston 4:1, Hampel 12:3, Swiderski 10:3, Schramm 5.
▲ *Won dramatic last-heat decider with Scott Nicholls crashing out when trying to pass Hampel.*

WOLVERHAMPTON (A) SKY TV
Monday, May 19
Won 48-43
Edward Kennett [G] 8:1, Miskowiak 8:1, Kroner 3:2, Johnston 4, Hampel 10, Swiderski 12:1, Schramm 3:1.
▲ *Fought back from eight down to go 38-27 up, and then fended off Wolves' tactical moves.*

POOLE (A)
Wednesday, May 21
Won 50-40
Chris Harris [G] 12:2, Miskowiak 4, Kroner 6, Johnston 2:1, Hampel 9:1, Swiderski 15:2, Schramm 2.
▲ *Completed marvellous week of away wins with Swiderski dropping one point in six rides, and Chris Harris proving a strong guest for Louis.*

BELLE VUE (H)
Thursday, May 22
Won 52-41
Rory Schlein [G] 5, Miskowiak 14:1, Kroner 5, Johnston 5:1, *rider replacement for Hampel*, Swiderski 17:1, Schramm 6:3.
▲ *Made it 13 points in eight days to go top of the table, with Miskowiak unbeaten except for a tapes exclusion in his second ride.*

POOLE (H) SKY TV
Thursday, June 9
Lost 41-51
Hampel 6:1 (TS0), Kroner 2, Swiderski 15:1 (4), *rider replacement for Louis*, Miskowiak 9:1, Johnston 9:1, Schramm 0.

BELLE VUE (A) SKY TV
Monday, June 23
Lost 38-52
Swiderski 9 (4), Kroner 5:1, Hampel 7:1, *rider replacement for Louis*, Miskowiak 6:2, Johnston 9, Schramm 2:1.

Weather...

Elite League
Wednesday, July 9 .... POOLE (A)
Monday, July 28 .... WOLVERHAMPTON (A)
Monday, September 1 .... WOLVERHAMPTON (A)
Challenge
Thursday, March 13 .... KING'S LYNN (H)

...beaten

PETERBOROUGH (H)
Thursday, June 26
Won 54-38
Rider replacement for Swiderski, Kroner 11:1, Hampel 12:2, Rory Schlein [G] 11:1, Miskowiak 10, Johnston 8:2, Schramm 2.
▼ *Swiderski ruled out due to throat infection with Rory Schlein taking a late call-up to guest for Louis as a result.*

COVENTRY (H)
Thursday, July 10
Won 50-43
Piotr Swiderski 14, *rider replacement for Louis*, Hampel 13:1, Johnston 2:1, Miskowiak 4:1, Kroner 13:1, Schramm 4:1.
▲ *Taken to a last heat decider having held a 12-point lead, with Swiderski and Hampel proving up to the challenge.*

SWINDON (H) SKY TV
Monday, July 21
Won 54-39
Swiderski 12:2, *rider replacement for Louis*, Hampel 11, Johnston 3:1, Miskowiak 12:1, Kroner 11:1, Schramm 5:2.

SWINDON (A)
Thursday, July 24
Lost 44-49
Swiderski 10:1, *rider replacement for Louis*, Hampel 15:1 (6), Johnston 4:1, Miskowiak 3:1, Kroner 10, Schramm 2.
▲▼ *Kroner in double figures despite starting with two lasts.*

LAKESIDE (A)
Friday, July 25
Lost 38-55
Swiderski 13:2, *rider replacement for Louis*, Davey Watt [G] 6, Johnston 4, Miskowiak 1:1, Kroner 12, Schramm 2.
▼▲ *Collapsed mid-meeting from 23-25 to 33-48, with Kroner scoring 11 from his first four rides.*

LAKESIDE (H)
Thursday, July 31
Lost 42-51
Swiderski 18:1 (6), *rider replacement for Louis*, Jan Graversen [G] 1, Johnston 4:1, Miskowiak 8:1, Kroner 7:1, Schramm 4:1.
▼ *Lakeside took advantage of Hampel's missed flight and replacement with Premier League man Jan Graversen.*

Rory Schlein became the fourth loanee to ride regularly for the Witches in 2008.

BELLE VUE (A)
Monday, August 4
Lost 42-48
Rider replacement for Swiderski, Kroner 4:3, Hampel 8, Miskowiak 2:1, Rory Schlein [G] 14, Johnston 9:2, Schramm 5.

BELLE VUE (H)
Thursday, August 7
Won 48-42
Rider replacement for Swiderski, Kroner 6:1, Hampel 16, Miskowiak 7:2, Edward Kennett [G] 9:1, Johnston 6:2, Schramm 4.

EASTBOURNE (A)
Saturday, August 16
Won 49-41
Swiderski 10:2, Kroner 7:1, Hampel 8, Miskowiak 1, Schlein 10:1, Johnston 10:1, Schramm 3:1.
▲ *Enhanced top four chances with clinical win. Schlein showing well in his first official match as a Witches rider.*

WOLVERHAMPTON (H)
Thursday, August 21
Won 49-41
Swiderski 9:3, Kroner 4, Hampel 12, Miskowiak 4:2, Schlein 8, Johnston 9:2, Schramm 3:2.
▲ *Witches let off the hook against the bottom club – Wolves led 35-31 but fell apart in the last four heats .*

COVENTRY(A) SKY TV
Monday, August 25
Drew 45-45
Swiderski 6:1, Kroner 6:2, Hampel 13, Miskowiak 5:1, Schlein 5, Johnston 4:1, Schramm 6.
▲ *Led 13-5 in the early stages but Hampel had to ride a blinder for second place in Heat 15 ahead of Hans Andersen to snatch a draw.*

COVENTRY (H)
Thursday, September 4
Abandoned.
Swiderski 0, Kroner 0, Hampel, Miskowiak, Schlein, Johnston, Schramm, did not ride.
● *Abandoned after an aborted start to Heat 1. Swiderski was flung over the fence after clipping Hans Andersen, and heavy rain during the delay forced the match off.*

POOLE (A)
Wednesday, September 10
Lost 34-59
Swiderski 12:1 (6), Kroner 5, *rider replacement for Hampel*, Brent Werner [G] 1, Schlein 11, Johnston 1:1, Schramm 4:1.
▼ *Hampel ill, Miskowiak unavailable and Witches tracked a heavily depleted team which conceded 5-1s in each of the first four races.*

LAKESIDE (H)
Thursday, September 11
Lost 44-48
Swiderski 16 (4), Kroner 0, *rider replacement for Hampel*, Simon Lambert [G] 0, Schlein 11:2 (TS0), Johnston 12:1, Schramm 5:2.
▼ *Problems intensified as Kroner crashed out with a broken finger in Heat 1.*

WOLVERHAMPTON (A) SKY TV
Monday, September 15
Won 52-40
Swiderski 15, *rider replacement for Kroner*, Hampel 9, Miskowiak 5:1, Schlein 13, Johnston 9:2, Schramm 1:1.
▲ *Hit back to form with a more usual side on-track – Swiderski was unbeatable, and Schlein won his first four races at the top of the scorechart.*

PETERBOROUGH (A)
Monday, September 22
Lost 40-52
Swiderski 5, *rider replacement for Kroner*, Hampel 9, Wilkinson 0, Schlein 12:2 (4), Johnston 6:2, Schramm 8.
▲ *Schramm won two races on his old Conference League track.*

POOLE (H)
Thursday, September 25
Won 52-38
Swiderski 6, *rider replacement for Kroner*, Chris Harris [G] 10:1, Miskowiak 10:2, Schlein 13:1, Johnston 9:3, Schramm 4:3, Wilkinson [no. 8].

COVENTRY (H)
Thursday, September 25
Drew 45-45
Swiderski 7, *rider replacement for Kroner*, Davey Watt [G] 8, Miskowiak 4:1, Schlein 12:1, Johnston 7, Schramm 7:3, Wilkinson [no. 8].
▼ *Required a 21-point win to overhaul Swindon, but had to settle for a draw after Schlein managed to split Bees guest Bjarne Pedersen and Harris in Heat 15. Hampel missing owing to Polish commitment.*

ELITE LEAGUE

	M	*W*	*D*	*L*	*PtsF*	*PtsA*	*Pts*
Poole	32	22	0	10	1600	1321	52
Lakeside	32	22	1	9	1551	1375	52
Swindon	32	17	2	13	1498	1434	41
IPSWICH	**32**	**16**	**3**	**13**	**1483**	**1439**	**40**
Eastbourne	32	15	0	17	1462	1472	34
Coventry	32	12	3	17	1418	1506	29
Belle Vue	32	13	2	17	1423	1491	28
Peterborough	32	13	1	18	1371	1528	28
Wolverhampton	32	8	0	24	1341	1581	16

Play offs

Semi Final
POOLE (A) SKY TV
Monday, September 29
Lost 33-59
Swiderski 5, *rider replacement for Kroner*, Kenneth Bjerre [G] 11 (4), Miskowiak 0, Schlein 10:1, Johnston 6:1, Schramm 1:1.
▼ *Hampel banned following his Thursday absence.*

2009 Squad

Jaroslaw **HAMPEL** (8.28), Piotr **SWIDERSKI** (7.65), Daniel **KING** (6.13), Tobias **KRONER** (5.67), Leigh **LANHAM** (5.08), Morten **RISAGER** (4.42), Dawid **STACHYRA** (4.00), *Carl* **WILKINSON** *(3.08)/Kozza* **SMITH** *(3.00)*, Jerran **HART** (3.00).

Knock Out Cup

First round, first leg
WOLVERHAMPTON (H)
Thursday, April 3
Won 50-42
Miskowiak 6, Swiderski 7:2, Louis 6:1, Johnston 6:2, Hampel 13, Schramm 3:1, Kroner 9.

First round, second leg
WOLVERHAMPTON (A)
Monday, April 7
Lost 38-54
Miskowiak 6:2, Swiderski 15 (4), Louis 4, Johnston 4:1, Hampel 6, Kroner 3, Shaun Tacey [G] 0.
Aggregate: Lost 88-94.

ELITE LEAGUE

	M	W	D	L	PtsF	PtsA	Pts
Poole	32	22	0	10	1600	1321	52
Lakeside	32	22	1	9	1551	1375	52
Swindon	32	17	2	13	1498	1434	41
IPSWICH	**32**	**16**	**3**	**13**	**1483**	**1439**	**40**
Eastbourne	32	15	0	17	1462	1472	34
Coventry	32	12	3	17	1418	1506	29
Belle Vue	32	13	2	17	1423	1491	28
Peterborough	32	13	1	18	1371	1528	28
Wolverhampton	32	8	0	24	1341	1581	16

Craven Shield

LAKESIDE (H)
Friday, March 21
Lost 43-47
Miskowiak 2, Swiderski 9:1, Louis 9:1, Johnston 6:1, Hampel 12, Schramm 1, Kroner 4:1.

LAKESIDE (A)
Friday, March 21
Won 52-40
Rider replacement for Miskowiak, Swiderski 14:2, Louis 8, Johnston 8:1, Hampel 11, Kroner 9:1, Schramm 2:1.

PETERBOROUGH (A)
Monday, March 24
Lost 43-47
Miskowiak 1, Swiderski 14, Louis 8, Johnston 5:2, Hampel 5:1, Kroner 6:1, Schramm 4:1.
▲ *Sensational Showground return for Swiderski, beaten only by Hans Andersen in Heat 15.*

PETERBOROUGH (H)
Thursday, March 27
Won 61-31
Miskowiak 7:2, Swiderski 13:1, Louis 10:1, Johnston 4:2, Hampel 12:1, Schramm 5:1, **Kroner 10:2**.
▲ *First-ever paid maximum in British speedway for Kroner.*

CRAVEN SHIELD
Eastern Group

	M	W	D	L	PtsF	PtsA	Pts
Lakeside	4	2	1	0	190	175	6
IPSWICH	**4**	**2**	**0**	**2**	**199**	**165**	**5**
Peterborough	4	1	1	2	158	207	3

Challenge

Thursday, October 16
YOUNG LIONS & EUROS 51
Tai Woffinden 13:1, Leon Madsen 8, James Wright 10:1, Linus Sundström 9:1, Chris Schramm 8, Sönke Petersen 3:1.
YOUNG EAGLES & ROOS 44
Krzysztof Stojanowski 10:1 (4), Marcin Liberski 6:1, Travis McGowan 16 (6), Trent Leveringon 3:1, Tom Madsen 8, Jerran Hart 1.
● *Polish youngsters Grzegorz Zengota and Pawel Miesiac were programmed to ride for the losing team but withdrew because of domestic commitments and were replaced by Tom Madsen and Jerran Hart.*

Stach-ing up

Dawid Stachyra joined the long list of Polish riders signed by Ipswich in recent seasons when he agreed terms shortly after he'd ridden in their 16 Lap Classic towards the end of October.

IPSWICH

Rider	M	R	Pts	BP	TPts	Ave	F	P	TR	TPts	TS	TSPts
Piotr SWIDERSKI	34	180	373	34	407	9.04	1	0	7	17	0	0
Jaroslaw HAMPEL	**29**	**145**	**298**	**15**	**313**	**8.63**	**0**	**0**	**1**	**3**	**1**	**0**
Rory SCHLEIN	10	56	105	8	113	8.07	0	0	1	2	1	0
Chris LOUIS	**11**	**47**	**75**	**5**	**80**	**6.81**	**0**	**0**	**0**	**0**	**0**	**0**
Steve JOHNSTON	39	189	252	50	302	6.39	0	0	2	3	0	0
Tobias KRONER	**33**	**160**	**228**	**27**	**255**	**6.37**	**0**	**1**	**0**	**0**	**0**	**0**
Robert MISKOWIAK	35	158	211	33	244	6.18	0	0	0	0	0	0
Chris SCHRAMM	**37**	**148**	**125**	**33**	**158**	**4.27**	**0**	**0**	**0**	**0**	**0**	**0**
Carl WILKINSON	1	4	0	0	0	0.00	0	0	0	0	0	0
Guests	***19***	***86***	***136***	***12***	***148***	***6.88***	***0***	***0***	***1***	***2***	***0***	***0***

For Rory SCHLEIN see Coventry; for Carl WILKINSON see Scunthorpe. Robbie KESSLER and Jan GRAVERSEN were both named as official number eight but did not ride.

Kim Jansson Benefit

Thursday, October 2

Kim Jansson's career ended on Saturday, August 16, when he was innocent party in a crash during Team Bikab's Swedish Division One match against Filbyterna.

He suffered two crushed vertebrae (lumbar 5 and 6) in his back and won't ride again.

Tragically it was his second major injury during 2008, having broken his thigh early in May.

It was only his fourth league meeting of the season and, while he wasn't expected to recover in time to race again again last season, he made a courageous and relatively swift comeback within three months.

Kim, a former moto-cross racer, had only started practising on the shale in 2000 and quickly forced his way into Swedish League side Kaparna.

He made his Elite League debut for Ipswich in September, 2002, and was a regular member of the Witches' squad until being overlooked at the beginning of 2008.

In all he made 186 official appearances for his only British club.

IPSWICH 51 (Scott Nicholls 13:1, Carl Wilkinson 6:1, Rory Schlein 10:2, Robert Miskowiak 11:2, Steve Johnston 6, Chris Schramm 5:1)
KIM JANSSON SELECT 44 (Oliver Allen 10 (6), David Howe 8:1, Nick Simmons 4:1, Daniel King 9:1 (4), Shane Parker 6, Krzysztof Stojanowski 7:1).

More than £8,000 was raised from the meeting.

Anyone wishing to contribute to his benefit fund can do so at Kim Jansson Fund (A/C 33333334; Nationwide Bank Sort Code: 07 00 93; Account Number: 0630/704006748).

Inter League Challenge

KING'S LYNN (A)
Wednesday, March 12
Won 58-34
Miskowiak 4:1, Swiderski 10:1, Louis 10:1, Johnston 7, **Hampel 15**, Kroner 5:1, Schramm 7:1.
▲ *Hampel marked his return to UK racing with a five-ride maximum.*

KING'S LYNN SELECT (H)
Friday, March 14
Won 61-31
Miskowiak 7:1, **Swiderski 13:2**, **Louis 15**, Johnston 8:2, Hampel 10, Schramm 1, Kroner 7:1.
▲ *Paid maximum for Swiderski on his home debut.*
Aggregate: Won 119-65.

Steve Johnston Testimonial

EVEN though he only spent half a season at Coventry Steve Johnston returned to Brandon for his testimonial meeting.

Stadium owner Avtar Sandhu had offered his facilities towards the end of the previous season and Johno gratefully accepted, pointing out: "It's the perfect place as it's central to all the tracks I've ridden."

Those tracks are Sheffield (1992), Long Eaton (1993-96), Ipswich (1997, 2008), Oxford (1998-2002), Belle Vue (2003),Swindon (2004), Wolverhampton (2005), Arena Essex (2006) and, of course, the Bees.

Johno actually completed 10 years as an asset of the BSPA in 2007, having originally been bought by the former Oxford owners Vanessa and Steve Purchase.

See Coventry for meeting scores.

Individual

ANGLIAN WILLHIRE 16 LAP CLASSIC
Thursday, October 23

Scott Nicholls won his hometown marathon for the third time – after proving his endurance in the 16-lap Grand Final.

He'd only been joint third top scorer from his four preliminary round races and owed his victory to Troy Batchelor running out of fuel on the last lap.

Witches' fans had their first glimpse of Poland's Dawid Stachyra who was swiftly offered a 2009 contract.

	1	2	3	4	Tot	BP	GF	Tot
1 Scott NICHOLLS	**3**	**2**	**2**	**1**	**8**	**2**	**14**	**24**
2 Troy BATCHELOR	2	3	1	1	7	0	12	19
3 Oliver ALLEN	2	3	R	3	8	2	8	18
4 Robert MISKOWIAK	3	1	3	3	10	2	4	16
5 Rory SCHLEIN	3	3	3	2	11	2	2	15
6 Dawid STACHYRA	0	0	3	2	5	0	10	15
7 David HOWE	1	0	1	3	5	0	6	11
8 Piotr SWIDERSKI	2	1	2	2	7	0	0	7
9 Kevin DOOLAN	1	2	2	0	5			
10 Steve JOHNSTON	1	2	1	1	5			
11 Chris SCHRAMM	R	1	N^2	0	1			
12 Chris MILLS	0	0	R	0	0			
13 Scott CAMPOS [R]	F				0			

The four top scorers in the qualifying competition started 15 metres behind and were awarded two Bonus Points to be added to the overall total. Final placings were determined on total points including qualifying races, Grand Final and bonus points. Grand Final points: 1 – 14; 2 – 12; 3 – 10; 4 – 8; 5 – 6; 6 – 4; 7 – 2; 8 – 0.

Roll of Honour

1979 .... Joe OWEN
1980 .... Billy SANDERS
1981 .... Phil CRUMP
1982 .... Phil CRUMP
1983 .... Kenny CARTER
1984 .... Phil CRUMP
1985 .... Kenny CARTER
1986 .... Hans NIELSEN
1987 .... Jan O. PEDERSEN
1989 .... Andy GALVIN
1990 .... Craig BOYCE
1991 .... Sam ERMOLENKO
1992 .... Chris LOUIS
1993 .... Hans NIELSEN
1995 .... Chris LOUIS
1996 .... Jason CRUMP
1997 .... Chris LOUIS
1998 .... Jason CRUMP
1999 .... Jason CRUMP
2000 .... Chris LOUIS
2002 .... Scott NICHOLLS
2003 .... Scott NICHOLLS
2004 .... Adam SHIELDS
2005 .... Chris LOUIS
2006 .... Adam SHIELDS
2007 .... Chris LOUIS
2008 .... Scott NICHOLLS

Elite League

LAKESIDE

TRACK FILE

Track: Arena Essex Raceway, A1306, Arterial Road, Thurrock, Essex, RM19 1AE.
Telephone: 01708 863443.
Hotline: 09068 664686.
Website: www.lakesidehammers.com
Track Length: 252 metres.
Track Record: 56.8 secs, Andreas Jonsson, May 30, 2008.
Promoters: Stuart Douglas and Jon Cook.
Colours: Red and blue with white crossed hammers logo.
Nickname: Hammers.

HISTORY

First meeting: April 5, 1984, Essex Radio Championship.
Leagues: Division One, 1992-95, 2004-09. Division Two, 1984-91, 1997-2003. Division Three, 1996.

HONOURS

Major honours: 3.
Division Two champions (1), 1991.
Division Two Knock Out Cup winners (1), 1991.
Division Two Four Team champions (1), 1991.

2008 REVIEW

AFTER making great strides away from their perennial basement position in 2007, the Hammers always looked to be in a good position to continue that momentum – especially when they persuaded Andreas Jonsson to commit to a full season in the Elite League.

Minimal changes were required from the team which had evolved over the previous 12 months, and early away wins at Wolverhampton, Coventry and Belle Vue were a clear statement of intent from the promotional duo of Stuart Douglas and Jon Cook.

As expected, Jonsson scored as an out-and-out number one; Adam Shields was also in the form of his career; Jonas Davidsson was finally producing the goods in the Elite League on a regular basis; and Joonas Kylmåkorpi enjoyed a stunning run after dropping to reserve.

The Hammers also bolstered their squad with Kauko Nieminen joining as number eight, which provided them initially with ample cover in the lower part of the team.

But as the season reached its crucial phase, they were rocked by a sequence of injuries which saw Shields and Kylmåkorpi ruled out for the rest of the season, Davidsson also facing time out – and Lubos Tomicek's appearances became rather more irregular

It didn't stop the Hammers from reaching the Play offs for the first time, nor indeed reaching the Grand Final, but their semi final win over Swindon was at the cost of losing the free-scoring Finn Nieminen with a broken collarbone.

And there was a heart-breaking end to a superb season when their patched up team was beaten both home and away by Poole in the Elite League championship decider.

Then, to ensure the Hammers missed out on what would have been their first top-flight trophy, Coventry did likewise to take away what would have been the consolation prize of the Craven Shield.

2008 RESULTS

Elite League

Final position..Second

BELLE VUE (A)
Monday, March 31
Lost 43-47
Jonsson 5, Lanham 6:2, Shields 9, Davidsson 7:2, Kylmåkorpi 3:1, Kling 3:1, Tomicek 10:1.
▼ *Jonsson crashed with teammate Lanham in Heat 11 and broke a finger, giving the Aces the opportunity to take a fortunate win with a 5-1 in the last race.*

SWINDON (H)
Friday, April 4
Won 50-45
Davey Watt [G] 8, Lanham 5:1, Shields 12, Kylmåkorpi 5:2, Davidsson 10, Kling 5:2, Tomicek 5:3.

POOLE (A)
Wednesday, April 9
Lost 38-54
Jaroslaw Hampel [G] 9, Lanham 1, Shields 14 (4), Kylmåkorpi 3:1, Davidsson 6, Kling 2:2, Tomicek 3.
▼ *Outgunned at reserve with homesters Zbigniew Suchecki and Freddie Eriksson rattling up 19 (paid 24) for the home side.*

SWINDON (A)
Thursday, April 10
Lost 40-53
Davey Watt [G] 7, Lanham 5:1, Shields 13, Kylmåkorpi 3:2, Davidsson 5, Kling 7:1, Tomicek 0.

POOLE (H)
Friday, April 11
Won 48-45
Chris Louis [G] 8, Lanham 8:2, Shields 8:1, Kylmåkorpi 1, Davidsson 8:1, Kling 3, Tomicek 12:1.

PETERBOROUGH (H)
Friday, April 18
Won 56-37
Jonsson 11, Lanham10:2, Shields 11:1, Kylmåkorpi 7:4, Davidsson 5:3, Kling 9, Tomicek 3:1.

WOLVERHAMPTON (A)
Monday, April 21
Won 49-41
Jonsson 8, Lanham 3:2, Shields 9:1, Kylmåkorpi 9:1, Davidsson 7:1, Kling 10:2, Tomicek 3:1.

IPSWICH (H)
Friday, May 2
Won 51-42
Jonsson 13, Lanham 6:2, Shields 12, Tomicek 6:2, Davidsson 6, Kling 2, Kylmåkorpi 6:4.

COVENTRY (A)
Monday, May 12
Won 49-41
Jonsson 17, Lanham 1:1, *rider replacement for Shields*, Tomicek 0, Davidsson 11, Kling 5:2, Kylmåkorpi 15:1.
▲ *First win at Brandon for four years spearheaded by Coventry old-boys Jonsson and Kylmåkorpi.*

SWINDON (A)
Thursday, May 15
Lost 39-53
Jonsson 7:1, Lanham 7:2, Shields 8, Tomicek 0, Davidsson 6, Kling 2:1, Kylmåkorpi 9:2 (4).
▼ *Had no answer to Swindon's top three riders.*

SQUAD
Leigh Lanham, Chris Mills.
Foreign: Jonas Davidsson, Andreas Jonsson, Ricky Kling, Krzysztof Jablonski, Tomasz Jedrzejak, Joonas Kylmåkorpi, Kauko Nieminen, Adam Shields, Lubos Tomicek.

Grand Final runners-up and beaten in the Craven Shield Final – Andreas Jonsson, Leigh Lanham, Tomasz Jedrzejak, Ricky Kling, Krzysztof Jablonski and Jonas Davidsson

EASTBOURNE (H)
Friday, May 16
Won 48-45
Jonsson 10, Lanham 10:3, Shields 3:1, *rider replacement for Tomicek*, Davidsson 6, Kling 1, Kylmåkorpi 18:2 (6), Rikki Mullins [G] (no. 8), did not ride.
▲ *Recovered from 16-26 deficit using rider replacement for flu victim Tomicek.*

POOLE (H)
Friday, May 30
Won 53-39
Jonsson 11:1, Lanham 8:3, Shields 9:1, *rider replacement for Tomicek*, Davidsson 5, Kling 6:2, Kylmåkorpi 14:1, Aaron Baseby [G] (no. 8), did not ride.

BELLE VUE (A)
Monday, June 2
Won 48-42
Jonsson 12, Lanham 7:2, Shields 7:1, Tomicek 5, Davidsson 4:2, Kling 1, Kylmåkorpi 12:2.
▲ *Kylmäkorpi featured in four 5-1s and sealed victory by partnering Tomicek to maximum points in Heat 14.*

EASTBOURNE (A) SKY TV
Monday, June 16
Lost 39-53
Jonsson 8, Lanham 0, Shields 12 (6), Tomicek 3:1, Davidsson 3, Kling 8:2, Kylmåkorpi 5:1.
▼ *Kylmäkorpi suffered a dislocated shoulder in an horrific Heat 14 collision with Cameron Woodward.*

PETERBOROUGH (H)
Friday, June 20
Won 50-42
Jonsson 14, Lanham 7:2, Shields 11, Tomicek 0, Davidsson 10:1, Kling 4:1, Mills 4:1.

COVENTRY (H) SKY TV
Monday, June 30
Won 63-29
Jonsson 14:1, Lanham 8:3, **Shields 15**, Tomicek 7:3, Davidsson 7:1, Kling 6, Kylmåkorpi 6:2.

BELLE VUE (H)
Friday, July 4
Won 54-39
Jonsson 13, Lanham 10:3, Shields 9:1, Kylmåkorpi 8:2, *rider replacement for Davidsson*, Kling 7, Tomicek 7:2, Jerran Hart [G] (no. 8), did not ride.

COVENTRY (A)
Monday, July 21
Won 51-42
Jonsson 13, Lanham 1:1, Shields 12:1, Kylmåkorpi 4:3, Davidsson 8:1, Kling 5:1, Tomicek 8:1.
▼ *Lost Lanham (concussion) in a Heat 8 crash but finished strongly.*

IPSWICH (H)
Friday, July 25
Won 55-38
Jonsson 10, Lanham 3:1, **Shields 14:1**, Davidsson 7:2, Kylmåkorpi 10:1, Kling 4:4, Tomicek 7:1.
▲ *Conceded maximum in Heat 1 but in front three races later, and won the match with four 5-1s in five heats after Heat 8*

EASTBOURNE (A)
Saturday, July 26
Lost 44-49
Jonsson 15:1 (6), *rider replacement for Lanham*, Shields 9:1, Davidsson 4:1, Kylmåklorpi 7:1, Kling 9:1, Robert Mear [G] 0, Rikki Mullins, did not ride.
▼ *Absence of Tomicek at reserve may have tipped the scales.*

COVENTRY (H)
Wednesday, July 30
Won 56-37
Jonsson 15, Lanham 6:3, Shields 11, Davidsson 6:1, Kylmåkorpi 4:1, Kling 7:2, Tomicek 7.

IPSWICH (A)
Thursday, July 31
Won 51-42
Jonsson 9, Lanham 2:1, Shields 13, Davidsson 6:1, Kylmåkorpi 6:2, Kling 13:1, Tomicek 2:1.
▲ *Good night to visit Foxhall with Jarek Hampel absent due to a delayed flight. Kling cleaned up at reserve.*

EASTBOURNE (H) SKY TV
Monday, August 4
Won 56-37
Jonsson 13, Lanham 6:1, Shields 9:2, Davidsson 9:1, Kylmåkorpi 7, Kling 7:3, Tomicek 5:3.
▲ *Took 5-1s in Heats 8, 9 and 10 to establish control of the meeting, although Jonsson dropped a surprise 5-1 to Scott Nicholls and Edward Kennett in Heat 13.*

POOLE (A)
Wednesday, August 6
Lost 42-50
Rider replacement for Jonsson, Lanham 2:1, Shields 14, Davidsson 12:1, Kylmåkorpi 4, Kling 9:1, Tomicek 1:1.
▼ *Already missing Jonsson on paternity leave, Kylmäkorpi crashed out in Heat 6 and suffered a recurrence of his shoulder injury.*

SWINDON (H)
Friday, August 8
Lost 41-49
Jonsson 8, Lanham 3:3, Shields 6, Davidsson 12:1, *rider replacement for Kylmåkorpi*, Nieminen 11:3, Chris Mills [G] 1:1.
▼ *Swindon reserve Jurica Pavlic scored an astonishing 21-point maximum on his first-ever visit to Purfleet. Leigh Adams also unbeaten in a two-man demolition job to end the last unbeaten home record in the Elite League.*

WOLVERHAMPTON (A)
Monday, August 11
Won 47-43
Edward Kennett [G] 6, Lanham 5:2, Shields 10:2, **Davidsson 14:1**, *rider replacement for Kylmåkorpi*, Kling 10:1, Tomicek 2:1.
▲ *Hit back from home setback to bank all three points*

even without Jonsson and Kylmäkorpi. Shields lost his maximum when timed out of Heat 15.

PETERBOROUGH (A)
Thursday, August 21
Drew 36-36
Jonsson 6, Lanham 4, Shields 7, Nieminen 6:1, *rider replacement for Davidsson*, Kling 13:2, Tomicek 0.
▼ *Shields taken to hospital with spinal injuries after heat 12 crash...meeting abandoned due to time curfew. Kylmäkorpi already ruled out for the season, Davidsson suffered internal injuries in Sweden two nights earlier.*

WOLVERHAMPTON (H)
Friday, August 22
Won 53-40
Jonsson 16, Lanham 12:3, *rider replacement for Shields*, Nieminen 7:3, Lewis Bridger [G] 7:1, Kling 4, Tomicek 7:1.
▲ *Heavily patched-up team put in determined display – the management rated this one of the best displays of the season.*

BELLE VUE (H)
Wednesday, September 10
Won 59-34
Rider replacement for Shields, Lewis Bridger [G] 8:3, Jonsson 16, Lanham 10:4, Edward Kennett [G] 12, Kling 6:1, Nieminen 7:1.
▲ *Aces arrived with virtually a one-man team as Jason Crump scored a maximum but the Hammers dominated every race in which he was not involved.*

IPSWICH (A)
Thursday, September 11
Won 48-44
Jonsson 15, Lanham 5:2, *rider replacement for Shields*, Tomas Topinka [G] 9:1, Edward Kennett [G] 3:1, Kling 0, Nieminen 16:1, Jerran Hart [G] (no. 8), did not ride.
▲ *Stunning display by Nieminen at reserve, as Kling crashed out in Heat 2. Jonsson romped to a maximum as Hammers again took advantage of arriving at Foxhall and finding the home side weakened.*

WOLVERHAMPTON (H)
Wednesday, September 17
Won 58-32
Jonsson 12, Lanham 11:3, *rider replacement Shields*, **Jedrzejak 13:2**, Rory Schlein [G] 7:2, Kling 6:2, Nieminen 9:2.
▲▼ *Terrific debut for Jedrzejak with a paid maximum as Hammers won easily despite Jonsson crashing out of his last two rides.*

PETERBOROUGH (A)
Thursday, September 18
Lost 37-56
Jonsson 13 (6), Lanham 5:2, *rider replacement for Shields*, Jedrzejak 4, Lewis Bridger [G] 10, Kling 2:1, Nieminen 3:1.
▼ *Jonsson did not complete the meeting after blowing both of his engines.*

PETERBOROUGH (H)
Friday, September 19
Won 49-41
Jonsson 18, Lanham 7:1, *rider replacement for Shields*, Jedrzejak 7, Edward Kennett [G] 13, Kling 2:2, Tomasz Piszcz [G] 2, Jerrard Hart [G] (no. 8).
▲ *Rounded off their regular season league fixtures with a hard-earned win against dogged opponents, Jonsson back on-form with six rides and six wins, and Edward Kennett guesting well.*

ELITE LEAGUE

	M	*W*	*D*	*L*	*PtsF*	*PtsA*	*Pts*
Poole	32	22	0	10	1600	1321	52
LAKESIDE	**32**	**22**	**1**	**9**	**1551**	**1375**	**52**
Swindon	32	17	2	13	1498	1434	41
Ipswich	32	16	3	13	1483	1439	40
Eastbourne	32	15	0	17	1462	1472	34
Coventry	32	12	3	17	1418	1506	29
Belle Vue	32	13	2	17	1423	1491	28
Peterborough	32	13	1	18	1371	1528	28
Wolverhampton	32	8	0	24	1341	1581	16

LAKESIDE

Rider	*M*	*R*	*Pts*	*BP*	*TPts*	*Ave*	*F*	*P*	*TR*	*TPts*	*TS*	*TSPts*
Andreas JONSSON	35	174	435	8	443	10.18	5	1	3	9	1	0
Adam SHIELDS	**32**	**155**	**322**	**17**	**339**	**8.75**	**1**	**1**	**3**	**7**	**0**	**0**
Kauko NIEMINEN	9	44	72	13	85	7.73	0	0	0	0	0	0
Joonas KYLMÅKORPI	**27**	**123**	**186**	**42**	**228**	**7.41**	**0**	**0**	**2**	**5**	**0**	**0**
Jonas DAVIDSSON	35	154	259	26	285	7.40	0	1	1	2	1	2
Tomasz JEDRZEJAK	**8**	**44**	**69**	**8**	**77**	**7.00**	**0**	**1**	**0**	**0**	**0**	**0**
Leigh LANHAM	44	193	247	77	324	6.71	0	0	0	0	0	0
Ricky KLING	**44**	**198**	**232**	**50**	**282**	**5.70**	**0**	**0**	**0**	**0**	**0**	**0**
Lubos TOMICEK	31	123	133	31	164	5.33	0	0	0	0	0	0
Chris MILLS	**2**	**7**	**4**	**1**	**5**	**2.86**	**0**	**0**	**0**	**0**	**0**	**0**
Krzysztof JABLONSKI	3	14	6	1	7	2.00	0	0	0	0	0	0
Guests	***24***	***116***	***177***	***11***	***188***	***6.48***	***0***	***0***	***2***	***6***	***0***	***0***

For Kauko NIEMINEN see Workington; for Chris MILLS see Reading.

Play offs

Semi Final
SWINDON (H) SKY TV
Monday, September 29
Won 56-33
Rider replacement for Shields, Jedrzejak 12:3, **Jonsson 15**, Lanham 10:2, Edward Kennett [G] 10:1, Kling 3:1, Nieminen 6.
▲ *Performed a demolition job on the Robins but victory came at the cost of Nieminen suffering a broken collarbone.*

FINAL, first leg
POOLE (H) SKY TV
Monday, October 6
Lost 42-48
Jonsson 15:1 (TS0), Lanham 6:1, *rider replacement for Shields*, Davidsson 10:1, Jedrzejak 8:1, Kling 2:1, Jablonski 1:1.
▲▼ *Jonsson won four races but the patched-up side was no match for an efficient Poole unit. Jonsson's tactical substitution ride in Heat 8 was unsuccessful.*

FINAL, second leg
POOLE (A)
Monday, October 13
Lost 33-60
Scott Nicholls [G] 11 (6), Lanham 1, *rider replacement for Shields*, Jedrzejak 7:1, Davidsson 11, Kling 0, Jablonski 3.
▼ *Completed a nightmare Final without Jonsson due to illness, and only scored eight points in the first six races.*
Aggregate: Lost 75-108.

Knock Out Cup

First round, first leg
PETERBOROUGH (A)
Thursday, June 19
Won 51-39
Jonsson 13:1, Lanham 6:1, Shields 9:1, Tomicek 4:1, Davidsson 9, Kling 10:2, Jerran Hart [G] 0.
▲ *Hammers' greatest-ever night at the Showground and achieved without ex-Panther Kylmåkorpi; Kling unbeaten before retiring from Heat 14.*

First round, second leg
PETERBOROUGH (H)
Friday, June 20
Won 50-42
Jonsson 14, Lanham 7:2, Shields 11, Tomicek 0, Davidsson 10:1, Kling 4:1, Mills 4:1.
Aggregate: Won 101-81.

Semi Final, first leg
EASTBOURNE (H)
Wednesday, August 13
Won 52-41
Rory Schlein [G] 11, Lanham 5:3, Shields 12:1, Davidsson 4:1, *rider replacement for Kylmåkorpi*, Kling 6:1, Tomicek 7:3, Nieminen (no. 8) 7:1.

Semi Final, second leg
EASTBOURNE (A)
Saturday, August 30
Lost 39-54
Rider replacement for Shields, Lanham 2, Rory Schlein [G] 16, Kevin Doolan [G] 7:1, Billy Janniro [G] 6, Kling 7:2, Tomicek 1.
▼ *Injuries caught up despite guest Rory Schlein's efforts, going out of the Cup after 5-1 in last race.*
Aggregate: Lost 91-95.

Craven Shield

IPSWICH (A)
Friday, March 21
Won 47-43
Jonsson 11:1, Lanham 5:2, Shields 10, Davidsson 6, Kylmåkorpi 7:2, Kling 3:1, Tomicek 5:1.
▲ *Perfect way to start the new season with victory in the first of a Good Friday double header.*

IPSWICH (H)
Friday, March 21
Lost 40-52
Jonsson 11, Lanham 6:2, Shields 6:1, Davidsson 7 (4), Kylmåkorpi 2:1, Kling 2, Tomicek 6:1.
▼ *Hammers were stunned at home with the visitors having the points safe with two heats to go.*

PETERBOROUGH (H)
Friday, March 28
Won 58-35
Jonsson 15, Lanham 9:3, Shields 6, Davidsson 9:1, Kylmåkorpi 7:2, Kling 5:2, Tomicek 7:2.
▲ *Made the best of difficult conditions despite skipper Shields falling in his first two rides.*

PETERBOROUGH (A)
Thursday, April 3
Drew 45-45
Davey Watt [G] 6, Lanham 2:2, Shields 12, Kylmåkorpi 4:1, Davidsson 7:1, Kling 14, Tomicek 0.
▲ *Confirmed as group winners after leading for much of the meeting at the Showground before conceding a 5-1 in Heat 15.*

CRAVEN SHIELD
Eastern Group

	M	W	D	L	PtsF	PtsA	Pts
LAKESIDE	**4**	**2**	**1**	**0**	**190**	**175**	**6**
Ipswich	4	2	0	2	199	165	5
Peterborough	4	1	1	2	158	207	3

Seeded to Craven Shield Final as highest scoring Group winners.

Weather...

Three abortive attempts to stage the home Elite League match against Wolverhampton.

Elite League
Friday, June 6 .... WOLVERHAMPTON (H)
Monday, July 7 .... WOLVERHAMPTON (A)
Friday, July 11 .... WOLVERHAMPTON (H)
Friday, September 5 .... WOLVERHAMPTON (H)

Knock Out Cup
Saturday, August 9 .... EASTBOURNE (A)

Craven Shield
Thursday, March 20 .... PETERBOROUGH (A)
Friday, October 17 .... COVENTRY (H)
Meeting postponed because of re-staging of Final Grand Prix.

...beaten

FINAL
First leg
COVENTRY (H)
Friday, October 16
Lost 43-47

Jonsson 15:1, Lanham 8:1, *rider replacement for Shields*, Davidsson 7:2, Jedrzejak 12, Kling 1, Mills 0.

▼ *Still suffering the hangover from Grand Final defeat, Hammers conceded the majority of heat winners and were completely out-gunned at reserve.*

FINAL
Second leg
COVENTRY (A)
Friday, October 24
Lost 35-58

Jonsson 18 (6), Lanham 3:1, *rider replacement for Shields*, Davidsson 5, Jedrzejak 6:1, Kling 1, Jablonski 2.

▼ *Ran out of steam at the end of the season with Jonsson receiving little consistent support from his teammates. A low-key end to what had been a successful year.*

Aggregate: Lost 78-105.

Late season arrival Krzysztof Jablonski missed the first leg of the Craven Shield Final

Challenge

SPRING TROPHY
First leg
POOLE (A)
Wednesday, March 12
Lost 37-53

Jonsson 9:1 (1), Kylmåkorpi 6, Shields 8, Lanham 3:1, Davidsson 2, Kling 6, Tomicek 3:1.

Second leg
POOLE (H)
Friday, March 14
Won 53-40

Jonsson 14, Kylmåkorpi 8:2, Shields 11:2, Davidsson 7:1, Lanham 5, Kling 5:1, Tomicek 3:2.

Aggregate: Lost 90-93.

PAUL HURRY TESTIMONIAL
Wednesday, July 18

Peter Karlsson returned to Britain to pay trbute to Paul Hurry who made his debut for Arena-Essex in 1991 when he was only 16.

An arm injury ended Hurry's hopes of riding again in 2008 but he was rewarded with a decent Purfleet crowd.

	1	2	3	4	Tot	SF	GF
1 Peter KARLSSON	**2**	**3**	**3**	**3**	**11**	**❐**	**3**
2 Leigh LANHAM	2	1	3	3	9	3	2
3 Lubos TOMICEK	3	3	1	2	9	2	1
4 Lewis BRIDGER	1	2	3	3	9	1	0
5 Troy BATCHELOR	3	2	3	1	9	F	
6 Cameron WOODWARD	3	3	1	2	9		
7 Oliver ALLEN	3	3	F		6		
8 Joe SCREEN	0	0	2	3	5		
9 Chris NEATH	1	2	1	1	5		
10 Simon STEAD	2	1	0	2	5		
11 David HOWE	1	2	2	0	5		
12 Tommy ALLEN	2	0	2	F	4		
13 Tom MADSEN	0	1	2	1	4		
14 Chris MILLS	1	0	0	2	3		
15 Chris KERR	0	1	1	1	3		
16 Josef FRANC	0	0	0	0	0		
17 Rodney McDONALD [R]	0				0		

2009 Squad

Adam **SHIELDS** (8.10), Lee **RICHARDSON** (7.96), Jonas **DAVIDSSON** (6.75), Joonas **KYLMÅKORPI** (5.96), Kauko **NIEMINEN** (4.54), Stuart **ROBSON** (3.51), Chris **MILLS** (3.00)/Phil **MORRIS** (3.00), Robert **MEAR** (3.00).

Elite League

PETERBOROUGH

TRACK FILE

Track: East of England Showground, Alwalton, Peterborough, PE2 6XE.
Telephone: 01384 635948.
Hotline: 09068 664681.
Website: www.peterboroughspeedway.net
Track Length: 336 metres.
Track Record: 59.1 secs, Hans Andersen, April 6, 2007.
Promoters: Rick Frost and Mick Bratley.
Team Sponsors: Muscle Finesse.
Colours: Red, black and white.
Nickname: Panthers.

HISTORY

First meeting: June 12, 1970, Peterborough v Rayleigh, Division Two.
Leagues: Division One, 1995-97, 1999-2009. Division Two, 1970-1994, 1998. Division Three, 1996-97, 2000-03.

HONOURS

Major honours: 20.
Division One champions (2), 1999, 2006.
Division One Knock Out Cup winners (2), 1999, 2001.
Division One Craven Shield (1), 1999.
Division One Four team champions (1), 1997.
Division One Elite Shield winners (1), 2007.
Division Two champions (2), 1992, 1998.
Division Two Knock Out Cup winners (1), 1992.
Division Two Four Team champions (6), 1977-78, 1988-89, 1992, 1998.
Division Two Pairs champions (1), 1998.
Division Two Premiership winners (1), 1993.
Division Three champions (2), 1997, 2002.

2008 REVIEW

THE 2008 season at the Showground could almost be the subject of a book in its own right with the Panthers, for the second time in four years, going through a summer change in ownership.

Their team was built around the strength of Hans Andersen and Kenneth Bjerre with the intention of the lower riders all improving their averages, but the team failed to fire and always appeared destined to be in the lower half of the table.

On their night, they could cause an upset - just as they did in early June when they pulled off a stunning 46-44 win at Poole, but off the track there were problems brewing with owner Colin Horton hitting financial trouble and skipper Andersen eventually going public over the monies he was owed.

Andersen departed and was signed by Coventry, whilst Horton's final act was to rebuild the team with former Panthers riders Ryan Sullivan, Lukas Dryml and Karol Zabik all returning ahead of the club being taken over by businessman Rick Frost.

That put them into calmer waters financially but their Elite League position was still a matter which needed to be addressed, and they were confident of escaping the bottom two with several home matches in hand.

But there was little room for error with Sullivan unavailable for two of their remaining away matches, and a surprise home defeat by Eastbourne was eventually the result which left them in eighth place behind Coventry and Peterborough.

Sullivan departed before the relegation race-off, but the Panthers had put together a team which performed well on home shale and they were always favourites to overcome Wolverhampton, especially when they only lost the away leg by a point. The return saw them run up an enormous 67-23 win to bring a turbulent season to a successful conclusion.

2008 RESULTS

Elite League

Final position...Eighth

EASTBOURNE (A)
Saturday, March 29
Lost 35-59
Andersen 16 (4), Simota 1, Bjerre 9, Risager 1:1, King 3, Moller 2, Vissing 3:1.

EASTBOURNE (H) SKY TV
Tuesday, April 8
Won 48-42
Andersen 12:2, Risager 6:1, Bjerre 7, Simota 2, King 9, Vissing 9, Moller 3:3.
▲ *Made a 5-1 start when Eagles' guest Chris Harris retired from Heat 1, but still had to come back from 20-22 down to take first win of the season.*

BELLE VUE (H)
Thursday, April 17
Won 47-45
Andersen 11, Risager 4, Bjerre 11, Simota 3, King 9, Vissing 7:2, Moller 2.
▲ *Hugely entertaining meeting with Bjerre's win over tactical substitute Jason Crump in Heat 12 crucial.*

LAKESIDE (A)
Friday, April 18
Lost 37-56
Andersen 16:1 (6), Risager 4:1, Bjerre 9, Simota 0, King 1, Vissing 6, Moller 1.
▼ *Disappointing away form continued as once again Andersen was called to take a tactical ride as early as Heat 5.*

SQUAD
James Cockle, Daniel King.
Foreign: Hans Andersen, Henning Bager, Kenneth Bjerre, Lukas Dryml, Henrik Moller, Tyron Proctor, Morten Risager, Zdenek Simota, Ryan Sullivan, Claus Vissing, Karol Zabik.

IPSWICH (H)
Monday, April 21
Won 49-41
Andersen 13:1, Risager 3, Bjerre 10, Simota 0, **King 12**, Vissing 9, Moller 2:1.
▲ *First-ever Elite League maximum for King as Panthers recovered from 21-27 down to complete a turnaround win.*

WOLVERHAMPTON (A)
Monday, April 28
Lost 33-59
Andersen 9 (4), Risager 3:1, Bjerre 11, Simota 2, King 5, Vissing 1, Craig Watson [G] 2.
▼ *Manager Trevor Swales threatened team changes after another disastrous away showing, with lower-order riders under threat.*

IPSWICH (A)
Thursday, May 5
Lost 31-60
Andersen 8:1 (TS2), Risager 4, Bjerre 5 (1), Vissing 1, King 8, Proctor 4:1, Moller 1:1.

POOLE (H)
Thursday, May 8
Lost 35-47
Andersen 3, Risager 4, Bjerre 14 (4), Vissing 4:2, King 6 (TS1), Carl Wilkinson [G] 4:1, Moller 0.

Henrik Moller, Daniel King, Claus Vissing, Hans Andersen, Morten Risager, Kenneth Bjerre and Zdenek Simota

▼ *Heavily beaten at home after Andersen was involved in a spectacular crash in Heat 6 and was withdrawn by the medical officer. Pirates scored three consecutive 5-1s to go 16 points clear.*

WOLVERHAMPTON (H)
Thursday, May 22
Won 48-42
Andersen 17:1, Bager 3:1, *rider replacement for Bjerre*, Vissing 6:1, King 14, Risager 6:1, Carl Wilkinson [G] 2:1.
▲▼ *Had to wait until Heat 14 to win the match, without broken leg victim Bjerre (hurt in previous night's Danish league match), against a team including four ex-Panthers.*

EASTBOURNE (A)
Saturday, May 31
Lost 44-46
Andersen 15, Bager 4:2, *rider replacement for Bjerre*, Vissing 8:2, King 8, Ryan Fisher [G] 4, Proctor 5:1.
▼ *Went into last heat two points down but hopes of a shock away win were ended by King's fall on the second bend, although Andersen won the race.*

POOLE (A)
Wednesday, June 4
Won 46-44
Andersen 16, Bager 7:1, *rider replacement for Bjerre*, Vissing 4:1, King 9:1, Risager 10:1, Proctor 0.
▲ *Sensational and unexpected away win anchored by Andersen, whose 5-1 with Bager in Heat 11 was big turning point.*

SWINDON (A)
Thursday, June 5
Lost 40-53
Andersen 18 (6), Bager 1:1, *rider replacement for Bjerre*, Vissing 2, King 6, Risager 3:2, Ryan Fisher [G] 10:1.

WOLVERHAMPTON (A)
Monday, June 9
Lost 38-54
Andersen 13 (4), Bager 6:1, *rider replacement for Bjerre*, Vissing 3:1, King 10, Ryan Fisher [G] 5:1, Proctor 1.
▼ *Andersen angered by Heat 13 exclusion after clash with Fredrik Lindgren.*

SWINDON (H)
Monday, June 23
Lost 42-48
Andersen 14, Bager 2, Bjerre 6, Vissing 4:2, King 8:1, Risager 5:1, Proctor 3:1.
▼ *Another crushing home defeat.*

IPSWICH (A)
Thursday, June 26
Lost 38-54
Andersen 8 (4), Bager 2:1, Bjerre 8, Vissing 2:2, King 8, Risager 9:1, Rusty Harrison [G] 1.
▼ *Andersen was limited to just one race win on his old home track and suffered two retirements.*

BELLE VUE (A)
Monday, June 30
Lost 41-52
Andersen 17 (6), Bager 1, Bjerre 4:1, Vissing 7, King 3, Risager 8:1, Andrew Tully [G] 1.
▲ *Andersen defeated Jason Crump on three occasions, the first time in five meetings at Kirkmanshulme Lane that Crump had dropped points.*

BELLE VUE (H)
Thursday, July 3
Won 52-42
Andersen 11, Vissing 8:2, Bjerre 11:1, Bager 6:2, King 7:1, Risager 6, Simon Lambert [G] 3:1.

BELLE VUE (A)
Monday, July 21
Lost 39-53
Rider replacement for Andersen, Vissing 0, Bjerre 10 (4), Bager 11:2, King 7, Risager 6, Proctor 5:1.
▼ *Used rider replacement for Andersen, who was in dispute with club owner Colin Horton due to a backlog of unpaid wages.*

COVENTRY (A) SKY TV
Monday, July 28
Lost 39-48
Bjarne Pedersen [G] 12, Vissing 4, Bjerre 9, Bager 4, King 5:2, Risager 5:1, *Proctor 3:1*.
▼ *Andersen serving a ban for withholding his services, and Bjarne Pedersen stood in to good effect.* ● *Result amended from 48-42 because of ineligibility of Ty Proctor (4-3:1) as replacement for Moller.*

SWINDON (A)
Thursday, July 31
Lost 36-43
Rory Schlein [G] 11, Vissing 2:1, Bjerre 12 (6), Bager 5:2, King 4:1, Risager 2:1, *Ryan Fisher [G] 0*.
▼ *The Speedway Control Bureau ruled that Ryan Fisher was used as an ineligible replacement for Henrik Moller. Peterborough claimed Moller was injured but were unable to produce any evidence to that effect. Fisher's eight points were deducted from the original 44-49 result. Krzysztof Stojanowski was also ruled as ineligible to guest for Swindon as he had previously ridden for them seven days earlier and his points were also deducted from the amended result.*

COVENTRY (H)
Thursday, August 7
Won 51-38
Sullivan 12, Dryml 4, Bjerre 12:1, Zabik 4:1, King 8, Bager 7:3, Vissing 4:3.
▲ *Sullivan returned to the Peterborough colours after a near two year absence and fellow new signing Zabik also made his seasonal bow in Panthers' colours.*

LAKESIDE (H)
Thursday, August 21
Drew 36-36
Simon Lambert [G] 0, Dryml 7, Bjerre 12, Zabik 2, King 6:1, Bager 3:1, Vissing 6:1.
▼ *Ryan Sullivan unavailable due to a Russian League*

commitment. Meeting abandoned after 12 heats because of time curfew following serious crash involving Lakeside's Adam Shields. Zabik dislocated his elbow

COVENTRY (A)
Friday, August 22
Lost 36-59
Kozza Smith [G] 2, Dryml 3:1, Bjerre 10 (6), *rider replacement for Zabik*, King 15 (TS4), Bager 3:2, Vissing 3.
▼ *Sullivan's absence and other underperformance prevented Panthers from taking advantage of Coventry's mid-meeting injury problems.*

POOLE (A)
Monday, August 25
Lost 36-54
Sullivan 4, Dryml 2, Bjerre 9, *rider replacement for Zabik*, King 11 (0), Proctor 6, Vissing 4:3, Casper Wortmann [G] (no.8).
▼ *Sullivan returned but had no success. King deprived Bjarne Pedersen of maximum, passing him in Heat 15.*

SWINDON (H)
Monday, September 1
Won 52-41
Sullivan 11:1, Dryml 7:1, Bjerre 10, Bager 5:3, King 6:2, Proctor 6:1, Vissing 7.
▲ *Moved off the bottom of the table with a solid all-round show, Sullivan leading well from number one.*

EASTBOURNE (H)
Thursday, September 4
Lost 39-54
Sullivan 3, Dryml 7:1 (TS0), Bjerre 13:1 (6), Bager 2, King 6, Proctor 2:1, Vissing 6.
▼ *Shock home defeat where little went right. King withdrew after his fourth rider complaining of tightness in his chest and dizziness, Sullivan's scoring restricted by toothache.*

POOLE (H) SKY TV
Monday, September 8
Won 47-43
Sullivan 7:1, Dryml 5:1, Bjerre 8:1, Bager 10:1, *rider replacement for King*, Zabik 11:2, Vissing 6:2.
▲▼ *5-1 from Bager and Zabik in Heat 14 finally ended Poole's 13-match winning run, Panthers having been pegged back from a 12-point lead. King missed out due to illness.*

COVENTRY (H)
Monday, September 15
Won 51-42
Sullivan 10:2, *rider replacement for Dryml*, Bjerre 10, Bager 6:2, King 9:1, Zabik 8:3, Vissing 8:1.
▲ *Had to wait until Heat 10 for the first 5-1 but this was a comfortable win as only the visiting top two offered resistance.*

LAKESIDE (H)
Thursday, September 18
Won 56-37
Tai Woffinden [G] 10, *rider replacement for Dryml*, Bjerre 11, Bager 6, King 12:1, Zabik 7:3, Vissing 10:4.
▲ *Defeated the Hammers for the first time in four Showground clashes this season, Tai Woffinden stepped in well for the absent Sullivan.*

LAKESIDE (A)
Friday, September 19
Lost 41-49
Chris Harris [G] 7:2, *rider replacement for Dryml*, Bjerre 13, Bager 5:2, King 8, Zabik 0, Vissing 8:2.

IPSWICH (H)
Monday, September 22
Won 52-40
Sullivan 8, Dryml 5, **Bjerre 14:1**, Bager 6:2, King 8, Zabik 5, Vissing 6:1.
▲ *Bjerre wrapped up his paid maximum by overhauling Rory Schlein in Heat 15. Panthers still set to finish in bottom two.*

WOLVERHAMPTON (H)
Thursday, September 25
Won 56-37
Sullivan 7:3, Dryml 9:1, Bjerre 14, Bager 5:3, King 9:1, Zabik 8:1, Vissing 4:1.

ELITE LEAGUE

	M	W	D	L	PtsF	PtsA	Pts
Poole	32	22	0	10	1600	1321	52
Lakeside	32	22	1	9	1551	1375	52
Swindon	32	17	2	13	1498	1434	41
Ipswich	32	16	3	13	1483	1439	40
Eastbourne	32	15	0	17	1462	1472	34
Coventry	32	12	3	17	1418	1506	29
Belle Vue	32	13	2	17	1423	1491	28
PETERBOROUGH	**32**	**13**	**1**	**18**	**1371**	**1528**	**28**
Wolverhampton	32	8	0	24	1341	1581	16

Relegation Play offs

First leg
WOLVERHAMPTON (A)
Tuesday, October 14
Lost 47-48
Rory Schlein [G] 14:1 (4), Dryml 0, Bjerre 14 (6), Bager 7, King 1:1, Zabik 9:1, Vissing 2.
▼ *Fought back from 14-points down in tricky conditions, Bager and Zabik taking a 5-1 in Heat 14, backed up by Bjerre and guest Schlein in the last race.*

Second leg
WOLVERHAMPTON (H)
Thursday, October 16
Won 67-23
Rory Schlein [G] 9:3, Dryml 9:2, Bjerre 13, Bager 5:3, King 4:2, **Zabik 14:1, Vissing 13:2**.
▼ *King suffered a broken foot and was taken to hospital after a Heat 11 crash after claiming he had been taken wide by Fredrik Lindgren.*
Aggregate: Won 114-71.

Hard times

For the second season in a row Colin Horton failed to see out the season as an Elite League promoter. In 2007 he closed down Oxford after only 13 home meetings and in 2008 he hit more financial problems before eventually selling out to new owner Rick Frost in August.

Knock Out Cup

First round, first leg
LAKESIDE (H)
Thursday, June 19
Lost 39-51
Andersen 12 (1), Bager 1, *rider replacement for Bjerre*, Vissing 6:1, King 7, Risager 10:3, Ryan Fisher [G] 3:1.
▼ *Described by manager Trevor Swales as one of the Panthers' worst-ever performances at the Showground.*

First round, second leg
LAKESIDE (A)
Friday, June 20
Lost 42-50
Bjarne Pedersen [G] 15 (4), Bager 9:4, *rider replacement for Bjerre*, Vissing 4, James Wright [G] 2:1, Risager 5, Proctor 7:2.
Aggregate: Lost 81-101.

Weather...

Attractive Bank Holiday double-header against Coventry washed out.

Elite League
Monday, May 26 ....COVENTRY (H)
Monday, May 26 ....COVENTRY (A)
Thursday, July 10 ....................WOLVERHAMPTON (H)

Craven Shield
Thursday, March 20....................................LAKESIDE (H)

...beaten

Craven Shield

IPSWICH (H)
Monday, March 24
Won 47-43
Andersen 14, Simota 1:1, Bjerre 11, Risager 3:2, King 8:1, Moller 1:1, Vissing 9:1.
▼ *New signings Simota, Risager and Moller failed to make any impact on official home debuts.*

IPSWICH (A)
Thursday, March 27
Lost 31-61
Andersen 14 (4), Simota 1, Bjerre 6, Risager 4:1, King 5, Moller 0, Vissing 1.

LAKESIDE (A)
Friday, March 28
Lost 35-58
Andersen 9, Simota 2:2, Bjerre 12:1 (6), Risager 6:1, King 1, Moller 2, Vissing 3.

LAKESIDE (H)
Thursday, April 3
Drew 45-45
Andersen 14:1, Risager 4, Bjerre 7, Simota 3:1, King 11:1, Vissing 4, Moller 2:2.
▼ *Six down with three heats left but secured a draw with last-heat 5-1 from Andersen and King. Result sentenced Panthers to bottom of group finish.*

CRAVEN SHIELD
Eastern Group

	M	W	D	L	PtsF	PtsA	Pts
Lakeside	4	2	1	0	190	175	6
Ipswich	4	2	0	2	199	165	5
PETERBOROUGH	**4**	**1**	**1**	**2**	**158**	**207**	**3**

PETERBOROUGH

Rider	*M*	*R*	*Pts*	*BP*	*TPts*	*Ave*	*F*	*P*	*TR*	*TPts*	*TS*	*TSPts*
Hans ANDERSEN	22	113	280	7	287	10.16	0	2	8	17	2	3
Kenneth BJERRE	**33**	**159**	**335**	**7**	**342**	**8.60**	**1**	**1**	**9**	**21**	**1**	**0**
Ryan SULLIVAN	8	36	62	7	69	7.67	0	0	0	0	0	0
Karol ZABIK	**10**	**46**	**68**	**12**	**80**	**6.96**	**0**	**1**	**0**	**0**	**0**	**0**
Daniel KING	38	180	277	17	294	6.53	1	0	1	0	1	2
Henning BAGER	**27**	**113**	**132**	**39**	**171**	**6.05**	**0**	**0**	**0**	**0**	**0**	**0**
Lukas DRYML	11	45	58	7	65	5.78	0	0	0	0	1	0
Claus VISSING	**40**	**178**	**204**	**39**	**243**	**5.46**	**0**	**0**	**0**	**0**	**0**	**0**
Morten RISAGER	24	106	121	20	141	5.32	0	0	0	0	0	0
Ty PROCTOR	**10**	**38**	**35**	**7**	**42**	**4.42**	**0**	**0**	**0**	**0**	**0**	**0**
Henrik MOLLER	11	39	16	8	24	2.46	0	0	0	0	0	0
Zdenek SIMOTA	**10**	**36**	**15**	**4**	**19**	**2.11**	**0**	**0**	**0**	**0**	**0**	**0**
Guests	***22***	***97***	***121***	***13***	***134***	***5.53***	***0***	***0***	***1***	***2***	***1***	***2***

For Hans ANDERSEN see Coventry; for Karol ZABIK see Poole; for Henning BAGER see Berwick and Birmingham; for Morten RISAGER see Wolverhampton; for Ty PROCTOR see Redcar. James COCKLE was named as official number eight but did not ride, see Mildenhall.

Ty PROCTOR rode illegally at Coventry on July 28, scoring 3:1 from four rides; Ryan FISHER rode illegally at Swindon as a guest on July 31 scoring 8 from five rides. Points were deducted by the Speedway Control Bureau but the above statistics include the appearance but with no rides and no points.

Inter League Challenge

MILDENHALL (H)
Thursday, March 13
Won 56-34

Andersen 8:1, Simota 8:1, **Bjerre 9**, Risager 4:2, King 8:1, Moller 3:1, Vissing 16.

▼ *Risager took no further part after suffering bruising in a Heat 9 crash with Robbie Kessler. Andersen and Bjerre took three rides each to allow extra track-time for the reserves.*

2009 Squad

Kenneth **BJERRE** (7.88), Niels-Kristian **IVERSEN** (7.80), Mads **KORNELIUSSEN** (6.94), Karol **ZABIK** (4.56), Kenneth **HANSEN** (3.57), Ales **DRYML** (4.53), Claus **VISSING** (4.47), Rene **BACH** (4.00), *Lee* **COMPLIN** *(3.64)/Andrew* **TULLY** *(3.40)*, Simon **LAMBERT** (3.00).

Pairs

READY POWER PAIRS CHAMPIONSHIP
Friday, October 24

1 Karol Zabik (18) and Tai Woffinden (17) 35; 2 Henning Bager (19) and Ulrich Østergaard (13) 32, 3 Lukas Dryml (22), Carl Wilkinson (5) and Peter Kilderman (2) 29, 4 Claus Vissing (17) and Lee Complin (10) 27, 5 Kenneth Bjerre (23) and Casper Wortmann (2) 25, 6 Lewis Bridger (18) and Richard Hall (5) 23, 7 Stuart Robson (14) and Rene Bach (4) 18.

▼ *Zabik and Tai Woffinden were popular winners of the event, having been able to afford Woffinden's mechanical failure in Heat 20 as the Pole won the race. Denmark's Rene Bach made his debut.*

Roll of Honour

2008................................Karol Zabik & Tai Woffinden

Early season signing HENNING BAGER

East of England Showground legend Ryan Sullivan returned to the Peterborough colours at the beginning of August but refused to stay on for the relegation play offs.

Elite League

POOLE

TRACK FILE

Track: Wave 105 Stadium, Wimborne Road, Poole, Dorset, BH15 2BP.
Telephone: 01202 681145.
Hotline: 09068 664683.
Website: www.poolespeedway.net
Track Length: 299.1 metres.
Track Record: 56.91 secs, Antonio Lindback, June 14, 2006.
Promoters: Matt Ford and Giles Hartwell.
Team Sponsors: Castle Cover.
Colours: Blue and white with skull and crossbones logo.
Nickname: Pirates.

HISTORY

First meeting: April 26, 1948, Poole v Great Yarmouth, National Trophy.
Leagues: Division One, 1956, 1958-59, 1965-1984, 1991-2009. Division Two, 1952-55, 1960-64, 1985-1990. Division Three, 1948-1951. Metropolitan League, 1964.

Poole have entered a team in the 2009 National League known as the Bournemouth Buccaneers.

HONOURS

Major honours: 21.
Division One champions (5), 1969, 1994, 2003-04, 2008.
Division One Knock Out Cup winners (2), 2003-04.
Division One Craven Shield winners (3), 2001-02, 2006.
Division One Four Team champions (1), 1994.
Division One Pairs champions (1), 2007.
Inter League Knock Out Cup winners (1), 2003.
Division Two champions (6), 1952, 1955, 1961-62, 1989, 1990.
Division Two Knock Out Cup winners (1), 1990.
Division Three champions (1), 1951.

2008 REVIEW

THE Pirates had been proved to be too top-heavy in 2007 when they tracked both Jason Crump and Bjarne Pedersen, and Crump was the man to make way to enable them to come inside the points limit.

The experts were of the opinion that Poole had got the balance right with their team building, and made them title favourites – even though it was something of a low-key start at Wimborne Road with a number of niggling injuries preventing them from gaining true momentum.

Pedersen was quickly joined at the top of the averages by Australian sensation Chris Holder in his first season in the Elite League, and fellow countryman Davey Watt wasn't too far off the pace of the top two either as the Pirates developed into a powerful unit.

Two changes proved to be the final pieces of the jigsaw, with Karol Zabik and an injured Zibi Suchecki replaced by club assets Magnus Zetterström and Daniel Davidsson, and there were positive contributions from both new faces after the setback of home defeats against Peterborough and Ipswich.

Zetterström and Adam Skornicki both became national champions alongside Holder, and a 13-match wining run took the Pirates to the top of the table.

The play-offs turned into a stroll for what had become one of the fastest-gating units ever seen in the Elite League, with Ipswich easily despatched at Wimborne Road, and the Pirates then easing all nerves by winning at Lakeside – not a previous happy hunting ground – in the first leg of the Grand Final.

The title celebrations were underway well before the end of the second leg as the best team in the Elite League were deservedly crowned champions - but there was disappointment right at the end when South coast rivals Eastbourne took the Knock Out Cup honours on the last weekend of the season.

■ Details of Poole's 2009 New Year Classic are at the foot of Swindon section, page 121.

Davey Watt, Krzysztof Kasprzak, Chris Holder, Adam Skornicki, Freddie Eriksson, team manager Neil Middleditch, Daniel Davidsson and Magnus Zetterström. Inset: Bjarne Pedersen

2008 RESULTS

Elite League

Final position........................CHAMPIONS (First)

WOLVERHAMPTON (A)
Monday, March 31
Lost 36-54
Pedersen 7, *rider replacement for Skornicki*, Watt 9, Zabik 0, Holder 6:1 (R), Suchecki 4:1, Eriksson 10:2.
▼ *Badly missed ex-Wolf Skornicki and Zabik retired in all three of his races.*

WOLVERHAMPTON (H)
Wednesday, April 2
Won 62-31
Pedersen 13:2, *rider replacement for Skornicki*, Watt 9, Zabik 11:2, Holder 12:2, Suchecki 8:1, Eriksson 9:1.
▲ *Pedersen back to form with a paid maximum after engine trouble in the early weeks of the season.*

BELLE VUE (A) SKY TV
Monday, April 7
Lost 43-50
Pedersen 8:1, *rider replacement for Skornicki*, Watt 6, Zabik 3:1, Holder 8, Suchecki 1:1, Eriksson 17:1 (6).
▼ *Pirates unhappy with decision to put all-four back into re-run of Heat 15 after Jason Crump had fallen. Aces took a 5-1 to clinch win.*

LAKESIDE (H)
Wednesday, April 9
Won 54-38
Pedersen 9, *rider replacement for Skornicki*, Watt 12:1, Zabik 6, Holder 8:1, Suchecki 8:1, Eriksson 11:4.
▼ *Zabik withdrew from the meeting after a Heat 9 crash with wrist problems.*

SQUAD
Jordan Frampton.
Foreign: Daniel Davidsson, Freddie Eriksson, Chris Holder, Krzysztof Kasprzak, Mark Lemon, Bjarne Pedersen, Adam Skornicki, Zbigniew Suchecki, Davey Watt, Karol Zabik, Magnus Zetterström.

LAKESIDE (A)
Friday, April 11
Lost 45-48
Pedersen 11 (6), Woodward 5, Watt 11, *rider replacement for Zabik*, Holder 10, Eriksson 7:1, Andrew Bargh [G] 1.
▼ *Battled back from 31-17 down to force a last-heat decider which Holder won, but Watt was kept at the back.*

COVENTRY (H)
Wednesday, April 16
Won 53-39
Pedersen 12:1, Mads Kornliussen [G] 3:2, Watt 8:2, *rider replacement for Skornicki*, **Holder 15**, Suchanek 2, Eriksson 13:3.
▲ *Holder's first Elite League maximum in his 12th appearance for the club – achieved on his spare bike after his first machine failed on parade.*

COVENTRY (A)
Friday, April 18
Lost 45-48
Pedersen 18 (6), Zabik 0, Watt 11:1, *rider replacement for Skornicki*, Holder 8, Eriksson 8:2, Suchecki 0.

EASTBOURNE (H)
Wednesday, April 23
Won 52-41
Pedersen 10, Eriksson 9:2, Holder 9, *rider replacement for Zabik*, Watt 10:1, Suchecki 0, Skornicki 13:2, Frampton [no.8] 1.
▼ *Suchecki suffered a broken femur when he crashed out of Heat 2, but Skornicki made a successful return from a broken scaphoid*

SWINDON (H)
Monday, May 5
Won 53-39
Kasprzak 10, Eriksson 7:2, Holder 14, *rider replacement for Zabik*, Watt 11:1, Craig Watson [G] 1:1, Skornicki 10:4.
▲ *Kasprzak returned as a short-term replacement for injured Pedersen and won two races in routine home win.*

PETERBOROUGH (A)
Thursday, May 8
Won 57-35
Kasprzak 10:1, Eriksson 4:2, Holder 13, *rider replacement for Zabik*, Watt 12, Craig Watson [G] 9:2, Skornicki 9:3.
▲ *Emphatic win made easier by Hans Andersen's second ride withdrawal. Pirates became first visiting team to win at Alwalton since Reading in September 2006.*

EASTBOURNE (A) SKY TV
Monday, May 12
Won 48-41
Kasprzak 8, Eriksson 3:2, Holder 11:1, Zetterström 7:1, *rider replacement for Davey Watt*, Davidsson 1:1, Skornicki 18:1.

BELLE VUE (H)
Wednesday, May 14
Abandoned 24-12.
Rain.
Kasprzak 3. Eriksson 4:1, Holder 4:1. Zetterström 3. Watt 3. Davidsson 2:1, Skornicki 5:1.
● *Davey Watt, Daniel Davidsson and Adam Skornicki were unbeaten by an opponent when referee Paul Carrington abandoned the meeting at the end of heat 6 because of heavy rain.*

BELLE VUE (A)
Monday, May 19
Lost 42-48
Kasprzak 5:1, Eriksson 7:1, *rider replacement for Holder*, Zetterström 6:2, Watt 13, Davidsson 3, Skornicki 8:2.

IPSWICH (H)
Wednesday, May 21
Lost 40-50
Kasprzak 5, Eriksson 5:1, Holder 5, Zetterström 4, Watt 12, Skornicki 6:2, Davidsson 3:1.
▼ *Holder withdrew after two rides following crash in Poland.*

SWINDON (A)
Thursday, May 22
Won 51-39
Kasprzak 16:1, Eriksson 4:2, *rider replacement for Holder*, Zetterström 12:1, Watt 8:1, Davidsson 3:1, Skornicki 8:1.
▲ *Stunning away win using rider replacement for Holder; Zetterström and Skornicki clinching win with a 5-1 in Heat 14.*

LAKESIDE (A)
Friday, May 30
Lost 39-53
Kasprzak 14, Eriksson 2, Holder 7, Skornicki 6:1, Watt 9 (4), Zetterström 0, Davidsson 1.
▼ *Kasprzak scored well on his farewell appearance, beaten only by Andreas Jonsson in Heat 1.*

PETERBOROUGH (H)
Wednesday, June 4
Lost 44-46
Holder 9, Eriksson 4:1, Pedersen 13, Skornicki 2, Watt 5:1, Zetterström 5, Davidsson 6.
▼ *Second successive home defeat against a Panthers team without the injured Kenneth Bjerre.*

IPSWICH (A) SKY TV
Monday, June 9
Won 51-41
Holder 13, Eriksson 4:2, Pedersen 12:1, Skornicki 2:1, Watt 7:1, Zetterström 4, Davidsson 9.
▲ *Revenge for home defeat with Holder and Watt equalling the fastest Foxhall time of the season.*

WOLVERHAMPTON (H)
Wednesday, June 11
Won 55-37
Holder 12:2, Eriksson 5:2, Pedersen 7, Skornicki 6:2, Watt 10:1, Zëtterström 15:2, Davidsson 0.
▼ *Daniel Davidsson withdrew from the meeting with a neck injury after a Heat 2 fall.*

WOLVERHAMPTON (A)
Monday, June 16
Won 46-44
Holder 11, Eriksson 5:1, Pedersen 12:2, Skornicki 6, Watt 5, Zetterström 5, Davidsson 2:1.

COVENTRY (H)
Wednesday, July 2
Won 54-36
Holder 10, Zetterström 7, Watt 11, Skornicki 5:2, Pedersen 8:1, Eriksson 7:1, Davidsson 6:1.

COVENTRY (A)
Friday, July 4
Won 56-37
Holder 8:4, Zetterström 11, Watt 8:1, Skornicki 5:2, Pedersen 14, Eriksson 10:1, Davidsson 0.

BELLE VUE (H)
Wednesday, July 23
Won 59-33
Holder 15, Zetterström 6:2, Watt 11:1, Skornicki 4:2, Pedersen 11:1, Eriksson 5, Davidsson 7:1.

Bjarne Pedersen completed his seventh season as a Poole rider and celebrates his testimonial in 2009.

EASTBOURNE (H)
Wednesday, July 30
Won 60-33
Holder 15, Zetterström 7:2, Watt 13:1, Skornicki 5:2, Pedersen 9, Eriksson 6:3, Davidsson 5.

LAKESIDE (H)
Wednesday, August 6
Won 50-42
Holder 11:1, Zetterström 7, Pedersen 11:1, Skornicki 6:1, Watt 10, Eriksson 1:1, Davidsson 4.
▲ *All riders bar Eriksson managed at least one race win.*

SWINDON (A)
Thursday, August 7
Won 51-42
Holder 9:2, Zetterström 10:1, Pedersen 11, Skornicki 3:1, Watt 8:1, Eriksson 7:3, Davidsson 3.

BELLE VUE (H) SKY TV
Monday, August 18
Won 50-31
Holder 10, Zetterström 6:1, Pedersen 11, Skornicki 4:2, Watt 9:1, Eriksson 3:1, Davidsson 7:2.
▼ *Heat-leaders were all in impressive form, holding full control apart from when they were facing Jason Crump. Abandonment after Heat 13 saved Aces from further damage. Result to stand.*

EASTBOURNE (A)
Saturday, August 23
Won 52-41
Holder 14:1, Zetterström 7, Pedersen 11, Skornicki 4, Watt 10:1, Davidsson 3:1, Eriksson 3:1.
▲ *Holder equalled Jason Crump's Arlington track record, clocking 54.8 seconds in the opening race.*

PETERBOROUGH (H)
Monday, August 25
Won 54-36
Holder 7:1, Zetterström 9:1, Pedersen 11:2, Skornicki 7, Watt 12, Eriksson 3:1, Davidsson 5.
▲ *Holder and Zetterström started proceedings with a first-race 5-1, and that allayed any fears that the Panthers could repeat their previous win at Wimborne Road.*

SWINDON (H)
Wednesday, August 27
Won 58-35
Holder 12:2, Zetterström 8, Pedersen 14, Skornicki 6:1, Watt 5:1, Eriksson 6:3, Davidsson 7:1.
▲ *Recorded 10 heat advantages on way to top-two finish and home draw in the Play off semi-finals.*

PETERBOROUGH (A) SKY TV
Monday, September 8
Lost 43-47
Holder 11:1, Zetterström 9:1, Pedersen 8, Skornicki 5:2, Watt 0, Eriksson 8, Davidsson 2:1.
▼ *Watt completed only one ride before withdrawing from meeting with foot injury.*

IPSWICH (H)
Wednesday, September 10
Won 59-34
Holder 17, Zetterström 11:3, Pedersen 13, Skornicki 7:2, *rider replacement for Watt*, Eriksson 6:2, Davidsson 5:1.

IPSWICH (A)
Thursday, September 25
Lost 38-52
Holder 9, Zetterström 8:1, Pedersen 9:1, Skornicki 2:1, Watt 6, Eriksson 4:1, Davidsson 0.

ELITE LEAGUE

	M	W	D	L	PtsF	PtsA	Pts
POOLE	**32**	**22**	**0**	**10**	**1600**	**1321**	**52**
Lakeside	32	22	1	9	1551	1375	52
Swindon	32	17	2	13	1498	1434	41
Ipswich	32	16	3	13	1483	1439	40
Eastbourne	32	15	0	17	1462	1472	34
Coventry	32	12	3	17	1418	1506	29
Belle Vue	32	13	2	17	1423	1491	28
Peterborough	32	13	1	18	1371	1528	28
Wolverhampton	32	8	0	24	1341	1581	16

POOLE

Rider	M	R	Pts	BP	TPts	Ave	F	P	TR	TPts	TS	TSPts
Bjarne PEDERSEN	42	194	436	26	462	9.53	1	2	5	11	0	0
Chris HOLDER	**47**	**227**	**480**	**28**	**508**	**8.95**	**3**	**1**	**1**	**0**	**1**	**0**
Davey WATT	47	211	415	26	441	8.36	1	2	1	2	1	1
Krzysztof KASPRZAK	**7**	**36**	**68**	**3**	**71**	**7.89**	**0**	**0**	**0**	**0**	**0**	**0**
Magnus ZETTERSTRÖM	31	136	217	31	248	7.29	0	1	0	0	0	0
Adam SKORNICKI	**41**	**185**	**272**	**57**	**329**	**7.11**	**0**	**0**	**0**	**0**	**0**	**0**
Freddie ERIKSSON	49	232	278	76	354	6.10	0	0	1	3	0	0
Daniel DAVIDSSON	**33**	**129**	**151**	**22**	**173**	**5.36**	**0**	**0**	**0**	**0**	**0**	**0**
Karol ZABIK	8	34	40	4	44	5.18	0	0	0	0	0	0
Zbigniew SUCHECKI	**10**	**40**	**36**	**5**	**41**	**4.10**	**0**	**0**	**0**	**0**	**0**	**0**
Jordan FRAMPTON	3	9	3	1	4	1.78	0	0	0	0	0	0
Guests	***8***	***35***	***25***	***6***	***31***	***3.54***	***0***	***0***	***0***	***0***	***0***	***0***

For Karol ZABIK see Peterborough; for Jordan FRAMPTON see Somerset.

Play offs

Semi Final
IPSWICH (H) SKY TV
Monday, September 29
Won 59-33
Holder 13, Zetterström 6:2, Pedersen 13:1, Skornicki 7:2, Watt 11, Eriksson 5:2, Davidsson 4:1.
▲ *Pirates made dream start with back-to-back 5-1s and there was never any chance of a slip-up as they reached their third Grand Final in six years.*

FINAL
First leg
LAKESIDE (A) SKY TV
Monday, October 6
Won 48-42
Holder 7, Zetterström 4:1, Pedersen 12:2, Skonerikci 10:1, Watt 7, Eriksson 2:1, Davidsson 6:1.
▲ *Stunned home crowd with 5-1s in Heats 2 and 3 and controlled meeting thereafter. Skornicki took three race wins, including one in Heat 14 to foil the Hammers' late comeback hopes.*

FINAL
Second leg
LAKESIDE (H) SKY TV
Monday, October 13
Won 60-33
Holder 12, Zetterström 8:2, **Pedersen 14:1**, Skornicki 4, Watt 8, Eriksson 4:3, Davidsson 10:3.
▲ *All too predictable for the neutrals – but nobody of a Pirates persuasion was complaining. Led 28-8 after six races against lacklustre opponents, and the procession continued in front of a bumper crowd.*
Aggregate: Won 108-75.

Knock Out Cup

Quarter Final, first leg
SWINDON (H)
Wednesday, June 18
Won 53-40
Holder 10:2, Eriksson 2:1, Pedersen 10, Skornicki 6:3, Watt 11:1, Frampton 1:1, Davidsson 13:1.
▲ *Davidsson's four race wins ensured Pirates could cover for injured Zetterström (knuckle problem).*

Quarter Final, second leg
SWINDON (A)
Thursday, June 19
Lost 40-50
Holder 9:1, Eriksson 5:2, Pedersen 9:1, Skornicki 5:1, Watt 7, Frampton 1, Davidsson 4:1.
▲ *Conceded 5-1s in Heats 12 and 13 to take the tie to the wire, but secured required 3-3 from last race.*
Aggregate: Won 93-90.

Semi Final, first leg
COVENTRY (A)
Monday, August 11
Drew 45-45
Holder 6:1, Zetterström 8:2, Pedersen 12, Skornicki 4:1, Watt 7, Eriksson 3, Davidsson 5.
▲ *Led most of the first leg but were happy with a draw, salvaged by Skornicki's pass of Billy Janniro in Heat 14 and Pedersen holding on for second place in the last race.*

Semi Final, second leg
COVENTRY (H)
Wednesday, August 13
Drew 45-45
Holder 13, Zetterström 0, Pedersen 3:1, Skornicki 7, Watt 6, Eriksson 6:4, Davidsson 10:1.
▲▼ *Dramatic finale as Holder overhauled a misfiring Harris on the last lap to snatch a replay in tricky conditions.*
Aggregate: Drew 90-90.

Semi Final Replay, first leg
COVENTRY (H)
Wednesday, September 3
Won 56-36
Holder 12:1, Zetterström 7:2, Pedersen 13, Skornicki 6:3, Watt 7:1, Eriksson 2:1, Davidsson 9:2.
▲ *Pirates dominated the first leg of the replay with five 5-1s.*

Semi Final Replay, second leg
COVENTRY (A)
Thursday, September 18
Won 54-38
Holder 11:1, **Zetterström 10:2**, Pedersen 10:1, Skornicki 8:1, Watt 11, Eriksson 0, Davidsson 4.
▲ *Had to wait until nearly 10pm to start the meeting, which was the second half of a double-header. Quickly put the tie to bed with Zetterström unbeaten.*
Aggregate: Won 110-74.

FINAL
First leg
EASTBOURNE (A)
Saturday, October 25
Lost 35-57
Holder 8 (TS0), Zetterström 7:1, Pedersen 12 (4), *rider replacement for Skornicki*, Watt 2, Eriksson 6:2, Davidsson 0.
▼ *Slipped to a surprisingly heavy defeat, and were unhappy with Holder's exclusion from Heat 5 after inside pass on Lee Richardson .*

FINAL
Second leg
EASTBOURNE (H)
Sunday, October 26
Drew 45-45.
Holder 12, Zetterström 3:1, Pedersen 5:1, Skornicki 9:1, Watt 9:1, Eriksson 3, Davidsson 4.
▼ *Wet conditions proved to be a great leveller, and Pirates could not conjure the sort of blistering opening which had been their trademark. Holder and Watt finished second and third in Heat 15 to salvage a draw on the day.*
Aggegate: Lost 80-102.

Weather...

Blessed with relatively good weather on South Coast.

Elite League
Wednesday, May 28 ....EASTBOURNE (H)
Wednesday, July 9 ....IPSWICH (H)

...beaten

Craven Shield

EASTBOURNE (H)
Friday, March 21
Won 51-43
Pedersen 5:2, Skornicki 8:1, Watt 11:2, Zabik 5:1, Holder 11, Suchecki 6, Eriksson 5:3.
▼ *Zabik suffered a wrist injury in a Heat 14 crash which caused him to miss the evening fixture at Arlington.*

EASTBOURNE (A)
Friday, March 21
Lost 42-52
Pedersen 13 (6), Skornicki 6:2, Watt 8 (TS2), *rider replacement for Zabik*, Holder 5:2, Suchecki 1, Eriksson 9:3.

SWINDON (H)
Wednesday, March 26
Won 54-39
Pedersen 12:1, Skornicki 6:1, Watt 10:1, Zabik 7, Holder 7:1, Suchecki 8:1, Eriksson 4:1.

SWINDON (A)
Thursday, March 27
Lost 44-46
Pedersen 8, Skornicki 6, Watt 9:2, Zabik 8, Holder 5, Suchecki 0, Eriksson 8:2.
▲ *Lost a four-point lead with three heats to go, but still qualified for the semi-finals as group winners on points difference, at the cost of a broken wrist for Skornicki.*

CRAVEN SHIELD
Southern Group

	M	W	D	L	PtsF	PtsA	Pts
POOLE	**4**	**2**	**0**	**2**	**191**	**180**	**4**
Eastbourne	4	2	0	2	189	182	4
Swindon	4	2	0	2	174	192	4

Semi Final, first leg
COVENTRY (H)
Wednesday, April 30
Won 58-34
Pedersen 8:2, Eriksson 6:1, Holder 12, *rider replacement for Zabik*, **Watt 15**, Craig Watson [G] 2:1, Skornicki 15:3.
▲ *Watt's first maximum as Pirates made light of Zabik's absence, out with broken ribs from a Swedish crash night before.*

Semi Final, second leg
COVENTRY (A)
Friday, May 2
Lost 32-58
Pedersen 4 (FX), *rider replacement for Zabik*, Holder 8, Eriksson 5, Watt 5:1, Craig Watson [G] 2, Skornicki 8.
▼ *Pedersen broke wrist when set for a tactical ride 8-1 with Skornicki in Heat 11, and Pirates dramatically collapsed thereafter to crash out of the competition.*
Aggregate: Lost 90-92.

Chris Holder scored more points in his first season in the top-flight than Jason Crump did in his initial full-time Poole campaign in 1994. Holder got 508 points (from 47 meetings) while Crump had scored 488 points from 41 matches.

Individual

60 YEAR DIAMOND JUBILEE
Sunday, March 9
World Champion Nicki Pedersen caused uproar when he revealed that he and his three fellow finalists had agreed to split the £60,000 first prize.

The Dane's victory was the perfect riposte after being left without an Elite League starting place and he recovered from an opening heat last place to put together five successful rides.

Among the full-house audience was then Portsmouth soccer boss Harry Redknapp.

Nicki Pedersen 12+3, Andreas Jonsson 13+2, Scott Nicholls 11+1, Leigh Adams 11+0, Hans Andersen 10, Chris Holder 10, Bjarne Pedersen 9, Jason Crump 9, Krzysztof Kasprzak 7, Emil Sajfutdinov 6, Kenneth Bjerre 6, Davey Watt 5, Rory Schlein 4, Adam Shields 3, Karol Zabik 2, Chris Harris 1, Zbigniew Suchecki [R] 0, Adam Skornicki [R] 0.

Challenges

Spring Trophy, first leg
LAKESIDE (H)
Wednesday, March 12
Won 53-37
Pedersen 4:2, Skornicki 14, Watt 4:1, Zabik 11, Holder 10, Suchecki 4:2, Eriksson 6:3.
▲ *Skornicki won his first four rides on his Pirates debut.*

Spring Trophy, second leg
LAKESIDE (A)
Friday, March 14
Lost 40-53
Pedersen 10:1 (6), Skornicki 9:1, Watt 10, Zabik 2, Holder 6, Suchecki 0, Eriksson 3:1.
Aggregate: Won 93-90.

Four Team Challenge

DRAPER TOOLS FOUR TEAM CHAMPIONSHIP
Wednesday, September 17
1 READ FABRICATION SELECT 29 (Oliver Allen 7, Davey Watt 7, Troy Batchelor 10, Claus Vissing 5, Karl Mason, did not ride), **2 CASTLE COVER PIRATES 25** (Chris Holder 10, Freddie Eriksson 5, Daniel Davidsson 6, Mark Lemon 4, Kyle Newman, did not ride), **3 C.E.F. PREMIER LEAGUE ALL STARS 24** (Kevin Doolan 3, Jason Doyle 10, Tai Woffinden 6, Shane Parker 5, Jerran Hart, did not ride), **4 WESSEX MARINE POLES 18** (Adam Skornicki 6, Daniel Jeleniewski 9, Karol Zabik 3, Sebastian Truminski 0, Brendan Johnson, did not ride).
▲ *Polish racer Daniel Jeleniewski, 25, was an impressive debutant, scoring nine points from four rides. He won two of his four races and finished in front of Mark Lemon, Chris Holder, Tai Woffinden, Troy Batchelor, Daniel Davidsson, Freddie Eriksson and Davey Watt (mechanical problems).*

2009 Squad
Bjarne **PEDERSEN** (9.13), Chris **HOLDER** (8.80), Joe **SCREEN** (6.03), Jason **DOYLE** (4.76), Daniel **DAVIDSSON** (4.05), Lukasz **JANKOWSKI** (4.00), Paul **HURRY** (4.00), *Carl* ***STONEHEWER*** *(3.64)/Tomasz* ***PISZCZ*** *(3.56)*, Kyle **LEGAULT** (3.49), Craig **WATSON** (3.00), Chris **NEATH** (3.54),

Elite League

SWINDON

TRACK FILE

Track: Abbey Stadium, Blunsdon, Swibndon, Wiltshire, SN25 4N.
Telephone: 07003 921235.
Hotline: 09068 664682.
Website: www.swindon-speedway.co.uk
Track Length: 363 metres.
Track Record: 64.21 secs, Leigh Adams, August 2, 2007.
Promoters: Terry Russell, Alun Rossiter and Gary Patchett.
Colours: Red and white.
Nickname: Robins.

HISTORY

First meeting: July 23, 1949, Swindon v Oxford, challenge.
Leagues: Division One, 1957-1992, 1995-98, 2004-09. Division Two, 1954-56, 1993-94, 1999-2003. Division Three, 1949-1951, 1996-97, 2002-04. Southern League, 1952-53.

HONOURS

Major honours: 10.
Division One champions (2), 1957, 1967.
Division One Pairs champions (2), 2004-05.
Division One Elite Shield winners (1), 2008.
Divison Two champions (1), 1956.
Division Two Knock Out Cup winners (1), 2000.
Division Two Young Shield winners (1), 2000.
Division Two Four Team champions (1), 2003.
Division Two Pairs champions (1), 1994.

2008 REVIEW

WIDELY tipped to struggle in the lower regions of the Elite League table, Swindon in fact enjoyed a campaign which exceeded expectations and again resulted in qualification for the Play offs.

Only two members of the line-up which finished as runners-up in 2007 remained, and the early question marks appeared to concern how they would back up skipper Leigh Adams with the Australian's average taking up such a percentage of the team total.

Both Mads Korneliussen and Troy Batchelor answered positively by pushing their own averages up significantly, and that ensured the Robins would largely maintain their dominance around Blunsdon – except, it seemed, when they raced against Poole, who inflicted their only two home defeats of the season, with Ipswich and Belle Vue also salvaging draws.

The Robins managed early away wins at Belle Vue and, controversially, Ipswich to establish themselves amongst the pace-setters, and their top four place was never seriously in doubt.

A foot injury to Sebastian Aldén could have derailed matters, but the Robins took the opportunity to give Croatian youngster Jurica Pavlic his first outings in the Elite League, and the teenager responded with some remarkable scores including a spectacular 21-point maximum at Lakeside, where he and Adams contributed 38 points of the team's winning total of 49.

Ultimately the Robins couldn't manufacture enough away wins to challenge the top two, which put them into an away Play off semi final back at Purfleet – and this time they failed to adapt to a slick surface and were well beaten 56-33.

An unwell Pavlic failed to score although Travis McGowan finished a troubled season on a high with paid 14, having previously lost his place in the team when Aldén returned only to break a collarbone at Coventry.

2008 RESULTS

Elite League

Final position..Third

BELLE VUE (H)
Thursday, April 3
Won 49-43
Adams 14, Wright 5:1, Batchelor 7:1, Korneliussen 9:1, McGowan 4, Gathercole 3:1, Aldén 7:2.

LAKESIDE (A)
Friday, April 4
Lost 45-50
Adams 17 (TS6), Wright 0, Batchelor 8:2, Korneliussen 14:1 (4), McGowan 2, Phil Morris [G] 4:1, Aldén 0.
▼ *Took seven heat wins at Purfleet but could not recover from going 25-11 down in the first six races.*

made him ineligible. Swindon had Shaun Tacey on standby but Parsons rode and scored paid 11. The subsequent appeal was turned down.

IPSWICH (H)
Thursday, April 17
Drew 45-45
Adams 13:2, Wright 7, Batchelor 11, McGowan 5, *rider replacement for Korneliussen*, Gathercole 0, Aldén 9.
▲ *Rescued by a Heat 15 5-1 from Batchelor and paid maximum man Adams having trailed throughout the meeting.*

BELLE VUE (A)
Monday, April 21
Won 51-42
Adams 10:1, Wright 9, Batchelor 6, McGowan 9:1, Korneliussen 6:1, Gathercole 9:1, Aldén 2:1.
▼ *Conceded an 8-1 in Heat 10 but held their nerve to pull clear again, wrapping up another away win.*

Theo Pijper, Troy Batchelor, Sebastien Aldén, Cory Gathercole, Leigh Adams, Mads Korneliussen, James Wright, Travis McGowan and team manager Alun Rossiter

LAKESIDE (H)
Thursday, April 10
Won 53-40
Adams 10:2, Wright 7, Batchelor 10:4, Korneliussen 13:1, McGowan 5, Gathercole 2:1, Aldén 6:1.

IPSWICH (A) SKY TV
Monday, April 14
Won 50-43
Adams 17 (6), Wright 5:1, Batchelor 6:2, Korneliussen 10:1, McGowan 5, Joel Parsons [G] 7:4, Aldén 0.
▲ *Ipswich protested over the use of Joel Parsons as a guest because his average had changed that afternoon and*

WOLVERHAMPTON (H)
Thursday, April 24
Won 50-42
Adams 14:1, Wright 3:1, Batchelor 9, McGowan 7:2, Korneliussen 9, Tomas Suchanek [G] 3:1, Aldén 5:1.

EASTBOURNE (H) SKY TV
Monday, April 28
Won 56-37
Adams 13:1, Wright 8:2, Batchelor 12:2, McGowan 4, Korneliussen 8:1, Gathercole 3:1, Aldén 8:1.
▲ *Best score of the season for Wright as Robins continued to defy pre-season predictions they would struggle at the bottom of the Elite League.*

EASTBOURNE (A)
Saturday, May 3
Lost 44-46
Adams 12, Wright 3:2, Korneliussen 5:1, McGowan 6, Batchelor 6, Pijper 2:1, Aldén 10:2.
▼ *Both led and trailed by four points in a dramatic meeting and went into the last race level, only for an Eagles 4-2 to see them snatch victory.*

POOLE (A)
Wednesday, May 5
Lost 39-53
Adams 15 (4), Wright 3:2, Korneliussen 7:1, McGowan 4:1, Batchelor 2, Pijper 1, Aldén 7:1.

COVENTRY (H)
Thursday, May 8
Won 49-43
Adams 13:1, Wright 5:1, Korneliussen 11, McGowan 3:1, Batchelor 10:1, Pijper 1, Aldén 6:1.
▲ *Adams and Batchelor secured a last-heat 5-1 after a Coventry revival set up a final race decider.*

BELLE VUE (A)
Monday, May 12
Lost 43-47
Adams 11:1, Wright 5, Korneliussen 5:1, McGowan 7:1, Batchelor 4, Pijper 6:1, Aldén 5:3.
▼ *Adams had beaten Jason Crump in Heat 13 but a close meeting went the Aces' way when Crump won Heat 15 with ex-Robin Charlie Gjedde in third place.*

LAKESIDE (H)
Thursday, May 15
Won 53-39
Adams 13:2, Wright 3, Korneliussen 11, McGowan 6:1, **Batchelor 15**, Pijper 1, Aldén 4.
▲ *Batchelor recorded his first Robins' maximum.*

POOLE (H)
Thursday, May 22
Lost 39-51
Adams 10:1 (TS1), Wright 2:1, Korneliussen 10, McGowan 1, Batchelor 9, Pijper 1, Aldén 6.

WOLVERHAMPTON (A) SKY TV
Monday, June 2
Won 48-42
Adams 14, Aldén 1:1, Korneliussen 8:1, McGowan 3:1, Batchelor 11:1, Pijper 0, Wright 11.

PETERBOROUGH (H)
Thursday, June 5
Won 53-40
Adams 13:1, Aldén 7:1, Korneliussen 10:2, McGowan 8, Batchelor 7:1, Pijper 0, Wright 8:2.
▲ *Went three points clear at the top of the table with a comfortable win, although Hans Andersen collected 18 points for the visitors.*

EASTBOURNE (A)
Saturday, June 7
Lost 43-50
Adams 17 (6), Aldén 0, Korneliussen 5, McGowan 3, Batchelor 6, Pijper 2:1, Wright 10:3.

SQUAD
James Wright.
Foreign: Leigh Adams, Sebastien Aldén, Troy Batchelor, Cory Gathercole, Manuel Hauzinger, Mads Korneliussen, Travis McGowan, Joel Parsons, Jurica Pavlic, Theo Pijper.

EASTBOURNE (H)
Thursday, June 12
Won 53-39
Adams 10:1, Aldén 3, Korneliussen 9, McGowan 8:2, Batchelor 7, Hauzinger 8, Wright 8:1.
▲ *Austrian Manuel Hauzinger makes a stunning Elite League debut, winning Heat 2 and ending his first night with eight points.*

PETERBOROUGH (A)
Monday, June 23
Won 48-42
Adams 13, Aldén 6:2, Korneliussen 14:1, McGowan 5:1, *rider replacement for Batchelor*, Hauzinger 0, Wright 10:1.

BELLE VUE (H)
Thursday, July 10
Drew 45-45
Adams 13, *rider replacement for Batchelor*, Korneliussen 12:1, Wright 8:1, McGowan 8:1, Hauzinger 1:1, Aldén 3:1.
▼ *Aldén breaks his foot in a Heat 7 crash and is initially ruled out for the season. Hauzinger was involved in a separate incident and could not continue.*

COVENTRY (A)
Friday, July 11
Lost 41-52
Adams 11, *rider replacement for Batchelor*, Korneliussen 10:1, Wright 7:1, McGowan 6:1, Paul Clews [G] 1:1, Krzysztof Stojanowski [G] 6:1.

IPSWICH (A) SKY TV
Monday, July 21
Lost 39-54
Adams 15:1 (6), McGowan 8:1, Korneliussen 4:1, Wright 2, Batchelor 3, Krzysztof Stojanowski [G] 6:2, Parsons 1.
▼ *Dropped 12 points down after Heat 4 with Batchelor struggling on his comeback – although there were two encouraging race wins for McGowan.*

Leigh's seventh heaven

Leigh Adams was voted Swindon's Rider of the Year – for a seventh time!
He had previously won the Swindon Advertiser award in 1991, 1992, 2004, 2005, 2006 and 2007.
Troy Batchelor picked up the Raytrapp Memorial Trophy as the Robins' Most Improved Rider and newcomer James Wright was crowned Pit Crew Bonus King Award.
A special Unsung Hero Award went to track helper Bob Crowether for his behind-the-scenes efforts.

IPSWICH (H)
Thursday, July 24
Won 49-44
Adams 13:1, Wright 8:1, Korneliussen 4:1, Batchelor 12:1, McGowan 5, James Holder [G] 1, Krzysztof Stojanowski [G] 6:1.

PETERBOROUGH (H)
Thursday, July 31
Won 43-36
Adams 11:1, Wright 11:1, Korneliussen 9:2, McGowan 7:1, Batchelor 5, Hauzinger 0, *Krzysztof Stojanowski 0.*
▲ *The Speedway Control Bureau ruled that Krzysztof Stojanowski was ineligible to guest for Swindon as he had previously ridden for them seven days earlier. His six (and 1 bonus) points were deducted from the original 49-44 result. Peterborough had also used Ryan Fisher (eight points) as an ineligible replacement for Henrik Moller.*

WOLVERHAMPTON (A)
Monday, August 4
Lost 46-47
Adams 19 (6), McGowan 3:1, Korneliussen 9:1, Wright 2:1, *rider replacement for Batchelor*, Hauzinger 2:1, Pavlic 11:1.
▲ *Pavlic sparking debut, taking seven rides, including a Heat 2 race-win.*

POOLE (H)
Thursday, August 7
Lost 42-51
Adams 17:1 (6), Wright 3, Korneliussen 5, McGowan 0, Batchelor 2, Hauzinger 3:1, Pavlic 12:1.
▼ *Another home defeat against the Pirates with a middle order that totally failed to fire despite Pavlic's excellent home debut.*

LAKESIDE (A)
Friday, August 8
Won 49-41
Adams 17:1, Wright 5, *rider replacement for Korneliussen*, McGowan 0, Batchelor 6, Hauzinger 0, **Pavlic 21**.
▲ *How to win with only two riders – Adams and Pavlic surpassed themselves with Pavlic wrapping up a wonderful first week in the Elite League with seven straight wins.*

COVENTRY (H)
Thursday, August 21
Won 51-39
Adams 13, Wright 3, Korneliussen 8:1, McGowan 3:1, Batchelor 12, Richard Sweetman [G] 2, Pavlic 1.
▲ *Batchelor put in a brilliant showing with wins over the Coventry top two to keep the Robins just ahead in a match which wasn't decided until Heat 14.*

POOLE (A)
Wednesday, August 27
Lost 35-58
Adams 14 (6), Wright 0, Korneliussen 5, McGowan 0, Batchelor 7, Richard Sweetman [G] 0, Pavlic 9.
▼ *Adams won three races as Robins struggled against the strength of the Pirates – with three riders unable to score a point between them.*

PETERBOROUGH (A) SKY TV
Monday, September 1
Lost 41-52
Adams 17 (6), Wright 4:2, Korneliussen 0, McGowan 1, Batchelor 7, Parsons 0, Pavlic 12.
▼ *Korneliussen was concussed in a heavy Heat 3 crash, and two race wins for Batchelor weren't enough to provide support for Adams and Pavlic.*

WOLVERHAMPTON (H)
Thursday, September 4
Won 63-29
Adams 13:2, Wright 7:2, *rider replacement for Korneliussen*, Aldén 8:1, **Batchelor 18**, Richard Sweetman [G] 3:1, **Pavlic 14:1**.
▲ *Aldén returned to the line-up after missing 10 matches with a broken foot. Replaced McGowan on a permanent basis.*

COVENTRY (A) SKY TV
Monday, September 22
Lost 43-52
Adams 15 (6), Wright 5:3, Pavlic 7:1, Batchelor 7 (TS4), Korneliussen 1, Joel Parsons [G] 2:1, Aldén 6.
● *Disastrous night with the Play offs just a week away, as Aldén broke collarbone when he clipped Oliver Allen in Heat 8, and Wright was lucky to escape injury as he was also caught in the incident.*

ELITE LEAGUE

	M	W	D	L	PtsF	PtsA	Pts
Poole	32	22	0	10	1600	1321	52
Lakeside	32	22	1	9	1551	1375	52
SWINDON	**32**	**17**	**2**	**13**	**1498**	**1434**	**41**
Ipswich	32	16	3	13	1483	1439	40
Eastbourne	32	15	0	17	1462	1472	34
Coventry	32	12	3	17	1418	1506	29
Belle Vue	32	13	2	17	1423	1491	28
Peterborough	32	13	1	18	1371	1528	28
Wolverhampton	32	8	0	24	1341	1581	16

Play offs

Semi Final
LAKESIDE (A) SKY TV
Lost 33-56
Monday, September 29
Adams 14 (TS1), Wright 0, Pavlic 0, Batchelor 3 (0), Korneliussen 2, Gathercole 1, McGowan 13:1.
Title hopes over after a heavy defeat. McGowan, dropped from the team, made a remarkable return, but Pavlic was unwell and the other middle-order riders failed to fire.

Pavlic's lucky number

Even though he was averaging more than six points a meeting in the Polish Ekstraliga, Jurica Pavlic was allowed to join Swindon on an assessed four point average after the promotion put a special argument to Management Committee.

It proved to be a masterstroke by the Robins' management team as the Croatian Champion went on to average twice that in his first spell racing in the Elite League.

Knock Out Cup

First round, first leg
POOLE (A)
Wednesday, June 18
Lost 40-53
Adams 18 (6), Aldén 3, Korneliussen 11 (TS1), McGowan 2:2, *rider replacement for Batchelor,* Hauzinger 2:2, Wright 4.

First round, second leg
POOLE (H)
Thursday, June 19
Won 50-40
Adams 14:1, Aldén 3:2, Korneliussen 10:3, McGowan 9, *rider replacement for Batchelor,* Hauzinger 0, Wright 14.
▼ *Needed 5-1 from last race for tie victory, but Korneliussen was kept out by Bjarne Pedersen and Chris Holder.*
Aggregate: Lost 90-93.

Craven Shield

EASTBOURNE (A)
Saturday, March 15
Lost 41-52
Adams 17 (6), Korneliussen 5:2, Batchelor 5, Wright 2:1, McGowan 5, Pijper 1:1, Aldén 6:2.

EASTBOURNE (H)
Thursday, March 20
Won 48-42
Adams 14:1, Korneliussen 7, Batchelor 8, Wright 6:1, McGowan 5, Pijper 3:1, Aldén 5:1.

POOLE (A)
Wednesday, March 26
Lost 39-54
Adams 16 (6), Wright 5:1, Batchelor 4:1, Korneliussen 5, McGowan 3, Pijper 0, Aldén 6.

POOLE (H)
Thursday, March 27
Won 46-44
Adams 13:1, Wright 1, Batchelor 7:1, Korneliussen 7:2, McGowan 9:1, Pijper 3:1, Aldén 6:2.
▼ *Last heat 4-2 from Adams and McGowan clinched the win, but not enough for overall progression.*

CRAVEN SHIELD
Southern Group

	M	*W*	*D*	*L*	*PtsF*	*PtsA*	*Pts*
Poole	4	2	0	2	191	180	4
Eastbourne	4	2	0	2	189	182	4
SWINDON	**4**	**2**	**0**	**2**	**174**	**192**	**4**

Elite Shield

COVENTRY (H)
Sunday, March 23
Won 57-35
Adams 13:2, Wright 5:1, Batchelor 7:1, Korneliussen 10:1, McGowan 10, Pijper 4:2, Aldén 8:1.

COVENTRY (A)
Monday, March 24
Lost 41-52
Adams 14 (6), Wright 2, Batchelor 7, Korneliussen 6, McGowan 2, Pijper 2, Aldén 8.
Aggregate: Won 98-87.
▲ *Won first top-flight team trophy since 1967.*

2009 Squad

Leigh **ADAMS** (10.48), Troy **BATCHELOR** (6.96), Simon **STEAD** (6.53), Travis **McGOWAN** (4.25), Jurica **PAVLIC** (4.00), *Ryan FISHER (3.70)/Cory GATHERCOLE (3.28),* Krzysztof **STOJANOWSKI** (3.42), Richard **SWEETMAN** (3.00).

SWINDON

Rider	*M*	*R*	*Pts*	*BP*	*TPts*	*Ave*	*F*	*P*	*TR*	*TPts*	*TS*	*TSPts*
Leigh ADAMS	39	192	543	24	567	11.81	1	10	11	32	4	6
Jurica PAVLIC	**9**	**50**	**96**	**6**	**102**	**8.16**	**1**	**1**	**0**	**0**	**0**	**0**
Mads KORNELIUSSEN	36	166	278	30	308	7.42	0	0	1	2	1	0
Troy BATCHELOR	**33**	**150**	**252**	**19**	**271**	**7.23**	**2**	**0**	**1**	**0**	**1**	**2**
James WRIGHT	39	173	209	34	243	5.62	0	0	0	0	0	0
Sebastian ALDÉN	**28**	**123**	**138**	**26**	**164**	**5.33**	**0**	**0**	**0**	**0**	**0**	**0**
Travis McGOWAN	37	162	182	21	203	5.01	0	0	0	0	0	0
Cory GATHERCOLE	**6**	**23**	**18**	**4**	**22**	**3.83**	**0**	**0**	**0**	**0**	**0**	**0**
Manuel HAUZINGER	9	27	16	5	21	3.11	0	0	0	0	0	0
Theo PIJPER	**13**	**42**	**21**	**6**	**27**	**2.57**	**0**	**0**	**0**	**0**	**0**	**0**
Joel PARSONS	2	7	1	0	1	0.57	0	0	0	0	0	0
Guests	***13***	***50***	***41***	***13***	***54***	***4.32***	***0***	***0***	***0***	***0***	***0***	***0***

For Cory GATHERCOLE see Isle of Wight; for Manuel HAUZINGER see Berwick; for Theo PIJPER see Mildenhall and Berwick; for Joel PARSONS see Sheffield.

Krzytsztof STOJANOWSKI rode illegally as a guest for Swindon against Peterborough on July 31, scoring 6:1 from five rides. His points were deducted by the Speedway Control Bureau but the above statistics include the appearance but with no rides and no points.

Weather...

Only one home meeting postponed because of rain.

Elite League
Thursday, June 26 ....................WOLVERHAMPTON (H)
Friday, September 5..................................COVENTRY (A)

...beaten

Four Team Challenge

Sunday, October 12
SWINDON SPROCKETS 22
Cory Gathercole 10, Charlie Saunders 0, Richard Sweetman 11, Danny Warwick 0, Ben Reade [R] 1.
OXFORD CHEETAHS 22
James Cockle 3, Kyle Hughes 5, *rider replacement for Jamie Courtney,* Lee Smart 9, Brendan Johnson [R] 5.
LEICESTER LIONS 27
Sergey Darkin 15, Simon Lambert 5, Luke Priest 3, Adam Lowe 4, Mark Thompson [R], did not ride.
BRISTOL BULLDOGS 37
Semen Vlasov 13, Mark Burrows 6, Mark Simmonds 7, Linus Sundström 11, Jordan Tyrer [R] 0.

International

Second Test
Thursday, September 11
ENGLAND UNDER 23 44
Lewis Bridger 8:1, Jason King 6:2, James Wright 8:1, Ben Barker 5:2, Tai Woffinden 11, Robert Mear 3, Joe Haines 3:1.
AUSTRALIAN UNDER 23 47
Troy Batchelor 13, Cory Gathercole 0, Chris Holder 17 (TS2), Robert Ksiezak 3:1, Cameron Woodward 5, Kozza Smith 2, Richard Sweetman 7.

Elite League Pairs Championship

1 COVENTRY (Hans Andersen & Chris Harris), **2 SWINDON** (Leigh Adams & Mads Korneliussen), **3 IPSWICH** (Piotr Swiderski & Rory Schlein), **3 BELLEVUE** (Jason Crump & Charlie Gjedde), **5 POOLE** (Bjarne Pedersen & Chris Holder), **6 WOLVERHAMPTON** (Fredrik Lindgren & Niels-Kristian Iversen), **7 PETERBOROUGH** (Kenneth Bjerre & Daniel King), **8 EASTBOURNE** (Lee Richardson & Cameron Woodward), **9 LAKESIDE** (Adam Shields & Jonas Davidsson).
Semi Final 1: Swindon 5 (Mads Korneliussen 3, Leigh Adams 2:1), Ipswich 4 (Rory Schlein 4, Piotr Swiderski 0).
Semi Final 2: Coventry 5 (Hans Andersen 3, Chris Harris 2:1), Belle Vue 4 (Jason Crump 4, Charlie Gjedde 0).
Final: Coventry 5 (Chris Harris 3, Hans Andersen 2:1), Swindon 4 (Mads Korneliussen 4, Leigh Adams 0).

For full details and complete Roll of Honour see Elite League.

EVEN though they have been League members since taking over Hull's Division Three fixtures in September, 1949, Swindon have only won three league titles – the most recent way back in 1967. Of the nine current Elite League clubs no-one has gone longer without being crowned champions at any level.

POOLE (continued from page 115)

CRAIG BOYCE FAREWELL
Wednesday, June 28

POOLE honoured long-serving Craig Boyce with a Farewell meeting after he'd announced his retirement towards the end of 2007.

The Australian had made his British debut for the Pirates when they were in the Second Division in 1988 and after three seasons at Wimborne Road stepped up to the top flight with Oxford in 1991.

He returned to Poole the following season and continued riding for the Pirates on and off until he was dropped from their line-up in October 2007, making a total of 472 official appearances for the Pirates and 748 overall.

BOURNEMOUTH BEDDING CENTRE 38 (Krzysztof Kasprzak 10, Chris Holder 10, David Howe 8, Jason Doyle 10), **ARGON WELDING 24** (**Jason Crump 12**, Jordan Frampton 5, Daniel King 4, Cory Gathercole 3), **INTER ESTATE 22** (Davey Watt 8, Lewis Bridger 6, Cameron Woodward 5, Rory Schlein 3), **SHARP RETAIL SYSTEMS 12** (Lee Richardson 3, James Holder 0, Steve Johnston 2, Edward Kennett 7).

NEW YEAR CLASSIC
Sunday, January 4, 2009

The traditional first event of the year moved to a new home at Poole.

And Coventry youngster Ben Barker warmed up the fans who braved one of the coldest Sundays on recent record.

Polish Champion Adam Skornicki was unbeaten in the qualifying races.

Rider							
1 Ben BARKER	**3**	**3**	**3**	**2**	**0**	**11**	**3**
2 Adam SKORNICKI	3	3	3	3	3	15	2
3 Lukasz JANKOWSKI	1	1	3	3	2	10	1
4 Edward KENNETT	2	3	1	1	3	10	0
5 Lewis BRIDGER	3	2	3	1	X	9	
6 Tomasz PISZCZ	3	1	2	2	1	9	
7 Mark LEMON	2	0	2	0	3	7	
8 Mads KORNELIUSSEN	1	3	1	0	2	7	
9 Emil KRAMER	2	1	0	3	1	7	
10 Jordan FRAMPTON	0	2	1	2	2	7	
11 Daniel KING	1	0	2	3	0	6	
12 Stuart ROBSON	1	1	2	F	2	6	
13 Nicolai KLINDT	E	0	0	2	3	5	
14 David HOWE	2	2	0	0	1	5	
15 Michael HADEK	0	2	1	1	0	4	
16 Jan HOLUB	0	0	0	1	1	2	
17 Karl MASON [R]	0					0	

Roll of Honour

1999 ....Robbie KESSLER
2000 ....Phil MORRIS
†2001 ....Paul FRY
2002 ....Michael COLES
2003 ....David HOWE
2004 ....Chris HARRIS
2005 ....Chris HARRIS
2006 ....Brent WERNER
2007 ....David HOWE
2008 ....Chris HARRIS
2009 ....Ben BARKER

Held at Newport 1999-2008. †Held on Sunday, December 30, 2000.

Elite League

WOLVERHAMPTON

TRACK FILE

Track: Monmore Green Stadium, Sutherland Avenue, Wolverhampton, WV2 2JJ.
Telephone: 01902 870400.
Hotline: 09068 664664.
Website: www.wolverhampton-speedway.com
Track Length: 264 metres.
Track Record: 54.55 secs, Leigh Adams, June 2, 2008.
Promoters: Chris Van Straaten and Peter Adams.
Team Sponsors: Parrys International.
Colours: Old gold and black with Wolves head logo.
Nickname: Wolves.

HISTORY

First meeting: May 30, 1928, Individual Championship.
Leagues: Division One, 1965-1980, 1984-2009. Division Two, 1953-54, 1961-64, 1981. Division Three, 1951, 1997, 2002-03. Southern League, 1952.

HONOURS

Major honours: 7.
Division One champions (3), 1991, 1996, 2002.
Division One Knock Out Cup winners (1), 1996.
Division One Premiership winners (2), 1992, 1997.
Division Two champions (1), 1963.

2008 REVIEW

MONMORE promoter Chris Van Straaten felt his re-vamped team would improve during the season and challenge strongly for a top four place – but it turned out to be one of the most trying campaigns of his time in charge.

The campaign never truly got off the ground for Wolverhampton, who proved to be highly vulnerable around their home circuit with an almost unprecedented total of eight defeats out of 16 on their own shale.

And as the home losses racked up, there was no compensation by way of success on the road as the Midlands club suffered a dispiriting run of away defeats which caused Van Straaten and manager Peter Adams to contemplate changes from an early stage in an admission that they had perhaps relied too much on inexperienced riders, Peter Karlsson and Billy Hamill having been among the winter departures.

Niels-Kristian Iversen proved to be a popular signing on loan from Peterborough, but he was unfortunate with injuries with a series of shoulder dislocations eventually ending his season, the Dane crashing out for the final time on his old home track in October.

Wolves had long since resigned themselves to appearing in the first-ever relegation race off, even having changed almost half of their team in the last two months with Jesper B Monberg, Morten Risager and Ludvig Lindgren all attempting to steady the ship.

After storming into a 16-point lead in the race-off against Peterborough and then remarkably being pegged back to a one-point margin, Wolves were demolished at the Showground in the second leg, and had to fight for their Elite League future against Premier League Champions Edinburgh – a mission they successfully accomplished after wins in both legs, but it was still undoubtedly a season to forget.

2008 RESULTS

Elite League

Final position...Ninth

POOLE (H)
Monday, March 31
Won 54-36
F. Lindgren 14:1, Dryml 5, Iversen 9:1, Hansen 5:2, Howe 13, Klindt 7, Hefenbrock 1.

POOLE (A)
Wednesday, April 2
Lost 31-62
F. Lindgren 4:1, Dryml 3, Iversen 13 (6), *rider replacement for Hansen*, Howe 7, Klindt 2, Hefenbrock 2:1.

EASTBOURNE (A)
Saturday, April 12
Lost 40-53
F. Lindgren 11, Dryml 3:1, Iversen 13:1 (6), Hansen 2:1, Howe 6, Hefenbrock 4:1, Klindt 1:1.

EASTBOURNE (H)
Monday, April 14
Won 50-39
F. Lindgren 12:1, Dryml 6, Iversen 6, Hansen 1:1, Howe 13:1, Hefenbrock 5:1, Klindt 7.

LAKESIDE (H) SKY TV
Monday, April 21
Lost 41-49
F. Lindgren 7:2, Dryml 7, **Iversen 15**, Hansen 0, Howe 7, Hefenbrock 3, Klindt 2:1.
▼ *Home riders with the exception of maximum man Iversen found conditions not to their liking as they went down to their first home defeat of the season.*

SQUAD
David Howe, Chris Neath.
Foreign: Ales Dryml, Kenneth Hansen, Christian Hefenbrock, Niels-Kristian Iversen, Nicolai Klindt, Fredrik Lindgren, Ludvig Lindgren, Jesper B. Monberg, Morten Risager.

SWINDON (A)
Thursday, April 24
Lost 42-50
F. Lindgren 11:2, Dryml 0, Iversen 10, *rider replacement for Hansen*, Howe 4, Hefenbrock 3:2, Klindt 14:2.
▼▲ *Threatened a shock win when pulling back to 37-37 after Heat 12, but conceded 5-1s in the next two races. Klindt's best Elite League display so far.*

PETERBOROUGH (H)
Monday, April 28
Won 59-33
F. Lindgren 11:1, Dryml 10:3, Iversen 11, Hansen 4:1, Howe 7:1, Hefenbrock 8:2, Klindt 8.
▲ *Iversen's exclusion for bringing Daniel King down in Heat 9 was the only blot on a hefty win.*

COVENTRY (H)
Monday, May 5
Lost 44-45
F. Lindgren 13, Dryml 6, Iversen 7, Klindt 6:2, Howe 3, Hefenbrock 2:1, Hansen 7.
▼ *Lost Howe with concussion after a Heat 11 tangle with teammate Hefenbrock. Required a 5-1 from Heat 15 but Iversen was beaten by Chris Harris.*

David Howe, Chris Neath, Christian Hefenbrock, Fredrik Lindgren, Niels-Kristian Iversen, Kenneth Hansen, Ales Dryml and Nicolai Klindt

Photo: JOHN HIPKISS

IPSWICH (A)
Thursday, May 8
Lost 38-53
F. Lindgren 13 (TS4), Dryml 1, Iversen 12:2 (4), Klindt 1, Howe 8, Hefenbrock 2, Hansen 1:1.

IPSWICH (H) SKY TV
Monday, May 19
Lost 43-48
F. Lindgren 16 (4), Dryml 4, Iversen 6:3, Klindt 3, Howe 7, Hefenbrock 5, Hansen 2:1.
▼ *Roared into a 16-8 lead but conceded a 5-0 in Heat 5 when both Klindt and Iversen were excluded, and fell apart.*

PETERBOROUGH (A)
Thursday, May 22
Lost 42-48
F. Lindgren 6:1, Howe 6, Iversen 10:1, Klindt 5:2, Dryml 0, Hefenbrock 6:1, Hansen 9:2.
▼ *Nightmare return for Panthers asset Dryml, while Iversen finished second in each of his five rides.*

BELLE VUE (H)
Monday, May 26
Won 48-45
F. Lindgren 10:1, Dryml 8:1, Edward Kennett [G] 10, Klindt 3:2, Howe 7:1, Hefenbrock 3, Hansen 7:2.

COVENTRY (A)
Friday, May 30
14-22, abandoned after six heats.
Lindgren 5, Dryml 1:1, Edward Kennett [G] 3, *rider replacement for Klindt*, Howe 1, Neath 0, Joel Parsons [G] 4.
● *Meeting abandoned after an hour's delay following a local power cut.*

SWINDON (H) SKY TV
Monday, June 2
Lost 42-48
F. Lindgren 9, Dryml 8, Edward Kennett [G] 10:1, Klindt 3:1, Howe 6, Hefenbrock 5, Neath 1.
▼ *Again saw a home lead whittled away and were facing a 5-1 reverse in Heat 15 when Lindgren fell on the third lap.*

PETERBOROUGH (H)
Monday, June 9
Won 54-38
F. Lindgren 11, Dryml 5:1, Chris Harris [G] 13:1, Klindt 8:1, Howe 8:1, Hefenbrock 7:2, Hansen 2:1.

POOLE (A)
Wednesday, June 11
Lost 37-55
F. Lindgren 9:1, Dryml 1:1, Chris Harris [G] 16 (6), Klindt 0, Howe 0, Hefenbrock 4:1, Hansen 7.

POOLE (H)
Monday, June 16
Lost 44-46
Rider replacement for F. Lindgren, Dryml 10, Iversen 11, Klindt 5:1, Howe 11:1, Hefenbrock 0, Hansen 7.
▼ *Went ahead in Heat 14 when Klindt was brought down by Magnus Zetterström – but Iversen crashed in the last race and Chris Holder produced a last-bend burst past Howe for a 5-1.*

EASTBOURNE (H)
Monday, July 21
Lost 45-48
F. Lindgren 12, Dryml 1, Iversen 14:1 (6), *rider replacement for Hefenbrock*, Howe 6, Hansen 7:1, Klindt 5:2.
▼ *Hefenbrock ruled out by the doctor before the meeting, and the home side then suffered a succession of mistakes and mechanical problems en route to another home defeat.*

COVENTRY (A)
Friday, July 25
Lost 45-48
F. Lindgren 12, Dryml 4, Iversen 8:1, *rider replacement for Hefenbrock*, Howe 6, Hansen 4:2, Klindt 11:2.
▼ *Defeat from the jaws of victory with Coventry on the ropes for long spells before Wolves faded disastrously.*

SWINDON (H)
Monday, August 4
Won 47-46
F. Lindgren 12:1, Dryml 6:2, Iversen 13:1, Monberg 3:1, Howe 7, Hansen 1:1, Klindt 5.
▲ *Survived late scare (Robins took 8-1 in Heat 14) for a much-needed win, clinched by Lindgren and Iversen shutting out Mads Korneliussen in the decider.*

LAKESIDE (H)
Monday, August 11
Lost 43-47
F. Lindgren 12, Dryml 2:1, Iversen 7:1, Monberg 6:1, Howe 2:1, Hansen 4, Klindt 10.
▼ *Led by eight points after Heat 5 but fell away spectacularly. Jonas Davidsson scored paid maximum and Adam Shields unbeaten but for a two minute exclusion.*

COVENTRY (H)
Monday, August 18
Won 47-43
F. Lindgren 13, Dryml 2, Iversen 11, Howe 3:2, Monberg 0, Neath 3:1, Klindt 15.
▼▲ *Monberg's Heat 4 crash also took out Simon Stead, and Wolves covered better with Klindt enjoying his best night in British speedway.*

IPSWICH (A)
Thursday, August 21
Lost 41-49
F. Lindgren 11, Dryml 3, Iversen 10, Howe 1, Monberg 9, Hansen 2:1, Klindt 5:1.
▼ *Frustratingly close to an away win as Monberg and Lindgren won their first three rides – Wolves led 35-31 but it all went wrong in the last four heats.*

LAKESIDE (A)
Friday, August 22
Lost 40-53
F. Lindgren 9:1, *rider replacement for Dryml*, Iversen 15:1 (6), Howe 6:1, Monberg 5, Chris Kerr [G] 4, Klindt 1.
▼ *Unable to take advantage of Lakeside's injury problems, although Iversen showed up well with three race wins.*

BELLE VUE (H)
Monday, August 25
Won 48-45
F. Lindgren 12:2, Dryml 8:2, Iversen 12:1, Howe 5:1, Monberg 3:1, Hansen 3:1, Klindt 5.
▲ *Sensational finale saw Iversen and Lindgren secure match-clinching 5-1 over Jason Crump in Heat 15 after the Aces had come from ten points down to lead 44-43.*

BELLE VUE (A)
Wednesday, August 27
Lost 30-60
F. Lindgren 8 (1), *rider replacement for Dryml*, Iversen 1, Joe Haines [G] 4, Howe 2, Chris Kerr [G] 3:1, Klindt 12.
▼ *Iversen dislocated his shoulder again in Heat 7 – and Lindgren also crashed in Heat 15. Dryml and Hansen were both absent with their time up for 2008.*

SWINDON (A)
Thursday, September 4
Lost 29-63
F. Lindgren 12 (4), Risager 4:2, *rider replacement for Iversen*, Howe 0, Monberg 6, L. Lindgren 3:2, Klindt 4.
▼ *Failed to provide even a single race winner at Blunsdon with new-look team struggling and Howe (ankle) crashing out in Heat 7.*

BELLE VUE (A)
Monday, September 8
Lost 41-49
F. Lindgren 13, Risager 8, *rider replacement for Iversen*, Howe 4:1, Monberg 7:1, Neath 2, Klindt 7:1.

IPSWICH (H) SKY TV
Monday, September 15
Lost 40-52
F. Lindgren 13:2 (TS4), Risager 5, Iversen 10:1, Howe 4:2, Monberg 2, L. Lindgren 5, Klindt 1:1.
▼ *Monberg's nightmare included two identical falls, and the bottom team were limited to just three heat winners around their own circuit.*

LAKESIDE (A)
Wednesday, September 17
Lost 32-58
F. Lindgren 8:1, Risager 7, Iversen 1 (FX), Howe 4, Monberg 5, L. Lindgren 1, Klindt 6.
▼ *Iversen had to withdraw with a hand injury after crashing with Hammers' guest Rory Schlein in Heat 7.*

COVENTRY (A)
Thursday, September 18
Lost 40-53
F. Lindgren 14, Risager 2, Iversen 13:1 (6), Howe 0, Monberg 7:1, L. Lindgren 1:1, Klindt 3:1.

PETERBOROUGH (A)
Thursday, September 25
Lost 37-56
F. Lindgren 9:2, Risager 2, Iversen 12 (6), Howe 1, Monberg 0, L. Lindgren 2:1, Klindt 11:1.
▼ *Klindt won two outings mid-meeting but Howe, Monberg and Risager all endured troubled and unproductive nights on their former home track.*

EASTBOURNE (A)
Sunday, October 19
Lost 27-63
Ricky Kling [G] 7 (1), Tyron Proctor [G] 3, *rider replacement for Iversen*, Howe 8:1, Chris Kerr [G] 3:1, L. Lindgren 3:1, Klindt 3:1.
▼ *Patched-up team was always expected to go down heavily, and guest Ty Proctor's points came courtesy of their sole race win of the afternoon.*

ELITE LEAGUE

	M	*W*	*D*	*L*	*PtsF*	*PtsA*	*Pts*
Poole	32	22	0	10	1600	1321	52
Lakeside	32	22	1	9	1551	1375	52
Swindon	32	17	2	13	1498	1434	41
Ipswich	32	16	3	13	1483	1439	40
Eastbourne	32	15	0	17	1462	1472	34
Coventry	32	12	3	17	1418	1506	29
Belle Vue	32	13	2	17	1423	1491	28
Peterborough	32	13	1	18	1371	1528	28
WOLVERHAMPTON	**32**	**8**	**0**	**24**	**1341**	**1581**	**16**

Relegation Play offs

First leg
PETERBOROUGH (H)
Tuesday, October 14
Won 48-47
F. Lindgren 10:1, Risager 8:1, Iversen 11, Howe 4:1, Monberg 6:1, L. Lindgren 4:1, Klindt 5.
▲▼ *Raced into a 26-10 lead after six races but were thrown completely by a rainstorm and finished off by conceding 5-1s in the last two races .*

Second leg
PETERBOROUGH (A)
Thursday, October 16
Lost 23-67
F. Lindgren 3, Risager 4, Iversen 3 (FX), *rider replacement for Howe*, Monberg 7, L. Lindgren 3, Klindt 3.
▼ *Disastrous night which summed up the season. Iversen dislocated his shoulder in Heat 7 and, four races later, Risager broke his wrist. Conceded 5-1s in each of the last six races. Howe missed the meeting due to illness.*

Aggregate: Lost 71-114.

FINAL, *first leg*
EDINBURGH (A)
Friday, October 24
Won 53-37
F. Lindgren 10:1, Howe 12:1, *rider replacement for Iversen*, James Grieves [G] 10:4, Monberg 14, L. Lindgren 0, Klindt 7:2.
▲ *Eased nerves with a 5-1 in Heat 1 from Howe and Fredrik Lindgren.*

FINAL second leg
EDINBURGH (H)
Monday, October 27
Won 53-39
F. Lindgren 7:2, Howe 7:1, *rider replacement for Iversen*,

Lewis Bridger [G] 8:1, Monberg 12, L.Lindgren 2, Klindt 11:1, Neath [no. 8] 6.

▲ *Secured Elite League status on a terrific night of racing – although major team changes are set to be in place for 2009 to ensure that Wolverhampton do not compete in this shoot-out again!*

Aggregate: Won 106-76.

Knock Out Cup

First round, first leg
IPSWICH (A)
Thursday, April 3
Lost 42-50
Lindgren 10:2, Dryml 7:1, Iversen 12 (4), *rider replacement for Hansen*, Howe 4:1, Klindt 7, Hefenbrock 0, Neath [no. 8] 2.

▲ *Gave number eight Neath three rides.*

First round, second leg
IPSWICH (H)
Monday, April 7
Won 54-38
F. Lindgren 8:1, Dryml 4:3, Iversen 14, Hansen 2, Howe 11:2, Klindt 8, Hefenbrock 7:3.

▲ *Secured progression via a 4-2 in Heat 14 with Klindt's second race win of the night.*

Aggregate: Won 96-88.

Quarter Final, first leg
EASTBOURNE (A)
Saturday, June 21
Lost 30-62
Rider replacement for F. Lindgren, Dryml 5, Iversen 12:1 (4), Klindt 3, Howe 6, Hefenbrock 4, Hansen 0.

▼ *Klindt suffered four last places before winning his last ride.*

Quarter Final, second leg
EASTBOURNE (H)
Monday, June 23
Won 52-40
Rider replacement for F. Lindgren, Dryml 9:1, Iversen 15, Klindt 3:1, Howe 9:2, Hefenbrock 7:1, Hansen 9:1.

▼ *Threatened the most amazing of second leg comebacks when they went 28-10 up after Heat 6, only for the visitors to wake up!*

Aggregate: Lost 82-102.

Craven Shield

COVENTRY (H)
Monday, March 17
Won 53-37
F. Lindgren 9:2, Dryml 7:1, Iversen 11, Hansen 2:1, Howe 11:1, Klindt 5, Hefenbrock 8:2.

▲ *Debut-men Dryml, Iversen and Klindt all won their opening rides, Iversen beaten only by Chris Harris in Heat 12.*

BELLE VUE (A)
Friday, March 21
Lost 41-49
F. Lindgren 3:1, Dryml 9:1, Iversen 11, Hansen 4:3, Howe 7, Klindt 6 [*6*], Hefenbrock 1.

● *Result changed from 44-49 defeat as Nicolai Klindt was ineligible to take a tactical ride in Heat 14 as a replacement for Hefenbrock. His race win stood but without scoring double points.*

COVENTRY (A)
Friday, March 21
Lost 33-59
Lindgren 5, Dryml 10:1 (4), Iversen 8, Hansen 1, Howe 2, Klindt 0, Hefenbrock 7:1.

▼ *Completed second meeting in a day with second defeat.*

BELLE VUE (H)
Monday, March 24
Won 48-44
F. Lindgren 11:1, Dryml 7:1, Iversen 10:1, Hansen 6, Howe 9:1, Klindt 1:1, Hefenbrock 4.

▼ *Required a hefty victory but 10 points was their maximum lead, which was pegged back in the closing stages.*

Ales Dryml, Christian Hefenbrock and Kenneth Hansen were all sacked by Wolverhampton during the season after a sluggish start to the campaign.

WOLVERHAMPTON

Rider	*M*	*R*	*Pts*	*BP*	*TPts*	*Ave*	*F*	*P*	*TR*	*TPts*	*TS*	*TSPts*
Niels-Kristian IVERSEN	35	166	357	18	375	9.04	1	0	11	24	0	0
Fredrik LINDGREN	**38**	**190**	**386**	**28**	**414**	**8.72**	**0**	**2**	**2**	**2**	**5**	**8**
David HOWE	41	175	235	22	257	5.87	0	0	0	0	0	0
Ales DRYML	**31**	**127**	**161**	**21**	**182**	**5.73**	**0**	**0**	**1**	**2**	**0**	**0**
Christian HEFENBROCK	24	91	98	19	117	5.14	0	0	0	0	0	0
Jesper B. MONBERG	**14**	**57**	**66**	**6**	**72**	**5.05**	**0**	**0**	**0**	**0**	**0**	**0**
Morten RISAGER	8	35	40	3	43	4.91	0	0	0	0	0	0
Nicolai KLINDT	**42**	**206**	**220**	**25**	**245**	**4.76**	**0**	**0**	**0**	**0**	**0**	**0**
Kenneth HANSEN	26	114	99	23	122	4.28	0	0	0	0	0	0
Ludvig LINDGREN	**8**	**37**	**22**	**6**	**28**	**3.03**	**0**	**0**	**0**	**0**	**0**	**0**
Chris NEATH	4	14	8	1	9	2.57	0	0	0	0	0	0
Guests	***10***	***52***	***73***	***4***	***77***	***5.92***	***0***	***0***	***2***	***3***	***0***	***0***

For Morten RISAGER see Peterborough; for Chris NEATH see Rye House.

CRAVEN SHIELD
Northern Group

	M	W	D	L	PtsF	PtsA	Pts
Coventry	4	2	0	2	192	175	4
Belle Vue	4	2	0	2	182	185	4
WOLVERHAMPTON	**4**	**2**	**0**	**2**	**175**	**189**	**4**

Year to forget

Wolverhampton had one of the worst seasons in the club's history as they collected the wooden spoon with only eight league wins all year. The only previous occasions that they have finished bottom of the table was in the 1951 National League Division Three and the 1999 Elite League.

Inter League Challenge

MIDLAND SHIELD, first leg
BIRMINGHAM (H)
Monday, September 22
Won 48-44
F. Lindgren 9:1, Klindt 6:3, Lewis Bridger [G] 7:2, Risager 6, Tai Woffinden [G] 7:1, L. Lindgren 7, Chris Kerr [G] 6.
▼ *Struggled to overcome their Premier League neighbours, who fought back from 12-points down to set up a fascinating second leg at Perry Barr.*

MIDLAND SHIELD, second leg
BIRMINGHAM (A)
Wednesday, October 15
Won 48-42
F. Lindgren 12, Risager 5:2, Howe 10, L. Lindgtren 6:1, Klindt 8, Jerran Hart [G] 4:1, Luke Priest [G] 3:1.
▲ *Retained the Shield having led for much of the evening at Perry Barr. Welcome return to form for Howe, and each of the last five races were shared.*

Aggregate: Won 96-86.

Anniversary Meeting

80th ANNIVERSARY MEETING
Monday, June 30
1 TEAM ERMOLENKO 28 (Adam Skornicki 12, Ales Dryml 7, Tai Woffinden, did not ride, Christian Hefenbrock 6, Ben Wilson [R] 3), **2 TEAM CORREY 24** (Chris Neath, did not ride, Fredrik Lindgren 11, David Howe 6, James Grieves 0, Krister Jacobsen [R] 7), **3 TEAM OLSEN 21** (Niels-Kristian Iversen 10, Ty Proctor 3, Nicolai Klindt 7, George Stancl 1, Richard Juul [R] 0), 4 **TEAM ADAMS 20** (Peter Karlsson 4, Magnus Karlsson 8, Joe Haines 1, Mikael Max 4, Tony Atkin [R] 3).

2009 Squad

Peter **KARLSSON** (8.66), Fredrik **LINDGREN** (8.32), Adam **SKORNICKI** (5.56), Tai **WOFFINDEN** (4.67), Nicolai **KLINDT** (4.48), Hynek **STICHAUER** (4.00), *Tyron* **PROCTOR** *(3.82)/Chris* **KERR** (3.24), Joe **HAINES** (3.00).

Individual

BANKS'S OLYMPIQUE
Monday, October 20
Wolverhampton's annual classic was a victim of lunchtime rain and there was no re-staging date.

It was only the second time in the competition's history that it was not held and the first season since 1996.

Roll of Honour

1966	Barry BRIGGS
1967	Anders MICHANEK
1970	Ole OLSEN
1971	Ole OLSEN
1972	Ole OLSEN
1973	Ole OLSEN
1974	Ole OLSEN
1975	Ole OLSEN
1976	Peter COLLINS
1977	Billy SANDERS
1978	Gordon KENNETT
1979	Phil CRUMP
1980	Les COLLINS
1981	Mitch SHIRRA
1982	Hans NIELSEN
1984	Hans NIELSEN
1987	Sam ERMOLENKO
1988	Hans NIELSEN
1989	Jan O. PEDERSEN
1990	Ronnie CORREY
1991	Greg HANCOCK
1992	Ronnie CORREY
1993	Joe SCREEN
1994	Jason CRUMP
1995	Greg HANCOCK
1997	Mikael MAX[1]
1998	Greg HANCOCK
1999	Peter KARLSSON
2000	Peter KARLSSON
2001	Mikael MAX[1]
2002	Mikael MAX[1]
2003	Mikael MAX
2004	David HOWE
2005	Fredrik LINDGREN
2006	Peter KARLSSON
2007	Fredrik LINDGREN

Mikael MAX[1] – rode as Mikael Karlsson.
● *Staged at Wolverhampton with the exception of the following seasons: 1966-1967 (Newcastle), 1981-1982 (Birmingham).*

Year to forget

Wolverhampton became the first top-flight team to have to face the leading side from the Premier League to preserve their Elite League status. They took on PL champions Edinburgh in home and away matches but were never in real danger of surrendering their status.

2009 FIXTURES

March

Sunday 15
Swindon: 60th Anniversary
Eastbourne: Dean Barker Testimonial
Monday 16
Wolverhampton v Coventry (Challenge)
Wednesday 18
Poole v Newcastle (Bjarne Pedersen Testimonial)
Thursday 19
Ipswich v Lakeside (Challenge)
Swindon v Lejonen, Sweden (International Challenge)
Peterborough v Danish Select (International Challenge)
Friday 20
Lakeside v Ipswich (Challenge)
Coventry v Wolverhampton (Challenge)
Sunday 22
Wolverhampton: Billy Hamill Farewell
Eastbourne v Poole (Elite Shield)
Wednesday 25
Poole v Eastbourne (Elite Shield)
Thursday 26
Swindon v Wolverhampton (KO Cup)
Peterborough v Coventry (KO Cup)
Ipswich v Belle Vue (KO Cup)
Friday 27
Lakeside v Eastbourne (KO Cup)
Coventry v Peterborough (KO Cup)
Saturday 28
Eastbourne v Lakeside (KO Cup)
Monday 30
Belle Vue v Glasgow (Challenge)
Poole v Swindon
Wolverhampton v Lakeside

April

Thursday 2
Swindon v Eastbourne
Peterborough v Lakeside
Ipswich v Coventry
Friday 3
Lakeside v Peterborough
Coventry v Belle Vue
Saturday 4
Eastbourne v Belle Vue
Monday 6
Belle Vue v Lakeside
Wolverhampton v Swindon (KO Cup)
Thursday 9
Swindon v Coventry
Peterborough v Ipswich
Friday 10
Belle Vue v Wolverhampton
Coventry v Swindon
Eastbourne v Poole
Ipswich v Lakeside
Lakeside v Ipswich
Poole v Eastbourne
Tuesday 14
Wolverhampton v Belle Vue
Wednesday 15
Poole v Coventry
Thursday 16
Swindon v Lakeside
Peterborough v Poole
Ipswich v Eastbourne
Friday 17
Lakeside v Eastbourne
Coventry v Poole
Saturday 18
Eastbourne v Lakeside
Monday 20
Wolverhampton v Poole
Belle Vue v Ipswich
Wednesday 22
Poole v Wolverhampton
Thursday 23
Swindon v Peterborough
Ipswich v Poole
Coventry: Reserved (KO Cup)
Friday 24
Lakeside: British Under-21 Final
Monday 27
Wolverhampton v Eastbourne
Belle Vue v Poole
Peterborough v Coventry
Wednesday 29
Poole v Ipswich
Thursday 30
Swindon v Belle Vue
Ipswich v Wolverhampton

May

Friday 1
Lakeside v Wolverhampton
Coventry v Peterborough
Saturday 2
Eastbourne v Ipswich
Monday 4
Wolverhampton v Coventry
Ipswich v Peterborough
Wednesday 6
Poole v Belle Vue
Thursday 7
Swindon: Reserved
Peterborough v Belle Vue
Coventry v Lakeside
Friday 8
Lakeside v Coventry
Monday 11
Belle Vue v Peterborough
Eastbourne v Swindon
Wolverhampton v Ipswich
Wednesday 13
Poole v Lakeside
Thursday 14
Swindon v Eastbourne
Peterborough v Poole
Ipswich v Coventry
Friday 15
Lakeside v Belle Vue
Coventry v Wolverhampton
Saturday 16
Eastbourne v Wolverhampton
Monday 18
Belle Vue v Ipswich
Lakeside v Coventry
Wolverhampton v Swindon
Wednesday 20
Poole: British Final
Thursday 21
Swindon v Wolverhampton
Peterborough v Coventry
Ipswich v Eastbourne
Friday 22
Lakeside v Swindon
Coventry v Eastbourne
Saturday 23
Eastbourne v Peterborough
Monday 25
Coventry v Ipswich
Peterborough v Swindon

Wolverhampton v Belle Vue
Wednesday 27
Belle Vue v Wolverhampton
Thursday 28
Swindon: Reserved
Peterborough v Eastbourne
Ipswich v Belle Vue

June

Monday 1
Belle Vue v Eastbourne
Ipswich v Swindon
Wolverhampton v Lakeside
Wednesday 3
Poole v Eastbourne
Thursday 4
Swindon v Ipswich
Peterborough v Lakeside
Friday 5
Coventry v Belle Vue
Lakeside v Poole
Saturday 6
Eastbourne v Coventry
Monday 8
Belle Vue: Reserved
Peterborough v Coventry
Thursday 11
Coventry: Reserved
Ipswich: Reserved
Swindon: Reserved
Lakeside: Reserved
Monday 15
Wolverhampton: Reserved KOC
Belle Vue v Poole (KO Cup or Elite League)
Wednesday 17
Poole v Lakeside
Thursday 18
Ipswich v Poole (KO Cup, provisional)
Swindon v Peterborough
Friday 19
Coventry v Swindon
Lakeside v Peterborough
Saturday 20
Eastbourne v Belle Vue
Monday 22
Belle Vue v Coventry
Wolverhampton v Poole
Wednesday 24
Poole v Belle Vue or Ipswich (KOP Cup)
Thursday 25
Ipswich v Lakeside
Peterborough v Wolverhampton
Swindon v Coventry
Friday 26
Lakeside v Belle Vue
Eastbourne v Swindon
Monday 29
Belle Vue v Lakeside
Eastbourne v Swindon
Wolverhampton v Peterborough

July

Wednesday 1
Poole v Wolverhampton
Thursday 2
Peterborough v Belle Vue
Swindon v Ipswich
Friday 3
Coventry v Peterborough
Lakeside: Reserved
Saturday 4
Eastbourne v Peterborough
Monday 6
Belle Vue v Swindon
Wolverhampton v Eastbourne
Wednesday 8
Poole v Ipswich
Thursday 9
Ipswich v Wolverhampton
Peterborough v Eastbourne
Swindon v Lakeside
Friday 10
Lakeside v Wolverhampton
Coventry v Ipswich
Monday 13
Peterborough: World Cup Event 2
Monday 20
Belle Vue v Eastbourne
Wolverhampton v Coventry
Wednesday 22
Poole v Peterborough
Thursday 23
Ipswich: Reserved
Peterborough v Wolverhampton
Swindon v Belle Vue
Friday 24
Coventry v Poole
Lakeside v Swindon
Saturday 25
Eastbourne v Lakeside
Monday 27
Belle Vue: Peter Craven Memorial Trophy
Coventry: Reserved
Peterborough v Swindon
Wolverhampton v Ipswich
Wednesday 29
Poole v Belle Vue
Thursday 30
Ipswich v Poole
Friday 31
Lakeside v Poole

August

Monday 3
Belle Vue v Swindon
Wolverhampton: Reserved
Wednesday 5
Poole v Coventry
Thursday 6
Ipswich v Peterborough
Swindon v Wolverhampton
Friday 7
Coventry v Wolverhampton
Lakeside v Eastbourne
Saturday 8
Eastbourne: Elite League Pairs Final
Monday 10
Belle Vue v Coventry
Wolverhampton v Peterborough
Wednesday 12
Poole v Swindon
Thursday 13
Ipswich: Reserved
Friday 14
Lakeside: Reserved
Monday 17
Belle Vue v Ipswich
Eastbourne v Coventry
Wolverhampton: Reserved
Wednesday 19
Poole v Swindon
Thursday 20
Ipswich v Belle Vue
Swindon v Poole

2009 FIXTURES

August (continued)

Friday 21
Coventry v Lakeside
Saturday 22
Eastbourne v Wolverhampton
Lakeside v Coventry
Sunday, August 23
Coventry: Oliver Allen Testimonial
Monday 24
Belle Vue v Poole (provisional)
Wolverhampton: Open
Thursday 27
Ipswich v Swindon
Friday 28
Eastbourne v Poole
Lakeside v Ipswich
Saturday 29
Swindon v Eastbourne (provisional)
Monday 31
Coventry v Eastbourne
Peterborough v Ipswich
Wolverhampton v Swindon

September

Friday 4
Coventry: Reserved
Saturday 5
Eastbourne v Ipswich
Monday 7
Belle Vue v Peterborough
Thursday 10
Coventry: Reserved
Friday 11
Lakeside: Reserved
Saturday 12
Provisional cut-off date for play off qualification.

October

Friday 2
Coventry: Elite League Riders' Final
Monday 19
Wolverhampton: Olympique

MAJOR EVENTS

ELITE LEAGUE RIDERS' FINAL
Coventry, Friday, October 2

ELITE LEAGUE PAIRS' FINAL
Eastbourne, Saturday, August 8

BRITISH FINAL
Poole, Wednesday, May 20

BRITISH UNDER 21 FINAL
Lakeside, Friday, April 24

KNOCK OUT CUP
First round
Ipswich v Belle Vue

Quarter Final
Eastbourne 88 Lakeside 100
Peterborough 80 Coventry 100
Poole v Ipswich or Belle Vue
Swindon v Wolverhampton

■ *Fixtures are subject to alteration and do not take into account dates for the end of season Play offs.*
All fixtures should be confirmed via the club's website, local press or Speedway Star before undertaking any journeys.
All meetings are Elite League unless stated otherwise.

PREMIER LEAGUE

		Home			Away					
	M	W	D	L	W	D	L	PtsF	PtsA	Pts
1 EDINBURGH	30	15	0	0	7	2	6	1562	1161	53
2 SOMERSET	30	15	0	0	6	0	9	1517	1223	48
3 KING'S LYNN	30	14	1	0	4	4	7	1624	1111	45
4 RYE HOUSE	30	15	0	0	4	0	11	1500	1232	42
5 WORKINGTON	30	12	2	1	5	0	10	1435.5	1300.5	41
6 BERWICK	30	13	2	0	3	0	12	1428	1316	37
7 REDCAR	30	12	0	3	4	1	10	1369	1374	37
8 SHEFFIELD	30	12	1	2	3	1	11	1381	1345	35
9 READING	30	12	1	2	3	0	12	1350	1405	34
10 SCUNTHORPE	30	12	0	3	3	0	12	1309	1434	33
11 ISLE OF WIGHT	30	14	0	1	1	0	14	1359	1390	31
12 BIRMINGHAM	30	9	0	6	4	0	11	1317.5	1401.5	30
13 STOKE	30	9	1	5	2	0	13	1307	1441	25
14 NEWCASTLE	30	8	0	7	2	0	13	1220	1501	22
15 GLASGOW	30	8	0	7	1	0	14	1297	1469	19
16 MILDENHALL	30	0	0	15	0	0	15	932	1804	0

The top four teams went into the title play-offs and the next eight went into the Young Shield.

EDINBURGH weren't going to let the most memorable season in their history fade into the mists of time.

The Monarchs, crowned league champions for only the second time in their history staged their own Champions' Dance at the end of the season and published a commemorative calendar as a lasting souvenir of a campaign none of their long-suffering fans will ever forget.

Victory in the end of season play-offs also brought the tantalising prospect of promotion to the Elite League and defeat against Wolverhampton both home and away did nothing to blunt the excitement that enveloped not only West Lothian but almost the whole of Scotland.

Their feats certainly caught the imagination with the austere Armadale Stadium figuratively bulging at its seems for the important tail-end of the season meetings.

Premier League promoters had decided at their annual conference that whoever finished top of the table would be officially declared champions – and the Monarchs were duly presented with their precious and hard-won trophy before completing the final meetings of their play-off campaign.

After a disappointing 2007, the Monarchs retained four of what many believed was an under-achieving squad and reaped their rewards for persevering with William Lawson, Matthew Wethers, Derek Sneddon and, in particular, Andrew Tully.

A sign of what was to follow came in the early weeks of the season – when they overcame what looked like a Premier League baptism of fire with a draw at King's Lynn.

Further victories at Mildenhall and Scunthorpe reinforced the belief that they could mount a genuine title challenge and the strength in depth they had shone through at almost every meeting.

Five of their regular seven – skipper Derek Sneddon and Aaron Summers were the exception – celebrated at least one maximum and Matthew Wethers and Tully, who began at reserve, scored a hefty 700-plus league points between them.

For much of the way – until defeat at Birmingham on September 24 in their final league match of the season – Somerset were in contention and still with a mathematical opportunity to finish on top.

Both challengers were unbeaten in 15 home matches but Edinburgh had the edge on the road, picking up five points more than the Rebels.

Rye House were the only other side to boast an unblemished home record but they generally struggled on their travels and it was King's Lynn, whose only dropped point at Saddlebow Road was in that early draw against the champions-elect, who made it a three-team race for much of the rain-affected summer but when push came to shove there was no-one capable of matching the flying Scotsmen.

PLAY-OFFS

ELITE League wooden spoonists Wolverhampton openly admitted they would rather take on Premier League champions Edinburgh than face a fearful trip to Norfolk.

Their preference was understandable given King's Lynn's home track advantage but while Wolves might have been treating a potential clash with the Stars with some trepidation, Edinburgh had no such fears and fought a valiant rearguard action to book their place in the first ever promotion-relegation play-off.

After brushing aside Somerset's challenge, they held a 17 point lead after the first leg but within eight races the margin was down to three points and they'd already used up their tactical ride option.

A Heat 10 maximum from Andrew Tully and guest James Brundle steadied the listing ship, and another 5-1 (Tully and Aaron Summers) in Heat 14 turned the final race into nothing more than a celebratory four laps for the Monarchs.

An understated Edinburgh co-promoter John Campbell said: "It's been a great year for us and we've said all along we wanted to be the team going in for the promotion-relegation match."

Semi Final

EDINBURGH 57 SOMERSET 36
SOMERSET 53 **EDINBURGH 39**
EDINBURGH win 96-89 on aggregate.

KING'S LYNN 56 RYE HOUSE 37
RYE HOUSE 52 **KING'S LYNN 41**
KING'S LYNN win 97-89 on aggregate.

FINAL

EDINBURGH 55 KING'S LYNN 38
KING'S LYNN 52 **EDINBURGH 38**

EDINBURGH ***win 93-90 on aggregate.***

Roll of Honour

1936 .... SOUTHAMPTON
1937 .... BRISTOL
1938 .... HACKNEY WICK
1939 .... Not completed
1940-1945 .... No competition
1946 .... MIDDLESBROUGH
1947 .... MIDDLESBROUGH
1948 .... BRISTOL
1949 .... BRISTOL
1950 .... NORWICH
1951 .... NORWICH
1952 .... POOLE
1953 .... COVENTRY
1954 .... BRISTOL
1955 .... POOLE
1956 .... SWINDON
1960 .... RAYLEIGH
1961 .... POOLE
1962 .... POOLE
1963 .... WOLVERHAMPTON
1964 .... NEWCASTLE
1968 .... BELLE VUE II
1969 .... BELLE VUE II
1970 .... CANTERBURY
1971 .... EASTBOURNE
1972 .... CREWE
1973 .... BOSTON
1974 .... BIRMINGHAM
1975 .... BIRMINGHAM
1976 .... NEWCASTLE
1977 .... EASTBOURNE
1978 .... CANTERBURY
1979 .... MILDENHALL
1980 .... RYE HOUSE
1981 .... MIDDLESBROUGH
1982 .... NEWCASTLE
1983 .... NEWCASTLE
1984 .... LONG EATON
1985 .... ELLESMERE PORT
1986 .... EASTBOURNE
1987 .... EASTBOURNE
1988 .... HACKNEY
1989 .... POOLE
1990 .... POOLE
1991 .... ARENA ESSEX
1992 .... PETERBOROUGH
1993 .... GLASGOW
1994 .... GLASGOW
1997 .... READING
1998 .... PETERBOROUGH
1999 .... SHEFFIELD
2000 .... EXETER
2001 .... NEWCASTLE
2002 .... SHEFFIELD
2003 .... EDINBURGH
2004 .... HULL
2005 .... RYE HOUSE
2006 .... KING'S LYNN
2007 .... RYE HOUSE
2008 .... EDINBURGH

Since 2006 the league championship has been determined by play-offs but in 2008 the team that were top of the Premier League going into the play-offs were actually declared champions.

Perhaps fortunately for the record books Edinburgh followed up their regular season table-topping feat with victory in the play-offs.

Between 1929 and 1931 there were two regional leagues operating, the Southern League and the Northern League (also known as the English League) – champions listed below.

From 1932 onwards there has been a easily recognisable tiered league competition and the Roll of Honour above is for what was the second highest level of league competition in each year, excluding the weekend Southern Area League (which is listed in the 2008 Conference League section).

In 1939 all racing ceased on September 3, 1939, at the declaration of the Second World War. At the time Newcastle led the table but were never officially declared champions.

The 1946 competition was officially the Northern League but included Norwich and Birmingham.

Roll of Honour

1929 .... STAMFORD BRIDGE (Southern)
1929 .... LEEDS (Norhern)
1930 .... WEMBLEY (Southern)
1930 .... BELLE VUE (Northern)
1931 .... WEMBLEY (Southern)
1931 .... BELLE VUE (Northern)

YOUNG SHIELD

IN AN effort to provide more meaning to the end of the season for those clubs missing out on the promotion-relegation play-offs, the Young Shield was given a make-over.

Teams who finished fifth to 12th were seeded to the competition and at least that guaranteed an ever wider spread of the major silverware.

Curiously enough two top ranked sides – fifth placed Workington and sixth in the table Berwick – made it through to the final and the Comets were rewarded for their higher placing by adding the Young Shield to both the Pairs and Fours in a successful rookie season for new promoter Keith Denham who had bought out Tony Mole during the winter.

Their triumph came despite losing number one Daniel Nermark for a huge chunk of the season although they were certainly indebted to his guest replacements, Tomas Topinka contributing a massive 44 points from three appearances.

Quarter Final

BIRMINGHAM 50 **BERWICK 42**
BERWICK 50 BIRMINGHAM 40
BERWICK win 92-90 on aggregate.

ISLE OF WIGHT 57 SHEFFIELD 36
SHEFFIELD 52 **ISLE OF WIGHT 41**
ISLE OF WIGHT win 98-88 on aggregate.

REDCAR 52 READING 40
READING 33 **REDCAR 60**
REDCAR win 112-73 on aggregate.

SCUNTHORPE 51 **WORKINGTON 39**
WORKINGTON 58 SCUNTHORPE 35
WORKINGTON win 97-86 on aggregate.

Semi Final

ISLE OF WIGHT 53 **BERWICK 42**
BERWICK 58 ISLE OF WIGHT 37
BERWICK win 100-90 on aggregate.

REDCAR 48 **WORKINGTON 43**
WORKINGTON 51 REDCAR 42
WORKINGTON win 94-90 on aggregate.

FINAL

WORKINGTON 58 BERWICK 34
BERWICK 55 **WORKINGTON 38**
WORKINGTON win 96-89 on aggregate.

Roll of Honour

1997 .... EXETER
1998 .... ISLE OF WIGHT
1999 .... SHEFFIELD
2000 .... SWINDON
2001 .... ISLE OF WIGHT
2002 .... SHEFFIELD
2004 .... HULL
2005 .... KING'S LYNN
2007 .... REDCAR
2008 .... WORKINGTON

KNOCK OUT CUP

THE 2008 Knock Out Cup will forever be tinged with sadness – and inextricably linked with the death of Newport promoter Tim Stone.

The Welshman absented himself from the Wasps' early round visit to Rye House so that he could visit his terminally ill mother in hospital.

Tim never even got to hear the result from Hoddesdon as he had a heart attack and was found to be dead on arrival at the hospital he had been visiting.

The second leg, due to be completed at the Welsh track the following afternoon, was cancelled and Newport never raced again.

Rye House were awarded a virtual bye to the last eight and eventually got as far as the semi finals before bowing out to Somerset, the West Country side then going on to the Final.

An unexpected success at Derwent Park saw them bring a three point first leg lead back to the Oak Tree Arena where they completed their first Knock Out Cup win with the minimum of fuss.

Round 1

SHEFFIELD 55 SCUNTHORPE 36
SCUNTHORPE 44 **SHEFFIELD 48**
SHEFFIELD win 103-80 on aggregate.

Round 2

EDINBURGH 54 BERWICK 38
BERWICK 42 **EDINBURGH 51**
EDINBURGH win 105-80 on aggregate.

GLASGOW 40 **BIRMINGHAM 52**
BIRMINGHAM 43 GLASGOW 47
BIRMINGHAM win 95-87 on aggregate.

NEWCASTLE 39 **SOMERSET 39**
SOMERSET 64 NEWCASTLE 28
SOMERSET win 103-67 on aggregate.

READING 59 **KING'S LYNN 34**
KING'S LYNN 55 READING 38
READING win 97-89 on aggregate.

REDCAR 53 MILDENHALL 40
MILDENHALL 40 **REDCAR 50**
REDCAR win 103-80 on aggregate.

RYE HOUSE 60 NEWPORT 30
RYE HOUSE win 60-30 on aggregate
Second leg not raced due to Newport promoter Tim Stone's death.

SHEFFIELD 52 **ISLE OF WIGHT 38**
ISLE OF WIGHT 54 SHEFFIELD 38
ISLE OF WIGHT win 92-90 on aggregate.

STOKE 42 **WORKINGTON 50**
WORKINGTON 54 STOKE 36
WORKINGTON win 104-78 on aggregate.

NUMBER ONE: Somerset's cup-winning squad celebrate. Left to right: injured skipper Simon Walker, Stefan Katt, Jordan Frampton, promoter Mike Golding, Emil Kramer, Brent Werner, Jason Doyle, team manager Garry May and Matthias Kröger

Quarter Finals

REDCAR 38 **EDINBURGH 55**
EDINBURGH 55 REDCAR 38
EDINBURGH win 110-76 on aggregate.

RYE HOUSE 62 BIRMINGHAM 30
BIRMINGHAM 42 **RYE HOUSE 51**
RYE HOUSE win 113-72 on aggregate.

SOMERSET 53 READING 39
READING 51 **SOMERSET 44**
SOMERSET win 97-90 on aggregate.

WORKINGTON 53 ISLE OF WIGHT 38
ISLE OF WIGHT 51 **WORKINGTON 43**
WORKINGTON win 96-89 on aggregate.

Semi Finals

EDINBURGH 49 **WORKINGTON 41**
WORKINGTON 53 EDINBURGH 39
WORKINGTON win 94-88 on aggregate.

SOMERSET 53 RYE HOUSE 38
RYE HOUSE 50 **SOMERSET 43**
SOMERSET win 96-88 on aggregate.

FINAL

WORKINGTON 43 **SOMERSET 46**
SOMERSET 52 WORKINGTON 41
SOMERSET win 98-87 on aggregate.

Roll of Honour

1960 .... BRISTOL
1961 .... CRADLEY HEATH
1962 .... EXETER
1963 .... CRADLEY HEATH
1964 .... NEWPORT
1968 .... CANTERBURY
1969 .... BELLE VUE
1970 .... IPSWICH
1971 .... IPSWICH
1972 .... CREWE
1973 .... BOSTON
1974 .... BIRMINGHAM
1975 .... EASTBOURNE
1976 .... NEWCASTLE
1977 .... EASTBOURNE
1978 .... EASTBOURNE
1979 .... RYE HOUSE
1980 .... BERWICK
1981 .... EDINBURGH
1982 .... NEWCASTLE
1983 .... EXETER
1984 .... HACKNEY
1985 .... EASTBOURNE
1986 .... EASTBOURNE
1987 .... EASTBOURNE
1988 .... HACKNEY
1989 .... BERWICK
1990 .... POOLE
1991 .... ARENA ESSEX
1992 .... PETERBOROUGH
1993 .... GLASGOW
1994 .... GLASGOW
1997 .... EDINBURGH
1998 .... READING
1999 .... EDINBURGH
2000 .... SWINDON
2001 .... HULL
2002 .... SHEFFIELD
2003 .... ISLE OF WIGHT
2004 .... HULL
2005 .... KING'S LYNN
2006 .... KING'S LYNN
2007 .... KING'S LYNN
2008 .... SOMERSET

The first stand-alone Knock Out Cup competition for second tier clubs wasn't introduced until the launch of the Provincial League in 1960.

Between 1948 and 1952 the National Trophy was open to teams from all leagues and each Division had its own Final before the winners went through to the next stage so the five teams who won their Divisional Finals can claim to have been that season's Cup winners.

Roll of Honour

1948 .... BIRMINGHAM
1949 .... BRISTOL
1950 .... HALIFAX
1951 .... NORWICH
1952 .... POOLE

PREMIER TROPHY

GROUP A

		Home			Away					
	M	*W*	*D*	*L*	*W*	*D*	*L*	*PtsF*	*PtsA*	*Pts*
1 EDINBURGH	6	3	0	0	2	0	1	320	231	12
2 WORKINGTON	6	3	0	0	1	0	2	287	264	9
3 GLASGOW	6	2	0	1	0	0	3	240	313	4
4 BERWICK	6	1	0	2	0	0	3	255	294	2

GROUP B

		Home			Away					
	M	*W*	*D*	*L*	*W*	*D*	*L*	*PtsF*	*PtsA*	*Pts*
1 SHEFFIELD	8	4	0	0	2	0	2	386	345	14
2 REDCAR	8	3	1	0	0	1	3	362	360	8
3 SCUNTHORPE	8	2	1	1	1	0	3	345	380	8
4 NEWCASTLE	8	3	0	1	0	1	3	364	367	8
5 STOKE	8	3	0	1	0	0	4	363	368	6

GROUP C

		Home			Away					
	M	*W*	*D*	*L*	*W*	*D*	*L*	*PtsF*	*PtsA*	*Pts*
1 BIRMINGHAM	6	2	0	1	2	0	1	243	194	10
2 RYE HOUSE	6	3	0	0	1	0	2	291	250	9
3 KING'S LYNN	6	2	0	1	1	0	2	245	211	7
4 MILDENHALL	6	1	0	2	0	0	3	203	327	2

GROUP D

		Home			Away					
	M	*W*	*D*	*L*	*W*	*D*	*L*	*PtsF*	*PtsA*	*Pts*
1 READING	6	2	0	1	2	0	1	300	248	10
2 SOMERSET	6	2	0	1	2	0	1	296	257	10
3 ISLE OF WIGHT	6	3	0	0	0	0	3	275	272	6
4 NEWPORT	6	1	0	2	0	0	3	226	320	2

Group winners qualify for the two leg semi finals.

Semi Finals

BIRMINGHAM 57 SHEFFIELD 37
SHEFFIELD 53 **BIRMINGHAM 37**
BIRMINGHAM win 94-90 on aggregate.

EDINBURGH 56 READING 34
READING 46 **EDINBURGH 44**
EDINBURGH win 100-80 on aggregate.

FINAL

EDINBURGH 65 BIRMINGHAM 24

BIRMINGHAM 41 **EDINBURGH 52**

EDINBURGH win 117-65 on aggregate.

EDINBURGH had virtually wrapped up the first leg of what they hoped would be a magical treble on Friday, August 15.

That night they were basking in the luxury of a 41-point lead after the first leg of the Premier Trophy Final – and were able to put their minds to both the league title and, at that time, a Knock Out Cup semi final against Workington.

The second leg, which wasn't raced until some six weeks later, was little more than a formality but the Monarchs refused to take their hand off the throttle.

And if Birmingham, who had beaten Somerset the previous week to ensure Edinburgh were the regular season champs, expected an easy ride they were mistaken.

Edinburgh simply set about them with another powerhouse performance – much to the delight of their travelling army who made the evening a night to remember by mixing happily with the Brummies followers, even regaling themselves in the red and yellow Birmingham scarves they bought, en masse, from the Perry Barr track shop.

A great night for Edinburgh...and speedway!

Roll of Honour

1999 .... NEWPORT
2000 .... HULL
2001 .... SHEFFIELD
2002 .... TRELAWNY
2003 .... *Not staged*
2004 .... EXETER
2005 .... RYE HOUSE
2006 .... KING'S LYNN
2007 .... KING'S LYNN
2008 .... EDINBURGH

PREMIER LEAGUE RIDERS' FINAL

Sheffield

Sunday, September 21

YET another glistening bauble made its way into Tai Woffinden's rapidly filling trophy cabinet.

And within minutes of becoming one of the youngest Premier League Riders' champions he was dedicating his latest victory to pal Darren Boocock, tragically killed in a motor-cycle road accident that also saw his wife Sharon perish.

"I didn't start the night off too well, admitted Woffy, revealing: "I sat down and I was thinking about Darren and then I thought 'I want to do this for Booey' and changed things.

"Thinking about him made me realise I had to get on with it. I found it a little weird with him not being there, we used to go to Sheffield every Thursday and he was always there."

The Rye House youngster had been beaten by Jason Bunyan in his opening rider and then pegged back in third place by Ben Barker and Jason Lyons second time out, but he recovered to win his next three, including the Grand Final that clinched the night's honours and what was to become one of three major titles.

He added: "The PLRC was one of my targets this season – the top riders from every team are in it so it's going to be a tough one."

	1	2	3	4	5	Tot	SF	GF
1 Tai WOFFINDEN	**2**	**1**	**3**	**3**	**3**	**12**	**–**	**3**
2 Jason DOYLE	1	3	2	2	3	11	2	2
3 Adrian RYMEL	2	2	3	3	2	12	–	1
4 Kauko NIEMINEN	3	3	3	2	FX	11	3	R
5 Ben BARKER	3	3	2	0	3	11	1	
6 Jason BUNYAN	3	3	2	2	2	12	0	
7 Shane PARKER	1	2	3	3	1	10		
8 Ulrich ØSTERGAARD	2	0	2	1	2	7		
9 Kevin DOOLAN	0	2	1	3	0	6		
10 Jason KING	1	1	1	2	1	6		
11 André COMPTON	3	1	FX	1	R	5		
12 Jason LYONS	E	2	0	1	2	5		
13 Magnus KARLSSON	2	1	0	1	1	5		
14 William LAWSON	0	0	0	R	3	3		
15 Gary HAVELOCK	1	R	1	0	1	3		
16 Scott RICHARDSON [R]	F	1	0			1		
17 Henning LOOF	R					0		
18 Ben TAYLOR [R]	0	0				0		

Roll of Honour

1936	George GREENWOOD (Nottingham)
1960	Trevor REDMOND (Bristol)
1961	Reg REEVES (Rayleigh)
1962	Len SILVER (Exeter)
1963	Ivan MAUGER (Newcastle)
1964	Ivan MAUGER (Newcastle)
1968	Graham PLANT (Middlesbrough)
1969	Geoff AMBROSE (Crayford)
1970	Dave JESSUP (Eastbourne)
1971	John LOUIS (Ipswich)
1972	Phil CRUMP (Crewe)
1973	Arthur PRICE (Boston)
1974	Carl GLOVER (Boston)
1975	Laurie ETHERIDGE (Crayford)
1976	Joe OWEN (Newcastle)
1977	Colin RICHARDSON (Eastbourne)
1978	Steve KOPPE (Canterbury)
1979	Ian GLEDHILL (Stoke)
1980	Wayne BROWN (Berwick)
1981	Mike FERREIRA (Canterbury)
1982	Joe OWEN (Newcastle)
1983	Steve McDERMOTT (Berwick)
1984	Ian BARNEY (Peterborough)
1985	Neil MIDDLEDITCH (Arena Essex)
1986	Paul THORP (Stoke)
1987	Andrew SILVER (Arena Essex)
1988	Troy BUTLER (Milton Keynes)
1989	Mark LORAM (Ipswich)
1990	Andy GRAHAME (Wimbledon)
1991	Jan STÆCHMANN (Long Eaton)
1992	Robert NAGY (Glasgow)
1993	Gary ALLEN (Swindon)
1994	Paul BENTLEY (Middlesbrough)
1997	Peter CARR (Edinburgh)
1998	Glenn CUNNINGHAM (Peterborough)
1999	Sean WILSON (Sheffield)
2000	Carl STONEHEWER (Workington)
2001	Carl STONEHEWER (Workington)
2002	Adam SHIELDS (Isle of Wight)
2003	Sean WILSON (Sheffield)
2004	André COMPTON (Sheffield)
2005	Sean WILSON (Sheffield)
2006	Magnus ZETTERSTRÖM (Somerset)
2007	James WRIGHT (Workington)
2008	Tai WOFFINDEN (Rye House)

PREMIER LEAGUE FOURS' FINAL

WORKINGTON
Saturday, July 26

WORKINGTON may make a habit of winning Premier League Fours Finals on their own Derwent Park track.

But, at least, they provide plenty of excitement which can more than douse the claims of home track advantage that invetiably follow their successes.

This time around it needed a stupendous effort from Kauko Nieminen to pass the previously unbeaten Tomas Topinka in a run-off after the two sides had finished level on 20 points each.

The experienced Czech had been sensational up until that vital decider but he was outfoxed on a robust turn two.

FINAL

	1	2	3	4	Tot	
WORKINGTON 20+3						
Charles WRIGHT	2	2	1		5	
Kauko NIEMINEN	3	3	0		6	3
Carl STONEHEWER	2	1	3		6	
Joe HAINES	0	R	3		3	
John BRANNEY [R]	did not ride					
KING'S LYNN 20+2						
Kevin DOOLAN	3	1	3		7	
Tomas TOPINKA	3	3	3		9	2
Shaun TACEY	1	0	1		2	
Simon LAMBERT	0	1	1		2	
John OLIVER [R]	did not ride					
SOMERSET 19						
Jason DOYLE	3	3	1		7	
Jordan FRAMPTON	2	2	R		4	
Stephan KATT	0	3	2		5	
Brent WERNER	2	1	0		3	
SCUNTHORPE 13						
Magnus KARLSSON	0	0	0		0	
Richard HALL	1	2	2		5	
Carl WILKINSON	1	2	2		5	
Viktor BERGSTRÖM	1	0	2		3	

SEMI FINAL 1

	1	2	3	4	Tot
KING'S LYNN 16					
Kevin DOOLAN	2	3			5
Tomas TOPINKA	3	3			6
Shaun TACEY	2	2			4
Simon LAMBERT	0	1			1
John OLIVER [R]	did not ride				
SCUNTHORPE 16					
Magnus KARLSSON	3	0			3
Richard HALL	2	2			4
Carl WILKINSON	3	1			4
Viktor BERGSTRÖM	2	3			5
NEWCASTLE 10					
George STANCL	3	1			4
Richard JUUL	0	2			2
Jason KING	0	3			3
Sean STODDART	1	0			1
READING 6					
Mark LEMON	1	2			3
Tom MADSEN	0	0			0
Chris MILLS	1	0			1
Tomas SUCHANEK	1	1			2
Jamie SMITH [R]	did not ride				

SEMI FINAL 1

	1	2	3	4	Tot
WORKINGTON 14					
Charles WRIGHT	2	1			3
Kauko NIEMINEN	2	3			5
Carl STONEHEWER	0	3			3
Joe HAINES	3	R			3
John BRANNEY [R]	did not ride				
SOMERSET 13					
Jason DOYLE	3	3			6
Jordan FRAMPTON	3	2			5
Stephan KATT	0	0			0
Brent WERNER	0	2			2
SHEFFIELD 11					
André COMPTON	1	2			3
Ricky ASHWORTH	1	3			4
Ben WILSON	0	2			2
Joel PARSONS	2	0			2
Paul COOPER [R]	did not ride				
EDINBURGH 10					
Andrew TULLY	1	0			1
Matthew WETHERS	2	1			3
Ryan FISHER	3	1			4
Thomas JONASSON	1	1			2
Aaron SUMMERS [R]	did not ride				

Roll of Honour

1976	NEWCASTLE
1977	PETERBOROUGH
1978	PETERBOROUGH
1979	ELLESMERE PORT
1980	CRAYFORD
1981	EDINBURGH
1982	NEWCASTLE
1983	NEWCASTLE
1984	MILDENHALL
1985	MIDDLESBROUGH
1986	MIDDLESBROUGH
1987	MILDENHALL
1988	PETERBOROUGH
1989	PETERBOROUGH
1990	STOKE
1991	ARENA ESSEX
1992	PETERBOROUGH
1993	EDINBURGH
1994	OXFORD
1997	LONG EATON
1998	PETERBOROUGH
1999	SHEFFIELD
2000	SHEFFIELD
2001	WORKINGTON
2002	BERWICK
2003	SWINDON
2004	WORKINGTON
2005	SOMERSET
2006	WORKINGTON
2007	ISLE OF WIGHT
2008	WORKINGTON

In 1979 and 1980 a Four Team competition involving teams from the two top Leagues was staged.

Roll of Honour

1979	HULL
1980	CRADLEY HEATH

PREMIER LEAGUE PAIRS' FINAL

SOMERSET
Friday, June 27

FANS fought their way through traffic jams on the motorways as the Severn Bridge played host to a caravan of supporters making their way from Cardiff to Somerset.

Workington regained the trophy by beating hosts Somerset in the Final but the real drama was reserved for a controversial semi final.

Reading chief Tim Sugar demanded to see a video replay of a tight finish in which referee Graham Flint angered the Berkshire contingent by awarding a vital third place to Jason Doyle rather than their own Mark Lemon.

That decision meant the Rebels went through but a furious Lemon claimed: "I'm appalled by the referee's decision. I had no doubts that I got there."

Doyle wasn't sure admitting: "It was on the line, half the people said it was a win to Lemo and half said it was a win to me!"

And the majory of the neutrals appeared to support Lemon's contention, the referee's decision being loudly greeted by boos and jeers.

1 WORKINGTON, 2 SOMERSET, 3 READING, 4 SHEFFIELD.

GROUP A

	1	2	3	4	Tot
SHEFFIELD 25					
André COMPTON	2	3	4	4	13
Ricky ASHWORTH	4	2	3	3	12:3
READING 21					
Ulrich ØSTERGAARD	4	4	4	4	16
Mark LEMON	R	R	3	2	5:1
RYE HOUSE 20					
Chris NEATH	3	4	0	4	11
Tommy ALLEN	2	2	2	3	9:2
EDINBURGH 15					
William LAWSON	0	3	2	0	5:1
Matthew WETHERS	3	4	0	3	10
BIRMINGHAM 9					
Jamie BIRKINSHAW	0	0	0	0	0
Craig WATSON	3	2	2	2	9

GROUP B

	1	2	3	4	Tot
SOMERSET 26					
Jason DOYLE	3	2	4	4	13:1
Emil KRAMER	4	4	2	3	13:1
WORKINGTON 23					
Daniel NERMARK	4	3	2	3	12:1
Kauko NIEMINEN	3	0	4	4	11:1
REDCAR 15					
Gary HAVELOCK	0	R	0	3	3:1
Tyron PROCTOR	2	3	3	4	12
ISLE OF WIGHT 14					
Glen PHILLIPS	0	2	0	0	2
Jason BUNYAN	4	4	2	2	12
NEWCASTLE 10					
Josef FRANC	0	2	0	R	2:1
Chistian HENRY	2	3	3	FX	8

Semi Final 1: Workington 6 (Daniel Nermark 4, Kauko Nieminen 2), Sheffield 3 (Ricky Ashworth 3, André Compton 0).
Semi Final 2: Somerset 5 (Emil Kramer 3, Jason Doyle 2:1), Reading 4 (Ulrich Østergaard 4, Mark Lemon 0).
Consolation Final: Reading 6 (Ulrich Østergaard 4, Mark Lemon 2), Sheffield 3 (André Compton 3, Ricky Ashworth 0).
Final: Workington 6 (Daniel Nermark 4, Kauko Nieminen 2), Reading 3 (Jason Doyle 3, Emil Kramer 0).

Roll of Honour

1975....NEWCASTLE
1976....ELLESMERE PORT
1977....BOSTON
1978....ELLESMERE PORT
1979....MILTON KEYNES
1980....MIDDLESBROUGH
1981....CANTERBURY
1982....WEYMOUTH
1983....WEYMOUTH
1984....STOKE
1985....ELLESMERE PORT
1986....EDINBURGH
1987....MILDENHALL
1988....STOKE
1989....STOKE
1990....HACKNEY
1994....SWINDON
1997....LONG EATON
1998....PETERBOROUGH
1999....WORKINGTON
2000....WORKINGTON
2001....WORKINGTON
2002....ISLE OF WIGHT
2003....WORKINGTON
2004....READING
2005....GLASGOW
2006....GLASGOW
2007....ISLE OF WIGHT
2008....WORKINGTON

SUPERNATIONAL SERIES

In 1982 the top eight Division Two teams at a September cut-off date were engaged in an end-of-season series.

In 1990 the competition was revived in a different form with the top nine sides as of Sunday, September 23, contesting.

Roll of Honour

1982....NEWCASTLE
1983....NEWCASTLE
1990....GLASGOW

DIVISION TWO PREMIERSHIP

An occasional competition between the previous season's Division Two champions and the Knock Out Cup winners.

Roll of Honour

1993....PETERBOROUGH
1994....EDINBURGH
2000....SHEFFIELD
2002....HULL

Premier League

BERWICK

TRACK FILE

Track: Shielfield Park Stadium, Tweedmouth, Berwick-upon-Tweed, TD15 2EF.
Telephone: 01289 307707 (race-nights only).
Hotline: 09068 664667.
Website: www.berwickspeedway.co.uk
Track Length: 368 metres.
Track Record: 64.02 secs, Sean Wilson, August 21, 1999.
Promoters: John Anderson, Ryan Anderson, Cameron Anderson.
Team Sponsor: F1 Finance (Scotland).
Colours: Black and gold.
Nickname: Bandits.

HISTORY

First meeting: May 18, 1968, Berwick v Newcastle, British League Division Two challenge.
Leagues: Division Two: 1968-1980; 1997-2009. Division Three, 1996-97.

● *Berwick also raced at Berrington Lough Stadium, near Ancroft, Northumberland.*
First meeting: April 24, 1982, Berwick v Edinburgh, Division Two challenge.
Leagues: Division One, 1991. Division Two, 1982-1990, 1992. Division Three, 1994-95.

HONOURS

Major honours: 7.
Division Two Knock Out Cup winners (2), 1980, 1989.
Division Two Four Team champions (1), 2002.
Division Three champions (2), 1994, 1995.
Division Three Knock Out Cup winners (1), 1995.
Youth Development League champions (1), 1998.

2008 REVIEW

EXPECTATIONS for the Bandits were limited at the start of the season – and the Bandits duly struggled in the Premier Trophy, winning just one of their six group matches.

However, Peter Waite's team ended the first month with an emphatic 61-29 Premier League win at Mildenhall, and that sparked a dramatic revival, helped by a series of team changes which turned the Bandits into a real force at this level.

Henning Bager set the ball rolling with a month-long contract, but the Bandits also profited from the sad loss of Newport during the season by picking up Paul Clews and, until ruled out due to injury, Tony Atkin.

With Adrian Rymel in the form of his life in the number one race jacket, the Bandits rose to the top of the Premier League table and spent most of the summer with a genuine bid for a play-off place within their grasp.

Eventually, a lack of away wins ended their bid to finish in the top four, but the victory at West Row was followed by notable successes at both Birmingham and Workington on their way to a sixth-place finish.

The Bandits' home form was the best of any team outside the top four as they remained unbeaten at Shielfield Park throughout the Premier League campaign, although both Edinburgh and King's Lynn did manage to secure draws.

Berwick then overcame Birmingham in a dramatic Young Shield quarter-final which went right down to the wire, and got the better of the Isle of Wight in the semis before losing out at the final hurdle against Workington.

There was serious uncertainty about the future come the end of the campaign as Waite signalled that his time at the club was at an end.

Fortunately a solution was found just in time for the BSPA AGM and the Bandits will run under a new promotion in 2009.

2008 RESULTS

Premier League

Final position .... Sixth

MILDENHALL (A)
Sunday, March 30
Won 61-29
Rymel 14, *rider replacement for Franchetti*, Bager 10:1, Aarnio 10:2, Makovsky 13:4, Magosi 10, McKinna 4:1.
▲ *Rymel broke the track record in Heat 1 in Berwick's biggest ever away win.*

NEWPORT (H)
Saturday, April 12
Won 55-38
Rymel 11:1, *rider replacement for Franchetti*, Bager 10, Magosi 3:1, **Makovsky 14:1**, Aarnio 12:2, McKinna 5:2.
✱ *Meeting subsequently declared void after Newport's closure.*
▼ *Paul Clews impressed with 16 for the visitors.*

SHEFFIELD (H)
Saturday, April 19
Won 52-41
Rymel 14:1, Magosi 9:1, Bager 7, Scott James [G] 0, **Makovsky 13:2**, Aarnio 8, McKinna 1.

REDCAR (A)
Thursday, May 1
Lost 41-51
Rymel 11, Magosi 3:1, Makovsky 11:1 (4), *rider replacement for Franchetti*, Gary Beaton [G] 0, Aarnio 13:2, Adam McKinna [G] 3, Martin Emerson [no. 8].
▼ *Beaton rode in place of delayed new signing Benny Johansson.*

KING'S LYNN (H)
Saturday, May 3
Drew 45-45
Rymel 12:1, Magosi 8:1, Makovsky 10:1, *rider replacement for Franchetti*, Johansson 1:1, Aarnio 13:1, McKinna 1:1, John MacPhail [no. 8].
▼ *Johansson struggled on debut, leaving the Bandits a four-man team who made sure of a draw when Rusty Harrison failed to leave the start-line in Heat 15.*

ISLE OF WIGHT (H)
Saturday, May 10
17-19, meeting abandoned
Rymel 2:1, Magosi 7, Makovsky 2:1, *rider replacement for Johansson*, Aarnio 1, Smith 3, McKinna 2:1, MacPhail [no. 8].
■ *Referee Peter Clarke abandoned the meeting after a Heat 7 incident in which Scott Smith and Paul Fry's machines went into the crowd. Fans Graham Sykes, Becky Hope and Becky Gray were all hurt and taken to hospital by ambulance.*

Did you know?

Michal Makovsky had more official rides – 235 – than any other Premier League regular.

SQUAD
Tony Atkin, Paul Clews, Adam McKinna, Scott Smith.
Foreign: Tero Aarnio, Henning Bager, Guglielmo Franchetti, Manuel Hauzinger, Benny Johansson, Norbert Magosi, Michal Makovsky, Adrian Rymel, Tamas Sike.

SOMERSET (A)
Friday, May 16
Lost 34-58
Rymel 13 (4), Magosi 5:1, Makovsky 3:1, *rider replacement for Johansson*, Aarnio 6, Jay Herne [G] 5, McKinna 2:1.

SCUNTHORPE (H)
Saturday, May 24
Won 48-42
Tomas Topinka [G] 14, *rider replacement for Magosi*, Makovsky 12:1, Atkin 7:2, Aarnio 3, Clews 12:2, Smith 0.
▲ *Scott Smith was forced to withdraw from the meeting with knee ligament damage. Magosi and Rymel missing on international duty, but new-look team pulled back from 19-11 down.*

ISLE OF WIGHT (H)
Saturday, May 31
Won 46-44
Rymel 14:1, Kozza Smith [G] 5, Makovsky 11:1, *rider replacement for Magosi*, Atkin 3:1, Clews 11, Adam McKinna [G] 2:2, John MacPhail [no. 8].

KING'S LYNN (A)
Wednesday, June 5
Lost 29-61
Rymel 11, Atkin 1:1, Makovsky 4 (FX), Aarnio 2, Magosi 0, Clews 11, Smith 0.
▼ *Scott Smith fell in Heat 2 and withdrew from meeting.*

GLASGOW (H)
Saturday, June 7
Won 54-39
Rymel 13:2, Magosi 10, Makovsky 12, *rider replacement for Aarnio*, Atkin 5:1, Clews 6:1, Smith 8:3, John MacPhail [no. 8].
▲ *Rymel's paid maximum moved the Bandits into the Premier League's top four, as they started the match with three 5-1s.*

READING (H)
Saturday, June 14
Won 61-32
Rymel 14:1, Atkin 7, Makovsky 7, Aarnio 8, Magosi 11:1, Clews 7:3, Smith 7:2.
▲ *Peter Waite's self-styled Dream Team took to the track for the first time and produced exactly what he had been hoping for!*

STOKE (A)
Saturday, June 29
Lost 37-55
Tomas Topinka [G] 15:1 (4), *rider replacement for Aarnio*, Makovsky 3, Atkin 5, Magosi 8, Clews 5, Smith 1, Jay Herne [G] [no. 8].

SCUNTHORPE (A)
Friday, July 4
Lost 41-52
Bager [G] 12 (6), Atkin 0, Makovsky 8, Aarnio 5, Magosi 7, Clews 4:1, Smith 5:2.
▼ *Atkin withdrew with a hand injury after Heat 1, and a 7-2 and 4-2 in Heats 12 and 13 briefly gave the Bandits hope of salvaging an away win.*

RYE HOUSE (H)
Saturday, July 12
Won 60-33
Rymel 14, *rider replacement for Magosi*, Makovsky 13, Atkin 5:3, Aarnio 8:3, Clews 10:2, Smith 10:4.
▲ *First league points in nearly a month with a comfortable win – referee Stuart Wilson having to give the match the go-ahead after an early track inspection*

NEWCASTLE (A)
Sunday, July 13
Lost 42-47
Rymel 12, *rider replacement for Magosi*, Makovsky 10, Atkin 2, Aarnio 7:1, Clews 11, Smith 0.
▲▼ *Rymel four wins and one exclusion, Makovsky three wins and one exclusion.*

BIRMINGHAM (H)
Saturday, July 19
Won 58-34
Rymel 11, Atkin 4:2, Makovsky 12, Aarnio 6:4, Magosi 8:3, Clews 9:1, Smith 8:1.
▲ *Meeting delayed by around 40 minutes with track work required, and the Bandits had only two last places, both falls.*

READING (A)
Monday, July 21
Lost 46-47
Rymel 17 (6), *rider replacement for Atkin*, Makovsky 7:2, Aarnio 7:2, Magosi 1:1, Clews 13:1, Smith 1.

ISLE OF WIGHT (A)
Tuesday, July 22
Lost 40-53
Rymel 15:1 (6), Kozza Smith [G] 9:2, Makovsky 5, Aarnio 3:1, *rider replacement for Magosi*, Clews 7:1, Smith 1.

RYE HOUSE (A)
Sunday, July 27
Lost 33-57
Rymel 0, *rider replacement for Atkin*, Makovsky 8:2, Aarnio 6, Magosi 2, Clews 11, Smith 0, Tom Brown [no. 8] 6 (FX).
▼ *Rymel forced to withdraw on medical advice before his second ride in Heat 5. Clews took credit at reserve – and named number eight Tom Brown notable Heat 8 winner.*

BIRMINGHAM (A)
Wednesday, July 30
Won 48-42
Rymel 15, Franchetti 0, Makovsky 5:1, Aarnio 8:1, Magosi 5, Clews 15:1, Smith 0.
▼ *Memorable away win with Rymel immense and Clews again showing his liking for Perry Barr. Bandits provided a remarkable 12 heat winners.*

EDINBURGH (H)
Saturday, August 2
Drew 45-45
Travis McGowan [G] 11, Clews 6:3, Makovsky 13:1, Magosi 0, Aarnio 2:1, Franchetti 4, Smith 9:1.
▲ *Bandits led by six, trailed by four, and finally snatched a draw with a last-heat 5-1 from guest Travis McGowan and Makovsky.*

SHEFFIELD (A)
Thursday, August 7
Lost 42-48
Rymel 12:1, *rider replacement for Magosi*, Makovsky 9, Clews 2:2, Aarnio 4, Franchetti 2:1, Smith 13.

MILDENHALL (H)
Saturday, August 9
Won 72-18
Rymel 13:2, *rider replacement for Magosi*, **Makovsky 18**, Clews 8:4, Aarnio 10:3, **Franchetti 11:1**, **Smith 12:3**.
▲ *The first race was shared when Clews crashed out – Aarnio, in Heat 11 was the only other Bandit to drop a point in this most one-sided of matches.*

NEWCASTLE (H)
Saturday, August 16
Won 62-31
Rymel 15, **Magosi 9:3**, **Makovsky 14:1**, Clews 6:1, Aarnio 8:1, Franchetti 4:1, Smith 6:3.

EDINBURGH (A)
Friday, August 22
Lost 33-59
Rymel 14 (4), *rider replacement for Magosi*, Makovsky 7, Clews 5:1, Aarnio 3:1, Franchetti 2, Smith 2.

WORKINGTON (H)
Saturday, August 23
Won 48-41
Rymel 15, *rider replacement for Magosi*, Makovsky 13, Clews 8:3, Paul Cooper [G] 0, Franchetti 6, Smith 6, MacPhail [no. 8].
▲ *Trailed by five points at halfway stage but mounted a strong fightback, led again by the top two and Clews, with the points all-but secured by a 4-2 in Heat 14.*

WORKINGTON (A)
Monday, August 25
Won 51-42
Rymel 7, *rider replacement for Magosi*, Makovsky 16, Clews 6:2, Paul Cooper [G] 8:1, Franchetti 14:3, Smith 0, John MacPhail [no. 8].
▲▼ *Smith withdrew after a fall in Heat 2 but Franchetti covered superbly.*

SOMERSET (H)
Saturday, August 30
Won 58-35
Rymel 13:1, *rider replacement for Magosi*, Makovsky 14, Clews 6:3, Aarnio 11:1, Franchetti 8:3, Smith 6:1, John MacPhail [no. 8].

Adrian Rymel twice went through three successive Premier League home matches without being beaten by an opponent.

GLASGOW (A)
Sunday, August 31
3-3, abandoned after Heat 1, rain
Rymel 3, *rider replacement for Magosi*, Makovsky, Clews 0, Paul Cooper [G], Franchetti, Smith.

STOKE (H)
Saturday, September 13
Won 52-41
Shane Parker [G] 10:1, *rider replacement for Magosi*, Makovsky 13, Clews 11:3, Aarnio 3, Danny Warwick [G] 8:1, Smith 7:2.
▼ *Aarnio crashed heavily in Heat 10 and was taken to hospital for precautionary tests on his spine.*

GLASGOW (A)
Sunday, September 14
Lost 43-50
Tomasz Piszcz [G] 18 (6), *rider replacement for Magosi*, Makovsky 10:1, Clews 3:1, Danny Warwick [G] 2, Franchetti 2:1, Smith 8:1.
▲▼ *Guests Tomasz Piszcz was hugely impressive as a replacement for Rymel, but only Makovsky won another race as the Bandits lacked heat advantages.*

REDCAR (H)
Saturday, September 20
Won 46-44
Tomasz Piszcz [G] 13, Sike 1, Makovsky 12:1, Clews 5:1, Aarnio 6:1, Franchetti 3:1, Smith 6:1.
▲ *Dramatic finale saw the Bears take 4-2s in Heats 13 and 14 to go ahead, only for guest Tomasz Piszcz and Makovsky to rescue the Bandits with a match-winning 5-1 in the decider.*

PREMIER LEAGUE

		M	W	D	L	PtsF	PtsA	Pts
1	Edinburgh	30	22	2	6	1562	1161	53
2	Somerset	30	21	0	9	1517	1223	48
3	King's Lynn	30	18	5	7	1624	1111	45
4	Rye House	30	19	0	11	1500	1232	42
5	Workington	30	17	2	11	1435.5	1300.5	41
6	**BERWICK**	**30**	**16**	**2**	**12**	**1428**	**1316**	**37**
7	Redcar	30	16	1	13	1369	1374	37
8	Sheffield	30	15	2	13	1381	1345	35
9	Reading	30	15	1	14	1350	1405	34
10	Scunthorpe	30	15	0	15	1309	1434	33
11	Isle of Wight	30	15	0	15	1359	1390	31
12	Birmingham	30	13	0	17	1317.5	1401.5	30
13	Stoke	30	11	1	18	1307	1441	25
14	Newcastle	30	10	0	20	1220	1501	22
15	Glasgow	30	9	0	21	1297	1469	19
16	Mildenhall	30	0	0	30	932	1804	0

Young Shield

Quarter Final, first leg
BIRMINGHAM (A)
Wednesday, October 1
Lost 42-50
Rymel 14:1, Richard Sweetman [G] 7, Makovsky 9, *rider replacement for Aarnio*, Clews 4:2, Franchetti 7:2, Smith 1:1.
▲▼ *Rymel finished second to his team-mate Sweetman when taking a tac. sub ride in Heat 8, but then dislocated his shoulder in a Heat 15 crash.*

Quarter Final, second leg
BIRMINGHAM (H)
Saturday, October 4
Won 50-40
Jason Doyle [G] 11, Lee Dicken [G] 5:3, Makovsky 10, *rider replacement for Aarnio*, Clews 10:1, Franchetti 4:1, Smith 10:2.
▲ *Dramatic finish saw the Bandits take the aggregate lead with a Heat 14 5-1 from Clews and Smith, and Makovsky then*

BERWICK

Rider	*M*	*R*	*Pts*	*BP*	*TPts*	*Ave*	*F*	*P*	*TR*	*TPts*	*TS*	*TSPts*
Adrian RYMEL	30	145	362	15	377	10.40	3	5	4	10	1	2
Michal MAKOVSKY	**44**	**235**	**470**	**29**	**499**	**8.49**	**1**	**2**	**6**	**13**	**0**	**0**
Paul CLEWS	31	166	241	46	287	6.92	0	0	0	0	0	0
Henning BAGER	**5**	**22**	**35**	**2**	**37**	**6.73**	**0**	**0**	**0**	**0**	**0**	**0**
Norbert MAGOSI	24	118	174	17	191	6.47	0	1	0	0	0	0
Tero AARNIO	**32**	**151**	**209**	**34**	**243**	**6.44**	**0**	**0**	**1**	**3**	**0**	**0**
Scott SMITH	30	122	147	32	179	5.87	0	1	0	0	0	0
Guglielmo FRANCHETTI	**21**	**92**	**93**	**20**	**113**	**4.91**	**0**	**1**	**0**	**0**	**0**	**0**
Tony ATKIN	10	42	39	10	49	4.67	0	0	0	0	0	0
Adam McKINNA	**13**	**59**	**35**	**8**	**43**	**2.91**	**0**	**0**	**0**	**0**	**0**	**0**
Benny JOHANSSON	1	4	1	1	2	2.00	0	0	0	0	0	0
Tamas SIKE	**1**	**3**	**1**	**0**	**1**	**1.33**	**0**	**0**	**0**	**0**	**0**	**0**
Manuel HAUZINGER	1	1	0	0	0	0.00	0	0	0	0	0	0
Guests	***35***	***156***	***237***	***19***	***256***	***6.56***	***1***	***0***	***4***	***8***	***2***	***2***

For Paul CLEWS and Tony ATKIN see Newport; for Henning BAGER see Birmingham and Peterborough; for Scott SMITH see Workington; for Adam McKinna see Buxton and Redcar (CL); for Manuel HAUZINGER see Swindon.

Spectacular stuff from Scott Smith

PISTOL-PACKING BANDITS – Paul Clews, Guglielmo Franchetti, team manager Kevin Bunney, Norbert Magosi, Adrian Rymel, Scott Smith, kneeling Tero Aarnio and Michal Makovsky

Continued from page 143.

split the Brummies pair in the decider.
Aggregate: Won 92-40.

Semi Final, first leg
ISLE OF WIGHT (A)
Tuesday, October 14
Lost 42-53
Jason Doyle [G] 16 (TS4), Lee Dicken [G] 2:1, Makovsky 15:1 (6), *rider replacement for Aarnio*, Clews 7:1, Franchetti 2, Smith 0.
▼ *Smith had to pull out of the meeting after a Heat 4 fall with a knee injury.*

Semi Final, second leg
ISLE OF WIGHT (H)
Saturday, October 18
Won 58-37
Jason Doyle [G] 13:1, Lee Dicken [G] 8:3, Makovsky 12, *rider replacement for Aarnio*, Clews 12:2, Franchetti 5:3, Smith 8:2.
▲ *Bandits trailed 11-13 but put in an emphatic response, confirming their impressive aggregate win when Clews repelled Jason Bunyan's tac. sub ride in Heat 14.*
Aggregate: Won 100-90.

FINAL, first leg
WORKINGTON (H)
Saturday, October 25
0-0, abandoned.
Tai Woffinden [G], Tom Brown [G], Makovsky, *rider replacement for Aarnio*, Clews, Frenchetti, Smith.
● *An attempt was made to run the meeting despite awkward track conditions but when Workington guest Tomas Topinka fell while leading the opening race the meeting was abandoned.*

FINAL, first leg
WORKINGTON (A)
Sunday, October 26
Lost 34-58
Tai Woffinden [G] 11 (TS1), Lee Dicken [G] 4:1, Makovsky 11 (4), *rider replacement for Aarnio*, Clews 0, Franchetti 5, Smith 3:1.
▼ *Guest Tai Woffinden won his last two races but the Bandits carded far too many last places and left themselves with a big uphill battle for the second leg.*

FINAL, second leg
WORKINGTON (H)
Wednesday, October 29
Won 55-38
Tai Woffinden [G] 13:1, Lee Dicken [G] 3:1, Makovsky 13, *rider replacement for Aarnio*, Clews 10:3, Franchetti 7:1, Smith 9:2.
▼ *Final meeting of the Peter Waite era could have provided a sensational aggregate comeback – but the Bandits fell just short after Jason Lyons had won a tactical ride.*
Aggregate: Lost 89-96.

Premier Trophy

EDINBURGH (H)
Saturday, March 15
Lost 42-48
Rymel 14, Franchetti 2, Makovsky 12, Aarnio 4:1, Greg Blair [G] 2, Magosi 6, McKinna 2:2.
▼ *Conference League Greg Blair was drafted in for new signing Hauzinger, who had broken his collarbone in practice.*

GLASGOW (A)
Sunday, March 16
Lost 43-47
Rymel 11, Franchetti 4:2, Makovsky 9:1, Aarnio 5:2, Greg Blair [G] 0, Magosi 12:1, McKinna 2.
▼ *Blair crashed Heat 4, breaking his leg.*

EDINBURGH (A)
Friday, March 21
†Lost 34-56
Rymel 9, Franchetti 0, Makovsky 9, Aarnio 2:1, Hauzinger 0, Magosi 6:1, McKinna 8:1.
● *Magosi illegally took a tactical ride in Heat 8 and finished third, scoring two points. The point was deducted by the Speedway Control Bureau. Original result was Edinburgh 56 Berwick 35 with Magosi scoring 7:1 (2).*
▼▼ *Franchetti crashed in Heat 1 and took no further part in the meeting. Hauzinger failed to complete Heat 4 before withdrawing.*

WORKINGTON (A)
Monday, March 24
Lost 40-53
Rymel 5, Jamie Robertson [G] 0, Makovsky 9:2, Aarnio 11 (6), *rider replacement for Hauzinger*, Magosi 15, McKinna 0.

WORKINGTON (H)
Saturday, March 22
Lost 44-46
Rymel 8:1, Jamie Robertson [G] 4, Makovsky 12:1, Aarnio 5:1, *rider replacement for Hauzinger*, Magosi 13:1, McKinna 2:1.

GLASGOW (H)
Saturday, March 29
Won 52-44
Rymel 12:2, *rider replacement for Franchetti*, Bager 4:1, Aarnio 8:1, Makovsky 14:2, Magosi 14:1, McKinna 0.

PREMIER TROPHY Group A

		M	W	D	L	PtsF	PtsA	Pts
1	Edinburgh	6	5	0	1	320	231	12
2	Workington	6	4	0	2	287	264	9
3	Glasgow	6	2	0	4	240	313	4
4	**BERWICK**	**6**	**1**	**0**	**5**	**255**	**294**	**2**

Did you know?
Berwick have never won a league title in 25 seasons based at Shielfield Park.

Knock Out Cup

Second round, first leg
EDINBURGH (A)
Friday, April 25
Lost 38-54
Rider replacement for Rymel, Magosi 4, Bager 11, Franchetti 1, Makovsky 14 (6), Aarnio 5, McKinna 3:1.

Second round, second leg
EDINBURGH (H)
Saturday, April 26
Lost 42-51
Rider replacement for Rymel, Magosi 8, Bager 3, John MacPhail [G] 0, Makovsky 15:1 (6), Aarnio 9:3, McKinna 7.

▼ *John McPhail deputised for planned guest Ben Powell, who broke down en route. Rymel absent on European Championship duty, and Bager's final appearance at the end of his short-term deal.*

Aggregate: Lost 80-105.

Tyne/Tweed Trophy

First leg
NEWCASTLE (H)
Saturday, March 8
Lost 43-46
Rymel 9, Franchetti 2, Aarnio 6, Stanislaw Burza [G] 9, Makovsky 12, Magosi 3:1, McKinna 2.

NEWCASTLE (A)
Sunday, March 9
Won 46-44
Rymel 12:1, Franchetti 1:1, Aarnio 1, Stanislaw Burza [G] 12:1, Makovsky 8, Magosi 10, McKinna 2:1.

Aggregate: Lost 89-90.

Individual

KARL FRIAR MEMORIAL TROPHY
Saturday, April 5
Michal Makovsky found the perfect way to start his birthday celebrations early – by winning the Karl Friar Memorial Trophy for the first time.

The Czech Republic ace dropped only one point in his five rides on the eve of turning 32.

	1	2	3	4	Tot	F
1 Michal MAKOVSKY	**3**	**3**	**2**	**3**	**11**	**3**
2 Magnus KARLSSON	2	2	3	3	10	2
3 Ben POWELL	2	2	2	2	8	1
4 Josef FRANC	3	3	3	3	12	0
5 Carl WILKINSON	1	3	2	2	8	
6 Henning BAGER	3	2	R	1	6	
7 Trent LEVERINGTON	0	1	3	1	5	
8 Joshua AUTY	0	1	1	2	4	
9 Tero AARNIO	1	1	1	1	4	
10 Shaun HARMATIUK	2	0	0	0	2	
11Tamas SIKE	1	0	0	0	1	
12 Adam McKINNA	R	R	1	0	1	

Roll of Honour

1997 . . . . . Paul BENTLEY
1999 . . . . . Paul BENTLEY
2000 . . . . . Jesper OLSEN
2001 . . . . . Paul BENTLEY
2002 . . . . . Claus KRISTENSEN
2004 . . . . . Rory SCHLEIN
2005 . . . . . Adrian RYMEL
2008 . . . . . Michal MAKOVSKY

2009 Squad

William **LAWSON** (7.84), Michal **MAKOVSKY** (7.65), Josef **FRANC** (7.44), Tero **AARNIO** (5.49), Paul **CLEWS** (5.41), Guglielmo **FRANCHETTI** (4.43), Danny **WARWICK** (4.09).

BORDERNAPOLIS
Saturday, September 27
Finn Tero Aarnio's season ended when he was unable to avoid Chris Kerr's stray machine after the American came off in Heat 4.

Fears he had broken his leg were allayed but the heavy bruising ruled him out of the Bandits' Young Shield campaign.

No-one could touch Elite Leaguer Rory Schlein, an easy and convincing winner of his five races, including the title deciding Final.

	1	2	3	4	Tot	SF	F
1 Rory SCHLEIN	**3**	**3**	**3**	**3**	**12**	**–**	**3**
2 Tomasz PISZCZ	2	3	3	2	10	3	2
3 Michal MAKOVSKY	3	3	1	3	10	–	1
4 Trent LEVERINGTON	0	2	2	2	6	2	0
5 David HOWE	2	2	3	3	10	1	
6 Mark LEMON	3	1	2	1	7	0	
7 Scott SMITH	1	0	2	2	5		
8 Peter JUUL	1	2	1	1	5		
9 Tero AARNIO	2	1			3		
10 Tamas SIKE [R]	1	1	0		2		
11 Shane PARKER	R	1			1		
12 Chris KERR	1	fx	fx	fx	1		
13 Carl WILKINSON	0	R	R		0		

Roll of Honour

1972 . . . . . Doug TEMPLETON
1973 . . . . . Robin ADLINGTON
1974 . . . . . Andy MELDRUM
1975 . . . . . Joe OWEN
1976 . . . . . Joe OWEN
1977 . . . . . Graham JONES
1978 . . . . . Benny ROURKE
1979 . . . . . Steve MCDERMOTT
1999 . . . . . Mark LORAM
2000 . . . . . Paul BENTLEY
2001 . . . . . Mark LORAM
2002 . . . . . Jason CRUMP
2003 . . . . . Chris HARRIS
2004 . . . . . Sam ERMOLENKO
2005 . . . . . Adrian RYMEL
2006 . . . . . Todd WILTSHIRE
2007 . . . . . *Not staged*
2008 . . . . . Rory SCHLEIN

Weather...

Berwick lost only two home meetings to the weather although two others were abandoned, one without a race being finished.

Premier League
Monday, May 26 . . . . . RYE HOUSE (A)
Saturday, June 21 . . . . . REDCAR (H)
Saturday, September 6 . . . . . REDCAR (H)

...beaten

Testimonial

DAVID MELDRUM
Saturday, October 18
Postponed because of involvement in Young Shield.

B

Premier League

BIRMINGHAM

TRACK FILE

Track: Perry Barr Stadium, Aldridge Road, Perry Barr, Birmingham, B42 2ET.
Telephone: 0121 356 4001 (stadium), 01691 774321 (Mon-Fri, 10-4).
Hotline: 09068 664660.
Website: www.birminghamspeedway.co.uk
Track Length: 292 metres.
Track Record: 56.6 secs, Jason Lyons, June 25, 2008; Kevin Doolan, July 2, 2008.
Promoters: Graham Drury, Anthony Mole, Redvers Mole.
Team Sponsors: BRC Roofing Co. Ltd.
Colours: Red with yellow B.
Nickname: Brummies.

HONOURS

Major honours: 6.
Division Two champions (2), 1974, 1975.
Division Two Knock Out Cup winners (1), 1974.
Division One Premiership winners (2), 1992, 1997.
Division Two champions (1), 1963.

■ *See following page for track history.*

2008 REVIEW

BRUMMIES promoter Graham Drury took the radical step of bringing a local psychic to Perry Barr mid-season in an attempt to exorcise an unprecedented injury jinx.

The highly-fancied Brummies saw Kyle Legault break his thigh in their second home match of the season, and both Phil Morris and James Birkinshaw had lengthy early season injury absences.

The team showed its potential by reaching the Premier Trophy Final, including an emphatic away win at King's Lynn which ruined the Stars' hopes of reaching a 100 successive home wins landmark.

Just when the Brummies were able to again put seven riders back on-track, it lasted less than one race as Morris and Adam Roynon – who had been flying – crashed out in Heat 1 at Rye House, and neither rode for the rest of the season.

The pattern had been set, and Drury had to perform several patch-up jobs with both Craig Watson and Tomasz Piszcz making an impression as mid-season signings.

But the effect of the changes was a top-heavy Brummies team with a long tail, especially as Birkinshaw suffered a string of further crashes (and was briefly dropped mid-season too), the returning Legault was injured again in an horrific smash at Sheffield, and promising youngster Jack Roberts took no further part after a crash at the end of August.

Brummies never got any momentum going at Perry Barr with a series of rain-offs, too, and they were regularly beaten on home shale – even though they were a force to be reckoned with on the road, with a total of four away wins.

The home fans were at least able to enjoy the continued excellence of skipper Jason Lyons, and a successful staging of the Elite League Riders' Championship at their well-appointed venue, even though that event, too, was initially a victim of the appalling summer-long weather.

2008 RESULTS

Premier League

Final position ....Twelfth

SCUNTHORPE (H)
Wednesday, April 9
Won 53-37
Rider replacement for Legault, Powell 6:1, **Lyons 18**, Roynon 11:3, Ben Barker [G] 4:3, Hargreaves 3, Smart 11:1.

▲ *Injury-hit side collected a comfortable win with Lyons going through the card from six rides.*

NEWPORT (A)
Sunday, April 13
4-2, abandoned, rain, waterlogged track
Rider replacement for Legault, Chris Schramm [G] 3, Lyons, Roynon, Smart, Mark Burrows [G] 0, Hargreaves, did not ride.

HISTORY

First meeting: July 12, 1928, individual events.
Leagues: Division One, 1949-1957. Division Two, 1947-48; 2007-09. Northern League, 1946. Open licence, 1928, 1960.
Meetings have also been held at the following Birmingham venues.

● *Motordrome Greet, Colebrook Road, Birmingham.*
First meeting: August 6, 1928, mixed event.
Leagues: Open licence, 1928-29.

● *Perry Barr Greyhound Stadium, Walsall Road, Birmingham.*
First meeting: April 13, 1929, individual events.
Leagues: Division One, 1976-1983. Division Two, 1971-75. Southern League, 1929-1930. Open licence, 1930.

● *Hall Green Greyhound Stadium, York Road, Hall Green, Birmingham.*
First meeting: August 3, 1928, Golden Helmet individual meeting.
Leagues: Division One, 1934. Division Two, 1938, Southern League, 1929-1930. Provincial League, 1937. Open licence, 1928, 1931.

● *Birmingham Wheels Project, Adderley Road South, Bordersley Green, Birmingham.*
First meeting: September 2, 1984, Junior Four Team Tournament, Birmingham v Cradley Heath v Long Eaton v Stoke.
Leagues: Division Two, 1985-86. Open licence, 1984.

SQUAD
Jamie Birkinshaw, Mattia Carpanese, James Cockle, Jack Hargreaves, Phil Morris, Jack Roberts, Adam Roynon, Lee Smart.
Foreign: Henning Bager, Jay Herne, Kyle Legault, Jason Lyons, Tomasz Piszcz, Ben Powell, Craig Watson.

SOMERSET (A)
Friday, April 18
Lost 45-48
Rider replacement for Legault, Smart 2:1, Lyons 14:1, James Holder [G] 1, Roynon 17 (6), Hargreaves 5, Jack Roberts [G] 6:3.

STOKE (A)
Saturday, May 3
Lost 36-56
Bager 3, Smart 5:1, Lyons 16:1 (6), *rider replacement for Morris*, Roynon 10, Hargreaves 0, Carpanese 1, Roberts [no. 8] 1.

NEWCASTLE (H)
Wednesday, May 7
Won 46-44
Bager 7:1, Smart 5:1, **Lyons 15**, *rider replacement for Morris*, Roynon 10:1, Jack Roberts [G] 6:2, Carpanese 3, Paul Starke [no. 8].

▼ *Hargreaves (ill) pulled out before the start of meeting.*

GLASGOW (H)
Wednesday, May 14
Won 52-40
Bager 8, Smart 8:3, **Lyons 15**, *rider replacement for Morris*, Roynon 11:1, Hargreaves 6, Jack Roberts [G] 4:1, Paul Starke [no. 8].

READING (A)
Monday, June 9
Lost 42-48
Rider replacement for Roynon, Krzysztof Stojanowski [G] 11:1, Lyons 15, Smart 1:1, Watson 5:1, Clews 9:1, Birkinshaw 1.

ISLE OF WIGHT (A)
Tuesday, June 10
Lost 41-51
Rider replacement for Roynon, Nick Simmons [G] 12 (4), Lyons 17, Smart 2:1, Watson 6, John Oliver [G] 4:1, Birkinshaw 0.

▼ *Injury jinx continued with Birkinshaw and Smart both pulling out after crashing during the meeting.*

WORKINGTON (H)
Wednesday, June 11
Won 47.5-42.5
Rider replacement for Roynon, Robert Ksiezak [G] 9:1, Lyons 13.5:1, Jason Bunyan [G] 4, Watson 7:1, Paul Clews [G] 9:1, Birkinshaw 5:1, Jack Roberts [no. 8].

▲ *Lyons dead-heated for second place with Carl Stonehewer.*

WORKINGTON (A)
Saturday, June 14
Lost 41-51
Rider replacement for Roynon, Andrew Tully [G] 3:2, Lyons 16, Rusty Harrison [G] 10:1 (6), Watson 5:1,

Lee Smethills [G] 3, Birkinshaw 4.

GLASGOW (A)
Sunday, June 15
Won 53-40
Rider replacement for Roynon, Andrew Tully [G] 7:1, Lyons 14, Rusty Harrison [G] 8:2, Watson 15:1, Lee Smethills [G] 4:1, Birkinshaw 5:4.

EDINBURGH (H)
Wednesday, June 18
Lost 40-51
Rider replacement for Roynon, Chris Mills [G] 5, Lyons 12 (2), Krzysztof Stojanowski [G] 9:1, Watson 4, Lee Smethills [G] 0, Birkinshaw 10:1, Jack Roberts [no. 8].

REDCAR (A)
Thursday, June 26
Lost 44-46
Rider replacement for Roynon, Smart 4, Tomas Topinka [G] 15, Watson 11, Andrew Tully [G] 6, Hargreaves 0, Birkinshaw 8:3.
▼ *Hargreaves and guest Andrew Tully joined casualty list.*

KING'S LYNN (H)
Wednesday, July 2
Lost 38-54
Rider replacement for Roynon, Chris Mills [G] 2:1, André Compton [G] 16:1 (4), Smart 0, Watson 8:1, Paul Clews [G] 10:1, Birkinshaw 2.
▼ *Dropped 2-10 down after two races and lost reserve Birkinshaw with suspected internal injuries after a Heat 4 crash with Kozza Smith.*

KING'S LYNN (A)
Friday, July 4
Lost 24-66
James Brundle [G] 5:1 (TS0), Smart 6:1 (1), Legault 6, *rider replacement for Morris*, Watson 0, Adam Lowe [G] 1, Darren Mallett [G][6.
▼ *Legault made his long-awaited comeback – but Watson forced to withdraw with a knee injury after falling in his first ride.*

READING (H)
Wednesday, July 16
Lost 40-49
Legault 6:1, Hargreaves 3:1, Lyons 12, Smart 4:1, Watson 9, Roberts 2, Birkinshaw 4:1.
▲▼ *Managed to track a full seven-man line-up but could take only five race wins on their own circuit, Watson being the pick of the home riders with three wins and a retirement.*

EDINBURGH (A)
Friday, July 18
Lost 29-52
Legault 8, Hargreaves 3:1, Lyons 12 (6), Smart 1, Watson 2, Roberts 3, Birkinshaw 0.
●▼ *Meeting abandoned after Edinburgh's Tomas H Jonasson fell in Heat 14.*
Result stands.

BERWICK (A)
Saturday, July 19
Lost 34-58
Legault 7, Hargreaves 2, Lyons 11 (6), Smart 1, Watson 9, Roberts 1, Birkinshaw 3.

NEWCASTLE (A)
Sunday, July 20
Won 46-44
Legault 5:1, Hargreaves 0, Lyons 11, Smart 6:1, Watson 10:1, Roberts 12:2, Arlo Bugeja [G] 2:1.
▲ *Roberts the hero with a stunning paid 14, Lyons and Watson put the finishing touches to a surprise win by sharing the points in Heat 15.*

REDCAR (H)
Wednesday, July 23
Won 46-45
Legault 12, Hargreaves 2, **Lyons 12**, Smart 3, Watson 9, Roberts 3, Josh Grajczonek [G] 5:2.
▲ *Legault put in his best display since his return, and Lyons scored a maximum before being rested from Heat 15.*

SCUNTHORPE (A)
Friday, July 25
Lost 44-49
Legault 6, Hargreaves 1, Lyons 13 (6), Smart 0, Watson 9:3, Roberts 9:1, Josh Grajczonek [G] 6.

BERWICK (H)
Wednesday, July 30
Lost 42-48
Rider replacement for Smart, Hargreaves 3:1, Lyons 10:2, Legault 6:1, Watson 9:2, Roberts 3:2, Birkinshaw 11:1, Jay Herne [no. 8].
▼ *Shock home defeat against a visiting side inspired by maximum man Adrian Rymel and flying reserve Paul Clews.*

MILDENHALL (A)
Saturday, August 2
Won 55-36
Legault 12, *rider replacement for Hargreaves*, Lyons 9, Smart 8:2, Watson 15:2, Roberts 7:1, Birkinshaw 4:1.
▼ *Easy win wasn't enough to save Birkinshaw, Smart and injured Hargreaves from post-meeting axe as manager Graham Drury acted to re-build his team.*

STOKE (H)
Wednesday, August 6
Lost 46-47
Lyons 18 (6), Roberts 3:1, Piszcz 2, Legault 13:1, Watson 5:1, Cockle 1, Herne 4.
▼ *Piszcz suffered dreadful debut as two-man Brummies lost out to their fierce local rivals, despite an 8-1 in Heat 13.*

SHEFFIELD (A)
Thursday, August 21
Won 44-40
Piszcz 8, Roberts 1, **Lyons 11:1**, Legault 8, Watson 8, Cockle 7:1, Herne 1:1.
▲▼ *Shock victory came at the cost of Legault's season-*

Birmingham ended the season without a trophy – despite winning seven away matches, four in the Premier League, two in the Premier Trophy and a Knock Out Cup tie. Countering that they lost 10 at home in all competitions.

ending crash in Heat 15. He was unable to avoid a fallen Ben Wilson, and he and André Compton tangled with Legault suffering a broken jaw.

SHEFFIELD (H)
Wednesday, August 24
Won 46-44
Piszcz 15:2 (TS2), Roberts 0, **Lyons 15**, *rider replacement for Legault*, Watson 13:1, Cockle 0, Herne 3.
▼▲ *Roberts (burns) joined the casualty list but Brummies mounted an amazing comeback from 28-37 down to snatch victory with a Lyons/Piszcz 5-1 in Heat 15.*

MILDENHALL (H)
Wednesday, August 27
Won 61-32
Piszcz 14:3, Ben Taylor [G] 5, Lyons 9, *rider replacement for Legault*, **Watson 17:1**, Cockle 8:3, Herne 7:1, Adam Lowe [no. 8] 1.
▲ *Youngsters Cockle and guest Ben Taylor make positive impression and Watson untroubled from six rides.*

RYE HOUSE (A)
Saturday, August 30
Lost 40-53
Piszcz 16 (6), Kyle Hughes [G] 1, Lyons 11:1, *rider replacement for Legault*, Watson 9, Cockle 0, Herne 3.

RYE HOUSE (H)
Wednesday, September 10
Lost 42-48
Piszcz 14, *rider replacement for Legault*, Lyons 11, Birkinshaw 7:2, Watson 6:1, Herne 1:1, Ben Taylor [G] 3:1.
▲ *Birkinshaw returned and gained speed throughout the meeting.*

ISLE OF WIGHT (H)
Wednesday, September 17
Won 52-38
Piszcz 14:2, *rider replacement for Legault*, Lyons 12, Birkinshaw 5:1, Watson 14, Herne 2:1, Ben Taylor [G] 5:2.
▲ *Spirited fightback from 12-18 down and a super show from Piszcz, Watson and Lyons with 11 heat wins between them.*

Weather...

Birmingham suffered dreadfully from a wet summer and had ten home team matches called off because of rain – most approaching start-time.

Premier League
Wednesday, April 16 .... SOMERSET (H)
Sunday, April 30 .... SOMERSET (H)
Sunday, May 4 .... STOKE (H)
Wednesday, July 9 .... ISLE OF WIGHT (H)
Wednesday, September 3 .... SOMERSET (H)

Premier Trophy
Friday, March 21 .... KING'S LYNN (A)
Friday, March 21 .... KING'S LYNN (H)
Sunday, April 27 .... KING'S LYNN (H)
Sunday, May 25 .... KING'S LYNN (H)
Wednesday, August 13 .... EDINBURGH (H)

Knock Out Cup
Wednesday, May 28 .... RYE HOUSE (H)

Individual
Wednesday, August 20 .... ELRC (H)

...beaten

SOMERSET (H)
Wednesday, September 24
Won 48-44
Piszcz 7:1, *rider replacement for Legault*, **Lyons 15**, Birkinshaw 5, Watson 10, Herne 9, Ben Taylor [G] 2.
▲ *Brummies' win confirmed Edinburgh as Premier League Champions, with Lyons and Watson the heroes with a match-clinching 4-2 in Heat 15.*

PREMIER LEAGUE

	M	W	D	L	PtsF	PtsA	Pts
1 Edinburgh	30	22	2	6	1562	1161	53
2 Somerset	30	21	0	9	1517	1223	48
3 King's Lynn	30	18	5	7	1624	1111	45
4 Rye House	30	19	0	11	1500	1232	42
5 Workington	30	17	2	11	1435.5	1300.5	41
6 Berwick	30	16	2	12	1428	1316	37
7 Redcar	30	16	1	13	1369	1374	37
8 Sheffield	30	15	2	13	1381	1345	35
9 Reading	30	15	1	14	1350	1405	34
10 Scunthorpe	30	15	0	15	1309	1434	33
11 Isle of Wight	30	15	0	15	1359	1390	31
12 BIRMINGHAM	**30**	**13**	**0**	**17**	**1317.5**	**1401.5**	**30**
13 Stoke	30	11	1	18	1307	1441	25
14 Newcastle	30	10	0	20	1220	1501	22
15 Glasgow	30	9	0	21	1297	1469	19
16 Mildenhall	30	0	0	30	932	1804	0

Young Shield

Quarter Final, first leg
BERWICK (H)
Wednesday, October 1
Won 50-42
Piszcz 11, *rider replacement for Legault*, Lyons 14, Lee Smart [G] 3, Watson 13:3, Herne 2:1, Krister Jacobsen [G] 7.

Quarter Final, second leg
BERWICK (A)
Saturday, October 4
Lost 40-50
Piszcz 11:1, *rider replacement for Legault*, Lyons 14, Anders Andersen [G] 1, Watson 11, Herne 0, Ben Taylor [G] 3.
▼ *Still held a six-point aggregate lead with four heats to go, but conceded 5-1s in Heats 13 and 14, and couldn't quite hit back with maximum points in the finale.*
Aggregate: Lost 90-92.

Premier Trophy

MILDENHALL (H)
Wednesday, March 26
Won 60-33
Legault 10:2, Birkinshaw 5, **Lyons 14:1**, Roynon 7:2, Morris 9:1, Hargreaves 8:1, Smart 7:2.

RYE HOUSE (H)
Wednesday, April 2
Won 50-36
Legault 2, Birkinshaw 0, **Lyons 12**, Roynon 7:2, Morris 5:2, Hargreaves 13:2, Smart 11:1.
▼ *Legault (fractured femur) crashed in Heat 6. Jamie*

Birkinshaw also involved and did not take his remaining rides.
● *Abandoned after Heat 14, time curfew.*

RYE HOUSE (A)
Saturday, April 5
Lost 36-54
Rider replacement for Legault, Jack Roberts [G] 2:1, Lyons 6:1, Roynon 7:1 (1), Morris 13, Hargreaves 7:1, Smart 1.

MILDENHALL (A)
Sunday, April 6
Won 42-32
Rider replacement for Legault, Jack Roberts [G] 3, Lyons 9, Roynon 6:2, Morris 9:1, Hargreaves 6:1, Smart 9:2.
▼▼ *Meeting abandoned after Heat 12 because of a lack of medical cover after Casper Wortmann was seriously injured. Lyons (arm) had already pulled out of the meeting before the Heat 13 crash which left Morris with broken ribs and punctured lung.*

KING'S LYNN (A)
Friday, April 11
Won 55-39
Rider replacement for Legault, Mark Burrows [G] 4:3, Lyons 14, Roynon 11:3, Ben Barker [G] 6:1, Hargreaves 3:1, Smart 17:2.
▲ *One of the results of the season as the patched-up Brummies adapted far better to wet conditions with Smart putting in a career-best performance.*

KING'S LYNN (H)
Sunday, October 19
Lost 43-47
Piszcz 6:1, *rider replacement for Legault*, **Lyons 15**, Birkinshaw 3, Watson 12, Herne 1:1, Ben Taylor [G] 6:1.
▼ *The long-delayed meeting finally went ahead and went to a last-heat decider – but whilst Lyons wrapped up his maximum, Watson was shut out by Kevin Doolan and Tomas Topinka.*

PREMIER TROPHY Group C

		M	W	D	L	PtsF	PtsA	Pts
1	BIRMINGHAM	6	4	0	2	243	194	10
2	Rye House	6	4	0	2	291	250	9
3	King's Lynn	6	3	0	3	245	211	7
4	Mildenhall	6	1	0	5	203	327	2

Semi Final, first leg
SHEFFIELD (H)
Wednesday, June 4
Won 57-37
Rider replacement for Roynon, Chris Mills [G] 9, Lyons 15, Smart 6:2, Watson 14, Hargreaves 2:1, Birkinshaw 11:2, Jack Roberts (no. 8).
▲ *Best home performance of season with Watson making an impressive home debut.*

Semi Final, second leg
SHEFFIELD (A)
Thursday, June 5
Lost 37-53
Rider replacement for Roynon, Chris Mills [G] 5:2, Lyons 9, Smart 0, Watson 13, Hargreaves 0, Birkinshaw 10:2.
Aggregate: Won 94-90.

FINAL, first leg
EDINBURGH (A)
Friday, August 15
Lost 24-65
Piszcz 5:1, Roberts 4, Lyons 2 (0), Legault 9, Watson 2, Cockle 2, Herne 0.
▼ *A thrashing at Armadale virtually ended Brummies hopes of Premier Trophy success.*

PHOTO: **Dave Valentine**

Birmingham: *Jack Hargreaves, Phil Morris, Jamie Birkinshaw, Jason Lyons, Kyle Legault, Lee Smart and Adam Roynon*

FINAL, second leg
EDINBURGH (H)
Sunday, September 28
Lost 41-52
Piszcz 11 (6), *rider replacement for Legault*, Lyons 12:1, Birkinshaw 1:1, Watson 12:1, Herne 0, Ben Taylor [G] 5.
▼ *Had no answer to the strength of the new Premier League Champions in an entertaining meeting. Birkinshaw (concussion) crashed out in Heat 6.*
Aggregate: Lost 65-117.

Knock Out Cup

Second round, first leg
GLASGOW (A)
Sunday, April 20
Won 52-40
Rider replacement for Legault, Smart 8, **Lyons 16:2**, Jason King [G] 11:1, Roynon 10:1, Hargreaves 1:1, Jack Roberts [G] 6:2.
▲ *Jason King an impressive guest as Brummies made virtually certain of reaching the quarter-finals.*

Second round, second leg
GLASGOW (H)
Wednesday, April 23
Lost 43-47
Rider replacement for Legault, Smart 5:2, Lyons 16:1, Chris Schramm [G] 5:2, Roynon 14, Hargreaves 3, Carpanese 0, Jack Roberts [no. 8] 0.
▼ *Shock home defeat included miserable Perry Barr debut for Carpanese – but overall progression was never in doubt.*
Aggregate: Won 95-87.

Quarter Final, first leg
RYE HOUSE (A)
Saturday, May 31
Lost 30-62
Roynon 0, Morris 0, Lyons 10, Smart 4:1, Watson 5, Hargreaves 3, Birkinshaw 8:1.
▼ *Roynon (broken leg) and Morris (shoulder) involved in a first heat crash.*

Quarter Final, second leg
RYE HOUSE (H)
Wednesday, June 25
Lost 42-51
Rider replacement for Roynon, Smart 3, Lyons 3, Watson 14:1, Robert Ksiezak [G] 10 (6), Hargreaves 1:1, Birkinshaw 11:2, Jack Roberts [no. 8] 0.
▲ *Lyons broke track record but then suffered a broken collarbone in an horrific Heat 5 crash.*
Aggregate: Lost 72-113.

Midland Shield

WOLVERHAMPTON (A)
Monday, September 22
Lost 44-48
Davey Watt [G] 13, Watson 4, Edward Kennett [G] 10, Piszcz 0, Lyons 12:1 (4), Birkinshaw 1, Ben Wilson [G] 4.

WOLVERHAMPTON (H)
Wednesday October 15
Lost 42-48
Piszcz 12, Watson 4, Lyons 11:1, Birkinshaw 2:2, James Wright [G] 9:1, Herne 3, Ben Taylor [G] 1:1.
Aggregate: Lost 86-96.

For details of Alan Hunt Memorial Trophy see page 244.

2009 Squad
Jason **LYONS** (9.98), Tomasz **PISZCZ** (7.11), Ludvig **LINDGREN** (7.00), Robert **KSIEZAK** (6.62), Richard **SWEETMAN** (5.00), Marek **MROZ** (3.50), Ben **TAYLOR** (3.00).

BIRMINGHAM

Rider	*M*	*R*	*Pts*	*BP*	*TPts*	*Ave*	*F*	*P*	*TR*	*TPts*	*TS*	*TSPts*
Jason LYONS	43	214	538.5	13	551.5	10.31	9	3	8	18	0	0
Adam ROYNON	**13**	**62**	**121**	**16**	**137**	**8.84**	**0**	**0**	**2**	**3**	**0**	**0**
Phil MORRIS	5	19	36	4	40	8.42	0	0	0	0	0	0
Tomasz PISZCZ	**13**	**69**	**134**	**9**	**143**	**8.29**	**0**	**1**	**2**	**6**	**1**	**1**
Craig WATSON	34	174	311	23	334	7.68	0	1	0	0	0	0
Kyle LEGAULT	**14**	**63**	**110**	**6**	**116**	**7.36**	**0**	**0**	**0**	**0**	**0**	**0**
Henning BAGER	3	12	18	1	19	6.33	0	0	0	0	0	0
Jamie BIRKINSHAW	**24**	**105**	**123**	**23**	**146**	**5.56**	**0**	**0**	**0**	**0**	**0**	**0**
Lee SMART	28	126	138	26	164	5.21	0	0	1	0	0	0
Jack ROBERTS	**12**	**53**	**48**	**8**	**56**	**4.23**	**0**	**0**	**0**	**0**	**0**	**0**
Jack HARGREAVES	23	97	75	12	87	3.59	0	0	0	0	0	0
James COCKLE	**6**	**25**	**18**	**4**	**22**	**3.52**	**0**	**0**	**0**	**0**	**0**	**0**
Jay HERNE	13	52	33	6	39	3.00	0	0	0	0	0	0
Mattia CARPANESE	**3**	**12**	**4**	**0**	**4**	**1.33**	**0**	**0**	**0**	**0**	**0**	**0**
Guests	***58***	***281***	***312***	***49***	***361***	***5.14***	***0***	***0***	***3***	***8***	***2***	***2***

For Craig WATSON see Newport; for Henning BAGER see Berwick and Peterborough; for Jamie BIRKINSHAW see Scunthorpe (CL); for Lee SMART see Mildenhall and Weymouth; for Jack ROBERTS see Buxton; for James COCKLE see Mildenhall, Peterborough, Boston and Redcar (CL); for Jay HERNE see Weymouth.

Premier League

EDINBURGH

TRACK FILE

Track: Armadale Stadium, 2 Bathgate Road, Armadale, West Lothian, EH48 2PD.
Telephone: 01501 734404.
Hotline: 09068 664675.
Website: www.edinburghspeedway.com
Track Length: 260 metres.
Track Record: 54.6 secs, Theo Pijper, September 22, 2006.
Promoters: John Campbell and Alex Harkess.
Team Sponsors: Scotwaste Recycling.
Colours: Royal blue and gold with crown.
Nickname: Monarchs.

HONOURS

Major honours: 11.
Division Two champions (2), 2003, 2008.
Division Two Knock Out Cup winners (3), 1981, 1997, 1999.
Division Two Premier Trophy winners (1), 2008.
Division Two Four Team champions (2), 1981, 1993.
Division Two Pairs champions (1), 1986.
Division Two Premiership winners (1), 1998.
Division Three Trophy winners (1), 2005 (as Armadale).

2008 CHAMPIONS PHOTO
www.sports-media-partnership.com

2008 REVIEW

MONARCHS made several crucial team-building decisions over the winter – and were rewarded for their judgement with arguably the greatest season in their history.

Key to the success of the Armadale side was the fact that all seven of their starting line-up had significant potential for improvement, and that was exactly how the campaign panned out.

Edinburgh's first major transfer move was to give American star Ryan Fisher his first-ever outings in the Premier League after a troubled time in the Elite with Belle Vue in 2007 – and Fisher proved to be a huge success.

Promising young Swede Thomas H. Jonasson also showed why he is such a hot prospect, although he missed the conclusion of the season due to a broken leg.

Number one rider William Lawson was another to be injury hit with a lengthy broken collarbone absence but the Monarchs always had the strength in depth to cover for absentees, with both Andrew Tully and Matthew Wethers recording spectacular scores during their outings at reserve.

The first serious signal of intent came when the Monarchs drew 45-45 at King's Lynn in mid-April, and a 58-34 win at fierce rivals Glasgow in the Premier Trophy further increased the feel-good factor.

Progress was sound in all competitions and as the title race came down to the Monarchs versus Somerset, it was the Scottish club's better away record which tipped the balance in their favour – seven wins and two draws on the road being hugely impressive.

They won the Premier Trophy, too, overcoming Birmingham in the Final by winning both legs although their hopes of a treble were ended by Workington in the Knockout Cup.

Monarchs also contested the first-ever promotion/relegation race-off and gave a strong account of themselves against Elite League basement club Wolverhampton before the top flight club prevailed.

SQUAD
William Lawson, Derek Sneddon, Andrew Tully.
Foreign: Ryan Fisher, Thomas H. Jonasson, Aaron Summers, Matthew Wethers.

HISTORY

First meeting: April 4, 1997, Edinburgh v Glasgow, Spring Trophy.
Leagues: Division Two, 1997-2009. Division Three, 2003-05 (raced as Armadale).
Meetings have also been held at the following Edinburgh venues.

● *Marine Gardens, Seafield Road, Portobello, Edinburgh.*
First meeting: May 19, 1928, Gold Helmet international.
Leagues: Northern League, 1930. Open licence, 1928-29, 1931, 1938-39.

● *Old Meadowbank Stadium, Clockmill Road, Edinburgh.*
First meeting: April 17, 1948, Edinburgh v Glasgow, Division Two.
Leagues: Division One, 1965-67. Division Two, 1948-54, 1960-64. Open licence, 1959.

■ *After the closure of Old Meadowbank at the end of the 1967 season, the Monarchs decamped and spent two seasons at*

● *Cliftonhill Stadium, Main Street, Coatbridge, Lanarkshire.*
First meeting: April 6, 1968, Monarchs v Glasgow, Champagne Derby.
Leagues: Division One, 1968-69.

● *Powderhall Stadium, Beaverhall Road, Edinburgh.*
First meeting: April 15, 1977, Edinburgh v Berwick, Division Two challenge.
Leagues: Division One, 1995. Division Two, 1977-1994.
Edinburgh also raced as the Scottish Monarchs at

● *Shawfield Stadium, Glasgow Road, Rutherglen, Glasgow.*
First meeting: April 24, 1996, Scottish Monarchs v Reading, Division One.
Leagues: Division One, 1996.

Did you know?

Reading's Mark Lemon made five guest appearances for Edinburgh in a 22 -day period in August – including four appearances at Armadale.

2008 RESULTS

Premier League

Final position........................CHAMPIONS (First)

REDCAR (A)
Thursday, April 10
26-28, abandoned after nine heats, rain.
Fisher 4, Sneddon 1:1, Jonasson 5, Lawson 1:1, Wethers 6, Tully 3, Summers 6.

KING'S LYNN (A)
Wednesday, April 16
Drew 45-45
Fisher 6:1, Sneddon 6:1, Jonasson 9:1, Lawson 9:2, Wethers 4:1, Summers 2:1, Tully 9:1.
▲*Came within one race of becoming the second visiting team in succession to win at the Norfolk Arena, only for Lawson and Jonasson to lose out to Tomas Topinka and Kevin Doolan in Heat 15 – but still a notable draw.*

KING'S LYNN (H)
Friday, May 2
Won 54-39
Lawson 14, *rider replacement for Jonasson*, Sneddon 10, Fisher 9:3, Wethers 9, Tully 7:4, Summers 5:1.
▲ *Lawson won his first four rides before being beaten by Stars guest Shane Parker in Heat 15 of a competitive meeting.*

READING (H)
Friday, May 9
Won 49-43
Sneddon 6:1, Fisher 12, Lawson 10, *rider replacement for Jonasson*, Wethers 7:2, Tully 5, Summers 9:3.
▲ *Had to wait until Heat 14 to confirm victory, Fisher crucially holding off the tactical substitute Ulrich Østergaard.*

RYE HOUSE (A)
Saturday, May 10
Lost 42-48
Lawson 8:1, *rider replacement for Jonasson*, Sneddon 0, Fisher 5:1, Wethers 11:1, Tully 13:2, Summers 5:1.

MILDENHALL (A)
Sunday, May 11
Won 60-30
Lawson 12:2, *rider replacement for Jonasson*, Sneddon 7:2, Fisher 9:1, Wethers 7:3, Tully 15, Summers 10:3.

SCUNTHORPE (H)
Friday, May 23
Won 68-22
Lawson 15, Jonasson 6:1, Sneddon 6:1, Fisher 8:3, **Wethers 11:4, Tully 15**, Summers 7:4.

SCUNTHORPE (A)
Monday, May 26
Won 53-39
Lawson 9:2, Jonasson 7:1, Sneddon 1:1, Fisher 13:1, Wethers 7:1, Tully 14:1, Summers 2.
▲*First nine heats finished 3-3 but Monarchs then scored*

two consecutive 5-1s to take command.

ISLE OF WIGHT (H)
Friday, June 6
Won 67-23
Tomas Topinka [G] 8:3, Fisher 14:3, Sneddon 8, *rider replacement for Jonasson*, Wethers 10:3, **Tully 21**, Summers 6.
▲ *Spectacular seven-ride maximum from reserve Tully, with Fisher beaten only once in six starts.*

SHEFFIELD (A)
Thursday, June 12
Lost 36-55
Lawson 6, Fisher 2:2, Sneddon 2:2, Jonasson 12 (4), Wethers 4, Tully 4, Summers 6:2.

BIRMINGHAM (A)
Wednesday, June 18
Won 51-40
Lawson 10:1, Jonasson 7:1, Sneddon 8, Wethers 5:2, Fisher 12:1, Tully 5:2, Summers 4.
▲ *Suffered falls and retirements in four of the first five races but dominated afterwards.*

SHEFFIELD (H)
Friday, June 20
Won 56-33
Lawson 15, Adam McKinna [G] 2, Sneddon 7:1, Wethers 10:2, Fisher 5:1, Tully 12:2, Summers 5:1.
▼ *Fisher suffered two exclusions and was unhappy to be adjudged the cause of Ricky Ashworth's fall in Heat 11.*

STOKE (H)
Friday, July 4
Won 54-39
Lawson 2, *rider replacement for Jonasson*, Tully 5:2, Fisher 13:1, Wethers 14:3, Sneddon 17, Summers 3:1.
▼ *Lawson crashed in Heat 6 and was ruled out with a broken collar bone.*

STOKE (A)
Saturday, July 5
28-26, match abandoned after nine heats, rain.
Ricky Ashworth [G] 3, *rider replacement for Jonasson*, Tully 6:1, Wethers 4:1, Fisher 7, Summers 1:1, Sneddon 7:1.

RYE HOUSE (H)
Friday, July 11
Won 47-46
Mark Lemon [G] 7, Jonasson 5:3, Tully 6, Fisher 4:1, Wethers 8:2, Sneddon 12, Summers 5:1.

READING (A)
Sunday, July 13
Won 48-41
Krzysztof Stojanowski [G] 6:2, Jonasson 12:1, Tully 3:1, Fisher 5:1, Wethers 4:2, Sneddon 14, Summers 4:1.
▲ *First team to win at Smallmead in Premier League.*

ISLE OF WIGHT (A)
Tuesday, July 15
Lost 32-60
Carl Stonehewer [G] 6, Jonasson 5, Tully 4:1, Fisher 9 (4), Wethers 5:1, Sneddon 3, Summers 0.

BIRMINGHAM (H)
Friday, July 18
Won 52-29
Carl Stonehewer [G] 8:1, Sneddon 8:2, Tully 7:3, Fisher 7:1, Wethers 6:2, Jonasson 8:1, Summers 8:1.
▼ *Meeting abandoned after Thomas H. Jonasson came off in Heat 14. Result to stand.*

REDCAR (H)
Friday, July 25
Won 55-37
Carl Stonehewer [G] 0, Jonasson 7:1, Tully 10:2, Fisher 11:1, Wethers 5:1, Sneddon 10, Summers 12:2.
▼ *Stonehewer brought down in Heat 1 and unfit to take part in the rest of the meeting.*

BERWICK (A)
Saturday, August 2
Drew 45-45
Josef Franc [G] 5:3, Sneddon 8, Jonasson 8, Wethers 7:2, Fisher 7, Tully 6, Summers 4.
▼ *Conceded last-gasp 5-1 with Jonasson and Wethers both being overtaken in Heat 15, and Jonasson subsequently coming to grief heavily.*

MILDENHALL (H)
Friday, August 8
Won 69-21
Mark Lemon [G] 9:1, Sneddon 12:1, *rider replacement for Jonasson*, Wethers 12:2, **Fisher 13:2**, Tully 16:3, Summers 7:2.

WORKINGTON (H) SKY TV
Monday, August 11
Won 59-30
Mark Lemon [G] 13:1, Sneddon 3:1, Jonasson 8:1, Wethers 7:2, Fisher 7:2, Tully 12:1, Summers 9:2.
▲ *Big crowd for TV fixture, which the Monarchs won much more easily than had been expected.*

WORKINGTON (A)
Saturday, August 16
Lost 39-53
Kyle Legault [G] 12 (4), Sneddon 2:1, *rider replacement for Jonasson*, Wethers 4:1, Fisher 13, Tully 8, Summers 0.

BERWICK (H)
Friday, August 22
Won 59-33
Mark Lemon [G] 7:2, Sneddon 6, Jonasson 6:1, Wethers 9, Fisher 12:2, Tully 10:2, Summers 9:2.

SOMERSET (A)
Wednesday, August 27
Lost 44-48
Mark Lemon [G] 8, Sneddon 3, Jonasson 6:1, Wethers 10:1, Fisher 14:1 (4), Tully 3:1, Summers 0.

SOMERSET (H)
Friday, August 29
Won 66-24
Mark Lemon [G] 9:1, Sneddon 8:3, Jonasson 4:1, Matthew Wethers 12:2, Ryan Fisher 11:3, Andrew Tully 14:2, Aaron Summers 8:1.

▲ *Monarchs showed exactly why they were title favourites with crushing success against their closest rivals, racking up ten 5-1s.*

STOKE (A)
Saturday, August 30
Won 57-36
Magnus Karlsson [G] 8:3, Sneddon 7:1, Jonasson 12, Wethers 9:1, Fisher 10, Tully 8:2, Summers 3:1.
▲ *Another big step towards the title, 14-4 up after Heat 3 and didn't give the home side a sniff.*

REDCAR (A)
Thursday, September 11
Lost 41-49
Lawson 4, Sneddon 9, *rider replacement for Jonasson*, Tully 10, Fisher 4, Wethers 7:2, Summers 7:3 (TS0).

NEWCASTLE (H)
Friday, September 12
Won 64-29
Lawson 8:3, Sneddon 11, *rider replacement for Jonasson*, **Tully 14:1**, Fisher 11:3, Wethers 12:3, Summers 8:3.

NEWCASTLE (A)
Sunday, September 14
Won 49-40
Lawson 12:1, Sneddon 2, *rider replacement for Jonasson*, Tully 4, Fisher 8, **Wethers 21**, Summers 2:1.
▲ *Career-best performance from Wethers, almost single-handedly responsible for this away victory with seven straight wins.*

GLASGOW (H)
Friday, September 19
Won 54-39
Lawson 14:1, Sneddon 7:1, *rider replacement for Jonasson*, Tully 9:1, Fisher 12:2, Wethers 9:3, Summers 3.
▲ *Not the Monarchs' best display of such a successful season, with track conditions tricky – but still enough to see off their local rivals, for whom Shane Parker (19) was superb.*

GLASGOW (A)
Sunday, October 12
Won 47-45
Lawson 4:1, *rider replacement for Jonasson*, Fisher 14:1 (4), Tully 7:1, Wethers 14:2, Sneddon 8, Summers 0.
▲ *Again won at Ashfield in stunning fashion, taking the last seven heats by a 28-14 margin with Fisher and Wethers gating to a 5-1 to complete the comeback in Heat 15.*

Play offs

Semi final, first leg
SOMERSET (H)
Friday, October 3
Won 57-36
Tomasz Piszcz [G] 6:3, *rider replacement for Jonasson*, Fisher 12:1, Tully 12:2, Wethers 9:2, Sneddon 9, Summers 9:1.
▲ *Roared into a 43-17 lead after 10 races before being pegged back by an 8-1 in Heat 11.*

Semi final, second leg
SOMERSET (A)
Wednesday, October 8
Lost 39-53
Lawson 1:1, *rider replacement for Jonasson*, Fisher 13:1 (4), Tully 6:2, Wethers 12, Sneddon 7:2, Summers 0.
▲ *Found themselves under early pressure with an 11-25 deficit on the night, but Fisher and Wethers sparked the revival.*

Aggregate: Won 96-89.

FINAL, first leg
KING'S LYNN (H)
Friday, October 17
Won 55-38
Lawson 7, *rider replacement for Jonasson*, Fisher 10:1, Tully 11:1, Wethers 14:1, Sneddon 0, Summers 13:5.
▼▲ *Sneddon fractured his jaw after crashing in Heat 2 and being unable to take his place in the re-run.*

FINAL, second leg
KING'S LYNN (A)
Friday, October 18
Lost 38-52
Lawson 4:1, *rider replacement for Jonasson*, Fisher 2 (FX), Tully 8:1, Weathers 7:1, James Brundle [G] 7:2, Summers 10.
▲ *Pressure was on when Fisher crashed on a tactical ride in Heat 8, but an eventual Summers/Tully 5-1 in Heat 14 secured the victory.*

Aggregate: Won 93-90.

PREMIER LEAGUE

		M	*W*	*D*	*L*	*PtsF*	*PtsA*	*Pts*
1	**EDINBURGH**	**30**	**22**	**2**	**6**	**1562**	**1161**	**53**
2	Somerset	30	21	0	9	1517	1223	48
3	King's Lynn	30	18	5	7	1624	1111	45
4	Rye House	30	19	0	11	1500	1232	42
5	Workington	30	17	2	11	1435.5	1300.5	41
6	Berwick	30	16	2	12	1428	1316	37
7	Redcar	30	16	1	13	1369	1374	37
8	Sheffield	30	15	2	13	1381	1345	35
9	Reading	30	15	1	14	1350	1405	34
10	Scunthorpe	30	15	0	15	1309	1434	33
11	Isle of Wight	30	15	0	15	1359	1390	31
12	Birmingham	30	13	0	17	1317.5	1401.5	30
13	Stoke	30	11	1	18	1307	1441	25
14	Newcastle	30	10	0	20	1220	1501	22
15	Glasgow	30	9	0	21	1297	1469	19
16	Mildenhall	30	0	0	30	932	1804	0

Promotion Play offs

First leg
WOLVERHAMPTON (H)
Friday, October 24
Lost 37-53
Lawson 4, *rider replacement for Jonasson*, Fisher 14 (F), Tully 6, Wethers 4, Chris Schramm [G] 7:3, Summers 2.
▲▼ *Fisher showed his pedigree against Elite League opponents and was unlucky to crash when on a tactical ride.*

Second leg
WOLVERHAMPTON (A)
Monday, October 27
Lost 39-53
Lawson 6, *rider replacement for Jonasson*, Fisher 16:1 (4), Tully 8:1, Wethers 0, James Brundle [G] 7:1, Summers 2:1.
▲▼ *Further enhanced their reputation with a battling showing on the Elite League track – with Fisher and Tully twice combining for 5-1s, and guest James Brundle sensationally heading home Fredrik Lindgren in Heat 6.*
Aggregate: Lost 76-106.

Premier Trophy

BERWICK (A)
Saturday, March 15
Won 48-42
Fisher 6:2, Sneddon 9:1, Jonasson 4:1, Lawson 10, Wethers 10, Summers 2:2, Tully 7:1.

BERWICK (H)
Friday, March 21
Won 56-35
Fisher 12:1, Sneddon 8:2, Jonasson 5:1, Lawson 9, Wethers 9:1, Summers 8:1, Tully 5:1.
▼ *Lawson's eight-race home winning run ended with engine failure in Heat 14.*

WORKINGTON (H)
Friday, March 28
Won 56-37
Fisher 7, Sneddon 9:2, *rider replacement for Jonasson*, Lawson 14:2, Wethers 10:1, Tully 10:1, Summers 6:2.
▼ *Visiting No.1 Daniel Nermark scored a five-ride maximum but a home win was never threatened.*

GLASGOW (H)
Friday, April 4
Won 57-36
Fisher 9:3, Sneddon 11:1, *rider replacement for Jonasson*, Lawson 16:1, Wethers 13:1, Tully 3:2, Summers 5:1.

WORKINGTON (A)
Saturday, April 5
Lost 45-48
Fisher 8, Sneddon 9:1, *rider replacement for Jonasson*, Lawson 11:2, Wethers 11:1, Tully 5:1, Summers 1:1.

GLASGOW (A)
Sunday, April 27
Won 58-34
Sneddon 7:1, Fisher 6:2, Lawson 10:2, Jonasson 10:1, Wethers 10:3, Tully 4:1, **Summers 11:1**.

PREMIER TROPHY Group A

		M	W	D	L	PtsF	PtsA	Pts
1	**EDINBURGH**	**6**	**5**	**0**	**1**	**320**	**231**	**12**
2	Workington	6	4	0	2	287	264	9
3	Glasgow	6	2	0	4	240	313	4
4	Berwick	6	1	0	5	255	294	2

Semi Final, first leg
READING (H)
Friday, June 16
Won 56-34
Lawson 11, Jonasson 0, Sneddon 7:3, Wethers 8:1, Fisher 12, Tully 13:4, Summers 5:1.

Semi Final, second leg
READING (A)
Monday, June 23
Lost 44-46
Lawson 8:1, Jonasson 6, Sneddon 8, Wethers 6:1, Fisher 12:1, Tully 4, Summers 0.
Aggregate: Won 100-80.

FINAL, first leg
BIRMINGHAM (H)
Friday, August 15
Won 65-24
Mark Lemon [G] 8:3, Sneddon 9, *rider replacement for Jonasson*, Wethers 12:2, Fisher 18, Tully 10:1, Summers 8:4.

FINAL, second leg
BIRMINGHAM (A)
Sunday, September 28
Won 52-41
Lawson 9:2, Sneddon 7, *rider replacement for Jonasson*, Tully 6:2, Fisher 17, Wethers 5:1, Summers 8:2.
Aggregate: Won 117-65.

Knock Out Cup

Second round, first leg
BERWICK (H)
Friday, April 25
Won 54-38
Sneddon 4:2, Fisher 14, James Grieves [G] 13:1, Jonasson 5:1, Wethers 9, Lee Dicken [G] 5:1, Summers 4:2.
▲ *James Grieves guested for Lawson, at the British U21 Final.*

Second round, second leg
BERWICK (A)
Saturday, April 26
Won 51-42
Sneddon 3:2, Fisher 12:1, Lawson 6:1, Jonasson 8:1, Wethers 12, Tully 6:2, Summers 4:1.
Aggregate: Won 105-80.

Quarter Final, first leg
REDCAR (A)
Thursday, May 29
Won 55-38
Tomas Topinka [G] 8:2, *rider replacement for Jonasson*, Sneddon 2:1, Fisher 16:1, Wethers 12, Tully 11:1, Summers 6:2.
▲ *Lawson (British Final) and Jonasson (U21 qualifier) absent.*

Quarter Final, second leg
REDCAR (H)
Friday, May 30
Won 55-38
Lawson 15, *rider replacement for Jonasson*, Sneddon 6, Fisher 13, Wethers 14:2, Sean Stoddart [G] 6:1,

Summers 1:1.

Aggregate: Won 110-76.

Semi Final, first leg
WORKINGTON (H)
Friday, September 26
Won 49-41
Lawson 6:2, Sneddon 10, *rider replacement for Jonasson*, Tully 12:1, Fisher 12, Wethers 8:2, Summers 1.
▼ *First-bend falls for Fisher (twice) and Tully didn't help the Monarchs' hopes of building a first-leg lead.*

Semi Final, second leg
WORKINGTON (A)
Saturday, September 27
Lost 39-53
Lawson 3, Sneddon 9, *rider replacement for Jonasson*, Tully 6:1, Fisher 12 (4), Wethers 9:1, Summers 0.
▼ *Hopes of a League and Cup double were ended despite a fine effort at Derwent Park. Aggregate scores were level with three heats to go but it was the Comets who took advantages in two of those races.*

Aggregate: Lost 88-94.

Individual

SCOTTISH OPEN CHAMPIONSHIP
Friday, August 1

Monarchs' hero Rory Schlein, who spent his formative years in Scotland, returned to Armadale to claim his second Scottish Open Championship.

Four years after his first victory he underlined his top-flight status with a peerless six-win performance to deny Andrew Tully what would have been an equally popular victory.

	1	*2*	*3*	*4*	*5*	*Tot*	*SF*	*F*
1 Rory SCHLEIN	**3**	**3**	**3**	**3**	**3**	**15**	**–**	**3**
2 Travis McGOWAN	3	0	1	3	3	10	3	2
3 Joe SCREEN	3	2	1	3	3	12	–	1
4 Andrew TULLY	3	3	2	2	2	12	2	0
5 Aaron SUMMERS	2	2	2	2	1	9	1	
6 Ryan FISHER	2	3	3	3	R	11	R	
7 Robert KSIEZAK	1	2	2	2	1	8		
8 George STANCL	2	1	3	1	0	7		
9 Trent LEVERINGTON	1	0	3	1	2	7		
10 Matthew WETHERS	F	1	F	2	3	6		
11 Tyron PROCTOR	1	3	0	1	1	6		
12 Michal MAKOVSKY	2	0	2	0	2	6		
13 Derek SNEDDON	R	2	1	1	2	6		
14 Tero AARNIO	1	1	0	0	0	2		
15 Anders ANDERSEN	0	1	0	0	F	1		
16 James GRIEVES	FN					0		

Roll of Honour

1960	Doug TEMPLETON
1961	Trevor REDMOND
1962	Doug TEMPLETON
1963	Maury MATTINGLEY
1964	George HUNTER
1965	Arne PANDER
1966	Bill LANDELS
1967	Barry BRIGGS
1968	Martin ASHBY
1969	Reidar EIDE
1970	Ivan MAUGER
1971	Ivan MAUGER
1972	Ivan MAUGER
1973	Ivan MAUGER
1975	Brian COLLINS
1976	Peter COLLINS
1977	Bert HARKINS
†1981	Wayne BROWN
§1983	Phil COLLINS
1984	Mitch SHIRRA
1985	Jamie LUCKHURST
1986	Les COLLINS
1987	Neville TATUM
1988	Steve LAWSON
1989	Todd WILTSHIRE
1990	Les COLLINS
1991	Greg HANCOCK
1992	Greg HANCOCK
1993	Michael COLES
1994	Ben HOWE
1995	Bobby OTT
1996	Shane PARKER
1997	Peter CARR
1998	Frede SCHØTT
1999	Peter CARR
2000	Peter CARR
2001	André COMPTON
2002	Peter CARR
2003	Sam ERMOLENKO
2004	Rory SCHLEIN
2005	David HOWE
2006	Stanislaw BURZA
2007	Daniel NERMARK
2008	Rory SCHLEIN

■ *Staged at Old Meadowbank (1960-67, 1973-76), Coatbridge (1968-69), Hampden Park, Glasgow (1970-71), Blantyre (1977), Powderhall (1981-1996) and Armadale (1997-2008).*
†Winner of Carlo Biagi Testimonial. §Winner of George Hunter Testimonial.

Four Team Challenge

EDINBURGH MONARCHS DIAMOND JUBILEE
Friday, May 16
OLD MEADOWBANK 18 (Ryan Fisher 3-3-R-2 8, Derek Sneddon 2-0-2-0- 4, Theo Pijper 0-1-1-2- 4, Jamie Birkinshaw 0-1-1-0), **COATBRIDGE 12** (Arlo Bugeja 1-0-0-0- 1, Thomas H. Jonasson 2-R-2-1- 5, Mark Burrows 2-2-FX-2- 6, Joni Keskinen 0-0-0-0- 0), **POWDERHALL 33** (Carl Stonehewer 3-3-3-2-1- 12, Robert Eriksson 0-2-2-3-2- 9, Andrew Tully 3-3-1-3-1-1- 12), **ARMADALE 33** (Jason Lyons 1-1-3-3- 8, Matthew Wethers 2-2-3-3- 10, Aaron Summers 1-3-1-3- 8, Trent Leverington 1-2-1-3- 7).
King of the Monarchs: 1 Carl Stonehewer, 2 Matthew Wethers, 3 Andrew Tully, 4 Ryan Fisher (fell, excluded).

Spring Trophy

GLASGOW (H)
Friday, March 14
Won 51-38
Fisher 10:1, Sneddon 10:2, Jonasson 1, **Lawson 15**, Wethers 5:2, Tully 6, Summers 4.
▲ *Monarchs dominated despite suffering four falls and two time exclusions.*

GLASGOW (A)
Sunday, March 23
Won 49-41
Fisher 14:1, Sneddon 5:1, Jonasson 5, Lawson 7, Wethers 10:1, Summers 3:1, Tully 5:3.

Aggregate: Won 100-79.

Celebrations at the Scotwaste Arena: *co-promoter Alex Harkess, Aaron Summers, Matthew Wethers, Andrew Tully, Ryan Fisher, William Lawson, Derek Sneddon and co-poromoter John Campbell acknowledge the fans' cheers*

Heading for the off: *Andrew Tully, Thomas H. Jonasson, Aaron Summers, Derek Sneddon, William Lawson, Ryan Fisher and Matthew Wethers*

PHOTOS: www.sports-media-partnership

EDINBURGH

Rider	M	R	Pts	BP	TPts	Ave	F	P	TR	TPts	TS	TSPts
Ryan FISHER	50	249	503	52	555	8.92	1	1	6	10	0	0
Matthew WETHERS	**50**	**251**	**460**	**72**	**532**	**8.48**	**1**	**2**	**0**	**0**	**0**	**0**
William LAWSON	32	156	292	29	321	8.23	3	0	1	3	0	0
Thomas H. JONASSON	**23**	**91**	**160**	**19**	**179**	**7.87**	**1**	**1**	**1**	**2**	**0**	**0**
Andrew TULLY	48	241	415	59	474	7.87	2	1	0	0	0	0
Derek SNEDDON	**49**	**215**	**345**	**37**	**382**	**7.11**	**0**	**0**	**0**	**0**	**0**	**0**
Aaron SUMMERS	50	202	255	65	320	6.34	0	2	1	0	0	0
Guests	**22**	**93**	**161**	**31**	**192**	**8.26**	**0**	**0**	**0**	**0**	**0**	**0**

For Aaron SUMMERS see Redcar (CL).

Statistics do not include the promotion play off matches against Elite League Wolverhampton.

Scottish Cup

GLASGOW (A)
Sunday, October 5
Won 45-44
Rider replacement for Lawson, Tomasz Piszcz [G] 5:1, **Fisher 17:1**, Tully 9:2, Wethers 3:1, Sneddon 7:1, Summers 4:2.

▲ *Dramatic finale saw Fisher and Tully collect a 5-0 in Heat 15 after the Tigers' pairing of Robert Ksiezak (fall) and Shane Parker (engine problems) disappeared completely.*

GLASGOW (H)
Friday, October 31
Won 64-26
Lawson 8:3, *rider replacement for Jonasson*, Wethers 12:2, Tully 13:2, Fisher 16:1, Theo Pijper [G] 7, Summers 8:2.

▲ *Finished best season in their history by beating essentially a Glasgow Select team.*

Aggregate: Won 109-70.

Roll of Honour

1951 .... EDINBURGH
1952 .... GLASGOW White City
1953 .... GLASGOW White City
1964 .... EDINBURGH
1965 .... GLASGOW
1966 .... GLASGOW
1967 .... EDINBURGH
1968 .... COATBRIDGE
1969 .... COATBRIDGE
1974 .... COATBRIDGE
1975 .... COATBRIDGE
1976 .... COATBRIDGE
1977 .... EDINBURGH
1978 .... GLASGOW
1979 .... GLASGOW
1984 .... EDINBURGH
1985 .... EDINBURGH
1989 .... EDINBURGH
1990 .... GLASGOW
1991 .... GLASGOW
1992 .... EDINBURGH
1993 .... GLASGOW
1994 .... GLASGOW[1]
1995 .... GLASGOW
1997 .... EDINBURGH[1]
1999 .... EDINBURGH
2000 .... EDINBURGH
2001 .... EDINBURGH
2002 .... EDINBURGH
2003 .... EDINBURGH
2004 .... EDINBURGH
2005 .... GLASGOW
2006 .... EDINBURGH
2007 .... EDINBURGH
2008 .... EDINBURGH

[1] *Only one leg completed.*

Weather...

Edinburgh had four home meetings washed out, including a couple against local rivals Glasgow.

Premier League
Friday, April 2 .... NEWCASTLE (H)
Sunday, August 17 .... GLASGOW (A)
Friday, September 5 .... GLASGOW (H)
Wednesday, October 15 .... KING'S LYNN (A)

Premier Trophy
Saturday, March 29 .... WORKINGTON (A)
Friday, April 11 .... NEWCASTLE (H)
Wednesday, August 13 .... BIRMINGHAM (A)

Scottish Cup
Friday, October 10 .... GLASGOW (H)

Spring Trophy
Sunday, March 9 .... GLASGOW (A)

...beaten

2009 Squad

Edinburgh's future at antiquated Armadale Stadium is short-lived after an early 2009 announcement that supermarket giants Sainsburys are planning a £23 million development of the site. With backing from West Lothian Council it is hoped to have a new venue by 2011.
Ryan **FISHER** (7.40), Tomas H. **JONASSON** (7.32), Matthew **WETHERS** (7.30), Andrew **TULLY** (6.80), Aaron **SUMMERS** (5.00), Michal **RAJKOWSKI** (4.37), Sean **STODDART** (3.59).

Premier League

GLASGOW

TRACK FILE

Track: Ashfield Stadium, 404 Hawthorn Street, Glasgow, G22 6RU.
Telephone: 0141 3364800.
Hotline: 09068 664685.
Website: www.glasgowspeedway.co.uk
Track Length: 302 metres.
Track Record: 57.3 secs, Shane Parker, August 26, 2007.
Promoters: Alan Dick and Stewart Dickson.
Team Sponsors: A-Plant.
Colours: Red and white stripes with tiger head.
Nickname: Tigers.

HONOURS

Major honours: 7.
Division Two champions (2), 1993, 1994.
Division Two Knock Out Cup winners (2), 1993, 1994.
Division Two National Series winner (1), 1990.
Division Two Pairs champions (2), 2005, 2006.

■ *See following page for track history.*

SQUAD

Ross Brady, Lee Dicken.

Foreign: Anders Andersen, Mitchell Davey, Josh Grajczonek, Peter Juul, Robert Kseizak, Peter Juul Larsen, Trent Leverington, Shane Parker.

2008 REVIEW

THE Ashfield season was in stark contrast to that enjoyed by their close rivals Edinburgh, as the Tigers had to suffer the pain of watching the Monarchs staging a dream campaign.

Glasgow's own prospects always appeared modest as the club entered a re-building phase, with two young Australians – Mitchell Davey and Josh Grajczonek – introduced for their debuts in British speedway.

The big blow, though, was the fact that captain Shane Parker had suffered from illness when back in Australia last winter and although he started the season, he quickly found himself on the sidelines with a broken collarbone in early May, and there were a number of complications with his recovery.

Parker was re-admitted to hospital with a chest complaint, and it was mid-August before he returned – by which time the Tigers were well and truly out of the chase for honours.

Grajczonek, in particular, showed a number of promising signs, but the rest of the team were largely inconsistent and injury-hit too with Ross Brady, in particular, seeing his appearances severely limited.

The Tigers were unable to get into a run of consistent form on their home circuit, and suffered a disappointing total of seven home defeats in the Premier League, the final one, most frustratingly, coming in a last-heat decider against Edinburgh, just a week after the Monarchs had won in similar circumstances in the Scottish Cup!

There was an early-season away win at Birmingham in the Knockout Cup – albeit not enough for an aggregate win – but a 56-35 win at Mildenhall was the Tigers' only other success on the road.

By the end of the year, the Tigers had done further work on boosting their asset base.

And young Danish rider Peter Juul Larsen is one on whom there are plenty of hopes for the future.

HISTORY

First meeting: April 19, 1949, Ashfield v Walthamstow, Division Two.
Leagues: Division Two, 1949-1952, 1999-2009. Division Three, 2000 (raced as Ashfield). Open licence, 1953.
Meetings have also been held at the following Glasgow venues.

● *Nelson Athletic Grounds, Porter Street, Camlachie, Glasgow.*
First meeting: April 9, 1928, Individual.
Leagues: Open licence, 1928, 1932.

● *Celtic Park, London Road, Glasgow.*
First meeting: April 28, 1928, Opening Handicap and Golden Gauntlet.
Leagues: Open licence, 1928.

● *Carntyne Greyhound Stadium, Myreside Street, Carntyne, Glasgow..*
First meeting: May 25, 1928, Individual.
Leagues: Open licence, 1928, 1930.

● *White City Stadium, Paisley Road Wet, Ibrox, Glasgow.*
First meeting: June 29, 1928, Individual.
Leagues: Division One, 1965-68. Division Two, 1947-1953, 1964. Northern League, 1930-31, 1946. Northern Shield, 1954. Open licence, 1928-29, 1940, 1945, 1956.

● *Hampden Park, Mount Florida, Glasgow.*
First meeting: April 11, 1969, Glasgow v King's Lynn, Division One.
Leagues: Division One, 1969-1972.

■ *In 1973 the Tigers' promotion switched home track to*

● *Cliftonhill Stadium, Main Street, Coatbridge, Lanarkshire.*
First meeting: March 39, 1973, Coatbridge v Halifax, Watson Bros. Trophy.
Leagues: Division One, 1973. Division Two, 1977 (mid-season).

● *Blantyre Sports Stadium Glasgow Road, Blantyre, near Glasgow.*
First meeting: July 8, 1977, Glasgow v Crayford, Division Two.
Leagues: Division Two, 1977-1981.

● *Craighead Park, Forrest Street, Blantyre, near Glasgow.*
First meeting: April 30, 1982, Glasgow v Rye House, Division Two challenge.
Leagues: Division Two, 1982-86.

● *Shawfield Stadium, Glasgow Road, Rutherglen, Glasgow.*
First meeting: April 15, 1988, Glasgow v Edinburgh, Convenor's Trophy.
Leagues: Division One, 1995. Division Two, 1988-1994, 1997-98.

■ *After the closure of Craighead Park at the end of the 1986 season the Tigers moved to Workington and raced as Glasgow Tigers until the end of July when they adopted the name Workington although still racing as the Tigers. They were expelled from the league on September 15 without completing their fixtures.*

● *Derwent Park, Workington.*
First meeting: May 1, 1987, Glasgow v Boston, Division Two.
Leagues: Division Two, 1987.

2008 RESULTS

Premier League

Final position..Fifteenth

KING'S LYNN (H)
Sunday, April 13
Lost 46-47
Parker 14:1 (TS2), Brady 2, Leverington 11:1 (4), Davey 0, Ksiezak 5:1, Grajczonek 4, Dicken 10:2.

NEWCASTLE (H)
Sunday, May 4
Lost 44-46
Leverington 5, Dicken 5:1, James Grieves [G] 13, Grajczonek 3:1, Ksiezak 11:1, Davey 0, Brady 7:1.
▼ *Shock home defeat saw Tigers concede a six-point lead and lose Davey (concussion) to join Parker on the injured list.*

Glasgow were able to track their original 2008 starting line-up in only one Premier League match.

NEWCASTLE (A)
Monday, May 5
Lost 42-53
Leverington 13 (6), Dicken 2:1, Grieves 13 (TS4), Grajczonek 0, Ksiezak 5, Gary Beaton [G] 1:1, Brady 8:2.
▼ *Grajczonek suffered a broken wrist in Heat 10 crash as Leverington and Grieves kept the score respectable.*

ISLE OF WIGHT (H)
Sunday, May 11
Won 51-42
Leverington 7:1, *rider replacement for Grajczonek*, Carl Stonehewer [G] 12:2, Dicken 6:1, Ksiezak 8:1, Gary Beaton [G] 2:1, Brady 16:1, James McBain [no. 8].
▲ *First league win despite conceding a 5-1 in the first race – Brady enjoying his best performance so far.*

BIRMINGHAM (A)
Wednesday, May 14
Lost 40-52
Leverington 2, *rider replacement for Grajczonek*, Carl Stonehewer [G] 14 (TS4), Dicken 0, Ksiezak 9, Davey 2:2, Brady 13:1, Ben Hopwood [no. 8].
▼ *Brady won three of the last four races but Tigers fell away in the final third of the meeting.*

SHEFFIELD (A)
Thursday, May 15
Lost 29-63
Leverington 4:1, *rider replacement for Grajczonek*, Tomas Topinka [G] 12 (4), Dicken 3:1, Ksiezak 5, Davey 3, Brady 1, Ben Hopwood [no. 8] [G] 1:1.
▼ *Brady aggravated an old injury in his second ride.*

SCUNTHORPE (H)
Sunday, May 18
Won 46-44
Leverington 5:2, *rider replacement for Grajczonek*, Kauko Nieminen [G] 14, Dicken 4:3, Ksiezak 11:1, Davey 1, Brady 11, Gary Beaton [no. 8].

REDCAR (H)
Sunday, May 25
Lost 42-48
Rider replacement for Leverington, Luke Priest [G] 1, Kauko Nieminen [G] 17, Dicken 8:1, Ksiezak 11, Davey 5:1, Brady 0, James McBain [no. 8].
▼ *Brady pulled out on medical advice after Heat 2 leaving Tigers vulnerable, with Adam McKinna scoring a remarkable paid 13 for the visitors.*

SHEFFIELD (H)
Sunday, June 1
6-6, Abandoned after two races
William Lawson [G] 3, *rider replacement for Leverington*, Andersen, did not ride, Dicken 0, Ksiezak, did not ride, Davey 2, Adam McKinna [G] 1:1, James McBain [no. 8].

BERWICK (A)
Saturday, June 7
Lost 39-54
Tomas Topinka [G] 15:1 (6), Leverington 4, *rider repalcement for Andersen*, Dicken 9:1, Ksiezak 9:1, Davey 1, Sam Martin [G] 1.

WORKINGTON (H)
Sunday, June 8
Lost 41-49
Adrian Rymel [G] 13, Leverington 8, *rider replacement for Andersen*, Dicken 7:1, Ksiezak 11, Davey 1, Adam McKinna [G] 1:1, James McBain [no. 8].

SOMERSET (A)
Friday, June 13
Lost 29-63
Craig Watson [G] 9 (4), Dicken 3:2, Andersen 3, Leverington 3, Ksiezak 8, Davey 3:1, Andrew Bargh [G] 0.

STOKE (A)
Saturday, June 14
Lost 43-49
Tomas Topinka [G] 15:1 (6), Dicken 1, Andersen 3, Leverington 7:1, Ksiezak 10:1, Davey 2, Kozza Smith [G] 5.

Ross BRADY

Mitchell DAVEY

BIRMINGHAM (H)
Sunday, June 15
Lost 40-53
Carl Stonehewer [G] 11 (TS1), Dicken 1:1, Andersen 1:1, Leverington 4, Ksiezak 15:1 (6), Davey 3, Grajczonek 5:1.
▼ *Fifth home defeat of the season against a Brummies side who displayed some wise choices of guests. The visitors included five ex-Tigers and Edinburgh's Andrew Tully!*

MILDENHALL (A)
Sunday, June 29
Won 56-35
Carl Stonehewer [G] 9:2, Dicken 5:2, Andersen 10:3, Leverington 8, Ksiozak 13, Davey 3, Grajczonek 8:3.

RYE HOUSE (A)
Saturday, July 5
Lost 27-65
Cory Gathercole [G] 5, Dicken 0, Andersen 3, Leverington 3, Ksiezak 13 (4), Davey 2:1, Grajczonek 1.

RYE HOUSE (H)
Sunday, July 13
Won 52-41
Carl Stonehewer [G] 9:1, Dicken 8:1, Andersen 5:4, Leverington 13, Ksiezak 4, Davey 3:2, Grajczonek 10:2.
▲ *First home meeting for four weeks, and first win since mid-May, starting well with two consecutive maximums.*

MILDENHALL (H)
Sunday, July 20
Won 55-37
Carl Stonehewer [G] 7:3, Dicken 8:1, Andersen 8:3, Leverington 14, Ksiezak 6, Davey 4:2, Grajczonek 8:2.
▲ *Best home tally of season with Leverington winning four rides before losing out to guest Ricky Ashworth (Heat 15).*

READING (H)
Sunday, July 27
Won 60-32
Magnus Karlsson [G] 8:1, Dicken 10, Ksiezak 14, Leverington 11:4, Andersen 6:1, Davey 7:1, Grajczonek 4:1.
▲ *Eclipsed their best result, limiting Racers to three heat wins with Leverington banking a full house.*

READING (A)
Monday, July 28
Lost 43-51
Magnus Karlsson [G] 17 (6), Dicken 4:1, Ksiezak 5, Leverington 1, Andersen 1, Davey 4:2, Grajczonek 11:1.

ISLE OF WIGHT (A)
Tuesday, July 29
Lost 42-51
Magnus Karlsson [G] 1, Dicken 9, Ksiezak 3:1, Leverington 15 (6), Andersen 2:1, Davey 0, Grajczonek 12:2.

Josh GRAJCZONEK

Robert KSIEZAK

▼ *Terrific effort on a tough away track, with Grajczonek really taking to the Smallbrook circuit and Leverington again in good form.*

SOMERSET (H)
Sunday, August 3
Won 51-39
Carl Stonehewer [G] 8, Dicken 5, Ksiezak 11:2, Leverington 8:1, Andersen 3:1, Davey 0, Grajczonek 16:2.
▲ *Red-letter day for young reserve Grajczonek as the Tigers inflicted major damage on the Rebels' title hopes.*

WORKINGTON (A)
Saturday, August 9
25-23, abandoned, heavy rain.
Ricky Ashworth [G] 2, Dicken 1, Ksiezak 4:1, Leverington 3, Andersen 2, Davey 9:2, Grajczonek 4.
● *Meeting abandoned after Heat 8 by referee Jim McGregor because of rain and a waterlogged track.*

SHEFFIELD (H)
Sunday, August 10
Lost 44-46
Carl Stonehewer [G] 3:1, Dicken 5, Ksiezak 10, Andersen 2, Leverington 1, Davey 7:1, Grajczonek 16:4.
▲ *Both Dicken and Leverington forced to withdraw from long-running meeting, as Sheffield snatched victory with a 4-2 in the last race.*

KING'S LYNN (A)
Wednesday, August 20
Lost 32-61
Ksiezak 7, Dicken 2:1, Parker 12 (6), Andersen 0, Leverington 6:1, Davey 1, Jerran Hart [G] 4.
▲ *Parker made his long-awaited comeback and rode as if he hadn't been away.*

REDCAR (A)
Thursday, August 21
Lost 38-55
Ksiezak 3, Dicken 4:1, Parker 15 (6), Andersen 3, Leverington 4, Davey 0, Klaus Jakobsen [G] 9:1.

STOKE (H)
Sunday, August 24
Won 56-36
Ksiezak 12:1, Dicken 6:1, **Parker 12**, Andersen 1, **Leverington 15**, Davey 5, Grajczonek 5:1.
▲ *Parker showed what the home fans had been missing with a 12-point maximum. Leverington went through the card from five rides and Ksiezak completed the top-end domination.*

SCUNTHORPE (A)
Monday, August 25
Lost 39-54
Ksiezak 10, Dicken 1, **Parker 17:1 (6)**, Andersen 2, Leverington 1, Davey 4:1, Grajczonek 4.

WORKINGTON (A)
Saturday, August 30
Lost 36-59
Ksiezak 12 (6), Dicken 0, Parker 10:1, Andersen 0, Leverington 4:1, Davey 2, Grajczonek 8:1.

BERWICK (H)
Sunday, August 31
3-3, abandoned after Heat 1, rain
Ksiezak 2, Dicken 1, Parker, Andersen, Leverington, Davey, Grajczonck, did not ride.
● *Abandoned after an aborted attempt to run Heat 2 when Grajczonek fell, and continuing rainfall made the decision a straightforward one.*

BERWICK (H)
Sunday, September 14
Won 50-43
Ksiezak 7:1, Dicken 7:1, Parker 12:1, *rider replacement for Grajczonek*, Leverington 13:1, Davey 4:1, Andersen 6:1, Adam McKinna [no. 8] 1.
▼▲ *Berwick guest Tomasz Piszcz scored an almost untroubled maximum, but the Tigers went eight points up after Heat 6 and were never in danger thereafter.*

EDINBURGH (A)
Friday, September 19
Lost 39-54
Rider replacement for Ksiezak, Dicken 5, Parker 19 (6), Tomas Suchanek [G] 0, Leverington 10:1, Davey 1:1, Andersen 4, Adam McKinna [no. 8] 0.

EDINBURGH (H)
Sunday, October 12
Lost 45-47
Parker 8:1, Dicken 11:2, Juul 4:1, *rider replacement for Ksiezak*, Leverington 11, Davey 3:1, Andersen 8:1, Adam McKinna [no. 8].
▲ *Dramatic late collapse by the Tigers, who led 31-19 and still by six points with three heats to go – only to concede two 4-2s and a final 5-1 in Heat 15.*

PREMIER LEAGUE

	M	*W*	*D*	*L*	*PtsF*	*PtsA*	*Pts*
1 Edinburgh	30	22	2	6	1562	1161	53
2 Somerset	30	21	0	9	1517	1223	48
3 King's Lynn	30	18	5	7	1624	1111	45
4 Rye House	30	19	0	11	1500	1232	42
5 Workington	30	17	2	11	1435.5	1300.5	41
6 Berwick	30	16	2	12	1428	1316	37
7 Redcar	30	16	1	13	1369	1374	37
8 Sheffield	30	15	2	13	1381	1345	35
9 Reading	30	15	1	14	1350	1405	34
10 Scunthorpe	30	15	0	15	1309	1434	33
11 Isle of Wight	30	15	0	15	1359	1390	31
12 Birmingham	30	13	0	17	1317.5	1401.5	30
13 Stoke	30	11	1	18	1307	1441	25
14 Newcastle	30	10	0	20	1220	1501	22
15 GLASGOW	**30**	**9**	**0**	**21**	**1297**	**1469**	**19**
16 Mildenhall	30	0	0	30	932	1804	0

Premier Trophy

BERWICK (H)
Sunday, March 16
Won 47-43
Parker 13:1, *rider replacement for Brady*, Leverington 13:1, Davey 3, Ksiezak 8:1, Grajczonek 3:2, Dicken 7.

With a youthful side Glasgow failed to make progress in any competition. They missed out on the play-offs, the Young Shield, the late stages of the Premier Trophy and were out of the Knock Out Cup at the first hurdle.

BERWICK (A)
Saturday, March 29
Lost 44-52
Parker 15:1 (TS6), Brady 4, Leverington 8:1, Davey 0, Ksiezak 9 (6), Grajczonek 4, Dicken 4:3.
▼ *Tigers pulled back from 12-down at halfway to go into a last-heat decider, but Parker and Leverington were beaten by Michal Makovsky and Adrian Rymel.*

WORKINGTON (H)
Sunday, March 30
Won 47-43
Parker 10, Brady 4:1, Leverington 8:2, Davey 2:2, Ksiezak 5:2, Grajczonek 6:2, Dicken 12:1.

EDINBURGH (A)
Friday, April 4
Lost 36-57
Parker 17 (6), Brady 0, Leverington 7, Davey 1:1, Ksiezak 2:1, Grajczonek 2:1, Dicken 7:1.
▼ *Brady fell in his opening ride and took no further part in the meeting.*

WORKINGTON (A)
Saturday, April 19
Lost 32-60
Parker 7, Brady 7:1, Leverington 6, Davey 1, Ksiezak 5, Grajczonek 4:1, Dicken 2.

EDINBURGH (H)
Sunday, April 27
Lost 34-58
Leverington 2, Ksiezak 4:2, Parker 19 (TS4), Dicken 1, Brady 1:1, Grajczonek 5, Davey 2.
▼ *Embarrassingly one-sided local derby with Leverington ruled out after being brought down by Ryan Fisher in Heat 1.*

PREMIER TROPHY Group A

		M	W	D	L	PtsF	PtsA	Pts
1	EDINBURGH	6	5	0	1	320	231	12
2	Workington	6	4	0	2	287	264	9
3	**GLASGOW**	**6**	**2**	**0**	**4**	**240**	**313**	**4**
4	Berwick	6	1	0	5	255	294	2

Knock Out Cup

Second round, first leg
BIRMINGHAM (H)
Sunday, April 20
Lost 40-52
Parker 16 (TS4), Brady 3:1, Leverington 8:1, Davey 0, Ksiezak 3:1, Grajczonek 5, Dicken 5.
▼ *Brady and Davey were both forced to withdraw after mid-meeting crashes.*

Second round, second leg
BIRMINGHAM (A)
Wednesday, April 23
Won 47-43
Parker 13, *rider replacement for Brady*, Leverington 8:1, Chris Mills [G] 8:1, Ksiezak 7:1, Grajczonek 9:2, Dicken 2:1.
Aggregate: Lost 87-95.

Scottish Cup

EDINBURGH (H)
Sunday, October 5
Lost 44-45
Parker 11, Dicken 5:3, Juul 4:1, Ksiezak 8, Leverington 4:1, Davey 6, Andersen 6.
▼ *Match swung both ways but Tigers led 44-40 only for Ksiezak to crash out of Heat 15 and race leader Parker then stopped on lap two and didn't have the power to coast around to salvage a draw.*

EDINBURGH (A)
Friday, October 31
Lost 26-64
James Grieves [G] 10, Robert McNeill [G] 1, Michal Makovsky [G] 9, *rider replacement for Ksiezak*, Leverington 0, Adam McKinna [G] 3, Charles Wright [G] 3.
▼ *Very strange-looking team with which to complete the season, with only one of the regular riders – and that man Leverington suffered a nightmare evening!*
Aggregate: Lost 70-109.

■ For Scottish Cup **Roll of Honour** see *Edinburgh*.

GLASGOW

Rider	*M*	*R*	*Pts*	*BP*	*TPts*	*Ave*	*F*	*P*	*TR*	*TPts*	*TS*	*TSPts*
Shane PARKER	17	90	229	7	236	10.49	1	1	5	15	5	10
Robert KSIEZAK	**39**	**171**	**291**	**20**	**311**	**7.27**	**0**	**0**	**6**	**13**	**0**	**0**
Trent LEVERINGTON	37	167	271	21	292	6.99	1	1	3	8	0	0
Josh GRAJCZONEK	**24**	**117**	**153**	**29**	**182**	**6.22**	**0**	**0**	**0**	**0**	**0**	**0**
Ross BRADY	14	58	77	9	86	5.93	0	0	1	2	0	0
Lee DICKEN	**38**	**160**	**189**	**33**	**222**	**5.55**	**0**	**0**	**0**	**0**	**0**	**0**
Anders ANDERSEN	20	76	71	16	87	4.58	0	0	0	0	0	0
Peter JUUL Larsen	**1**	**5**	**4**	**1**	**5**	**4.00**	**0**	**0**	**0**	**0**	**0**	**0**
Mitchell DAVEY	35	136	80	20	100	2.94	0	0	0	0	0	0
Guests	***35***	***161***	***259***	***18***	***277***	***6.88***	***0***	***0***	***4***	***10***	***4***	***7***

For Robert KSIEZAK see Belle Vue.

Despite an injury-hit season Glasgow skipper Shane Parker still scored more than 200 points.

David McAllan Farewell

Sunday, September 7

Riders got on with proceedings despite poor weather conditions as a large crowd turned out in support of David McAllan who was forced into retirement through injury.

David made his competitive debut for then Conference League Berwick in 1996 and a year later made his first Premier League appearance for the Bandits.

A Scotland international, he rode for all three local clubs (Berwick 1996-98, 2001; Glasgow 2002-04, 2006-07; Edinburgh 2005) as well as Linlithgow, Boston, Sheffield, Newcastle, Stoke and Workington.

His last meeting was for the Tigers against Birmingham on October 14, 2007, when he suffered severe internal injuries.

GLASGOW 42 (Steve Johnston 8, Trent Leverington 10:4, Shane Parker 7:1, Robert Ksiezak 2, Mitchell Davey 8:1, James Grieves 6, James McBain 1), **WORKINGTON 35** (Kevin Doolan 11, Jeremiah Thelaus 0, Kauko Nieminen 13, James Cockle 4:1, Jamie Birkinshaw 4, Richard Lawson 3), **EDINBURGH 31** (William Lawson 3, Robert Eriksson 0, Andrew Tully 7, Derek Sneddon 6:1, Michal Makovsky 8:2, George Stancl 7:1, James McBain 0).

2009 Squad

Shane **PARKER** (9.01), James **GRIEVES** (8.63), Peter JUUL **Larsen** (7.00), Josh **GRAJCZONEK** (5.25), Ross **BRADY** (5.11), Anders **ANDERSEN** (3.74), Mitchell **DAVEY** (3.00).

Weather...

Home Premier League meetings against Redcar, Edinburgh and Stoke (twice) fell victim of the Glasgow rain.

Premier League

Sunday, April 6 .... REDCAR (H)
Saturday, June 21 .... WORKINGTON (A)
Sunday, June 22 .... STOKE (H)
Thursday, July 3 .... STOKE (H)
Sunday, August 17 .... EDINBURGH (H)
Friday, September 5 .... EDINBURGH (A)

Scottish Cup

Friday, October 10 .... EDINBURGH (A)

Spring Trophy

Sunday, March 9 .... EDINBURGH (H)

Individual

Sunday, October 19 .... *Heathersfield Golden Helmet (H)*

...beaten

Individual

HEATHERSFIELD GOLDEN HELMET

Sunday, October 26

After finishing runner-up in 2007, Adam McKinna went through the card to win the re-arranged junior event (the original staging on Sunday, October 19 was called off) with a maximum to become the third Scottish winner of the trophy.

	1	2	3	4	5	6	Tot
1 Adam McKINNA	**3**	**3**	**3**	**3**	**3**		**15**
2 Richard LAWSON	2	3	3	3	3		14
3 Gary BEATON	1	2	3	3	2		11
4 Robert McNEIL	3	0	1	2	3		9
5 Craig COOK	3	2	2	FX	0		7
6 Michael PICKERING	0	3	2	0	2		7
7 John MacPHAIL	1	2	2	1	1		7
8 Stuart PARNABY	2	1	FX	1	2		6
9 Jack HIRST	1	1	1	2	1		6
10 James McBAIN	2	1	1				4
11 Steven MORRIS [R]	0	0	0	1	2	0	3
12 Rickylee BEECROFT	FX						0
13 Jonny GREY	FN						0

Roll of Honour

2004 .... Sean STODDART
2005 .... Gary FLINT
2006 .... Matej KUS
2007 .... Gary BEATON
2008 .... Adam McKINNA

Spring Trophy

EDINBURGH (A)
Friday, March 14
Lost 38-51
Parker 8, Andreas Bergtstöm [G] 3:2, Leverington 6:1, Davey 0, Ksiezak 7:1, Grajczonek 6:1, Dicken 8.

EDINBURGH (H)
Sunday, March 23
Lost 41-49
Parker 4, *rider replacement for Brady*, Leverington 13:1, Davey 4:2, Ksiezak 10, Grajczonek 10:3, Dicken 0.
Aggregate: Lost 79-100.

Premier League

ISLE OF WIGHT

TRACK FILE

Track: Wave 105 Smallbrook Stadium, Ashey Road, Ryde, Isle of Wight, PO33 4BH.
Telephone: 01983 811180.
Hotline: 09068 664673.
Website: www.islandspeedway.co.uk
Track Length: 385 metres.
Track Record: 66.3 secs, Jason Bunyan, April 15, 2008.
Promoters: Dave Pavitt and Martin Newnham
Team Sponsors: Wightlink.
Colours: White and red.
Nickname: Islanders.

HISTORY

First meeting: May 13, 1996, Island Individual Championship.
Leagues: Division Two, 1997-2008. Division Three, 1996-97, 2009.
■ *In 1997 Skegness moved to complete their Division Two fixtures at Smallbrook Stadium and rode as Isle of Wight.*

The Isle of Wight have entered the 2009 National League.

HONOURS

Major honours: 6.
Division Two Knock Out Cup winners (1), 2003.
Division Two Young Shield winners (2), 1998, 2001.
Division Two Four Team champions (1), 2007.
Division Two Pairs champions (2), 2002, 2007.

2008 REVIEW

IT was always likely to be something of a different season at the Smallbrook Stadium as the Islanders' out-and-out number one of the previous season, Chris Holder, had unsurprisingly moved up into the Elite League with Poole.

That led to the promotion's decision not to directly replace the Australian, but to build a side based on all-round strength, headed up by skipper Jason Bunyan.

It was no surprise that that proved to be a successful policy for home matches, as the Islanders continued their recent tradition for pulling off a number of convincing home wins.

Bunyan was far from the only track specialist in the team, with Glen Phillips and Krzysztof Stojanowski typically consistent at home, and Cory Gathercole providing plenty of thrills despite over a month out with injury.

But the Islanders were far less successful away from home, and the home record of one defeat out of 15 was exactly mirrored by the away record of just one win and, as that came at Mildenhall, it wasn't a result which saw the Islanders gain any ground on their opponents.

And with three points being awarded for an away win and no aggregate point either, the Islanders slipped down the table as a result, finishing 11th out of 16 – losing out on a top ten finish when they were dramatically beaten 49-41 at home by title chasing Somerset in mid-September.

They were still expected to be strong in the Young Shield, but having impressively got the better of Sheffield in the quarter-finals, Berwick blocked their route to the Final.

And the minimal crowd in attendance for the Bandits' match ensured that the Islanders' time as a second-tier club has come to an end for the time being at least, as they look ahead to a future in the new National League.

2008 RESULTS

Premier League

Final position..Eleventh

RYE HOUSE (A)
Saturday, April 12
Lost 24-66
Rider replacement for Stojanowski, Gathercole 7:1, Bunyan 1 (0), Fry 5, Phillips 7, Bargh 0, Holder 4.

MILDENHALL (A)
Sunday, April 20
Won 52-41
Bunyan 7:2, Gathercole 11:2, Stojanowski 8:1, Fry 7:1, Phillips 6:2, Bargh 4:3, Holder 9.
▲ *First away win of the season was set-up by going 21-9 up in the first five races.*

WORKINGTON (H)
Tuesday, April 22
Won 49-44
Stojanowski 2:1, Gathercole 11, Phillips 9:1, Fry 7, Bunyan 10, Bargh 1, Holder 9:3.

READING (A)
Monday, May 5
Lost 44-46
Stojanowski 10:2, Gathercole 6:1, Phillips 9, Fry 3, Bunyan 7:1, Bargh 5, Holder 4.
▼ *Frustratingly close to an away win but Stojanowski and Bunyan were beaten by Mark Lemon and Ulrich Østergaard in Heat 15 as the home side completed a comeback.*

SQUAD
Jason Bunyan, Paul Fry, Glen Phillips.
Foreign: Andrew Bargh, Cory Gathercole, James Holder, Krzysztof Stojanowski, Richard Sweetman.

READING (H) SKY TV
Tuesday, May 6
Won 58-34
Rider replacement for Stojanowski, Gathercole 9, Phillips 15:1, Fry 11:2, Bunyan 10:1, Bargh 6:1, Holder 7:3.
▲ *Islanders turned on the style in front of the cameras with each of their six riders winning at least one race.*

BERWICK (A)
Saturday, May 10
19-17, Abandoned before the completion of Heat 7
Rider replacement for Stojanowski, Gathercole 6, Phillips 3, Fry 2:1, Bunyan 5, Bargh 0, Holder 3:1, Johnny Grey [no. 8]

GLASGOW (A)
Sunday, May 11
Lost 42-51
Rider replacement for Stojanowski, Gathercole 13 (6), Phillips 3:1, Tero Aarnio [G] 12, Bunyan 12:1, Bargh 0, Holder 2.

REDCAR (H)
Tuesday, May 20
Won 53-40
Bunyan 6:2, Gathercole 12:1, Phillips 9:1, *rider replacement for Fry*, Stojanowski 9, Bargh 5, Holder 12:2.

BERWICK (A)
Saturday, May 31
Lost 44-46
Bunyan 8:1, Gathercole 7:3, Phillips 8, *rider*

Isle of Wight 2008: James Holder, Glen Phillips, Paul Fry, Cory Gathercole, Andrew Bargh, captain Jason Bunyan and Krzysztof Stojanowski

replacement for Fry, Stojanowski 14, Bargh 3:1, Holder 4.

EDINBURGH (A)
Friday, June 6
Lost 23-67
Bunyan 8 (0), Gathercole 2 (TS0), Phillips 2, *rider replacement for Fry*, Stojanowski 2, Bargh 4, Holder 5, James McBain [no. 8].

BIRMINGHAM (H)
Tuesday, June 10
Won 51-41
Bunyan 12:1, Gathercole 8:2, Phillips 10:1, *rider replacement for Fry*, Stojanowski 11:2, Bargh 2:1, Holder 8:2.

SHEFFIELD (A)
Thursday, June 19
Lost 33-59
Bunyan 1:1, Gathercole 10 (4), Phillips 4:1, Fry 7:1, Stojanowski 4, Bargh 4:1, Holder 3.

SHEFFIELD (H)
Tuesday, June 24
Won 54-39
Bunyan 6:2, Gathercole 13:1, Phillips 11, Fry 3:2, Stojanowski 8, Bargh 4:1, Holder 9:1.
▼▲ *Fry suffered two exclusions after falls but the Islanders took control with 5-1s in Heats 6, 8 and 9.*

MILDENHALL (H)
Tuesday, July 1
Won 65-28
Bunyan 14:1, Gathercole 8:2, Phillips 6:1, Fry 8:1, Stojanowski 11, Bargh 5:2, **Holder 13:2**.
▲ *First maximum in British Speedway for Holder – with Bunyan also unbeaten in this one-sided fixture.*

SCUNTHORPE (H)
Tuesday, July 8
Won 60-32
Bunyan 13:1, Gathercole 0, Phillips 9:2, Stojanowski 10:1, Fry 11:3, Bargh 8:1, Holder 9:1.
▲ *Gathercole crashed out in the first race and suffered a wrist injury.*

WORKINGTON (A)
Saturday, July 12
Lost 32-58
Bunyan 5:2, *rider replacement for Gathercole*, Phillips 6:1, Fry 8:1, Stojanowski 4 (R), Bargh 5:1, Holder 4.
▼ *Rider replacement for Gathercole gleaned just five points, and Bargh collected the Islanders' only win of the night in Heat 2.*

EDINBURGH (H)
Tuesday, July 15
Won 60-32
Bunyan 18, *rider replacement for Gathercole*, Phillips 8, **Fry 15:3**, Stojanowski 8:2, Bargh 4, Holder 7:1, Kyle Newman [no. 8].

The Islanders' final Premier League home match was a defeat – ending a run of 26 successive wins.

BERWICK (H)
Tuesday, July 22
Won 53-40
Bunyan 6:2, Holder 9:1, Phillips 5:1, Fry 12, Stojanowski 12, Bargh 6:3, Sweetman 3.
▲▼ *Sweetman won Heat 2 on debut before being hit by carburettor problems.*

GLASGOW (H)
Tuesday, July 29
Won 51-42
Bunyan 13:2, Holder 5:1, Phillips 6, Fry 9, Stojanowski 11, Bargh 2, Sweetman 5:2.
▲ *Biggest crowd of the season as Glasgow fought all the way and were one point adrift with four heats to go.*

NEWCASTLE (H)
Tuesday, August 5
Won 68-22
Bunyan 10:2, Holder 9:1, Phillips 9:1, **Fry 14:1**, Stojanowski 8:3, **Bargh 10:2**, Sweetman 8:1.

REDCAR (A)
Thursday, August 7
Lost 41-52
Bunyan 6, Holder 3:1, Phillips 4:1, Fry 13:1, Stojanowski 9, Bargh 2:1, Sweetman 4:1.

SCUNTHORPE (A)
Friday, August 8
Lost 40-53
Bunyan 10:1 (6), Holder 6, Phillips 1, Fry 8, Stojanowski 4, Bargh 6:2, Sweetman 5:1.
▼ *Threatened rare away win as they went into a 10-2 lead, but it was an advantage they couldn't maintain.*

KING'S LYNN (H)
Tuesday, August 12
Won 49-41
Bunyan 12, Holder 1, Phillips 10:1, Fry 6:1, Stojanowski 9:1, Bargh 2, Sweetman 9.

SOMERSET (A)
Friday, August 15
Lost 22-67
Bunyan 5, Holder 4:1, Phillips 5, Fry 2, Stojanowski 4 (1), Bargh 0, Sweetman 2:1.

STOKE (H)
Tuesday, September 2
Won 56-37
Bunyan 11:2, Holder 4:3, Stojanowski 9:1, Fry 8:1, Phillips 12, Bargh 5, Sweetman 7.
▲ *Eventful contest with Fry denied a paid maximum by being adjudged at fault in a heavy crash with Mark Burrows in Heat 14, and Phillips scuppered by a Heat 11 retirement.*

KING'S LYNN (A)
Wednesday, September 3
Lost 23-68
Bunyan 5 (2), Holder 0, Stojanowski 3, Fry 1, Phillips 2, Bargh 0, Sweetman 12.
▼ *Sweetman's performance was the only respite on a bad night, the young Aussie's win in Heat 11 being the sole Islanders' success.*

RYE HOUSE (H)
Tuesday, September 16
Won 51-42
Bunyan 12:1, Gathercole 10:2, Stojanowski 9, Fry 8, Phillips 6, Bargh 4, Sweetman 2:1.

BIRMINGHAM (A)
Wednesday, September 17
Lost 38-52
Bunyan 6, Gathercole 4:1, Stojanowski 10, Fry 2:2 (FX), Phillips 3:1, Bargh 3, Sweetman 10:2.
▼ *Led by six points after Heat 5 but faded spectacularly with no answer to the home team's top three riders.*

NEWCASTLE (A)
Monday, September 22
Lost 42-48
Bunyan 9:2, Gathercole 6, Stojanowski 7:1, Fry 6, Phillips 4, Bargh 5:1, Sweetman 5.
▼ *Led by two points with three heats to go but the match turned quickly with 5-1 reverses in Heats 13 and 14.*

SOMERSET (H)
Tuesday, September 23
Lost 41-49
Bunyan 11:1, Gathercole 4:1, Stojanowski 3:2, Fry 9, Phillips 6, Bargh 5:2, Sweetman 3:1.
▼ *Lost their unbeaten home record in their last match with Brent Werner doing damage at reserve and Jason Doyle involved in key 5-1s in Heats 11 and 15. Stojanowski crashed in Heat 9, was unable to take part in the re-run and withdrew from the meeting.*

STOKE (A)
Saturday, September 27
Lost 40-53
Bunyan 16 (6), Gathercole 6:2 (TS0), Stojanowski 9, Fry 3:1, Phillips 4, Bargh 0, Sweetman 2.

PREMIER LEAGUE

		M	W	D	L	PtsF	PtsA	Pts
1	Edinburgh	30	22	2	6	1562	1161	53
2	Somerset	30	21	0	9	1517	1223	48
3	King's Lynn	30	18	5	7	1624	1111	45
4	Rye House	30	19	0	11	1500	1232	42
5	Workington	30	17	2	11	1435.5	1300.5	41
6	Berwick	30	16	2	12	1428	1316	37
7	Redcar	30	16	1	13	1369	1374	37
8	Sheffield	30	15	2	13	1381	1345	35
9	Reading	30	15	1	14	1350	1405	34
10	Scunthorpe	30	15	0	15	1309	1434	33
11	**ISLE OF WIGHT**	**30**	**15**	**0**	**15**	**1359**	**1390**	**31**
12	Birmingham	30	13	0	17	1317.5	1401.5	30
13	Stoke	30	11	1	18	1307	1441	25
14	Newcastle	30	10	0	20	1220	1501	22
15	Glasgow	30	9	0	21	1297	1469	19
16	Mildenhall	30	0	0	30	932	1804	0

Did you know?

Isle of Wight used only one guest in an official match. Berwick's Finnish rider Tero Aarnio replaced the injured Paul Fry in their Premier League visit to Glasgow on Sunday, May 11.

The Islanders used rider replacement in 16 matches but only named a number eight three times – Kyle Newman (at home to Edinburgh and away at Reading) and James McBain who was on stand-by at Armadale.

Young Shield

Quarter Final, first leg
SHEFFIELD (H)
Tuesday, October 7
Won 57-36
Bunyan 13:2, Gathercole 7, Phillips 5:4, Fry 10, Stojanowski 10, Bargh 3:1, Sweetman 9:1.
▲ *Raced in far from ideal conditions after heavy rain, and Islanders held the advantage in most departments to run up a good first leg lead.*

Quarter Final, second leg
SHEFFIELD (A)
Thursday, October 9
Lost 41-52
Bunyan 11:1 (6), Gathercole 4:1, Phillips 1, Fry 7, Stojanowski 3, Bargh 2:1, Sweetman 13.
▲ *Pre-match nerves were dispelled by Sweetman, who won three of the first five races.*
Aggregate: Won 98-88.

Semi Final, first leg
BERWICK (H)
Tuesday, October 14
Won 53-42
Rider replacement for Phillips, Gathercole 8:2, Bunyan 16, Fry 8:3, Stojanowski 13, Bargh 1, Sweetman 7:1.
▲ *Delicately poised at halfway with the visitors well-served by guest Jason Doyle and Michal Makovsky. The most the Islanders ever led by was 14 points.*

BERWICK (A)
Saturday, October 18
Lost 37-58
Rider replacement for Phillips, Gathercole 4, Bunyan 10 (TS4), Fry 0, Stojanowski 14 (6), Bargh 0, Sweetman 9:1.
▼ *Fry crashed out in Heat 7 as the Islanders lost their early momentum, and 5-1s to Berwick in Heats 10 and 11 left the visitors fighting a losing battle – despite Stojanowski's three wins.*
Aggregate: Lost 90-100.

Weather...

Lost three home meetings and four away.

Premier League
Sunday, June 1 .... NEWCASTLE (A)
Tuesday, June 3 .... STOKE (H)
Saturday, June 21 .... STOKE (A)
Wednesday, July 9 .... BIRMINGHAM (A)
Saturday, August 16 .... STOKE (A)
Tuesday, September 9 .... SOMERSET (H)

Knock Out Cup
Tuesday, April 29 .... SHEFFIELD (H)

...beaten

Premier Trophy

NEWPORT (H)
Tuesday, April 1
Won 46-43
Bunyan 8, Gathercole 7:3, Stojanowski 5, Fry 7:1, Phillips 12, Holder 3:2, Bargh 4.

SOMERSET (A)
Friday, April 4
Lost 39-54
Bunyan 10:2, Gathercole 10:1 (6), Stojanowski 0, Fry 5, Phillips 7, Holder 4:2, Bargh 3.
▼ *Stojanowski withdrawn from meeting by paramedic after a Heat 3 crash.*

NEWPORT (A)
Sunday, April 6
Lost 42-47
Bunyan 5:2, Gathercole 8:2, *rider replacement for Stojanowski*, Fry 7:1, Phillips 9, Holder 6:1, Bargh 7:1.
▼ *Islanders threw away a 25-16 advantage and conceded the last four heats by an 18-6 margin.*

SOMERSET (H)
Tuesday, April 8
Won 58-34
Rider replacement for Stojanowski, Gathercole 10, Bunyan 15, Fry 3:1, Phillips 14:1, Bargh 7:1, Holder 9:3.
▼ *Bunyan was denied a maximum by a faulty spark plug in the final race.*

READING (A)
Monday, April 14
Lost 40-52
Rider replacement for Stojanowski, Gathercole 3:2, Bunyan 16 (6), Fry 5, Phillips 13, Bargh 0, Holder 3, Kyle Newman [no. 8].

READING (H)
Tuesday, April 15
Won 50-42
Stojanowski 6:3, Gathercole 8:1, Bunyan 11, Fry 6:1, Phillips 13, Bargh 1, Holder 5:1.
▲ *Bunyan and Phillips both won their first three races, Bunyan breaking the track record in Heat 3.*

PREMIER TROPHY Group D

		M	W	D	L	PtsF	PtsA	Pts
1	READING	6	4	0	2	300	248	10
2	Somerset	6	4	0	2	296	257	10
3	**ISLE OF WIGHT**	**6**	**3**	**0**	**3**	**275**	**272**	**6**
4	Newport	6	1	0	5	226	320	2

Knock Out Cup

Second round, first leg
SHEFFIELD (A)
Thursday, April 24
Lost 38-52
Stojanowski 2:1, Gathercole 8, Phillips 7, Fry 7:1, Bunyan 6:1, Bargh 1, Holder 7:2.
▼ *Conceded the last five heats by a 21-9 margin to make the second leg tougher than it might otherwise have been.*

Second round, second leg
SHEFFIELD (H)
Tuesday, May 13
Won 54-38
Stojanowski 6, Gathercole 11:3, Phillips 11, *rider replacement for Fry*, Bunyan 11:1, Bargh 6:1, Holder 9:1.
▲ *Dramatic aggregate win was confirmed when André Compton, riding as a tactical substitute, was excluded from Heat 14 for bringing Bargh down.*
Aggregate: Won 92-90.

Quarter Final, first leg
WORKINGTON (A)
Saturday, June 7
Lost 38-53
Bunyan 4, *rider replacement for Fry*, Phillips 8:2 (TS4), Gathercole 8:1, Stojanowski 10 (1), Bargh 3:1, Holder 5.

Quarter Final, second leg
WORKINGTON (H)
Tuesday, June 17
Won 51-43
Bunyan 12:1, Gathercole 9:1, Phillips 7:1, Fry 6:1, Stojanowski 9:1, Bargh 2:1, Holder 6:2.
▼ *Ahead on aggregate after Heat 8 but pegged back when Holder crashed in Heat 12 resulting in a Comets' maximum.*
Aggregate: Lost 89-96.

ISLE OF WIGHT

Rider	*M*	*R*	*Pts*	*BP*	*TPts*	*Ave*	*F*	*P*	*TR*	*TPts*	*TS*	*TSPts*
Jason BUNYAN	44	219	418	39	457	8.35	1	3	7	13	1	2
Cory GATHERCOLE	**33**	**153**	**252**	**36**	**288**	**7.53**	**0**	**0**	**3**	**8**	**2**	**0**
Krzysztof STOJANOWSKI	38	166	286	22	308	7.42	0	0	4	3	0	0
Paul FRY	**37**	**160**	**257**	**30**	**287**	**7.17**	**0**	**2**	**2**	**3**	**0**	**0**
Glen PHILLIPS	42	188	306	25	331	7.04	0	0	0	0	1	2
James HOLDER	**35**	**159**	**207**	**37**	**244**	**6.14**	**0**	**1**	**0**	**0**	**0**	**0**
Richard SWEETMAN	18	88	115	13	128	5.82	0	0	0	0	0	0
Andrew BARGH	**44**	**181**	**150**	**29**	**179**	**3.96**	**0**	**1**	**0**	**0**	**0**	**0**
Guests	***1***	***6***	***12***	***0***	***12***	***8.00***	***0***	***0***	***0***	***0***	***0***	***0***

For Cory GATHERCOLE see Swindon; for Andrew BARGH see Weymouth.

Inter League Challenge

EASTBOURNE (A)
Saturday, April 26
Lost 37-57
Davey Watt [G] 14 (6), Gathercole 5:1 (TS4), Bunyan 3, Tomas Suchanek [G] 5:1, Stojanowski 2, Bargh 3:1, Holder 5.
▲ *Took a surprise lead after Heat 2 but the Elite League side advanced to a predictably comfortable win.*

WEYMOUTH (A)
Saturday, September 6
Won 48-45
Bunyan 15, Bargh 5:1, **Gathercole 14:1**, Sweetman 9:1, Nick Simmons [G] 2, Gary Cottham [G] 2, Russell Barnett [G] 1.

PLYMOUTH (A)
Friday, October 3
Lost 43-47
Bunyan 15, Gathercole 5, Phillips 8:2, Sweetman 3, Fry 4, Bargh 8:1, Danny Stoneman [G] 0.
▼ *Went down to a surprise defeat in Devon despite missing only Stojanowski (replaced by reserve Danny Stoneman) of their normal Premier League side.*

Challenge

CHALFONT COACHES EASTER CHALLENGE
First leg
READING (H)
Saturday, March 22
Won 48-47
Bunyan 7:1, Gathercole 6, Stojanowski 8:1, Fry 7:2, Phillips 13, Holder 3:1, Bargh 4:1.

Second leg
READING (A)
Sunday, March 23
Lost 36-56
Bunyan 8, Gathercole 4:1, Stojanowski 11 (4), Fry 4:2, Phillips 5, Holder 3:1, Bargh 1:1.
Aggregate: Lost 84-103.

Did you know?

In their opening match of the season, a Premier League visit from Newport, the Islanders lined up: 1 Jason Bunyan, 2 Cory Gathercole, 3 Krzysztof Stojanowski, 4 Paul Fry, 5 Glen Phillips, 6 James Holder, 7 Andrew Bargh. And that was the final rankings of the team in their overall averages!

New start, new faces in 2009

DANIEL BERWICK (above) has joined the Isle of Wight from Sittingbourne for their first season in the National League and TOM BROWN (right) has left Plymouth to become an Islander

2009 Squad

Daniel **BERWICK**, Andrew **BRAITHWAITE**, Tom **BROWN**, Ben **HOPWOOD**, Brendan **JOHNSON**, Chris **JOHNSON**, Scott **MEAKINS**, Ryan **SEDGMEN**, Nick **SIMMONS**.
Competing in the 2009 National League.

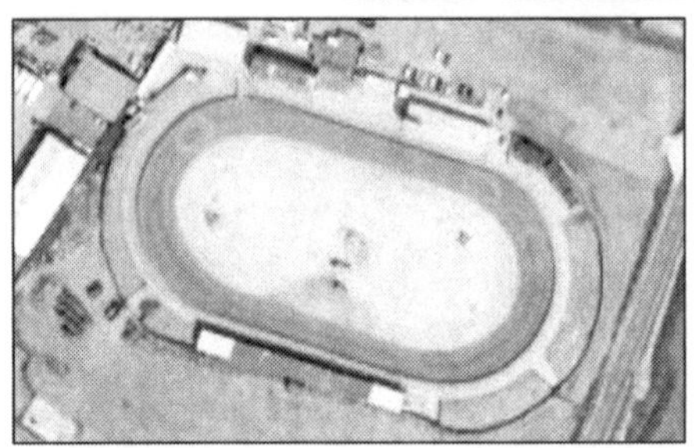

Premier League

KING'S LYNN

TRACK FILE

Track: Norfolk Arena, Saddlebow Road, King's Lynn, Norfolk, PE34 3AG.
Telephone: 01553 771111.
Hotline: 09066 555929.
Website: www.norfolkarena.co.uk
Track Length: 342 metres.
Track Record: 57.8 secs, Tomas Topinka, September 3, 2003.
Promoters: Keith and Jonathan Chapman.
Colours: Blue and yellow.
Nickname: Stars.

HISTORY

First meeting: May 23, 1965, Lynn Trophy.
Leagues: Division One, 1966-1995, 1997-2002. Division Two, 2003-09. Division Three, 1998 (as Norfolk), 1999, 2002, 2004, 2009. Open licence, 1965.
The venue was also used as a home track by Division Three Boston, 2000-08.

King's Lynn have also entered the 2009 National League racing as the Barracudas.

HONOURS

Major honours: 10.
Division One Knock Out Cup winners (2), 1977, 2000.
Division One Premiership winners (1), 2001.
Inter League Knock Out Cup winners (2), 1978, 1980.
Division Two champions (1), 2006.
Division Two Knock Out Cup winners (1), 2005, 2006, 2007.
Division Two Young Shield winners (1), 2005.
Division Two Trophy winners (2), 2006, 2007.

2008 REVIEW

THE Stars have been one of the big-hitters in the Premier League for several seasons – but on this occasion, a strong season was not quite backed up with silverware on the table.

By midway through the campaign, their traditional home strength was being seen on a weekly basis at the Norfolk Arena.

But at that stage their hopes had already been dented by a Premier Trophy home defeat against Birmingham – ending the chance of a 100-win milestone, and a draw against Edinburgh in the League which enabled the Monarchs to steal an early march.

Typically, the Stars were good value on their travels and were involved in a series of close matches but it was their misfortune that three points were awarded for a win in the season when they remarkably drew four matches away from home and had to settle for a single point on each occasion.

A rare hammering away from home came at Reading in the Knock Out Cup, a deficit which they could not overcome in the return fixture, but four away wins in the League ensured a comfortable top-four finish in third place.

Their results were based around the top-end power of Tomas Topinka and Kevin Doolan, but there were injury problems lower down, and the loss of Shaun Tacey and Rusty Harrison (forced to retire due to illness) put the Stars on the back foot for the promotion play-offs.

They overcame perennial rivals Rye House in the semi finals, and were well fancied to give Wolverhampton a run for their money – if they could make it past Edinburgh first.

But it was the League champions who had the final say on a dramatic night at the Norfolk Arena, with Lynn left to rue mechanical failures and a Heat 14 spill for Simon Lambert which left them just short of the Monarchs.

2008 RESULTS

Premier League

Final position..Third

WORKINGTON (A)
Saturday, April 12
Drew 45-45
Topinka 6:2, Tacey 8, Doolan 14, Smith 2:1, Harrison 7, Oliver 8, Lambert 0.

GLASGOW (A)
Sunday, April 13
Won 47-46
Topinka 5, Tacey 11:1, Doolan 14, Smith 4:2, Harrison 7, Oliver 4:1, Lambert 2.

EDINBURGH (H)
Wednesday, April 16
Drew 45-45
Topinka 15, Tacey 6:1, Doolan 13:1, Smith 0, Harrison 3, Oliver 5, Lambert 3:1.

SHEFFIELD (A)
Thursday, April 17
Lost 40-48
Topinka 9:1, Tacey 4:2, Doolan 12, Smith 1, Harrison 6:1, Oliver 3, Lambert 5.
▼ *Oliver was excluded for bringing down Paul Cooper in Heat 14 and Lambert fell in the re-run.*

EDINBURGH (A)
Friday, May 2
Lost 39-54
Shane Parker [G] 10 (TS0), Tacey 5:1, Topinka 15 (6), Lambert 0, Harrison 5, Oliver 3:1, Smith 1.

SQUAD
Simon Lambert, Shaun Tacey.
Foreign: Kevin Doolan, Rusty Harrison, John Oliver, Kozza Smith, Tomas Topinka.

BERWICK (A)
Saturday, May 3
Drew 45-45
Shane Parker [G] 0, Tacey 7:1, Topinka 14, Lambert 5:1, Harrison 8, Oliver 2:1, Smith 9.
▼ *Shane Parker was involved in a Heat 1 crash in which he broke his wrist and collarbone. He was unable to take his place in the re-run but was not adjudged to be at fault in the first bend incident by referee Christina Turnbull. Last-heat mechanical failure for Harrison denied Stars a possible win.*

RYE HOUSE (H)
Wednesday, May 14
Won 62-31
Doolan 12, Tacey 8:2, Topinka 13, Lambert 6:2, Harrison 9:1, Oliver 6:2, Smith 8:2.

NEWCASTLE (H)
Wednesday, May 28
Won 65-27
Doolan 9, **Tacey 12:3**, **Topinka 14:1**, Lambert 8:1, Harrison 8:3, Oliver 7:1, Smith 7:2.

WORKINGTON (H)
Wednesday, June 4
Won 61-31
Doolan 14, Tacey 6, **Topinka 13:2**, Lambert 8:1, Harrison 9:1, Oliver 5:1, Smith 6:3.
▲ *Daniel Nermark was limited to just two heat wins on his return to the Norfolk Arena as the 2009 Stars dominated,*

PHOTO: Steve HONE

KINGS LYNN 2008: Rusty Harrison, John Oliver, Tomas Topinka (on bike), Simon Lambert, Shaun Tacey. Kneeling - Kevin Doolan, Kozza Smith

going 31-11 up inside seven races.

REDCAR (H)
Wednesday, June 11
Won 66-27
Doolan 15, Tacey 7:3, **Topinka 11:1**, Lambert 11:2, Harrison 10:1, Oliver 4:1, Smith 8:1.

REDCAR (A)
Thursday, June 12
Won 47-43
Doolan 9:1, Tacey 7, Topinka 12, Lambert 2:1, Harrison 6, Oliver 5:2, Smith 6:2.

NEWCASTLE (A)
Sunday, June 22
Lost 42-50
Doolan 15 (4), Tacey 7:3, Topinka 7, Lambert 1:1, Harrison 4:1, Oliver 8:2, Adam McKinna [G] 0.
▼ *Failed to build on a Heat 1 5-1 from Doolan and Tacey, and will have regarded this meeting as points dropped in the title chase.*

BERWICK (H)
Wednesday, June 25
Won 61-29
Doolan 14:1, Tacey 8:2, Topinka 12, Lambert 6:3, Harrison 9:1, Oliver 7:1, Smith 5:2.

BIRMINGHAM (A)
Wednesday, July 2
Won 54-38
Doolan 15, Tacey 6:1, Topinka 6:1, Lambert 8:2, Harrison 9, Oliver 4:1, Smith 6:1.
▲ *Doolan equalled the Perry Barr track record on his way to a maximum.*

BIRMINGHAM (H)
Friday, July 4
Won 66-24
Doolan 9, Tacey 8:2, **Topinka 14:1**, **Lambert 10:2**, Harrison 9:2, Oliver 6:3, Smith 10.
▼▲ *Doolan fell in Heat 1 but was then unbeaten, and there were only two other last places recorded by a rampant home side.*

SOMERSET (H)
Friday, July 16
Won 68-25
Doolan 15, Tacey 7:3, **Topinka 10:2**, **Lambert 10:2**, Harrison 7:2, Oliver 7:2, Smith 12.

SCUNTHORPE (A)
Friday, July 18
Lost 43-46
Doolan 14, Tacey 3:2, Topinka 13, Lambert 5, Harrison 3, Oliver 2, Smith 3.

STOKE (A)
Saturday, July 19
Drew 45-45
Doolan 10:1, Tacey 4:2, Topinka 10:2, Lambert 5:1, Harrison 6, Oliver 1:1, Smith 9.
▼ *Two points dropped as they held a 5-1 position in the deciding Heat 15, only for Doolan to lose power and be overhauled by Ben Barker and Andrew Moore.*

SCUNTHORPE (H)
Wednesday, July 23
Won 63-28
Doolan 15, Tacey 8:2, Topinka 13:1, Lambert 5:3, Harrison 8:1, Oliver 8:1, Smith 6:1.

SOMERSET (A)
Friday, July 25
Lost 40-53
Doolan 16 (6), Tacey 1:1, Topinka 12:1 (TS0), Lambert 2, Harrison 3, Oliver 3:1, Smith 3.

MILDENHALL (H)
Wednesday, July 30
Won 72-18
Doolan 12, Tacey 7:3, **Topinka 10:2**, **Lambert 11:1**, **Harrison 9:3**, Oliver 12:2, Smith 11:3.
▲ *Quite simply, no contest. Graversen the only Fen Tigers man to beat an opponent, and he won Heat 15 against the Stars reserves.*

RYE HOUSE (A)
Saturday, August 2
Lost 41-49
Doolan 11, Tacey 2:1, Topinka 11, Lambert 5:1, Harrison 4, Oliver 1, Smith 7:1.

SHEFFIELD (H)
Wednesday, August 6
Won 59-35
Doolan 14:1, Tacey 0, **Topinka 15**, Lambert 7:1, **Harrison 11:1**, Oliver 7, Smith 5:2.
▼ *Damaging night with Tacey ruled out after a first-race crash, and Smith and Ben Powell also involved in a heavy smash.*

ISLE OF WIGHT (A)
Tuesday, August 12
Lost 41-49
Doolan 15:2 (6), Tacey 2, Topinka 10, Lambert 0, Harrison 5:1, Oliver 3, Smith 6.
▼ *Doolan beaten only by Jason Bunyan in Heat 1, but the second-strings struggled and an unusual 3-0 was conceded in Heat 8 when both Tacey and Smith fell.*

GLASGOW (H)
Wednesday, August 20
Won 61-32
Doolan 14, Tacey 5:2, **Topinka 13:2**, Lambert 8, Harrison 4, Oliver 9:2, Smith 8:3.

READING (A)
Monday, August 25
Drew 45-45
Doolan 10:2, Tacey 4, Topinka 12, Lambert 4, Harrison 6, Oliver 3, Smith 6:2.

STOKE (H)
Wednesday, August 27
Won 67-25
Doolan 14:1, Tacey 7, **Topinka 12:3**, Lambert 9:1, Harrison 6:2, Oliver 11:1, Smith 8:3.
▼ *Tacey's broken collarbone in Heat 10, when he clashed with*

Ben Barker, put a dampener on an otherwise entertaining evening despite the scoreline.

ISLE OF WIGHT (H)
Wednesday, September 3
Won 68-23
Doolan 14:1, *rider replacement for Tacey*, **Topinka 13:2**, **Lambert 13:2**, Harrison 3:1, Oliver 15:3, Smith 10:1.
▼ *Harrison withdrawn after complaining of pains in his legs after Heat 12. He was diagnosed with suspected deep vein thrombosis and forced into reluctant retirement.*

READING (H)
Wednesday, September 10
Won 59-31
Doolan 13, Jan Graversen [G] 5:2, Topinka 13:2, Lambert 11:2, *rider replacement for Harrison*, Oliver 9:1, Smith 8:2.
▲ *Doolan recorded the fastest time of the season.*

MILDENHALL (A)
Sunday, September 14
Won 67-23
Doolan 15, Chris Mills [G] 4:1, **Topinka 14:1**, Lambert 10:1, *rider replacement for Harrison*, **Oliver 14:4**, Smith 10:2.
▲ *Reserves took centre stage with Oliver's six-ride paid maximum backed up by Smith being unbeaten until a Heat 14 exclusion.*

PREMIER LEAGUE

		M	W	D	L	PtsF	PtsA	Pts
1	Edinburgh	30	22	2	6	1562	1161	53
2	Somerset	30	21	0	9	1517	1223	48
3	**KING'S LYNN**	**30**	**18**	**5**	**7**	**1624**	**1111**	**45**
4	Rye House	30	19	0	11	1500	1232	42
5	Workington	30	17	2	11	1435.5	1300.5	41
6	Berwick	30	16	2	12	1428	1316	37
7	Redcar	30	16	1	13	1369	1374	37
8	Sheffield	30	15	2	13	1381	1345	35
9	Reading	30	15	1	14	1350	1405	34
10	Scunthorpe	30	15	0	15	1309	1434	33
11	Isle of Wight	30	15	0	15	1359	1390	31
12	Birmingham	30	13	0	17	1317.5	1401.5	30
13	Stoke	30	11	1	18	1307	1441	25
14	Newcastle	30	10	0	20	1220	1501	22
15	Glasgow	30	9	0	21	1297	1469	19
16	Mildenhall	30	0	0	30	932	1804	0

Play offs

Semi Final, first leg
RYE HOUSE (H)
Wednesday, October 8
Won 56-37
Doolan 11:2, Joe Haines [G] 9:1, Topinka 15:1, Lambert 4, *rider replacement for Harrison*, Oliver 6:2, Smith 11:4.

Semi Final, second leg
RYE HOUSE (A)
Saturday, October 11
Lost 41-52
Doolan 15 (6), Viktor Bergström [G] 3:1, Topinka 12, Lambert 1, *rider replacement for Harrison*, Oliver 3:1, Smith 7:1.
▲ *Confirmed aggregate win with an 8-1 from Doolan and guest Viktor Bergström in Heat 11, backed up by 3-3s in the next two races.*
Aggregate: Won 97-89.

FINAL, first leg
EDINBURGH (A)
Friday, October 17
Lost 38-55
Doolan 11:1 (TS1), Lee Dicken [G] 1, Topinka 18 (6), Lambert 0, *rider replacement for Harrison*, Oliver 7:1, Smith 1:1.
▼ *Tried every tactical move to restrict the damage, Topinka winning four races, but middle-order weaknesses allowed Monarchs to build up a healthy advantage.*

FINAL, second leg
EDINBURGH
Saturday, October 18
Won 52-38
Doolan 13, Chris Mills [G] 2:1, **Topinka 17:1**, Lambert 2:1, *rider replacement for Harrison*, Oliver 10:1, Smith 8:1.
▼ *So close to turning things around but Doolan ran out of fuel in Heat 10 to concede a 5-1, and then Lambert crashed heavily due to a jammed throttle in Heat 14, which ended the Stars' hopes.*
Aggregate: Lost 90-93.

Top star Kevin Doolan

As well as racing in the 2009 Premmier League, King's Lynn have also entered a team in the 2009 National League, running on a Saturday night. Squad members: Adam ALLOTT, Scott CAMPOS, Benji COMPTON, Jake KNIGHT, Adam LOWE, Darren MALLETT, Rhys NAYLOR, Jamie SMITH.

Premier Trophy

MILDENHALL (H)
Wednesday, March 19
Won 66-24
Topinka 13:1, Tacey 8:2, Doolan 14, Smith 6:1, Harrison 7:2, Oliver 8:3, **Lambert 10:2**.
▲ *Nine 5-1s but Lambert was the only maximum scorer as Kaj Laukkanen collected half of the Fen Tigers' total.*

RYE HOUSE (H)
Wednesday, March 26
Won 61-31
Topinka 9:1, Tacey 9:2, **Doolan 14:1**, Smith 5:2, Harrison 7:1, Oliver 1:1, **Lambert 16:2**.
▲ *Six-ride paid maximum at reserve for Lambert, and Doolan also unbeaten.*

BIRMINGHAM (H)
Friday, April 11
Lost 39-55
Topinka 14:1 (TS2), Tacey 3, Doolan 14:1 (6), Smith 0, Harrison 0, Oliver 5, Lambert 3:1.
▼ *Had been looking to move on to 99 consecutive home victories against Premier League opposition – but well beaten in wet and heavy conditions.*

RYE HOUSE (A)
Saturday, April 19
Lost 35-55
Topinka 9 (4), Tacey 8:2, Doolan 2, Smith 0, Harrison 3:1, Oliver 6, Lambert 7:2.
▼ *Doolan forced to withdraw Heat 6 crash, which resulted in a Rockets' 5-0.*

MILDENHALL (A)
Saturday, April 26
Lost 44-46
Topinka 11, Lambert 3:2, Doolan 11, Harrison 5, Tacey 4, Oliver 3, Smith 7:2.
▼ *Shock defeat against struggling local rivals ended all hopes of qualifying for the Premier Trophy semi-finals. It was the only win Mildenhall recorded all season.*

BIRMINGHAM (A)
Sunday, October 19
Won 47-43
Doolan 12, Luke Priest [G] 1, Topinka 14:1, Mark Baseby [G] 1, *rider replacement for Harrison*, Oliver 8:2, Smith 11:1.
▲ *Consolation away win set up by a 5-1 in Heat 14 from reserves Smith and Oliver, and confirmed by Doolan and Topinka taking second and third places in the last race.*

PREMIER TROPHY Group C

		M	W	D	L	PtsF	PtsA	Pts
1	Birmingham	6	4	0	2	243	194	10
2	Rye House	6	4	0	2	291	250	9
3	**KING'S LYNN**	**6**	**3**	**0**	**3**	**245**	**211**	**7**
4	Mildenhall	6	1	0	5	203	327	2

King's Lynn raced their final Premier Trophy group match at Birmingham with 176 days between their last two matches in the competition.

Knock Out Cup

Second round, first leg
READING (A)
Monday, April 28
Lost 34-59
Topinka 13 (TS2), Lambert 0, Doolan 1, Harrison 9:1 (4), Tacey 2, Oliver 5, Smith 4.
● *Kevin Doolan withdrew after one race on medical advice and the paramedic insisted Kozza Smith was unfit to ride after falling six times in six rides.*

Second round, second leg
READING (H)
Wednesday, May 7
Won 55-38
Billy Janniro [G] 10, Tacey 4:2, Topinka 14, Lambert 7:1, Harrison 10:1, Oliver 8:2, Smith 2.
▼ *Former Stars man Chris Mills prevented Lynn from gaining momentum with two wins in the first eight heats.*
Aggregate: Lost 89-97.

King's Lynn never made a single change to the line-up throughout the summer.

2009 Squad
Tomas **TOPINKA** (9.37), Christian **HENRY** (6.91), Chris **SCHRAMM** (5.76), Emiliano **SANCHEZ** (5.58), Kozza **SMITH** (5.38), Darcy **WARD** (5.00), Jan **GRAVERSEN** (4.18).

KING'S LYNN

Rider	*M*	*R*	*Pts*	*BP*	*TPts*	*Ave*	*F*	*P*	*TR*	*TPts*	*TS*	*TSPts*
Kevin DOOLAN	39	186	485	16	501	10.77	6	5	5	14	1	0
Tomas TOPINKA	**42**	**212**	**506**	**33**	**539**	**10.17**	**2**	**11**	**3**	**8**	**3**	**2**
Shaun TACEY	34	134	198	46	244	7.28	0	1	0	0	0	0
Rusty HARRISON	**35**	**141**	**225**	**28**	**253**	**7.18**	**0**	**2**	**1**	**2**	**0**	**0**
Simon LAMBERT	41	167	233	43	276	6.61	0	6	0	0	0	0
John OLIVER	**42**	**189**	**252**	**48**	**300**	**6.35**	**0**	**1**	**0**	**0**	**0**	**0**
Kozza SMITH	41	190	247	49	296	6.23	0	0	0	0	0	0
Guests	***12***	***44***	***46***	***6***	***52***	***4.73***	***0***	***0***	***0***	***0***	***1***	***0***

For Simon LAMBERT see Boston.

Individual

PRIDE OF THE EAST

Wednesday, September 24

Kevin Doolan was the star turn in the 20 qualifying races in King's Lynn's long-time classic Pride of the East.

But it was Poole's Davey Watt who came out on top to lift the major awardx, winning the Grnnd Final to head an all-Australian top three.

Watt, a previous winner in both 2004 and 2006, admitted he had to make clutch adjustments before the deciding race and didn't even have time to make a practice start in his haste to avoid a two minute exclusion.

	1	2	3	4	5	Tot	GF
1 Davey WATT	**3**	**1**	**3**	**3**	**3**	**13**	**3**
2 Troy BATCHELOR	3	3	3	3	1	13	2
3 Kevin DOOLAN	3	2	3	3	3	14	1
4 Tomas TOPINKA	2	3	2	3	2	12	0
5 Tai WOFFINDEN	3	2	2	2	3	12	
6 Rory SCHLEIN	2	2	2	2	2	10	
7 Darcy WARD	1	3	0	1	2	7	
8 Oliver ALLEN	2	1	3	0	1	7	
9 Leigh LANHAM	1	2	2	2	0	7	
10 James BRUNDLE	1	3	1	1	0	6	
11 Shane PARKER	0	R	1	R	3	4	
12 Kozza SMITH	0	F	0	2	2	4	
13 Richard SWEETMAN	1	1	1	0	1	4	
14 Chris SCHRAMM	0	1	1	1	1	4	
15 Simon LAMBERT	2	0	0	1	0	3	
16 Jerran HART	0	0	0	0	0	0	
17 Darren MALLETT [R]				did not ride			

Roll of Honour

1957 . . . . Ove FUNDIN
1958 . . . . Peter CRAVEN
1959 . . . . Peter CRAVEN
1960 . . . . Björn KNUTSSON
1961 . . . . Peter CRAVEN
1962 . . . . Björn KNUTSSON
1963 . . . . Björn KNUTSSON
1966 . . . . Colin PRATT
1967 . . . . Bengt LARSSON
1968 . . . . Terry BETTS
1969 . . . . Howard COLE
1970 . . . . Ole OLSEN
1971 . . . . Ole OLSEN
1972 . . . . Ole OLSEN
1973 . . . . Anders MICHANEK
1974 . . . . Ivan MAUGER
1975 . . . . John LOUIS
1976 . . . . Peter COLLINS
1977 . . . . Ole OLSEN
1978 . . . . Ole OLSEN
1979 . . . . Dave JESSUP
1980 . . . . Dave JESSUP
1981 . . . . Michael LEE
1982 . . . . Tommy KNUDSEN
1983 . . . . Michael LEE
1984 . . . . Hans NIELSEN
1985 . . . . Jan ANDERSSON
1986 . . . . Sam ERMOLENKO
1987 . . . . Kelvin TATUM
1989 . . . . Martin DUGARD
1990 . . . . Kelvin TATUM
1991 . . . . Henrik GUSTAFSSON
1982 . . . . Henrik GUSTAFSSON
1983 . . . . Tony RICKARDSSON
1984 . . . . Craig BOYCE
1989 . . . . Chris LOUIS
1998 . . . . Chris LOUIS
1989 . . . . Lee RICHARDSON
2003 . . . . Simon STEAD
2004 . . . . Davey WATT
2006 . . . . Davey WATT
2007 . . . . Chris HOLDER
2008 . . . . Davey WATT

†*From 1957 until 1963 the meeting was held at Norwich.*

British Under 21 Championship

QUALIFYING ROUND

Wednesday, April 2

Joe Haines 14+□+3, 2 Sean Stoddart 12+3+2, Charles Wright 11+2+1, Andrew Tully 14+□+FX,
Byron Bekker 9+F, Sam Martin 11+R, Jerran Hart 9, Simon Lambert 8, Adam Lowe 7, Guy Kendrew 6, Scott Campos 4, Keiran Morris 4, Scott Whittington 3
Scott Richardson 3 Oliver Rayson 2, Ben Hannon0 Richard Franklin [R] 0.

● *Grand Final was awarded after a crash on the third lap when Andrew Tully got out of shape approaching turn four and collided with Charles Wright*

Did you know?

Only one visiting team – Reading – prevented at least one home rider from recording maximum points in official competitions.

And they did it twice – in both the Premier League and the Premier Trophy.

The Stars didn't have an unbeaten rider in their Premier League home match against Rye House but Kevin Doolan had a paid full house in the early season Rockets' Premier Trophy visit.

Inter League Challenge

IPSWICH (H)
Wednesday, March 12
Lost 34-58
Topinka 11, Tacey 2, Doolan 12 (4), Smith 3, Harrison 2:1, Oliver 3, Lambert 1.

IPSWICH (A)
Friday, March 14
Lost 31-61
Troy Batchelor [G] 3, Tacey 5:1, Topinka 10 (4), Harrison 3:1, Doolan 7, Oliver 2, Smith 1:1, Lambert [no. 8] 0.

Challenge

ASHLEY JONES MEMORIAL

Wednesday, June 18

YOUNG LIONS 37 (Lewis Bridger 2, Darren Rolph 2, James Brundle 14, Darren Mallett 2:1, Simon Lambert 7:1, Jerran Hart 6, Josh Grajczonek 4:1).

YOUNG ROOS 53 (**Tai Woffinden 15**, Ty Proctor 7:1, Kozza Smith 10, James Holder 6:1, John Oliver 7, Mitchell Davey 7:2, Arlo Bugeja 1).

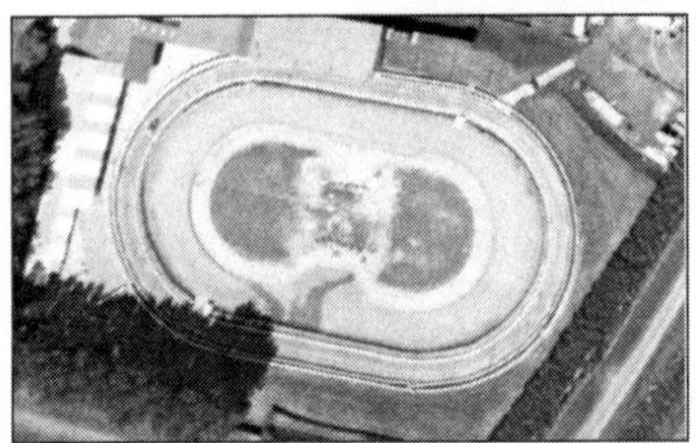

Premier League

MILDENHALL

TRACK FILE

Track: Mildenhall Stadium, Hayland Drove, West Rowm, Mildenhall, Suffolk, IP28 8QU.
Telephone: 01638 711777.
Hotline: 09068 664674.
Website: www.mildenhallspeedway.com
Track Length: 260 metres.
Track Record: 49.81 secs, Kenneth Bjerre, October 21, 2007.
Promoters:John Bailey.
Colours: Yellow and black.
Nickname: Fen Tigers.

HISTORY

First meeting: May 18, 1975, Mildenhall v Scunthorpe, Division Two.
Leagues: Division Two, 1975-1989, 1992, 2006-08. Division Three, 1994-2006, 2009.
Operated as a training track from April 8, 1973, until joining Division Two in 1975.

Mildenhall have entered the 2009 National League.

HONOURS

Major honours: 12.
Division Two champions (1), 1979.
Division Two Four Team champions (2), 1984, 1987.
Division Two Pairs champions (1), 1987.
Division Three champions (2), 2003, 2004.
Division Three Knock Out Cup winners (2), 2003, 2004.
Division Three Trophy winners (2), 002, 2004.
Division Three League Cup winners (1), 2000.
Division Three Four Team champions (1), 2004.

2008 REVIEW

THE bare statistics of the Fen Tigers' efforts tell the story of one of the most disastrous seasons for any club in the sport's history.

And the only consolation for long-suffering Mildenhall fans was that they still had a club to support come the end of the campaign – even if a noise abatement order needed to be lifted to keep them in business for 2009.

The Fen Tigers, initially under the promotion of Simon Barton as the leader of a shareholders' consortium, lost all 30 of their Premier League matches, conceding almost double the number of points that they scored.

No fewer than 18 riders were declared as Mildenhall team members during the season, and young Dane Jan Graversen finished the season as captain having recorded easily the most appearances of any Fen Tigers' rider.

On three occasions they conceded over 70 points, the trips to Berwick, King's Lynn and Somerset seeing them muster a score of just 18. Their best display on the road stood as a 42-48 reverse at Scunthorpe.

At home, things were little better – and Berwick, Edinburgh, King's Lynn, Rye House and Sheffield all recorded 60-plus wins at West Row.

There was one dramatic success in the early season – the Fen Tigers' sole win of the season, which came with a shock last-race 5-1 from Robbie Kessler and Kaj Laukkanen giving them a 46-44 home win over local rivals King's Lynn in the Premier Trophy.

But that competition, too, had its disastrous moments, none more so than a crash in the home fixture against Birmingham which left Casper Wortmann fighting for his life.

Thankfully, the Dane recovered and even resumed his position in the team, which for the last three matches came under the control of King's Lynn promoters Keith and Jonathan Chapman who at least ensured that the club completed their miserable season.

2008 RESULTS

Premier League

Final position..Sixteenth

BERWICK (H)
Sunday, March 30
Lost 29-61
Laukkanen 6:1 (0), John Oliver [G] 7:1, Graversen 6:1, *rider replacement for Kessler*, Wortmann 2, Baseby 5, Cockle 3.

ISLE OF WIGHT (H)
Sunday, April 20
Lost 41-52
Laukkanen 17 (6), Makinen 2:1, Graversen 11, *rider replacement for Wortmann*, Chris Schramm [G] 8:1, Baseby 2, Cockle 1:1.
▲▼ *Laukkanen's superb showing lifted some gloom as the injury-hit Fen Tigers lost Baseby with ankle ligament damage after a Heat 5 incident.*

Jan GRAVERSEN

EDINBURGH (H)
Sunday, May 11
Lost 30-60
Mikael Rajkowski 3, Graversen 1, Laukkanen 6:1, Loof 4, Kessler 11 (1), Kyle Hughes [G] 2, Makinen 3.
▼ *Defeat was mathematically ensured as early as Heat 10, with Kessler's showing on his return from injury offering the only real glimmer of hope.*

SOMERSET (H)
Sunday, June 1
Lost 37-55
Rajkowski 3, Graversen 10:1 (4), Laukkanen 7, Makinen 0, Kessler 9:1, Kyle Hughes [G] 6, Loof 2:1.
▲ *Kessler won his last two rides and Rajkowski his third, sandwiched by three last places.*

REDCAR (A)
Thursday, June 5
Lost 40-53
Rajkowski 3, Graversen 1, Laukkanen 16 (6), Makinen 4:1, Kessler 8, Baseby 7, Loof 1.

SQUAD
Mark Baseby, James Cockle, Shane Colvin, Barrie Evans, Paul Lee, Luke Priest, Lee Smart, Matthew Wright.
Foreign: Jan Graversen, Robbie Kessler, Kaj Laukkanen, Henning Loof, Jari Makinen, Marek Mroz, Theo Pijper, Michal Rajkowski, Sebastian Truminski, Casper Wortmann.

NEWCASTLE (H)
Saturday, June 7
Lost 39-53
Rajkowski 4, Graversen 10:1 (6), Laukkanen 4:1, Makinen 1, Kessler 9, Baseby 8:2, Loof 3.
▼ *Hauled themselves back from 14-28 to 33-35 before the meeting ended in anti-climax.*

REDCAR (H)
Sunday, June 15
Lost 35-58
Rajkowski 2:1, Graversen 11 (6), Laukkanen 9, Makinen 2, Kessler 7:1, Baseby 2, Loof 2:1.
▼ *Could make no inroads even though their opponents were suffering themselves from unavailable riders – described as one of the worst-ever performances by a Mildenhall team!*

READING (A)
Monday, June 16
Lost 33-60
Rajkowski 9, Graversen 5, Laukkanen 16, Makinen 0, *rider replacement for Kessler*, Jay Herne [G] 2, Loof 1.

SCUNTHORPE (A)
Friday, June 20
Lost 42-48
Rajkowski 7:1, Graversen 5:3, Laukkanen 12, Tomas Suchanek [G] 9:2, *rider replacement for Kessler*, Loof 1, Baseby 8.
▲ *Needed a 5-1 from Heat 15 to snatch draw. Laukkanen and guest Suchanek were close before conceding a 4-2 in what one of the best displays of the season.*

SCUNTHORPE (H)
Sunday, June 22
Lost 40-53
Rajkowski 14 (6), *rider replacement for Kessler*, Laukkanen 4, Tomas Suchanek [G] 11:1, Graversen 8 (TS0), Loof 2, Baseby 1, Ben Hopwood [no. 8].
●▼ *Both teams' promoters and managers hauled into the office by referee Barbara Horley after a first bend clash between Graversen and Carl Wilkinson spilled over. Mark Baseby injured in Heat 12.*

GLASGOW (H)
Sunday, June 29
Lost 35-56
Chris Schramm [G] 9:2 (1), Rajkowski 11, *rider replacement for Kessler*, Andrew Bargh [G] 2:2, Graversen 11 (TS4), Baseby 1, Wright 1.

MILDENHALL'S 2008 PREMIER LEAGUE RECORD

Home..L L L L L L L L L L L L L L

Away..L L L L L L L L L L L L L L

ISLE OF WIGHT (A)
Tuesday, July 1
Lost 28-65
Chris Schramm [G] 13 (6), Rajkowski 4:1, Pijper 7, Graversen 2, *rider replacement for Kessler*, Baseby 2:1, Wright 0.
▲ *Guest Chris Schramm and Rajkowski made the Fen Tigers' only heat advantage, collecting shock Heat 11 8-1.*

SHEFFIELD (A)
Thursday, July 3
Lost 27-65
Chris Schramm [G] 9 (4), Rajlkowski 3, Pijper 8, *rider replacement for Kessler*, Graversen 2, Baseby 2, Wright 3:1.

SHEFFIELD (H)
Sunday, July 6
Lost 27-65
Chris Schramm [G] 7 (4), Rajkowski 4:1, Pijper 5:1, *rider replacement for Kessler*, Graversen 2, Nicki Glanz [G] 9:1, Wright 0, Ben Hopwood [no. 8].
▼ *Fen Tigers' worst-ever home defeat was made even more painful by the fact that the meeting took three and a half hours to run due to a variety of delays.*

WORKINGTON (A)
Saturday, July 19
Lost 28-64
Ricky Ashworth [G] 12 (4), Rajkowski 4:2, *rider replacement for Kessler*, Mroz 2, Graversen 5, Luke Priest [G] 2, Wright 2, Adam McKinna [G] 1.

GLASGOW (A)
Sunday, July 20
Lost 37-55
Ricky Ashworth [G] 16 (6), Mroz 4:1, *rider replacement for Kessler*, Rajkowski 7, Graversen 7, Adam McKinna [G] 2, Wright 1:1, John MacPhail [no. 8].

WORKINGTON (H)
Sunday, July 27
Lost 31-53
Chris Schramm [G] 6:1, Mroz 7, *rider replacement for Kessler*, Arlo Bugeja [G] 5:1, Graversen 9, Andrew Bargh [G] 2:1, Wright 2, Ben Hopwood [no. 8].
● *Abandoned after Heat 14, rain.*

KING'S LYNN (A)
Wednesday, July 30
Lost 18-72
Truminski 2, *rider replacement for Rajkowski*, Pijper 2, Mroz 3, Graversen 6 (R), Darren Mallett [G] 4, Wright 1.
▼ *Graversen beat Shaun Tacey in Heat 6 and the Lynn reserves in Heat 15 – apart from that, it was a total whitewash!*

Fen Tigers used 18 contracted riders in official fixtures.

BIRMINGHAM (H)
Sunday, August 2
Lost 36-55
Truminski 8 (2), Nicki Glanz [G] 8:1, Pijper 5, *rider replacement for Rajkowski*, Graversen 1, Mroz 12:2, Wright 2.

EDINBURGH (A)
Friday, August 8
Lost 21-69
Truminski 4, Smart 3, Pijper 9, *rider replacement for Rajkowski*, Graversen 3, Mroz 1, Mitchell Davey [G] 1.
▼ *Pijper managed a race win on his old home circuit but Mroz suffered lower back damage in a Heat 8 crash.*

BERWICK (A)
Saturday, August 9
Lost 18-72
Truminski 5, Smart 2:1, Pijper 5 (1), *rider replacement for Rajkowski*, Graversen 1, Mroz 1, Adam McKinna 4, Ben Hopwood [no. 8] 0.
▼ *Mroz retired after one ride following his Friday crash, and others also appeared to have thrown the towel in during another near-whitewash defeat.*

NEWCASTLE (A)
Sunday, August 10
Lost 22-68
Truminski 5 (0), Smart 2, Pijper 9, *rider replacement for Rajkowski*, Graversen 4, Luke Priest [G] 1, Adam McKinna [G] 1.

RYE HOUSE (H)
Sunday, August 17
Lost 27-65
Truminski 11 (4), *rider replacement for Graversen*, Wortmann 1:1, Evans 4, Smart 1, Mroz 4, Arlo Bugeja [G] 6.

BIRMINGHAM (A)
Wednesday, August 27
Lost 32-61
Truminski 4:3, Smart 15, *rider replacement for Mroz*, Wortmann 3:1, Graversen 3, Luke Priest [G] 3, Evans 4, Paul Starke [no. 8] 0.
▼ *Smart, who lost his place at Perry Barr earlier in the month, provided a rare high double-figure score.*

READING (H)
Sunday, August 31
Lost 42-51
Truminski 11, Barrie Evans 9:2, Lee 5, Smart 3:1, Graversen 5, Loof 6:2, Wortmann 3:1.
● *First match in charge for new promoters Keith and Jonathan Chapman. After six heats Mildenhall led 23-13.*

RYE HOUSE (A)
Saturday, September 13
Lost 23-66
Truminski 2, Wortmann 3, Lee 5, Graversen 4:1,

Evans 7, Loof 1:1, Priest 1.

KING'S LYNN (H)
Sunday, September 14
Lost 23-67
Truminski 4, Wortmann 1, Lee 3, Graversen 3:1, Evans 6, Loof 1:1, Priest 5.

▼ *The size of the crowd gave some cheer, but this was the biggest of a catalogue of enormous home defeats.*

SOMERSET (A)
Friday, September 19
Lost 18-72
Rider replacement for Truminski, Karl Mason [G] 2, Lee 2, Richard Sweetman [G] 5 (1), Wortmann 6, Mark Thompson [G] 0, Priest 3.

▼ *Embarrassed with no team manager, no race jackets and no hope as their only points were taken off Conference League youngster Kyle Newman.*

STOKE (H)
Sunday, September 28
Lost 34-56
Kozza Smith [G] 12:1 (1), Wortmann 0, *rider replacement for Truminski*, Daniel Halsey [G] 0, Richard Sweetman [G] 12:1, James Cockle [G] 2, Priest 8:1, Mark Thompson [no. 8].

▼ *Had been hoping to include Travis McGowan as a post-deadline signing – that was turned down, and the season was concluded with a 30th league defeat out of 30.*

PREMIER LEAGUE

	M	W	D	L	PtsF	PtsA	Pts
1 Edinburgh	30	22	2	6	1562	1161	53
2 Somerset	30	21	0	9	1517	1223	48
3 King's Lynn	30	18	5	7	1624	1111	45
4 Rye House	30	19	0	11	1500	1232	42
5 Workington	30	17	2	11	1435.5	1300.5	41
6 Berwick	30	16	2	12	1428	1316	37
7 Redcar	30	16	1	13	1369	1374	37
8 Sheffield	30	15	2	13	1381	1345	35
9 Reading	30	15	1	14	1350	1405	34
10 Scunthorpe	30	15	0	15	1309	1434	33
11 Isle of Wight	30	15	0	15	1359	1390	31
12 Birmingham	30	13	0	17	1317.5	1401.5	30
13 Stoke	30	11	1	18	1307	1441	25
14 Newcastle	30	10	0	20	1220	1501	22
15 Glasgow	30	9	0	21	1297	1469	19
16 MILDENHALL	**30**	**0**	**0**	**30**	**932**	**1804**	**0**

Mildenhall became the first team to go through an entire league season without picking up at least one match point, losing all 30 matches, most by a heavy margin.

MILDENHALL

Rider	M	R	Pts	BP	TPts	Ave	F	P	TR	TPts	TS	TSPts
Kaj LAUKKANEN	19	92	198	8	206	8.96	0	0	7	18	0	0
Robbie KESSLER	**10**	**50**	**93**	**2**	**95**	**7.60**	**0**	**0**	**2**	**2**	**0**	**0**
Barrie EVANS	5	25	30	2	32	5.12	0	0	0	0	0	0
Theo PIJPER	**8**	**41**	**50**	**1**	**51**	**4.98**	**0**	**0**	**1**	**0**	**1**	**0**
Jan GRAVERSEN	35	172	197	11	208	4.84	0	0	7	12	3	2
Michal RAJKOWSKI	**15**	**73**	**82**	**6**	**88**	**4.82**	**0**	**0**	**1**	**3**	**0**	**0**
Sebastian TRUMINSKI	10	49	56	3	59	4.82	0	0	3	3	0	0
Marek MROZ	**8**	**34**	**34**	**3**	**37**	**4.35**	**0**	**0**	**1**	**0**	**0**	**0**
Lee SMART	6	27	26	2	28	4.15	0	0	2	3	0	0
Luke PRIEST	**4**	**21**	**17**	**1**	**18**	**3.43**	**0**	**0**	**1**	**0**	**0**	**0**
Mark BASEBY	14	68	53	5	58	3.41	0	0	0	0	0	0
Paul LEE	**4**	**19**	**15**	**0**	**15**	**3.16**	**0**	**0**	**1**	**0**	**0**	**0**
Henning LOOF	15	63	41	8	49	3.11	0	0	1	0	0	0
Casper WORTMANN	**12**	**55**	**36**	**6**	**42**	**3.05**	**0**	**0**	**0**	**0**	**0**	**0**
Jari MAKINEN	12	45	22	4	26	2.31	0	0	0	0	0	0
James COCKLE	**6**	**27**	**12**	**1**	**13**	**1.93**	**0**	**0**	**0**	**0**	**0**	**0**
Matthew WRIGHT	9	40	12	2	14	1.40	0	0	0	0	0	0
Shane COLVIN	**1**	**2**	**0**	**0**	**0**	**0.00**	**0**	**0**	**0**	**0**	**0**	**0**
Guests	***50***	***229***	***241***	***24***	***265***	***4.63***	***0***	***0***	***6***	***7***	***0***	***0***

For Robbie KESSLER see Coventry; for Barrie EVANS see Stoke; for Theo PIJPER see Swindon and Berwick; for Michal RAJKOWSKI see Belle Vue; for Sebastian TRUMINSKI and Marek MROZ see Newport; for Lee SMART see Birmingham and Weymouth; for Luke PRIEST see Weymouth; for Mark BASEBY see Sittingbourne; for Henning LOOF see Somerset; for James COCKLE see Birmingham and Peterborough; for Matthew WRIGHT see Boston and Weymouth.

The unlucky Casper Wortmann (above) was seriously hurt when he crashed against Birmingham on April 6 and was expected to be out for the season but made a brave comeback in August, riding in the Fen Tigers' last seven matches of the year

Kaj Laukkanen (left) was top of the averages when he stunned the Fen Tigers by retiring from Premier League racing to spend more time at home in Finland with his wife and family

Photos: **STEVE DIXON.**

MILDENHALL'S last roll-call before the rescue by King's Lynn owners Keith and Jonathan Chapman. Left to right: Blayne Scroggins (assistant team manager), Sebastian Truminski, Henning Loof, Jan Graversen, Luke Priest, Lee Smart, Laurence Rogers (team manager) and Barrie Evans

Premier Trophy

KING'S LYNN (A)
Wednesday, March 19
Lost 24-66
Laukkanen 12, Colvin 0, Graversen 4 (X), *rider replacement for Kessler*, Wortmann 4, Baseby 2:1, Cockle 2, Adam Lowe [no. 8].

▼ *Colvin damaged his knee in a Heat 3 fall, and Graversen was excluded for tangling with Rusty Harrison when on a tactical ride.*

RYE HOUSE (A)
Monday, March 24
Lost 33-59
Laukkanen 7:1, Lee Smart [G] 4, Graversen 12, Wortmann 6:2, *rider replacement for Kessler*, Baseby 1, Cockle 2, Aaron Baseby [no. 8] 1.

▼ *Two race wins for Graversen gave Fen Tigers something to cheer after dropping 6-30 down after six races.*

BIRMINGHAM (A)
Wednesday, March 26
Lost 33-60
Laukkanen 13 (6), Jamie Smith [G] 6:2, Graversen 4, Wortmann 6:1, *rider replacement for Kessler*, Baseby 2, Cockle 1, Rob Smith [no. 8] 1.

BIRMINGHAM (H)
Sunday, April 6
Lost 32-42
Laukkanen 7, Barrie Evans [G] 3:2, Graversen 8 (4), *rider replacement for Kessler*, Wortmann 1, Baseby 10, Cockle 3, Aaron Baseby [no. 8].

● *Abandoned after Heat 12, insufficient medical cover remaining after Casper Wortmann taken to hospital following fall.*

KING'S LYNN (H)
Saturday, April 26
Won 46-44
Graversen 5, Loof 6, Laukkanen 11:2, *rider replacement for Wortmann*, Kessler 16, Matthew Wright [G] 7, Makinen 1.

▲ *Mildenhall's only victory of the season, Kessler and Laukkanen sending West Row into ecstasy with a last-heat match-winning 5-1 over Tomas Topinka and Kevin Doolan. Loof, signed from Somerset, makes terrific debut.*

RYE HOUSE (H)
Sunday, May 4
Lost 35-56
Rider replacement for Wortmann, Graversen 4:1, Laukkanen 12, Loof 4:1, Kessler 10 (4), Matthew Wright [G] 1:1, Makinen 4.

PREMIER TROPHY Group C

		M	W	D	L	PtsF	PtsA	Pts
1	Birmingham	6	4	0	2	243	194	10
2	Rye House	6	4	0	2	291	250	9
3	King's Lynn	6	3	0	3	245	211	7
4	**MILDENHALL**	**6**	**1**	**0**	**5**	**203**	**327**	**2**

Weather...

Mildenhall's had two local derbies against neighbours King's Lynn rained off.

Premier League
Sunday, May 25 .... READING (H)
†Sunday, July 13 .... STOKE (H)
Sunday, August 24 .... KING'S LYNN (H)
Friday, September 5 .... SOMERSET (A)
Friday, September 5 .... SOMERSET (A)
Sunday, September 7 .... STOKE (H)

Premier Trophy
Sunday, March 16 .... RYE HOUSE (H)
Sunday, March 23 .... KING'S LYNN (H)
Sunday, April 13 .... RYE HOUSE (H)

†Meeting postponed because of damage to the track by stock cars and electrical problems.

...beaten

Knock Out Cup

Second round, first leg
REDCAR (A)
Thursday, April 24
Lost 40-53
Graversen 9:1, Makinen 1:1, Laukkanen 14:1 (6), *rider replacement for Wortmann*, Kessler 10, Ben Taylor [G] 2:1, Matthew Wright [G] 4.

Second round, second leg
REDCAR (H)
Sunday, April 27
Lost 40-50
Rider replacement for Wortmann, Graversen 8, Laukkanen 13:1, Loof 4:1 (0), Kessler 7, Matthew Wright [G] 5, Makinen 3:1.
Aggregate: Lost 80-103.

Inter League Challenge

PETERBOROUGH (A)
Thursday, March 13
Lost 34-56
Laukkanen 7:1, Smith 6:1 (2), Graversen 8:1, Wortmann 5:1, Kessler 1, Baseby 3:1, Cockle 4:1.

▲▼ *Graversen the Fen Tigers' only heat winner, taking the flag twice in an impressive UK debut. Kessler concussed in a Heat 9 crash.*

Did I really say that?

'We had a brilliant full scale practice'

Mildenhall manager Laurence Rogers before the Fen Tigers embarked on the first ever pointless league campaign

2009 Squad

New promoters **John Bailey** (who left before their first meeting) and **Ray Maskall** took over in February, 2009: Leigh **BOUJOS**, Gary **COTTHAM**, Barrie **EVANS**, Dean **FELTON**, Joe **JACOBS**, David **MASON**, Oliver **RAYSON** and Mark **THOMPSON**.

Premier League

NEWCASTLE

TRACK FILE

Track: Newcastle Stadium, Brough Park, Fossway, Newcastle-upon-Tyne, NE6 2XJ.
Telephone: 0191 2656581.
Hotline: 09068 664679.
Website: www.newcastlespeedway.net
Track Length: 300 metres.
Track Record: 62.1 secs, Kenneth Bjerre, July 20, 2003.
Promoters: George English, Darryl Illingworth and Darren Bond.
Team Sponsors: Sapphire Engineering.
Colours: Black with white diamond.
Nickname: Diamonds.

HISTORY

First meeting: May 17, 1929, Individual.
Leagues: Division One, 1965-1970, 1984. Division Two, 1938-39, 1947-1951, 1961-64, 1975-1983, 1986=87, 1989-1994, 1997-2009. Northern League, 1946. Division Three, 2002-04, English Dirt Track League, 1929. Open licence, 1930, 1945.

Speedway was also held at

- *Gosforth Park, Great North Road, Newcastle-upon-Tyne.*

First meeting: June 1, 1929,Individual.
Leagues: Northern League, 1930. Open licence, 1929,1931.

HONOURS

See facing page.

2008 REVIEW

FAILURE even to reach the Young Shield competition by finishing outside the Premier League's top 12 meant it was a hugely disappointing season at Brough Park.

The Diamonds were expected to be in and around the highly-competitive mid-table area of the Premier League, and if they had known the strides that were to be taken by new signing Jason King, they would probably have expected a top-six finish.

But while King, acquired over the winter from Mildenhall, went forward at a great rate, the story for a number of their other riders was one of far less success.

The team were quickly forced to concentrate on their League campaign with no progress in the Premier Trophy or Knock Out Cup, where they were brushed aside by Somerset.

And things started in relatively encouraging fashion with the Diamonds picking up an early away win at Glasgow, albeit being edged out in a home thriller against Somerset – despite being eight points up with two heats to go!

Diamonds' only other away win, though, came at struggling Mildenhall, and in the meantime there were several other setbacks around their home circuit, where they were beaten a total of seven times, which was never going to be enough for even a top 12 finish.

King put two points on his average, but the remaining members of the top four saw their performances fall away, and George Stancl's season came to an end in early September.

The club made a number of changes as the season moved on, with Jerran Hart showing plenty of talent at reserve despite an injury lay-off – and Danish youngster Kenni Arendt Larsen made a real impact in the closing weeks.

Long-serving rider Richard Juul is now set to move into a managerial role as the Diamonds attempt to re-capture their glory days after a difficult season.

2008 RESULTS

Premier League

Final position....................................Fourteenth

WORKINGTON (H)
Sunday, April 13
Lost 42-48
Franc 11, *rider replacement for Stancl*, Henry 11, Powell 4:1, King 6:1, Robertson 6:1, Stoddart 4:1.
▼ *Rider replacement for the injured Stancl proved costly, collecting just five points.*

GLASGOW (A)
Sunday, May 4
Won 46-44
Franc 13, *rider replacement for Stancl*, Henry 10:1, King 10:3, Powell, did not arrive, Robertson 2:1, Stoddart 11:1.
● *Ben Powell failed to turn up after vehicle problems and was initially suspended by the Diamonds before being released. Five-man Diamonds mounted splendid fightback to secure the points, Henry holding on for second place in Heat 15.*

GLASGOW (H)
Monday, May 5
Won 53-42
Franc 15, *rider replacement for Stancl*, Henry 14, King 8:3, Aaron Summers [G] 1:1, Robertson 3:1, Stoddart 12:2.
▲ *Completed profitable weekend, Stoddart scored 23 (paid 26) from 14 rides across the two meetings against the Tigers.*

BIRMINGHAM (A)
Wednesday, May 7
Lost 44-46
Franc 12, *rider replacement for Stancl*, Henry 10, King 8:3, Daniel Giffard [G] 5, Robertson 0, Stoddart 9:4.
▼ *Jamie Robertson withdrew after being hurt in Heat 2. Diamonds beaten by a 5-1 in a last heat decider when Henry touched the tapes. Henry required treatment after colliding with Jason Lyons – before the start of Heat 3!*

SCUNTHORPE (A)
Friday, May 16
Lost 36-56
Tomas Topinka [G] 18 (4), Daniel Giffard [G] 1, *rider replacement for Stancl*, King 8, Henry 4:1, Robertson 0, Stoddart 5:1.

SOMERSET (H)
Sunmday, May 18
Lost 47-48
Franc 12:2, Juul 4, *rider replacement for Stancl*, King 11:1, Henry 12:1, Robertson 1, Stoddart 7:1.
▼ *Led 37-25 after Heat 10 only to be pulled back in when Jason Doyle made a successful Heat 14 tactical substitute.*

HONOURS

Major honours: 15.
Division Two champions (5†), 1964, 1976, 1982, 1983, 2001.
Division Two Knock Out Cup winners (2), 1976, 1982.
Division Two Supernational winners (2), 1982, 1983.
Division Two Four Team champions (3), 1976, 1982, 1983.
Division Two Pairs champions (1), 1975.
Division Two Gold Cup winners (2), 1991, 1992.
†Newcastle were top of Division Two when racing was suspended at the outbreak of the Second World Wat in 1939 but never officially declared champions.

SQUAD
Jerran Hart, Jason King, Jamie Robertson, Sean Stoddart.
Foreign: Josef Franc, Christian Henry, Matyas Hlavacek, Richard Juul, Kenni Arendt Larsen, Ben Powell, George Stancl.

KING'S LYNN (A)
Wednesday, May 28
Lost 27-65
Franc 3:1, Juul 4, Stancl 5, King 10 (6), Henry 1, Hart 2:1, Stoddart 2.

SOMERSET (A)
Friday, June 6
Lost 25-65
Franc 8, Stoddart 2:1, Stancl 1:1, King 5 (0), Henry 3, Hart 6, Juul 0.
▼ *Received an even bigger beating than their 36-point Cup defeat at the Oak Tree Arena, only race win of the night coming from Franc in Heat 15. Juul was forced to withdraw with rib injury after crashing in Heat 2.*

MILDENHALL (A)
Saturday, June 7
Won 53-39
Franc 10:2, Stoddart 3:1, Stancl 8:2, King 12, Henry 9, Hart 7:2, Arlo Bugeja [G] 4.
▲ *Withstood a surprising Mildenhall fightback in mid-meeting to take 5-1s in three of the last four races.*

STOKE (H)
Sunday, June 8
Won 48-42
Rider replacement for Franc, Stoddart 3, Stancl 11:2, **King 18**, Henry 10, Hart 5:2, Arlo Bugeja [G] 1.
▲ *King scored a fabulous maximum as the Diamonds secured victory even without Franc, on European Championship duty.*

READING (H)
Sunday, June 15
Won 45-44
Franc 11:1, Stoddart 3, Stancl 6:2, King 12, Henry 8,

Hart 4, Paul Clews [G] 1:1.

▲ *Took a dramatic victory when Mark Lemon was excluded from Heat 15 for unfair riding when he impeded Franc on the second bend.*

KING'S LYNN (H)
Sunday, June 22
Won 50-42
Franc 11, Stoddart 2, Stancl 9, King 11:3, Henry 8:1, Hart 6, Jesper Kristiansen [G] 3:1.

BERWICK (H)
Sunday, July 13
Won 47-42
Franc 6, Juul 4:3, Stancl 5.1, King 10:2, Henry 12, Hart 3:1, Stoddart 7.

BIRMINGHAM (H)
Sunday, July 20
Lost 44-46
Franc 7, Juul 3:1, Stancl 8:2, King 13:1, Henry 8, Jonathon Grey [G] 0, Stoddart 5.

▼ *Youngster Jack Roberts inflicted plenty of damage as the Diamonds threw away a four-point lead and Stancl could make no headway in Heat 15 .*

SHEFFIELD (A)
Thursday, July 24
Lost 38-55
Franc 12 (6), Juul 3:1, Stancl 3, King 16, *rider replacement for Henry*, Luke Priest [G] 3, Stoddart 1.

▲ *King's display reported as the best by a visiting rider at Owlerton so far in the season. Franc was the only man to provide any back-up.*

SHEFFIELD (H)
Sunday, July 27
Won 48-41
Stancl 9:2, *rider replacement for Henry*, Franc 6:1, Juul 7:2, King 14, Jonathan Bethell [G] 0, Stoddart 12:1.

▲ *Trailed by four points with three heats to go but stunned the Tigers with a 5-1 in Heat 13 and a 5-0 in Heat 14.*

REDCAR (H)
Sunday, August 3
Lost 42-48
Stancl 7, *rider replacement for Henry*, Franc 10, Juul 1, King 14, Adam McKinna [G] 1, Stoddart 9:1.

▼ *Rider replacement for Henry accounted for just one point as the Diamonds again faded in the second half of a meeting.*

READING (A)
Monday, August 4
Lost 32-60
Stancl 2, *rider replacement for Henry*, Franc 8, Juul 6:2, King 14 (6), Luke Priest [G] 2:1, Stoddart 0.

ISLE OF WIGHT (A)
Tuesday, August 5
Lost 22-68
Stancl 3, *rider replacement for Henry*, Franc 6:1, Stoddart 0, King 11 (1), Luke Priest [G] 0, Juul 2.

Danish youngster Kenni Larsen confused some fans because he was also known as Kenni Arendt.

MILDENHALL (H)
Sunday, August 10
Won 68-22
Stancl 12, Stoddart 8:2, Franc 10:1, King 9:2, Henry 9:1, Hart 11:3, Juul 9:3.

▲ *Record home win in the Premier League era for the Diamonds, although Theo Pijper and Sebastian Truminski ensured only Stancl would go unbeaten.*

REDCAR (A)
Thursday, August 14
Lost 33-59
Stancl 9 (4), Stoddart 1, Franc 4, King 11, Henry 0, Hart 3, Juul 5.

▼ *Henry's appearance lasted just one ride as he aggravated his shoulder injury.*

BERWICK (A)
Saturday, August 16
Lost 31-62
Stancl 6, Stoddart 2:1, Franc 7:1, King 12 (6), *rider replacement for Henry*, Hart 0, Juul 4.

EDINBURGH (A)
Friday, September 12
Lost 29-64
Franc 5:1, Stoddart 4, King 11 (6), Stancl 1, Henry 6, Hart 0, Juul 2.

WORKINGTON (A)
Saturday, September 13
Lost 31-61
Franc 9:1 (4), Stoddart 0, King 6, *rider replacement for Stancl*, Henry 7:1, Hart 7:2, Juul 2.

▼ *Stancl would undoubtedly have scored more than rider replacement (four), but bright spot was Hart.*

EDINBURGH (H)
Sunday, September 14
Lost 40-49
Franc 9, Stoddart 2, King 9, *rider replacement for Stancl*, Henry 11, Hart 1:1, Juul 8:3.

▼ *Destroyed by a remarkable 21-point maximum by Monarchs reserve Matthew Wethers.*

RYE HOUSE (H)
Sunday,September 14
Lost 33-41
Franc 8, Stoddart 3, King 11 (6), *rider replacement for Stancl*, Henry 3, Hart 4, Juul 4.

●▼ *Meeting abandoned after Heat 12 due to time restrictions. Result to stand. Juul broke collarbone in Heat 8.*

ISLE OF WIGHT (H)
Monday, September 22
Won 48-42
Franc 7:1, Stoddart 6:1, King 7:1, Larsen 8, Henry 12, Hart 3, John Branney [G] 5:3.

STOKE (A)
Saturday, September 20
Lost 38-54
Franc 13:1 (4), Stoddart 2:1, King 6, Larsen 6, Henry 10:1, Hart 0, Mark Baseby [G] 1.

▲▼ *Debutant Larsen showed his talent with two wins as well as two exclusions.*

NEWCASTLE

Rider	M	R	Pts	BP	TPts	Ave	F	P	TR	TPts	TS	TSPts
Kenni Arendt LARSEN	4	19	38	2	40	8.42	0	0	1	3	1	0
Josef FRANC	**38**	**189**	**371**	**19**	**390**	**8.25**	**0**	**1**	**7**	**17**	**0**	**0**
Jason KING	40	198	375	30	405	8.18	1	0	8	18	0	0
Christian HENRY	**34**	**151**	**262**	**13**	**275**	**7.28**	**0**	**0**	**0**	**0**	**0**	**0**
George STANCL	22	95	159	14	173	7.28	1	0	1	2	0	0
Ben POWELL	**11**	**42**	**46**	**11**	**57**	**5.43**	**0**	**1**	**0**	**0**	**0**	**0**
Richard JUUL	17	78	69	15	84	4.31	0	0	0	0	0	0
Sean STODDART	**39**	**181**	**166**	**23**	**189**	**4.18**	**0**	**0**	**0**	**0**	**0**	**0**
Jamie ROBERTSON	15	56	38	15	53	3.79	0	0	0	0	0	0
Jerran HART	**18**	**87**	**66**	**12**	**78**	**3.59**	**0**	**0**	**0**	**0**	**0**	**0**
Guests	***21***	***89***	***61***	***8***	***69***	***3.10***	***0***	***0***	***1***	***2***	***0***	***0***

For Ben POWELL see Scunthorpe (PL); for Jamie ROBERTSON see Scunthorpe (CL); for Jerran HART see Newport and Sittingbourne.

Bright smiles but a miserable season: the 2008 Newcastle starting squad – George Stancl, Jamie Robertson, Josef Franc, Ben Powell and Sean Stoddart. Kneeling at front Christian Henry and Jason King. Only four of the squad survived the season with Stancl, Robertson and Powell all being replaced before the end of the summer.

Newcastle went on a run of one win in 12 Premie League and Tyne Tees Trophy matches in a nine-week spell between August 3 and September 22.

RYE HOUSE (A)
Friday, September 26
Lost 34-59
Franc 8, Stoddart 0, King 5, Larsen 11:1 (6), Henry 2, Hart 4, Mark Baseby [G] 4.
▼ *Larsen's win in Heat 7 was some relief as the score was 6-30 at that stage.*

SCUNTHORPE (H)
Sunday, October 12
Lost 46-47
Franc 15 (6), Stoddart 0, King 7:1, Larsen 13:1 (TSX), Henry 8:1, Hart 0, Mark Baseby [G] 3.
▼ *Fell one point short of successfully coming back from 10 points down – but ex-Diamond Ben Powell was involved in an unsavoury incident with Larsen, when he aimed his bike at his rival after an on-track clash.*

PREMIER LEAGUE

	M	W	D	L	PtsF	PtsA	Pts
1 Edinburgh	30	22	2	6	1562	1161	53
2 Somerset	30	21	0	9	1517	1223	48
3 King's Lynn	30	18	5	7	1624	1111	45
4 Rye House	30	19	0	11	1500	1232	42
5 Workington	30	17	2	11	1435.5	1300.5	41
6 Berwick	30	16	2	12	1428	1316	37
7 Redcar	30	16	1	13	1369	1374	37
8 Sheffield	30	15	2	13	1381	1345	35
9 Reading	30	15	1	14	1350	1405	34
10 Scunthorpe	30	15	0	15	1309	1434	33
11 Isle of Wight	30	15	0	15	1359	1390	31
12 Birmingham	30	13	0	17	1317.5	1401.5	30
13 Stoke	30	11	1	18	1307	1441	25
14 NEWCASTLE	**30**	**10**	**0**	**20**	**1220**	**1501**	**22**
15 Glasgow	30	9	0	21	1297	1469	19
16 Mildenhall	30	0	0	30	932	1804	0

Premier Trophy

STOKE (H)
Sunday, March 16
Won 51-42
Henry 9:1, Powell 3:1, Franc 13:1, King 9:2, Stancl 12, Robertson 2:2, Stoddart 3.
▲ *Franc's only defeat was at the hands of newcomer Jesper Kristiansen in Heat 12.*

REDCAR (H)
Sunday, March 23
Won 52-38
Henry 8, Powell 2:2, Franc 9, King 8:1, Stancl 14, Robertson 2:1, Stoddart 9:1.
● *Match completed despite mid-afternoon snowstorm caused the top surface to be scraped off.*

REDCAR (A)
Thursday, March 27
Drew 45-45
Henry 6, Powell 3:1, Franc 13, King 4, Stancl 10:1, Robertson 4:3, Stoddart 5:1.

SHEFFIELD (H)
Sunday, March 30
Won 63-27
Henry 10:2, **Powell 10:2**, **Franc 14:1**, King 8:2, Stancl 10:1, Robertson 5:1, Stoddart 6.

SCUNTHORPE (A)
Friday, April 4
Lost 38-55
Henry 5:1, Powell 3, Franc 2, King 15 (6), Stancl 8, Robertson 1, Stoddart 4.

SCUNTHORPE (H)
Monday, April 21
Lost 43-47
Franc 10:1, *rider replacement for Stancl*, Henry 10, Powell 11, King 4:1, Robertson 5:1, Stoddart 3:1.
▼ *Defeat effectively ended the Diamonds' chances of reaching the semi-finals, with Henry and Franc unable to take the 5-1 which was needed from Heat 15.*

SHEFFIELD (A)
Thursday, May 1
Lost 33-59
Franc 13 (4), *rider replacement for Stancl*, Henry 5, Powell 3:1, King 8:1, Robertson 4:1, Stoddart 0.

STOKE (A)
Saturday, May 10
Lost 39-54
Franc 16 (6), Daniel Giffard [G] 4:1, *rider replacement for Stancl*, King 6:2, Henry 6:1, Scott Richardson [G] 0, Stoddart 7.

PREMIER TROPHY Group B

	M	W	D	L	PtsF	PtsA	Pts
1 Sheffield	8	6	0	2	386	345	14
2 Redcar	8	3	2	3	362	360	8
3 Scunthorpe	8	3	1	4	345	380	8
4 NEWCASTLE	**8**	**3**	**1**	**4**	**364**	**367**	**7**

Knock Out Cup

Second round, first leg
SOMERSET (A)
Friday, April 25
Lost 28-64
Franc 12 (4), *rider replacement for Stancl*, Henry 5, Powell 2, King 3, Robertson 1:1, Danny Warwick [G] 5.

Second round, second leg
SOMERSET (H)
Sunday, April 27
Drew 39-39
Franc 13, *rider replacement for Stancl*, Henry 10, Powell 5:3, King 5, Robertson 2:2, Stoddart 4:1.
● *Meeting abandoned after Heat 13 because of rain. Result to stand.*
Aggregate: Lost 67-103.

2009 Squad

Steve BOXALL (7.45), Jason KING (7.24), Kenni Arendt LARSEN (7.00), Derek SNEDDON (6.44), Trent LEVERINGTON (6.33), Craig BRANNEY (3.98), Casper WORTMANN (3.00).

Challenge

TYNE TWEED TROPHY
First leg
BERWICK (A)
Saturday, March 8
Won 46-43
Henry 5:1, Powell 5, Franc 11, King 4, Stancl 12:1, Robertson 4, Stoddart 5:2.

TYNE TWEED TROPHY
Second leg
BERWICK (H)
Sunday, March 9
Lost 44-46
Henry 6:1, Powell 4:1, Franc 10, King 2:1, Stancl 12, Robertson 2:1, Stoddart 8:2.
Aggregate: Won 90-89.

TYNE TEES TROPHY
First leg
REDCAR (H)
Sunday, August 24
Lost 42-48
Stancl 12:2, Stoddart 4, *rider replacement for Franc*, Hlavacek 0, King 15, Hart 2:1, Juul 9:1.
▼ *Franc was missing due to the re-arranged European Championship Final, and new-boy Hlavacek was off the pace, with the Bears taking full advantage.*

TYNE TEES TROPHY
Second leg
REDCAR (A)
Thursday, August 28
Lost 31-50
Stancl 8, Stoddart 0, Franc 13, Hlavacek 0, King 6, Harty 0, Mitchell Davey [G] 4.
▼ *Hlavacek sparked a Heat 14 tangle also involving guest Davey and Chris Kerr, which forced the abandonment of the meeting due to the curfew.*
Aggregate: Lost 73-98.

Individual

SAPPHIRE ENGINEERING JUNIOR CHAMPIONSHIP
Sunday, May 11
REDCAR'S Australian Scott James didn't put a foot wrong in five rides as he coasted to an unbeaten maximum.

James, who actually made his UK debut at Brough Park six years ago, had three points to spare although runner-up Paul Starke shone on his Byker bow, winning his last three rides.

Scott James 15, Paul Starke 12, Jonathan Bethell 12, Brendan Johnson 11, Scott Richardson 11, Luke Priest 9, Steven Jones 9, Martin Emerson 7, Jonathan Grey 6, Mike Pickering 6, David Wallinger 5, Keiron Morris 5, Jitendra Duffill 4, Guy Kendrew 4, Gary Irving 2, Scott Meakins 1.

Roll of Honour
2008 .... Scott JAMES

SAPPHIRE ENGINEERING PRECISION TROPHY
Sunday, September 28
JOSEF Franc overcame a tape-touching 15 metre handicap last place third ride to top the scorecard.

Unbeaten in his other four rides, he had a point to spare after runner-up Christian Henry (three race wins) coould only finish third behind impressive Danish new boy Kenni Arendt Larsen and John Branney.

Josef Franc 12, Christian Henry 11 Kenni Arendt Larsen 11+3, Ty Proctor 11+2, John Branney 10, Carl Wilkinson 7, Craig Branney 7, Ben Wilson 6, Jason King 5, Emiliano Sanchez 4, Chris Kerr 4, Jerran Hart 2.

Roll of Honour
2008 .... Josef FRANC

NEWCASTLE OPEN CHAMPIONSHIP
Sunday, October 19
JASON Doyle rounded off Newcastle's season with victory in their second major individual meeting of the year.

He was beaten by Berwick's Michal Makovsky in Heat 2 but that was the only point he dropped all night as he won his last five rides.

Originally the meeting was to be contested by 16 riders over the conventional 20 heat format but withdrawals through a variety of reasons – some genuine, others less so – prompted the promotion to reduce the races to 15 and an all-important Grand Final.

That the event clashed with Reading's big End of an Era meeting at Smallmead added to the problems in attracting a big-name line-up.

Jason Doyle 14+3, Carl Wilkinson 9+2, Christian Henry 11+1, Josef Franc 10+0, Lee Complin 9, Trent Leverington 9, Michal Makovsky 9, Craig Branney 5, Jason King 4, John Branney 4, Jerran Hart 4, Lee Dicken 1.

Roll of Honour
2008 .... Jason DOYLE

SPARKLING DIAMOND Jason King

Premier League

NEWPORT

TRACK FILE

Track: Hayley Stadium, Plover Close, Nash Mead, Queensway Meadows, Newport NP19 4SZ.
Hotline: 09068 664676.
Track Length: 285 metres.
Track Record: 58.38 secs, Craig Watson,. August 3, 2003.
Promoters: Steve Mallett and Nick Mallett.
Colours: Yellow and black.
Nickname: Wasps.
The track closed down temporarily on April 26, 2008, after the sudden death of sole promoter Tim Stone.

HISTORY

First meeting: May 4, 1997, Newport v Exeter, Division Two.
Leagues: Division Two, 1997-2009. Division Three, 1997-2006.
Speedway was also held at
● *Somerton Park, Newport, Gwent, South Wales.*
First meeting: April 17, 1964, Newport v Cradley Heath, Southern League challenge.
Leagues: Division One, 1965-1976. Division Two, 1964, 1977.
Newport have also entered the 2009 National League, racing as the Hornets.

HONOURS

Major honours: 3.
Division Two Knock Out Cup winners (1), 1964.
Division Two Trophy winners (1), 1999.
Division Three champions (1), 1999.

Testimonial

NICK SIMMONS TESTIMONIAL
Sunday, March 16
Lewis Bridger 11+3, Chris Harris 13+2, Billy Janniro 14+1, Mads Korneliussen 14+0, Niels-Kristian Iversen 11, Leigh Lanham 10, Krzysztof Stojanowski 8, Rusty Harrison 7, Tony Atkin 7, Marek Mroz 7, Michael Coles 6, Chris Schramm 3, David Mason 3, Chris Mills 2, Karl Mason 2, Paul Fry 0.

2008 REVIEW

FOR the second season running, a club in one of Britain's top two divisions did not see out the season as the Wasps were forced out of the Premier League in tragic circumstances.

Promoter Tim Stone ran what amounted to a one-man show at the Hayley Stadium, and was the man fully responsible for the return of the sport to the South Wales town just over a decade ago.

Crowds had dipped in recent years due to poor results on-track, and Stone had made a further attempt to drag the Wasps away from the basement of the Premier League with a new look team for 2008 including the welcome return of one old face in Australian star Craig Watson.

The Premier Trophy results weren't wholly encouraging as both Somerset and Reading took away wins from the Wasps, who were happy to defeat the Isle of Wight at home and come close themselves to a shock away win at the Smallbrook Stadium thanks to a stunning performance from reserve Nick Simmons.

They were also set to go out of the Knock Out Cup after a 60-30 first leg defeat at Rye House at the end of April – but that paled into insignificance with the remainder of events that weekend.

Stone had not attended the Hoddesdon meeting as he was visiting his ill mother, and he planned to watch that evening's Slovenian Grand Prix on TV but he suffered a heart attack and died in the vicinity of the Royal Gwent Hospital.

The tragedy did not become apparent until riders started to arrive at the stadium for the Sunday meeting, and the sad story continued with his mother Marion Wood passing away that day.

Following the funeral, Wasps riders and officials remained optimistic that the legalities could be completed in time to allow the club to fulfil their 2008 fixtures, but this proved to be impossible and they were forced to withdraw from the Premier League.

2008 RESULTS

Premier League

Final position..Withdrew

BERWICK (A)
Saturday, April 12
Lost 38-55
Watson 3:2, Clews 16 (6), Mroz 5, *rider replacement for Atkin,* Truminski 8:1, Hart 1:1, Simmons 5.

BIRMINGHAM (H)
Sunday, April 13
2-4, abandoned rain, waterlogged track.
Watson 0, Clews 2, Mroz, Truminski, Hart, Simmons, did not ride, *rider replacement for Atkin.*
● *After Jack Hargreaves came down twice in an aborted Heat 2, rain returned and the meeting was called off.*

REDCAR (H)
Sunday, April 20
Lost 46-47
Watson 13:1 (6), Simmons 8:3, Truminski 9:1, *rider replacement for Atkin,* Clews 7:1, Hart 1, Mroz 8:1.
▼ *Visitors were reduced to four riders but still held on to win as Watson and Truminski were beaten by Gary Havelock in Heat 15.*

Premier Trophy

SOMERSET (H)
Sunday, March 23
Lost 43-50
Watson 11 (TS2), Clews 5, Mroz 2:1, Atkin 10, Truminski 10 (4), Simmons 4:1, Hart 1.
▼ *Never really recovered from disastrous start which saw the Rebels go into a 12-point lead after eight races.*

SOMERSET (A)
Friday, March 28
Lost 26-67
Watson 14 (6), Clews 2, Mroz 0, Atkin 4, Truminski 3, Simmons 3, Hart 0.

READING (H)
Sunday, March 30
Lost 34-56
Watson 7 (1), Clews 4:1, Mroz 4:2, Atkin 6:1, Truminski 8:1, Hart 0, Simmons 5.
▼ *Scoreline went from 15-15 to 22-38 in the space of five races as the Wasps suffered a heavy home defeat.*

ISLE OF WIGHT (A)
Tuesday, April 1
Lost 43-46
Watson 10, Clews 3:1, Mroz 0, Atkin 8, Truminski 3:1, Hart 3:1, Simmons 16:2.
▲ *Stunning showing from Simmons on his old home circuit, Atkin and Watson also contributing two race wins apiece in encouraging performance.*

ISLE OF WIGHT (H)
Sunday, April 6
Won 47-42
Watson 9:2, Clews 5, Mroz 5:1, Atkin 0, Truminski 12,

SQUAD
Tony Atkin, Paul Clews, Jerran Hart, Nick Simmons.
Foreign: Marek Mroz, Sebastian Truminski, Craig Watson.

Hart 4, Simmons 12:2.
▼▲ *Tony Atkin crashed in Heat 3 and withdrew from the meeting with broken ankle. First win of the season, coming back from nine points down.*

READING (A)
Monday, April 7
Lost 33-59
Watson 1, Clews 9, Mroz 4:1, *rider replacement for Atkin,* Truminski 12 (4), Hart 6:2, Simmons 1:1.

PREMIER TROPHY Group D

		M	W	D	L	PtsF	PtsA	Pts
1	Reading	6	4	0	2	300	248	10
2	Somerset	6	4	0	2	296	257	10
3	Isle of Wight	6	3	0	3	275	272	6
4	**NEWPORT**	**6**	**1**	**0**	**5**	**226**	**320**	**2**

Knock Out Cup

Second round, first leg
RYE HOUSE (A)
Saturday, April 26
Lost 30-60
Watson 5, Simmons 1:1, Truminski 4 (1), *rider replacement for Atkin,* Clews 7:1, Hart 4, Mroz 9:1.
▼ *The last meeting raced by Newport as the second leg the following afternoon was called off after the death of sole promoter Tim Stone.*

Second round, second leg
RYE HOUSE (H)
Sunday, April 27
Cancelled.
The passing of promoter Tim Stone only became clear in the build-up to the meeting, which was called off around an hour before start-time.

Individual

NEW YEAR CLASSIC
Sunday, January 6, 2008
Chris Harris 14+3, Brent Werner 11+2, Leigh Lanham 9+1, Ritchie Hawkins 10+0, Paul Fry 8, Krzysztof Stojanowski 8, Adam Roynon 7, Phil Morris 7, Lewis Bridger 6, Ricky Ashworth 4, Marek Mroz 3, Marcin Kozdras 1.
■ *The New Year Classic was traditionally held at Newport until owner Tim Stone's death. First staged on Sunday, January 2, 1999, it became the annual outdoor winter meeting, the only one sanctioned by the Speedway Control Bureau.*

For Roll of Honour see Elite League Poole.

2009 Squad
Mark LEMON (7.41), Craig WATSON (6.89), Chris KERR (6.47), Jordan FRAMPTON (6.33), Paul FRY (6.19), Brent WERNER (5.57), James HOLDER (5.22), Nick SIMMONS (4.16).

NEWPORT

Rider	M	R	Pts	BP	TPts	Ave	F	P	TR	TPts	TS	TSPts
Craig WATSON	9	43	73	5	78	7.25	0	0	3	6	1	1
Sebastian TRUMINSKI	**9**	**44**	**69**	**4**	**73**	**6.64**	**0**	**0**	**3**	**4**	**0**	**0**
Tony ATKIN	5	18	28	1	29	6.44	0	0	0	0	0	0
Nick SIMMONS	**9**	**43**	**55**	**10**	**65**	**6.05**	**0**	**0**	**0**	**0**	**0**	**0**
Paul CLEWS	9	43	58	4	62	5.77	0	0	1	3	0	0
Marek MROZ	**9**	**38**	**37**	**7**	**44**	**4.63**	**0**	**0**	**0**	**0**	**0**	**0**
Jerran HART	9	41	20	4	24	2.34	0	0	0	0	0	0

Averages relate to two Premier League matches, six Premier Trophy matches and one Knock Out Cup match. All results were expunged from official records.

For Craig WATSON see Birmingham; for Sebastian TRUMINSKI and Marek MROZ see Mildenhall; for Tony ATKIN and Paul CLEWS see Berwick; for Nick SIMMONS see Belle Vue; for Jerran HART see Newcastle and Sittingbourne.

TIMOTHY STONE

Born: June 26, 1953.

Died: April 26, 2008.

TIM Stone lived, breathed and eventually died for speedway – and the sport will be poorer for his passing....

The man who brought racing back to Gwent was only 54 – but he had seen through his driving ambition to re-establish the sport in his hometown: a quest that took more than five years.

Tim – like all of us – had his faults: he was obsessive, reluctant to delegate and a man of staunch views and opinions.

He fell out with people but no-one ever questioned whether he had his heart in speedway and he will be sadly missed by everyone, not least those who worked alongside him at Queensway Meadows and the riders who wore the Wasps' race-jacket.

He had been a fan since he was 11, making his first visit to Somerton Park when speedway was first introduced there in 1964 after Mike Parker and Charles Foot had opened the track to huge crowds at the home of the then Football League side Newport County.

As soon as he was old enough he was helping out in the pits, initially as a mechanic to Bob Coles, later with Phil Crump, father of two times World Champion Jason.

He even had a go himself, practising on the sands down in Devon and making weekend trips to the Sunday afternoon training track at Mildenhall.

But he was never going to be Wales' second World Champion and after a nasty prang at West Row decided his riding days were over.

One of his saddest days was when the Wasps dropped out of the top-flight at the end of 1976, the team transferred to Bristol's Eastville Stadium.

It was the beginning of the end.

After a year racing in the old National League, the Wasps closed down and, for many, that was the end of a glorious era.

Tim became an infrequent follower, his interest dulled but never extinguished by Newport's sad demise. Even though he was working in Germany – he was an engineer, specialising in book binding – he still watched as many meetings as he could, on the grass, on the ice and the shale.

He returned to Wales in the late nineties and, flushed with a successful career, promised himself he would revive speedway where he was born and lived.

He began searching the area for a possible site...and his passion was rekindled. Others had the same idea but it was Tim who had the fortitude and drive to see his ambition through.

He began travelling down to Exeter where he struck up a firm friendship with the late Colin Hill – another super enthusiast who poured his heart into speedway – and sometimes they would travel together to away meetings.

Tim would talk long into the night about his dream of one day standing on the centre green of his own stadium to see Newport Wasps race on.

In 1993 the old Somerton Park home went under the hammer, and Tim bought the old grandstand seats, lights and turnstiles.

He stored them while he continued his search for a new site and was probably the only man in Wales who still believed in his project.

Finally he reached agreement with the Welsh Development Agency for a 125 year lease on a 7.3 acre site bordering the old Llanwern Steelworks.

It was absolutely perfect situation on a new industrial-cum-retail park and work started on building a stadium from scratch in December, 1996.

Five months later Tim realised his dream as he stood on the centre green, drenched by a Bank Holiday cloudburst, watching Paul Fry win the first-ever race at the Hayley Stadium.

The meeting only got as far as heat seven when referee Ronnie Allan was forced to call it off with the Wasps leading by half a dozen points.

It was hardly the opener he wanted but Tim quickly endeared himself to the new and old fans by offering a reduction in admission to the following week's meeting!

He also became something of a pioneer, running teams in both the Premier and Conference League; staging a winter event which has become an annual date on the supporters' calendar; hosting pre and post British Grand Prix meetings surrounding the Cardiff bonanza.

And, perhaps even more important, he was an absolutely tireless worker, being at his track early some mornings, late other nights, and when the winter has been at its harshest.

Except for the early days it has invariably been a financial struggle – so much so that at one time to help meet his bills Tim worked a night shift stacking shelves at a local supermarket.

But the one thing I have never, ever heard anyone say about Newport is that they were owed money.

He always met his commitments and that reflects the inner honesty of the man who will never ever be forgotten for what he did for Newport Speedway.

The club's future is now in limbo and there must be serious doubts about what will happen.

Tim missed the Wasps' Saturday night trip to Hertfordshire because he was visiting his ill mother Marion Wood in Newport's Royal Gwent Hospital.

Tragically she died within 24 hours of her son suffering that fatal heart attack.

No-one within the sport really knows if Tim had any next-of-kin and it is up to his solicitors to inform the British Speedway Promoters' Association whether he made a will and, if he did, what provision he made for the continuance of racing at Queensway Meadows.

Tim gave the best years of his life to Newport Speedway.

It would be an unforgiveable crime if his death was also to spell the end of his beloved Wasps....

Peter Oakes
Speedway Star,
May 3, 2008

Premier League

READING

TRACK FILE

Track: Reading Stadium, A33 Relief Road, Smallmead, Reading, Berkshire, RG2 0JL
Telephone: 01189 867343 (from 3pm racedays), 07796 666984 (all other times).
Hotline: 09068 664662.
Website: www.readingspeedway.com
Track Length: 304 metres.
Track Record: 58.1 secs, Per Jonsson, October 12,1987.
2008 Promoters: Mark Legg and Malcolm Holloway.
Colours: Blue and white.
Nickname: Racers.

HISTORY

First meeting: April 28, 1975, Reading v Hull, Division One.
Leagues: Division One, 1975-1996, 2006-2007. Division Two, 1997-2005, 2008. Division Three, 1996-97.
Speedway was also held at
● *Reading Greyhound Stadium, Oxford Road, Tilehurst, Reading.*
First meeting: June 17, 1968, Reading v Nelson, Division Two.
Leagues: Division One, 1971-73. Division Two, 1968-1970.

HONOURS

Major honours: 12.
Division One champions (4), 1973, 1980, 1990, 1992.
Division One Knock Out Cup winners (1), 1990,
Division One Premiership winners (2), 1991, 1993.
Division One Four Team champions (1), 1993.
Inter League Knock Out Cup winners (1), 1992.
Division Two champions (1), 1997.
Division Two Knock Out Cup winners (1), 1998.
Division Two Pairs champions (1), 2004.

2008 REVIEW

AFTER a financially-disastrous flirtation with the Elite League, the Racers dropped back into the second tier and appeared to have built a team with real potential for honours.

However, their story was one of under-achievement as a promising start to the campaign fizzled out in the second half of the season.

A much-changed team was well led by Danish star Ulrich Østergaard, who more than confirmed his status as one of the top riders in the Premier League, but too often he was left at the head of the scorechart on his own as riders such as Mark Lemon, Chris Mills and Tomas Suchanek saw their averages dip.

Racers qualified for the semi-finals of the Premier Trophy, mainly due to a spectacular away win at Somerset after the Rebels had themselves taken the points at Smallmead.

But they were knocked out of that competition by Edinburgh after going down by 22 points in the first leg of the semi-final, and Somerset gained some revenge too with victory in the Knock Out Cup tie between the teams – Reading looking set to go through but being hit by an 8-1 setback in Heat 14 of the second leg.

The League campaign promised much with away wins at Redcar and Birmingham keeping the Racers well in touch but these were not added to, and dropped points at home against the top sides left the club outside their hoped-for top four place.

Their last win turned out to be on September 1 against Scunthorpe and the last-ever team meeting at Smallmead was an unmitigated disaster as their Young Shield bid ended with an embarrassing 60-33 home defeat against Redcar.

Reading are now set to take the 2009 season out of the sport as they await the construction of a new stadium which will hopefully see them back in action in the following campaign.

2008 RESULTS

Premier League

Final position..Ninth

WORKINGTON (H)
Monday, April 21
Won 54-39
Lemon 7:1, Mills 6:1, Østergaard 14, Suchanek 8:1, Madsen 6:2, Smith 10:1, Warwick 3:2.

ISLE OF WIGHT (H)
Monday, May 5
Won 46-44
Lemon 10:1, Mills 6:1, **Østergaard 15**, Suchanek 3, Madsen 6, Smith 0, Nicki Glanz [G] 6.
▲ *Racers trailed 37-41 and then 41-43 before Østergaard and Lemon sent the Bank Holiday crowd home happy with a last-heat 5-1. Jamie Smith withdrew with concussion.*

ISLE OF WIGHT (A) SKY TV
Tuesday, May 6
Lost 34-58
Lemon 9, Mills 2, Østertgaard 12:1 (4), Suchanek 2:1, Madsen 5, Jay Herne [G] 1, Joe Haines [G] 3.
▼ *Started encouragingly but quickly faded after the first four heats and were well beaten in front of the TV cameras.*

EDINBURGH (A)
Friday, May 9
Lost 43-49
Lemon 12 (6), Mills 4:1, Østergaard 13:1 (TS2), Suchanek 6:2, Madsen 4, Gary Beaton [G] 0, Ross Brady [G] 4.
▼ *One of the best showings of an away team at Armadale but undone by a four-race mid-meeting spell which they conceded 18-5.*

WORKINGTON (A)
Saturday, May 10
Lost 36-54
Lemon 9, Mills 3, Østergaard 13, Suchanek 0, Madsen 8, Tom Brown [G] 3:1, Ross Brady [G] 0.
▼ *Handicap of being without their two regular reserves too much, despite a fine show from ex-Comet Østergaard.*

SHEFFIELD (H)
Monday, May 12
Won 60-33
Lemon 10:1, Mills 6:1, **Østergaard 15**, Suchanek 7:1, Madsen 9:1, Nicki Glanz [G] 4:2, Joe Haines [G] 9:1.

REDCAR (H)
Monday, May 19
Won 57-35
Lemon 9:1, Mills 7:2, Østergaard 14, Suchanek 7:1, Madsen 12:1, Smith 4:1, Nicki Glanz [G] 4.

RYE HOUSE (H) SKY TV
Tuesday, May 27
Won 47-46
Lemon 9, Mills 6:2, Østergaard 11, Suchanek 8:2, Madsen 7, Smith 4:1, Nicki Glanz [G] 2:2.

SQUAD
Chris Mills, Jamie Smith, Danny Warwick.
Foreign: Mark Lemon, Tom Madsen, Ulrich Østergaard, Tomas Suchanek.

▲ *Suchanek and Smith took a match-clinching 5-1 in Heat 14 after Racers' ten-point lead had been eradicated.*

STOKE (H)
Monday, June 2
Won 54-41
Lemon 8:2, Mills 7:1, **Østergaard 15**, Suchanek 5:2, Madsen 13:1, Smith 2, Nicki Glanz [G] 4.

BIRMINGHAM (H)
Monday, June 9
Won 48-42
Lemon 11:2, Mills 9:2, Østergaard 6, Suchanek 6, Madsen 3, Smith 12, Nicki Glanz [G] 1.

BERWICK (A)
Saturday, June 14
Lost 32-61
Lemon 14 (6), Mills 5:1, Østergaard 9, Suchanek 0, *rider replacement for Madsen*, Smith 4, Nicki Glanz [G] 0.
▼ *Former Bandits Madsen and Warwick both missed their return to Shielfield Park due to injury.*

NEWCASTLE (A)
Sunday, June 15
Lost 44-45
Lemon 6, Mills 5:1, Østergaard 10:3, Suchanek 7, Madsen 6:1, Smith 5, Nicki Glanz [G] 5:2.
▼ *Thought they had snatched a draw with a 4-2 in Heat 15 but Lemon had been excluded for a first-bend incident which caused the retirement of Josef Franc – even though the Australian kept on racing.*

MILDENHALL (H)
Monday, June 16
Won 60-33
Lemon 10:2, Mills 10, Østergaard 9:2, Suchanek 12:1, Madsen 6:1, Smith 7:3, Nicki Glanz [G] 6:1.
▲ *Dominated from start to finish with even the home fans grateful to Kaj Laukkanen (16) for providing some opposition.*

REDCAR (A)
Thursday, June 19
Won 48-42
Lemon 7:1, Mills 8:1, Østergaard 12, Suchanek 6:2, Madsen 3:1, Smith 7, Nicki Glanz [G] 5:3.

EDINBURGH (H)
Sunday, July 13
Lost 41-48
Lemon 12:1, Madsen 7:2, Østergaard 11:1, Suchanek 2, Mills 4:1, Smith 5:1, Nicki Glanz [G] 0.
▼ *Six points behind when Østergaard crashed out of Heat 5.*

BIRMINGHAM (A)
Wednesday, July 16
Won 49-40
Lemon 10:1, Madsen 9, Josef Franc [G] 8:1, Suchanek 6, Mills 7, Smith 5, Nicki Glanz [G] 4:1.

BERWICK (H)
Monday, July 21
Won 47-46
Lemon 9:3, Madsen 9:1, Jason Doyle [G] 13, Suchanek 2:1, Mills 7, Smith 3, Nicki Glanz [G] 4:2.

GLASGOW (A)
Sunday, July 27
Lost 32-60
Lemon 8:1, Madsen 4:1, Kevin Doolan [G] 10 (4), Suchanek 0, Mills 2, Smith 4, Nicki Glanz [G] 4.

GLASGOW (H)
Monday, July 28
Won 51-43
Lemon 7:1, Madsen 10:1, **Østergaard 15**, Suchanek 7:2, Mills 8, Smith 1, Nicki Glanz [G] 3:2.
▲ *Østergaard made a successful return from injury although Smith crashed out and suffered shoulder damage.*

SOMERSET (A)
Friday, August 1
Lost 31-62
Lemon 8, Madsen 2:1, Østergaard 14 (6), Suchanek 1, Mills 3, Nicki Glanz [G] 1, Warwick 2:1.
▼ *Østergaard's tactical ride win in Heat 7 was nowhere near enough to turn the match.*

NEWCASTLE (H)
Monday, August 4
Won 60-32
Lemon 15, Madsen 7:4, **Østergaard 14:1**, Suchanek 4:1, Mills 5:1, Nicki Glanz 9:1, Warwick 6:1.

SOMERSET (H)
Sunday, August 10
5-1, abandoned after Heat 1, rain.
Lemon 2:1, Suchanek 3, Østergaard, Mills, Madsen, Nicki Glanz [G], Warwick, did not ride.
● *Meeting was delayed by nearly 90 minutes for track work but the circuit was deemed unfit after an aborted attempt to run Heat 2, with Glanz suffering a shoulder injury.*

SHEFFIELD (A)
Thursday, August 14
Lost 42-51
Lemon 9, Suchanek 4:1, Østergaard 16:1 (6), Mills 4, Madsen 1, Benji Compton [G] 3:1, Warwick 5:1.

RYE HOUSE (A)
Saturday, August 16
Lost 39-54
Lemon 6, Suchanek 6, Østergaard 16 (6), Mills 4:1, Madsen 4:1, Jamie Courtney [G] 2, Warwick 1.

KING'S LYNN (H)
Monday, August 25
Drew 45-45
Lemon 6:1, Suchanek 4, **Østergaard 15**, Mills 6:1, Madsen 8, Jamie Courtney [G] 2, Andrew Bargh [G] 4:1.

MILDENHALL (A)
Sunday, August 31
Won 51-42
Lemon 9, Suchanek 6:1, Østergaard 17 (6), Mills 6:2, Madsen 5:2, Matthew Wright [G] 6:1, Warwick 2.
▼▲ *Appeared set for a humiliating defeat against the whipping boys, but Østergaard's tactical ride win started the comeback, and Mills and guest Matthew Wright wrapped up a nervous victory in Heat 14.*

SCUNTHORPE (H)
Monday, September 1
Won 49-44
Lemon 8:1, Suchanek 6:3, **Østergaard 15**, Mills 3:1, Madsen 7:1, Jamie Courtney [G] 0, Warwick 10.

SOMERSET (H)
Monday, September 8
Lost 39-53
Lemon 6:1, Suchanek 7:1, Østergaard 16 (TS4), Mills 3, Madsen 3, Ben Taylor [G] 1:1, Warwick 3:1.
▼ *Last-ever league meeting at Smallmead. Østergaard only Racer to perform despite unfair riding exclusion in Heat 15.*

KING'S LYNN (A)
Wednesday, September 10
Lost 31-59
Lemon 7, Suchanek 0, Østergaard 13 (1), Mills 4, Madsen 3, Darren Mallett [G] 2, Warwick 2.
▼ *Østergaard again saved the Racers from embarrassment, despite a blip in Heat 7 tactical ride when he lost out to Tomas Topinka and John Oliver.*

SCUNTHORPE (A)
Friday, September 26
Lost 40-53
Lemon 5, Suchanek 4:1, **Østergaard 18 (6)**, Mills 0, Madsen 5:1, Ben Taylor [G] 0, Warwick 8:1.
▲▼ *Østergaard reeled off five classy wins but there was disappointment elsewhere again as the Racers could not continue from a 13-11 lead after four races.*

STOKE (A)
Sunday, October 26
Lost 40-51
Lemon 15, *rider replacement for Suchanek*, Nicolai Klindt [G] 14:1 (4), Mills 5:1, Madsen 3, Ben Taylor [G] 3:1, Warwick 0.
▲▼ *Delayed final match of the season saw Lemon in fine form, with five straight wins.*

PREMIER LEAGUE

		M	*W*	*D*	*L*	*PtsF*	*PtsA*	*Pts*
1	Edinburgh	30	22	2	6	1562	1161	53
2	Somerset	30	21	0	9	1517	1223	48
3	King's Lynn	30	18	5	7	1624	1111	45
4	Rye House	30	19	0	11	1500	1232	42
5	Workington	30	17	2	11	1435.5	1300.5	41
6	Berwick	30	16	2	12	1428	1316	37
7	Redcar	30	16	1	13	1369	1374	37
8	Sheffield	30	15	2	13	1381	1345	35
9	**READING**	**30**	**15**	**1**	**14**	**1350**	**1405**	**34**
10	Scunthorpe	30	15	0	15	1309	1434	33
11	Isle of Wight	30	15	0	15	1359	1390	31
12	Birmingham	30	13	0	17	1317.5	1401.5	30
13	Stoke	30	11	1	18	1307	1441	26
14	Newcastle	30	10	0	20	1220	1501	22
15	Glasgow	30	9	0	21	1297	1469	19
16	Mildenhall	30	0	0	30	932	1804	0

Young Shield

Quarter Final, first leg
REDCAR (A)
Thursday, October 2
Lost 40-52
Lemon 10, *rider replacement for Suchanek*, Østergaard 15 (4), Mills 6:3, Madsen 2, Klaus Jakobsen [G] 6:2, Warwick 1.
▲ *Good containment job with four riders putting in commendable performances. Østergaard lost out to Ty Proctor.*

Quarter Final, second leg
REDCAR (H)
Monday, October 6
Lost 33-60
Lemon 7, Suchanek –, Østergaard 16 (6), Mills 0, Madsen 6, Andrew Bargh [G] 1, Warwick 3.
Aggregate: Lost 73-112.
▼ *Suchanek refused to return to England because of a conflicting Czech Republic fixture. Reading did not use a replacement rider and went into three races with only one rider. Embarrassing end to the final team campaign at Smallmead with a record home defeat. PA announcer Bob Radford described the performance, with the exception of Østergaard as "disgusting."*

Gaming International Limited, owners of Smallmead, have planning permission to build a new stadium and Casino on an adjacent Island Road site and hope to start work in mid 2009, in time for a 2010 opening.

Premier Trophy

NEWPORT (A)
Sunday, March 30
Won 56-34
Lemon 5, Suchanek 7, **Østergaard 14:1**, Mills 7, Madsen 9:2, Smith 8:1, Mark Burrows [G] 6:3.
▲ *Racers hit form in the second half of the meeting and took 12 heat wins from this away fixture.*

SOMERSET (H)
Monday, March 31
Lost 44-49
Lemon 5:1, Suchanek 6, Østergaard 20 (6), Mills 0, Madsen 6:1, Smith 0, Mark Burrows [G] 7:2.
▼*Lemon's crash in Heat 13 resulting in hip injury, effectively ended chances.*

NEWPORT (H)
Monday, April 7
Won 59-33
Lemon 10:1, Mills 10:2, **Østergaard 15**, Suchanek 8:2, Madsen 8:1, Smith 0, Warwick 8:1.

SOMERSET (A)
Friday, April 11
Won 47-42
Lemon 11:1, Mills 3:2, Østergaard 13, Suchanek 5:1, Madsen 5:1, Jay Herne [G] 2, Warwick 8:1.
▲ *Took dramatic revenge over the Rebels despite the loss of Madsen (concussion) after the Heat 6 crash and*

PHOTO: Les Aubrey

Reading: co-promoter Malcolm Holloway, Chris Mills, Danny Warwick, Jamie Smith, Mark Lemon, Ulrich Østergaard, Tomas Suchanek, Tom Madsen and team manager Tim Sugar

Weather...

Reading only managed to complete their Premier League match away to Stoke at the fourth attempt after three late season rain-offs.

Premier League
Sunday, May 25 .... MILDENHALL (A)
Monday, July 7 .... KING'S LYNN (H)
Wednesday, July 9 .... KING'S LYNN (A)
Friday, September 5 .... SCUNTHORPE (A)
Saturday, September 6 .... STOKE (A)
Saturday, October 4 .... STOKE (A)
Saturday, October 25 .... STOKE (A)

Young Shield
Sunday, October 5 .... REDCAR (H)

Knock Out Cup
Wednesday, April 30 .... KING'S LYNN (A)
Monday, May 26 .... SOMERSET (H)

Thames Valley Trophy
Monday, March 10 .... RYE HOUSE (H)

...beaten

subsequent 'afters' which saw Jason Doyle excluded from the rest of the meeting.

ISLE OF WIGHT (H)
Monday, April 14
Won 52-40
Lemon 10:2, Mills 6:1, **Østergaard 15**, Suchanek 5, Madsen 6, Jay Herne [G] 3:2, Warwick 7:2.

ISLE OF WIGHT (A)
Tuesday, April 15
Lost 42-50
Lemon 9, Mills 5:1, Østergaard 14:1 (4), Suchanek 3:1, Madsen 4, Smith 6, Warwick 1:1.
▲ *Did enough to qualify for semi-finals as group winners, on points difference from Somerset.*

PREMIER TROPHY Group D

		M	W	D	L	PtsF	PtsA	Pts
1	**READING**	**6**	**4**	**0**	**2**	**300**	**248**	**10**
2	Somerset	6	4	0	2	296	257	10
3	Isle of Wight	6	3	0	3	275	272	6
4	Newport	6	1	0	5	226	320	2

Semi Final, first leg
EDINBURGH (A)
Friday, June 13
Lost 34-56
Lemon 10 (FX), Mills 2:1, Østergaard 8:1, Suchanek 2, Madsen 4, Smith 2:1, Nicki Glanz [G] 6:1

Semi Final, second leg
EDINBURGH (H)
Monday, June 23
Won 46-44
Lemon 7:1, Mills 7:2, Østergaard 14, Suchanek 6:1, Madsen 4:1, Smith 4:1, Nicki Glanz [G] 4:1.
▲ *Østergaard's Heat 15 win secured victory although the overall aggregate position was well beyond them.*
Aggregate: Lost 80-100.

Knock Out Cup

Second round, first leg
KING'S LYNN (H)
Monday, April 28
Won 59-34
Lemon 15, Mills 7:2, Østergaard 11:1, Suchanek 7:1, Madsen 7:1, Smith 12:3, Warwick 0.
▲ *Controversial meeting but emphatic win, Lemon winning five races out of five and Østergaard denied by a Heat 15 exclusion for bringing down Rusty Harrison.*

Second round, second leg
KING'S LYNN (A)
Wednesday, May 7
Lost 38-55
Lemon 5, Mills 11:1 (6), Østergaard 12 (TSF), Suchanek 1, Madsen 6, Jay Herne [G] 0, Sam Martin [G] 3.
▲ *Did just enough to qualify for the quarter-finals, race wins from Østergaard and Mills, as well as Lemon in Heat 13.*
Aggregate: Won 97-89.

Quarter Final, first leg
SOMERSET (A)
Friday, May 30
Lost 39-53
Lemon 12 (4), Mills 2, Østergaard 12:1 (TS0), Suchanek 0, Madsen 6, Smith 6:1, Nicki Glanz [G] 1.
▼ *Attempted tactical substitute ride from Østergaard in Heat 14 failed to pay off.*

Quarter Final, second leg
SOMERSET (H)
Monday, June 29
Won 51-44
Lemon 7:3, Madsen 10:1, Østergaard 13, Suchanek 4:2, Mills 6:1, Smith 2:1, Nicki Glanz [G] 9:1.
▼ *Moved ahead on aggregate in Heat 12 but conceded an 8-1 in Heat 14 when Jason Doyle came through from 15m. Doyle won last race too.*
Aggregate: Lost 90-97.

Did you know?

Even though he rode in a total of 21 matches for Reading in official competitions, Nicki Glanz was never named in the Racers' line-up and every single appearance was as a Conference League guest.
Everyone assumed that he had been included in the Berkshire club's 1-7.
He made his Racers' debut against the Isle of Wight on May 5 and was a regular until injury cut short his season.
He scored 101 points in those meetings, averaging 4.12

Challenge

RYE HOUSE (A)
First leg
Saturday, March 15
19-26, abandoned, rain
Lemon 4, Suchanek 1, Østergaard 8 (6), Mills 1:1, Madsen 2, Smith 3, Warwick 0.

● *Meeting abandoned after Heat 7, heavy rain. With the schedule first leg (at Smallmead on the previous Monday) having been postponed the meeting was never re-staged.*

SOMERSET (H)
Monday, March 17
Won 54-37
Lemon 13:1, Suchanek 8:1, Østergaard 10:1, Mills 6:1, Madsen 7:1, Warwick 0, Smith 10:2.

▼ *Warwick suffered ankle ligament damage in Heat 2 and had to withdraw. Smith looked a potent scorer at reserve in his first home meeting.*

SOMERSET (A)
Friday, March 21
Lost 41-52
Lemon 10, Suchanek 3:1, Østergaard 14:1 (6), Mills 4:2, Madsen 5:1, Smith 3:1, Robert Mear [G] 2.
Aggregate: Won 95-89.

CHALFONT COACHES EASTER CHALLENGE
First leg
ISLE OF WIGHT (A)
Saturday, March 22
Lost 47-48
Lemon 15 (4), Suchanek 3:1, Østergaard 17:1 (TS6), Mills 4, Madsen 3, Smith 2, Sam Martin [G] 3.

Second leg
ISLE OF WIGHT (H)
Sunday, March 23
Won 56-36
Lemon 15, Suchanek 5, **Østergaard 14:1**, Mills 4:1, Madsen 10:1, Smith 6, Sam Martin [G] 2.
Aggregate: Won 103-84.

Individual

END OF AN ERA
Sunday, October 19

ULRICH Østergaard had been at the vanguard of what could turn out to be Reading's final season.

And, fittingly, he won the last ever race at Smallmead, the Racers' home for 33 years.

With work yet to start on the promised new stadium there are genuine fears that the Berkshire town will join the ever-growing list of former homes for speedway.

But at least the fans can look back to the early seventies when they were also left without the sport after the closure of their original Tilehurst Stadium.

They had to decamp to Newcastle for a year but then returned to what was their pristine new home on the opposite side of town.

Now that stadium, too, has gone for redevelopment and it was a tearful send-off with a galaxy of Racers' legends in attendance.

Probably the greatest Reading rider of all – ex-World Champion Anders Michanek – was there along with that great and loyal servant Jan Andersson.

But it was Østergaard who had the honour of winning that farewell race to clinch overall victory.

One of the more nostalgic voices to be heard came loud and clear over the tannoy as former Racers' promoter and one-time voice of ITV speedway, Dave Lanning provided his own inimitable commentary of one of the heats.

	1	*2*	*3*	*4*	*5*	*Tot*	*SF*	*F*
1 Ulrich ØSTERGAARD	**3**	**3**	**3**	**1**	**3**	**13**	**3**	**3**
2 Chris NEATH	2	2	1	3	2	10	3	2
3 Jordan FRAMPTON	1	2	X	2	3	8	2	1
4 Linus SUNDSTRÖM	1	3	3	3	1	11	2	0
5 Mark LEMON	2	3	2	3	3	13	1	
6 Richard SWEETMAN	2	1	1	0	3	7	1	
7 Mads KORNELIUSSEN	3	3	3	3	2	14	X	
8 Krzysztof STOJANOWSKI	1	2	2	2	2	9	0	
9 Tom MADSEN	3	1	2	F	1	7		
10 Emil KRAMER	0	2	1	2	2	7		
11 Tomas SUCHANEK	3	0	1	1	1	6		
12 Danny WARWICK	2	0	3	0	0	5		
13 Shawn McCONNELL	1	1	0	1	1	4		
14 Paul CLEWS	0	1	2	0	0	3		
15 Marc ANDREWS [R]	0	0	2			2		
16 Cory GATHERCOLE	0	F	F	FX		0		
17 Ben READE [R]	0	0	0			0		
18 Robert MEAR	did not ride							

READING

Rider	*M*	*R*	*Pts*	*BP*	*TPts*	*Ave*	*F*	*P*	*TR*	*TPts*	*TS*	*TSPts*
Ulrich ØSTERGAARD	40	204	540	15	555	10.88	9	2	9	22	6	8
Mark LEMON	**44**	**207**	**394**	**30**	**424**	**8.19**	**3**	**0**	**5**	**8**	**0**	**0**
Tom MADSEN	43	173	258	31	289	6.68	0	0	0	0	0	0
Chris MILLS	**44**	**182**	**227**	**38**	**265**	**5.82**	**0**	**0**	**1**	**3**	**0**	**0**
Tomas SUCHANEK	41	167	190	33	223	5.34	0	0	0	0	0	0
Jamie SMITH	**24**	**101**	**113**	**15**	**128**	**5.07**	**0**	**0**	**0**	**0**	**0**	**0**
Danny WARWICK	18	72	70	12	82	4.56	0	0	0	0	0	0
Guests	***50***	***209***	***198***	***37***	***235***	***4.50***	***0***	***0***	***2***	***4***	***0***	***0***

For Chris MILLS see Lakeside; for Tomas SUCHANEK see Eastbourne; for Jamie SMITH see Boston.

Premier League

REDCAR

TRACK FILE

Track: South Tees Motorpark, Dormey Way, Southbank Road, Middlesbrough, TS6 6HX.
Telephone: 07796 441850.
Hotline: 09068 664665.
Website: www.redcarspeedway.co.uk
Track Length: 271 metres.
Track Record: 53.2 secs, Ricky Ashworth, July 15, 2008; Daniel Nermark, July 24, 2008.
Promoter: Brian Havelock.
Team Sponsors: NEBT/Simpson Racing UK.
Colours: Red and white
Nickname: Bears.
†See Redcar (Conference League).

HISTORY

First meeting: April 13, 2006, Redcar v Sheffield, Premier Trophy.
Leagues: Division Two, 2006-09.
Speedway was also held at
● *Cleveland Park, Stockton Road, Middlesbrough.*
First meeting: August 23, 1928, Stockton Handicap.
Leagues: Division One, 1995-96. Division Two, 1939, 1947-48, 1961-64, 1968-1994. Division Three, 1994-95 (raced as Cleveland). English Dirt-Track League, 1929. Northern League, 1946, 1966. Open licence: 1928, 1930-31, 1936-38, 1945, 1953-55, 1965.

HONOURS

Major honours: 7.
Division Two champions (2), 1947, 1981.
Division Two Young Shield winners (1), 2007.
Division Two Pairs champions (1), 1980.
Division Two Four Team champions (2), 1985, 1986.
Northern League champions (1), 1946.

2008 REVIEW

IT was a traumatic season on Teesside, where just reaching the end of the campaign with the club intact had to be regarded as something of an achievement.

Former co-promoter Glyn Taylor took control of the club over the winter looking to build on the Young Shield success of 2007, but he hit financial problems and in mid-season took the momentous decision to axe skipper Gary Havelock for cost-cutting reasons.

The public outcry and outside assistance resulted in the 1992 World Champion being swiftly re-instated, but it served to underline the precarious situation at the South Tees Motorsports Park.

This was a great pity, because on the track the Bears were one of the more entertaining units in the Premier League, even if their true potential was not seen for some time due to injuries.

Chris Kerr broke his leg in March and was ruled out until mid-season, while reserve Daniel Giffard saw his campaign effectively over by the end of May.

On the positive side, the Bears had unearthed a star in young Australian Ty Proctor, and he gave strong support to Havelock as the Bears maintained a respectable home record despite the absence of Kerr.

Somerset, King's Lynn and Reading did emerge from South Tees with the points, but with close to a full team on show, the Bears showed what might have been when they won at both Newcastle and Stoke, and were close at Berwick in their last Premier League fixture.

Their fine form made them among the favourites for the Young Shield again, and an emphatic 60-33 win at Reading did nothing to dispel that theory.

But Workington defended well in the first leg of the semi final to limit the Bears to a five-point lead, and this proved to be just enough as the Comets went through by four and ended the Redcar season – and Glyn Taylor's spell as promoter, a consortium including team boss Brian Havelock taking over.

2008 RESULTS

Premier League

Final position..Seventh

EDINBURGH (H)
Thursday, April 10
28-26, abandoned after nine heats, rain.
Havelock 0, *rider replacement for Kerr*, Grieves 8, Auty 2:1, Proctor 7, Bugeja 6:3, Giffard 5.

NEWPORT (A)
Sunday, April 20
Won 47-46
Havelock 14, *rider replacement for Kerr*, Grieves 6, Auty 2:1, Proctor 11, Bugeja 4:1, Aaron Summers [G] 10:2.
▲ *Gary Havelock the hero in Heat 15 after injuries to James Grieves and Josh Auty in a Heat 10 crash put the Bears down to four riders.*

BERWICK (H)
Thursday, May 1
Won 51-41
Havelock 7:1, *rider replacement for Kerr*, Grieves 14, Auty 2, Proctor 15:1, Bugeja 7:2, Giffard 6:1, Jitendra Duffill [no. 8].
▲ *Fifth straight win to end the Bandits' 100 per cent start to the Premier League campaign and give the Bears a boost in their first Premier League home match of the year.*

SQUAD
Joshua Auty, Daniel Giffard, James Grieves, Gary Havelock.
Foreign: Arlo Bugeja, Chris Kerr, Joni Keskinen, Tyron Proctor.

SOMERSET (H)
Thursday, May 8
Lost 39-54
Havelock 12 (6), *rider replacement for Kerr*, Grieves 10, Giffard 2:1, Proctor 9:1 (TS1), Bugeja 0, Auty 6.

READING (A)
Monday, May 19
Lost 35-57
Havelock 13, Keskinen 0, Grieves 10 (4), Giffard 1, Proctor 3, Auty 6:1, Bugeja 2:2.

ISLE OF WIGHT (A)
Tuesday, May 20
Lost 40-53
Havelock 18 (6), Keskinen 1, Grieves 9, Giffard 3:1, Proctor 4 (TSFX), Auty 5, Bugeja 0.

GLASGOW (A)
Sunday, May 25
Won 48-42
Havelock 12, Keskinen 0, Grieves 11, Giffard 5:1, Proctor 4:1, Adam McKinna [G] 11:2, Bugeja 5:1.
▲ *Guest Adam McKinna with his highest Premier League score helped Bears to an away win.*

PHOTO: Tim Helm

Redcar: Brian Havelock (team manager), Joshua Auty, Chris Kerr, Tyron Proctor, James Grieves, promoter Glyn Taylor. Front – Daniel Giffard, Gary Havelock, Arlo Bugeja

MILDENHALL (H)
Thursday, June 5
Won 53-40
Havelock 10, *rider replacement for Giffard*, Grieves 14, Keskinen 3:1, Proctor 9:3, Auty 10, Bugeja 5:1, Adam McKinna [G] [no. 8] 2:1.

SCUNTHORPE (A)
Friday, June 6
Lost 41-52
Havelock 15 (6), *rider replacement for Giffard*, Grieves 8, Keskinen 0, Proctor 5:1, Auty 7:1, Bugeja 4, Adam McKinna [no. 8] 2.

KING'S LYNN (A)
Wednesday, June 11
Lost 27-66
Havelock 12 (6), *rider replacement for Kerr*, Grieves 4, Adam McKinna [G] 0, Proctor 2:1, Auty 7, Bugeja 2.
▼ *Bears' only race win in the 15 heats came when Havelock donned the black-and-white helmet colour in Heat 11.*

KING'S LYNN (H)
Thursday, June 12
Lost 43-47
Havelock 14, Adam McKinna [G] 0, Grieves 10, *rider replacement for Keskinen*, Proctor 11:1 (TSFX), Auty 5:2, Bugeja 3.

MILDENHALL (A)
Sunday, June 15
Won 58-35
Havelock 14, James Cockle [G] 7:2, Grieves 13:1, Brent Werner [G] 5, *rider replacement for Proctor*, Kozza Smith [G] 13:2, Bugeja 6:2.
▲ *Proctor and Auty absent due to World Under 21 Championship semi finals.*

READING (H)
Thursday, June 19
Lost 42-48
Havelock 12:1, *rider replacement for Keskinen*, Grieves 12, Byron Bekker [G] 1, Proctor 13, Auty 4:1, Scott Richardson [G] 0.
▼ *Bugeja out with broken wrist suffered at King's Lynn in the Ashley Jones Memorial meeting 24 hours earlier.*

BIRMINGHAM (H)
Thursday, June 26
Won 46-44
Havelock 9:2, *rider replacement for Keskinen*, Grieves 9, John Branney [G] 1, Proctor 15:1, Auty 9:1, Scott James [G] 3:1.
▲ *Havelock broke track record in Heat 1. Tyron Proctor secured the vital second place in Heat 15 after the injury-hit Brummies had threatened to come away with a draw.*

SCUNTHORPE (H)
Thursday, July 3
Won 50-40
Havelock 10:1, *rider replacement for Keskinen*, Grieves 12:2, Auty 6:1, Proctor 16, Scott James [G] 1:1, James Cockle [G] 5:2.
▼ *Match overshadowed by the bombshell news that number one Havelock was set to leave the club as promoter Glyn Taylor could not afford to pay him.*

WORKINGTON (A)
Saturday, July 5
Lost 44-49
Havelock 16 (6), *rider replacement for Keskinen*, Grieves 9, Auty 4, Proctor 10:1, Scott James [G] 2, James Cockle [G] 3:2.
▲ *Havelock continued as extra backing was sought to pay his wages – and he was unbeaten until conceding a 5-1 in Heat 15 which clinched the match for the Comets.*

SHEFFIELD (A)
Thursday, July 10
Drew 45-45
Havelock 12, Auty 3:1, Grieves 10, Kerr 3:1, Proctor 11:2, Bugeja 1, Klaus Jakobsen [G] 5.

SHEFFIELD (H)
Tuesday, July 15
Won 54-39
Havelock 12:1, Auty 8:1, Grieves 8, Kerr 7:1, Proctor 9:1, Giffard 1, Bugeja 9:2.
▼ *Giffard suffered a broken shoulder in his comeback meeting.*

RYE HOUSE (H)
Thursday, July 17
Won 50-43
Havelock 6, Auty 7:3, Grieves 13:1, Kerr 6:2, Proctor 13, James Cockle [G] 1:1, Bugeja 4.

RYE HOUSE (A)
Saturday, July 19
Lost 26-65
Havelock 5, Kerr 3:1, Grieves 9 (4), Auty 3:1, Proctor 3:1, Benji Compton [G] 1, Bugeja 2.
▼ *Amazingly went 6-30 down in the first six races, with only Grieves summoning up consistent resistance.*

BIRMINGHAM (A)
Wednesday, July 23
Lost 45-46
Havelock 12, Kerr 4, Grieves 10:2, Auty 7:1, Proctor 6, Benji Compton [G] 6:1, Bugeja 0.
▼ *Mechanical problems for Grieves and a fall for Kerr proved extremely costly for the Bears.*

WORKINGTON (H)
Thursday, July 24
Won 47-43
Havelock 10:1, Auty 3, Grieves 13, Kerr 4:2, Proctor 9, Benji Compton [G] 2, Bugeja 6.
▲ *Daniel Nermark's Heat 11 crash was the turning point.*

Redcar ran a team in the Conference League in 2008 but will not be operating in the new National League.

Grieves and Havelock took advantage with a last race 5-1 to take the points.

EDINBURGH (A)
Friday, July 25
Lost 37-55
Havelock 7:1, Auty 4, Grieves 10, Kerr 3:1, Proctor 10 (4), Benji Compton [G] 3, Bugeja 0.

NEWCASTLE (A)
Sunday, August 3
Won 48-42
Havelock 6:3, Auty 10:1, *rider replacement for Grieves*, Proctor 14:2, Kerr 13, Benji Compton [G] 0, Bugeja 5:1.
▲ *Stunning away win achieved without track specialist Grieves, who crashed in Edinburgh's Scottish Open 48 hours previously.*

ISLE OF WIGHT (H)
Thursday, August 7
Won 52-42
Havelock 11:1, Auty 9:2, Grieves 11, Proctor 7:2, Kerr 10, Benji Compton [G] 3, Bugeja 1.

SOMERSET (A)
Friday, August 8
Lost 42-48
Havelock 12:1, Auty 6:1, Grieves 3:1, Proctor 11, Kerr 7:1, Jay Herne [G] 1, Bugeja 2.

NEWCASTLE (H)
Thursday, August 15
Won 59-33
Havelock 12:2, Auty 8:3, Grieves 8, Kerr 7:3, **Proctor 15**, Benji Compton [G] 5, Bugeja 4:1.
▼ *Proctor finally secured the full house he had been waiting for.*

GLASGOW (H)
Thursday, August 21
Won 55-38
Havelock 13:1, Auty 5:1, Grieves 12:2, Kerr 9:1, Proctor 9:1, Benji Compton [G] 3:1, Bugeja 4.

EDINBURGH (H)
Thursday, September 11
Won 49-41
Havelock 12:1, Auty 1:1, Grieves 10:1, Kerr 7:1, Proctor 11:1, Benji Compton [G] 5:1, Bugeja 3.
▲ *Grieves and Proctor both won three races.*

STOKE (A)
Sunday, September 14
Won 48-41
Havelock 11:1, Auty 0, Grieves 9:1, Kerr 8:3, Proctor 9, Benji Compton [G] 9, Bugeja 2:1.
▲ *Havelock unbeaten apart from a tapes exclusion.*

STOKE (H)
Thursday, September 18
Won 51-40
Havelock 13:2, Auty 5:1, Grieves 14, Kerr 5, Proctor 11, Benji Compton [G] 0, Bugeja 3:1.
▲ *Just six points in it before Proctor and Havelock virtually wrapped things up with a 5-1 in Heat 13.*

BERWICK (A)
Saturday, September 20
Lost 44-46
Havelock 8, *rider replacement for Proctor*, Grieves 14, Auty 3, Kerr 11, Benji Compton [G] 1, Bugeja 7:1.
▲ *Led going into the last race but Grieves and Kerr lost out to Tomasz Piszcz and Michal Makovsky.*

PREMIER LEAGUE

		M	*W*	*D*	*L*	*PtsF*	*PtsA*	*Pts*
1	Edinburgh	30	22	2	6	1562	1161	53
2	Somerset	30	21	0	9	1517	1223	48
3	King's Lynn	30	18	5	7	1624	1111	45
4	Rye House	30	19	0	11	1500	1232	42
5	Workington	30	17	2	11	1435.5	1300.5	41
6	Berwick	30	16	2	12	1428	1316	37
7	**REDCAR**	**30**	**16**	**1**	**13**	**1369**	**1374**	**37**
8	Sheffield	30	15	2	13	1381	1345	35
9	Reading	30	15	1	14	1350	1405	34
10	Scunthorpe	30	15	0	15	1309	1434	33
11	Isle of Wight	30	15	0	15	1359	1390	31
12	Birmingham	30	13	0	17	1317.5	1401.5	30
13	Stoke	30	11	1	18	1307	1441	25
14	Newcastle	30	10	0	20	1220	1501	22
15	Glasgow	30	9	0	21	1297	1469	19
16	Mildenhall	30	0	0	30	932	1804	0

● *Glyn Taylor was in charge at the South Tees Motorsports Park for 25 meetings.*

REDCAR

Rider	*M*	*R*	*Pts*	*BP*	*TPts*	*Ave*	*F*	*P*	*TR*	*TPts*	*TS*	*TSPts*
Gary HAVELOCK	46	214	482	31	513	9.59	1	2	6	17	0	0
James GRIEVES	**43**	**204**	**457**	**18**	**475**	**9.31**	**2**	**0**	**4**	**10**	**1**	**1**
Tyron PROCTOR	44	216	416	31	447	8.28	3	0	1	2	5	0
Chris KERR	**24**	**104**	**178**	**21**	**199**	**7.65**	**0**	**0**	**1**	**3**	**1**	**0**
Joshua AUTY	44	210	246	39	285	5.43	0	0	0	0	0	0
Daniel GIFFARD	**18**	**76**	**66**	**14**	**80**	**4.21**	**0**	**0**	**0**	**0**	**0**	**0**
Arlo BUGEJA	42	183	136	29	165	3.61	0	0	0	0	0	0
Joni KESKINEN	**8**	**25**	**6**	**2**	**8**	**1.28**	**0**	**0**	**0**	**0**	**0**	**0**
Guests	***36***	***152***	***125***	***21***	***146***	***3.84***	***0***	***0***	***0***	***0***	***0***	***0***

For Ty PROCTOR see Peterborough.

Young Shield

Quarter Final, first leg
READING (H)
Thursday, October 2
Won 52-40
Havelock 6, Auty 7:2, Grieves 9:1, Kerr 8:1, **Proctor 15**, Benji Compton [G] 5, Bugeja 2:1.
▲▼ *Ulrich Østergaard and Mark Lemon kept the Racers in contention but Proctor was superb, and the Bears' gained their lead thanks to three 4-2s in the last three races.*

Quarter Final, second leg
READING (A)
Monday, October 6
Won 60-33
Havelock 8:2, Auty 8:2, Grieves 10:1, Kerr 9:1, Proctor 13, Benji Compton [G] 6:2, Bugeja 6:2.
▲ *Dominant away win raising further hopes of retaining the Young Shield. Bears opened with two 5-1s and never let up the pressure in a true seven-man team performance.*
Aggregate: Won 112-73.

Semi Final, first leg
WORKINGTON (H)
Thursday, October 16
Won 48-43
Havelock 7, Auty 3:2, Grieves 9:1, Kerr 7:2, **Proctor 15**, Benji Compton [G] 7, Bugeja 0.
▲ *Second successive home maximum for Proctor, but Jason Doyle and Joe Haines kept the Comets in the tie, as the Bears missed out on their target of a 12-point lead.*

Semi Final, second leg
WORKINGTON (A)
Saturday, October 18
Lost 42-51
Havelock 9:2, Auty 2:2, Grieves 7:1, Kerr 14 (6), Proctor 7 (TS0), Benji Compton [G] 3, Bugeja 0.
▼ *Kerr and Havelock kept the Bears in the tie for long spells, but they did not secure the advantages required to cut back the deficit caused by conceding Heats 4 to 6 by a 13-5 margin.*
Aggregate: Lost 90-94.

Premier Trophy

STOKE (A)
Saturday, March 22
Lost 41-49
Havelock 8, Proctor 4, Grieves 11, Auty 3, Kerr 7, Bugeja 3:3, Giffard 5:1.
▼ *Bears led by four points at half-way stage but lost out to an all-round Potters display.*

NEWCASTLE (A)
Sunday, March 23
Lost 38-52
Havelock 6:1, Proctor 7:1, Grieves 12, Auty 2:1, Kerr 10 (TS1), Bugeja 0, Giffard 1.
▼ *Gary Havelock's tapes exclusion in Heat 5 put the Diamonds in the clear.*

NEWCASTLE (H)
Thursday, March 27
Drew 45-45
Havelock 9:2, Proctor 8:1, Grieves 7:1, Auty 3, Kerr 10, Bugeja 5, Giffard 3:1.
▼ *Grieves withdrew after three rides due to chest infection. Havelock crashed out of Heat 15 but Kerr saved the draw by winning re-run.*

SCUNTHORPE (A)
Sunday, March 30
Drew 45-45
Havelock 11:1, Proctor 10:4, *rider replacement for Grieves*, Auty 11, Kerr 6, Bugeja 0, Giffard 7:2.
▼ *Proctor's Heat 15 win secured a draw, but at the cost of a broken leg for Kerr in Heat 9.*

SHEFFIELD (A)
Thursday, April 3
Lost 39-53
Havelock 17 (4), Tomas Suchanek [G] 3:2, *rider replacement for Grieves*, Auty 10:2, Proctor 3, Bugeja 5, Giffard 1, David Wallinger [no. 8].
▼ *Grieves ruled out due to illness and planned guest Jamie Birkinshaw injured on the previous evening.*

SHEFFIELD (H)
Thursday, April 12
Won 47-43
Havelock 13, *rider replacement for Kerr*, Grieves 12:1, Auty 3:1, Proctor 10, Bugeja 4:2, Giffard 5:1.

SCUNTHORPE (H)
Saturday, May 3
Won 55-35
Havelock 12:2, *rider replacement for Kerr*, **Grieves 15**, Auty 9, Proctor 10:1, Bugeja 6:2, Giffard 3, David Wallinger [no. 8].

STOKE (H)
Thursday, May 15
Won 52-38
Havelock 10:1, Keskinen 0, **Grieves 15**, Giffard 4, Proctor 13, Auty 7:1, Bugeja 3:2.
▼ *New signing Keskinen failed to impress.*

PREMIER TROPHY Group B

		M	W	D	L	PtsF	PtsA	Pts
1	Sheffield	8	6	0	2	386	345	14
2	**REDCAR**	**8**	**3**	**2**	**3**	**362**	**360**	**8**
3	Scunthorpe	8	3	1	4	345	380	8
4	Newcastle	8	3	1	4	364	367	7
5	Stoke	8	3	0	5	363	368	6

2009 Squad

A consortium headed by team manager Brian Havelock guaranteed the club's future when they bought out former promoter Glyn Taylor shortly before Christmas.
Gary **HAVELOCK** (8.73), Ty **PROCTOR** (7.63), Carl **STONEHEWER** (7.28), Ben **WILSON** (6.44), Robbie **KESSLER** (5.79), Arlo **BUGEJA** (3.03), Benji **COMPTON** (3.00).

Knock Out Cup

Second round, first leg
MILDENHALL (H)
Thursday, April 24
Won 53-40
Havelock 13, *rider replacement for Kerr*, Grieves 10, Auty 6:2, Proctor 11:1, Bugeja 6, Giffard 7:2, David Wallinger [no. 8].

Second round, second leg
MILDENHALL (A)
Sunday, April 27
Won 50-40
Havelock 6, *rider replacement for Kerr*, Grieves 13, Auty 5, Proctor 14, Bugeja 5, Giffard 7:1.
Aggregate: Won 103-80.

Quarter Final, first leg
EDINBURGH (H)
Thursday, May 29
Lost 38-55
Havelock 7, Keskinen 1:1, Grieves 15:1 (6), Giffard 3, Proctor 8 (TS1), Auty 4, Bugeja 0.

Quarter Final, second leg
EDINBURGH (A)
Friday, May 30
Lost 38-55
Havelock 4, Keskinen 1, Grieves 13 (6), Giffard 2:2, Proctor 4:1, Auty 10, Bugeja 4:2.
Aggregate: Lost 76-110.

Challenge

TYNE TEES TROPHY
First leg
NEWCASTLE (A)
Sunday, August 24
Won 48-42
Havelock 10, Autty 6:4, Grieves 13, Kerr 6:1, Proctor 7, Benji Compton [G] 1:1, Bugeja 5.

Second leg
NEWCASTLE (H)
Thursday, August 28
Won 50-31
Havelock 7:1, Auty 8:2, **Grieves 12**, Kerr 4:1, Proctor 10, Scott James [G] 4:2, Bugeja 5.
▼ *Meeting abandoned after a Heat 14 crash involving Matyas Hlavacek and Mitchell Davey.*
Aggregate: Won 98-73.

WORKINGTON (A)
Saturday, October 18
Lost 42-51
Havelock 9:2, Auty 2:2, Grieves 7:1, Kerr 14 (6), Proctor 7 (TS0), Benji Compton [G] 3, Bugeja 0.

Individual

SOUTH TEES SILVER HELMET
Thursday, October 23

JASON Crump was the class of the strongest field to be assembled at the South Tees Motorsports Park, winning all five of his races.

It was the final meeting of Glyn Taylor's season-long reign as the Redcar promoter had run into financial problems mid-season.

The young Swede Ludvig Lindgren also showed up well for third place to clinch a full-time Premier League berth at Birmingham in 2009.

	1	2	3	4	5	Tot	RO
1 Jason CRUMP	**3**	**3**	**3**	**3**	**3**	**15**	
2 Josef FRANC	2	3	3	3	2	13	
3 Ludvig LINDGREN	3	1	2	1	3	10	
4 Tai WOFFINDEN	3	1	1	2	3	10	
5 Ricky KLING	3	1	3	0	2	9	
6 Ty PROCTOR	0	3	1	3	1	9	
7 Peter KILDEMAND	2	2	1	3	1	9	
8 Stuart ROBSON	1	2	3	2	1	9	
9 Jason LYONS	0	2	2	1	3	8	
10 Jason KING	1	3	0	1	2	7	
11 Gary HAVELOCK	2	0	2	2	N2	6	
12 Chris KERR	F	2	0	2	2	6	
13 Benji COMPTON	1	1	2	0	0	4	
14 Ryan FISHER	2	F	F	1	N2	3	
15 Richard HALL	1	0	1	0	0	2	
16 Arlo BUGEJA [R]	1					1	
17 Christian ISOMETTÄ	0	0	0	0	0	0	

Roll of Honour

1968 .... Dave SCHOFIELD
1969 .... Geoff AMBROSE
1970 .... Graeme SMITH
1971 .... Bruce FORRESTER
1972 .... John JACKSON
1973 .... Lou SANSOM
1974 .... Dave DURHAM
1975 .... Alan EMERSON
1976 .... Joe OWEN
1977 .... Nigel CLOSE
1978 .... Brian HAVELOCK
1979 .... Steve WILCOCK
1980 .... Steve WILCOCK
1981 .... Steve WILCOCK
1985 .... Steve WILCOCK
1989 .... Darren SUMNER
2006 .... Richard HALL
2007 .... Peter KARLSSON
2008 .... Jason CRUMP

■ *Prior to 2006, meeting held at Middlesbrough's Cleveand Park Stadium.*

Weather...

Five of Redcar's first seven home meetings either didn't start or failed to last the distance.

Premier League
Sunday, April 6 .... GLASGOW (A)
Thursday, April 17 .... SCUNTHORPE (H)
Saturday, June 21 .... BERWICK (A)
Friday, July 11 .... SHEFFIELD (H)
Saturday, July 12 .... STOKE (A)
Thursday, July 31 .... NEWCASTLE (H)
Saturday, September 6 .... BERWICK (A)

Young Shield
Sunday, October 5 .... READING (A)

Premier Trophy
Monday, March 24 .... STOKE (H)
Friday, March 28 .... SCUNTHORPE (A)
Friday, April 4 .... SHEFFIELD (H)

...beaten

Premier League

RYE HOUSE

TRACK FILE

Track: Rye Road, Hoddesdon, Hertfordshire, EN11 0EH
Telephone: 01992 440400.
Hotline: 09066 555948.
Website: www.ryehouse.com
Track Length: 262 metres.
Track Record: 55.6 secs, Tai Woffinden, September 29, 2007.
Promoters: Len Silver and Hazal Naylor.
Team Sponsors: Silver Ski Holidays Ltd.
Colours: Blue and gold with white rocket.
Nickname: Rockets.
†See also Rye House (Conference League).

HISTORY

First meeting: August 3, 1958, August Trophy.
Leagues: Division Two, 1974-1993, 2002-09. Division Three, †1999, 2000-09. Southern Area League, 1959. Open licence: 1958, 1960-66, 1969-1973.
Speedway was held at an adjoining stadium at the same address.
First meeting: *†May 27, 1934 (this is the first recorded meeting but it is believed meetings were held priot to this date.*
Leagues: Sunday Dirt-Track League, 1938, Southern Area League, 1954-57. Open licence, 1935-37, 1939-43, 1943-53.

HONOURS

Major honours: 9.
Division Two champions (3), 1980, 2005, 2007.
Division Two Knock Out Cup winners (1), 1979.
Division Two Trophy winners (1), 2005.
Division Three Four Team champions (1), 2003.
Southern Area League champions (3), 1954, 1955, 1956.

2008 REVIEW

THE reigning champions were once again a force to be reckoned with in the Premier League, but they never quite produced the consistency to be able to retain their title.

In 2007, they had taken the crown via the play-offs after eventual runners-up Sheffield had despatched King's Lynn in the semi-finals, but in 2008 they finished 13 points off top spot having mounted a late surge into the top four.

Once again, the Rockets' form around their Hoddesdon circuit was hugely impressive, and few visiting sides were able to threaten an away win – only Edinburgh and King's Lynn finishing within ten points as Rye maintained an unblemished home record.

Away from home, however, three of their four wins came in the closing weeks of league competition, and that allowed the likes of Edinburgh and Somerset to move well clear during the summer, and left the Rockets initially looking set for the Young Shield.

Wins at Mildenhall, Scunthorpe and Newcastle were eventually added to success at Birmingham, but the Rockets' hopes of reaching the promotion/relegation play-off were immediately extinguished by King's Lynn – and the further cost of that semi-final was a serious back injury suffered by Stefan Ekberg in the first leg.

Injuries affected several other members of the team, including wonderkid Tai Woffinden, and his absence from the second leg of the Knock Out Cup semi final against Somerset proved costly.

Woffinden did, however, provide one of the season's biggest highlights with his team-riding alongside partner Tommy Allen in a televised fixture at Reading being worthy of the highest praise.

The only full-time team change during the season came when Danny Betson retired from the sport, which gave an opportunity to Daniel Halsey, and the Rockets seem set to continue to base their future mainly around home-grown riders.

2008 RESULTS

Premier League

Final position ....Fourth

ISLE OF WIGHT (H)
Saturday, April 12
Won 66-24
Neath **15:3**, Bowen 11:1, **Woffinden 14:1**, **Allen 12:3**, *rider replacement for Ekberg*, Betson 4:1, Mear 10.
▲ *Three unbeaten riders – a cruise for the Rockets.*

WORKINGTON (A)
Saturday, May 3
Lost 44-46
Neath 4:1, Josh Grajczonek [G] 9, Woffinden 10:1, *rider replacement for Allen*, Ekberg 13:1, Daniel Halsey [G] 0, Mear 8:3.

WORKINGTON (H)
Monday, May 5
Won 52-40
Neath 4, Bowen 4, Woffinden 13, *rider replacement for Allen*, Ekberg 12:1, Daniel Halsey [G] 3:2, Mear 16:3, Lee Strudwick [no. 8].
▲ *Sensational display from Mear as Rockets won despite skipper Neath suffering mechanical problems in his first two rides.*

SOMERSET (A)
Friday, May 9
Lost 27-66
Neath 3, Bowen 1, Woffinden 17 (6), *rider replacement for Allen*, Ekberg 3, Daniel Halsey [G] 0, Mear 3, Matt Bates [no. 8].

EDINBURGH (H)
Saturday, May 10
Won 48-42
Neath 12:1, Mear 9:1, Woffinden 11:1, *rider replacement for Allen*, Ekberg 9, Daniel Halsey [G] 1, Bowen 6:1, Gary Cottham [no. 8].

KING'S LYNN (A)
Wednesday, May 14
Lost 31-62
Neath 3:1, Mear 4, Woffinden 13 (6), *rider replacement for Allen*, Ekberg 9, Daniel Halsey [G] 0, Bowen 2, Adam Lowe [no. 8].

READING (A) SKY TV
Tuesday, May 27
Lost 46-47
Neath 6:2, Mear 6, Woffinden 15:1 (6), Allen 2:1, Ekberg 11, Betson 0, Bowen 6.
▲ *Woffinden earned high praise in front of Sky cameras for his tactical ride win in Heat 7 in which he also team-rode Allen home for an 8-1.*

SCUNTHORPE (H)
Saturday, June 21
Won 54-38
Rider replacement for Ekberg, Mear 11:3, Woffinden 8, Allen 9:1, Neath 14:1, Daniel Halsey [G] 3:2, Bowen 9:1.

SQUAD
Tommy Allen, Danny Betson, Luke Bowen, Daniel Halsey, Robert Mear, Chris Neath, Tai Woffinden.
Foreign: Stefan Ekberg.

SHEFFIELD (H)
Sunday, June 29
Won 61-32
Rider replacement for Ekberg, Mear 9, **Woffinden 16:2**, **Allen 15:3**, Neath 8:2, Halsey 5:3, Bowen 8, Rob Smith [no. 8].

GLASGOW (H)
Saturday, July 5
Won 65-27
Rider replacement for Ekberg, Mear 11, Tomas Topinka [G] 13:4, Allen 16:1, Neath 12, Halsey 6:1, Bowen 7:4, Gary Cottham [no. 8].
▲ *Halsey made his official Premier League debut, having been named as a replacement for Daniel Betson.*

EDINBURGH (A)
Friday, July 11
Lost 46-47
Ekberg 4, Mear 1, **Woffinden 17:1 (6)**, Allen 5, Neath 12, Halsey 6:3, Bowen 1.
▼ *Mear pulled out after crashing in his second ride in Heat 5. Needed a 5-1 from the last race to take a shock away win, but although Woffinden took the win required, Neath was beaten by Matthew Wethers.*

BERWICK (A)
Saturday, July 12
Lost 33-60
Ekberg 3, Mear 5:2, Woffinden 17 (6), Allen 3, Neath 2, Halsey 0, Bowen 3.

GLASGOW (A)
Sunday, July 13
Lost 41-52
Ekberg 7, Mear 0, Woffinden 17 (6), Allen 0, Neath 8:1, Halsey 1, Bowen 8:1.
▼ *Allen forced to withdraw from the meeting after crashing in Heat 3.*

REDCAR (A)
Thursday, July 17
Lost 43-50
Ekberg 7, *rider replacement for Mear*, Tomas Topinka [G] 18 (6), Allen 1, Neath 8:1, Halsey 0, Bowen 9:2.
▲ *Tomas Topinka deputised superbly for Woffinden, and his terrific tactical substitute win in Heat 14 gave the Rockets a glimmer – only for that hope to be extinguished in Heat 15.*

REDCAR (H)
Saturday, July 19
Won 65-26
Ekberg 6:2, Mear 10:1, **Woffinden 14:1**, **Allen 10:2**, **Neath 14:1**, Halsey 5:1, Bowen 6:3.
▲ *Banged in six 5-1s in the first six races to leave the Bears facing a damage limitation exercise.*

BERWICK (H)
Sunday, July 27
Won 57-33
Ekberg 13:1, Mear 6:2, Woffinden 9, Allen 6:3, Neath 12, Halsey 5:1, Bowen 6.
▼ *Mear withdrew after a Heat 10 tumble.*

KING'S LYNN (H)
Saturday, August 2
Won 49-41
Ekberg 9:2, Mear 6, Woffinden 12:1, Allen 5:1, Neath 8:1, Halsey 1:1, Bowen 8.
▲ *Taken right to wire and needed two points from Heat 15 to clinch victory – Ekberg and Woffinden responded with a 5-1.*

READING (H)
Saturday, August 16
Won 54-39
Ekberg 7:1, Mear 6:1, Woffinden 10:1, Allen 10:2, Neath 7, Halsey 5:1, Bowen 9:2.
▲ *Rockets blasted into a maximum 30-6 lead after six races – but Ulrich Østergaard won his last four rides.*

MILDENHALL (A)
Sunday, August 17
Won 65-27
Ekberg 8:3, Mear 9:1, Woffinden 13:1, Allen 11:3, Neath 11, Halsey 6:1, Bowen 7:1.

STOKE (A)
Saturday, August 23
Lost 35-54
Ekberg 7:1, Mear 7:1, Woffinden 6:1, Allen 3 (1), Neath 8:1, Halsey 0, Bowen 4.

STOKE (H)
Monday, August 25
Won 55-37
Ekberg 10:3, Mear 9:2, *rider replacement for Woffinden*, Allen 8, Neath 14, Halsey 2, Bowen 11:2, Rob Smith [no. 8] 1:1.
▼ *Halsey and Allen both crashed in the first three races but Rockets took the lead in Heat 4.*

SHEFFIELD (A)
Thursday, August 28
Lost 36-54
Ekberg 9 (X), Mear 5, Tomas Topinka [G] 7, Allen 7:2, Neath 5, Halsey 0, Bowen 3:1.
▲ *Race winners in three of the first five heats but Ekberg's tactical ride ended with a crash in Heat 11, and the match was over as a contest.*

BIRMINGHAM (H)
Saturday, August 30
Won 53-40
Ekberg 4:1, Mear 8, Tomas Topinka [G] 13:1, Allen 6:1, Neath 7, Halsey 6:2, Bowen 9:3.
▼▲ *Won match with a blistering mid-meeting surge that saw them outscore Brummies 24-6 between Heats 5 and 9.*

BIRMINGHAM (A)
Wednesday, September 10
Won 48-42
Neath 6:1, Ekberg 9:1, Woffinden 12, Mear 3, Allen 6, Halsey 7, Ben Powell [G] 5:3.
▲▼ *Woffinden crashed in his first ride but then won his next four, including the last-heat decider. Allen won his first two but did not re-appear after clashing with team-mate Halsey and Jason Lyons in Heat 9.*

MILDENHALL (H)
Saturday, September 13
Won 66-23
Neath 5:1, **Ekberg 16:2**, **Woffinden 15**, Mear 6:3, *rider replacement for Allen*, Halsey 13:1, **Bowen 11:4**, Rob Smith [no. 8].
▼ *Expected outcome despite problems for Neath, who failed to finish two of his races. Red-letter day for reserves Bowen and Halsey.*

SOMERSET (H)
Saturday, September 13
Won 65-25
Neath 12:3, **Ekberg 14:1**, Woffinden 10:2, Mear 9, *rider replacement for Allen*, Halsey 6:2, Bowen 14:1, Rob Smith [no. 8].
▲ *Ekberg and Neath unbeaten and Bowen denied second maximum by a tapes exclusion.*

NEWCASTLE (A)
Sunday, September 14
Won 41-33
Neath 6:2, Ekberg 9:1, Woffinden 9, Mear 7:1, *rider replacement for Allen*, Halsey 1, Bowen 9.
▼● *Woffinden crashed and was excluded from Heat 12 causing significant fence damage, which was repaired in time to allow the re-run. Because of a double header programme it was agreed to abandon the match, the result to stand.*

ISLE OF WIGHT (A)
Tuesday, September 16
Lost 42-51
Neath 5:1, Ekberg 12:1 (TS0), Woffinden 15 (6), Mear 5, *rider replacement for Allen*, Halsey 0, Bowen 5:1.
▼ *Woffinden won three races and Ekberg also gave the home side plenty to think about, but the Islanders had the all-round strength to control the meeting.*

SCUNTHORPE (A)
Friday, September 19
Won 53-40
Neath 6:2, Ekberg 15, Woffinden 14, Mear 9:2, *rider replacement for Allen*, Halsey 0, Bowen 9:1.
▲ *Continued their late-season charge towards the top four with Woffinden and Ekberg again spearheading the performance – Rockets were 16-points up after Heat 11.*

NEWCASTLE (H)
Friday, September 26
Won 59-34
Neath 13:2, Ekberg 8:3, Woffinden 8:1, Mear 8:1, Allen 8, Halsey 5:2, Bowen 9:1.
▲ *Confirmed a top four finish and a place in the play offs by starting the meeting with six successive 5-1s. Former rider Dave Jessup stood in as referee after the nominated official failed to turn up.*

PREMIER LEAGUE

		M	W	D	L	PtsF	PtsA	Pts
1	Edinburgh	30	22	2	6	1562	1161	53
2	Somerset	30	21	0	9	1517	1223	48
3	King's Lynn	30	18	5	7	1624	1111	45
4	**RYE HOUSE**	**30**	**19**	**0**	**11**	**1500**	**1232**	**42**
5	Workington	30	17	2	11	1435.5	1300.5	41
6	Berwick	30	16	2	12	1428	1316	37
7	Redcar	30	16	1	13	1369	1374	37
8	Sheffield	30	15	2	13	1381	1345	35
9	Reading	30	15	1	14	1350	1405	34
10	Scunthorpe	30	15	0	15	1309	1434	33
11	Isle of Wight	30	15	0	15	1359	1390	31
12	Birmingham	30	13	0	17	1317.5	1401.5	30
13	Stoke	30	11	1	18	1307	1441	25
14	Newcastle	30	10	0	20	1220	1501	22
15	Glasgow	30	9	0	21	1297	1469	19
16	Mildenhall	30	0	0	30	932	1804	0

Play offs

Semi Final, first leg
KING'S LYNN (A)
Wednesday, October 8
Lost 37-56
Ekberg 0, Neath 9, Woffinden 15 (4), Mear 3:2, Allen 8 (TS2), Halsey 1, Bowen 1.
▼ *Ekberg crashed in the opening heat and suffered back injuries that could be career ending.*

KING'S LYNN (H)
Saturday, October 11
Won 52-41
Rider replacement for Ekberg, Neath 12:2, Woffinden 14, Mear 7:1, Allen 10:1, Halsey 1, Bowen 8:1.
▼ *Went 16-points up on the night but were immediately hit by a 1-8 reverse in Heat 11 from Kevin Doolan and guest Viktor Bergström which all-but ended their hopes of aggregate victory.*
Aggregate: Lost 89-97.

Premier Trophy

MILDENHALL (H)
Monday, March 24
Won 59-33
Neath 6:1, Bowen 8:1, Woffinden 11:1, Allen 7:2, Ekberg 12, Betson 8:1, Mear 7:2.

KING'S LYNN (A)
Wednesday, March 26
Lost 31-61
Neath 13 (6), Bowen 1, Woffinden 0, Allen 5, Ekberg 5, Betson 2, Mear 5:3.
▼ *Woffinden withdrew with a hand injury after Heat 3 crash.*

BIRMINGHAM (A)
Wednesday, April 2
Lost 36-50
Neath 13:1 (4), Bowen 1, *rider replacement for Woffinden*, Allen 7:1, Ekberg 5, Betson 5, Mear 5:3, Jack Roberts [G].
▼ *Meeting abandoned after Heat 14, result stands. Reduced to five riders when Bowen crashed out in Heat 3 (hand).*

BIRMINGHAM (H)
Saturday, April 5
Won 54-36
Neath 5:1, Bowen 4:1, **Woffinden 14:1**, Allen 11:2, Ekberg 6:1, Betson 10:1, Mear 4:3.

KING'S LYNN (H)
Saturday, April 19
Won 55-35
Neath 7:1, Bowen 0, Woffinden 12, Allen 5:2, Ekberg 12:1, Betson 9:1, Mear 10:2.
▼ *Bowen suffered arm and shoulder injuries in a Heat 1 crash and an eventful meeting saw both sides collect a 5-0!*

MILDENHALL (A)
Sunday, May 4
Won 56-35
Neath 5:1, Joe Haines [G] 4, Woffinden 12:2, *rider replacement for Allen*, Ekberg 17, Daniel Halsey [G] 6:1, Mear 12:1.
▼ *Victory at West Row wasn't enough to put the Rockets into the next stage of the competition.*

PREMIER TROPHY Group C

		M	W	D	L	PtsF	PtsA	Pts
1	Birmingham	6	4	0	2	243	194	10
2	**RYE HOUSE**	**6**	**4**	**0**	**2**	**291**	**250**	**9**
3	King's Lynn	6	3	0	3	245	211	7
4	Mildenhall	6	1	0	5	203	327	2

CHRIS NEATH TESTIMONIAL
Saturday, September 20
CHRIS Neath celebrated his 11 seasons in the sport as a Wolverhampton asset, having signed for the club he supported as a schoolboy in 1998.

He made his competitive debut on May 9, 1998, scoring six, paid seven from four rides, for Conference League Newport against St. Austell.

His first Premier League experience came six days later in Newport's Knock Out Cup visit to Arena Essex and he had his first taste of Elite League action for Wolves against Ipswich on March 25, 2002. Has spent the bulk of his career on loan to Premier League outfits Newport, Swindon and Rye House.

Fredrik Lindgren 12, Tai Woffinden 11+3, Chris Neath 11+0, Luke Bowen 8, Daniel King 8, Mads Korneliussen 8, Davey Watt 8, Leigh Lanham 8, Kevin Doolan 8, David Howe 7, Stuart Robson 6, Stefan Ekberg 6, Paul Lee 5, Steve Johnston 5, Robert Mear 5, Daniel Halsey [R] 4, Brent Werner 0.

Knoclk Out Cup

Second round, first leg
NEWPORT (H)
Saturday, April 26
Won 60-30
Neath 12:1, Daniel Halsey [G] 4, **Woffinden 13:2**, *rider replacement for Allen*, Ekberg 11:1, Betson 0, Mear 19:1, Gary Cottham [no. 8] 1.
▼ *Betson crashed and suffered elbow damage in his opening ride in Heat 2 and did not continue.*

The second leg was never raced following the sudden death of Newport promoter Tim Stone.

Quarter Final, first leg
BIRMINGHAM (H)
Saturday, May 31
Won 62-30
Neath 8:1, Mear 8:3, **Woffinden 13:2**, Allen 7:1, **Ekberg 14:1**, Betson 2, Bowen 10.
▼ *Opponents were reduced to five riders as early as Heat 1 allowing Rockets to virtually wrap up the tie.*

Quarter Final, second leg
BIRMINGHAM (A)
Wednesday, June 25
Won 51-42
Rider replacement for Ekberg, Mear 12:3, James Wright [G] 14:1, Allen 7:2, Neath 9:1, Daniel Halsey [G] 6:1, Luke Bowen 3:1, Rob Smith [no. 8].
Aggregate: Won 113-72.

Semi Final, first leg
SOMERSET (A)
Friday, August 22
Lost 38-53
Ekberg 2:1, Mear 5, Woffinden 11:1 (4), Allen 8:1, Neath 5, Halsey 0, Bowen 7:2.
▼ *Ekberg concussed in a crash with Jordan Frampton.*

Semi Final, second leg
SOMERSET (H)
Monday, August 25
Won 50-43
Ekberg 11:2, Mear 7:2, *rider replacement for Woffinden*, Allen 10:3, Neath 7:1, Halsey 5, Bowen 10:1, Rob Smith [no. 8].
▲▼ *Managed to take ten points off the deficit in first four races, but Jason Doyle then won a tactical ride and Rockets conceded a 5-1 in the last race when they needed maximum points to draw the tie.*
Aggregate: Lost 88-96.

Performances in the first leg of the Knock Out Cup against Newport are included in the Rye House averages even though the second leg never took place following the death of Wasps owner Tim Stone.

2009 Squad

Chris **NEATH** (7.08), Linus **SUNDSTRÖM** (7.00), Tommy **ALLEN** (6.55), Robert **MEAR** (5.78), Joe **HAINES** (5.36), Luke **BOWEN** (5.32), Andrew **SILVER** (5.00). *Silver is making a full-time comeback after being out of racing since early 1994.*

Weather...

A Premier League double header against Newcastle and Somerset was among victims of the weather.

Premier League
Saturday, May 17 .... SOMERSET (H)
Monday May 26 .... BERWICK (H)
Sunday, July 6 .... NEWCASTLE (A)
Sunday, August 31 .... NEWCASTLE (A)
Saturday, September 6 .... NEWCASTLE (H)
Saturday, September 6 .... SOMERSET (H)
Friday, September 12 .... SCUNTHORPE (A)
Wednesday, October 1 .... KING'S LYNN (A)

Premier Trophy
Sunday, March 16 .... MILDENHALL (A)
Sunday, April 13 .... MILDENHALL (A)
Wednesday, May 28 .... BIRMINGHAM (A)
Saturday, March 29 .... KING'S LYNN (H)

Knock Out Cup
Saturday, August 9 .... SOMERSET (H)

Challenge
Monday, March 10 .... READING (A)
Saturday, March 22 .... LAKESIDE (H)

...beaten

Individual

SAINSBURY'S ACE OF HERTS CHAMPIONSHIP
Saturday, October 18

DAVID Howe received a late, late call-up after Edward Kennett withdrew through illness and made the trip well worthwhile by getting better as the meeting progressed.

Even though he failed to win a race in the 20-heat qualifying section he won both his semi final and final, on each occasion finishing ahead of Lewis Bridger.

	1	2	3	4	5	Tot	SF	F
1 David HOWE	**2**	**2**	**2**	**2**	**2**	**10**	**3**	**3**
2 Lewis BRIDGER	3	2	0	3	3	11	2	2
3 Oliver ALLEN	3	1	3	0	1	8	3	1
4 Robert MEAR	2	2	2	2	0	8	2	X
5 Stuart ROBSON	1	1	3	3	3	11	1	
6 Luke BOWEN	2	1	1	0	2	6	1	
7 Chris NEATH	0	3	3	3	3	12	0	
8 Linus SUNDSTRÖM	1	3	2	1	1	8	0	
9 Tai WOFFINDEN	3	3	0	1		7		
10 Tommy ALLEN	1	0	1	2	2	6		
11 Daniel HALSEY	0	0	1	0	1	2		
12 Shawn McCONNELL [R]	1					1		
13 Andrew SILVER	0	0	0	0	0	0		

Roll of Honour

1965 .... Malcolm SIMMONS
1966 .... Brian LEONARD
1969 .... John HIBBEN
1970 .... Nigel RACKETT
1972 .... Stan STEVENS
2002 .... Leigh LANHAM
2003 .... Brent WERNER
2004 .... Stuart ROBSON
2006 .... Edward KENNETT
2007 .... Tommy ALLEN
2008 .... David HOWE

World Under 21 Championship

Semi Final
Sunday, June 15
1 Troy Batchelor 15, 2 Tai Woffinden 13, 3 Chris Holder 12+3, 4 Morten Risager 12+2, 5 Grzegorz Zengota 9, 6 Lewis Bridger 8, 7 William Lawson 8, 8 Ludvig Lindgren 8, 9 Simon Gustafsson 7+3, 10 Mateusz Szczepaniak 7+2, 11 Linus Eklöf 7+1, 12 Ricky Wells 6, 13 Tobias Busch 3, 14 Tyron Proctor [R] 2, 15 Max Dilger 1, 16 Robert Kapsrzak 1, 17 Joshua Auty [R] 1, 18 Kim Nilsson 0.

Challenge

THAMES VALLEY TROPHY
READING (H)
Saturday, March 15
26-19, abandoned after Heat 7, rain.
Neath 6, Bowen 4:2, Woffinden 5, Allen 0, Ekberg 4:1, Betson 2:2, Mear 5.

For comprehensive details of Rye House Cobras see Conference League section.

Photo: Jeff B. HIGGOTT/SEQUELLA.co.uk

ROCKET MEN: *Stefan Ekberg, Chris Neath, Tai Woffinden, Robert Mear, Tommy Allen, Daniel Halsey and Luke Bowen*

RYE HOUSE

Rider	M	R	Pts	BP	TPts	Ave	F	P	TR	TPts	TS	TSPts
Tai WOFFINDEN	35	169	430	24	454	10.75	1	7	9	25	0	0
Chris NEATH	**43**	**195**	**361**	**39**	**400**	**8.20**	**0**	**4**	**2**	**5**	**0**	**0**
Stefan EKBERG	37	178	329	32	361	8.11	0	3	1	0	1	0
Tommy ALLEN	**31**	**136**	**228**	**38**	**266**	**7.82**	**0**	**3**	**1**	**0**	**1**	**1**
Robert MEAR	42	203	310	53	363	7.15	0	0	0	0	0	0
Luke BOWEN	**39**	**184**	**248**	**37**	**285**	**6.20**	**0**	**1**	**0**	**0**	**0**	**0**
Danny BETSON	9	35	40	4	44	5.03	0	0	0	0	0	0
Daniel HALSEY	**25**	**101**	**82**	**16**	**98**	**3.88**	**0**	**0**	**0**	**0**	**0**	**0**
Guests	***22***	***91***	***119***	***20***	***139***	***6.11***	***0***	***0***	***0***	***0***	***1***	***3***

For Chris NEATH see Wolverhampton; for Robert MEAR, Danny BETSON and Daniel HALSEY see Rye House (CL).

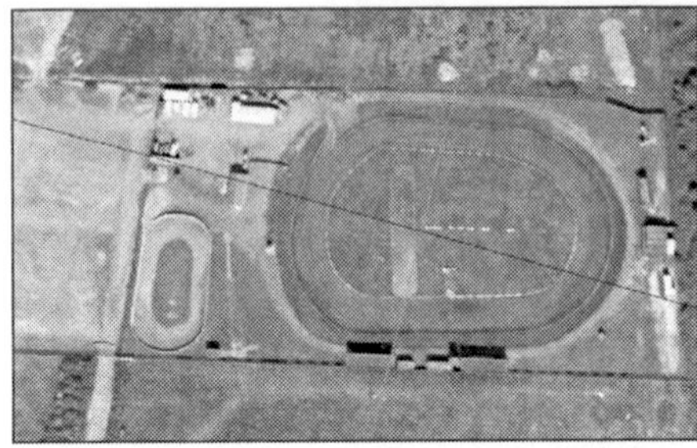

Premier League

SCUNTHORPE

TRACK FILE

Track: Eddie Wright Raceway, Normanby Road, Scunthorpe, North Lincolnshire, DN15 8QZ.
Telephone: 01724 848899.
Hotline: 09066 555923.
Website: www.scunthorpespeedway.com
Track Length: 285 metres.
Track Record: 56.39 secs, Richard Hall, August 25, 2008.
Promoters: Rob Godfrey and Kenny Smith.
Team Sponsors: Jotun Paints.
Colours: White with blue trim and black scorpion.
Nickname: Scorpions.

HISTORY

First meeting: March 27, 2005, Grand Opening Individual meeting.
Leagues: Division Two, 2009. Division Three, 2005-09.
Meetings were also held at
● *Quibell Park, Brumby Wood Lane, Scunthorpe.*
First meeting: May 3, 1971, Scunthorpe v Hull, Humberside Trophy.
Leagues: Division Two, 1972-78.
● *Ashby Ville Stadium off Queensway, Adshby, Scunthorpe.*
First meeting: May 6, 1979, Scunthorpe v Middlesbrough, Division Two challenge.
Leagues: Division Two, 1979-1985.

HONOURS

Major honours: 9.
Division Three champions (2), 2006, 2007.
Division Three Knock Out Cup winners (2), 2006, 2007.
Division Three Shield winners (1), 2006.
Division Three Trophy winners (2), 2006, 2007.
Division Three Four Team champions (1), 2007.
Division Three Pairs champions (1), 2006.

2008 REVIEW

THE newcomers to the Premier League quickly established a reputation for providing some of the best racing in the country at the Eddie Wright Raceway.

Numerous Scorpions meetings went to last heat deciders, and they were eventually beaten three times on their own shale, but it was still a good first season at this level.

By the end of the campaign, the club's management were reflecting on the fact that they lacked an out-and-out big-hitter, relying on their best results coming when all seven riders clicked together on the same night.

And that left them a little short on their away trips, although they did win back-to-back matches on the road at Stoke and Mildenhall in June.

However, they had to wait until their last match of the season to add the other away win, at Newcastle, and by that stage they had already been knocked out of the Young Shield by eventual winners Workington.

The win at Brough Park was overshadowed by the controversial incident which saw mid-season signing Ben Powell aim his bike at Kenni Arendt Larsen after the two had clashed in Heat 12.

Powell was immediately released from the club, his late-season individual meeting bookings were taken away, and he was eventually handed a one-year ban by the SCB.

Swedish star Magnus Karlsson finished top of the Scorpions' averages with a figure of just over eight, while Richard Hall and Carl Wilkinson were both over the seven mark.

The main disappointment was the fact that they appeared to suffer some kind of jinx against local rivals Sheffield, who won at the Eddie Wright Raceway on all three of their visits, including knocking the Scorpions out of the Cup at the first round stage.

The club also staged the British Under-18 Championship at the end of the season, which was won by former home favourite Tai Woffinden.

2008 RESULTS

Premier League

Final position ....Tenth

BIRMINGHAM (A)
Wednesday, April 9
Lost 37-53
Karlsson 5:1, Wilkinson 8, Moore 13 (TS1), Bergström 0, Hall 6, Bekker 4, Compton 1.

SOMERSET (A)
Friday, May 2
Lost 29-63
Moore 0, Wilkinson 8, Karlsson 14, Compton 0, Hall 5, Bekker 0, Bergström 2.

SOMERSET (H)
Monday, May 5
Won 51-39
Moore 8, Wilkinson 4:3, Karlsson 9:2 (4), Compton 3, Hall 14, Bekker 3:1, Bergström 10:1.
▲ *Recovered well from Oak Tree Arena thrashing, despite losing Compton with a shoulder injury after spectacular Heat 5 crash.*

WORKINGTON (H)
Friday, May 9
Won 47-43
Moore 9:1, Wilkinson 8:2, Karlsson 11, Compton 1, Hall 9:1, Bergström 6:1, Bekker 3:2.
▲ *Bergstrom's win in Heat 14 ensured the Scorpions would not face a nervous final race – which the Comets duly took a 5-1 from!*

NEWCASTLE (H)
Friday, May 16
Won 56-36
Moore 6:2, Wilkinson 9, Karlsson 13, Compton 4:2, Hall 11, Bergström 5, **Bekker 8:4**.
▲ *Reserve Bekker became the first Scorpion to score a Premier League maximum by finishing second in each of his four rides.*

WORKINGTON (A)
Saturday, May 17
Lost 39-54
Moore 4, Wilkinson 9 (6), Karlsson 7, Compton 0, Joel Parsons [G] 8, Bergström 5:4, Bekker 6:1.

GLASGOW (A)
Sunday, May 18
Lost 44-46
Moore 8:2, Wilkinson 9:2, Karlsson 14, Compton 1, *rider replacement for Hall*, Bergström 9:1, Bekker 3:1.

EDINBURGH (A)
Friday, May 23
Lost 22-68
Moore 2:1, Wilkinson 5, Karlsson 9 (1), Scott Richardson [G] 0, Hall 4 (TS1), Scott James [G] 1, Bekker 1.
▲▼ *Karlsson won two races after five years away from Armadale but his team-mates struggled throughout.*

SQUAD
Richard Hall, Andrew Moore, Carl Wilkinson
Foreign: Byron Bekker, Viktor Bergström, Magnus Karlsson, Ben Powell, Emiliano Sanchez.

BERWICK (A)
Saturday, May 24
Lost 42-48
Moore 11:2, Wilkinson 5, Karlsson 10, Scott Richardson [G] 1:1, Hall 6:1, Adam McKinna [G] 6:1, Bekker 3.
▼ *Provided winners in the first five races but saw their eight-point lead eradicated, and were beaten by Heat 14*

EDINBURGH (H)
Monday, May 26
Lost 39-53
Moore 3:2, Wilkinson 8, Karlsson 10, Scott Richardson [G] 1:1, Hall 10 (TS4), Adam McKinna [G] 1:1, Bekker 6:4.
▼ *Had to use Conference League guests for Compton and Bergström, but did manage to hold the scores level for the first nine races – all of which were shared!*

REDCAR (H)
Friuday, June 6
Won 52-41
Hall 10, Wilkinson 7:1, Karlsson 10:1, **Bergström 9:3**, Moore 2:1, Powell 9:1, Bekker 5:1.
▼ *Scorpions trailed early on but turned things around despite Moore crashing out of his final appearance in Heat 11.*

STOKE (A)
Saturday, June 7
Won 47-43
Hall 2:1, Wilkinson 11, **Karlsson 14:1**, Bergström 11:2, *rider replacement for Moore*, Powell 5, Bekker 4.
▲ *Karlsson completed paid maximum by winning the last-heat decider.*

MILDENHALL (H)
Friday, June 20
Won 48-42
Hall 11:1, Wilkinson 6:2, Karlsson 10:1, Bergström 7, Sanchez 8:1, Powell 2, Bekker 4:1.

RYE HOUSE (A)
Saturday, June 21
Lost 38-54
Hall 4:1, Wilkinson 4:1, Karlsson 13 (4), Bergström 5:1, Sanchez 4:1, Powell 6:2, Bekker 2.

MILDENHALL (A)
Sunday, June 22
Won 53-40
Hall 6:1, Wilkinson 9:1, Karlsson 10:1, Bergström 7, Sanchez 10:3, Powell 3:1, Bekker 8:2.

REDCAR (A)
Thursday, July 3
Lost 40-50
Hall 7, Wilkinson 6:2, Karlsson 8:1, Bergström 7:1,

For comprehensive details of Scunthorpe Saints see Conference League section.

Sanchez 4, Powell 7:1, Bekker 1.

BERWICK (H)
Friday, July 4
Won 52-41
Hall 13:1, Wilkinson 7:1, Karlsson 4:1, Bergström 11:2, Sanchez 9:1, Powell 4:1, Bekker 4.

ISLE OF WIGHT (A)
Tuesday, July 8
Lost 32-60
Hall 12:1 (4), Wilkinson 6, *rider replacement for Karlsson*, Bergström 5:1, Sanchez 4, Powell 3:3, Bekker 2.

▼ *Struggled on their first ever visit, with only Hall really coming to terms with the track with two race wins.*

KING'S LYNN (H)
Friday, July 18
Won 46-43
Hall 7, Wilkinson 5:1, Karlsson 5:2, Bergström 12, Sanchez 9:1, Powell 1, Bekker 7:3.

▲ *Sanchez provided an heroic ride to beat Kevin Doolan in Heat 11.*

KING'S LYNN (A)
Wednesday, July 23
Lost 28-63
Hall 9 (4), Wilkinson 0, Karlsson 5, Bergström 3, Sanchez 6:1, Powell 4, Darren Mallett [G] 1:1.

BIRMINGHAM (H)
Friday, July 25
Won 49-44
Hall 10:1, Bergström 7:1, Karlsson 11, Sanchez 6:3, Wilkinson 6:1, Scott Richardson [G] 1:1, Powell 8.

ISLE OF WIGHT (H)
Friday, August 8
Won 53-40
Hall 9, Bergström 7:1, **Karlsson 14:1**, Sanchez 3:1, Wilkinson 12:2, Gary Irving [G] 3, Powell 5.

▲ *Conceded 5-1s in the first two races but mounted a spirited comeback with six successive heat advantages to take control.*

SHEFFIELD (H)
Friday, August 15
Lost 43-47
Hall 7:2, Bergström 4, Karlsson 6:2, Sanchez 4:1, Wilkinson 8, Bekker 4:2, Powell 10:1.

▼ *Sheffield jinx struck again as the Tigers carded 4-2s in the last two races after the home side had made a strong comeback from 10 points down.*

GLASGOW (H)
Monday, August 25
Won 54-39
Hall 11, Bergström 7:4, Karlsson 11, Sanchez 3:1, Wilkinson 7, Bekker 9, Powell 6:1.

▲ *Hall broke the track record in Heat 1.*

PHOTO: Steve Dixon

Scunthorpe: Team manager Kenny Smith, Richard Hall, Byron Bekker, Magnus Karlsson (kneeling), Ben Powell, mascot Reece Downes, Emiliano Sanchez [kneeling), Carl Wilkinson and Viktor Bergström

STOKE (H)
Friday, August 29
Won 46-44
Hall 8, Bergström 6, Karlsson 6:1, Sanchez 8, Wilkinson 8, Powell 6:2, Bekker 4:2.

READING (A)
Monday, September 1
Lost 44-49
Hall 6, Bergström 5:2, Karlsson 13 (6), Sanchez 1, Wilkinson 9:1, Powell 7:2, Bekker 3.
▲▼ *Came back from 10 points down to force a last-heat decider, but had no answer to Ulrich Østergaard in the finale, with Mark Lemon taking second place.*

SHEFFIELD (A)
Thursday, September 18
Lost 38-52
Hall 10 (TS0), Sanchez 2:1, Karlsson 7 (F), Bergström 5, Wilkinson 8:1, Powell 5:1, Bekker 1:1.
▼ *Karlsson received an astonishing tapes exclusion in Heat 15 when Joel Parsons was the rider at fault.*

RYE HOUSE (H)
Friday, September 19
Lost 40-53
Hall 12 (6), Sanchez 3:1, Karlsson 8:1 (TS0), Bergström 5:2, Wilkinson 4, Powell 1, Bekker 7.
▼ *Tai Woffinden did plenty of damage to the Scorpions on his return, beaten only by Karlsson and that due to a puncture.*

READING (H)
Friday, September 26
Won 53-40
Hall 12, Sanchez 7:3, Karlsson 11:1, Bergström 8:3, Wilkinson 8:1, Powell 3:1, Bekker 4:1.

NEWCASTLE (A)
Sunday, October 12
Won 47-46
Hall 7, Sanchez 6:2, Karlsson 10:1, Bergström 5, Wilkinson 8:1, Powell 6, Bekker 5:2.

Ben Powell (above) was involved in an incident in Heat 12 in which he aimed his bike at Newcastle's Kenni Arendt Larsen after the Dane had brought him down. He was fined £300 by the meeting referee and and sacked by Scunthorpe.
At a subsequent Speedway Control Bureau hearing he was suspended for 12 months

PREMIER LEAGUE

	M	W	D	L	PtsF	PtsA	Pts
1 Edinburgh	30	22	2	6	1562	1161	53
2 Somerset	30	21	0	9	1517	1223	48
3 King's Lynn	30	18	5	7	1624	1111	45
4 Rye House	30	19	0	11	1500	1232	42
5 Workington	30	17	2	11	1435.5	1300.5	41
6 Berwick	30	16	2	12	1428	1316	37
7 Redcar	30	16	1	13	1369	1374	37
8 Sheffield	30	15	2	13	1381	1345	35
9 Reading	30	15	1	14	1350	1405	34
10 SCUNTHORPE	**30**	**15**	**0**	**15**	**1309**	**1434**	**33**
11 Isle of Wight	30	15	0	15	1359	1390	31
12 Birmingham	30	13	0	17	1317.5	1401.5	30
13 Stoke	30	11	1	18	1307	1441	25
14 Newcastle	30	10	0	20	1220	1501	22
15 Glasgow	30	9	0	21	1297	1469	19
16 Mildenhall	30	0	0	30	932	1804	0

Young Shield

Quarter Final, first leg
WORKINGTON (H)
Friday, October 3
Won 51-39
Hall 14, Sanchez 5:2, Karlsson 9:1, Bergström 7, Wilkinson 7, Powell 6:2, Bekker 3:1.
▼ *Scorpions started well and were 13-5 up but struggled to further extend their lead, and were grateful for a Heat 14 5-1 from Bergstrom and Powell to move further clear.*

Quarter Final, second leg
WORKINGTON (A)
Sunday, October 5
Lost 35-58
Hall 4 (TS2), Sanchez 5, Karlsson 11 (4), Bergström 4:2, Wilkinson 8, Powell 1, Bekker 2:2.
▼ *First leg lead proved to be nowhere near enough with Karlsson the Scorpions' only race winner in Heat 12 as their official season came to a disappointing end.*

Aggregate: Lost 86-97.

Weather...

Scunthorpe had four Premier League level home meetings fall victim to rain.

Premier League
Friday, June 13 .... STOKE (H)
Friday, July 11 .... KING'S LYNN (H)
Sunday, August 17 .... NEWCASTLE (A)
Thursday, September 4 .... SHEFFIELD (A)
Friday, September 5 .... READING (H)
Sunday, September 7 .... NEWCASTLE (A)
Friday, September 12 .... RYE HOUSE (H)

Young Shield
Saturday, October 4 .... WORKINGTON (A)

Premier Trophy
Friday, March 28 .... REDCAR (H)
Saturday, March 29 .... STOKE (A)
Sunday, April 6 .... NEWCASTLE (A)
Friday, April 17 .... REDCAR (A)

...beaten

■ *Scunthorpe ran amateur meetings throughout the year – see Amateur Speedway section for details.*

Premier Trophy

SHEFFIELD (A)
Thursday, March 20
Lost 36-57
Moore 7, Wilkinson 0, Karlsson 11, Bergström 2, Hall 10 (6), Bekker 0, Compton 6:1.
▲▼ *Revived club debut at Premier League level gleaned four heat wins – two each from Karlsson and Hall.*

SHEFFIELD (H)
Friday, March 21
Lost 41-48
Moore 6:1, Wlkinson 6, Karlsson 7, Bergström 3:3, Hall 9:1, Bekker 7, Compton 3:2.

REDCAR (H)
Sunday, March 30
Drew 45-45
Moore 7:1, Wilkinson 6:1, Karlsson 13, Bergström 0, Hall 10:1, Bekker 5:2, Compton 4:1.
▼*Bergstrom suffered a chipped bone in his shoulder in a Heat 9 crash with Chris Kerr.*

NEWCASTLE (H)
Friday, April 4
Won 55-38
Karlsson 6, *rider replacement for Bergström*, Moore 10, Wilkinson 11:1, Hall 17, Bekker 5:1, Compton 6:2, Scott Richardson [no. 8].

STOKE (H)
Friday, April 18
Won 47-43
Moore 6:2, Wilkinson 9, Karlsson 12, Bergström 8:1, Hall 8, Bekker 2, Compton 2.
▼▲ *Karlsson blew an engine in his first ride but won his remaining four outings, securing victory in a shared Heat 15.*

STOKE (A)
Saturday, April 19
Lost 39-51
Moore 9, Wilkinson 2:2, Karlsson 12, Bergström 4:1, Hall 6, Bekker 0, Compton 6:1.

NEWCASTLE (A)
Monday, April 21
Won 47-43
Moore 9:1, Wilkinson 10:1, Karlsson 7, Bergström 6:1, Hall 6, Bekker 5, Compton 4:2.
▲ *First-ever win on Tyneside, Wilkinson winning his last three races including Heat 15 on his old home track.*

REDCAR (A)
Saturday, May 3
Lost 35-55
Moore 5, Wilkinson 8:2, Karlsson 6, Compton 0, Hall 7, Bekker 1, Bergström 8:2 (1).

PREMIER TROPHY Group B

		M	W	D	L	PtsF	PtsA	Pts
1	Sheffield	8	6	0	2	386	345	14
2	Redcar	8	3	2	3	362	360	8
3	**SCUNTHORPE**	**8**	**3**	**1**	**4**	**345**	**380**	**8**
4	Newcastle	8	3	1	4	364	367	7
5	Stoke	8	3	0	5	363	368	6

Knock Out Cup

First round, first leg
SHEFFIELD (A)
Thursday, April 10
Lost 36-55
Karlsson 4:1, Wilkinson 7 (2), Moore 6, Bergström 4:1, Hall 9 (TS0), Bekker 0, Compton 6.

First round, second leg
SHEFFIELD (H)
Friday, April 11
Lost 44-48
Karlsson 1:1, Wilkinson 11:1, Moore 14, Bergström 2:1, Hall 10 (TS4), Bekker 5:2, Compton 1.
Aggregate: Lost 80-103.

2009 Squad

David **HOWE** (10.00), Magnus **KARLSSON** (7.75), Carl **WILKINSON** (6.05), Simon **LAMBERT** (5.89), Viktor **BERGSTRÖM** (5.63), Byron **BEKKER** (3.86), Jerran **HART** (3.00).

SCUNTHORPE

Rider	*M*	*R*	*Pts*	*BP*	*TPts*	*Ave*	*F*	*P*	*TR*	*TPts*	*TS*	*TSPts*
Magnus KARLSSON	41	197	377	21	398	8.08	0	2	7	9	1	0
Richard HALL	**40**	**193**	**348**	**13**	**361**	**7.48**	**0**	**0**	**3**	**8**	**7**	**7**
Andrew MOORE	21	90	145	16	161	7.16	0	0	0	0	1	0
Carl WILKINSON	**42**	**187**	**297**	**31**	**328**	**7.02**	**0**	**0**	**2**	**4**	**0**	**0**
Viktor BERGSTRÖM	38	160	221	42	263	6.57	0	1	1	0	0	0
Emiliano SANCHEZ	**20**	**81**	**107**	**23**	**130**	**6.42**	**0**	**0**	**0**	**0**	**0**	**0**
Ben POWELL	22	94	108	19	127	5.40	0	0	0	0	0	0
Byron BEKKER	**39**	**156**	**146**	**36**	**182**	**4.67**	**0**	**1**	**0**	**0**	**0**	**0**
Benji COMPTON	17	67	48	11	59	3.52	0	0	0	0	0	0
Guests	***10***	***36***	***23***	***6***	***29***	***3.22***	***0***	***0***	***0***	***0***	***0***	***0***

For Andrew MOORE and Emiilano SANCHEZ see Stoke; for Carl WILKINSON see Ipswich; for Ben POWELL see Newcastle; for Byron BEKKER see Scunthorpe (CL); for Benji COMPTON see Redcar (CL) and Scunthorpe (CL).

Individual

BRITISH UNDER 18 FINAL
Monday, October 27
1 Tai Woffinden 15+3, 2 Joshua Auty 12+3+2, 3 Jerran Hart 11+2+1, 4 Joe Haines 14+0, 5 Ben Taylor 12+1, 6 Ben Hopwood 10+0, 7 Marc Owen 8, 8 Richard Franklin 7, 9 Brendan Johnson 6, 10 Paul Starke 6, 11 Jamie Pickard 6, 12 Aaron Basbey 5, 13 James Sarjeant 2, 14 Chris Widman 2. John Resch and Jason Garrity, did not arrive.
See British Championship for full details.

HALLOWE'EN TROPHY
Friday, October 31
DAVID Howe ended Scunthorpe's season with another reminder of what a powerful force he can be in the Premier League.

In a 12-rider line-up that included two other Elite League regulars – Piotr Swiderski and Troy Batchelor – he saved the best till last, winning both the semi final and final of the Halloween Trophy.

	1	2	3	4	Tot	SF	F
1 David HOWE	**2**	**1**	**2**	**3**	**8**	**3**	**3**
2 Tai WOFFINDEN	X	3	2	2	7	3	2
3 Troy BATCHELOR	3	2	3	3	11	2	1
4 Richard HALL	3	2	3	1	9	2	0
5 Carl WILKINSON	3	2	1	1	7	1	
6 Paul COOPER	0	R	3	2	5	1	
7 Piotr SWIDERSKI	2	R	2	3	7	R	
8 Stuart ROBSON	1	3	R	2	6	0	
9 Joshua AUTY	1	1	1	1	4		
10 Magnus KARLSSON	2	0	1	0	3		
11 Viktor BERGSTRÖM	0	3	0	0	3		
12 Craig WATSON	1	1	0	R	2		

Roll of Honour
2008 .... David HOWE

TOP of the averages Magnus Karlsson became a full-blown Scunthorpe asset during the winter.

After a successful season on loan he agreed to a permanent transfer from Elite League Wolverhampton.

Did you know?

Racing at Division Two level Scunthorpe have never won a Knock Out Cup tie – they have had defeats against Crewe, Birmingham, Coatbridge, Middlesbrough (three times), Berwick (twice), Edinburgh, Eastbourne, Oxford, Peterborough, Newcastle and Sheffield.

South African Byron Bekker had a successful first season in the Premier League and is back at Normanby Road in 2009

Premier League

SHEFFIELD

TRACK FILE

Track: Owlerton Stadium, Penistone Road, Sheffield, S6 2DE.
Telephone: 00114 2853142.
Hotline: 09068 664670.
Website: www.sheffieldspeedway.com
Track Length: 361 metres.
Track Record: 59.3 secs, Chris Holder, September 6, 2007.
Promoters: Neil Machin, David Hoggart and Eric Boocock.
Team Sponsors: Sheffield Window Centre.
Colours: Blue and yellow.
Nickname: Tigers.

HISTORY

First meeting: March 30, 1929, Golden Helmet Individual.
Leagues: Division One, 1933, 1965-1988, 1995-96. Division Two, 1938-39, 1947-1950, 1960-64, 1991-94, 1997-2009. Division Three 1996, 2000-04. English Dirt-Track League, 1929. Northern League, 1930-31, 1946. Speedway National Association Trophy, 1932. Open licence, 1945, 1951-52.

HONOURS

Major honours: 13.
Division One Knock Out Cup winners (1), 1974.
Division Two champions (2), 1999, 2002.
Division Two Knock Out Cup winners (1), 2002.
Division Two Trophy winners (1), 2001.
Division Two Young Shield winners (2), 1999, 2002.
Division Two British Speedway Cup winners (1), 1947.
Division Two Four Team champions (2), 1999, 2000.
Division Two Premiership winners (1), 2000.
Division Three champions (2), 2000, 2001.

2008 REVIEW

TIGERS were one of the popular pre-season tips for the Premier League title – but this was a season which completely failed to live up to expectations.

It was a winter of little change with five of the 2007 team recalled, and the appointment of the experienced Eric Boocock as team manager was well received by supporters.

But the Owlerton side had to be content with a mid-table finish and most remarkable was the fact that their generally unblemished home record was cracked on several occasions.

Both Birmingham and Workington emerged from their trips to Yorkshire with away wins, and Redcar collected a 45-45 draw – and yet, the fact that the Tigers defeated all of the top three shows that they did have the ability to do better.

Their away wins were limited to strugglers Glasgow and Mildenhall, with success at Scunthorpe being one of their better results alongside a draw at Workington.

Tigers' number one André Compton saw his average fall, and before the end of the season he had announced that it would be his last campaign in the sport as his other business commitments took priority – a decision he later reversed to join Workington after there was no vacancy at Owlerton.

And there were problems at reserve with both Sam Martin and Kyle Hughes having stints in a difficult number six spot, and Lee Smethills missed huge parts of the season due to injury.

Ricky Ashworth, who offered important heat-leader support as back-up to Compton, had a consistent season, but crashed out at Glasgow in August, and that left the Tigers vulnerable in their closing fixtures.

By then, hopes of a high finish in the Premier League had fallen by the wayside, and the Tigers were out of the Premier Trophy too, beaten by Birmingham in the semi-finals, and looking set for a major re-build for 2009 with Compton gone and long-serving Ben Wilson off to Redcar.

2008 RESULTS

Premier League

Final position...Eighth

KING'S LYNN (H)
Thursday, April 17
Won 48-40
Ashworth 3, Parsons 11:1, Compton 12, Cooper 5:2, Wilson 8, Martin 1:1, Smethills 8:1.
▲ *Arranged at short notice and went ahead despite pre-meeting rain, Cooper and Smethills collecting a Heat 14 5-0.*

BERWICK (A)
Saturday, April 19
Lost 41-52
Ashworth 6, Parsons 2:2, Compton 13:1 (6), Cooper 5, Wilson 3, Martin 4, Smethills 8:3.

READING (A)
Monday, May 12
Lost 33-60
Ashworth 10:1, Parsons 4, Compton 12 (6), Smethills 0, Wilson 1, Martin 1, Cooper 5.

GLASGOW (H)
Thursday, May 15
Won 63-29
Ashworth 12, Parsons 10:2, **Compton 12**, Smethills 8:2, Wilson 9, Martin 3:1, Cooper 9:3.

WORKINGTON (H)
Thursday, May 22
Lost 40-50
Ashworth 5:1, Parsons 4:2, Compton 11, Smethills 3:2, Wilson 10, Martin 1:1, Cooper 6.
▼ *Worst home defeat since losing 33-57 againt Peterborough on October 16, 1998, in Young Shield semi final.*

WORKINGTON (A)
Saturday, May 31
Drew 45-45
Ashworth 7, Parsons 4, Compton 12, Smethills 6:1, Wilson 8, Ben Hopwood [G] 0, Cooper 8:2.
▲ *Gained some revenge for home defeat by coming back from 38-34 down to force a draw. Took 4-2s in Heats 13 and 14, and Compton then won Heat 15.*

GLASGOW (A)
Sunday, June 1
6-6, abandoned, waterlogged track.
Ashworth 2, Parsons 1:1, Compton, Cooper, Wilson, Ben Hopwood [G] 0, Smethills 3.
● *Meeting abandoned after Heat 2 because of torrential rain.*

EDINBURGH (H)
Thursday, June 12
Won 55-36
Ashworth 12, Parsons 7:4, Compton 13, Cooper 3, Wilson 12, Hughes 0, Smethills 8:1.
▲▼ *Hughes made his debut as a replacement for Martin. Held sway throughout against the Premier League's form team, winning 13 of the races.*

SQUAD
Ricky Ashworth, André Compton, Kyle Hughes, Paul Cooper, Lee Smethills, David Speight, Ben Wilson.
Foreign: Sam Martin, Joel Parsons.

ISLE OF WIGHT (H)
Thursday, June 19
Won 59-33
Ashworth 14:1, Parsons 6:1, **Compton 12**, Cooper 7:1, Wilson 13, Hughes 1, Smethills 6:2.
▲ *Ashworth clocked the fastest time of the season on his way to a paid maximum.*

EDINBURGH (A)
Friday, June 20
Lost 33-56
Ashworth 7:1, Parsons 6 (TS1), Compton 10 (1), Cooper 0, Wilson 4:1, Hughes 4, Smethills 2:1.
▼ *Ashworth withdrew after being brought down by Ryan Fisher in Heat 11.*

ISLE OF WIGHT (A)
Tuesday, June 24
Lost 39-54
Ashworth 15 (6), Parsons 2, Compton 5:2, Cooper 5, Wilson 8:1, Hughes 0, Smethills 4.

RYE HOUSE (A)
Sunday, June 29
Lost 32-61
Ashworth 10, Parsons 3:1, Compton 11 (6), Cooper 0, Wilson 2, Hughes 3, Smethills 3.

MILDENHALL (H)
Thursday, July 3
Won 65-27
Ashworth 15, Parsons 8:2, Compton 9, Smethills 8:1, **Wilson 13:2**, Hughes 4:1, Cooper 8:2.
▲ *Compton denied a full house when he was excluded for clattering Chris Schramm in Heat 5.*

SOMERSET (A)
Friday, July 4
Lost 30-60
Ashworth 3 (FX), Parsons 2, Compton 11, Smethills 3, Wilson 5, Hughes 1:1, Cooper 5.
▼ *A night when most of the Tigers riders would rather have been somewhere else, having heard of the death of Darren and Sharon Boocock – friends of all at Owlerton – earlier in the day.*

MILDENHALL (A)
Sunday, July 6
Won 65-27
Ashworth 10:2, **Parsons 13:2**, **Compton 10:2**, Smethills 3, **Wilson 13:2**, Hughes 2, Cooper 14:2.
▼ *Smethills suffered internal injuries after crashing in Heat 7 and was taken to hospital, the meeting being delayed for 40 minutes while he was being treated.*

REDCAR (H)
Thursday, July 10
Drew 45-45
Ashworth 8:1, *rider replacement for Smethills*, Compton 10, Parsons 6:3, Wilson 7, Hughes 0, Cooper 14:1.

▼ *Thriller in poor conditions, and the water got into Ashworth's bike in the last race just when it seemed the Tigers would complete their comeback from six points down.*

REDCAR (A)
Tuesday, July 15
Lost 39-54
Ashworth 5, *rider replacement for Smethills*, Compton 9:1 (6), Parsons 8:1, Wilson 10 (TS1), Hughes 4:1, Cooper 3:1.

NEWCASTLE (H)
Thursday, July 24
Won 55-38
Ashworth 13, *rider replacement for Smethills*, Compton 12:1, Parsons 8:1, Wilson 4:1, Hughes 5:2, Cooper 13:3.

NEWCASTLE (A)
Sunday, July 27
Lost 41-48
Ashworth 9, *rider replacement for Smethills*, Compton 9, Parsons 7:1, Wilson 3:1, Hughes 1, Cooper 12.
▼ *Parsons and Cooper were both excluded from an eventful Heat 14 which handed victory to the Diamonds – after Sheffield had led 38-34.*

STOKE (A)
Saturday, August 2
Lost 34-58
Ashworth 13 (6), Parsons 1, Compton 5:1, Cooper 3, Wilson 2, Hughes 0, Powell 10.

KING'S LYNN (A)
Wednesday, August 6
Lost 35-59
Ashworth 4:1, Parsons 13:1 (TS4), Compton 9:1 (4), Cooper 3:1, Wilson 4, Hughes 1, Ben Powell [G] 1.

BERWICK (H)
Thursday, August 7
Won 48-42
Ashworth 4, Parsons 6, Compton 9:3, Cooper 13:1, Wilson 6:1, Hughes 0, John Oliver [G] 10:1.
▼▲ *Scott Smith (13) did plenty of damage against old club but Tigers just held control, despite two Ashworth stoppages.*

GLASGOW (A)
Sunday, August 10
Won 46-44
Ashworth 6, Parsons 5, **Compton 15**, Cooper 10:3, Wilson 3:2, Hughes 2, Scott Smith [G] 5:1.
▲▼ *Victory with a Heat 15 4-2 from Compton and Cooper marred by Ashworth's nasty crash with Trent Leverington which saw him sustain a season-ending broken wrist.*

READING (H)
Thursday, August 14
Won 51-42
Rider replacement for Ashworth, Cooper 8:3, Compton 10:1, Parsons 14:1, Wilson 14, Hughes 1, Josh Grajczonek [G] 4:2.
▲ *Parsons and Wilson blasted right back to form as Tigers covered well for Ashworth's absence.*

SCUNTHORPE (A)
Friday, August 15
Won 47-43
Rider replacement for Ashworth, Cooper 8:1, Compton 12:1, Parsons 11:1, Wilson 9, Hughes 1, Josh Grajczonek [G] 6.
▲ *Compton and Parsons collected the all-important 4-2 in Heat 15 after Tigers' early 10 point lead had been pegged back to all-square with two races to go. Guest Josh Grajczonek crashed heavily with Viktor Bergstrom in Heat 8 and took no futher part.*

BIRMINGHAM (H)
Thursday, August 21
Lost 40-44
Rider replacement for Ashworth, Cooper 6, Compton 7:1, Parsons 10:2, Wilson 7:1, Hughes 1:1, Ben Powell [G] 9:2.
▼ *Meeting abandoned after Ben Wilson, André Compton and Birmingham's Kyle Legault fell in Heat 15 and there was a lengthy delay for medical treatment.*

BIRMINGHAM (A)
Sunday, August 24
Lost 44-46
Rider replacement for Ashworth, Cooper 7:1, Mark Lemon [G] 11, Parsons 7:4, Wilson 9:1, Hughes 5, Ben Powell [G] 5:3.
▲ *Nine points up with four heats to go, the home side finished with a 5-2 and two 5-1s.*

RYE HOUSE (H)
Thursday, August 28
Won 54-36
Rider replacement for Ashworth, Parsons 10:2, Compton 13:2, Cooper 8:1, Wilson 10:1, Hughes 3:1, Smethills 10.
▲ *Smethills won his first three rides against a Rockets team who badly missed the injured Tai Woffinden.*

SOMERSET (H)
Thursday, September 11
Won 50-40
Rider replacement for Ashworth, Parsons 8:3, Compton 16, Cooper 4, Wilson 8:2, Hughes 5, Smethills 9:1.
▲ *Compton reeled off five wins after a first-ride third place, including Heats 9 and 10.*

SCUNTHORPE (H)
Thursday, September 18
Won 52-38
Rider replacement for Ashworth, Parsons 9:1, **Compton 18**, Cooper 5:1, Wilson 8:1, Hughes 0, Smethills 12:1, David Speight [no. 8].
▲ *Faultless showing from Compton as Tigers held sway against a team who had been expected to push them all the way.*

STOKE (H)
Thursday, September 25
Won 52-38
Rider replacement for Ashworth, Parsons 12:1, Compton 12:1, Cooper 10:3, Wilson 10, Speight 0, Smethills 8.
▲ *Compton and Wilson both recovered from sluggish starts to pull the Tigers clear after their visitors remained in touch until past the half-way stage.*

PREMIER LEAGUE

		M	W	D	L	PtsF	PtsA	Pts
1	Edinburgh	30	22	2	6	1562	1161	53
2	Somerset	30	21	0	9	1517	1223	48
3	King's Lynn	30	18	5	7	1624	1111	45
4	Rye House	30	19	0	11	1500	1232	42
5	Workington	30	17	2	11	1435.5	1300.5	41
6	Berwick	30	16	2	12	1428	1316	37
7	Redcar	30	16	1	13	1369	1374	37
8	**SHEFFIELD**	**30**	**15**	**2**	**13**	**1381**	**1345**	**35**
9	Reading	29	15	1	13	1310	1354	34
10	Scunthorpe	30	15	0	15	1309	1434	33
11	Isle of Wight	30	15	0	15	1359	1390	31
12	Birmingham	30	13	0	17	1317.5	1401.5	30
13	**Stoke**	**29**	**10**	**1**	**18**	**1256**	**1401**	**23**
14	Newcastle	30	10	0	20	1220	1501	22
15	Glasgow	30	9	0	21	1297	1469	19
16	Mildenhall	30	0	0	30	932	1804	0

Young Shield

Quarter Final, first leg
ISLE OF WIGHT (A)
Tuesday, October 7
Lost 36-57
Rider replacement for Ashworth, Parsons 4:1, Compton 14 (6), Cooper 8:1, Wilson 8:1 (TS0), Speight 0, Smethills 2, Ben Hopwood [no. 8].

Quarter Final, second leg
ISLE OF WIGHT (H)
Thursday, October 9
Won 52-41
Compton 14, Cooper 13:1, *rider replacement for Ashworth*, Wilson 12:2, Parsons 8:2, Benji Compton [G] 4:1, Smethills 1:1.
▼ *Compton announced his retirement prior to the meeting, although he will be seen again in 2009!*
Aggregate: Lost 88-98.

Premier Trophy

SCUNTHORPE (H)
Thursday, March 20
Won 57-36
Ashworth 12:1, Parsons 11:2, Compton 9:1, Cooper 6:2, Wilson 8, Martin 1, Smethills 10.

SCUNTHORPE (A)
Friday, March 21
Won 48-41
Compton 12:1, Parsons 9, Ashworth 11:1, Cooper 5, Wilson 7, Martin 0, Smethills 4:2.
▲ *All of the Tigers top five won at least one race – with Ashworth, Parsons and Compton winning three apiece!*

STOKE (H)
Thursday, March 27
Won 51-41
Ashworth 14:1, Parsons 5, **Compton 15**, Cooper 6:1, Wilson 8, Martin 0, Smethills 3:1.
▲ *Compton and Ashworth saw Tigers home, both completing maximums in Heat 15.*

NEWCASTLE (A)
Sunday, March 30
Lost 27-63
Ashworth 2, Parsons 6, Compton 8 (1), Cooper 2, Wilson 1, Martin 2, Simon Lambert [G] 6:2.
▼ *Wilson withdrawn by the track doctor after his third ride.*

REDCAR (H)
Thursday, April 3
Won 53-39
Ashworth 7, Parsons 8:2, **Compton 14:1**, Cooper 5:1, Wilson 8:2, Martin 3, Simon Lambert [G] 8:1.
▲ *Back to form despite three retirements with guest Lambert impressing at reserve.*

PHOTO: Chris Spires

Sheffield: Back – Paul Cooper, Ricky Ashworth, skipper André Compton, team manager Eric Boocock, Joel Parsons, Ben Wilson. Front – Lee Smethills and Sam Martin

STOKE (A)
Tuesday, April 5
Won 48-45
Ashworth 10, Parsons 8:4, Compton 11:1, Cooper 6:2, Wilson 8, Martin 3, Simon Lambert [G] 2:1.
▲ *Came through a nervy finale with a 39-25 lead being cut back to 45-42 before Ben Barker crashed out of the decider against Compton and Parsons.*

REDCAR (A)
Saturday, April 12
Lost 43-47
Ashworth 6:1, Parsons 6:1, Compton 7, Cooper 7, Wilson 10, Martin 1, Smethills 6:2.
▲▲ *Still on course for semi-finals despite losing in a last-heat decider when they required a 5-1 to draw.*

NEWCASTLE (H)
Thursday, May 1
Won 59-33
Ashworth 11:2, Parsons 7:3, **Compton 15**, Smethills 4, Wilson 10, Martin 3, Cooper 9:1.
▲ *Booked their place in the last four of the Premier Trophy with an all-round display which limited the Diamonds to just two heat winners.*

PREMIER TROPHY Group B

		M	W	D	L	PtsF	PtsA	Pts
1	**SHEFFIELD**	**8**	**6**	**0**	**2**	**386**	**345**	**14**
2	Redcar	8	3	2	3	362	360	8
3	Scunthorpe	8	3	1	4	345	380	8
4	Newcastle	8	3	1	4	364	367	7
5	Stoke	8	3	0	5	363	368	6

Semi Final, first leg
BIRMINGHAM (A)
Wednesday, June 4
Lost 37-57
Ashworth 11 (4), Parsons 4, Compton 14:1 (TS4), Cooper 1, Wilson 2, Hughes 1:1, Smethills 4.
▼ *Ashworth was excluded from Heat 1 for bringing Craig Watson down, and the Tigers never truly recovered from going 6-18 down in the first four races.*

Semi Final, second leg
BIRMINGHAM (H)
Thursday, June 5
Won 53-37
Ashworth 5:3, Parsons 6, Compton 13, Cooper 4:1, Wilson 11, Hughes 3:1, Smethills 11.
▼ *Could make no impact on the aggregate position for the first two-thirds of the meeting thanks to Craig Watson and ex-Tiger James Birkinshaw.*
Aggregate: Lost 90-94.

Knock Out Cup

First round, first leg
SCUNTHORPE (H)
Thursday, April 10
Won 55-36
Ashworth 11:2, Parsons 9, Compton 8:1, Cooper 5, Wilson 11:2, Martin 1, Smethills 10:2.

First round, second leg
SCUNTHORPE (A)
Friday, April 11
Won 48-44
Ashworth 6:2, Parsons 10:1, Compton 9, Cooper 6, Wilson 10:1, Martin 4:1, Smethills 3.
Aggregate: 103-80.

Second round, first leg
ISLE OF WIGHT (H)
Thursday, April 24
Won 52-38
Ashworth 7:3, Parsons 12:1, Compton 14, Cooper 4:1, Wilson 8:1, Martin 5:1, Smethills 2.

Second round, second leg
ISLE OF WIGHT (A)
Tuesday, May 13
Lost 38-54
Ashworth 8, Parsons 2:2, Compton 7:1 (TSX), Smethills 1, Wilson 14 (4), Martin 1, Cooper 5:1.
▼ *Compton rode as a tactical substitute in Heat 14 but scored no points after being excluded for bringing down Andrew Bargh, and a tie-clinching 5-1 to the Islanders was awarded.*
Aggregate: Lost 90-92.

SHEFFIELD

Rider	*M*	*R*	*Pts*	*BP*	*TPts*	*Ave*	*F*	*P*	*TR*	*TPts*	*TS*	*TSPts*
André COMPTON	45	224	503	25	528	9.43	6	2	8	17	2	2
Ricky ASHWORTH	**36**	**159**	**312**	**24**	**336**	**8.45**	**2**	**3**	**4**	**8**	**0**	**0**
Joel PARSONS	46	213	332	58	390	7.32	0	1	0	0	2	2
Ben WILSON	**46**	**211**	**359**	**26**	**385**	**7.30**	**1**	**2**	**1**	**2**	**2**	**0**
Paul COOPER	46	215	299	44	343	6.38	0	0	0	0	0	0
Lee SMETHILLS	**31**	**131**	**170**	**24**	**194**	**5.92**	**0**	**0**	**0**	**0**	**0**	**0**
Sam MARTIN	17	61	34	5	39	2.56	0	0	0	0	0	0
Kyle HUGHES	**23**	**93**	**44**	**7**	**51**	**2.19**	**0**	**0**	**0**	**0**	**0**	**0**
David SPEIGHT	2	6	0	0	0	0.00	0	0	0	0	0	0
Guests	***16***	***68***	***85***	***16***	***101***	***5.94***	***0***	***0***	***0***	***0***	***0***	***0***

For Joel PARSONS see Swindon; for Sam MARTIN see Scunthorpe (CL); for Kyle HUGHES see Plymouth.

André Compton rode in 339 official matches for Sheffield and was unbeaten by an opponent in 70 meetings – and all-time club record, putting him well clear of Doug Wyer (50) and Reg Wilson (40).

Challenge

COMPTON'S LAST STAND
Thursday, October 16
BRADFIELD BREWERY
OWLERTON OUTLAWS (H)
Lost 34-44
Compton 12, Cooper 5, *rider replacement for Ashworth,* Wilson 9, Parsons 0, Ben Hopwood [R] 6:1, Smethills 2.
OUTLAWS
Lee Complin 9:1, James Birkinshaw 4:1, Tomasz Piszcz 9, Carl Wilkinson 3:2, Richard Hall 7, Scott Smith 12:3, Byron Bekker 0.

▼ *Parsons and Bekker were involved in a three-rider Heat 4 crash (Smethills was the other party) that caused a 40 minute hold up and neither took any further part in the meeting. Ref Dave Dowling was forced to abandon the event after Heat 13 because of the time curfew. A distressing season-ending for Tigers and their fans.*

Inter League Challenge

COVENTRY (H)
Thursday, March 13
Lost 37-56
Compton 6, Parsons 3, Ashworth 15:1 (6), Wilson 8, Cooper 3, Smethills 2, Martin 0.

Ashworth won his last three races to prevent the Elite League team from reaching the 60-point mark.

COVENTRY (A)
Friday March 14
Lost 31-61
Compton 7, Richard Hall [G] 3:1, Tai Woffinden [G] 9:1, Ashworth 1, Wilson 3:1, Parsons 8, Cooper 0.

Aggregate: Lost 68-117.

2009 Squad

Ricky **ASHWORTH** (7.57), Richard **HALL** (6.83), Joel **PARSONS** (6.06), Ritchie **HAWKINS** (5.44), Paul **COOPER** (5.51), Chris **MILLS** (4.93), Joshua **AUTY** (4.55).

Weather...

Sheffield lost three home team meetings to the weather and three away meetiungs, including two derbies againt Redcar.

Premier League
Friday, July 11 .... REDCAR (A)
Thursday, July 17 .... SOMERSET (H)
Thursday, July 31 .... STOKE (H)
Thursday, September 4 .... SCUNTHORPE (H)

Knock Out Cup
Tuesday, April 29 .... ISLE OF WIGHT (A)

Premier Trophy
Friday, April 4 .... REDCAR (A)

...beaten

PREMIER LEAGUE RIDERS' FINAL
Sunday, September 21

	1	2	3	4	5	Tot	SF	F
1 Tai WOFFINDEN	**2**	**1**	**3**	**3**	**3**	**12**		**3**
2 Jason DOYLE	1	3	2	2	3	11	2	2
3 Adrian RYMEL	2	2	3	3	2	12		1
4 Kai NIEMINEN	3	3	3	2	FX	11	3	R
5 Ben BARKER	3	3	2	0	3	11	1	
6 Jason BUNYAN	3	3	2	2	2	12		
7 Shane PARKER	1	2	3	3	1	10		
8 Ulrich ØSTERGAARD	2	0	2	1	2	7		
9 Kevin DOOLAN	0	2	1	3	0	6		
10 Jason KING	1	1	1	2	1	6		
11 André COMPTON	3	1	FX	1	R	5		
12 Jason LYONS	E	2	0	1	2	5		
13 Magnus KARLSSON	2	1	0	1	1	5		
14 William LAWSON	0	0	0	R	3	3		
15 Gary HAVELOCK	1	R	1	0	1	3		
16 Scott RICHARDSON [R]	F	1	0			1		
17 Henning LOOF	R					0		
18 Ben TAYLOR [R]	0	0				0		

See Premier League for Roll of Honour

THE 2008 TOP GUN
Thursday, October 2

1 Darcy WARD	**3**	**3**	**3**	**3**	**FX**	**12**	**2**	**3**
2 Ben TAYLOR	3	3	0	3	3	12		2
3 Scott RICHARDSON	3	3	2	FX	3	11	3	1
4 Ben HOPWOOD	3	3	1	3	3	13		0
5 Daniel HALSEY	2	2	3	2	2	11	1	
6 Rob SMITH	2	2	3	3	0	10	0	
7 Gareth ISHERWOOD	1	2	3	2	1	9		
8 Adam McKINNA	1	1	2	1	3	8		
9 Luke PRIEST	1	0	2	2	2	7		
10 David SPEIGHT	2	1	1	1	2	7		
11 Gary IRVING	0	1	2	2	1	6		
12 Mark THOMPSON	1	0	0	0	2	3		
13 Andrew ALDRIDGE	0	2	0	0	1	3		
14 Leigh BOUJOS	2	0	1	R		3		
15 Darren SMITH	R	1	E	1	1	3		
16 Adam WRATHALL	0	FX	1	1	FX	2		
17 Scott WHITTINGTON [R]	0					0		
17 Andrew BLACKBURN [R]	0					0		

Roll of Honour
1994 .... Peter SCULLY
1997 .... Jamie BIRKINSHAW
2004 .... Ben WILSON
2006 .... Joshua AUTY
2007 .... Adam ROYNON
2008 .... Darcy WARD

YorkshireCup

HULL (H)
Thursday, May 8
Won 52-37
Ashworth 11, Cooper 6:1, **Compton 15**, Smethills 6, Wilson 8, Martin 1, Jamie Birkinshaw [G] 5:1.
HULL 37
Joel Parsons 10, Robbie Kessler 6, Tai Woffinden 8:1, Emiliano Sanchez 1, Paul Thorp 0, Lee Dicken 7:1, Barrie Evans 5:2.

▲ *Compton completed a maximum in an incident-filled challenge match, despite a heavy crash when brought down by Robbie Kessler in Heat 5.*

Premier League

SOMERSET

TRACK FILE

Track: Oak Tree Arena, Edithmead, near Highbridge, Somerset, TA9 4HA.
Telephone: 07860 718630.
Hotline: 09068 664684.
Website: www.somerset-rebels.co.uk
Track Length: 300 metres.
Track Record: 56.08 secs, Leigh Adams, March 23, 2007.
Promoters: Debbie Hancock, Dave Pavitt and Peter Toogood.
Team Sponsors: Sharp Retail Systems.
Colours: White with US Confederate Stainless Banner flag.
Nickname: Rebels.

HISTORY

First meeting: June 2, 2000, Somerset v St. Austell, Conference League Cup.
Leagues: Division Two, 2002-09. Division Three, 2000-01

HONOURS

Major honours: 4.
Division Two Knock Out Cup winners (1), 2008.
Division Two Four Team champions (1), 2005.
Division Three Knock Out Cup winners (1), 2001.
Division Three Trophy winners (1), 2001.

Simon Walker, Emil Kramer and the KO Cup

2008 REVIEW

THE Rebels raised a few eyebrows when they built a team without former skipper Magnus Zetterström – but they turned everything to their advantage and enjoyed their best season in the sport.

Somerset fought Edinburgh almost neck-and-neck for the Premier League title, with the outcome in doubt right to the end of their final fixture.

An unblemished home record saw them score almost double the number of points that they conceded around the Oak Tree Arena as they genuinely turned their home track into a fortress.

On the road, the last of six away wins came at the Isle of Wight in their penultimate fixture as they smashed the Islanders' own unbeaten home record.

That kept the Rebels in contention, and a win at Birmingham the following night would have forced Edinburgh to draw their last match at Glasgow to take the title.

But on a stormy night at Perry Barr, the Rebels were edged out in a last-heat decider, and had to be content with a still-praiseworthy second place.

Consolation came in the form of the Knock Out Cup, where the runners-up of the last two years finally got their hands on the silverware with aggregate wins over Newcastle, Rye House and Workington.

It was a stunning season of achievement, led from the front by Jason Doyle, whose return to the Premier League was hugely successful.

A solid middle-order was enhanced by the early-season signing of Matthias Kröger to replace Henning Loof, and the Rebels also had to cope with the absence all year of Ritchie Hawkins, injured in a pre-season German indoor meeting, and skipper Simon Walker crashing out in late June.

The year ended in uncertainty after a dispute between landowner Bill Hancock and promoter Mike Golding, and that left fans facing an anxious winter before Dave Croucher was installed as the new promoter.

2008 RESULTS

Premier League

Final position..Second

BIRMINGHAM (H)
Friday, April 18
Won 48-45
Doyle 10, Loof 5:1, Kramer 13, Katt 5:2, Frampton 4, Walker 8:1, Werner 3:1.
▼ *Astonishing finale saw Rebels' 39-21 lead slashed to 43-38, before Walker eased the nerves by winning Heat 14.*

SCUNTHORPE (H)
Friday, May 2
Won 63-29
Doyle 9:2, Frampton 8:2, Kramer 9:1, Kröger 11:3, Katt 14, Walker 6:3, Werner 6:2.

SCUNTHORPE (A)
Monday, May 5
Lost 39-51
Doyle 10, Frampton 3:2, Kramer 8:1, Kröger 3, Katt 0, Walker 6, Werner 9:1.

REDCAR (A)
Thursday, May 8
Won 54-39
Doyle 15, Frampton 8:3, Kramer 9, Kröger 5:3, Katt 4, Walker 3:1, Werner 10:1.
▲ *Doyle only the third visiting rider to record a 15-point maximum at the South Tees Motorsports Park.*

RYE HOUSE (H)
Friday, May 9
Won 66-27
Doyle 10:1, Frampton 8:3, Kramer 13, Kröger 7:3, Katt 10:1, Walker 11:2, Werner 7:4.

BERWICK (H)
Friday, May 16
Won 58-34
Doyle 10:1, Frampton 11:2, Kramer 10, Kröger 4:2, Katt 7:1, **Walker 12**, Werner 4:1.
▲ *Maintained top place in Premier League table with an opening four-race blitz which produced a 19-5 advantage.*

NEWCASTLE (A)
Sunday, May 18
Won 48-47
Doyle 19:1 (TS6), Katt 1, Kramer 13 (4), Kröger 1:1, Frampton 4:1, Werner 9:1, Walker 1.
▲ *Doyle won Heats 11, 13 and 14 (as a tactical substitute) and then partnered Kramer to a Heat 15 5-1 to turn around a 12-point deficit with five races to go.*

STOKE (H)
Friday, May 23
Won 68-22
Doyle 11, Katt 6:1, **Kramer 14:1**, Kröger 7:2, **Frampton 9:3**, **Walker 13:2**, Werner 8:2.
▲ *Three riders scored paid maximums, Frampton completing his first Premier League full house when Ben Barker slid off in Heat 15.*

SQUAD
Jordan Frampton, Simon Walker.
Foreign: Jason Doyle, Stefan Katt, Emil Kramer, Matthias Kröger, Henning Loof, Brent Werner.

MILDENHALL (A)
Sunday, June 1
Won 55-37
Doyle 12:1, Katt 2, Kramer 8, Kröger 6:1, Frampton 12:1, Werner 7:1, Walker 8:2.

NEWCASTLE (H)
Friday, June 6
Won 65-25
Doyle 10:2, Katt 10:2, Kramer 14, Kröger 6:2, Frampton 9, **Walker 11:1**, Werner 5:2.

GLASGOW (H)
Friday, June 13
Won 63-29
Doyle 12, Katt 9:1, Kramer 7, **Kröger 12:3**, Frampton 9, Walker 8:1, Werner 6:3.
▲ *First three races were all Somerset 5-1s and Kroger enjoyed his first maximum, albeit fortuitously in Heat 15 when Craig Watson fell on lap two.*

SHEFFIELD (H)
Friday, July 4
Won 60-30
Doyle 12, Katt 10:1, Kramer 8:2, *rider replacement for Walker*, Frampton 7:1, Kröger 14:2, Werner 9:1, Matt Bates [no. 8].
▲ *Doyle unbeaten save for a nasty crash in his second ride, as the Rebels coasted to a surprisingly straightforward win.*

WORKINGTON (H)
Friday, July 11
Won 57-36
Doyle 15, Katt 7:1, Kramer 8, *rider replacement for Walker*, Frampton 10:2, Kröger 9:1, Werner 8:3, Matt Bates [no. 8].
▲ *Doyle underlined his increasing class with a fine maximum as the Rebels recorded their biggest-ever win over the Comets.*

KING'S LYNN (A)
Wednesday, July 16
Lost 25-68
Doyle 12 (6), Katt 3, Kramer 0, *rider replacement for Walker*, Frampton 2:1, Werner 4, Kroger 4.
▼ *Home promoters Keith and Jonathan Chapman hit out at the poor display of the Rebels – saying they would have sacked their own riders had they performed so badly!*

KING'S LYNN (H)
Friday, July 25
Won 53-40
Doyle 14, Katt 8:1, *rider replacement for Kramer*, Chris Neath [G] 5:3, Frampton 12:1, Kröger 12:1, Werner 2, Jay Herne [no. 8].
▲ *Gained some revenge from their Norfolk Arena disaster, with only Werner having an off-night as the Stars were totally reliant on their top two.*

STOKE (A)
Sunday, July 27
Won 45-43
Doyle 17, Katt 4:1, *rider replacement for Kramer*, Craig Watson [G] 6:2, Frampton 5:1, Werner 8:1, Kröger 5, Jay Herne [no. 8].
▼ *Would have wrapped up victory but for Kröger's exclusion from Heat 14 due to a defective silencer.*

READING (H)
Friday, August 1
Won 62-31
Doyle 15, Kröger 8:1, Kramer 8:2, *rider replacement for Walker*, Frampton 12:3, Katt 13:2, Werner 6:2, Brendan Johnson [no. 8].

WORKINGTON (A)
Saturday, August 2
Lost 44-46
Doyle 12:1, Ben Taylor [G] 0, Kramer 2:1, *rider replacement for Walker*, Frampton 10, Katt 15, Werner 5:1.
▼ *Handed the chance of a win by Craig Branney's puncture in Heat 14, but Frampton fell chasing.*

GLASGOW (A)
Sunday, August 3
Lost 39-51
Doyle 16 (TS1), Kröger 3:1, Kramer 4:1, *rider replacement for Walker*, Frampton 7, Werner 8:1, Ben Taylor [G[1:1.
▼ *Failed to take an expected away win, even though Doyle was unbeaten but for unsuccessful tactical substitute ride in Heat 14.*

REDCAR (H)
Friday, August 8
Won 48-42
Doyle 12:1, *rider replacement for Walker*, Kramer 7, Kröger 1:1, Frampton 9, Katt 14:4, Werner 5:2.
▼ *Kröger fell in Heat 1 and subsequently withdrew after failing to finish his third ride in Heat 5.*

READING (A)
Sunday, August 10
1-5, abandoned, rain.
Doyle 1, *rider replacement for Walker*, Kramer, Craig Watson [G], Frampton, Katt 0, Werner.

ISLE OF WIGHT (H)
Friday, August 15
Won 67-22
Doyle 9, *rider replacement for Walker*, **Kramer 13:2**, Kröger 9:1, **Frampton 15:3**, Katt 8:2, **Werner 13:2**.

EDINBURGH (H)
Wednesday, August 27
Won 48-44
Doyle 11, *rider replacement for Walker*, Kramer 9, Kröger 7:1, Frampton 7:1, Katt 7:3, Werner 7:1, Kyle Newman [no. 8].
▼ *A large Wednesday night crowd witnessed a thrilling contest, with the Rebels making sure of the points by sharing Heat 14 after their title rivals had stubbornly remained in touch.*

EDINBURGH (A)
Friday, August 29
Lost 24-66
Doyle 7 (TS1), *rider replacement for Walker*, Kramer 4 (1), Kröger 3, Frampton 6, Werner 2, Katt 2, Keiran Morris [no. 8].
▼ *Again struggled away from home to top-four rivals, and Doyle finished the meeting with an injured wrist after crashing in his last two rides.*

BERWICK (A)
Saturday, August 30
Lost 35-58
Doyle 16 (6), *rider replacement for Walker*, Kramer 6, Kröger 4, Frampton 6, Werner 3:1, Adam McKinna [G] 0.
▼ *Never fully recovered from the damage done at Edinburgh, although Doyle bravely raced on and dropped just two points in five rides.*

READING (A)
Monday, September 8
Won 53-39
Doyle 12:2, *rider replacement for Walker*, Kramer 10:1, Katt 6, Frampton 13:2, Kröger 0, Werner 12:2.
▲ *Maintained title hopes with an emphatic away win, Frampton enjoying one of his best away performances.*

SHEFFIELD (A)
Thursday, September 11
Lost 40-50
Doyle 8 (FX), *rider replacement for Walker*, Kramer 8:1, Katt 4:2, Frampton 11, Werner 1, Kröger 8:1.
▼ *Doyle's tactical ride in Heat 13 looked set to spark big comeback but he crashed heavily on turn two.*

RYE HOUSE (A)
Saturday, September 13
Lost 25-65
Joel Parsons [G] 1, *rider replacement for Walker*, Kramer 4, Robert Ksiezak,[G] 6 (0), Frampton 9, Ben Powell [G] 4:1, Werner 1:1.

MILDENHALL (H)
Friday, September 19
Won 72-18
Doyle 11:1, *rider replacement for Walker*, **Kramer 10:2, Katt 9:3, Frampton 11:1, Kröger 12:3, Werner 14:1**, Kyle Newman [no. 8] 5:1.
▲ *Kyle Newman was given all four of Simon Walker's rider replacement outings and was the only Somerset rider to be beaten by an opponent, finishing third in heats 1, 6 and 10.*

ISLE OF WIGHT (A)
Tuesday, September 23
Won 49-41
Doyle 14, *rider replacement for Walker*, Kramer 2:1, Katt 3, Frampton 14:2, Kröger 5:1, Werner 11:2, Brendan Johnson [no. 8].
▼ *Kept title hopes alive with last heat decider win.*

BIRMINGHAM (A)
Wednesday, September 24
Lost 44-48
Doyle 15:1 (TS4), *rider replacement for Walker*,

Kramer 9:1, Katt 4, Frampton 5:2, Kröger 5:1, Werner 6:1, Kyle Newman [no. 8].

▼ *Fortunes ebbed and flowed and it was 40-40 with two heats to go, only for the home side to secure two 4-2s to end the Rebels' title dreams.*

PREMIER LEAGUE

		M	W	D	L	PtsF	PtsA	Pts
1	Edinburgh	30	22	2	6	1562	1161	53
2	**SOMERSET**	**30**	**21**	**0**	**9**	**1517**	**1223**	**48**
3	King's Lynn	30	18	5	7	1624	1111	45
4	Rye House	30	19	0	11	1500	1232	42
5	Workington	30	17	2	11	1435.5	1300.5	41
6	Berwick	30	16	2	12	1428	1316	37
7	Redcar	30	16	1	13	1369	1374	37
8	Sheffield	30	15	2	13	1381	1345	35
9	Reading	30	15	1	14	1350	1405	34
10	Scunthorpe	30	15	0	15	1309	1434	33
11	Isle of Wight	30	15	0	15	1359	1390	31
12	Birmingham	30	13	0	17	1317.5	1401.5	30
13	Stoke	30	11	1	18	1307	1441	25
14	Newcastle	30	10	0	20	1220	1501	22
15	Glasgow	30	9	0	21	1297	1469	19
16	Mildenhall	30	0	0	30	932	1804	0

Play offs

Semi Final, first leg
EDINBURGH (A)
Friday, October 3
Lost 36-57
Doyle 15 (6), *rider replacement for Walker*, Kramer 8, Katt 0, Frampton 2, Krøger 5, Werner 6:1.

▼ *Doyle and Werner gave the Rebels a glimmer of hope with an 8-1 in Heat 11.*

Semi Final, second leg
EDINBURGH (H)
Wednesday, October 8
Won 53-39
Doyle 12, *rider replacement for Walker*, Kramer 12:1, Katt 11:3, Frampton 11:1, Danny Warwick [G] 1, Werner 6, Kyle Newman [no. 8].

▲ *Clawed back 14 points of their deficit after Heat 5 but the Monarchs dug in and it was virtually all over when the Monarchs took a 5-1 in Heat 12*

Aggregate: Lost 89-96.

Premier Trophy

NEWPORT (A)
Sunday, March 23
Won 50-43
Doyle 12:1, Walker 4:1, Kramer 14, Loof 3, Werner 3:1, Katt 10:1, Frampton 4.

NEWPORT (H)
Friday, March 28
Won 67-26
Doyle 15, Loof 1, Kramer 13, Walker 7:4, Werner 8:1, Frampton 10:2, Katt 13:3.

▼ *Loof withdrew due to concussion and Craig Watson scored over half of Newport's total.*

READING (A)
Monday, March 31
Won 49-44
Doyle 11:2, *rider replacement for Loof*, Kramer 12:1, Walker 3:3, Werner 3:1, Katt 11, Frampton 9:2.

ISLE OF WIGHT (H)
Friday, April 4
Won 54-39
Doyle 14, Loof 0, Kramer 12:1, Walker 5:1, Werner 6, Frampton 10:3, Katt 7:2.

ISLE OF WIGHT (A)
Tuesday, April 8
Lost 34-58
Doyle 12:1 (4), Loof 0, Kramer 4, Walker 2:1, Werner 5:1, Katt 4, Frampton 7:1.

READING (H)
Friday, April 11
Lost 42-47
Doyle 3, Loof 0, Kramer 11, Walker 9:1, Werner 3:1, Frampton 9:1, Katt 7:1.

▼ *Somerset finished with five riders after Loof and Doyle were ruled out. Loof crashed in the opening race and was*

ON PARADE: Emil Kramer, Matthias Kröger, Jason Doyle, Jordan Frampton, Stefan Katt. Front – Brent Werner, Simon Walker, mascot Henry Atkins

PHOTO: Mike Manning

withdrawn and Doyle crashed in his second ride in Heat 6 and was expelled from meeting by referee Dave Watters.

PREMIER TROPHY Group D

		M	W	D	L	PtsF	PtsA	Pts
1	Reading	6	4	0	2	300	248	10
2	**SOMERSET**	**6**	**4**	**0**	**2**	**296**	**257**	**10**
3	Isle of Wight	6	3	0	3	275	272	6
4	Newport	6	1	0	5	226	320	2

Knock Out Cup

First round, first leg
NEWCASTLE (H)
Friday, April 25
Won 64-28
Doyle 14:1, Frampton 8:2, Kramer 12, Kröger 6:3, Katt 7:2, **Walker 14:1**, Werner 3.
▲ *Paid maximums for Doyle and Walker – and in the last seven races, the Rebels scored 34 points out of 35 available.*

First round, second leg
NEWCASTLE (A)
Sunday, April 27
Drew 39-39
Doyle 8, Kröger 3, **Kramer 12**, Katt 0, Frampton 6:2, Walker 1:1, Werner 9.
● *Meeting abandoned after Heat 13, rain. Result to stand.*

Aggregate: Won 103-67.

Quarter Final, first leg
READING (H)
Friday, May 30
Won 53-39
Doyle 12:1, Katt 7, Kramer 9, Kröger 4:1, Frampton 6:2, Walker 11:1, Werner 4:2.

Quarter Final, second leg
READING (A)
Monday, June 29
Lost 44-51
Doyle 20:1 (TS6), Katt 5, Kramer 11, Kröger 2:1, Frampton 3, Werner 0, Walker 3.

Aggregate: Won 97-90.
▲ *After Heat 10 Somerset were 18 points down on the leg and trailed Reading by two points overall but Doyle took a tactical substitute ride in Heat 14 and recorded a tie-winning 8-1 with Kröger.*

Semi Final, first leg
RYE HOUSE (H)
Friday, August 22
Won 53-38
Doyle 13:2, *rider replacement for Walker*, Kramer 12, Kröger 9:1, Frampton 5, Katt 8:1, Werner 6:1, Andrew Braithwaite [no. 8].
▲ *Had all 15 heat winners – although a painful end for Doyle, who landed on the fence in Heat 13.*

Semi Final, second leg
RYE HOUSE (A)
Monday, August 25
Lost 43-50
Doyle 17 (6), *rider replacement for Walker*, Kramer 8:2, Kröger 0, Frampton 8, Katt 1, Werner 9:1, Kyle Newman [no. 8].
▲ *Successful defence of first leg lead, although it went right down to the last race before Doyle and Kramer defeated Stefan Ekberg and Tommy Allen.*

Aggregate: Won 96-88.

FINAL, first leg
WORKINGTON (A)
Saturday, October 11
Won 46-43
Doyle 10:1, *rider replacement for Walker*, Kramer 10:1, Katt 9, Frampton 9, Kröger 6:1, Werner 2.
▲ *Led by eight points halfway before pegged back to 39-39. Gained 5-0 in Heat 14 to ensure a first leg lead.*

FINAL, second leg
WORKINGTON (H)
Friday, October 17
Won 52-41
Doyle 14, *rider replacement for Walker*, Kramer 11:1, Katt 1, Frampton 7:3, Kröger 9:3, Werner 10.
▲ *In total control with 5-1s in the first two races, and while the Comets remained in touch throughout, there was little doubt that the Rebels would be celebrating the silverware after near-misses in 2006 and 2007.*

Aggregate: Won 98-84.

SOMERSET

Rider	*M*	*R*	*Pts*	*BP*	*TPts*	*Ave*	*F*	*P*	*TR*	*TPts*	*TS*	*TSPts*
Jason DOYLE	45	218	558	24	582	10.68	4	4	5	11	5	8
Emil KRAMER	**44**	**207**	**401**	**25**	**426**	**8.23**	**1**	**3**	**3**	**5**	**1**	**0**
Simon WALKER	21	86	146	27	173	8.05	1	3	0	0	0	0
Jordan FRAMPTON	**46**	**233**	**370**	**56**	**426**	**7.31**	**0**	**3**	**0**	**0**	**0**	**0**
Stefan KATT	43	197	286	42	328	6.66	0	1	0	0	0	0
Brent WERNER	**46**	**210**	**282**	**51**	**333**	**6.34**	**0**	**2**	**0**	**0**	**0**	**0**
Matthias KRÖGER	36	166	215	45	260	6.26	0	2	0	0	0	0
Henning LOOF	**6**	**16**	**9**	**1**	**10**	**2.50**	**0**	**0**	**0**	**0**	**0**	**0**
Guests	***10***	***44***	***29***	***8***	***37***	***3.36***	***0***	***0***	***1***	***0***	***0***	***0***

For Jordan FRAMPTON see Poole; for Brent WERNER see Eastbourne; for Henning LOOF see Mildenhall.

2009 Squad

Steve JOHNSTON (10.70), Emil KRAMER (7.64), Cory GATHERCOLE (6.55), Simon WALKER (6.52), Justin SEDGMEN (5.00), Tom BROWN (3.00), Jay HERNE (3.00)/Brendan JOHNSON (3.00).

Challenge

READING (A)
Monday, March 17
Lost 37-54
Doyle 5:2, Walker 4, Kramer 10 (1), Loof 0, Werner 6:2, Katt 8, Frampton 4:1.
▼ *New No.1 Doyle failed to finish in his first two rides.*

READING (H)
Friday, March 21
Won 52-41
Doyle 9, Loof 0, Kramer 9:1, Walker 7, Werner 10:1, Frampton 7:2, Katt 10.
▲ *Impressive home debut for Werner as Rebels pulled clear having been just 36-33 up with four heats to go.*
Aggregate: Won 99-95.

International

Friday, September 12
ENGLAND Under 23 22
James Wright 4, Jordan Frampton 3, Edward Kennett 5, Ben Barker 1:1, Lewis Bridger 5, Joshua Auty 3:1, Ben Taylor 1.
AUSTRALIA Under 23 26
Troy Batchelor 3, Cory Gathercole 4:1, Chris Holder 6, Robert Ksiezak 0, Cameron Woodward 5, Ty Proctor 4, Kozza Smith 4:1.
● *Meeting abandoned after eight heats, rain.*

Friday, September 26
ENGLAND Under 23 40
James Wright 5, Jordan Frampton 4:1, Edward Kennett 9, Ben Barker 7:2 (4), Lewis Bridger 7, Joshua Auty 1, Ben Wilson 7:1.
AUSTRALIA Under 23 52
Chris Holder 11, Cory Gathercole 5:1, Troy Batchelor 13:1, Tyron Proctor 6:1, Jason Doyle 13:1, Richard Sweetman 0, Kozza Smith 4.

Weather...

Three times Somerset had official meetings at Rye House postponed because of rain.

Premier League
Wednesday, April 16 .... BIRMINGHAM (A)
Wednesday, April 30 .... BIRMINGHAM (A)
Saturday, May 17 .... RYE HOUSE (A)
Thursday, July 17 .... SHEFFIELD (A)
Friday, September 5 .... MILDENHALL (H)
Wednesday, September 3 .... BIRMINGHAM (A)
Saturday, September 6 .... RYE HOUSE (A)
Tuesday, September 9 .... ISLE OF WIGHT (A)

Knock Out Cup
Monday, May 26 .... READING (A)
Saturday, August 9 .... RYE HOUSE (A)

Individual
Friday, June 20 .... *EXMOOR CHASE (H*

...beaten

Individual

EXMOOR CHASE INDIVIDUAL CHAMPIONSHIP
Friday, July 18 (Postponed Friday, June 20)
Ben Barker came within half a second of Leigh Adams all-time Oak Tree Arena track record in his opening ride win but lost out to home favourite Jason Doyle in a title-deciding Heat 15.

	1	2	3	4	5	Tot	RO
1 Jason DOYLE	**3**	**3**	**3**	**3**	**3**	**15**	
2 Ben BARKER	3	3	3	2	3	14	
3 Simon WALKER	3	1	3	1	2	10	3
4 Joe HAINES	2	2	1	2	3	10	2
5 Paul COOPER	2	1	2	2	3	10	1
6 Jason BUNYAN	0	3	2	3	2	10	0
7 Ben WILSON	3	2	3	0	1	9	
8 Brent WERNER	0	2	2	3	2	9	
9 Krzysztof STOJANOWSKI	2	3	1	1	1	8	
10 Manuel HAUZINGER	1	2	1	3	0	7	
11 Jerran HART	1	1	2	1	0	5	
12 Stephan KATT	2	0	1	1	0	4	
13 Matthias KRÖGER	1	R	0	2	1	4	
14 Jay HERNE	1	1	0	0	1	3	
15 Jordan FRAMPTON	0	N2	R	0	2	2	
16 Kyle NEWMAN [R]	X	X	0	0		0	
17 Emil KRAMER	0					0	
18 Andrew BRAITHWAITE [R]	E					0	

Roll of Honour
2008 .... Jason DOYLE

SOMERSET JUNIOR CHAMPIONSHIP
Friday, October 3
Australian teenage star Darcy Ward looked a class act on his first competitive visit to Somerset.

	1	2	3	4	5	Tot	GF
1 Darcy WARD	**3**	**3**	**3**	**3**	**3**	**15**	
2 Mark BASEBY	3	3	3	2	2	13	3
3 Ben HOPWOOD	2	2	3	3	3	13	2
4 Gareth ISHERWOOD	3	2	2	3	1	11	
5 Jerran HART	2	3	3	2	0	10	
6 Luke PRIEST	2	2	2	3	1	10	
7 Rob SMITH	3	3	1	X	2	9	
8 Terry DAY	1	0	2	2	2	7	
9 Matt BATES	0	2	0	1	3	6	
10 Andy BRAITHWAITE	2	1	1	2	FX	6	
11 Harland COOK	1	1	2	1	0	5	
12 Aaron BASEBY	1	0	1	1	2	5	
13 Andrew ALDRIDGE	0	0	0	0	3	3	
14 Jamie PICKARD	0	1	0	1	1	3	
15 Michael BOVIS	1	0	1	0	0	2	
16 Gary COTTHAM	0	1	0	0	1	2	
17 James WILLIAMS [R]				did not ride			

Roll of Honour
2005 .... Lee DICKEN
2008 .... Darcy WARD

Four Team Challenge

KINGSWOOD HOTEL SOUTH WEST FOURS
Weymouth, Saturday, July 26
4 SOMERSET 12
Kyle Newman 5, Brendan Johnson 2, David Gough 3, Andrew Braithwaite 2.
1 WEYMOUTH 30, 2 BRISTOL 28, 3 EXETER 24

For full details of the Premier League Pairs Championship see start of Premier League section.

Premier League

STOKE

TRACK FILE

Track: Loomer Road Stadium, Newcastle-under-Lyme, Staffordshire, ST5 7LB.
Telephone: 01782 562184.
Hotline: 09068 664669.
Website: www.potterspower.com
Track Length: 312 metres.
Track Record: 60.06 secs, Lee Complin, September 8, 2007.
Promoter: David Tattum.
Team Sponsors: Easy Rider.
Colours: White with red stars logo
Nickname: Potters.

HISTORY

First meeting: April 12, 1973, Stoke v Birmingham, Division Two challenge.
Leagues: Division Two, 1973-1992, 1996-2009. Division Three, 1994-95, 2003-07.
†*Training was held at the track in 1972 before its official opening the following year.*
Meetings were also held at

● *Hanley Stadium, Sun Street, Hanley, Staffordshire.*
First meeting: April 11, 1929, Golden Helmet Individual.
Leagues: Division Two, 1939, 1950-53, 1960-63. Division Three, 1947-49. English Dirt-Track League, 1929.

HONOURS

Major honours: 6.
Division Two Four Team champions (1), 1990.
Division Two Pairs champions (3), 1984, 1988, 1989.
Division Three champions (1), 1949.
Division Three Four Team champions (1), 2006.

2008 REVIEW

STOKE took a major gamble at the start of the season by handing their top two places in the team to a pair of untried Danish riders, Klaus Jakobsen and Jesper Kristiansen.

Promoter Dave Tattum didn't expect them to maintain their assessed averages but although both displayed promising signs and certainly had their moments, they finished with averages of around five-and-a-half, and that left the Potters heavily reliant on improvement elsewhere.

It came in particular from Ben Barker, who started the season with an average of under six and finished it above eight after easily his best-ever season in the sport – and he also took over as captain too, albeit in most unfortunate circumstances.

The return to racing of Lee Complin after a five-year absence had been one of the best stories of 2007, but Complin's hopes of a successful season were wrecked by a serious road accident in May which left him initially in a critical condition.

He made a remarkable recovery before going through a frustrating wait before being cleared for a return, which he finally did for the final four matches of the season.

So the Potters spent the majority of the summer booking guests, and opposing teams took a strong liking to the Loomer Road circuit, where Stoke suffered five home defeats.

They went through a particularly miserable spell in the second half of the season, losing ten consecutive matches between August 24 and September 19, the Potters hardly helped by having to cram in their fixtures after a succession of rain-offs.

Knock Out Cup progress was ended early by Workington, and the Potters were also unsuccessful in the Premier Trophy – so despite the general high quality of the racing, it was not a season to be remembered with any great fondness by the Staffordshire club.

2008 RESULTS

Premier League

Final position ....Thirteenth

BIRMINGHAM (H)
Saturday, May 3
Won 56-36
Complin 9:1, Burrows 7, Barker 10, Jakobsen 3:1, Sanchez 8:2, Evans 10, Kristiansen 9:2.
▲ *Biggest score of the season highlighted by 19 (paid 21) at reserve compared to the Brummies' one!*

MILDENHALL (H)
Saturday, May 17
Won 54-39
Complin 14, Burrows 3:1, Barker 13:1, Evans 5:2, Sanchez 7, Luke Priest [G] 2:1, **Kristiansen 10:2**.
▲*Kristiansen scored his first maximum in British speedway.*

SOMERSET (A)
Friday, May 23
Lost 22-68
Complin 4, Burrows 1, Barker 7 (1), Evans 1:1, Sanchez 7, Jakobsen 0, Kristiansen 2.
▼ *Match started 40 minutes late after rain – and Potters must have wished the downpour had continued!*

WORKINGTON (H)
Saturday, May 24
Lost 36-59
Complin 9 (6), Burrows 4:1, Barker 12 (TS4), Evans 0, Sanchez 6, Jakobsen 1:1, Kristiansen 4:1.

READING (A)
Monday, June 2
Lost 41-54
Kauko Nieminen [G] 10 (6), Burrows 4:1, Barker 13 (TS4), Evans 2:1, Sanchez 5, Jakobsen 1, Kristiansen 6.

SCUNTHORPE (H)
Saturday, June 7
Lost 43-47
Craig Watson [G] 9, Burrows 5:3, Ryan Fisher [G] 10:1, Evans 4:1, Sanchez 3:1, Jakobsen 7:1, Kristiansen 5:2.
▼*Provided only four heat wins on their own circuit and patched-up team needed a 5-1 in last-heat decider, but conceded a 4-2.*

NEWCASTLE (A)
Sunday, June 8
Lost 42-48
Matthew Wethers [G] 5:1, Burrows 8:1, Ryan Fisher [G] 11, Evans 2:1, Sanchez 7:1, Jakobsen 4:1, Kristiansen 5:1.

GLASGOW (H)
Saturday, June 14
Won 49-43
Magnus Karlsson [G] 9, Burrows 3:1, Barker 13:1, Evans 4, Moore 8, Jakobsen 8:1, Kristiansen 4.
▲ *A win at last after six straight defeats despite Glasgow's late comeback causing some nervous moments.*

SQUAD
Ben Barker, Mark Burrows, Lee Complin, Barrie Evans, Andrew Moore (see Scunthorpe).
Foreign: Krister Jacobsen, Klaus Jakobsen, Jesper Kristiansen, Emiliano Sanchez (see Scunthorpe).

BERWICK (H)
Sunday, June 29
Won 55-37
George Stancl [G] 4:2, Burrows 8:1, Barker 12:1, Evans 5:3, Moore 7:1, Jakobsen 12:1, Kristiansen 7:1.
▲ *Jakobsen put in his best-ever Potters performance, winning his first three rides including victory over tactical-ride Tomas Topinka in Heat 11.*

EDINBURGH (A)
Friday, July 4
Lost 39-54
George Stancl [G] 9, Burrows 1:1, Barker 13 (6), Kristiansen 1:1, Moore 5:3, Evans 3, Jakobsen 7.

EDINBURGH (H)
Saturday, July 5
26-28, abandoned rain.
Magnus Karlsson [G] 4, Burrows 3:2, Barker 7, Kristiansen 2:1, Moore 4, Evans 1:1, Jakobsen 5
● *Meeting abandoned after Heat 9 because of rain. Result does not stand.*

KING'S LYNN (H)
Saturday, July 19
Drew 45-45
Ryan Fisher [G] 8, Burrows 3, Barker 10:1, Kristiansen 2, Moore 12:1, Evans 0, Jakobsen 10:2.
▲ *Potters levelled the scores with a 4-2 in Heat 9 and every remaining race was shared, the home side helped in Heat 15 by Kevin Doolan seemingly losing power.*

SOMERSET (H)
Sunday, July 27
Lost 43-45
Ryan Fisher [G] 12:1, Burrows 1, Barker 11, Kristiansen 5, Moore 7, Kozza Smith [G] 6:1, Gareth Isherwood [G] 1.
▼ *Remarkable conclusion saw Somerset take two 3-2s in Heats 13 and 14 after a series of exclusions – and Barker and guest Ryan Fisher couldn't stop Jason Doyle in the decider.*

SHEFFIELD (H)
Saturday, August 2
Won 58-34
Nicolai Klindt [G] 9:2, **Burrows 10:2**, **Barker 15**, Kristiansen 6:1, Moore 10, Benji Compton [G] 1, Jakobsen 7:2.
▼ *Full maximum for Barker and stunning paid maximum for veteran Burrows.*

BIRMINGHAM (A)
Wednesday, August 6
Won 47-46
Mark Lemon [G] 6, Burrows 6:3, Barker 12, Kristiansen 4:2, Moore 6:1, Charles Wright [G] 3:1, Jakobsen 10:1.

▲ *Eye-catching show on the road from reserve Jakobsen, who had full control over that department after finishing second in Heat 2.*

KING'S LYNN (A)
Wednesday, August 13
Lost 25-67
Richard Hall [G] 3, Jacobsen 1, Barker 5 (TS0), Kristiansen 3, Moore 12 (6), Burrows 0, Jakobsen 1.

RYE HOUSE (H)
Saturday, August 23
Won 54-35
Nicolai Klindt [G] 6, Jacobsen 5, Barker 5:1, Kristiansen 6:1, Moore 12:1, Burrows 5:1, **Jakobsen 15**.
▲ *Reserve Jakobsen scored inspirational maximum, Stoke having been put under pressure by Barker's two early mechanical failures.*

GLASGOW (A)
Sunday, August 24
Lost 36-56
Ryan Fisher [G] 6, Jacobsen 1:1, Barker 11:1 (4), Kristiansen 5:2, Moore 6, Burrows 1:1, Jakobsen 6.

RYE HOUSE (A)
Monday, August 25
Lost 37-55
Ryan Fisher [G] 16 (4), Jacobsen 1:1, Barker 9, Kristiansen 3:1, Moore 1, Burrows 5, Jakobsen 2:1.
▲ *Ryan Fisher starred as a guest with four wins and Barker won Heat 12 and was promptly whisked off to Coventry's late-afternoon match with Ipswich!*

SCUNTHORPE (A)
Friday, August 29
Lost 44-46
Joel Parsons [G] 8:2, Jacobsen 6:2, **Barker 15**, Kristiansen 2, Moore 6, Burrows 2, Jakobsen 5:1.
▲ *Marvellous performance by Barker kept the Potters in contention for an away win, but they dropped a 5-1 in the penultimate race, and Richard Hall kept guest Parsons at bay in Heat 15.*

EDINBURGH (H)
Saturday, August 30
Lost 36-57
Mark Lemon [G] 7, Jacobsen 1, Barker 18 (6), Kristiansen 1, Moore 4, Burrows 3, Jakobsen 2:1.
▼ *Jacobsen suffered hip and leg injuries in Heat 6.*

ISLE OF WIGHT (A)
Tuesday, September 2
Lost 37-56
Mark Lemon [G] 11 (6), Jacobsen 1, Barker 7 (TSX), Burrows 5:1, *rider replacement for Moore*, Kristiansen 9, Jakobsen 4.
▼ *Unusual Heat 8 saw tac. sub Barker fail to beat the time allowance and therefore be sent back 10 yards further – only to drop a chain as the race got underway!*

BERWICK (A)
Saturday, September 13
Lost 41-52
Rider replacement for Complin, Jacobsen 2, Barker 16:1 (6), Burrows 6:2, Moore 13, Kristiansen 2, Jakobsen 2:2.
▼ *Kristiansen withdrew after tangling with Scott Smith in Heat 2.*

REDCAR (H)
Sunday, September 14
Lost 41-48
Jason Bunyan [G] 3:2, Jacobsen 11, Barker 10:1, Burrows 2, Moore 5, Kristiansen 5:2, Jakobsen 5.

REDCAR (A)
Thursday, September 18
Lost 40-51
Shane Parker [G] 7, Burrows 2:1, Barker 13 (TS2),

STOKE 2008: Klaus Jakobsen, Mark Burrows, Lee Complin, Emiliano Sanchez, Barrie Evans, front – Jesper Kristiansen, mascot Sam Ward and Ben Barker

Jacobsen 1, Moore 4:1, Kristiansen 1, Jakobsen 12:1.

▼ *Jakobsen impressed at reserve, but Barker wasn't quite able to make up a 15-metre handicap when taking a tac. sub ride in Heat 14.*

WORKINGTON (A)
Friday, September 19
Lost 34-59
Chris Kerr [G] 9, Burrows 1, Barker 11:1 (6), Jacobsen 4, Moore 2, Kristiansen 1, Jakobsen 6.

▼▲ *Barker fell in his first ride but recovered to win his next for double points*

NEWCASTLE (H)
Saturday, September 20
Won 54-38
Magnus Karlsson [G] 5:1, Burrows 6:3, **Barker 15**, Jacobsen 6:1, Moore 5:1, Kristiansen 9:1, Jakobsen 8:2.

SHEFFIELD (A)
Thursday, September 25
Lost 38-52
Complin 4, Burrows 3:2, Barker 7 (TS0), Kristiansen 2, Moore 11, Jacobsen 2:2, Jakobsen 9:1.

▲ *Long-awaited comeback for Complin netted two second places.*

ISLE OF WIGHT (H)
Saturday, September 27
Won 53-40
Complin 8, Burrows 4:3, Barker 11, Kristiansen 6:2, Moore 9, Jakobsen 9, Jacobsen 6:1.

▲▼ *Complin took the first race win of his comeback in Heat 6. Barker won three races but crashed out of Heat 5.*

MILDENHALL (A)
Sunday, September 28
Won 56-34
Complin 5:2, Burrows 7:2, **Barker 15**, Kristiansen 4:1, Moore 7:1, Jacobsen 7:2, Jakobsen 11:1.

● *Stoke's win completed a pointless Premier League season for Mildenhall. Barker outstanding and Jakobsen unbeaten but for a last-place in his second ride.*

READING (H)
Sunday, October 26
Won 51-40
Complin 7:1, Kristiansen 9:1, Barker 4:1, *rider replacement for Burrows*, Moore 8:2, Gareth Isherwood [G] 6:2, Jakobsen 17:1.

▲*Finished a difficult season on a high with Jakobsen only beaten in Heat 15. Mark Lemon scored a maximum for the visitors.*

PREMIER LEAGUE

		M	W	D	L	PtsF	PtsA	Pts
1	Edinburgh	30	22	2	6	1562	1161	53
2	Somerset	30	21	0	9	1517	1223	48
3	King's Lynn	30	18	5	7	1624	1111	45
4	Rye House	30	19	0	11	1500	1232	42
5	Workington	30	17	2	11	1435.5	1300.5	41
6	Berwick	30	16	2	12	1428	1316	37
7	Redcar	30	16	1	13	1369	1374	37
8	Sheffield	30	15	2	13	1381	1346	35
9	Reading	30	15	1	14	1350	1405	34
10	Scunthorpe	30	15	0	15	1309	1434	33
11	Isle of Wight	30	15	0	15	1359	1390	31
12	Birmingham	30	13	0	17	1317.5	1401.5	30
13	**STOKE**	**30**	**11**	**1**	**18**	**1307**	**1441**	**25**
14	Newcastle	30	10	0	20	1220	1501	22
15	Glasgow	30	9	0	21	1297	1469	19
16	Mildenhall	30	0	0	30	932	1804	0

Andrew Moore arrived at Loomer Road in June after a swap that saw Emiliano Sanchez move to Scunthorpe

STOKE

Rider	*M*	*R*	*Pts*	*BP*	*TPts*	*Ave*	*F*	*P*	*TR*	*TPts*	*TS*	*TSPts*
Ben BARKER	38	194	409	13	422	8.70	4	1	7	13	8	10
Lee COMPLIN	**17**	**79**	**155**	**11**	**166**	**8.40**	**0**	**0**	**4**	**9**	**0**	**0**
Andrew MOORE	22	99	160	12	172	6.95	0	0	2	2	0	0
Emiliano SANCHEZ	**17**	**72**	**102**	**13**	**115**	**6.39**	**0**	**0**	**0**	**0**	**0**	**0**
Mark BURROWS	39	159	181	43	224	5.63	0	1	0	0	0	0
Jesper KRISTIANSEN	**40**	**158**	**185**	**36**	**221**	**5.59**	**0**	**1**	**0**	**0**	**0**	**0**
Klaus JAKOBSEN	37	169	204	29	233	5.51	0	0	0	0	0	0
Barrie EVANS	**21**	**81**	**87**	**15**	**102**	**5.04**	**0**	**0**	**0**	**0**	**0**	**0**
Krister JACOBSEN	15	56	55	10	65	4.64	0	0	0	0	0	0
Guests	***30***	***133***	***210***	***17***	***227***	***6.83***	***0***	***0***	***3***	***8***	***0***	***0***

For Ben BARKER see Coventry; for Andrew MOORE and Emiliano SANCHEZ see Scunthorpe (PL); for Barrie EVANS see Mildenhall.

Premier Trophy

NEWCASTLE (A)
Sunday, March 16
Lost 42-51
Jakobsen 0, Barker 10, Kristiansen 6:2, Complin 12, Sanchez 4, Evans 6, Burrows 4.
▲ *Five Potters won at least one race, debutant Kristiansen defeating Josef Franc in Heat 12.*

REDCAR (H)
Saturday, March 22
Won 49-41
Rider replacement for Jakobsen, Barker 9:1, Kristiansen 2:1, Complin 15:1, Sanchez 9, Evans 7:2, Burrows 7.
▲ *Heat 14 5-1 from Complin and Evans secured first win of the season*

SHEFFIELD (A)
Thursday, March 27
Lost 41-51
Jakobsen 2:2, Barker 9 (4), Kristiansen 4:1, Complin 11, Sanchez 7, Evans 4:1, Burrows 4:2.

SHEFFIELD (H)
Saturday, April 5
Lost 45-48
Jakobsen 2, Barker 13 (TS4), Kristiansen 1:1, Complin 15 (6), Sanchez 5, Evans 2, Burrows 7:3.
▼*Trailed by 14 points with four heats to go but forced last-heat decider but Barker crashed trying to pass André Compton*

SCUNTHORPE (A)
Friday, April 18
Lost 43-47
Jakobsen 0, Barker 4:1, Kristiansen 6:1, Complin 6:2, Sanchez 10:1, Evans 2:1, Burrows 15.
▲▼ *Burrows was outstanding against one of his old clubs but he and Sanchez could not get the better of Magnus Karlsson in a last-heat decider.*

SCUNTHORPE (H)
Saturday, April 19
Won 51-39
Jakobsen 3, **Barker 14:1**, Kristiansen 6:2, Complin 13:1, Sanchez 4:2, Evans 8, Burrows 3:1.
▲ *Barker collected his first paid maximum for the club with Kristiansen showing his most encouraging signs so far.*

NEWCASTLE (H)
Saturday, May 10
Won 54-39
Complin 10:2, Burrows 7:1, Barker 14, Jakobsen 3:1, Sanchez 6:2, Evans 9, Kristiansen 5:2.
▲ *Potters took a comfortable win in a meeting which was academic as far as the overall group situation was concerned.*

REDCAR (A)
Thursday, May 15
Lost 38-52
Complin 5:1 (1), Burrows 5:2, Barker 10, Evans 3, Sanchez 6, Jakobsen 2:2, Kristiansen 7:1.
▲▼*Barker was the only man to challenge the Bears' top three, losing out to James Grieves but ending the maximum hopes of Gary Havelock and Ty Proctor.*

PREMIER TROPHY Group B

		M	W	D	L	PtsF	PtsA	Pts
1	Sheffield	8	6	0	2	386	345	14
2	Redcar	8	3	2	3	362	360	8
3	Scunthorpe	8	3	1	4	345	380	8
4	Newcastle	8	3	1	4	364	367	7
5	**STOKE**	**8**	**3**	**0**	**5**	**363**	**368**	**6**

Knock Out Cup

First round, first leg
WORKINGTON (H)
Sunday, April 27
Lost 42-50
Complin 8, Burrows 7:1, Barker 7, Jakobsen 4:1, Sanchez 3:2, Evans 6:1, Kristiansen 7:1.

First round, second leg
WORKINGTON (A)
Monday, May 26
Lost 36-54
Adam Roynon [G] 8, Burrows 6:2, Barker 6 (0), Evans 4:1, Sanchez 5:2, Jakobsen 4:1, Kristiansen 3.
▼ *Roynon was used as a guest for Complin, who was seriously injured in a weekend road accident.*
Aggregate: Lost 78-104.

Ben Barker had a great year for both Stoke and Elite League Coventry

Weather...

Stoke's opening meeting of the season was rained-off – one of 10 home matches that didn't start.

Premier League

Sunday, May 4 .... BIRMINGHAM (A)
Tuesday, June 3 .... ISLE OF WIGHT (A)
Friday, June 13 .... SCUNTHORPE (A)
Saturday, June 21 .... ISLE OF WIGHT (H)
Sunday, June 22 .... GLASGOW (A)
Saturday, July 12 .... REDCAR (H)
Thursday, July 3 .... GLASGOW (A)
†Sunday, July 13 .... MILDENHALL (A)
Thursday, July 31 .... SHEFFIELD (A)
Saturday, August 9 .... NEWCASTLE (H)
Wednesday, August 13 .... KING'S LYNN (A)
Saturday, August 16 .... ISLE OF WIGHT (H)
Saturday, September 5 .... WORKINGTON (A)
Sunday, September 6 .... READING (H)
Saturday, October 4 .... READING (H)
Saturday, October 25 .... READING (H)

†Meeting postponed because of damage to the track by stockcars and electrical problems.

Premier Trophy

Saturday, March 15 .... NEWCASTLE (H)
Saturday, March 29 .... SCUNTHORPE (H)
Saturday, April 12 .... NEWCASTLE (H)

Knock Out Cup

Saturday, April 26 .... WORKINGTON (A)

...beaten

Conference League Fours

Saturday, October 18
Semi Final 1

1 REDCAR 19 (Scott James 6, Adam McKinna 6, James Cockle 5, Richard Lawson 2), **2 SITTINGBOURNE 12** (Mark Baseby 3, Aaron Baseby 2, Dean Felton 2, Ricky Scarboro 5), **3 PLYMOUTH 9** (Tom Brown 2, Paul Starke 4, Jamie Pickard 3, David Gough 0), **4 BOSTON 7** (Adam Lowe 2, Darren Rolph 2, Darren Mallett 2, Adam Allott 1).

Semi Final 2

1 WEYMOUTH 15 (Lee Smart 6, Jay Herne 3, Brendan Johnson 2, Karl Mason 4), **2 SCUNTHORPE 13** (Scott Richardson 4, Ben Hopwood 5, Gary Irving 2, Stuart Parnaby 2), **3 RYE HOUSE 12** (Rob Smith 3, Gary Cottham 2, Richard Franklin 4, Andrew Aldridge 3), **4 BUXTON 7** (Ben Taylor 2, Gareth Isherwood 5, Paul Burnett 0, Scott Whittington 0).

FINAL

1 WEYMOUTH 13
Lee Smart 6, Jay Herne 3, Brendan Johnson 3, Karl Mason 1), **2 REDCAR 12** (Scott James 3, Adam McKinna 2, James Cockle 3, Richard Lawson 4), **3 SITTING-BOURNE 7** (Mark Baseby 4, Aaron Baseby 0, Dean Felton 2, Ricky Scarboro 1), **4 SCUNTHORPE 4** (Scott Richardson 0, Ben Hopwood 1, Gary Irving 1, Stuart Parnaby 1, Scott Whittington 1).

See Conference League for race-by-race details and Roll of Honour.

Neil Collins Farewell

Saturday, October 11

NEIL Jeffrey Collins made his debut on March 31, 1978, and completed his final competitive ride on Sunday, September 17, 2006.

His was a career that scaled the heights of a World Cup call-up for England when he rode alongside his brothers, 1976 World Champion Peter and Phil, to win a silver medal at the 1984 final in Leszno, Poland.

A member of speedway's most famous family – another brother Les was runner-up in the 1982 World Final and youngest sibling Stephen became the fifth brother to follow the shale trail – he first rode for Ellesmere Port and finished his career at Newport.

With ports of call at Sheffield, Cradley Heath, Belle Vue, Leicester, Wolverhampton and Peterborough in the top-flight and campaigns with Division Two Long Eaton, Workington, Edinburgh, Glasgow, Stoke, Swindon, Somerset and Hull, he made a staggering total of 1,088 official appearances. He won 20 England caps, was a nine times British Finalist and finished fifth in the 1980 European Under 21 Championship.

At his Farewell meeting brothers Peter, Les and Phil joined him for a nostalgic final four laps of Loomer Road.

STOKE SELECT 49 (Jason Bunyan 11, Paul Fry 4:2, Barker 10:1, Moore 3, David Howe 4, Burrows 8, Adam Allott 9:1), **NEIL COLLINS SELECT 34** (George Stancl 7, Shawn McConnell 3:1, Stuart Robson 8 (R), Craig Branney 6, Neil Collins 5 (TS0), Scott Richardson 4:1, Aidan Collins 1:1).

Under 16s

THREE TEAM TOURNAMENT
Saturday, May 31
HOME COUNTIES 26
Rider replacement for Michael Bovis, Joe Newey 3, Joseph Jacobs 11:2, Jake Knight 11, Sam Woods 1:1.
NORTH 33
Dale Lamb 3:2, Jason Garrity 8:2, Jack Hurst 4:1, James Sarjeant 14, Montana Jowett 4:1.
MIDLANDS & WEST 30
Ashley Morris 4:1, Claire Frays 2, Daniel Greenwood 13:1, Scott Meakins 10:2, Jack Butler 1:1.

British Under 15 Championship

Sunday, July 20

500cc: John Resch 12, Daniel Greenwood 9, Jason Garrity 8, Joe Jacobs 7, James Sarjeant 7, Jack Butler 6, Jack Hirst 3, Cameron Hoskins 3, Ashley Morris 2, Scott Day 0.

250cc: Nathan Stoneman 11+3, Marc Owen 12+R, Conor Dwyer 8+2, Lloyd Barrett 6+1, Daniel I'Anson 4, Ben Morley 3, Jack Cornes 3, Daniel Sibson 0.

See British Championship for full details.

2009 Squad

Lee **COMPLIN** (7.27), Jason **BUNYAN** (7.08), Glen **PHILLIPS** (6.39), Tom P. **MADSEN** (6.04), Phil **MORRIS** (5.88), Klaus **JAKOBSEN** (4.87), Jesper **KRISTIANSEN**[2] (4.67).

Premier League

WORKINGTON

TRACK FILE

Track: Derwent Park Stadium, Workington, Cumbria, CA14 2HG.
Telephone: 01900 608071 (race nights only). 01943 878448 (9am-5pm, Mon-Fri).
Hotline: 09068 664671.
Website: www.workingtonspeedway.com
Track Length: 364 metres.
Track Record: 63.2 secs, Simon Stead, September 23, 2006.
Promoters: Keith Denham and Ian Thomas.
Team Sponsors: Thomas Armstrong (Holdings) Ltd.
Colours: Blue and white quarters with blue C.
Nickname: Comets.

HISTORY

First meeting: April 3, 1970, Workington v Berwick, Border Trophy.
Leagues: Division Two, 1970-1981, 1987, 1999-2009. Open licence, 1985
In 1987 Glasgow used Derwent Park as their home track and raced as Glasgow Tigers until the end of July when they adopted the name Workington although still racing as the Tigers. They were expelled from the league on September 15 without completing their fixtures.

HONOURS

Major honours: 10.
Division Two Young Shield winners (1), 2008.
Division Two Four Team champions (4), 2001, 2004, 2006, 2008.
Division Two Pairs champions (5), 1999, 2000, 2001, 2003, 2008.

2008 REVIEW

THE Comets started the season under new ownership after former sponsor Keith Denham took over from Tony Mole, but Ian Thomas remained on board to run the team.

Thomas elected to track a side high on top-end strength and picked up the signing of Daniel Nermark from King's Lynn to form a quality top-three alongside skipper Kauko Nieminen and long-serving Carl Stonehewer – and there was plenty of excitement ,too, with the arrival of youngster Joe Haines.

However, there was a blow before the start of the season when Craig Branney broke his leg in the Telford ice event in February, and that was a gap which the Comets took some time to plug.

They initially snapped up former Sheffield star Scott Smith, but he was quickly replaced by Barry Burchatt, who suffered multiple injuries in a grass track crash and could not contemplate a return.

Eventually, Finnish rider Tomi Reima filled the void, but that was not without its problems due to domestic issues.

However, the team were a competitive force and for most of the season they looked like top-four material, even if they were generally some way behind Edinburgh and Somerset in terms of a title challenge and dropped four points at home.

Five away wins, though, left them fifth in the table and in pole position for the Young Shield competition with first choice of opponents.

They duly overcame Scunthorpe and holders Redcar en route to the Final, where they proved to be too strong for Berwick with a powerful performance in the first leg at Derwent Park.

It brought seven-man team silverware to the club for the first time since the re-launch of the sport in 1999, and that added to two triumphs earlier in the season as the Comets collected both the Premier League Fours and Premier League Pairs titles.

2008 RESULTS

Premier League

Final position..Fifth

KING'S LYNN (H)
Saturday, April 12
Drew 45-45
Nermark 10:1, Smith 2, Stonehewer 4:1., Wright 10, Nieminen 9:1, Haines 4:2, Branney 6:1.
▲ *Dramatic draw with Comets looking set for defeat, then going 43-41 up before Kevin Doolan and Tomas Topinka, split by Nermark, took a 4-2 in Heat 15.*

NEWCASTLE (A)
Sunday, April 13
Won 48-42
Nermark 11, Smith 1:1, Stonehewer 10, Wright 0, Nieminen 11:2, Haines 6:1, Branney 9.

READING (A)
Monday, April 21
Lost 39-54
Nermark 15 (6), Smith 0, Nieminen 12, Wright 0, Stonehewer 6, Haines 4:1, Branney 2:1.

ISLE OF WIGHT (A)
Tuesday, April 22
Lost 44-49
Nermark 17:1 (6), Smith 1, Nieminen 11, Wright 4:1, Stonehewer 7, Haines 2, Branney 2.
▲▼ *Paid maximum-man Nermark won four races and Nieminen three but comeback only ever brought the Comets to within five points of home side.*

RYE HOUSE (H)
Saturday, May 3
Won 46-44
Nermark 12, Burchatt 1, Nieminen 8, Wright 5:1, Stonehewer 8:1, Haines 7:1, Branney 5:1.
▲ *Comets fought back from eight points down and secured their victory when Nermark won Heat 15.*

RYE HOUSE (A)
Monday, May 5
Lost 40-52
Nermark 3, Burchatt 4:1, Nieminen 13, Wright 0, Stonehewer 10, Haines 8:1, Branney 2:2.
▼ *Nieminen's tactical ride in Heat 12 was neutralised by Tai Woffinden, and Nermark forced to withdraw with broken thumb.*

SCUNTHORPE (A)
Friday, May 9
Lost 43-47
James Wright [G] 12:1, Burchatt 2, Nieminen 13, Wright 2:2, Stonehewer 1:1, Haines 12, Branney 1.
▼ *Ex-Comet Wright made a guest appearance but Stonehewer had three retirements.*

READING (H)
Saturday, May 10
Won 54-36
James Wright [G] 10, Burchatt 4:2, Nieminen 11:1, Wright 5:1, Stonehewer 10:2, Haines 8:1, Branney 6:2.
▲ *Biggest win of the season so far.*

SQUAD
John Branney, Barry Burchatt, Joe Haines, Scott Smith, Carl Stonehewer, Charles Wright.
Foreign: Daniel Nermark, Kauko Nieminen, Tomi Reima.

SCUNTHORPE (H)
Saturday, May 17
Won 54-39
Nermark 15, *rider replacement for Burchatt*, Nieminen 10, Wright 5:2, Stonehewer 11:1, Haines 9:1, Branney 4:1, Gary Irving [no. 8].
▲ *Perfect return from injury for Nermark.*

SHEFFIELD (A)
Thursday, May 22
Won 50-40
Nermark 13, *rider replacement for Burchatt*, Nieminen 9, Wright 4:1, Stonehewer 12:2, Haines 10:2, Branney 2:1.
▲ *Comets' result of the season with five riders wining races, and Stonehewer rolling back the years.*

STOKE (A)
Saturday, May 24
Won 59-36
Nermark 14:1, *rider replacement for Burchatt*, Nieminen 12:1, Wright 6:4, Stonehewer 8, Haines 13:2, Branney 6:2.

SHEFFIELD (H)
Saturday, May 31
Drew 45-45
Nermark 8:2, Reima 5, Nieminen 13, Wright 3, *rider replacement for Stonehewer*, Haines 14:1, Branney 2:1.
▼ *Held to a draw in the match of the season at Derwent Park, Nieminen and Nermark beaten by Andre Compton in Heat 15.*

KING'S LYNN (A)
Wednesday, June 4
Lost 32-61
Nermark 14 (6), Reima 1:1, Nieminen 0, Haines 9, *rider replacement for Stonehewer*, Wright 8, Branney 0.
▼ *Nieminen failed to complete a single race and Haines suffered an arm injury when crashing out of Heat 15.*

GLASGOW (A)
Sunday, June 8
Won 49-41
Nermark 14, Reima 3, Nieminen 12, *rider replacement for Haines*, Stonehewer 8, Wright 3:2, Branney 9:1.

BIRMINGHAM (A)
Wednesday, June 11
Lost 42.5-47.5
Nermark 13, Reima 2, Nieminen 10:2, Haines 3, Stonehewer 6.5, Wright 6, Branney 2:1.
● *Stonehewer and Jason Lyons could not be separated by referee Mike Posselwhite in the race for second place in*

Heat 9.

BIRMINGHAM (H)
Saturday, June 14
Won 51-41
James Wright [G] 11, Reima 7:2, Nieminen 13, Haines 4:1, Stonehewer 9:3, Wright 5:1, Branney 2.
▲ *Secured first official victory over the Brummies in the modern era at the sixth attempt.*

REDCAR (H)
Saturday, July 5
Won 49-44
Kevin Doolan [G] 6:1, *rider replacement for Haines*, Nieminen 14, Kozza Smith [G] 3:1, Stonehewer 14:1, Wright 8, Branney 4:1.

SOMERSET (A)
Friday, July 11
Lost 36-57
Nermark 15 (6), *rider replacement for Reima*, Nieimen 9:2, Haines 5, Stonehewer 1, Wright 4, Branney 2.

ISLE OF WIGHT (H)
Saturday, July 12
Won 58-32
Nermark 15, *rider replacement for Reima*, **Nieminen 14:1**, Haines 8:2, Stonehewer 10:1, Wright 6:1, Branney 5:2.

MILDENHALL (H)
Saturday, July 19
Won 64-28
André Compton [G] 5:3, *rider replacement for Reima*, **Nieminen 14:1**, Haines 10:2, Stonehewer 12:2, Wright 9:1, Branney 14:1.

REDCAR (A)
Thursday, July 24
Lost 43-47
Nermark 3, *rider replacement for Reima*, Nieminen 12, Haines 8, Stonehewer 9, Wright 10:2, Branney 1.
▼ *Nermark crashed in Heat 11 and suffered an ankle injury which kept him out until the end of August when he clipped Ty Proctor's back wheel*

MILDENHALL (A)
Sunday, July 27
Won 53-31
Tomas Topinka [G] 8:1, Viktor Bergtström [G] 8, Nieminen 13, Haines 10, *rider replacement for Stonehewer*, Wright 9:1, Branney 5:2.

SOMERSET (H)
Saturday, August 2
Won 46-44
Gary Havelock [G] 10:1, Gary Beaton [G] 1, Nieminen 12:1, Haines 6, Stonehewer 8, Wright 1:1, Branney 8:2.
▲ *Fought back from early deficit and took a two-point lead into Heat 15, where Nieminen and guest Gary Havelock claimed match-winning 3-3.*

GLASGOW (H)
Saturday, August 9
23-25, abandoned, heavy rain and waterlogged track.
Tomas Topinka [G] 6, Ben Taylor [G] 2, Nieminen 2:1, Haines 6, Stonehewer 4, Wright 2, Branney1:1.
● *Meeting started 40 minutes late due to rain, and further persistent downpours led to abandonment after Heat 8, result does not stand.*

EDINBURGH (A) SKY TV
Monday, August 11
Lost 30-59
Tai Woffinden [G] 7 (X), Ben Taylor [G] 2, Nieminen 8, Haines 3:1, Stonehewer 2:1, Wright 8, Branney 0.
▼ *Sequence of falls, exclusions and mechanical failures dogged the Comets from start to finish leaving them well beaten in televised fixture.*

EDINBURGH (H)
Saturday, August 16
Won 53-39
Jason Doyle [G] 7:1, Reima 6:2, **Nieminen 15**, Haines 5:1, Stonehewer 9:1, Wright 4:2, Branney 7:2.

BERWICK (A)
Saturday, August 23
Lost 41-48
Ryan Fisher [G] 8:1, Reima 3:1, Nieminen 11:1, Haines 6, Stonehewer 7:1, Wright 5, Branney 1.
▼ *Unable to bring things home from a 26-21 lead. Bandits took two straight 5-1s to overturn matters.*

BERWICK (H)
Monday, August 25
Lost 42-51
Gary Havelock [G] 13 (TS1), Reima 2:2, Nieminen 11:1 (6), Haines 2, Stonehewer 5:1, Wright 4, Branney 5:1.
▼ *Shock home defeat but there was no doubt that Berwick deserved their win having adapted better to heavy track conditions. Michal Makovsky (16) and Guglielmo Franchetti (14+3) did the main damage.*

GLASGOW (H)
Saturday, August 30
Won 59-36
Nermark 12:2, Reima 7:1, Nieminen 12:1, Haines 8, Stonehewer 8, Wright 6:2, Branney 6.

NEWCASTLE (H)
Saturday, September 13
Won 61-31
Tomas Topinka [G] 13:2, Wright 9:1, **Nieminen 15**, Haines 7:1, Stonehewer 9, Ben Taylor [G] 3:1, Branney 5.
▲ *Comprehensive victory featured 28 points out of the first 30 available, and all 15 heat winners provided by the Comets.*

STOKE (H)
Friday, September 19
Won 59-34
Tomas Topinka [G] 14:1, Wright 9:1, Nieminen 12, Haines 6:1, Stonehewer 9:1, Ben Taylor [G] 3, Branney 6:2.
▲ *Another strong top-end performance with 12 heat winners, although Ben Barker and Chris Kerr did their best to provide some entertainment.*

PREMIER LEAGUE

		M	W	D	L	PtsF	PtsA	Pts
1	Edinburgh	30	22	2	6	1562	1161	53
2	Somerset	30	21	0	9	1517	1223	48
3	King's Lynn	30	18	5	7	1624	1111	45
4	Rye House	30	19	0	11	1500	1232	42
5	**WORKINGTON**	**30**	**17**	**2**	**11**	**1435.5**	**1300.5**	**41**
6	Berwick	30	16	2	12	1428	1316	37
7	Redcar	30	16	1	13	1369	1374	37
8	Sheffield	30	15	2	13	1381	1345	35
9	Reading	30	15	1	14	1350	1405	34
10	Scunthorpe	30	15	0	15	1309	1434	33
11	Isle of Wight	30	15	0	15	1359	1390	31
12	Birmingham	30	13	0	17	1317.5	1401.5	30
13	Stoke	30	11	1	18	1307	1441	25
14	Newcastle	30	10	0	20	1220	1501	22
15	Glasgow	30	9	0	21	1297	1469	19
16	Mildenhall	30	0	0	30	932	1804	0

Young Shield

Quarter Final, first leg
SCUNTHORPE (A)
Friday, October 3
Lost 39-51
Tomas Topinka [G] 15, Wright 4, *rider replacement for Nieminen*, Haines 1, Stonehewer 6, Reima 8:1, Branney 5:2.
▼ *Tomas Topinka proved a sterling guest after conceding a 5-1 in the first race, and reserves did an important job in a damage limitation effort.*

Quarter Final, second leg
SCUNTHORPE (H)
Sunday, October 5
Won 58-35
Tomas Topinka [G] 18, Wright 2, *rider replacement for Nieminen*, Haines 11:1, Stonehewer 11:2, Reima 8, Branney 8:1.
▲ *Six faultless rides from guest Tomas Topinka at the head of an emphatic performance in a meeting put back by 24 hours.*
Aggregate: Won 97-86.

Semi Final, first leg
REDCAR (A)
Thursday, October 16
Lost 43-48
Jason Doyle [G] 17 (TS2), Wright 0, *rider replacement for Nieminen*, Haines 10:2, Stonehewer 4, Reima 7:1, Branney 5:2.
▼ *Guest Jason Doyle won his first three races and gained a point as a tactical sub.*

Semi Final, second leg
REDCAR (H)
Saturday, October 18
Won 51-42
Jason Lyons [G] 6:2, Wright 9:1, *rider replacement for Nieminen*, Haines 8:1, **Stonehewer 18**, Reima 6, Branney 4:2.
▲ *Recorded ten race winners with Stonehewer in vintage form. Took the aggregate lead in Heat 6 and never let it slip.*
Aggregate: Won 94-90.

FINAL, first leg
BERWICK (A)
Saturday, October 25
0-0, abandoned, waterlogged track.
Tomas Topinka [G], Wright, *rider replacement for Nieminen*, Haines, Stonehewer, Reima, Branney.
● *The meeting was called off because of track conditions after Workington guest Tomas Topinka fell while leading Heat 1.*

FINAL, first leg
BERWICK (H)
Sunday, October 26
Won 58-34
Tomas Topinka [G] 11:2, Wright 10:1, *rider replacement for Nieminen*, Haines 13:1, Stonehewer 14:1, Reima 5:1, Branney 5:2.
▲ *Became the first leg after wash-out at Shielfield Park the previous evening, and after an uncertain start the Comets racked up a big advantage, suffering only three last places and winning eleven races.*

FINAL, second leg
BERWICK (A)
Wednesday, October 29
Lost 38-55
Jason Lyons [G] 18 (6), Wright 5:1, *rider replacement for Nieminen*, Haines 4:1, Stonehewer 5, Reima 1:1, Branney 5.
▼ *Survived a few nervous moments in difficult track conditions to finish the season with silverware. Not the best of all-round performances, with the Comets heavily reliant on guest Jason Lyons to see them through.*
Aggregate: Won 96-89.

Premier Trophy

BERWICK (A)
Saturday, March 22
Won 46-44
Nermark 14:1, Smith 6:2, Stonehewer 9, Wright 4:1, Nieminen 10, Haines 0, Branney 3.
▲ *Away win in first meeting thanks to Nermark's paid maximum, including crucial victory in Heat 15.*

BERWICK (H)
Monday, March 24
Won 53-40
Nermark 10:1, Smith 3:1, **Stonehewer 15**, Wright 2, Nieminen 13:1, Haines 6:2, Branney 4:1.
▲ *Dream return home for Stonehewer after 32-month injury lay-off with five winning rides.*

EDINBURGH (A)
Friday, March 28
Lost 37-56
Nermark 18 (6), Smith 1, Stonehewer 7, Wright 2, Nieminen 7, Haines 2, Branney 0.

GLASGOW (A)
Sunday, March 30
Lost 43-47
Nermark 15, Smith 3, Stonehewer 11, Wright 1, Nieminen 9, Haines 3, Branney 1:1.
▲ *Second successive unbeaten away performance from Nermark not quite enough to give the Comets victory.*

EDINBURGH (H)
Saturday, April 5
Won 48-45
Nermark 15, Smith 3:1, Stonehewer 8:1, Wright 6:1, Nieminen 8, Haines 4, Branney 4:1.
▲ *Led by 10 with four heats to go but conceded an 8-1 in Heat 12. Took a 4-2 from Nermark and Stonhewer in the last-heat decider.*

GLASGOW (H)
Saturday, April 19
Won 60-32
Nermark 13:1, Smith 6:1, **Nieminen 15**, Wright 5:2, Stonehewer 9, Haines 8:1, Branney 4:1.

PREMIER TROPHY Group A

	M	W	D	L	PtsF	PtsA	Pts
1 Edinburgh	6	5	0	1	320	231	12
2 WORKINGTON	**6**	**4**	**0**	**2**	**287**	**264**	**9**
3 Glasgow	6	2	0	4	240	313	4
4 Berwick	6	1	0	5	255	294	2

Knock Out Cup

First round, first leg
STOKE (A)
Sunday, April 27
Won 50-42
Nermark 15, Smith 0, Nieminen 16:2 (4), Wright 7, Stonehewer 8, Haines 1, Branney 3.
▲ *Astonishing comeback from the Comets, who were 32-22 down with six heats to go and were inspired by Nieminen and Nermark in closing stages.*

First round, second leg
STOKE (H)
Saturday, May 26
Won 54-36
Nermark 14:1, *rider replacement for Burchatt*, Nieminen 12, Wright 7:3, Stonehewer 6, Haines 7:1, Branney 8:3.
Aggregate: Won 104-78.

Quarter Final, first leg
ISLE OF WIGHT (H)
Won 53-38
Nermark 15, Reima 7:2, Nieminen 9, *rider replacement for Haines*, Stonehewer 12:1, Wright 4:1, Branney 6:2, David Haigh [no. 8].

Quarter Final, second leg
ISLE OF WIGHT (A)
Tuesday, June 17
Lost 43-51
Nermark 0, Reima 4:1, Nieminen 12:1 (4), Haines 5:1, Stonehewer 17 (TS4), Wright 5, Branney 0.
▲ *Stonehewer showed all of his experience and won the deciding race as the Comets held on without Nermark, missing due to a Swedish League fixture.*
Aggregate: Won 96-89.

Semi Final, first leg
EDINBURGH (A)
Friday, September 26
Lost 41-49
Tomas Topinka [G] 6, Wright 5, Nieminen 11:1, Haines 7:2, Stonehewer 4:1, Reima 1:1, Branney 7:1.
▲▼ *Threatened a shock first-leg away win when they led 32-28 with five heats to go*

Semi Final, second leg
EDINBURGH (H)
Saturday, September 27
Won 53-39
Tomas Topinka [G] 13:1, Wright 1, **Nieminen 14:1**, Haines 6, Stonehewer 7:1, Reima 4:2, Branney 8.
▲ *Moved into the Final with an exciting finale, Nieminen and guest Tomas Topinka teaming up for a 5-1 in Heat 15 .*
Aggregate: Won 94-88.

FINAL, first leg
SOMERSET (H)
Saturday, October 11
Lost 43-46
Jason Lyons [G] 17, Wright 3:1, *rider replacement for Nieminen*, Haines 9:1, Stonehewer 8:2, Reima 1:1, Branney 5, Craig Cook [no 8].
▲ *Never led during the meeting and conceded a 5-0 in Heat 14 when Branney crashed and Haines retired. Jason Lyons was another successful guest.*

FINAL, second leg
SOMERSET (A)
Friday, October 17
Lost 41-52
Jason Lyons [G] 17 (6), Wright 4:1, *rider replacement for Nieminen*, Haines 8:1, Stonehewer 3, Reima 8:1, Branney 1.
▼ *Made a poor start when they really needed a good one, although the sterling efforts of guest Jason Lyons backed by Haines and Reima at least made a match of it – even if it was overall disappointment.*
Aggregate: Lost 84-98.

Weather... beaten

Workington escaped major weather problems on the road – but were hit by five Derwent Park rain-offs.

Premier League
Saturday, June 21 ....GLASGOW (H)
Friday, September 5 ....STOKE (H)

Premier Trophy
Saturday, March 29.................................EDINBURGH (H)

Knock Out Cup
Saturday, April 26...STOKE (H)

Young Shield
Saturday, October 4 ....SCUNTHORPE (H)

Did you know?

In all six Premier Trophy group matches at least one Workington rider was unbeaten by an opponent! Daniel Nermark (four), Carl Stonehewer (one) and Kauko Nieminen (one) all scored maximums.

CARL Stonehewer (seen with the late Darren Boocock) ended his Workington career when he was told he didn't feature in their 2009 plans.

It brought the chequered flag down on a momentous era in which he became the first and only British-born Premier League rider to qualify as a regular member of the Grand Prix series between 2000 and 2003.

He initially signed for the Comets on the return of racing at Derwent Park in 1999 and along the way became the club's all-time record holder for both appearances and points, overtaking Lou Sansom's figures even though he missed 2006 and much of 2007 through injury.

In all he rode in 361 matches for the Cumbrian club, scoring 4,598.5 points, including 56 full and paid maximums.

His first match for Workington was at Stoke on April 4, 1999, and his final official appearance was helping them win the Young Shield at Berwick on Saturday, October 29, 2008.

Premier League Fours

Saturday, July 26

Semi Final 1

1 WORKINGTON 14
Charles Wright 3, Kauko Nieminen 5, Carl Stonehewer 3, Joe Haines 3, John Branney [R].

2 SOMERSET 13
Jason Doyle 6, Jordan Frampton 5, Stephan Katt 0, Brent Werner 2.

3 SHEFFIELD 11
André Compton 3, Ricky Ashworth 4, Ben Wilson 2, Joel Parsons 2, Paul Cooper [R].

4 EDINBURGH 10
Andrew Tully 1, Matthew Wethers 3, Ryan Fisher 4, Thomas Jonasson 2, Aaron Summers [R].

Semi Final 2

1 KING'S LYNN 16
Kevin Doolan 5, **Tomas Topinka 6**, Shaun Tacey 4, Simon Lambert 1, John Oliver [R].

1 SCUNTHORPE 16
Magnus Karlsson 3, Richard Hall 4, Carl Wilkinson 4, Viktor Bergström 5.

3 NEWCASTLE 10
George Stancl 4, Richard Juul 2, Jason King 3, Sean Stoddart 1.

4 READING 6
Mark Lemon 3, Tom Madsen 0, Chris Mills 1, Tomas Suchanek 2, Jamie Smith [R].

Final

1 WORKINGTON 20+3
Charles Wright 5, Kauko Nieminen 6+3, Carl Stonehewer 6, Joe Haines 3, John Branney [R].

2 KING'S LYNN 20+2
Kevin Doolan 7, Tomas Topinka 9+2, Shaun Tacey 2, Simon Lambert 2, John Oliver [R].

3 SOMERSET 19
Jason Doyle 7, Jordan Frampton 4, Stephan Katt 5, Brent Werner 3.

4 SCUNTHORPE 13
Magnus Karlsson 0, Richard Hall 5, Carl Wilkinson 5, Viktor Bergström 3.

See Premier League for race-by-race details and Roll of Honour.

2009 Squad

Kevin **DOOLAN** (10.32), Adrian **RYMEL** (9.73), André **COMPTON** (8.48), Charles **WRIGHT** (4.29), John **BRANNEY** (3.68), Richard **LAWSON** (3.00), Luke **PRIEST** (3.00).

WORKINGTON

Rider	*M*	*R*	*Pts*	*BP*	*TPts*	*Ave*	*F*	*P*	*TR*	*TPts*	*TS*	*TSPts*
Daniel NERMARK	26	125	333	11	344	11.01	7	4	5	15	0	0
Kauko NIEMINEN	**42**	**205**	**475**	**21**	**496**	**9.68**	**3**	**3**	**3**	**7**	**2**	**2**
Carl STONEHEWER	47	213	395.5	29	424.5	7.97	2	0	0	0	1	2
Joe HAINES	**47**	**223**	**310**	**37**	**347**	**6.22**	**0**	**0**	**0**	**0**	**0**	**0**
Charles WRIGHT	50	222	244	40	284	5.12	0	0	0	0	0	0
Tomi REIMA	**21**	**93**	**96**	**21**	**117**	**5.03**	**0**	**0**	**0**	**0**	**0**	**0**
John BRANNEY	50	218	215	47	262	4.81	0	0	0	0	0	0
Barry BURCHATT	**4**	**15**	**11**	**3**	**14**	**3.73**	**0**	**0**	**0**	**0**	**0**	**0**
Scott SMITH	11	39	26	6	32	3.28	0	0	0	0	0	0
Guests	***30***	***146***	***282***	***19***	***301***	***8.25***	***1***	***2***	***3***	***6***	***2***	***2***

For Kauko NIEMINEN see Lakeside; for Joe HAINES see Boston; for John BRANNEY see Buxton; for Barry BURCHATT see Sittingbourne; for Scott SMITH see Berwick.

Photo: DEREK FRY

WORKINGTON 2008: James Wright, Joe Haines, Kauko Nieminen, Daniel Nermark, John Branney, Scott Smith and Carl Stonehewer

BIRMINGHAM (from page 152)

Individual

ALAN HUNT MEMORIAL TROPHY

Sunday, March 16

David Howe 15, Daniel King 12+3, Steve Johnston 12+2, Jason Lyons 11, Ulrich Østergaard 11, Kauko Nieminen 10, Kyle Legault 10, Phil Morris 8, Brent Werner 7, Adam Roynon 6, Lubos Tomicek 6, Ricky Ashworth 5, Jamie Birkinshaw 3, Lee Smart 2, Shawn McConnell 1, Jack Hargreaves 1, Jack Roberts [R] 0, Adam Lowe [R], did not ride.

Roll of Honour

1963 .... Ivor BROWN
1964 .... Ivan MAUGER
1965 .... Nigel BOOCOCK
1966 .... Barry BRIGGS
1968 .... Hasse HOLMKVIST
1969 .... Bernt PERSSON
1970 .... Ole OLSEN
1971 .... Ole OLSEN
1972 .... Peter JARMAN
2007 .... André COMPTON
2008 .... David HOWE

■ *Meeting was held at Cradley Heath from 1963 until 1972. In 1967 it was combined with the Ivor Hughes Memorial Trophy but was never staged, being rained off twice.*

SKY SPORTS ELITE LEAGUE

SKY SPORTS covered a total of 45 live matches throughout 2008, headlined by the Grand Prix series which ended in such bizarre fashion.

Sky actually had their team in place for all 12 rounds, including the abandoned German GP at Gelsenkirchen.

The first of the season's transmissions went out on Monday, March 31, when armchair viewers witnessed the previous season's treble winners Coventry beaten at home by Eastbourne.

A total of 30 domestic meetings – 27 Elite League and three Premier League – were screened live throughout the year and the calendar produced only eight away wins.

Changes to the format saw Jonathan Green leave for new pastures early in the season and subsequently the pits studio was given a make-over with Nigel Pearson and former Great Britain skipper Kelvin Tatum (pictured together) fronting the show.

There was also a change of personel in the pits: Sarra Rees replacing Sophie Blake on a regular basis after her brief stint in 2007.

GRAND PRIX

Saturday, April 26: **Slovenian GP.**
Saturday, May 10: **European GP.**
Saturday, May 24: **Swedish GP.**
Saturday, June 14: **Danish GP.**
Saturday, June 28: **British GP.**
Saturday, August 2: **Czech Republic GP.**
Saturday, August 16: **Scandinavian GP.**
Saturday, August 30: **Latvian GP.**
Saturday, September 13: **Polish GP.**
Saturday, September 27: **Italian GP.**
Saturday, October 11: **German GP.**
Saturday, October 18: **Final Grand Prix.**

SPEEDWAY WORLD CUP

Saturday, July 12: **Event 1 – Australia v Russia v Hungary v Poland.**
Monday, July 14: **Event 2 – Great Britain v Sweden v Czech Republic v Denmark.**
Thursday, July 17: **Race-off – Great Britain v Sweden v Poland v Russia.**
Saturday, July 19: **FINAL – Denmark v Australia v Sweden v Poland.**

ELITE LEAGUE

Monday, March 31: **Coventry v Eastbourne.**
Monday, April 7: **Belle Vue v Poole.**
Tuesday, April 8: **Peterborough v Eastbourne.**
Monday, April 14: **Ipswich v Swindon.**
Monday, April 21: **Wolverhampton v Eastbourne.**
Monday, April 28: **Swindon v Eastbourne.**
Monday, May 12: **Eastbourne v Poole.**
Monday, May 19: **Wolverhampton v Ipswich.**
Monday, June 2: **Wolverhampton v Swindon.**
Monday, June 9: **Ipswich v Poole.**
Monday, June 16: **Eastbourne v Lakeside.**
Monday, June 23: **Belle Vue v Ipswich**
Monday, June 30: **Lakeside v Coventry.**
Monday, July 7: **Belle Vue v Coventry**
Monday, July 21: **Ipswich v Swindon.**
Monday, July 28: **Coventry v Peterborough.**
Monday, August 4: **Lakeside v Eastbourne.**
Monday, August 18: **Poole v Belle Vue.**
Monday, August 25: **Coventry v Ipswich.**
Monday, September 1: **Peterborough v Swindon.**
Monday, September 8: **Peterborough v Poole.**
Monday, September 15: **Wolverhampton v Ipswich.**
Monday, September 22: **Coventry v Swindon.**
Monday, September 29: **Lakeside v Swindon, play-off, semi-final.**
Monday: September 29: **Poole v Ipswich, play-off, semi-final.**
Monday, October 6: **Lakeside v Poole, Grand Final, first leg.**
Monday, October 13: **Poole v Lakeside, Grand Final, second leg.**

PREMIER LEAGUE

Tuesday, Tuesday, May 6: **Isle of Wight v Reading.**
Monday, May 27: **Reading v Rye House.**
Monday, August 11: **Edinburgh v Workington.**

2009 FIXTURES

March

Sunday 15
Newport: Prince of Wales Trophy
Rye House v Birmingham (PT)
Sheffield: Ozchem Classic
Wednesday 18
Birmingham: Alan Hunt Memorial
Friday 20
Scunthorpe v Sheffield (Challenge)
King's Lynn: Tom Madsen Testimonial
Saturday 21
Berwick v Newcastle (Tweed-Tyne Trophy)
Rye House v Newport (PT)
Stoke v Birmingham (Challenge)
Sunday 22
Glasgow v Belle Vue (Challenge)
Newcastle v Berwick (Tweed-Tyne Trophy)
Newport v Somerset (Severn Bridge Trophy)
Sheffield v Scunthorpe (Challenge)
Wednesday 25
Birmingham v Rye House (PT)
King's Lynn v Edinburgh (Challenge)
Thursday 26
Redcar v Newcastle (Challenge)
Friday 27
Edinburgh v Glasgow (Spring Trophy)
Scunthorpe v Stoke (PT)
Somerset v Newport (Severn Bridge Trophy)
Saturday 28
Berwick v Sheffield (PT)
Rye House v Somerset (PT)
Stoke v King's Lynn (PT)
Workington v Newcastle (PT)
Sunday 29
Glasgow v Edinburgh (Spring Trophy)
Newcastle v Redcar (Challenge)
Newport v Rye House (PT)
Sheffield: Ben Fund Bonanza

April

Wednesday 1
Birmingham v Newport (PT)
King's Lynn v Rye House (PT)
Thursday 2
Redcar v Berwick (PT)
Sheffield v Edinburgh (PT)
Friday 3
Edinburgh v Sheffield (PT)
Scunthorpe v Birmingham (PT)
Somerset v Rye House (PT)
Saturday 4
Berwick v Edinburgh (PT)
Rye House v King's Lynn (PT)
Stoke v Somerset (PT)
Workington v Glasgow (PT)
Sunday 5
Glasgow v Redcar (PT)
Newcastle v Sheffield (PT)
Newport v Scunthorpe (PT)
Wednesday 8
King's Lynn v Scunthorpe (PT)
Thursday 9
Sheffield v Redcar (PT)
Friday 10
Birmingham v Stoke (PT)
Edinburgh v Newcastle (PT)
Redcar v Sheffield (PT)
Somerset v Scunthorpe (PT)
Saturday 11
Berwick v Workington (PT)
Stoke v Rye House (PT)
Sunday 12
Glasgow v Newcastle (PT)
Newport v King's Lynn (PT)
Monday 13
Newcastle v Glasgow (PT)
Rye House v Stoke (PT)
Scunthorpe v Somerset (PT)
Workington v Berwick (PT)
Wednesday 15
Birmingham v Scunthorpe (PT)
King's Lynn v Somerset (PT)
Thursday 16
Redcar v Workington (PT)
Sheffield v Newcastle (PT)
Friday 17
Edinburgh v Workington (PT)
Scunthorpe v Rye House (PT)
Somerset v Birmingham (PT)
Saturday 18
Berwick: Meldrum's Milestone (Testimonial)
Rye House v Scunthorpe (PT)
Stoke v Birmingham (PT)
Workington v Redcar (PT)
Sunday 19
Glasgow v Workington (PT)
Newcastle v Berwick (PT)
Newport v Stoke (PT)
Wednesday 22
Birmingham v Somerset (PT)
King's Lynn v Newport (PT)
Thursday 23
Redcar v Glasgow (PT)
Sheffield v Workington (PT)
Friday 24
Edinburgh v Berwick (PT)
Scunthorpe v King's Lynn (PT)
Somerset v Stoke (PT)
Saturday 25
Berwick v Glasgow (PT)
Stoke v Scunthorpe (PT)
Workington v Edinburgh (PT)
Sunday 26
Glasgow v Berwick (PT)
Newcastle v Edinburgh (PT)
Newport v Birmingham (PT)
Tuesday 28
Somerset v King's Lynn
Wednesday 29
Birmingham v Rye House (KO Cup)
King's Lynn v Stoke (PT)
Thursday 30
Redcar v Edinburgh (PT)
Sheffield v Glasgow (PT)

May

Friday 1
Edinburgh v Redcar (PT)
Scunthorpe: Open
Somerset v King's Lynn (PT)
Saturday 2
Berwick v Newcastle (PT)
Stoke v Workington
Sunday 3
Birmingham v King's Lynn (PT)
Glasgow v Sheffield (PT)
Newcastle v Workington (PT)
Newport v Somerset (PT)
Monday 4
Rye House v Berwick
Scunthorpe v Newport (PT)
Workington v Stoke

Wednesday 6
Berwick v Stoke (KO Cup)
King's Lynn v Birmingham (PT)
1 ***Thursday 7***
Redcar v Stoke
Sheffield v Edinburgh (KO Cup)
Friday 8
Edinburgh v Sheffield (KO Cup)
Scunthorpe v Newcastle (KO Cup)
Somerset v Glasgow (KO Cup)
Saturday 9
Rye House v Birmingham (KO Cup)
Stoke v Berwick (KO Cup)
Workington v Sheffield (PT)
Sunday 10
Glasgow v Somerset (KO Cup)
Newcastle v Scunthorpe (KO Cup)
Newport: Open
Wednesday 13
Birmingham: Reserved
King's Lynn: Open
Thursday 14
Redcar v Newport (KO Cup)
Sheffield v Berwick (PT)
Friday 15
Edinburgh v Glasgow (PT)
Scunthorpe v Berwick
Somerset v King's Lynn (PT)
Saturday 16
Berwick v Redcar (PT)
Stoke v Newport (PT)
Workington: Open
Sunday 17
Glasgow v Edinburgh (PT)
Newcastle: 80th Anniversary meeting
Newport v Redcar (KO Cup)
Rye House: World Under-21 Championship qualifying round
Wednesday 20
Birmingham v Redcar (PT)
King's Lynn: Open
Thursday 21
Redcar v Newcastle (PT)
Sheffield: Open
Friday 22
Edinburgh v Scunthorpe
Somerset v Newport (PT)
Saturday 23
Berwick v Scunthorpe
Stoke v Newcastle
Workington v Rye House
Sunday 24 Birmingham v Sheffield
Glasgow v King's Lynn
Newcastle v Redcar (PT)
Newport v Workington
Monday 25
Rye House v Workington
Scunthorpe v Edinburgh
Wednesday 27
Birmingham: Reserved
King's Lynn v Redcar
Thursday 28
Redcar v King's Lynn
Sheffield: Open
Friday 29
Edinburgh v Stoke
Scunthorpe v Glasgow
Somerset v Berwick
Saturday 30
Berwick: Junior meeting
Rye House v Sheffield
Stoke v Somerset
Workington v Birmingham
Sunday 31
Glasgow v Workington
Newcastle v Birmingham
Newport v Berwick

June

Wednesday 3
Birmingham v Scunthorpe
King's Lynn v Sheffield
Somerset v Edinburgh
Thursday 4
Redcar v Glasgow
Sheffield v Edinburgh
Friday 5
Edinburgh v Rye House
Scunthorpe v Somerset
Saturday 6
Berwick v Rye House
Stoke v Redcar
Workington v Somerset
Sunday 7
Glasgow v Rye House
Newcastle v Somerset
Newport: Open
Wednesday 10
Birmingham v Somerset
King's Lynn v Workington
Thursday 11
Redcar v Newport
Sheffield v Birmingham
Friday 12
Edinburgh v Newcastle
Newport v Glasgow
Scunthorpe v Birmingham
Somerset v Birmingham or Rye House (KO Cup)
Saturday 13
Berwick v Sheffield
Rye House v Glasgow or Somerset (KO Cup)
Stoke v Scunthorpe
Workington v Newport
Sunday 14
Glasgow v Newport
Newcastle v King's Lynn
Wednesday 17
Birmingham v Glasgow or Somerset (KO Cup)
King's Lynn v Berwick or Stoke (KO Cup)
Thursday 18
Redcar v Scunthorpe or Newcastle (KO Cup)
Sheffield v Workington (KO Cup)
Friday 19
Edinburgh v Workington (KO Cup)
Scunthorpe v Newport or Redcar (KO Cup)
Somerset v Newcastle
Saturday 20
Berwick v King's Lynn (KO Cup)
Rye House v Newcastle
Stoke v King's Lynn (KO Cup)
Workington v Sheffield or Edinburgh
Sunday 21
Glasgow v Birmingham or Rye House (KO Cup)
Newcastle v Newport or Redcar (KO Cup)
Newport v Scunthorpe or Newcastle (KO Cup)
Wednesday 24
Birmingham v Newcastle
King's Lynn: Open
Thursday 25
Redcar v Birmingham
Sheffield v Scunthorpe
Friday 26
Somerset: Premier League Pairs Final
Sunday 28
Newcastle: Open
Newport: Welsh Open Championship
Rye House v Glasgow
Stoke v Berwick

July

Wednesday 1
Birmingham v Stoke (Challenge)
King's Lynn v Rye House
Thursday 2
Redcar: Open
Sheffield v King's Lynn
Friday 3
Edinburgh v Newport
Scunthorpe v Workington
Somerset v Sheffield
Saturday 4
Berwick v Newport
Rye House v Edinburgh
Stoke v Birmingham
Workington v Glasgow
Sunday 5
Glasgow v Stoke
Newcastle v Sheffield
Newport v Rye House
Wednesday 8
Birmingham v Berwick
King's Lynn v Newcastle
Thursday 9
Redcar v Workington
Sheffield v Berwick
Friday 10
Edinburgh v King's Lynn
Scunthorpe v Stoke
Somerset v Glasgow
Saturday 11
Berwick v Newcastle
Stoke v Glasgow
Workington v King's Lynn
Sunday 12
Glasgow v Sheffield
Newcastle v Berwick
Newport v Edinburgh
Wednesday 15
Birmingham v Workington
King's Lynn v Scunthorpe
Thursday 16
Redcar v Newcastle
Sheffield v Newport
Friday 17
Edinburgh v Somerset
Scunthorpe v Newport
Saturday 18
Berwick v Somerset
Rye House v Scunthorpe
Stoke v Edinburgh
Workington v Sheffield
Sunday 19
Glasgow v Somerset
Newcastle v Redcar
Newport v Birmingham
Wednesday 22
Birmingham v Glasgow
King's Lynn v Stoke
Thursday 23
Redcar v Berwick
Sheffield v Newcastle
Friday 24
Edinburgh v Redcar
Scunthorpe v King's Lynn
Somerset v Stoke
Saturday 25
Workington: Premier League Four Team Final
Sunday 26
Glasgow v Scunthorpe
Newcastle v Workington
Newport v Sheffield
Wednesday 29
Birmingham v Edinburgh
King's Lynn v Somerset
Thursday 30
Redcar v Somerset
Sheffield v Rye House
Friday 31
Edinburgh: Scottish Open
Scunthorpe v Redcar
Somerset v Birmingham

August

Saturday 1
Berwick v Redcar
Rye House v Birmingham
Stoke v Sheffield
Workington v Scunthorpe
Sunday 2
Glasgow: Reserved (KO Cup)
Newcastle v Scunthorpe
Newport v King's Lynn
Wednesday 5
Birmingham v Newport
King's Lynn: Reserved (KO Cup)
Thursday 6
Redcar: Open
Sheffield v Stoke
Friday 7
Edinburgh v Sheffield
Scunthorpe v Newcastle
Somerset v Redcar
Saturday 8
Berwick v Edinburgh
Rye House v King's Lynn
Stoke: Reserved (KO Cup)
Workington: Reserved (KO Cup)
Sunday 9
Glasgow v Edinburgh
Newcastle: Reserved (KO Cup)
Newport: Reserved (KO Cup)
Wednesday 12
Birmingham: Reserved (KO Cup)
King's Lynn v Edinburgh
Thursday 13
Redcar v Edinburgh
Sheffield: Reserved (KO Cup)
Friday 14
Edinburgh: Reserved (KO Cup)
Scunthorpe v Rye House
Somerset: Reserved (KO Cup)
Saturday 15
Berwick: Reserved (KO Cup)
Rye House v Redcar
Stoke v King's Lynn
Workington v Newcastle
Sunday 16
Glasgow: Ashfield Classic
Newcastle v Stoke
Newport v Redcar
Wednesday 19
Birmingham v Rye House
King's Lynn v Glasgow
Thursday 20
Redcar: Reserved (KO Cup)
Sheffield v Glasgow
Friday 21
Edinburgh v Birmingham
Scunthorpe: Reserved (KO Cup)
Somerset v Workington
Saturday 22
Berwick v Birmingham
Rye House v Somerset
Stoke v Newport

Workington v Edinburgh
Sunday 23
Glasgow v Birmingham
Newcastle v Edinburgh
Newport v Scunthorpe
Wednesday 26
Birmingham v Stoke
King's Lynn v Berwick
Thursday 27
Redcar v Scunthorpe
Sheffield v Workington
Friday 28
Edinburgh v Glasgow
Scunthorpe: Open
Somerset v Rye House
Saturday 29
Berwick v Workington
Stoke v Rye House
Sunday 30
Birmingham v King's Lynn
Glasgow v Newcastle
Newport v Somerset
Monday 31
Newcastle v Glasgow
Rye House v Stoke
Scunthorpe v Sheffield
Workington v Berwick

September

Wednesday 2
King's Lynn v Birmingham
Thursday 3
Sheffield v Redcar
Friday 4
Edinburgh v Workington
Redcar v Sheffield
Scunthorpe: Open
Somerset v Newport
Saturday 5
Berwick v King's Lynn
Rye House: Open
Stoke: Open
Workington: Open
Sunday 6
Glasgow v Berwick
Newcastle v Rye House
Newport v Stoke
Wednesday 9
King's Lynn v Newport
Thursday 10
Redcar v Rye House
Sheffield v Somerset
Friday 11
Edinburgh: Open
Scunthorpe: Open
Somerset v King's Lynn
Saturday 12
Berwick v Stoke
Rye House v Newport
Stoke: Open
Workington v Redcar
Sunday 13
Glasgow v Redcar
Newcastle: Open
Newport: Open
Wednesday 16
Birmingham: Open
King's Lynn: Open
Thursday 17
Redcar: Open
Sheffield: Open
Friday 18
Edinburgh v Berwick
Somerset v Scunthorpe
Saturday 19
Berwick v Glasgow
Rye House: Open
Stoke: Open
Workington: Open
Sunday 20
Glasgow v Edinburgh (Scottish Cup)
Newcastle: Open
Newport: Open
Wednesday 23
Birmingham v Buxton (Challenge)
King's Lynn: Open
Thursday 24
Redcar: Open
Sheffield: Open
Friday 25
Edinburgh v Glasgow (Scottish Cup)
Scunthorpe: Open
Somerset: Open
Saturday 26
Rye House: National League Riders' Championship
Stoke: Open
Workington: Open
Sunday 27
Sheffield: Premier League Riders' Championship
Wednesday 30
Birmingham: Second City Trophy
King's Lynn: Open

October

Friday 30
Edinburgh: Fireworks Farewell
Scunthorpe: Halloween Trophy
Saturday 31
Rye House: Ace of Herts (Individual)

■ *Fixtures subject to alteration and do not take into account dates for the end of season play-offs and Young Shield competition. All fixtures should be confirmed via the club's website, local press or Speedway Star before undertaking any journeys. KO Cup = Knock Out Cup.*

MAJOR EVENTS

PREMIER LEAGUE RIDERS' FINAL
Sheffield, Sunday, September 27

PREMIER LEAGUE PAIRS' FINAL
Somerset, Friday, June 26

PREMIER LEAGUE FOUR TEAM FINAL
Workington, Saturday, July 25

KNOCK OUT CUP
First round
Berwick v Stoke
Birmingham v Rye House
Edinburgh v Sheffield
Redcar v Newport
Scunthorpe v Newcastle
Somerset v Glasgow
Quarter Final
Birmingham/Rye House v Somerset/Glasgow
Berwick/Stoke v King's Lynn
Edinburgh/Sheffield v Workington
Newcastle/Scunthorpe v Redcar/Newport

CONFERENCE LEAGUE

	M	Home W	Home D	Home L	Away W	Away D	Away L	PtsF	PtsA	Pts
1 PLYMOUTH	14	7	0	0	2	0	5	709	569	20
2 BOSTON	14	6	1	0	2	0	5	713	565	19
3 REDCAR	14	7	0	0	1	1	5	657	614	18
4 WEYMOUTH	14	7	0	0	1	0	6	688	588	17
5 SCUNTHORPE	14	7	0	0	1	0	6	637	629	17
6 BUXTON	14	6	0	1	1	0	6	605	669	15
7 RYE HOUSE	14	6	0	1	0	0	7	614	663	12
8 SITTINGBOURNE	14	1	0	6	0	0	7	472	798	2

The top four teams went into the title play-offs.

Semi Finals

PLYMOUTH 46 **WEYMOUTH 44**
WEYMOUTH 56 PLYMOUTH 38
WEYMOUTH win 100-84 on aggregate.

REDCAR 45 **BOSTON 48**
BOSTON 44 REDCAR 46
BOSTON win 92-91 on aggregate.

FINAL

WEYMOUTH 67 BOSTON 23

BOSTON 45 **WEYMOUTH 46**

WEYMOUTH win 113-68 on aggregate and are 2008 Conference League champions.

WEYMOUTH carved their own huge slice of history with the first league title in their chequered history.

And they also became the first team to be crowned champions after finishing FOURTH in the table!

Curiously when they took on Plymouth in the second leg of the play-off semi-final the Wildcats were going into action on the back of four successive defeats but they certainly didn't have any inferiority complex.

They were bouyed by a fighting first leg display that ranks among their finest: losing by only two points in Devon.

While Plymouth had pushed them close on earlier visits, this time the home side were rampant, rattling up nearly 60 points to go through.

Having knocked out the team that had finished top of the pile during the regular season, they were in no mood to let the ultimate prize slip out of their grasp.

They simply destroyed Boston's hopes in a one-sided first leg, running up their biggest total of the season.

Any hope the Staffsmart Barracudas had of bowing out of league racing with the league crown disappeared that remarkable night in Dorset.

The absence of both Darcy Ward – back home in Australia – and Joe Haines (needed by Premier League side Workington the following night for their Young Shield Final at long-away Berwick) was a bitter double blow for the Cudas.

Karl Mason becomes the first Weymouth captain to get his hands on a league championship trophy after being presented with it byConference League co-ordinator Peter Morrish after the second leg of the play-off Grand Final at Boston

Their only hope was to hold the Wildcats to a recoverable margin but they had no answer to the powerful Lee Smart-Matthew Wright pairing who totalled 26, paid 30, between them.

The triumphant Wildcats – – team manager Jem Dicken, Jay Herne, Matthew Wright, Andrew Bargh, Lee Smart and club chairman Phil Bartlett Kneeling: Karl Mason, Brendan Johnson, Tim Webster and, holding the photo of Kyle Newman, Jon Armstrong

Skipper Simon Lambert tried to stem the flow but was handicapped by a broken bone in his wrist which should have sidelined him until the end of the season.

The return, scheduled for 24 hours later, was called off (much to Weymouth's consternation) and re-arranged for the following Wednesday, by which time Kyle Newman had already flown out to spend a few months racing in Australia.

But he wasn't forgotten on the night – his teammates arriving with a huge poster portrait which was constantly gazing over them as they made sure of that first ever league championship.

And for Plymouth, who would have been champions prior to 2006, the consolation of two other trophies.

Roll of Honour

1947 .... EASTBOURNE
1948 .... EXETER
1949 .... STOKE
1950 .... OXFORD
1951 .... POOLE
1952 .... RAYLEIGH
1953 .... †RAYLEIGH
1994 .... BERWICK
1995 .... BERWICK
1996 .... LINLITHGOW
1997 .... PETERBOROUGH
1998 .... ST. AUSTELL
1999 .... NEWPORT
2000 .... SHEFFIELD
2001 .... SHEFFIELD
2002 .... PETERBOROUGH
2003 .... MILDENHALL
2004 .... MILDENHALL
2005 .... OXFORD
2006 .... SCUNTHORPE
2007 .... SCUNTHORPE
2008 .... WEYMOUTH

Since 2006 the league championship has been determined by play-offs.
†In 1953 Exeter finished top of the table at the end of the season but Rayleigh protested over a refereeing ruling that allowed the Falcons to change their line-up for a crucial match at the County Ground. The Speedway Control Board upheld the protest and declared the match null and void, handing the title to Rayleigh.
From 1954 until 1957 a virtual amateur weekend Southern Area League was staged involving a maximum of six tracks.

Roll of Honour

1954 .... RYE HOUSE
1955 .... RYE HOUSE
1956 .... RYE HOUSE
1957 .... RAYLEIGH ROVERS

Heat 11, Knock Out Cup Final with Adam Allott, Seemond Stephens, Chris Widman and Kyle Hughes at the tapes

KNOCK OUT CUP

PLYMOUTH had waited more than 50 years to win a major trophy – and finally ended up with two!

Having already beaten Boston in the final of the truncated Conference Trophy, the Devils completed the big event double over their East Anglian rivals.

While their success in the Trophy had been built on the foundations of a convincing home win in the first leg, the ties were reversed.

And Boston were well pleased with a late flourish that saw them pull away in the final three races at Saddlebow Road.

Devils' mini-bus of travellers were almost breaking open the champagne at the end of Heat 12 when only one point separated the two sides.

But successive 5-1s and then a last race 4-2 saw Boston travel down to the deepest West with a precious 11 point lead, something that had seemed impossible a few races earlier.

They needed a bright, brisk start in the second leg – but had to send a makeshift side the 650 miles from their Norfolk Base to Devon.

Simon Lambert and Joe Haines were both missing – and gone was the spark of hope.

Quarter Final

BOSTON 51 REDCAR 43
REDCAR 45 **BOSTON 45**
BOSTON win 96-88 on aggregate.

RYE HOUSE 59 SITTINGBOURNE 33
SITTINGBOURNE 42 **RYE HOUSE 47**
RYE HOUSE win 106-75 on aggregate.

SCUNTHORPE 52 BUXTON 41
BUXTON 50 **SCUNTHORPE 41**
SCUNTHORPE win 93-91 on aggregate.

WEYMOUTH 47 **PLYMOUTH 45**
PLYMOUTH 51 WEYMOUTH 42
PLYMOUTH win 96-89 on aggregate.

Semi Final

BOSTON 56 SCUNTHORPE 35
SCUNTHORPE 45 **BOSTON 48**
BOSTON win 104-80 on aggregate.

PLYMOUTH 57 RYE HOUSE 36
RYE HOUSE 56 **PLYMOUTH 37**
PLYMOUTH win 94-92 on aggregate.

FINAL

BOSTON 50 **PLYMOUTH 39**
PLYMOUTH 59 BOSTON 33
PLYMOUTH win 98-83 on aggregate.

The first stand-alone Knock Out Cup competition for second tier clubs wasn't introduced until the launch of the Conference League in 1995.

Between 1948 and 1952 the National Trophy was open to teams from all leagues and each Division had its own Final before the winners went through to the next stage so the five teams who won their Divisional Finals can claim to have been that season's Cup winners.

Roll of Honour

1948 .... SOUTHAMPTON
1949 .... STOKE
1950 .... OXFORD
1951 .... EXETER
1952 .... PLYMOUTH
1995 .... BERWICK
1996 .... LINLITHGOW
1998 .... ST. AUSTELL
1999 .... ST. AUSTELL
2000 .... BOSTON
2001 .... SOMERSET
2002 .... BUXTON
2003 .... MILDENHALL
2004 .... MILDENHALL
2005 .... WEYMOUTH
2006 .... SCUNTHORPE
2007 .... SCUNTHORPE
2008 .... PLYMOUTH

CONFERENCE TROPHY

ONLY four teams entered the Conference Trophy – but at least it let Plymouth win their first major trophy in more than half a century.

The Devils last put out the bunting after they were crowned 1952 Southern League National Trophy winners after beating Aldershot, Exeter and Rayleigh.

This time – 56 years later – they faced only two opponents, Weymouth and Boston.

Defending a 22 point lead from the home leg the Devils put in a stunning performance at Radipole Lane and built up such a huge first leg lead in the Final that their visit to Norfolk was relatively carefree despite a heavy defeat.

Reserve Paul Starke had been their star at home, recording a career best 19, paid 21, in seven reserve rides to maintain his unbeaten record in the two ties at the St. Bonface's Arena.

Ironically, the return when Plymouth made sure of their place in Conference League history was the only meeting that he missed all season, ruled out withy a leg injury.

After losing out to Scunthorpe in both the Knock Out Cup and Conference Trophy in 2007 it was a welcome victory for the Devon outfit in only their third season back in action.

A delighted Devils' boss Mike Bowden beamed: "We have been so near yet so far – but the side we have now is capable of beating any team in the country over two legs."

Semi Final

BOSTON 60 BUXTON 34
BUXTON 49 **BOSTON 41**
BOSTON win 101-83 on aggregate.

PLYMOUTH 57 WEYMOUTH 35
WEYMOUTH 46 **PLYMOUTH 45**
PLYMOUTH win 102-81 on aggregate.

FINAL

PLYMOUTH 63 BOSTON 28
BOSTON 60 **PLYMOUTH 31**

PLYMOUTH *win 94-88 on aggregate.*

Roll of Honour

2000 .... MILDENHALL
2001 .... SOMERSET
2002 .... MILDENHALL
2003 .... BOSTON
2004 .... MILDENHALL
2005 .... ARMADALE
2006 .... SCUNTHORPE
2007 .... SCUNTHORPE
2008 .... PLYMOUTH

CONFERENCE SHIELD

A one-season league competition involving six Conference League tracks, meeting each other once home and away.

Roll of Honour

2006 .... SCUNTHORPE

2009...2009...2009...2009

THE Conference League is no more as the third tier of competition ungoes yet another re-branding.

The competition was originally launched in 1994 and since then has undergone a series of name changes and, from 2009, will be known as the National League, it's fourth different title in 15 seasons.

- BRITISH ACADEMY LEAGUE – 1994-1995.
- CONFERENCE LEAGUE – 1996, 1998-2008.
- AMATEUR LEAGUE – 1997

And there have been fundamental changes in the way the league will operate with an open door policy now extended to Commonwealth riders.

British Speedway Promoters' Association Management Committee member Dave Pavitt was charged with drawing up the new regulations and his initial target was to have at least ten teams competing.

With Boston having announced they would not be continuing their nomadic life, operating out of King's Lynn's Norfolk Arena, Sittingbourne and Redcar indicating they would not be entering the new set-up there will be a drastic new-look to the fixture lists.

Premier League Isle of Wight, with Pavitt at the helm, have dropped down to become founder members of the National League and there's be a name totally new to speedway with Poole running a junior side under the name Bournemouth Buccaneers.

Teams entering the new National League for 2009 are:

BOURNEMOUTH Buccaneers
BUXTON Hitmen
ISLE OF WIGHT Islanders
KING'S LYNN Barracudas
MILDENHALL Fen Tigers
NEWPORT Hornets
PLYMOUTH Devils
RYE HOUSE Cobras
SCUNTHORPE Saints
WEYMOUTH Wildcats

Team will meet home and away with the top four qualifying for the play-offs.

Buxton, Isle of Wight, Mildenhall, Plymouth and Weymouth will face each other home and away in the Conference Trophy.

The Knock Out Cup draw is

Round 1: Bournemouth v Newport, King's Lynn v Mildenhall.

Round 2: Buxton v Rye House, Plymouth v Isle of Wight, Bournemouth or Newport v Weymouth, King's Lynn or Mildenhall v Scunthorpe.

A big attraction will be a five match Under 21 series between Great Britain and Australasia at Weymouth (July 10), King's Lynn (July 11), Isle of Wight ((July 14), Plymouth (July 17) and Buxton (July 19).

Major meeting dates are Riders' Championship Final (Rye House, Saturday, September 26), Pairs Championship (Isle of Wight, Tuesday, August 18) and the Bronze Helmet (Weymouth, Friday, July 24).

CONFERENCE LEAGUE RIDERS' FINAL

RYE HOUSE
Saturday, September 27

AUSTRALIAN Darcy Ward probably spent his winter wondering how he missed out on the Conference League Riders' crown.

He looked to have the title in one hand as he beat eventual champion Benji Compton in spectacular fashion, coming from the back after a slip at the start, and followed that with two more wins.

But the championship slipped from his grasp in a fateful Heat 14 when he fell while chasing race leader Jay Herne.

Having also come from fourth to first in his second ride he was more than capable of overhauling his fellow Commonwealth racer but it was not to be.

And the unsung Compton, who actually made his Conference League debut for Newcastle in 2002, capitalised on Ward's misfortune.

He had to do what his rival couldn't: pass Herne and he did it cleanly in his last ride to avoid the trauma of a race-off against runner-up Byron Bekker.

Said a delighted Compton: "You know when your mind is set on something so far you can actually do it. And that's what I did!

"It's a really good feeling to have finally won something."

	1	2	3	4	5	Tot	RO
1 Benji COMPTON	**2**	**3**	**3**	**3**	**3**	**14**	
2 Byron BEKKER	1	3	3	3	3	13	
3 Darcy WARD	3	3	3	FX	3	12	3
4 Daniel HALSEY	0	3	3	3	3	12	2
5 Jay HERNE	3	2	2	3	2	12	1
6 Ben TAYLOR	3	2	1	2	1	9	
7 Rob SMITH	FX	2	2	2	1	7	
8 Gareth ISHERWOOD	2	0	2	2	1	7	
9 Kyle HUGHES	3	1	2	FX		6	
10 Dean FELTON	1	1	1	1	2	6	
11 Gary COTTHAM [R]	0	1	2	2		5	
12 Simon LAMBERT	2	1	0	1	0	4	
13 Tom BROWN	1	2	FX			3	
14 Harland COOK [R]	1	1	0	1		3	
15 Scott RICHARDSON	F	FX	0	2	FX	2	
16 Richard LAWSON	2	FX				2	
17 Aaron BASEBY	F	1	0	N2		1	
18 Kyle NEWMAN	FX	0	1	0	0	1	

Roll of Honour

1994 .... Andy HOWE (Cleveland)
1995 .... Kevin LITTLE (Berwick)
1996 .... Mike HAMPSON (Buxton)
1997 .... Jon ARMSTRONG (Buxton)
1998 .... Steve BISHOP (St. Austell)
1999 .... Jonathan SWALES (Linlithgow)
2000 .... Scott PEGLER (Newport)
2001 .... David MASON (Rye House)
2002 .... Jamie BIRKINSHAW (Boston)
2003 .... Barrie EVANS (Rye House)
2004 .... James WRIGHT (Buxton)
2005 .... Steve BOXALL (Rye House)
2006 .... Adam ROYNON (Rye House)
2007 .... Tai WOFFINDEN (Rye House)
2008 .... Benji COMPTON (Redcar)

CONFERENCE LEAGUE FOURS' FINAL

STOKE
Saturday, October 18

THERE was no mistaking the joy as Weymouth celebrated their unexpected victory.

And equally there was no disguising the rancour in the Redcar pits as the Cubs were robbed of a possible success by the incessant ticking of the clock.

Referee Chris Durno was forced to abandon the Final with two important races left because racing had reached the Loomer Road time curfew.

Redcar still had Adam McKinna and James Cockle – who had dropped only two points between them in their previous three races – and Weymouth were left with their youngest rider Brendan Johnson and Karl Mason to come.

Cubs boss Jason Pipe grumbled: "It's not the ideal situation and I feel we were robbed. It's not a nice way to lose out."

Conference League Co-ordinator Peter Morrish admitted: "To run 24 heats in two hours might have been ambitious and maybe we should have started at 7 pm but hindsight is a wonderful thing!"

A succession of tumbles – there were nine exclusions and seven re-runs – was mainly to blame for the delays.

FINAL

	1	2	3	4	Tot
1 WEYMOUTH 13					
Lee SMART	3	3			6
Jay HERNE	FX	3			3
Brendan JOHNSON	3				3
Karl MASON	1				1
2 REDCAR 12					
Scott JAMES	3	FX			3
Adam McKINNA	2				2
James COCKLE	3				3
Richard LAWSON	2	2			4
3 SITTINGBOURNE 7					
Mark BASEBY	2	2			4
Aaron BASEBY	0				0
Dean FELTON	2				2
Ricky SCARBORO	1	0			1
4 SCUNTHORPE 4					
Scott RICHARDSON	FX				0
Ben HOPWOOD	FX	1			1
Gary IRVING	1				1
Stuart PARNABY	1				1
Scott WHITTINGTON [TR]	1				1

SEMI FINAL 1

	1	2	3	4	Tot
REDCAR 19					
Scott JAMES	3	3			6
Adam McKINNA	3	3			6
James COCKLE	2	3			5
Richard LAWSON	FX	2			2
SITTINGBOURNE 12					
Mark BASEBY	3	FX			3
Aaron BASEBY	1	1			2
Dean FELTON	0	2			2
Ricky SCARBORO	3	2			5

PLYMOUTH 9			
Tom BROWN	2	R	2
Paul STARKE	1	3	4
Jaimie PICKARD	2	1	3
David GOUGH	0	0	0
BOSTON 7			
Adam LOWE	0	2	2
Darren ROLPH	1	1	2
Darren MALLETT	2	FX	2
Adam ALLOTT	1	0	1

SEMI FINAL 2

WEYMOUTH 15			
Lee SMART	3	3	6
Jay HERNE	FX	3	3
Brendan JOHNSON	1	1	2
Karl MASON	3	1	4
SCUNTHORPE 13			
Scott RICHARDSON	2	2	4
Ben HOPWOOD	2	3	5
Gary IRVING	FX	2	2
Stuart PARNABY	0	2	2
RYE HOUSE 12			
Rob SMITH	2	1	3
Gary COTTHAM	1	1	2
Richard FRANKLIN	1	3	4
Andrew ALDRIDGE	3	0	3
BUXTON 7			
Ben TAYLOR	2	0	2
Gareth ISHERWOOD	3	2	5
Paul BURNETT	0	0	0
Scott WHITTINGTON	0	0	0

Roll of Honour

2003 .... RYE HOUSE
2004 .... MILDENHALL
2005 .... WEYMOUTH
2006 .... STOKE
2007 .... SCUNTHORPE
2008 .... WEYMOUTH

CONFERENCE LEAGUE PAIRS' FINAL

WEYMOUTH
Saturday, May 31

HOME favourites Weymouth saw their hopes of the Conference League Pairs Championship driven out of the Wessex Stadium in the back of an ambulance.

Once Jon Armstrong was ruled out with a season-ending broken leg, the Wildcats had no hope of celeberating their staging of the major event.

Armstrtong had been unable to avoid his fallen teammate Jay Herne in Heat 7 and in the re-run the Aussie was ruled out leaving Weynouth without a score as track reserve Brendan Johnson's points didn't count.

Boston retained their title with a clever team riding stategy, allowing Cleveland's Aaron Summers – unbeaten in all five rides on his first visit to Radipole Lane – to take the chequered flag while they kept out Scott James' challenge .

1 BOSTON, 2 REDCAR, 3 SITTINGBOURNE, 4 SCUNTHORPE.

GROUP A

	1	2	3	4	Tot
REDCAR 18					
Scott JAMES	2	2	2		6
Aaron SUMMERS	4	4	4		12
SITTINGBOURNE 14					
Dean FELTON	R	3	0		3:1
Jerran HART	3	4	4		11
BUXTON 12					
Ben TAYLOR	0	3	2		5:1
Jack ROBERTS	4	FX	3		7
WEYMOUTH 9					
Jon ARMSTRONG	2	FN			2
Jay HERNE	3	FX	4		7
Brendan JOHNSON [TR]	–	*2*	*0*		*2*

GROUP B

	1	2	3	4	Tot
BOSTON 17					
Simon LAMBERT	R	2	3		5:1
James COCKLE	4	4	4		12
SCUNTHORPE 14					
Byron BEKKER	4	3	4		11
Jonathan BETHELL	3	R			3:1
Tim WEBSTER [TR]	–	–	*2*		*2*
PLYMOUTH 14					
Kyle HUGHES	3	4	3		10
Paul STARKE	2	2	FX		4:1
RYE HOUSE 7					
Gary COTTHAM	2	3	0		5
Terry DAY	FX	0	2		2

Semi Final 1: Redcar 7 (Aaron Summers 4, Scott James 3:1), Scunthorpe 2 (Tim Webster [TR] 2, Byron Bekker 0).

Semi Final 2: Boston 7 (James Cockle 4, Simon Lambert 3:1), Sittingbourne 2 (Jerran Hart 2, Dean Felton FX).

Consolation Final: *Awarded to Sittingbourne over Scunthorpe by ballot after neither team had riders to contest the race.*

Final: Boston 5 (James Cockle 3, Simon Lambert 2:1), Redcar 4 (Aaron Summers 4, Scott James 0).

Roll of Honour

2004 .... WIMBLEDON
2005 .... WIMBLEDON
2006 .... SCUNTHORPE
2007 .... BOSTON
2008 .... BOSTON

YOUTH DEVELOPMENT LEAGUE

Contested by Elite and Premier League clubs to encourage young riders and limited in age and experience. A total of 17 different clubs entered and were allowed to organise their own matches, against whoever they wished, with league positions being decided on a percentage basis.

Roll of Honour

1998 .... BERWICK

YOUTH DEVELOPMENT LEAGUE RIDERS' FINAL

Roll of Honour

1998 .... Simon STEAD (Peterborough)

Conference League

BOSTON

TRACK FILE

Track: Norfolk Arena, Saddlebow Road, King's Lynn, Norfolk, PE34 3AG.
Telephone: 01553 771111.
Hotline: 09066 555969.
Website: www.bostonspeedway.net
Track Length: 342 metres.
Track Record: 60 secs, Trevor Harding, June 15, 2003.
2008 Promoters: Dale Allitt, Michael Smith and Stephen Lambert.
Team Sponsors: Staffsmart.
Colours: Blue, red and silver.
Nickname: Barracudas.

HISTORY

First meeting: April 1, 2000, Boston v Mildenhall, Division Three challenge.
Leagues: Division Three, 2000-2008.
Meetings were also held at
● *Boston Sports Stadium, New Hammond Beck Road, Boston, Lincolnshire.*
First meeting: August 16, 1970, Boston v Peterborough, Inter Counties Challenge Cup.
Leagues: Division Two, 1970-1984, 1986-87.
■ *See also King's Lynn for further track details.*

HONOURS

Major honours: 6.
Division Two champions (1), 1973.
Division Two Knock Out Cup winners (1), 1973.
Division Two Pairs champions (1), 1977.
Division Three Knock Out Cup winners (1), 2000.
Division Three Trophy winners (1), 2003.
Division Three Pairs champions (3), 2007, 2008.

2008 REVIEW

SECOND place can be the most frustrating place to finish in sport - and Boston had plenty of experience of being runners-up in 2008.

It had to be recorded as a successful season on-track, and there was some team silverware on the mantelpiece as well as Simon Lambert and James Cockle clinched victory in the Conference League Pairs at Weymouth.

But there was also sadness for the hard-trying club, established in an attempt to bring speedway back to the town whilst operating from King's Lynn's Norfolk Arena.

Those hopes finally faded during 2008, and with crowd levels minimal, the Barracudas were disbanded at the end of the season, although King's Lynn do intend to run a third-tier set-up with several of the Boston staff involved in 2009.

Long-serving manager Malcolm Vasey left for Scunthorpe, but the 2008 Barracudas boasted a strong spearhead in Lambert and Joe Haines, backed up by Australian teenager Darcy Ward, who hit a nine-point average in his debut season.

That sort of scoring was enough to see the Barracudas sail through the first three-quarters of the season, eventually settling for second place in the regular League standings having been held to a dramatic home draw (46-46) by Redcar.

A sensational play off semi final saw the Barracudas overcome the Cubs by a single point on aggregate as both teams won on each others' circuits - but Boston's problems were just beginning.

The final three matches were the most important, but the team was severely weakened with Ward back in Australia, Lambert injured and Haines having Premier League commitments.

The outcome was a 59-33 defeat in the second leg of the Knockout Cup Final at Plymouth for a 15-point aggregate defeat, and overall League hopes were ended with a crushing 67-23 loss at Weymouth in the first leg of the Final – an unfortunate way for the club to finish.

2008 RESULTS

Conference League

Final position..Second

SCUNTHORPE (A)
Monday, March 24
Lost 43-46
Thompson 3:2, Mallett 5, Wright 7, Lambert 12:1, Smith 8, Lowe 7:1, Rayson 1:1.

PLYMOUTH (A)
Friday, May 9
Lost 32-60
Rider replacement for Thompson, Rolph 2, Wright 5:1, Lambert 15 (4), Mallett 5:1, Lowe 4:1, Rayson 1.
▼ *Struggled to make an impression in absence of Smith and Haines due to their Premier League commitments.*

RYE HOUSE (H)
Wednesday, May 21
Won 54-39
Lambert 14:1, Mallett 7:2, Wright 0, Smith 0, **Haines 14:1**, Lowe 12:1, Rayson 7:1.
▼ *Wright crashed in his opening ride, was not excluded but ruled out for remainder of the meeting. Crash in Heat 3 also caused Smith to withdraw later on.*

SITTINGBOURNE (A)
Sunday, June 1
Won 55-35
Cockle 7:1, Mallett 10:1, Wright 13, *rider replacement for Thompson*, **Lambert 18**, Lowe 3, Rayson 4.

SITTINGBOURNE (H)
Sunday, June 29
Won 62-25
Cockle 5:1, Rolph 11:1, **Haines 14:1**, Mallett 7, **Lambert 14:1**, Lowe 4:1, Rayson 7:3.
▼ *Meeting delayed for 30 minutes due to visibility problems, and tricky conditions saw six exclusions and five other fallers during the 15 races.*

SCUNTHORPE (H)
Sunday, July 13
Won 60-33
Lambert 14:1, Rolph 9:3, Cockle 5:1, Mallett 11, **Haines 14:1**, Lowe 1, Rayson 6:1.
▲ *Barracudas took victory over their former boss Malcolm Vasey.*

BUXTON (H)
Sunday, July 20
Won 63-29
Lambert 15, Rolph 7:3, Cockle 9, Mallett 2, **Haines 13:2**, Lowe 11:2, Rayson 6:1.
▲ *Another rampant home performance with a surprise win for Lewis Dallaway in Heat 14 being the only time a visiting rider took the flag.*

Did you know?

Simon Lambert was unbeaten in five of his six Conference League home meetings while Joe Haines was denied a similar return by an engine failure in his last race against Weymouth!

SQUAD
Adam Allott, Scott Campos, James Cockle, Joe Haines, Simon Lambert, Adam Lowe, Darren Mallett, Oliver Rayson, Darren Rolph, Jamie Smith, Mark Thompson, Chris Widman, Matthew Wright.
Foreign: Sam Martin, Darcy Ward.

BUXTON (A)
Sunday, July 27
Won 47-42
Lambert 15, Mallett 5, Cockle 8:1, Ward 7, Rolph 4:1, Lowe 4:1, Widman 4:1.
▲ *Barracudas were in front throughout with Lambert in unstoppable form.*

PLYMOUTH (H)
Friday, August 1
Won 64-30
Lambert 11:1, Mallett 10:1, Cockle 10:1, Ward 9:1, **Haines 14:1**, Lowe 6:1, Widman 4:2.
▲ *Opened up with three 5-1s and limited the visitors to just one race win from Tom Brown.*

WEYMOUTH (A)
Saturday, August 2
Lost 39-54
Rider replacement for Lambert, Ward 15 (4), Cockle 9:1, Rolph 8:2 (TS2:1), Mallett 4, Lowe 1, Widman 2.
▲ *Ward impressed on his first visit to the Wessex Stadium.*

REDCAR (H)
Friday, August 22
Drew 46-46
Lambert 12:1, Mallett 9:1, Haines 9, Rolph 6:1, Ward 5, Lowe 5, Widman 0.
▼ *Dropped a point at home as Mallett suffered chain failure when third in Heat 15, and leader Lambert slowed to a crawl – two of several mechanical failures.*

REDCAR (A)
Thursday, September 4
Lost 44-46
Lambert 10:1, *rider replacement for Thompson*, Haines 16, Mallett 1, Ward 12:2, Lowe 2, Rayson 3.

WEYMOUTH (H)
Monday, September 15
Won 64-28
Lambert 14:1, Rolph 8:2, Haines 12, Mallett 7:2, Ward 12, Lowe 5:2, Rayson 6:1.
▲ *Re-arranged after rain-off three days earlier, and each of the first seven races resulted in Boston heat advantages.*

RYE HOUSE (A)
Sunday, September 21
Lost 40-52
Lambert 4 (TSFX), Rolph 4:2, **Haines 18 (6)**,

Mallett 0, Ward 10, Lowe 1, Widman 3:1.

▼▲ *Injury scare for Lambert, who fell heavily in Heat 8 having been introduced as a tactical substitute, but escaped with heavy brusing.*

CONFERENCE LEAGUE

	M	W	D	L	PtsF	PtsA	Pts
Plymouth	14	9	0	5	709	569	20
BOSTON	**14**	**8**	**1**	**5**	**713**	**565**	**19**
Redcar	14	8	1	5	657	614	18
Weymouth	14	8	1	6	688	588	17
Scunthorpe	14	8	1	6	637	629	17
Buxton	14	7	1	7	605	669	15
Rye House	14	6	1	8	614	663	12
Sittingbourne	14	1	0	13	472	798	2

PLAY-OFFS

Semi Final, first leg
REDCAR (A)
Thursday, September 25
Won 48-45
Haines 17:1, *rider replacement for Thompson*, Lambert 3, Rolph 2, Ward 19:1 (TS6), Gary Irving [G] 7, Lowe 0.

▲ *Ward and Haines gave brilliant displays to give the club one foot in the Final, the duo combining for a 5-1 in the last race to complete a comeback from 29-34 down.*

Semi Final, second leg
REDCAR (H)
Tuesday, October 14
Lost 44-46
Haines 14, Rolph 5:1, Lambert 8:3, Mallett 6, Allott 9, Widman 0, Rayson 2.

▲ *Seemed set to be going out as nothing less than a 5-1 in Heat 15 would do – and they took it when Aaron Summers shed a chain on the start-line.*

Aggregate: Won 92-91.

FINAL, first leg
WEYMOUTH (A)
Saturday, October 25
Lost 23-67
Allott 5 (TS0), Lowe 1, Lambert 7 (1), Mallett 3, Rolph 6, Widman 1, Naylor 0.

▼ *Conceded 5-1s in nine of the 15 heats and were left wishing they had been able to track the likes of Haines and a fully-fit Lambert, who rode with injured wrist.*

FINAL, second leg
WEYMOUTH (H)
Wednesday, October 29
Lost 45-46
Allott 7:1, Lowe 3, Lambert 15 (TS2), Mallett 11:2, Rolph 3, Naylor 4:2, Widman 2.

Aggregate: Lost 68-113.

British Under 21 Championship

Qualifying round
Wednesday, April 2
Joe Haines 14+❐+3, Sean Stoddart 12+3+2, Charles Wright 11+2+1, Andrew Tully 14+❐+FX, Byron Bekker 9+F, Sam Martin 11+R, Jerran Hart 9, Simon Lambert 8, Adam Lowe 7, Guy Kendrew 6, Scott Campos 4, Keiran Morris 4, Scott Whittington 3, Scott Richardson 3, Oliver Rayson 2, Ben Hannon 2, Richard Franklin [R] 0.

Knock Out Cup

Quarter Final, first leg
REDCAR (H)
Sunday, June 8
Won 51-43
Cockle 7, Rolph 6:2, Smith 10:1, Mallett 8:2, Lambert 12, Campos 3:2, Rayson 5.

▼ *Held 14-point lead after seven races but Cubs fought back with the help of tactical moves.*

Quarter Final, second leg
REDCAR (A)
Saturday, June 14
Drew 45-45
Cockle 8:2, Mallett 7:2, *rider replacement for Wright*, Lambert 16, Rolph 7:1, Rayson 3, Lowe 4.

▲ *Led almost throughout the whole of the second leg in an efficient defence of first leg eight-point advantage.*

Semi Final, first leg
SCUNTHORPE (H)
Sunday, September 28
Won 56-35
Haines 15, Rolph 5:1, **Lambert 12**, Mallett 7:1, **Ward 13:2**, Widman 1:1, Lowe 3.

▲ *Favourites for the Final with a completely unbeaten showing from the three heat-leaders, and second-strings providing valuable support.*

Semi Final, second leg
SCUNTHORPE (A)
Friday, October 10
Won 48-45
Haines 15, Lowe 0, **Lambert 20:1 (TS6)**, Mallett 2, Allott 7:1, Widman 2:1, Rayson 2.

▲ *Came back from eight points down to snatch victory in the last race thanks to unbeaten Haines and Lambert.*

Aggregate: Won 104-80.

FINAL, first leg
PLYMOUTH (H)
Sunday, October 19
Won 50-39
Haines 16, Rolph 4, *rider replacement for Lambert*, Mallett 15:2, Allott 10:1, Widman 0, Rayson 5:2.

▲ *Withdrawal of injured Lambert was a body blow in building a lead, but Mallett won the last two races as part of a run of two 5-1s and a 4-2 from Heats 13 to 15.*

FINAL, second leg
PLYMOUTH (A)
Friday, October 24
Lost 33-59
Allott 13 (4), Naylor 0, *rider replacement for Lambert*, Rolph 7:1 (TS0), Mallett 5, Widman 0, Lowe 8:2.

▼ *Dropped only two points in the first three races, but could not maintain momentum.*

Aggregate: Lost 83-98.

Did you know?

Boston had six rain-offs at their home track during the season – but none away.

Conference Trophy

BUXTON (H)
Sunday, May 11
Won 60-34
Lambert 15, Mallett 6, Wright 5:1, **Haines 14:1**, Rolph 4:2, Lowe 13, Rayson 3:1.

BUXTON (A)
Sunday, May 25
Lost 41-49
Cockle 6:1, Rolph 10:2, Wright 3:1, Mallett 5, Haines 10, Lowe 4:1, Rayson 3:1.
▲ *Did enough to qualify for Final on aggregate, holding onto their first leg led despite defeat.*
Aggregate: Won 101-83.

FINAL, first leg
PLYMOUTH (A)
Friday, June 6
Lost 28-63
Cockle 7 (4), Martin 5:1, Wright 4 (TS0), Mallett 2, Rolph 5, Lowe 0, Rayson 5:1.
▼ *Badly lacked the influential Lambert, who was away on international duty, replacement Martin securing their only race win.*

FINAL, second leg
PLYMOUTH (H)
Sunday, August 31
Won 60-31
Lambert 14:1, Rolph 6:1, **Haines 15**, Mallett 5:1, Ward 9, Lowe 5:1, Rayson 6:2.
▼ *Nearly pulled off an epic comeback but were just held up in Heats 13 and 14, when the visitors escaped with a 2-3 and 3-3.*
Aggregate: Lost 88-94.

Challenge

REDCAR (H)
Wednesday, April 9
Won 55-38
Lambert 13, Mallett 5:1, Wright 8:1, Haines 11:2, Cockle 9:1, Lowe 6:1, Rayson 3:1.

Weather...

Lost six home matches throughout a sodden season.

Conference League
Sunday, April 20 .... RYE HOUSE (H)
Sunday, August 3 .... WEYMOUTH (H)
Friday, September 12 .... WEYMOUTH (H)

Conference League Play off
Sunday, October 5.......... REDCAR (H)
Sunday, October 26 .... WEYMOUTH (H)

Knock Out Cup
Sunday, September 7 .... SCUNTHORPE (H)

...beaten

BOSTON

Rider	M	R	Pts	BP	TPts	Ave	F	P	TR	TPts	TS	TSPts
Joe HAINES	17	86	240	8	248	11.53	4	7	1	3	0	0
Simon LAMBERT	**23**	**116**	**290**	**13**	**303**	**10.45**	**5**	**7**	**2**	**2**	**3**	**4**
Darcy WARD	10	49	111	7	118	9.63	1	1	1	2	1	3
Adam ALLOTT	**6**	**28**	**51**	**3**	**54**	**7.71**	**0**	**0**	**1**	**2**	**1**	**0**
James COCKLE	11	51	81	9	90	7.06	0	0	1	2	0	0
Jamie SMITH	**3**	**11**	**18**	**1**	**19**	**6.91**	**0**	**0**	**0**	**0**	**0**	**0**
Darren ROLPH	22	96	129	26	155	6.46	0	2	0	0	2	1
Darren MALLETT	**27**	**121**	**165**	**18**	**183**	**6.05**	**0**	**0**	**0**	**0**	**0**	**0**
Matthew WRIGHT	7	29	37	3	40	5.52	0	0	0	0	1	0
Scott CAMPOS	**1**	**4**	**3**	**2**	**5**	**5.00**	**0**	**0**	**0**	**0**	**0**	**0**
Mark THOMPSON	1	4	3	2	5	5.00	0	0	0	0	0	0
Oliver RAYSON	**18**	**76**	**75**	**14**	**89**	**4.68**	**0**	**0**	**0**	**0**	**0**	**0**
Adam LOWE	25	104	107	14	121	4.65	0	0	0	0	0	0
Chris WIDMAN	**12**	**43**	**19**	**6**	**25**	**2.33**	**0**	**0**	**0**	**0**	**0**	**0**
Rhys NAYLOR	3	12	4	2	6	2.00	0	0	0	0	0	0
Guests												
Sam MARTIN	1	4	5	1	6	6.00	0	0	0	0	0	0
Gary IRVING	**1**	**5**	**7**	**0**	**7**	**5.60**	**0**	**0**	**0**	**0**	**0**	**0**

For Joe HAINES see Workington; for Simon LAMBERT see King's Lynn; for James COCKLE see Mildenhall, Berwick and Redcar (CL); for Jamie SMITH see Reading; for Matthew WRIGHT see Mildenhall and Weymouth.

The Boston team that reached the Play-off Final: Darcy Ward, Adam Lowe, Simon Lambert (on bike), Darren Rolph, Oliver Rayson. Kneeling – Darren Mallett, Joe Haines

And the side that just missed out on championship glory: co-chairman Stephen Lambert, Chris Widman, Darren Mallett, Simon Lambert, team manager Dale Allitt, Adam Lowe, Adam Allott, co-chairman Mick Smith. Kneeling - Darren Rolph, mascot Jack Butler and Rhys Naylor

PHOTOS: Steve HONE

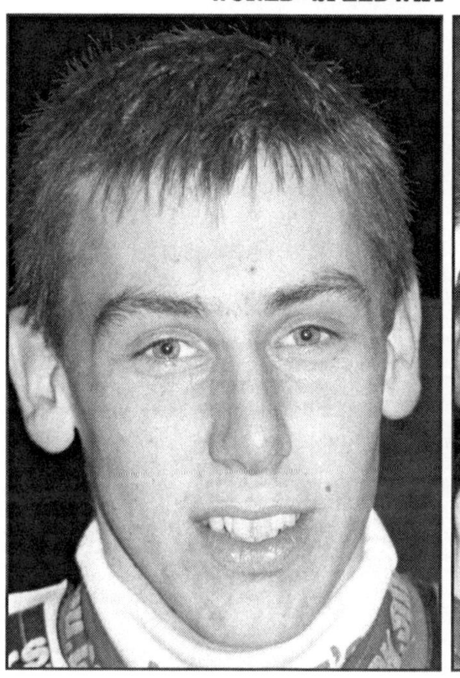

SIMON LAMBERT

DARREN ROLPH

Spectacular Australian discovery Darcy Ward

PHOTO: **Steve HONE**

TRACK FILE

Track: Hi-Edge Raceway, Dale Head Lane, Axe Edge, near Buxton, Derbyshire.
Telephone: 01298 72271.
Hotline:
Website: www.hitmen2000.co.uk
Track Length: 240 metres.
Track Record: 52.9 secs, James Wright, June 27, 2004.
Promoters: Jayne and Richard Moss.
Colours: Gold, black and red.
Nickname: Hitmen.

HISTORY

First meeting: May 19, 1996, Buxton v Mildenhall, Division Three.
Leagues: Division Three, 1996-2009.
Meetings were also held at an adjacent stock car circuit

● *Buxton Raceway, off A53, Buxton, Derbyshire.*
First meeting: August 28, 1994, Buxton v Stoke, Peak-Potteries Challenge Trophy.
Leagues: Division Three, 1994-95.

HONOURS

Major honours: 1.
Division Three Knock Out Cup winners (1), 2002.

Conference League

BUXTON

2008 REVIEW

WHEN it comes to commitment to youth development over a decade and more of racing, Buxton are one of British speedway's benchmark clubs.

The Derbyshire outfit cannot offer riches to their team members and have only once finished in the top three of the Conference League - but they play a vital part in rider progression, James Wright being a recent example of their work.

2008 saw the Hitmen more than playing their part in what was a close-fought league, and the club were rightly proud that several of the more-vaunted teams left the Hi-Edge Raceway pointless.

Only Boston managed to breach the Hitmen's defences at home, and there were excellent close matches against Plymouth and Weymouth for the supporters to enjoy in the final part of the season.

If there was a disappointment, it was that Buxton were rarely able to track a settled one-to-seven, frequently being forced to use rider replacement to cover the Premier League call-ups of Jack Roberts and Ben Taylor - a sign of both riders' progress - and John Branney's regular commitments with Workington.

All too often it left them short-handed on their travels, although they did manage a narrow win at Sittingbourne and were close at Scunthorpe.

Sixth place overall with a record of seven wins and seven defeats was probably a fair reflection of their team strength, but their achievements should not be under-estimated.

Roberts and Taylor made great strides, and at reserve Gareth Isherwood was a regular high scorer, including a sensational paid maximum at home to Plymouth.

The season, though, was tinged with sadness as the Hitmen had intended to track 19-year-old New Zealander Andrew Tree, who was relishing the prospect of making his British debut. But just a month before the campaign, he tragically died in his sleep at his Invercargill home.

2008 RESULTS

Conference League

Final position..Sixth

REDCAR (A)
Saturday, April 12
Lost 32-56
Rider replacement for Branney, Hodgson 3, Roberts 13, Burnett 1:1, Taylor 9, Whittington 5:1, Dallaway 1.
▼ *Branney and McKinna out due to Premier League commitments.*

SITTINGBOURNE (A)
Sunday, June 15
Won 46-44
Rider replacement for Branney, Burnett 0, Taylor 7:2, Dallaway 7, Roberts 15, Whittington 0, Isherwood 17:2.
▲ *Isherwood enjoyed the meeting of his career; Roberts was unbeaten after suffering a retirement in first ride.*

RYE HOUSE (H)
Sunday, June 22
Won 65-26
Branney 12, Burnett 8:4, Taylor 15, Dallaway 7:2, **Roberts 13:2**, Whittington 0, **Isherwood 10:2**.
▲ *Five riders went through the card in this emphatic win – Whittington missing out completely after crashing three times.*

RYE HOUSE (A)
Saturday, July 12
Lost 34-59
Rider replacement for Branney, Burnett 2, Taylor 8, Dallaway 1, Roberts 18 (6), Whittington 1, Isherwood 4.
▲ *Roberts showed his potential with five race wins, but most of his teammates struggled.*

SITTINGBOURNE (H)
Sunday, July 13
Won 61-31
Branney 8:1, Burnett 5, **Taylor 14:1**, Dallaway 8:2, **Roberts 15**, Whittington 1, **Isherwood 10:2**.
▲ *Completed the double over the bottom club with Taylor and Roberts unbeaten.*

SCUNTHORPE (A)
Friday, July 18
Lost 41-50
Branney 15:1 (4), Burnett 4:1, Taylor 0, Dallaway 6, *rider replacement for Roberts*, Whittington 0, Isherwood 16.
▲▼ *Isherwood won three of the last four races as the Hitmen were left to wonder what might have been had Roberts been available.*

BOSTON (A)
Sunday, July 20
Lost 29-63
Branney 11 (4), Burnett 1, Taylor 7, Dallaway 5:2, *rider replacement for Roberts*, Whittington 2:1, Isherwood 3:1.

BOSTON (H)
Sunday, July 27
Lost 42-47
Rider replacement for Branney, Burnett 5:1, Taylor 14, Dallaway 3:2, Roberts 7, Whittington 1, Isherwood 12:2.
▲ *Trailed all afternoon and looked to get back in touch with a 5-1 in Heat 14 only for Darcy Ward to split Isherwood and Dallaway to virtually secure victory.*

Quarter Final, first leg
SCUNTHORPE (H)
Sunday, August 10
Won 53-38
Branney 12:1, Burnett 5:1, **Taylor 14:1**, Dallaway 5, Roberts 9, Whittington 0, Isherwood 8:1.
▲ *Saw an early 12-point lead cut back to three, but the Hitmen top three were all in good form.*

Quarter Final, second leg
REDCAR (H)
Sunday, August 17
Won 52-40
Rider replacement for Branney, Burnett 2, **Taylor 16:2**, Dallaway 4:1, Roberts 15, Whittington 1, Isherwood 14:1.
▲ *Hugely impressive three-man show from unbeaten Taylor, Roberts and reserve Isherwood, which allowed Hitmen to cover for problems elsewhere.*

PLYMOUTH (H)
Sunday, August 24
Won 48-44
Branney 13:1, Burnett 4:1, Taylor 12:1, Dallaway 2:1, *rider replacement for Roberts*, Whittington 0, **Isherwood 17:1**.
▲ *Amazing paid maximum from Isherwood inspired the Hitmen to this win – and his Heat 14 win was crucial as Plymouth took a 5-1 in the last race.*

PLYMOUTH (A)
Friday, August 29
Lost 28-63
Rider replacement for Branney, Kyle Newman [G] 3, Taylor 15 (6), Dallaway 1, Isherwood 7, Whittington 2, Richard Andrews [G] 0.
▼ *Could not track anything like their strongest team and suffered a heavy defeat – Dallaway failed to finish five of his six rides!Guest Richard Andrews withdrew after a Heat 2 crash.*

WEYMOUTH (A)
Saturday, August 30
Lost 28-64
Rider replacement for Branney, Dixon 0, Taylor 11:1 (4), Dallaway 2:1, Isherwood 11, Whittington 1:1, Braithwaite 3.

SQUAD
John Branney, Paul Burnett, Lewis Dallaway, Jamie Dixon, Danny Hodgson, Gareth Isherwood, Adam McKinna, Jack Roberts, Ben Taylor, Scott Whittington.
Foreign: Grant Tregoning.

▼ *Difficult weekend continued with another heavy defeat, and again 28 points was the sum total of the Hitmen efforts – Isherwood taking their only win and Braithwaite was caught at the tapes three times by referee Dave Watters!*

WEYMOUTH (H)
Sunday, September 14
Won 46-44
Branney 15:1, Burnett 2, Taylor 10, Dallaway 5:3, *rider replacement for Roberts*, Whittington 0, Isherwood 14.
▲ *Never more than two points between the teams, Hitmen going in front with a 5-1 in Heat 14 from Isherwood and Dallaway, with Branney taking the flag in the decider.*

CONFERENCE LEAGUE

	M	W	D	L	PtsF	PtsA	Pts
Plymouth	14	9	0	5	709	569	20
Boston	14	8	1	5	713	565	19
Redcar	14	8	1	5	657	614	18
Weymouth	14	8	1	6	688	588	17
Scunthorpe	14	8	1	6	637	629	17
BUXTON	**14**	**7**	**1**	**7**	**605**	**669**	**15**
Rye House	14	6	1	8	614	663	12
Sittingbourne	14	1	0	13	472	798	2

Did you know?

New Zealander Grant Tregoning rode in only two matches for Buxton on successive nights. He had to return home because he didn't have the right paperwork for a work permit to race in the Premier League with Mildenhall.

Knock Out Cup

First round, first leg
SCUNTHORPE (A)
Monday, May 26
Lost 41-52
Roberts 13 (TS0), Dalaway 1, Taylor 7, Grant Tregoning 13 (6), McKinna 0, Whitington 1, Isherwood 6.
▼ *Remained in contention despite Roberts' exclusion for bringing down Scott Richardson when riding as a tactical substitute in Heat 12.*

First round, second leg
SCUNTHORPE (H)
Sunday, June 8
Won 50-41
Roberts 4, Burnett 12, Taylor 15:1, Dallaway 9:4, *rider replacement for Branney*, Whittington 2, Isherwood 8:2.
▼ *Agonisingly missed out on aggregate progression having levelled the aggregate scores with three heats to go.*
Aggregate: Lost 91-93.

Conference Trophy

Semi Final, first leg
BOSTON (A)
Sunday, May 11
Lost 34-60
Branney 11 (TS4), Hodgson 0, Taylor 12 (6), McKinna 4:1, Roberts 7, Isherwood 0, Dallaway 0.

Semi Final, second leg
BOSTON (H)
Sunday, May 25
Won 49-41
Branney 15, Dallaway 1:1, Taylor 10, Tregoning 6, Roberts 6, Whittington 1, Isherwood 10:2.
▲ *First Dalehead meeting of the season was cliffhanger.*
Aggregate: Lost 83-101.

BUXTON

Rider	*M*	*R*	*Pts*	*BP*	*TPts*	*Ave*	*F*	*P*	*TR*	*TPts*	*TS*	*TSPts*
John BRANNEY	9	47	112	5	117	9.96	2	0	2	4	1	2
Jack ROBERTS	**12**	**59**	**135**	**2**	**137**	**9.29**	**1**	**1**	**1**	**3**	**1**	**0**
Grant TREGONING	2	9	19	0	19	8.44	0	0	1	3	0	0
Ben TAYLOR	**18**	**97**	**196**	**10**	**206**	**8.49**	**1**	**3**	**3**	**8**	**0**	**0**
Gareth ISHERWOOD	17	91	167	16	183	8.04	0	3	0	0	0	0
Paul BURNETT	**13**	**56**	**51**	**9**	**60**	**4.29**	**0**	**1**	**0**	**0**	**0**	**0**
Adam McKINNA	2	5	4	1	5	4.00	0	0	0	0	0	0
Lewis DALLAWAY	**18**	**87**	**68**	**18**	**86**	**3.95**	**0**	**0**	**0**	**0**	**0**	**0**
Andrew BRAITHWAITE	1	5	3	0	3	2.40	0	0	0	0	0	
Danny HODGSON	**2**	**8**	**3**	**0**	**3**	**1.50**	**0**	**0**	**0**	**0**	**0**	**0**
Scott WHITTINGTON	17	64	18	3	21	1.31	0	0	0	0	0	0
Jamie DIXON	**1**	**3**	**0**	**0**	**0**	**0.00**	**0**	**0**	**0**	**0**	**0**	**0**
Guests												
Kyle NEWMAN	1	4	3	0	3	3.00	0	0	0	0	0	0
Richard ANDREWS	**1**	**1**	**0**	**0**	**0**	**0.00**	**0**	**0**	**0**	**0**	**0**	**0**

For John BRANNEY see Workington; for Jack ROBERTS see Birmingham; for Adam McKINNA see Berwick and Redcar (CL).

encounter, Hitmen confirming win on the day with a 5-1 from home debutant Tregoning and Isherwood in Heat 14.

Aggregate: Lost 83-101.

Reserve Gareth Isherwood was unbeaten by an opponent in three home matches.

Under 16 Challenge

CARMARTHEN (H)
Sunday, October 19
Lost 44-46

Jason Garrity 21, *rider replacement*, Cameron Hoskins 1, Ashley Morris 0, *rider replacement*, Lloyd Barrett 5:1, Kyle Howarth 17:1.

CARMARTHEN 46

Rider replacement, Scott Meakins 10:1, James Sarjeant 17, Jack Hirst 8:3, *rider replacement*, Richard Andrews 10:5, Jack Butler 1:1.

Sunday,

● *This Under-16 challenge was hit by late withdrawals with both sides operating double rider-replacement – which must surely be a speedway first!*

Weather...

Made three unsuccessful attempts to race Belle Vue.

Conference League
Sunday, July 6 .... REDCAR (H)
Sunday, September 7 .... WEYMOUTH (H)

Challenge
Sunday, April 27 .... BELLE VUE (H)
Sunday, May 4 .... BELLE VUE (H)
†Sunday, October 26 .... BELLE VUE (H)

†Cancelled because Belle Vue unable to raise a team.

...beaten

2009 Squad

Craig **COOK**, Lewis **DALLAWAY**, Jason **GARRITY**, Gareth **ISHERWOOD**, Scott **JAMES**, Jade **MUDGWAY**, Lee **SMETHILLS**,

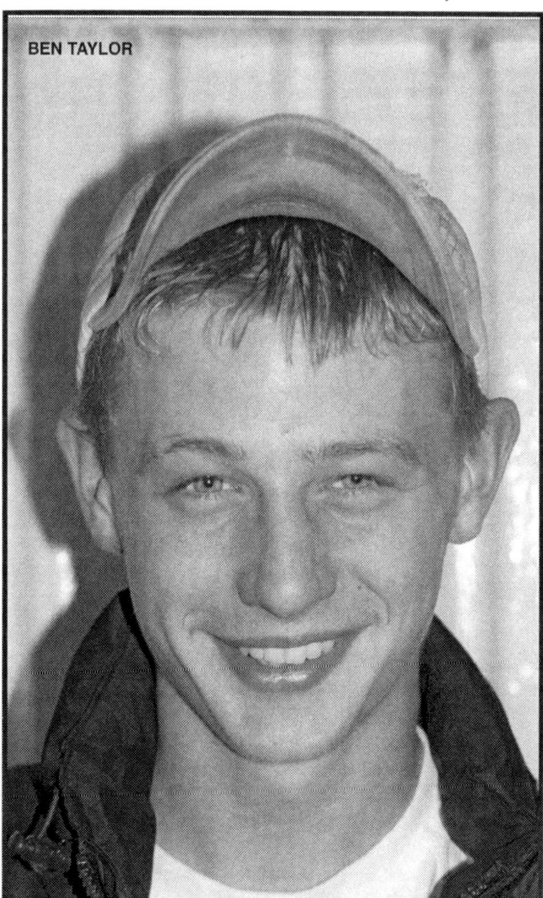

BEN TAYLOR

The current Buxton track (right) and the original circuit within the stock car complex

Scott James returns to Hi-Edge in 2009

Conference League

PLYMOUTH

TRACK FILE

Track: St. Boniface's Arena, Coypool Road, Plymouth, PL7 4NW.
Telephone: 01752 345146.
Hotline: 09068 664668.
Website: www.plymouthdevils.co.uk
Track Length: 216 metres.
Track Record: 50.43 secs, Jason Bunyan, October 3, 2008.
Promoter: Mike Bowden.
Team Sponsors: GT Motorcycles.
Colours: Yellow with red Devil.
Nickname: Devils.

HISTORY

First meeting: April 21, 2006, Plymouth v USA Dream Team, challenge.
Leagues: Division Three, 2006-09.
Meetings have also been held at the following Plymouth venue.

● *Pennycross Stadium, Pennycross, Plymouth.*
First meeting: June 13, 1931, Plymouth v Exeter, challenge.
Leagues: Division One, 1932-34. Division Two, 1936, 1950, 1954, 1961-62, 1968-69. Division Three, 1947-49, 1951. Southern League, 1952-53. Open licence, 1931, 1935, 1937, 1960, 1970.

HONOURS

Major honours: 3.
Division Three Knock Out Cup winners (1), 2008.
Division Three Trophy winners (1), 2008.
Southern League Trophy winners (1), 1952.

2008 REVIEW

PLYMOUTH finally put major silverware on the table after two years of going close - even if the major prize still eluded the men from Devon.

The Devils had been forced to play second fiddle to Scunthorpe in 2006 and 2007 but proved to be the class of the league in the regular stages on this occasion, before agonisingly missing out in the play-offs.

After a narrow opening defeat at Redcar, the Devils won their next four matches to move up amongst the early pace-setters, and away wins at Rye House and Sittingbourne were enough to secure first place with a 20-point total.

Weymouth were also defeated in the first round of the Knockout Cup as well as the Conference Trophy - so perhaps there was a degree of inevitability that the Wildcats would take some revenge right at the death.

By then, Plymouth had lost Nicki Glanz to a broken collarbone sustained when riding for Reading, and they survived a scare to win the Conference Trophy, being grateful for their 63-28 first leg lead over Boston as they lost the return 60-31.

But it always looked a step to far when Weymouth held them to a 46-44 win in the first leg of the play-off semi-final, and so it proved as the Wildcats dominated the return fixture - much to the frustration of the management, who felt the leaders after the league stage should take the title.

Consolation came in the form of Cup success against Boston, with the second leg being staged at home on this occasion, and it was fitting that comeback man Mark Simmonds rounded off the season with a paid maximum.

37-year-old Simmonds made a splendid return after four seasons out, and Tom Brown remained a fans' favourite for his all-action style. Simmonds and fellow veteran Seemond Stephens are both inked in for the Devils' National League campaign in 2009.

2008 RESULTS

Conference League

Final position...First

REDCAR (A)
Saturday, May 3
Lost 43-47
Stephens 12:1, Hughes 7:1, Brown 7, Hopwood 4:2, Glanz 6, Starke 2, Pickard 5:1.
▼ *Starke was excluded from Heat 2 for not making an attempt to race, when the Devils would have taken a 5-0.*

BOSTON (H)
Friday, May 9
Won 60-32
Stephens 8:1, Hughes 11:1, **Glanz 12**, Hopwood 6:3, Brown 6:1, Pickard 5:1, Starke 12:2.
▲ *Devils opened their League programme with a convincing win against a visiting team for whom Simon Lambert scored 15 of their 32 points.*

RYE HOUSE (A)
Saturday, June 7
Won 47-42
Stephens 2, Hughes 2, Glanz 9:3, Hopwood 9:1, Brown 12:1, Pickard 2:1, Starke 11:1.
▼ *Kyle Hughes was forced to pull out of the meeting after a Heat 8 spill.*

RYE HOUSE (H)
Friday, June 13
Won 56-34
Stephens 9:1, Hughes 8:1, **Brown 12**, White-Williams 1, Simmonds 14, Pickard 2, Starke 10:3.

SCUNTHORPE (H)
Friday, June 27
Won 58-34
Stephens 8:2, Hughes 11:1, **Glanz 15**, Pickard 1, **Simmonds 12**, White-Williams 5:1, Starke 6:1.
▲ *Moved top of the league with a convincing win with both Glanz and Simmonds scoring full maximums.*

WEYMOUTH (A)
Saturday, July 12
Lost 41-49
Glanz 9:2, Hughes 8, Brown 12:1, White-Williams 1, Stephens 6, Stoneman 1:1, Starke 4.

SITTINGBOURNE (H)
Friday, July 25
Won 60-31
Simmonds 12:3, Hughes 8:1, **Brown 12**, Gough 2, **Stephens 12**, White-Williams 2, **Starke 12:3**.
▲ *Provided 14 heat winners on a red-letter night for reserve Starke with a maximum – and similar outcomes for three other Devils riders.*

BOSTON (A)
Friday, August 1
Lost 30-64
Simmonds 5, Hughes 8:1 (4), Brown 10 (TS4), Pickard 1, Stephens 4, White-Williams 2:1, Starke 0.
▼ *Reserve Starke suffered an injured wrist in Heat 4, which made a difficult task even harder – Devils were already 3-15 down.*

SITTINGBOURNE (A)
Sunday, August 3
Won 59-33
Simmonds 11:1, White-Williams 2, Brown 8:2, **Glanz 14:1**, **Stephens 15**, Pickard 1:1, Starke 8:1.
▲ *Top three riders all in dominant form as the Devils cruised to a straightforward away win, taking the lead for the first time in Heat 3.*

REDCAR (H)
Friday, August 8
Won 58-34
Simmonds 14:1, Hughes 8:2, **Glanz 15**, White-Williams 2, Stephens 9, Stoneman 2:1, Starke 8:3.

WEYMOUTH (H)
Friday, August 22
Won 51-42
Simmonds 13:1, Hughes 7, **Brown 12**, White-Williams 0, Stephens 10:1, Pickard 1:1, Starke 8:1.
▲ *Top-order race wins got the better of strength-in-depth as far as the Wildcats were concerned – Simmonds, Brown and Stephens won ten heats between them.*

BUXTON (A)
Sunday, August 24
Lost 44-48
Simmonds 16:1 (4), White-Williams 0, *rider replacement for Glanz*, Brown 6, Stephens 13:2, Pickard 3, Starke 6:4.
▼ *Were unable to stop the Hitmen's flying reserve Gareth Isherwood, as the efforts of Simmonds and Stephens in particular were in vain.*

SCUNTHORPE (A)
Monday, August 25
Lost 39-51
Simmonds 7:1, Hughes 6:1, Brown 13, White-Williams 1, Stephens 9:1, Pickard 0, Starke 3:1.
▼ *Disappointing weekend ended pointless after two away wins had been targeted. Devils' only heat advantage of the afternoon came in the very first race.*

BUXTON (H)
Friday, August 29
Won 63-28
Simmonds 12, Gough 5:2, Brown 11:2, Hughes 8:2, **Stephens 14:1**, White-Williams 11:1, Starke 2:1.
▲▼ *Found life fairly straightforward against a weakened Buxton side to book their place in the play-offs with a 100 per cent home record. Starke withdrew after a Heat 2 crash.*

SQUAD
Richard Andrews, Tom Brown, Nicki Glanz, David Gough, Ben Hopwood, Kyle Hughes, Jamie Pickard, Jason Prynne, Paul Starke, Mark Simmonds, Seemond Stephens, Danny Stoneman, Jamie White-Williams.

CONFERENCE LEAGUE

	M	W	D	L	PtsF	PtsA	Pts
PLYMOUTH	**14**	**9**	**0**	**5**	**709**	**569**	**20**
Boston	14	8	1	5	713	565	19
Redcar	14	8	1	5	657	614	18
Weymouth	14	8	1	6	688	588	17
Scunthorpe	14	8	1	6	637	629	17
Buxton	14	7	1	7	605	669	15
Rye House	14	6	1	8	614	663	12
Sittingbourne	14	1	0	13	472	798	2

PLAY-OFFS
Semi Final, first leg
WEYMOUTH (H)
Friday, October 10
Won 46-44
Simmonds 14, Gough 0, Brown 12:2, Hughes 7:1, Stephens 7, White-Williams 1, Starke 5:2.
▲ *Trailing for much of the meeting and only salvaged a narrow first-leg lead thanks to 5-1s in Heat 14, and in Heat 15 from Simmonds and Brown after Lee Smart had crashed.*

Semi Final, second leg
WEYMOUTH (A)
Saturday, October 11
Lost 38-56
Simmonds 13 (4), Gough 0, Brown 13, Hughes 1, Stevens 9, White-Williams 0, Starke 2.
▼ *First leg lead proved to be nowhere near enough – were 12 points down on aggregate at the halfway stage and the efforts of the top three were not enough to spark a fightback.*
Aggregate: Lost 84-100.

Conference Trophy

Semi Final, first leg
WEYMOUTH (H)
Friday, May 23
Won 57-35
Stephens 9:2, Hughes 13:1, Glanz 8, Hopwood 3:3, Brown 11:2, Pickard 4:1, **Starke 9:3**.

WEYMOUTH (A)
Saturday, May 24
Lost 45-46
Stephens 9, Hughes 5:1, Glanz 9, Hopwood 1, Brown 9:2, Pickard 6:1, Starke 6.
Aggregate: Won 102-81.
▼ *Referee Jim McGregor issued a public warning to both club chairman about the conduct of their riders as the meeting threatened to get out of hand.*

FINAL, first leg
BOSTON (H)
Friday, June 6
Won 63-28
Stephens 10:2, Hughes 9:2, Glanz 9, Hopwood 5:2, Brown 7, Pickard 4, **Starke 19:2**.
▲ *Took control of the silverware with an emphatic first leg performance, and a memorable night for Starke with paid 21 at reserve.*

BOSTON (A)
Sunday, August 31
Lost 31-60
Simmonds 11 (4), Gough 3:1, Brown 5:1 (TSF) Hughes 8:1, Stephens 2, White-Williams 0, Andrews 2.
▲ *Hughes took the flag in Heat 14 to clinch the silverware at the end of a nervous meeting in which the Devils needed almost all of their massive first leg advantage.*
Aggregate: Won 94-88.

Knock Out Cup

Quarter Final, first leg
WEYMOUTH (A)
Saturday, June 21
Lost 45-47
Stephens 14:1 (6), White-Williams 4, Brown 1:1, Glanz 9, Simmonds 12, Pickard 1, Starke 4:2.
▲ *Recovered strongly from going 12 points down, race wins for Stephens and Simmonds leading the comeback.*

Quarter Final, second leg
WEYMOUTH (H)
Friday, July 11
Won 51-42
Rider replacement for Simmonds, White-Williams 3, Brown 10:3, Glanz 17, **Stephens 15**, Stoneman 1:1, Starke 5:2.
▲ *Had to wait to secure aggregate win and a place in the semi-finals, but the strength of Glanz and Stephens was the determining factor.*
Aggregate: Won 96-89.

Semi Final, first leg
RYE HOUSE (H)
Friday, July 18
Won 57-36
Simmonds 14, Pickard 1, **Brown 12:3**, Glanz 10, Stephens 9:1, White-Williams 2:1, Starke 9:2.
▲ *More than useful first-leg advantage which effectively had to be built on two occasions after Daniel Halsey and Rob Smith worked hard to keep the Cobras in it.*

Semi Final, second leg
RYE HOUSE (A)
Sunday, July 27
13-11, abandoned after Heat 4, waterlogged track following thunderstorm.

Semi Final, second leg
RYE HOUSE (A)
Sunday, August 10
Lost 37-56
Simmonds 17 (6), Reade 0, *rider replacement for Glanz*, Brown 8, Stephens 11:1, White-Williams 0, Starke 1.
▼ *Simmonds' winning tactical ride in Heat 11 was crucial and he then split the Rob Mear/Daniel Halsey combination in Heat 15 to take the Devils narrowly into the Final.*
Aggregate: Won 94-92.

FINAL, first leg
BOSTON (A)
Sunday, October 19
Lost 39-50
Stephens 7, Hughes 5:1, Brown 10, Gough 1, Simmonds 9, Pickard 1, Starke 6:1.
▲ *Could have got even closer but for conceding 14 points in the last three races, and that ensured there would still be a job to do in the second leg.*

FINAL, second leg
BOSTON (H)
Friday, October 24
Won 59-33
Stephens 10, Hughes 12:2, Brown 13:1, Gough 2, **Simmons 11:1**, Pickard 3:1, Starke 8:3.
▲ *Went in front on aggregate midway through the meeting, and when Simmonds defeated the double-points Adam Allott in Heat 11 the Devils were virtually home and dry for the silverware.*
Aggregate: Won 98-83.

Inter League Challenge

ISLE OF WIGHT (H)
Friday, October 3
Won 47-43
Simmonds 9:1, Gough 1:1, Brown 8:2, Hughes 7:2, Stephens 10, Prynne 6:2, Starke 6.
▲ *Eye-catching result as the Devils got the better of an almost full-strength Premier League Isle of Wight outfit – and had the result confirmed even before Heat 15.*

2009 Squad

Marc **ANDREWS**, Matt **BATES**, David **GOUGH**, Kyle **HUGHES**, Jason **PRYNNE**, Mark **SIMMONDS**, Paul **STARKE**, Seemond **STEPHENS**, Danny **STONEMAN**.

Backers SilverlineTaxis presented a trophy to the fastest rider of the night at all of Plymouth's 2008 home meetings.
The recipients are listed below with their respective winning times.

Date	*Time (secs)*	*Rider*
April 18	**52.18**	**Kyle Hughes**
April 26	**51.91**	**Jack Roberts**
May 9	**52.35**	**Nicki Glanz**
May 23	**52.78**	**Kyle Hughes**
June 6	**51.12**	**Nicki Glanz**
June 13	**53.32**	**Mark Simmonds**
June 27	**51.53**	**Kyle Hughes**
July 11	**52.00**	**Nicki Glanz**
July 18	**51.50**	**Mark Simmonds**
July 25	**51.78**	**Kyle Hughes**
August 8	**52.66**	**Mark Simmonds**
August 22	**52.37**	**Mark Simmonds**
August 29	**53.08**	**Ben Taylor**
September 12	**52.75**	**Seemond Stephens**
September 18	**51.00**	**Mark Simmonds**
October 3	**50.43**	**Jason Bunyan**
October 10	**52.96**	**Mark Simmonds**
October 24	**53.00**	**Kyle Hughes**

Weather...

Only one official fixture was postponed because of rain – but that happened twice! Three other rain offs affected composite meetings.

Knock Out Cup
Friday, June 20..........WEYMOUTH (H)
Friday, July 4 ....WEYMOUTH (H)

Other meetings
Friday, May 16..........PAIRS TROPHY (H)
Friday, May 30..........PAIRS TROPHY (H)
Friday, September 5 ..FOUR TEAM TOURNAMENT (H)

...beaten

PLYMOUTH

Rider	*M*	*R*	*Pts*	*BP*	*TPts*	*Ave*	*F*	*P*	*TR*	*TPts*	*TS*	*TSPts*
Mark SIMMONDS	18	87	217	9	226	10.39	2	4	4	9	0	0
Nicki GLANZ	**13**	**60**	**142**	**6**	**148**	**9.87**	**3**	**1**	**0**	**0**	**0**	**0**
Seemond STEPHENS	26	114	243	17	260	9.12	3	2	1	3	0	0
Tom BROWN	**24**	**114**	**232**	**22**	**254**	**8.91**	**3**	**1**	**0**	**0**	**4**	**4**
Kyle HUGHES	20	85	152	20	172	8.09	0	1	1	2	0	0
Paul STARKE	**25**	**114**	**166**	**38**	**204**	**7.16**	**0**	**3**	**0**	**0**	**0**	**0**
Ben HOPWOOD	6	23	28	11	39	6.78	1	0	0	0	0	0
Jaimie PICKARD	**17**	**70**	**41**	**8**	**49**	**2.80**	**0**	**0**	**0**	**0**	**0**	**0**
Richard ANDREWS	1	3	2	0	2	2.67	0	0	0	0	0	0
David GOUGH	**7**	**25**	**13**	**3**	**16**	**2.54**	**0**	**0**	**0**	**0**	**0**	**0**
Danny STONEMAN	3	11	4	3	7	2.54	0	0	0	0	0	0
Jamie WHITE-WILLIAMS	**18**	**70**	**37**	**4**	**41**	**2.34**	**0**	**0**	**0**	**0**	**0**	**0**
Ben READE	1	3	0	0	0	0.00	0	0	0	0	0	0

For Kyle HUGHES see Sheffield; for Ben HOPWOOD see Scunthorpe.

Challenge

DEVON-DORSET TROPHY
First leg
WEYMOUTH (H)
Friday, April 18
Won 61-29
Stephens 9:2, Hughes 12:2, **Brown 12**, Hopwood 4:1, Glanz 13:1, Starke 7:2, Pickard 4.
▲ *Four-ride maximum for Brown, with three other riders dropping just one point.*

Second leg
WEYMOUTH (A)
Saturday, April 19
Won 49-39
Stephens 10:1, Hughes 7, Brown 6, Hopwood 6:1, Glanz 10:1, Starke 4:2, Pickard 6:1.

CONFERENCE LEAGUE ALL STARS (H)
Saturday, April 26
Won 50-40
Stephens 9:1, Hughes 10:2, Brown 7:1, Hopwood 4:1, Glanz 12, Starke 8:1, Pickard 0.
CONFERENCE LEAGUE ALL STARS 40
Mark Simmonds 9:2, Jack Roberts 10, Ben Taylor 6:1, Luke Priest 1, Dean Felton 2:1, Scott Meakins 2:1, Shaun Harmatiuk 10:1.

BRISTOL (H)
Friday, September 12
Won 63-26
Simmonds 11:1, Gough 7:2, **Brown 12:3**, Hughes 8, **Stephens 12**, Stoneman 4:2, Starke 9:1.
▼ *Simmonds crashed in Heat 1 when he tangled with Prynne, but only Prynne and Priest secured race wins for the Bulldogs. Best score yet for Gough.*

For BRISTOL scorers see Blasts from the Past.

British Under 21 Championship

Qualifying Round
Friday, April 11
Harland Cook 8, Daniel Betson 8, Jack Roberts 7, Kyle Hughes 7, Robert Mear 7, Paul Starke 6, Nicki Glanz 6, Jamie Courtney 6, Ben Taylor 4, Jaimie Pickard 4, Rob Smith 2, Ben Reade 2, 13 Chris Widman 2, Nicky Mallett 2, Scott Meakins 1, Daniel Blake 0, Russell Barnett [R], did not ride.
● *Abandoned after Heat 13 due to a heavy downpour so positions were allocated based on the order after Heat 12.*
See British Championship for full details.

Four Team Challenge

WEST COUNTRY FOURS
Friday, September 19
KENT CRUSADERS 23
Dean Felton 7, Harland Cook 7, Gary Cottham 5, Daniel Berwick 4.
WELSH WIZARDS 20
Tom Brown 9, David Gough 4, Jamie White-Williams 3, Jamie Pickard 4.
PLYMOUTH DEVILS 29
Seemond Stephens 9, Jason Prynne 10, Kyle Hughes 9, Danny Stoneman 1.
DEVON SELECT 24
Ben Reade 3, Mark Simmonds 12, Paul Starke 9, Richard Andrews 0.
● ***Postponed, Friday, September 5.***

Pairs

SILVERLINE TAXIS PERPETUAL PAIRS TROPHY
Friday, August 15
1 Harland Cook 13 & Dean Felton 12:1 = 25, 2 Seemond Stephens 11 & Jason Prynne 13:1 = 24, 3 Gary Cottham 8:1 & Paul Starke 15 = 23, 4 Ben Reade 9:3 & Jamie Pickard 13 = 22, 5 Mark Simmonds 20 & Danny Stoneman 2 = 22, 6 David Gough 9 & Jamie White-Williams 8:1 = 17.
● ***Postponed, Friday, May 16 and Friday, May 30.***

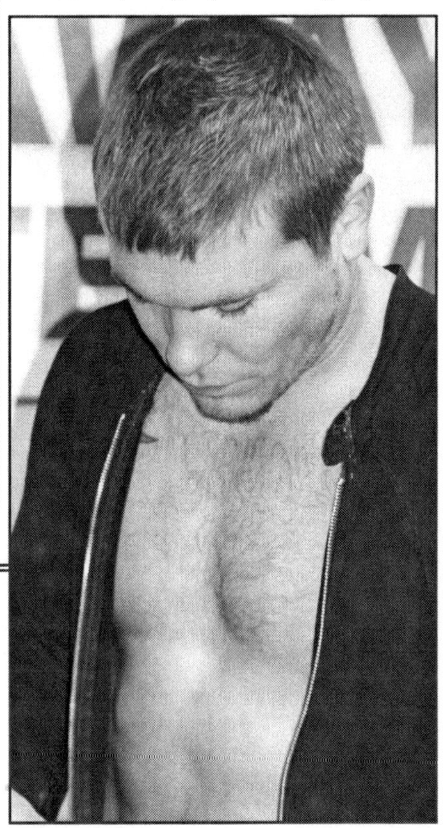

A worried Tom Brown deep in thought in between races

PLYMOUTH 2008: Kyle Hughes, Jaimie Pickard, Seemond Stephens, Tom Brown, Ben Hopwood, Paul Starke, mascot David Abrahams and Nicki Glanz

PHOTO: **Julie MARTIN**

Mark Simmonds leaves the Boston pits before a vital race in the Knock Out Cup Final

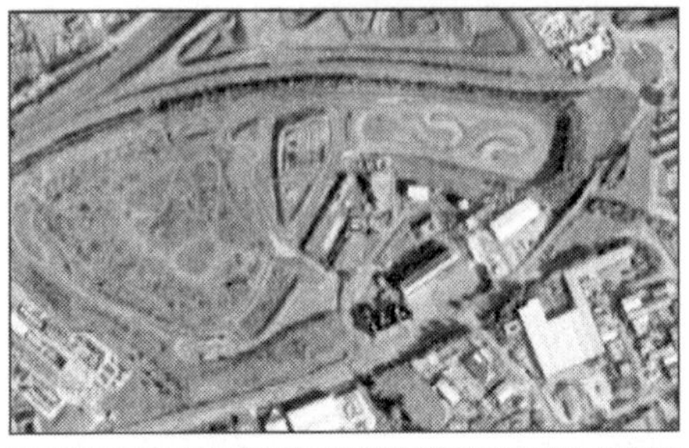

Conference League

REDCAR

TRACK FILE

Track: South Tees Motorpark, Dormey Way, Southbank Road, Middlesbrough, TS6 6HX.
Telephone: 07796 441850.
Hotline: 09068 664665.
Website: www.redcarspeedway.co.uk
Track Length: 271 metres.
Track Record: 55.6 secs, Aaron Summers, June 14, 2008.
2008 Promoters: Glyn Taylor and Chris Van Straaten.
Team Sponsors: TLS Vehicle Rental of Billingham/Simpson Racing UK.
Colours: Red and white
Nickname: Cubs.

HISTORY

First meeting: August 28, 2006, Cleveland v Scunthorpe, Conference Shield.
Leagues: Division Three, 2006-08.
†See Redcar (Premier League).

The aerial photograph above shows the site of the Redcar track before it was constructed.

HONOURS

Major honours: 7.
Division Two champions (2), 1947, 1981.
Division Two Young Shield winners (1), 2007.
Division Two Pairs champions (1), 1980.
Division Two Four Team champions (2), 1985, 1986.
Northern League champions (1), 1946.

2008 REVIEW

A NEW name at Conference League level but familiar faces as the former Cleveland Bays took the same branding as their second-tier colleagues.

It was a season where the club were so near, yet so far, from success despite an early setback when Greg Blair was ruled out even before the Cubs' campaign had started, whilst a number of other injuries forced something of a rebuilding job.

One rider to make an astonishing impact - and clearly one to look out for in the future - was former moto-cross rider Richard Lawson, who made a remarkable start to his speedway career with paid 17 on his debut at Sittingbourne.

Scott James was ever present and consistent home and away, and the Cubs did use a large number of riders as they juggled their resources around their squad's Premier League commitments. When Aaron Summers was available, he proved to be every inch a Conference League class act, and the Edinburgh man partnered James to second place in the Pairs.

There was glory for another mid-season acquisition, Benji Compton, who won the Conference League Riders' Championship at Rye House.

The League campaign saw the Cubs finish third in the table, unbeaten at home and scoring on the road at Sittingbourne (win) and Boston (draw).

It was Boston again in the play-offs, and the Cubs' home record fell to a late Barracudas onslaught, giving the Lincolnshire men a 48-45 lead to defend.

Yet before the last race of the return, the Cubs were assured of a win on the night and were favourites to go through, only for the unbeaten Summers to shed a chain on the start-line - and Boston edged to a one-point aggregate success.

It wasn't the only time the Cubs had that empty feeling, as they also felt robbed of gold in the Conference League Fours, sitting just one point behind Weymouth when the meeting was curtailed early.

2008 RESULTS

Conference League

Final position...Third

BUXTON (H)
Saturday, April 12
Won 56-32
James 15, Emerson 3:1, Beaton 2, Mudgway 7:1, **Summers 13:2**, Wallinger 6:2, Kendrew 10:1.
▲ *James became the first Cubs rider to score a full maximum, and Summers also unbeaten from five rides.*

SCUNTHORPE (A)
Saturday, April 26
Lost 39-49
James 13:1, *rider replacement for Summers*, Beaton 5, Emerson 8, Mudgway 5:1, Wallinger 8:2, Kendrew 0, Scott Whittingon [G] [no. 8].
▼ *Lost despite leading 37-34 with three heats to go. Wallinger and Emerson both crashed in match-changing Heat 14.*

PLYMOUTH (H)
Saturday, May 3
Won 47-43
James 8:1, Jones 6:1, Beaton 7:1, Emerson 4:1, Summers 19:1 (TS6), Wallinger 0, Kendrew 3.
▼ *Taken to last-heat decider but secured a 4-2 from Summers and James. Wallinger withdrew with foot injury after Heat 2 tumble.*

SCUNTHORPE (H)
Thursday, May 22
Won 49-43
James 11:1, Jones 7:2, Beaton 9, Emerson 2:1, **Summers 15**, Wallinger 5:1, Kendrew 0.
▲ *Moved top of the table thanks to Summers completing his maximum in Heat 15 when the Saints required a 5-1 to draw.*

RYE HOUSE (A)
Saturday, May 24
Lost 40-49
James 7, Mudgway 6:1, Beaton 6:1, Emerson 4, Jones 5:1, Wallinger 6:2, Kendrew 6:1.

PLYMOUTH (A)
Friday, August 8
Lost 34-58
James 7, Jones 3:2, *rider replacement for Summers*, Mudgway 10:1 (4), Compton 4:1, Mitchell 0, Beaton 7, Lawson [no. 8] 3:1.
▲ *Mudgway didn't win a race but was involved in much of the best action, and also figured in only two heat advantages.*

SITTINGBOURNE (A)
Sunday, August 10
Won 54-36
James 9, Jones 7:3, Beaton 6, Mudgway 9:2, Compton 6, Mitchell 1, Lawson 16:1.
▲ *Remarkable debut for Lawson with five straight wins in his first five outings, while James and Compton were both unbeaten in the races they finished.*

SQUAD
Gary Beaton, James Cockle, Benji Compton, Jitendra Duffill, Martin Emerson, Guy Kendrew, Steven Jones, Richard Lawson, Adam McKinna, Michael Mitchell, David Wallinger.
Foreign: Leigh Boujos, Scott James, Jade Mudgway, Aaron Summers.

WEYMOUTH (A)
Saturday, August 16
Lost 37-56
James 12:2 (6), Beaton 8:3, rider replacement for Summers, Mudgway 7, Compton 8, Ben Reade [G] 0, Daniel Greenwood [G] 2.
▼▼ *James won an early tactical ride to set up an 8-1 with Beaton, but this was the only respite as the Wildcats won comfortably. Guest reserve Ben Reade withdrawn after a Heat 2 fall.*

BUXTON (A)
Sunday, August 17
Lost 40-52
James 14:1 (4), Jones 3:3, *rider replacement for Summers*, Mudgway 7:1, Compton 10:1, Mitchell 0, Beaton 6.
▼ *Another disastrous start; James' tactical ride repelled.*

BOSTON (A)
Friday, August 22
Drew 46-46
James 14:2 (6), *rider replacement for Summers*, Cockle 9, Boujos 1, McKinna 10:1, Mudgway 6:3, Lawson 6:1.
▼ *Came back from 35-24 down to snatch a draw with 4-2 in Heat 14 and 5-1 in Heat 15 after both home riders hit mechanical trouble, McKinna and James cashing in.*

RYE HOUSE (H)
Thursday, September 4
Won 56-37
James 9:1, Jones 7:2, McKinna 11, Boujos 5, Mudgway 7:2, Beaton 9:2, Lawson 8:2.
▲ *Overcame a heavy deluge an hour before the start to rack up a comfortable win and maintain play-off hopes.*

BOSTON (H)
Thursday, September 4
Won 46-44
James 1, McKinna 9:1, Cockle 5:1, Compton 6, Summers 10, Mudgway 6:4, Lawson 9:1.
▲ *Trailed 38-40 but took a Heat 14 5-1 from Compton and Mudgway, and Summers was then the hero in Heat 15 – after being excluded in Heat 4 for not having a dirt deflector!*

Did you know?

Redcar went 75 days without a Conference League fixture between away matches at Rye House on May 24 and Plymouth on August 8.

WEYMOUTH (H)
Saturday, September 13
Won 53-37
James 9, *rider replacement for Summers*, Cockle 5:2, **Compton 15**, McKinna 9:1, Beaton 4, Lawson 11:1.
▲ *First 15-point maximum of Compton's career and Lawson also showed why he was quickly becoming a sought-after rider.*

SITTINGBOURNE (H)
Saturday, September 13
Won 60-32
James 11:1, Boujos 3, Cockle 7:4, Compton 11, **McKinna 12**, Jones 6:3, Lawson 10:1.
▲ *Cubs booked their play-off place with, as expected, a comfortable win although Mark Baseby prevented Compton from completing the day unbeaten.*

CONFERENCE LEAGUE

	M	W	D	L	PtsF	PtsA	Pts
Plymouth	14	9	0	5	709	569	20
Boston	14	8	1	5	713	565	19
REDCAR	**14**	**8**	**1**	**5**	**657**	**614**	**18**
Weymouth	14	8	1	6	688	588	17
Scunthorpe	14	8	1	6	637	629	17
Buxton	14	7	1	7	605	669	15
Rye House	14	6	1	8	614	663	12
Sittingbourne	14	1	0	13	472	798	2

PLAY-OFFS
Semi Final, first leg
BOSTON (H)
Thursday, September 25
Lost 45-48
James 7:3, McKinna 5:1, *rider replacement for Cockle*, Compton 8, Summers 9:1, Jones 8:2, Lawson 8:2.
▼ *Lost a five-point lead in the closing stages and conceded a 5-1 in Heat 15 to leave an uphill battle for the second leg – having not dropped a point at home all season.*

Semi Final, second leg
BOSTON (A)
Tuesday, October 14
Won 46-44
Cockle 1, Summers 12, James 5:2, Compton 7, McKinna 8, Jones 3, Lawson 10:2.
▼ *Heartbreaking end to the season when aggregate victory seemed certain. Two points were required from the last race but the unbeaten Summers never left the start-line due to chain failure.*
Aggregate: Lost 91-92.

Knock Out Cup

First round, first leg
BOSTON (A)
Sunday, June 8
Lost 43-51
James 9 (4), Jones 1, Beaton 7, Mudgway 6:1, Summers 17:1 (TS4), Kendrew 0, Wallinger 3.
▲▼ *Did well to recover from going 22-8 down in the first five races, Summers helping the Cubs to restrict the home side.*

First round, second leg
BOSTON (H)
Saturday, June 14
Drew 45-45
James 10:1, Jones 5:1, Beaton 8, Mudgway 0, **Summers 14:1**, Duffill 1, Emerson 7:1.
▲▼ *Summers broke track record but Mudgway's participation was ended by a first-ride mechanical failure.*
Aggregate: Lost 88-96.

It's all over for the Cubs – manager Jason Pipe, Adam McKinna and Benji Compton console each other after their dramatic play-off semi final defeat against Boston

Challenge

BOSTON (A)
Wednesday, April 9
Lost 38-55
James 3, Emerson 2:2, Mudgway 2, Beaton 8 (4), Summers 17 (TS4), Wallinger 3, Kendrew 3.

Weather...

Redcar had four team meetings called off because of rain – all of them away from home.

Conference League
Sunday, May 25 .... SITTINGBOURNE (A)
Sunday, July 6 .... BUXTON (A)
Saturday, August 9 .... WEYMOUTH (A)

Conference League Play-offs
Sunday, October 5 .... BOSTON (A)

...beaten

Former moto cross star Richard Lawson switched to the shale and was an instant success with Redcar
The son of ex-Glasgow legend Steve Lawson he did well enough in only nine appearances to be offered a team place in Workington's 2009 line-up

REDCAR

Rider	M	R	Pts	BP	TPts	Ave	F	P	TR	TPts	TS	TSPts
Aaron SUMMERS	8	43	109	6	115	10.70	1	2	0	0	2	5
Richard LAWSON	**9**	**43**	**81**	**12**	**93**	**8.65**	**0**	**0**	**0**	**0**	**0**	**0**
Scott JAMES	18	88	171	16	187	8.50	1	1	4	10	0	0
Adam McKINNA	**7**	**34**	**64**	**4**	**68**	**8.00**	**1**	**0**	**0**	**0**	**0**	**0**
Benji COMPTON	9	41	75	2	77	7.51	1	0	0	0	0	0
Jade MUDGWAY	**12**	**53**	**76**	**17**	**93**	**7.02**	**0**	**0**	**1**	**2**	**0**	**0**
Steven JONES	12	47	61	20	81	6.89	0	0	0	0	0	0
James COCKLE	**5**	**21**	**27**	**7**	**34**	**6.48**	**0**	**0**	**0**	**0**	**0**	**0**
Gary BEATON	13	57	84	7	91	6.39	0	0	0	0	0	0
David WALLINGER	**6**	**24**	**28**	**7**	**35**	**5.83**	**0**	**0**	**0**	**0**	**0**	**0**
Martin EMERSON	6	27	28	4	32	4.74	0	0	0	0	0	0
Guy KENDREW	**6**	**26**	**19**	**2**	**21**	**3.23**	**0**	**0**	**0**	**0**	**0**	**0**
Leigh BOUJOS	3	13	9	0	9	2.77	0	0	0	0	0	0
Jitendra DUFFILL	**1**	**3**	**1**	**0**	**1**	**1.33**	**0**	**0**	**0**	**0**	**0**	**0**
Michael MITCHELL	3	10	1	0	1	0.40	0	0	0	0	0	0
Guests												
Daniel GREENWOOD	1	7	2	0	2	1.14	0	0	0	0	0	0
Ben READE	**1**	**1**	**0**	**0**	**0**	**0.00**	**0**	**0**	**0**	**0**	**0**	**0**

For Aaron SUMMERs see Edinburgh; for Adam McKINNA see Berwick and Buxton; for Benji COMPTON see Scunthorpe (PL and CL); for James COCKLE see Mildenhall, Birmingham and Boston.

Conference League

RYE HOUSE

TRACK FILE

Track: Rye Road, Hoddesdon, Hertfordshire, EN11 0EH
Telephone: 01992 440400.
Hotline: 09066 555948.
Website: www.ryehouse.com
Track Length: 262 metres.
Track Record: 55.6 secs, Tai Woffinden, September 29, 2007.
Promoters: Len Silver and Hazal Naylor.
Team Sponsors: Rye House Kart Raceway.
Colours: Blue and gold with cobra logo.
Nickname: Rye House Kart Raceway Cobras.
See also Rye House (Premier League).

HISTORY

First meeting: August 3, 1958, August Trophy.
Leagues: Division Three, †1999, 2000-09.
†In 1999 the Rye House Rockets were a nomadic team, racing their home matches at Eastbourne, King's Lynn and Mildenhall.

HONOURS

Major honours: 1.
Division Three Four Team champions (1), 2003.

2009 Squad

Daniel **BLAKE**, Michael **BOVIS**, Jamie **COURTNEY**, Daniel **HALSEY**, Ben **MORLEY**, Rob **SMITH**, Lee **STRUDWICK**.

2008 REVIEW

RYE House have always been staunch supporters of the third tier as they seek to unearth fresh talent to come into their Premier League set-up.

But their patience was sorely tested during an altogether disappointing campaign in which the management admitted they had to question the desire and commitment of some of their squad.

The year started with a fresh look as the Raiders were re-named the Cobras, and it was always expected that they would be able hold their own on their home circuit.

They could do little more than that and were never amongst the front runners, even after the confidence-booster of a comfortable KO Cup win over Sittingbourne in their opening fixtures.

The Cobras lost six of their first seven Conference League fixtures, two of them at home, and a series of heavy away defeats left them some way behind the front-runners.

Ironically one of the best performances came in a 56-37 home Cup win over Plymouth with the Cobras so close to overturning a 21-point first leg deficit.

But they needed to win their last two away matches to reach the play-offs and ended up winning neither - even allowing Sittingbourne their sole success in a 46-44 defeat in their penultimate fixture, conceding a 5-1 in the last race.

On the riding staff, skipper Daniel Halsey was beyond criticism and was voted rider of the year, and there were promising signs too from Lee Strudwick and Richard Franklin - but several others were left to reflect on campaigns which were at best inconsistent. Four riders each scored one maximum during the season.

Halsey had hoped to win the Conference League Riders' Championship on his home circuit but had to settle for fourth place, paying dearly for a last place in his first ride.

2008 RESULTS

Conference League

Final position..Seventh

BOSTON (A)
Wednesday, May 21
Lost 39-54
Rider replacement for Betson, Smith 2, Aldridge 1:1, Day 10:1, Halsey 12 (6), Franklin 3:1, Cottham 11:1.
▼ *Aldridge withdrew with a shoulder injury after a Heat 3 crash, and three other riders suffered falls during the meeting.*

REDCAR (H)
Saturday, May 24
Won 49-40
Betson 12:1, Smith 3, Aldridge 6, Day 0, **Halsey 13:2**, Cottham 1, Strudwick 14:1.
▲ *Trailed 24-30 after nine races but Strudwick, Halsey and Betson did enough to turn things around.*

SCUNTHORPE (A)
Friday, May 30
Lost 34-58
Betson 3, Cottham 5:1, Halsey 11:1 (4), Aldridge 4:1, Day 3, Franklin 4, Strudwick 4.
▼ *Lost the services of reserve Strudwick after he hit the fallen Scott Richardson in Heat 4, but battled hard after going 3-15 down.*

PLYMOUTH (H)
Saturday, June 7
Lost 42-47
Betson 5:1, Cottham 5, **Halsey 15**, Aldridge 5, Day 5, Greenwood 7, Franklin 0.
▼ *Franklin suffered a broken wrist in a crash in Heat 2 so Greenwood took seven rides on his Conference League debut.*

PLYMOUTH (A)
Friday, June 13
Lost 34-56
Rider replacement for Betson, Smith 8:1 (1), Halsey 12:1, Aldridge 6:1, Day 1:1, Greenwood 1:1, Cottham 6.
▼ *Day suffered knee and elbow injuries when he crashed in Heat 4.*

WEYMOUTH (A)
Saturday, June 14
Lost 31-62
Rider replacement for Betson, Smith 2, Halsey 13 (6), Aldridge 3:1, Day 10, Greenwood 1, Cottham 2.
▼ *Former Weymouth rider Day returned and won two races, as did Halsey, but defeat brought a disappointing weekend to a close.*

BUXTON (A)
Sunday, June 22
Lost 26-65
Smith 3, Cottham 4:1, Halsey 7 (4), Aldridge 5:1, Day 2, Greenwood 5, Strudwick 0.
▲▼*Aldridge won Heat 14 at the end of a difficult afternoon when five of the Buxton riders went unbeaten by a Cobra.*

SQUAD
Daniel Betson, Daniel Blake, Gary Cottham, Terry Day, Richard Franklin, Daniel Greenwood, Danny Halsey, Nick Laurence, Robert Mear, Rob Smith, Lee Strudwick.
Foreign: Andrew Aldridge.

SCUNTHORPE (H)
Sunday, June 29
Won 54-36
Rider replacement for Betson, Smith 6, Halsey 13, Aldridge 7:3, Day 7:1, **Cottham 19:2**, Greenwood 2.
▲ *Cottham collected a seven-ride paid maximum although he received a stroke of fortune in Heat 15 when leader Byron Bekker hit trouble on the third lap.*

BUXTON (H)
Saturday, July 12
Won 59-34
Smith 10:4, Cottham 16:1, *rider replacement for Halsey*, Aldridge 12:2, Day 6, Laurence 5:3, Strudwick 10:1, Greenwood [no. 8] 0.
▲ *Cobras promotion offered free admission for this meeting – a straightforward win despite efforts of Jack Roberts and Ben Taylor.*

SITTINGBOURNE (H)
Saturday, August 23
Won 54-35
Smith 13:2, Strudwick 11, Cottham 4:1, Aldridge 9, Day 7:1, Greenwood 3, Franklin 7:2.
▲ *Scores level after three heats, but Cobras took control with five 5-1s in the next seven races.*

REDCAR (A)
Thursday, September 4
Lost 37-56
Smith 3, Cottham 3:1, Halsey 17 (6), Aldridge 2, Strudwick 5, Robert McNeil [G] 1, Franklin 6.
▼ *Only Halsey offered consistent resistance, being beaten by Adam McKinna in Heat 3 but then reeling off four straight wins.*

BOSTON (H)
Sunday, September 21
Won 52-40
Smith 9:1, Cottham 7:1, Halsey 8:2, Aldridge 6, Day 2:1, Franklin 10:1, Strudwick 10:2.
▲ *Reserves took centre stage as both Franklin and Strudwick earned nominations for Heat 15.*

SITTINGBOURNE (A)
Sunday, September 28
Lost 44-46
Smith 11, Strudwick 5, Cottham 5:1, Aldridge 8:1, Day 5, Blake 4:1, Franklin 6:2.

WEYMOUTH (H)
Sunday, October 12
Won 59-34
Mear 15, Cottham 9:3, Halsey 10:1, Aldridge 6:2,

Smith 6:1, Franklin 8:2, Strudwick 5:1.

▲ *Cobras showed fine form to start with four 5-1s, another indication of the form which they had been unable to display consistently during the season.*

CONFERENCE LEAGUE

	M	*W*	*D*	*L*	*PtsF*	*PtsA*	*Pts*
Plymouth	14	9	0	5	709	569	20
Boston	14	8	1	5	713	565	19
Redcar	14	8	1	5	657	614	18
Weymouth	14	8	1	6	686	588	17
Scunthorpe	14	8	1	6	637	629	17
Buxton	14	7	1	7	605	669	15
RYE HOUSE	**14**	**6**	**1**	**8**	**614**	**663**	**12**
Sittingbourne	14	1	0	13	472	798	2

Knock Out Cup

Quarter Final, first leg
SITTINGBOURNE (H)
Saturday, May 3
Won 59-33

Smith 7, *rider replacement for Betson*, **Aldridge 16:2**, **Strudwick 16:2**, Day 3:1, Franklin 7:3, Cottham 10, Nick Laurence [no. 8].

▲ *New Zealander Aldridge and Strudwick both unbeaten from six rides to put the newly re-named Cobras into a strong position in the tie.*

Quarter Final, second leg
SITTINGBOURNE (A)
Sunday, May 11
Won 47-42

Halsey 9:1, Smith 2, Aldridge 6:1, Day 4, Strudwick 13, Franklin 3, Cottham 10:3.

▲ *Comfortable win on aggregate.*

Aggregate: Win 106-75.

Did you know?

Rye House were the only team to lose a Conference League match at Sittingbourne all season. Top scorers Rob Smith and Andrew Aldridge were unable to pass Mark Baseby in the decider.

Semi Final, first leg
PLYMOUTH (A)
Friday, July 18
Lost 36-57

Rider replacement for Betson, Smith 10, Halsey 13 (6), Aldridge 3:1, Day 6:1, Greenwood 0, Cottham 3:1, David Gough [G] [no. 8] 1:1.

▼ *Left with plenty to do in second leg as they relied heavily on two riders and conceded 5-1s in the last two races.*

Semi Final, second leg
PLYMOUTH (H)
Sunday, July 27
11-13 abandoned after Heat 4, waterlogged track following thunderstorm.

Rider replacement for Mear, Smith 3, Halsey 1, Aldridge 1, Day 0, Cottham 3, Strudwick 3:1.

▼ *Torrential downpour during Heat 4 caused a winning time seven seconds slower than the previous race, with the inevitable decision.*

Semi Final, second leg
PLYMOUTH (H)
Sunday, August 10
Won 56-37

Mear 14:1, Smith 9:1, Halsey 11, Aldridge 4:2, Day 3:1, Cottham 9:1, Strudwick 6:3.

▼ *Narrowly failed to pull off a shock aggregate win as Halsey was just denied by veteran Mark Simmonds for second place in the decider – a 5-1 would have set up a replay.*

Aggregate: Lost 92-94.

RYE HOUSE

Rider	*M*	*R*	*Pts*	*BP*	*TPts*	*Ave*	*F*	*P*	*TR*	*TPts*	*TS*	*TSPts*
Robert MEAR	2	10	29	1	30	12.00	1	1	0	0	0	0
Daniel HALSEY	**14**	**70**	**164**	**8**	**172**	**9.83**	**1**	**1**	**6**	**16**	**0**	**0**
Lee STRUDWICK	12	53	99	10	109	8.23	0	1	0	0	0	0
Nick LAURENCE	**1**	**4**	**5**	**3**	**8**	**8.00**	**0**	**0**	**0**	**0**	**0**	**0**
Danny BETSON	3	13	20	2	22	6.77	0	0	0	0	0	0
Andrew ALDRIDGE	**18**	**77**	**109**	**19**	**128**	**6.65**	**0**	**0**	**0**	**0**	**0**	**0**
Gary COTTHAM	18	90	129	18	147	6.53	0	1	0	0	0	0
Rob SMITH	**16**	**70**	**104**	**10**	**114**	**6.51**	**0**	**0**	**1**	**0**	**0**	**0**
Richard FRANKLIN	10	45	54	11	65	5.78	0	0	0	0	0	0
Danny BLAKE	**1**	**4**	**4**	**1**	**5**	**5.00**	**0**	**0**	**0**	**0**	**0**	**0**
Terry DAY	16	67	74	8	82	4.90	0	0	0	0	0	0
Daniel GREENWOOD	**8**	**35**	**19**	**1**	**20**	**2.29**	**0**	**0**	**0**	**0**	**0**	**0**
Robert McNEIL	1	3	1	0	1	1.33	0	0	0	0	0	0
Guests												
David GOUGH	1	1	1	1	2	8.00	0	0	0	0	0	0

For Robert MEAR, Daniel HALSEY and Danny BETSON see Rye House (PL).

Individual

CONFERENCE LEAGUE RIDERS' FINAL
Saturday, September 27

1 Benji Compton 14, 2 Byron Bekker 13, 3 Darcy Ward 12+3, 4 Daniel Halsey 12+21, 5 Jay Herne 12+1, 6 Ben Taytor 9, 7 Gareth Isherwood 7, 8 Rob Smith 7, 9 Kyle Hughes 6, 19 Dean Felton 6, 11 Gary Cottham [R] 5, 12 Simon Lambert 4, 13 Tom Brown 3, 14 Harland Cook [R] 3, 15 Scott Richardson 2, 16 Richard Lawson 2, 17 Aaron Baseby 1, 18 Kyle Newman 1.

For race-by-race details and Roll of Honour see Conference League.

Weather...

Two home matches fell by the wayside as well as an intriguing challenge against Elite League Lakeside's juniors.

Conference League

Sunday, April 20 .... BOSTON (A)
Sunday, September 7 .... SITTINGBOURNE (A)
Saturday, October 4 .... WEYMOUTH (H)

Challenge

Saturday, March 22 .... LAKESIDE (H)

...beaten

Daniel GREENWOOD

Richard FRANKLIN – and in action right

Conference League

SCUNTHORPE

TRACK FILE

Track: Eddie Wright Raceway, Normanby Road, Scunthorpe, North Lincolnshire, DN15 8QZ.
Telephone: 01724 848899.
Hotline: 09066 555923.
Website: www.scunthorpespeedway.com
Track Length: 285 metres.
Track Record: 56.39 secs, Richard Hall, August 25, 2008.
Promoters: Rob Godfrey and Kenny Smith.
Colours: Blue with white trim and Saint logo.
Nickname: Saints.
See Scunthorpe (Premier League).

HISTORY

First meeting: March 27, 2005, Grand Opening Individual meeting.
Leagues: Division Two, 2008-09. Division Three, 2005-09.

HONOURS

Major honours: 9.
Division Three champions (2), 2006, 2007.
Division Three Knock Out Cup winners (2), 2006, 2007.
Division Three Shield winners (1), 2006.
Division Three Trophy winners (2), 2006, 2007.
Division Three Four Team champions (1), 2007.
Division Three Pairs champions (1), 2006.

2008 REVIEW

THERE was a change of emphasis for Scunthorpe's Conference League set-up in 2008 as the club made the big step into Premier League racing.

Under the management of former Boston boss Malcolm Vasey, the priority now was to work on developing new talent which could make its way eventually towards the PL side - and that spelt the end of the club's domination of the third tier.

Re-named the Saints, it was virtually an all-new team with the likes of Tai Woffinden, Josh Auty and Joe Haines - all outstanding talents - moving on, and their replacements being riders at different stages of their development.

Even so, the team were a match for virtually everyone in what was a closely-fought division, and they could consider themselves somewhat unfortunate to miss out on the play-offs having finished fifth, just three points off the top.

The season got off to a strong start with a series of home wins, although they never really threatened to succeed on the road until running up 60 points at Sittingbourne in July.

Byron Bekker, who was also racing for the PL side, reeled off several maximums, and the club were particularly impressed with the steady progress of Cumbrian youngster Gary Beaton.

Knockout Cup progress was ensured with a narrow aggregate win over Buxton, but the regular campaign was to end in disappointment as they were unable to secure the one more away win needed to break into the top four.

And the team's lengthy and impressive home record was finally ended in their final outing of the season, when Boston gained some revenge for several defeats in previous seasons by taking the local derby Cup semi-final by winning both legs.

Bekker finished runner-up in the Conference League Riders' Championship, and the team also reached the Final of the Fours but were placed fourth.

2008 RESULTS

Conference League

Final position..Fifth

BOSTON (H)
Monday, March 24
Won 46-43
Compton 5, Anderson 0, Bethell 4:1, Bekker 11, Martin 6:3, Irving 3:1, Richardson 17.
▲ *Richardson was the trump card at reserve although he crashed out of Heat 14 – but Saints successfully shared the decider.*

REDCAR (H)
Saturday, April 26
Won 49-39
Compton 11, Anderson 1:1, Bethell 5:2, Bekker 13:1, Martin 8:1, Irving 5:2, Richardson 6:1.
▲ *Result in doubt until the Saints secured a 5-0 in Heat 14, having been three points down with three races to go.*

WEYMOUTH (H)
Monday, May 5
Won 48-45
Rider replacement for Compton, Anderson 6:2, Bethell 9:3, Bekker 16, Martin 2:2, Irving 6:2, Richardson 9.

REDCAR (A)
Thursday, May 22
Lost 43-49
Rider replacement for Compton, Anderson 0, Bethell 2:1, Bekker 15 (6), Robertson 7:1, Irving 5:2, Richardson 12:2, Pickering [no. 8] 2.
▼ *Suffered first defeat in last-heat decider having taken an 8-1 in Heat 14 to close to within four points of Cubs.*

RYE HOUSE (H)
Friday, May 30
Won 58-34
Bekker 11:1, Anderson 9:1, Bethell 8:1, **Compton 11:1**, Martin 5, Irving 5:3, Richardson 9:2.
▲▼ *Opened with three 5-1s to take control. Martin was forced to withdraw after crash with Irving in Heat 7.*

PLYMOUTH (A)
Friday, June 27
Lost 34-58
Bekker 11 (4), Parnaby 4:2, *rider replacement for Bethell,* Richardson 5:1, Scarboro 6:1, Irving 5, Pickering 2, Danny Stoneman [G] [no. 8] 1:1.
▲▼ *Major team changes in place with Bethell and Anderson injured and the club having parted company with Compton and Martin.*

RYE HOUSE (A)
Sunday, June 29
Lost 36-54
Bekker 8:1 (1), Parnaby 6:2, *rider replacement for Bethell,* Richardson 4:1, Scarboro 4:1, Irving 9:1, Pickering 5.
▼ *Bekker pushed home for over a lap in Heat 15 after suffering mechanical trouble with Terry Day having already crashed out.*

SQUAD
Scott Anderson, Jonathan Bethell, Jamie Birkinshaw, Benji Compton, Ben Hopwood, Gary Irving, Stuart Parnaby, Mike Pickering, Scott Richardson, Adam Wrathall.
Foreign: Byron Bekker, Sam Martin.

SITTINGBOURNE (A)
Sunday, July 6
Won 60-32
Bekker 17:1,Parnaby 8:4, *rider replacement for Bethell,* Richardson 15, Scarboro 8:1, Irving 8:1, Pickering 4:2.
▲ *Dominated at the Old Gun site with a 5-1 and a 5-0 in the first two races and a sparkling display from Bekker.*

BOSTON (A)
Sunday, July 13
Lost 33-60
Bekker 11 (TS4), Parnaby 3:1, Richardson 5:1, Hopwood 0, Scarboro 3, Irving 8:1 (4), Pickering 3:1.
▼▲ *Bekker's retirement from Heat 1 set the tone for the day, with the Saints' number one recording their only race win in Heat 5. New signing Hopwood debuted.*

BUXTON (H)
Friday, July 18
Won 50-41
Bekker 12, Hopwood 6, Bethell 10, Pickering 5:3, Richardson 7:1, Irving 8, Wrathall 2:1.
● *Spirited show from Buxton reserve Gareth Isherwood (16).*

SITTINGBOURNE (H)
Friday, August 1
Won 62-30
Bethell 14, Pickering 8:3, Richardson 9, Parnaby 8:2, Hopwood 10:2, Irving 8:1, Wrathall 5:1.
▲ *Promotion attracted 1,400 crowd for free-admission fixture, and Saints put on a convincing display.*

BUXTON (A)
Sunday, August 10
Lost 38-53
Bethell 6, Pickering 1:1, Richardson 7, Parnaby 9:2 (4), Hopwood 5, Irving 5, Wrathall 5:3.
▼ *Remained in touch until the final four heats, but were never likely to win with only two heat winners.*

WEYMOUTH (A)
Saturday, August 23
Lost 29-52
Bekker 10:1 (6), Hopwood 1, Bethell 4:1, Parnaby 1, Richardson 8, Irving 5:1, Wrathall 0.
●▼ *Meeting abandoned after Heat 13, heavy rain. Result to stand. Disappointing performance with Bekker and Richardson taking the only race wins, including a 5-1 in Heat 13 – the last race before rain forced a halt.*

PLYMOUTH (H)
Monday, August 25
Won 51-39
Birkinshaw 8:2, Hopwood 8:1, Bethell 4:2, Richardson 10,

Weather...

Their only forfeited meeting was a planned trip to Norfolk to face Boston in the KO Cup.

Knock Out Cup
Sunday, September 7 ....BOSTON (A)

...beaten

Bekker 10, Irving 8:1, Wrathall 3:1.

▲ *Back to winning ways somewhat against the formbook – a determined show from the Saints, whose 5-1 from Bekker and debutant Birkinshaw in Heat 13 was crucial.*

CONFERENCE LEAGUE

	M	W	D	L	PtsF	PtsA	Pts
Plymouth	14	9	0	5	709	569	20
Boston	14	8	1	5	713	565	19
Redcar	14	8	1	5	657	614	18
Weymouth	14	8	1	6	688	588	17
SCUNTHORPE	**14**	**8**	**1**	**6**	**637**	**629**	**17**
Buxton	14	7	1	7	605	669	15
Rye House	14	6	1	8	614	663	12
Sittingbourne	14	1	0	13	472	798	2

2009 Squad

Byron **BEKKER**, Jamie **BIRKINSHAW**, Richard **FRANKLIN**, Kyle **HOWARTH**, Gary **IRVING**, Simon **LAMBERT**, Ashley **MORRIS**, Stuart **PARNABY**, Scott **RICHARDSON**, James **SARJEANT**, Adam **WRATHALL**.

Knock Out Cup

Quarter Final, first leg
BUXTON (H)
Monday, May 26
Won 52-41
Bekker 13, Anderson 5:1, Bethell 9:1, *rider replacement for Compton*, Martin 9:1, Irving 5:2, Richardson 10, Pickering [no. 8] 1.

Quarter Final, second leg
BUXTON (A)
Sunday, June 8
Lost 41-50
Bekker 12 (4), Anderson 0, *rider replacement for Bethell*, Richardson 7:1, Scarboro 4, Irving 6:1, Pickering 12.

▲▼ *Under pressure with a 34-19 deficit, but clawed their way back on aggregate thanks to Bekker's win in Heat 15. Anderson crashed in opening heat and was eligible for the re-run but ruled out through injury*

Aggregate: Won 93-91.

Semi Final, first leg
BOSTON (A)
Sunday, September 28
Lost 35-56
Bekker 5:1 (TSX), *rider replacement for Bethell*, Richardson 8, Hopwood 2:2, Parnaby 7, Wrathall 0, Irving 13:2 (4).

▼ *Uphill battle to reach the Final, reserve Irving performing well but Saints being unable to hold any of the Barracudas' top three.*

SCUNTHORPE

Rider	*M*	*R*	*Pts*	*BP*	*TPts*	*Ave*	*F*	*P*	*TR*	*TPts*	*TS*	*TSPts*
Byron BEKKER	16	83	183	7	190	9.16	1	2	5	10	2	2
Benji COMPTON	**3**	**13**	**27**	**1**	**28**	**8.61**	**0**	**1**	**0**	**0**	**0**	**0**
Jamie BIRKINSHAW	1	5	8	2	10	8.00	0	0	0	0	0	0
Jamie ROBERTSON	**1**	**4**	**7**	**1**	**8**	**8.00**	**0**	**0**	**0**	**0**	**0**	**0**
Jonathan BETHELL	11	46	75	12	87	7.56	0	0	0	0	0	0
Sam MARTIN	**5**	**21**	**30**	**7**	**37**	**7.05**	**0**	**0**	**0**	**0**	**0**	**0**
Scott RICHARDSON	18	94	153	11	164	6.98	0	0	0	0	0	0
Gary IRVING	**18**	**85**	**124**	**23**	**147**	**6.92**	**0**	**0**	**2**	**4**	**0**	**0**
Stuart PARNABY	9	39	52	15	67	6.87	0	0	1	2	0	0
Mike PICKERING	**10**	**37**	**43**	**10**	**53**	**5.73**	**0**	**0**	**0**	**0**	**0**	**0**
Ben HOPWOOD	8	33	38	7	45	5.45	0	0	0	0	0	0
Scott ANDERSON	**7**	**20**	**21**	**5**	**26**	**5.20**	**0**	**0**	**0**	**0**	**0**	**0**
Ricky SCARBORO	5	24	25	3	28	4.67	0	0	0	0	0	0
Adam WRATHALL	**7**	**28**	**22**	**7**	**29**	**4.14**	**0**	**0**	**0**	**0**	**0**	**0**
Craig COOK	1	3	1	1	2	2.67	0	0	0	0	0	0
Guests												
Danny STONEMAN	*1*	*1*	*1*	*1*	*2*	*8.00*	*0*	*0*	*0*	*0*	*0*	*0*

For Byron BEKKER see Scunthorpe (PL); for Benji COMPTON see Scunthorpe (PL) and Redcar (CL); for Jamie BIRKINSHAW see Birmingham; for Jamie ROBERTSON see Newcastle; for Sam MARTIN see Sheffield; for Ben HOPWOOD see Plymouth; for Ricky SCARBORO see Sittingbourne.

Semi Final, second leg
BOSTON (H)
Friday, October 10
Lost 45-48
Bekker 8:1, Cook 1:1, Richardson 5:1, Parnaby 6:2, Hopwood 6:2, Wrathall 7:1, Irving 12:2.
▲ *Run of consecutive home wins ended in the 49th fixture with Joe Haines and Simon Lambert taking a 5-1 in Heat 15 for the Barracudas, whose aggregate win was never in doubt.*
Aggregate: Lost 80-104.

Jonathan Bethell (left) joined the Saints from Conference League rivals Buxton while Scott Richardson (above) was an everpresent in all the Lincolnshire side's 18 official fixtures

PHOTOS: **Steve Dixon**

Scunthorpe: back – Jonathan Bethell, Byron Bekker, skipper Benji Compton, team manager Malcolm Vasey, Sam Martin, Gary Irving, Scott Richardson. Front – Adam Wrathall, Scott Anderson

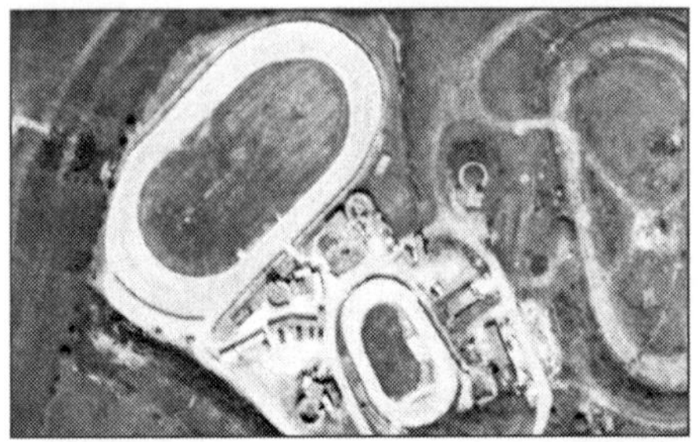

Sittingbourne

Conference League

SITTINGBOURNE

TRACK FILE

Track: The Old Gun Site, Raspberry Hill Lane, Iwade, Kent, ME9 8SP.
Telephone: 01795 430014.
Hotline: 07857 849551.
Website: www.sittingbournespeedway.co.uk
Track Length: 251 metres.
Track Record: 58 secs, Paul Hurry, October 30, 2005.
2008 Promoters: Graham Arnold and Chris Hunt.
Colours: Blue and yellow.
Nickname: Crusaders.

HISTORY

First meeting: November 5, 1972, Training School Championship.
Leagues: Division Three, †1994, 1995-96, 2004-08. Open licence, 1972-1993, 1997-2003.
Operated as a training track in 1970 and 1971.
†Entered Division Three but withdrew after completing only one away meeting.

HONOURS

Major honours: 0.

2008 REVIEW

IT could well turn out to be the Crusaders' final season - and it was a largely forgettable campaign which appeared destined for disappointment from the word go.

Ironically enough, the perennial strugglers felt they had put themselves in with a good chance by putting together a tidy initial line-up. The problem was that this team was broken up even before they turned a wheel.

An inherent danger of Conference League racing is that riders will be picked up to race in the higher tier, and this turned out to be exactly the case for Barry Burchatt and Jerran Hart - with any chance of appearances for Burchatt being removed by his awful grasstrack accident which appears to have ended his career.

Mark Baseby, another heat-leader with PL aspirations, hurt his ankle in a British U21 qualifier, and he only returned to the club's colours in mid-September.

So the rest of the team battled on with a hefty collection of riders used, but the only time they got close to a win in the Conference League was when Buxton were limited to just a two-point win at the Old Gun site in June.

That was until the very last match of the season against Rye House, when Baseby and Harland Cook combined for a last-heat 5-1 to bring some joy with a 46-44 win.

It was Baseby's younger brother Aaron who took most of the individual plaudits with an ever-present record, and although his average was still a shade under five, there was the feeling that he had made genuine progress.

Unexpected highlights arrived in two of the major events, with the Crusaders placed third in both the Conference League Fours and the Pairs - the latter being somewhat controversial as they took it from Scunthorpe on the drawing of lots when the consolation final could not be raced.

2008 RESULTS

Conference League

Final position..Eighth

WEYMOUTH (A)
Saturday, May 10
Lost 31-61
Felton 3, Cook 7:1, Cunningham 0, Hart 11 (6), Cross 2, Berwick 2, Baseby 6:3.
▼ *Hart's tactical ride win was the Crusaders' sole success of the evening.*

BOSTON (H)
Sunday, June 1
Lost 35-55
Felton 5:1, Cunningham 3:1, Irwin 3:1, Cook 13, *rider replacement for M. Baseby,* Berwick 4, Baseby 7.

BUXTON (H)
Sunday, June 15
Lost 44-46
Felton 12:1, Cunnibngham 6:1, Irwin 10:1, A. Baseby 8, *rider replacement for M. Baseby,* Andrews 2:1, Berwick 6:2.
▼ *Denied victory or even a point in a last-heat decider after the Hitmen's Jack Roberts collected a 4-2 with Lewis Dallaway.*

BOSTON (A)
Sunday, June 29
Lost 25-62
Felton 5, Cunningham 1, Irwin 3:1, Cook 6:1, Hart 4, Andrews 4:1, A. Baseby 2.
▼ *Failed to provide a heat winner as Crusaders struggled in difficult track conditions.*

SCUNTHORPE (H)
Sunday, July 6
Lost 32-60
Felton 12 (6), Cunningham 4:1, Irwin 3, A. Baseby 6:1, Cook 4, Andrews 1, Berwick 2:1.
▼ *Trailed 10-1 after two disastrous opening races leading to a heavy defeat – consolation being an 8-1 from Felton and Cunningham in Heat 6.*

BUXTON (A)
Sunday, July 13
Lost 31-61
Felton 10:1 (4), Cunningham 4:1, Irwin 2, *rider replacement for M. Baseby,* A. Baseby 7, Berwick 7, Andrews 1:1.
▼ *Felton won Heat 1 but that was as good as it got for the Crusaders, who again conceded 60-plus points.*

WEYMOUTH (H)
Sunday, July 20
Lost 31-60
Felton 11:1 (4), Cunninbgham 5:1, *rider replacement for M. Baseby,* Cook 7, A. Baseby 1, Andrews 1, Berwick 6, Mullins [no. 8] 0.
▼ *Crusaders suffered a remarkable series of falls, exclusions and retirements to make it easy for the Wildcats.*

SQUAD
Marc Andrews, Aaron Baseby, Mark Baseby, Daniel Berwick, Harland Cook, Andre Cross, Dean Felton, Jerran Hart, Nathan Irwin, Rikki Mullins, Ricky Scarboro, Niall Strudwick.
Foreign: Alex Cunningham.

PLYMOUTH (A)
Friday, July 25
Lost 31-60
Felton 11 (4), Cunningham 2:2, *rider replacement for M. Baseby,* Cook 9:1, A. Baseby 4:1, Andrews 0, Berwick 5:1.
▼ *Only advantages came with a 5-3 in Heat 5 and a 5-1 from Cook and Berwick in Heat 14, by which time the match was long-since lost.*

SCUNTHORPE (A)
Friday, August 1
Lost 30-62
Felton 9:1, Cunningham 3:1, Cook 10, Mullins 0, A. Baseby 3, Andrews 1, Berwick 4:1.
▲▼ *Cook improved and won two races, but this was a contest dominated by the home side.*

PLYMOUTH (H)
Sunday, August 3
Lost 33-59
Felton 11 (4), Cunningham 3:3, Cook 6, Andrews 1:1, A. Baseby 3, Mullins 0, Berwick 9:1.
▼ *Berwick picked up a win in Heat 2 but this turned out to be the Crusaders' sole success. They were a beaten side by Heat 12.*

REDCAR (H)
Sunday, August 10
Lost 36-54
Felton 8:1, Cunningham 2, Cook 8:1 (4), *rider replacement for M. Baseby,* A. Baseby 11, Mullins 3:1, Berewick 4:1.
▼ *Crusaders were level after Heat 4 but had no answer to Redcar's debutant Richard Lawson, who racked up an impressive paid 17.*

RYE HOUSE (A)
Saturday, August 23
Lost 35-54
Felton 2, M. Baseby 7:1, Cook 6, Hart 10:1 (0), Scarboro 3, A. Baseby 7, Berwick 0.
▼ *Held the home side to 24-18 after Heat 7, but conceded three straight 5-1s before Hart and the Baseby brothers finished the meeting well.*

REDCAR (A)
Saturday, September 13
Lost 32-60
Felton 1:1, Cunningham 3 (TS0), M. Baseby 16 (4), *rider replacement for Cook,* Scarboro 5:2, A. Baseby 1, Berwick 6.
▼ *Mark Baseby impressed with wins in each of his last three races, but neither younger brother Aaron (leg) or skipper Felton (abrasions) were able to complete the meeting which saw Crusaders fail to pick up an away point all season.*

RYE HOUSE (H)
Sunday, September 28
Won 46-44
Felton 7, A. Baseby 6, Cook 9:3, **M. Baseby 15**, Scarboro 6, Strudwick 0, Berwick 3.

▲ *Snatched their only win of the year in their last fixture of the season, Mark Baseby ensuring that Cook's engine failure would not affect the final result by taking the flag to scenes of celebration in Heat 15.*

CONFERENCE LEAGUE

	M	W	D	L	PtsF	PtsA	Pts
Plymouth	14	9	0	5	709	569	20
Boston	14	8	1	5	713	565	19
Redcar	14	8	1	5	657	614	18
Weymouth	14	8	1	6	688	588	17
Scunthorpe	14	8	1	6	637	629	17
Buxton	14	7	1	7	605	669	15
Rye House	14	6	1	8	614	663	12
SITTINGBOURNE	**14**	**1**	**0**	**13**	**472**	**798**	**2**

JERRAN HART

Knock Out Cup

Quarter Final, first leg
RYE HOUSE (A)
Saturday, May 3
Lost 33-59
Felton 6:2, Cook 8, *rider replacement for Burchatt*, Hart 11 (6), Berwick 2:1, Cunningham 1, A. Baseby 5:1, Mullins [no. 8].

▼ *Hart and former Rye House man Cook were the top Crusaders, but they were 9-26 down after six races.*

Quarter Final, second leg
RYE HOUSE (H)
Sunday, May 11
Lost 42-47
Felton 13:2, Cook 6:2, *rider replacement for M. Baseby*, Hart 12, Cunningham 1, A. Baseby 8:1, Mullins 2:1.

▲▼ *Never a question of aggregate win but a creditable showing from the Crusaders before finally going down in Heat 14.*

Aggregate: Lost 75-106.

Weather...

Lost two home matches to the elements.

Conference League
Sunday, May 25 ....REDCAR (H)
Sunday, September 7 ....RYE HOUSE (H)

...beaten

SITTINGBOURNE'S chequered career took another downturn during the winter when the decision was reached not to contest the 2009 National League.
Even though there'll be no league racing at the Old Gun Site they will continue to run training schools and corporate dates.

SITTINGBOURNE

Rider	M	R	Pts	BP	TPts	Ave	F	P	TR	TPts	TS	TSPts
Mark BASEBY	3	15	38	1	39	10.40	1	0	1	2	0	0
Jerran HART	**5**	**26**	**48**	**1**	**49**	**7.54**	**0**	**0**	**3**	**6**	**0**	**0**
Dean FELTON	16	82	126	11	137	6.68	0	0	6	11	1	2
Harland COOK	**13**	**65**	**99**	**9**	**108**	**6.65**	**0**	**0**	**2**	**2**	**0**	**0**
Aaron BASEBY	16	78	84	7	92	4.67	0	0	0	0	0	0
Nathan IRWIN	**5**	**23**	**21**	**3**	**24**	**4.17**	**0**	**0**	**0**	**0**	**0**	**0**
Ricky SCARBORO	3	14	14	2	16	4.57	0	0	0	0	0	0
Daniel BERWICK	**14**	**67**	**60**	**8**	**68**	**4.06**	**0**	**0**	**0**	**0**	**0**	**0**
Alex CUNNINGHAM	14	61	39	11	50	3.28	0	0	0	0	1	0
André CROSS	**1**	**3**	**2**	**0**	**2**	**2.67**	**0**	**0**	**0**	**0**	**0**	**0**
Ricky MULLINS	5	14	5	2	7	2.00	0	0	0	0	0	0
Marc ANDREWS	**8**	**32**	**11**	**4**	**15**	**1.87**	**0**	**0**	**0**	**0**	**0**	**0**
Niall STRUDWICK	1	3	0	0	0	0.00	0	0	0	0	0	0

For Mark BASEBY see Mildenhall; for Jerran HART see Newport and Newcastle; for Ricky SCARBORO see Scunthorpe (CL).

Conference League

WEYMOUTH

TRACK FILE

Track: Wessex Stadium, Radipole Lane, Weymouth, Dorset, DT4 9XJ.
Telephone: 07841 042475.
Hotline: 09068 644663.
Website: www.wildcatsweymouth.co.uk
Track Length: 223 metres.
Track Record: 51.3 secs, Jason Bunyan, September 6, 2008.
Promoter: Phil Bartlett.
Sponsors: Doonans Building Materials Limited
Colours: Broad red and white stripes with wildcat logo.
Nickname: Wildcats.

HISTORY

First meeting: March 26, 2004, Wessex Rosebowl Individual Trophy.
Leagues: Division Three, 2004-09.
Meetings were also held at

- *Wessex Stadium, Radipole Lane, Weymouth, Dorset.*

First meeting: August 4, 1954, Young England vYoung Overseas.
Leagues: Division Two, 1955, 1968, 1974-1984. Metropolitan League, 1964. Open licence, 1954, 1962-63, 1965, 1971-73, 1985.

HONOURS

Major honours: 6.
Division Two Pairs champions (2), 1982, 1983.
Division Three champions (1), 2008.
Division Three Knock Out Cup winners (1), 2005.
Division Three Four Team champions (2), 2005, 2008.

Top – site of the Weymouth track with the football ground at bottom of aerial photo.

2008 REVIEW

THE Wildcats enjoyed the highest point of their 54-year history as they finally secured a league championship title.

Life for the South coast club has rarely been straightforward, and they had to wait nearly two decades to even bring the sport back after closing in 1984 - and even then, they had to fight on to extend their stadium lease.

But 2008 was the year in which it all came right in the end, culminating in an emphatic play-off final triumph against Boston.

The Wildcats were by no means certainties for the crown, having finished fourth in an eight team league, albeit just three points behind first-placed Plymouth, after a somewhat inconsistent run of regular results.

Their home record was unblemished and they were frequently comfortable winners, only Plymouth themselves keeping the margin below ten points.

But on the road it was a different story as the Wildcats only won at basement boys Sittingbourne, although there were frustrating near-misses at Scunthorpe and Buxton.

The Plymouth semi-final saw the Devils limited to just a 46-44 first leg win and the Wildcats put the tie to bed in the return - whilst in the Final it was a demolition job over an admittedly weakened Boston, who were routed 67-23 at the Wessex Stadium with the Wildcats then refusing to let up, and winning away as well.

Lee Smart put his Premier League troubles behind him to head the averages as Jon Armstrong suffered a broken leg, but Jay Herne and skipper Karl Mason weren't far behind in a true all-round effort.

Unluckiest team member at the end was 16-year-old Kyle Newman - handed a dream opportunity to experience life and speedway in Australia, but ruled out of the second leg due to the timing of his flight out.

Wildcats also triumphed in the Conference League Fours at Stoke, edging out Redcar by a single point having held the lead when the meeting had to be terminated early.

2008 RESULTS

Conference League

Final position....................CHAMPIONS (Fourth)

SCUNTHORPE (A)
Monday, May 5
Lost 45-48
Armstrong 16:1 (6), Johnson 4:2, Priest 3:2, Mason 6, J. Herne 9, Webster 6, Newman 1.
▼ *Needed a 4-2 in the last race to win, but Herne fell on the first turn as their chances came to an end.*

SITTINGBOURNE (H)
Saturday, May 10
Won 61-31
Armstrong 11:1, Johnson 9:1, Priest 10:2, **Mason 11:1**, J. Herne 10:1, Webster 6:2, Newman 4.
▲ *Armstrong and Mason both scored four-ride paid maximums as the Wildcats had things all their own way.*

RYE HOUSE (H)
Saturday, June 14
Won 62-31
Bargh 10:1, Johnson 6:2, Priest 12, Mason 9:2, J. Herne 9:2, Webster 9:2, Newman 7:2.
▲ *Six straight home wins, the Wildcats kicking the meeting off with three successive 5-1s.*

PLYMOUTH (H)
Saturday, July 12
Won 49-41
L. Herne 9, Johnson 5, Priest 4:1, Mason 9, J. Herne 11:1, Webster 6:2, Newman 5:3.
▲ *Biggest ever win for the Wildcats over the Devils in an eventful meeting with a good crowd, match being decided by a Heat 14 5-1 from Mason and Webster.*

SITTINGBOURNE (A)
Sunday, July 20
Won 60-31
Bargh 13, Johnson 6:2, Priest 9:2, Mason 10:1, **Herne 11:1**, Webster 7:1, Newman 4:1.
▲ *Almost the perfect away display – 12 race wins and seven 5-1s meaning the points were never in doubt.*

BOSTON (H)
Saturday, August 2
Won 54-39
Bargh 8, Johnson 3:1, Priest 11:1, **Mason 11:1**, J. Herne 10:1, Webster 3:1, Newman 8:2.
▼ *Webster came off in Heat 11 in a crash also involving Darren Mallett who was excluded. He broke his leg.*

REDCAR (H)
Saturday, August 16
Won 56-37
Rider replacement for Bargh, Wright 11:1, Priest 8:1, Mason 10, **J. Herne 15**, Johnson 2, Newman 10:1.
▲ *Successful debut for Wright, unbeaten from his first four rides.*

SQUAD
Jon Armstrong, Matt Bates, Brendan Johnson, Karl Mason, Alex McLeod, Kyle Newman, Luke Priest, Matt Wright, Lee Smart, Tim Webster.
Foreign: Andrew Bargh, Jay Herne, Lee Herne.

PLYMOUTH (A)
Friday, August 22
Lost 42-51
Bargh 11:2 (TS4), Mason 5:1, Priest 6, Wright 8:2 (4), J. Herne 7, Johnson 1:1, Newman 4:1.
▼ *Newman won Heat 2 and Bargh took two later race wins, but Wildcats struggled to hold the Devils' top men.*

SCUNTHORPE (H)
Saturday, August 23
Won 52-29
Bargh 8, Wright 8:1, Priest 5:3, Mason 8, J. Herne 7, Johnson 5:2, **Newman 11:1**.
▲▼ *Abandoned after Heat 13 (result stands) due to rain as Newman celebrated his maiden paid maximum, despite a painful crash with Adam Wrathall in Heat 4.*

BUXTON (H)
Saturday, August 30
Won 64-28
Bargh 9:3, Wright 11:1, **Priest 15, Mason 12:3**, *rider replacement for J. Herne*, Johnson 6:1, Newman 11:1.
▲ *Completed faultless home campaign with routine win.*

REDCAR (A)
Saturday, September 13
Lost 37-53
Bargh 12, Mason 0, Smart 5:1 (0), Wright 9:1, J. Herne 6, Johnson 2, Newman 3:1.
▼ *Bargh's two late race wins were mere consolation from a meeting in which the Wildcats were unable to make a significant impression.*

BUXTON (A)
Sunday, September 14
Lost 44-46
Bargh 0, Mason 11, Smart 12:1, Wright 2:1, J. Herne 8:1, Johnson 9:2, Newman 2:1.
▼ *Dreadful day for Bargh was probably the difference between the teams as the Wildcats were beaten despite leading with two heats to go.*

BOSTON (A)
Monday, September 15
Lost 28-64
Bargh 0, Mason 6, Smart 11:1 (4), Wright 3, Herne 3, Johnson 1, Newman 4:1.
▼ *Disappointing weekend ended on a low note, the only race win coming from Wright – after he had failed to score from his first three outings!*

RYE HOUSE (A)
Sunday, October 12
Lost 34-59
Smart 7:2, Wright 5, Bargh 12 (6), Mason 1, J. Herne 5:1, Johnson 2:1, Newman 2:1.
▼ *Took no chances in a 'dead rubber' fixture, with Bargh, Smart and Herne winning a race apiece against an in-*

form home side.

CONFERENCE LEAGUE

	M	W	D	L	PtsF	PtsA	Pts
Plymouth	14	9	0	5	709	569	20
Boston	14	8	1	5	713	565	19
Redcar	14	8	1	5	657	614	18
WEYMOUTH	**14**	**8**	**1**	**6**	**688**	**588**	**17**
Scunthorpe	14	8	1	6	637	629	17
Buxton	14	7	1	7	605	669	15
Rye House	14	6	1	8	614	663	12
Sittingbourne	14	1	0	13	472	798	2

PLAY-OFFS

Semi Final, first leg
PLYMOUTH (A)
Friday, October 10
Lost 44-46
Smart 7:1, Wright 7:2, Bargh 6:1, Mason 5:1, J. Herne 8:1, Johnson 6:1, Webster 5:2.
▲ *Led 42-36 with two heats to go and were delighted with the result despite conceding 5-1s in both Heat 14 and 15.*

Semi Final, second leg
PLYMOUTH (H)
Saturday, October 11
Won 56-38
Smart 10:1, Wright 9:1, Bargh 8:2, Mason 8:1, J. Herne 9, Johnson 8:2, Newman 4:1.
▲ *Went through comfortably, extending their lead through the early stages and seeing off both of the Devils' major tactical moves.*
Aggregate: Won 100-84.

FINAL, first leg
BOSTON (H)
Saturday, October 25
Won 67-23
Smart 12:3, Wright 14:1, Bargh 7:3, Mason 10, Herne 10, Johnson 9:2, Newman 5:2.
▲ *Job done in the first leg against injury-hit opponents, with only Adam Allott winning a race for the Barracudas.*

FINAL, second leg
BOSTON (A)
Wednesday, October 29
Won 46-45
Smart 10, Wright 2:1, Bargh 7, Mason 9:1, J. Herne 9:1, Webster 1:1, Johnson 8:1.
▲ *Let the celebrations begin as Wildcats embrace first league title in their history.*
Aggregate: Won 113-68.

Conference Trophy

Semi Final, first leg
PLYMOUTH (A)
Friday, May 23
Lost 35-57
Armstrong 11, Johnson 5:2, Priest 8 (4), Mason 2:1, J. Herne 5, Webster 4, Newman 0.
▼ *Hoped to limit home side to six-point lead but suffered problems with Newman withdrawing with troublesome wrist injury.*

Lee Smart

Semi Final, second leg
PLYMOUTH (H)
Saturday, May 24
Won 46-45
Armstrong 14, Johnson 6, Priest 5, Mason 7, J. Herne 7:1, Webster 7:3, Bates 0.
▲ *Armstrong took dramatic last-bend win in Heat 15 over Nicki Glanz to secure win on the night.*
Aggregate: Lost 81-102.

Knock Out Cup

Quarter Final, first leg
PLYMOUTH (H)
Saturday, June 21
Won 47-45
L. Herne 7, Johnson 7:2, Priest 5:1, Mason 7:1, J. Herne 7, Webster 2:1, Newman 12.

Quarter Final, second leg
PLYMOUTH (A)
Friday, July 11
Lost 42-51
L. Herne 7, Johnson 1:1, Priest 3:2, Bargh 13 (6), J. Herne 7:1, Webster 9:2, Newman 2:1.
▲ *Kept in the tie for long spells, but a 5-1 reverse in Heat 12 turned out to be a damaging blow.*
Aggregate: Lost 89-96.

Inter League Challenge

ISLE OF WIGHT (H)
Saturday, September 6
Lost 45-48
Smart 9:1, Wright 2, Priest 8, Mason 5:2, J. Herne 7:1, Johnson 5:2, Newman 9:2.

Challenge

DEVON-DORSET TROPHY
First leg
PLYMOUTH (A)
Friday, April 18
Lost 29-61
Armstrong 5 (1), Johnson 2:2, Priest 5, Mason 3:1, J. Herne 7, Webster 7, McLeod 0.
▲▼ *Herne won his first two rides but crashed heavily in Heat 9 and scored just one point thereafter.*

DEVON-DORSET TROPHY
Second leg
PLYMOUTH (H)
Saturday, April 19
Lost 39-49
Armstrong 11 (R), Johnson 0, Priest 6:1, Mason 4, J., Herne 9:2, Webster 7:1, Bates 2.
Aggregate: Lost 68-110.
●▲▼ *Referee Jim McGregor officially warned both sides about their conduct in a stormy affair. Armstrong won three races but fell when on a tactical ride in Heat 13.*

NEWPORT (H)
Saturday, April 26
Won 50-42
Armstrong 11, Johnson 6:3, Priest 8:1, Mason 4, J. Herne 9:1, Webster 12:1, McLeod 0.
NEWPORT 42
Andrew Bargh 9, Nathan Irwin 3, Matthew Wright 5, Darren Mallett 5, Tom Brown 8:1, Oliver Gay 1:1, Terry Day 11:2 (4).

SOMERSET (H)
Saturday, May 3
Won 53-38
Armstrong 12:1, Johnson 7:2, Priest 3:1, Mason 10:3, J. Herne 9, Webster 10, McLeod 2:1.
SOMERSET 38
Shaun Harmatiuk 11, Marc Andrews 1, Mark Simmonds 6, Ben Taylor 3:1, Andrew Bargh 12:1 (TS4), Jamie White-Williams 4:2, Andy Braithwaite 1:1.
▲ *Armstrong, Mason and Webster all in double-figures with Andrew Bargh and Shaun Harmatiuk impressing for Somerset.*

WIMBLEDON (H)
Saturday, May 17
29-25, abandoned after Heat 9, rain.
Armstrong 6:1, Johnson 6, *rider replacement for Priest*, Mason 5, J. Herne 9, Webster 3:1, Newman 0.
For WIMBLEDON scorers see Blasts from the Past.

BRISTOL (H)
Saturday, June 7
Won 54-38
Rider replacement for Armstrong, Johnson 7:2, Priest 6:2, Mason 13, J. Herne 14, Webster 9:1, Newman 5:1.
For BRISTOL scorers see Blasts from the Past.

OXFORD (H)
Saturday, September 20
Won 61-32
Bargh 6:1, Mason 9, Smart 9:1, Wright 10:1, J. Herne 14, Johnson 7:3, Newman 6:2.
For OXFORD scorers see Blasts from the Past.

EXETER (H)
Friday, September 26
Won 60-34
Bargh 13:1, Mason 5:2, Smart 10:1, Wright 5:3, **J. Herne 12**, Johnson 9:1, Newman 6:1.
For EXETER scorers see Blasts from the Past.

Individual

CONFERENCE LEAGUE BRONZE HELMET
Saturday, July 19
1 Tom Brown 9+3+3, 2 Jay Herne 11++2, 3 Darren Mallett 7+2, 4 Paul Starke 9+1, 5 Gary Cottham 8+0, 6 Karl Mason 6, 7 Jade Mudgway 6, 8 Byron Bekker 5, 9 Scott Richardson 5, 10 Gareth Isherwood 5, 11 Terry Day 4, 12 Dean Felton 3, 13 Kyle Newman [R] 1, 14 Jerran Hart 0, 15 Brendan Johnson [R] 0.
■ *Riders finishing second to fifth in the qualifying races competed for a place in the Final against the top-scoring rider who was automatically seeded.*
For race by race details, see Conference League.

British Under 21 Championship

Qualifying Round
Saturday, April 12
Lee Smart 15+–+3, Daniel Halsey 12+3+2, Lee Strudwick 12+–+1, Gareth Isherwood 11+2, Barry Burchatt 11+1, Kyle Newman 11+FX, Matt Bates 7, Tim Webster 6, Nick Laurence 6, Adam Chandler 6, Aaron Baseby 5, Andrew Braithwaite 5, Niall Strudwick 4, John MacPhail [R] 3, Brendan Johnson [R] 2, Oliver Gay 1, Gary Irving 0, Mark Baseby 0.
● *Ex-Wildcat Lee Smart made a winning return to the Wessex Stadium in an eventful meeting – there were a total of 20 crashes in the 22 heats!*
See British Championship for full details and Roll of Honour.

Weather...

Four home meetings and five away were lost to the weather.

Conference League
Friday, July 4 ....PLYMOUTH (A)
Sunday, August 3 ....BOSTON (A)
Saturday, August 9 ....REDCAR (H)
Sunday, September 7 ....BUXTON (A)
Friday, September 12 ....BOSTON (A)
Saturday, October 4 ....RYE HOUSE (A)

Conference League Play-offs
Sunday, October 26 ....BOSTON (A)

Knock Out Cup
Friday, June 20............PLYMOUTH (A)

Challenge
Saturday, July 5 ....SWINDON (H)
Friday, October 3............SWINDON (H)

...beaten

Pairs

CONFERENCE LEAGUE PAIRS CHAMPIONSHIP
Saturday, May 31

1 BOSTON 5 (Simon Lambert 3, James Cockle 2:1).
2 REDCAR 4 (Aaron Summers 4, Scott James 0).
3 SITTINGBOURNE
4 SCUNTHORPE
Third place was decided by ballot.

QUALIFYING
Group 1
WEYMOUTH 8 (Jon Armstrong 2:1, Jay Herne 6), **BUXTON 12** (Ben Taylor 5:1, Jack Roberts 7), **REDCAR 18** (Scott James 6, Aaron Summers 12), **SITTINGBOURNE 14** (Dean Felton 3:1, Jerran Hart 11). *Reserve: Brendan Johnson 2.*
Group 2
BOSTON 17 (Simon Lambert 5:1, James Cockle 12), **PLYMOUTH 14** (Kyle Hughes 10, Paul Starke 4:1), **RYE HOUSE 7** (Gary Cottham 5, Terry Day 2), **SCUNTHORPE 14** (Byron Bekker 11, Jonathan Bethell 3:1). *Reserve: Tim Webster 2.*

Semi Final 1
REDCAR 7 (Scott James 3:1, Aaron Summers 4), **SCUNTHORPE 2** (*Tim Webster [R] 2*, Byron Bekker 0).

Semi Final 2
BOSTON 7 (Simon Lambert 3:1, James Cockle 4), **SITTINGBOURNE 2** (Dean Felton FX, Jerran Hart 2).
▼ *Home star Jon Armstrong broke his leg in a crash in Heat 7 and was taken to the Dorset County Hospital in Dorchester where he had surgery.*
For race by race details, see Conference League.

2009 Squad

Jon **ARMSTRONG**, James **COCKLE**, Terry **DAY**, Lee **SMART**, Tim **WEBSTER**, Jamie **WHITE-WILLIAMS**, Matthew **WRIGHT**.

Four Team Challenge

KINGSWOOD HOTEL SOUTH WEST FOURS
Saturday, July 26
WEYMOUTH 30
Lee Herne 10, **Jay Herne 12**, Luke Priest 2, Karl Mason 6.
2 BRISTOL 28, 3 EXETER 24, 4 SOMERSET 12
Kyle Newman 5, Brendan Johnson 2, David Gough 3, Andrew Braithwaite 2.
For BRISTOL and EXETER scorers see Blasts from the Past.

British Under 15 Championship

Round Three
Saturday, September 13
500cc
1 Marc Owen 11, 2 Joe Jacobs 10, 3 Jason Garrity 9, 4 James Sarjeant 9, 5 John Resch 7, 6 Scott Day 5, 7 Jack Butler 4, 8 Cameron Hoskins 4, 9 Scott Gibbons 3.
250cc
1 Ben Morley 12, 2 Rhys Naylor 10+3, 3 Brendan Freemantle 10+2, 4 Nathan Stoneman 8, 5 Connor Dwyer 7, 6 Lloyd Barrett 6, 7 Jack Cornes 5, 8 Tyler Govier 4.
For race by race details, see British Under 15 Championship.

Brendan Johnson

WEYMOUTH

Rider	M	R	Pts	BP	TPts	Ave	F	P	TR	TPts	TS	TSPts
Jon ARMSTRONG	4	19	52	2	54	11.37	0	1	2	6	0	0
Lee SMART	**8**	**37**	**74**	**10**	**84**	**9.08**	**0**	**1**	**2**	**2**	**0**	**0**
Andrew BARGH	15	68	124	12	136	8.00	0	0	2	6	1	1
Jay HERNE	**21**	**93**	**173**	**12**	**185**	**7.96**	**1**	**1**	**0**	**0**	**0**	**0**
Karl MASON	21	86	157	14	171	7.95	0	3	0	0	0	0
Luke PRIEST	**14**	**61**	**104**	**15**	**119**	**7.80**	**1**	**0**	**1**	**2**	**0**	**0**
Lee HERNE	3	12	23	0	23	7.67	0	0	0	0	0	0
Matthew WRIGHT	**12**	**53**	**89**	**12**	**101**	**7.62**	**0**	**1**	**1**	**2**	**0**	**0**
Tim WEBSTER	12	52	65	17	82	6.31	0	0	0	0	0	0
Kyle NEWMAN	**19**	**81**	**100**	**20**	**120**	**5.93**	**0**	**1**	**0**	**0**	**0**	**0**
Brendan JOHNSON	22	93	110	26	136	5.85	0	0	0	0	0	0
Matt BATES	**1**	**3**	**0**	**0**	**0**	**0.00**	**0**	**0**	**0**	**0**	**0**	**0**

For Lee SMART see Birmingham and Mildenhall; for Andrew BARGH see Isle of Wight; for Matthew WRIGHT see Boston and Mildenhall; for Jay HERNE see Birmingham; for Luke PRIEST see Mildenhall.

2009 FIXTURES

April

Tuesday 7
Isle of Wight v Bournemouth (Challenge)
Friday 10
King's Lynn v Mildenhall (KO)
Plymouth: Open
Weymouth v Isle of Wight (Challenge)
Saturday 11
Rye House v Mildenhall
Weymouth: Open
Sunday 12
Mildenhall v King's Lynn (KO)
Monday 13
Newport v Mildenhall
Scunthorpe v Weymouth
Tuesday April 14
Isle of Wight: British Under 21 Championship semi final
Friday 17
Plymouth: Open
Saturday 18
King's Lynn v Scunthorpe
Tuesday 21
Isle of Wight v Weymouth (Challenge)
Thursday 23
Bournemouth v Isle of Wight (Challenge)
Friday 24
Plymouth v Weymouth (Challenge)
Saturday 25
Rye House v King's Lynn
Weymouth v Plymouth (Challenge)
Sunday 26
Mildenhall v Isle of Wight
Newport v Bournemouth (KO)
Thursday 30
Bournemouth v Nerwport (KO)
Friday 31
Plymouth: Open

May

Saturday 2
King's Lynn v Plymouth
Rye House v Isle of Wight
Sunday 3
Buxton v Plymouth
Monday 4
Scunthorpe v Newport
Friday 8
Plymouth v Isle of Wight (KO Cup)
Weymouth v Rye House
Saturday 9
King's Lynn v Weymouth
Sunday 10
Mildenhall v Rye House
Tuesday 12
Isle of Wight v King's Lynn
Friday 15
Plymouth v Rye House
Weymouth v Bournemouth or Newport (KO)
Sunday 17
Buxton v King's Lynn
Mildenhall: Reserved
Newport v Weymouth
Thursday 21
Bournemouth v King's Lynn
Friday 22
King's Lynn v Rye House
Weymouth v Scunthorpe
Saturday 23
Rye House v Bournemouth
Sunday 24
Buxton v Scunthorpe
Monday 25
Newport v Isle of Wight
Rye House v Buxton (KO Cup)
Scunthorpe v Plymouth
Tuesday, May 26
Isle of Wight v Plymouth (KO Cup)
Thursday 28
Bournemouth v Weymouth
Friday 29
Plymouth v Newport
Weymouth v Buxton
Sunday 31
Mildenhall v King's Lynn

June

Friday 5
Newport v Buxton
Scunthorpe v Isle of Wight
Saturday 6
Rye House v Scunthorpe
Weymouth v Plymouth
Sunday 7
Buxton v Bournemouth
Mildenhall v Weymouth
Tuesday 9
Isle of Wight v Newport
Thursday 11
Bournemouth v Scunthorpe
Friday 12
King's Lynn v Isle of Wight
Scunthorpe v Bournemouth
Saturday 13
King's Lynn v Isle of Wight
Weymouth: British Under 15 Championship
Sunday 14
Buxton v Mildenhall
Newport v Plymouth
Friday 19
Plymouth v King's Lynn
Weymouth v Bournemouth
Sunday 21
Buxton v Rye House
Mildenhall v Newport
Tuesday 23
Isle of Wight v Rye House
Thursday 25
Bournemouth v Isle of Wight
Friday 26
Plymouth v Buxton
Sunday, June 28
King's Lynn v Newport
June 30
Isle of Wight v Mildenhall

July

Friday 3
Plymouth v Scunthorpe
Weymouth v Mildenhall
Sunday 5
Buxton v Isle of Wight
Mildenhall v Bournemouth
Newport v Rye House
Tuesday 7
Isle of Wight v Weymouth (NT)
Friday 10
Newport: Reserved
Plymouth v Isle of Wight (NT)
Scunthorpe v Mildenhall
Weymouth: Great Britain U21 v Australiasia
Saturday 11
King's Lynn: Great Britain U21 v Australiasia

Rye House v Weymouth
Sunday 12
Mildenhall v Buxton
Tuesday 14
Isle of Wight: Great Britain U21 v Australiasia
Thursday 16
Bournemouth v Plymouth
Friday 17
Plymouth: Great Britain U21 v Australiasia
Weymouth: Open
Saturday 18
King's Lynn v Bournemouth
Sunday 19
Buxton: Great Britain U21 v Australiasia
Mildenhall v Scunthorpe
Tuesday 21
Isle of Wight: Smallbrook Spectacular
Thursday 23
Bournemouth v Newport
Friday 24
Weymouth: Bronze Helmet
Saturday 25
Buxton: British Under 15 Championship
Tuesday 28
Isle of Wight v Buxton
Thursday 30
Isle of Wight v Scunthorpe
Friday 31
Weymouth v Mildenhall

August

Sunday 2
Buxton: Reserved
Mildenhall v Plymouth
Newport v King's Lynn
Tuesday 4
Isle of Wight v Bournemouth
Thursday 6
Bournemouth v Rye House
Isle of Wight v Plymouth (NT)
Friday 7
Plymouth v Weymouth
Saturday 8
King's Lynn v Buxton
Weymouth v Newport
Sunday 9
Buxton v Newport
Mildenhall: Reserved
Tuesday 11
Isle of Wight v Weymouth
Friday 14
Newport: Reserved
Plymouth v Isle of Wight
Scunthorpe v Rye House
Weymouth v King's Lynn
Saturday 15
Mildenhall v Bournemouth
Sunday 16
Buxton v Plymouth (NT)
Tuesday 18
Isle of Wight: National League Pairs Final
Thursday 20
Bournemouth v Buxton
Isle of Wight v Mildenhall (NT)
Friday 21
Plymouth v Mildenhall
Scunthorpe v King's Lynn
Weymouth v Buxton (NT)
Sunday 23
Buxton v Rye House
Mildenhall v Weymouth (NT)
Newport v Scunthorpe
Tuesday 25
Isle of Wight v Buxton (NT)
Thursday 27
Bournemouth v Mildenhall
Friday 28
Plymouth v Bournemouth
Weymouth v Isle of Wight
Saturday 29
Rye House v Newport
Sunday 30
Buxton v Weymouth
Monday 31
Newport v Bournemouth
Rye House v Plymouth
Scunthorpe v Buxton

September

Friday 4
Plymouth v Buxton (NT)
Saturday 5
Rye House v Buxton
Weymouth v Plymouth (NT)
Sunday 6
Mildenhall v Buxton (NT)
Tuesday 8
Isle of Wight v Plymouth (NT)
Friday 11
Plymouth v Weymouth (NT)
Saturday 12
King's Lynn v Mildenhall
Weymouth v Isle of Wight (NT)
Sunday 13
Buxton v Mildenhall (NT)
Tuesday 15
Weymouth: Reserved
Friday 18
Plymouth v Mildenhall (NT)
Weymouth: Reserved
Sunday 20
Buxton v Isle of Wight (NT)
Friday 25
Plymouth v Buxton (NT)
Weymouth: Reserved
Saturday 26
Rye House: National League Riders' Final
Sunday 27
Buxton v Weymouth (NT)
Mildenhall v Isle of Wight (NT)

October

Sunday 4
Mildenhall v Plymouth (NT)
Sunday 11
Mildenhall: Reserved
Sunday 18
Mildenhall: Reserved
Sunday 25
Mildenhall: Reserved

Unless otherwise stated all fixtures National League. KO = Knock Out Cup; NT = National Trophy.

NATIONAL LEAGUE NEWCOMERS

BOURNEMOUTH *(see pages 110-115)*
Aaron **BASEBY**, Andrew **ALDRIDGE**, Mark **BASEBY**, Jerran **HART**, Jay **HERNE**, Kyle **NEWMAN**, Luke **PRIEST**.

ISLE OF WIGHT *(see pages 168-173)*
Daniel **BERWICK**, Andrew **BRAITHWAITE**, Tom **BROWN**, Ben **HOPWOOD**, Brendan **JOHNSON**, Scott **MEAKINS**, Ryan **SEDGMEN**, Nick **SIMMONS**.

KING'S LYNN *(see pages 174-179)*
Adam **ALLOTT**, Scott **CAMPOS**, Benji **COMPTON** ,Jake **KNIGHT**, Adam **LOWE**, Darren **MALLETT**, Rhys **NAYLOR**, Jamie **SMITH**, Chris **WIDMAN**.

MILDENHALL *(see pages 180-185)*
Leigh **BOUJOS**, Barrie **EVANS**, Joe **JACOBS**, David **MASON**, Oliver **RAYSON**, Mark **THOMPSON**.

NEWPORT *(see pages 192-195)*
Richard **ANDREWS**, Tony **ATKIN**, Russell **BARNETT**, Lee **DICKEN**, Sam **HURST**, Karl **MASON**, Jaimie **PICKARD**, Shelby **RUTHERFORD**, Grant **TREGONING**, Tom **YOUNG**.

■ ***For Buxton, Plymouth, Rye House, Scunthorpe and Weymouth 2009 teams see Conference League section.***

AMATEUR SPEEDWAY

IN recent years there has been a spiralling growth in amateur speedway – and there are now increasing opportunities for riders who are either not good enough or have no desire to take part in competitive league racing.

The three major organisations are the Scunthorpe Speedway promotion at their Normanby Road track, the long-operating Southern Track Riders' Amateur Speedway Club and the Welsh-based Dragons Amateur Speedway Club.

SCUNTHORPE AMATEUR SPEEDWAY

TOWARDS the end of 2007, amateur rider, Andy Harrison, persuaded the club that running amateur meetings would be a good idea.

The first meeting was run on January 26, 2008 and, largely due to the commitment of the large band of volunteers that run them, they have proven to be an overwhelming success.

An eight round Summer Championship was arranged and a six round Winter Series.

Meeting entry fee: £35,
Enquiries: Richard Hollingsworth.
Tel: 07832-402167.
E-mail: richard@scunthorpespeedway.com
Website: www.scunthorpespeedway.com/amateur

CLASSES

Open
Second half to league standard.

Support
Beginners to second half standard.

Youth 500
As per Speedway Control Bureau regulations.

Youth 250
As per Speedway Control Bureau regulations.

SOUTHERN TRACK RIDERS' AMATEUR SPEEDWAY CLUB

SOUTHERN Track Riders, now in its 16th year, is a non profit making club which prides itself on offering track time to members who otherwise may not be given the opportunity to ride.

The club caters for riders of all abilites with a range of classes available although in order to participate in the main racing events riders must be 15 years of age or above.

All riders must hold a Speedway Control Bureau Speedway Permit that can be purchased by contacting The ACU at ACU House, Wood Street, Rugby, Warks, CV21 2YX TEL:-01788 566400.

Non-Riding members are most welcome and not only help to top up club funds but can help out on the administration side and/or at meetings as flag marshall etc.

All STR events are held on SCB Licensed Tracks on hire to the club from various promoters.

Annual Membership Fee: £15.
Meeting Entry Fee: £30.
Meeting Secretary: Linda Taylor, Greenglaze Cottage, Outwell Road, Emneth, Wisbech, Cambridgeshire, PE14 8BG.
Tel: 01945 772429; 07875 140019.
E-mail: linda@southerntrackriders.co.uk
Training Officer: Steve Cook 07950446394.
Website: www.southerntrackriders.co.uk

CLASSES

Novice
Any rider with league experience will be excluded from this class. Any new member declaring themselves a novice will be allowed entry but will be assessed on the day and may be requested to move to a different class if needed. This class is for the less experienced.

Intermediate
For riders with more experience who are not yet ready for the open class.

Open
For the more experienced riders and those excluded from other classes.

Over 40s & Over 50s
Governed by age on the day of the meeting only.

DRAGONS AMATEUR SPEEDWAY CLUB

FOUNDED to provide racing experience for riders based in South Wales and the West Country they ran regular meetings at Newport until it's closure in 2008 but are hoping to resume regular activity in 2009

Meeting Secretary: Julie Tutton, 149 Medway Road, Newport, NP20 7XT.
Tel: 01633 858899, 07920 002785.
E-mail:j.tutton@tiscali.co.uk

SCUNTHORPE
2008 Summer Championship
Open class

OPEN CLASS

Overall Standings: 1 Stuart Parnaby 64, 2 Jitendra Duffill 57, 3 Mike Pickering 53, 4 Andrew Blackburn 50, 5 Lee Geary 46, 6 David Lidgett 41, 7 Ben Hannon 39, 8 Leigh Boujos 31 (3), 9 Dean Hancox 30, 10 Gary O'Hare 27, 11 Richard Walsh, 12 Greg Walsh 23, 13 Chris Widman 21, 14 Michael Faulkner 20, 15 Dan Lead 20, 16 Daniel Mitchell 18, 17 Linus Sundström 16, 18 Jade Mudgway 15, 18 Gary Beaton 15, 20 Kye Norton 14, 20 Ben Hopwood 14, 22 Chris Widman 13, 23 Jon Stevens 12, 23 Jonathan Bethell 12, 23 Josh Auty 12, 26 John MacPhail 11, 26 Tom Hill 11, 28 Neil Painter 10, 29 Oliver Gay 9, 30 Jack Hirst 8, 31 Martin Emerson 7, 32 Matt Davis 6, 32 Brendan Coughlan 6, 32 Darren Smith 6, 35 Russell Barnett 5, 36 Michael Mitchell 4, 37 James Fear 3, 37 Glyn Edwards 3.

Points awarded according to finishing positions in eight rounds 16-15-14-13-12-11-10-9-8-7-6-5-4-3-2-1. Best four scores to count.

Saturday, January 26: 1 Gary Beaton, 2 Gary Irving, 3 Stuart Parnaby, 4 David Wallinger.

Saturday, February 16: 1 David Wallinger, 2 Gary Irving, 3 Danny Halsey, 4 Gary Beaton.

Saturday, March 1: 1 Danny Halsey, 2 Scott Richardson, 3 Simon Lambert, 4 Matthew Wright.

Saturday, April 12: 1 Stuart Parnaby, 2 Michael Faulkner, 3 Jitendra Duffill, 4 David Lidgett.
Viktor Bergström won the meeting but didn't compete for the trophies.

Saturday, May 3: 1 Mike Pickering, 2 Stuart Parnaby, 3 John MacPhail, 4 Jitendra Duffill.

Saturday, July 5: 1 Jitendra Duffill, 2 Lee Geary, 3 Andrew Blackburn, 4 David Lidgett.

Saturday, August 2: 1 Stuart Parnaby, 2 Jade Mudgway, 3 Kye Norton, 4.Jitendra Duffill.

Saturday, August 30: 1 Stuart Parnaby, 2 Leigh Boujos, 3 Ben Hopwood, 4 Gary O'Hare.

Saturday, September 20: 1 Stuart Parnaby, 2 Gary Beaton, 3 Gary O'Hare, 4 Ben Hannon

Saturday, October 11: 1 Linus Sundström, 2 Stuart Parnaby, 3 Mike Pickering, 4 Andrew Blackburn.

PHOTO: *Open Class champion Stuart Parnaby, Swedish Under 21 international Linus Sundström and third placed Mike Pickering.*

Support class

Overall Standings: 1 Montana Jowett 64, 2 Duncan Towler 61, 3 Chris Baldwin 59, 4 Craig Osborne 47, 5 James Culbert 44, 6 Jeff Halford 42, 7 Andy Lauder 38, 8 Andy Harrison 38, 9 Ben Holloway 36, 10 Mark Whitehead 35, 11 Adam Oughtibridge 35, 12 Adam Kenyon 32, 13 Tony Mitchell 30, 14 Andy Saxby 22, 15 Marc Stevenson 21, 16 Craig Whitehead 22, 17 Michael Osborne 20, 18 Dan Moulson 20, 19 Willy Kennis 16, 20 Wim Kennis 15, 20 Jack Hirst 15, 22 Derek Holt 15, 23 Jessica Lamb 12, 23 Ian Leverington 12, 25 Kevin Thrift 12, 26 Peter Robinson 11, 27 Philip Lane 10, 28 Jamie Roberts 9, 29 Robert Pallister 8, 30 Joe Burdekin 6, 31 Darren Hartman 4, 32 Howard Hirst 3, 32 Neil Roberts 3, 34 Kev Armitage 2.

Points awarded according to finishing positions in eight rounds 16-15-14-13-12-11-10-9-8-7-6-5-4-3-2-1. Best four scores to count.

Saturday, January 26: 1 Greg Walsh, 2 Dan Lead, 3 Andy Harrison, 4 Ian Leverington.

Saturday, February 16: 1 Glyn Picken, 2 Andy Harrison, Chris Baldwin, 4 Lee Harris.

Saturday, March 1: 1 Dan Lead, 2 Montana Jowett, 3 Andy Harrison, 4 Adam Oughtibridge.

Saturday, April 12: 1 Montana Jowett, 2 Chris Baldwin, 3 Andy Lauder, 4 Mark Stevenson.

Saturday, May 3: 1 Montana Jowett, 2 Chris Baldwin, 3 Duncan Towler, 4 Andy Saxby.

Saturday, July 5: 1 Duncan Towler, 2 Mark Whitehead, 3 Craig Osborne, 4 Andy Lauder.

Saturday, August 2: 1 Willy Kennis, 2 Wim Kennis, 3 Adam Oughtibridge, 4 Andy Harrison.

Saturday, August 30: 1 Duncan Towler, 2 Chris Baldwin, 3 Craig Osborne, 4 Montana Jowett.

Saturday, September 20: 1 Montana Jowett, 2 Jack Hirst, 3 Chris Baldwin, 4 Duncan Towler.

Saturday, October 11: 1 Montana Jowett, 2 Duncan Towler, 3 Ben Holloway, 4 Andy Harrison.

PHOTO: *Champion Montana Jowett with runner-up Duncan Towler (left) and bronze medallist Chris Baldwin.*

Youth 500 class

Overall Standings: 1 James Sarjeant 16, Jack Butler 12, 2 Cameron Hoskins 12, 3 Kyle Howarth 10, 4 Shane Hazleden 7, 5 Ashley Morris 6, 6 Josh Birkett 5, 7 Chris Bint 4.

Points awarded according to finishing positions in four rounds 8-7-6-5-4-3-2-1. Best two scores to count.

Saturday, January 26: 1 James Sarjeant, 2 Oliver Rayson, 3 Montana Jowett.

Saturday, March 8: 1 James Sarjeant, 2 Chris Bint, 3 Jack Butler.

Saturday, April 12: 1 James Sarjeant, 2 Jack Butler, 3 Cameron Hoskins.

Saturday, August 2: 1 James Sarjeant, 2 Shane Hazelden, 3 Cameron Hoskins.

Saturday, September 20: 1 James Sarjeant, 2 Kyle Howarth, 3 Ashley Morris.

PHOTO: *Championship top three – Cameron Hoskins, James Sarjeant and Jack Butler.*

Intermediate class

Saturday, March 8: 1 Mike Pickering, 2 Lee Geary, 3 Dean Hancox, 4 Greg Walsh.

Rounds on Saturday, June 1, Saturday, December 13 and Saturday, December 20 postponed, weather.

Youth 250 class

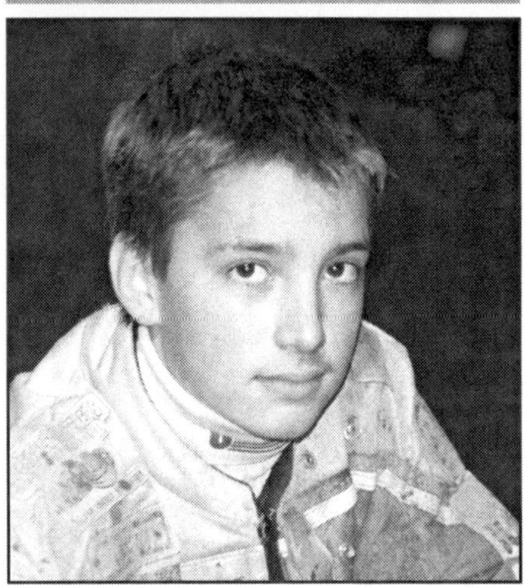

Overall Standings: 1 Marc Owen 16, 2 Conor Dwyer 15, 3 Adam Portwood 14, 4 Robert Lambert 8, 5 Jack Cornes 6.

Points awarded according to finishing positions in four rounds 8-7-6-5-4-3-2-1. Best two scores to count.

Saturday, February 16: 1 Marc Owen, 2 Tom Stokes, 3 Rhys Naylor.

Saturday, March 8: 1 Rhys Naylor, 2 Tom Stokes, 3 Adam Portwood.

Saturday, May 3: 1 Marc Owen, 2 Adam Portwood, 3 Conor Dwyer.

Saturday, July 5: 1 Marc Owen, 2 Conor Dwyer.

Saturday, August 30: 1 Conor Dwyer, 2 Adam Portwood, 3 Jack Cornes.

Saturday, October 11: 1 Robert Lambert.

PHOTO: *250 champion Marc Owen.*

2008-09 Winter Championship

Winter champions Reece Downes, Richard Franklin, Kyle Howarth and Montana Jowett

OPEN

Final Standings

Richard Franklin 45, Adam Wrathall 42, James Sarjeant 40, Jack Hirst 34, Robert McNeil 34, Stuart Parnaby 31, Gary Beaton 29, Richard Andrews 26, Scott Meakins 23, Jordan Tyrer 22, Kyle Howarth 20, Michael Faulkner 17, Craig Cook 16, Paul Starke 15, Andrew Blackburn 15, Richard Lawson 14, Darren Mallett 13, Ben Hannon 13, Daniel Mitchell 13, Tom Hill 12, Adam Lowe 11, Gary O'Hare 10, Martin Møller 10, James White-Williams 9, Byron Bekker 9, Jake Knight 7, Lee Geary 7, Aaron Pease 5, Oliver Gay 4, Rhys Naylor 3, Rikki Mullins 2, Robert Goodfellow 2, Rune Knudsen 1.

SUPPORT

Final Standings

Montana Jowett 48, Mark Whitehead 43, Sam Woods 42, Adam Kenyon 37, James Culbert 32, Steve Cook 31, Andy Harrison 29, Luke Chessell 27, Robert Pallister 25, Tony Mitchell 23, Gary Colin 23, Craig Whitehead 21, Adam Oughtibridge 20, Jeff Halford 19, Nick Calvert 18, Derek Holt 17, David Farley 16, Dave Lambert 16, Rhys

Naylor 15, Ben Holloway 15, Liam Rumsey 14, David Lidgett 9, Lee Harris 5.

YOUTH 500
Final standings
Kyle Howarth 24, Josh Birkett 21, Tom Stokes 18, Jack Butler 15, Tom Woolley 15, Cameron Hoskins 14, Ben Morley 12, Ashley Morris 7, Dale Lamb 4, Daniel I'Anson 4, Lloyd Barrett 3.

YOUTH 250
Final Standings
Reece Downes 23, Jack Cornes 22, Robert Lambert 8.

ROUND-BY-ROUND

Saturday, November 15
Open: 1 James Sarjeant, 2 Stuart Parnaby, 3.Richard Franklin, 4 Gary Beaton.
Support: 1 David Farley, 2. Montana Jowett, 3 Sam Woods, 4 Andy Harrison.
Youth 500: 1 Kyle Howarth, 2 Tom Woolley, 3 Josh Birkett.

Saturday, January 10
Open: 1 Craig Cook, 2. Richard Franklin, 3. Richard Lawson, 4 Scott Meakins.
Support: 1 Montana Jowett, 2 Rhys Naylor, 3 Sam Woods, 4 Mark Whitehead.
Youth 500: 1 Kyle Howarth, 2 Jack Butler, 3 Josh Birkett.
Youth 250: 1 Jack Cornes, 2 Reece Downes.

Saturday, January 31
Open: 1= Stuart Parnaby, 1= Richard Franklin, 1= Adam Wrathall, 4 Darren Mallett.
Support: 1 Steve Cook, 2 Mark Whitehead, 3 Liam Rumsey, 4 Andy Harrison.
Youth 500: 1 Kyle Howarth, 2 Josh Birkett, 3 Ben Morley.
Youth 250: 1 Robert Lambert, 2 Jack Cornes, 3 Reece Downes.

Saturday, February 9
Open: 1 Stuart Parnaby, 2 Adam Wrathall, 3 Richard Franklin, 4 Darren Mallett.
Support:: 1 Steve Cook, 2 Mark Whitehead, 3 Liam Rumsey, 4 Andy Harrison.
Youth 500: 1 Kyle Howarth, 2 Josh Birkett, 3 Ben Morley, 4 Tom Stokes.
Youth 250: 1 Robert Lambert, 2 Jack Cornes, 3 Reece Downes.

Saturday, March 14
Open: 1 Scott Richardson, 2 Paul; Starkem, 3 Richard Franklin, 4 Kyle Howarth.
Support:: 1 Montana Jowett, 2 Adam Kenyon, 3 Sam Woods, 4 Luke Chessell.
Youth 500: 1 Tom Stokes, 2 Cameron Hoskins.
Youth 250: 1 Reece Downes, 2 Jack Cornes.

2009 Summer Championship

Round 1: Saturday, April 11.
Round 2: Saturday, May 9.
Round 3: Sunday, June 7.
Round 4: Sunday, July 5.
Round 5: Saturday, August 1.
Round 6: Saturday, August 29.
Round 7: Saturday, September 26.
Round 8: Saturday, October 17.

SOUTHERN TRACK RIDERS

King's Lynn, Sunday, March 2
Novice Pairs: Liam Rumsey 20 & Lee Coley 12:2 = 32, Andy Harrison 11:2 & James Fear 16 = 27, Pete Shakespeare 13:1 & Phil Hindley 13:3 = 26, Ben Holloway 5:2 & Kieren Higgins 17 = 22, Su Marshall 3:1 & Sarah Cook 12 = 15, Clive Marshall 7 & Joe Burdekin 2 = 9.
Intermediate Pairs: Matt Jarman 14:1 & Steve Oakey 17:2 = 31, Steve Cook 9:1 & Dave Johnson 18:1 = 27, Paul Chester 18:1 & Nigel Knott 8 = 26, Gary Fawdrey 11 & Sid Higgins 14:3 = 25, Andy Lauder 8 & Montana Jowett 5 = 13.
Open Support: Dean Garrod 13, Scott Meakins 12.

King's Lynn, Sunday, April 6
Novice: Tony Venables 14, Ian Hart 13, Montana Jowett 13, Pete Shakespeare 11, Phil Hindley 10, Bill Smith 10, Lee Coley 8, Graeme Platten 7, Mark Anderson 7, Adi Bursil 7, Clive Marshall 7, Dan Howett 4, Craig Everitt 3, Su Marshall 3, Joe Burdeki 2, Norman Hornblow 1.
Intermediate: Dave Johnson 12, Steve Oakey 10, Matt Jarman 10, Paul Chester 9, Alec Gooch 7, Richard Davison 6, Nigel Knott 5, James Fear 4, Liam Rumsey 3, Andy Lauder 3, Shayne Denny 2, Sam Howett 0.
Open: Mike Holding 11, Chris Widman 10, Kevin Garwood 7, Dean Garrod 7, Andrew Blackburn 6, Jason Taylor 5, Rod Woodhouse 4, Russell Paine 0, Scott Anderson 0, Wayne Dunworth 0.
Youth 250: Rhys Naylor 12, Tom Stokes 7, Adam Portwood 7, Conor Dwyer 3, Matt Allitt 1.

Scunthorpe, Saturday, April 19
Novice: Andy Lauder 11, Andy Harrison 11, Montana Jowett 10, Adam Oughtibridge 8, James Luckman 8, Pete Shakespeare 7, Bill Smith 5, Sarah Cook 5, Clive Marhsall 5, Lee Coley 2, Su Marshall 0, Richard Lewin 0.
Open: Rod Woodhouse 14, Wayne Dunworth 14, Jittendra Duffill 14, Oliver Gay 11, Daniel Blake 11, Andrew Blackburn 7, Chris Widman 7, Liam Rumsey 7, Steve Oakey 6, Sid Higgins 6, Kevin Garwood 6, Matt Jarman 6, Paul Chester 5, Nigel Knott 3, Dave Lidgett 2.
Youth 250: Rhys Naylor 8+3, Adam Portwood 7+2, Joe Newey 1+1, Tom Stokes 7+0, Matt Allitt 1.

King's Lynn, Sunday, May 11
Novice challenge: ALEC'S ACES 64 (Pete Shakespeare 17, Sarah Cook 4:1, Bill Smith 9, Dan Howett 5:4, Adam Oughtibridge 10:1, Mark Anderson 11:2, Alec Jones 8:2, *rider replacement*), TONY'S TIGERS 55 (Richard Lewin 5, Su Marshall 0, Tony Venables 13:1, Norman Hornblow 1:1, Dennis Cairns 6:1, *rider replacement*, Derek Jones 18, Phil Hindley 12:4).
Intermediate challenge: STEVE'S STARS 52 (Graham Wilson 13, Lee Harris 4:2, Sid Higgins 9, Graeme Platten 0, Steve Oakey 9:1, Andy Harrison 5:1, Liam Rumsey 0, Ian Leverington 12), PAUL'S PIRATES 68 (Dave Johnson 0, Andy Lauder 8:2, Paul Chester 15:1, Adi Bursill 4:2, Matt Jarman 11, *rider replacement*, Montana Jowett 12:2, Ross Buchanan 18:1).
Open Challenge: ROD'S ROCKETS 41 (Karl White 12:1, Niall Strudwick 4, Jason Taylor 1, Daniel Blake 9, Mike Holding 11, Rod Woodhouse 4:1), DUNNIE'S DEVILS 48 (James Walker 4:2, Oliver Gay 10, Chris Widman 12:3, John Resch 12, Wayne Dunworth 10:1, *rider replacement*).

Scunthorpe, Saturday, May 24

Novice: Adam Oughtibridge 9+3, Pete Shakespeare 11+2, Dennis Cairns 11+1, Clive Marshall 8+N, Alec Jones 7+3, Joe Burdekin 7+2, Su Marshall 3+1, Lee Coley 6+R.

Open Pairs: Wayne Dunworth 19 & Dave Lidgett 9:1 = 28, Dean Hancox 16:1 & Montana Jowett 10:2 = 26, Chris Widman 18 & Adi Bursill 4 = 22, Oliver Gay 19 & Shayne Denny 2 = 21, Andrew Blackburn 17 & Nigel Knott 4:1 = 21, Lee Geary 8 & Sid Higgins 9:2 = 17.

Youth 250: Rhys Naylor 14, Conor Dwyer 11, Tom Stokes 10, Joe Newey 9, Adam Portwood 9, Matt Allitt 6.

Rye House, Sunday, June 8

Novice: Andy Lauder 12, Dennis Cairns 11, Mark Anderson 11, Pete Shakespeare 9, Derek Jones 9, Sam Howett 8, Adam Oughtibridge 7, Bill Smith 7, Alec Jones 6, Lee Coley 4, Joe Burdekin 4, James Luckman 3, Norman Hornblow 3, Pat Doyle 1, Dan Howett 1, Roger Curtis 0.

Intermediate: Ross Buchanan 11, Paul Chester 11, Charlie Gates 10, Montana Jowett 8, Steve Lockyer 8, Ashley Pearce 7, Sid Higgins 6, Steve Oakey 6, Matt Jarman 5, Shayne Denny 5, Liam Rumsey 5, Adi Bursill 4, Steve Edwards 4, Lee Harris 3, Tony Venables 2, Andy Harrison 0.

Open: Karl White 11, Chris Widman 11, James Walker 9, Daniel Blake 8, Niall Strudwick 7, Mike Holding 5, Graham Wilson 5, Andrew Blackburn 5, Glyn Edwards 4, Rod Woodhouse 3, Jason Taylor 2, Russell Paine 0.

King's Lynn, Sunday, June 15

Novice: Clive Marshall 8, Lee Coley 7, Martin Pearce 6, Simon Pearce 6, Pay Doyle 5, Norman Hornblow 5, Tony Raybould 4, Su Marshall 2, Richard Lewin 1.

Intermediate Challenge: THE TIGERS 41 (**Steve Lockyer 12**, Graeme Platten 0, Matt Jarman 13:1, Richard Davison 7, Adi Bursill 2, Tony Venables 4, Bill Smith 3:1), THE REBELS 49 (Sid Higgins 10, Shayne Denny 7:1, James Fear 10:2, Pete Shakespeare 7:2, Ian Hart 6:2, Mark Anderson 4:1, Phil Hindley 5:1).

Open Challenge: THE BEES 38 (**Karl White 12**, Jason Taylor 1, Wayne Dunworth 6:2, Ross Buchanan 0, Mike Holding 5, Paul Chester 3, Charlie Heatley 5:2, Oliver Rayson 6), THE PANTHERS 34 (Chris Widman 7, Rod Woodhouse 6:2, Oliver Gay 8, Charlie Gates 3:1, John Resch 6, Kevin Garwood 1:1, Ian Leverington 3).

Mildenhall, Saturday, June 21

Novice: Mark Anderson 8+3, Sam Howett 11+2, Clive Marhsall11 +1, Lee Coley 9+0, Adam Oughtibridge 8+3, Joe Burdekin 6+2, Alec Jones 7+1, Dan Howett 4+0, Tony Raybould 3+3, Su Marshall 1+2, Dave Lambert 3, Tony Venables 1,

Intermediate: Shayne Denny 8+3, Ted Ede 10+2, Montana Jowett 10+1, Sid Higgins 11+0, Liam Rumsey 6+3, Oliver Kinsley 7+2, Simon Pearce 4+1, Andy Lauder 4+N, Martin Pearce 3+3, Pete Shakespeare 4+2, Dave Lambert N+1,

Open: Chris Widman 10+3, Karl White 10+2, James Walker 12+1, Ross Buchanan 9+0, Wayne Dunworth 8+3, Mike Holding 4+2, Matt Jarman 4+1, Rod Woodhouse 7+R, Graham Wilson 3+3, Paul Chester 2.

Youth 250: Adam Portwood 15+3, Tom Stokes 10+2.

King's Lynn, Sunday, July 13

Novice: Adi Bursill 14, Phil Hindley 13, Mark Anderson 12, Pete Shakespeare 12, Lee Harris 11, Graeme Platten 9, Andy Harrison 8, Tony Venables 8, Steve Edwards 8, Pat Doyle 6, Alec Jones 5, Lee Coley 4, Sam Woods 3, Andrew Johnson 3, Norman Hornblow 2, Tony Raybould 2.

Intermediate: John Freeman 7+3, Shayne Denny 7+2, Matt Jarman 10+1, Liam Rumsey 9+F, Martin Pearce 4+3, Sid Higgins 4 +2, Simon Pearce 2+1, Richard Davison 3.

Open Pairs: Oliver Rayson 18 & Kevin Howse 10:3 = 28, Ian Leverington 11:3 & Steve Lomas 13 = 24, Karl White 19 & Andrew Blackburn 4 = 23, Niall Strudwick 16 & Charlie Gates 4:2 = 20, Chris Widman 19 & Jason Taylor 0 = 19, Wayne Dunworth 3 & Dean Garrod 14:1 = 17, .

Youth 250: Rhys Naylor 15, Tom Stokes 9, Conor Dwyer 6, Matt Allitt 0.

Rye House, Sunday, July 20

Over 50s: Sid Higgins 11+3, Steve Cook 12+2, Dennis Cairns 7+1, Pete Shakespeare 7+0, Phil Hindley 7+3, Derek Jones 7+2, Alec Jones 3+1, Pat Doyle 3+0, Richard Lewin 2+3, Norman Hornblow 1+2,

Open: Daniel Blake 11+3, Oliver Gay 7+2, Chris Widman 11+1, Wayne Dunworth 8+F, Niall Strudwick 5+3, Andrew Blackburn 2+2, Dean Garrod 4+1, Karl White 6+N, Daniel Greenwood [G] 12, Graham Wilson 2, Scott Anderson 1.

Intermediate Pairs: Matt Jarman 17:1 & Mark Anderson 12:2 = 29, Martin Pearce 7:2 & Ian Leverington 19 = 26, Shayne Denny 17 & Sam Howett 8:2 = 25, Charlie Gates 16 & Tony Venables 4 = 20, Liam Rumsey 16 & Ben Holloway 4:1 = 20, Simon Pearce 15 & Dan Howett 0 = 15.

King's Lynn, Sunday, August 3

Novice: Sam Howett 14, Richard Cawthorne 14, Pete Shakespeare 14, Graeme Platten 12, Adam Oughtibridge 10, Phil Hindley 10, Sam Woods 6, Lee Coley 6, Joe Miullarkey 6, Pat Doyle 6, Alec Jones 5, Joe Burdekin 5, Clive Marshall 5, Andrew Johnson 4, Dan Howett 2, Su Marshall 1.

Intermediate: Shayne Denny 11, Lee Harris 10, Liam Rumsey 10, Steve Cook 9, Matt Jarman 8, Steve Lockyer 6, Simon Pearce 6, Tony Venables 4, Montana Jowett 3, Martin Pearce 2, Sid Higgins 2.

Open: Shane Henry 11, Oliver Gay 10, Darren Smith 9, Dean Garrod 7, Tom Hill 7, Nially Strudwick 6, Robert Henry 2, Ben Hannon 0.

Rye House, Sunday, September 7

Over 40s: Wayne Dunworth 12, Ian Leverington 7, Kevin Garwood 7, Shayne Denny 7, Lee Harris 5, Andy Harrison 5, Tony Venables 4, Mark Anderson 2, Adi Bursill 1, Graham Wilson [G] 10, John Freeman [G] 9, Matt Jarman [G] 3.

Over 50s: Steve Cook 14, Steve Lockyer 13, Paul Chester 11, Sid Higgins 11, Pete Shakespeare 10, Dennis Cairns 7, Graeme Platten 7, Pat Doyle 5, Phil Hindley 5, Clive Marshall 3, Richard Lewin 3, Alec Jones 2, Tony Raybould 2,,Rob Hollingworth [G] 15, Ted Ede [G] 9, Steve Banting [G] 2.

Novice: Sam Woods 15, Lee Coley 10, Sarah Cook 3, Su Marshall 2.

Support: Chris Widman 14, Rhys Naylor 9, Liam Rumsey 6, Lee Geary 1.

Youth 250: Ben Morley 14, Tom Stokes 11, Adam Portwood 4.

King's Lynn, Sunday, September 28
Novice: Derek Jones 13, Sam Woods 12, Andy Harrison 10, Adam Oughtibridge 10, Graeme Platten 10, Michael Osborne 10, Phil Hindley 9, Pete Shakespeare 7, Richard Davison 7, Tony Raybould 5, Lee Coley 4, Alec Jones 3, Su Marshall 3, Paul Robinson [G] 9, Chris Archer [G] 2, David Witt [G] 1.
Intermediate: Rhys Naylor 15, Kevin Garwood 14, Liam Rumsey 13, Dave Lidgett 11, Montana Jowett 10, Shayne Denny 9, Steve Lockyer 9, Simon Pearce 8,Matt Jarman 7, Sid Higgins 6, Graham Wiloson 5, Nigel Knott 2, Lee Harris 1, Martin Pearce 1.
Open: Chris Widman 14, Mike Holding 11, Rod Woodhouse 4, Andrew Blackburn 1.
Youth 250: Ben Morley 14, Adam Portwood 10, Tom Stokes 5, Conor Dwyer 1.

King's Lynn, Sunday, October 19
Novice: Michael Osborne 11, Bill Smith 11, Richard Davison 9, Clive Marshall 7, Alec Jones 7, Richard Lewin 6, Pat Doyle 6, Gary Upchurch 5, Su Marshall 3, Gary Wood 1.
Support: Rob Hollingworth 12, Glyn Edwards 9, Steve Lockyer 9, Shayne Denny 9, Simon Pearce 7, Martin Pearce 7, Matt Jarman 6, Steve Oakey 5, Lee Harris 3, Charlie Gates 0.
Open Fours: 1 IT'S ONLY A TROPHY 41 (Kevin Garwood 10, Mark Anderson [R] 7, Oliver Gay 8, Pete Shakespeare 4, Liam Rumsey 12), **2 MARTIN'S MARAUDERS 45** (Chris Widman 15, Rhys Naylor 13, Russell Paine 12, Tony Venables 3, Adam Oughtibridge [R] 2), **3 CINDERS RECRUITS 34** (Mike Holding 11, Rod Woodhouse 10, Sid Higgins 8, Derek Jones 3, Sam Woods [R] 2), **4 TIGERS 30** (Dave Lidgett 8, Andy Harrison 6, Montana Jowett 8, Graeme Platten [R] 1, Andrew Blackburn 7).
Youth 250: Ben Morley 15, Adam Portwood 10.

Rye House, Sunday, November 9
Novice: Mark Baldock 12, Sam Howlett 11, Mark Bishop 9, Richard Lewin 9, Steve Banting 8, Gary Upchurch 7, Dan Howett 4, Pat Doyle 4, Alec Jones 4, Tony Raybould 3, Ian Jones 1, Su Marshall 0.
Support: Ian Olson 12, Ben Holloway 10, Richard Cawthorne 9, Sam Woods 8, Paul Robinson 7, Lee Harris 7, Andy Harrison 7, Mark Anderson 4, Pete Shakespeare 3, Tony Venables 3, Clive Marshall 1.
Open/Intermediate: Chris Widman 12, Oliver Gay 8, Jim Wannell 8, Rhys Naylor 8, Steve Lockyer 8, Liam Rumsey 7, Sid Higgins 6, Shayne Denny 5, Martin Pearce 4, Steve Cook 3, Steve Oakey 2, Simon Pearce 0.
Youth 250: Ben Morley 15, Adam Portwood 10.

The spread of ages of regular competitors in Southern Track Riders' Club meetings is an astonishing 60 years.
The oldest regular competitor is Norman Hornblow who was 73 on his last birthday, on September 18. He's actually 11 days older than fellow competitor Alec Jones who was 73 on September 29. At the other end of the scale the youngest rider in their Youth 250cc class in 2008 was Adam Portwood who was 13 on July 1.

Training Tracks

IN ADDITION to the three Amateur organisations previously listed, a number of tracks and organisations run training days and corporate race-days.

The following venues all have the approval of the speedway authorities and will operate with insurance and medical cover.

BUXTON SPEEDWAY
Track: Dale Head Lane, Axe Edge, near Buxton, Derbyshire.
Contact: Jayne Moss.
Tel: 01298 77299, 07979 640198.
E-mail: jayne@moss2828.fsworld.co.uk

EASTBOURNE SPEEDWAY
Track: Arlington Stadium, Arlington Road West, Hailsham, East Sussex, BH27 3RE.
Contact: Mike Bellerby.
Tel: 07899 987436.
E-mail:mike.bellerby@tiscali.co.uk

NORTHSIDE TRAINING TRACK
Track: Dale Head Lane, Axe Edhe, near Buxton.
Contact: Judith Lomas.
Tel: 01900 603032, 07748 574274.
E-mail: michjaellomas@btinternet.com

POWER SLIDE TRAINNG SCHOOL
Track: Norfolk Arena, Saddlebow Road, King's Lynn, PE34 3AG.
Contact: Keith Chapman.
Tel:01553 771111.
E-mail: info@norfolkarena.co.uk

SCUNTHORPE SPEEDWAY
Track: Scunthorpe Raceway, Normanby Road, Scunthorpe, Lincolnshire, DN15 9YG.
Contact: Rob Godfrey.
Tel: 01724 271851, 07832 138983.
E-mail: richard@scunthorpespeedway.com

SITTINGBOURNE SPEEDWAY
Track: The Old Gun Site, Old Ferry Road, Iwade, near Sittingbourne, Kent, ME9 8SP.
Contact: Graham Arnold.
Tel: 01227 451911.
E-mail: theoldgunsite@googlemail.com

STOKE SPEEDWAY
Track: Loomer Road Stadium, Newcastle-under-Lyme, Staffordshire, ST5 7LB.
Contact: Dave Tattum.
Tel: 01782 786021.

BLASTS FROM THE PAST

IN recent seasons nostalgia has come to the fore – with long forgotten tracks being reborn, principally by enthusiasts clinging onto the hope of seeing their favourite clubs being revived.

Throughout 2008 a number of current circuits staged challenge matches representing clubs that no longer have a home venue.

Weymouth staged the majority of these meetings, bringing back to life four former clubs.

BRISTOL Bulldogs

THERE'S been no racing in Bristol since the final meeting at the city's Eastville Stadium on October 27, 1978.

A brief but hugely successful two season revival was brought to an abrupt end on Thursday, December 14, when stadium managing director Ian Stevens gave an undertaking in closed session in the High Court in London not to allow any more meetings after noise objections from local residents.

Fan Andy Hewlett, who is hoping to find a new site in the city to build a new stadium, revived the side who wore the once familiar Bulldog motif race-jacket.

WEYMOUTH (A)
Saturday, June 7
Lost 38-54
James Cockle 5, Ben Reade 1, **Mark Simmonds 18 (6)**, Jade Mudgway 5:1, Michael Coles 4, Oliver Gay 3, Paul Derrick 2:1.

▲ *Mark Simmonds scored an 18-point maximum for the Bristol team, nearly 30 years since the Bulldogs were lost to the sport*

KINGSWOOD HOTEL SOUTH WEST FOURS
Saturday, July 26
2 BRISTOL 28 (Matthew Wright 9, Jade Mudgway 8, Ryan Sedgman 6, Justin Sedgman 5), 1 **WEYMOUTH 30, 3 EXETER 24, 4 SOMERSET 12.**

PLYMOUTH (A)
Friday, September 12
Lost 26-63
Rider replacement for Danny Warwick, Jason Prynne 6:2, Marc Andrews 1, Luke Priest 10, Ben Hopwood 7, Richard Andrews 2, Paul Derrick 0.

BRISTOL REVIVED: The first Bulldogs team since 1978 – manager Glenn Cunningham, Ben Reade, Paul Derrick, Andy Hewlett, Jade Mudgway, James Cockle. Front – Mark Simmonds, skipper Michael Coles and Oliver Gay

OXFORD Cheetahs

HOPES that the Cheetahs could return to regular league racing in 2008 were dashed when stadium owners refused to grant a long term lease to Allen Trump, who had saved the club from closure in 2007.

Efforts by Tony Mole, Jon Cook and Nick Andrews to resurrect the team for 2009 also failed but at least they did compete in one meeting, at Weymouth where they managed to use both Kyle Hughes and Matt Bates who had ridden for the Cheetahs in 2007.

WEYMOUTH (A)
Saturday, September 20
Lost 32-61
Dean Felton 3, Richard Andrews 1, Luke Priest 9, Terry Day 1, Kyle Hughes 14 (6), Harland Cook 4:1, Matt Bates 0.

WIMBLEDON Dons

THERE have to be serious doubts whether racing will ever return to Wimbledonb's Plough Lane stadium.

The South London venue, still a bouyant greyhound racing home, hasn't staged a meeting since October 5, 2005.

Talks over a new lease for the following season floundered and while there have been tentative inquires about resuming the reaction from the Greyhound Racing Association – the stadium owners – have been lukewarm and expensive.

Meanwhile the Dons have continued to race the occasional challenge match on Conference League circuits.

WEYMOUTH (A)
Saturday, May 17
25-29, abandoned after Heat 9, rain.
Andrew Bargh 2:1, Jerran Hart 6:1, Tom Brown 3, Nathan Irwin 0, Matthew Wright 4:1, Lee Strudwick 4:1, Terry Day 6:1.

DUBLIN

Huge crowds used to follow speedway at Dublin's Shelbourne Park. Now one-time promoter Stuart Cosgrave is keen to revive the sport in the Republic of Ireland

STUART Cosgrave is the driving force behind a new initiative to re-establish speedway in Ireland.

Cosgrave, who runs what is reputed to be the biggest indoor karting centre in Dublin, was promoter at Shelbourne Park in 1970 and 1971 – the last meeting at the greyhound track was on June 20 –and has applied for planning permission to build a new circuit in the city.

He is also keen to run an Irish Grand Prix by constructing a temporary circuit within the Royal Dublin Showground and has already had preliminary talks with the rights holders IMG.

He also has hopes that other tracks will spring up both north and south of the Irish border. There's a prospective site in Limerick and there are other possible venues in Northern Ireland although Cosgrave's priority is to re-establish speedway in Dublin.

Gareth Rogers, David Lucas and Glyn Taylor – all instrumental in the opening of Redcar – have been taken on board as advisors and there are genuine hopes that at least one Irish club will be staging challenge matches against National League visitors in 2009.

EXETER Falcons

ALLEN Trump was convinced he would have Exeter Falcons back in full flight for the 2009 season after getting planning permission to build a new stadium at the Exeter Racecourse.

But complicatioons over the length and some terms of the lease saw the project delayed although he still hopes to have his hometown club back in league racing in 2010.

The now desolate County Ground (pictured right) staged its End of an Era meeting on Monday, October 10, 2005, when legend Ivan Mauger completed the final four laps on a track that had first opened in 1929 and staged regular league racing for 45 successive seasons.

Trump has spent the last three years battling to find a new site in the Devon city and the day after Teingbridge District Council passed a planning application to build a circuit in the middle of the Jockey Club owned racecourse at Haldon – a few miles outside Exeter – he was in joyful mood.

A faint outline of the old track and its infamous banking is still just about discernible at the County Ground

WEYMOUTH (A)
Friday, September 26
Lost 34-60
Kyle Hughes 12 (4), Gary Cottham 4:1, Terry Day 4, Tim Webster 1, Luke Priest 11:1 (TS4), Richard Andrews 1:1, Matt Bates 1.

KINGSWOOD HOTEL SOUTH WEST FOURS
Saturday, July 26
1 WEYMOUTH 30, 2 BRISTOL 28, 3 EXETER 24 (Kyle Hughes 6, Tim Webster 4, Terry Day 8, Gary Cottham 6), **4 SOMERSET 12.**

FALCONS FLY AGAIN: The Exeter team that raced a challenge match at Weymouth. Left to right: promoter Allen Trump, Richard Andrews, Terry Day, Kyle Hughes, Matt Bates, Gary Cottham, Tim Webster and co-promoter David Short

PHOTO: ***Julie MARTIN***

FOURSOME FALCONS: The Falcons quartet who took part in the Flur Team Tournament at Weymouth – Matthew Wright, promoter Allen Trump, Kyle Hughes, Terry Day and Gary Cottham

PHOTO: ***Julie MARTIN***

SITTINGBOURNE

PREMIER League promoters extended their 2009 deadline in the hope that racing could start at Sittingbourne's plush Central Park Stadium in 2009.

But even though Swale Council granted tempoary planning permission to build a circuit at the greyhound stadium, prospective promoter Roger Cearns – a member of the family that used to run Wimbledon Stadium – had to shelve his league plans for at least a season because of time constraints.

However he does hope to get the green light to stage several open meetings in 2009 before a full-time excursion into the Premier League in 2010.

He said: "The most likely scenario is we will be looking to hold some meetings in the late summer."

INTERNATIONALS

ENGLAND UNDER 23

v

AUSTRALIA UNDER 23

AUSTRALIA proved too strong for a full-strength England squad in a three match Under 23 series.

But it was a close run thing with England winning the opening Test at Monmore Green before the Aussies won the last two meetings at Swindon and Somerset.

They were helped in the last two by the presence of Chris Holder who had missed the opening clash at Blunsdon.

The England team was in the charge of Dave Croucher, one third of the new Under 21 set-up which took over at the beginning of the season.

And he picked a strong side for all the matches, including the aborted attempt to run the match at Somerset.

Continuous rain caused it to be called off after eight heats, Australian leading 26-22 at the point where referee Chris Durno called time on the action.

Elite League regulars James Wright and Lewis Bridger rode in all three completed matches but Edward Kennett, who top-scored at both Wolverhampton and Somerset missed the middle tie in the rubber.

It's almost certain that had he been available that England would have added to their opening victory and they missed his points.

Eleven different riders won caps – with Joe Haines Robert Mear and Jordan Frampton getting their first taste of international competition.

Australia, with fewer riders to choose from, also restricted their pick to 11 different riders with Troy Batchelor, Cory Gathercole and exciting young reserve Richard Sweetman everpresent throughout the series.

Debutant Frampton certainly enjoyed his baptism at this level – inflicting one of only two defeats suffered by Holder in his 10 rides.

He got the better of him in the opening heat at the Oak Tree Arena and in the early stages it inspired his team-mates as England built up a six point lead that was gradually whittled away before the Aussies stormed away, underlining their victory with a last race maximum.

First Test
Wolverhampton, Monday, September 8

ENGLAND U23 48			
James Wright	1 2 2 2	7	1
Tai Woffinden	3 3 0 F	9	
Edward Kennett	2 1 3 2 3	11	1
Ben Barker	0 2 2 3	7	1
Lewis Bridger	3 0 3 0	6	
Josh Auty	1 2 0 1	4	1
Joe Haines	2 0 2 0	4	1
AUSTRALIA U23 43			
Troy Batchelor	2 3 2 2 3	12	
Cory Gathercole	R 0 1 1	2	1
Cameron Woodward	3 1 3 3 2	12	
Tyron Proctor	1 3 1 2	7	
Matthew Wethers	2 FX 0 1	3	
Aaron Summers	0 1 1 1	3	1
Richard Sweetman	3 1 0 0	4	1

Referee: Dave Robinson.

Second Test
Swindon, Thursday, September 11

ENGLAND U23 44			
Lewis Bridger	2 3 2 1 0	8	1
Jason King	1 1 3 1	6	2
James Wright	2 1 3 2	8	1
Ben Barker	1 2 2 F	5	2
Tai Woffinden	3 2 2 2 2	11	
Robert Mear	2 0 0 1	3	
Joe Haines	0 1 2 0	3	1
AUSTRALIA U23 47			
Troy Batchelor	3 3 3 3 1	13	
Cory Gathercole	FX 0 F	0	
Chris Holder	3 3 3 2 3 3	17	
Robert Ksiezak	0 1 0 2	3	1
Cameron Woodward	2 2 1 0	5	
Kozza Smith	1 0 0 1	2	
Richard Sweetman	3 0 1 3	7	

Referee: Graham Reeve.

Third Test
Somerset, Friday, September 26

ENGLAND U23 40			
James Wright	0 2 1 1 1	5	
Jordan Frampton	3 1 0 R	4	1
Edward Kennett	3 2 2 2	9	
Ben Barker	1 1 1 4	7	2
†Lewis Bridger	3 2 2 0 0	7	
Joshua Auty	1 0 0	1	
Ben Wilson	3 1 2 0 1	7	1
AUSTRALIA U23 52			
†Chris Holder	2 3 3 3	11	
Cory Gathercole	1 0 3 1	5	1
Troy Batchelor	2 3 3 3 2	13	1
Tyron Proctor	0 1 2 3	6	1
Jason Doyle	2 3 3 2 3	13	1
Richard Sweetman	0 R 0	0	
Kozza Smitrh	2 0 1 1 0	4	

Referee: Jim Lawrence.

AUSTRALIA won series 2-1.

Original staging of Third Test abandoned after eight races. For details - see Somerset.

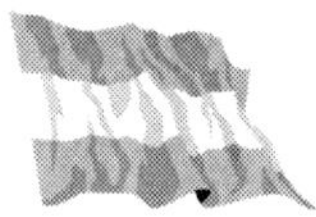

ARGENTINE

ARGENTINE INTERNATIONAL CHAMPIONSHIP

The Argentine Championship is an open championship with riders from other countries competing in the winter series.

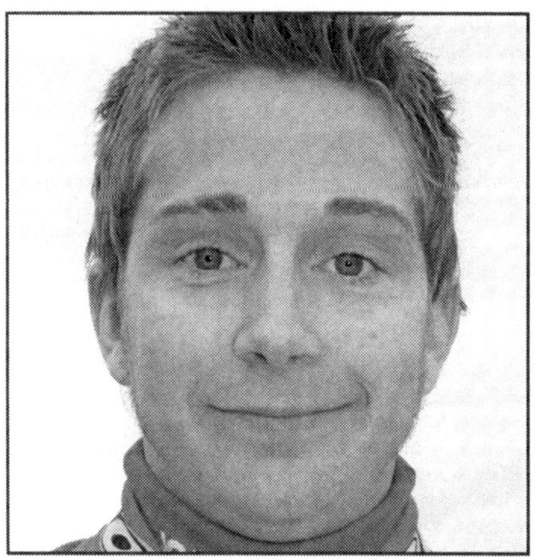

CANADIAN Kyle Legault joined the relatively small club of riders to have won national titles in more than one country.

The former Canadian Champion added the Argentine crown to his collection after taking a grip on the 13-round winter series.

Augmented from the influx of riders from Europe the series was raced at five different circuits.

The midget car track at Aldea Romana played host to the majority of the meetings – often in opposition to the longer established circuit at San Martin and clearly crowds at both Bahia Blanca venues were affected by the clash.

Other rounds were held at Daireaux, Carlos Casares (some 200 miles from the capital), Carhue (more than 300 miles away) and at Freyre, Cordoba.

Final Standings

1 Kyle LEGAULT 180, 2 Lee COMPLIN 154, 3 Guglielmo FRANCHETTI 151, 4 Emiliano SANCHEZ 141, 5 Mattia CARPANESE 133, 6 Matias LOPEZ 120, 7 Nicolas COVATTI 90, 8 Lucas ALLENDE 72, 9 Julio ROMANO 61, 10 Lisandro HUSMAN 54, 11 Alejandro RUIZ 42, 12 Jonathan ITURRE 34, 13 Cristian CARRICA 26, 14 Facundo GRUAT 19, 15 Micaela BAZAN 18, 16 Gianfranco RISSONE 17, 17 Pablo MENDEZ 13, 18 Sebastian CLEMENTE 11, 19 Claudio SCHMIDT 8, 20 Flavio HUSMAN 8, 21 Wilson FANFLIET 6, 22 Oscar MAUREL 5, 23 Antonio MOYANO 4, 24 Carlos SILVA 4, 25 Gustavo CURZIO 2, 26 Fernando GARCIA 2, 27 Maximilliano WESTDORP 1, 28 Diego ELENO 0.

Round 1

Aldea Romana, Bahia Blanca, Sunday, December 21, 2008

1 Emiliano Sanchez 19, 2 Lee Complin 16, 3 Kyle Legault 15, 4 Guglielmo Franchetti 10, 5 Lucas Allende 8, 6 Nicolas Covatti 8, 7 Matias Lopez 7, 8 Alejandro Ruiz 4, 9 Julio Rojano 3, 10 Sebastian Clemente 3, 11 Mattia Carpanese 3, 12 Gianfranco Rissone 2, 13 Micaela Bazan 2, 14 Jonathan Iturre 0.

Round 2

Aldea Romana, Bahla Blanca, Sunday, December 28, 2008

1 Lee Complin 18, 2 Guglielmo Franchetti 13, 3 Nicolas Covatti 13, 4 Matias Lopez 13, 5 Emiliano Sanchez 11, 6 Mattia Carpanese 7, 7 Kyle Legault 5, 8 Lucas Allende 5, 9 Alejandro Ruiz 5, 10 Julio Romano 3, 11 Sebastian Clemente 3, 12 Gianfranco Rissone 1, 13 Pablo Mendez 1, 14 Micaela Bazan 0, 15 Jonathan Iturre 0.

Round 3

Daireaux, Friday, January 2

1 Kyle Legault 18, 2 Matias Lopez 17, 3 Guglielmo Franchetti 12, 4 Nicolas Covatti 11, 5 Julio Romano 9, 6 Lucas Romano 9, 6 Lucas Allende 6, 7 Alejandro Ruiz 6, 8 Lee Complin 4, 9 Oscar Maurel 3, 10 Flavio Husman 3, 11 Pablo Mendez 3, 12 Emiliano Sanchez 3, 13 Micaela Bazan 1, 14 Mattia Carpanese 1, 15 Sebastian Clemente 0.

Round 4

Aldea Romana, Bahia Blanca, Sunday, January 4

1 Mattia Carpanese 19, 2 Lee Complin 16, 3 Kyle Legault 14, 4 Nicolas Covatti 12, 5 Matias Lopez 11, 6 Lucas Allende 8, 7 Guglielmo Franchetti 6, 8 Julio Romano 4, 9 Emiliano Sanchez 4, 10 Oscar Maurel 2, 11 Pablo Mendez 2, 12 Micaela Bazan 2, 13 Sebastian Clemente 0, 14 Gianfranco Rissone 0.

Round 5

Aldea Romana, Bahia Blanca, Sunday, January 11

1 Mattia Carpanese 19, 2 Guglielmo Franchetti 16, 3 Lee Complin 13, 4 Kyle Legault 11, 5 Nicolas Covatti 11, 6 Matias Lopez 9, 7 Lucas Allende 7, 8 Julio Romano 4, 9 Jonathan Iturre 4, 10 Alejandro Ruiz 2, 12 Micaela Bazan 2, 12 Pablo Mendez 2, 13 Gianfranco Rissone 2, 14 Facundo Gruat 0, 15 Sebastian Clemente 0.

Final staged on January 18 after rain prevented it being run on January 11.

Round 6

Carlos Casares, Friday, January 16

1 Matias Lopez 17, 2 Nicolas Covatti 16, 3 Lee Complin 13, 4 Julio Romano 11, 5 Guglielmo Franchetti 8, 6 Kyle Legault 7, 7 Mattia Carpanese 5, 8 Facundo Gruat 5, 9 Lucas Allende 4, 10 Micaela Bazan 3, 11 Gianfranco

Rissone 2, 12 Maximilliano Westdorp 1, 13 Diego Eleno 0.

Round 7

Aldea Romana, Bahia Blanca, Sunday, January 18

1 Gugiielmo Franchetti 18, 2 Mattia Carpanese 17, 3 Kyle Legault 13, 4 Nicolas Covatti 12, 5 Lucas Allende 10, 6 Lee Complin 9, 7 Matias Lopez 8, 8 Alejandro Ruiz 7, 8 Facundo Gruat 6, 10 Gianfranco Rissone 4, 11 Julio Romano 3, 12 Pablo Mendez 3, 13 Jonathan Iturre 3, 14 Sebastian Clemente 2, 15 Carlos Silva 2, 16 Micaela Bazan 1.

Round 8

Carhue, Friday, January 23

1 Emiliano Sanchez 18, 2 Kyle Legault 17, 3 Lisandro Husman 11, 4 Lee Complin 11, 5 Nicolas Covatti 7, 6 Mattia Carpanese 6, 7 Jonathan Iturre 6, 8 Guglielmo Franchetti 6, 9 Julio Romano 6, 10 Cristian Carrica 5, 11 Flavio Husman 4, 12 Lucas Allende 4, 13 Claudio Schmidt 3, 14 Sebastian Clemente 2, 15 Micaela Bazan 2, 16 Matias Lopez 1, 17 Pablo Mendez 1, 16 Alejandro Ruiz 1, 19 Gianfranco Rissone 1, 20 Facundo Gruat 0.

Round 9

Aldea Romana, Bahia Blanca, Sunday, January 25

1 Emiliano Sanchez 18, 2 Mattia Carpanese 17, 3 Guglielmo Franchetti 13, 4 Lee Complin 13, 5 Kyle Legault 12, 6 Matias Lopez 9, 7 Wilson Fanfliet 6, 8 Claudio Schmdit 5, 9 Cristian Carrica 4, 10 Lisandro Husman 4, 11 Alejandro Ruiz 4, 12 Julio Romano 3, 13 Jonathan Iturre 3, 14 Gianfranco Rissone 3, 15 Facundo Gruat 2, 16 Lucas Allende 1, 17 Gustavo Curzio 1, 18 Sebastian Clemente 0, 19 Pablo Mendez 0, 20 Micaela Bazan 0.

Round 10

Freyre, Cordoba, Friday, January 30

1 Guglielmo Franchetti 18, 2 Emiliano Sanchez 17, 3 Kyle Legault 13, 4 Lisandro Husman 12, 5 Lee Complin 11, 6 Matias Lopez 10, 7 Lucas Allende 6, 8 Jonathan Iturre 6, 9 Alejandro Ruiz 5, 10 Cristian Carrica 4, 11 Julio Romano 4, 12 Facundo Gruat 3, 13 Mattia Carpanese 2, 14 Antonio Moyano 2, 15 Gianfranco Rissone 1, 16 Micaela Bazan 1, 17 Sebastian Clemente 1, 18 Carlos Silva 1, 19 Flavio Husman 1, 20 Gustavo Curzio 1, 21 Pablo Mendez 0.

Round 11

Freyre, Cordoba, Saturday, January 31

1 Kyle Legault 19, 2 Emiliano Sanchez 15, 3 Mattia Carpanese 13, 4 Lisandro Husman 11, 5 Lee Complin 11, 6 Matias Lopez 9, 7 Guglielmo Franchetti 8, 8 Cristian Carrica 6, 9 Jonathan Iturre 6, 10 Lucas Allende 5, 11 Julio Romano 5, 12 Alejandro Ruiz 4, 13 Facundo Gruat 2, 14 Antonio Moyana 2, 15 Gianfranco Rissone 1, 16 Pablo Mendez 1, 17 Carlos Silva 1, 18 Sebastian Clemente 0, 19 Micaela Bazan 0, 20 Flavio Husman 0.

Freyre – venue for two rounds of the championship

Round 12

Daireaux, Saturday, February 7

1 Emiliano Sanchez 19, 2 Kyle Legault 17, 3 Guglielmo Franchetti 13, 4 Lisandro Husman 11, 5 Mattia Carpanese 10, 6 Lee Complin 8, 7 Matias Lopez 6, 8 Alejandro Ruiz 5, 9 Jonathan Iturre 4, 10 Micaela Bazan 3, 11 Julio Romano 2, 12 Fernando Garcia 2, 13 Diego Eleno 0, 14 Maximilliano Westdorp 0,15 Facundo Gruat 0.

Round 13

Aldea Romana, Bahia Blanca, Sunday, February 8

1 Kyle Legault 19, 2 Emiliano Sanchez 17, 3 Mattia Carpanese 14, 4 Lee Complin 11, 5 Lucas Allende 8, 6 Guglielmo Franchetti 8, 7 Cristian Carrica 7, 8 Lisandro Husman 5, 9 Matias Lopez 3, 10 Julio Romano 4, 11 Jonathan Iturre 2, 12 Micaela Bazan 1, 13 Facundo Gruat 1, 14 Gustavo Curzio 0, 15 Sebastian Clemente 0, 16 Gianfranco Rissone 0, Pablo Mendez 0.

2008

FINAL STANDINGS

1 Nicolas Covatti 195, 2 Manuel Hauzinger 141, 3 Julio Romano 131, 4 Lisandro Husman 111, 5 Lucas Allende 83, 6 Flavio Husman 70, 7 Luciano Goycochea 60, 8 Daniel Keegan 48, 9 Micaela Bazan 45, 10 Gustavo Curzio 45, 11 Enrique Salas 43, 12 Martin Albanesse 41, 13 Manuel Novotny 39, 14 Claudio Schmidt 38, 15 Daniel Finochiaro 33, 16 Matias Lopez 30, 17 Carlos Silva 25, 18 Wilson Fanfliet 14, 19 Rafael Gismondi 11, 20 Sebastian Clemente 9, 21 Gabriel Catafi 7, 22 Rodrigo Montuelle 7, 23 Fabian Orlando 5, 24 Alejandro Ruiz 4, 25 Rodolfo Pereyra 3, 26 Santiago Martinez 1,

Roll of Honour

1930	Roberto SIGRAND
1931	Juan PAGANO
1934	Juan PAGANO
1936	Juan SALATINO
1937	Juan SALATINO
1938	Juan SALATINO
1939	Juan SALATINO
1955	Hector SANTIN
1956	Julio ZECCHI
1962	Edgar CASTELLANOS
1975	Horacio ILACQUA
1983	Juan Carlos CURZIO
1985	Juan Carlos CURZIO
1986	Heinrich SCHATZER (Austria)
1987	Peter HEHLERT (East Germany)
1988	Luis Alberto VALLEJOS
1989	Luis Alberto VALLEJOS
1990	Luis Alberto VALLEJOS
1991	Luis Alberto VALLEJOS
1992	Heinrich SCHATZER (Austria)
1993	Luis Alberto VALLEJOS
1994	Luis Alberto VALLEJOS
1995	Luis Alberto VALLEJOS
1996	Zoltan ADORJAN (Hungary)
1997	Marcel GERHARD (Switzerland)
1998	Luis Alberto VALLEJOS

1999 ....Armandon CASTAGNA (Italy)
2000 ....Emiliano SANCHEZ
2001 ....Antonin SVAB II (Czech Republic)
2002 ....Emiliano SANCHEZ
2003 ....Carlos SILVA
2004 ....Luis Alberto VALLEJOS
2005 ....Lisandro HUSMAN
2006 ....Lisandro HUSMAN
2007 ....Manuel HAUZINGER (Austria)
2008 ....Nicolas COVATTI
2009 ....Kyle LEGAULT (Canada)

FINAL STANDINGS
500cc B CLASS

1 Maximiliano Westdorp 165, 2 Diego Elena 124, 3 Diego Genchi 74, 4 Fernando Garcia 71, 5 Facundo Gruat 53, 6 Martin Melchior 46, 7 Carlos Zubelda 17, 8 Nestor Mansilla 14, 9 Gustavo Sproviero 13, 10 Santiago Quadro 10.

ARGENTINE CHAMPIONSHIP
2008-09 Summer Series

Round 1
Bahia Blanca, Sunday, December 21, 2008
1 Claudio Schmidt 19, 2 Cristian Carrica 17, 3 Gustavo Curzio 15, 4 Luciano Goycochea 12, 5 Enrique Salas 9, 6 Oscar Maurel 8, 7 Daniel Finochiaro 1, 8 Santiago Martinez 1, 9 Antonio Moyano 0.

Round 2
Bahia Blanca, Sunday, December 28, 2008
1 Flavio Husman 19, 2 Cristian Carrica 16, 3 Claudio Schmidt 14, 4 Gustavo Curzio 9, 5 Luciano Guycochea 9, 6 Oscar Maurel 6, 7 Enrique Salas 6, 8 Antonio Moyano 3, 9 Santiago Martinez 1, 10 Daniel Finochiaro 0.

Round 3
Bahia Blanca, Sunday, January 4
1 Wilson Fanfliet 19, 2 Cristian Carrica 16, 3 Claudio Schmidt 14, 4 Flavio Husman 11, 5 Enrique Salas 7, 6 Gustavo Curzio 3, 7 Daniel Finochiaro 1, 8 Santiago Martinez 1, 9 Antonio Moyano 0.

Round 4
Bahia Blanca, Sunday, January 11
1 Cristian Carrica 18, 2 Flavio Husman 17, 3 Gustavo Curzio 14, 4 Antonio Moyano 11, 5 Daniel Finochiaro 8, 6 Santiago Martinez 7, 7 Enrique Salas 2, 8 Adrian Rossi 1.

Round 5
Bahia Blanca, Sunday, January 18
1 Cristian Carrica 19, 2 Gustavo Curzio 14, 3 Luciano Goycochea 13, 4 Flavio Husman 11, 5 Daniel Finochiaro 9, 6 Enrique Salas 8, 7 Antonio Moyano 1, 8 Adrian Rossi 1, 9 Santiago Martinez 0.

Round 6
Bahia Blanca, Sunday, January 25
1 Luciano Goycochea 19, 2 Flavio Husman 13, 3 Enrique Salas 13, 4 Daniel Finochiaro 12, 5 Antonio Moyano 10, 6 Santiago Martinez 8, 7 Roberto Cabral 1.

ARGENTINE CHAMPIONSHIP
Winter Series

The series, which does not usually include professional riders who are committed to a full season of racing elsewhere, will be run over 10 rounds throughout the South American winter.

Lisandro Husman took part and won the second round in his final meeting before heading for Europe.

Rounds are expected to be held at Daireaux and Colonia Baron as well as Bolivar and the long-established circuit at Carhue.

Standings after two rounds:
Jonathan Iturre 33, Matias Lopez 28, Julio Romano 18, Lisandro Husman 18, Sebastian Clement 12, Pablo Mendez 12, Gianfranco Rissone 12, Maximiliano Westdorp 10, Cristian Carrica 10, Daniel Finochiaro 6, Santiago Martinez 1.

Round 1
Carhue, Friday, February 27
Jonathan Iturre, 2 Julio Romano, 3 Matias Lopez, 4 Sebastian Clemente, 5 Pablo Mendez.

Round 2
Carhue, Sunday, March 15
1 Lisandro Husman, 2 Jonathan Iturre, 3 Cristian Carrico, 4 Matias Lopez, 5 Maximiliano Westdorp.

Round 3: Sunday, April 5, Bolivar.
Round 4: Friday, May 1, venue to be confirmed.
Round 5: Saturday, June 6, venue to be confirmed.
Round 6: Sunday, July 5, venue to be confirmed.
Round 7: Sunday, August 2, venue to be confirmed.
Round 8: Sunday, Spetember 6, venue to be confirmed.
Round 9: Sunday, October 4, venue to be confirmed.
Round 10: Sunday, November 1, venue to be confirmed.

AUSTRALIA

AUSTRALIAN CHAMPIONSHIP

The Australian Championship has often been held over the course of two years with their main racing season running from Autumn to Spring. The year listed refers to the end of the season in question rather than the beginning.
Therefore the 2009 Australian Championship covers the 2008-09 season.

LEIGH Adams made it a perfect 10 – as he returned to the Australian Championship.

After sitting out last year's series the world number six was back doing what he does best – showing his back wheel to his rivals.

And he did it in overpowering style as he further enhanced his reputation as the best Australian rider never to be crowned World Champion.

The Mildurian won his first senior national title way back in 1992 and emphasised his enduring qualities with an unbeatable performance over the three round series.

He began by winning all six races at Newcastle and went through the card in subsequent rounds at his hometown track and then Gillman, near Adelaide.

Adams took 18 races throughout the week-long series and won every one to end Chris Holder's ambitions to successfully retain the title he won, in Adams' absence, a year earlier.

With Jason Crump again opting not to contest the championship, Adams will have looked back with some optimism as the new breed of young, thrusting Aussies began to make their mark.

FINAL STANDINGS – OVERALL

	R1	*R2*	*R3*	*Tot*
1 Leigh ADAMS	20	20	20	60
2 Chris HOLDER	17	18	17	52
3 Rory SCHLEIN	18	15	15	48
4 Troy BATCHELOR	10	17	18	45
5 Davey WATT	13	14	16	43
6 Cameron WOODWARD	15	13	13	41
7 Tyron PROCTOR	14	12	11	37
8 Jason DOYLE	16	16		32
9 Darcy WARD	6	11	14	31
10 Cory GATHERCOLE	12	4	12	28
11 Kozza SMITH	7	10	10	27
12 Josh GRAJCZONEK	4	9	9	22
13 Jay HERNE	11	3	3	17
14 Justin SEDGMEN	3	7	4	14
15 Aaron SUMMERS	2	6	6	14
16 Lee HERNE	9	2	2	13
17 James HOLDER			7	7

Round scoring: 20-18-17-16-15-14-13-12-11-10-9-7-6-4-3-2.

Rory Schlein was runner-up in New South Wales but didn't make the Grand Final at either Mildura or Gillman, allowing Holder to overhaul him in the race for the silver medal.

There were encouraging displays from Ty Proctor and teenager Darcy Ward (a qualifier from the preliminary round at Gosford) who both finished in the top 10.

Adams' victory means he is now way out in front on the Roll of Honour.

He's won four titles more than Billy Sanders and half a dozen more than Jim Airey – and that is a true measure of his dominance at a time when Australian stock has rarely been higher.

Taking into account his early victories in both the Under 16 and Under 21 challenges, the Swindon skipper now has a total of 15 Australian titles – an all-time record that is unlikely to be broken.

He said: "I wanted to clean-sweep it, and I knew it was going to be tough with the competition that was there – I had some real battles with a lot of guys right throughout the series.

"It's great, and it's good for Australian speedway that they're catching up. Even though I went through undefeated they are right there, I promise you!"

Round 1

Newcastle, New South Wales, Saturday, January 3

1 Leigh Adams 15+□+3, 2 Rory Schlein 12+□+2, 3 Chris Holder 11+3+1, 4 Jason Doyle 12+□+0, 5 Cameron Woodward 11+2, 6 Ty Proctor 7+1, 7 Davey Watt 10+0, 8 Cory Gathercole 7, 9 Jay Herne 6, 10 Troy Batchelor 6, 11 Lee Herne 6, 12 Kozza Smith 5, 13 Darcy Ward 5, 14 Josh Grajczonek 4, 15 Justin Sedgmen 3, 16 Aaron Summers 0, James Holder [R], Hugh Skidmore [R], did not ride.

Round 2

Mildura, Victoria, Wednesday, January 7

1 Leigh Adams 15+□+3, 2 Chris Holder 11+3+2, 3 Troy Batchelor 12+□+1, 4 Jason Doyle 12+□+0, 5 Rory Schlein 11+2, 6 Davey Watt 11+1, 7 Cameron Woodward 10+0, 8 Ty Proctor 8, 9 Darcy Ward 8, 10 Kozza Smith 6, 11 Justin Sedgmen 4, 12 Josh Grajczonek 3, 13 Jay Herne 3, 14 Aaron Summers 3, 15 Lee Herne 2, 16 Cory Gathercole 1, James Holder [R], Hugh Skidmore [R], did not ride.

Round 3

Gillman, South Australia, Saturday, January 10

1 Leigh Adams 15+□+3, 2 Troy Batchelor 10+3+2, 3 Chris Holder 13+□+1, 4 Davey Watt 12+□+0, 5 Rory Schlein 11+2, 6 Darcy Ward 11+1, 7 Cameron Woodward 9+0, 8 Cory Gathercole 9, 9 Ty Proctor 6, 10 Kozza Smith 5, 11 Aaron Summers 5, 12 Josh Grajczonek 5, 13 Justin Sedgmen 5, 14 James Holder 3, 15 Jay Herne 1, 16 Lee Herne 0, Arlo Bugeja [R], Ryan Sedgmen [R], did not ride.

Qualifying Round

Gosford, New South Wales, Friday, January 2

Kozza Smith 14, Aaron Summers 13, Darcy Ward 12, Justin Sedgmen 11, Jay Herne 11, Lee Herne 10, James Holder 9, Hugh Skidmore 8, Sam Masters 7, Richard Sweetman 6, Arlo Bugeja 6, Michael Penfold 5, Jake Anderson 2, Kurt Shields 2, Ryan Sedgmen 2, Mitchell Davey 2.

Roll of Honour

1926 .... Pat HAMILTON
1927 .... Paddy DEAN
1928 .... Sig SCHLAM
1928 .... Alby TAYLOR
1929 .... Frank PEARCE
1929 .... Max GROSSKREUTZ
1929 .... Frank DUCKETT
1929 .... Sig SCHLAM
1930 .... Jack CHAPMAN
1930 .... Reg WEST
1930 .... Arthur ATKINSON
1931 .... Harold HASTINGS
1931 .... Ray TAUSER (USA)
1932 .... Bill ROGERS
1932 .... Arnold HANSEN
1932 .... Wally LITTLE
1933 .... Larry BOULTON
1934 .... Vic HUXLEY
1935 .... Bluey WILKINSON
1936 .... Max GROSSKREUTZ
1937 .... Jack MILNE (USA)
1938 .... Jack PARKER (England)
1938 .... Bluey WILKINSON
1940 .... Cordy MILNE (USA)
1941 .... Vic DUGGAN
1946 .... Frank DOLAN
1947 .... Vic DUGGAN
1947 .... Andy MENZIES
1947 .... Bill ROGERS
1948 .... Vic DUGGAN
1949 .... Vic DUGGAN
1949 .... Aub LAWSON
1950 .... Bill KITCHEN (England)
1950 .... Aub LAWSON
1950 .... Jack PARKER (England)
1951 .... Jack PARKER (England)
1952 .... Lionel LEVY
1952 .... Keith RYAN
1952 .... Aub LAWSON
1953 .... Aub LAWSON
1953 .... Lionel LEVY

Until 1954 the Australian Championship was held over a variety of distances and engine capacities and there is no true guide to an undisputed national champion for many of the pre-1954 seasons.

1954 .... Aub LAWSON
1955 .... Aub LAWSON
1956 .... Ulf ERICSSON (Sweden)
1961 .... Bob SHARP
1962 .... Mike BROADBANK (England)
1964 .... Ken McKINLAY (Scotland)
1965 .... Bob SHARP
1966 .... Chum TAYLOR
1967 .... Jack SCOTT
1968 .... Jim AIREY
1969 .... Jim AIREY
1970 .... Jim AIREY
1971 .... John BOULGER
1972 .... Jim AIREY
1973 .... John BOULGER
1974 .... Steve REINKE
1975 .... Phil CRUMP
1976 .... Ole OLSEN (Denmark)
1977 .... John TITMAN
1978 .... Billy SANDERS
1979 .... Phil CRUMP
1980 .... Billy SANDERS
1981 .... Billy SANDERS
1982 .... Billy SANDERS
1983 .... Billy SANDERS
1984 .... Phil CRUMP
1985 .... Billy SANDERS
1986 .... Troy BUTLER
1987 .... Steve REGELING
1988 .... Phil CRUMP
1989 .... Glenn DOYLE
1990 .... Glenn DOYLE
1991 .... Craig BOYCE
1992 .... Leigh ADAMS
1993 .... Leigh ADAMS
1994 .... Leigh ADAMS
1995 .... Jason CRUMP
1996 .... Craig BOYCE
1997 .... Craig BOYCE
1998 .... Leigh ADAMS
1999 .... Todd WILTSHIRE
2000 .... Leigh ADAMS
2001 .... Todd WILTSHIRE
2002 .... Leigh ADAMS
2003 .... Leigh ADAMS
2004 .... Ryan SULLIVAN
2005 .... Leigh ADAMS
2006 .... Leigh ADAMS
2007 .... Jason CRUMP
2008 .... Chris HOLDER
2009 .... Leigh ADAMS

AUSTRALIAN UNDER 21 CHAMPIONSHIP

DARCY Ward overhauled Kozza Smith in the Final to take victory in the Australian Under-21 Championship.

Ward scored 14 points from his qualifying rides, dropping his only point to Smith, while his 2009 King's Lynn teammate finished on 13 after a third place in Heat 10 when he lost out to Richard Sweetman and Alex Davies, son of former Peterborough rider Stephen Davies.

FINAL

Gosford, New South Wales, Saturday, January 31

1 Darcy WARD 14+□+3, 2 Kozza SMITH 13+□+2, 3 Aaron SUMMERS 12+□+1, 4 Justin SEDGMEN 7+3+0, 5 Richard SWEETMAN 11+2, 6 Mitchell DAVEY 9+1, 7 Josh GRAJCZONEK 11+0, 8 Sam MASTERS 7, 9 Alex DAVIES 6, 10 Hugh SKIDMORE 5, 11 Todd KURTZ 5, 12 Tom HEDLEY 5, 13 Ryan SEDGMEN 4, 14 Jake ANDERSON 3, 15 Ricky WALLACE [R] 3, 16 Michael PENFOLD 3, 17 Taylor POOLE 1, 18 Daniel BEGLEY [R] 1.

Roll of Honour

1987	Gary ALLAN
1988	Leigh ADAMS
1989	Craig HODGSON
1990	Leigh ADAMS
1991	Leigh ADAMS
1992	Leigh ADAMS
1993	Ryan SULLIVAN
1996	Ryan SULLIVAN
1997	Adam SHIELDS
1998	Travis McGOWAN
1999	Nigel SADLER
2000	Travis McGOWAN
2001	Russell HARRISON
2002	Travis McGOWAN
2003	Rory SCHLEIN
2004	Rory SCHLEIN
2005	Chris HOLDER
2006	Chris HOLDER
2007	Chris HOLDER
2008	Chris HOLDER
2009	DARCY WARD

State Championships

NEW SOUTH WALES

Nepean, Saturday, October 25, 2008

1 Hugh SKIDMORE 15+3, 2 Darcy WARD 12+2, 3 Justin SEDGMEN 11+1, 4 Tom HEDLEY 10+0, 5 Sam MASTERS 10, 6 Michael PENFOLD 9, 7 Anthony PERKS 9, 8 Alex DAVIES 8, 9 Jackson MILNE 8, 10 Jake ANDERSON 7, 11 Michael DYER 7, 12 Ryan SEDGMEN 3, 13 Elliott MYERS 3, 14 James BEVAN 2, 15 Nick ROWE 2, 16 Ricky WALLACE 2.

QUEENSLAND

Ayr, Saturday, November 29, 2008

1 Darcy WARD 13+3, 2 Josh GRAJCZONEK 13+2, 3 Kozza SMITH 15+1, 4 Mitchell DAVEY 12+0, 5 Steven REID 10, 6 Hugh SKIDMORE 9, 7 Kyle NEWMAN 8, 8 Damien KOPPE 8, 9 Ashley CATHCART 7, 10 Mitchell WEISMANTEL 7, 11 Kurt PALMER 3, 12 Ryan McMANUS 3, 12 Matt PILCHER 3.

SOUTH AUSTRALIA

Gillman, Saturday, January 24

1 Troy BATCHELOR 14+□+3, 2 Rory SCHLEIN 15+□+2, 3 Aaron SUMMERS 13+□+1, 4 Justin SEDGMEN 10+3+0, 5 Robert KSIEZAK 9+2, 6 Tom HEDLEY 8+1, 7 Ryan SEDGMEN 9+0, 8 Todd KURTZ 8, 9 Arlo BUGEJA 7, 10 Taylor POOLE 7, 11 Sam MASTERS 6, 12 Shelby RUTHERFORD 3, 13 Ben TURNER 3, 14 Brock GATES 3, 15 Samsurry PILGRAM 2, 16 Damien KOPPE 1, 17 Jake ANDERSON [R] 1, Adam BRIGGS [R], did not ride.

VICTORIA

Mildura, Saturday, November 29, 2008

1 Cameron WOODWARD 15+3, 2 Ty PROCTOR 14+2, 3 Aaron SUMMERS 11+1, 4 Tom HEDLEY 11+3+0, 5 Jason STEWART 11+2, 6 Justin SEDGMEN 9, 8 Michael PENFOLD 9, 9 Brock GATES 8, 10 Jackson MILNE 5, 11 Jake ANDERSON 4, 12 Arlo BUGEJA 4, 13 Matt JONES 4, 14 Mitch GOODWIN 4, 14 Bob STONEHAM 0, 15 Kurt SHIELDS 0.

WESTERN AUSTRALIA

Perth, Saturday, December 6, 2008

1 Frank SMART 15+3+3, 2 Shelby RUTHERFORD 11+2+2, 3 David CHESHIRE 14+3+1, 4 Samsurry PILGRAM 7+2+0, 5 Brady WEBB 10+1, 6 Michael STONEHAM 7+F, 7 Stewart RUSSELL 9+FX, 8 Daniel WINCHESTER 7+R, 9 Leigh BOUJOS 6, 10 Alan CASS 6, 11 Jason KETTERINGHAM 6, 13 Jason BURTON 5, 14 Trevor WILLIAMS 4, 15 Andy FENDLEY 4, 16 Carley GITTUS 0.

Under 21 State Championships

NEW SOUTH WALES

Gosford, Saturday, December 6, 2008

1 Chris HOLDER 15+3, 2 Kozza SMITH 13+2, 3 Lee HERNE 11+1, 4 James HOLDER 12+0, 5 Richard SWEETMAN 10, 6 Sam MASTERS 9, 7 Jay HERNE 9, 8 Kurt SHIELDS 9, 9 Michael PENFOLD 8, 10 Alex DAVIES 6, 11 Hugh SKIDMORE 6, 12 Tim HEFFERMAN 4, 13 Todd KURTZ 3, 14 Taylor POOLE 2, 15 Michael DYER 1, 16 Ricky WALLACE 1, 17 Nick ROWE [R] 0.

QUEENSLAND
Brandon, Ayr, Saturday, November 15, 2008
1 Josh GRAJCZONEK 14+3, 2 Darcy WARD 15+2, 3 Scott SMITH 13+1, 4 Mitchell DAVEY 12+0, 5 Ashley CATHCART 9, 6 Ricky BARNEY 9, 7 Steven REID 7, 8 Harley HORWOOD 7, 9 Damien KOPPE 6, 10 Kurt PALMER 5, 11 Mitchell WEISMANTEL 5, 12 Kyle NEWMAN 4, 13 Chris FERGUSON [R] 4, 14 Roy STOUT 3, 15 Ryan McMANUS 3, 16 Matt PILCHER 3, 17 Wes JENKINS 1.

Individual

2008

DAVE BOOTH MEMORIAL
Gold Coast, Queensland, Saturday, November 8
Abandoned, rain. Wet weather prevented the re-staging and the third annual Memorial meeting was cancelled.

JACK YOUNG CUP
Gillman, South Australia, Saturday, December 6
Aaron Summers 9+3, Arlo Bugeja 8+2, Nigel Sadler 8+3+1, Rory Schlein 12+R, Tom Hedley 5+2, Justin Sedgmen 6+1, Jake Anderson 5+0, Sam Martin 1, Kyle Newman 0.

2009

RON JOHNSON MEMORIAL
Pinjar Park, Perth, Saturday, January 17
Frank Smart 15+3+3, Daniel Winchester 9+3+2, Alan Cass 7+2+1, Shelby Rutherford 10+2+F, Glenn Gordon 8+1, Leigh Boujos 8+1, Brady Webb 10+0, David Cheshire 8+0, Corey Blackman 7, Tim Boujos 7, Trevor Williams 6, Carley Gittus 5, Stewart Russell 3, Andy Fendley 2, Ethan Ballentine 2.

STAR OF THE COAST
Labrador, Queensland, Saturday, January 17
Kozza Smith 8+3+3, Mitchell Davey 8+2+2, Michael Penfold 6+3+1, Damien Koppe 9+2+R, Richard Sweetman 12+1, Alex Davies 7+1, Scott Smith 8+0, Trent Leverington 7+R, Guy Mallett 4, Todd Groves 3, Tim Murray 1.

WESTERN BIG ONE
Pinjar Park, Perth, Saturday, January 31
Leigh Adams 15+3, Simon Stead 13+2, Chris Holder 14+1, Steve Johnston 12+3+0, Ty Proctor 8+2, Frank Smart 11+1, Daniel Winchester 7+0, Leigh Boujos 7, Cory Gathercole 6, David Cheshire 5, James Holder 5, Lee Herne 5, Corey Blackman 4, Brady Webb 2, Shelby Rutherford 2, Samsurry Pilgram 1, Stewart Russell [R] 1.

GILLMAN CHAMPIONSHIP
Gillman, Adelaide, Saturday, February 7
Tyron Proctor 11+□+3, Robert Ksiezak 5+3+2, Frank Smart 10+□+1, Aaron Summers 10+□+0, Justin Sedgmen 6+2, Ryan Sedgmen 8+1, Leigh Boujos 4+0, Jackson Milne 4, Ben Turner 2, Brady Webb 1.

Ivan Mauger Golden Helmet

2008 SERIES

IVAN Mauger's annual series was reduced to five meetings after the late cancellation of two scheduled rounds.

A meeting at Cairns was called off by the local motorcycle club at late notice after they discovered they could not use the stadium because it had been double-booked for a rock concert which brought in better financial rewards.

And a meeting at Ayr, Queensland, was cancelled by Motorcycling Queensland when they refused to give the Ayr club a permit because the date clashed with their Awards' Night in Brisbane.

A furious Mauger said: "The meeting was 1,600 kilometres (1,000 miles) north of Brissy - this is another example of Motorcycling Australia and their state authorities strangling domestic speedway.

"They seem to live on the fact that Jason Crump and Leigh Adams are well up the Grand Prix list but are oblivious to the problems of domestic racing in Australia."

Mauger resisted importing big names for the series, instead offering racing opportunities to local talent at all five meetings run under his banner.

Renmark, South Australia, Saturday, November 1
Jake Anderson 11+□+4, Justin Sedgmen 11+□+3, Brock Gates 5+3+2, Jason Stewart 9+□+1, Ryan Sedgmen 3+2+0, Sam Martin 5+1, Seane Chapman 3+0, Daniel Mutton 1.

Gillman, South Australia, Saturday, November 8
Justin Sedgmen 11+□+3, Jake Anderson 9+5+2, Todd Kurtz 10+□+1, Hugh Skidmore 10+□+0, Jason Stewart 5+4, Kyle Newman 5+3, Brock Gates 5+2, Shelby Rutherford 5+1, Ryan Sedgmen 6+0, Sam Martin 4, Damien Koppe 2, Daniel Mutton 0.

Baccus Marsh, Victoria, Saturday, November 15
Ty Proctor 11+3+3, Richard Sweetman 8+2+2, Jackson Milne 7+2+1, James Holder 10-+3+X, Sam Masters 8+F+3, Jake Anderson 8+F+2, Josh Munro 5+1+1, Wayne Morrinson 4+0+0, Matt Jones 3, Mitch Goodwin 3, Tony Nagle [R] 3, Bob Stoneham 1, Tim Holford 0.

Newcastle, New South Wales, Saturday, November 22
Jay Herne 12+3, Michael Penfold 13+2, Kozza Smirth 13+1, James Holder 13+0, Alex Davies 9+3, Taylor Poole 10+2, Sam Masters 9+R, Hugh Skidmore 9+N, James Bevan 7, Tim Hefferman 6, Ricky Wallace 5, Michael Dyer 5, Lee Herne 3, Michael Rowe 3.

Gold Coast, Queensland, Saturday, December 13
Darcy Ward 10+□+3, Josh Grajczonek 5+3+2, Trent Leverington 11+□+1, Taylor Poole 8+2+0, Sam Taylor 7+1, Mitchell Davey 4+0, Harley Horwood 1.

AUSTRALIAN UNDER 16 CHAMPIONSHIP

FINAL

Undera Park, Victoria, Saturday, January 17

1 Arthur SISSIS 15+3, 2 Nick MORRIS 10+3+2, 3 Mason CAMPTON 12+1, 4 Dane CARTWRIGHT 13+0, 5 Robert MEDSON 12+R, 6 Brady KURTZ 10+R, 7 Clinton DENNIS 9+X, 8 Cameron HEEPS 8, 9 Cooper RIODAN 7, 10 Matthew DAY 6, 11 Luke MITCHELL 5, 12 Dylan BLAIN 4, 13 JAcl FALLON 4, 14 Max FRICKE 3, 15 Braydon MUNRO 1, 16 Ellis PERKS 1, Sam ANDERSON [R], Blake RUSSELL [R], did not ride.

Roll of Honour

1982 .... Paul SNADDEN
1983 .... Craig HODGSON
1984 .... Michael CARTER
1985 .... Shane PARKER
1986 .... Leigh ADAMS
1987 .... Jason HAWKES
1988 .... Jason HAWKES
1989 .... Brett TOMKINS
1990 .... Jason CRUMP
1991 .... Ryan SULLIVAN
1992 .... Troy WYTEN
1993 .... Travis McGOWAN
1994 .... Nigel SADLER
1995 .... Russell HARRISON
1996 .... Brendon MACKAY
1997 .... Russell HARRISON
1998 .... Jaye STEVENS
1999 .... Mark JONES
2000 .... Rory SCHLEIN
2001 .... Mark JONES
2002 .... Trevor HARDING
2003 .... Troy BATCHELOR
2004 .... Aaron SUMMERS
2005 .... Jason NORMAN
2006 .... Ryan SEDGMEN
2007 .... Dakota NORTH
2008 .... Arthur SISSIS
2009 .... Arthur SISSIS

350cc CHAMPIONSHIP FINAL

Tamworth, New South Wales, South Australia Saturday, February 28

1 Tyson NELSON 15+3+3, 2 Mason CAMPTON 14+3+2, 3 Nick MORRIS 12+2+1, 4 Bryce JOHNSTON 10+2+0, 5 Brenton BARNFIELD 10+1, 6 Fletcher TYDD 7+1, 7 Robert BRANFORD 7+0, 8 Dylan BLAIN 5+0, 9 Jake MOORE 5, 10 Dane CARTWRIGHT 4, 11 Harley BRIGDEN 2, 12 Braydon ELLIOTT 1, 13 Hayden BARR 0.

Under 16 State Championships

NEW SOUTH WALES

Somerseby, Saturday, November 15, 2008

1 Mason CAMPTON, 2 Brady KURTZ, 3 Dane CARTWRIGHT, 4 Sean McLELLAN, 5 Tyler KING, 6 Mitchell WATSON, 7 Jack HOLDER, 8 Corey TAGGART.

QUEENSLAND

Brandon, Ayr, Saturday, November 15, 2008

1 Nick MORRIS 11+3, 2 Clinton DENNIS 11+2, 3 Dylan BAIN 14+1, 4 Matthew DAY 12+0, 5 Jayden O'MALLEY 11, 6 Glen SQUIRES 8, 7 Jack McLEAN 8, 8 Jake MOORE 8, 9 Zaine KENNEDY 7, 10 Harley BRIGDEN 7, 11 Tyler MOON 6, 12 Hayden BARR 5, 13 Scott SCHOFIELD 5, 14 Michael DETENON 4, 15 Robert GOTTARDI [R] 3, 16 Brandon COGLIN 1, 17 Brodie OATS 0.

SOUTH AUSTRALIA

Wingfield, Adelaide, Saturday, November 15, 2008

1 Arthur SISSIS 11+3, 2 Robert MEDSON 12+2, 3 Luke MITCHELL 9+1, 4 Cameron HEEPS 8+0, 5 Blake RUSSELL 6, 6 Joel PELLICONE 6, 7 Dakota BALLANTYNE 5, 8 Damon WHELAN 5, 9 Jake MITCHELL 4, 10 Nathan COCKAYNE 3, 11 Tony PELLICONE 3, 12 Kane TURNER 23, 13 Seth HICKEY 0.

NEW SOUTH WALES 350cc CHAMPIONSHIP

Nepean, Saturday, October 25, 2008

1 Tyson NELSON 13+3, 2 Mason CAMPTON 12+2, 3 Todd KURTZ 7+1, 4 Nick MORRIS 14+F, 5 Daniel BEGLEY 6, 6 Bryce JOHNSON 4, 7 Fletcher TYDD 2, 8 Mitchell WATSON 1.

The next generation....

ARTHUR SISSIS (b15.6.1995) is Australia's brightest under age talent, having won the Under 16 national championship two years in a row.

He only saw his first speedway meeting at the 2002 Junior Championship at the Adelaide Sidewinders Club and immediately decided he wanted to have a go.

He was a member of the Melbourne Stunt Squadron at the 2005 Calder Park round of the Yamaha Super Motard Championships in 2005.

An all-round motor-cyclist he has also competed at dirt track, moto cross and motard racing and could well be lost to speedway because of his ambition to compete in Moto GP.

He haas already taken a major step in that direction by qualifying for the 2009 Red Bull Rookies Cup in Europe.

He won a bronze medal in the 2008 FIM Speedway Youth Gold Trophy 80cc Final at Skærbæk, Denmark – the first Australian to get on the rostru,

NICK MORRIS (b7.6.1994) only started racing speedway in February, 2005, although he was a regular spectactor with his father from thre agte of four.

An accomplished sportsman, he played club level soccer and rugby league before concentrating on shale.

After winning the 2009 Queensland Under 16 Championship he was runner-up to Arthur Sissis in the national championship.

MASON CAMPTON (b4.10.1993) has already declared that he wants to race in Europe.

His father raced speedway sidecars and he has been riding on the shale since he was 11.

He is a member of the Central Coast Junior Motorcycle Club and the Kurri Kurri club.

Winner of the 2007 Victorian Under 16 State Championship, he won the New South Wales Under 16 title in 2008 and was third in the 2009 national championship.

AUSTRIA

AUSTRIAN CHAMPIONSHIP

The Austrian Championship is part of the tri-national competition also involving riders from Croatia and Slovenia.
The highest scoring Austrian rider is the national champion.

MANUEL Hauzinger reigns supreme as the highest-ranked Austrian and continues to impress on the continent.

Even though he has struggled to hold down a regular team place in Britain he was crowned Austrian champion for a fifth successive season and for the seventh time overall.

That triumph means he has now overtaken Andreas Bössner as the most decorated Austrian of all time at domestic level.

Final standings
1 Manuel HAUZINGER 114, 2 Manuel NOVOTNY 98, 3 Lukas SIMON 73, 4 Heinrich SCHATZER 66, 5 Josef FASCHING 64, 6 Christoph FINK 56, 7 Christian PELLIKAN 43, 8 Daniel GAPPMAIER 37, 9 Friedrich [Fritz] WALLNER 20, 10 Martin FIALA 18, 11 Anton WANNASEK 14, 12 Johannes FIALA 1.

Roll of Honour

1930 .... Leopold KILLMEYER
1948 .... Fritz DIRTL
1951 .... Fritz DIRTL
1952 .... Leopald KILLMEYER
1953 .... Josef KAMPER
1955 .... Josef KAMPER
1957 .... Josef KAMPER
1958 .... Josef KAMPER
1959 .... Josef KAMPER
1960 .... Erich LUTHER
1961 .... Wilfried VACANO
1962 .... Josef BÖSSNER
1963 .... Josef BÖSSNER
1964 .... Alfred SITZWOHL
1965 .... Johann KEHR
1970 .... Alfred RINZNER
1971 .... Josef HAIDER
1973 .... Josef BÖSSNER
1974 .... Josef HAIDER
1975 .... Adolf [Adi] FUNK
1976 .... Hubert FISCHBACHER
1977 .... Herbert SZERECZ
1978 .... Herbert SZERECZ
1979 .... Hubert FISCHBACHER
1980 .... Adolf [Adi] FUNK
1981 .... Adolf [Adi] FUNK
1982 .... Adolf [Adi] FUNK
1983 .... Antoni PILOTTO
1984 .... Antoni PILOTTO
1985 .... Siegfried EDER
1986 .... Heinrich SCHATZER
1987 .... Heinrich SCHATZER
1988 .... Heinrich SCHATZER
1989 .... Antoni PILOTTO
1990 .... Heinrich SCHATZER
1991 .... Andreas BÖSSNER
1992 .... Andreas BÖSSNER
1993 .... Andreas BÖSSNER
1994 .... Franz LEITNER
1995 .... Franz LEITNER
1996 .... Andreas BÖSSNER
1997 .... Andreas BÖSSNER
1998 .... Andreas BÖSSNER
1999 .... Antoni PILOTTO
2000 .... Walter NEBEL
2001 .... Walter NEBEL
2002 .... Manuel HAUZINGER
2003 .... Fritz WALLNER
2004 .... Manuel HAUZINGER
2005 .... Manuel HAUZINGER
2006 .... Manuel HAUZINGER
2007 .... Manuel HAUZINGER
2008 .... Manuel HAUZINGER

AUSTRIAN-CROATIAN-SLOVENIAN CHAMPIONSHIP

Round 1
Krsko, Slovenia, Sunday, March 30
1 Matej Zagar 13+3, 2 Jernej Kolenko 13+2, 3 Izak Santej 12+3, 4 Jurica Pavlic 12+2, 5 Maks Gregoric 11, 6 Manuel Hauzinger 11, 7 Denis Stojs 7, 8 Matija Duh 7, 9 Nikola Martinec 6, 10 Manuel Novotny 6, 11 Ivan Vargek 5, 12 Heinrich Schatzer 4, 13 Aleksander Conda 3, 14 Dino Kovacic [R] 3, 15 Matic Voldrih 3, 15 Fritz Wallner 2, 17 Nikola Pigac 2.
Group B: Kreso Petkovic 12, Dino Kovacic 11, Renato Cvetko 10, Simon Lukas 9, Josef Fasching 7, Andrej Kezman 6, Daniel Gappmaier 6, Aljosa Remih 5, Christopher Fink 4, Johannes Fiala 2, Martin Fiala 2, Ales Kraljic 0.

AUSTRIAN-CROATIAN-SLOVENIAN CHAMPIONSHIP

Round 2
Natschbach-Loipersbach, Austria, Saturday, April 5
1 Jernej Kolenko 15, 2 Jurica Pavlic 14, 3 Matej Zagar 13, 4 Izak Santej 12, 5 Manuel Hauzinger 9, 6 Denis Stojs 9, 7 Aleksander Conda 8, 8 Maks Gregoric 8, 9 Manuel Novotny 7, 190 Nikola Martinec 7, 11 Matija Duh 5, 12 Heinrich Schatzer 4, 13 Dino Kovacic 4, 14 Ivan Vargek 4, 15 Renato Cvetko 1, 16 Kreso Petkovic 0.

Group B: Matic Voldrih 12, Nikola Pigac 11, Lukas Simon 10, Aljosa Remih 8, Josef Fasching 7, Anton Wannasek 7, Andrej Kezman 6, Christopher Fink 6, Daniel Gappmaier 4, Christian Pelliikan 3, Martin Fiala 0.

Round 3
Prelog, Croatia, Sunday, April 13
1 Jurica Pavlic 15, 2 Matej Zagar 14, 3 Aleksander Conda 11, 4 Denis Stojs 10, 5 Manuel Hauzinger 10, 6 Izak Santej 9, 7 Nikola Pigac 7, 8 Matic Voldrih 7, 9 Matija Duh, 10 Dino Kovacic 6, 11 Ivan Vargek 5, 12 Jernej Kolenko 4, 13 Maks Gregoric 4, 14 Manuel Novotny 4, 15 Heinrich Schatzer 2, 16 Aljosa Remih [R] 2, 17 Nikola Martinec 0, 18 Lukas Simon [R] 0.

Group B: Kreso Petkovic 11, Renato Cvetko 10, Lukas Simon 8, Andrej Kezman 7, Aljosa Remih 6, Christopher Funk 3, Josef Fasching 2, Christian Pellikan 1.

Round 4
Ljubljana, Slovenia, Sunday, September 21
1 Matej Zagar 15, 2 Maks Gregoric 14, 3 Jurica Pavlic 13, 4 Izak Santej 12, 5 Denis Stojs 9, 6 Dino Kovacic 9, 7 Matic Voldrih 9, 8 Aleksander Conda 7, 9 Nikola Pigac 7, 10 Matija Duh 5, 11 Renato Cvetko 5, 12 Ivan Vargek 5, 13 Manuel Novotny 4, 14 Manuel Hauzinger 2, 15 Christian Pellikan 2, 16 Lukas Simon 1, 17 Christopher Fink 0.

Group B: Ales Kraljic 9, Marko Vlah 8, Dalibor Bot 7, Ladislav Vida 6, Daniel Gappmaier 5, Jasmin Ilijas 5, Josef Fasching 5, Christian Pellikan 2.

FINAL STANDINGS – OVERALL

		R1	*R2*	*R3*	*R4*	*Tot*
1	Matej ZAGAR	40	35	37	40	152
2	Jurica PAVLIC	33	37	40	35	145
3	Izak SANTEJ	35	33	30	33	131
4	Denis STOJS	29	30	33	31	123
5	Maks GREGORIC	31	28	24	37	120
6	Aleksander CONDA	23	29	35	28	115
7	Manuel HAUZINGER	30	31	31	22	114
8	Matija DUH	28	25	27	26	106
9	Dino KOVACIC	22	23	26	30	101
10	Jernej KOLENKO	37	40	23	–	100
11	Manuel NOVOTNY	26	27	22	23	98
12	Ivan VARGEK	25	22	25	24	96
13	Matic VOLDRIH	21	17	28	29	95
14	Nikola PIGAC	19	16	29	27	91
15	Renato CVETKO	17	21	16	25	79
16	Lukas SIMON	16	19	18	20	73
17	Nikola MARTINEC	27	26	19	–	72
18	Heinrich SCHATZER	24	24	20	–	68
19	Josef FASCHING	15	18	13	18	64
20	Christopher FINK	11	12	14	19	56
21	Krešo PETKOVIC	18	20	17	–	55
22	Aljosa REMIH	12	15	21	–	48
23	Christian PELLIKAN	–	10	12	21	43
24	Andrej KEZMAN	14	13	15	–	42
25	Daniel GAPPMAIER	13	11	–	13	37
26	Ales KRALJIC	8	–	–	17	25
27	Fritz WALLNER	20	–	–	–	20
28	Martin FIALA	9	9	–	–	18
29	Marko VLAH	–	–	–	16	16
30	Dalibor BOT	–	–	–	15	15
31	Anton WANNASEK	–	14	–	–	14
32	Ladislav VIDA	–	–	–	14	14
33	Jasmin ILIJAS	–	–	–	12	12
34	Johannes FIALA	10	–	–	–	10

Scoring: 40-37-35-33-31-30-29-28-27-26-25-24-23-22-21-20-19-18-17-16-15-14-13-12-11-10-9.
A qualifying tournament (Group B) was held prior to the main event to find qualifiers. Riders competing were also awarded championship points.

AUSTRIA-CROATIA-HUNGARY- SLOVENIA JUNIOR CHAMPIONSHIP

AUSTRIAN U21 CHAMPIONSHIP

The Austrian Championship is part of the four nation competition also involving riders from Croatia, Hungary and Slovenia.
The highest scoring Austrian rider is the national champion.

Final standings
1 Lukas SIMON 34, 2 Hans Peter KULTERER 11, Manuel NOVOTNY 11, Christopher FINK 11, 5 Daniel Gappmaier 10, 6 Anton HACKL 9, Christian PELLIKAN 5, 8 Markus OBERHOFER 4, 9 Ernst SZUDECZ 3.

Roll of Honour
2007 .... Manuel NOVOTNY
2008 .... Lukas SIMON

Round 1
Gorican, Croatia, Sunday, April 27
1 Aleksander Conda 15, 2 Matic Voldrih 12+3, 3 Kreso Petkovic 12+2, 4 Matija Duh 11, 5 Nikola Pigac 10, 6 Renato Cvetko 10, 7 Roland Kovacs 10, 8 Dino Kovacic 8, 9 Tamas Szilagyi 8, 10 Andrej Kezman 7, 11 Aljosa Remih 6, 12 Daniel Gappmaier 4, 13 Dalibor Bot 3, 14 Ladislav Vida [R] 2, 15 Hans Peter Kulterer 1, 16 Attila Lorincz 0, 16 Lukas Simon 0.

FINAL STANDINGS - OVERALL

	R1	R2	R3	R4	R5	R6	Tot
1 Aleksander Conda	20	15	16	20	16	20	107
2 Matic Voldrih	18	16	15	16	18	15	98
3 Dino Kovacic	11	14	13	18	20	16	92
4 Nikola Pigac	14	13	18	11	12	18	86
5 Roland Kovacs	12	11	14	15	14	13	79
6 Matija Duh	15	18	20	–	15	–	68
7 Renato Cvetko	13	8	12	6	13	12	64
8 Aljosa Remih	8	12	9	9	–	14	52
9 Kreso Petkovic	16	2	6	8	6	–	38
10 Lukas Simon	3	–	11	10	10	–	34
11 Tamas Szilagyi	10	9	2	5	8	–	34
12 Dalibor Bot	6	–	10	3	7	8	34
13 Zsolt Nagy	–	–	8	13	–	11	32
14 Ladislav Vida	5	5	5	4	3	9	31
15 Roland Benko	–	10	–	14	–	–	24
16 Jozsef Tabaka	–	20	–	–	–	–	20
17 Andrej Kezman	9	6	4	–	–	–	19
19 Attila Lorincz	2	–	–	7	–	10	19
19 Attila Molnar	–	–	–	12	–	–	12
20 Manuel Novotny	–	–	–	–	11	–	11
21 Hans Peter Kulterer	4	–	7	–	–	–	11
22 Christopher Fink	–	7	–	–	4	–	11
23 Daniel Gappmaier	7	–	3	–	–	–	10
24 Anton Hackl	–	–	–	–	9	–	9
25 Jasmin Ilijas	–	–	–	–	–	7	7
26 Christian Pellikan	–	–	–	–	5	–	5
27 Markus Oberhofer	–	4	–	–	–	–	4
28 Ernst Szudecz	–	3	–	–	–	–	3
29 Robert Szegvari	–	–	–	2	–	–	2

Scoring: 40-37- 35-33-31-30-29-28-27-26-25-24-23-22-21-20-19-18-17-16-15-14-13-12-11-10-9.

Round 2
Debrecen, Hungary, Thursday, May 1
Jozsef Tabaka 15, Matija Duh 14, Matic Voldrih 12, Aleksander Conda 11, Dino Kovacic 11, Nikola Pigac 9, Aljosa Remih 8, Roland Kovacs 8, Roland Benko [R] 7, Tamas Szilagyi 7, Renato Cvetko 5, Christopher Fink 4, Andrej Kezman 3, Ladisav Vida 1, Markus Oberhofer 1, Ernst Szudecz 0, Kreso Petkovic 0.

Round 3
Lendava, Slovenia, Saturday June 14
Matihja Duh 15, Nikola Pigac 14, Aleksander Conda 13, Matic Voldrih 12, Roland Kovacs 11, Dino Kovacic 9, Renato Cvetko 8, Lukas Simon 7, Dalibor Bot 6, Aljosa Remih [R] 5, Zsolt Nagy 5, Hans Peter Kulterer 4, Kreso Petkovic 3, Ladislav Vida 3, Andrej Kejman 3, Daniel Grappmaier 1, Tamas Szilagyi 0.

Round 4
Gyula, Hungary, Sunday, July 27
Aleksander Conda 15, Dino Kovacic 14, Matic Voldrih 13, Roland Kovacs 12, Roland Benko 9, Zsolt Nagy 9, Attila Molnar 9, Nikola Pigac 7, Lukas Simon 7, Aljosa Remih 6, Kreso Petkovic 6, Attila Lorincz 4, Renato Cvetko 4, Tamas Szilagyi 2, Ladislav Vida 1, Dalibor Bot 1, Robert Szegvari [R] 0.

Round 5
Mureck, Austria, Sunday, September 7
Dino Kovacic 14, Matic Voldrih 13+3, Aleksander Conda 13+2, Matija Duh 12, Roland Kovacs 10, Renato Cvetko 10, Nikola Pigac 9, Manuel Novotny 7, Lukas Simon 6, Anton Hackl 6, Tamas Szilagyi 4, Dalibor Bot 4, Kreso Petkovic 3, Christian Pellikan 3, Christopher Fink 2, Ladislav Vida 2.

Round 6
Krsko, Slovenia, Saturday, October 18
Aleksander Conda 11, Nikola Pigac 10+3, Dino Kovacic 10+2, Matic Voldrih 9, Aljosa Remih 7, Roland Kovacs 6, Renato Cvetko 6, Zsolt Nagy 5, Attila Lorincz 5, Ladislav Vida 4, Dalibor Bot 4, Jasmin Ilijas 1.

AUSTRIA-CROATIA-HUNGARY-SLOVENIA TEAM CHAMPIONSHIP

FINAL STANDINGS

	M	Pts
1 SLOVENIA	3	136+0
2 HUNGARY	3	132+3
3 AUSTRIA	**3**	**93**
4 CROATIA	3	60

Round 1
Lendava, Slovenia, Saturday, May 3
1 HUNGARY 56 (Matej Ferjan 14, Laszlo Szatmari 12, Jozsef Tabaka 12, Robert Nagy 10, Sandor Tihanyi 8), **2 SLOVENIA 55** (**Matej Zagar 15**, Izak Santej 12, Maks Gregoric 10, Aleksander Conda 9, Denis Stojs 9), **3 AUSTRIA 16** (Matih Duh [G] 8, Fritz Wallner 7, Manuel Novotny 1, Daniel Gappmaier 0), 4 **CROATIA 15** (Dino Kovacic 4, Ivan Vargek 3, Nikola Pigac 3, Renato Cvetko 3, Nikola Martinec 2).

Round 2
St. Johann-im-Pongau, Austria, Saturday, July 26
1 AUSTRIA 57 (**Manuel Hauzinger 15**, Fritz Wallner 14, Frank Facher [G] 14, Martin Smolinski [G] 12, Manuel Novotny 2), **2 SLOVENIA 40** (Aleksander Conda 15, Maks Gregoric 9, Ales Kraljic 7, Denis Stojs 6, Matic Voldrih 3), **3 HUNGARY 35** (Jozsef Tabaka 9, Sandor Tihanyi 8, Laszlo Szatmari 8, Daniel Gappmaier [G] 7, Marcel Helfer [G] 3), 4 **CROATIA 8** (Dino Kovacic 4, Renato Cvetko 2, Ivan Vargek 1, Nikola Pigac 1, Hans Peter Kulterer [G] 0),

Round 3
Gorican, Croatia, Friday, August 15
1 HUNGARY 41+3 (Matej Ferjan 13+3, Robert Nagy 6, Laszlo Szatmari 3, Sandor Tihanyi 10, Jozsef Tabaka 9), **2 SLOVENIAN 41+X** (Matija Duh 9, Maks Gregoric 12+X, Denis Stojs 3, Ales Krajlic 10, Aleksander Conda 7), **3 CROATIA 37** (**Jurica Pavlic 15**, Ivan Vargek 6, Nikola Pigac 3, Kreso Petkovic 4, Dino Kovacic 9), **4 AUSTRIA 20** (**Manuel Hauzinger 9**, Andreas Maida [G] 4, Fritz Wallner 4, Renato Cvetko [G] 1, Lukas Simon 2).

AUSTRIA AVERAGES

Rider	M	R	Pts	Ave	FM
Manuel HAUZINGER	2	9	24	12.00	2
Fritz WALLNER	**3**	**13**	**25**	**7.69**	**0**
Manuel NOVOTNY	2	7	3	1.71	0
Lukas SIMON	**1**	**4**	**2**	**2.00**	**0**
Daniel GAPPMAIER	1	4	0	0.00	0
Guests					
Frank FACHER	1	5	14	11.20	0
Martin SMOLINSKI	**1**	**5**	**12**	**9.60**	**0**
Matija DUH	1	5	8	6.40	0
Andrea MAIDA	**1**	**3**	**4**	**5.33**	**0**
Renato CVETKO	1	5	1	0.80	0

International

Natsbach-Loipersbach, Saturday, May 10

AUSTRIĄ 72 (Fritz Wallner 16, Manfred Betz [G] 7, Manuel Hauzinger [G] 16, Matija Duh [G] 8, Manuel Novotny 13, Ronny Weis [G] 12, Hans-Peter Kulterer, did not ride), **CZECH REPUBLIC 36** (Adam Vandirek 7, Jan Holub III 2, Hynek Stichauer 17, Pavel Hucko 0, Martin Gavenda 8, Michal Dudek 1, Vladimir Visvader 1).

Individual

JOSEF BÖSSNER MEMORIAL
Sunday, October 19, Mureck
Manuel Hauzinger 15, Norbert Magosi 13, Marcel Kajzer 12+3, Michael Hadek 12+2, Sandor Tihanyi 11, Jan Holub II 8, Denis Stojs 8, Manuel Novotny 8, Ales Kraljic 7, Marcel Helfer 6, Marcin Nowaczyk 5, Lukas Simon 5, Zsolt Bencze 3, Denis Helfer 3, Christoopher Fink 2, Christian Pellikan 2.

2009 Fixtures

WORLD CHAMPIONSHIP

Sunday, June 7: World Championship qualifying round, Wiener Neustadt.

EUROPEAN CHAMPIONSHIP

Saturday, May 2: Individual qualifying round, Mureck.
Saturday, May 16: Individual semi final, Natschbach-Loipersbach.

AUSTRIAN CHAMPIONSHIP
Round 1
Sunday, March 22: Mureck.
Round 2
Sunday, September 20: Wiener Neustadt.
Round 3
Saturday, September 26: Natschbach-Loipersbach.
Round 4
Saturday, October 3: St. Johann-im-Pongau..

INTERNATIONAL
Saturday, April 4: Natschbach-Loipersbach.
Saturday, June 20: Josef Kamper Memorial, Natschbach-Loipersbach.
Sunday, June 21: Wiener Neustadt.
Saturday, September 5: Natschbach-Loipersbach.
Sunday, October 18: Josef Bössner Memorial, Mureck.
Monday, October 26: Natschbach-Loipersbach.

Continued from opposite page

2001 .... Carlos VILLAR (Argentine)
2002 .... John KEHOE
2003 .... Kyle LEGAULT
2004 .... Kyle LEGAULT
2005 .... Nick FAFARD
2006 .... Kyle LEGAULT
2007 .... Aaron HESMER

CANADIAN LONG TRACK CHAMPIONSHIP
Belleville, Saturday, August 16
1 Jeff OROSZ 10+5, 2 Rob DIXON 8+4, 3 Terry RIDEOUT 3+3,4 Tim MURRAY 5+2, 5 Gary MOODY 1+1, 6 John BENNETT 3+0.

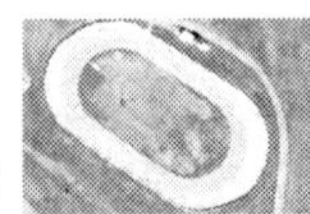

PARIS SPEEDWAY
Address: Paris Fair Grounds, 139 Silver Street, Paris, Ontario, N3L 3E7.
Tel:(001) 519 4422823.
Website: www.parisfairgrounds.com
Racing is on the half-mile track at the Fairgrounds

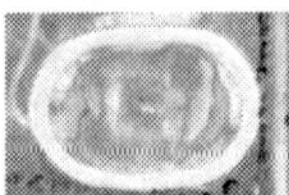

WELLAND SPEEDWAY
Address: Niagara Motorcycle Raceway, 603, Netherby Road, R.R4, Welland, Ontario, ON L3B 5N7, Canada.
Tel: 9(001) 05 8923594.
Website: www.wellandmotorcycleclub.com

CANADA

THE prestigious Canadian Championship fell foul to the weather – called off an hour before start-time.

Because of fixture problems it was never re-staged so theoretically Aaron Hesmer remained the champion, having won the title in 2007.

Favourite for the Welland event among the home riders was almost certainly the dominant Jeff Orosz who was chasing his first crown since 1997.

American promoter Jason Bonsignore brought three riders to the Final – Shawn McConnell, Shaun Harmatiuk and Mikey Buman but the heavy rain forced referee Ian March to call off the meeting.

Attempts were made to re-run it at the Paris track but they fell through so there was no official 2008 Canadian Champion.

Orosz proved to be the top rider over the season, gaining the coveted number one plate based on performance at the two tracks at Paris and Welland.

Speedway was given a huge fillip with the Paris Agricultural Society promoting events at the showground although they admitted their initial mistake in staging meetings to a Sunday afternoon.

They switched to a Saturday night when Welland's short season came to an end and were rewarded with much bigger crowds and more riders.

Welland was run by the Canadian Speedway Riders' Association amd ran regular Saturday night meets during the height of the summer.

During Welland's season the CSRA rented the Paris track to put on five weeks of practice and they brought through not only some out-of-retirement old names but a handful of new competitors, the most prominent of which were 17-year-old Jeremy Zelaska (who sadly ended the season with a broken leg) and exciting lady rider Nicole DeVeau.

One-time British competitor Stan Bradbury (a Canadian Hall of Famer) provided some of his own bikes for the sessions and also built a 175cc junior bike. Division Two, Division Three and 85cc Championships were held during the Saturday of the August Paris Fair, the respective winners being Corinne Franic, Zelaska and Matt Sehl. On the Sunday Joe Heye took the final ahead of Orosz in front of a big Fair crowd although the day was marred by Zelaska's nasty crash.

Paris, Sunday, May 25
Chris Hesmer 13+3, Terry Rideout 9+2, Fred Legault 9+1, Aaron DeVeau 3+0.

Paris, Sunday, June 1
Joe Heye 10+3, Terry Rideout 10+2, Chris Hesmer 3+1, Fred Legault 6+R, Aaron DeVeau 1.

Paris, Sunday, June 15
Joe Heye, Jeff Orosz, Terry Rideout, Aaron Hesmer.

Welland, Saturday, June 7
Jeff Orosz 12+4, Aaron Hesmer 10+3, Rob Dixon 6+2, Chris Hesmer 10+1, John Kehoe 9+0, Terry Rideout 5, Joe Heye 4, Gary Hesmer 2, Tim Murray 1, Drew Kehoe 1.

Welland, Saturday, June 14
1 Jeff Orosz 8+4, Aaron Hesmer 7+3, John Kehoe 6+2, Joe Heye 6+1, Chris Hesmer 5+0, Terry Rideout 0+3, Gary Hesmer 2+2, Rob Dixon 4+1, Tim Murray 1+0.

Welland, Saturday, June 21
Aaron Hesmer 6+4, Jeff Orosz 8+3, Chris Hesmer 8+2, Joe Heye 4+3+1, John Kehoe 6+0, Rob Dixon 4+2+4, Terry Rideout 2+3, Tim Murray 0+2, John Bennett 0+1, Katalina Davis 2+0.

Welland, Saturday, July 5
Jeff Orosz 8+4, Aaron Hesmer 6+3, Joe Heye 6+2, Terry Rideout 4+1, Rob Dixon 7+0, Katalin Davis 4, Drew Kehoe 0.

Welland, Saturday, July 26
Jeff Orosz 7+4, Chris Hesmer 7+3, Fred Legault 2+2, Terry Rideout 2+1, Rob Dixon 2+0.

Paris, Saturday, August 23
Jioe Heye, Jeff Orosz, Aaron Hesmer, Chris Hesmer.

Paris, Sunday, August 31
Joe Heye, Jeff Orosz, Terry Rideout, Terry DeVeau.

CANADIAN CHAMPIONSHIP

Roll of Honour

1930 .... Jimmy GIBB
1934 .... Eric CHITTY
1963 .... Yvon Du HAMEL
1974 .... Roger YAKELEY
1975 .... George KALAMAROFF (USA)
1976 .... Gary FORD
1977 .... Gary FORD
1978 .... Tony ARMSTRONG
1979 .... Timmy Joe SHEPARD (USA)
1980 .... Gary FORD
1981 .... Gary FORD
1982 .... Gary FORD
1983 .... Len DILLON
1984 .... Len DILLON
1985 .... Gary FORD
1986 .... Gary FORD
1987 .... Len DILLON
1989 .... Len DILLON
1990 .... Len DILLON
1991 .... Lenny McBRIDE
1992 .... Len DILLON
1993 .... Len DILLON
1994 .... Len DILLON
1995 .... John KEHOE
1996 .... John KEHOE
1997 .... Jeff OROSZ
1998 .... Chris HESMER
2000 .... John KEHOE

Continued on previous page

CROATIA

CROATIAN CHAMPIONSHIP

The Croatian Championship is part of the tri-national competition also involving riders from Austria and Slovenia.
The highest scoring Croatian rider is the national champion.
For full details of the rounds see Austria.

SWINDON'S Jurica Pavlic clinched his sixth Croatian title in a row after finishing runner-up to Matej Zagar in the Tri-nations championship.

He won the one round on home soil at his father's Gorican track but a poor opening round cost him his chance of overall victory in the four-meeting series.

Final Standings
1 Jurica PAVLIC 145, 2 Dino KOVACIC 101, 3 Ivan VARGEK 98, 4 Nikola PIGAC 91, 5 Renato CVETKO 79, 6 Nikola MARTINEC 72, 7 Kreso PETKOVIC 55, 8 Andrej KEZMAN 42, 9 Marko VLAH 16, 10 Jasmin ILIJAS 12.

Round 3
Gorican, Croatia, Sunday, April 13
1 Jurica Pavlic 15, 2 Matej Zagar 14, 3 Aleksander Conda 11, 4 Denis Stojs 10, 5 Manuel Hauzinger 10, 6 Izak Santej 9, 7 Nikola Pigac 7, 8 Matic Voldrih 7, 9 Matija Duh, 10 Dino Kovacic 6, 11 Ivan Vargek 5, 12 Jernej Kolenko 4, 13 Maks Gregoric 4, 14 Manuel Novotny 4, 15 Heinrich Schatzer 2, 16 Aljosa Remih [R] 2, 17 Nikola Martinec 0, 18 Lukas Simon [R] 0.
Group B: Kreso Petkovic 11, Renato Cvetko 10, Lukas Simon 8, Andrej Kezman 7, Aljosa Remih 6, Christopher Fink 3, Josef Fasching 2, Christian Pellikan 1.

Roll of Honour

1992	Zlatko KRZNARIC
1993	Renato KUSTER
1994	Zlatko KRZNARIC
1995	Zlatko KRZNARIC
1996	Zlatko KRZNARIC
1997	Zeljko FEHER
1998	Zeljko FEHER
1999	Zlatko KRZNARIC
2000	Zlatko KRZNARIC
2002	Marko VLAGH
2003	Jurica PAVLIC
2004	Jurica PAVLIC
2005	Jurica PAVLIC
2006	Jurica PAVLIC
2007	Jurica PAVLIC
2008	Jurica PAVLIC

Croatia declared its independence in 1991, having been part of the Socialist Federal Republic of Yugoslavia. Other Yugoslavian countries to subsequently declare their independence included Slovenia (see separate section).

FEDERAL REPUBLIC OF YUGOSLAVIA

1959	Valent MEDVED
1960	Drago REGVART
1961	Valent MEDVED
1962	Franc BABIC
1963	Drago REGVART
1964	Franc BABIC
1965	Franc BABIC
1966	Drago REGVART
1967	Franc BABIC
1970	Ivan MOLAN
1971	Ivan MOLAN
1972	Drasko ORSIC
1973	Stefan KEKEC
1974	Stefan KEKEC
1975	Stefan KEKEC
1976	Vlado KOCUVAN
1977	Vlado KOCUVAN
1978	Stefan KEKEC
1979	Vlado KOCUVAN
1980	Vlado KOCUVAN
1981	Vlado KOCUVAN
1982	Stefan KEKEC
1983	Joze ZIBERT
1984	Albert KOCMUT
1985	Kreso OMERZEL
1986	Zvonko PAVLIC
1987	Artur HORVAT
1988	Zvonko PAVLIC
1989	Gregor PINTAR
1990	Gregor PINTAR
1991	Gregor PINTAR

AUSTRIA-CROATIA-HUNGARY-SLOVENIA TEAM CHAMPIONSHIP

FINAL STANDINGS

	M	Pts
1 SLOVENIA	3	136+0
2 HUNGARY	3	132+3
3 AUSTRIA	3	93
4 CROATIA	**3**	**60**

CROATIA AVERAGES

Rider	M	R	Pts	Ave	M
Jurica PAVLIC	1	5	15	12.00	1
Dino KOVACIC	**3**	**14**	**17**	**4.86**	**0**
Kreso PETKOVIC	1	5	4	3.20	0
Ivan VARGEK	**3**	**15**	**10**	**2.67**	**0**
Nikola PIGAK	3	13	7	2.15	0
Renato CVETKO	**2**	**10**	**5**	**2.00**	**0**
Nikola MARTINEC	1	5	2	1.60	0
Guests					
Hans Peter KULTERER	1	2	0	0.00	0

Round 3

Gorican, Croatia, Friday, August 15

1 HUNGARY 41+3 (Matej Ferjan 13+3, Robert Nagy 6, Laszlo Szatmari 3, Sandor Tihanyi 10, Jozsef Tabaka 9), **2 SLOVENIAN 41+X** (Matija Duh 9, Maks Gregoric 12+X, Denis Stojs 3, Ales Krajlic 10, Aleksander Conda 7), **3 CROATIA 37** (**Jurica Pavlic 15**, Ivan Vargek 6, Nikola Pigac 3, Kreso Petkovic 4, Dino Kovacic 9), **4 AUSTRIA 20** (**Manuel Hauzinger 9**, Andreas Maida [G] 4, Fritz Wallner 4, Renato Cvetko [G] 1, Lukas Simon 2).

Individual

PRIZE OF PRELOG

Prelog, Croatia, Sunday, June 29

1 Martin Smolinski 11+2+3, 2 Jurica Pavlic 14+3+3, 3 Manuel Hauzinger 11+2+1, 4 Thomas Stange 13+3+0, 5 Robert Mikolajczak 12+1, 6 Dino Kovacic 10+1, 7 Johannes Kikkenborg 9+0, 8 Jozsef Tabaka 8+0, 9 Matija Duh 7, 10 Aleksander Conda 6, 11 Claes Nedermark 4, 12 Kreso Petkovic 4, 13 Sandor Tihanyi 4, 14 Joakim Kugelmann 3, 15 Manuel Novotny 2, 16 Renato Cvetko 1.

CROATIAN U21 CHAMPIONSHIP

The Croatian Championship is part of the national competition also involving riders from Austria, Hungary and Slovenia.

The highest scoring Croatian rider is the national champion.

For full details of the rounds see Austria.

Final standings

1 Dino KOVACIC 92, 2 Nikola PIGAC 86, 3 Renato CVETKO 64, 4 Kreso PETKOVIC 38, 5 Andrej KEZMAN 19, 6 Jasmin ILIJAS 7.

Round 1

Gorican, Sunday, April 27

1 Aleksander Conda 15, 2 Kreso Petkovic 12+3, 3 Matic Voldrih 12+2, 4 Matija Duh 11, 5 Nikola Pigac 10, 6 Renato Cvetko 10, 7 Roland Kovacs 10, 8 Dino Kovacic 8, 9 Tamas Szilagyi 8, 10 Andrej Kezman 7, 11 Aljosa Remih 6, 12 Daniel Gappmaier 4, 13 Dalibor Bot 3, 14 Ladislav Vida [R] 2, 15 Hans Peter Kulterer 1, 16 Attila Lorincz 0, 16 Lukas Simon 0.

Roll of Honour

2007 .... Nikola MARTINEC
2008 .... Dino KOVACIC

2009 FIXTURES

CROATIA-SLOVENIA CHAMPIONSHIP

Round 1: Sunday, April 19, Gorican, Croatia.
Round 2: Saturday, August 15, Gorican, Croatia.
Round 3: Saturday, September 5, Lendava, Slovenia.
Round 4: Saturday, October 10, Krsko, Slovenia.

CROATIA-HUNGARY-SLOVENIA UNDER 21 CHAMPIONSHIP

Round 1: Saturday, April 11, Ljubljana, Slovenia.
Round 2: Sunday, April 12, Krsko, Slovenia.
Round 3: Saturday, April 18, Lendava, Slovenia.
Round 4: Saturday, July 25, Gyula, Hungary.
Round 5: Saturday, August 8, Debrecen, Hungary.
Round 6: Sunday, September 6, Prelog, Croatia.

THE superb stadion Milenium at Donji Kraljevec, Gorican, was officially opened on August 14, 2005 – the brainchild of former Yugoslavian Champion Zvonko Pavlic who built the track at the back of the head offices of his road building company.

Even though Donja Kraljevec has a population of only 2,000, stadion Milenium is now one of the best appointed permanent tracks in the world and Pavlic plans to increase its capacity to 10,000 and hopes to stage a Croatian Grand Prix in 2010 or beyond.

The track is the home of Klub Unia Gorican – founded in 2004 – which has eight riders old enough to compete in senior or Under 21 meetings this year.

They are Jurica Pavlic (19), Ivan Vargek (25), Renato Cvetko (19), Nikola Pigac (18), Andrej Kezman (17), Dino Kovacic (15), Jasmin Ilijas (14) and Dario Vugrinec (14).

Track: Murska 58, 40320 Donja Kraljevec, Croatia.
Track Length: 320 metres.
Track Record: 59.46 secs, Jurica Pavlic, August 19, 2006.
Website: www.speedway-unia.hr

THE only other venue in Croatia is at Prelog which opened on May 15, 1964.

Their leading riders are Marko Vlah (24), Nikola Martinec (18) and Kreso Petkovic (17).

Track: Sajmlsna bb, HR-40323 Prelog, Croatia.
Telephone: (0385) 40654309.
Track Length: 342 metres.
Track Record: 62.2 secs, Nikola Martinec, September 2, 2007.
Website: www.speedway-klub-prelog.hr

CZECH REPUBLIC

New champion Lukas Dryml flanked by brother Ales and Lubos Tomicek

CZECH REPUBLIC CHAMPIONSHIP

LUKAS Dryml, whose father was Czechoslovakian Champion in 1984, beat his younger brother Ales to win his second national title.

Held over three rounds, the 2008 Grand Prix regular took top spot in the second meeting with maximum points and was runner-up in the first and third rounds.

Final Standings
1 Lukas Dryml 40, 2 Ales Dryml[2] 38, 3 Lubos Tomicek 35, 4 Adrian Rymel 31, 5 Filip Sitera 31, 6 Matej Kus 27, 7 Martin Vaculik (Slovakia) 25, 8 Josef Franc 23, 9 Hynek Stichauer 19, 10 Richard Wolff 18, 11 Adrian Pluska (Poland) 16, 12 Jan Jaros 15, 13 Martin Malek 13, 14 Adam Vandirek 12, 15 Pavel Ondrasik 10, 16 Martin Gavenda 3, 17 Vladimir Visvader 3, 18 Michael Hadek 1.

Semi Final
Koprivnice, Thursday, May 1
Jan Jaros 12, Matej Kus 11+3, Hynek Stichauer 11+2, Richard Wolff 9, Martin Malek 9, Lubos Tomicek III 8, Vladimir Visvader 8, Adam Vandirek 8, Adrian Pluska 7+3, Michael Hadek 7+2, Martin Gavenda 6, Jaroslav Petrak 5, Tomas Suchanek 5, Antonin Galliani 4, Michal Dudek 4, Jan Holub III 2, Krzysztof Nowacki 2, Petr Babicka 1, Lukas Hromadka 1, Jaromir Otruba 0.

Final, Round 1
Prague, Tuesday, May 13
Lubos Tomicek 14, Lukas Dryml 12, Filip Sitera 11+3, Adrian Rymel 11+2, Ales Dryml[2] 11+R, Martin Vaculik 10, Matej Kus 9, Josef Franc 8, Jan Jaros 7, Hynek Stichauer 7, Adam Vandirek 5, Pavel Ondrasik 5, Adrian Pluska 4, Martin Malek 4, Vladimir Visvader 1, Michael Hadek [R] 1, Richard Wolff 0, Martin Gavenda [R], did not ride.

Final, Round 2
Pardubice, Wednesday, May 14
Lukas Dryml 15, Richard Wolff 13+3, Ales Dryml 13+E, Martin Vaculik 11, Lubos Tomicek 11, Filip Sitera 10, Adrian Rymel 9, Josef Franc 7, Matej Kus 6, Adrian Pluska 5, Adam Vandirek 5, Martin Malek 4, Hynek Stichauer 4, Pavel Ondrasik 4, Vladimir Visvader 2, Jan Jaros 1. Michael Hadek [R], Martin Gavenda [R], did not ride.

Final, Round 3
Liberec, Saturday, July 26
Ales Dryml 14, Lukas Dryml 13, Matej Kus 12, Adrian Rymel 11, Lubos Tomicek 10, Filip Sitera 10, Josef Franc 8, Hynek Stichauer 8, Jan Jaros 7, Adrian Pluska 7, Martin Malek 5, Richard Wolff 5, Martin Vaculik 4, Martin Gavenda [R] 3, Adam Vandirek 2, Pavel Ondrasik 1, Vladimir Visvader 0.

Roll of Honour

1993	Bohumil BRHEL
1994	Antonin KASPER[2]
1995	Zdenek TESAR
1996	Tomas TOPINKA
1997	Antonin KASPER[2]
1998	Bohumil BRHEL
1999	Michal MAKOVSKY

■ *Lubos TOMICEK[1] (b16.8.1934-d20.10.1968), Lubos TOMICEK[2] (b10.7.1956), Jan HOLUB[1] (b12.8.1942), Jan HOLUB[2] (b24.1.1968), Jan HOLUB[3] (b7.8.1991), Jiri STANCL[1] (b18.11.1949), Jiri [George] STANCL[2] (b19.8.1975), Ales DRYML[1] (b10.6.1953), Antonin KASPER[2] (b5.12.1962-d31.7.2006), Vaclav MILIK[1] (b23.2.1960), Vaclav MILIK[2] (b22.5.1993).*

2000 .... Bohumil BRHEL
2001 .... Bohumil BRHEL
2002 .... Antonin KASPER[2]
2003 .... Tomas TOPINKA
2004 .... Bohumil BRHEL
2005 .... Lukas DRYML
2006 .... Adrian RYMEL
2007 .... Martin VACULIK
2008 .... Lukas DRYML

On January 1, 1993, Czechoslovakia split into its constituent states, the Czech Republic and Slovakia.

CZECHOSLOVAKIA CHAMPIONSHIP

Roll of Honour

1949 .... Hugo ROSAK
1950 .... Rudolf HAVELKA
1954 .... Hugo ROSAK
1955 .... Hugo ROSAK
1956 .... Hugo ROSAK
1957 .... Rudolf HAVELKA
1958 .... Richard JANICEK
1959 .... Frantisek RICHTER
1960 .... Jaroslav MACHAC
1961 .... Lubos TOMICEK[1]
1962 .... Lubos TOMICEK[1]
1963 .... Lubos TOMICEK[1]
1964 .... Lubos TOMICEK[1]
1965 .... Lubos TOMICEK[1]
1966 .... Antonin SVAB
1967 .... Antonin SVAB
1968 .... Jan HOLUB[1]
1969 .... Jan HOLUB[1]
1970 .... Jiri STANCL[1]
1971 .... Vaclav VERNER
1972 .... Jiri STANCL[1]
1973 .... Jiri STANCL[1]
1974 .... Jiri STANCL[1]
1975 .... Jiri STANCL[1]
1976 .... Jiri STANCL[1]
1977 .... Jiri STANCL[1]
1978 .... Jiri STANCL[1]
1979 .... Jiri STANCL[1]
1980 .... Jiri STANCL[1]
1981 .... Jiri STANCL[1]
1982 .... Ales DRYML[1]
1983 .... Jiri STANCL[1]
1984 .... Ales DRYML[1]
1985 .... Antonin KASPER[2]
1986 .... Antonin KASPER[2]
1987 .... Antonin KASPER[2]
1988 .... Roman MATOUSEK
1989 .... Petr VANDIREK
1990 .... Antonin KASPER[2]
1991 .... Vaclav MILIK[1]
1992 .... Bohumil BRHEL

CZECH REPUBLIC UNDER 21 CHAMPIONSHIP

MATEJ Kus could afford to miss the final round of the championship – after establishing an unassailable lead by winning three of the first four rounds!

Missing two of the first three rounds cost Filip Sitera his chance of becoming only the third rider to complete a hat-trick of crowns in the competition's long history, dating back to 1969.

He was, over the course of the first four meetings, the

Matej Kus missed the final round of the Under 21 championship but was presented with the trophy at an official prize-giving ball when he was also handed his Under 19 Championship silverware.

sole rider to beat Kus who dropped one point in 20 races.

Final Standings

1 Matej Kus 73, 2 Hynech Stichauer 52, 3 Martin Gavenda 47, 4 Michael Hadek 40, 5 Jan Holub[3] 37, 6 Michal Dudek 37, 7 Marcin Piekarski (Poland) 33, 8 Pavel Pucko 30, 9 Martin Vaculik (Slovakia) 27, 10 Filip Sitera 25, 11 Adam Vandirek 22, 12 Mateusz Kowalczyk (Poland) 20, 13 Petr Babicka 15, 14 Jakub Fencl 13, 15 Pavel Fuksa 12, 16 Vaclav Milik[2] 10, 17 Marcel Kajzer (Poland) 10, 18 Kamil Cieslar (Poland) 8, 19 Roman Cejka 6, 20 Lukas Hromadka 6, 21 Miroslav Horak 5, 22 Rastislav Bandzi (Slovakia) 5, 23 Grzegorz Strozyk (Poland) 2, 24 Rene Vidner 1, 25 Jiri Vonasek 1, 26 Lubos Velinsky 0..

Round 1
Pardubice, Saturday, April 12
Matej Kus 15, Martin Vaculik 14, Hynek Stichauer 13, Marcin Piekarski 12, Martin Gavenda 8, Adam Vandirek 8, Michal Dudek 8, Michael Hadek 8, Pavel Pucko 7, Mateusz Kowalczyk 7, Pavel Fuksa 6, Jan Holub 5, Ratislav Bandzi 4, Miroslav Horak 2, Jakub Fencl 1, Petr Babicka 0.

Round 2
Prague, Tuesday, June 10
Filip Sitera 15, Matej Kus 14, Martin Vaculik 13, Marcin Piekarski 11, Hynek Stichauer 11, Adam Vandirek 10,

Michael Hadek 9, Martin Gavenda 7, Jan Holub 7, Michal Dudek 6, Petr Babicka 6, Pavel Pucko 5, Jakub Fencl 3, Ratislav Bandzi 1.

Round 3
Koprivnice, Friday, June 27
Matej Kus 15, Hynek Stichauer 14, Mateusz Kowalczyk 13, Martin Gavenda 11, Jan Holub 10, Pavel Pucko 10, Kamil Cieslar 8, Michal Dudek 8, Lukas Hromadka 6, Jakub Fencl 3, Miroslav Horak 3, Grzegorz Strozyk 1.

Round 4
Mseno, Friday, July 25
Matej Kus 15, Hynek Stichauer 134, Michael Hadek 11, Filip Sitera 10, Marcel Kajzer 10, Marcin Piekarski 10, Martin Gavenda 9, Pavel Pucko 8, Michal Dudek 7, Pavel Fuksa 6, Jan Holub 5, Petr Babicka 4, Jakub Fencl 4, Adam Vandirek 4, Jiri Vonasek 1.

Round 5
Slany, Friday, September 26
1 Matej Kus 14+3, 2 Michael Hadek 12+2, 3 Martin Gavenda 12+1, 4 Jan Holub[3] 12+F, 5 Roman Cejka 6+3, 6 Vaclav Milik 10+2, 7 Michael Dudek 8+1, 8 Petr Babicka 5+F, 9 Jakub Fencl 2, 10 Rene Vidner 1, 11 Lubos Velinsky 0. Miroslav Horak [R], did not ride.

Roll of Honour

1993 .... Jiri STANCL II
1994 .... Marian JIROUT
1995 .... Pavel ONDRASIK
1996 .... Pavel ONDRASIK
1997 .... Richard WOLFF
1998 .... Josef FRANC
1999 .... Josef FRANC
2000 .... Josef FRANC
2001 .... Miroslav FENCL
2002 .... Tomas SUCHANEK
2003 .... Tomas SUCHANEK
2004 .... Miroslav FENCL
2005 .... Martin MALEK
2006 .... Filip SITERA
2007 .... Filip SITERA
2008 .... Matej KUS

CZECHOSLOVAKIA UNDER 21 CHAMPIONSHIP

Roll of Honour

1974 .... Jiri JIROUT
1975 .... Stefan ELIAS
1976 .... Lubos TOMICEK II
1977 .... Pavel KARNAS
1978 .... Josef JUZA
1979 .... Jaroslav DRAHOS
1979 .... Antonin KASPER II
1980 .... Antonin KASPER II
1981 .... Antonin KASPER II
1982 .... Petr KUBICEK
1983 .... Petr VANDIREK
1984 .... Ivan PACAK
1985 .... Bohumil BRHEL
1986 .... Jan HOLUB II
1987 .... Vladimir KALINA
1988 .... Gaspar FORGAC
1989 .... Borivoj HADEK
1990 .... Jiri HURYCH
1991 .... Jan FEJFAR
1992 .... Tomas TOPINKA

CZECH REPUBLIC UNDER 19 CHAMPIONSHIP

MATEJ Kus completed what was to become the first leg of a junior championship double when he was unbeaten from his four rides.

FINAL
Plzen, Wednesday, June 25
1 Matej Kus 12, 2 Michael Hadek 11+3, 3 Pavel Pucko 11+FX, 4 Jan Holub[3] 7, 5 Michal Dudek 7, 6 Pavel Fuksa 5, 7 Petr Babicka 3, 8 Vaclav Lacina 2, 9 Jakub Fencl 2, 10 Jiri Lang 0.

Roll of Honour

1999 .... Milan NOSEK
2001 .... Miroslav FENCL
2005 .... Hynek STICHAUER
2006 .... Filip SITERA
2007 .... Filip SITERA
2008 .... Matej KUS

CZECH REPUBLIC PAIRS CHAMPIONSHIP

FINAL
Brezolupy, Saturday, September 27
1 AK SLANY 7 (Karol Zabik 4, Martin Malek 3:1), **2 PSK OLYMP PRAGUE 2** (Adrian Rymel 2, Josef Franc 0), **3 JII VINTER TEAM BREZOLUPY 6** (Matej Ferjan 4, Martin Gavenda 2), **4 PK PLZEN 3** (Jan Holub[3] 3, Michael Hadek 0).

Group A: 1 AK SLANY 22 (Karol Zabik 4-4-4-4- 16, Martin Malek 2-2-0-2- 6), 2 JIRI VINTER TEAM BREZOLUPY 22 (Matej Ferjan 4-3-4-3- 14, Martin Gavenda 3-0-3-2- 8:3), 3 SOND-PO SPEEDWAY CLUB MILETICE 21 (Marcin Nowaczyk 2-3-3-4- 12:1, Marcel Kajzer F-4-2-3- 9:2), 4 AK MARKETA PRAGUE 13 (Lubos Tomicek[3] 2-4-3-4- 13, Pavel Ondrasik 0-0-0-0- 0), 5 FOTO RUDNA 12 (Kamil Cieslar 0-3-2-2- 7, Mateusz Kowalczyk 3-2-0-0- 5:1).
Group B: 1 PSK OLYMP PRAGUE 25 (Josef Franc 4-4-4-3- 15:1, Adrian Rymel 3-3-X-4- 10:2), 2 PK PLZEN 22 (Michael Hadek 2-4-3-2- 11:2, Jan Holub[3] 3-3-2-3- 11:2), 3 HBC@VRATES SPEEDWAY – RSC MV 20 (Richard Wolff F-3-3-0- 6:2, Filip Sitera 4-4-4-2- 14), 4 ZP PARDUBICE 12 (Hynek Stichauer 2-2-4-4- 12, Tomas Suchanek F-F- 0), 5 OTRUBA-BANDZI 11 (Jaromir Otruba 0-0-2-2- 4:1, Rastislav Bandzi 2-2-0-3- 7).
Semi Final 1: AK SLANY 7 (Martin Malek 3:1, Karol Zabik 4), PK PLZEN 2 (Michael Hadek 2, Jan Holub 0).
Semi Final 2: PSK OLYMP PRAGUE 5 (Adrian Rymel 3, Josef Franc 2:1), JIRI VINTER TEAM BREZOLUPY 4 (Matej Ferjan 4, Martin Gavenda 0).

Roll of Honour

2002 .... MPM KOPRIVNICE
2004 .... Grepl PDK MSENO
2005 .... AK SLANY
2006 .... PSK OLYMP PRAGUE
2007 .... PSK OLYMP PRAGUE
2008 .... AK SLANY

For Czechoslovakia champions see page 541

Extraleague champions Pardubice: co-manager Martin Kratochvil, Matej Ferjan, Ales Dryml, Lukas Dryml, Hynek Stichauer, coach Frantisek Kalina. Kneeling: Vaclav Milik and Jaroslav Petrak.

CZECH REPUBLIC UNDER 21 PAIRS CHAMPIONSHIP

FINAL TABLE

	M	*RPts*	*Pts*
1 PRAGUE	4	82	17
2 MSENO	4	74	15
3 PLZEN	4	58	12
4 PARDUBICE	4	53	9
5 SLANY	4	41	7

[Scoring: 5-4-3-2-1].

Round 1
Slany, Saturday, April 26
1 PRAGUE 23 (Matej Kus 14, Adam Vandirek 8:1, Marvin Gavenda 1), 2 PLZEN 19 (Michael Hadek, did not ride, Jan Holub³ 4, Filip Sitera 15:1), 3 SLANY 16 (Martin Vaculik 13, Michal Dudek 3:1, Petr Babicka, did not ride), 4 PARDUBICE 12 (Hynek Stichauer 11, Pavel Pucko 1:1), 5 MSENO 4 (Pavel Fuksa 4, Miroslav Horak 0).

Round 2
Prague, Tuesday, April 29
Postponed, rain.

Round 3
Mesno, Saturday, June 21
1 MSENO 27 (Marcin Piekarski [Poland] 11:2, Marcel Kajzer [Poland] 14, Pavel Fuksa 2), 2 PRAGUE 21 (Martin Gavenda 14:1, Adam Vandirek 7:2, Jakub Fencl 0), 3 PLZEN 11 (Jan Holub³ 11, Jiri Vonasek 0, Vaclav Lacina 0), 4 SLANY 11 (Petr Babicka 3:2, Michal Dudek 8), 5 PARDUBICE 8 (Pavel Pucko 6, Lubos Velinsky 2:2).

Round 4
Pardubice, Wednesday, August 13
1 PRAGUE 22 (Matej Kus 16, Martin Gavenda 6:4, Pavel Pucko, did not ride), 2 MSENO 22 (Marcin Piekarski [Poland] 9:3, Daniel Pytel [Poland] 13, Pavel Fuksa, did not ride), 3 PLZEN 15 (Michael Hadek 9, Jan Holub³ 6), 4 PARDUBICE 13 (Hynek Stichauer 13, Vaclav Milik² 0), 5 SLANY 6 (Petr Babicka 3:1, Michal Dudek 3).

Round 5
Plzen, Wednesday, September 3
1 MSENO 21 (Daniel Pytel [Poland] 13, Marcel Kajzer 8:4 [Poland]), 2 PARDUBICE 20 (**Hynek Stichauer 18**, René Vidner 2), 3 PRAGUE 16 (Martin Gavenda 9, Pavel Pucko 7:3), 4 PLZEN 13 (Jiri Lang 1, Jan Holub³ 12), 5 SLANY 8 (Petr Babicka 3:1, Michal Dudek 3, Roman Cejka 2:1).

EXTRALEAGUE

A POWERFUL Pardubice squad were relative runaway winners of the Czech Republic Extra League.

A side embracing the Dryml brothers, Lukas and Ales, and hot prospect Hynek Stichauer, was strengthened by regular appearances from Matej Ferjan and occasional outings for Jesper B. Monberg and Adrian Gomolski.

While Olymp Prague dominated the qualifying rounds – to eliminate only struggling Slany –the Golden Helmet club were comfortable victors in all four of the final rounds which decided the title.

FINAL STANDINGS

	M	*RPts*	*Pts*
1 PARDUBICE	4	187	19
2 MSENO	4	145+3	12
3 PRAGUE	4	123	11
4 PLZEN	4	131+2	8

[Scoring: 4-3-2-1].

PRELIMINARY ROUND STANDINGS

	M	*RPts*	*Pts*
1 PRAGUE	4	174	13
2 PARDUBICE	4	178	11
3 MSENO	4	137	11
4 PLZEN	4	153	8
5 SLANY	4	127	7

[Scoring: 4-3-2-1. The top four teams progressed to the finals rounds and took match points forward as follows: 4-3-2-1].

Round 1
Prague, Tuesday, April 15
1 PRAGUE 54 (Lubos Tomicek 12, Adrian Rymel 13, Matej Kus 12, Richard Wolff 8, Josef Franc 9, Adam Vandirek, did not ride), **2 PLZEN 45** (Filip Sitera 14, Matthias Schultz 12, Zdenek Simota 7, Daniel Jeleniewski 11 (6), Michael Hadek 1, Jan Holub³, did not ride), **3 SLANY 29** (Slawomir Drabik 13, Michal Dudek 0, Martin Malek 6, Adrian Pluska 4, Martin Vaculik 6 (0), Petr Babicka, did not ride), **4 MSENO 25** (Tomas Topinka 7 (R), Norbert Kosciuch

12, Dariusz Lowicki 2, Tomasz Bajerski 4, Pavel Fuksa 0, Miroslav Horak, did not ride).

Round 2
Pardubice, Wednesday, April 30
1 PARDUBICE 64 (Hynek Stichauer 10, Tomas Suchanek 10, Lukas Dryml 14, **Ales Dryml 15**, **Matej Ferjan 15**, Lubos Velinsky, did not ride), **2 PRAGUE 42** (Adrian Rymel 10, Matej Kus 9 (2), Josef Franc 8, Pavel Ondrasik 6, Lubos Tomicek 9, Martin Gavenda, did not ride), **3 MSENO 27** (Norbert Kosciuch 12, Filip Sitera 9 (0), Ronnie Jamrozy 4, Dariusz Lowicki 1, Vladimir Visvader 1, Pavel Fuksa 0), **4 SLANY 21** (Martin Malek 3, Martin Vaculik 6, Mariusz Puszakowski 12 (6), Michal Dudek 0, Adrian Pluska 0, Petr Babicka, did not ride).

Round 3
Plzen, Wednesday, May 28
1 MSENO 43 (Ronnie Jamrozy 11, Jan Jaros 9, Adam Vandirek 8, Norbert Kosciuch 12, Vladimir Visvader 3, Pavel Fuksa, did not ride) **2 PLZEN 42** (Michael Hadek 8, Jiri Stobl 0, Filip Sitera 9, Mathias Schultz 17 (6), Grzegorz Zengota 8, Jan Holub[3] 0), **3 SLANY 38** (Martin Malek 6, Adrian Pluska 3, Martin Vaculik 12, Sebastian Ulamek 16 (6), Michal Dudek 1, Petr Babicka, did not ride), **4 PARDUBICE 33** (Matej Ferjan 12, Tomas Suchanek 9, Manuel Novotny 0, Hynek Stichauer 9, Jaroslav Petrak 3, Vaclav Milkik[2], did not ride).

Round 4
Slany, Wednesday, June 18
1 PRAGUE 41 (Adrian Rymel 9, Josef Franc 9, Richard Wolff 6, Lubos Tomicek 12, Matej Kus 5, Martin Gavenda, did not ride), **2 PARDUBICE 40** (Ales Dryml 8, Hynek Stichauer 14, Jaroslav Petrak 2, Matej Ferjan 13, Tomas Suchanek 3, Lubos Velinsky, did not ride), **3 SLANY 39** (Michal Dudek 0, Patrik Linhart 1, Martin Malek 5, Karol Zabik 17 (6), Martin Vaculkik 16, Petr Babicka, did not ride), **4 PLZEN 35** (Filip Sitera 10, Jiri Strobl 1, Miroslaw Jablonski 10 (4), Jan Holub[3] 2, Daniel Jelenewski 11, Michael Hadek 1).

Round 5
Mseno, Thursday, July 10
1 MSENO 42 (Tomas Topinka 11, Jan Jaros 9, Pavel Fuksa 1, Piotr Protasiewicz 14, Norbert Kosciuch 7, Miroslav Horak, did not ride), **2 PARDUBICE 41** (Hynek Stichauer 7, Matej Ferjan 15, Jesper B. Monberg 14, Tomas Suchanek 4, Jaroslav Petrak 1, Lubos Velinskiy, did not ride), **3 PRAGUE 37** (Adrian Rymel 9, Josef Franc 5, Lubos Tomicek 9 (0), Richard Wolff 2, Matej Kus 12, Martin Gavenda 0), **4 PLZEN 31** (Michael Hadek 1, Jiri Strobl 0, Mathias Schultz 11, Filip Sitera 5, Daniel Jeleniewski 11 (2), Jan Holub[3] 3).

Final 1
Mseno, Friday, August 8
1 PARDUBICE 57 (Ales Dryml 12, **Matej Ferjan 15**, Lukas Dryml 13, Hynek Stichauer 6, Adrian Gomolski 11, Vaclav Milik[2], did not ride), **2 PRAGUE 39** (Richard Wolff 10, Adrian Rymel 4, Lubos Tomicek[3] 8, Josef Franc 5, Matej Kus 12 (6), Martin Gavenda, did not ride), **3 MSENO 35** (Vladimir Visvader 0, AdamVandirek 1, Ronnie Jamrozy 5, Tomas Topinka 12, Piotr Protasiewicz 17 (6), Pavel Fuksa 0), **4 PLZEN 26** (Michael Hadek 4, Jan Holub[3] 1, Mathias Schultz 6, Filip Sitera 13 (4), Grzegorz Zengota 2, Vaclav Lacina, did not ride).

Final 2
Plzen, Wednesday, August 27
1 PARDUBICE 39 (Adrian Gomolski 9, Ales Dryml[2] 4, Tomas Suchanek 5, Hynek Stichauer 10, Matej Ferjan 11, Lubos Velinsky, did not ride), **2 PLZEN 34** (Jiri Strobl 0, Grzegorz Klopot 3, Filip Sitera 12, Michael Hadek 7, Daniel Jeleniewski 11, Jan Holub[3] 1), **3 MSENO 30** (Petr Vandirek 3, Daniel Pytel 9, Piotr Protasiewicz 11, Jan Jaros 6, Pavel Fuksa 1, Miroslav Horak, did not ride), **4 PRAGUE 16** (Lubos Tomicek[3] 1, Adrian Rymel 2 (0), Josef Franc 10, Richard Wolff 1, Martin Gavenda 2, Pavel Pucko, did not ride).

Final 3
Pardubice, Wednesday, September 10
1 PARDUBICE 46 (Jaroslaw Petrak 2, Hynek Stichauer 8, Lukas Dryml 12, Ales Dryml[2] 10, Matej Ferjan 14, Vaclav Milik[2], did not ride), **2 MSENO 40+3** (Vladimir Visvader 1, Pavel Fuksa 1, Norbert Kosciuch 10, Piotr Protasiewicz 20 (6)+3, Jan Jaros 8, Miroslav Horak, did not ride), **3 PLZEN 40+2** (Daniel Jeleniewski 13+2, Jan Holub[3] 4, Michael Hadek 5, Filip Sitera 11, Grzegorz Zengota 7, Jiri Lang, did not ride), **4 PRAGUE 30** (Adrian Rymel 9, Josef Franc 5, Richard Wolff 13 (6), Pavel Ondrasik 2, Martin Gavenda 1, Pavel Pucko, did not ride).

Final 4
Prague, Wednesday, September 24
1 PARDUBICE 45 (Ales Dryml 12, Hynek Stichauer 6, Jesper B. Monberg 13, Matej Ferjan 11, Tomas Suchanek 3, Vaclav Milik[2], did not ride), **2 MSENO 40** (Piotr Protasiewicz 13, Pavel Fuksa 0, Jan Jaros 7, Norbert Kosciuch 11, Tomas Topinka 9, Miroslav Horak, did not ride), **3 PRAGUE 38** (Lubos Tomicek[3] 3, Adrian Rymel 7, Josef Franc 11, Matej Kus 12 (6), Richard Wolff 5, Martin Gavenda, did not ride), **4 PLZEN 31** (Jan Holub[3] 1, Filip Sitera 12, Daniel Jeleniewski 11 (2), Miroslaw Jablonski 5, Michael Hadek 2, Jiri Lang, did not ride).

Roll of Honour

1993 ....Olymp PRAGUE
1994 ....Cetrans Marco Polo PLZEN
1995 ....Olymp PRAGUE
1996 ....Olymp PRAGUE
1997 ....Olymp PRAGUE
1998 ....Olymp PRAGUE
1998 ....Racek PARDUBICE
1999 ....Golden Helmet PARDUBICE
2000 ....Olymp PRAGUE

2001 ....Golden Helmet PARDUBICE
2002 ....Golden Helmet PARDUBICE
2003 ....Olymp PRAGUE
2004 ....Golden Helmet PARDUBICE
2005 ....AK SLANY
2006 ....AK SLANY
2007 ....PK PLZEN
2008 ....Golden Helmet PARDUBICE

CZECHOSLOVAKIA

Roll of Honour

1956....................Red Star PRAGUE
1957....................Red Star PRAGUE
1958....................Red Star PRAGUE
1959....................Red Star PRAGUE
1960....................Red Star PRAGUE
1961....................Red Star PRAGUE
1962....................Red Star PRAGUE
1968....................Red Star PRAGUE
1969 ....Bateria SLANY
1970....................Red Star PRAGUE
1971....................Red Star PRAGUE
1972....................Red Star PRAGUE
1973....................Red Star PRAGUE
1974....................Red Star PRAGUE
1975....................Red Star PRAGUE
1976....................Red Star PRAGUE
1977....................Red Star PRAGUE
1978 ....Golden Helmet PARDUBICE
1979....................Red Star PRAGUE
1980....................Red Star PRAGUE
1981....................Red Star PRAGUE
1982 ....Golden Helmet PARDUBICE
1983....................Red Star PRAGUE
1984 ....SVS PARDUBICE
1985 ....SVS PARDUBICE
1986....................Red Star PRAGUE
1987....................Red Star PRAGUE A
1988....................Olymp PRAGUE B
1989 ....SVS PARDUBICE
1990 ....Olymp PRAGUE
1991 ....Olymp PRAGUE
1992 ....Olymp PRAGUE

†In 1967 Victoria Prague won unoffical championship.

LEAGUE FOR THREE MEMBERS

FINAL STANDINGS

	M	*RPts*	*Pts*
1 PRAGUE	**8**	**248**	**26**
2 LIBEREC	**8**	**240**	**25**
3 BREZOLUPY	**8**	**209+2**	**18**
4 PARDUBICE	**8**	**163+3**	**11**

Round 1
Prague, Tuesday, May 27
1 LIBEREC 33 (Pavel Ondrasik 9:1, Dariusz Lowicki 5:2, Ronny Weis 4:1, **Martin Vaculik 15**), **2 PRAGUE 28** (Richard Wolff 10:1, Matej Kus 12:1, Adam Vandirek 6:3, Martin Gavenda, did not ride), **3 BREZOLUPY 24** (Antonin Galliani 5:1, Michael Hadek 4:1, Martin Malek 15:1, Pavel Pucko 0), **4 PARDUBICE 23** (Roman Andrusiv 0, Hynek Stichauer 19, Jaroslav Petrak 4:1).

Round 2
Svitavy, Saturday, May 31
1 LIBEREC 33 (Dariusz Lowicki 11:1, Pavel Ondrasik 14, Ronny Weis 8:5, Vladimir Visvader 0), **2 PRAGUE 28** (Matej Kus 18, Martin Gavenda 5:2, Adam Vandirek 5, Jakub Fencl, did not ride), **3 BREZOLUPY 26** (Krzysztof Nowacki 0, Martin Malek 17:2, Antonin Galliani 9:3), **4 PARDUBICE 21** (Jaroslav Petrak 2:1, Pavel Fuksa 3, Hynek Stichauer 16, Lubos Velinsky 0).

Round 3
Brezolupy, Saturday, June 14
1 PRAGUE 42 (Martin Gavenda 10:5, **Matej Kus 18**, Jan Jaros 12:2, Adam Vandirek 2:1), **2 BREZOLUPY 29** (Martin Malek 13:2, Antonin Galliani 9, Michael Hadek 3:2, Grzegorz Strozyk 4:1), **3 LIBEREC 28** (Pavel Ondrasik 6:1, Dariusz Lowicki 5:2, Martin Vaculik 17, Jan Holub[3], did not ride), **4 PARDUBICE 8** (Jaroslaw Petrak 6, Lubos Velinsky 2).

Round 4
Liberec, Saturday, July 5
1 PRAGUE 29 (Jan Jaros 15, Martin Gavenda 8, Adam Vandirek 6), **2 PARDUBICE 28** (Pavel Fuksa 2, Jaroslav Petrak 9:3, Hynek Stichauer 17), **3 LIBEREC 26** (Dariusz Lowicki 10:1, Adrian Pluska 9, Pavel Ondrasik 7:2, Jan Holub[3] 0), **BREZOLUPY 23** (Martin Malek 16, Antonin Galliani 7:1).

Round 5
Brezolupy, Sunday, August 9
1 PRAGUE 37 (Richard Wolff 14:1, Matej Kus 13:1, Martin Gavenda 10:5), **2 LIBEREC 29** (Martin Vaculik 14:1, Filip Sitera 12, Adrian Pluska 2:1, Dariusz Lowicki 1), **3 BREZOLUPY 22** (Martin Malek 4:1, Antonin Galliani 2, Michael Hadek 7, Adam Pawliczek 9:1), **4 PARDUBICE 20** (Pavel Fuksa 4:1, Hynek Stichauer 14, Jaroslaw Petrak 2).

Round 6
Svitavy, Saturday, September 13
1 BREZOLUPY 34 (Martin Malek 14:1, Michael Hadek 6:1, Adam Pawliczek 14:1), **2 PRAGUE 27** (Jan Jaros 13:1, Martin Gavenda 10:1, Pavel Pucko 4:2, Jiri Brummer, did not ride), **3 LIBEREC 25** (Dariusz Lowicki 4:1, Martin Vaculik 19, Adrian Pluska 0, Vladimir Visvader 2), **4 PARDUBICE 21** (Hynek Stichauer 15, Jaroslav Petrak 3, Pavel Fuksa 3).

Round 7
Prague, Tuesday, September 16
1 LIBEREC 33 (Pavel Ondrasik 8:2, Filip Sitera 17, Jan Holub III 8:1, Vladimir Visvader 0), **2 PRAGUE 31** (Richard Wolff 11:2, Martin Gavenda 5:2, Jan Jaros 15:1, Pavel Pucko, did not ride), **3 PARDUBICE 22+3** (Hynek Stichauer 17+3, Jaroslav Petrak 3, Vaclav Milik[2] 2, René Vidner 0), **45 BREZOLUPY 22+2** (Martin Malek 7:2+2, Michael Hadek 10, Antonin Galliani 5:1).

Round 8
Liberec, Saturday, September 20
1 LIBEREC 33 (Martin Vaculik 13:1, Filip Sitera 15:2, Jan Holub[3] 4:2, Dariusz Lowicki 1), **2 BREZOLUPY 29** (Martin Malek 14:1, Antonin Galliani 6:1, Michael Hadek 9:2), **3 PRAGUE 26** (Jan Jaros 10, Martin Gavenda 4:1, René Vidner 0, Matej Kus 12:1), **4 PARDUBICE 20** (Jaroslav Petrak 4, Vaclav Milik[2] 1:1, Hynek Stichauer 15).

Roll of Honour

2007 ....LIBEREC
2008 ....Marketa PRAGUE

In 2007 the League for Three Members replaced the old Division One.

Roll of Honour

1999 .... Marketa PRAGUE
2001 .... SVITAVY
2002 .... SLANY
2003 .... SVITAVY
2004 .... Golden Helmet PARDUBICE II
2005 .... Golden Helmet PARDUBICE II
2006 .... MSENO

CZECHOSLOVAKIA

Roll of Honour

1956 .... BRNO
1958 .... CESKE BUDEJOVICE
1959 .... USTI NAD LABEM
1960 .... PARDUBICE & HRADEC KRALOVE
1961 .... KV SVAZARMU
1980 .... Red Star PRAGUE B
1981 .... ZARNOVICA
1985 .... Red Star PRAGUE B
1991 .... PLZEN

Individual

JIRI HURYCH MEMORIAL

Chabarovice June 21

1 Jan Jaros 15+3+3, 2 Ronny Weis 12+3+2, 3 Szymon Kielbasa 11+2+X, 4 Tadeusz Kostro 11+2+X, 5 Pawel Gwozdz 8+1, 6 Mateusz Mikorski 12+X, 7 Marcel Helfer 9+R, 10 Janusz Baniak 8+X, 11 Lukasz Cyran 5, 11 Sergei Malyschew 5, 12 Denis Wienke 5, 13 Dennis Helfer 5, 14 Kamil Fleger 2, 15 Marcel Kalms 0, 16 Danny Krakowski 0.

CZECH REPUBLIC LONG TRACK FINAL

Marianske Lazne, Sunday, July 27

1Zdenek Schneiderwind18+5, 2 Sirg Schützbach 18+4, 3 Nynke de Jong 14+3, 4 Alessandro Milanese 17+2, 5 Richard Wolff 16+1, 6 Pavel Ondrasik 19+0, 7 Daniel Winterton 7+3, 8 Francesco Barbetta 7+2, 9 Anton Wannasek 11+0, 10 Karel Kadlec 13, 11 David Speight 10, 12 Stefan Drofa 7, 13 Silvano Soatin.

DIVISOV GRAND PRIX

Divisov, Saturday, August 2

Jan Jaros 13+3, Hynek Stichauer 13+2, Lukas Cyran 12, Janusz Baniak 11, Richard Wolff 10, Tadeusz Kostro 10, Michael Hadek 10, Maciej Cesielski 9, Martin Malek 9, Mateusz Kowalczyk 6, Jan Holub[3] 5, Mateusz Mikorski 4, Vladimir Visvader 3, Michal Dudek 3, Petr Babicka 1, Tomasz Halicki 1.

ANTONIN VILDE MEMORIAL

Slany, Saturday, August 23

1 MILETICE 27 (Martin Malek 12:3, Marcel Kajzer 15:2), 2 GORZOW 26 (Mateusz Sikorski 13:3, Mateusz Kowalczyk 13:2), 3 PLZEN 18+3 (Michael Hadek 12+3, Jan Holub[3] 6:1), 4 TARNOW 18+2 (Tadeusz Kostro 11+2, Maciej Cesielski 7:2), 5 LIBEREC 15 (Vladimir Visvader 6:1, Pavel Pucko 9:2), 6 ZIELONA GORA 13 (Janusz Baniak 13, Patryk Dudek 0), 7 SLANY 6 (Petr Babicka 6, Michal Dudek 0).

MICHAL MATULA MEMORIAL

Koprivnice, Saturday, September 28

Richard Wolff 11+3+3, Martin Malek 6+3+2, Adam Pawliczek 11+2+1, Rafal Fleger 6+2+0, Kamil Cieslar 9+1, Mateusz Kowalczyk 6+1, Tomasz Szmidt 9+N, Pavel Ondrasik 6+0, Piotr Rembas 5, Vladimir Visvader 1, Martin Gavenda 1, Rastislav Bandzi 0.

2009 FIXTURES

2010 GRAND PRIX QUALIFIER

Divisov, Sunday, June 7.

CZECH REPUBLIC CHAMPIONSHIP

Semi Final: Prague, Tuesday, June 23.
Final 1: Divisov, Saturday, August 1.
Final 2: Pardubice, Friday, September 11.
Final 3: Svitavy, Saturday, September 12.

PAIRS CHAMPIONSHIP

Final: Liberec, Saturday, August 8.

UNDER 21 CZECH REPUBLIC CHAMPIONSHIP

Round 1: Slany, Saturday, April 11.
Round 2: Prague, Tuesday, May 26.
Round 3: Divisov, Saturday, August 29.
Round 4: Liberec, Monday, September 28.

UNDER 19 CZECH REPUBLIC CHAMPIONSHIP

Final: Pardubice, Thursday, August 7.

EXTRALIGA

Round 1: Pardubice, Wednesday, April 29.
Round 2: Prague, Tuesday, May 12.
Round 3: Slany, Friday, May 29.
Round 4: Slany, Wednesday, June 17.
Round 5: Plzen, Wednesday, June 24.
Final 1: venue to be confirmed, Wednesday, August 19.
Final 2: venue to be confirmed, Wednesday, September 2.
Final 3: venue to be confirmed, Wednesday, September 16.
Final 4: venue to be confirmed, Wednesday, September 30.

LEAGUE FOR THREE MEMBERS

Round 1: Svitavy, Friday, May 8.
Round 2: Kopřivnice, Saturday, May 9.
Round 3: Liberec, Saturday, May 23.
Round 4: Slany, Friday, May 29.
Round 5: Brezolupy, Saturday, June 13.
Round 6: Slany, Monday, July 6.
Round 7: Brezolupy, Saturday, July 25.
Round 8: Svitavy, Saturday, August 15.
Round 9: Liberec,Friday, August 21.
Round 10: Prague, Tuesday, September 8.

UNDER 21 TEAM CHAMPIONSHIP

Round 1: Slany, Sunday, April 12.
Round 2: Plzen, Wednesday, May 13.
Round 3: Prague, Tuesday, June 9.
Round 4: Mseno, Sunday, July 5.
Round 5: Pardubice, Friday, August 28.

INDIVIDUAL

Emil Sova Memorial, Mseno, Friday, May 1.
Jiri Hurych Memorial, Chabarovice, Saturday, June 27.
Koprivnice, Saturday, September 5.
Antonin Vilde Memorial, Slany, Saturday, September 19.
Brezolupy, Saturday, September 26.
Golden Helmet, Pardubice, Saturday October 3-Sunday, October 4.
Lubos Tomicek Memorial, Prague, Monday, October 5.

AUTOKLUB v ACR BREZOLUPY

Czech Division One

BREZOLUPY

Final Division position.................................Third

Rider	M	R	Pts	BP	TPts	Ave	F	P
Adam PAWLICZEK	2	11	23	2	25	9.09	0	0
Martin MALEK	**8**	**50**	**102**	**10**	**112**	**8.96**	**0**	**0**
Grzegorz STROZYK	1	3	4	1	5	6.67	0	0
Michael HADEK	**6**	**32**	**39**	**6**	**45**	**5.63**	**0**	**0**
Antonin GALLIANI	7	37	43	7	50	5.41	0	0
Pavel PUCKO	**1**	**2**	**0**	**0**	**0**	**0.00**	**0**	**0**
Krzysztof NOWACKI	1	2	0	0	0	0.00	0	0

For Pavel PUCKO see also Prague.

Staged only three meetings throughout the year – two rounds of the Division One Championship and the final of the Czech Republic Pairs Championship.

Relied heavily on Polish riders although youngster Michael Hadek, grandson of Jan and son of Borivoj, rode regularly and improved the longer the season went on.

In 2009 they will stage their major individual meeting on September 26 and will again compete in Division One with two home rounds of the championship.

Brezolupy
Antonin Galliani, Martin Malek and team manager Milos Plzak. Kneeling: Krzysztof Nowacki and his mechanic brother

Czech Division One

LIBEREC

Final Division position . . . . .Runners up

Liberece drafted in the big guns in their bid to successfully retain their First League title.

And it was a move that very nearly came off with Marketa Prague just scraping through.

The capital city side would have missed out if they had finished fourth in the final round.

Only three senior meetings were held at the track – their two home rounds in Division One and the third and final round of the Czech Republic Championship.

Slovakian number one Martin Vaculik was their principal points scorer in their encouraging bid for Division One honours and Filip Sitera provided handsome support in the three meetings in which he took part.

Look out for teenager Jan Holub whose grandfather raced in Britain at Exeter from 1969 to 1970.

Liberec – Dariusz Lowicki, Pavel Pluska, Filip Sitera and Martin Vaculik

Rider	M	R	Pts	BP	TPts	Ave	F	P
Martin VACULIK	5	30	78	2	80	10.67	1	0
Filip SITERA	**3**	**18**	**44**	**2**	**46**	**10.22**	**0**	**0**
Pavel ONDRASIK	5	27	44	6	50	7.41	0	0
Ronny WEIS	**2**	**10**	**12**	**6**	**18**	**7.20**	**0**	**0**
Dariusz LOWICKI	7	32	37	7	44	5.50	0	0
Jan HOLUB[3]	**4**	**11**	**12**	**3**	**15**	**5.45**	**0**	**0**
Pavel PLUSKA	3	10	11	1	12	4.80	0	0
Vladimir VISVADER	**3**	**5**	**2**	**0**	**2**	**1.60**	**0**	**0**

Czech Extra League

MSENO

Final Extra League position ....Runners up

Mesno had been tipped to stay at the bottom of the Extra League but they came closest to toppling Pardubice.

It was a remarkable transition within a season and much of the credit should go to coach Petr Vandirek and club officials who agreed to sign Poland's Piotr Protasiewicz.

The former Grand Prix star was a revelation – and finished in top spot in the Extra League averages as he sparked Mseno's unexpected title challenge.

Fellow Pole Norbert Kosciuch was also an impressive import, generally improving on his 2007 performances as Mseno used 12 different riders throughout the year.

Individual

Emil Sova Memorial
Thursday, May 1
Matej Kus 15, Marcin Piekarski 13, Hynek Stichauer 12+3, Adrian Pluska 12+2, Dariusz Lowicki 11, Martin Malek 10, Marcin Nowaczyk 9, Michael Hadek 8, Vladimir Visvader 7, Pavel Fuksa 6, Michal Dudek 5, Pavel Pucko 4, Jan Holub[3] 4, Jaromir Otruba 3, Miroslav Horak 0.

Antonin Kasper Memorial
Friday, August 1
Hynek Stichauer 14, Matej Kus 13+3, Tomasz Piszcz 13+F, Jan Jaros 12, Richard Wolff 12, Marcin Piekarski 9, Michael Hadek 9, Martin Gavenda 8, Adam Vandirek 6, Martin Malek 6, Jaroslaw Petrak 5, Ronny Weis 4, Marcel Kalms 3, Jan Holub[3] 3, Pavel Pucko 3, Vladimir Visvader 0, Jaromir Otruba [R], did not ride.

Super Prix
Saturday, October 11
Zbigniew Suchecki 15, Richard Wolff 14, Norbert Kosciuch 13, Jan Jaros 12, Filip Sitera 11, Ronny Weis 10, Jan Holub[3] 8, Michal Dudek 7, Vaclav Milik[2] 7, Marcel Kajzer 6, Jaromir Otruba 5, Roman Cejka 5, Vladimir Visvader 3, Marcel Kalms 0.

Rider	*M*	*R*	*Pts*	*BP*	*TPts*	*Ave*	*F*	*P*	*TR*	*TPts*
Piotr PROTASIEWICZ	5	26	78	0	78	12.00	0	0	2	6
Norbert KOSCIUCH	**6**	**32**	**64**	**0**	**64**	**8.00**	**0**	**0**	**0**	**0**
Daniel PYTEL	1	5	9	0	9	7.20	0	0	0	0
Tomas TOPINKA	**4**	**22**	**39**	**0**	**39**	**7.09**	**0**	**0**	**0**	**0**
Jan JAROS	5	24	39	0	39	6.50	0	0	0	0
Filip SITERA	**1**	**6**	**9**	**0**	**9**	**6.00**	**0**	**0**	**1**	**0**
Ronnie JAMROZY	3	16	20	0	20	5.00	0	0	0	0
Adam VANDIREK	**3**	**11**	**12**	**0**	**12**	**4.36**	**0**	**0**	**0**	**0**
Tomasz BAJERSKI	1	6	4	0	4	2.67	0	0	0	0
Dariusz LOWICKI	**2**	**8**	**3**	**0**	**3**	**1.50**	**0**	**0**	**0**	**0**
Vladimir VISVADER	4	17	5	0	5	1.18	0	0	0	0
Pavel FUKSA	**7**	**23**	**3**	**0**	**3**	**0.52**	**0**	**0**	**0**	**0**

Non-riding appearances: Miroslav HORAK (5), Pavel FUKSA (1). For Filip Sitera see also Plzen.

Grepl PDK Mseno
Back, left to right Norbert Kosciuch, Jan Jaros, Pavel Fuksa and coach Petr Vandirek. Kneeling Miroslav Horak, Tomas Topinka and Piotr Protasiewicz.

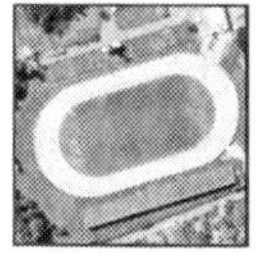

Czech Extra League

PARDUBICE

Final Extra League position..............Champions

Final Division One position ....Fourth

The Extra League trophy returned to Pardubice after a gap of three years as the Golden Helmet club were crowned champions for the fourth time in eight seasons.

Matej Ferjan and Wolverhampton-bound Hynek Stichauer were everpresents throughout the campaign with the Slovenian (now racing on a Hungarian licence) ending the year as overall top points scorer, topping the century mark with a string of double figure scores. Ferjan proved himself on the big track, finishing third in the annual Golden Helmet.

That the consistent Ales Dryml could only claim to be fifth in the Pardubice averages indicated how well they had done as a team although brother Lukas, Jesper B. Monberg and Poland's Adrian Gomolski only managed a total of seven appearances between them.

Rider	M	R	Pts	BP	TPts	Ave	F	P	TR	TPts
Lukas DRYML	3	15	39	0	39	10.40	0	0	0	0
Matej FERJAN	**8**	**41**	**106**	**0**	**106**	**10.34**	**2**	**0**	**0**	**0**
Jesper B. MONBERG	2	11	27	0	27	9.82	0	0	0	0
Adrian GOMOLSKI	**2**	**9**	**20**	**0**	**20**	**8.89**	**0**	**0**	**0**	**0**
Ales DRYML[2]	6	29	61	0	61	8.41	1	0	0	0
Hynek STICHAUER	**8**	**41**	**70**	**0**	**70**	**6.83**	**0**	**0**	**0**	**0**
Tomas SUCHANEK	6	30	34	0	34	4.53	0	0	0	0
Jaroslav PETRAK	**4**	**16**	**8**	**0**	**8**	**2.00**	**0**	**0**	**0**	**0**
Manuel NOVOTNY	1	3	0	0	0	0.00	0	0	0	0

Non-riding appearances: Vaclav MILIK[2] (4) and Lubos VELINSKY (4).

Individual

GOLDEN HELMET
Sunday, October 5

1 HANS ANDERSEN, 2 Leigh Adams, 3 Matej Ferjan, 4 Peter Karlsson, 5 Karol Zabik, 6 Wieslaw Jagus, 7 Jurica Pavlic, 8 Jesper B. Monberg, 9 Adrian Miedzinski, 10 Lukas Dryml, 11 Kenneth Bjerre, 12 Martin Vaculik.

Group 1: Rory Schlein 9, Matej Kus 9, Christian Hefenbrock 8, Martin Malek 6, Andy Smith 4, Tomas Suchanek 0.

Group 2: Josef Franc 10, Denis Gizatullin 8, Jan Jaros 7, Martin Smolinski 7, Tai Woffinden 6, Mattia Carpanese 1.

Group 3: Adrian Miedzinski 10, Martin Vaculik 8, Manuel Hauzinger 8, Lubos Tomicek[3] 7, Izak Santej 5, Vladimir Dubinin 3, Jaroslav Petrak [R] 1.

Group 4: Wieslaw Jagus 10, Steve Johnston 9, Filip Sitera 8, Mathias Schultz 6, Ludvig Lindgren 3, Alessandro Milanase 2, Jaroslav Petrak [R] 0.

Quarter Final 1: Karol Zabik 10, Jurica Pavlic 9, Hans Andersen 8, Denis Gizatullin 6, Rory Schlein 3, Manuel Hauzinger 0.

Quarter Final 2: Wieslaw Jagus 10, Kenneth Bjerre 9, Peter Karlsson 8, Matej Kus 6, Ales Dryml[2] 5, Jan Jaros 2, Jaroslav Petrak [R] 0.

Quarter Final 3: Jesper B. Monberg 10, Lukas Dryml 8, Adrian Miedzinski 6, Rune Holta 5, Christian Hefenbrock 4, Steve Johnston 3.

Quarter Final 4: Matej Ferjan 10, Leigh Adams 9, Martin Vaculik 7, Filip Sitera 6, Matej Zagar 5, Josef Franc 1.

Semi Final 1: Matej Ferjan 10, Hans Andersen 9, Karol Zabik 7, Kenneth Bjerre 7, Lukas Dryml 5, Martin Vaculik 2.

Semi Final 2: Leigh Adams 10, Peter Karlsson 9, Wieslaw Jagus 8, Adrian Miedzinski 5, Jurica Pavlic 4, Jesper B. Monberg 1.

Consolation Final: Jurica Pavlic, Jesper B. Monberg, Adrian Miedzinski, Lukas Dryml, Kenneth Bjerre, Martin Vaculik.

FINAL: Hans Andersen, Leigh Adams, Matej Ferjan, Peter Karlsson, Karol Zabik, Wieslaw Jagus.

GOLDEN RIBBON
Friday, October 3

1 Martin Vaculik 14+4+5, 2 Grzegorz Zengota 9+3+4, 3 Nicolai Klindt 14+4+3, 4 Tai Woffinden 10+3+2, 5 Michael Hadek 9+2+1, 6 Hynek Stichauer 11+2+X, 7 Kevin Wölbert 14+1, 8 Ben Barker 13+1, 9 Adrian Szewczykowski 11+0, 10 Filip Sitera 9+0, 11 Matej Kus 8, 12 Ludvig Lindgren 8, 13 Kenneth Hansen 6, 14 Jan Holub[3] 6, 15 Martin Gavenda 6, 16 Simon Nielsen 5, 17 Tobias Busch 3, 18 Manuel Novotny 2, 19 Vaclav Milik[2] 1, 20 Matijah Duh 0.

Division One

Rider	M	R	Pts	BP	TPts	Ave	F	P
Hynek STICHAUER	7	46	116	0	116	10.09	0	0
Jaroslav PETRAK	**8**	**45**	**33**	**5**	**38**	**3.38**	**0**	**0**
Pavel FUKSA	4	23	12	1	13	2.26	0	0
Vaclav MILIK[2]	**2**	**10**	**3**	**1**	**4**	**1.60**	**0**	**0**
Lubos VELENSKY	2	8	2	0	2	1.00	0	0
René VIDNER	**1**	**2**	**0**	**0**	**0**	**0.00**	**0**	**0**

Czech Extra League

PLZEN

Final Extra League position......................Fourth

Plzen had a miserable fall from grace after the 2007 highs of winning the Extra League championship.

Stocking their squad with a string of Polish signings, only Daniel Jeleniewski really lived up to expectations and the home of Pilsener beer had little to celebrate by the end of the season.

They scraped into the final stages of the championship by just a single point over Slany and finished bottom of the pile twice in the four round, despite some hefty scoring from their top Czech Filip Sitera.

The youngster outscored everyone else but they had no proven spearhead to cope with their rivals although there were bright signs from both Michael Hadek and Jan Holub, both of whom come from long established racing stock.

AK Plzen
Jan Holub, Filip Sitera, Mathias Schultz, Jiri Strobl, Michael Hadek and Grzegorz Zengota

Rider	M	R	Pts	BP	TPts	Ave	F	P	TR	TPts
Daniel JELENIEWSKI	6	34	70	0	70	8.24	0	0	3	5
Mathias SCHULTZ	**4**	**24**	**46**	**0**	**46**	**7.67**	**0**	**0**	**1**	**3**
Filip SITERA	8	45	86	0	86	7.64	0	0	1	2
Miroslaw JABLONSKI	**2**	**11**	**15**	**0**	**15**	**5.45**	**0**	**0**	**1**	**2**
Zdenek SIMOTA	1	6	7	0	7	4.67	0	0	0	0
Grzegorz ZENGOTA	**3**	**16**	**17**	**0**	**17**	**4.25**	**0**	**0**	**0**	**0**
Michael HADEK	8	29	29	0	29	4.00	0	0	0	0
Grzegorz KLOPOT	**1**	**4**	**3**	**0**	**3**	**3.00**	**0**	**0**	**0**	**0**
Jan HOLUB III	8	22	12	0	12	2.18	0	0	0	0
Jiri STROBL	**4**	**5**	**1**	**0**	**1**	**0.80**	**0**	**0**	**0**	**0**

Non-riding appearances: Jiri LANG (2) and Vaclav LACINA (1). For Filip Sitera see also Mseno.

International

Natsbach-Loipersbach, Austria
Saturday, May 10
AUSTRIA 72 (Fritz Wallner 16, Manfred Betz 7, Manuel Hauzinger 16, Matija Duh 8, Manuel Novotny 13, Ronny Weis 12, Hans-Peter Kulterer, did not ride), CZECH REPUBLIC 36 (Adam Vandirek 7, Jan Holub[3] 2, Hynek Stichauer 17, Pavel Hucko 0, Martin Gavenda 8, Michal Dudek 1, Vladimir Visvader 1).

Thanks go to Antonin Skach and Pavel Fiser for their help in compiling the Czech Republic information.
Besides publishing the annual reference book Ceska Plochodrazni Rocenka they also run the informative speedwayA-z website (www.speedwaya-z.cz) which carries all the latest information from the Czech Republic and elsewhere.

Czech Extra League

PRAGUE

Final Extra League position ....Third

Final Division One position ....Champions

Three regulars in Prague's Division One line-up – Martin Gavenda, Matej Kus and Richard Wolff

Rider	*M*	*R*	*Pts*	*BP*	*TPts*	*Ave*	*F*	*P*	*TR*	*TPts*
Matej KUS	6	31	62	0	62	8.00	0	0	3	7
Lubos TOMICEK[3]	**7**	**33**	**54**	**0**	**54**	**6.55**	**0**	**0**	**1**	**0**
Adrian RYMEL	8	39	63	0	63	6.46	0	0	1	0
Josef FRANC	**8**	**42**	**62**	**0**	**62**	**5.90**	**0**	**0**	**0**	**0**
Richard WOLFF	7	34	45	0	45	5.29	0	0	1	3
Pavel ONDRASIK	**2**	**7**	**8**	**0**	**8**	**4.57**	**0**	**0**	**0**	**0**
Martin GAVENDA	2	8	3	0	3	1.50	0	0	0	0

Non-riding appearances: Martin GAVENDA (4), Pavel PUCKO (2), Adam VANDIREK (1).

PSK Olymp Praha: Martin Gavenda, Matej Kus, Lubos Tomicek, Richard Wolff, Josef Franc and Adrian Rymel.

Individual

Lubos Tomicek I Memorial. Prague, Monday, October 6

1 Greg Hancock 14+4, 2 Grzegorz Walasek 10+3, Marcin Jedrzejewski 9+2, 4 Lubos Tomicek[3] 13+1, 5 Matej Ferjan 13+X, 6 Ludvig Lindgren 9, 7 Filip Sitera 9, 8 Karol Zabik 8, 9 Tai Woffinden 7, 10 Matej Kus 6, 11 Jan Holub[3] 4, 12 Josef Franc 4, 13 Maks Gregoric 4, 14 Mathias Schultz 4, 15 Richard Wolff 4, 16 Mattia Carpanese 2. ***Qualifying:*** Maks Gregoric 10, Marcin Jedrzejewski 9, Jan Holub[3] 6, Martin Gavenda 5, Mathias Bartz 4, Alessandro Milanese 2.

PRAGUE were the only club to rely solely on home-grown riders – and paid the price with their third place finish.

Scorning the trend to bring in big name stars from other countries, Olymp stuck with the riders who had come through the ranks.

Unfortunately it was a bold decision that didn't reap rewards although there was the spin-off of the lower league title.

Czech Division One

PRAGUE

Division One

Rider	M	R	Pts	BP	TPts	Ave	F	P
Matej KUS	5	29	73	3	76	10.48	2	0
Jan JAROS	**5**	**29**	**65**	**4**	**69**	**9.52**	**0**	**0**
Richard WOLFF	3	18	35	4	39	8.67	0	0
Martin GAVENDA	**7**	**42**	**52**	**16**	**68**	**6.48**	**0**	**0**
Adam VANDIREK	4	18	19	4	23	5.11	0	0
Pavel PUCKO	**1**	**6**	**4**	**2**	**6**	**4.00**	**0**	**0**
René VIDNER	1	1	0	0	0	0.00	0	0

Non-riding appearances: Jiri BRUMMER (1), Jakub FENCL (1), Pavel PUCKO (1).

Czech Extra League

SLANY

Final Extra League position ....Fifth

Woeful Slany had four of the best riders in the Extra League – unfortunately they never ever rode in the same team!

And it was no surprise that the team was the one to miss out on the final rounds.

Slovakia's Martin Vaculik was the only rider to offer real assistance to the Polish imports with Martin Malek struggling.

AK Slany
Petr Babicka, Michal Dudek, Sebastian Ulamek, Martin Vaculik, Adrian Pluska, Martin Malek and coach Milan Mach

Rider	M	R	Pts	BP	TPts	Ave	F	P	TR	TPts
Karol ZABIK	1	5	17	0	17	13.60	0	0	0	0
Sebastian ULAMEK	**1**	**6**	**16**	**0**	**16**	**10.67**	**0**	**0**	**1**	**3**
Slawomir DRABIK	1	6	13	0	13	8.67	0	0	0	0
Mariusz PUSZAKOWSKI	**1**	**6**	**12**	**0**	**12**	**8.00**	**0**	**0**	**1**	**3**
Martin VACULIK	4	24	40	0	40	6.67	0	0	1	0
Martin MALEK	**4**	**22**	**20**	**0**	**20**	**3.64**	**0**	**0**	**0**	**0**
Adrian PLUSKA	3	13	7	0	7	2.15	0	0	0	0
Patrik LINHART	**1**	**4**	**1**	**0**	**1**	**1.00**	**0**	**0**	**0**	**0**
Michal DUDEK	4	13	1	0	1	0.31	0	0	0	0

Non-riding appearances: Petr BABICKA (4).

See page 541 for further Track information

DENMARK

DANISH CHAMPIONSHIP

NICKI Pedersen regained his domestic crown after missing out on the Danish Championship in 2007– – claiming his fifth title.

The destination of the title wasn't decided until the 42nd race when he took the Grand Final ahead of chief challenger Hans Andersen.

Andersen got the best of their first meeting in the opening race of the first leg of the Final.

But that was the only time in four clashes that the Danish skipper came out on top although both were, surprisingly, beaten by Niels-Kristian Iversen in Heat 17 of the second leg.

The top six riders in the first leg of the Final were offered spots in the 2009 Grand Prix qualifying tournament but Nicki Pedersen and Hans Andersen turned down the places which went to the seventh and eighth placed riders at Holsted.

Overall

1 Nicki PEDERSEN 31, 2 Hans ANDERSEN 28, 3 Niels-Kristian IVERSEN 26, 4 Kenneth BJERRE 22, 5 Mads KORNELIUSSEN 22, 6 Nicolai KLINDT 18, 7 Patrick HOUGAARD 17, 8 Jesper B. MONBERG 17, 9 Charlie GJEDDE 15, 10 Henning BAGER 12, 11 Claus VISSING 12, 12 Ulrich ØSTERGAARD 9, 13 Leon MADSEN 7, 14 Dannie SØDERHOLM 5, 15 Klaus JAKOBSEN 3, 16 Peter Juul LARSEN 2, Henrik MOLLER 0.

Final, First leg
Holsted, Sunday, May 17

	1	*2*	*3*	*4*	*5*	*Tot*	*RO*	*F*
1 Nicki PEDERSEN	**2**	**3**	**3**	**3**	**3**	**14**		**3**
2 Hans ANDERSEN	3	3	2	3	3	14		2
3 Niels-Kristian IVERSEN	3	1	3	3	2	12		1
4 Mads KORNELIUSSEN	3	2	3	0	3	11		0
5 Kenneth BJERRE	2	2	3	2	2	11		
6 Jesper B. MONBERG	1	0	2	3	3	9	3	
7 Charlie GJEDDE	2	2	2	1	2	9	2	
8 Nicolai KLINDT	3	1	2	2	1	9	1	
9 Patrick HOUGAARD	2	3	0	2	1	8		
10 Henning BAGER	1	3	1	1	1	7		
11 Leon MADSEN	1	1	1	1	1	5		
12 Claus VISSING	0	0	0	2	2	4		
13 Ulrich ØSTERGAARD	0	2	1	0	0	3		
14 Dannie SØDERHOLM	1	1	1	0	0	3		
15 Klaus JAKOBSEN	0	0	0	1	0	1		
16 Peter Juul LARSEN	0	0	0	0	0	0		
17 Henrik MOLLER [R]	0					0		

Final, Second leg
Outrup, Friday, August 8

	1	*2*	*3*	*4*	*5*	*Tot*	*RO*	*F*
1 NICKI PEDERSEN	**3**	**3**	**3**	**3**	**2**	**14**		**3**
2 Niels Kristian IVERSEN	3	1	2	3	3	12		2
3 Hans ANDERSEN	3	3	3	3	1	13		1
4 Kenneth BJERRE	1	3	3	2	2	11		0
5 Mads KORNELIUSSEN	2	2	1	3	3	11		
6 Patrick HOUGAARD	1	3	0	2	3	9		
7 Nicolai KLINDT	3	1	2	2	1	9		
8 Jesper B. MONBERG	2	2	0	1	3	8		
9 Claus VISSING	2	2	1	2	1	8		
10 Ulrich STERGAARD	0	1	2	1	2	6		
11 Charlie GJEDDE	0	2	2	0	2	6		
12 Henning BAGER	0	1	3	0	1	5		
13 Klaus JAKOBSEN	2	0	0	0	0	2		
14 Peter Juul LARSEN	1	0	1	0	0	2		
15 Leon MADSEN	0	0	1	1	0	2		
16 Dannie SØDERHOLM	1	0	0	1	0	2		
17 Henrik MOLLER [R]	0	0	0			0		

Semi Final
Grindsted, Monday, May 5

Charlie Gjedde 14, Ulrich Østergaard 11, Leon Madsen 11, Peter Juul Larsen 10, Henning Bager 9, Nicolai Klindt 9, Claus Vissing 9, Dannie Søderholm 8+3, Klaus Jakobsen 8+2, Henrik Moller 7, Morten Risager 6, Anders Andersen 5, Jan Graversen 5, Patrick Nørgaard 4, Jesper Kristiansen 3, Kenneth Hansen 1.

Roll of Honour

1931 .... Erik ENGSTROM
1947 .... Orla KNUDSEN
1948 .... Bent JENSEN
1949 .... Orla KNUDSEN
1950 .... Svend NISSEN
1951 .... Kiehn BERTHELSEN
1952 .... Leif BECH
1953 .... Kiehn BERTHELSEN
1954 .... Leif BECH
1955 .... Kiehn BERTHELSEN

1956 .... Arena PANDER
1957 .... Sven NISSEN
1958 .... Arne PANDER
1959 .... Erik KASTEBO
1960 .... Kurt Walter PEDERSEN
1961 .... Kurt Walter PEDERSEN
1962 .... Kurt Walter PEDERSEN
1963 .... Kurt Walter PEDERSEN
1964 .... H.P. BOISEN
1965 .... Erik KASTEBO
1966 .... Godtfred ANDREASEN
1967 .... Ole OLSEN
1968 .... Ole OLSEN
1969 .... Ole OLSEN
1970 .... Ole OLSEN
1971 .... Ole OLSEN
1972 .... Ole OLSEN
1973 .... Ole OLSEN
1974 .... Bent NØRREGAARD Jensen
1975 .... Ole OLSEN
1976 .... Ole OLSEN
1977 .... Ole OLSEN
1978 .... Hans NIELSEN
1979 .... Ole OLSEN
1980 .... Bo PETERSEN
1981 .... Ole OLSEN
1982 .... Hans NIELSEN
1983 .... Erik GUNDERSEN
1984 .... Erik GUNDERSEN
1985 .... Erik GUNDERSEN
1986 .... Erik GUNDERSEN
1987 .... Hans NIELSEN
1988 .... Jan O. PEDERSEN
1989 .... Erik GUNDERSEN
1990 .... Hans NIELSEN
1991 .... Jan O. PEDERSEN
1992 .... Gert HANDBERG
1993 .... Hans NIELSEN
1994 .... Hans NIELSEN
1995 .... Brian ANDERSEN
1996 .... Brian KARGER
1997 .... Tommy KNUDSEN
1998 .... Brian KARGER
1999 .... Brian ANDERSEN
2000 .... Brian KARGER
2001 .... Hans CLAUSEN
2002 .... Nicki PEDERSEN
2003 .... Nicki PEDERSEN
2004 .... Bjarne PEDERSEN
2005 .... Nicki PEDERSEN
2006 .... Nicki PEDERSEN
2007 .... Hans ANDERSEN
2008 .... Nicki PEDERSEN

The majority of Danish tracks do not officially record track length or track records in their programme information even though times are announced at meetings.

Riders themselves have asked for this information but it has not usually been forthcoming from club officials!

Where known these details have been included in the track-by-track information on the following pages.

If any reader has a collective or individual list of this information we would be grateful if they could contact us so it can be included in all future editions of the World Speedway Yearbook.

DANISH UNDER 21 CHAMPIONSHIP

FINAL

Fjelsted, Sunday, August 17

NICOLAI Klindt dropped just one point on his way to a second Danish Under 21 victory.

Beaten by exciting newcomer Rene Bach in the second of the two semi finals, he made no mistake at Fjelsted.

After stringing together five conclusive heat wins in the qualifying races, he regained his title with success over Patrick Hougaard, Peter Kildemand and 18-year-old surprise package Bach in the Grand Final.

Eleven of the 16 finalists had or were to shortly have experience of racing in the UK.

	1	2	3	4	5	Tot	F
1 Nicolai KLINDT	**3**	**3**	**3**	**3**	**3**	**15**	**3**
2 Patrick HOUGAARD	3	3	1	3	2	12	2
3 Peter KILDEMAND	2	1	3	2	3	11	1
4 René BACH	3	3	3	1	1	11	0
5 Morten RISAGER	3	3	1	3	0	10	
6 Leon MADSEN	1	2	2	2	2	9	
7 Krister JACOBSEN	2	1	3	0	2	8	
8 Kenneth HANSEN	2	0	2	1	3	8	
9 Kenni Arendt LARSEN	1	2	2	1	1	7	
10 Jan GRAVERSEN	1	1	0	3	1	6	
11 Dannie SØDERHOLM	0	1	0	2	2	5	
12 Peter Juul LARSEN	0	0	2	2	0	4	
13 Steffen JESPERSEN	1	2	0	0		3	
14 Patrick NØRGAARD	0	2	1	0	0	3	
15 Klaus JAKOBSEN	2	0	0	0	1	3	
16 Simon NIELSEN [R]	3					3	
17 Anders ANDERSEN	0	0	1	1	0	2	
18 Tommy PEDERSEN [R]	did not ride						

Semi Final

Holstebro, Saturday, July 26

Kenni Arendt Larsen 14, Krister Jacobsen 12, Jan Graversen 12, Peter Kildemand 11, Steffen Jespersen 11, Peter Juul Larsen 11, Dannie Søderholm 9+3, Steffen Andersen 9+F, Claes Nedermark 8, Tommy Pedersen 6, Jeppe Schmidt 5, Ricco Niewick 4, Chris H. Jacobsen 3,

Dennis Spicker Thøstesen 3, Simon Frahm 1, Jesper Kristiansen 0.

Semi Final

Holstebro, Saturday, July 26

Nicolai Klindt 14, Morten Risager 13, Kenneth Hansen 11, Anders Andersen 11, Leon Madsen 11, René Bach 11, Patrick Nørgaard 10+3, Simon Nielsen 10+2, Klaus Jakobsen 6, Patrick Bjerregard 5, Michael Vissing 5, Nicki Barrett 5, Morten Frahm 3, Michael Palm Toft 3, Mads Kobak 1, Morten Ludvigsen 0.

The two semi finals were run on the same day at Holstebro.

Roll of Honour

1965 .... Ole OLSEN
1966 .... Hans Walter JOHANSSON
1967 .... Bent NØRREGAARD Jensen
1968 .... Preben ROSENKILDE
1969 .... Bent LARSEN
1970 .... Niels Schelde HANSEN
1971 .... Ervin Juul HANSEN
1972 .... Ole HERMANSEN
1973 .... Finn THOMSEN
1974 .... Michael LOHMANN
1975 .... Finn Rune JENSEN
1976 .... Hans NIELSEN
1977 .... Erik GUNDERSEN
1978 .... Tommy KNUDSEN
1979 .... Hans Albert KLINGE
1980 .... John ESKILDSEN
1981 .... Sam NIKOLAJSEN
1982 .... Erik HOLM
1983 .... Aksel JEPSEN
1984 .... Jan JAKOBSEN
1985 .... Ole HANSEN
1986 .... Gert HANDBERG
1987 .... Kenneth ARNFRED
1988 .... Jan MIKKELSEN
1989 .... John JØRGENSEN
1990 .... Bo ERIKSEN
1991 .... Kim BRANDT
1992 .... Ronni PEDERSEN
1993 .... Carsten HANSEN
1994 .... Klaus RASMUSSEN
1995 .... Charlie GJEDDE
1996 .... Hans ANDERSEN
1997 .... Claus KRISTENSEN
1998 .... Ronnie HENNINGSEN
1999 .... Mads KORNELIUSSEN
2000 .... Kenneth BJERRE
2001 .... Sabrina BØGH
2002 .... Niels-Kristian IVERSEN
2003 .... Kenneth BJERRE
2004 .... Kenneth BJERRE
2005 .... Kenneth BJERRE
2006 .... Nicolai KLINDT
2007 .... Patrick HOUGAARD
2008 .... Nicolai KLINDT

When Sabrina Bøgh won the 2001 Danish Under 21 Championship on her home track at Holsted she became the first female rider to win a national title anywhere in the world.

She was crowned champion with a 15 point maximum and was actually one of two girls in the meeting, Maria Mobjerg finished tenth.

The line-up included Ulrich Østergaard (who was third) and Steen Jensen who had a short spell riding for Eastbourne in the Elite League.

Sabrina had made her Danish Under 21 Final debut the previous season when she was 14th with three points.

Winner of that season's final was Kenneth Bjerre, who qualified as a regular for the 2009 Grand Prix series.

Sabrina also became the first female to qualify for a major championship final, reaching the 2001 European Under 19 Final at Pardubice, Czech Republic.

She scored two points – four last places and a second – to finish 15th, ahead of Russian Renat Gafurov.

Among her rivals in the pits that day were Bjerre, Krzysztof Kasprzak, Niels-Kristian Iversen and reserve Matej Zagar, all of whom went on to reach the Grand Prix series.

Sabrina retired shortly after her appearance in the European Under 19 Final and never went on to a higher standard despite her pedigree and past record.

Individual

EUROPEAN UNDER 19 CHAMPIONSHIP

Nordic Final

Fjelsted, Friday, June 16

Patrick Hougaard 14, Peter Kildemand 13, Kim Nilsson 11, Jonas Messing 10+3, Simon Nielsen 10+2, Linus Eklöf 10+1, Dennis Andersson 10+0, Peter Juul Larsen 9, Linus Sundström 8, Nicklas Larsson 7, Patrick Nørgaard 5, Klaus Jakobsen 4, Niko Siltaniemi 4, Jari Mäkinen 3, Kalle Katajisto 1, Tord Solberg 0. Rene Bach [R], Nicky Barrett [R] did not ride.

For full details of the European Under 19 Championship see Europe (page 53).

ERIK JENSEN 50 YEAR JUBILEE

Herning, Friday, April 18

1 Nicki Pedersen 3+3, 2 Jesper B. Monberg 2+2, 3 Henning Bager 2+1, 4 Anders Andersen 3+0, 5 Niels-Kristian Iversen 1, Peter Juul Larsen 1, 7 Ulrich Østergaard 0, 8 Daniel Pytel X^2.

Uhre Best Pairs

Herning, Friday, April 18

1 Sebastian Ulamok 17 & Kjelle Greve 4 = 21, 2 Henning Bager 14 & Peter Juul Larsen 6+3 = 20+3, 3 Nicki Pedersen 18 & Mads Skov 2+2 = 20+2, 4 Jesper B. Monberg 15 & Tommy Pedersen 5+1 = 20+1, 5 Niels-Kristian Iversen 13 & Simon Nielsen 3 = 16, 6 Ulrich Østergaard 10 & Carsten Hansen 4 = 14, 7 Daniel Pytel 8 & Anders Andersen 6 = 14.

Danish Speedway League

BROVST

2008 RESULTS

Final position...Sixth

OUTRUP (A)
Wednesday, May 14
Lost 40-44
Zabik 11, Østergaard 13:1, Mikolajczak 6, Nørgaard 7:1 [8:2), Trasborg 3:2.
■ Result amended from 41-43 because of using ineligible Patrick Nørgaard in heat 13. His point deducted from final score and Steffen Andersen upgraded by one point.

GRINDSTED (A)
Monday, May 19
Won 44-40
Kosciecha 6, Nieminen 13:1, Rempala 11:1, Nørgaard 14:2, Trasborg 0.

HOLSTED (H)
Wednesday, May 21
Lost 39-48
Kosciecha 17:1 (6), Østergaard 11:1, Rempala 5, Georgsen 2, Trasborg 4:1.

HOLSTED (A)
Wednesday, May 28
Won 44-40
Dobrucki 14, Nieminen 11:1, Østergaard 8:3, Nørgaard 10:2, Trasborg 1.
Aggregate: Lost 83-88 .

OUTRUP (H)
Wednesday, June 4
Won 27-24
Zabik 13:1, Henrik Vedel [G] 3, Østergaard 9:1, Nørgaard 2, Trasborg 0.
Abandoned after eight heats, result stands.
Aggregate: Lost 67-68.

ESBJERG (A)
Wednesday, June 11
Lost 39-48
Zabik 6:1, Rempala 16:1, Østergaard 15:1, Rene Madsen [G] 0, Lasse Jensen [G] 2.

GRINDSTED (H)
Wednesday, June 18
Won 46-39
Østergaard 13:2, Mikolajczak 12:1, Klaus Jakobsen [G] 8:3, Nørgaard 13:1, Georgsen 0.
Aggregate: Won 90-79.

TRACK FILE

Track: Brovst Speedway Club, Over Søen 10, 9460 Brovst, Denmark.
Telephone: 0045 98235452.
Website: www.brovst-speedway-club.dk

SQUAD
Mads Georgsen, Patrick Nørgaard, Ulrich Østergaard, Jeppe Schmidt, Jens Trasborg.
Foreign: Rafal Dobrucki, Robert Kosciecha, Robert Mikolajczak, Kauko Nieminen, Jacek Rempala, Karol Zabik.

FJELSTED (A)
Wednesday, June 25
Won 42-41
Dobrucki 15, Østergaard 9, Nieminen 8:3, Nørgaard 8:3, Georgsen 2.

ESBJERG (H)
Wednesday, July 2
Won 47-39
Zabik 13:1, Østergaard 12:2, Nieminen 11:1, Norgaard 11:3, Georgsen 0.
Aggregate: Lost 86-87.

SLANGERUP (H)
Wednesday, August 6
Lost 42-45
Zabik 16:1, Østergaard 9:1, Nieminen 8:3, Nørgaard 9:1, Georgsen 0.

HOLSTEBRO (H)
Wednesday, August 20
Won 46-38
Adrian Miedzinski [G] 14:1, Nørgaard 9, Østergaard 10:1, Mikolajczak 10, Schmidt 3:1.

HOLSTEBRO (A)
Friday, September 17
Lost 37-49
Charlie Gjedde [G] 14 (4), Nørgaard 9:2, Østergaard 7:1, Klaus Jakobsen [G] 5:1, Schmidt 2:1.
Aggregate: Lost 83-87.

SLANGERUP (A)
Wednesday, September 24
Lost 31-56
Østergaard 13, Mikolajczak 6:1, Rempala 7:1, Schmidt 5:1, Jørgen Krogh [G] 0.
Aggregate: Lost 73-101.

FJELSTED (H)
Friday, October 3
Lost 40-47
Nieminen 16:1, Nørgaard 11:1, Østergaard 8:1, Mikolajczak 4:1, Schmidt 1.
Aggregate: Lost 82-88.

DANISH LEAGUE

	M	W	D	L	PTsF	PtsA	BP	TPts
Slangerup	14	11	0	3	660	538	7	43
Esbjerg	14	8	1	5	645	558	5	36
Holsted	14	8	1	5	602	591	4	35
Fjelsted	14	5	0	9	601	594	5	29
Grindsted	14	6	0	8	592	609	3	29
BROVST	**14**	**6**	**0**	**8**	**582**	**616**	**1**	**27**
Holstebro	14	6	0	8	565	624	1	27
Outrup	14	5	0	9	542	659	2	26

Brovst's glory days – when Hans Nielsen was their top man – are long gone but they will be anxious to improve on their sixth place.

They have kept changes to a minimum and will be tracking the bulk of their 2008 side which won only four of their seven home matches.

Rafal Dobrucki, Karol Zabik and Ulrich Østergaard are all back along with Adrian Miedzinski who made one guest appearance for them last year.

Rider	*M*	*R*	*Pts*	*BP*	*TPts*	*Ave*	*F*	*P*	*TR*	*TPts*
Rafal DOBRUCKI	2	12	29	0	29	9.67	0	0	0	0
Kauko NIEMINEN	**6**	**37**	**70**	**9**	**79**	**8.54**	**0**	**0**	**1**	**3**
Karol ZABIK	5	30	59	4	63	8.40	0	0	2	6
Ulrich ØSTERGAARD	**13**	**79**	**134**	**15**	**149**	**7.54**	**0**	**0**	**1**	**3**
Patrick NØRGAARD	11	65	104	17	121	7.45	0	0	0	0
Robert KOSCIECHA	**2**	**13**	**23**	**1**	**24**	**7.38**	**0**	**0**	**1**	**3**
Jacek REMPALA	4	26	39	3	42	6.46	0	0	0	0
Robert MIKOLAJCZAK	**5**	**29**	**38**	**3**	**41**	**4.00**	**0**	**0**	**0**	**0**
Jeppe SCHMIDT	4	14	11	3	14	4.00	0	0	0	0
Jens TRASBORG	**5**	**18**	**8**	**3**	**11**	**2.44**	**0**	**0**	**0**	**0**
Mads GEORGSEN	5	19	4	0	4	0.84	0	0	0	0
Guests										
Adrian MIEDZINSKI	1	6	14	1	15	10.00	0	0	0	0
Charlie GJEDDE	**1**	**7**	**14**	**0**	**14**	**8.00**	**0**	**0**	**1**	**2**
Klaus JAKOBSEN	2	11	13	4	17	6.18	0	0	0	0
Henrik VEDEL	**1**	**4**	**3**	**0**	**3**	**3.00**	**0**	**0**	**0**	**0**
Lasse Raun JENSEN	1	4	2	0	2	2.00	0	0	0	0
Rene MADSEN	**1**	**3**	**0**	**0**	**0**	**0.00**	**0**	**0**	**0**	**0**
Jørgen KROGH	1	3	0	0	0	0.00	0	0	0	0

For Jacek REMPALA see also Holstebro.

Jan Graversen is back with Brovst in 2009

2009 FIXTURES

Wednesday, April 22 .... Esbjerg (a)
Wednesday, May 6 .... Vojens (a)
Wednesday, May 13 .... Slangerup (a)
Wednesday, May 20 .... SLANGERUP (H)
Wednesday, June 3 .... ESBJERG (H)
Wednesday, June 10 .... Fjelsted (a)
Wednesday, June 17 .... GRINDSTED (H)
Wednesday, July 1 .... VOJENS (H)
Wednesday, August 5 .... FJELSTED (H)
Wednesday, August 19 .... Holsted (a)
Wednesday, August 26 .... HOLSTED (H)
Wednesday, September 2 .... HOLSTEBRO (H)
Monday, September 14 .... Grindsted (a)
Wednesday, September 20 .... Holstebro (a)

2009 SQUAD

A – Rafal DOBRUCKI, Adrian MIEDZINSKI, Ulrich ØSTERGAARD, Karol ZABIK.
B – Jan GRAVERSEN, Leon MADSEN, Robert MIKOLAJCZAK, Daniel PYTEL.
C – Christian AGÖ, Jari MÄKINEN.
D – Thomas JØRGENSEN.

Danish Speedway League

ESBJERG

2008 RESULTS

Final position....................................Second

SLANGERUP (H)
Wednesday, April 23
Won 46-38
Bjerre 14, Lyngsø 12:2, Korneliussen 12, Jacobsen 7:1, Nilsson 1.

FJELSTED (A)
Wednesday, April 30
Won 55-31
Bjerre 14:1, Lyngsø 12:1, **Korneliussen 17:1**, Jacobsen 11:3, Nilsson 1.

FJELSTED (H)
Wednesday, May 21
Won 46-41
Bjerre 5, Lyngsø 10:1, Korneliussen 16, Jacobsen 7:2, Nilsson 8:1.
Aggregate: Won 101-72.

OUTRUP (A)
Wednesday, May 28
Won 52-35
Korneliussen 18, Kröger 8:1, Lyngso 14:2, Jacobsen 11, Kikkenborg 1.

BROVST (H)
Wednesday, June 11
Won 48-39
Korneliussen 11:1, Kröger 7:1, **Lyngsø 18**, Jacobsen 10, Kikkenborg 2.

HOLSTED (A)
Wednesday, June 18
Lost 38-46
Bjerre 11:1, Kröger 3, Lyngsø 14, Jacobsen 9:2, Nilsson 1.

GRINDSTED (H)
Wednesday, June 25
Won 54-33
Kosciuch 11:3, **Lyngsø 16:2**, Korneliussen 13:1, Jacobsen 9:2, Nilsson 5:1.

BROVST (A)
Wednesday, July 2
Lost 39-47
Kosciuch 16:3 (4), Henrik Vedel [G] 2, Korneliussen 13, Kikkenborg 3:1, Nilsson 5:2.
Aggregate: Won 87-86.

TRACK FILE

Track: Korskro Motorcentrum, Tinghedevej, 6715 Esbjerg, Denmark.
Telephone: 0045 51328032.
Website: www.esbjergmotorsport.dk
Track length: 310 metres.

SQUAD
Kenneth Bjerre, Krister Jacobsen, Johannes Kikkenborg, Mads Korneliussen, Brian Lyngsø, Bjarne Nilsson.
Foreign: Tobias Busch, Norbert Kosciuch, Mathias Kröger, Kevin Wölbert.

GRINDSTED (A)
Monday, August 4
Lost 40-46
Adam Skornicki [G] 17, Tobias Busch 13:1, Klaus Jakobsen [G] 3, Jacobsen 3, Nilsson 4:2.
Aggregate: Won 94-79.

OUTRUP (H)
Wednesday, August 27
Won 56-30
Bjerre 17:1, **Busch 15:3**, Lyngsø 13:2, Nilsson 3:1, Kikkenborg 8.
Aggregate: Won 108-70.

SLANGERUP (A)
Wednesday, September 3
Lost 38-48
Kosciuch 14 (4), Busch 8:1, Lyngsø 6, Jacobsen 9:1, Nilsson 1:1.
Aggregate: Lost 84-86.

HOLSTEBRO (A)
Sunday, September 7
Lost 42-45
Bjerre 15, Kikkenborg 4:2, Wölbert 8, Manuel Hauzinger [G] 10:1, Nilsson 5:1.

HOLSTEBRO (H)
Wednesday, September 10
Won 49-37
Bjerre 17:1, Busch 10, Korneliussen 10, Jacobsen 5, Nilsson 7:2.
Aggregate: Won 91-82.

HOLSTED (H)
Wednesday, September 17
Drew 42-42
Bjerre 13, Kevin Wölbert 12:1, Korneliussen 9:1, Kikkenborg 3:1, Nilsson 5:1.
Aggregate: Lost 80-88.

DANISH LEAGUE

	M	W	D	L	PTsF	PtsA	BP	TPts
Slangerup	14	11	0	3	660	538	7	43
ESBJERG	**14**	**8**	**1**	**5**	**645**	**558**	**5**	**36**
Holsted	14	8	1	5	602	591	4	35
Fjelsted	14	5	0	9	601	594	5	29
Grindsted	14	6	0	8	592	609	3	29
Brovst	14	6	0	8	582	616	1	27
Holstebro	14	6	0	8	565	624	1	27
Outrup	14	5	0	9	542	659	2	26

After finishing runners-up in 2008, Esbjerg were determined to build a side that can take over top spot.

They had talks with both Jason Crump and Greg Hancock and when they turned down contracts successfully switched their sights to Tomasz Gollob who has agreed to ride in three matches.

Having lost Kenneth Bjerre to Vojens they have brought in a more than adequate replacement in Niels-Kristian Iversen but it is Gollob's arrival that will attract all the attention and publicity.

Rider	M	R	Pts	BP	TPts	Ave	F	P	TR	TPts
Kenneth BJERRE	8	44	106	4	110	10.00	0	2	0	0
Brian LYNGSØ	**9**	**52**	**115**	**8**	**123**	**9.46**	**1**	**1**	**0**	**0**
Norbert KOSCIUCH	3	20	41	6	47	9.40	0	0	2	4
Mads KORNELIUSSEN	**9**	**54**	**119**	**4**	**123**	**9.11**	**1**	**1**	**0**	**0**
Tobias BUSCH	4	26	46	5	51	7.85	0	1	0	0
Krister JACOBSEN	**10**	**55**	**81**	**13**	**94**	**6.84**	**0**	**0**	**0**	**0**
Kevin WÖLBERT	2	12	20	1	21	7.00	0	0	0	0
Mathias KRÖGER	**3**	**17**	**18**	**3**	**21**	**4.94**	**0**	**0**	**0**	**0**
Bjarne NILSSON	12	60	46	12	58	3.87	0	0	0	0
Johannes KIKKENBORG	**6**	**29**	**21**	**4**	**25**	**3.45**	**0**	**0**	**0**	**0**
Guests										
Adam SKORNICKI	1	7	17	0	17	9.71	0	0	0	0
Manuel HAUZINGER	**1**	**6**	**10**	**1**	**11**	**7.33**	**0**	**0**	**0**	**0**
Klaus JAKOBSEN	1	5	3	0	3	2.67	0	0	0	0
Henrik VEDEL	**1**	**3**	**2**	**0**	**2**	**2.67**	**0**	**0**	**0**	**0**

Top scorer Kenneth Bjerre

2009 FIXTURES

Wednesday, April 22 ....BROVST (H)
Wednesday, May 6....................................Fjelsted (a)
Wednesday, May 20 ....FJELSTED (H)
Wednesday, May 27 ....Vojens (a)
Wednesday, June 3 ....Brovst (a)
Wednesday, June 10 ....HOLSTEBRO (H)
Wednesday, June 17.....................GRINDSTED (H)
Friday, July 3 ....Holstebro (a)
Monday, August 10 ....Grindsted (a)
Wednesday, August 19 ....VOJENS (H)
Wednesday, August 26 ....SLANGERUP (H)
Wednesday, September 2 ....Holsted (a)
Wednesday, September 16................HOLSTED (H)
Wednesday, September 20....................Holstebro (a)

2009 SQUAD

A – Niels-Kristian IVERSEN, Mads KORNELIUSSEN, Norbert KOSCIUCH.
B – Tobias BUSCH, Manuel HAUZINGER, Krister JACOBSEN, Adam KAJOCH, Brian LYNGSØ.
C – Johannes KIKKENBORG, Bjarne NILSSON, Dannie SØDERHOLM.

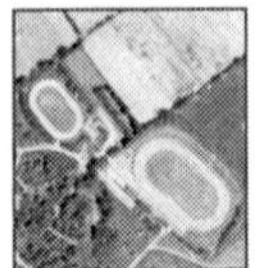

Danish Speedway League

FJELSTED

2008 RESULTS

Final position ....Fourth

HOLSTEBRO (A)
Sunday, April 27
Lost 38-48
Trojanowski 16 (6), Vissing 12:1, Hauzinger 7:1, Kildemand 1, Barrett 2.

ESBJERG (H)
Wednesday, April 30
Lost 31-55
Trojanowski 14 (4), Vissing 7:2, Hauzinger 1, Bach 4:1, Barrett 5.

SLANGERUP (H)
Wednesday, May 14
Lost 41-43
Andersen 18, Bach 8:1, Nowaczyk 7:2, Kildemand 6, Barrett 2.

ESBJERG (A)
Wednesday, May 21
Lost 41-46
Ulamek 21:1 (6), Kajoch 8, Hauzinger 4:1, Kildemand 7:1, Barrett 1.
Aggregate: Lost 72-101.

GRINDSTED (H)
Wednesday, May 28
Won 54-33
Andersen 18, Klaus Jakobsen [G] 6:1, Vissing 13:3, Bach 10:2, Barrett 7.

HOLSTED (A)
Wednesday, June 4
Lost 40-44
Ulamek 16, Bach 6:3, Kajoch 7:2, Kildemand 10:1, Barrett 1:1.

GRINDSTED (A)
Monday, June 9
Lost 39-47
Ulamek 14, Bach 5, Kajoch 5:1, Kildemand 3, Barrett 12:1 (6).
Aggregate: Won 93-80.

Outrup's Piotr Protasiewicz was the only rider to lower Hans Andersen's colours in his four Danish League outings for Fjelsted. Hans was unbeaten in three matches but finished behind the Pole in Heat 7 of the clash on August 6.

TRACK FILE

Track: Hele Fyns Speedwaycenter, Ridderstien 31, Harndrup, Denmark 5463.
Telephone: 0045 64881617.
Website: www.fjelsted-speedway.dk

SQUAD
Hans Andersen, René Bach, Nicki Barrett, Peter Kildemand, Claus Vissing.
Foreign: Manuel Hauzinger, Adam Kajoch, Marcin Nowaczyk, Rafal Trojanowski, Sebastian Ulamek.

SLANGERUP (A)
Wednesday, June 18
Lost 36-51
Ulamek 17 (6), Jan Graversen [G] 6, Vissing 6, Bach 6:2, Barrett 1.
Aggregate: Lost 77-94.

BROVST (H)
Wednesday, June 25
Lost 41-42
Ulamek 15, Kildemand 6:1, Vissing 8:1, Bach 4:1, Barrett 8:1.

OUTRUP (A)
Wednesday, July 30
Won 52-34
Andersen 16:2, Bach 14, Vissing 11, Kildemand 7:2, Barrett 4:1.

OUTRUP (H)
Wednesday, August 6
Lost 42-44
Andersen 16:1, Jan Graversen [G] 7:1, Vissing 9, Bach 7, Barrett 3.
Aggregate: Won 94-78.

HOLSTEBRO (H)
Wednesday, August 27
Won 48-32
Ulamek 11, Bach 8:1, **Vissing 17:1**, Kildemand 10:2, Barrett 2.
Aggregate: Won 86-80.

BROVST A)
Friday, September 3
Won 47-40
Ulamek 18, Kildemand 8:1, Vissing 11:1, Barrett 0, Henrik Vedel [G] 10:2.
Aggregate: Won 88-82.

HOLSTED (H)
Wednesday, September 10
Won 51-35
Ulamek 18, Bach 11, Vissing 12:1, Kildemand 4:1, Dannie Søderholm [G] 6:1.
Aggregate: Won 91-79.

DANISH LEAGUE

	M	*W*	*D*	*L*	*PTsF*	*PtsA*	*BP*	*TPts*
Slangerup	14	11	0	3	660	538	7	43
Esbjerg	14	8	1	5	645	558	5	36
Holsted	14	8	1	5	602	591	4	35
FJELSTED	**14**	**5**	**0**	**9**	**601**	**594**	**5**	**29**
Grindsted	14	6	0	8	592	609	3	29
Brovst	14	6	0	8	582	616	1	27
Holstebro	14	6	0	8	565	624	1	27
Outrup	14	5	0	9	542	659	2	26

Fjelsted will have to carry the pre-season tag of the team most likely to finish with the wooden spoon having lost Hans Andersen during the winter.

Their A Grade riders are hardly of the same class or standing although Sebastian Ulamek had a superb 2008 at the club.

Fellow Pole Ronnie Jamrozy, though, is a poor replacement for the Denmark skipper.

Peter Kildemand, Claus Vissing and René Bach will have a huge job to do to bring any sort of success in League racing.

Rider	*M*	*R*	*Pts*	*BP*	*TPts*	*Ave*	*F*	*P*	*TR*	*TPts*
Hans ANDERSEN	4	24	68	3	71	11.83	2	1	1	2
Sebastian ULAMEK	**8**	**49**	**130**	**1**	**131**	**10.69**	**2**	**0**	**2**	**6**
Rafal TROJANOWSKI	2	14	30	0	30	8.57	0	0	2	5
Claus VISSING	**10**	**61**	**106**	**10**	**116**	**7.61**	**0**	**1**	**0**	**0**
Marcin NOWACZYK	1	6	7	2	9	6.00	0	0	0	0
Adam KAJOCH	**3**	**18**	**20**	**3**	**23**	**5.11**	**0**	**0**	**0**	**0**
Peter KILDEMAND	10	56	62	9	71	5.07	0	0	0	0
René BACH	**11**	**65**	**72**	**10**	**82**	**5.05**	**0**	**0**	**0**	**0**
Nicki BARRETT	13	55	48	5	53	3.85	0	0	1	3
Manuel HAUZINGER	**3**	**17**	**12**	**2**	**14**	**3.29**	**0**	**0**	**0**	**0**
Guests										
Henrik VEDEL	1	5	10	2	12	9.60	0	0	0	0
Klaus JAKOBSEN	**1**	**5**	**6**	**1**	**7**	**5.60**	**0**	**0**	**0**	**0**
Dannie SØDERHOLM	1	5	6	1	7	5.60	0	0	0	0
Jan GRAVERSEN	**2**	**12**	**13**	**1**	**14**	**4.67**	**0**	**0**	**0**	**0**

Hans Andersen will be missing from the 2009 line-up

2009 FIXTURES

Friday, April 24 .... Grindsted (a)
Wednesday, May 6 .... ESBJERG (H)
Friday, May 15 .... Holstebro (a)
Wednesday, May 20 .... Esbjerg (a)
Wednesday, May 27 .... HOLSTED (H)
Wednesday, June 10 .... BROVST (H)
Wednesday, June 17 .... Vojens (a)
Wednesday, June 24 .... SLANGERUP (H)
Wednesday, July 1 .... Holsted (a)
Wednesday, August 5 .... Brovst (a)
Wednesday, August 12 .... HOLSTEBRO (H)
Wednesday, August 26 .... GRINDSTED (H)
Wednesday, September 2 .... Slangerup (a)
Wednesday, September 9 .... VOJENS (H)

2009 SQUAD

A – Ronnie JAMROZY, Sebastian ULAMEK.
B – René BACH, Marcel KAJZER, Peter KILDEMAND, Marcin NOWACZYK, Hynek STICHAUER, Claus VISSING.
C – Nicki BARRETT, Maciej FAJFER.
D – Nicklas SONNE.

Danish Speedway League

GRINDSTED

2008 RESULTS

Final position .... Fifth

OUTRUP (H)
Monday, April 28
Won 47-38
Gustafsson 7:1, Kristiansen[2] 9:1, Bager 14:1, Andersen 9:1, Larsen 8:1.

HOLSTED (A)
Wednesday, April 30
Lost 41-45
Lindbäck 17 (6), Andersen 3, Kristiansen[2] 7, Petersen 6:3, Larsen 8:3.

SLANGERUP (A)
Wednesday, May 7
Lost 37-47
Laukkanen 9:2, Larsen 9, Kristiansen[2] 4:2, Andersen 8:1, Tero Aarnio [G] 7:1.

BROVST (H)
Monday, May 19
Lost 40-44
Bager 8:3, Larsen 11, Gustafsson 10:1, Kristiansen[2] 7:1, Andersen 4:1.

FJELSTED (A)
Wednesday, May 28
Lost 33-54
Bager 10, Larsen 11:1 (6), Kevin Wölbert [G] 6, Kristiansen[2] 4:2, Andersen 2.

FJELSTED (H)
Monday, June 9
Won 47-39
Joonas Kylmåkorpi [G] 13:1, Larsen 9:4, Gustafsson 13, Kristiansen[2] 10:1, Skov 2:1.
Aggregate: Lost 80-93.

BROVST (A)
Wednesday, June 18
Lost 39-46
Bager 12:1. Larsen 10 (2), Gustafsson 15:2, Kristiansen[2] 0, Andersen 2:1.
Aggregate: Lost 79-90.

ESBJERG (A)
Wednesday, June 25
Lost 33-54
Bager 7:2, Larsen 7, Kevin Wölbert [G] 14 (6), Kristiansen[2] 2, Andersen 3:1.

TRACK FILE

Track: Blbjergvej 1, 7200 Grindsted, Denmark.

Website: www.grindsted-speedway.dk

SQUAD
Henning Bager, Jesper Kristiansen[1], Peter Juul Larsen, Mads E. Skov.
Foreign: Henrik Gustafsson, Billy Janniro, Niklas Klingberg, Kaj Laukkanen, Antonio Lindbäck, Sönke Pedersen.

SLANGERUP (H)
Monday, June 30
Lost 42-44
Lindbäck 20 (6), Kevin Wölbert [G] 9:2, Gustafsson, did not ride, Larsen 8, Skov 5:2.
Aggregate: Lost 79-82.

ESBJERG (H)
Monday, August 4
Won 46-40
Gustafsson 6:2, Janniro 14, Bager 13:2, Larsen 7:2, Andersen 6:2.
Aggregate: Lost 79-94.

OUTRUP (A)
Wednesday, August 20
Won 49-38
Peter Ljung [G] 13:1, Bager 11:1, Gustafsson 13:1, Larsen 9:4, Skov 3:1.
Aggregate: Won 96-76.

HOLSTEBRO (A)
Sunday, August 24
Lost 41-43
Gustafsson 10:2, Janniro 14, Bager 10:2, Larsen 4:1, Petersen 3:3.

HOLSTED (H)
Monday, August 25
Won 47-40
Klingberg 11:1, Bager 15, Gustafsson 11:1, Larsen 9:1, Skov 1.
Aggregate: Won 88-85.

HOLSTEBRO (H)
Saturday, September 20
Won 50-37
Klingberg 12, Bager 15:1, Gustafsson 14:2, Larsen 6:1, Skov 3:2.
Aggregate: Won 91-80.

There are two licensed riders of the name Jesper KRISTIANSEN. See also Slangerup.

DANISH LEAGUE

	M	W	D	L	PTsF	PtsA	BP	TPts
Slangerup	14	11	0	3	660	538	7	43
Esbjerg	14	8	1	5	645	558	5	36
Holsted	14	8	1	5	602	591	4	35
Fjelsted	14	5	0	9	601	594	5	29
GRINDSTED	**14**	**6**	**0**	**8**	**592**	**609**	**3**	**29**
Brovst	14	6	0	8	582	616	1	27
Holstebro	14	6	0	8	565	624	1	27
Outrup	14	5	0	9	542	659	2	26

Grindsted celebrate their 25-year anniversary in 2009 and have brought in two big-hitters – Andreas Jonsson and Charlie Gjedde – to make it a season to remember.

They lacked a genuine number one in 2008 and have clearly tackled that particular subject with the dual signing of their two new A Grade stars.

They've plenty of experience lower down the order with Swedish veteran Henrik Gustafsson and new signing Robert Johansson on board as well as a return for Henning Bager.

Rider	*M*	*R*	*Pts*	*BP*	*TPts*	*Ave*	*F*	*P*	*TR*	*TPts*
Antonio LINDBÄCK	2	13	37	0	37	11.38	0	0	2	6
Billy JANNIRO	**2**	**12**	**28**	**0**	**28**	**9.33**	**0**	**0**	**0**	**0**
Henrik GUSTAFSSON	9	53	99	12	111	8.38	0	0	0	0
Henning BAGER	**10**	**62**	**115**	**13**	**128**	**8.26**	**0**	**0**	**0**	**0**
Niklas KLINGBERG	2	12	23	1	24	8.00	0	0	0	0
Kaj LAUKKANEN	**1**	**7**	**9**	**2**	**11**	**6.29**	**0**	**0**	**0**	**0**
Peter Juul LARSEN	14	86	116	18	134	6.23	0	0	2	4
Sönke PETERSEN	**2**	**10**	**9**	**6**	**15**	**6.00**	**0**	**0**	**0**	**0**
Anders ANDERSEN	8	35	37	7	44	5.03	0	0	0	0
Jesper KRISTIANSEN[1]	**8**	**42**	**43**	**7**	**50**	**4.76**	**0**	**0**	**0**	**0**
Mads E. SKOV	5	22	14	6	20	3.64	0	0	0	0
Guests										
Joonas KYLMÅKORPI	1	6	13	1	14	9.33	0	0	0	0
Peter LJUNG	**1**	**6**	**13**	**1**	**14**	**9.33**	**0**	**0**	**0**	**0**
Kevin WÖLBERT	2	12	20	0	20	6.67	0	0	0	0
Tero AARNIO	**1**	**6**	**7**	**1**	**8**	**5.33**	**0**	**0**	**0**	**0**

Henrik GUSTAFSSON was programmed in the meeting against Slangerup on Monday, June 30, but did not ride, his races being taken by the reserves.

Henning Bager scored 128 points for Grindsted

2009 FIXTURES

Friday, April 24 .... FJELSTED (H)
Monday, May 11 .... HOLSTEBRO (H)
Wednesday, May 20 .... Holsted (a)
Friday, May 29 .... HOLSTED (H)
Wednesday, June 3 .... Vojens (a)
Wednesday, June 10 .... Slangerup (a)
Friday, June 12 .... Holstebro (a)
Wednesday, June 17 .... Brovst (a)
Monday, June 29 .... SLANGERUP (H)
Monday, August 10 .... ESBJERG (H)
Wednesday, August 12 .... Esbjerg (a)
Wednesday, August 26 .... Fjelsted (a)
Friday, August 28 .... VOJENS (H)
Monday, September 14 .... BROVST (H)

2009 SQUAD

A – Charlie GJEDDE, Henrik GUSTAFSSON, Andreas JONSSON.
B – Henning BAGER, Robert JOHANSSON, Jesper KRISTIANSEN[1] Peter Juul LARSEN, Sönke PETERSEN.
C – Anders ANDERSEN, Steffen BREDAHL, Sebastian CARLSSON, Robert PETTERSSON.
D – Claus LAURIDSEN, Mads E. SKOV.

Danish Speedway League

HOLSTEBRO

2008 RESULTS

Final position..Seventh

FJELSTED (H)
Sunday, April 27
Won 48-38
Pedersen 17:1, Madsen 10:1, Bajerski 8:2, Larsen 8:2, Nedermark 5.

HOLSTED (H)
Sunday, May 18
Won 43-41
Adrian Miedzinski [G] 14, Madsen 11:1, Bajerski 5:2, Larsen 5, Nedermark 8:1.

SLANGERUP (A)
Wednesday, May 21
Lost 31-55
Ferjan 13 (4), Bajerski 6:1, Madsen 5:1, Larsen 6, Hansen 1.

OUTRUP (A)
Wednesday, June 18
Lost 37-48
David Ruud [G] 10:1, Schultz 11:1 (2), Madsen 8, Nedermark 4:2, Larsen 4.

OUTRUP (H)
Wednesday, June 25
Won 44-40
Pedersen 18, Nedermark 5:1, Schultz 11:2, Madsen 6, Larsen 4.
Aggregate: Lost 81-88.

SLANGERUP (H)
Wednesday, July 2
Lost 41-46
Ferjan 20 (6), Madsen 9:1, Schultz 3:2, Larsen 3, Nedermark 6:1.
Aggregate: Lost 72-101.

BROVST (A)
Wednesday, August 20
Lost 38-46
Ferjan 12, Madsen 10:2, Moller 5:1, Larsen 11, Vissing 0.

GRINDSTED (H)
Sunday, August 24
Won 43-41
Karpov 7:2, Rempala 10:1, Madsen 15, Larsen 11, Sørensen 0.

TRACK FILE

Track: Holstebro Speedway Stadion, Hesselåvej 41b, Skave, 7500 Holstebro, Denmark.
Website: www.hosk.dk

SQUAD
Morten Hansen, Kenni Arendt Larsen, Leon Madsen, Henrik Moller, Claes Nedermark, Bjarne Pedersen, Thomas Sørensen, Michael Vissing.
Foreign: Tomasz Bajerski, Matej Ferjan, Rafael Fleger, Andrey Karpov, Jacek Rempala, Mathias Schultz.

FJELSTED (A)
Wednesday, August 27
Lost 32-48
Karpov 8, Madsen 12:1, Schultz 3, Larsen 9, Vissing 0.
Aggregate: Lost 80-86.

ESBJERG (H)
Sunday, September 7
Won 45-42
Ferjan 20:1 (6), Moller 4:1, Madsen 10:2, Larsen 11:1, Vissing 0.

ESBJERG (A)
Wednesday, September 10
Lost 37-49
Rempala 9, Larsen 6, Madsen 8:2, Schultz 13:2 (4), Fleger 1.
Aggregate: Lost 82-91.

HOLSTED (A)
Monday, September 15
Lost 40-43
Pedersen 16, Madsen 8:1, Rempala 5:1, Larsen 9:1, Vissing 2.
Aggregate: Lost 83-84.

BROVST (H)
Wednesday, September 17
Won 49-37
Pedersen 18, Moller 4, Madsen 13:1, Larsen 14:1, Vissing 0.
Aggregate: Won 87-83.

GRINDSTED (A)
Saturday, September 20
Lost 37-50
Pedersen 12:1 (6), Moller 3:1, Madsen 14, Tommy Pedersen [G] 8, Per Lind [G] 0.
Aggregate: Lost 80-91.

DANISH LEAGUE

	M	W	D	L	PTsF	PtsA	BP	TPts
Slangerup	14	11	0	3	660	538	7	43
Esbjerg	14	8	1	5	645	558	5	36
Holsted	14	8	1	5	602	591	4	35
Fjelsted	14	5	0	9	601	594	5	29
Grindsted	14	6	0	8	592	609	3	29
Brovst	14	6	0	8	582	616	1	27
HOLSTEBRO	**14**	**6**	**0**	**8**	**565**	**624**	**1**	**27**
Outrup	14	5	0	9	542	659	2	26

Bjarne Pedersen has been Holstebro's skipper since they returned to league racing in 2007 and is back for another season.

He's been joined by newcomers Marcin Sekula, Tommy Pedersen, German teenager Rene Deddens and Michael Vissing.

But perhaps most attention will be focused on Claes Nedermark who was the highest ranked D Grade rider in 2008 and has, as a result, been notched up to a C grade for 2009.

Kenni Larsen is also someone to improve yet again.

Rider	*M*	*R*	*Pts*	*BP*	*TPts*	*Ave*	*F*	*P*	*TR*	*TPts*
Bjarne PEDERSEN	5	30	81	2	83	11.07	2	1	1	3
Matej FERJAN	**4**	**27**	**65**	**1**	**66**	**9.78**	**0**	**0**	**3**	**8**
Leon MADSEN	14	87	139	13	152	6.99	0	0	1	0
Jacek REMPALA	**3**	**17**	**24**	**2**	**26**	**6.18**	**0**	**0**	**0**	**0**
Mathias SCHULTZ	5	32	41	7	48	6.00	0	0	1	1
Kenni Arendt LARSEN	**13**	**72**	**101**	**4**	**105**	**5.83**	**0**	**0**	**0**	**0**
Claes NEDERMARK	5	24	28	5	33	5.50	0	0	0	0
Tomasz BAJERSKI	**3**	**18**	**19**	**5**	**24**	**5.33**	**0**	**0**	**0**	**0**
Andrey KARPOV	2	13	15	2	17	5.23	0	0	0	0
Henrik MOLLER	**4**	**22**	**16**	**3**	**19**	**3.45**	**0**	**0**	**0**	**0**
Rafael FLEGER	1	3	1	0	1	1.33	0	0	0	0
Michael VISSING	**5**	**17**	**2**	**0**	**2**	**0.47**	**0**	**0**	**0**	**0**
Thomas SØRENSEN	1	5	0	0	0	0.00	0	0	0	0
Guests										
Adrian MIEDZINSKI	1	6	14	0	14	9.33	0	0	0	0
David RUUD	**1**	**7**	**10**	**1**	**11**	**6.29**	**0**	**0**	**0**	**0**
Tommy PEDERSEN	1	6	8	0	8	5.33	0	0	0	0
Per LIND	**1**	**3**	**0**	**0**	**0**	**0.00**	**0**	**0**	**0**	**0**

For Jacek REMPALA see also Brovst; for Henriik MOLLER see also Holsted.

Despite his Elite League Wednesday race-night, Bjarne Pedersen still managed five matches for Holstebro

2009 FIXTURES

Friday, April 24 .... SLANGERUP (H)
Monday, May 11 .... Grindsted (a)
Friday, May 15 .... FJELSTED (H)
Wednesday, May 27 .... Slangerup (a)
Wednesday, June 3 .... Holsted (a)
Wednesday, June 10 .... Esbjerg (a)
Friday, June 12 .... GRINDSTED (H)
Friday, August 3 .... ESBJERG (H)
Wednesday, August 5 .... Vojens (a)
Wednesday, August 12 .... Fjelsted (a)
Wednesday, September 2 .... Brovst (a)
Friday, September 4 .... VOJENS (H)
Wednesday, September 9 .... HOLSTED (H)
Sunday, September 20 .... BROVST (H)

2009 SQUAD

A – Matej FERJAN, Bjarne PEDERSEN.
B – Andrey KARPOV, Mathias SCHULTZ, Marcin SEKULA.
C – Rene DEDDENS, Kenni Arendt LARSEN, Claes NEDERMARK, Tommy PEDERSEN.
D – Per LIND, Michael VISSING.

Danish Speedway League

HOLSTED

2008 RESULTS

Final position..Third

GRINDSTED (H)
Wednesday, April 30
Won 45-41
N. Pedersen 15, Hougaard 11:2, Moller 10, T. Pedersen [G] 4:1, Hansen 5:1.

HOLSTEBRO (A)
Sunday, May 18
Lost 41-43
Iversen 14, Moller 10:1, Vaculik 14:2, T. Pedersen 0, Hansen 3.

BROVST (A)
Wednesday, May 21
Won 48-39
Balinski 16, Jan Graversen [G] 12:1, Hougaard 13:1, Raun 0, Hansen 7:1.

BROVST (H)
Wednesday, May 28
Lost 40-44
N. Pedersen 17, Moller 7:1, Hougaard 9, Nielsen 1, Hansen 6.
Aggregate: Won 88-83.

FJELSTED (H)
Wednesday, June 4
Won 44-40
Balinski 12:2, Vaculik 15:1, Hougaard 12:1, Slawomir Musielak [G] 2, Hansen 3:1.

ESBJERG (H)
Wednesday, June 18
Won 46-38
Iversen 17:1, Stephan Katt [G] 6:1, Hougaard 12:1, Nielsen 8, Hansen 3:2.

SLANGERUP (A)
Wednesday, June 25
Lost 37-49
Balinski 11:1, Hougaard 16:2 (4), Vaculik 6:1, Hansen 0, Nielsen 4.

OUTRUP (A)
Wednesday, July 2
Won 48-39
N. Pedersen 18, Hougaard 10:1, Vaculik 8:1, Hansen 5:1, Nielsen 7:2.

TRACK FILE

Track: Hedevejen 1, 6670 Holsted, Denmark.
Tel: 0045 7539230900.
Website: www.holsted-speedway.dk
Track Length: 300 metres.
Track Record: 56.8 secs, Nicki Pedersen, 2007.

SQUAD
Patrick Bjerregaard, Morten G. Hansen, Patrick Hougaard, Niels-Kristian Iversen, Henrik Moller, Simon Nielsen, Nicki Pedersen, Tommy Pedersen.
Foreign: Damian Balinski, Lubos Tomicek, Martin Vaculik.

SLANGERUP (H)
Wednesday, August 20
Won 44-40
Balinski 15:1, Vaculik 11:2, Hougaard 15, Nielsen 2, Hansen 1.
Aggregate: Lost 81-89.

GRINDSTED (A)
Monday, August 25
Lost 40-47
Balinski 21:1 (6), Piotr Swist [G] 9, Tomicek 2, Nielsen 5:1, Hansen 3:1.
Aggregate: Lost 85-88.

OUTRUP (H)
Wednesday, September 3
Won 49-38
N. Pedersen 18, Vaculik 10:2, Hougaard 13:3, Nielsen 7:1, Hansen 1.
Aggregate: Won 97-77.

FJELSTED (A)
Wednesday, September 10
Lost 35-51
Hougaard 15:1, Adam Czechowicz [G] 8, Vaculik 6, Anders Andersen [G] 0, Nielsen 6.
Aggregate: Lost 79-91.

HOLSTEBRO (H)
Monday, September 15
Won 43-40
Balinski 8:2, Vaculik 11:1, Hougaard 15:1, Nielsen 6:1, Bjerregaard 3:1.
Aggregate: Won 84-83.

ESBJERG (A)
Wednesday, September 17
Drew 42-42
N. Pedersen 20, Vaculik 7:1, Hougaard 8:1, Nielsen 6:2, Bjerregaard 1.
Aggregate: Won 88-80.

DANISH LEAGUE

	M	W	D	L	PTsF	PtsA	BP	TPts
Slangerup	14	11	0	3	660	538	7	43
Esbjerg	14	8	1	5	645	558	5	36
HOLSTED	**14**	**8**	**1**	**5**	**602**	**591**	**4**	**35**
Fjelsted	14	5	0	9	601	594	5	29
Grindsted	14	6	0	8	592	609	3	29
Brovst	14	6	0	8	582	616	1	27
Holstebro	14	6	0	8	565	624	1	27
Outrup	14	5	0	9	542	659	2	26

Loyal Nicki Pedersen will begin his sixth successive season at Holsted and is joined by another club stalwart, Poland's Damian Balinski who has been a regular for many years.

Outrup's demise has seen Nicolai Klindt move in and he's one of five B grade riders including Poles Dawid Lampart, Dawid Stachyra and Krystian Klecha.

Former FIM Gold Cup champion Simon Nielsen, 18, is the most exciting prospect among the lower order although Henrik Moller could be key after being downgraded after a poor 2008.

Rider	M	R	Pts	BP	TPts	Ave	F	P	TR	TPts
Nicki PEDERSEN	5	31	88	0	88	11.35	2	0	0	0
Niels-Kristian IVERSEN	**2**	**12**	**31**	**1**	**32**	**10.67**	**0**	**1**	**0**	**0**
Damian BALINSKI	6	38	83	7	90	9.47	0	0	1	3
Patrick HOUGAARD	**12**	**73**	**149**	**14**	**163**	**8.93**	**0**	**0**	**2**	**5**
Marcin VACULIK	9	54	88	11	99	7.33	0	0	0	0
Simon NIELSEN	**10**	**59**	**52**	**8**	**60**	**4.07**	**0**	**0**	**0**	**0**
Lubos TOMICEK	1	2	2	0	2	4.00	0	0	0	0
Morten G. HANSEN	**11**	**52**	**37**	**7**	**44**	**3.38**	**0**	**0**	**0**	**0**
Patrick BJERREGAARD	2	7	4	1	5	2.86	0	0	0	0
Tommy PEDERSEN	**2**	**7**	**4**	**1**	**5**	**2.86**	**0**	**0**	**0**	**0**
Jonas RAUN	1	4	0	0	0	0.00	0	0	0	0
Guests										
Adam CZECHOWICZ	1	6	89	0	8	5.33	0	0	0	0
Piotr SWIST	**1**	**7**	**9**	**0**	**9**	**5.14**	**0**	**0**	**0**	**0**
Stephan KATT	1	6	6	1	7	4.67	0	0	0	0
Slawomir MUSIELAK	**1**	**4**	**2**	**0**	**2**	**2.00**	**0**	**0**	**0**	**0**
Anders ANDERSEN	1	2	0	0	0	0.00	0	0	0	0

For Henrik MOLLER see also Holstebro; for Morten G. HANSEN see also Outrup.

Ex-Swindon ace Damian Balinski will be spending another summer at Holsted

2009 FIXTURES

Wednesday, April 29 ....Vojens (a)
Wednesday, May 13..............................VOJENS (H)
Wednesday, May 20 ....GRINDSTED (H)
Wednesday, May 27.................................Fjelsted (a)
Friday, May 29 ....Grindsted (a)
Wednesday, June 3 ....HOLSTEBRO (H)
Wednesday, June 17 ....Slangerup (a)
Wednesday, July 1............................FJELSTED (H)
Wednesday, August 5 ....SLANGERUP (H)
Wednesday, August 19........................BROVST (H)
Wednesday, August 26...............................Brovst (a)
Wednesday, September 2.................ESBJERG (H)
Wednesday, September 9......................Holstebro (a)
Wednesday, September 16 ....Esbjerg (a)

2009 SQUAD

A – Damian BALINSKI, Nicki PEDERSEN, Martin VACULIK.

B – Patrick HOUGAARD, Krystian KLECHA, Nicolai KLINDT, Dawid LAMPART, Dawid STACHYRA.

C – Henrik MOLLER, Simon NIELSEN.

D – Patrick BJERREGAARD, Niklas PORSING, Jeppe SCHMIDT.

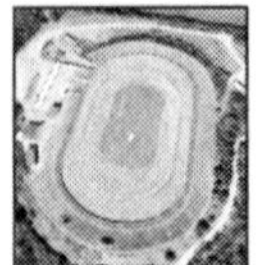

Danish Speedway League

OUTRUP

2008 RESULTS

Final position..Eighth

GRINDSTED (A)
Monday, April 28
Lost 38-47
Jamrozy 14 (4), Kamil Zielinski [G] 7:2, Jablonski 7:1, Georgsen 5, Andersen 5.

BROVST (H)
Wednesday, May 14
Won 44-40
Buczkowski 19, Jablonski 7:1, Klindt 14:5, Georgsen 1, Andersen 3 [2].
■ Result amended from 43-41 because Brovst used ineligible Patrick Nørgaard in heat 13. His point deducted from final score and Steffen Andersen upgraded by one point.

ESBJERG (H)
Wednesday, May 28
Lost 35-52
Buczkowski 14:1 (6), Sekula 12:1, Jablonski 3, Andersen 0, Jespersen 6:1.

BROVST (A)
Wednesday, June 4
Lost 24-27
Gjedde 7, Sekula 7:1, Klindt 5, Husman 3:1, Jespersen 2.
■ Abandoned after eight heats, result stands.
Aggregate: Won 68-67.

HOLSTEBRO (H)
Wednesday, June 18
Won 48-37
Gjedde 14:1, **Sekula 14:4**, Klindt 14, Erik Pudel [G] 3, Jespersen 3.

HOLSTEBRO (A)
Wednesday, June 25
Lost 40-44
Gjedde 11, Klindt 9:2, Sekula 10, Husman 8:1, Andersen 2.
Aggregate: on 88-81.

HOLSTED (H)
Wednesday, July 2
Lost 39-48
Gjedde 9:1, Klindt 18:1 (6), Sekula 10:1, Lukasz Loman [G] 1, Jespersen 1.

TRACK FILE

Track: Hennevej 35, 6855 Outrup, Denmark.
Website: www.outrup-speedway.dk
The new Outrup track was opened in 1986 and is alongside the old circuit which had been in existence since 1976, three years after the Outrup club was first formed by a group of local enthusiasts.

SQUAD
Steffen Andersen, Tommy Georgsen, Morten Frahm Hansen, Steffen B. Jespersen, Jesper Jørgensen, Nicolai Klindt.
Foreign: Krzysztof Buczkowski, Lisandro Husman, Miroslaw Jablonski, Ronnie Jamrozy, Piotr Protasiewicz, Marcin Sekula, Richard Speiser.

FJELSTED (H)
Wednesday, July 30
Lost 34-52
Gjedde 12:1, Klindt 18:1 (6), Sekula 2:1, Damian Sperz [G] 0, Andersen 2.

FJELSTED (A)
Wednesday, August 6
Won 44-42
Protasiewicz 15, Sekula 4, Klindt 9:1, Speiser 10:2, Jespersen 6:1.
Aggregate: Lost 78-94.

SLANGERUP (A)
Wednesday, August 13
Lost 29-57
Klindt 17 (4), Mattias Nilsson [G] 3, Sekula 5:2, Jørgensen 0, Hansen 4.

GRINDSTED (H)
Wednesday, August 20
Lost 38-49
Protasiewicz 12:1 (6), Jablonski 14:1, Klindt 10, Hansen 2, Jørgensen 0.
Aggregate: Lost 76-96.

ESBJERG (A)
Wednesday, August 27
Lost 30-56
Paluch 0, Jablonski 11 (4), Sekula 8, Hansen 2, Tommy Pedersen [G] 9:1.
Aggregate: Lost 65-108.

HOLSTED (A),
Wednesday, September 3
Lost 38-49
Matej Zagar [G] 9, Jablonski 16 (6), Klindt 9:1, Anders Mellgren [G] 2:1, Jespersen 2.
Aggregate: Lost 77-97.

SLANGERUP (H)
Wednesday, September 10
Won 43-41
Greg Hancock [G] 15, Jablonski 3, Klindt 11:1, Speiser 10:1, Jespersen 4:2.
Aggregate: Lost 72-98.

Outrup are not competing in the 2009 Danish Super League.

Rider	M	R	Pts	BP	TPts	Ave	F	P	TR	TPts
Krzysztof BUCZKOWSKI	2	14	30	1	31	8.86	0	0	0	0
Piotr PROTASIEWICZ	**2**	**13**	**27**	**1**	**28**	**8.62**	**0**	**0**	**1**	**3**
Nicolai KLINDT	11	68	134	12	146	8.59	0	0	3	8
Charlie GJEDDE	**5**	**28**	**53**	**3**	**56**	**8.00**	**0**	**0**	**0**	**0**
Ronnie JAMROZY	1	7	14	0	14	8.00	0	0	1	2
Richard SPEISER	**2**	**12**	**20**	**3**	**23**	**7.67**	**0**	**0**	**0**	**0**
Marcin SEKULA	9	56	72	10	82	5.86	0	1	0	0
Miroslaw JABLONSKI	**7**	**44**	**61**	**3**	**64**	**5.82**	**0**	**0**	**2**	**5**
Lisandro HUSMAN	2	9	11	2	13	5.78	0	0	0	0
Steffen B. JESPERSEN	**7**	**31**	**24**	**4**	**28**	**3.61**	**0**	**0**	**0**	**0**
Tommy GEORGSEN	2	9	6	0	6	2.67	0	0	0	0
Steffen ANDERSEN	**5**	**18**	**11**	**0**	**11**	**2.44**	**0**	**0**	**0**	**0**
Morten F. HANSEN	3	14	4	0	4	1.14	0	0	0	0
Jesper JØRGENSEN	**2**	**7**	**0**	**0**	**0**	**0.00**	**0**	**0**	**0**	**0**
Piotr PALUCH	1	2	0	0	0	0.00	0	0	0	0
Guests										
Greg HANCOCK	1	6	15	0	15	10.00	0	0	0	0
Matej ZAGAR	**1**	**6**	**9**	**0**	**9**	**6.00**	**0**	**0**	**0**	**0**
Kamil ZIELINSKI	1	6	7	2	9	6.00	0	0	0	0
Tommy PEDERSEN	**1**	**7**	**9**	**1**	**10**	**5.71**	**0**	**0**	**0**	**0**
Anders MELLGREN	1	4	2	1	3	3.00	0	0	0	0
Mattias NILSSON	**1**	**6**	**3**	**0**	**3**	**2.00**	**0**	**0**	**0**	**0**
Erik PUDEL	1	6	3	0	3	2.00	0	0	0	0
Lukasz LOMAN	**1**	**4**	**1**	**0**	**1**	**1.00**	**0**	**0**	**0**	**0**
Damian SPERZ	1	3	0	0	0	0.00	0	0	0	0

DANISH LEAGUE

	M	W	D	L	PTsF	PtsA	BP	TPts
Slangerup	14	11	0	3	660	538	7	43
Esbjerg	14	8	1	5	645	558	5	36
Holsted	14	8	1	5	602	591	4	35
Fjelsted	14	5	0	9	601	594	5	29
Grindsted	14	6	0	8	592	609	3	29
Brovst	14	6	0	8	582	616	1	27
Holstebro	14	6	0	8	565	624	1	27
OUTRUP	**14**	**5**	**0**	**9**	**542**	**659**	**2**	**26**

Poland's Piotr Protasiewicz was a steady scorer in his two meetings for Outrup

Danish Speedway League

SLANGERUP

2008 RESULTS

Final position..First

ESBJERG (A)
Wednesday, April 23
Lost 38-46
Monberg 14:3, Risager 12, K. Hansen 7:2, Kus 3, Kristiansen[1] 2.

GRINDSTED (H)
Wednesday, May 7
Won 47-37
Monberg 14:1, Risager 15:1, **K. Hansen 16:2**, C. Hansen 0, Kristiansen[1] 2.

FJELSTED (A)
Wednesday, May 14
Won 43-41
Monberg 12:1, K. Hansen 10:2, Risager 13, Søderholm 4, Kristiansen[1] 4:1.

HOLSTEBRO (H)
Wednesday, May 21
Won 55-31
Monberg 13:2, **K. Hansen 15:3**, **Risager 17:1**, Kus 5, Kristiansen[1] 5:1.

FJELSTED (H)
Wednesday, June 18
Won 51-36
Monberg 16:1, K. Hansen 13:2, Risager 13:1, Frankow 8:2, Spicker 1.
Aggregate: Won 94-77.

HOLSTED (H)
Wednesday, June 25
Won 49-37
Monberg 13:1, K. Hansen 14:2, Risager 13, Frankow 9:4, Spicker 0.

GRINDSTED (A)
Monday, June 30
Won 44-42
Monberg 13, Lindgren 12:2, K. Hansen, did not ride, Frankow 14:1, Spicker 5:1.
Aggregate: Won 91-79.

There are two licensed riders of the name Jesper KRISTIANSEN. See also Grindsted.

TRACK FILE

Track: Frederikssundsvej 6a, 3550 Slangerup, Denmark.
Tel: 0045 47 38 03 66.
Website: www.slangerupspeedway.dk

SQUAD
Carsten Hansen, Kenneth K. Hansen, Jesper Kristiansen[2], Jesper B. Monberg, Morten Risager, Dannie Søderholm, Dennis Spicker Thøstesen.
Foreign: Mariusz Frankow, Matej Kus, Ludvig Lindgren.

HOLSTEBRO (A)
Wednesday, July 2
Won 46-41
Monberg 16:1, K. Hansen 12, Risager 9:1, Frankow 8, Spicker 1.
Aggregate: Won 101-72.

BROVST (A)
Wednesday, August 6
Won 45-42
Monberg 15:1, K. Hansen 12:1, Risager 6:1, Frankow 10, Spicker 2.

OUTRUP (H)
Wednesday, August 13
Won 57-29
Monberg 9, Risager 16, K. Hansen 11:3, Frankow 14:1, Spicker 7:3.

HOLSTED (A)
Wednesday, August 20
Lost 40-44
Monberg 17, Risager 8:1, Hansen 7, Frankow 6:4, Spicker 2:1.
Aggregate: Won 89-81.

ESBJERG (H)
Wednesday, September 3
Won 48-38
Monberg 15:1, K. Hansen 14:1, Risager 13:1, Frankow 3, Spicker 3:1.
Aggregate: Won 86-84.

OUTRUP (A)
Wednesday, September 10
Lost 41-43
Monberg 10:1, K. Hansen 14:2, Risager 9, Frankow 8, Spicker 0.
Aggregate: Won 98-72.

BROVST (H)
Wednesday, September 24
Won 56-31
Monberg 17:1, **Risager 16:2**, **K. Hansen 15:3**, Kristiansen[1] 6:1, Spicker 2.
Aggregate: Won 101-73.

DANISH LEAGUE

	M	W	D	L	PTsF	PtsA	BP	TPts
SLANGERUP	**14**	**11**	**0**	**3**	**660**	**538**	**7**	**43**
Esbjerg	14	8	1	5	645	558	5	36
Holsted	14	8	1	5	602	591	4	35
Fjelsted	14	5	0	9	601	594	5	29
Grindsted	14	6	0	8	592	609	3	29
Brovst	14	6	0	8	582	616	1	27
Holstebro	14	6	0	8	565	624	1	27
Outrup	14	5	0	9	542	659	2	26

The major winter move has seen Hans Andersen switch to the reigning Danish League champions from Fjelsted.

Despite his arrival, Jesper B. Monberg, an everpresent in 2008, will remain as club captain but will find his opportunities restricted as natural second choice to Andersen.

Slangerup have retained the core of the title-winning squad but have released Poland's Mariusz Frankow.

Another newcomer is the Czech Republic's Lubos Tomicek who will be hoping to get more Danish meetings than last year when he rode in only one match for Holsted.

Rider	M	R	Pts	BP	TPts	Ave	F	P	TR	TPts
Jesper B. MONBERG	14	83	194	14	208	10.02	0	1	0	0
Kenneth HANSEN	**13**	**78**	**160**	**23**	**183**	**9.38**	**0**	**3**	**0**	**0**
Morten RISAGER	13	78	160	9	169	8.67	0	2	0	0
Mariusz FRANKOW	**9**	**53**	**80**	**12**	**92**	**6.94**	**0**	**0**	**0**	**0**
Jesper KRISTIANSEN[2]	5	25	19	3	22	3.52	0	0	0	0
Matej KUS	**2**	**10**	**8**	**0**	**8**	**3.20**	**0**	**0**	**0**	**0**
Dannie SØDERHOLM	1	5	4	0	4	3.20	0	0	0	0
Dennis SPICKER Thøstesen	**10**	**46**	**23**	**6**	**29**	**2.52**	**0**	**0**	**0**	**0**
Carsten HANSEN	1	5	0	0	0	0.00	0	0	0	0
Guests										
Ludvig LINDGREN	1	6	12	2	14		0	0	0	0

Kenneth HANSEN was programmed in the meeting at Grindsted on Monday, June 30, but did not ride, his races being taken by the reserves.

Morten Risager helped Slangerup win the Anti-Rust Danish League title, missing only one match

2009 FIXTURES

Friday, April 24 .... Holstebro (a)
Wednesday, May 20 .... Brovst (a)
Wednesday, May 13 .... BROVST (H)
Wednesday, May 27 .... HOLSTEBRO (H)
Wednesday, June 10 .... GRINDSTED (H)
Wednesday, June 17 .... HOLSTED (H)
Wednesday, June 24 .... Fjelsted (a)
Monday, June 29 .... Grindsted (a)
Wednesday, August 5 .... Holsted (a)
Wednesday, August 12 .... VOJENS (H)
Wednesday, August 19 .... ESBJERG (H)
Wednesday, August 26 .... Esbjerg (a)
Wednesday, September 2 .... FJELSTED (H)
Wednesday, September 16 .... Vojens (a)

2009 SQUAD

A – Hans ANDERSEN, Jesper B. MONBERG.
B – Kenneth HANSEN, Ludvig LINDGREN, Morten RISAGER, Lubos TOMICEK.
C – Robin ASPELUND, Jesper KRISTIANSEN[2], Henrik VEDEL.
D – Dennis SPICKER Thøstesen, Philip Barkhus TIRSDAL.

Open licence

VOJENS

TRACK FILE

Track: Vojens Speedway Center, Tinglykke 9, 6500 Vojens, Skyrdstrup, Denmark.
Telephone: 0045 74 50 44 41.
Website: www.speedway.dk
Track Length: 300 metres.
Track Record: 57.2 secs,Nicki Pedersen, October 4, 2008.

Vojens Speedway Club is the new team in Russeting ANTI NEGLIGIBLE Speedway League in 2009, when they replace Outrup Speedway Club.

Their return to league racing ends several seasons in the wilderness when they were saddled with huge debts, including outstanding payments to the Danish Motor Union.

However, after talks with Ole Olsen, who designed and built the track, they will go into the new campaign on a sound footing and have built up what looks like a crowd-pleasing squad including a top four of Kenneth Bjerre, Russian Emil Sajfutdinov and exciting young Brits Edward Kennett and Tai Woffinden.

Bjerre opted to move from former club Esbjerg to Vojens and will no doubt use his new home track knowledge when one of the two Danish Grands Prix is held there during the summer.

Their squad is filled with huge but questionable talent, particularly in the lower levels.

2009 FIXTURES

Wednesday, April 29 .... HOLSTED (H)
Wednesday, May 6 .... BROVST (H)
Wednesday, May 13 .... Holsted (a)
Wednesday, May 27 .... ESBJERG (H)
Wednesday, June 3 .... GRINDSTED (H)
Wednesday, June 17 .... FJELSTED (H)
Wednesday, July 1 .... Brovst (a)
Wednesday, August 5 .... HOLSTEBRO (H)
Wednesday, August 12 .... Slangerup (a)
Friday, August 21 .... Esbjerg (a)
Friday, August 28 .... Grindsted (a)
Friday, September 4 .... Holstebro (a)
Wednesday, September 9 .... Fjelsted (a)
Wednesday, September 16 .... SLANGERUP (H)

2009 SQUAD

A – Kenneth BJERRE, Edward KENNETT, Emil SAJFUTDINOV, Tai WOFFINDEN.
B – Klaus JAKOBSEN, Michal MITKO, Patrick NØRGAARD, Kevin WÖLBERT.
C – Lars HANSEN, Casper WORTMANN.
D – Lasse BJERRE, Rene HOLM, Michael Jepsen JENSEN, Thomas SORENSEN.

Vojens at night

ANTI-RUST RINGEN SPEEDWAY LEAGUE STANDINGS

	M	W	D	L	PTsF	PtsA	BP	TPts
SLANGERUP	14	11	0	3	660	538	7	43
Esbjerg	14	8	1	5	645	558	5	36
Holsted	14	8	1	5	602	591	4	35
Fjelsted	14	5	0	9	601	594	5	29
Grindsted	14	6	0	8	592	609	3	29
Brovst	14	6	0	8	582	616	1	27
Holstebro	14	6	0	8	565	624	1	27
Outrup	14	5	0	9	542	659	2	26

A RESURGENCE in interest in Denmark – principally on the back of Nicki Pedersen's Grand Prix exploits – ended the recent decline.

The Anti-Rust Danish League – a Superleague in all but name – saw eight teams contest the season long competition with sides meeting once home and away and the title being decided on the conventional basis without play-offs.

Esbjerg and Fjelsted returned to league competition and Grindsted stepped up into the top-flight for the first time in their history.

A grading system – A Grade to D grade – was introduced in an attempt to keep sides balanced and a look at the final league table suggests it was successful with champions Slangerup losing three of their 14 matches and bottom of the table Outrup winning five.

Unfortunately the wooden spoonists struggled for crowds and dropped out of the league at the end of the season but the return of a now debt-free Vojens compensated and saw the league remain at its eight-club strength.

Each club was allowed to nominate an 11 rider squad although for each meeting they could only track a maximum of one A Grade rider (assessed at eight point), but any combination of B Grade (six), C Grade (four) and D Grade (one) providing the overall combined total did not exceed 25.

Slangerup lost their opening match at Esbjerg but nine successive wins saw them go top of the table and they had a seven point winning margin over their opening day conquerors.

All the top Danish riders took part in the competition – mainly run on Wednesday nights – despite relatively poor financial rewards, a tribute to their willingness to help the sport domestically.

International

Vojens, Saturday, October 4

DENMARK 36 (Nicki Pedersen 12 (6), Niels-Kristian Iversen 6:1 (2), Hans Andersen 6, Mads Korneliussen 3:1, Bjarne Pedersen 6:1, Kenneth Bjerre 3:1) **REST OF THE WORLD 40** (Jason Crump 9, Rune Holta 0, Andreas Jonsson 11, Fredrik Lindgren 5:2, Leigh Adams 9, Scott Nicholls 6:2).

▲ *Nicki Pedersen broke Jason Crump's five-year-old track record before a Heat 12 abandonment.*

Roll of Honour

1958 .... AMAGER
1967 .... ESBJERG
1968 .... FREDERICIA
1969 .... ESBJERG
1970 .... ESBJERG
1971 .... ESBJERG
1972 .... ESBJERG
1973 .... ARHUS
1974 .... FREDERICIA
1975 .... FREDERICIA
1976 .... HOLSTED
1977 .... HOLSTED
1978 .... HOLSTED
1979 .... HOLSTED
1980 .... ESBJERG
1981 .... ESBJERG
1983 .... Kulsvierne FREDERIKSBORG
1984 .... Vikingerne ESBJERG
1985 .... Blabjergdrengene OUTRUP
1986 .... FJELSTED
1987 .... FREDERICIA
1988 .... SLANGERUP
1989 .... FREDERICIA
1990 .... BROVST
1991 .... HSK HOLSTED
1992 .... FJELSTED
1993 .... FREDERICIA
1994 .... HOLSTED
1995 .... FJELSTED
1996 .... HOLSTED
1997 .... HOLSTEBRO
1998 .... BROVST
1999 .... OUTRUP
2000 .... BROVST
2001 .... OUTRUP
2002 .... HOLSTED
2003 .... HOLSTED
2005 .... FREDERICIA
2006 .... HOLSTED
2007 .... HOLSTED
2008 .... SLANGERUP

2009 START TIMES

The traditional start-times and race-days of the eight competing Danish League clubs are:

Brovst, Wednesday, 7 pm; Esbjerg, Wednesday, 6.30 pm; Fjelsted, Wednesday, 6.30pm; Grindsted, Monday or Friday, 6.00pm; Holstebro, Friday, 6.00pm; Holsted, Wednesday, 7.00pm; Slangerup, Wednesday, 6.30pm; Vojens, Wednesday, 7.00.

All times are local.

Nearly 500 different riders were graded to compete in the 2009 Danish League. Full gradings list are:

A GRADE

Leigh Adams, Sebastian Aldén, Oliver Allen, Tommy Allen, Hans Andersen, Eric Andersson, Ricky Ashworth, Damian Balinski, Ben Barker, Troy Batchelor, Kenneth Bjerre, Maksim Bogdanovs, Lewis Bridger, Jason Bunyan, Krzysztof Buczkowski, Kamil Brzozowski, Tomasz Chrzanowski, Dawid Cieslewicz, Lee Complin, André Compton, Jason Crump, Sergey Darkin, Daniel Davidsson, Jonas Davidsson, Rafal Dobrucki, Kevin Doolan, Jason Doyle, Slawomir Drabik, Ales Dryml, Lukas Dryml, Stefan Ekberg, Freddie Eriksson, Robert Eriksson, Matej Ferjan, Ryan Fisher, Billy Forsberg, Josef Franc, Paul Fry, Renat Gafurov, Tomasz Gapinski, Cory Gathercole, Denis Gizatullin, Charlie Gjedde, Tomasz Gollob, Adrian Gomolski, James Grieves, Henrik Gustafsson, Simon Gustafsson, Richard Hall, Jaroslaw Hampel, Greg Hancock, Chris Harris, Juha Hautamåki, Gary Havelock, Christian Hefenbrock, Christian Henry, Pawel Hlib, Chris Holder, Rune Holta, David Howe, Niels-Kristian Iversen, Krzysztof Jablonski, Miroslaw Jablonski, Wieslaw Jagus, Ronnie Jamrozy, Lukasz Jankowski, Billy Janniro, Maciej Janowski, Tomasz Jedrzejak,Marcin Jedrzejewski, Daniel Jeleniewski, Steve Johnston, Thomas H. Jonasson, Tomas Jonasson, Andreas Jonsson, Matej Kus, Brian Karger, Magnus Karlsson, Peter Karlsson, Krzysztof Kasprzak, Robert Kasprzak, Edward Kennett, Robbie Kessler, Daniel King, Jason King, Ricky Kling, Niklas Klingberg, Janusz Kolodziej, Mads Korneliussen, Robert Kosciecha, Norbert Kosciuch, Emil Kramer, Tobias Kroner, Robert Ksiezak, Maciej Kuciapa, Joonas Kylmåkorpi, Artem Laguta, Grigori Laguta, Leigh Lanham, Kaj Laukkanen, William Lawson, Kyle Legault, Mark Lemon, Antonio Lindbäck, Fredrik Lindgren, Peter Ljung, Chris Louis, Michal Makovsky, Mikael Max, Travis McGowan, Pawel Mesiac, Adrian Miedzinski, Robert Miskowiak, Borys Miturski, Jesper B. Monberg, Phil Morris, Chris Neath, Scott Nicholls, Kauko Nieminen, Kim Nilsson, Rafal Okoniewski, Ulrich Østergaard, Piotr Paluch, Shane Parker, Jurica Pavlic, Patryk Pawlaszczyk, Przemszyslaw Pawlicki, Bjarne Pedersen, Nicki Pedersen, Glen Phillips, Tomasz Piszcz, Roman Povazhny, Tyron Proctor, Piotr Protasiewicz, Mariusz Puszczakowski, Jacek Rempala, Marcin Rempala, Lee Richardson, Adam Roynon, David Ruud, Adrian Rymel, Emil Sajfutdinov, Rory Schlein, Joe Screen, Adam Shields, Adam Skornicki, Krzysztof Slabon, Martin Smolinski, Derek Sneddon, George Stancl, Pawel Staszek, Simon Stead, Krzysztof Stojanowski, Ryan Sullivan, Piotr Swiderski, Mateusz Szczepaniak, Michal Szczepaniak, Tomas Topinka, Rafal Trojanowski, Andrew Tully, Sebastian Ulamek, Martin Vaculik, Grzegorz Walasek, Simon Walker, Craig Watson, Davey Watt, Mariusz Wegrzyk, Matthew Wethers, Ben Wilson, Tai Woffinden, Cameron Woodward, James Wright, Karol Zabik, Matej Zagar, Grzegorz Zengota, Magnus Zetterström.

B GRADE

Tero Aarnio, Jonas Andersson, Tony Atkin, Joshua Auty, René Bach, Henning Bager, Tomasz Bajerski, Karol Baran, Andrew Bargh, Byron Bekker, Andreas Bergström, Viktor Bergström, Daniel Betson, Jamie Birkinshaw, Luke Bowen, Ross Brady, John Branney, Sebastian Brucheiser, James Brundle, Mark Burrows, Tobias Busch, Stanislaw Burza, Damian Celmer, Roman Chromik, Tomasz Cieslewicz, Paul Clews, Paul Cooper, Adam Czechowicz, Zbigniew Czerwinski, Stefan Dannö, Slawomir Drabowski, Lee Dicken, Max Dilger, Wojciech Druchniak, Patryk Dudek, Piotr Dym, Piotr Dziatkowiak, Linus Eklöf, Barrie Evans, Frank Facher, Kiril Filinov, Rafal Fleger, Jordan Frampton, Guglielmo Franchetti, Mariusz Frankow, Ruslan Gatiatov, Martin Gavenda, Viatcheslav Gerutsky, Nicki Glanz, Jacek Gollob, Josh Grajczonek, Jan Graversen, Maks Gregoric, Aleksey Guzajev, Michael Hadek, Joe Haines, Daniel Halsey, Kenneth Hansen, Jack Hargreaves, Rusty Harrison, Roberto Haupt, Manuel Hauzinger, Jame Holder, Patrick Hougaard, Kai Huckenback, Lisandro Husmann, Emil Idziorek, Christian Isomettä, Roman Ivanov, Krister Jacobsen, Klaus Jakobsen, Jan Jaros, Robert Johansson, Peter Juul (Larsen), Richard Juul, Adam Kajoch, Marcel Kajzer, Evgeny Karavatskaya, Andrey Karpov, Bartosz Kasprowiak, Stephan Katt, Chris Kerr, Aleksey Kharchenko, Szymon Kielbasa, Peter Kildemand, Krystian Klecha, Nicolai Klindt, Grzegorz Klopot, Danny Knakowski, Grzegorz Knapp, Vladimir Kolody [sen], Andrej Korolev, Alexander Kosolapkin, Jesper Kristiansen[2] (Grindsted), Matthias Kröger, Simon Lambert, Dawid Lampart, Mateusz Lampkowski, Rene Lehtinen, Andreas Lekander, Trent Leverington, Marcin Liberski, Ludvig Lindgren, Michal Lopaczewski, Tomasz Lukaszewicz, Brian Lyngsø, Leon Madsen, Norbert Magosi, Martin Malek, Alan Marcinkowski, Robert Mear, Steffen Mell, Anders Mellgren, Andreas Messing, Jonas Messing, Robert Mikolajczak, Chris Mills, Michal Mitko, Andrew Moore, Artur Mroczka, Marek Mroz, Lars Munkedal, Slawomir Musielak, Lenar Nigmatyanov, Olof Nilsson, Patrick Nørgaard, Marcin Nowaczyk, John Oliver, Joel Parsons, Leonids Paura, Adam Pawliczek, Sönke Petersen, Maciej Piaszczynski, Theo Pijper, Ben Powell, Erik Pudel, Kjastas Puodzhuks, Slawomir Pyszny, Daniel Pytel, Michal Rajkowski, Tomi Reima, Piotr Rembas, Tomasz Rempala, Morten Risager, Jack Roberts, Herbert Rudolf, Denis Sajfutdinov, Emiliano Sanchez, Izak Santej, Tomasz Schmid, Chris Schramm, Mathias Schultz, Marcin Sekula, Filip Sitera, Krzysztof Slabon, Lee Smart, Lee Smethills, Jamie Smith, Kozza Smith, Scott Smith (UK), Rune Sola, Richard Speiser, Damian Sperz, Dawid Stachyra, Thomas Stange, Hynek Stichauer, Sean Stoddart, Tomas Suchanek, Zbigniew Suchecki, Aaron Summers, Linus Sundström, Richard Sweetman, Piotr Swist, Laszlo Szatmari, Adrian Szewczykowski, Rafal Szombierski, Mateusz Szostek, Grzegorz Szyszka, Cyprian Szymko, Jozsef Tabaka, Sean Tacey, Jeremia Thelaus, Lubos Tomicek, Sebastian Truminski, Adam Vandirek, Claus Vissing, Semen Vlasov, Artem Vodyakov, Friedrich Wallner, Danny Warwick, Ronny Weis, Brent Werner, Carl Wilkinson, Kevin Wölbert, Richard Wolff, Charles Wright, Kamil Zielinski.

C GRADE

Christian Agö, Anders Andersen, Dennis Andersson, Kenni Arendt (Larsen), Robin Aspegren, Nicki Barrett, Mathias Bartz, Mark Baseby, Robin Bergkvist, Manfred Betz, Arlo Bugeja, Barry Burchatt, Sebastian Carlsson, James Cockle, Benji Compton, Dennis Dahlborg, Mitchell Davey, Rene Deddens, Christoph Demmel, Sebastian Eckerle, Dennis Fagerkrantz, Maciej Fajfer, Daniel Giffard, Tommy Georgsen, Carsten Hansen, Lars Hansen, Jerran Hart, Marcel Helfer, Jay Herne, Kyle Hughes, Steffen Jespersen, Joni Keskinen, Johannes Kikkenborg, Dan Kjellberg, Vladimir Kolody [jun], Jesper Kristiansen[1] (Slangerup), Stefan Kurz, Arne Ledwig, Henning Loof, Piotr Machnik, Rene Madsen, Jari Mäkinen, Sam Martin, Adam McKinna, Maciej Michaluk, Dominik Möller, Hans-Jörg Müller, Claes Nedermark, Niels Nielsen, Simon Nielsen, Tomas Olsson, Vladimir Omelian, Tommy Pedersen, Magnus Persson, Robert Pettersson, Pawel Ratajszczak, Daniel Rath, Jamie Robertson, Anton Rosén, Sirg Schützbach, Nick Simmons, Zdenek Simota, Dannie Søderholm, Ramon Stanek, Bartosz Szymura, Robin Törnqvist, Henrik Vedel, Denis Wienke, Franz Winklhofer, Casper Wortmann, Matthew Wright,

D GRADE

Jesper Andersen, Nicklas Sonne Ingemann Andersen, Nicolai Alm Andersen, Steffen Skovgård Andersen, Kasper Rønnow Back, Patrick Bjerregaard, Anders Thorbjørn Clausen, Mads Georgsen, Kalle Greve, Thomas Grimm, Kasper Klit Hansen, Morten Frahm Hansen, Morten Graakjær Hansen,

Denmark continued on opposite page

EUROPE

MACEC CUP

ALEXANDRU Toma retained his MACEC Cup title – principally because he rode in all four rounds of the competition.

Restricted to riders from Eastern Europe, the MACEC Cup gives some of the lesser lights the chance to shine and is raced over rounds in Hungary, Poland, Romania and Ukraine.

Toma didn't get on the rostrum at any of the meetings and had either Kiril Cukanov (Russia) or Poland's Tomasz Lukaszewicz ridden in the opening round they would surely have overtaken the defending champion.

A total of 38 riders from nine different countries – Bulgaria, Croatia, Germany, Hungary, Poland, Romania, Russia, Slovakia and Ukraine - took part in a series that began in July and ended in October.

Final Standings

	1	*2*	*3*	*4*	*Tot*
1 ALEXANDRU TOMA	**10**	**9**	**11**	**10**	**40**
2 Kiril CUKANOV	–	14	12	12	38
3 Tomasz LUKASZEWICZ	–	14	14	7	35
4 Milan MANEV	6	10	7	6	29
5 Vladimir DUBININ	–	13	13	–	26
6 Attila MOLNAR	7	8	10	–	25
7 Attila LORINCZ	7	8	6	–	21
8 Piotr MACHNIK	–	8	5	5	18
9 Sergey BORISENKO	6	4	5	1	16
10 Maciej MICHALUK	9	–	–	7	16
11 Tomasz PISZCZ	15	–	–	–	15
11 Zoltan ADORJAN	–	–	–	15	15
13 Jaroslav POLIUCHOVIC	–	–	14	–	14
13 Dino KOVACIC	–	–	–	14	14
15 Grzegorz KNAPP	13	–	–	–	13
16 Dawid STACHYRA	12	–	–	–	12
16 Rafal KLIMEK	12	–	–	–	12
18 Sebastian TRUMINSKI	10	–	–	–	10
18 Ronny WEIS	–	10	–	–	10
18 Nikola PIGAC	–	–	–	10	10
21 Rastislav BANDZI	4	2	–	3	9
22 Vladimir TEJGAL	4	–	4	–	8
23 Michail ONESHKO	–	–	8	–	8
23 Sandor FEKETE	–	–	–	8	8
23 Roland BENKO	–	–	–	8	8
26 Marian GHEORGHE	–	7	–	–	7
26 Adrian GHEORGHE	–	7	–	–	7
26 Zsolt BENCZE	–	–	–	7	7
29 Petr FEDIK	2	–	–	3	5
30 Stanislav OGORODNIK	–	–	5	–	5
31 Fanica POPA	–	4	0	–	4
32 Lubos DORICA	2	–	–	–	2
33 Aleksandr GAJKOVSKY	–	–	2	–	2
33 Zsolt NAGY	–	–	–	2	2
35 Patrik Kotta KIS	1	–	–	–	1
35 Stefan POPA	–	1	–	–	1
35 Florian BARABASU	–	1	–	–	1
35 Mate SZEGEDI	–	–	–	1	1

Round 1
Lublin, Poland, Saturday, July 26
Tomasz Piszcz 15, Grzegorz Knapp 13, Dawid Stachyra 12, Rafal Klimek 12, Sebastian Truminski 10, Alexandru Toma 10, Maciej Michaluk 9, Attila Molnar 7, Attila Lorincz 7, Sergey Borisenko 6, Milan Manev 6, Rastislav Bandzi 4, Valdimir Tejgal 4, Petr Fedik 2, Lubos Dorica 2, Patrik Kotta Kis 1, Fanic Popa, did not ride.

Round 2
Braila, Romania, Saturday, September 20
Tomasz Lukaszewicz 14, Kiril Cukanov 14, Vladimir Dubinin 13, Ronny Weis 10, Milan Manev 10, Alexandru Toma 0, Attila Molnar 8, Attil Lorincz 8, Piotr Machnik 8, Marian Gheorghe 7, Andrian Gheorghe 7, Sergey Borisenko 4, Fanica Popa 4, Rastislav Bandzi 2, Stefan Popa 1, Florian Barabasu 1, Daniel Marin, did not ride.

Round 3
Lvov, Ukraine, Sunday, September 28
Tomasz Lukaszewicz 14+3, Jaroslav Poliuchovic 14+2, Vladimir Dubinin 13, Kiril Cukanov 12, Alexandru Toma 11, Attila Molnar 10, Michail Oneshko 8, Milan Manev 7, Attila Lorincz 6, Sergey Borisenko 5, Piotr Machnik 5, Stanislav Ogorodnik 5, Vladimir Tejgal 4, Aleksandr Gajkovsky 2, Fanica Popa 0.

Round 4
Debrecen, Hungary, Saturday, October 25
Zoltan Adorjan 15, Dino Kovacic 14, Kiril Cukanov 12, Alexandru Toma 10, Nikola Pigac 10, Sandor Fekete 8, Roland Benko 8, Tomasz Lukaszewski 7, Maciej Michaluk 7, Zsolt Bencze 7, Milan Manev 6, Piotr Machnik 5, Rastislav Bandzi 3, Petr Fedik 3, Zsolt Nagy [R] 2, Mate Szegedi 1, Sergey Borisenko 1, Sandor Konya [R] 0.

Roll of Honour

2004 .... Pawel BARAN (Poland)
2005 .... Daniel JELENIEWSKI (Poland)
2006 .... Andrey KARPOV (Ukraine)
2007 .... Alexandru TOMA (Romania)
2008 .... Alexandru TOMA (Romania)

Denmark continued from opposite page

Simon Frahm Hansen, Claus Hedergaard, Amalie Hermansen, Daniel Høbjerg, Karsten Højhus, Rene Holm, Thomas Frank Irming, Chris Halskov Jacobsen, Anders Agergård Jensen, Jacob Jensen, Lasse Raun Jensen, Stefanie Jensen, Jesper Jørgensen, Nanna Warning Jørgensen, Thomas Jørgensen, Nick Kjellerup, Mads Kølbæk, Michael Kristensen, Steen Frederik Larsen, Claus Lauridsen, Per Lind, Morten Ludvigsen, Mikkel Madsen, Michael Melchiorsen, Paw Mikkelsen, Erling Mogensen, Dennis Møller, Martin Møller, Rene Mortensen, Rasmus Nørskov-Nielsen, Steven Nielsen, Thomas Gotfred Nielsen, Ricco Mahlenfeldt Niewick, Bjarne Nilsson, Mads Olsen (Slangerup), Karsten Pagh, Dan Erik Pedersen, Kim S. Pedersen, Ole Rom Pedersen, Daniel Vesterkov Puck, Cebine Randrup, Alex Richardy, Jeppe Schmidt, Mads Eberhart Skov, Andy Sørensen, Thomas Sørensen, Michael Staal, Thomas Bo Stage, Dennis Spicker Thøstesen, Philip Barkhus Tirsdal, Michael Palm Toft, Jens Trasborg, Anders Vad, Shanchajan Vasantharajan, Lars Vedsted, Michael Vissing.

FINLAND

FINNISH CHAMPIONSHIP

FINAL

Haapajärvi, Saturday, July 26

JUHA Hautamäki established his growing reputation as Finland's number one by successfully retaining his national title – his third victory in the last four years.

The 26-year-old from Seinäjokli turned down several approaches to race in Britain during the year but is clearly a talented performer.

He survived a Heat 9 stoppage – when he was up against three rivals who all finished in the bottom half of the field – to secure his seeded place in the title decider, the top two scorers being spared a semi-final shoot-out.

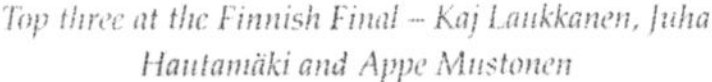

Top three at the Finnish Final – Kaj Laukkanen, Juha Hautamäki and Appe Mustonen

It took his gold medal collection – individual, team and pairs – to 13 and despite a bunch of younger rivals coming along he seems certain to add to that tally over the coming years.

Even though he did race in Sweden (Griparna) and Poland (Opole) what he clearly needs now is wider experience racing elsewhere and he gave hints towards the end of the season that he could be interested in racing in the Premier League in future.

Kaj Laukkanen failed in his bid for a ninth championship that would have seen him draw level with Kai Niemi who won nine titles between 1977 and 1990.

	1	2	3	4	5	Tot	SF	F
1 Juha HAUTAMÄKI	**3**	**3**	**R**	**3**	**3**	**12**	**–**	**3**
2 Kaj LAUKKANEN	3	2	2	1	3	11	3	2
3 Appe MUSTONEN	2	3	3	3	2	13	–	1
4 Tomi REIMA	3	2	3	2	2	12	2	0
5 Tero AARNIO	0	3	0	3	3	9	1	
6 Timo LAHTI	0	3	3	3	1	10	0	
7 Rene LEHTINEN	3	1	1	2	2	9		
8 Niko SILTANIEMI	2	2	1	1	3	9		
9 Teemu LAHTI	1	2	2	2	2	9		
10 Kalla KATAJISTO	2	1	3	1	1	8		
11 Aleksey POPTSOV	1	0	1	2	1	5		
12 Markku AUTIO	1	1	2	0	0	4		
13 Joni KESKINEN	1	0	2	X	1	4		
14 Juha MÄKELÄ	2	1	R	0	0	3		
15 Aarni HAIKKILÄ	0	0	1	1	0	2		
16 Petteri KOIVUNEN	0	0	0	0	0	0		

Qualifying Round

Pori, Saturday, July 5

1 Appe Mustonen 15, 2 Kalle Katajisto 13, 3 Markku Autio 11+3, 4 Timo Lahti 11+2, 5 Niko Siltaniemi 9, 6 Teemu Lahti 9, 7 Joni Keskinen 9, 8 Juha Mäkelä 8, 9 Marko Suojanen 8, 10 Aleksey Poptsov 7, 11 Aarni Heikkilä 7, 12 Petteri Koivunen 6, 13 Jani Eerikäinen 4, 14 Juho Ruuska 1, 15 Jukka Nieminen 1, Petri Koskela 0.

Roll of Honour

1949 .... Raine LAMPINEN
1955 .... Kauko JOUSANEN
1956 .... Antti PAJARI
1957 .... Antti PAJARI
1958 .... Antti PAJARI
1959 .... Pertti MIKKOLA
1960 .... Kalevi LAHTINEN
1961 .... Timo LAINE
1962 .... Timo LAINE
1963 .... Timo LAINE
1964 .... Kalevi LAHTINEN
1965 .... Kalevi LAHTINEN
1966 .... Olavi TURUNEN
1967 .... Matti OLIN
1968 .... Matti OLIN
1969 .... Kalevi LAHTINEN
1970 .... Kalevi LAHTINEN
1971 .... Matti OLIN
1972 .... Matti OLIN
1973 .... Matti OLIN
1974 .... Kari VUORISTO
1975 .... Ila TEROMAA
1976 .... Ila TEROMAA
1977 .... Kai NIEMI
1978 .... Kai NIEMI
1979 .... Kai NIEMI
1980 .... Kai NIEMI
1981 .... Kai NIEMI
1982 .... Kai NIEMI
1983 .... Ari KOPONEN
1984 .... Kai NIEMI
1985 .... Ari KOPONEN
1985 .... Juha MOKSUNEN
1986 .... Juha MOKSUNEN
1987 .... Ari KOPONEN
1988 .... Kai NIEMI
1989 .... Juha MOKSUNEN
1990 .... Kai NIEMI
1991 .... Vesa YLINEN
1992 .... Vesa YLINEN
1993 .... Mika PELLINEN
1994 .... Roy MALMINHEIMO
1995 .... Vesa YLINEN
1996 .... Vesa YLINEN
1997 .... Kaj LAUKKANEN
1998 .... Vesa YLINEN
1999 .... Kaj LAUKKANEN
2000 .... Kaj LAUKKANEN
2001 .... Kaj LAUKKANEN
2002 .... Kaj LAUKKANEN

Champions Kotkat

Rene Lehtinen, Petteri Koivunen, Juha Hautamäki, Kaj Laukkanen and team manager Mikko Koskinen

Best of the young Finns at Haapajärvi. Timo Lahti leads Niko Siltaniemi

A happy champ Teemu Lahti (centre) flanked by brother Timo and Kalle Katajisto after the Under 21 Final at Hyvinkä

2003 ..... Kaj LAUKKANEN
2004 ..... Kaj LAUKKANEN
2005 ..... Juha HAUTAMÄKI
2006 ..... Kaj LAUKKANEN
2007 ..... Juha HAUTAMÄKI
2008 ..... Juha HAUTAMÄKI

FINNISH U21 CHAMPIONSHIP

FINAL
Hyvinkää, Saturday, July 12

TEEMU Lahti upstaged brother Timo to regain his Under 21 title – despite being beaten three times in the qualifying races.

The 20-year-old Lahti ace lost out to his brother, Kalle Katajisto and Russian youngster Fedor Poptsov (twice) in the preliminaries but made no mistake in the final.

Timo, who had been unbeaten in the earlier stages, missed out when it really mattered, being outgated by Teemu and then passed on the last lap by ex-Edinburgh rider Katajisto.

	1	2	3	4	5	Tot	SF	F
1 Teemu LAHTI	**2**	**3**	**2**	**2**	**3**	**12**	**2**	**3**
2 Kalle KATAJISTO	3	3	3	3	R	12	–	2
3 Timo LAHTI	3	3	3	3	3	15	–	1
4 Fedor POPTSOV	0	2	3	3	3	11	3	FX
5 Apple MUSTONEN	2	2	2	3	3	12	1	
6 Niko SILTANIEMI	1	3	3	2	2	11	0	
7 Joni KITALA	3	2	1	1	2	9		
8 Markku AUTIO	3	1	1	2	2	9		
9 Aleksander EDBERG	2	1	2	2	1	8		
10 Aarni HEIKKILÄ	1	2	0	1	2	6		
11 Jere MATTILA	0	1	2	1	1	5		
12 Jukka NIEMINEN	1	1	1	0	1	4		
13 Ario TUOMISTO	0	0	1	1	1	3		
14 Olli HEIKKILÄ	0	0	1	1	1	3		
15 Jonas MESSING	did not ride							
16 Jens OSKARSSON	did not ride							

Roll of Honour

1990 ..... Esa EINOLA
1991 ..... Petri NURMESNIEMI
1992 ..... Mika LAUKKANEN
1993 ..... Kaj LAUKKANEN
1994 ..... Pasi PULLIAINEN
1995 ..... Kaj LAUKKANEN
1996 ..... Juha RISTIHARJU
1997 ..... Joonas KYLMÅKORPI
1998 ..... Kauko NIEMINEN
1999 ..... Kauko NIEMINEN
2000 ..... Kauko NIEMINEN
2001 ..... Mico BROTKIN
2002 ..... Jonas DAVIDSSON
2003 ..... Juha HAUTAMÄKI
2004 ..... Tero AARNIO
2005 ..... Tero AARNIO
2006 ..... Teemu LAHTI
2007 ..... Jari MÄKINEN
2008 ..... Teemu LAHTI

EXTRALIIGA

Round 1
Seinäjoki, Friday, May 9

KOTKAT 13 (Kaj Laukkanen 2, Juha Hautamäki 6, Rene Lehtinen 3, Petteri Koivunen 2), PAHOLAISET 10 (Jari Mäkinen 3, Petri Koskela 1, Marko Suajanen 4, Alexander Edberg 2), JOKERIT 8 (Kalle Katajisto 1, Jani Eerikäinen 2, Timo Villanen 1, Markku Autio 4), HAUKAT-ROYALS 5 (Tomi Reima 3, Juha Mäkelä 2, Joni Kitala 0, Aarni Heikkilä 0).

Meeting abandoned after a crash in Heat 7 in which Jokerit's Timo Villanen suffered serious back injuries, broken ribs and a punctured lung.

Round 2
Kuusankosi, Saturday, June 14

1 KOTKAT 41 (**Juha Hautamäki 12**, **Rene Lehtinen 12**, Benny Johansson 11, Niko Siltaniemi 6), 2 PAHOLAISET 31 (Cezary Owizyc 3, Petri Koskela 4, Marko Suojanen 10 (1), Appe Mustonen 14), 3 JOKERIT 22 (Kalle Katajisto 7 (1), Jani Eerikäinen 9, Markku Autio 5, Jan-Eric Korkeamäki 1), 4 KEITTIÖPISTE 16 (Teemu Lahti 5 (0), Aleksey Poptsov 1, Toni Stenberg 0, Timo Lahti 10).

Round 3
Kauhajoki, Saturday, June 28

1 KEITTIÖPISTE 32 (Teemu Lahti 10, Niklas Larsson 3, Sami Lahti 1, Timo Lahti 18), 2 HAUKAT-ROYALS 31 (Viktor Bergström 12, Juha Mäkelä 11, Joni Kitala 1, Aarni Heikkilä 7), 3 PAHOLAISET 26 (Marko Suojanen 8, Petri Koskela 2, Alex Edberg 6, Appe Mustonen 10), 4 JOKERIT 21 (Kalle Katajisto 12 (2), Jani Eerikäinen 0, Markku Autio 9, Jan-Eric Korkeamäki 0).

Round 4 (re-staged)
Lahti, Sunday, July 13

1 KEITTIÖPISTE 33 (Teemu Lahti 9, Toni Stenberg 0, Aleksey Poptsov 8, Timo Lahti 16), 2 KOTKAT 32 (Kaj Laukkanen 13, Rene Lehtinen 14, Petterio Koivunen 3, Niko Siltaniemi 2), 3 HAUKAT-ROYALS 30 (Tomi Reima 12, Juha Mäkelä 9, Joni Kitala 4, Aarni Heikkilä 5), 4 JOKERIT 13 (Kalle Katajisto 7, Jani Eerikäinen 1, Markku Autio 4, Jan-Eric Korkeamäki 1).

Original staging on Sunday, June 15 postponed because of a waterlogged track at Lahti.

EXTRALIIGA FINAL TABLE

	M	1	2	3	4	RPts	Pts
1 KOTKAT	8	6	1	0	1	303	36
2 KEITTIÖPOSTE	8	3	1	3	1	220	30
3 HAUKAT-ROYALS	8	0	4	3	1	223	27
4 PAHOLAISET	8	0	3	2	3	199	24
5 JOKERIT	8	1	1	2	4	182	23

[Match points scoring: 1 = 5 points; 2nd = 4 pts; 3rd = 3 pts; 4th = 2 pts].

Round 5 (re-staged)
Kauhajoki, Sunday, July 20
1 KOTKAT 39 (**Juha Hautamâki 15**, **Kaj Laukkanen 15**, Joni Keskinen 5, Niko Siltaniemi 4), 2 HAUKAT-ROYALS 32 (Tomi Reima 14 (2), Juha Mäkelä 8, Joni Kitala 6, Aarni Heikkilä 4), 3 JOKERIT 25 (Kalle Katajisto 16 (2), Jani Eerikäinen 0, Markku Autio 8, Jan-Eric Korkeamäki 1), 4 PAHOLAISET 18 (Petri Koskela 4, Cesary Owizyc 4, Marko Suojanen 10 (2), Jukka Nieminen 0).

Round 6
Pori, Saturday, July 19
1 KOTKAT 42 (Kaj Laukkanen11, Joni Keskinen 10, **Juha Hautamäki 12**, Niko Siltaniemi 9), 2 PAHOLAISET 27+3 (Cesary Owizyc 5, Petri Koskela 3, Marko Suojanen 18 (3)+3, Tomi Kauppa 1), 3 KEITTIÖPISTE 27+2 (Teemu Lahti 12 (2), Toni Stenberg 1, Aleksey Poptsov 6, Timo Lahti 8+2), 4 HAUKAT-ROYALS 18 (Tomi Reima 10 (1), Juha Mäkelä 2, Joni Kitala 6, Aarni Heikkilä 0).

Round 7
Seinäjoki, Saturday, August 2
1 KOTKAT 44 (**Juha Hautamäki 12**, **Kaj Laukkanen 15**, Joni Keskinen 10, Niko Siltaniemi 7), 2 JOKERIT 32 (Fedor Poptsov 5, Kalle Katajisto 14 (2), Markku Autio 9, Jani Eerikäinen 4), 3 KEITTIÖPISTE 20 (Teemu Lahti 11 (2), Aleksey Poptsov 2, Timo Lahti 7, Toni Stenberg 0), 4 PAHOLAISET 19 (Cesary Owizyc 0, Marko Suojanen 1, Appe Mustonen 14 (3), Petri Koskela 4).

Round 8
Kauhajoki, Sunday, August 3
1 JOKERIT 33 (Fedor Poptsov 4, Kalle Katajisto 12, Markku Autio 10, Jani Eerikäinen 7), 2 KEITTIÖPISTE 31 (Teemu Lahti 11, Aleksey Poptsov 9, Timo Lahti 11 (2), Toni Stenberg 0), 3 HAUKAT-ROYALS 29 (Tomi Reima 19 (3), Juha Mäkela 5, Joni Kitala 3, Aarni Heikkilä 2), 4 PAHOLAISET 23 (Cesary Owizyc 5, Marko Suojanen 7, Appe Mustonen 9 (3), Petri Koskela 2).

Round 9
Lahti, Sunday, August 10
KOTKAT 37 (Juha Hautamäki 14, Rene Lehtinen 12, Joni Keskinen 5, Niko Siltaniemi 6), 2 HAUKAT-ROYALS 30 (Tomi Reima 14, Juha Mäkela 2, Jonas Andersson 9, Joni Kitala 5), 3 KEITTIÖPISTE 25 (Teemu Lahti 8, Aleksey Poptsov 3, Timo Lahti 14 (3), Toni Stenberg 0), 4 JOKERIT 21 (Fedor Poptsov 2, Kalle Katajisto 12 (2), Markku Autio 5, Jani Eerikäinen 2).

Round 10
Kuusankoski, Tuesday, September 9
1 KEITTIÖPISTE 36 (Teemu Lahti 7, Tero Aarnio 14, Timo Lahti 11, Aleksey Poptsov 4), 2 HAUKAT-ROYALS 28 (Tomi Reima 16 (3), Juha Mäkela 5, Joni Kitala 4, Aarni Heikkilä 3), 3 PAHOLAISET 26 (Appe Mustonen 9, Marko Suojanen 12 (2), Jari Mäkinen 4, Cesary Owizyc 1), 4 KOTKAT 25 (Niko Siltaniemi 7, Rene Lehtinen 16 (3), Joni Keskinen 2, Petteri Koivunen 0).

Round 11
Pori, Saturday, September 20
1 KOTKAT 43 (Juna Hautamäki 14, **Kaj Laukkanen 15**, **Rene Lehtinen 12**, Petteri Koivunen 2), 2 PAHOLAISET 29 (Appe Mustonen 11 (1), Jari Mäkinen 6, Marko Suojanen 2, Cesary Owizyc 10), 3 HAUKAT-ROYALS 25 (Tomi Reima 10, Juha Mäkelä 8, Joni Kitala 3, Aarni Heikkilä 4), 4 JOKERIT 15 (Fedor Poptsov, did not ride, Kalle Katajisto 11 (3), Jani Eerikäinen 4, Teemu Mattila 0).

Roll of Honour

1954 .... Haukat LAHTI
1955 .... Haukat LAHTI
1957 .... Hakkapelitat TAMPERE
1976 .... Assat TAMPERE
1977 .... Haukat LAHTI
1978 .... Haukat LAHTI
1979 .... Assat TAMPERE
1980 .... Assat TAMPERE
1981 .... Assat TAMPERE
1982 .... Pizza Team VARKAUS
1983 .... Team Pizzeria VARKAUS
1984 .... Assat TAMPERE
1985 .... Kotkat SEINÄJOKI
1986 .... Kotkat SEINÄJOKI
1987 .... Haukat LAHTI
1988 .... Haukat LAHTI
1989 .... Tiikerit KARHULA
1990 .... Kotkat SEINÄJOKI
1991 .... Ankkurit VARKAUS
1991 .... Ankkurit VARKAUS
1992 .... Ankkurit VARKAUS
1993 .... Sand Blowers HYVINKAA
1994 .... Ankkurit VARKAUS
1995 .... Kotkat SEINÄJOKI
1996 .... Paholaiset Haukat PORI/LAHTI
1997 .... Wasamat TAMPERE
1998 .... Kotkat SEINÄJOKI
1998 .... Ankkurit VARKAUS
1999 .... Kotkat SEINÄJOKI
2000 .... Neva ST. PETERSBURG (Russia)
2001 .... Hanavalinta HYVINKAA
2002 .... Hanavalinta HYVINKAA
2003 .... Keittioenet KUUSANKOSKI
2004 .... LEIJONAHAUKAT
2005 .... Kotkat SEINÄJOKI
2006 .... Keittiöpiste PORI
2007 .... Keittiöpiste KUSANKOSKI
2008 .... Kotkat SEINÄJOKI

EXTRALIIGA AVERAGES

Rider	Club	M	R	Pts	Ave	FM	TR	TPts
Juha HAUTAMÄKI	Kotkat	6	27	79	11.70	4	0	0
Tero AARNIO	**Kettiöpiste**	**1**	**5**	**14**	**11.20**	**0**	**0**	**0**
Kaj LAUKKANEN	Kotkat	5	25	69	11.04	3	0	0
Rene LEHTINEN	**Kotkat**	**5**	**24**	**66**	**11.00**	**2**	**1**	**3**
Tomi REIMA	Haukat-Royals	7	39	95	9.74	0	4	10
Viktor BERGSTRÖM	**Haukat-Royals**	**1**	**5**	**12**	**9.60**	**0**	**0**	**0**
Jonas ANDERSSON	Haukat-Royals	1	4	9	9.00	0	0	0
Benny JOHANSSON	**Kotkat**	**1**	**5**	**11**	**8.80**	**0**	**0**	**0**
Kalle KATAJISTO	Jokerit	8	46	91	7.91	0	6	12
Timo LAHTI	**Kettiöpiste**	**8**	**50**	**97**	**7.76**	**0**	**2**	**5**
Appe MUSTONEN	Paholaiset	6	35	67	7.66	0	3	7
Marko SUOJANEN	**Paholaiset**	**8**	**40**	**71**	**7.10**	**0**	**4**	**8**
Teemu LAHTI	Kettiöpiste	8	42	73	6.95	0	3	4
Joni KESKINEN	**Kotkat**	**5**	**21**	**32**	**6.10**	**0**	**0**	**0**
Alexander EDBERG	Paholaiset	1	4	6	6.00	0	0	0
Markku AUTIO	**Jokerit**	**7**	**34**	**50**	**5.88**	**0**	**0**	**0**
Juha MÄKELÄ	Haukat-Royals	8	36	50	5.56	0	0	0
Niko SILTANIEMI	**Kotkat**	**7**	**33**	**44**	**5.33**	**0**	**0**	**0**
Jari MÄKINEN	Paholaiset	2	8	10	5.00	0	0	0
Aleksey POPTSOV	**Kettiöpiste**	**7**	**28**	**33**	**4.71**	**0**	**0**	**0**
Cesary OWIZYC	Paholaiset	7	28	28	4.00	0	0	0
Fedor POPTSOV	**Jokerit**	**3**	**11**	**11**	**4.00**	**0**	**0**	**0**
Joni KITALA	Haukat-Royals	8	34	32	3.76	0	0	0
Aarni HEIKKILÄ	**Haukat-Royals**	**7**	**29**	**25**	**3.45**	**0**	**0**	**0**
Jani EERIKÄINEN	Jokerit	8	33	27	3.27	0	0	0
Petri KOSKELA	**Paholaiset**	**6**	**24**	**19**	**3.17**	**0**	**0**	**0**
Niklas LARSSON	Kettiöpiste	1	4	3	3.00	0	0	0
Tomi KAUPPE	**Paholaiset**	**1**	**3**	**1**	**1.33**	**0**	**0**	**0**
Sami LAHTI	Kettiöpiste	1	3	1	1.33	0	0	0
Jan-Eric KORKEAMÄKI	**Jokerit**	**4**	**13**	**3**	**0.92**	**0**	**0**	**0**
Petteri KOIVUNEN	Kotkat	3	9	2	0.89	0	0	0
Toni STENBERG	**Kettiöpiste**	**6**	**15**	**1**	**0.27**	**0**	**0**	**0**
Jukka NIEMINEN	Paholaiset	1	3	0	0.00	0	0	0
Teemu MATTILA	**Jokerit**	**1**	**6**	**0**	**0.00**	**0**	**0**	**0**

Statistics for Marko SUOJANEN and Timo LAHTI include points scored in run-off in Round 5.

Jokerit
Kalle Katajisto, Markku Autio, Jan-Eric Korkeamäki and Jani Eerikäinen

ABOVE: League silver medallists Keittiöpiste (KMMK) – Teemu Lahti, Toni Stenberg, Timo Lahti, Aleksey Poptsov and team manager Jorma Mäkikunnas

RIGHT: Paholaiset (PMK) – Alex Edberg, Petri Koskela, Jari Mäkinen, team manager Tomi Kauppi and Marko Suojanen

Finland Under 21 squad: coach Mikael Teurnberg, Teemu Lahti, Joni Keskinen, Joni Kitala, Timo Lahti, Kalle Katajisto, Aarni Heikkilä and coach Jyri Palomäki. Kneeling: Niko Siltaniemi and Jari Mäkinen

KAUPUNKI CUP FINAL TABLE

	M	1	2	3	4	5	6	RPts	Pts
1 PORI	6	4	1	0	0	0	1	116	39
2 FORSSA I	6	1	2	2	0	1	0	103+3	33
3 HAAPAJÄRVI	6	1	2	1	1	1	0	109	31
4 KAUHAJOKI	6	0	1	3	1	0	1	94+2	27
5 LAHTI	6	0	0	0	4	2	0	77	22
6 FORSSA II	6	0	0	0	0	2	4	53	13

[Match points scoring: 1 = 8 points; 2nd = 6 pts; 3rd = 5 pts; 4th = 4 pts; 5th = 3 pts; 6th = 2 pts].
†Haapajärvi (June 8), Pori (August 24) and Forssa II (Septembner 21) were deducted one point for fielding only one rider in a round.

KAUPUNKI CUP

Round 1
Pori, Sunday, September 21
1 PORI 24 (Juoni Viljanen 5:2, **Appe Mustonen 12**, **Jari Mäkinen 7:2**), 2 HAAPAJÄRVI 21 (Niko Siltaniemi 13, Juho Ruuska 8:4), 3 KAUHAJOKI 18 (Jere Mattila 11, Teemu Mattila 7:3), 4 LAHTI 11 (Jukka Nieminen 4:1, Markku Weckman 7), 5 FORSSA I 10 (Reima Heikilä 1, Jari Tapani 9), 6 FORSSA II 6 (Johan Ahponen 6).
Original staging on Monday, May 5 postponed because of a waterlogged track at Pori.

Round 2
Hyvinkää, Saturday, May 24
1 PORI 20 (Jouni Viljanen 3:1, Appe Mustonen 11, Petri Koskela 6:2), 2 FORSSA I 19+3 (Aarni Heikkilä 14+3, Tommi Ahlgren 4:2, Reimi Heikkilä 1:1), 3 KAUHAJOKI 19+2 (Jan-Eric Korkeamäki 8:2, Markku Autio 8:1+2, Jere Mattila 3:1), 4 HAAPAJÄRVI 14 (Niko Siltaniemi 14, Juho Ruuska 0), 5 LAHTI 11 (Jukka Nieminen 5:1, Markku Weckman 6:1), 6 FORSSA II 7 (Ari Tuomisto 6, Johan Ahponen 1:1).

Round 3
Kauhajoki, Sunday, June 8
1 PORI 20 (Jouni Viljanen 6:2, Marko Suojanen 14), 2 KAUHAJOKI 16 (Jan-Eric Korkeamäki 11, Jere Mattila 0, Olli Heikkilä 5:4), 3 FORSSA I 15 (**Aarni Heikkilä 15**, Reima Heikkilä 0), 4 LAHTI 13 (Jukka Nieminen 0, Markku Autio 13), 5 HAAPAJÄRVI 12 (Petteri Koivunen 12), 6 FORSSA II 11 (Ari Tuomisto 8, Johan Ahponen 3:3).

Round 4
Lathti, Sunday, July 13
1 PORI 27 (Jouni Viljanen 5:1, **Appe Mustonen 15**, **Kalle Kalajisto 7:2**), 2 HAAPAJÄRVI 24 (Niko Siltaniemi 16, Petteri Koivunen 8:3), 3 FORSSA I 20 (Aarni Heikkilä 9:1, Timo Lahti 6, Toni Stenberg 5:2), 4 ST. PETERSBURG NEVA 18 (Fedor Poptsov 6, Aleksey Poptsov 12:2), 5 LAHTI 14 (Jukka Nieminen 6, Markku Weckman 1:1, Joni Kitala 7), 6 FORSSA II 11 (Tommi Ahlgren 6:1, Ari Tuomisto 5), 7 KAUHAJOKI 10 (Jan Eric-Korkeamäki 9, Olli Heikkilä 0, Jere Mattila 1).

Round 5
Haapajärvi, Sunday, August 24
1 HAAPAJÄRVI 21 (**Niko Siltaniemi 15**, Juho Ruuska 6:2), 2 FORSSA I 19 (Aarni Heikkilä 13, Markku Larronmaa 6:3), 3 KAUHAJOKI 17 (Markku Autio 14, Olli Heikkilä 3), 4 LAHTI 15 (Jukka Nieminen 3:1, Joni Kitala 12), 5 FORSSA II 10 (Jari Tapani 8, Johan Ahponen 2), 6 PORI 7 (Juoni Viljanen 7).

Round 6
Hyvinkää, Saturday, August 30
1 FORSSA I 20 (Aarni Heikkilä 14, Jari Tapani 6:2), 2 PORI 18 (**Appe Mustonen 15**, Jouni Viljanen 3:1), 3 HAAPAJÄRVI 17 (Juho Ruuska 12, Petteri Koivunen 5:3), 4 KAUHAJOKI 14 (Jan-Eric Korkeamäki 9, Olli Heikkilä 0, Jere Mattila 5:1), 5 LAHTI 13 (Jukka Nieminen 1, Joni Kitala 12), 6 FORSSA II 8 (Johan Ahponen 3:1, Ari Tuomisto 5).

Roll of Honour
2008 ....PORI

FINNISH PAIRS CHAMPIONSHIP

Kauhajoki, Saturday, August 16
1 SEINÄJOEN MOOTTORIKERHO I 28 (Kaj Laukkanen 13:4, Juha Hautamäki 13:1, Petteri Koivunen [R] 2:1), **2 VARKAUS RACING TEAM 27** (Kalle Katajisto 17:1, Appe Mustonen 10:3), **3 KUUSANKOSKEN MOOTTORIM-IESKERHO 19** (Teemu Lahti 8:2, Timo Lahti 11), **4 SAINÄJOEN MOOTTORIKERHO II 18** (Niko Siltaniemi 7:2, Joni Keskinen 11:1), **5 PORIN MOOTTORIKERHO 17** (Marko Suojanen 12:1, Cesary Owyzic 5), **6 KAUHAJOEN MOOTTORIKERHO I 11** (Markku Autio 9, Jan-Eric Korkeamäki 2:1), **7 KAUHAJOEN MOOTTORIKERHO II 6** (Olli Heikkilä 1, Jere Mattila 5).

Roll of Honour
1999..SEINÄJOKI
2005 ....KUUSANKOSKI
2008 ....SEINÄJOEN

Representative

Hällstavik, Sunday, April 20
STJÄRNORNA (Sweden) 45 (Linus Jansson 8:2, Andreas Westlund 8:2, Niklas Larsson 1, Jens Oskarsson 11, Robin Burestad 3:2, Peter Wall 5:1, Jonas Messing 9, Harald Andersson, did not ride), **FINLAND 51** (Rene Lehtinen 7:2, Joni Keskinen 5, Teemu Lahti 12, Kalle Katajisto 12, Tomi Reima 6, Timo Lahti 0, Niko Siltaniemi 6, Aarni Heikkilä 3).

Hallstavik, Sweden, Saturday, September 6
STJÄRNORNA 47 (David Hillborg 6:1, Jens Oskarsson 8:1, Emil Lindqvist 9, Andreas Westlund 3:2, Andreas Messing 12, Robin Burestad 5:1, Peter Wall 4:1), **FINLAND UNDER 21 49** (Kalle Katajisto 12, Niko Siltaniemi 7:1, Timo Lahti 6, Jari Mäkinen 1, Teemu Lahti 10:1, Aarni Heikkilä 0, Joni Kitala 3, Joni Keskinen 10:1).

Eskilstuna, Sweden, Sunday, September 7
TEAM BIKAB 61 (Eric Andersson 13:1, Jimmy Jansson 5:1, Henrik Karlsson 6, Robin Berkvist 6:2, Daniel

KAUPUNKI CUP AVERAGES

Rider	M	R	Pts	BP	TPts	Ave	F	P
Jari MÄKINEN	1	3	7	2	9	12.00	0	1
Kalle KATAJISTO	**1**	**3**	**7**	**2**	**9**	**12.00**	**0**	**1**
Appe MOSTONEN	4	18	53	0	53	11.78	3	0
Marko SUOJANEN	**1**	**5**	**14**	**0**	**14**	**11.20**	**0**	**0**
†Markku AUTIO	3	13	35	1	36	11.08	0	0
Niko SILTANIEMI	**4**	**21**	**58**	**0**	**58**	**11.05**	**1**	**0**
Petri KOSKELA	1	3	6	2	8	10.67	0	0
†Aarni HEIKKILÄ	**5**	**26**	**68**	**1**	**69**	**10.62**	**1**	**0**
Joni KITALA	3	13	31	0	31	9.54	0	0
Aleksey POPTSOV	**1**	**6**	**12**	**2**	**14**	**9.33**	**0**	**0**
Toni STENBERG	1	3	5	2	7	9.33	0	0
Jan-Eric KORKEAMÄKI	**4**	**19**	**39**	**2**	**41**	**8.63**	**0**	**0**
Juho RUUSKA	4	16	26	6	32	8.00	0	0
Teemu MATTILA	**1**	**5**	**7**	**3**	**10**	**8.00**	**0**	**0**
Petteri KOIVUNEN	3	16	25	6	31	7.75	0	0
Markku LARRONMAA	**1**	**5**	**6**	**3**	**9**	**7.20**	**0**	**0**
Jari TAPANI	3	15	23	2	25	6.67	0	0
Jere MATTILA	**5**	**14**	**20**	**2**	**22**	**6.29**	**0**	**0**
Jouni VILJANEN	6	25	29	7	36	5.76	0	0
Tommi AHLGREN	**2**	**10**	**10**	**3**	**13**	**5.20**	**0**	**0**
Markku WECKMAN	3	13	14	2	16	4.92	0	0
Ari TUOMISTO	**4**	**21**	**24**	**0**	**24**	**4.57**	**0**	**0**
Fedor POPTSOV	1	6	6	0	6	4.00	0	0
Jukka NIEMINEN	**6**	**27**	**19**	**3**	**22**	**3.26**	**0**	**0**
Johan AHPONEN	5	25	15	5	20	3.20	0	0
Olli HEIKKILÄ	**4**	**17**	**8**	**4**	**12**	**2.82**	**0**	**0**
Reima HEIKKILÄ	3	6	2	1	3	2.00	0	0

†Includes points scored in race-off for second place in Round 2.

Representative

Henderson 13:1, Rasmus Eklöf 3, Alexander Edberg 15:1) **FINLAND UNDER 21 35** (Kalle Katajisto 11, Niko Siltaniemi 7:1, Timo Lahti 2:1, Jari Mäkinen 3, Teemu Lahti 0, Aarni Heikkilä 3, Joni Kitala 4, Joni Keskinen 5).

Seinäjoki, Saturday, August 23
WEST 49 (**Juha Hautamäki 18**, Joni Keskinen 10:2, Markku Autio 6:2, Niko Siltaniemi 13, Petteri Koivunen 2:2), **EAST 38** (Kalle Katajisto 15, Juha Mäkelä 12 (6), Aarni Heikkilä 2:1, Joni Kitala 9:1, *rider replacement for Jani Eerikäinen*).

Individual Championship
Semi Final: Joni Keskinen, Markku Autio, Joni Kitala, Kalle Katajisto.
Final: Juha Hautamäki, Joni Keskinen, Niko Siltaniemi, Markku Autio.

Yyteri, Saturday, May 17
1 Kalle Katajisto 11+□+3, 2 Tomi Reima 10+3+2, Marko Suojanen 11+□+1, 4 Appe Mustonen 11+2+0, 5 Niko Siltaniemi 11+1, 6 Niklas Larsson 11+0, Timo Lahti 10, Jens Oskarsson 9, Alexander Edberg 7, Markku Autio 6, Juho Ruuska 6, Teemu Lahti 5, Aarni Heikkilä 4, Jukka Nieminen 3, Jouni Viljanen 2.

Individual

XXI Kemppi Speedway, Lahti, Sunday, June 1
1 Kalle Katajisto 15+r+3, 2 Robert Henderson 12+3+2, 3 Timo Lahti 14+2+1, 4 Joni Kitala 9+r+0, 5 Aarni Heikkilä 10+1, 6 Teemu Lahti 12+FX, 7 Aleksey Poptsov 9, 8 Jan-Eric Korkeamäki 8, 9 Fedor Poptsov 6, 10 Alexander Edberg 6, 11 Markku Weckman 5, 12 Jukka Nieminen 4, 13 Reima Heikkilä 3, Jere Mattila, Juha Mäkelä, did not ride.

III Kauhajoki Cup, Kauhajoki, Saturday, June 7
1 Rene Lehtinen 14+3, 2 Timo Lahti 13+2, 3 Markku Autio 14+1, 4 Petri Koskela 11+0, 5 Jani Eerikäinen 10+3, 6 Aarni Heikkilä 11+2, 7 Petteri Koivunen 10+1, 8 Jan-Eric Korkeamäki 9+0, 9 Jere Mattila 7, 10 Toni Stenberg 6, 11 Markku Larronmaa 5, 12 Olli Heikkilä 3, 13 Reima Heikkilä 3.

For 2009 information see page 541

Photographs by
PETTERI POHJOLA
Editor
Speedway Sanomat

FRANCE

FRENCH CHAMPIONSHIP

FINAL

Lamothe Landeron, Saturday, June 14

FLYING Dutchman Theo Pijper – racing on a French licence – became a dual national champion with three unbeaten rides.

The domestic championship was run as part of a major open meeting at Lamothe Landeron and the troubled Pijper, who had an unsettled season in Britain, dominated, restricting the Tresarrieu siblings Stephane and Sébastien to rostrum places.

The final was contested by only ten riders, the other nine being France nationals.

	1	2	3	Tot
1 THEO PIJPER	**5**	**5**	**5**	**15**
2 Stephane TRESARRIEU	4	4	5	13
3 Sébastien TRESARRIEU	5	4	4	13
4 Theo DI PALMA	3	3	4	10
5 Jerome LESPINASSE	2	2	3	7
6 Sebastian BROUSSILOU	1	2	3	6
7 Gabriel DUBERNAUD	2	1	2	5
8 Maxime MAZEAU	3	0	0	3
9 Jerome TURANI	0	1	1	2
10 Guillaume COMBLON	0	0	1	1

Roll of Honour

1928 .... Charles BELLISENT
1929 .... Fernand MEYNIER
1930 .... Fernand MEYNIER
1931 .... Fernand MEYNIER
1932 .... Fernand MEYNIER
1948 .... Charles BELLISENT
1950 .... Jean LANDRU
1953 .... Robert FLUIMANI
1957 .... Ted CONNOR (England)
1958 .... Keith MORRISON (England)
1959 .... Claude BOSTON
1960 .... Jean Du BARDINE
1961 .... Ray LISTON (Australia)
1962 .... Roger BEGASSE
1984 .... Patrice BLONDY
1992 .... Christophe DUBERNARD
1996 .... Philippe BERGÉ
2007 .... Mathieu TRESARRIEU
2008 .... Theo PIJPER (Holland)

Individual

FRENCH INTERNATIONAL OPEN

Lamothe Landeron, Saturday, June 14

1 Adam Skornicki 19+6+6, 2 Ricky Ashworth 19+5+5, 3 Adam Shields 21+5+4, 4 Joe Screen 19+3+3, 5 Steve Johnston 20+2+2, 6 Matej Ferjan 21+6+0 [R], 7 Cory Gathercole 17+3, 8 Travis McGowan 14+4, 9 Glen Phillips 12+4, 10 Adrian Szewczykowski 14+1, 11 Joonas Kylmåkorpi 13+1, 12 Theo Pijper 11+2, 13 Filip Sitera 9, 14 Stephane Tresarrieu 9, 15 Grzegorz Knapp 9, 16 Sébastian Tresarrieu 8, 17 Richard Wolff 7, 18 Ben Wilson 5.

[Scoring: 6-5-4-3-2-1-0 for non-finisher. Top 12 scorers to two semi finals; top six scorers to Grand Final].

FRENCH INTERNATIONAL OPEN

Lamothe Landeron, Saturday, October 11

1 Matej Ferjan 35 [29+6], 2 Oliver Allen 31 [26+5], 3 Grzegorz Knapp 29 [26+3], 4 Maks Gregoric 29 [25+4], 5 Cory Gathercole 25 [23+2], 6 Mark Lemon 24 [23+1], 7 Joel Parsons 21, 8 Piotr Swist 19, 9 Theo Pijper 15, 10 Glen Phillips 14, 11 Sébastien Tresarrieu 13, 12 Mateusz Mikorski 13, 13 Tom Madsen 11, 14 Emil Idziorek 8, 15 Lee Complin (*pictured above*) 8, 16 Jerome Léspinasse 7, 17 Richard Sweetman 6, 18 Mathieu Tresarrieu 4, 19 Stephane Tresarrieu 0.

[Scoring: 6-5-4-3-2-1. The top 12 riders from a 12-heat qualifying competition went into two six rider semi finals and the top six overall points scorers went into the six rider Grand Final].

GERMANY

GERMAN CHAMPIONSHIP

FINAL

Diedenbergen, Sunday, September 14

EX-KING'S Lynn flop Thomas Stange looked a nailed on certainty to make home track advantage pay off.

The Diedenbergen skipper won his first three rides but an engine failure fourth time out dramatically changed the complexion of the meeting.

And when he was blamed for a crash involving both Tobias Busch and Kevin Wölbert his hopes of a first senior national title to add to his 2006 junior crown were over.

With ten points out of 12, Richard Speiser held the initiative going into the final four races but nerves got the better of the 21-year-old Bavarian and he suffered a surprise defeat against Erik Pudel.

It left the title wide open with Kevin Wölbert, defending champion Martin Smolinski, Stange and even Tobias Busch still in with a genuine opportunity of being crowned.

Smolinski and Wölbert duly booked their places in a title run-off with race wins but Busch's third place ruled him out.

In the race-off, Wölbert made the crucial start, holding off Smolinski's spirited challenge.

The 19-year-old said: "Getting the silver medal in the European Team Championship was very pleasing – but this means so much more to me."

	1	2	3	4	5	Tot	RO
1 Kevin WÖLBERT	**1**	**2**	**3**	**3**	**3**	**12**	**3**
2 Martin SMOLINSKI	3	2	2	2	3	12	2
3 Richard SPEISER	3	3	1	3	2	12	1
4 Frank FACHER	1	3	1	3	3	11	
5 Roberto HAUPT	0	3	2	3	2	10	
6 Tobias BUSCH	3	1	3	2	1	10	
7 Thomas STANGE	3	3	3	R	FX	9	
8 Mathias SCHULTZ	2	2	2	1	2	9	
9 Max DILGER	2	1	2	2		7	
10 Erik PUDEL	1	0	0	2	3	6	
11 Sönke PETERSEN	0	2	3	0	1	6	
12 Steffen MELL	2	R	1	1	1	5	
13 Mathias BARTZ	0	1	0	1	2	4	
14 René DEDDENS	2	0	1	0	0	3	
15 Hans-Jorg MÜLLER	1	0	0	1	FX	2	
16 Manfred BETZ	R	1	0	0	0	1	
17 Sebastian ECKERLE [R]	1					1	

Roll of Honour

1992 .... Gerd RISS
1993 .... Marvyn COX (England)
1994 .... Gerd RISS
1995 .... Marvyn COX (England)
1996 .... Gerd RISS
1997 .... Todd WILTSHIRE (Australia)
1998 .... Todd WILTSHIRE (Australia)
1999 .... Mirko WOLTER
2000 .... Robert BARTH
2001 .... Robert BARTH
2002 .... Mirko WOLTER
2003 .... Mathias SCHULTZ
2004 .... Mirko WOLTER
2005 .... Mathias SCHULTZ
2006 .... Christian HEFENBROCK
2007 .... Martin SMOLINSKI
2008 .... Kevin WÖLBERT

The divided Germany staged independent championships until the end of 1991.

The old West and East Germany were re-united after 40 years in October, 1990 and since 1992 an all-embracing championship has been held.

FEDERAL REPUBLIC of GERMANY (West Germany)

1979 .... Egon MÜLLER
1980 .... Georg GILGENREINER
1981 .... Egon MÜLLER
1982 .... Josef AIGNER
1983 .... Egon MÜLLER
1984 .... Egon MÜLLER
1985 .... Egon MÜLLER
1986 .... Gerd RISS
1987 .... Tommy DUNKER
1988 .... Klaus LAUSCH
1989 .... Klaus LAUSCH
1990 .... Klaus LAUSCH

GERMAN DEMOCRATIC REPUBLIC (East Germany)

1962 .... Jurgen HEHLERT
1963 .... Jochen DINSE
1964 .... Jochen DINSE
1965 .... Jochen DINSE
1966 .... Jurgen HEHLERT
1967 .... Jochen DINSE
1968 .... Jochen DINSE
1969 .... Peter LIEBING
1970 .... Hans Jurgen FRITZ
1971 .... Hans Jurgen FRITZ
1972 .... Hans Jurgen FRITZ
1973 .... Jochen DINSE
1974 .... Dieter TETZLAFF
1975 .... Clemens BEVER
1976 .... Dieter TETZLAFF
1977 .... Hartmut ERNST
1978 .... Dieter TETZLAFF
1979 .... Dieter TETZLAFF
1980 .... Dieter TETZLAFF
1981 .... Diethelm TRIEMER
1982 .... Diethelm TRIEMER
1983 .... Diethelm TRIEMER
1984 .... Diethelm TRIEMER
1985 .... Diethelm TRIEMER
1986 .... Diethelm TRIEMER

1987 .... Diethelm TRIEMER
1988 .... Herbert MUSSEHL
1989 .... Joachim MELL
1990 .... Mike OTT
1991 .... Thomas DIEHR

UNDER 21 CHAMPIONSHIP

FINAL

Herxheim. Sunday, August 31

GERMAN Champion Kevin Wölbert arrived at Herxheim straight from the previous night's European Under 19 Final.

And Richard Speiser came with the silver medal he had won at the European Grass Track Final in Holland just 24 hours earlier.

Both were on a high – but while they both figured on the rostrum neither claimed the winner's spot, the title going to Max Dilger.

A grippier than expected track caused problems for most of the competitors with a string of falls and exclusions with referee Frank Ziegler incurring the wrath of the big contingent of Olching fans cheering on Frank Facher.

His late exclusion effectively cost him the title as a win in his final race would have seen him finish with 13 points, one ahead of Dilger and Speiser who met in a race-off for the silver medal.

Disappointed Facher even missed out on bronze, Wölbert beating Tobias Busch in another run-off.

Newly-crowned champion Dilger said: "Simply super – my first big title.

"In the Final I was faster over the four laps than Richard [Speiser], but I could not find a way past him until the last bend when I had a little gap I could go through!"

Speiser added: "I was perhaps caught out not concentrating. Max caught me out – that's speedway, finished, out!"

	1	2	3	4	5	Tot	RO
1 Max DILGER	**1**	**3**	**3**	**2**	**3**	**12**	**3**
2 Richard SPEISER	3	1	3	2	3	12	2
3 Kevin WÖLBERT	3	2	2	3	1	11	3
4 Tobias BUSCH	2	3	1	3	2	11	2
5 Kai HUCKENBECK	3	2	0	3	2	10	
6 Frank FACHER	2	3	3	2	FX	10	
7 Erik PUDEL	2	2	FX	3	3	10	
8 Sönke PETERSEN	3	2	3	X	2	10	
9 Manfred BETZ	2	3	2	FX	1	8	
10 René DEDDENS	0	1	2	1	3	7	
11 Denis WIENKE	1	0	0	1	2	4	
12 Marcel HELFER	FX	1	1	2	0	4	
13 Christoph DEMMEL	R	0	2	1	1	4	
14 Ramon STANEK	1	1	1	1	FX	4	
15 Franz WINKELHOFER	1	R	R	0	1	2	
16 Arne LEDWIG	0	0	0	0	0	0	

QUALIFYING

Group North

Round 1, Güstrow, Friday, May 9

Sönke Petersen 15, Tobias Busch 14, Erik Pudel 13, Robert Baumann 11, Ramon Stanek 10, Rene Deddens 9, Denis Wienke 7, Arne Ledwig 7, Marcel Kalms 7, Sergej Malyschew 7, Fritz Riemer 5, Toni Brosowski 4, Domingo Krecklow 4, Danny Maaßen 3, Nils Hesse 2, Marco Gaschka 1, Clemens Sommer 1, Henk Koonstra 0.

Round 2, Teterow, Saturday, June 14

Kevin Wölbert 15, Erik Pudel 14, Rene Deddens 13, Sönke Petersen 12, Denis Wienke 11, Toni Brosowski 10, Robert Baumann 8, Kai Huckenbeck 8, Arne Ledwig 6, Ramon Stanek 4, Marcel Kalms 4, Henk Koonstra 4, Domingo Krecklow 4, Sergej Malyschew 3, Bernd Dinklage 2, Danny Maaßen 1, Fritz Riemer[R] 1.

Round 3, Norden, Sunday, August 3

Tobias Busch 14, Ramon Stanek 13, Sönke Petersen 12, Kai Huckenbeck 12, Rene Deddens 12, Arne Ledwig 10, Fritz Riemer 8, Henk Koonstra 7, Danny Maaßen 7, Nils Hesse 6, Bernd Dinklage 6, Clemens Sommer 4, Marco Gaschka 4, Denis Wienke 2.

Group South

Round 1, Landshut, Sunday, April 13

Frank Facher 15, Sönke Petersen 13, Richard Speiser 12, Sebastian Mack 11, Marcel Helfer 10, Manfred Betz 10, Franz Winkelhofer 8, Max Dilger 8, Arne Ledwig 6, Christoph Demmel 6, Ramon Stanek 5, Sebastian Eckerle 5, Dennis Helfer 3, Marcel Dachs 3, Friedrich Ruf 3, Stefan Drofa 0.

Round 2, Abensberg, Saturday, August 16

Richard Speiser 11+3, Frank Facher 12+2, Max Dilger 10+1, Marcel Helfer 6+0, Manfred Betz 8+3, Christoph Demmel 3+2, Franz Winkelhofer 7+1, Marcel Dachs 4+0, Friedrich Ruf 5, Dennis Helfer 3, Sebastian Eckerle 2, Stefan Drofa 1.

Roll of Honour

1992 .... Robert KESSLER
1993 .... Robert KESSLER
1994 .... Sebastian MAAG
1995 .... Mirko WOLTER
1996 .... Mirko WOLTER
1997 .... Stefan BACHHUBER
1998 .... Ales DRYML[2] (Czech Republic)
1999 .... Ales DRYML[2] (Czech Republic)
2000 .... Matthias SCHULTZ
2001 .... Christian HEFENBROCK
2002 .... Thomas STANGE
2003 .... Martin SMOLINSKI
2004 .... Matthias SCHULTZ
2005 .... Christian HEFENBROCK
2006 .... Thomas STANGE
2007 .... Tobias BUSCH
2008 .... Max DIILGER

FEDERAL REPUBLIC of GERMANY (West Germany)

1983 .... Gerd RISS
1987 .... Robert BARTH
1988 .... Robert BARTH
1989 .... Uwe FIENHAGE

GERMAN DEMOCRATIC REPUBLIC (East Germany)

1964 .... Paul Gerhard FRITZ
1966 .... Paul Gerhard FRITZ
1969 .... Jurgen STREHLOW
1972 .... Jurgen STREHLOW
1973 .... Hartmut ERNST
1977 .... Udo KAMMANN
1979 .... Udo KAMMANN
1982 .... Wolfgang BUSKE
1983 .... Mike OTT
1984 .... Ralf PETERS
1985 .... Dirk MUHLENFELD
1989 .... Maik EBENSING
1990 .... Thomas HOPP
1991 .... Matthias KOCH

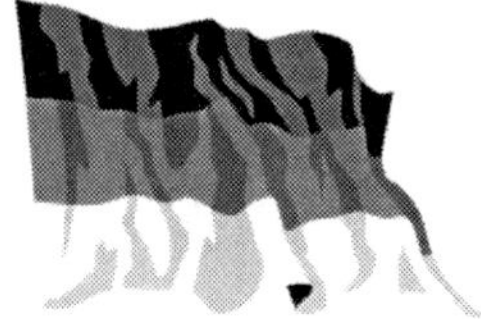

SPEEDWAY BUNDESLIGA
speedway-bundesliga.de

FINAL

Wolfslake, Friday, October 3

1 MSC OLCHING 37						
Martin SMOLINSKI	2	1	2	3	1	9
Matej ZAGAR	2	2	3	3	0	10
Frank FACHER	0	1	1	3	2	7
Manuel HAUZINGER	2	1	2	1	3	9
Manfred BETZ	*2*	*A*	*2*	*2*		*2*
Ch. RINKENBURGER	*0*	*0*	*0*	*0*		*0*
2 MSC DIEDENBERGEN 34						
Thomas STANGE	1	2	0	1	0	4
Piotr SWIDERSKI	3	3	3	1	3	13
Ronny WEIS	0	A	1	0	1	2
Tomasz JEDRZEJAK	1	3	3	2	2	11
Denis WEINKE	*0*	*2*	*1*	*0*		*1*
Rene DEDDENS	*2*	*3*	*3*	*3*		*3*
3 ST WOLFSLAKE 33						
Marcin SEKULA	2	0	2	2	0	6
Matej FERJAN	3	3	R	0	1	7
Sebastian ULAMEK	3	2	2	3	1	11
Pawel HLIB	1	0	1	2	3	7
Robert BAUMANN	*1*	*1*	*0*	*1*		*0*
Erik PUDEL	*3*	*2*	*2*	*2*	*2*	*2*
4 AC LANDSHUT 28						
Christian HEFENBROCK	1	1	0	0	2	4
Piotr PROTASIEWICZ	3	3	3	2	3	14
Adam SKORNICKI	0	2	1	1	2	6
Stefan KURZ	0	0	0	0	0	0
Richard SPEISER	*3*	*3*	*3*	*3*		*3*
Marcel HELFER	*1*	*1*	*1*	*1*		*1*

Throughout the competition each team had to include both an Under 21 and Under 19 rider in their line-up. They had four races and the highest points scorer was awarded three points, second highest scorer 2 points, third highest scorer 1 point, lowest scorer 0 pts to be included in overall team total. In the statistics that follow for the qualifying competition, points scored from the four races are included in parenthesis in team details.

FINAL QUALIFYING TABLE

	M	RPts	MPts
1 WOLFSLAKE	4	162	9
2 Olching	4	148	9
3 Landshut	4	147	8
4 Diedenbergen	4	139	7
5 Brokstedt	4	134	5
6 Neuenknick	4	109	4
7 Pfaffenhofen	4	75	0

Match points: 1= 3pts, 2= 2pts, 3= 1 pt; 4= 0 pts.

Roll of Honour

1991 .... LANDSHUT
1992 .... OLCHING
1993 .... LANDSHUT
1994 .... DIEDENBERGEN
1995 .... DIEDENBERGEN
1996 .... DIEDENBERGEN
1997 .... BROKSTEDT
1998 .... DIEDENBERGEN
1999 .... LANDSHUT
2000 .... LANDSHUT
2001 .... DIEDENBERGEN
2002 .... GÜSTROW
2003 .... GÜSTROW
2004 .... PARCHIM/WOLFSLAKE
2005 .... DIEDENBERGEN
2006 .... OLCHING
2007 .... OLCHING
2008 .... OLCHING

FEDERAL REPUBLIC of GERMANY (West Germany)

1973 .... NEUMÜNSTER
1974 .... BOPFINGEN
1975 .... KRUMBACH
1976 .... KRUMBACH
1997 .... LANDSHUT
1978 .... LANDSHUT
1979 .... LANDSHUT
1980 .... BROKSTEDT
1981 .... BROKSTEDT
1982 .... LANDSHUT
1983 .... KRUMBACH
1984 .... LANDSHUT
1985 .... DIEDENBERGEN
1986 .... LANDSHUT
1987 .... DIEDENBERGEN
1988 .... DIEDENBERGEN
1989 .... LANDSHUT
1990 .... DIEDENBERGEN

GERMAN DEMOCRATIC REPUBLIC (East Germany)

1965 .... MEISSEN
1966 .... GÜSTROW
1967 .... GÜSTROW
1968 .... GÜSTROW
1969 .... Dynamo ROSTOCK
1970 .... Dynamo ROSTOCK
1971 .... Dynamo ROSTOCK
1972 .... GÜSTROW
1973 .... GÜSTROW
1974 .... GÜSTROW
1975 .... GÜSTROW
1976 .... MEISSEN
1977 .... GÜSTROW
1978 .... GÜSTROW
1979 .... GÜSTROW
1980 .... GÜSTROW
1981 .... GÜSTROW
1982 .... GÜSTROW
1983 .... GÜSTROW
1984 .... GÜSTROW
1985 .... GÜSTROW

1986 .... GÜSTROW
1987 .... GÜSTROW
1988 .... NEUBRANDENBURG
1989 .... GÜSTROW
1990 .... GÜSTROW

MAJOR GERMAN CLUBS

MSC ABENSBERG
Track: Postfach 1252, 93321 Abensberg, Germany. **Telephone:** 0049 09443 905510. **Website:** www.speedway-abensberg.de

ST BERLIN-WOLFSLAKE
Track: c/o Fritz Mauer, Bäckerweg 7, 14621 Schönwalde, Germany. **Telephone:** 0049 033230 50289. **Website:** www.speedwayteam-wolfslake.de

MSC BROKSTEDT
Track: Postfach 1236, 25543 Kellinghusen, Germany. **Telephone:** 0049 04822 2344. **Website:** www.mscbrokstedt.de

MSC DIEDENBERGEN
Track: Wildsachsenerstraße, 65719 Hofheim-Diedenbergen, Germany. **Telephone:** 0049 06192 31395. **Website:** www.msc-diedenbergen.de

MC GÜSTROW
Track: Plauer Chaussee, 18273 Güstrow, Germany. **Telephone:** 0049 03843 684685. **Website:** www.mcguestrow.de

AC LANDSHUT
Track: Stadion Ellermühle, Flugplatzstrasse 10, D-84034, Landshut, Germany.
Telphone: 0049 08765332.
Website: acl-neu.landshut.org

MC MEISSEN
Track: Speedway Stadion, Zaschendorfer Straßer, 01662, Meißen, Germany. **Telephone:** 0049 03521 733208. **Website:** www.mc-meissen.de

MSC MOORWINKELSDAMM
Track: Weißenmoorstraße 20, 26345 Bockhorn, Germany. **Telephone:** 0049 04453 71378. **Website:** www.mscm.de

SC NEUENKNICK e.V. im ADAC,
Track: Karl-Heinrich König, Am Brokenkamp 9, 32469, Petershagen, Germany. **Telephone:** 0049 05768 490. **Website:** www.sc-neuenknick.homepage.t-online.de

MSC NORDSTERN STRALSUND
Track: Paul-Greifzu-Stadiion, Bartherstraße 58, 18473 Stralsund, Germany. **Telephone:** 0049 03831 292777. **Website:** www.mcn-stralsund.de

MSC PFAFFENHOFEN
Track: Altenstadt 1a, 825276, Pfaffenhofen, Germany. **Telephone:** 0049 08441 785104. **Website:** www.msc-paf.de

MC POCKING
Track: Postfach 1107, 94052 Pocking, Germany. **Telephone:** 0049 08531 8383. **Website:** www.msc-pocking.de

MC BERGRING TETEROW
Track: Appelhäger Chaussee 1, 17166 Teterow, Germany. **Telephone:** 0049 03996 172935. **Website:** www.bergring-teterow.de

Bundesliga

BERLIN WOLFSLAKE

2008 RESULTS

SQUAD
Steffen Mell, Tomasz Schmidt.
Under 21: Robert Baumann, Clemens Sommer, Fritz Riemer.
Under 19: Erik Pudel.
Foreign: Matej Ferjan, Pawel Hlib, Marcin Sekula, Sebastian Ulamek, Karol Zabik.

Round 1
Brokstedt, Sunday, April 20
3 WOLFSLAKE 32 (Sekula 8, Mell 5, Hlib 7, Zabik 9, Baumann 1 [4], Pudel 2 [8]), 1 LANDSHUT 36+3, 2 BROKSTEDT 36+2, 3 NEUENKNICK 28.

Round 2
Pfaffenhofen, Sunday May 4
2 WOLFSLAKE 36+3 (Schultz 7, Sekula 9, Schmidt 6, Ferjan 11+3, Sommer 0 [2], Pudel 3 [11]), 1 OLCHING 40, 2 LANDSHUT 36+2, 3 PFAFFENHOFEN 20.

Round 6
Diedenbergen, Saturday, July 26
1 WOLFSLAKE 51 (Sekula 8, Ferjan 13, Hlib 13, Ulamek 14, Fritz Riemer 0 [1], Pudel 3 [12]), 2 DIEDENBERGEN 38+3, 3 BROKSTEDT 38+2, 4 PFAFFENHOFEN 5.

Round 7
Wolfslake, Saturday, August 2
1 WOLFSLAKE 43 (Sekula 6, Ferjan 12, Hlib 11, Ulamek 11, Baumann 1 [4], Pudel 2 [6]), 2 NEUENKNICK 32, 3 DIEDENBERGEN 31, 4 BROKSTEDT 26.

Rider	*M*	*R*	*Pts*	*Ave*	*FM*
Sebastian ULAMEK	3	15	36	9.60	0
Matej FERJAN	**4**	**21**	**46**	**8.76**	**0**
Pawel HLIB	4	20	38	7.60	0
Karol ZABIK	**1**	**5**	**9**	**7.20**	**0**
Marcin SEKULA	5	25	37	5.92	0
Matthias SCHULTZ	**1**	**5**	**7**	**5.60**	**0**
Tomasz SCHMIDT	1	5	6	4.80	0
Steffen MELL	**1**	**5**	**5**	**4.00**	**0**
Under 21					
Clemens SOMMER	1	4	4	4.00	0
Robert BAUMANN	**2**	**8**	**7**	**3.50**	**0**
Fritz RIEMER	1	4	1	1.00	0
Under 19					
Erik PUDEL	5	20	46	9.20	1

Bundesliga

BROKSTEDT

2008 RESULTS

SQUAD
Stephan Katt, Matthias Kröger, Tobias Kroner.
Under 21: Sönke Petersen, Kristian Drossman.
Under 19: Ramon Stanek.
Foreign: Henning Bager, Charlie Gjedde, Joonas Kylmåkorpi.

Round 1
Brokstedt, Sunday, April 20
2 BROKSTEDT 36+2 (Kröger 5, Katt 4, Kroner 11, Gjedde 13+2, Petersen 3 [12], Stanek 0 [1]), 1 LANDSHUT 36+3, 3 WOLFSLAKE 32, 4 NEUENKNICK 28.

Round 3
Neuenknick, Sunday, June 15
2 BROKSTEDT 34 (Kröger 4, Gjedde 10, Kylmåkorpi 7, Kroner 9, Petersen 3 [12], Stanek 1 [3]), 1 DIEDENBERGEN 40, 3 NEUENKNICK 33, 4 OLCHING 25.

Round 6
Diedenbergen, Saturday, July 26
3 BROKSTEDT 38+2 (Kröger 7, Gjedde 8, Kroner 11+2, Bager 8, Petersen 3 [12], Stanek 1 [4]), 1 WOLFSLAKE 51, 2 DIEDENBERGEN 38+3, 4 PFAFFENHOFEN 5.

Round 7
Wolfslake, Saturday, August 2
4 BROKSTEDT 26 (Kröger 3, Petersen 4, Kroner 5, Kylmåkorpi 10, Drossman 3 [10], Stanek 1 [5], 1 WOLFSLAKE 43, 2 NEUENKNICK 32, 3 DIEDENBERGEN 31.

See page 542 for details of opening 2009 fixture.

Rider	M	R	Pts	Ave	FM
Charlie GJEDDE	3	16	33	8.25	0
Tobias KRONER	**4**	**21**	**38**	**7.24**	**0**
Joonas KYLMÅKORPI	2	10	17	6.80	0
Henning BAGER	**1**	**5**	**8**	**6.40**	**0**
Matthias KRÖGER	4	20	19	3.80	0
Stephan KATT	**1**	**5**	**4**	**3.20**	**0**
Sönke PETERSEN	1	5	4	3.20	0
Under 21					
Sönke PETERSEN	3	12	36	12.00	3
Kristian DROSSMANN	**1**	**4**	**10**	**10.00**	**0**
Under 19					
Ramon STANEK	4	16	13	3.25	0

Bundesliga

DIEDENBERGEN

2008 RESULTS

SQUAD
Ronny Weis, Thomas Stange,
Under 21: Sergej Malyschew, Denis Wienke.
Under 19: Rene Deddens.
Foreign: Patrick Hougaard, Tomasz Jedrzejak, Robert Kosciecha, Piotr Swiderski, Grzegorz Walasek.

Round 3
Neuenknick, Sunday, June 15
1 DIEDENBERGEN 40 (Weis 4, Swiderski 13, Jedrzejak 12, Stange 8, Wienke 0 [3], Deddens 3 [12]), 2 BROKSTEDT 34, 3 NEUENKNICK 33, 4 OLCHING 25.

Round 4
Landshut, Saturday, July 12
3 DIEDENBERGEN 30 (Kosciecha 7, Weis 2, Stange 7, Jedrzejak 11, Wienke 0 [1], Deddens 3 [10], 1 OLCHING 39, 2 LANDSHUT 38, 4 PFAFFENHOFEN 25.

Round 6
Diedenbergen, Saturday, July 26
2 DIEDENBERGEN 38+3 (Stange 9, Hougaard 10, Walasek 12+3, Weis 4, Wienke 1 [3], Deddens 2 [8]), 1 WOLFSLAKE 51, 3 BROKSTEDT 38+2, 4 PFAFFENHOFEN 5.

Round 7
Wolfslake, Saturday, August 2
3 DIEDENBERGEN 31 (Weis 5, Walasek 11, Stange 7, Jedrzejak 8, Malyschew 0 [4], Deddens 0 [4]), 1 WOLFSLAKE 43, 2 NEUENKNICK 32, 4 BROKSTEDT 26.

See page 542 for details of opening 2009 fixture.

Rider	M	R	Pts	Ave	FM
Piotr SWIDERSKI	2	10	26	10.40	0
Grzegorz WALASEK	**2**	**11**	**26**	**9.45**	**0**
Tomasz JEDRZEJAK	4	20	42	8.40	0
Patrick HOUGAARD	**1**	**5**	**10**	**8.00**	**0**
Thomas STANGE	5	25	35	5.60	0
Robert KOSCIECHA	**1**	**5**	**7**	**5.60**	**0**
Ronny WEIS	5	25	17	2.72	0
Under 21					
Sergej MALYSCHEW	1	4	4	4.00	0
Denis WIENKE	**4**	**16**	**10**	**2.50**	**0**
Under 19					
Rene DEDDENS	5	20	45	9.00	1

Bundesliga

LANDSHUT

2008 RESULTS

SQUAD
Christian Hefenbrock, Herbert Rudolph, Sirg Schützbach. **Under 21:** Sebastian Mack, Richard Speiser, Stefan Kurz. **Under 19:** Marcel Helfer.
Foreign: Eric Andersson, Antonio Lindbäck, Robert Miskowiak, Piotr Protasiewicz, Adam Skornicki, Simon Stead.

Round 1
Brokstedt, Sunday, April 20
1 LANDSHUT 36+3 (Lindbäck 13+3, Hefenbrock 11, Speiser 7, Schützbach 2, Mack 2 [5], Helfer 1 [3]), 2 BROKSTEDT 36+2, 3 WOLFSLAKE 32, 4 NEUENKNICK 28.

Round 2
Pfaffenhofen, Sunday May 4
3 LANDSHUT 36+2 (Stead 13+2, Andersson 6, Speiser 9, Rudolph 6, Mack 1 [5], Helfer 1 [2]), 1 OLCHING 40, 2 WOLFSLAKE 36+3, 4 PFAFFENHOFEN 20.

Round 4
Landshut, Saturday, July 12
2 LANDSHUT 38 (Hefenbrock 8, Lindbäck 11, Protasiewicz 11, Kurz 0, Speiser 3+3 [12], Helfer 2 [8]), 1 OLCHING 39, 3 DIEDENBERGEN 30, 4 PFAFFENHOFEN 25.

Round 5
Olching, Sunday, July 20
2 LANDSHUT 37 (Hefenbrock 10, Speiser 11, Rudolph 4, Miskowiak 11, Kurz 0 [1], Helfer 1 [5]), 1 OLCHING 44, 3 NEUENKNICK 26, 4 PFAFFENHOFEN 25.

Rider	*M*	*R*	*Pts*	*Ave*	*FM*
Piotr PROTASIEWICZ	2	10	25	10.00	0
Simon STEAD	**1**	**6**	**15**	**10.00**	**0**
Antonio LINDBÄCK	2	11	27	9.82	0
Robert MISKOWIAK	**1**	**5**	**11**	**8.80**	**0**
Richard SPEISER	4	15	30	8.00	0
Christian HEFENBROCK	**4**	**20**	**33**	**6.60**	**0**
Eric ANDERSSON	1	5	6	4.80	0
Adam SKORNICKI	**1**	**5**	**6**	**4.80**	**0**
Herbert RUDOLPH	2	10	10	4.00	0
Sirg SCHÜTZBACH	**1**	**5**	**2**	**1.60**	**0**
Stefan KURZ	2	9	0	0.00	0
Under 21					
Richard SPEISER	2	8	24	12.00	2
Sebastian MACK	**2**	**8**	**10**	**5.00**	**0**
Stefan KURZ	1	4	1	1.00	0
Under 19					
Marcel HELFER	5	20	22	4.40	0

Bundesliga

NEUENKNICK

2008 RESULTS

SQUAD
Toni Kröger, Dominik Möller, Kevin Wölbert
Under 21: Tobias Busch, Arne Ledwig.
Under 19: Max Dilger, Kai Huckenbeck.
Foreign: Mariusz Frankow, Adrian Gomolski, Brian Lyngsø, Alan Marcinkowski, Adrian Miedzinski, Rafal Okoniewski, David Ruud.

Round 1
Brokstedt, Sunday, April 20
4 NEUENKNICK 28 (Wölbert 10, Ruud 7, Marcinkowski 8, Möller 0, Ledwig 0 [2], Dilger 3 [12]), 1 LANDSHUT 36+3, 2 BROKSTEDT 36+2, 3 WOLFSLAKE 32.

Round 3
Neuenknick, Sunday, June 15
3 NEUENKNICK 33 (Wölbert 5, Möller 1, Okoniewski 11, Miedzinski 12, Ledwig 2 [5], Huckenbeck 2 [8]), 1 DIEDENBERGEN 40, 2 BROKSTEDT 34, 4 OLCHING 25.

Round 5
Olching, Sunday, July 20
3 NEUENKNICK 26 (Wölbert 4, Frankow 7, Lyngsø 9, Möller 0, Busch 3 [9], Dilger 3 [12]), 1 OLCHING 44, 2 LANDSHUT 38, 4 PFAFFENHOFEN 25.

Round 7
Wolfslake, Saturday, August 2
2 NEUENKNICK 32 (Wölbert 6, Kröger 1, Gomolski 8, Okoniewski 12, Busch 2 [6], Dilger 3 [9]), 1 WOLFSLAKE 43, 3 DIEDENBERGEN 31, 4 BROKSTEDT 26.

Rider	*M*	*R*	*Pts*	*Ave*	*FM*
Rafal OKONIEWSKI	2	10	23	9.20	0
Adrian MIEDZINSKI	**1**	**5**	**12**	**9.60**	**0**
Brian LYNGSØ	1	5	9	7.20	0
Adrian GOMOLSKI	**1**	**5**	**8**	**6.40**	**0**
Alan MARCINKOWSKI	1	5	8	6.40	0
Mariusz FRANKOW	**1**	**5**	**7**	**5.60**	**0**
David RUUD	1	5	7	5.60	0
Kevin WÖLBERT	**4**	**20**	**25**	**5.00**	**0**
Toni KRÖGER	1	5	1	0.80	0
Dominik MÖLLER	**3**	**14**	**1**	**0.29**	**0**
Under 21					
Tobias BUSCH	2	8	15	7.50	0
Arne LEDWIG	**2**	**8**	**7**	**3.50**	**0**
Under 19					
Max DILGER	3	12	33	11.00	2
Kai HUCKENBECK	**1**	**4**	**8**	**8.00**	**0**

Bundesliga

OLCHING

2008 RESULTS

SQUAD
Frank Facher, Martin Smolinski.
Under 21: Manfred Betz.
Under 19: Dennis Helfer, Sebastian Kapser, Christian Rinkenburger.
Foreign: Michael Hadek, Manuel Hauzinger, Billy Janniro, Pawel Staszek, Matej Zagar.

Round 2
Pfaffenhofen, Sunday May 4
1 OLCHING 40 (Smolinski 12, Hauzinger 9, Hadek 6, Facher 11, Betz 2 [6], Kapser 0 [2]), 2 WOLFSLAKE 36+3, 3 LANDSHUT 36+2, 4 PFAFFENHOFEN 20.

Round 3
Neuenknick, Sunday, June 15
4 OLCHING 25 (Smolinski 9, Hauzinger 5, Facher 6, Staszek 4, Betz 1 [4], Helfer 0 [1]), 1 DIEDENBERGEN 40, 2 BROKSTEDT 34, 3 NEUENKNICK 33.

Round 4
Landshut, Saturday, July 12
1 OLCHING 39 (Zagar 12, Smolinski 14, Hauzinger 6, Facher 6, Betz 1 [4], Helfer 0 [2]), 2 LANDSHUT 38, 3 DIEDENBERGEN 30, 4 PFAFFENHOFEN 25.

Round 5
Olching, Sunday, July 20
1 OLCHING 44 (Smolinski 14, Hauzinger 11, Facher 8, Janniro 9, Betz 2 [8], Rinkenburger 0 [1]), 2 LANDSHUT 37, 3 NEUENKNICK 26, 4 PFAFFENHOFEN 25.

Rider	*M*	*R*	*Pts*	*Ave*	*FM*
Charlie GJEDDE	3	16	33	8.25	0
Tobias KRONER	**4**	**21**	**38**	**7.24**	**0**
Joonas KYLMÅKORPI	2	10	17	6.80	0
Henning BAGER	**1**	**5**	**8**	**6.40**	**0**
Matthias KRÖGER	4	20	19	3.80	0
Stefan KATT	**1**	**5**	**4**	**3.20**	**0**
Sönke PETERSEN	1	5	4	3.20	0
Under 21					
Sönke PETERSEN	3	12	36	12.00	3
Kristian DROSSMANN	**1**	**4**	**10**	**10.00**	**0**
Under 19					
Ramon STANEK	4	16	13	3.25	0

Bundesliga

PFAFFENHOFEN

2008 RESULTS

SQUAD
Roberto Haupt, Danny Knakowski, Daniel Rath.
Under 21: Christoph Dremmel, Marcel Kalms.
Under 19: Franz Winkelhofer.
Foreign: Ales Dryml, David Howe, Krystian Klecha, Matej Kus, Jesper B. Monberg, Marcin Nowaczy, Tomasz Rempala, Cameron Woodward.

Round 2
Pfaffenhofen, Sunday May 4
4 PFAFFENHOFEN 20 (Woodward 7, Knakowski 6, Haupt 0, Klecha 2, Demmel 3 [11], Winkelhofer 2 [6]), 1 OLCHING 40, 2 WOLFSLAKE 36+3, 3 LANDSHUT 36+2.

Round 4
Landshut, Saturday, July 12
4 PFAFFENHOFEN 25 (Monberg 9, Haupt 4, Kus 7, Rath 2, Demmel 2 [7], Winkelhofer 1 [4]), 1 OLCHING 39, 2 LANDSHUT 38, 3 DIEDENBERGEN 30.

Round 5
Olching, Sunday, July 20
4 PFAFFENHOFEN 25 (Howe 6, Haupt 7, Rath 2, Dryml 7, Demmel 1 [6], Winkelhofer 2 [6]), 1 OLCHING 44, 2 LANDSHUT 37, 3 NEUENKNICK 26.

Round 6
Diedenbergen, Saturday, July 26
4 PFAFFENHOFEN 5 (Rempala 1, Haupt 0, Nowaczyk 1, Kalms 1, Demmel 2 [8], Winkelhofer 0 [0]), 1 WOLFSLAKE 51, 2 DIEDENBERGEN 38+3, 3 BROKSTEDT 38+2.

Rider	*M*	*R*	*Pts*	*Ave*	*FM*
Jesper B. MONBERG	1	5	9	7.20	0
Ales DRYML	**1**	**5**	**7**	**5.60**	**0**
Matej KUS	1	5	7	5.60	0
Cameron WOODWARD	**1**	**5**	**7**	**5.60**	**0**
David HOWE	1	5	6	4.80	0
Danny KNAKOWSKI	**1**	**5**	**6**	**4.80**	**0**
Roberto HAUPT	4	17	11	2.59	0
Daniel RATH	**2**	**10**	**4**	**1.60**	**0**
Krystian KLECHA	1	5	2	1.60	0
Marcin NOWACZYK	**1**	**5**	**1**	**0.80**	**0**
Marcel KALMS	1	5	1	0.80	0
Tomasz REMPALA	**1**	**5**	**1**	**0.80**	**0**
Under 21					
Christoph DREMMEL	4	16	32	8.00	0
Under 19					
Franz WINKELHOFER	4	16	16	4.00	0

INTERNATIONAL

AUTOHOUSE CUP
Meißen, Saturday, April 26
1 CZECH REPUBLIC 24 (Richard Wolff 16, Pavel Ondrasik 8), **2 POLAND 22** (Robert Mikolajczak 12, Bartosz Kasprowiak 10), **3 GERMANY 21** (Ronny Weis 15, Tobias Busch 6), **4 AUSTRIA 19** (Friedrich Wallner 12, Manuel Novotny 7), **5 DENMARK 18** (Jonas Andersson 13, Jörg Tebbe [G] 5), **6 SWEDEN 14** (Kalle Lindgren 12, Leif Karlsson 2), **7 HOLLAND 8** (Henk Bos 8, Erik Eijbergen 0).

Stralsund, Saturday, May 3
GERMANY 57 (Mathias Schultz 15, Tobias Busch 15, Steffen Mell 14, Erik Pudel 10, Robert Haupt 3), **POLAND 31** (Mariusz Puszakowski 14, Bartosz Kasprowiak 9, Daniel Rath [G] 5, Lukasz Loman 3, Grzegorz Klopot 0).

Landshut, Saturday, August 23
1 POLAND 46 (Tomasz Bajerski 20, Piotr Swist 17, Max Dilger [G] 9), **2 SLOVENIA 44** (Izak Santej 18, Maks Gregoric 14, Matija Duh 12), **3 SWEDEN 35** (Robert Henderson 13, Andreas Bergström 10, Frank Facher [G] 12), **4 AC LANDSHUT 34** (Joakim Kugelmann 11, Eric Andersson 19, Herbert Rudolph 4), **5 AUSTRIA 21** (Manuel Hauzinger 17, Manfred Betz [G] 3, Manuel Novotny 1).

Dohren, Saturday, October 18
1 POLAND 33 (Kamil Brzozowski 7, Marcin Sekula 8, Daniel Pytel 9, Miroslaw Jablonksi 9), **2 GERMANY 29** (Kevin Wölbert 11, Sönke Petersen 10, Jörg Tebbe 8, Nils Hesse 0), **3 DENMARK 17+3** (Anders Andersen 6+3, Peter Juul Larsen 1, Steffen Jespersen 4, Jesper Kristiansen 6), 4 **HOLLAND 17+2** (Thomas Sørensen [G] 5, Henk Bos 5+2, Dirk Fabriek 5, Mark Stiekema 2).

Challenge

Güstrow, Saturday, July 12
GÜSTROW 53 (Mathias Schultz 13, Tobias Busch 10, Steffen Mell 10, Kevin Wölbert 9, Erik Pudel 8, Robert Baumann 3), **STAL GORZOW (POLAND) 37** (Pawel Hlib 13, Mateusz Mikorski 7, Adrian Szewczykowski 7, Slawomir Dabrowski 5, Lukasz Cyran 4, Marcin Kozdras 1).

Landshut, Saturday, September 20
LANDSHUT 56 (Christian Hefenbrock 14, Sirg Schützbach 4, Richard Speiser 7, Manfred Betz 6, Herbert Rudolph 5, Hans-Jörg Müller 12, Frank Facher 8), **LONIGO 40** (Alessandro Milanese 3, Andrea Baroni 3, Armando Castagna 12, Mattia Cavicchiloi 4, Mattia Carpanese 12, Simone Tadiello 6, Alessandro Novello 0).

Individual

Nordhastedt, Thursday, May 1
Manuel Hauzinger 14+3, Ronny Weis 14+2, Marcin Sekula 13, Simon Nielsen 11, Rene Deddens 10, Thomas Sørensen 9, Toni Kröger 9, Thomas Nielsen 9, Kristian Drossmann 8, Nanna Jørgensen 6, Dominik Möller 3, Sjörd Rozenberg 3, Malte Zyweck 3, Thomas Lata 2, Karel Kadlec 0.

MASTER OF SPEEDWAY
Moorwinkelsdamm, Saturday, May 3
Fredrik Lindgren 9+3+5, Martin Smolinski 6+1+4, Kevin Wölbert 4+2+3, Joe Screen 4+3+2, Matthias Kröger 0+1, Jonas Davidsson 6+1+0, Marcin Nowaczik 5+0, Stephan Katt 3, Sönke Petersen 3, Manuel Hauzinger 1, Jannick de Jong 0.

Teterow, Saturday, May 10
Sebastian Ulamek 14+3+5, Christian Hefenbrock 10+1+4, Matej Ferjan 12+2+3, Grzegorz Walasek 13+1+2, David Ruud 10+3+1, Troy Batchelor 9+2+0, Niklas Klingberg 9+0, Kenneth Hansen 8+0, Joonas Kylmåkorpi 8, Tobias Kroner 7, Martin Smolinski 6, Patrick Hougaard 5, Edward Kennett 5, Mathias Schultz 2, Karol Zabik 2, Matthias Kröger 0.

Güstrow, Sunday, May 11
David Ruud 14, Mathias Schultz 13, Steffen Mell 11, Peter Ljung 10, Troy Batchelor 10, Karol Zabik 8, Henning Bager 8, Nicolai Klindt 6, Slawomir Drabik 6, Sebastian Aldén 6, Manuel Hauzinger 5, Patrick Hougaard 5, Ilya Bondarenko 5, Daniel Jeleniewski 5, Grzegorz Zengota 4, Tobias Busch 3.

GERMAN OPEN
Olching, Thursday, May 22
Martin Smolinski 15, Matej Ferjan 13, Norbert Magosi 12, Pawel Staszek 10, Richard Wolff 9, Grzegorz Walasek 9, Jurica Pavlic 8, Joakim Kugelmann 7, Richard Speiser 7, Michael Hadek 7, Manfred Betz 6, Manuel Hauzinger 6, Hans-Jörg Müller 3, Laszlo Szatmari 2, Christoph Demmel [R] 2, Sebastian Mack 1, Andrew Appleton 1.

25 YEAR ANNIVERSARY
Brokstedt, Sunday, June 22
Charlie Gjedde 8+2+5, Tomasz Bajerski 7+3+4, Matthias Kröger 4+1+3, Henning Bager 8+2+2, Brian Lyngsø 7+3+FX, Thomas Stange 6+1+R, Sönke Petersen 4+0, Stephan Katt 4+0, Peter Juul Larsen 4, Lukasz Kasperek 1, Niklas Klingberg 1, Simon Walker 0.

Biesenthal b. Berlin, Friday, June 27
1 Tomasz Piszcz, 2 Sönke Petersen, 3 Peter Juul Larsen, 4 Marcin Sekula, 5 Kevin Wölbert, 6 Erik Pudel, 7 Piotr Swist, 8 Tobias Kroner, 9 Mathias Schultz, 10 Christian Hefenbrock, 11 Maksim Bogdanovs, 12 Ronny Weis.

Meißen, Saturday, July 5
Ronny Weis 12+5, Manfred Betz 9+4, Steffen Mell 11+3, Denis Wienke 8+2, Henk Bos 9+1, Marcel Helfer 8+0, Dennis Helfer 3+5, Vladimir Visvader 3+4, Marcel Kalms 4+3, Nanna Jørgensen 4+2, Karel Kadlec 1+1, Grzegorz Grocki 0.

Wolfslake, Saturday, July 5
Pawel Hlib 12+3, Marcin Sekula 12+2, Andrej Korolev 11+1, Leonids Paura 9+0, Manuel Hauzinger 9, Kalle Lindgren 8, Roberto Haupt 7, Maks Gregoric 7, Peter Juul Larsen 5, Robert Mikolajczak 5, Mateusz Kowalczyk 3, Mathias Bartz 2.

MECKLENBURG REGIONAL CHAMPIONSHIP
Senior Championship
1 Erik Pudel 61 (16-25-20), 2 Steffen Mell 52 (18-18-16), 3 Danny Knakowski 50 (12-20-18), 4 Mathias Schultz 40 (25-N-15), 5 Robert Baumann 36 (10-12-14), 6 Tobias Busch 27 (15-N-12), 7 Sergej Malyschew 26 (6-10-10), 8 Roberto Haupt 25 (N-N-25), 9 Rene Deddens 24 (8-16-N), 10 Mathias Bartz 22 (8-14-N), 11 Fritz Riemer 21 (6-8-7), 12 Kevin Wölbert 20 (20-N-N), 13 Toni Brosowski 20

(4-8-8), 14 Marcel Lebich 19 (5-6-8), 15 Denis Wienke 19 (7-7-5), 16 Marcel Kalms 19 (7-5-7), 17 Clemens Sommer 16 (5-5-6), 18 Daniel Rath 15 (N-15-N), 19 Domingo Krecklow 15 (3-7-5), 20 Ronny Weis 14 (14-N-N), 21 Christian Seligert 13 (3-4-6), 22 Kevin Gevert 9 (2-3-4), 23 Thomas Lata 8 (N-4-4), 24 Arne Ledwig 6 (N-6-N), 25 Kristina Gradert 4 (4-N-N).

Under 21 Championship
1 Erik Pudel, 2 Robert Baumann, 3 Tobias Busch, 4 Sergej Malyschew, 5 Rene Deddens, 6 Fritz Riemer, 7 Kevin Wölbert, 8 Toni Brosowski, 9 Denis Wienke, 9 Marcel Kalms, 11 Clemens Sommer, 12 Ronny Weis, 13 Kevin Gevert, 14 Arne Ledwig, 15 Kristina Gradert.

Under 16 Championship
1 Rene Deddens, 2 Fritz Riemer, 3 Clemens Sommer, 4 Kevin Gevert.

Held over three rounds at Güstrow (Saturday, April 12), Teterow (Saturday, April 26) and Stralsund (Saturday, June 7). Points scoring 25-20-18-16-15-14-12-10-8-8-7-6-5-4-3-2-0.

Teterow, Friday, August 22
1 Tobias Kroner, 2 Niklas Klingberg, 3 Joe Screen, 4 Matej Ferjan, 5 Patrick Hougaard, 6 Kevin Wölbert.

Preliminary Round
Group 1: Matej Ferjan 8+10, Mathias Schultz 7+2, Erik Pudel 4+3, Mariusz Frankow 4, Enrico Sonnenberg 0.
Group 2: Tobias Kroner 5+12, Niklas Klingberg 5+8, Eric Andersson 4+10, Tobias Busch 1.
Group 3: Joe Screen 8+9, Patrick Hougaard 7+10, Kevin Wölbert 5+11, Robert Baumann 2, Toni Brosowski 1.
Group 4: Kjastas Puodzhuks 6+7, Marcin Sekula 5+5, Sönke Petersen 3+2, Steffen Mell 2.

● *In the initial Group stages riders had three heats each with their two best scores counting. The top three riders then went through to a second series of three races.*

BERGHAUPTEN SUPERCUP
Berghaupten, Saturday, September 6
Thomas Stange 14+3, Marcin Sekula 12+2, Kozza Smith 12+1, Max Dilger 15+R, Richard Speiser 9, Bernd Diener 8, Marcel Helfer 7, Frank Facher 7, Alessandro Milanese 7, Manfred Betz 6, Hans-Jörg Müller 6, Marcel Dachs 5, Paul Cooper 4, Rene Schafer 3, Friedrich Ruf 3, Charlie Saunders 0.

Leipzig, Saturday, September 13
Manuel Hauzinger 14, Maks Gregoric 13, Kjastas Puodzhuks 12, Mathias Schultz 10, Steffen Mell 10, Marcin Sekula 10, Tobias Busch 9, Roberto Haupt 9, Jan Holub[3] 8, Ronny Weis 7, Thomas Sørensen 6, Marcel Kalms 5, Christopher Fink 2, Krzysztof Nowacki 2.

SILVER STEEL SHOE
Meißen, Friday, October 3
Maks Gregoric 14+3, Ronny Weis 14+2, Vladimir Dubinin 12, Grzegorz Strozyk 11, Kalle Lindgren 10, Mathias Bartz 10, Henk Bos 9, Attila Molnar 7, Alexandru Toma 6, Thomas Sørensen 6, Attilia Lorincz 5, Marcel Kalms 5, Jaroslav Petrak 5, Milan Manev 3, Sergey Borisenko 3.

GERMAN GOLDEN BAND
Olching, Sunday, October 12
Frank Facher 14, Martin Smolinski 13, Manuel Hauzinger 12, Mathias Schultz 11, Richard Speiser 11, Kevin Wölbert 11, Sönke Petersen 8, Roberto Haupt 8, Michael Hadek 6, Tobias Busch 5, Alexander Conda 5, Hans-Jörg Müller 5, Manfred Betz 4, Manuel Novotny 3, Norbert Magosi 2, Franz Winkelhofer 1.

Ludwigslust, Saturday, November 1
Christian Hefenbrock 12, Kevin Wölbert 10, Piotr Swist 9, Mathias Schultz 8, Dannie Søderholm 6, Erik Pudel 7, Roberto Haupt 7, Steffen Jespersen 5, Ronny Weis 4, Tobias Busch 1, Robert Baumann 1, Fritz Riemer 0.

German Under 21 champion Max Dilger

2009 MAJOR FIXTURES

BUNDESLIGA 1
Sunday, March 22, Diedenbergen 46 Brokstedt 41.
Friday, May 1, Brokstedt v Güstrow.
Thursday, May 21, Wolfslake v Diedenbergen.
Saturday, June 6, Landshut v Güstrow.
Saturday, July 4, Wolfslake v Brokstedt.
Saturday, July 25, Güstrow v Diedenbergen.
Saturday, July 25, Landshut v Wolfslake.
Sunday, August 2, Brokstedt v Landshut.
Friday, August 21, Güstrow v Wolfslake.
Sunday, August 30, Diedenbergen v Landshut.

FINAL
Saturday, October 3, to be confirmed.

GERMAN CHAMPIONSHIP
FINAL
Saturday, September 19, Landshut.

GERMAN UNDER 21 CHAMPIONSHIP

Northern Group
Thursday, May 28, Güstrow.
Monday, June 1, Norden.
Saturday, June 20, Teterow.
Sunday, August 2, Brokstedt.

Southern Group
Saturday, April 11, Pocking.
Sunday, April 12, Pocking.
Saturday, May 16, Landshut.
Sunday, August 16, Abensberg.

FINAL
Sunday, September 13, Norden.

HOLLAND

DUTCH OPEN CHAMPIONSHIP

STUDENT Jannick de Jong, who has to combine his racing with studies, edged closer to becoming a Dutch legend with his fourth championship success in the last five seasons.

De Jong, 21, was virtually unchallenged throughout the six round series, winning the first five and then, with the title already assured, finishing runner up in the last round at Lelystad.

Half of the rounds were actually held outside Holland – two meetings being staged across the German border at Moorwinkelsdamm and another at Zolder in Belgium.

The series was also open to non-Dutch riders, the best-placed being Denmark's Thomas Sørensen who took the bronze medal.

Final standings

	1	*2*	*3*	*4*	*5*	*6*	*Tot*
1 JANNICK DE JONG	**50**	**50**	**50**	**50**	**50**	***47***	**250**
2 Henk BOS	47	47	36	–	47	50	227
3 Thomas SØRENSEN	–	37	47	47	45	45	221
4 Mark STIEKEMA	45	*39*	45	45	41	41	217
5 Henry van der STEEN	38	38	41	41	40	–	198
6 Nick LOURENS	37	40	39	43	*34*	39	198
7 Pascal SWART	*35*	43	37	39	39	38	196
8 Roy KLAASSENS	*33*	34	43	35	43	40	195
9 Berry de VOS	39	41	40	36	38	–	194
10 Benjamin BORGERS	32	35	*31*	40	37	43	187
11 Jer. van der VEEN	34	36	*30*	38	30	37	175
12 Lars ZANDVLIET	–	–	32	37	36	–	105
13 Dirk FABRIEK	43	45	–	–	–	–	88
14 Sjoerd ROZENBERG	40	–	38	–	–	–	78
15 Stefan BLAUW	–	–	–	–	35	35	70
16 Dennis NOORDMAN	–	–	34	34	–	–	68
17 Isaak-Jacob MULDER	–	–	–	–	32	34	66
18 Erik EIJBERGEN	41	–	–	–	–	–	41
19 Den. van der TANG	36	–	–	–	–	–	36
19 Jeffrey WORTMAN	–	–	–	–	–	36	36
21 Jan Okke LOONSTRA	–	–	35	–	–	–	35
22 Bernd DINKLAGE	–	–	33	–	–	–	33
23 Kevin KREMER	–	–	–	–	31	–	31

[Scoring: 50-47-45-43-41-40-39-38-37-36-35-34-33-32-31-30. Best five totals only count. Where applicable, dropped score in italics].

Round 1

Moorwinkelsdamm, Germany, Sunday, April 13

Jannick de Jong 12+3, Henk Bos 11+2, Dirk Fabriek 10+1, Mark Stiekema 9+0, Erik Eijbergen 9, Sjoerd Rozenberg 7, Henry van der Steen 7, Berry de Vos 7, Dennis van der Tang 6, Nick Lourens 6, Pascal Swart 4, Roy Klaassens 3, Jeroen van der Veen 3, Benjamin Jan Borgers 1, Jan Okke Loonstra 0, Thomas Sørensen 0.

Round 2

Zolder, Belgium, Sunday, April 27

Jannick de Jong 12+3, Henk Bos 10+2, Dirk Fabriek 8+1, Pascal Swart 8+0, Berry de Vos 8, Nick Lourens 7, Thomas Sørensen 6, Mark Stiekema 5, Henry van der Steen 5, Jeroen van der Veen 2, Banjamin Jan Borgers 1, Roy Klaassens 1.

Round 3

Vledderveen, Holland, Saturday, May 10

Jannick de Jong 11+3, Thomas Sørensen 11+2, Mark Stiekema 10+1, Roy Klaassens 9+0, Henry van der Steen 9, Sjoerd Rozenberg 7, Berry de Vos 7, Nick Lourens 7, Henk Bos 5, Pascal Swart 5, Jan Okke Loonstra 5, Dennis Noordman 4, Bernd Dinklage 2, Benjamin Jan Borgers 1, Jeroen van der Veen 1, Lars Zandvliet 1.

Round 4

Lelystad, Holland, Sunday, June 8

Jannick de Jong 11+3, Thomas Sørensen 8+2, Mark Stiekema 9+1, Nick Lourens 8+0, Henry van der Steen 8, Benjamin Jan Borgers 6, Pascal Swart 5, Jeroen van der Veen 4, Lars Zandvliet 4, Berry de Vos 3, Roy Klaassens 3, Dennis Noordman 1.

Round 5

Moorwinkelsdamm, Germany, Sunday, June 29

Jannick de Jong 12+3, Henk Bos 10+2, Thomas Sørensen 9+1, Roy Klaassens 9+0, Mark Stiekema 8, Henry van der Steen 8, Pascal Swart 8, Berry de Vos 8, Benjamin Jan Borgers 5, Lars Zandvliet 4, Nick Lourens 3, Dennis Noordman 3, Stefan Blauw 3, Isaak-Jacob Mulder 2, Jeroen van der Veen 2, Kevin Kremer 2.

Round 6

Lelystad, Holland, Sunday, September 14

Henk Bos 9+3, Jannick de Jong 8+2, Thomas Sørensen 11+1, Benjamin Jan Borgers 7+0, Mark Stiekema 7, Pascal Swart 7, Roy Klaassens 7, Nick Lourens 7, Jeroen van der Veen 4, Jeffrey Woortman 3, Stefan Blauw 2, Isaak-Jacob Mulder 0.

Roll of Honour

1948 .... Henk STEMAN
1949 .... Tinus METZELAAR
1950 .... Co BOEF
1951 .... Henk STEMAN I
1953 .... Henk STEMAN I
1954 .... Tonny KROEZE
1955 .... Thei BISSCHOPS
1956 .... Thei BISSCHOPS
1972 .... Henny KROEZE
1973 .... Gerry KROEZE
1974 .... Henny KROEZE
1975 .... Henny KROEZE
1976 .... Henk STEMAN II
1977 .... Frits KOPPE
1978 .... Henny KROEZE
1978 .... Sjörd DIJKEMA
1979 .... Rudy MUTS
1980 .... Henny KROEZE
1981 .... Henk STEMAN II
1982 .... Henny KROEZE
1983 .... Henny KROEZE
1984 .... Henny KROEZE
1985 .... Henny KROEZE
1986 .... Henny KROEZE
1987 .... Henk STEMAN II
1988 .... Henk STEMAN II
1989 .... Rene ELZINGA
1990 .... Robert Jan MUNNECOM
1991 .... Rene ELZINGA
1992 .... Rob STEMAN
1993 .... Ron KOPPE
1994 .... Rob STEMAN
1995 .... Patrick VERBRUGGE
1996 .... Ralf STRACK (GERMANY)
1997 .... Roy VERBRUGGE
1998 .... Patrick VERBRUGGE
1999 .... Maik GROEN
2000 .... Ralf STRACK (Germany)
2001 .... Jim GROEN
2002 .... Henk BOS
2003 .... Ralf STRACK (Germany)
2004 .... Jannick De JONG
2005 .... Henk BOS
2006 .... Jannick de JONG
2007 .... Jannick de JONG
2008 .... Jannick de JONG

Individual

DUTCH GOLDEN HELMET

Veenord, Saturday, September 27

1 Jonas Andersson 11+2+3, 2 Manuel Hauzinger 11+3+0, 3 Richard Hall 11+1+2,4 Kalle Lindgren 10+1+0, 5 Dirk Fabriek 9, 6 Sönke Petersen 9, 7 Thomas Sørensen 7, 8 Mark Stiekema 7, 9 Henk Bos 7, 10 Maciej Jader 7, 11 Paul Cooper 5, 12 Roy Klaassens 5, 13 Jannick de Jong 5, 14 Henry dan der Steen 4, 15 Sjoerd Rozenberg 4, 16 Erik Eijbergen 4, 17 Nick Lourens 2, 18 Jeroen van der Veen 1, 18 Berry de Vos 1, 20 Pascal Swart 0.

2009 DUTCH CHAMPIONSHIP

Round 1: Moorwinkelsdamm (Germany), Sunday, March 22.
Round 2: Lelystad, Sunday, May 3.
Round 3: Vledderveen, Saturday, May 30.
Round 4: Veenoord, Saturday, July 18.
Round 5: Norden (Germany), Sunday, August 2.
Round 6: Lelystad, Sunday, September 13.
DUTCH GOLDEN HELMET
Veenoord, Saturday, September 26

GERMANY

Continued from page 373

AFTER 36 seasons of a Four Team Championship, the Bundesliga has adopted the more traditional league formula.

Five clubs – Brokstedt, Diedenbergen, Güstrow, Landshut and Wolfslake – will meet home and away with three points for the winners of each meeting.

There are restrictions of team format and each club must include a German rider under the age of 21 in their five man line-up.

Teams are allowed a maximum of two riders from each category.

Team trailing by eight points may nominate a rider as a Joker, his points being doubled and teams can also use a tactical substitute when they are six down.

The two top teams will face each other in a Grand Final to decide the 2009 Bundelsiga champions.

Bundesliga champions Olching, Neuenknick and Pfaffenhofen all withdrew from the competition, Olching in particular being vigorous opponents of the sweeping changes.

BROKSTEDT VIKINGS

A – Mads Korneliussen, Martin Vaculik, Leon Madsen.
B – Matthias Kröger, Sönke Petersen U21). Kai Huckenbeck (U21).
C – Stephan Katt, Marco Gaschka, Danny Maaßen.

DIEDENBERGEN ROCKETS

A – Christian Hefenbrock, Tomasz Jedrzejak, Tomasz Chrzanowski, Thomas Stange.
B – Grzegorz Zengota, Maciej Janowski, Frank Facher (U21).
C – Rene Deddens (U21), Denis Wienke (U21).

GÜSTROW

A – Mathias Schultz, Adrian Gomolski, Kevin Wölbert.
B – Steffen Mell, Maksim Bogdanovs, Roberto Haupt, Tobias Busch (U21).
C – Robert Baumann, Arne Ledwig (U21).

LANDSHUT

A – Tobias Kroner, Martin Smolinski, Piotr Protasiewicz.
B – Richard Speiser, Max Dilger (U21).
C – Hans-Jörg Müller, Sirg Schützbach, Marcel Helfer (U21).

WOLFSLAKE WOLVES

A – Matej Ferjan, Adrian Miedzinski, Pawel Hlib, Maks Gregoric, Kjastas Puodzhuks.
B – Matej Kus, Erik Pudel, Marcin Sekula, Tomasz Schmidt.
C – Mathias Bartz, Ronny Weis, Ramon Stanek (U21).

HUNGARY

HUNGARIAN CHAMPIONSHIP

MATEJ Ferjan won his fifth Hungarian title in six seasons, reigning over a change of the guard.

Veteran Sandor Tihanyi slipped down the rankings as bright young thing Jozsef Tabaka, 19, established himself as his country's top home-grown prospect with a fighting fifth place in a field otherwise dominated by adopted licence-holders rather than genuine Magyars.

Plans to stage two further rounds were scrapped, leaving Ferjan as champion for a third successive year.

FINAL

Debrecen, Saturday, May 31

1 Matej Ferjan 19 (13+3+3), 2 Maks Gregoric 16 (12+2+2), 3 Laszlo Szatmari 15 (14+1), 4 Maciej Kuciapa 14 (11+3+0), 5 Jozsef Tabaka 14 (11+2+1), 6 Sandor Tihanyi 12 (11+1), 7 Tomasz Rempala 9 (9+0), 8 Robert Nagy 9 (9+0), 9 Aleksander Conda 8, 10 Tamas Szilagyi 5, 11 Matija Duh 4, 12 Attila Lorincz 3, 13 Roland Kovacs 3, 14 Attila Molnar 3, 15 Zsolt Nagy 2, 16 Zsolt Bencze 0, 17 Patrik Kott Kis 0, 18 Norbert Magosi 0.

Roll of Honour

1949 ... Janos KESJAR
1950 ... Sandor LEVAI
1951 ... Sandor LEVAI
1952 ... Sandor LEVAI
1953 ... Sandor LEVAI
1954 ... Sandor LEVAI
1955 ... Sandor LEVAI
1956 ... Sandor LEVAI
1957 ... Laszlo NANDORI
1958 ... Lajos VOROS
1959 ... Lajos VOROS
1960 ... Lajos VOROS
1961 ... Lajos VOROS
1962 ... Istvan DAJKA
1963 ... Ferenc RADACSI
1964 ... Ferenc RADACSI
1965 ... Pal PERENYI
1966 ... Barnabas GYEPES
1967 ... Barnabas GYEPES
1968 ... Barnabas GYEPES
1969 ... Barnabas GYEPES
1970 ... Barnabas GYEPES
1971 ... Janos SZOKE
1972 ... Janos SZOKE
1973 ... Barnabas GYEPES
1974 ... Sandor CSATHO
1975 ... Istvan SZIRACZKI
1976 ... Istvan SZIRACZKI
1977 ... Istvan SZIRACZKI
1978 ... Istvan SZIRACZKI
1979 ... Laszlo MESZAROS
1980 ... Istvan SZIRACZKI
1981 ... Istvan SZIRACZKI
1982 ... Zoltan HAJDU
1983 ... Zoltan ADORJAN
1984 ... Zoltan ADORJAN
1985 ... Zoltan ADORJAN
1986 ... Zoltan ADORJAN
1987 ... Zoltan ADORJAN
1988 ... Zoltan ADORJAN
1989 ... Zoltan ADORJAN
1990 ... Zoltan ADORJAN
1991 ... Zoltan ADORJAN
1992 ... Jozsef PETRIKOVICS
1993 ... Robert NAGY
1994 ... Zoltan ADORJAN
1995 ... Zoltan ADORJAN
1996 ... Zoltan ADORJAN
1997 ... Zoltan ADORJAN
1998 ... Robert NAGY
1999 ... Sandor TIHANYI
2000 ... Robert NAGY
2001 ... Robert NAGY
2002 ... Attila STEFANI
2003 ... Matej FERJAN
2004 ... Matej FERJAN
2005 ... Sandor TIHANYI
2006 ... Matej FERJAN
2007 ... Matej FERJAN
2008 ... Matej FERJAN

HUNGARIAN TEAM CHAMPIONSHIP

Debrecen, Monday, May 12

1 SIMON & WOLF SC 55 (Jozsef Tabaka 16, Maciej Kuciapa 23, Sandor Tihanyi 16), **2 GYULAI SC 36** (Roland Benko 4, Maks Gregoric 17, Robert Nagy 15), **3 DUNA HOUSE-LUIGI TEAM 33** (Tamas Szilagyi 1, Matej Ferjan 18, Izan Santej 14), **4 MISKOLC SE 32** (Attila Molnar 3, Tomasz Rempala 14, Laszlo Szatmari 15), **5 HAJDU SE 32** (Roland Kovacs 8, Pawel Miesiac 18, Rafal Trojanowski 6).

Roll of Honour

1974 ... MISKOLC
1975 ... MISKOLC
1976 ... MISKOLC
1977 ... MISKOLC
1978 ... MISKOLC
1979 ... MISKOLC
1980 ... MISKOLC
1981 ... DEBRECEN
1982 ... DEBRECEN
1983 ... MISKOLC
1984 ... DEBRECEN
1985 ... DEBRECEN
1986 ... DEBRECEN
1987 ... NYIREGYHAZA
1988 ... HAJDU
1989 ... DEBRECEN
1990 ... TISZA
1991 ... DEBRECEN
1992 ... DEBRECEN
1993 ... HAJDU
1994 ... DEBRECEN
2004 ... DEBRECEN
2005 ... DEBRECEN
2006 ... DEBRECEN
2007 ... DEBRECEN
2008 ... DEBRECEN

UNDER 18 CHAMPIONSHIP

OVERALL

	1	2	3	4	5	6	Tot
1 ROLAND BENKO	**14**	**18**	**18**	**21**	**21**	**14**	**106**
2 Roland KOVACS	6	21	21	18	16	16	98
3 Tamas SZILAGYI	21	12	16	12	6	21	88
4 Zsolt NAGY	10	16	14	14	14	18	86
5 Attila MOLNAR	18	14	12	16	12	12	84
6 Attila LORINCZ	12	10	10	8	18	8	66
7 Patrik KOTTA KIS	16	6	8	4	–	–	34
8 Robert SZEGVARI	8	–	4	10	10	–	32
9 Sandor KONYA	–	–	–	2	8	10	20
10 Robert FEHER	–	8	6	6	–	–	20
11 Gyula MOLNAR	–	–	–	–	14	–	14
12 Laszlo MITRU	–	–	–	–	–	10	10
13 Tamas BIHARI	–	–	–	–	–	6	6
14 Tamas BANYAI	–	–	–	–	2	–	2

[Meetings raced over qualifying heats, top three scorers going through to the A Final, the next three to the B Final and the bottom three to the C Final. Winner of the C Final and B Final both progressed to the subsequent race. Championship score: 21-18-16-14-12-10-8-6-4-2].

Round 1
Gyula, Saturday, March 22
1 Tamas Szilagyi, 2 Attila Molnar, 3 Patrik Kotta Kis, 4 Roland Benko, 5 Attila Lorincz, 6 Zsolt Nagy, 7 Robert Szegvari, 8 Roland Kovacs.

Round 2
Debrecen, Saturday, June 7
1 Roland Kovacs 9+3, 2 Roland Benko 9+2, 3 Zsolt Nagy 6+1, 4 Attila Molnar 4+3+0, 5 Tamas Szilagyi 6+2, 6 Attila Lorincz 4+1, 7 Robert Feher 2+3+0, 8 Patrik Kotta Kis 3+2, 9 Zsolt Nagy, did not ride.

Round 3
Debrecen, Friday, July 4
1 Roland Kovacs 8+3, 2 Roland Benko 9+2, 3 Tamas Szilagyi 7+1, 4 Zsolt Nagy 6+3+0, 5 Attila Molnar 3+2, 6 Attila Lorincz 5+1, 7 Patrick Kotta Kis 0+3+R, 8 Robert Feher 2+2, 9 Robert Szegvari 1+1.

Round 4
Gyula, Saturday, July 19
1 Roland Benko, 2 Roland Kovacs, 3 Attila Molnar, 4 Zsolt Nagy, 5 Tamas Szilgayi, 6 Robert Szegvari, 7 Attila Lorincz, 8 Robert Feher, 9 Patrik Kotta Kis, 10 Sandor Konya.

Round 5
Gyula, Saturday, October 11
1 Roland Benko, 2 Attila Lorincz, 3 Roland Kovacs, 4 Gyula Molnar, 5 Zsolt Nagy, 6 Attila Molnar, 7 Robert Szegvari, 8 Sandor Konya, 9 Tamas Szilagyi, 10 Tamas Banyai.

Round 6
Debrecen, Sunday, October 26
1 Tamas Szilagyi, 2 Zsolt Nagy, 3 Roland Kovacs, 4 Roland Benko, 5 Attila Molnar, 6 Laszlo Mitru, 7 Sandor Konya, 8 Tamas Bihari, 9 Attila Lorincz.

Hungarian club side Miskolc will again compete in the Polish Second League in 2009. For full details of their fixtures see Poland section.

HUNGARIAN U21 CHAMPIONSHIP

Final standings
1 Roland Kovacs 79, 2 Tamas Szilagyi 34, 3 Zsolt Nagy 32, 4 Roland Benko 24, 5 Jozsef Tabaka 20, 6 Attila Lorincz 19, 7 Attila Molnar 12, 8 Robert Szegvari 2.

Roll of Honour

2007 .... Attila LORINCZ
2008 .... Roland KOVACS

■ For full round-by-round details see **AUSTRIA**.

Round 2
Debrecen, Hungary, Thursday, May 1
Jozsef Tabaka 15, Matija Duh 14, Matic Voldrih 12, Aleksander Conda 11, Dino Kovacic 11, Nikola Pigac 9, Aljosa Remih 8, Roland Kovacs 8, Roland Benko [R] 7, Tamas Szilagyi 7, Renato Cvetko 5, Christopher Fink 4, Andrej Kezman 3, Ladisav Vida 1, Markus Oberhofer 1, Ernst Szudecz 0, Kreso Petkovic 0.

Round 4
Gyula, Hungary, Sunday, July 27
Aleksander Conda 15, Dino Kovacic 14, Matic Voldrih 13, Roland Kovacs 12, Roland Benko 9, Zsolt Nagy 9, Attila Molnar 9, Nikola Pigac 7, Lukas Simon 7, Aljosa Remih 6, Kreso Petkovic 6, Attila Lorincz 4, Renato Cvetko 4, Tamas Szilagyi 2, Ladislav Vida 1, Dalibor Bot 1, Robert Szegvari [R] 0.

2009 FIXTURES

HUNGARIAN CHAMPIONSHIP
Round 1: Friday, April 24, Miskolc.
Round 2: Saturday, April 25, Gyula.
Round 3: Sunday, May 24, Debrecen.

HUNGARIAN UNDER 21 CHAMPIONSHIP
Run in conjunction with the Croatia-Hungary-Slovenia tournament. Two rounds in Hungary.
Round 4: Saturday, July 25, Gyula.
Round 5: Saturday, August 8, Debrecen.
See Croatia and Slovenia for full details of other dates and venues.

INDIVIDUAL
Friday, May 1, Debrecen.

Polish Second League

MISKOLC

2008 RESULTS

Polish Second League

Final position ....Runners-up (First)

OPOLE (H)
Sunday, April 13
Won 53-37
Rymel 6, Magosi 1:1, **Bajerski 14:1**, Rempala 11:3, Szatmari 10, Szilagyi, did not ride, Stichauer 1, Tabaka 10:1.

KROSNO (A)
Sunday, April 20
Won 51-39
Rempala 4:1, Rymel 11:1, Bajerski 13, **Magosi 11:4**, Szatmari 10, Szilagyi, did not ride, Stichauer 0, Tabaka 2.

LODZ (H)
Thurday, May 1
Won 45-44
Rempala 6:2, Dubinin 6, Bajerski 9:2, Tihanyi 7, Szatmari 9, Lorincz, did not ride, Gavenda 0, Tabaka 8.

RIVNE (A)
Sunday, May 4
Lost 38-48
Rempala 14, Dubinin 0, Szatmari 7, Tihanyi 2:1, Bajerski 5, Szilagyi 0, Gavenda 10:1.

GNIEZNO (H)
Sunday, June 1
Lost 44-49
Bajerski 11:1, Magosi 1, Rempala 6:1, Rymel 13:1, Szatmari 11:1, Kovacs, did not ride, Gavenda 0, Tabaka 2.

GNIEZNO (A)
Sunday, June 15
Won 49-41
Rempala 10:2, Rymel 8:1, Bajerski 4:1, Magosi 12, Szatmari 4, Tabaka 1, Stichauer 10.
Aggregate: Won 93-90.

LODZ (A)
Sunday, July 20
Won 46-44
Rempala 12, Szatmari 3:1, Bajerski 2:1, Magosi 10, Rymel 10:1, Tabaka 8, Stichauer 1.
Aggregate: Won 91-88.

RIVNE (H)
Thursday, July 31
Won 50-40
Rempala 7:2, Szatmari 8, Bajerski 12:1, Magosi 5, Rymel 7:1, Szilagyi, did not ride, Stichauer 3:1, Tabaka 8:1.
Aggregate: Drew 88-88.

OPOLE (A)
Sunday, August 3
Won 47-43
Rempala 4, Szatmari 1, Bajerski 8:1, Magosi 9, **Rymel 14:1**, Tabaka 0, Stichauer 11:2.
Aggregate: Won 100-80

KROSNO (H)
Sunday, August 10
Won 65-25
Bajerski 7:1, Rempala 6:2, **Magosi 12**, Szatmari 6:2,. Rymel 13, Molnar 2:1, Stichauer 9:2, **Tabaka 10:2**.
Aggregate: Won 116-64.

Play offs

LODZ (H)
Sunday, August 24
Won 57-34
Magosi 10:1, Rempala 1, Bajerski 14, Szatmari 4:2, Rymel 11, Molnar, did not ride, Stichauer 11:2, Tabaka 6.
■ Result amended from 58-34 as Norbert Magosi ruled ineligible to ride in Heat 14.

GNIEZNO (A)
Sunday, August 31
Lost 34-58
Magosi 1, Szatmari 4:1, Bajerski 14 (4), Szilagyi, did not ride, Rempala 3, Molnar, did not ride, Stichauer 10, Tabaka 2:1.

RIVNE (H)
Sunday, September 7
Won 65-25
Bajerski 14:1, Rempala 11:1, Magosi 7:2, Szatmari 10:1, Rymel 11:3, Molnar, did not ride, Stichauer 7:1, Tabaka 5:2.

RIVNE (A)
Thursday, September 25
Lost 42-48
Rempala 6:2, Magosi 2, Bajerski 6:1, Szatmari 2, Rymel 8, Molnar, did not ride, Stichauer 5, Tabaka 13:1.
Aggregate: Won 107-73.

TRACK FILE

Track: Gyertyan Str. 30, 3535, Miskolc, Hungary.
Telephone: 0036 305383230.
Website: www.rso.hu
Track Length: 367 metres.

SQUAD
Zsolt Bencze, Patrik Kotta Kis, Attila Lorincz, Norbert Magosi, Attila Molnar, Laszlo Szatmari, Tamas Szilagyi, Jozef Tabaka, Sandor Tihanyi.
Foreign: Ricky Ashworth, Tomasz Bajerski, Karol Baran, Vladimir Dubinin, Stefan Ekberg, Martin Gavenda, Evgeny Gomozov, Igor Kononov, Marcin Les, Tomasz Rempala, Adrian Rymel, Derek Sneddon, Hynek Stichauer, Radik Tibeev,Ben Wilson,

Rider	M	R	Pts	BP	TPts	Ave	F	P	TR	TPts
Adrian RYMEL	12	59	120	10	130	8.81	0	1	1	1
Tomasz BAJERSKI	**15**	**67**	**126**	**12**	**138**	**8.24**	**0**	**2**	**1**	**2**
Tomasz REMPALA	15	69	113	15	128	7.42	0	0	0	0
Norbert MAGOSI	**13**	**59**	**100**	**9**	**109**	**7.39**	**1**	**1**	**1**	**2**
Hynek STICHAUER	12	48	74	10	84	7.00	0	0	0	0
Jozsef TABAKA	**14**	**54**	**81**	**9**	**90**	**6.67**	**0**	**1**	**0**	**0**
Laszlo SZATMARI	15	69	89	9	98	5.68	0	0	0	0
Vladimir DUBININ	**2**	**5**	**6**	**0**	**6**	**4.80**	**0**	**0**	**0**	**0**
Sandor TIHANYI	2	9	9	1	10	4.44	0	0	0	0
Martin GAVENDA	**3**	**10**	**10**	**1**	**11**	**4.40**	**0**	**0**	**0**	**0**
Atilla MOLNAR	3	4	2	1	3	3.00	0	0	0	0
Tamas SZILAGYI	**1**	**2**	**0**	**0**	**0**	**0.00**	**0**	**0**	**0**	**0**

LODZ (A)
Sunday, September 28
Lost 37-54
Rempala 4, Szatmari 6:2, Bajerski 3:1, Magosi 6, Rymel 8:1 (2), Szilagyi, did not ride, Stichauer 6:1, Tabaka 4:1.
Aggregate: Won 94-88

GNIEZNO (H)
Sunday, October 5
Lost 34-58
Bajerski 0, *rider replacement for Rymel*, Szatmari 5, Magosi 12 (4), Rempala 13, Molnar 0, Gavenda 0, Tabaka 4.
Aggregate: Lost 68-116.

DIVISION ONE PLAY-OFF

GRUDZIADZ (H & A)
Miskolc defaulted.

SECOND LEAGUE (after play-offs)

	M	W	D	L	BP	Pts
Gniezno	16	12	1	3	7	32
MISKOLC	**16**	**10**	**0**	**6**	**6**	**26**
Rivne	16	9	0	7	3	21
Lodz	16	4	1	11	3	12

SECOND LEAGUE (regular season)

	M	W	D	L	BP	Pts
MISKOLC	**10**	**8**	**0**	**2**	**4**	**20**
Gniezno	10	7	0	3	4	18
Rivne	10	6	0	4	2	14
Lodz	10	3	0	7	3	9
Opole	10	3	0	7	1	7
Krosno	10	3	0	7	0	6

2009 Squad

Sandor **FEKETE**, Roland **KOVACS**, Attila **LORINCZ**, Norbert **MAGOSI**, Laszlo **SZATMARI**, Tamas **SZILAGYI**, Jozsef **TABAKA**.
Foreign: Sergey **DARKIN**, Vladimir **DUBININ**, Stefan **EKBERG**, Martin **GAVENDA**, Manuel **HAUZINGER**, Klaus **JAKOBSEN**, Sergey **KARACHINTSEV**, Jaroslav **POLUICHOVIC**, Adrian **RYMEL**, Joe **SCREEN**, Denis **STOJS**, Tomas **SUCHANEK**, Semen **VLASOV**.

Challenge

RZESOW (H)
Sunday, March 16
Won 74-37
Szatmari 14, Zsolt 3, Bajerski 7, Tihanyi 12, Rempala 10, Tabaka 11, Stichauer 12, Kovacs 5.

Other meetings

SZEGEDI OPEN
Szeged-Algyo, Sunday, May 11
Jaroslav Poliuchovic 14, Adam Vandirek 12, Ronny Weis 11+3, Vladimir Visvader 11+2, Marcel Helfer 9, Vladimir Trofimov 9, Dennis Helfer 6, Tamas Sike 6, Jaromir Otruba 5, Karel Kadlec 4, Jan Holub[3] 0, Istvan Barna 0.

DEBRECEN INTERNATIONAL
Debrecen, Wednesday, August 20
Jozsef Tabaka 12+3, Maciej Kuciapa 12+2, Hynek Stichauer 11+3, Maks Gregoric 11+R, Rafal Trojanowski 11+N, Tomasz Rempala 10, Manuel Hauzinger 10, Sandor Tihanyi 9, Dino Kovacic 9, Manuel Novotny 5, Andrea Maida 5, Matic Voldrih 4, Nikola Pigac 2, Roland Kovacs 2, Mate Szegedi [R] 1, Tamas Szilagyi 0, Zsolt Nagy [R] 0.

AUSTRIA-CROATIA-HUNGARY-SLOVENIA TEAM CHAMPIONSHIP

FINAL STANDINGS

	M	Pts
1 SLOVENIA	3	136+0
2 HUNGARY	**3**	**132+3**
3 AUSTRIA	3	93
4 CROATIA	3	60

HUNGARY AVERAGES

Rider	M	R	Pts	Ave	FM
Matej FERJAN	2	11	30	10.91	0
Jozsef TABAKA	**3**	**15**	**30**	**8.00**	**0**
Sandor TIHANYI	3	14	26	7.43	0
Robert NAGY	**2**	**9**	**16**	**7.11**	**0**
Laszlo SZATMARI	3	13	23	7.08	0
Guests					
Daniel GRAPPMAIER	1	5	7	5.60	0
Marcel HELFER	**1**	**5**	**3**	**2.40**	**0**

position in the higher division as a consequence.

ITALY

ITALIAN CHAMPIONSHIP

MATTIA Carpanese made it a hat-trick of Italian titles with victories in each of the two rounds.

He was beaten only twice in 12 championship rides – once in each of the qualifying stages before dominating the sudden death finals at Lonigo and Terenzano.

The championship also doubled as the Italian Under 21 Championship with 18-year-old Mattia Tadiello – a surprise runner-up in the overall contest – taking the honours.

Round 1

Lonigo, Saturday, April 12

1 Mattia Carpanese 14+3, 2 Mattia Tadiello 11+2, 3 Antonin Galliani 12+1, 4 Andrea Maida 11+FX, 5 Alessandro Milanese 11, 6 Marco Gregnanin 10, 7 Massimo Mora 10, 8 Joakim Kugelmann 10, 9 Daniele Tessari 7, 10 Christian Miotello, 11 Massimo Zambon 5, 12 Alessandro Novello 5, 13 Mattia Cavicchioli 4, 14 Jonatha Seren 2, 15 Mario Marzotto 1, 16 Maurizio Betali 1, 17 Federico Stevanni, Stefano Mazzali.

Round 2

Terenzano, Sunday, September 21

1 Mattia Carpanese 14+3, 2 Andrea Maida 13+2, 3 Mattia Tadiello 11+1, 4 Alessandro Milanese 12+0, 5 Marco Gregnanin 10, 6 Massimo Zambon 10, 7 Daniele Tessari 10, 8 Simone Tadiello 9, 9 Antonin Galliani 7, 10 Jonatha Seren 6, 11 Alessandro Novello 5, 12 Mattia Cavicchioli 3, 13 Mario Marzotto 3, 14 Pier Paolo Scagnetti 3, 15 Francesco Barbetta 2, 16 Andrea Baroni 2, 17 Giovanni Boggian 2.

OVERALL

	R1	*R2*	*Tot*
1 Mattia CARPENESE	**25**	**25**	**50**
2 Mattia TADIELLO	22	20	42
3 Andrea MAIDA	20	22	42
4 Alessandro MILANESE	18	18	36
5 Marco GREGNANIN	16	16	32
6 Daniele TESSARI	12	12	24
7 Massimo ZAMBON	10	14	24
8 Alessandro NOVELLO	9	8	17
9 Jonatha SEREN	7	9	16
10 Mattia CAVICCHIOLI	8	7	15
11 Massimo MORA	14	–	14
12 Mario MARZOTTO	6	6	12
13 Christian MIOTELLO	11	–	11
14 Simone TADIELLO	–	11	11
15 Maurizio BETTALI	5	–	5
16 Pier Paolo SCAGNETTI	–	5	5
17 Federico STEVANINI	4	–	4
18 Stefano MAZZALI	3	–	3
19 Andreas BARONI	–	3	3
20 Giovanni BOGGIAN	–	2	2
21 Antonin GALLIANI	*0*	*0*	*0*
22 Joakim KUGELMANN	*0*	–	*0*
23 Francesco BARBETTA	–	*0*	*0*

[Scoring: 25-22-20-18-16-14-12-11-10-9-8-7-6-5-4-3-2].

Points scored by the Czech Republic's Antonin Galliani, Germany's Joakim Kugelmann and Francesco Barbetta (who raced on a Czech Republic licence) did not count towards the official championship.

Roll of Honour

1967 .... Domenico PIETROGRANDE
1968 .... Giordano BON
1969 .... Giuseppe PIZZO
1970 .... Ermanno FEDELE
1971 .... Annibale PRETTO
1972 .... Gianni PIZZO
1973 .... Annibale PRETTO
1975 .... Giuseppe MARZOTTO
1976 .... Giuseppe MARZOTTO
1977 .... Giuseppe MARZOTTO
1978 .... Giuseppe MARZOTTO
1979 .... Francesco BIGINATO
1980 .... Francesco BIGINATO
1981 .... Mauro FERRACCIOLI
1982 .... Francesco BIGINATO
1983 .... Giuseppe MARZOTTO
1984 .... Armando CASTAGNA
1985 .... Armando CASTAGNA
1986 .... Armando CASTAGNA
1987 .... Valentino FURLANETTO
1988 .... Armando CASTAGNA
1989 .... Valentino FURLANETTO
1990 .... Armando CASTAGNA
1991 .... Armando CASTAGNA
1992 .... Armando CASTAGNA
1993 .... Armando CASTAGNA
1994 .... Armando CASTAGNA
1995 .... Armando CASTAGNA
1996 .... Andrea MAIDA
1997 .... Andrea MAIDA

1998 .... Stefano ALFONSO
1999 .... Andrea MAIDA
2000 .... Armando CASTAGNA
2001 .... Armando CASTAGNA
2002 .... Andrea MAIDA
2003 .... Andrea MAIDA
2004 .... Emiliano SANCHEZ
2005 .... Emiliano SANCHEZ
2006 .... Mattia CARPANESE
2007 .... Mattia CARPANESE
2008 .... Mattia CARPANESE

UNDER 21 CHAMPIONSHIP

Roll of Honour

1977 .... Stefano BORON
1978 .... Mario ANDRIOLO
1979 .... Piermario ZANIN
1980 .... Giorgio ZARAMELLA
1981 .... Giuliano BERGAMINI
1982 .... Armando CASTAGNA
1983 .... Alessandro TOFFANIN
1984 .... Paolo SALVATELLI
1985 .... Paolo FACCIO
1986 .... Amerigo MILANESE
1987 .... Mariano CASTAGNA
1988 .... Alessandro MILANESE
1989 .... Gabriele MASINA
1990 .... Remo dal BOSCO
1991 .... Paolo MONTICOLO
1992 .... John BARBETTA
1993 .... Stefano SPAGNOLO
1994 .... Alessandro DALLA VALLE
1995 .... Simome TADIELLO
1996 .... Marco SALIMISTRARO
1997 .... Graziano FRANCHETTI
1998 .... Andrea MAESTRELLI
1999 .... Simone TERENZANI
2000 .... Francesco ULIAN
2001 .... Christian MIOTELLO
2002 .... Daniele TESSARI
2003 .... Marco GREGNANIN
2004 .... Mattia CARPANESE
2005 .... Mattia CARPANESE
2006 .... Mattia CARPANESE
2007 .... Andrea BARONI
2008 .... Mattia TADIELLO

TEAM CHAMPIONSHIP

FINAL STANDINGS

	Pts
1 MC LONIGO	**155**
2 MC La Favorita	**148**
3 MC Olimpia	**103**
4 ASM Abato KLM	**103**
5 Team Titano	**84**

Round 1

Terenzano, Sunday, April 13

1 MC LONIGO 37 (Mattia Carpanese 10, Daniele Tessari 9, Steve Johnston 18), 2 MC LA FAVORITA (Montello) 34 (Alessandro Milanese 5, Thomas Stange 13, Emiliano Sanchez 16), 3 ASM ABATO KLM 19 (Marco Gregnanin 9, Marcin Piekarski 8, Maurizio Bettali 2), 4 MC OLIMPIA (Terenzano) 18 (Joakim Kugelmann 10, Andrea Maida 0, Mattia Cavicchioli 8), 5 TEAM TITANO (Lonigo) 12 (Alessandro Novello 2, Mattia Tadiello 6, Antonin Galliani 4).

Round 2

Lonigo, Saturday, May 3

1 MC LA FAVORITA (Montello) 34 (Piotr Swist 15, Massimo Mora 13, Alessandro Milanese 6), 2 MC LONIGO 30 (Steve Johnston 15, Daniele Tessari 9, Simone Tadiello 6), 3 ASM ABATO KLM 26 (Marco Gregnanin 17, Marcin Piekarski 8, Mauriziio Bettali 1), 4 MC OLIMPIA (Terenzano) 18 (Joakim Kugelmann 13, Christian Miotello 4, Mattia Cavicchioli 1), 5 TEAM TITANO (Lonigo) 11 (Massimo Zambon 7, Mattia Tadiello 2, Alessandro Novello 2).

Round 3

Giavera del Montello, Saturday, May 10

1 MC LA FAVORITA (Montello) 40 (Massimo Mora 12, Alessandro Milanese 17, Rafal Dobrucki 11), 2 MC LONIGO 30 (Mattia Carpanese 6, Simone Tadiello 7, Steve Johnston 17), 3 MC OLIMPIA (Terenzano) 20 (Andrea Baroni 3, Mattia Cavicchioli 7, Joakim Kugelmann 10), 4 ASM ABATO KLM 17 (Adam Czechowicz 8, Marco Gregnanin 8, Maurizio Bettali 1), 5 TEAM TITANO (Lonigo) 13 (Mattia Tadiello, did not ride, Alessandro Novello 7, Antonin Galliani 6).

Round 4

Lonigo, Saturday, July 26

1 MC OLIMPIA (Terenzano) 30+3 (Joakim Kugelmann 13+3, Guglielmo Franchetti 9, Andrea Maida 8), 2 MC LONIGO 30+2 (Steve Johnston 14+2, Daniele Tessari 7, Mattia Carpanese 9), 3 TEAM TITANO (Lonigo) 25 (Jesper B. Monberg 16, Mattia Tadiello 7, Alessandro Novello 2), 4 MC LA FAVORITA (Montello) 19 (Emiliano Sanchez 9, Mads Korneliussen 7, Massimo Mora 3), 5 ASM ABATO KLM 14 (Marco Gregnanin 8, Marcin Piekarski 5, Mattia Cavicchioli 1).

Round 5

Terenzano, Sunday, October 19

1 MC LONIGO 28 (Mattia Carpanese 10, Daniele Tessari 9, Steve Johnston 9), 2 ASM ABATO KLM 27 (Filip Sitera 14, Marco Gregnanin 7, Mattia Cavicchioli 6), 3 TEAM TITANO (Lonigo) 23 (Simone Tadiello 5, Alessandro Novello 1, Jesper B. Monberg 17), 4 MC LA FAVORITA (Montello) 21 (Alessandro Milanese 4, Sebastian Ulamek 17, Emiliano Sanchez, did not ride), 5 MC OLIMPIA (Terenzano) 19 (Grzegorz Strozyk 3, Andrea Maida 9, Guglielmo Franchetti 7).

Roll of Honour

1970 .... AMF di TARCENTO
1985 .... LONIGO
1989 .... ROVIGO
1991 .... CASTELMASSA
1993 .... TERENZANO
1994 .... TERENZANO
1999 .... TERENZANO
2001 .... BADIA CALAVENA
2002 .... BADIA CALAVENA
2003 .... MONTELLO
2004 .... LONIGO
2005 .... MONTELLO
2006 .... LONIGO
2007 .... TERENZANO
2008 .... LONIGO

TRIVENETO CHAMPIONSHIP

OVERALL

	1	2	3	4	5	6	7	8	9	10	11	Tot
1 Armando CASTAGNA	**25**	**25**	**18**	**25**	**25**	**25**	**25**	**14**	**20**	**25**	–	**227**
2 Andrea MAIDA	12	–	22	22	20	22	18	20	25	16	25	202
3 Mattia CARPANESE	18	14	16	20	12	18	20	25	*9*	22	22	187
4 Marco GREGNANIN	22	22	11	16	11	16	*2*	12	22	18	16	166
5 Mattia TADIELLO	20	–	25	–	18	14	14	18	16	20	14	159
6 Massimo ZAMBON	16	16	20	14	16	20	11	16	18	*6*	12	159
7 Mattia CAVICCHIOLI	11	12	10	12	14	11	*9*	9	14	14	10	117
8 Simone TADIELLO	10	–	14	–	10	12	16	11	11	12	18	114
9 Alessandro NOVELLO	9	18	12	8	7	*6*	10	7	7	11	11	100
10 Daniele TESSARI	14	–	–	18	–	–	12	22	–	–	20	86
11 Jonatha SEREN	6	11	8	9	5	*4*	6	8	10	9	7	79
12 Andrea BARONI	4	–	9	7	8	10	7	10	12	7	–	74
13 Mario MARZOTTO	5	–	7	11	6	8	5	6	8	4	9	69
14 Federico STEVANINI	3	10	6	10	4	5	4	4	–	5	6	57
15 Guglielmo FRANCHETTI	–	–	–	–	22	9	22	–	–	–	–	53
16 Maurizio BETTALI	2	8	–	–	9	7	8	–	–	–	–	34
17 Massimo MORA	8	20	–	–	–	–	3	–	–	–	–	31
18 Stefano MAZZALI	1	–	–	–	–	–	–	5	6	10	8	30
19 Giovanni BOGGIAN	–	–	–	–	3	3	1	2	5	8	5	27
20 Lorenzo FRANCHETTI	–	9	–	–	–	–	–	–	–	–	–	9
21 Alessandro MILANESE	7	–	–	–	–	–	–	–	–	–	–	7
22 Giuseppe FURLAN	–	–	–	–	–	–	–	3	4	–	–	7

[Scoring: 25-22-20-18-16-14-12-11-10-9-8-7-6-5-4-3-2-1]. Riders drop their worst score (in italics)

ARMANDO Castagna – 45 last birthday – is a man of many parts.

He's a high-ranking FIM official, technical director of the Italian Federation and still his country's top rider!

He's only a part-time racer these days but he was still good enough to retain his Thursday afternoon Triveneto Championship.

He actually launched the competition to give increrased competition to his riders but still proved he's virtually unbeatable on track.

He won seven of the ten rounds in which he competed and had wrapped up the title before the last round, allowing him to sit it out as Andrea Maida pipped Italian Champion Mattia Carpanese for the runners-up spot.

Round 1

Lonigo, Thursday, April 3

1 Armando Castagna 14+3, 2 Marco Gregnanin 13+2, 3 Mattia Carpanese 12+0, 4 Mattia Tadiello 11+1, 5 Massimo Zambon 10, 6 Daniele Tessari 9, 7 Andrea Maida 8, 8 Mattia Cavicchioli 8, 9 Simone Tadiello 8, 10 Alessandro Novello 7, 11 Massimo Mora 6, 12 Alessandro Milanese 4, 13 Jonatha Seren [R] 3, 14 Mario Marzotto 2, 15 Andrea Baroni 2, 16 Federico Stevanini [R] 1, 17 Stefano Mazzali 1, 18 Maurizio Bettali 1.

Round 3

Lonigo, Thursday, May 22

1 Mattia Tadiello 12+3, 2 Andrea Maida 11+2, 3 Massimo Zambon 11+1, 4 Armando Castagna 15+F, 5 Mattia Carpanese 11, 6 Simone Tadiello 10, 7 Alessandro Novello 10, 8 Marco Gregnanin 9, 9 Mattia Cavicchioli 7, 10 Andrea Baroni 5, 11 Jonatha Seren 5, 12 Mario Marzotto 5, 13 Federico Stevanini 4.

Round 4

Lonigo, Thursday, May 29

1 Armando Castagna 9+3, 2 Andrea Maida 9+2, 3 Mattia Carpanese 11+1, 4 Daniele Tessari 10+FX, 5 Marco Gregnanin 7, 6 Massimo Zambon 6, 7 Mattia Cavicchioli 4, 8 Mario Marzotto 3, 9 Federico Stevanini 2, 10 Jonatha Seren 2, 11 Alessandro Novello 1,12 Andrea Baroni 1.

Round 6

Lonigo, Thursday, July 3

1 Armando Castagna, 2 Andrea Maida, 3 Massimo

Zambon, 4 Mattia Carpanese, 5 Marco Gregnanin, 6 Mattia Tadiello, 7 Simone Tadiello, 8 Mattia Cavicchioli, 9 Andrea Baroni, 10 Guglielmo Franchetti, 11 Mario Marzotto, 12 Maurizio Bettali, 13 Alessandro Novello, 14 Federico Stevanini, 15 Jonatha Seren, 16 Giovanni Boggian. ■ *Individual scores not available.*

Round 5

Lonigo, Thursday, July 10

1 Armando Castagna 15+3, 2 Guglielmo Franchetti 14+2, 3 Andrea Maida 12+1, 4 Mattia Tadiello 11+N, 5 Massimo Zambon 9, 6 Mattia Cavicchioli 9, 7 Mattia Carpanese 9, 8 Marco Gregnanin 7, 9 Simone Tadiello 7, 10 Maurizio Bettali 7, 11 Andrea Baroni 6, 12 Alessandro Novello 5, 13 Mario Marzotto 4, 14 Jonatha Seren 3, 15 Federico Stevanini 2, 16 Giovanni Boggian 0.

Round 7

Lonigo, Thursday, July 17

1 Armando Castagna 14+3, 2 Guglielmo Franchetti 14+2, 3 Mattia Carpanese 13+1, 4 Andrea Maida 12+0, 5 Simone Tadiello 9, 6 Mattia Tadiello 9, 7 Daniele Tessari 9, 8 Massimo Zambon 8, 9 Alessandro Novello 7, 10 Mattia Cavicchioli 6, 11 Maurizio Bettali 6, 12 Andrea Baroni 5, 13 Jonatha Seren 3, 14 Mario Marzotto 3, 15 Federico Stevanini [R] 2, 16 Massimo Mora 0, 17 Marco Gregnanin 0, 18 Giovanni Boggian [R], did not ride.

Round 8

Lonigo, Thursday, September 4

1 Mattia Carpanese 15+3, 2 Dániele Tessari 14+2, 3 Andrea Maida 13+1, 4 Mattia Tadiello 11+0, 5 Massimo Zambon 10, 6 Armando Castagna 9, 7 Marco Gregnanin 9, 8 Simone Tadiello 8, 9 Andrea Baroni 7, 10 Mattia Cavicchioli 5, 11 Jonatha Seren 5, 12 Alessandro Novello 4, 13 Mario Marzotto 4, 14 Stefano Mazzaili 2, 15 Federic Stevanini 2, 16 Giuseppe Furlan [R] 2, 17 Giovanni Boggian 0.

Round 9

Lonigo, Thursday, September 11

1 Andrea Maida 14+3, 2 Marco Gregnanin 12+2, 3 Armando Castagna 15+1, 4 Massimo Zambon 12+0, 5 Mattia Tadiello 9, 6 Mattia Cavicchioli 9, 7 Andrea Baroni 9, 8 Simone Tadiello 8, 9 Jonatha Seren 8, 10 Mattia Carpanese 5, 11 Mario Marzotto 5, 12 Alesssandro Novello 4, 13 Stefano Mazzali 4, 14 Giovanni Boggian 3, 15 Giuseppe Furlan 1.

Round 10

Lonigo, Thursday, October 9

1 Armando Castagna 15+3, 2 Mattia Carpanese 12+2, 3 Mattia Tadiello 12+1, 4 Marco Gregnanin 13+R, 5 Andrea Maida 11, 6 Mattia Cavicchioli 11, 7 Simone Tadiello 9, 8 Alesssandro Novello 7, 9 Stefano Mazzali 6, 10 Jonatha Seren 6, 11 Giovanni Boggian 5, 12 Andrea Baroni 4, 13 Massimo Zambon 3, 14 Federico Stevanini 1, 15 Mario Marzotto 0.

Round 11

Lonigo, Thursday, October 16

1 Andrea Maida 13+3, 2 Mattia Carpanese 11+2, 3 Daniele Tessari 10 +1, 4 Simone Tadiello 14+0, 5 Marco Gregnanin 10, 6 Mattia Tadiello 9, 7 Massimo Zambon 9, 8 Alesssandro Novello 9, 9 Mattia Cavicchioli 8, 10 Mario Marzotto 6, 11 Stefano Mazzali 5, 12 Jonatha Seren 5, 13 Federico Stevanini 4, 14 Giovanni Boggian 3.

INTERNATIONAL

Natschback-Loipersbach, Austria

Saturday, October 25

1 POLAND 39 (Marcin Jedrzejewski 15, Mateusz Kowalczyk 5, Marcel Kajzer 12, Lukas Simon [Austria] 6, Christopher Funk [Austria] 1), **2 ITALY 35** (Andrea Maida 10, Marco Gregnanin 12, Matti Cavicchioli 2, Sandor Tihanyi [Hungary] 11, Gernot Schneebacher [Austria] 0), 3 NATSCHBACH-LOIPERSBACH 31 (Manuel Hauzinger 10, Manuel Novotny 8, Denis Stojs [Slovenia] 6, Franz Winklhofer [Germany] 7), 4 CZECH REPUBLIC 21 (Michael Hadek 5, Jan Holub 5, Michal Dudek 5, Vaclav Milik[2] 3, Roman Cejka 3).

Challenge

Landshut, Germany, Saturday, September 20

LANDSHUT 56 (Christian Hefenbrock 14, Sirg Schützbach 4, Richard Speiser 7, Manfred Betz 6, Herbert Rudolph 5, Hans-Jörg Müller 12, Frank Facher 8), **LONIGO 40** (Alessandro Milanese 3, Andrea Baroni 3, Armando Castagna 12, Mattia Cavicchiloi 4, Mattia Carpanese 12, Simone Tadiello 6, Alessandro Novello 0).

2009 FIXTURES

ITALIAN CHAMPIONSHIP

Round 1: Monday, June 1, Giavera del Montello.
Round 2: Sunday, June 21, Terenzano.
Round 3: Saturday, July 11, Lonigo.
Round 4: Saturday, October 3, Giavera del Montello.
Round 5: Saturday, October 10, Lonigo.

ITALIAN TEAM CHAMPIONSHIP

Five teams will complete in the 2009 Team Championship based at four different tracks – Team Titano also use Lonigo as their base – over four rounds with race points determining the champions.

MC LONIGO
Track: Via Santa Marina, Casella Postale 65, 36045, Lonigo, Italy.
Telephone: 0039 0444 0835144.
Track Length: 334 metres.
Track Record: 59.8 secs, Tony Rickardsson, June 1, 1996.

MC OLIMPIA DI TERENZANO
Track: Piazza Terenzio 1, 33050, Terenzano, Italy.
Telephone: 0039 0432 553230.
Track Length: 400 metres.
Track Record: 69.6 secs, Valentino Furlanetto.

MC MONTELLO
Track: Via Stazione, 31040 Giavera del Montello, Italy.
Telephone: 0039 0422 776271.
Track Length: 396 metres.

MC LA FAVORITA
Track: Via Monticello di Fara 33, 36040 Sarego, Italy.
Telephone: 0039 0444-832683

MC ABATO
Track: Badia Calavena, Verona, Italy.
Telephone: 0039 045 7000118.
Track Length: 295 metres.
Track Record: Tony Rickardsson, 1998.

Round 1: Sunday, May 10, Lonigo.
Round 2: Saturday, May 30, Terenzano.
Round 3: Saturday, September 19, Lonigo.
Round 4: Sunday, October 18, Terenzano.

ITALIAN PAIRS CHAMPIONSHIP

Sunday, March 22, Lonigo.

LATVIA

LATVIAN CHAMPIONSHIP

FINAL

Daugapils, Sunday, July 13

RUSSIAN Grigori Laguta, the mainstay of the Daugavpils Polish League side and a regular in the Latvian Grand Prix, won his first national championship.

Even though he was surprisingly beaten by veteran Pole Piotr Swist in Heat 9, he went on to gain his revenge in the final, points from which went towards the top four riders' overall total.

Swist, who lost to Tomasz Piszcz and Leonids Paura, needed to win the last race to make up the leeway but was well beaten by the home track favourite.

One-time Oxford rider Kjastas Puodzhuks, the defending champion, was absent having suffered a broken leg in a horror crash in which his bike went into the crowd at the Lokomotiv Stadium during the European Pairs Championship on May 31.

The Under 21 championship – decided on points scored in the senior competition – went to 19-year-old Maksim Bogdanovs who was third overall, and the top ranked Latvian in the line-up.

Bogdanovs admitted: "I was glad to get gold in the juniors but I wanted to win the senior championship."

And the new champ claimed: "I hope it's not my last Latvian title!"

Riders under the age of 21 are listed in the scorechart in italics.

	1	2	3	4	5	6	Tot
1 GRIGORI LAGUTA	**3**	**3**	**2**	**3**	**3**	**3**	**17**
2 Piotr SWIST	2	2	3	3	3	1	14
3 Maksim BOGDANOVS	*2*	*1*	*3*	*2*	*3*	*2*	*13*
4 Leonids PAURA	3	FX	2	3	3	0	11
5 Tomasz PISZCZ	2	3	1	2	2	10	
6 Viatcheslav GERUTSKY	*1*	*1*	*3*	*2*	*2*	*9*	
7 Sergey DARKIN	2	3	3	1	0	9	
8 Zbigniew CZERWINSKI	1	1	2	3	1	8	
9 Pawel MIESIAC	3	2	1	1	1	8	
10 Andrej KOROLEV	3	0	R	2	2	7	
11 Evgenyi KARAVATSKAYA	*0*	*3*	*2*	*0*	*1*	*6*	
12 Ilya BONDARENKO	1	2	1	1	0	5	
13 Vladimir DUBININ	E	2	0	0	1	3	
14 Ruslan GATYATOV	0	0	1	0	2	3	
15 Semen VLASOV	0	1	0	1	0	2	
16 Evgeny PETUKHOV	*1*	*0*	*0*	*0*	*0*	*1*	
17 Maris KURSITIS [R]	*0*					*0*	

Roll of Honour

1965 .... Rejno VIJDAS (Estonia)
1966 .... Anatoli PETROVSKY
1967 .... Juri STUPAKOV
1970 .... Anatoli PETROVSKY
1976 .... Anatoli KUZMIN
1977 .... Anatoli KUZMIN
1978 .... Valeri CHARITONOV
1979 .... Ivan RYBNIKOV
1980 .... Sergey DOWZENKO
1982 .... Vladimir TKACZUK
1983 .... Oleg ISAEEV
1984 .... Vladimir RYBNIKOV
1985 .... Vladimir RYBNIKOV
1986 .... Sergey DANU
1987 .... Vladimir RYBNIKOV
1988 .... Valeri SOKOLOV
1990 .... Nikołai KOKIN
1991 .... Andrey KOROLEV
1992 .... Nikołai KOKIN
1993 .... Vladimir VORONKOV
1994 .... Nikołai KOKIN
1995 .... Andrey KOROLEV
1997 .... Andrey KOROLEV
1998 .... Vladimir VORONKOV
1999 .... Adam SKORNICKI (Poland)
2000 .... Andrey KOROLEV
2001 .... Andrey KOROLEV
2003 .... Robert MIKOŁAJCZAK (Poland)
2004 .... Kjastas PUODZHUKS
2005 .... Sławomir DUDEK (Poland)
2006 .... Marcin JEDRZEJEWSKI (Poland)
2007 .... Kjastas PUODZHUKS
2008 .... Grigori LAGUTA (Russia)

UNDER 21 CHAMPIONSHIP

Roll of Honour

1965 .... Anatoli PETROVSKY
1966 .... Anatoli PETROVSKY
1970 .... Anatoli KUZMIN
1976 .... Dmitri VASILEEV
1977 .... Valeri CHARITONOV
1978 .... Valeri CHARITONOV
1979 .... Vladimir TKACZUK
1980 .... Sergey DANU
1982 .... Vladimir RYBNIKOV
1983 .... Vasili MATVIEJEV
1984 .... Igor JEMELIANOV
1985 .... Juri BRAUCEJS
1986 .... Andris MATISANS
1987 .... Juri BRAUCEJS
1990 .... Normunds DOBURMS
1991 .... Aleksandr BIZNIA
1992 .... Aleskandr BIZNIA
1993 .... Aleksandr BIZNIA
1994 .... Maksim ANDRIEJEV
1995 .... Maksim ANDRIEJEV
1997 .... Maksim ANDRIEJEV
1998 .... Maksim ANDRIEJEV
1999 .... Maksim ANDRIEJEV
2000 .... Denis POPOVIC
2001 .... Leonids PAURA
2003 .... Kjastas PUODZHUKS
2004 .... Kjastas PUODZHUKS
2005 .... Kjastas PUODZHUKS
2006 .... Kjastas PUDOZHUKS
2007 .... Maksim BOGDANOVS
2008 .... Maksim BOGDANOVS

■ ***Chairman of Daugavpils is three-times Latvian Champion Vladimir Rybnikov.***

Daugavpils – the only club in Latvia – will compete in the Polish First League in 2009 and will, once again, stage the Latvian Grand Prix at their Lokomotiv Stadium. They have released all their Polish riders from 2008 as well as Sergey Darkin.

Polish
First League

DAUGAVPILS

2008 RESULTS

First League

Final position..................................Fifth (Sixth)

GDANSK (A)
Sunday, April 6
Lost 39-53
Puodzhuks 5:2, Swist 2, Miesiac 5, Piszcz 0, G. Laguta 13:1 (4), A. Laguta 7, Bogdanovs 7:1, Gerutsky, did not ride.

RYBNIK (H)
Sunday, April 13
Won 56-37
Puodzhuks 7, Paura 4:1, Swist 9, Miesiac 9:2, G. Laguta 13:1, A. Laguta 8:1, Bogdanovs 5:2, Gerutsky 1.

POZNAN (A)
Sunday, April 20
Lost 29-60
Puodzhuks 2:1, Swist 9:1, Miesiac 11, Paura 0, G. Laguta 0, Gerutsky 0, Bogdanovs 0, A. Laguta 7.

OSTROW (H)
Thursday, May 1
Lost 43-49
Puodzhuks 5, Piszcz 5:3, Swist 0, Miesiac 17 (4), G. Laguta 7, Karavatskaya, did not ride, Bogdanovs 3:2, A. Laguta 6.

RAWICZ (H)
Sunday, May 4
Won 60-32
Puodzhuks 8:2, Piszcz 5:1, Gerutsky 3, Miesiac 9, G. Laguta 9, Karavatskaya 4:1, Bogdanovs 11:1, A. Laguta 11:1.

BYDGOSZCZ (A)
Sunday, May 11
Lost 32-60
G. Laguta 10, Puodzhuks 1, Piszcz 0, Swist 3:1, Miesiac 4:2, Karavatskaya 1, Bogdanovs 2, A. Laguta 11:1 (4).

GRUDZIADZ (A)
Sunday, June 8
Lost 28-62
G. Laguta 11, Korolev 1:1, Piszcz 1, Swist 6, Miesiac 4, Gerutsky 0, Bogdanovs 3:1, A. Laguta 2 (0).

GRUDZIADZ (H)
Friday, June 13
Won 52-40
G. Laguta 13, Paura 2, Swist 3:1, Darkin 12, Miesiac 10:1, Karavatskaya 1:1, Bogdanovs 11:2, Gerutsky 0.
Aggregate: Lost 80-102.

TRACK FILE

Track: Lokomotiv Stadium, ul. Jelgavas 54, 5404 Daugavpils, Latvia.
Telephone: 00371 5440580.
Website: www.latvijasspidvejs.lv
Track Length: 373 metres.
Track Record: 67.74 secs, Grigori Laguta, June 13, 2008.

BYDGOSZCZ (H)
Sunday, June 22
Won 47-43
G. Laguta 8:1, *rider replacement for A. Laguta*, Korolev 10, Darkin 5:4, Miesiac 7:1, Karavatskaya, did not ride, Gerutsky 2, Bogdanovs 15.
Aggregate: Lost 79-103.

RAWICZ (A)
Sunday, July 6
Won 48-42
G. Laguta 11:1, Korolev 3:1, Swist 7:2, Darkin 3, Miesiac 5, Karavatskaya, did not ride, A. Laguta 12:1, Bogdanovs 7:1.
Aggregate: Won 108-74.

OSTROW (A)
Sunday, July 20
Lost 28-62
G. Laguta 7, Korolev 0, Swist 6, Piszcz 0, Miesiac 7, Karavatskaya 0, A. Laguta 3:1, Bogdanovs 5:1.
Aggregate: Lost 71-109.

POZNAN (H)
Sunday, July 27
Won 58-34
G. Laguta 14, Korolev 8:2, Swist 7:1, Darkin 8:1, Miesiac 4:1, Gerutsky 5:1, Bogdanovs 12:2, Karavatskaya, did not ride.
Aggregate: Lost 87-94.

RYBNIK (A)
Sunday, August 3
Lost 32-58
G. Laguta 11 (R), Korolev 2:1, Swist 9, Darkin 2:1, Miesiac 7, Gerutsky 0, A. Laguta 1, Bogdanovs 0.
Aggregate: Lost 88-95.

GDANSK (H)
Sunday, August 10
Lost 44-46
G. Laguta 12:1, Darkin 3:2, Korolev 4:1, Miesiac 2:1, Swist 7, Gerutsky, did not ride, A. Laguta 6, Bogdanovs 10:2.
Aggregate: Lost 83-99.

Play offs

GRUDZIADZ (A)
Sunday, August 24
Won 50-42
G. Laguta 12:3, Puodzhuks 6, Korolev 7, Miesiac 1, Swist 6:1, Gerutsky 0, A. Laguta 9, Bogdanovs 9:2.

SQUAD
Maksim Bogdanovs, Viatcheslav Gerutsky, Evgenyi Karavatskaya, Andrey Korolev, Leonids Paura, Evgeny Petukhov, Kjastas Puodzhuks.
Foreign: Ilya Bondarenko, Sergey Darkin, Roman Ivanov, Pawel Miesiac, Artem Laguta, Grigori Laguta, Tomasz Piszcz, Piotr Swist.

RYBNIK (A)
Sunday, August 31
Lost 36-54
G. Laguta 5, Puodzhuks 1, Korolev 3:1, Miesiac 9, Swist 3:1, Karavatskaya 0, no rider at seven, Bogdanovs 15.

RAWICZ (A)
Sunday, September 7
Won 49-41
G. Laguta 11:1, Puodzhuks 1, Korolev 1, Miesiac 8, Swist 9:2, Gerutsky, did not ride, A. Laguta 11, Bogdanovs 8:2.

RAWICZ (H)
Sunday, September 21
Won 61-29
G. Laguta 11:1, Gerutsky 4:1, **Korolev 11:1**, Puodzhuks 8:3, Swist 3, Karavatskaya 3, **Bogdanovs 12**, A. Laguta 9.
Aggregate: Won 110-70.

GRUDZIADZ (H)
Sunday, September 28
Won 60-30
G. Laguta 9, Karavatskaya 6:1, Korolev 7, Puodzhuks 7:1, Miesiac 2, Gerutsky 9:3, Bogdanovs 10:1, A. Laguta 10:1.
Aggregate: Won 110-72.

RYBNIK (H)
Sunday, October 5
Won 60-33
G. Laguta 11:1, Karavatskyi 7:3, Korolev 9:1, Puodzhuks 9:1, Paura 2, Gerutski 2, **Bogdanovs 12**, A. Laguta 8.
Aggregate: Won 96-87.

POLISH FIRST LEAGUE

	M	*W*	*D*	*L*	*BP*	*Pts*
Bydgoszcz	20	16	0	4	10	42
Gdansk	20	13	1	6	6	33
Ostrow	20	13	0	7	7	26
Poznan	20	8	1	11	4	21
DAUGAVPILS	**20**	**11**	**0**	**9**	**4**	**26**
Rybnik	20	9	0	11	6	24
Grudziadz	20	8	0	12	3	19
Rawicz	20	1	0	19	0	2

Challenge

GNIEZNO (H)
Tuesday, March 25
Won 74-46
Puodzhuks 14:1, Gerutsky 2, Korolev 7:2, Paura 5, **Miesiac 9**, Karavatskaya 8:1, A. Laguta 9:3, Bogdanovs 6, Swist 11, Piszcz 3:1.

Roman Povazhny, a 2009 Daugavpils newcomer

2009 Squad

Maksim **BOGDANOVS**, Viatcheslav **GERUTSKY**, Evgeny **KARAVATSKAYA**, Andrey **KOROLEV**, Leonids **PAURA**, Kjastas **PUODZHUKS**, Evgeny **PETUKHOV**, Evgeny **SAMKOV**.
Foreign: Christian **HEFENBROCK**, Artem **LAGUTA**, Grigori **LAGUTA**, Roman **POVAZHNY**.

Rider	*M*	*R*	*Pts*	*BP*	*TPts*	*Ave*	*F*	*P*	*TR*	*TPts*
Grigori LAGUTA	20	98	198	11	209	8.53	1	2	2	2
Maksim BOGDANOVS	**20**	**89**	**158**	**18**	**176**	**7.91**	**2**	**0**	**0**	**0**
Artem LAGUTA	16	66	121	6	127	7.70	0	0	2	2
Sergey DARKIN	**6**	**24**	**33**	**8**	**41**	**6.83**	**0**	**0**	**0**	**0**
Pawel MIESIAC	18	82	121	8	129	6.29	0	0	1	2
Kjastas PUODZHUKS	**12**	**45**	**60**	**10**	**70**	**6.22**	**0**	**0**	**0**	**0**
Piotr SWIST	16	67	88	11	99	5.91	0	0	0	0
Andrey KOROLEV	**13**	**50**	**66**	**7**	**73**	**5.84**	**0**	**1**	**0**	**0**
Evgenyi KARAVATSKAYA	8	20	22	6	28	5.60	0	0	0	0
Viatcheslav GERUTSKY	**13**	**28**	**26**	**6**	**32**	**4.57**	**0**	**0**	**0**	**0**
Tomasz PISZCZ	6	19	11	4	15	3.16	0	0	0	0
Leonids PAURA	**4**	**13**	**8**	**1**	**9**	**2.77**	**0**	**0**	**0**	**0**

NEW ZEALAND

NEW ZEALAND CHAMPIONSHIP

FINAL

Palmerston North, Sunday, January 4

INVETERATE winter traveller Jason Bunyan made it six of the best as he retained his New Zealand title for a fifth time.

The Milton Keynes-born former Isle of Wight skipper, warmed up for his new career at Stoke by coming out on top at Palmerston North just four days into the New Year.

Bunyan won the Friday night qualifier and went through the card at Sunday's re-staging after the initial Saturday night meet had been postponed because of heavy rain.

	1	2	3	4	5	Tot	RO
1 Jason BUNYAN	**3**	**3**	**3**	**3**	**3**	**15**	
2 Jade MUDGWAY	2	3	3	3	3	14	
3 Larry ROSS	3	2	2	3	3	13	
4 Andrew ALDRIDGE	3	3	2	0	2	10	
5 Sean COX	1	2	2	2	3	10	
6 Craig RAMSAY	2	3	3	0	1	9	
7 John TUFFLEY	0	2	2	3	2	9	
8 Sean MASON	1	1	3	2	2	9	
9 Dylan MOOHAN	3	2	1	1	0	7	
10 John ROSS	2	1	1	2	0	6	
11 Alex CUNNINGHAM	2	0	0	2	1	5	
12 Jamie MOOHAN	1	1	1	1	1	5	
13 Haydon BAGSHAW	0	0	0	1	2	3	
14 Paul HABIB	1	0	0	1	1	3	
15 Jason McKAY	0	1	1	0	0	2	

Roll of Honour

1929 .... Dave MANAGH
1930 .... Alf MATSON
1931 .... Alf MATSON
1936 .... Wally KILMISTER
1941 .... Charlie BUCHANAN
1945 .... Jack HUNT
1946 .... Len PERRY
1947 .... Gillbert CRAVEN (England)
1948 .... Jack HUNT
1949 .... Harold FAIRHURST
1950 .... Bruce ABERNETHY
1951 .... Bruce ABERNETHY
1952 .... Ron JOHNSTON
1954 .... Harold FAIRHURST
1956 .... Ronnie MOORE
1958 .... Maury DUNN
1959 .... Barry BRIGGS
1960 .... Charlie NEW
1961 .... Charlie NEW
1962 .... Ronnie MOORE
1963 .... Barry BRIGGS
1964 .... Geoff MARDON
1965 .... Murray BURT
1966 .... Bob ANDREWS (England)
1967 .... Howard COLE (Wales)
1968 .... Ronnie MOORE
1969 .... Ronnie MOORE
1970 .... Chris BAILEY (England)
1971 .... Frank SHUTER
1972 .... Bruce CRIBB
1973 .... Gary PETERSON
1974 .... Ivan MAUGER
1975 .... Dave MORTON (England)
1976 .... Larry ROSS
1977 .... Larry ROSS
1978 .... Larry ROSS
1979 .... Larry ROSS
1980 .... Larry ROSS
1981 .... Ivan MAUGER
1982 .... Mitch SHIRRA
1983 .... Mitch SHIRRA
1984 .... Mitch SHIRRA
1985 .... Larry ROSS
1986 .... David BARGH
1987 .... David BARGH
1988 .... Larry ROSS
1989 .... Larry ROSS
1990 .... Larry ROSS
1991 .... David BARGH
1992 .... Gary ALLAN
1993 .... Mark THORPE
1994 .... Mark THORPE
1995 .... Andy WALKER
1996 .... Mark THORPE
1997 .... Chris PENNY
1998 .... Paul ATKINS
1999 .... Mark JAMIESON
2000 .... David BARGH
2001 .... Graham HARTSHORNE
2002 .... Andrew APPLETON (England)
2003 .... Sam TAYLOR
2004 .... Jason BUNYAN (England)
2005 .... Jason BUNYAN (England)
2006 .... Jason BUNYAN (England)
2007 .... Jason BUNYAN (England)
2008 .... Jason BUNYAN (England)
2009 .... Jason BUNYAN (England)

QUALIFYING ROUND

Palmerston North, Friday, January 2

Jason Bunyan 8, Jade Mudgway 8, Grant Tregoning 8, Andrew Aldridge 8, Larry Ross 7, John Tuffley 7, Craig Ramsay 6, Dylan Moohan 6, Kody Tocher 6, Alex Cunningham 6, Jamie Moohan 5, Sean Mason 5, Ryan

Moss 5, Paul Habib 4, Haydon Bagshaw 4, John Ross 3. ***Non-qualifiers:*** Sean Cox, Mitchell McHardy, James Miller, Josh O'Docherty, Ryan Bagshaw.

NEW ZEALAND UNDER 21 CHAMPIONSHIP

FINAL
Palmerston North, Friday, January 2

GRANT Tregoning retained his national Under-21 title – but luck was on his side.

Redcar's Jade Mudgway looked to have the championship in his hands when he was well ahead in both the opening and last heat of the final round of races.

His primary chain snapped in both races and he was handicapped by his throttle coming off at the start of the second Final heat.

Even though he was some 80 metres behind he held the throttle onto the handlebars with his thumb and passed the retiring Jamie Moohan, Ryan Moss and Michael Patey to claim third place.

His misfortune allowed Andrew Aldridge to take advantage and his only defeat came when Moohan took the lead after Mudgway had ground to a halt coming off the last bend.

An impressive fourth place went to Michael Patey in only his fourth meeting on a 500cc bike.

	Q	*Q*	*F1*	*F2*	*F3*	*Tot*
1 Grant TREGONING	**4**	**4**	**5**	**5**	**4**	**14**
2 Kody TOCHER	4	3	4	4	3	11
3 Jamie MOOHAN	3	4	3	R	5	8
4 Michael PATEY	2	3	2	2	2	6
5 Jade MUDGWAY	4	4	R	3	R	3
6 Ryan MOSS	3	2	1	1	1	3
7 Sean MASON	3	1				
8 Ryan BAGSHAW	0	3				
9 Chris JENNINGS	2	1				
10 Hayden BAGSHAW	1	2				
11 Josh O'DOUGHERTY	1	2				
12 Karl BAGSHAW	R	1				
13 Dylan HANCOCK	N	R				
14 Cory LANG	0	0				
15 Mitchell McHARDY	did not ride					

[Contested over six qualifying races (4-3-2-1-0) with the top six scorers going into a series of three Finals (5-4-3-2-1-0) and finishing positions behind decided over the three Finals].

Roll of Honour

1987 .... Dean SULLIVAN
1989 .... Mark THORPE
1990 .... Mark THORPE
1991 .... Justin MONK
1992 .... Rhys HAMBURGER
1993 .... Rhys HAMBURGER
1994 .... Daniel BURBERRY
1995 .... Andy WALKER
1996 .... Graham HARTSHORNE
1997 .... Graham HARTSHORNE
1998 .... Graham HARTSHORNE
1999 .... Kris JEMMET
2000 .... Sam TAYLOR
2001 .... Joshua BLOMQUIST
2002 .... Sam TAYLOR
2003 .... Andrew ALDRIDGE
2004 .... Grant TREGONING
2005 .... Andrew BARGH
2006 .... Andrew ALDRIDGE
2007 .... Andrew ALDRIDGE
2008 .... Grant TREGONING
2009 .... Grant TREGONING

Stamp of approval

ON February 4, 2009, the New Zealand Post Service issued a commemorative series of new stamps honouring five of the country's Champions of World Motorsport.

And speedway legend Ivan Mauger was included in the special issue alongside motor racing greats Bruce McLaren, Denny Hulme and Scott Dixon as well as World GP motorcyclist Hugh Anderson.

The colourful stamp (above at 150% its actual size), which also included Mauger's autograph, came in various denominations while an unique first day cover (below at 50% of actual size) included a tribute to the six-times World Speedway Champion's Long Track record speed of 144.666 miles an hour (232.8 kilometres per hour), set at Auckland's Alexander Park.

Mauger became the first New Zealand speedway rider ever to appear on his country's stamps.

Individual

NEW ZEALAND GRAND PRIX
Meeanee, Napier, Saturday, January 31, 2009
1 Andrew Bargh, 2 Jade Mudgway, 3 Andrew Aldridge, 4 Craig Ramsay, 5 Sean Mason.

NORTH ISLAND CHAMPIONSHIP
Waikaraka Park, Auckland, Saturday, January 24, 2009
1 Jason Bunyan 12+2+3, 2 Andrew Bargh 11+3+2, 3 Jamie Moohan 9+2+1, 4 Jade Mudgway 10+3+0, 5 Mitchell McHardy 9+0+3, 6 Karl Bagshaw 8+3+1+2, 7 Craig Ramsay 11+1+1, 8 Dylan Moohan 6+0+N, Paul Habib 8+2, Sean Mason 7, Hayden Bagshaw 5, Ryan Bagshaw 5, Jason McKay 3, Jay Lucas 3, Daniel Hanley 3, Steve Mudgway 3, Colin Pearce 2, Ben Antunovich 1, Kim Stevens 1, Chris Jennings 0, Darrin Wilson, did not ride.

SOUTH ISLAND CHAMPIONSHIP
Oreti Park, Invercargill, Saturday, March 14, 2009
Larry Ross 15, Grant Tregoning 14, Alex Cunnigham 11, Paul Hayes 10, John Tuffley 10, Cory Lang 8, Adam Wilson 8, Matt Smith 8, John Ross 7, Craig Blackett 6, Ryan Moss 6, Paul Highsted 5, James Miller 5, Barry O'Brien 2, Doug Stenning 2, Jamie Moohan 0.

ROLLY INN PAIRS
Moore Park, Christchurch, Sunday, October 26
1 John Ross 4 & Larry Ross 3:1, 2 Ryan Moss 2 & Grant Tregoning 0.

BERT MUNRO CHALLENGE SPECTACULAR
Oreti Park, Invercargill, Saturday, November 29
1 Grant Tregoning, 2 Andrew Aldridge, 3 Alex Cunningham, 4 Paul Hayes , 5 Cory Lang, 6 Craig Blackett.

ASRC SUMMER CUP
Rosebank, Auckland, Sunday, December 14
Jason Bunyan 9+3+3, Dylan Moohan 6+2+2, Jade Mudgway 8+1+1, Andrew Bargh 5+3+0, Sean Mason 7+0+3 , Barry Free 6+2+2, Ben Antunovich 1+3+1, Ryan Bagshaw 3+1+N, Andrew Aldridge 3+1+3, Karl Bagshaw 1+2+2, Hayden Bagshaw 1+0+1, Dylan Hancock 3+0+N.

SOUTHLAND CHAMPIONSHIP
Oreti Park, Invercargill, Saturday, Janury 24, 2009
Grant Tregoning 14, Alex Cunningham 9, Andrew Aldridge 8, Kody Tocher 5, Paul Hayes 4, John Tuffley 3. ***Non-qualifiers:*** Jamie Moohan, Craig Blackett, Doug Stenning.

Pairs

BEST PAIRS
Rosebank, Auckland, Sunday, November 2
1 Jason McKay 3 & Brendon Manu 2:1, 2 Jade Mudgway 4 & Sean Mason F, 3.
Qualifying scorers: Jade Mudgway 16 & Sean Mason 10:2 = 26, Jason McKay 11+3 & Brendon Manu 10:2+F = 21+3, Daniel Hanley 13+F & Karl Bagshaw 0+N = 13+0, Dylan Moohan 11 & Ben Antunovich 2 = 13, Barry Free 5 & Ryan Bagshaw 7 = 12.

Challenge matches

Rosebank, Auckland, Sunday, October 12
AUCKLAND 42 (Sean Mason 15, Ben Antunovich 6:3, Daniel Hanley 8:3, Karl Bagshaw 3, Ryan Bagshaw 5, Dean Ruding, did not ride, Rob Campbell 4:2, Dylan Hancock 1), **PALMERSTON NORTH 46** (**Jade Mudgway 15**, Jason McKay 4:1, Steve Mudgway 4, David Bargh 11:1, James Smith 3:1, Brendon Manu 9:2).

IVAN MAUGER SERIES
First leg
Moore Park, Christchurch, Friday, January 9, 2009
SOUTH ISLAND 53 (Andrew Aldridge 17, Alex Cunninghan 12, Kody Tocher 12, Adam Wilson 4, Ryan Moss 4, Matt Smith 4) **NORTH ISLAND 55** (Jade Mudgway 16, Jamie Moohan 14, Dylan Moohan 11, Sean Mason 10, Craig Blackett 2, James Smith 2).

Second leg
Oreti Park, Invercargill, Sunday, January 11, 2009
NORTH ISLAND 51 (Jade Mudgway 15, Dylan Moohan 8, Jamie Moohan 6, Paul Hayes 9, Sean Mason 6, John Tuffley 7), **SOUTH ISLAND 56** (Andrew Aldridge 17, Adam Wilson 4, Ryan Moss 1, Alex Cunningham 11, Kody Tocher 8, Matt Smith 0, Grant Tregoning 15).

TRACKS

CHRISTCHURCH (South Island)
Track: Moore Park, Weedons Ross Road, West Melton, Christchurch. **Telephone:** 0064 0273200977.
Website: www.moorepark.co.nz

Track: Ruapuna Speedway, Hasketts Road, Templton, Christchurch. **Telephone:** 0064 033497727.
Website: www.ruapunaspeedway.co.nz
Track Length: 406 metres.

GISBORNE (North Island)
Track: Eastland Group Raceway, Awapuni Road, Gisborne. **Telephone:** 0064 068684917.
Website: www.gisbornespeedway.co.nz
Track Length: 389 metres.

MEEANEE (North Island)
Track: Sandy Road, Meeanee, Napier.
Telephone: 0064 06 834 4655.
Website: www.hbspeedway.co.nz
Track Length: 400 metres.

INVERCARGILL (South Island)
Track: Oreti Park, Pitt Road, Otatara, Invercargill.
Telephone: 0064 0276554005.
Website: www.oretiparkspeedway.racing.org.nz
Track Length: 408 metres.

PALMERSTON NORTH (North Island)
Track: Arena Manawatu, corner Cuba and Pascal Streets, Palmerston North. **Telephone:** 0064 063588838.
Website: www.pnspeedway.co.nz
Track Length: 431 metres.

AUCKLAND (North Island)
Track: Rosebank Domain, 126, Patiki Road, Avondale, Auckland. **Telephone:** 0064 098282173.
Website: www.rosebankspeedway.co.nz
Track Length: 320 metres.

Track: Waikaraka Park, Neilson Street, Onehunga, Auckland. **Telephone :** (0064) 096365014.
Website: www.waikarakafamilyspeedway.co.nz
Track Length: 460 metres.

WESTPORT (South Island)
Track: Sunset Speedway, Craddock Drive, North Beach, Westport. **Telephone:** 0064 037897801.
Track Length: 302 metres.

NORWAY

NORWEGIAN CHAMPIONSHIP

FINAL
Elgane, Saturday, August 23

RUNA Sola made it a birthday to remember with a hat-trick of victories even though he was beaten twice in six rides.

Sola certainly wasn't suffering any hangovers after celebrating his 24th birthday on the eve of the championship final.

He has been top Norwegian since the retirement of veteran Arnt Førland but at least there are signs he will soon be challenged by teenager Lars Daniel Gunnestad, son of ten-times title-winner Lars.

	1	2	3	4	Tot	SF	F
1 Rune SOLA	**3**	**3**	**3**	**3**	**12**	**2**	**3**
2 Carl Johan RAUGSTAD	3	2	2	3	10	3	2
3 Mikke BJERK	3	3	3	2	11	2	1
4 Tage SKRETTING	2	2	2	3	9	3	0
5 Inge BJERK	2	1	3	2	8	1	
6 Lars Daniel GUNNESTAD	1	1	3	2	7	1	
7 Henrik Bauer HANSEN	2	2	0	1	5	0	
8 Tord SOLBERG	0	0	2	1	3	0	
9 Patrick HEROLD	0	1	1	1	3		
10 Remi UELAND	1	R	1	1	3		
11 Stian HANSEN	1	F	0	0	1		
12 Lars Filip HELLER	F	0	0	0	0		

Roll of Honour

1938 Leif Basse HVEEM
1939 Thorleif ANDREASSEN
1940 Leif Basse HVEEM
1946 Leif Basse HVEEM
1947 Leif Basse HVEEM
1948 Leif Basse HVEEM
1949 Leif Basse HVEEM
1950 Henry ANDERSEN
1951 Leif Basse HVEEM
1952 Leif Basse HVEEM
1953 Leif Basse HVEEM
1954 Reidar KRISTOFFERSEN
1955 Arne Herman KURLSRUD
1957 Aage HANSEN
1958 Aage HANSEN
1959 Aage HANSEN
1960 Aage HANSEN
1961 Aage HANSEN
1962 Sverre HARRFELDT
1963 Aage HANSEN
1964 Sverre HARRFELDT
1965 Sverre HARRFELDT
1966 Sverre HARRFELDT
1967 Reidar EIDE
1968 Reidar EIDE
1969 Reidar EIDE
1970 Reidar EIDE
1971 Reidar EIDE
1972 Ulf LOVAAS
1973 Dag LOVAAS
1974 Dag LOVAAS
1975 Jan Terje GRAVNINGEN
1976 Edgar STANGELAND
1977 Audun Ove OLSEN
1978 Kjell Arvid GIMRE
1979 Audun Ove OLSEN
1980 Dag HÅLAND
1981 Audun Ove OLSEN
1982 Trond Helge SKRETTING
1983 Dag HÅLAND
1984 Einar KYLLINGSTAD
1985 Einar KYLLINGSTAD
1986 Arne SVENDSEN
1987 Tor Einar HIELM
1988 Lars GUNNESTAD
1989 Arnt FØRLAND
1990 Lars GUNNESTAD
1991 Lars GUNNESTAD
1992 Lars GUNNESTAD
1993 Lars GUNNESTAD
1994 Rune HOLTA
1995 Lars GUNNESTAD
1996 Rune HOLTA
1997 Rune HOLTA
1998 Lars GUNNESTAD
1999 Lars GUNNESTAD
2000 Rune HOLTA
2001 Lars GUNNESTAD
2002 Mikke BJERK
2003 Lars GUNNESTAD
2004 Arnt FØRLAND
2005 Arnt FØRLAND
2006 Rune SOLA
2007 Rune SOLA
2008 Rune SOLA

2009 MAJOR DATES

NORWEGIAN CHAMPIONSHIP
Saturday, August 15, Lunner, Oslo.

NORWEGIAN PAIRS CHAMPIONSHIP
DSaturday, July 25, Drammen.

NORWEGIAN TEAM CHAMPIONSHIP
Saturday, September 13, Riska.

PAIRS CHAMPIONSHIP

FINAL
Vinsvoli, Drammen, Saturday August 30
1 RISKA 22 (Rune Sola 13:1, Carl Johan Raugstad 9:3), **DRAMMEN 22** (Bjørn Guddal Hansen 8:4, Marius Røkeberg 14), **OSLO 17** (Henrik Bauer Hansen 4:1, Lars Daniel Gunnestad 13), **4 DRAMMEN II 11** (Morten Hvamstad 10, Miclos Nemeth 1), **5 GRENLAND 9** (Hasse Prytz 0, Sverre Omsland 9), **6 GRENLAND/RISKA 9** (Helge Groven 2:1, Patrick Herold 7).

OSLO (Kristian Magaji and Lars Filip Heller), did not compete.

NORWEGIAN LEAGUE

FINAL LEAGUE STANDINGS

	M	RPts	Pts
1 RISKA	6	186	26
2 ELGANE	6	169	23
3 OSLO	6	139	17
4 DRAMMEN	6	134	16
5 GRENLAND	6	82	7

[Scoring: 5-4-3-2-1].

Round 1
Geitryggen, Sunday, May 4
1 ELGANE 32 (Remi Ueland 7, Mikke Bjerk 16:1, Inge Bjerk 9:3), 2 RISKA 29 (Rune Sola 16, Carl Johan Raugstad 12:4, Patrik Herold 1), 3 DRAMMEN 24 (Bjørn G. Hansen 8:3, Benny Johansson 12, Kenneth Borgenhaug 4:3), 4 OSLO 21 (Lars Daniel Gunnestad 5, Lisandro Husman 15, Lars Fillip Heller 1), 5 GRENLAND 14 (Emil Omsland 4, Ronni Bergan 8, Tord Solberg 2).

Round 2
Elgane, Sunday, June 22
1 ELGANE 31 (Tage Skretting 12:2, Mikke Bjerk 14:1, Inge Bjerk 5:2), 2 OSLO 29 (Lisandro Husman 17, Lars Daniel Gunnestad 10:1, Christian Magaji 2:1), 3 DRAMMEN 23+3 (Bjørn G. Hansen 11, Marius Røkeberg 5:1, Kenneth Borgenhaug 7:1+3), 4 RISKA 23+R (Rune Sola 13+R, Carl Johan Raugstad 8, Patrick Herold 2), 5 GRENLAND 13 (Emil Omsland 1, Ronny Bergan 9, Tord Solberg 3:2).

Round 3
Riska, Sunday, August 3
1 RISKA 36 (**Rune Sola 15:3**, **Carl Johan Raugstad 17:1**, Patrick Herold 4:1), 2 ELGANE 34 (Mikke Bjerk 9:3, Remi Ueland 10, Inge Bjerk 15:2), 3 OSLO 22 (Lars Daniel Gunnestad 7, Christian Magaji 7:1, Tarald Håland 8:1), 4 GRENLAND 20 (Emil Omsland 5:3, Sverre Omsland 4, Tord Solberg 11), 5 DRAMMEN 0, did not compete.
Drammen were not awarded a match point.

Round 4
Drammen, Saturday, August 9
DRAMMEN 36 (Bjørn G. Hansen 14, Benny Johansson 15, Marius Røkeberg 7), 2 RISKA 31 (Rune Sola 16, Carl Johan Raugstad 13, Patrick Herold 2), 3 ELGANE 25 (Tage Skretting 12, Remi Ueland 8, Inge Bjerk 5), 4 OSLO 18 (Lars Daniel Gunnestad 8, Jeremia Thelaus 9, Christian Magaji 1), 5 GRENLAND 9 (Emil Omsland 5, Sverre Omsland 1, Tord Solberg 3).

Round 5
Lunner, Sunday, August 17
1 RISKA 31 (Rune Sola 13:2, Carl Johan Raugstad 14:1, Patrick Herold 4:1), 2 OSLO 28+3 (Lars Daniel Gunnestad 11:2, Jeremia Thelaus 15+3, Christian Magaji 2), 3 DRAMMEN 28+2 (Bjørn G. Hansen 12:2+2, Benny Johansson 8:1, Marius Røkeberg 8:2), 4 ELGANE 19 (Tage Skretting 1, Inge Bjerk 5:1, Remi Ueland 13:1), 5 GRENLAND 14 (Emil Omsland 4:1, Tord Solberg 10, Lars Filip Heller 0).

Round 6
By, Sunday, September 14
1 RISKA 36 (Rune Sola 17, Carl Johan Raugstad 14:3, Patrick Herold 5:1), 2 ELGANE 28 (Mikke Bjerk 14:2, Inge Bjerk 6:1, Remi Ueland 8), 3 DRAMMEN 23 (Marius Røkeberg 6:2, Kim Rudi Mortensen 3:1, Morten Hvamstad 14), 4 OSLO 21 (Lars Daniel Gunnestad 13, Henrik B. Hansen 7, Lars F. Heller 1), 5 GRENLAND 12 (Tord Solberg 10, Sverre Omsland 2, Helge Groven 0).

Roll of Honour

1984 .... SANDNES & JAEREN
1985 .... SANDNES & JAEREN
1991 .... ELGANE
1997 .... OSLO
1998 .... RISKA
1999 .... DRAMMEN
2000 .... OSLO
2001 .... ELGANE
2003 .... RISKA
2004 .... ELGANE
2005 .... ELGANE
2006 .... ELGANE
2007 .... ELGANE
2008 .... RISKA

2009 Squads

The 2009 Norwegian League will be run on familiar lines with each of the five clubs staging a home round of the competition with three riders in each team.

Round 1: Friday, May 1, Elgane.
Round 2: Saturday, May 2, Riska.
Round 3: Saturday, June 20, Drammen.
Round 4: Sunday, June 21, Skien.
Round 5: Saturday, August 8, Lunner, Oslo.

DRAMMEN
Kenneth **BORGENHAUG**, Bjørn Guddal **HANSEN**, Morten **HVAMSTAD**, Kim Rudi **MORTENSEN**, Marius **RØKEBERG**.
Foreign: Benny **JOHANSSON**.

ELGANE
Inge **BJERK**, Mikke **BJERK**, Trond **SKRETTING**, Remi **UELAND**.

GRENLAND
Ronny **BERGAN**, Helge **GROVEN**, Stian **HANSEN**, Emil **OMSLAND**, Sverre **OMSLAND**, Tord **SOLBERG**.

OSLO
Lars Daniel **GUNNESTAD**, Tarald **HÅLAND**, Lars Filip **HELLER**, Krister **LANGELAND**, Christian **MAGAJI**.
Foreign: Lisandro **HUSMAN**, Jeremia **THELAUS**

RISKA
Patrick **HEROLD**, Stein Roar **PEDERSEN**, Carl Johan **RAUGSTAD**, Rune **SOLA**, Willy **TJESSEM**.

NORWEGIAN LEAGUE AVERAGES

Rider	Club	M	R	Pts	BP	TPts	Ave	FM	PM
Lisandro HUSMAN	Oslo	2	12	32	0	32	10.67	0	0
Mikke BJERK	**Elgane**	**4**	**23**	**53**	**7**	**60**	**10.43**	**0**	**0**
Rune SOLA	Riska	6	35	90	5	95	10.27	1	0
Carl Johan RAUGSTAD	**Riska**	**6**	**35**	**78**	**9**	**87**	**9.94**	**0**	**1**
Tarald HÅLAND	Oslo	1	4	8	1	9	9.00	0	0
Bjørn Guddal HANSEN	**Drammen**	**4**	**25**	**47**	**5**	**52**	**8.32**	**0**	**0**
Jeremia THELAUS	Oslo	2	13	27	0	27	8.31	0	0
Benny JOHANSSON	**Drammen**	**3**	**18**	**35**	**1**	**36**	**8.00**	**0**	**0**
Kim Rudi MORTENSEN	Drammen	1	2	3	1	4	8.00	0	0
Inge BJERK	**Elgane**	**6**	**30**	**45**	**9**	**54**	**7.20**	**0**	**0**
Morten HVAMSTAD	Drammen	1	8	14	0	14	7.00	0	0
Remi UELAND	**Elgane**	**5**	**27**	**46**	**1**	**47**	**6.96**	**0**	**0**
Tage SKRETTING	Elgane	3	16	25	2	27	6.75	0	0
Marius RØKEBERG	**Drammen**	**4**	**19**	**26**	**5**	**31**	**6.53**	**0**	**0**
Lars Daniel GUNNESTAD	Oslo	6	36	54	3	57	6.33	0	0
Kenneth BORGENHAUG	**Drammen**	**2**	**10**	**11**	**4**	**15**	**6.00**	**0**	**0**
Ronny BERGAN	Grenland	2	12	17	0	17	5.67	0	0
Tord SOLBERG	**Grenland**	**6**	**31**	**39**	**2**	**41**	**5.29**	**0**	**0**
Henrik Bauer HANSEN	Oslo	1	6	7	0	7	4.67	0	0
Christian MAGAJI	**Oslo**	**4**	**17**	**12**	**2**	**14**	**3.29**	**0**	**0**
Patrick HEROLD	Riska	6	25	17	3	20	3.20	0	0
Emil OMSLAND	**Grenland**	**5**	**29**	**19**	**4**	**23**	**3.17**	**0**	**0**
Sverre OMSLAND	Grenland	3	16	7	0	7	1.75	0	0
Lars Filip HELLER	**Oslo & Grenland**	**3**	**10**	**2**	**0**	**2**	**0.80**	**0**	**0**
Helge GROVEN	Grenland	1	2	0	0	0	0.00	0	0

Statistics for Kenneth BORGENHAUG, Bjørn G. HANSEN, Carl Johan RAUGSTAD and Jeremia THELAUS include rides and points in race-offs.

TEAM CHAMPIONSHIP

FINAL
Oslo, Saturday, September 27
1 ELGANE 29 (Mikke Bjerk 15:1, Inge Bjerk 10:1, Remi Ueland 4:3), **2 DRAMMEN 28** (Bjørn G. Hansen 12:1, Marius Røkeberg 10:2, Morten Hvamstad 6:2), **3 RISKA 24+3** (Rune Sola 16, Carl Johan Raugstad 6+3, Patrick Herold 2), **4 OSLO 24+2** (Lars Daniel Gunnestad 14+2, Jeremia Thelaus 10:3, Krister Langeland 0), **5 GRENLAND 14** (Tord Solberg 8, Sverre Omsland 5:1, Lars Filip Heller 1:1).

NORWAY'S stock as a leading Scandinavian speedway nation has fallen in recent years and, arguably, they are now ranked fourth behind Denmark, Sweden and even Finland.

Their cause hasn't been helped by the retirement of Lars Gunnestad and the defection of Rune Holta who now rides under a Polish licence.

The hoped for spin-off from staging Grand Prix rounds between 2002 and 2004 failed to materialise although there are some brighter signs.

There's a relatively bouyant 80cc set-up and a new vibrant promotion at NMK Oslo although the fruits of this endeavour is unlikely to be felt for several years with Lars Daniel Gunnestad leading the revival.

Photo: **Paul PAULSEN**, www.nmkdrammen.com

Runners-up Drammen – Morten Hvamstad, team manager Kenneth Borgenhaug, Marius Røkeberg and Bjørn Guddal Hansen

POLAND

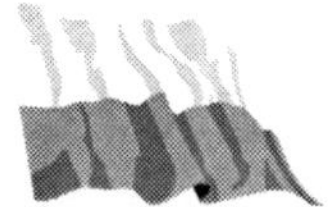

POLISH CHAMPIONSHIP

FINAL

Leszno, Saturday, August 9

ADAM Skornicki enjoyed the greatest day of his career – winning the Polish Championship with a 15-point maximum at Leszno.

The unsung Skornicki crowned what was probably his best ever season by finishing two points clear of his rivals, including Grand Prix regulars Tomasz Gollob, Krzysztof Kasprzak and Rune Holta.

Unfancied in his own country, Skornicki, who was probably not even given a second thought when Marek Cieslak picked his Speedway World Cup squad, joined the list of shock winners of the biggest domestic event in the Polish calendar.

Defending champion Rune Holta, racing with a broken collarbone, pulled out after crashing in his fourth ride at a stage when he had scored only one point after a first race win.

A delighted Skornicki beamed: "This is the biggest achievement in my career, my dreams have been granted and I am very happy.

"To win it the way I did [with a maximum] is great and they cannot say I owed my victory to the starts because I had to come from behind in my last race."

	1	2	3	4	5	TotRO
1 ADAM SKORNICKI	**3**	**3**	**3**	**3**	**3**	**15**
2 Jaroslaw HAMPEL	2	3	3	2	3	13
3 Grzegorz WALASEK	2	2	3	3	2	12
4 Tomasz GOLLOB	3	2	1	3	2	11
5 Damian BALINSKI	FX	3	2	3	1	9
6 Krzysztof KASPRZAK	3	1	1	1	2	8
7 Piotr PROTASIEWICZ	0	1	3	2	1	7
8 Robert KOSCIECHA	R	1	2	2	2	7
9 Tomasz JEDRZEJAK	0	0	1	2	3	6
10 Sebastian ULAMEK	2	X	2	1	1	6
11 Janusz KOLODZIEJ	1	2	2	FX	1	6
12 Rune HOLTA	3	1	0	X		4
13 Dawid STACHYRA [R]	1	3				4
14 Adrian GOMOLSKI	0	3	0	0	0	3
15 Michal SZCZEPANIAK	2	0	1	0	0	3
16 Slawomir DRABIK	1	2	R	R	X	3
17 Krzysztof JABLONSKI	1	0	0	1	0	2
18 Jacek REMPALA [R]	0					0
19 Adrian MIEDZINSKI [R]	did not ride					
19 Piotr SWIDERSKI [R]	did not ride					

Quarter Final, Opole, Thursday, June 5

1 Sebastian Ulamek 13, 2 Grzegorz Zengota 11, 3 Tomasz Jedrzejak 11, 4 Michal Szczepaniak 11, 5 Piotr Swiderski 10, 6 Robert Miskowiak 10, 7 Adam Czechowicz 9, 8 Krzysztof Buczkowski 7, 9 Adam Pawliczek 6, 10 Karol Zabik 6, 11 Mateusz Szczepaniak 6, 12 Marcin Jedrzejewski 5, 13 Tomasz Piszcz 5, 14 Michael Mitko 4, 15 Piotr Rembas 4, 16 Patryk Pawlaszczyk 2.

Quarter Final, Gniezno, Thursday, June 5

1 Jaroslaw Hampel 14, 2 Robert Kosciecha 13, 3 Adam Skornicki 12, 4 Adrian Gomolski 10, 5 Krzysztof Slabon 10, 6 Dawid Cieslewicz 8, 7 Roman Chromik 7+3, 8 Daniel Pytel 7+E, 9 Pawel Staszek 7+N, 10 Robert Kasprzak 6, 11 Lukasz Jankowski 6, 12 Pawel Hlib 6, 13 Mariusz Puszakowski 5, 14 Grzegorz Klopot 5, 15 Miroslaw Jablonski 3, 16 Marcel Kajzer 1.

Quarter Final, Gdansk, Thursday, June 5

1 Zbigniew Czerwinski 14, 2 Tomasz Chrzanowski 12, 3 Krzysztof Jablonski 11, 4 Grzegorz Knapp 11, 5 Slawomir Drabik 10+3, 6 Adrian Miedzinski 10+2, 7 Wieslaw Jagus 10+1, 8 Rafal Okoniewski 8, 9 Artur Mroczka 6, 10 Norbert Kosciuch 6, 11 Adam Kajoch 6, 12 Ronnie Jamrozy 5, 13 Piotr Swist 4, 14 Kamil Idziorek 3, 15 Damian Sperz 2, 16 Piotr Dym 2, 17 Cyprian Szymko [R] 0.

Quarter Final, Krosno, Thursday, June 5

1 Piotr Protasiewicz 14, 2 Tomasz Gapinski 13, 3 Dawid Stachyra 12, 4 Roman Povazhny 11, 5 Jacek Rempala 11, 6 Maciej Kuciapa 11, 7 Rafal Trojanowski 9, 8 Stanislaw Burza 8, 9 Pawel Miesiac 8, 10 Maciej Piaszczynski 6, 11 Tomasz Lukaszewicz 6, 12 Bartos Kasprowiak 3, 13 Wojciech Druchniak 3, 14 Piotr Machnik [R] 1, 15 Marcin Les [R] 1, 16 Marcin Rempala 1, 17 Borys Miturski 1, 18 Karol Baran 0, 19 Grzegorz Szyszka [R] 0.

Semi Final, Gorzow, Thursday, July 3

1 Jaroslaw Hampel 12, 2 Rune Holta 12, 3 Adrian Gomolski 11, 4 Krzysztof Kasprzak 11, 5 Adam Skornicki 11, 6 Piotr Protasiewicz 10, 7 Robert Kosciecha 9, 8 Grzegorz Walasek 8, 9 Dawid Stachyra 6+3, 10 Jacek Rempala 6+2, 11 Daniel Jeleniewski 6+R, 12 Roman Povazhny 5, 13 Rafal Dobrucki 4, 14 Krzysztof Slabon 3, 15 Rafal Trojanowski 2, 16 Maciej Kuciapa 1, 17 Tomasz Gapinski [R], did not ride.

Semi Final, Bydgoszcz, Thursday, July 3

1 Tomasz Gollob 14, 2 Krzysztof Jablonski 12, 3

Sebastian Ulamek 12, 4 Tomasz Jedrzejak 11, 5 Adrian Miedzinski 8, 7 Slawomir Drabik 8, 8 Piotr Swiderski 8, 9 Janusz Kolodziej 6+3, 10 Damian Balinski 6+2, 11 Tomasz Chrzanowski 6+1, 12 Grzegorz Zengota 5, 13 Krystian Klecha 4, 14 Grzegorz Knapp 4, 15 Robert Miskowiak 3, 16 Zbigniew Czerwinski 1, 17 Wieslaw Jagus [R], Adam Czechowicz [R], did not ride.

Roll of Honour

1932 .... Alfred WEYL
1933 .... Alfred WEYL
1935 .... Jan WITKOWSKI
1947 .... Boleslaw DOBROWOLSKI
1949 .... Alfred SMOCZYK
1950 .... Jozef OLEJNICZAK
1951 .... Wlodzimierz SZWENDROWSKI
1952 .... Edward KUPCZYNSKI
1954 .... Mieczyslaw POLUKARD
1955 .... Wlodzimierz SZWENDROWSKI
1956 .... Florian KAPALA
1957 .... Marian KAISER
1958 .... Stanislaw TKOCZ
1959 .... Stefan KWOCZALA
1960 .... Konstanty POCIEJKOWICZ
1961 .... Florian KAPALA
1962 .... Florian KAPALA
1963 .... Henryk ZYTO
1964 .... Andrzej WYGLENDA
1965 .... Stanislaw TKOCZ
1966 .... Antoni WORYNA
1967 .... Zygmunt PYTKO
1968 .... Andrzej WYGLENDA
1969 .... Andrzej WYGLENDA
1970 .... Edmund MIGOS
1971 .... Jerzy GRYT
1972 .... Zenon PLECH
1973 .... Andrzej WYGLENDA
1974 .... Zenon PLECH
1975 .... Edward JANCARZ
1976 .... Zdzislaw DOBRUCKI
1977 .... Boguslaw NOWAK
1978 .... Bernard JADER
1979 .... Zenon PLECH
1980 .... Bernard JADER
1981 .... Roman JANKOWSKI
1982 .... Andrzej HUSZCZA
1983 .... Edward JANCARZ
1984 .... Zenon PLECH
1985 .... Zenon PLECH
1986 .... Maciej JAWOREK
1987 .... Wojciech ZABIALOWICZ
1988 .... Roman JANKOWSKI
1989 .... Wojciech ZALUSKI
1990 .... Zenon KASPRZAK
1991 .... Slawomir DRABIK
1992 .... Tomasz GOLLOB
1993 .... Tomasz GOLLOB
1994 .... Tomasz GOLLOB
1995 .... Tomasz GOLLOB
1996 .... Slawomir DRABIK
1997 .... Jacek KRZYZANIAK
1998 .... Jacek GOLLOB
1999 .... Piotr PROTASIEWICZ
2000 .... Jacek GOLLOB
2001 .... Tomasz GOLLOB
2002 .... Tomasz GOLLOB
2003 .... Rune HOLTA
2004 .... Grzegorz WALASEK
2005 .... Janusz KOLODZIEJ
2006 .... Tomasz GOLLOB
2007 .... Rune HOLTA
2008 .... Adam SKORNICKI

POLISH UNDER 21 CHAMPIONSHIP

FINAL

Rybnik, Tuesday, August 19

DANIEL Pytel came close to pulling off the biggest shock in the competition's 42-season history.

He wasn't even included in the list of 16 starters but came into the line-up when Adam Kajoch and Borys Miturski crashed in Heat 1.

He took five rides but his performance provoked controversy as he never met several riders, including Adrian Gomolski.

Victory, in the end, went to the impressive Maciej Janowski who won five of his six rides, including the crunch decider against Pytel.

The Atlas Wroclaw teenager's only defeat came in Heat 16 when he was third behind pre-meeting favourite Grzegorz Zengota and Pytel.

	1	*2*	*3*	*4*	*5*	*Tot*	*R*
1 Maciej JANOWSKI	**3**	**3**	**3**	**1**	**3**	**13**	**3**
2 Daniel PYTEL [R]	2	3	2	3	3	13	2
3 Grzegorz ZENGOTA	2	3	2	3	2	12	
4 Przemyslaw PAWLICKI	3	3	2	3	0	11	
5 Adrian GOMOLSKI	3	3	FX	3	1	10	
6 Patryk PAWLASZCZYK	2	1	3	2	2	10	
7 Robert KASPRZAK	2	1	3	2	1	9	
8 Artur MROCZKA	0	2	2	2	2	8	
9 Mateusz SZCZEPANIAK	2	0	1	1	3	7	
10 Ad. SZEWCZYKOWSKI	3	2	0	0	1	6	
11 Michal MITKO	1	1	1	1	2	6	
12 Marcin JEDRZEJEWSKI	1	2	1	1	0	5	
13 Dawid LAMPART [R]	0	1	3	R		4	
14 Mateusz SZOSTEK	1	X	2	0	FX	3	
15 Borys MITURSKI	1	X				1	
16 Michal LOPACZEWSKI	0	R	R	R	N	0	
17 Kamil BRZOZOWSKI	0	R	R	R		0	
18 Adam KAJOCH	FX					0	

Semi Final, Poznan, Thursday, July 10

1 Patryk Pawlaszczyk 13, 2 Grzegorz Zengota 13, 3 Kamil Brzozowski 12, 4 Adam Kajoch 11, 5 Maciej Janowski 10, 6 Michal Mitko 10, 7 Adrian Szewczykowski 9, 8 Artur Mroczka 8, 9 Daniel Pytel 7+3, 11 Damian Celmer 7+2, 12 Slawomir Musielak 4, 13 Mateusz Lampkowski 4, 14 Marcel Kajzer 3, 15 Marcin Piekarski 2, 16 Mateusz Mitorski [R] 1, 17 Janusz Baniak [R] 0, 18 Piotr Dziatkowiak 0.

Semi Final, Tarnow, Thursday, July 10

1 Robert Kasprzak 14, 2 Przemyslaw Pawlicki 14, 3 Adrian Gomolski 13, 4 Mateusz Szczepaniak 10, 5 Borys Miturski 8, 6 Marcin Jedrzejewski 8, 7 Michal Lopaczewski 8, 8 Mateusz Szostek 8, 9 Dawid Lampart 7+3, 10 Szymon Kielbasa 7+R, 11 Rafal Fleger 6, 12 Maciej Piaszynski 5, 13 Slawomir Pyszny [R] 3, 14 Bartosz Szymura 3, 15 Slawomir Dabrowski 3, 16 Grzegorz Szyszka 2, 17 Kacper Gomolski [R] 1, 18 Marcin Liberski 0, 19 Emil Idziorek [R] 0.

Roll of Honour

1967 .... Zbigniew JADER
1968 .... Zdzislaw DOBRUCKI
1969 .... Zdzislaw DOBRUCKI
1970 .... Stanislaw KASA
1971 .... Jerzy WILIM
1972 .... Bernard JADER

1973 ..... Zbigniew FILIPIAK
1974 ..... Jerzy REMBAS
1975 ..... Boleslaw PROCH
1976 ..... Wieslaw PATYNEK
1977 ..... Marek ZIARNIK
1978 ..... Wieslaw PATYNEK
1979 ..... Mariusz OKONIEWSKI
1980 ..... Miroslaw BERLINSKI
1981 ..... Stanislaw POGORZELSKI
1982 ..... Maciej JAWOREK
1983 ..... Piotr PAWLICKI
1984 ..... Wojciech ZALUSKI
1985 ..... Zbigniew BLAZEJCZAK
1986 ..... Ryszard DOLOMISIEWICZ
1987 ..... Piotr SWIST
1988 ..... Piotr SWIST
1989 ..... Piotr SWIST
1990 ..... Tomasz GOLLOB
1991 ..... Tomasz GOLLOB
1992 ..... Tomasz GOLLOB
1993 ..... Tomasz BAJERSKI
1994 ..... Grzegorz REMPALA
1995 ..... Rafal DOBRUCKI
1996 ..... Tomasz BAJERSKI
1997 ..... Grzegorz WALASEK
1998 ..... Robert DADOS
1999 ..... Rafal OKONIEWSKI
2000 ..... Rafal OKONIEWSKI
2001 ..... Jaroslaw HAMPEL
2002 ..... Artur BOGINCZUK
2003 ..... Lukasz ROMANEK
2004 ..... Janusz KOLODZIEJ
2005 ..... Adrian MIEDZINSKI
2006 ..... Karol ZABIK
2007 ..... PAWEL HLIB
2008 ..... Maciej JANOWSKI

POLISH PAIRS CHAMPIONSHIP

FINAL

Torun, Friday, September 5

1 TORUN 24 (Wieslaw Jagus 12:1, Robert Kosciecha 12:4, Adrian Miedzinski, did not ride), **2 LESZNO 23+3** (Damian Balinski 9:3, Krzysztof Kasprzask 14:1+3, Robert Kasprzak, did not ride), **3 ZIELONA GORA 23+2** (Grzegorz Walasek 16:1+2, Grzegorz Zengota 7:1), **4 CZESTOCHOWA 21** (Sebastian Ulamek 14:1, Michal Szczepaniak 7:2, Tomasz Gapinski, did not ride), **5 POZNAN 15** (Adam Skornicki 14, Alan Marcinkowski 0, Daniel Pytel 1), **6 GRUDZIADZ 10** (Mariusz Puszakowski 6, Pawel Staszek 1:1, Kamil Brzozowski 3), **7 RYBNIK 9** (Michal Mitko 1, Maciej Kuciapa 8).

Qualifying Round, Rawicz, Saturday, July 26

1 CZESTOCHOWA 20 (Michal Szczepaniak 13:1, Tomasz Gapinski 7:2), **2 POZNAN 20** (Adam Skornicki 13:1, Zbigniew Suchecki 6:1, Norbert Kosciuch 1), **3 GORZOW 16** (Pawel Hlib 9, Adrian Szewczykowski 7:1), **4 RAWICZ 15** (Marcel Kajzer 5:1, Piotr Dym 10:1, Marcin Nowaczyk 0), **5 RAWICZ II 10** (Grzegorz Knapp 6:1, Pawel Ratajszczak 4:1), **6 OPOLE 9** (Rafal Fleger 8, Pawel Chudy 1:1).

Qualifying Round, Gdansk, Friday, August 22

1 RYBNIK 19 (Piotr Swiderski 10:2, Maciej Kuciapa 9), **2 LESZNO 19** (Krzysztof Kasprzak 9:3, Damian Balinski 10:1), **3 GDANSK 18** (Tomasz Chrzanowski 7:2, Krzysztof Jablonski 11:1), **4 TARNOW 13** (Marcin Rempala 4:3, Krystian Klecha 9), **5 BYDGOSZCZ 12** (Rafal Okoniewski 10, Krzysztof Buczkowski 1:1, Marcin Jedrzejewski 1), **6 GDANSK 9** (Damian Sperz 8, Cyprian Szymko 1, Marcl Szymko 0).

Qualifying Round, Grudziadz, Friday, August 22

1 ZIELONA GORA 22 (Grzegorz Walasek 12:3, Rafal Dobrucki 9, Grzegorz Zengota 1), **2 GRUDZIADZ 19** (Mariusz Puszakowski 8:2, Pawel Staszek 11:2, Jacek Krzyzaniak, did not ride), **3 WROCLAW 17** (Tomasz Jedrzejak 9, Daniel Jeleniewski 8:2), **4 OSTROW 15** (Adrian Gomolski 8:2, Robert Miskowiak 7:1), **5 GRUDZIADZ II 12** (Kamil Brzozowski 8, Artur Mroczka 2:1, Wojciech Zurawski 2:1)**6 GNIEZNO 5** (Lukasz Loman 3:1, Marcin Kozdras 2).

Roll of Honour

1974 ..... BYDGOSZCZ
1975 ..... GORZOW
1976 ..... GORZOW
1977 ..... GORZOW
1978 ..... GORZOW
1979 ..... ZIELONA GORA
1980 ..... LESZNO
1981 ..... GORZOW
1982 ..... ZIELONA GORA
1983 ..... ZIELONA GORA
1984 ..... LESZNO
1985 ..... GDANSK
1986 ..... TORUN
1987 ..... LESZNO
1988 ..... LESZNO
1989 ..... LESZNO
1990 ..... BYDGOSZCZ
1991 ..... BYDGOSZCZ
1992 ..... GORZOW
1993 ..... BYDGOSZCZ
1994 ..... BYDGOSZCZ
1995 ..... BYDGOSZCZ
1996 ..... BYDGOSZCZ
1997 ..... BYDGOSZCZ
1998 ..... GORZOW
1999 ..... BYDGOSZCZ
2000 ..... BYDGOSZCZ
2001 ..... WROCLAW
2002 ..... BYDGOSZCZ
2003 ..... LESZNO
2004 ..... TORUN
2005 ..... RZESZOW
2006 ..... CZESTOCHOWA
2007 ..... TARNOW
2008 ..... TORUN

DIVISION TWO

1974 ..... OPOLE
1975 ..... TORUN

Despite the competition's title, the Polish Pairs Championship has, since 1983, embraced three riders from each club.
The first champions, in 1974, were the Bydgoszcz duo of Henryk Glucklich and Stanislaw Kaza while Jerzy Rembas won the first of his four titles – with three different partners – in 1975.
Brothers Tomasz and Jacek Gollob represented Bydgoszcz in their gold medal winning performances in 1993, 1994, 1995, 1996, 1997 and 2002 with a variety of third partners.

POLISH UNDER 21 PAIRS CHAMPIONSHIP

FINAL
Gorzow, Sunday, August 17
1 RYBNIK 21 (Rafal Fleger, did not ride, Michal Mitko 12:2, Patryk Pawlaszczyk 9:3), **2 OSTROW 19+3** (Adrian Gomolski 16+3, Marcin Liberski 3:1, Emil Idziorek, did not ride), **3 RZESZOW 19+2** (Dawid Lampart 10:1+2, Mateusz Szostek, did not ride, Martin Vaculik 9), **4 GORZOW 18** (Adrian Szewczykowski 15, Lukasz Cyran 3:2, Mateusz Mikorski, did not ride), **5 LESZNO 18** (Robert Kasprzak 5:1, Przemyslaw Pawlicki 13:1, Adam Kajoch 0), **6 ZIELONA GORA 17** (Grzegorz Zengota 15, Patryk Dudek 1:1, Janusz Baniak 1), **7 CZESTOCHOWA 14** (Mateusz Szczepaniak 14, Borys Miturski, did not ride, Marcin Piekarskio 0).

Eliminating Round, Bydgoszcz, Thursday, May 29
1 ZIELONA GORA 16 (Grzegorz Zengota 12, Patryk Dudek 4:1, Pawel Gwozdz, did not ride), **2 LESZNO 14** (Robert Kasprzak 8, Adam Kajoch 5:1, Przemyslaw Pawlicki 1), **3 BYDGOSZCZ 13** (Marcin Jedrzejewski 10, Michal Lopaczewski 3:1, Damian Adamczak, did not ride), **4 GDANSK 9** (Damian Sperz 9, Cyprian Szymko 0, Marcel Szymko 0), **5 GNIEZNO 8** (Slawomir Musielak 5, Kacper Gomolski 3:2, Arkadiusz Sturomski 0).

Eliminating Round, Czestochowa, Sunday, June 29
1 CZESTOCHOWA 24 (Mateusz Szczepaniak 11:1, **Borys Miturski 9:3**, Marcin Piekarski 4), **2 RYBNIK 21** (Michal Mitko 10:2, Rafal Fleger, did not ride, Patryk Pawlaszczyk 11:2), **3 TORUN 15** (Damian Celmer 7:2, Oskar Pieniazek 8, Adam Wisniewski, did not ride), **4 TARNOW 14** (Kamil Zielinski 7:1, Szymon Kielbasa 6:1, Lukasz Kielbasa 1), **5 RAWICZ 9** (Marcel Kajzer 9, Pawel Ratajszczak 0), **6 CZESTOCHOWA II 7** (Mateusz Kowalczyk 5, Cezary Romanczuk 1:1, Adrian Osmolski 1).

Eliminating Round, Ostrow, Sunday, June 29
1 OSTROW 22 (**Adrian Gomolski 12**, Maciek Piaszczynski 6:2, Emil Idziorek 4), **2 RZESZOW 17** (Dawid Lampart 11, Mateusz Szostek 6:2), **3 WROCLAW 16** (Maciej Janowski 13, Grzegorz Strozyk 3:1), **4 GRUDZIADZ 15** (Kamil Brzozowski 10, Artur Mroczka 5:1), **5 POZNAN 12** (Daniel Pytel 8, Piotr Dziatkowiak 4:1), **5 OPOLE 7** (Slawomir Dabrowski 7).

Roll of Honour

1980 .... BYDGOSZCZ
1981-82 .... *Not staged*
1983 .... RYBNIK
1984 .... OPOLE
1985 .... GORZOW
1986 .... GORZOW
1987 .... GORZOW
1988 .... ZIELONA GORA
1989 .... GDANSK
1990 .... TORUN
1991 .... TORUN
1992 .... TORUN
1993 .... TORUN
1994 .... TARNOW
1995 .... PILA
1996 .... LESZNO
1997 .... LESZNO
1998 .... PILA
1999 .... OSTROW
2000 .... PILA
2001 .... ZIELONA GORA
2002 .... PILA
2003 .... RYBNIK
2004 .... TARNOW
2005 .... LESZNO
2006 .... RZESZOW
2007 .... TORUN
2008 .... RYBNIK

GOLDEN HELMET

The Golden Helmet (Zloty Kask) is an individual competition open to riders of any age and is the equivalent of Britain's Elite League Riders' Final.

Wroclaw, Saturday, October 25
1 Damian Balinski 14, 2 Jaroslaw Hampel 13, 3 Adrian Miedzinski 11, 4 Piotr Swiderski 9, 5 Roman Povazhny 8, 6 Adam Skornicki 8, 7 Tomasz Jedrzejak 8, 8 Daniel Jeleniewski 8, 9 Norbert Kosciuch 8, 10 Grzegorz Walasek 8, 11 Piotr Protasiewicz 7, 12 Grzegorz Zengota 6, 13 Slawomir Drabik 5, 14 Jacek Rempala 4, 15 Rafal Trojanowski 3.

Roll of Honour

1961 .... Florian KAPALA
1962 .... Marian KAISER
1963 .... Joachim MAJ
1964 .... Andrzej WYGLENDA
1965 .... Stanislaw TKOCZ
1966 .... Andrzej POGORZELSKI
1967 .... Antoni WORYNA
1968 .... Pawel WALOSZEK
1969 .... Edward JANCARZ
1970 .... Jan MUCHA
1971 .... Antoni WORYNA
1972 .... Edward JANCARZ
1973 .... Zenon PLECH
1974 .... Zenon PLECH
1975 .... Edward JANCARZ
1976 .... Marek CIESLAK
1977 .... Jerzy REMBAS
1978 .... Zenon PLECH
1979 .... Robert SLABON
1980 .... Robert SLABON
1981 .... Boleslaw PROCH
1982 .... Roman JANKOWSKI
1983 .... Jan KRZYSTYNIAK
1984 .... Roman JANKOWSKI
1985 .... Roman JANKOWSKI
1986 .... Wojciech ZABIALOWICZ
1987 .... Zenon KASPRZAK
1988 .... Piotr SWIST
1989 .... Wojciech ZALUSKI
1990 .... Miroslaw KORBEL
1991 .... Slawomir DRABIC
1992 .... Tomasz GOLLOB
1993 .... Dariusz SLEDZ
1994 .... Tomasz GOLLOB
1995 .... Tomasz GOLLOB
1996 .... Jacek GOLLOB
1997 .... Tomasz GOLLOB
1998 .... Jacek GOLLOB
1999 .... Jacek KRZYZANIAK
2000 .... Tomasz GOLLOB
2001 .... Piotr PROTASIEWICZ
2002 .... Tomasz GOLLOB
2003 .... Rafal OKONIEWSKI
2004 .... Wieslaw JAGUS
2005 .... Janusz KOLODZIEJ
2006 .... Tomasz GOLLOB
2007 .... Grzegorz WALASEK
2008 .... Damian BALINSKI

SILVER HELMET

The Silver Helmet (Srebrny Kask) is an individual competition open to riders under the age of 21 and is a prestigious title, won by many young riders who went on to attain world status, including second season winner Edward Jancarz.

In 1971, Zenon Plech, Grzegorz Kuzniar and Zbigniew Marcinkowski were declared joint winners after a six round series with the best four scores counting.

An expected run-off to decide the medal positions did not take place after the final round at Rzeszow.

FINAL

Rzeszow, Friday, October 10

1 Maciej Janowski 12, 2 Grzegorz Zengota 11+3, 3 Patryk Pawlaszczyk 11+2, 4 Mateusz Szczepaniak 11+FN, 5 Dawid Lampart 11+FX, 6 Michal Mitko 10, 7 Marcin Jedrzejewski 9, 8 Adrian Szewczykowski 8, 9 Daniel Pytel 8, 10 Szymon Kielbasa 8, 11 Slawomir Musielak 6, 12 Marcin Piekarski 6, 13 Patryk Dudek 3, 14 Damian Celmer 2, 15 Kamil Brzozowski 1, 16 Rafal Fleger 0, 17 Grzegorz Szyszka [R] 0, Adrian Gomolski [R], Przemyslaw Pawlicki [R], did not ride. *Track reserve: Mateusz Szostek 3.*

Semi Final, Czestochowa, Thursday, August 21

1 Maciej Janowski 15, 2 Damian Celmer 12, 3 Mateusz Szczepaniak 11, 4 Michal Mitko 11, 5 Adrian Szewczykowski 10, 6 Marcin Piekarski 9, 7 Patryk Pawlaszczyk 9, 8 Kamil Brzozowski 7+3, 9 Grzegorz Szyszka 7+2, 10 Maciej Piaszczynski 6, 11 Slawomir Pyszny 6, 12 Mateusz Mikorski 5, 13 Marcin Liberski 4, 14 Artur Mroczka 3, 15 Pawel Gwodz 2, 16 Damian Sperz, did not ride.

Semi Final. Opole, Thursday, August 21

1 Adrian Gomolski 15, 2 Dawid Lampart 12, 3 Marcin Jedrzejewski 12, 4 Przemyslaw Pawlicki 11, 5 Rafal Fleger 10, 6 Slawomir Musielak 9, 7 Daniel Pytel 9, 8 Szymon Kielbasa 8+3, 9 Grzegorz Zengota 8+X, 10 Robert Kasprzak 7, 11 Patryk Dudek 6, 12 Emil Idziorek 3, 13 Piotr Dziatkowiak [R] 3, 14 Janusz Baniak 3, 15 Marcel Kajzer 2, 16 Slawomir Dabrowski 2, 17 Maciej Fajfer 0.

Roll of Honour

1966 .... Zygfryd FRIEDEK
1967 .... Edward JANCARZ
1968 .... Piotr BRUZDA
1969 .... Jerzy SZCZAKIEL
1970 .... Zbigniew MARCINKOWSKI
1971 .... Zenon PLECH,
1971 .... Grzegorz KUZNIAR
1971 .... Zbigniew MARCINKOWSKI
1972 .... Andrzej TKOCZ
1973 .... Zbigniew FILIPIAK
1974 .... Gerard STACH
1975 .... Boleslaw PROCH
1976 .... Mariusz OKONIEWSKI
1977 .... Andrzej HUSZCZA
1978 .... Andrzej HUSZCZA
1979 .... Roman JANKOWSKI
1980 .... Maciej JAWOREK
1981 .... Miroslaw BERLINSKI
1982 .... Maciej JAWOREK
1983 .... Wojciech ZALUSKI
1984 .... Ryszard DOLOMISIEWICZ
1985 .... Ryszard FRANCZYSZYN
1986 .... Ryszard DOLOMISIEWICZ
1987 .... Ryszard DOLOMISIEWICZ
1988 .... Jaroslaw OLSZEWSKI
1989 .... Piotr SWIST
1990 .... Tomasz GOLLOB
1991 .... Jacek REMPALA
1992 .... Tomasz GOLLOB
1993 .... Tomasz KRUK
1994 .... Piotr BARON
1995 .... Rafal DOBRUCKI
1996 .... Wieslaw JAGUS
1997 .... Rafal DOBRUCKI
1998 .... Rafal OKONIEWSKI
1999 .... Mariusz FRANKOW
2000 .... Jaroslaw HAMPEL
2001 .... Rafal OKONIEWSKI
2002 .... Krzysztof KASPRZAK
2003 .... Robert MISKOWIAK
2004 .... Adrian MIEDZINSKI
2005 .... Janusz KOLODZIEJ
2006 .... Karol ZABIK
2007 .... Marcin JEDRZEJEWSKI
2008 .... Maciej JANOWSKI

BRONZE HELMET

The Bronze Helmet (Brazowy Kask) is an individual competition open to riders under the age of 19.

FINAL

Gdansk, Friday, September 26

1 Artur Mroczka 13, 2 Maciej Janowski 12, 3 Adrian Szewczykowski 11+3, 4 Damian Sperz 11+R, 5 Rafal Fleger 10, 6 Patryk Dudek 9, 7 Michal Lopaczewski 8, 8 Kacper Gomolski 7, 9 Dawid Lampart 6, 10 Slawomir Musielak 6, 11 Slawomir Pyszny 5, 12 Borys Miturski 5, 13 Marcin Piekarski 5, 14 Damian Celmer 4, 15 Maciej Piaszczynski 3, 16 Mateusz Szostek 2, 17 Mateusz Kowalczyk [R] 0, 17 Mateusz Lampkowski [R] 0.

Semi Final, Ostrow, Tuesday, September 9

1 Borys Miturski 13, 2 Dawid Lampart 12, 3 Damian Celmer 12, 4 Maciej Janowski 10, 5 Kacper Gomolski 10, 6 Michal Lopaczewski 8, 7 Mateusz Szostek 8, 8 Maciej Piaszczynski 7+3, 9 Mateusz Lampkowski 7+2, 10 Oskar Pieniazek 7+1, 11 Mateusz Mikorski 6, 12 Emil Idziorek 6, 13 Marcel Szymko 6, 14 Piotr Szostak [R] 3, 15 Piotr Machnik 2, 16 Karol Sroka 2, 17 Pawel Zmarzlik [R] 1, 18 Cyprian Szymko 0.

Semi Final, Gniezno, Tuesday, September 9

1 Rafal Fleger 12, 2 Slawomir Musielak 12, 3 Artur Mroczka 11, 4 Marcin Piekarski 10, 5 Slawomir Pyszny 10, 6 Patryk Dudek 10, 7 Adrian Szewczykowski 10, 8 Damian Sperz 9+3, 9 Przemyslaw 9+N, 10 Lukasz Cyran 7, 11 Szymon Kielbasa 5, 12 Mateusz Kowalczyk 4, 13 Marcel Kajzer 4, 14 Tadeusz Kostro 4, 15 Adam Wisniewski 3, 16 Kamil Cieslar [R] 0, 17 Maciej Fajfer 0, 18 Pawel Paliga [R] 0.

Roll of Honour

1976 .... Alfred SIEKIERKA
1977 .... Mieczyslaw KMIECIAK
1978 .... Mieczyslaw KMIECIAK
1979 .... Jozef KAFEL
1980 .... Marek KEPA
1981 .... Miroslaw BERLINSKI
1982 .... Not staged
1983 .... Ryszard FRANCZYSZYN
1984 .... Ryszard DOLOMISIEWICZ

1985 .... Zbigniew BLAZEJCZAK
1986 .... Piotr SWIST
1987 .... Piotr SWIST
1988 .... Jaroslaw OLSZEWSKI
1989 .... Jacek REMPALA
1990 .... Robert KUZDZAL
1991 .... Adam LABEDZKI
1992 .... Maciej BARGIEL
1993 .... Piotr BARON
1994 .... Waldemar WALCZAK
1995 .... Rafal DOBRUCKI
1996 .... Damian BALINSKI
1997 .... Rafal OKONIEWSKI
1998 .... Rafal OKONIEWSKI
1999 .... Rafal OKONIEWSKI
2000 .... Roman CHROMIK
2001 .... Rafal SZOMBIERSKI
2002 .... Robert UMINSKI
2003 .... Janusz KOLODZIEJ
2004 .... Adrian MIEDZINSKI
2005 .... Patryk PAWLASZCZYK
2006 .... Mateusz SZCZEPANIAK
2007 .... Adam KAJOCH
2008 .... Artur MROCZKA

Under 21 Team Championship

FINAL

Leszno, Thursday, September 4

1 LESZNO 45 (Slawomir Musielak 9, Adam Kajoch 10, Robert Kasprzrak 11, **Przemyslaw Pawlicki 15**, Pawel Ratajszczak, did not ride), **2 RYBNIK 31** (Patryk Pawlaszczyk 6, Slawomir Pyszny 6, Rafal Fleger 9, Pawel Paliga 0, Michal Mitko 10), **3 CZESTOCHOWA 22** (Mateusz Szczepaniak 11, Mateusz Kowalczyk 5, Kamil Cieslar 2, Marcin Piekarski 4, Adrian Osmolski, did not ride), **4 ZIELONA GORA 21** (Grzegorz Zengota 11, Janusz Baniak 2, Patryk Dudek 8, Tomasz Halicki 0).

GROUP 1

Round 1, Poznan, Thursday, June 12

1 LESZNO 31 (Robert Kasprzak 10, Adam Kajoch 9, Przemyslaw Pawlicki 5, Slawomir Musielak 7, Pawel Ratajszczak, did not ride), 2 POZNAN 28 (Piotr Dziatkowiak 5, Marcel Kajzer 3, Maciej Janowski 10, Daniel Pytel 10), 3 OSTROW 27 (Maciej Piaszczynski 7, Marcin Liberski 8, Emil Idziorek 2, Adrian Gomolski 9, Karol Sroka 1), 4 GNIEZNO 8 (Kacper Gomolski 5, Marcin Kozdras 3, Arkadiusz Sturomski 0).

Round 2, Leszno, Thursday, June 26

1 LESZNO 40 (Przemyslaw Pawlicki 11, Slawomir Musielak 9, Adam Kajoch 10, Robert Kasprzak 10, Pawel Ratajszczak, did not ride), 2 OSTROW 27 (Emil Idziorek 4, Adrian Gomolski 11, Maciej Piaszczynski 6, Marcin Liberski 6, Karol Sroka, did not ride), 3 POZNAN 24 (Daniel Pytel 9, Maciej Janowski 7, Piotr Dziatkowiak 5, Marcel Kajzer 3), 4 TORUN 5 (Damian Celmer 1, Oskar Pieniazek 0, Adam Wisniewski 0, Robert Ksiezak 4).

Round 3, Ostrow, Tuesday, July 8

1 OSTROW 40 (Marcin Liberski 11, Emil Idziorek 11, Adrian Gomolski 8, Maciej Piaszczynski 10), 2 POZNAN 27 (Daniel Pytel 6, Maciej Janowski 10, Marcel Kajzar 6, Piotr Dziatkowiak 5), 3 TORUN 20 (Damian Celmer 7, Adam Wisniewski 5, Oskar Pieniazek 6, Mateusz Lampkowski 2, Emil Pulczynski 0), 4 GNIEZNO 7 (Kacper Gomolski 3, Arkadiusz Sturomski 2, Marcin Kozdras 2).

Round 4, Torun, Thursday, July 24

1 LESZNO 43 (Robert Kapsrzak 11, Przemyslaw Pawlicki 11, **Adam Kajoch 12**, Slawomir Musielak 9, Pawel Ratajszczak, did not ride), 2 POZNAN 27 (Daniel Pytel 9, Marcel Kajzer 6, Piotr Dziatkowiak 5, Maciej Janowski 7), 3 TORUN 19 (Oskar Pieniazek 2, Damian Celmer 9, Mateusz Lampkowski 5, Adam Wisniewski 2, Emil Pulczynski 1), 4 GNIEZNO 6 (Marcin Kozdras 3, Kacper Gomolski 2, Maciej Fajfer 1, Arkadiusz Sturomski 0).

Round 5, Gniezno, Thursday, August 7

1 LESZNO 39 (Przemyslaw Pawlicki 9, Robert Kasprzak 11, Adam Kajoch 9, Slawomir Musielak 10, Pawel Ratajszczak, did not ride), 2 OSTROW 31 (Adrian Gomolski 11, Emil Idziorek 6, Marcin Liberski 9, Maciej Piaszczynski 5, Karol Sroka, did not ride), 3 GNIEZNO 15 (Kacper Gomolski 3, Maciej Fajfer 6, Arkadiusz Sturomski 2, Marcin Kozdras 4), 4 TORUN 11 (Oskar Pieniazek 1, Kamil Pulczynski 3, Damian Celmer 6, Adam Wisniewski 1, Emil Pulczynski 0).

GROUP 1 TABLE

	M	*RPts*	*Pts*
1 LESZNO	**4**	**153**	**12**
2 OSTROW	4	125	8
3 POZNAN	4	106	7
4 TORUN	4	55	2
5 GNIEZNO	4	36	1

GROUP 2

Round 1, Zielona Gora, Thursday, June 12

1 ZIELONA GORA 39 (**Grzegorz Zengota 12**, Patryk Dudek 9, Janusz Baniak 9, Pawel Gwozdz 9), 2 GORZOW 24 (Pawel Zmarzlik 8, Adrian Szewczykowski 9, Mateusz Mikorski 7), 3 BYDGOSZCZ 18 (Marcin Jedrzejewski 10, Michal Lopaczewski 7, Damian Adamczak 1), 4 GDANSK 13 (Damian Sperz 6, Cyprian Szymko 5, Marcel Szymko 1, Kamil Poplawski 1).

Round 2, Bydgoszcz, Thursday, June 26

1 ZIELONA GORA 30 (Patryk Dudek 3, Grzegorz Zengota 11, Janusz Baniak 6, Pawewi Gwozdz 10), 2 GRUDZIADZ 21 (Artur Mroczka 11, Kamil Brzozowski 10, Pawel Kaczorowski 0), 3 GORZOW 21 (Adrian Szewczykowski 6, Pawel Zmarzlik 3, Mateusz Mikorski 6, Lukasz Cyran 6), 4 BYDGOSZCZ 17 (Marcin Jedrzejewski 10, Michal Lopaczewski 7, Damian Adamczak 0).

Round 3, Gorzow, Tuesday, July 8

1 ZIELONA GORA 23 (Grzegorz Zengota 10, Janusz Baniak 7, Pawel Gwozdz 6), 2 GRUDZIADZ 23 (Artur Mroczka 11, Kamil Brzozowski 12), 3 GORZOW 20 (Adrian Szewczykowski 7, Lukasz Cyran 4, Mateusz Mikorski 9), 4 GDANSK 19 (Damian Sperz 9, Cyprian Szymko 5, Marcel Szymko 5).

Round 4, Grudziadz, Thursday, July 24

1 ZIELONA GORA 34 (Grzegorz Zengota 11, Tomasz Halicki 7, Janusz Baniak 9, Patryk Dudek 7), 2 GRUDZIADZ 23 (Artur Mroczka 12, Kamil Brzozowski 11), 3 BYDGOSZCZ 17 (Marcin Jedrzejewski 9, Michal Lopaczewski 8), 4 GDANSK 14 (Damian Sperz 3, Cyprian Szymko 2, Marcel Szymko 5, Kamil Poplawski 4).

POLAND staged a series of qualifying rounds to decide their entrants for the major World Championship and European Championship events.

While many other countries automatically seeded the top scorers from the domestic national championships the PZM (Polski Zwiazek Motorowy [Polish Motor Federation]) organised a series of early season qualifying events.

The competition to enter the 2009 Grand Prix qualification series also served as a domestic qualifier for the European Championship and was run over two semi finals and a final.

The competition to represent Poland in the World Under 21 Championship was also staged over two semi finals and a final while the qualifier for the European Junior (Under 19) Championship was a one-off final.

Sebastian Ulamek

2009 GRAND PRIX
2008 European Championship
Semi Final
Poznan, Thursday, April 10

1 Grzegorz Walasek 15, 2 Rafal Dobrucki 13, 3 Michal Szczepaniak 11, 4 Tomasz Gapinski 11, 5 Daniel Jeleniewski 11, 6 Krzysztof Kasprzak 10, 7 Piotr Swiderski 9, 8 Janusz Kolodziej [R] 5+3+3, 9 Krzysztof Slabon 5+3+2, 10 Lukasz Jankowski 5+2+3+1, 11 Krzysztof Jablonski 5+1+2+R, 12 Krystian Klecha 5+2+1, 13 Rafal Okoniewski 4, 14 Alan Marcinkowski 3, 15 Rafal Trojanowski 3, 16 Daniel Pytel 3, 17 Mateusz Szczepaniak 1, 18 Grzegorz Klopot [R] 0, 19 Rafal Szombierski 0.

Semi Final
Torun, Tuesday, April 15

1 Sebastian Ulamek 13, 2 Tomasz Jedrzejak 12, Robert Kosciecha 11, Krzysztof Buczkowski 11, 5 Jaroslaw Hampel 10, 6 Adrian Miedzinski 10, 7 Karol Zabik 9, 8 Piotr Protasiewicz 7+3, 9 Grzegorz Zengota [R] 7+2, 10 Dawid Stachyra 6, 11 Adrian Gomolski 6, 12 Pawel Staszek 5, 13 Mariusz Puszakowski 4, 14 Marcin Jedrzejewski 3, 15 Pawel Hlib 3, 16 Damian Celmer [R] 2, 17 Adam Wisniewski [R] 1, 18 Mateusz Lampkowski [R] 0, 19 Tomasz Piszcz 0.

FINAL
Zielona Gora, Monday, April 21

1 Adrian Miedzinski 13, 2 Sebastian Ulamek 12, 3 Janusz Kolodziej 11, 4 Grzegorz Walasek 11, 5 Rafal Dobrucki 11, 6 Tomasz Jedrzejak 10, 7 Michael Szczepaniak 8+3, 8 Piotr Swiderski 8+2, 9 Jaroslaw Hampel 8+FX, 10 Krzysztof Kasprzak 6, 11 Tomasz Gapinski 5, 12 Piotr Protasiewicz 5, 13 Robert Kosciecha 4, 14 Krzysztof Buczkowski 3, 15 Daniel Jeleniewski 2, 16 Karol Zabik 2, Krzysztof Jablonski [R], Grzegorz Rempala [R], did not ride.

WORLD UNDER 21 CHAMPIONSHIP
Semi Final, Grudziadz, Tuesday, April 22

1 Grzegorz Zengota 12, 2 Adrian Gomolski 12, 3 Daniel Pytel 11, 4 Marcin Piekarski 10, 5 Kamil Brzozowski 10, 6 Bartosz Szymura 10, 7 Marcin Jedrzejewski 10, 8 Damian Sperz 8, 9 Pawel Zmarzlik 7, 10 Artur Mroczka 6, 11 Sebastian Brucheiser 5, 12 Przemyslaw Zarzycki 4, 13 Michal Lopaczewski 4, 14 Adrian Szewczykowski 3, 15 Rafal Fleger 3, 17 Pawel Gwozdz 2, Mateuesz Mikorski [R], Adam Wisniewski [R], Cyprian Szymko [R], did not ride.

Semi Final, Ostrow, Wednesday, April 23

1 Mateusz Szczepaniak 15, 2 Maciej Piaszczynski 13, 3 Adam Kajoch 12, 4 Robert Kasprzak 11, 5 Slawomir Dabrowski 11, 6 Michal Mitko 9, 7 Patryk Pawlaszczyk 9, 8 Maciej Janowski 8+3, 9 Slawomir Pyszny 8+2, 10 Borys Miturski 6, 11 Kamil Zielinski 6, 12 Emil Idziorek 4, 13 Dawid Lampart 3, 14 Marcel Kajzer 3, 15 Szymon Kielbasa 1, 16 Mateusz Kowalczyk 1, Pawel Paliga [R] 0, Pawel Ratajszczak [R], Karol Stroka [R], did not ride.

FINAL
Tarnow, Thursday, April 24

1 Adrian Gomolski 14, 2 Grzegorz Zengota 13, 3 Mateusz Szczepaniak 12, 4 Patryk Pawlaszczyk 10, 5 Adam Kajoch 10, 6 Michal Mitko 9, 7 Kamil Brzozowski 8, 8 Robert Kasprzak 8, 9 Marcin Jedrzejewski 7, 10 Slawomir Dabrowski 6, 11 Maciej Janowski 6, 12 Maciej Piaszczynski 5, 13 Bartos Szymura 4, 14 Marcin Piekarski 3, 15 Damian Sperz 3, 16 Daniel Pytel 2, Pawel Zmarzlik [R], Slawomir Pyszny [R], did not ride.

European Under 19 Championship
Rawicz, Wednesday, April 9

1 Marcel Kajzer 15, 2 Artur Mroczka 13, 3 Maciej Janowski 12, 4 Michael Lopaczewski 10, 5 Borys Miturski 9, 6 Pawel Zmarzlik 8+3, 7 Adrian Szewczykowski 8+2, 8 Bartosz Szymura 8+N, 9 Rafal Fleger 7, 10 Maciej Piaszczynski 7, 11 Marcin Piekarski 7, 12 Emil Idziorek 4, 13 Pawel Gwozdz 4, 14 Szymon Kielbasa [R] 3, 15 Mateusz Kowalczyk 2, 16 Dawid Lampart 2, 17 Mateusz Mikorski [R] 1, Piotr Korbel 0.

Round 5, Gdansk, Thursday, August 7
1 GDANSK 27 (Damian Sperz 10, Cyprian Szymko 6, Marcl Szymko 6, Andriej Kobrin 5, Kamil Poplawski, did not ride), 2 GORZOW 23 (Adrian Szewczykowski 9, Lukasz Cyran 8,Mateuesz Mikorski 6), 3 GRUDZIADZ 22 (Artur Mroczka 8, Kamil Brzozowski 11, Pawel Kaczorowski 3), 4 BYDGOSZCZ 19 (Marcin Jedrzejewski 11, Michal Lopaczewski 8).

GROUP 2 TABLE

	M	*RPts*	*Pts*
1 ZIELONA GORA	**4**	**126**	**11.5**
2 GRUDZIADZ	4	89	7
3 GORZOW	4	85	6.5
4 GDANSK	4	73	3
5 BYDGOSZCZ	4	71	2

GROUP 3

Round 1, Rzeszow, Thursday, June 12
1 RYBNIK 32 (Slawomir Pyszny 3, Bartosz Szymura 5, Rafal Fleger 3, Michal Mitko 11, Patryk Pawlaszczyk 10), 2 CZESTOCHOWA 28 (Mateusz Szczepaniak 11, Borys Miturski 7, Marcin Piekarski 6, Mateusz Kowalczyk 4, Kamil Cieslaw, did not ride), 3 RZESZOW 21 (Martin Vaculik 11, Mateusz Szostek 9, Karol Polak 1), 4 KROSNO 10 (Grzegorz Szyszka 5, Piotr Machnik 0, Kamil Fleger 5).

Round 2, Krosno, Thursday, June 26
1 CZESTOCHOWA 32 (Mateusz Szczepaniak 11, Mateusz Kowlaczyk 6, Marcin Piekarski 7, Borys Miturski 8), 2 TARNOW 29 (Tadeusz Kostro 4, Maciej Ciesielski 9, Szymon Kielbasa 9, Lukasz Kielbasa 7), 3 RZESZOW 21 (Karol Polak 1, **Dawid Lampart 12**, Mateusz Szostek 8), 4 KROSNO 10 (Grzegorz Szyszka 6, Kamil Fleger 2, Piotr Machnik 2).

Round 3, Rybnik. Tuesday, July 8
1 RYBNIK 40 (Slawomir Pyszny 11, Rafal Fleger 9, Mariusz Konsek 0, Michal Mitko 11, Patryk Pawlaszczyk 9), 2 CZESTOCHOWA 31 (Mateusz Szczepaniak 11, Marcin Piekarski 2, Borys Miturski 9, Mateus Kowalczyn 8, Kamil Zieslar 1), 3 TARNOW 13 (Szymon Kielbasa 5, Tadeusz Kostro 4, Maciej Ciesielski 4, *Mateusz Chochlinski [G] 1*), 4 KROSNO 6 (*Bartosz Szymura [G] 5*, Grzegorz Szyszka 3, Piotr Machnik 3).

Round 4, Czestochowa, Thursday, July 24
1 RYBNIK 35 (Slawomir Pyszny 6, Michal Mitko 9, Pawel Paliga 1, Rafal Fleger 8, Patryk Pawlaszczyk 11), 2 CZESTOCHOWA 28 (Marcin Piekarski 6, Borys Miturski 9, Mateusz Kowalczyk 4, Kamil Cieslar, did not ride, Mateusz Szczepaniak 9), 3 TARNOW 14 (Szymon Kielbasa 7, Maciej Ciesielski 3, Tadeusz Kostro 4, *Cezary Romanczuk [G] 2*), 4 RZESZOW 14 (Dawid Lampart 7, Karol Polak 1, Mateusz Szostek 6).
Points scored by guests do not count.

Round 5, Tarnow, Thursday, August 7
1 RYBNIK 44 (Michael Mitko 11, Slawomir Pyszny 5, Pawel Paliga 6, Rafal Fleger 11, Patryk Pawlaszczyk 11), 2 TARNOW 22 (Szymon Kielbasa 8, Tadeusz Kostro 6, Maciej Cielsielski 8), 3 KROSNO 11 (Piotr Machnik 4, Grzegorz Szyszka 7), 4 RZESZOW 10 (Mateusz Szostek 7, Karol Polak 3, Dawid Lampart, did not ride).

GROUP 3 TABLE

	M	*RPts*	*Pts*
1 RYBNIK	**4**	**151**	**12**
2 CZESTOCHOWA	**4**	**119**	**9**
3 TARNOW	4	78	5.5
4 RZESZOW	4	78	5.5
5 KROSNO	4	37	1

■ *Group winners and best placed runners-up to final.*

Roll of Honour

1978	LESZNO
1979	LESZNO
1980	ZIELONA GORA
1981-82	Not staged
1983	GDANSK
1984	LUBLIN
1985	TORUN
1986	GORZOW
1987	ZIELONA GORA
1988	ZIELONA GORA
1989	BYDGOSZCZ
1990	TORUN
1991	TARNOW
1992	TORUN
1993	TARNOW
1994	RZESZOW
1995	RZESZOW
1996	CZESTOCHOWA
1997	GRUDZIADZ
1998	GNIEZNO
1999	GORZOW
2000	CZESTOCHOWA
2001	LESZNO
2002	RYBNIK
2003	PILA
2004	TORUN
2005	TORUN
2006	RZESZOW
2007	RYBNIK
2008	LESZNO

POLAND'S superb record at Under 21 and Under 19 level can be easily related to their foresight of their clubs and governing body in providing meaningful competition for their young riders.

Other than the compulsory use of riders under the age of 21 in team line-ups (albeit there has in recent years been no nationalist restriction) they also run Under 21 championships for individuals, pairs and teams.

Additionally there is also the Silver Helmet (for riders under 21) and the Bronze Helmet (under 19), both of which are staged over a series of qualifying rounds.

They provide plenty of racing opportunities for the youngsters attached to not only the Ekstraliga outfits but also much lower down the pecking order.

In 2009, 15 different clubs were involved in the Polish Under 21 Team Championship and 10 of them had representation in the Polish Under 21 Pairs Championship.

That Leszno and Rbynik were victorious respectively in the Team Championship and Pairs Championship illustrates the depth of talent.

2009 MAJOR EVENTS

2010 GRAND PRIX QUALIFICATION
(and 2009 European Championship)
POLISH FINAL: Tuesday, April 7, Gdansk.

WORLD UNDER 21 CHAMPIONSHIP
Polish Semi Final 1: Wednesday, April 15, Poznan.
Polish Semi Final 2: Wednesday, April 15, Rzeszow.
POLISH FINAL: Tuesday, April 21, Gorzow.

EUROPEAN UNDER 19 CHAMPIONSHIP
POLISH FINAL: Tuesday, March 31, Tarnow.

POLISH CHAMPIONSHIP
Quarter Final 1: Thursday, June 18, Gniezno.
Quarter Final 2: Thursday, June 18, Krosno.
Quarter Final 3: Thursday, June 18, Lodz.
Quarter Final 4: Thursday, June 18, Pila.
Semi Final 1: Wednesday, July 1, Opole.
Semi Final 2: Wednesday, July 1, Rawicz.
FINAL: Saturday, July 25, Torun.

POLISH UNDER 21 CHAMPIONSHIP
Semi Final 1: Wednesday, July 15, Gniezno.
Semi Final 2: Wednesday, July 15, Ostrow.
Semi Final 3: Wednesday, July 15, Rybnik.
FINAL: Friday, August 7, Leszno.

POLISH PAIRS CHAMPIONSHIP
Semi Final 1: Thursday, July 23, Krosno.
Semi Final 2: Thursday, July 23, Lodz.
Semi Final 3: Thursday, July 23, Pila.
FINAL: Thursday, September 17, Leszno.

POLISH UNDER 21 PAIRS CHAMPIONSHIP
Semi Final 1: Wednesday, June 17, Grudziadz.
Semi Final 2: Wednesday, June 17, Opole.
Semi Final 3: Wednesday, June 17, Rawicz.
FINAL: Friday, August 14, Rybnik.

POLISH UNDER 21 TEAM CHAMPIONSHIP
Group Rounds: Wednesday, May 27; Thursday, July 9; Thursday, July 30; Thursday, August 13.
FINAL: Thursday, August 27, venue to be confirmed.

ZLOTY KASK (Golden Helmet)
FINAL: Saturday, October 10, Zielona Gora.

SREBRNY KASK (Silver Helmet)
Semi Final 1: Wednesday, August 5, Bydgoszcz.
Semi Final 2: Wednesday, August 5, Rzeszow.
FINAL: Friday, September 25, Czestochowa.

BRAZOWA KASK (Bronze Helmet)
Semi Finalo 1: Thursday, August 20, Grudziadz.
Semi Final 2: Thursday, August 20, Poznan.
FINAL: Friday, September 11, Wroclaw.

EKSTRALIGA REGULAR SEASON STANDINGS

	M	W	D	L	PtsF	PtsA	BP	Pts
1 CZESTOCHOWA	14	12	0	2	767	514	7	31
2 TORUN	14	12	0	2	734	535	5	30
3 LESZNO	14	10	1	3	721	559	4	25
4 ZIELONA GORA	14	7	0	7	633	640	3	17
5 GORZOW	14	6	1	7	622	658	3	16
6 WROCLAW	14	4	0	10	621	657	4	12
7 RZESZOW	14	3	0	11	511	766	1	7
8 TARNOW	14	1	0	13	501	781	0	2

EKSTRALIGA PLAY OFF STANDINGS

	M	W	D	L	PtsF	PtsA	BP	Pts
1 TORUN	2	2	0	0	113	68	–	4
2 CZESTOCHOWA	2	2	0	0	113	71	–	4
3 LESZNO	2	1	0	1	94	87	–	2
4 ZIELONA GORA	2	1	0	1	87	94	–	2
5 WROCLAW	2	0	0	2	71	113	–	0
6 GORZOW	2	0	0	2	68	113	–	0

FINAL STANDINGS

1 TORUN
2 LESZNO
3 ZIELONA GORA
4 CZESTOCHOWA
5 WROCLAW
6 GORZOW
7 RZESZOW
8 TARNOW

CZESTOCHOWA only lost two of their first 14 Ekstraliga matches – but their form slipped when it really mattered.

And the Lions failed to win their first league title since 2003, going out to eventual beaten finalists Leszno in the play-offs.

Their demise allowed second placed Torun to come through with a devastating play-off series in which they lost only one of six matches.

They were even able to compensate for a pointless performance from Karol Zabik in the first leg of the final at Leszno where Wieslaw Jagus was unbeaten.

Taking an eight point lead into the second leg, they were actually run closer on their home circuit!

Roll of Honour

1948 WARSAW
1949 LESZNO
1950 LESZNO
1951 LESZNO
1952 LESZNO
1953 LESZNO
1954 LESZNO
1955 BYDGOSZCZ
1956 RYBNIK
1957 RYBNIK
1958 RYBNIK
1959 CZESTOCHOWA
1960 RZESZOW
1961 RZESZOW
1962 RYBNIK
1963 RYBNIK
1964 RYBNIK
1965 RYBNIK
1966 RYBNIK
1967 RYBNIK
1968 RYBNIK
1969 GORZOW
1970 RYBNIK
1971 BYDGOSZCZ
1972 RYBNIK
1973 GORZOW
1974 CZESTOCHOWA
1975 GORZOW
1976 GORZOW
1977 GORZOW
1978 GORZOW
1979 LESZNO
1980 LESZNO
1981 ZIELONA GORA
1982 ZIELONA GORA
1983 GORZOW
1984 LESZNO
1985 ZIELONA GORA
1986 TORUN
1987 LESZNO
1988 LESZNO
1989 LESZNO
1990 TORUN
1991 ZIELONA GORA
1992 BYDGOSZCZ
1993 WROCLAW
1994 WROCLAW
1995 WROCLAW
1996 CZESTOCHOWA
1997 BYDGOSZCZ
1998 BYDGOSZCZ
1999 PILA
2000 BYDGOSZCZ
2001 TORUN
2002 BYDGOSZCZ
2003 CZESTOCHOWA
2004 TARNOW
2005 TARNOW
2006 WROCLAW
2007 LESZNO
2008 TORUN

PLAY OFFS...PLAY-OFFS...PLAY-OFFS...PLAY-OFFS...PLAY-OFFS...PLAY-OFFS

ROUND 1
Wroclaw 32 Czestochowa 60
Czestochowa 53 Wroclaw 39
Wroclaw 71 CZESTOCHOWA 113.

Gorzow 43 Torun 47
Torun 66 Gorzow 25
Gorzow 68 TORUN 113.

Zielona Gora 49 Leszno 40
Leszno 54 Zielona Gora 38
Zielona Gora 87 LESZNO 94.

ROUND 2
Top four places
Zielona Gora 48 Torun 42
Torun 57 Zielona Gora 36
Zielona Gora 84 TORUN 99.

Leszno 52 Czestochowa 41
Czestochowa 40 Leszno 50
LESZNO 102 Czestochowa 81.

Seventh place
Tarnow 42 Rzeszow 48
Rzeszow 51 Tarnow 41
Tarnow 83 RZESZOW 99.

ROUND 3
Third place
Zielona Gora 62 Czestochowa 28
Czestochowa 51 Zielona Gora 41
ZIELONA GORA 103 Czestochowa 79.

Championship
Leszno 41 Torun 49
Torun 47 Leszno 43
Leszno 84 TORUN 96.

2009 FIXTURES

Sunday, April 5
Bydgoszcz v Wroclaw
Gdansk v Torun
Leszno v Gorzow
Zielona Gora v Czestochowa
Monday, April 13
Czestochowa v Leszno
Gorzow v Bydgoszcz
Gdansk v Wroclaw
Torun v Zielona Gora
Sunday, April 19
Bydgoszcz v Torun
Gdansk v Gorzow
Leszno v Zielona Gora
Wroclaw v Czestochowa
Sunday, May 3
Czestochowa v Bydgoszcz
Gorzow v Wroclaw
Torun v Leszno
Zielona Gora v Gdansk
Sunday, May 10
Bydgoszcz v Zielona Gora
Gorzow v Czestochowa
Gdansk v Leszno
Wroclaw v Torun
Sunday, May 24
Gdansk v Bydgoszcz
Leszno v Wroclaw
Torun v Czestochowa
Zielona Gora v Gorzow
Sunday May 31
Bydgoszcz v Leszno
Czestochowa v Gdansk
Gorzow v Torun
Wroclaw v Zielona Gora
Sunday, June 14
Gdansk v Bydgoszcz
Leszno v Wroclaw
Torun v Czestochowa
Zielona Gora v Gorzow
Sunday, June 21
Bydgoszcz v Gdansk
Czestochowa v Torun
Gorzow v Zielona Gora
Wroclaw v Leszno
Sunday, June 28
Czestochowa v Gorzow
Leszno v Gdansk
Torun v Wroclaw
Zielona Gora v Bydgoszcz
Sunday, July 5
Bydgoszcz v Czestochowa
Gdansk v Zielona Gora
Leszno v Torun
Wroclaw v Gorzow
Sunday, July 19
Czestochowa v Wroclaw
Gorzow v Gdansk
Torun v Bydgoszcz
Zielona Gora v Leszno
Sunday, July 26
Bydgoszcz v Gorzow
Gdansk v Wroclaw
Leszno v Czestochowa
Zielona Gora v Torun
Sunday, August 2
Czestochowa v Zielona Gora
Gorzow v Leszno
Torun v Gdansk
Wroclaw v Bydgoszcz

PLAY-OFFS

Round 1
Sunday, August 16: *6 v 1, 5 v 2, 4 v 3.*
Sunday, August 30: 1 v 6, 2 v 5, 3 v 4.

Round 2
Sunday, September 6
Sunday, September 13

Third place race off
Sunday, September 27
Sunday, October 4

CHAMPIONSHIP RACE OFF
Sunday, October 11
Sunday, October 18 (or Sunday, October 25).

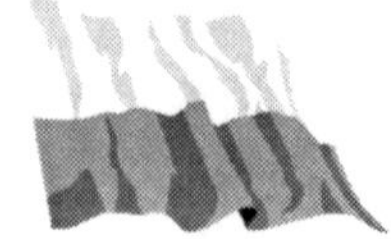

Polish Ekstraliga

CZESTOCHOWA

2008 RESULTS

Ekstraliga

Final position ....Fourth (First)

LESZNO (A)
Sunday, April 6
Lost 42-50
Hancock 7, Gapinski 4:1, Ulamek 11:3, Richardson 1:1, Pedersen 17 (4), Mateusz Szczepaniak 2:1, Miturski 0.

TARNOW (H)
Sunday, April 13
Won 69-23
Hancock 14:1, Michal Szczepaniak 7:3, **Ulamek 15**, Gapinski 9:4, **Pedersen 15**, Mateusz Szczepaniak 5:1, Bridger 4:2.

GORZOW (A)
Sunday, April 20
Won 50-40
Hancock 12:1, Michal Szczepaniak 2, Ulamek 8, Gapinski 9:1, Pedersen 13:1, Mateusz Szczepaniak 5, Woffinden 1.

TORUN (H)
Thursday, May 1
Lost 41-50
Michal Szczepaniak 0, Richardson 0, Ulamek 1, Gapinski 12:2, Pedersen 20 (6), Mateusz Szczepaniak 5, Woffinden 3:1.

ZIELONA GORA (H)
Friday, May 16
Won 49-41
Gapinski 7:1, Ulamek 3, **Pedersen 15:3**, *rider replacement for Richardson*, Hancock 16, Mateusz Szczepaniak 5, Woffinden 3.

WROCLAW (A)
Sunday, June 1
Won 50-40
Gapinski 9:3, *rider replacement for Richardson*, Hancock 13, Ulamek 5:2, Pedersen 17, Mateusz Szczepaniak 6, Woffinden 0.

RZESZOW (A)
Friday, June 6
Won 60-32
Gapinski 9:4, *rider replacement for Richardson*, **Hancock 17:1**, Ulamek 14:2, **Pedersen 14:1**, Miturski 0, Mateusz Szczepaniak 6.

TRACK FILE

Track: Arena Czestochowa, ul. Olsztynska 79, ul. Faradaya 53, 42-200, Czesthchowa, Poland.
Telephone: 0048 0343616785.
Website: www.ckmwlokniarz.pl.
Track Length: 368 metres.
Track Record: 61.85 secs, Nicki Pedersen, September 28, 2008.

SQUAD
Przemyslaw Dadela, Slawomir Drabik, Tomasz Gapinski, Mateusz Kowalczyk, Kamil Mistygacz, Borys Miturski, Marcin Piekarski, Damian Romanczuk, Mateusz Szczepaniak, Michal Szczepaniak, Sebastian Ulamek.
Foreign: Lewis Bridger, Jamie Courtney, Greg Hancock, Edward Kennett, Antonio Lindbäck, Nicki Pedersen, Lee Richardson, Tai Woffinden.

WROCLAW (H)
Sunday, June 8
Won 60-33
Gapinski 10:3, Richardson 6:2, Hancock 12:2, Ulamek 10:1, **Pedersen 15**, Mateusz Szczepaniak 2:1, Woffinden 5:1.
Aggregate: Won 110-73.

ZIELONA GORA (A)
Friday, June 20
Won 52-38
Hancock 14:2, Richardson 8, Ulamek 12:3, *rider replacement for Gapinski*, Pedersen 15, Mateusz Szczepaniak 1, Bridger 2.
Aggregate: Won 101-79.

RZESZOW (H)
Sunday, July 6
Won 65-26
Ulamek 10:2, **Richardson 12:3**, **Hancock 14:1**, Michal Szczepaniak 6:1, **Pedersen 15**, Mateusz Szczepaniak 5, Miturski 3:2.
Aggregate: Won 125-58.

TORUN (A)
Sunday, July 20
Won 59-34
Hancock 13:2, Richardson 10:1, Ulamek 11:1, *rider replacement for Gapinski*, Pedersen 15:2, Mateusz Szczepaniak 9:1, Woffinden 1.
Aggregate: Won 100-84.

GORZOW (H)
Sunday, July 27
Won 55-38
Ulamek 12, Richardson 9:1, Pedersen 13, Michal Szczepaniak 4:1, Hancock 10:1, Mateusz Szczepaniak 4:1, Miturski 3.
Aggregate: Won 105-78.

TARNOW (A)
Sunday, August 3
Won 59-33
Hancock 12, Michal Szczepaniak 3:1, Ulamek 8:1,

Richardson 13:2, **Pedersen 15**, Miturski 5, Woffinden 3:1.

Aggregate: Won 128-56.

LESZNO (H)
Sunday, August 10
Won 56-36
Ulamek 13:3, *rider replacement for Gapinski*, Hancock 13:2, Richardson 9:1, Pedersen 16, Woffinden 5:1, Miturski, did not ride.

Aggregate: Won 98-86.

Play offs

Quarter Final first leg
WROCLAW (H)
Sunday, August 31
Won 53-39
Pedersen 11, Gapinski 4:1, Ulamek 10:1, Richardson 10:3, Hancock 14, Mateusz Szczepaniak 4:1, Bridger 0.

Quarter Final, second leg
WROCLAW (A)
Monday, September 1
Won 60-32
Hancock 15, Gapinski 8:2, Ulamek 8:2, Richardson 10:2, **Pedersen 14:1**, Mateusz Szczepaniak 4:1, Bridger 1.

Aggregate: Won 113-71.

Semi Final, first leg
LESZNO (A)
Sunday, September 7
Lost 41-52
Hancock 10:1, Gapinski 1, Ulamek 1, Richardson 7, **Pedersen 21 (6)**, Mateusz Szczepaniak 1, Woffinden 0.

Semi Final, second leg
LESZNO (H)
Sunday, September 28
Lost 40-50
Hancock 12:1, Michal Szczepaniak 2:1, Ulamek 7, Richardson 0, Pedersen 14, Mateusz Szczepaniak 3, Woffinden 2:1.

Aggregate: Lost 81-102.

EKSTRALIGA	*M*	*W*	*D*	*L*	*BP*	*Pts*
CZESTOCHOWA	**14**	**12**	**0**	**2**	**7**	**31**
Torun	14	12	0	2	6	30
Leszno	14	10	1	3	4	25
Zielona Gora	14	17	0	7	3	17
Gorzow	14	6	1	7	3	16
Wroclaw	14	4	0	10	4	12
Rzeszow	14	3	0	11	1	7
Tarnow	14	1	0	13	0	2

Third place decider, first leg
ZIELONA GORA (A)
Sunday, October 5
Lost 28-62
Hancock 10, Bridger 5, Ulamek 4, Michal Szczepaniak 0, Pedersen 8, Miturski 0, Mateusz Szczepaniak 1.

Third place decider, second leg
ZIELONA GORA (H)
Sunday, October 12
Won 51-41
Ulamek 11, Bridger 8:3, **Hancock 15**, Kennett 2, Richardson 11, Miturski 1:1, Woffinden 3.

Aggregate: Lost 79-103.

Challenge

TARNOW (H)
Saturday, March 15
Won 60-30
Pedersen 12, Drabik 6:3, **Ulamek 12**, Michal Szczepaniak 8:2, Gapinski 14, Miturski 1, Piekarski 1, Kowalczyk 0.

TARNOW (A)
Sunday, March 16
Lost 38-50
Piekarski 0, Gapinski 12, Michal Szczepaniak 7:2, Ulamek 6, Pedersen 9, Mateusz Szczepaniak 3, Kowalczyk 1.

RYBNIK (H)
Wednesday, March 19
Won 28-8
Pedersen 2:1, Michal Szczepaniak 3, Gapinski 5:1, Drabik 4, **Ulamek 6**, Woffinden 4, **Mateusz Szczepaniak 4:2**, Piekarski, Kowalczyk, Courtney, did not ride.

CZESTOCHOWA

Rider	*M*	*R*	*Pts*	*BP*	*TPts*	*Ave*	*F*	*P*	*TR*	*TPts*
Nicki PEDERSEN	19	102	283	8	291	11.41	4	3	3	8
Greg HANCOCK	**19**	**103**	**243**	**15**	**258**	**10.02**	**1**	**3**	**0**	**0**
Lee RICHARDSON	13	61	106	16	122	8.00	0	2	0	0
Sebastian ULAMEK	**20**	**102**	**174**	**21**	**195**	**7.65**	**1**	**0**	**0**	**0**
Tomasz GAPINSKI	11	56	82	22	104	7.43	0	0	0	0
Lewis BRIDGER	**6**	**18**	**20**	**5**	**25**	**5.56**	**0**	**0**	**0**	**0**
Michal SZCZEPANIAK	8	28	24	7	31	4.43	0	0	0	0
Mateusz SZCZEPANIAK	**17**	**75**	**68**	**7**	**75**	**4.00**	**0**	**0**	**0**	**0**
Borys MITURSKI	8	16	12	3	15	3.75	0	0	0	0
Tai WOFFINDEN	**11**	**35**	**26**	**5**	**31**	**3.54**	**0**	**0**	**0**	**0**
Edward KENNETT	1	4	2	0	2	2.00	0	0	0	0

RAWICZ (A)
Monday, March 31
Drew 48-48
Michal Szczepaniak 12, Piekarski 3:1, Mateusz Szczepaniak 10, Kowalczyk 1, Andrzej Zieja [G] 9, Miturski 5:1, Robert Mikolajczak [G] 8:1.

WROCLAW (A)
Tuesday, April 1
Won 46-44
Drabik 4, Gapinski 9:1, Ulamek 10:1, Michal Szczepaniak 7:3, Pedersen 14, Mateusz Szczepaniak 2, Bridger 0, Miturski 0.

GDANSK (H)
Friday, April 11
Won 60-18
Hancock 11, Gapinski 6:3, Michal Szczepaniak 9:2, Richardson 9:2, **Ulamek 11:1**, **Mateusz Szczepaniak 7:2**, **Woffinden 7:2**.

HOT HEARTS CUP
Sunday, October 26
DRABIK SELECT 48 (J. Rempala 10:2, Kowalczyk 7, **Drabik 12**, S. Kielbasa 3, Romanczuk 2, Osmolski 3, Bajerski 11), **CIESLAK SELECT 42** (Jeleniewski 12, Mistygacz 0, Trojanowski 9, Zielinski 1:1, Chromik 11, Cieslar 2:1, Mitko 7:3).

Individual

ZLOMREX CUP
Sunday, April 27
Sullivan 13, Pedersen 13, Adams 13, T. Gollob 11, Jedrzejak 10, Krzysztof Kasprzak 9, Drabik 8, Walasek 7, Hancock 7, Holta 7, Ulamek 6, Screen 5, Michal Szczepaniak 5, Gapinski 2, Hampel 2, Mateusz Szczepaniak 2.

GRAND PRIX QUALIFYING ROUND
Sunday, June 15
Walasek 14, Lukas Dryml 13, Peter Karlsson 11, Richardson 10, Ales Dryml 10, Ulamek 10, Nermark 9, Emil Sajfutdinov 8, Gizatullin 7, Hampel 7, Kolodziej 6, Oliver Allen 5, Bogdanovs 4, Klindt 3, Karpov 3, Paura 1, Miturski 0.

SILVER HELMET
Semi Final
Thursday, August 21
Janowski 15, Celmer 12, Mateusz Szczepaniak 11, Mitko 11, Szewczykowski 10, Piekarski 9, Pawlaszczyk 9, Brzozowski 7, Szyszka 7, Piaszczynski 6, Pyszny 6, Mikorski 5, Liberski 4, Mroczka 3, Gwozdz 2.

Czestochowa have kept team changes to an absolute minimum despite a winter of rumours about the club's financial state. The restriction on clubs having more than two Grand Prix riders saw the departure of Sebastian Ulamek to Tarnow.

PHOTO: Grzegorz Przygodzinski

CZESTOCHOWA 2008: Tai Woffinden, team manager Piotr Zyto, Michal Szczepaniak, Mateusz Szczepaniak, Sebastian Ulamek. Front kneeling Tomasz Gapinski, Lee Richardson and Nicki Pedersen

Polish Ekstraliga

GORZOW

2008 RESULTS

Ekstraliga

Final position....................................Sixth (Fifth)

WROCLAW (H)
Saturday, April 12
Won 53-40
Gollob 10:2, Monberg 8:2, Karlsson 12, Ferjan 3:1, Holta 12:1, Szewczykowski 0, Jonasson 8:1.

ZIELONA GORA (A)
Sunday, April 13
Lost 39-53
Gollob 14:1 (4), Monberg 0, Karlsson 8:2, Ferjan 6, Holta 10, Jonasson 0, Szewczykowski 1.

CZESTOCHOWA (H)
Sunday, April 20
Lost 40-50
Karlsson 6, Monberg 7:3, Gollob 10:1, Ferjan 1:1, Holta 13, Jonasson 3, Szewczykowski 0.

TARNOW (A)
Thursday, May 1
Won 47-46
Gollob 11:1, Hlib 7, Karlsson 6, Monberg 4:1, Holta 13, Jonasson 6, Zmarzlik 0.

LESZNO (H)
Sunday, May 4
Won 48-42
Gollob 15, Hlib 4:1, Karlsson 11, Monberg 2:1, Holta 12:1, Jonasson 4, Szewczykowski 0.

RZESZOW (H)
Sunday, May 11
Won 51-41
Gollob 12:2, Hlib 3, Karlsson 12, Ferjan 5:1, Holta 13, Szewczykowski 5, Hansen 1.

TORUN (A)
Sunday, June 1
Lost 30-61
Gollob 11, Monberg 5:1, Karlsson 0, Ferjan 2, Holta 7 (2), Jonasson 4, Szewczykowski 1.

TORUN (H)
Sunday, June 8
Lost 43-47
Gollob 16, Hlib 0, Karlsson 6, Monberg 3:1, Holta 10:1, Szewczykowski 1, Jonasson 7:1.
Aggregate: Lost 73-108.

TRACK FILE

Track: Edward Jancarz Stadium, ul. Kwiatowa 55, 66-400 Gorzow Wlkp, Poland.
Telephone: 0048 0957356245.
Website: www.stalgorzow.pl
Track Length: 430 metres.
Track Record: 61.16 secs, Tomasz Gollob, May 4, 2008.

SQUAD
Lukasz Cyran, Tomasz Gollob, Pawel Hlib, Rune Holta, Slawomir Dabrowski, Mateusz Mikorski, Adrian Szewczykowski, Pawel Zmarzlik.
Foreign: Matej Ferjan, Kenneth Hansen, Jesper B Monberg, Thomas H. Jonasson, Peter Karlsson, Jari Mäkinen.

RZESZOW (A)
Friday, June 20
Won 48-44
Gollob 13:2 (4), Monberg 4, Karlsson 11:1, Ferjan 8:1, Holta 9:2, Szewczykowski 2, Jonasson 1.
Aggregate: Won 99-85.

LESZNO (A)
Sunday, July 6
Drew 45-45
Gollob 16, Monberg 1:1 Karlsson 8:1, Ferjan 5, Holta 3:1, Szewczykowski 0, Jonasson 12:1.
Aggregate: Won 93-87.

TARNOW (H)
Sunday, July 20
Won 60-32
Hlib 4:1, **Gollob 9**, Ferjan 12:2, Karlsson 10:2, Holta 11, Szewczykowski 5:1, Jonasson 9:2.
Aggregate: Won 107-78.

CZESTOCHOWA (A)
Sunday, July 27
Lost 38-55
Gollob 9:1, Hlib 0, Karlsson 5:2, Ferjan 8, Holta 15 (6), Szewczykowski 1.
Aggregate: Lost 78-105.

ZIELONA GORA (H)
Sunday, August 3
Lost 41-49
Gollob 16, Monberg 2:1, Ferjan 2, Karlsson 7:1, Holta 11, Szewczykowski 2, Jonasson 1
Aggregate: Lost 80-102.

WROCLAW (A)
Sunday, August 10
Lost 39-53
Gollob 14 (4), Monberg 8:2, Karlsson 7:2, Ferjan 6, Hlib 2, Szewczykowski 2, Hansen 0.
Aggregate: Lost 92-93.

EKSTRALIGA

	M	W	D	L	BP	Pts
Czestochowa	14	12	0	2	7	31
Torun	14	12	0	2	6	30
Leszno	14	10	1	3	4	25
Zielona Gora	14	17	0	7	3	17
GORZOW	**14**	**6**	**1**	**7**	**3**	**16**
Wroclaw	14	4	0	10	4	12
Rzeszow	14	3	0	11	1	7
Tarnow	14	1	0	13	0	2

Play offs

Quarter Final, first leg
TORUN (H)
Sunday, August 24
Lost 43-47
Gollob 11:1, Monberg 0, Karlsson 10:2, Ferjan 7:1, Holta 10:1, Szewczykowski 0 Jonasson 5.

Quarter Final, second leg
TORUN (A)
Sunday, August 31
Lost 25-66
Gollob 4, Cyran 0, Karlsson 4, Ferjan 2, Holta 8 (2), Szewczykowski 3, Jonasson 4:1.

Aggregate: Lost 68-113.

Challenge

TORUN (A)
Thursday, March 20
Lost 33-44
Gollob 6, Smarzlik 4, Hlib 8, Mikorski 1, Holta 6, Jonasson 6, Szewczykowski 2.

LESZNO (A)
Thursday, March 27
Won 50-40
Gollob 12, Monberg 5:2, Karlsson 8:2, Ferjan 8, Holta 10, Szewczykowski 4:2, Hlib 3, Zmarzlik 0.

BYDGOSZCZ (A)
Tuesday, April 1
Won 43-41
Holta 10, Mikorski 0, Hlib 4:1, Monberg 10, Ferjan 11, Szewczykowski 5, Zmarzlik 3:1.

GÜSTROW, GERMANY (A)
Saturday, July 12
Lost 37-53
Hlib 13, Mikorski 7, Szewczykowski 7, Dabrowski 5, Cyran 4, Marcin Kozdras 1.

Individual

POLISH CHAMPIONSHIP
Semi Final
Thursday, July 5
Hampel 12, Holta 12, Skornicki 11, K. Kasprzak 11, Gomolski 11, Protasiewicz 10, Kosciecha 9, Walasek 8, Stachrya 6+3, J. Rempala 6+2, Jeleniewski 6+F, Povazhny 5, Dobrucki 4, Slabon 3, Trojanowski 2, Kuciapa 1, Gapinski [R], did not ride.

EDWARD JANCARZ MEMORIAL
Saturday, June 21
Crump 13+3, N. Pedersen 15+2, K. Kasprzak 11+1, Gollob 11+0, Balinski 10, Adams 9, Jagus 8, Dobrucki 8, Holta 8, Ulamek 6, Karlsson 5, Kolodziej 4, Zabik 4, Zetterström 3, Hlib 2, Szewczykowski [R] 1,Zmarzlik [R], did not ride.

Number two Rune Holta

GORZOW

Rider	M	R	Pts	BP	TPts	Ave	F	P	TR	TPts
Tomasz GOLLOB	16	82	191	11	202	9.85	2	0	3	6
Rune HOLTA	**15**	**82**	**157**	**7**	**164**	**8.00**	**0**	**0**	**3**	**5**
Peter KARLSSON	16	75	123	13	136	7.25	0	0	0	0
Jesper B. MONBERG	**12**	**45**	**44**	**13**	**57**	**5.07**	**0**	**0**	**0**	**0**
Matej FERJAN	13	62	67	7	74	4.77	0	0	0	0
Thomas H. JONASSON	**13**	**62**	**65**	**5**	**70**	**4.52**	**0**	**0**	**0**	**0**
Pawel HLIB	7	30	20	3	23	3.07	0	0	0	0
Adrian SZEWCZYKOWSKI	**15**	**34**	**22**	**2**	**24**	**2.82**	**0**	**0**	**0**	**0**
Kenneth HANSEN	2	5	1	0	1	0.80	0	0	0	0
Pawel ZMARZLIK	**1**	**1**	**0**	**0**	**0**	**0.00**	**0**	**0**	**0**	**0**
Lukasz CYRAN	1	1	0	0	0	0.00	0	0	0	0

Polish Ekstraliga

LESZNO

2008 RESULTS

Ekstraliga

Final position ....Runners-up (Third)

CZESTOCHOWA (H)
Sunday, April 6
Won 50-42
Adams 11, Batchelor 1, K.Kasprzak 7:1, Balinski 9:1, Hampel 11, Kajoch 2:1, Pavlic 9:3.

RZESZOW (A)
Sunday, April 13
Won 65-27
Adams 14:1, Shields 10:1, K. Kasprzak 10:2, **Balinski 10:2**, **Hampel 14:1**, Kajoch 2, Batchelor 5.

TARNOW (H)
Sunday, April 20
Won 67-26
Adams 12, Shields 7:4, K. Kasprzak 11:2, Balinski 9:2, Hampel 8:3, R. Kasprzak 10:3, Pavlic 10:1.

WROCLAW (A)
Thursday, May 1
Won 47-46
Adams 7:2, Shields 11:1, K. Kasprzak 11, Balinski 5:1, Hampel 9, R. Kasprzak 0, Pavlic 4:1.

GORZOW (A)
Sunday, May 4
Lost 42-48
Adams 10, Shields 2:1, K. Kasprzak 3:1, Balinski 6:1, Hampel 9, R. Kasprzak 2:1, Pavlic 10:2.

TORUN (H)
Friday, May 16
Lost 43-47
Hampel 10, Pavlic 1:1, K. Kasprzak 10:1, Balinski 7:2, Adams 10, R. Kasprzak 4:1, Batchelor 1:1.

ZIELONA GORA (A)
Sunday, June 1
Won 57-36
Adams 12, Shields 2:1, K. Kasprzak 12:2, Balinski 10:4, Hampel 12:1, R. Kasprzak 0, Pavlic 9:2.

ZIELONA GORA (H)
Sunday, June 8
Won 50-40
Adams 12:1, Batchelor 0, K. Kasprzak 8:1, Balinski 9:2, Hampel 14, R. Kasprzak 2:1, Pavlic 5:1.
Aggregate: Won 107-76.

TRACK FILE

Track: Alfred Smoczyk Stadium, ul. Strzelecka 7, 64-100 Leszno, Poland.
Telephone: 0048 0655299977.
Website: www.unialeszno.pl
Track Length: 342.5metres.
Track Record: 58.4 secs, Krzysztof Kasprzak, May 3, 2007.

SQUAD
Damian Balinski, Jaroslaw Hampel, Krzysztof Kasprzak, Adam Kajoch, Robert Kasprzak, Slawomir Musielak, Przemyslaw Pawlicki, Damian Perz, Pawel Ratajszczak.
Foreign: Leigh Adams, Troy Batchelor, Travis McGowan, Jurica Pavlic, Adam Shields.

TORUN (A)
Friday, June 20
Won 46-44
Hampel 14:1, Kajoch 1, K. Kasprzak 4, Balinski 12, Adams 11:3, R. Kasprzak 0, Pavlic 4.
Aggregate: Lost 89-91.

GORZOW (H)
Sunday, July 6
Drew 45-45
Adams 13, Shields 5:2, K. Kasprzak 9:1, Balinski 5:1, Hampel 9, R. Kasprzak 2, Pavlic 2:2.
Aggregate: Lost 87-93.

WROCLAW (H)
Sunday, July 20
Won 61-29
Balinski 2:1, K. Kasprzak 11:1, Hampel 11:2, Shields 7:2, **Adams 11:1**, Pawlicki 11, Pavlic 8:3.
Aggregate: Won 108-75.

TARNOW (A)
Sunday, July 27
Won 53-40
Adams 13:1, Batchelor 5, K. Kasprzak 9:1, Balinski 7:1, Hampel 9:2, Pawlicki 1, Pavlic 9.
Aggregate: Won 120-66.

RZESZOW (H)
Sunday, August 3
Won 59-33
K. Kasprzak 9:2, Balinski 10:1, Hampel 12:1, Shields 8:3, Adams 11:1, Kajoch 6, Pavlic 3.
Aggregate: Won 124-60.

CZESTOCHOWA (A)
Sunday, August 10
Lost 36-56
Adams 6, Shields 4:1, Kasprzak 16 (6), Balinski 1:1,

Hampel 7, Pawlicki 0, Kajoch 2.
Aggregate: Lost 86-98.

EKSTRALIGA

	M	*W*	*D*	*L*	*BP*	*Pts*
Czestochowa	14	12	0	2	7	31
Torun	14	12	0	2	6	30
LESZNO	**14**	**10**	**1**	**3**	**4**	**25**
Zielona Gora	14	17	0	7	3	17
Gorzow	14	6	1	7	3	16
Wroclaw	14	4	0	10	4	12
Rzeszow	14	3	0	11	1	7
Tarnow	14	1	0	13	0	2

Play offs

Quarter Final, first leg
ZIELONA GORA (A)
Thursday, August 28
Lost 40-49
Adams 9:2, Batchelor 0, K. Kasprzak 10:1, Balinski 6:1, Hampel 11:1 (FX), R. Kasprzak 1, Pavlic 3.

Quarter Final, second leg
ZIELONA GORA (H)
Sunday, August 31
Won 54-38
K. Kasprzak 10:2, Balinski 8, Adams 8:2, Batchelor 7:1, Hampel 8:1, Pawlicki 11:1, Pavlic 2:1.
Aggregate: Won 94-87.

Semi Final, first leg
CZESTOCHOWA (H)
Sunday, September 7
Won 52-41
K. Kasprzak 10:1, Balinski 5:2, Adams 11:1, Batchelor 5:1, Hampel 9:2, Pawlicki 8:2, Pavlic 4:1.

Semi Final, second leg
CZESTOCHOWA (A)
Sunday, September 28
Won 50-40
Adams 10, Batchelor 3:1, K. Kasprzak 12:1, Balinski 6:2, Hampel 12, R. Kasprzak 1, Pavlic 6:2.
Aggregate: Won 102-81.

FINAL, first leg
TORUN (H)
Sunday, October 12
Lost 41-49
K. Kasprzak 4:1, Balinski 7:1, Adams 8:1, Batchelor 5:1, Hampel 10:1, R. Kasprzak 2, Pavlic 5.

For team photograph see end of Ekstraliga section

FINAL, second leg
TORUN (A)
Sunday, October 19
Lost 43-47
Adams 9:1, Batchelor 3:1, K. Kasprzak 5, Balinski 7:1, Hampel 10:1, R. Kasprzak 1, Pavlic 8:1.
Aggregate: Lost 84-96.

Challenge

OSTROW (A)
Saturday, March 15
Won 47-43
K. Kasprzak 13:2, Balinski 12:1, Pavlic 13, Ratajszczak 0, Kajoch 3, R. Kasprzak 4, Musielak 2.

OSTROW (H)
Monday, March 17
Won 50-28
K. Kasprzak 10:2, Balinski 8:1, Kajoch 10:1, Ratajszczak 1:1, **Hampel 11:1**, R. Kasprzak 9:1, Musielak 1.

GORZOW (H)
Thursday, March 27
Lost 40-50
K.Kasprzak 10, R. Kasprzak 0, Shields 7:1, Hlib 4, Balinski 11, Musielak 5, Kajoch 3.

ZIELONA GORA (H)
Wednesday, April 2
Won 46-44
K. Kasprzak 12, R. Kasprzak 3:1, Balinski 14, Musielak 1, Hampel 12:1, Kajoch 4, Ratajszczak 0.

Individual

POLISH FINAL
Saturday, August 9
Skornicki 15, Hampel 13, Walasek 12, T. Gollob 11, Balinski 9, K. Kasprzak 9, Protasiewicz 7, Kosciecha 7, Jedrzejak 6, Ulamek 6, Kolodziej 6, Stachyra 4, Holta 4, A. Gomolski 3, Mi.Szczepaniak 3, Drabik 3, K. Jablonski 2, J. Rempala 0.

58th ALFRED SMOCZYK MEMORIAL
Saturday, March 29
Adams 13, Hampel 12, Dobrucki 11, Holta 10, Jagus 10, Balinski 9, Okoniewski 8, Walasek 8, Batchelor 8, K. Kasprzak 7, Ulamek 6, Jedrzejak 6, Kajoch 5, Chrzanowski 3, Zabik 2, Shields 2, R. Kasprzak 0, Musielak 0.

YOUTH EXTRALEAGUE FINAL
Tuesday, August 26
Janowski 15, R. Kasprzak 13, Pawlicki 13, Mateusz Szczepaniak 12, Zengota 10, Szewczykowski 9, Dudek 8, Vaculik 7, Kajoch 7, Strozyk 7, Celmer 6, S. Kielbasa 5, Pieniazek 4, Kostro 2, Kowalczyk 1, Zmarzlik 1.

Rider	*M*	*R*	*Pts*	*BP*	*TPts*	*Ave*	*F*	*P*	*TR*	*TPts*
Jaroslaw HAMPEL	20	99	210	16	226	9.13	0	1	1	0
Leigh ADAMS	**20**	**99**	**208**	**17**	**225**	**9.09**	**1**	**2**	**0**	**0**
Krzysztof KASPRZAK	20	99	181	21	202	8.16	0	0	1	3
Adam SHIELDS	**9**	**39**	**56**	**16**	**72**	**7.38**	**0**	**0**	**0**	**0**
Damian BALINSKI	20	92	141	27	168	7.30	0	1	0	0
Przemyslaw PAWLICKI	**5**	**20**	**31**	**3**	**34**	**6.80**	**0**	**0**	**0**	**0**
Jurica PAVLIC	18	76	102	21	123	6.47	0	0	0	0
Robert KASPRZAK	**12**	**26**	**24**	**7**	**31**	**4.77**	**0**	**0**	**0**	**0**
Troy BATCHELOR	11	37	35	6	41	4.43	0	0	0	0
Adam KAJOCH	**5**	**15**	**13**	**1**	**14**	**3.73**	**0**	**0**	**0**	**0**

Polish Ekstraliga

RZESZOW

2008 RESULTS

Ekstraliga

Final position ....Seventh (Seventh)

TORUN (A)
Sunday, April 6
Lost 28-63
Stachyra 4, Povazhny 1, Watt 6, Zagar 6, Bjerre 8:1 (2), Lampart 1:1, Vaculik 2.

LESZNO (H)
Sunday, April 13
Lost 27-65
Watt 12 (4), Povazhny 1, Bjerre 8:1, Stachyra 3, *rider replacement for Nicholls*, Szostek 0, Vaculik 3.

WROCLAW (H)
Sunday, April 20
Won 47-43
Watt 10:1, Woodward 6:4, Nicholls 8, Bjerre 12:2 (6), Zagar 8:1, Lampart 3, Szostek 0.

ZIELONA GORA (A)
Thursday, May 1
Lost 39-52
Nicholls 10:1 (2), Povazhny 7:2, Watt 3, Bjerre 2, Zagar 12, Lampart 3, Vaculik 2.

GORZOW (A)
Sunday, May 11
Lost 41-51
Zagar 16:1 (4), Povazhny 5:1, Nicholls 6:3, Bjerre 8:1, Watt 4, Lampart 0, Vaculik 2.

TARNOW (H)
Sunday, June 1
Won 51-37
Nicholls 10, Stachyra 8:3, Watt 10, Povazhny 4:1, Zagar 9:2, Vaculik 10:2, Lampart 0.

CZESTOCHOWA (H)
Friday, June 6
Lost 32-60
Watt 5:1, Woodward 0, Zagar 3:1, Stachyra 8 (4), Nicholls 5, Vaculik 10:1, Lampart 1.

TARNOW (A)
Sunday, June 8
Won 47-44
Nicholls 9, Stachyra 5, Watt 4, Povazhny 13:1, Zagar 10, Lampart 0, Vaculik 6:1.
Aggregate: Won 98-81.

TRACK FILE

Track: Municipal Stadium, ul. Hetmańska 69 Rzeszó, Poland.
Telephone: 0048 017 8541592.
Website: www.stal.rzeszow.pl
Track Length: 395 metres.
Track Record: 64.27 secs, Grzegorz Walasek, July 20, 2008.

SQUAD
Dawid Lampart, Dawid Stachyra, Mateusz Szostek.
Foreign: Kenneth Bjerre, Scott Nicholls, Roman Povazhny, Martin Vaculik, Davey Watt, Cameron Woodward, Matej Zagar.

GORZOW (H)
Friday, June 20
Lost 44-48
Zagar 9, Watt 6:1, Bjerre 11:1, Stachyra 2:1, Nicholls 10, Lampart 6, Vaculik 0.
Aggregate: Lost 85-99.

CZESTOCHOWA (A)
Sunday, July 6
Lost 26-65
Zagar 1, Stachyra 3, Watt 6, Szostek 1, Bjerre 2, Lampart 5:1 (2), Vaculik 8.
Aggregate: Lost 58-125.

ZIELONA GORA (H)
Sunday, July 20
Lost 33-59
Nicholls 4:1, Stachyra 5, Watt 1, Zagar 12 (4), Bjerre 4, Lampart 3, Vaculik 4:1.
Aggregate: Lost 72-111.

WROCLAW (A)
Sunday, July 27
Lost 30-62
Bjerre 6, Watt 0, Nicholls 6:2, Stachyra 5:1, Zagar 12 (4), Lampart 0, Vaculik 1.
Aggregate: Lost 77-105.

LESZNO (A)
Sunday, August 3
Lost 33-59
Stachyra 8:1, Nicholls 11 (4), Zagar 8:1, Woodward 1, no rider at number 5, Szostek 0, Vaculik 5.
Aggregate: Lost 60-124.

TORUN (H)
Sunday, August 10
Lost 33-58
Nicholls 8:1, Povazhny 2, Stachyra 4:1, Watt 8, Zagar 6 (2), Vaculik 5:1, Szostek 0.
Aggregate: Lost 61-121.

For team photograph see end of Ekstraliga section

Relegation Play-off

First leg
TARNOW (A)
Sunday, September 7
Won 48-42
Zagar 7:1, Povazhny 3:1, Watt 12, Stachyra 10, Nicholls 9:2, Lampart 1, Vaculik 6:1.

Second leg
TARNOW (H)
Sunday, September 28
Won 51-41
Zagar 9:1, Woodward 4:1, Stachyra 8:3, Watt 12, Nicholls 11, Vaculik 6:1, Lampart 1.
Aggregate: Won 99-83.

First leg
GDANSK (A)
Sunday, October 12
Lost 37-54
Zagar 12:1, Povazhny 2:1, Watt 6, Stachyra 1:1, Nicholls 8, Lampart 3, Vaculik 5:1.

Second leg
GDANSK (H)
Sunday, October 19
Won 47-45
Zagar 9, Stachyra 2:2, Watt 10, Woodward 3:1, Nicholls 13:1, Vaculik 5, Lampart 5:1.
Aggregate: Lost 84-99.

EKSTRALIGA

	M	*W*	*D*	*L*	*BP*	*Pts*
Czestochowa	14	12	0	2	7	31
Torun	14	12	0	2	6	30
Leszno	14	10	1	3	4	25
Zielona Gora	14	17	0	7	3	17
Gorzow	14	6	1	7	3	16
Wroclaw	14	4	0	10	4	12
RZESZOW	**14**	**3**	**0**	**11**	**1**	**7**
Tarnow	14	1	0	13	0	2

Challenge

MISKOLC (Hungary) (A)
Sunday, March 16
Lost 37-74
Kuciapa 6 [G], Szostek 2, Marcin Les [G] 8, Lukasz Ciesielski [G]2, Povazhny 9, Lampart 4, Tamas Szilagyi [G] 2, L. Kielbasa [G] 4.

TARNOW (H)
Saturday, March 29
Won 52-38
Povazhny 9:1, Piszcz 5, Stachyra 9:1, Les 2, T. Rempala 8, Lampart 9:2, Szostek 9:2, Miesiac 1.

TARNOW (A)
Sunday, March 30
Lost 36-54
Povazhny 5, T. Rempala 3, Woodward 6:1, Les 2, Stachyra 10, Szostek 2, Lampart 2, Piszcz 6.

RYBNIK (A)
Monday, March 31
Lost 39-50
Povazhny 12, Piszcz 1, Stachyra 9:1, Henrik Moller [G] 2:1, Miesiac 9, Lampart 5:1, Szostek 1:1.

Individual

SILVER HELMET FINAL
Friday, October 10
Janowski 12, Zengota 11, Pawlaszczyk 11, Mateusz Szczepaniak 11, Lampart 11, Mitko 10, Jedrzejewski 9, Szewczykowski 8, Pytel 8, S. Kielbasa 8, Musielak 6, Piekarski 6, Szostek 3, Dudek 3, Celmer 2, Brzozowski 1, Szyszka 0, Fleger 0.

EUGENIUSZ NAZIMEK MEMORIAL
Friday, September 26
Zagar 13, Skornicki 11, Kuciapa 11, Zabik 10, Dobrucki 10, Miedzinski 10, Watt 9, Lindbäck 9, Jeleniewski 8, Trojanowski 8, Stachyra 7, Woodward 5, Miesiac 4, Vaculik 4, Mitko 1, Szyszka 0.

Rider	*M*	*R*	*Pts*	*BP*	*TPts*	*Ave*	*F*	*P*	*TR*	*TPts*
Matej ZAGAR	15	74	129	8	137	7.41	0	0	4	7
Scott NICHOLLS	**13**	**65**	**106**	**11**	**117**	**7.20**	**0**	**0**	**2**	**3**
Kenneth BJERRE	9	44	61	6	67	6.09	0	0	2	4
Davey WATT	**15**	**69**	**99**	**3**	**102**	**5.91**	**0**	**0**	**1**	**2**
Dawid STACHYRA	13	63	73	9	82	5.21	0	0	1	2
Martin VACULIK	**15**	**62**	**70**	**8**	**78**	**5.03**	**0**	**0**	**0**	**0**
Roman POVAZHNY	8	34	36	6	42	4.94	0	0	0	0
Cameron WOODWARD	**4**	**16**	**11**	**5**	**16**	**4.00**	**0**	**0**	**0**	**0**
Dawid LAMPART	12	39	23	2	25	2.56	0	0	1	1
Mateusz SZOSTEK	**6**	**15**	**2**	**0**	**2**	**0.53**	**0**	**0**	**0**	**0**

Relegation to the 2009 First League cost Rzeszow dear on the rider front with a host of defections during the winter.
Of their seven 2008 foreign riders only Australian Cameron Woodward remains – with Dawid Stachyra and juniors Dawid Lampart and Mateusz Szostek also still at the club.

For details of 2009 squad see First League

Polish Ekstraliga

TARNOW

2008 RESULTS

Ekstraliga

Final position .... Eighth (Eighth)

CZESTOCHOWA (A)
Sunday, April 13
Lost 23-69
Dryml 5:1, Klecha 0, Ljung 3, M. Rempala 1, Kolodziej 9 (4), Zielinski 1, Hougaard 4

ZIELONA GORA (H)
Monday, April 14
Lost 41-49
Ljung 4:2, M. Rempala 10:2, J. Rempala 8, Doolan 2, Kolodziej 10, Zielinski 6:2, Hougaard 1:1.

LESZNO (A)
Sunday, April 20
Lost 26-67
Kolodziej 16 (6), M. Rempala 0, J. Rempala 2, Klecha 2, Dryml 4, Zielinski 1, Busch 1.

GORZOW (H)
Thursday, May 1
Lost 46-47
Drabik 2, Dryml 4:2, J. Rempala 12, M. Rempala 6, Kolodziej 19 (6), Zielinski 1:1, Busch 2.

TORUN (A)
Sunday, May 4
Lost 26-66
Kolodziej 10 (4), M. Rempala 1, Dryml 1, Ljung 7, J. Rempala 2, Hougaard 4, Zielinski 1

WROCLAW (H)
Friday, May 16
Won 57-36
Drabik 6:1, Ljung 8:2, J. Rempala 10, M. Rempala 6:2, Kolodziej 10:3, **Hougaard 15**, Zielinski 2:1.

RZESZOW (A)
Sunday, June 1
Lost 37-51
Ljung 4, Ivanov 5, Drabik 5, Doolan 4:1, Kolodziej 17, Hougaard 0, Zielinski 2:1.

RZESZOW (H)
Sunday, June 8
Lost 44-47
Drabik 6, M. Rempala 9:1, J. Rempala 0, Ljung 13:1, Kolodziej 9:2, Hougaard 5:1, Zielinski 2.
Aggregate: Lost 81-98.

TRACK FILE

Track: ul. Zbylitowska 1, 33-101 Tarnow, Poland.

Telephone: 0048 014 6330201.

Website: www.unia-tarnow.pl.

Track Length: 392 metres.

Track Record: 59.69 secs, Janusz Kolodziej, August 11, 2008.

SQUAD
Krystian Klecha, Janusz Kolodziej, Jacek Rempala, Marcin Rempala, Maciej Ciesielski, Lukasz Kielbasa, Szymon Kielbasa, Tadeusz Kostro, Kamil Zielinski.
Foreign: Steve Boxall, Tobias Busch, Kevin Doolan, Ales Dryml, Patrick Hougaard, Daniil Ivanov, Peter Juul Larsen, Peter Ljung, James Wright.

WROCLAW (A)
Friday, June 20
Lost 29-61
M. Rempala 7, Doolan 0, Kolodziej 7 (2), Ivanov 2, Ljung 7, Busch 0, S. Kielbasa 6.
Aggregate: Lost 86-97.

TORUN (H)
Sunday, July 6
Lost 38-53
Drabik 1, M. Rempala 13 (2), Ljung 8:1, J. Rempala 5, Kolodziej 8:1, S. Kielbasa 1:1, Hougaard 2.
Aggregate: Lost 64-119.

GORZOW (A)
Sunday, July 20
Lost 32-60
M. Rempala 6:1, Klecha 0, J. Rempala 5, Ljung 5:1, Kolodziej 13 (4), S. Kielbasa 0, Larsen 3.
Aggregate: Lost 78-107.

LESZNO (H)
Sunday, July 27
Lost 40-53
M. Rempala 4:1, Klecha 0, J. Rempala 9:1, Drabik 2, Kolodziej 19 (6), S. Kielbasa 6:1, Hougaard 0.
Aggregate: Lost 66-120.

CZESTOCHOWA (H)
Sunday, August 3
Lost 33-59
M. Rempala 3:2, Ljung 13 (4), J. Rempala 3, Drabik 4:1, Kolodziej 9:1, S. Kielbasa 1, Larsen 0.
Aggregate: Lost 56-128.

ZIELONA GORA (A)
Sunday, August 10
Lost 29-63
Kolodziej 14:1 (4), J. Rempala 0, Drabik 4:1, M. Rempala 2, Ljung 0, S. Kielbasa 3, Hougaard 6.
Aggregate: Lost 70-112.

For details of 2009 squad see First League

Relegation Play offs

First leg
RZESZOW (H)
Sunday, September 7
Lost 42-48
J. Rempala 9, M. Rempala 2:1, Drabik 7:1, Klecha 9:1, Kolodziej 13, S. Kielbasa 0, Hougaard 2.

Second leg
RZESZOW (A)
Sunday, September 28
Lost 41-51
Rider replacement for M. Rempala, Doolan 1, Drabik 16 (4), Klecha 2, Kolodziej 13:3, Hougaard 9:1, S. Kielbasa 0.
Aggregate: Lost 83-99.

EKSTRALIGA

	M	*W*	*D*	*L*	*BP*	*Pts*
Czestochowa	14	12	0	2	7	31
Torun	14	12	0	2	6	30
Leszno	14	10	1	3	4	25
Zielona Gora	14	17	0	7	3	17
Gorzow	14	6	1	7	3	16
Wroclaw	14	4	0	10	4	12
Rzeszow	14	3	0	11	1	7
TARNOW	**14**	**1**	**0**	**13**	**0**	**2**

Challenge

CZESTOCHOWA (A)
Saturday, March 15
Lost 30-60
J. Rempala 6, M. Rempala 0, Klecha 7, Doolan 8:2, Larsen 4:2, Zielinski 0, Hougaard 5, S. Kielbasa, did not ride.

CZESTOCHOWA (H)
Sunday, March 16
Won 50-38
J. Rempala 6:2, Doolan 9:1, M. Rempala 10:1, Klecha 7:1, Larsen 4:1, Hougaard 9:1, Zielinski 5.

OSTROW (A)
Friday, March 28
Lost 37-53
J. Rempala 8, Klecha 4:2, M. Rempala 7, Ljung 3, Kolodziej 12, Hougaard 2, Zielinski 1.

RZESZOW (A)
Saturday, March 29
Lost 38-52
Dryml 3, Klecha 2:1, M. Rempala 8:1, Ivanov 8, Kolodziej 10:1, Larsen 0, Zielinski 1, Ljung 5, S. Kielbasa 1.

RZESZOW (H)
Sunday, March 30
Won 54-36
Dryml 7:1, Ivanov 7:1, Doolan 7, J. Rempala 10:1, Kolodziej 4, S. Kielbasa 0, Busch 5, M. Rempala 6:2, Klecha 4:1, Ljung 1, Hougaard 3.

Individual

WORLD UNDER 21 CHAMPIONSHIP
Qualifying
POLISH FINAL
Thursday, April 24
A. Gomolski 14, Zengota 13, Mateusz Szczepaniak 12, Pawlaszczyk 10, Kajoch 10, Mitko 9, Brzozowski 8, R. Kasprzak 8, Jedrzewski 7, Dabrowski 6, Janowski 6, Piaszczynski 5, Szymura 4, Piekarski 3, Sperz 3, Pytel 2.

POLISH U21 CHAMPIONSHIP
Semi Final
Thursday, July 10
R. Kasprzak 14, Pawlicki 14, A. Gomolski 13, Mateusz Szczepaniak 10, Miturski 8, Jedrzejewski 8, Lopaczewski 8, Szostek 8, Lampart 7, S. Kielbasa 7, R. Fleger 6, Piaszczynski 5, Pyszny 3, Szymura 3, Dabrowski 3, Szyszka 2, K. Gomolski 1, Liberski 0, Idziorek 0.

Wednesday, March 19
J. Rempala 15, M. Rempala 14, Ivanov 12, Klecha 10, Larsen 10, Tihanyi 9, Baran 9, Busch 9, Zielinski 8, J. Wright 8, Ciesielski 5, L. Kielbasa 4, Szilagyi 3, Les 2, Piszcz 0, S.Kielbasa 0.

SZCZEPAN BUKOWSKI MEMORIAL
Saturday, October 25
Hougaard 14+3, S. Kielbasa 12+2, Busch 13+1, Lampart 10+FX, Zielinski 10, Pudel 10, R. Henderson 10, Gavenda 9, Skov 7, D. Henderson 6, Spicker 5, R. Fleger 4, Bjerregaard 4, Kostro 2, Lorincz 2, Molnar 2, K. Fleger 0.

Rider	*M*	*R*	*Pts*	*BP*	*TPts*	*Ave*	*F*	*P*	*TR*	*TPts*
Janusz KOLODZIEJ	16	94	196	11	207	8.81	0	0	8	18
Peter LJUNG	**11**	**54**	**72**	**7**	**79**	**5.85**	**0**	**0**	**1**	**2**
Slawomir DRABIK	10	41	53	4	57	5.56	0	0	1	2
Jacek REMPALA	**12**	**54**	**65**	**1**	**66**	**4.89**	**0**	**0**	**0**	**0**
Marcin REMPALA	14	67	70	9	79	4.72	0	0	1	1
Patrick HOUGAARD	**11**	**45**	**48**	**2**	**50**	**4.44**	**1**	**0**	**0**	**0**
Kamil ZIELINSKI	8	20	16	6	22	4.40	0	0	0	0
Ales DRYML	**4**	**18**	**14**	**3**	**17**	**3.78**	**0**	**0**	**0**	**0**
Daniil IVANOV	2	8	7	0	7	3.50	0	0	0	0
Szymon KIELBASA	**9**	**29**	**17**	**2**	**19**	**2.62**	**0**	**0**	**0**	**0**
Krystian KLECHA	6	22	13	1	14	2.55	0	0	0	0
Kevin DOOLAN	**4**	**13**	**7**	**0**	**7**	**2.15**	**0**	**0**	**0**	**0**
Peter Juul LARSEN	2	6	3	0	3	2.00	0	0	0	0
Tobias BUSCH	**3**	**10**	**3**	**0**	**3**	**1.20**	**0**	**0**	**0**	**0**

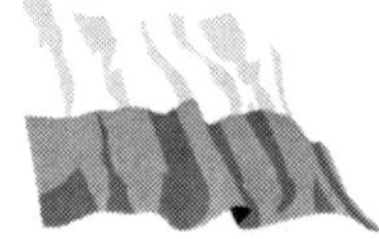

Polish
Ekstraliga

TORUN

TRACK FILE

Track: Marian Rose Stadion, ul. Falata 98/102, 87-100 Torun, Poland.
Telephone: 0048 056 6518066.
Website: www.speedway.torun.pl
Track Length: 333 metres.
Track Record: 59.03 secs, Tony Rickardsson, April 24, 2005.

2008 RESULTS

Ekstraliga

Final position....................Champions (Second)

RZESZOW (H)
Sunday, April 6
Won 63-28
Jagus 12:1, Miedzinski 10:2, Andersen 12, Zabik 5:3, **Sullivan 14:1**, Holder 9:2, Celmer 1.

WROCLAW (A)
Sunday, April 13
Won 48-41
Andersen 9, Kosciecha 8:3, Jagus 8:2, Miedzinski 6:1, Sullivan 7:1, Holder 10:2, Celmer 0.

ZIELONA GORA (H)
Sunday, April 20
Won 56-34
Jagus 13, Miedzinski 5:1, Andersen 9:2, Kosciecha 9:1, Sullivan 11, Holder 9:2, Celmer 0.

CZESTOCHOWA (A)
Thursday, May 1
Won 50-41
Jagus 12, Miedzinski 8:3, Andersen 9, Kosciecha 4:1, Sullivan 9, Celmer 0, Holder 8:4.

TARNOW (H)
Sunday, May 4
Won 66-26
Jagus 14, Kosciecha 8:4, Andersen 11:1, Miedzinski 6:3, **Sullivan 13:2**, Celmer 0, Holder 14:1.

LESZNO (A)
Friday, May 16
Won 47-43
Jagus 17, Kosciecha 5:2, Sullivan 1, Miedzinski 5, Andersen 7, Ksiezak 0, Holder 12:2.

GORZOW (H)
Sunday, June 1
Won 61-30
Jagus 9:2, Miedzinski 12:1, Andersen 4:1, Sullivan 13:1, Kosciecha 11:3, Lampkowski 2, Holder 10:4.

GORZOW (A)
Sunday, June 8
Won 47-43
Jagus 8:2, Miedzinski 9:3, Andersen 11, Sullivan 6:1, Kosciecha 3:2, Lampkowski 0, Holder 10.
Aggregate: Won 108-73.

SQUAD
Damian Celmer, Wieslaw Jagus, Robert Kosciecha, Alan Marcinkowski, Adrian Miedzinski, Kamil Pulczynski, Damian Stachowiak, Karol Zabik, Marcin Nowakowski, Mateusz Lampkowski, Lukasz Lipinski, Oskar Pieniazek.
Foreign: Hans Andersen, Simon Gustafsson, Chris Holder, Robert Ksiezak, Ryan Sullivan, Robin Törnqvist.

LESZNO (H)
Friday, June 20
Lost 44-46
Jagus 6:1, Miedzinski 7:1, Sullivan 11, Andersen 3:2, Kosciecha 9:3, Ksiezak 1, Holder 7:1.
Aggregate: Won 91-89.

TARNOW (A)
Sunday, July 6
Won 53-38
Kosciecha 13:1, Zabik 4, Miedzinski 10:1, Andersen 10:2, Sullivan 10, Celmer 0, Holder 6:1.
Aggregate: Won 119-64.

CZESTOCHOWA (H)
Sunday, July 20
Lost 34-59
Jagus 1, Miedzinski 2, Sullivan 6, Andersen 14:2 (6), Kosciecha 3:2, Lampkowski 0, Holder 8.
Aggregate: Lost 84-100.

ZIELONA GORA (A)
Sunday, July 27
Won 58-32
Kosciecha 2, Miedzinski 10:1, Andersen 10:2, **Sullivan 12:3, Jagus 15**, Celmer 2, Holder 7:2.
Aggregate: Won 114-66.

WROCLAW (H)
Sunday, August 3
Won 49-41
Andersen 8:3. Kosciecha 12, Sullivan 7:2, Zabik 5, Jagus 9, Celmer 3, Holder 5.
Aggregate: Won 97-82.

RZESZOW (A)
Sunday, August 10
Won 58-33
Andersen 9:1, Kosciecha 11:2, Sullivan 11:2, Zabik 3, Jagus 10:2, Celmer 1, Holder 13:1.
Aggregate: Won 121-61.

Play offs

Quarter Final, first leg
GORZOW (A)
Sunday, August 24
Won 47-43
Andersen 12, Kosciecha 2:2, Sullivan 10, Pulczynski, did not ride, Jagus 10:1, Celmer 5:1, Holder 8:1.

Quarter Final, second leg
GORZOW (H)
Sunday, August 31
Won 66-25
Andersen 6:2, **Kosciecha 13:2**, Sullivan 13:1, Miedzinski 10:2, **Jagus 15**, Celmer 0, Holder 9:3.
Aggregate: Won 113-68.

Semi Final, first leg
ZIELONA GORA (A)
Sunday, September 7
Lost 42-48
Andersen 7:2, Kosciecha 4:1, Sullivan 9, Miedzinski 6:2, Jagus 8:1, Celmer 0, Holder 8.

Semi Final, second leg
ZIELONA GORA (H)
Friday, September 19
Won 57-36
Sullivan 12:1, Miedzinski 9:3, Andersen 13, Kosciecha 3:1, Jagus 9:1, Celmer 0, Holder 11:2.
Aggregate: Won 99-84.

FINAL, first leg
LESZNO (A)
Sunday, October 12
Won 49-41
Andersen 10, Zabik 0, Sullivan 11:1, Miedzinski 1, **Jagus 16:2**, Celmer 0, Holder 11.

FINAL, second leg
LESZNO (H)
Sunday, October 19
Won 47-43
Sullivan 9:1, Miedzinski 9:2, Andersen 6, Kosciecha 2:1, Jagus 7:1, Celmer 0, Holder 14:1.
Aggregate: Won 96-84.

■ **TORUN were the 2008 Ekstraliga champions.**

EKSTRALIGA

	M	*W*	*D*	*L*	*BP*	*Pts*
Czestochowa	14	12	0	2	7	31
TORUN	**14**	**12**	**0**	**2**	**6**	**30**
Leszno	14	10	1	3	4	25
Zielona Gora	14	17	0	7	3	17
Gorzow	14	6	1	7	3	16
Wroclaw	14	4	0	10	4	12
Rzeszow	14	3	0	11	1	7
Tarnow	14	1	0	13	0	2

Continued on page 424

PHOTO: Mariusz Murawski, www.emdwa.pl

The entire 2008 squad celebrate winning the Ekstraliga title after the two-leg final against Leszno

TORUN

Rider	*M*	*R*	*Pts*	*BP*	*TPts*	*Ave*	*F*	*P*	*TR*	*TPts*
Wieslaw JAGUS	19	96	199	16	215	8.96	2	1	0	0
Ryan SULLIVAN	**20**	**97**	**195**	**17**	**212**	**8.74**	**0**	**3**	**0**	**0**
Chris HOLDER	20	103	189	28	217	8.43	0	0	0	0
Hans ANDERSEN	**20**	**98**	**180**	**19**	**199**	**8.12**	**0**	**0**	**1**	**3**
Adrian MIEDZINSKI	17	79	125	26	151	7.65	0	0	0	0
Robert KOSCIECHA	**18**	**83**	**122**	**32**	**154**	**7.42**	**0**	**1**	**0**	**0**
Karol ZABIK	5	20	17	3	20	4.00	0	0	0	0
Damian CELMER	**15**	**20**	**12**	**1**	**13**	**2.60**	**0**	**0**	**0**	**0**
Mateusz LAMPKOWSKI	3	4	2	0	2	2.00	0	0	0	0
Robert KSIEZAK	**2**	**2**	**1**	**0**	**1**	**2.00**	**0**	**0**	**0**	**0**

Polish Ekstraliga

WROCLAW

2008 RESULTS

Ekstraliga

Final position..............................Fifth (Seventh)

GORZOW (A)
Saturday, April 12
Lost 40-53
Max 5, Jeleniewski 4, Jedrzejak 5:1, Schlein 2, Crump 20 (6), Janowski 1, Sitera 3.

TORUN (H)
Sunday, April 13
Lost 41-48
Max 0, Jeleniewski 7, **Jedrzejak 15**, Schlein 2:1, Crump 11, Janowski 2, Sitera 4:1.

RZESZOW (A)
Sunday, April 20
Lost 43-47
Jedrzejak 11, Slabon 4, Jeleniewski 4, Wegrzyk 2, **Crump 15**, Janowski 1, Sitera 6:1.

LESZNO (H)
Thursday, May 1
Lost 46-47
Jedrzejak 14 (6), Slabon 2:1, Jeleniewski 2, Wegrzyk 8:2, Crump 14, Janowski 5:1, Sitera 1.

ZIELONA GORA (H)
Sunday, May 4
Won 53-40
Jedrzejak 14, Slabon 3:1, Jeleniewski 11:1, Wegrzyk 7:2, **Crump 14:1**, Janowski 2:1, Sitera 2.

TARNOW (A)
Friday, May 16
Lost 36-57
Jedrzejak 9:1, Slabon 1, Jeleniewski 4:1, Wegrzyk 0, Crump 17 (6), Janowski 0, Sitera 5:1.

CZESTOCHOWA (H)
Sunday, June 1
Lost 40-50
Jedrzejak 10, Slabon 0, Jeleniewski 8:1, *rider replacement for Sledz*, Crump 15, Janowski 6:1, Sitera 1:1.

CZESTOCHOWA (A)
Sunday, June 8
Lost 33-60
Jedrzejak 6:1, Wegrzyk 5, Jeleniewski 1, Schlein 3, Crump 14 (6), Janowski 3:1, Madsen 1:1.
Aggregate: Lost 73-110.

TRACK FILE

Track: Olympic Stadium, ul. Ignacego Jana Padarewskiego 35, Wroclaw, Poland.
Telephone: 0048 071 3729210.
Website: www.wts.pl
Track Length: 387 metres.
Track Record: 61.1 secs, Jason Crump, June 1, 2008.

SQUAD
Tomasz Jedrzejak, Daniel Jelenlewski, Krzysztof Slabon, Maciej Janowski, Marcin Podlaszewski, Dariusz Sledz, Grzegorz Strozyk, Mariusz Wegrzyk.
Foreign: Ben Barker, Jason Crump, Mikael Max, Leon Madsen, Rory Schlein, Filip Sitera, Andy Smith.

TARNOW (H)
Friday, June 20
Won 61-29
Jedrzejak 10, Slabon 5:2, **Jeleniewski 14:1**, **Wegrzyk 11:4**, **Crump 15**, Janowski 5, Sitera 1.
Aggregate: Won 97-86.

ZIELONA GORA (A)
Sunday, July 6
Lost 43-47
Jedrzejak 9:1, Schlein 4:1, Jeleniewski 6, Wegrzyk 1:1, Crump 14:1, Janowski 9:1, Madsen 0.
Aggregate: Won 96-87.

LESZNO (A)
Sunday, July 20
Lost 29-61
Jedrzejak 6, Schlein 3, Jeleniewski 7, Wegrzyk 3, Slabon 6:1, Janowski 3, Sitera 1.
Aggregate: Lost 75-108.

RZESZOW (H)
Sunday, July 27
Won 62-30
Jedrzejak 12, Slabon 7:1, **Jeleniewski 15**, Wegrzyk 6:1, **Crump 13:2**, Janowski 7, Sitera 2:1.
Aggregate: Won 105-77.

TORUN (A)
Sunday, August 3
Lost 41-49
Jedrzejak 5:1, Slabon 0, Jeleniewski 5, Wegrzyk 2, Crump 16, Janowski 12:2, Sitera 1:1.
Aggregate: Lost 82-97.

GORZOW (H)
Sunday, August 10
Won 53-39
Jedrzejak 8:1, Slabon 6, Jeleniewski 10:3, Wegrzyk 8:1, Crump 12:1, Janowski 5:2, Barker 4.
Aggregate: Won 93-92.

Play offs

Quarter Final, second leg
CZESTOCHOWA (A)
Sunday, August 31
Lost 39-53
Jedrzejak 6:2, Slabon 7, Jeleniewski 4, Wegrzyk 0, Crump 15 (4), Janowski 6:1, Strozyk 1:1.

Quarter Final, second leg
CZESTOCHOWA (H)
Monday, September 1
Lost 32-60
Jedrzejak 5:1, Slabon 5:1, Jeleniewski 4, Wegrzyk 3, Crump, did not ride, Janowski 13:1 (4), Strozyk 2:1.
Aggregate: Lost 71-113.

Individual

GOLDEN HELMET FINAL
Saturday, October 25
Balinski 14, Hampel 13, Miedzinski 11, Swiderski 8, Povazhny 8, Skornicki 8, Jedrzejak 8, Jeleniewski 8, Kosciuch 8, Walasek 8, Protasiewicz 7, Zengota 6, Drabik 5, J. Rempala 4, Trojanowski 3.

Challenge

ZIELONA GORA (A)
Saturday, March 15
Drew 45-45
Jeleniewski 9:1, Wegrzyk 11:1, Slabon 3:1, Jedrzejak 9, no rider, Sitera 9:1, Janowski 4.

ZIELONA GORA (H)
Sunday, March 16
Won 31-29
Jeleniewski 2, Wegrzyk 5, Jedrzejak 8, Slabon 4:2, no rider, Janowski 5:1, Sitera 7.

BYDGOSZCZ (H)
Friday, March 28
Won 58-32
Jeleniewski 11:2, Wegrzyk 10:2, Jedrzejak 13, Slabon 7:2, Max 11, Janowski 3, Sitera 3.

CZESTOCHOWA (H)
Tuesday, April 1
Lost 44-46
Jeleniewski 8, Slabon 5, Jedrzejak 9:1, Schlein 4, Max 4:2, Janowski 4:1, Sitera 4, Wegrzyk 6:1.

WROCLAW 2008
Jason Crump, Daniel Jeleniewski, Mariusz Wegrzyk, Krzysztof Slabon, Filip Sitera, Maciej Janowski, Tomasz Jedrzejak

Rider	M	R	Pts	BP	TPts	Ave	F	P	TR	TPts
Jason CRUMP	14	77	205	5	210	10.91	2	2	4	11
Ben BARKER	**1**	**2**	**4**	**0**	**4**	**8.00**	**0**	**0**	**0**	**0**
Tomasz JEDRZEJAK	16	85	145	9	154	7.25	1	0	1	3
Daniel JELENIEWSKI	**16**	**75**	**106**	**7**	**113**	**6.03**	**1**	**1**	**0**	**0**
Maciej JANOWSKI	16	63	80	11	91	5.78	0	0	0	0
Mariusz WEGRZYK	**13**	**55**	**56**	**10**	**66**	**4.80**	**0**	**1**	**0**	**0**
Krzysztof SLABON	12	50	46	7	53	4.24	0	0	0	0
Filip SITERA	**11**	**35**	**27**	**6**	**33**	**3.77**	**0**	**0**	**0**	**0**
Grzegorz STROZYK	2	6	3	2	5	3.33	0	0	0	0
Rory SCHLEIN	**5**	**21**	**14**	**2**	**16**	**3.05**	**0**	**0**	**0**	**0**
Mikael MAX	2	8	5	0	5	2.50	0	0	0	0
Leon MADSEN	**2**	**5**	**1**	**1**	**2**	**1.60**	**0**	**0**	**0**	**0**

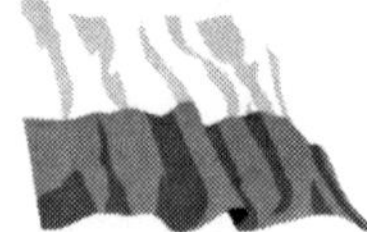

Polish Ekstraliga

ZIELONA GORA

2008 RESULTS

Ekstraliga

Final position..................................Third (Fourth)

GORZOW (H)
Sunday, April 13
Won 53-39
Walasek 10:1, Iversen 5:1, Protasiewicz 12:1, F. Lindgren 6:2, Dobrucki 11:1, Zengota 7:1, Kling 2:1.

TARNOW (A)
Monday, April 14
Won 49-41
Protasiewicz 11:1, Vodyakov 4, Dobrucki 14, Gwozdz, did not ride, Walasek 11, Zengota 5, Kling 4.

TORUN (A)
Sunday, April 20
Lost 34-56
Walasek 12, F. Lindgren 0, Protasiewicz 7, Iversen 3, Dobrucki 6 (0), Zengota 4, Kling 2:1.

RZESZOW (H)
Thursday, May 1
Won 52-39
Walasek 13:1, F. Lindgren 8, Protasiewicz 11:1, Iversen 2:1, Dobrucki 13, Zengota 4, Kling 1.

WROCLAW (A)
Sunday, May 4
Lost 40-53
Walasek 17 (6), F. Lindgren 1:1, Protasiewicz 6:1, Iversen 4, Dobrucki 4, Zengota 8:2, Kling 0.

CZESTOCHOWA (A)
Friday, May 16
Lost 41-49
Walasek 11:1, Iversen 2:2, Protasiewicz 11:1, F. Lindgren 2:1, Dobrucki 11:1, Klindt 0, Zengota 4:1.

LESZNO (H)
Sunday, June 1
Lost 36-57
Walasek 5, *rider replacement for Iversen*, Protasiewicz 1, F. Lindgren 4, Dobrucki 14:1 (6), Zengota 10:1, Vodyakov 2:1.

LESZNO (A)
Sunday, June 8
Lost 40-50
Dobrucki 7:3, Protasiewicz 9, F. Lindgren 9, Kling 2, Walasek 8, Zengota 5:1, Vodyakov 0.
Aggregate: Lost 76-107.

TRACK FILE

Track: Municipal Stadium, ul. Wroclawska 69, 65-218, Zielona Gora, Poland.
Telephone: 0048 068 4538911.
Website: www.zkzssa.pl
Track Length: 340 metres.
Track Record: 60.68 secs, Grzegorz Walasek, June 22, 2006.

SQUAD
Rafal Dobrucki, Adam Kulczynski, Piotr Protasiewicz, Mariusz Staszewski, Grzegorz Walasek, Janusz Baniak, Pawel Gwozdz, Mateusz Lukowiak, Przemyslaw Zarzycki, Grzegorz Zengota.
Foreign: Charlie Gjedde, Niels-Kristian Iversen, Fredrik Lindgren, Ludvig Lindgren, Nicolai Klindt, Ricky Kling, Alexander Kosolapkin, Artem Vodyakov.

CZESTOCHOWA (H)
Friday, June 20
Lost 38-52
Protasiewicz 6:1, Dobrucki 6:1, Iversen 10, Baniak, did not ride, Walasek 5:1, Zengota 7:2, Klindt 4:1.
Aggregate: Lost 79-101.

WROCLAW (H)
Sunday, July 6
Won 47-43
Rider replacement for Dobrucki, Iversen 2, Protasiewicz 12:2, F. Lindgren 13, Walasek 13:1, Zengota 4:1, Kling 3.
Aggregate: Lost 87-100.

RZESZOW (A)
Sunday, July 20
Won 59-33
Rider replacement for Dobrucki, Iversen 14:2, Protasiewicz 13, F. Lindgren 7:1, **Walasek 18**, Zengota 2:1, Kling 5.
Aggregate: Won 111-72.

TORUN (H)
Sunday, July 27
Lost 32-58
Dobrucki 7, Iversen 2, Protasiewicz 5, F. Lindgren 3:1, Walasek 4:1, Zengota 11:1, Kling 0.
Aggregate: Lost 66-114.

GORZOW (A)
Sunday, August 3
Won 49-41
Dobrucki 12:1, Iversen 3, Protasiewicz 5:1, F. Lindgren 9:2, Walasek 9, Zengota 8:1, Kling 3.
Aggregate: Won 102-80.

TARNOW (H)
Sunday, August 10
Won 63-29
Dobrucki 6:2, Iversen 14, Protasiewicz 9:1, **F. Lindgren 11:4, Walasek 10:2**, Zengota 13:1, Baniak 0.
Aggregate: Won 112-70.

Play offs

Round 1, first leg
LESZNO (H)
Thursday, August 28
Won 49-40
Rider replacement for Dobrucki, Baniak 0, Protasiewicz 11:1, F. Lindgren 9:2, Walasek 15, L. Lindgren 3:1, Zengota 11:1.

Round 1, second leg
LESZNO (A)
Sunday, August 31
Lost 38-54
Rider replacement for Dobrucki, Vodyakov 0, Protasiewicz 13:2, F. Lindgren 4, Walasek 16 (4), Zengota 2, Kling 3:2.
Aggregate: Lost 87-94.

Semi Final, first leg
TORUN (H)
Sunday, September 7
Won 48-42
Rider replacement for Dobrucki, L. Lindgren 0, Protasiewicz 13:1, F. Lindgren 14:1, Walasek 17, Kling 3, Zengota 1.

Semi Final, second leg
TORUN (A)
Friday, September 19
Lost 36-57
Dobrucki 1, Iversen 4, Protasiewicz 3, F. Lindgren 11:1, Walasek 13 (6), Vodyakov 3, Zengota 1.
Aggregate: Lost 84-99.

Third place, first leg
CZESTOCHOWA (H)
Sunday, October 5
Won 62-28
Rider replacement for Dobrucki, Iversen 14:2, Protasiewicz 9:5, F. Lindgren 13:3, Walasek 14:2, Zengota 10:1, Vodyakov 2:1.

Third place, second leg
CZESTOCHOWA (A)
Sunday, October 12
Lost 41-51
Rider replacement for Dobrucki, Iversen 0, Protasiewicz 14 (4), F. Lindgren 5, Walasek 11:1, Zengota 6:1, Vodyakov 5:3.
Aggregate: Won 103-79.

EKSTRALIGA

	M	W	D	L	BP	Pts
Czestochowa	14	12	0	2	7	31
Torun	14	12	0	2	6	30
Leszno	14	10	1	3	4	25
ZIELONA GORA	**14**	**17**	**0**	**7**	**3**	**17**
Gorzow	14	6	1	7	3	16
Wroclaw	14	4	0	10	4	12
Rzeszow	14	3	0	11	1	7
Tarnow	14	1	0	13	0	2

Challenges

WROCLAW (H)
Saturday, March 15
Drew 45-45
Walasek 11:1, Klindt 1, Protasiewicz 13, Gjedde 2, Dobrucki 11, Zengota 3, Kling 4:3, Gwozdz, did not ride.

WROCLAW (A)
Sunday, March 16
Lost 29-31
Walasek 7, Kling 1, **Dobrucki 6**, Gjedde 4:1, Protasiewicz 3, Zengota 7, Gwozdz 1:1, Zarzycki 0.

LESZNO (A)
Wednesday, April 2
Lost 44-46
Walasek 11, Kling 3, Dobrucki 6, Gjedde 6:1, Protasiewicz 9, Zengota 8:1, Zarzycki 1, Vodyakov 0.

PAIRS, Sunday, October 26
Walasek (10:2) & Zengota (7) 17, Protasiewicz (11) & Dudek (2:1) 13, Miedzinski (10) & Zabik (1) 11, Suchecki (8) & Baniak (3:2) 11, F. Lindgren (7) & L. Lindgren (1:1) 8.

Individual

Saturday, March 29
Iversen 14, F. Lindgren 12, Suchecki 12, Zengota 9, Pytel 8, Marcinkowski 8, Kosciuch 8, A. Andersen 7, Baniak 7, Klindt 7, Protasiewicz 6, Dziatkowiak 5, Lukowiak 5, Kling 4, Gwozdz 4, Zarzycki 2, Trojanowski 1.

GRZEGORZ WALASEK 15-YEAR TESTIMONIAL
Sunday, March 30
Dobrucki 14, Hampel 13, Iversen 11, Walasek 11, Kuciapa 11, Holta 10, Miedzinski 9, Protasiewicz 8, Gapinski 7, Swist 6, F. Lindgren 5, Richardson 5, Zengota 4, Gizatullin 4, Slabon 3, Karpov 0.

Rider	*M*	*R*	*Pts*	*BP*	*TPts*	*Ave*	*F*	*P*	*TR*	*TPts*
Grzegorz WALASEK	20	113	232	11	243	8.60	1	1	3	8
Rafal DOBRUCKI	**13**	**64**	**112**	**10**	**122**	**7.63**	**0**	**0**	**2**	**3**
Piotr PROTASIEWICZ	20	107	181	19	200	7.48	0	0	1	2
Fredrik LINDGREN	**18**	**89**	**129**	**19**	**148**	**6.65**	**0**	**1**	**0**	**0**
Grzegorz ZENGOTA	20	97	123	16	139	5.73	0	0	0	0
Niels-Kristian IVERSEN	**14**	**64**	**79**	**8**	**87**	**5.44**	**0**	**0**	**0**	**0**
Artem VODYAKOV	7	18	16	5	21	4.67	0	0	0	0
Ricky KLING	**12**	**35**	**28**	**5**	**33**	**3.77**	**0**	**0**	**0**	**0**
Nicolai KLINDT	2	6	4	1	5	3.33	0	0	0	0
Ludvig LINDGREN	**2**	**7**	**3**	**1**	**4**	**2.29**	**0**	**0**	**0**	**0**
Janusz BANIAK	2	4	0	0	0	0.00	0	0	0	0

PHOTO: fotospeedway.pl

LESZNO 2008: Sporting Director Slawomir Kryjom, Krzysztof Kasprzak, Jurica Pavlic (kneeling), Adam Kajoch, Jaroslaw Hampel, Leigh Adams, coach Czeslaw Czernicki, Troy Batchelor, Damian Balinski, club president Jozef Dworakowski

photo: SEBASTIAN MACIEJKO (courtesy of Rzeszow)

RZESZOW 2008: Martin Vaculik, Matej Zagar, Roman Povazhny, Davey Watt, Dawid Stachyra, Scott Nicholls

2009 SQUADS

EIGHT teams will compete in the Polish top-flight with all meeting each other home and away.

The top six then go into the title play-offs with the bottom two racing in.a series of play-offs to avoid relegation to the First League.

Each team must track two riders under the age of 21 and every side now has to include at least three Polish-born riders in their line-up for each official match.

BYDGOSZCZ

Krzysztof **BUCZKOWSKI**, *Tomasz* **CHRZANOWSKI**, *Marcin* **JEDRZEJEWSKI**.
Foreign: *Daniel* **DAVIDSSON**, *Jonas* **DAVIDSSON**, *Andreas* **JONSSON**, *Antonio* **LINDBÄCK**.
UNDER 21
Damian **ADAMCZAK**, *Mikolaj* **CYRULO**, *Miroslaw* **KONIECZNY**, *Michal* **LOPACZEWSKI**, *Szymon* **WOZNIAK**.
Foreign: *Jonas* **ANDERSSON**, *Emil* **SAJFUTDINOV**.

CZESTOCHOWA

Michal **CIURA**, *Slawomir* **DRABIK**, *Tomasz* **GAPINSKI**, *Jordan* **JURCZYNSKI**, *Kamil* **LYKO**, *Rafal* **OSUMEK**, *Sebastian* **PYDZIK**, *Mateusz* **SZCZEPANIAK**, *Michal* **SZCZEPANIAK**, *Artur* **TOMCZYK**.
Foreign: *Greg* **HANCOCK**, *Nicki* **PEDERSEN**, *Lee* **RICHARDSON**.
UNDER 21
Dawid **BAK**, *Marcin* **BUBEL**, *Kamil* **MISTYGACZ**, *Borys* **MITURSKI**, *Adrian* **OMOLSKI**, *Marcin* **PIEKARSKI**, *Czesary* **ROMANCZUK**, *Damian* **ROMANCZUK**.
Foreign: *Lewis* **BRIDGER**, *Jamie* **COURTNEY**, *Alexander* **EDBERG**, *Tai* **WOFFINDEN**.

GDANSK

Marek **MROZ**, *Tomasz* **PISZCZ**, *Adam* **SKORNICKI**.
Foreign: *Hans* **ANDERSEN**, *Kenneth* **BJERRE**, *Renat* **GAFUROV**, *Tobias* **KRONER**, *Joonas* **KYLMÄKORPI**, *Magnus* **ZETTERSTRÖM**.
UNDER 21
Pawel **JACKIEWICZ**, *Damian* **POPLAWSKI**, *Dariusz* **RYBAKOWASKI**, *Damian* **SPERZ**.
Foreign: *Joshua* **AUTY**, *Billy* **FORSBERG**, *Andrey* **KOBRIN**, *Sönke* **PETERSEN**, *Martin* **VACULIK**.

GORZOW

Jacek **GOLLOB**, *Tomasz* **GOLLOB**, *Rafal* **OKONIEWSKI**, *Michal* **RAJKOWSKI**.
Foreign: *Rune* **HOLTA**, *Peter* **KARLSSON**, *David* **RUUD**, *Matej* **ZAGAR**.
UNDER 21
Lukasz **CYRAN**, *Mateusz* **MIKORSKI**, *Adrian* **SZEWCZYKOWSKI**, *Pawel* **ZMARZLIK**.
Foreign: *Thomas H.* **JONASSON**.

LESZNO

Damian **BALINSKI**, *Jaroslaw* **HAMPEL**, *Krzysztof* **KASPRZAK**, *Robert* **KASPRZAK**.
Foreign: *Leigh* **ADAMS**, *Troy* **BATCHELOR**, *Adam* **SHIELDS**.
UNDER 21
Mateusz **JURGA**, *Mateusz* **LUKASZEWSKI**, *Slawomir* **MUSIELAK**, *Przemyslaw* **PAWLICKI**, *Pawel* **RATAJSZCZAK**.
Foreign: *Jurica* **PAVLIC**, *Richard* **SWEETMAN**, *Justin* **SEDGMEN**, *Ryan* **SEDGMEN**.

WROCLAW

Daniel **JELENIEWSKI**, *Tomasz* **JEDRZEJAK**.
Foreign: *Jason* **CRUMP**, *Scott* **NICHOLLS**, *Davey* **WATT**.
UNDER 21
Maciej **JANOWSKI**, *Marek* **LOZOWICKI**.
Foreign: *Dennis* **ANDERSSON**, *Ben* **BARKER**, *Leon* **MADSEN**.

TORUN

Tomasz **BAJERSKI**, *Wieslaw* **JAGUS**, *Robert* **KOSCIECHA**, *Alan* **MARCINKOWSKI**, *Adrian* **MIEDZINSKI**.
Foreign: *Chris* **HOLDER**, *Martin* **SMOLINSKI**, *Ryan* **SULLIVAN**.
UNDER 21
Damian **CELMER**, *Mateusz* **LAMPKOWSKI**, *Lukasz* **LIPINSKI**, *Marcin* **NOWAKOWSKI**, *Oskar* **PIENIAZEK**, *Emil* **PULCZYNSKI**, *Kamil* **PULCZYNSKI**.
Foreign: *Matej* **KUS**, *Darcy* **WARD**.

ZIELONA GORA

Rafal **DOBRUCKI**, *Adam* **KULCZYNSKI**, *Piotr* **PROTASIEWICZ**, *Grzegorz* **WALASEK**.
Foreign: *Niels-Kristian* **IVERSEN**, *Fredrik* **LINDGREN**.
UNDER 21
Patryk **DUDEK**, *Janusz* **BANIAK**, *Pawel* **GWOZDZ**, *Tomasz* **HALICKI**, *Mateusz* **LUKOWIAK**, *Przemyslaw* **ZARZYCKI**, *Grzegorz* **ZENGOTA**.
Foreign: *Ludvig* **LINDGREN**, *Artem* **VODYAKOV**.

Tai Woffinden – back at Czestochowa

TORUN (continued from page 417)

Challenge

GDANSK (A)
Saturday, March 15
Lost 38-40
Jagus 8:1, Miedzinski 7:1, Zabik 8, Kosciecha 4:1, Sullivan 7, Celmer 3, Wisniewski 1:1.

GDANSK (H)
Sunday, March 16
Won 67-25
Andersen 8, Zabik 8:2, Jagus 10:1, Miedzinski 9:2, **Sullivan 11:1**, Holder 9:1, Celmer 3:1, Kosciecha 9:2.

GORZOW (H)
Thursday, March 20
Won 44-33
Jagus 9, Wisniewski 0, Kosciecha 11, Miedzinski 7, **Sullivan 9**, Ksiezak 5, Celmer 1, Lampkowski 2, Lipinski 0.

GDANSK (H)
Thursday, March 27
Drew 39-39
Kosciecha 8, Lampkowski 3, **Jagus 9**, Miedzinski 6:1, Sullivan 7, Celmer 3, Wisniewski 3:1, Lipinski 0.

Individual

GRAND PRIX QUALIFIER
POLISH SEMI-FINAL
Tuesday, April 15
Ulamek 13, Jedrzejak 12, Kosciecha 11, Buczkowski 11, Hampel 10, Miedzinski 10, Zabik 9, Protasiewicz 7, Zengota 7, Stachrya 6, A. Gomolski 6, Staszek 5, Puszakowski 4, Jedrzejewski 3, Hlib 3, Celmer 2, Wisniewski 1, Lampkowski 0, Piszcz 0.
Meeting also served as a domestic qualifying round for the European Championship.

Marcin Celmer rode in 15 matches as Chris Holder's reserve partner – and failed to score in ten of those Ekstraliga matches!

FIRST LEAGUE 2009 FIXTURES

Sunday, April 5
Daugavpils v Grudziadz
Gniezno v Rybnik
Poznan v Tarnow
Rzeszow v Ostrow
Monday, April 13
Grudziadz v Gniezno
Ostrow v Poznan
Rybnik v Rzeszow
Tarnow v Daugavpils
Sunday, April 19
Gniezno v Ostrow
Poznan v Daugavpils
Rybnik v Tarnow
Rzeszow v Grudziadz
Sunday, May 3
Daugavpils v Rzeszow
Grudziadz v Poznan
Ostrow v Rybnik
Tarnow v Gniezno
Sunday, May 10
Gniezno v Daugavpils
Poznan v Rzeszow
Rybnik v Grudziadz
Tarnow v Ostrow
Sunday, May 31
Daugavpils v Rybnik
Rzeszow v Tarnow
Poznan v Gniezno
Grudziądz v Ostrow
Thursday, June 11
Gniezno v Rzeszow
Ostrow v Daugavpils
Rybnik v Poznan
Tarnow v Grudziadz
Sunday June 14
Daugavpils v Ostrow
Grudziadz v Tarnow
Poznan v Rybnik
Rzeszow v Gniezno
Sunday, June 21
Gniezno v Poznan
Ostrow v Grudziadz
Rybnik v Daugavpils
Tarnow v Rzeszow
Sunday, June 28
Daugavpils v Gniezno
Grudziadz v Rybnik
Ostrow v Tarnow
Rzeszow v Poznan
Sunday, July 5
Gniezno v Tarnow
Poznan v Grudziadz
Rybnik v Ostrow
Rzeszow v Daugavpils
Sunday, July 19
Daugavpils v Poznan
Grudziadz v Rzeszow
Ostrow v Gniezno
Tarnow v Rybnik
Sunday, July 26
Daugavpils v Tarnow
Gniezno v Grudziadz
Poznan v Ostrow
Rzeszow v Rybnik
Sunday, August 2
Grudziadz v Daugavpils
Ostrow v Rzeszow
Rybnik v Gniezno
Tarnow v Poznan

PLAY-OFFS

Quarter Final
Sunday, August 9: 6-1; 5-2; 4-3.
Sunday, August 16: 1-6; 2-5; 3-4.

Semi Final
Sunday, August 30
Sunday, September 6

Championship play-off (positions 1-4)
Sunday, September 13
Sunday, September 27

FIRST LEAGUE REGULAR SEASON STANDINGS

	M	W	D	L	PtsF	PtsA	BP	Pts
1 BYDGOSZCZ	14	11	0	3	744	531	7	29
2 GDANSK	14	10	1	3	647	535	4	25
3 †OSTROW	14	11	0	3	718	514	6	21
4 POZNAN	14	6	1	7	629	642	4	17
5 RYBNIK	14	6	0	8	636	598	4	17
6 DAUGAVPILS (Latvia)	14	6	0	8	596	678	1	13
7 GRUDZIADZ	14	5	0	9	586	687	2	12
8 RAWICZ	14	0	0	14	449	820	0	0

FIRST LEAGUE FINAL STANDINGS (after play-off rounds)

	M	W	D	L	PtsF	PtsA	BP	Pts
1 BYDGOSZCZ	20	16	0	4	1059	761	10	42
2 GDANSK	20	13	1	6	938	793	6	33
3 †OSTROW	20	13	0	7	969	808	7	26
4 POZNAN	20	8	1	11	864	952	4	21
5 DAUGAPILS (Latvia)	20	11	0	9	912	907	4	26
6 RYBNIK	20	9	0	11	926	854	6	24
7 GRUDZIADZ	20	8	0	12	847	973	3	19
8 RAWICZ	20	1	0	19	673	1140	0	2

● *OSTROW were deducted seven points after being involved in a 2007 bribery case.*

PROMOTION PLAY-OFF

Gdansk 54 Rzeszow 37
Rzeszow 47 Gdansk 45
Aggregate: Gdansk 99 Rzeszow 84
Gdansk win promotion to the 2009 Ekstraliga.

■ **For full details of Daugavpils see LATVIA.**

BYDGOSZCZ'S stay in the First League mercifully lasted only a season as they dominated the second tier following their 2007 relegation.

And they will be joined in the top flight by runners-up Gdansk who came out on top in their promotion-relegation battle against Ekstraliga Rzeszow.

One defeat in their first eight matches set Tomasz Gollob's old club off on the right foot and they lost only a further two matches to finish on top of the regular season standings.

And in the play-offs they were again an impressive force, with their only defeat coming, surprisingly, at Poznan.

Roll of Honour

1948 ....BYTOM
1949 ....BYDGOSZCZ
1955 ....RYBNIK
1956 ....SWIETOCHLOWICE
1957 ....RZESZOW
1958 ....GNIEZNO
1959 ....RZESZOW
1960 ....WROCLAW
1961 ....GORZOW
1962 ....SWIETOCHLOWICE
1963 ....TARNOW
1964 ....CZESTOCHOWA
1965 ....CZESTOCHOWA
1966 ....LESZNO
1967 ....SWIETOCHLOWICE
1968 ....SWIETOCHLOWICE
1969 ....OPOLE
1970 ....TARNOW
1971 ....ZIELONA GORA
1972 ....LESZNO
1973 ....WROCLAW
1974 ....OPOLE
1975 ....ZIELONA GORA
1976 ....LUBLIN
1977 ....ZIELONA GORA
1978 ....WROCLAW
1979 ....GNIEZNO
1980 ....OPOLE
1981 ....RZESZOW
1982 ....LUBLIN
1983 ....RYBNIK
1984 ....SWIETOCHLOWICE
1985 ....TARNOW
1986 ....GNIEZNO
1987 ....OPOLE
1988 ....OSTROW
1989 ....LUBLIN
1990 ....TARNOW
1991 ....RZESZOW
1992 ....RYBNIK
1993 ....GDANSK
1994 ....PILA
1995 ....GNIEZNO
1996 ....LESZNO
1997 ....GRUDZIADZ
1998 ....WROCLAW
1999 ....CZESTOCHOWA
2000 ....ZIELONA GORA
2001 ....GDANSK
2002 ....ZIELONA GORA
2003 ....RYBNIK
2004 ....GDANSK
2005 ....RZESZOW
2006 ....ZIELONA GORA
2007 ....GORZOW
2008 ....BYDGOSZCZ

Polish First League

BYDGOSZCZ

2008 RESULTS

First League

Final position..........................Champions (First)

RYBNIK (A)
Sunday, April 6
Won 55-38
Okoniewski 10:2, Buczkowski 10:2, Davidsson 7, Stead 9:1, *rider replacement for Jonsson*, Jedrzejeweski 8, E. Sajfutdinov 11:2, Lopaczewski, did not ride.

GDANSK (H)
Sunday, April 13
Won 48-42
Okoniewski 6, Davidsson 3:2, Stead 1:1, Buczkowski 12, Jonsson 4, Jedrzejewski 8:2, E. Sajfutdinov 14, Lopaczewski, did not ride.

OSTROW (A)
Sunday, April 20
Lost 43-46
Okoniewski 6:2, Davidsson 8:2, Buczkowski 2:1, Stead 3, Jonsson 13, Jedrzejewski 4, E. Sajfutdinov 7:1, Lopasczewski, did not ride.

GRUDZIADZ (H)
Thursday, May 1
Won 59-34
Okoniewski 5, Hefenbrock 0, Buczkowski 9:3, Davidsson 9:1, **Jonsson 14:1**, Jedrzejewski 7:2, **E. Sajfutdinov 15**, Lopaczewski 0.

POZNAN (A)
Sunday, May 4
Won 46-44
Okoniewski 4, Hefenbrock 4:1, Buczkowski 3:2, Davidsson 11:1, Jonsson 9, Jedrzejewski 2:1, E. Sajfutdinov 13:1, Lopaczewski, did not ride.

DAUGAVPILS (H)
Sunday, May 11
Won 60-32
Okoniewski 5, Hefenbrock 4:2, Davidsson 11, Buczkoiwski 5:2, **Jonsson 13:2**, Jedrzejewski 7:2, **E. Sajfutdinov 15**, Lopaczewski 0.

RAWICZ (A)
Sunday, June 1
Won 49-41
Okoniewski 13, Stead 1, Davidsson 1, Buczkowski 9:1, Jonsson 12:1, Jedrzejewski 3, E. Sajfutdinov 10:3. Lopaczewski, did not ride.

TRACK FILE

Track: Polonia Stadion, ul. Sportowa 2, 85-091 Bydgoszcz, Poland.
Telephone: 0048 052 5830030.
Website: www.polonia.bydgoszcz.pl
Track Length: 348 metres.
Track Record: 60.11 seconds, Tomasz Gollob, June 29, 1999.

SQUAD
Damian Adamczak, Krzysztof Buczkowski, Jacek Gollob, Rafal Okoniewski, Marcin Jedrzejewski, Michal Lopaczewski.
Foreign: Jonas Davidsson, Christian Hefenbrock, Andreas Jonsson, Denis Sajfutdinov, Emil Sajfutdinov, Simon Stead, Linus Sundström.

RAWICZ (H)
Sunday, June 8
Won 73-17
Okoniewski 13:2, Adamczak, did not ride, **Davidsson 10:2**, **Buczkowski 13:2**, **Jonsson 14:1**, **Jedrzejewski 12:3**, **E. Sajfutdinov 9:3**, Lopaczewski 2:1.
Aggregate: Won 122-58.

DAUGAVPILS (A)
Sunday, June 22
Lost 43-47
Okoniewski 7, Buczkowski 1, Gollob 0, Davidsson 6, Jonsson 14, Jedrzejewski 4:1, E. Sajfutdinov 11:1, Lopaczewski, did not ride.
Aggregate: Won 103-79.

POZNAN (H)
Sunday, July 6
Won 58-35
Okoniewski 12:1, Buczkowski 12:2, Davidsson 6:2, Gollob 11:2, Jonsson 10:1, Lopaczewski 2, Jedrzejewski 5:1.
Aggregate: Won 104-79.

GRUDZIADZ (A)
Sunday, July 20
Won 55-35
Okoniewski 8:1, Gollob 2:1, Buczkowski 11, Davidsson 10:2, Jonsson 12:1, Lopaczewski, did not ride, Jedrzejewski 5, E. Sajfutdinov 7:1.
Aggregate: Won 114-69.

OSTROW (H)
Sunday, July 27
Won 56-36
Okoniewski 8, Gollob 3:1, Davidsson 10:1, Buczkowski 5:1, **Jonsson 14:1**, Lopaczewski, did not ride, Jedrzejewski 3:1, **E. Sajfutdinov 13:2**.
Aggregate: Won 99-82.

GDANSK (A)
Sunday, August 3
Lost 43-47
Okoniewski 6:2, Stead 3, Davidsson 9, Buczkowski 4, Jonsson 12, Lopaczewski, did not ride, Jedrzejewski 0, E. Sajfutdinov 9.
Aggregate: Won 91-89.

RYBNIK (H)
Sunday, August 10
Won 56-37
Okoniewski 9:1, Gollob 5, Davidsson 9:1, Buczkowski 11:1, Jonsson 7:1, Lopaczewski, did not ride, Jedrzejewski 3:1, E. Sajfutdinov 12:2.
Aggregate: Won 111-75.

Play offs

POZNAN (H)
Sunday, August 24
Won 65-28
Okoniewski 17:1, Buczkowski 13:3, **Jonsson 15:3**, Gollob 0, *rider replacement for Davidsson*, Adamczak, did not ride, Jedrzejewski 6:2, E. Sajfutdinov 14.

GDANSK (A)
Sunday, August 31
Won 52-39
Buczkowski 5, *rider replacement for Davidsson*, Okoniewski 13:1, Gollob 5:1, Jonsson 9:1, Jedrzejewski 6:1, E. Sajfutdinov 14:2, Adamczak, did not ride.

OSTROW (A)
Sunday, September 7
Won 47-42
Buczkowski 9:2, *rider replacement for Davidsson*, Jonsson 14:3, Gollob 0, Okoniewski 6:1, Jedrzejewski 6, E. Sajfutdinov 12, Adamczak, did not ride.

OSTROW (H)
Sunday, September 21
Won 57-34
Buczkowski 2, *rider replacement for Davidsson*, Okoniewski 13:1, Gollob 8:2, Jonsson 10:1, Jedrzejewski 11, Adamczak 0, **E. Sajfutdinov 13:2**.
Aggregate: Won 104-76.

POZNAN (A)
Sunday, September 28
Lost 38-51
Okoniewski 10, Gollob 3, Davidsson 1, Adamczak 0, Jonsson 4, Jedrzejewski 3:1, E. Sajfutdinov 17.
Aggregate: Won 103-79.

GDANSK (H)
Sunday, October 5
Won 56-36
Okoniewski 12:1, Gollob 4:2, Davidsson 7:1, Adamczak 0, **Jonsson 14:1**, Jedrzejewski 5:1, **E. Sajfutdinov 14:1**.
Aggregate: Won 108-75.

FIRST LEAGUE

	M	W	D	L	BP	Pts
BYDGOSZCZ	**20**	**16**	**0**	**4**	**10**	**42**
Gdansk	20	13	1	6	6	33
Ostrow	20	13	0	7	7	26
Poznan	20	8	1	11	4	21
Daugavpils	20	11	0	9	4	26
Rybnik	20	9	0	11	6	24
Grudziadz	20	8	0	12	3	19
Rawicz	20	1	0	19	0	2

Challenges

WROCLAW (A)
Friday, March 28
Lost 32-58
Okoniewski 8, Lopaczewski 0, Buczkowski 5:1, Jedrzejewski 8, D. Sajfutdinov 1, E. Sajfutdinov 10.

GORZOW (H)
Tuesday, April 1
Lost 41-43
E. Sajfutdinov 8, D. Sajfutdinov 5:1, Okoniewski 8, no rider, Buczkowski 9:1, Jedzejewski 8:1, Lopaczewski 3.

Other meetings

POLISH CHAMPIONSHIP
Semi Final, Thursday, July 3
1 T. Gollob 14, 2 Jablonski 12, 3 Ulamek 12, 4 Jedrzejak 11, 5 Miedzinski 8, 7 Drabik 8, 8 Swiderski 8, 9 Kolodziej 6+3, 10 Balinski 6+2, 11 Chrzanowski 6+1, 12 Zengota 5, 13 Klecha 4, 14 Knapp 4, 15 Miskowiak 3, 16 Czerwinski 1, 17 Jagus [R], Czechowicz [R], did not ride.

POLISH UNDER 21 PAIRS CHAMPIONSHIP
Eliminating Round, Thursday, May 29
1 ZIELONA GORA 16 (Zengota 12, Dudek 4:1, Gwozdz, did not ride), **2 LESZNO 14** (R. Kasprzak 8, Kajoch 5:1, Pawlicki 1), **3 BYDGOSZCZ 13** (Jedrzejewski 10, Lopaczewski 3:1, Adamczak, did not ride), **4 GDANSK 9** (Sperz 9, C. Szymko 0, M. Szymko 0), **5 GNIEZNO 8** (Musielak 5, K. Gomolski 3:2, Sturomski 0).

■ *For Polish and Final Grand Prix see Grand Prix section. Polish Under 21 Team Championship results see early Poland section.*

Rider	M	R	Pts	BP	TPts	Ave	F	P	TR	TPts
Andreas JONSSON	19	90	213	19	232	10.31	0	6	0	0
Emil SAJFUTDINOV	**19**	**99**	**231**	**20**	**251**	**10.14**	**2**	**4**	**0**	**0**
Rafal OKONIEWSKI	20	98	183	16	199	8.12	0	2	0	0
Krzysztof BUCZKOWSKI	**18**	**83**	**136**	**23**	**159**	**7.66**	**0**	**1**	**0**	**0**
Jonas DAVIDSSON	16	72	118	15	133	7.39	0	1	0	0
Marcin JEDRZEJEWSKI	**20**	**78**	**108**	**19**	**127**	**6.51**	**0**	**1**	**0**	**0**
Christian HEFENBROCK	3	9	8	3	11	4.89	0	0	0	0
Jacek GOLLOB	**11**	**44**	**41**	**9**	**50**	**4.55**	**0**	**0**	**0**	**0**
Simon STEAD	5	19	17	2	19	4.00	0	0	0	0
Michal LOPACZEWSKI	**6**	**6**	**4**	**1**	**5**	**3.33**	**0**	**0**	**0**	**0**
Damian ADAMCZAK	3	4	0	0	0	0.00	0	0	0	0

Polish First League

GDANSK

2008 RESULTS

First League

Final position..Second

DAUGAVPILS (H)
Sunday, April 6
Won 53-39
Chrzanowski 12, Gafurov 5:3, Pedersen 13:1, Jablonski 6:1, Zetterström 11:1, Szymko, did not ride, Forsberg 6:1, Sperz 0.

BYDGOSZCZ (A)
Sunday, April 13
Lost 42-48
Chrzanowski 11, Gafurov 1:1, Zetterström 7:1, Jablonski 8:1, Pedersen 13, Szymko, did not ride, Karpov 2:1, Sperz 0.

GRUDZIADZ (A)
Sunday, April 20
Won 52-38
Chrzanowski 14, Gafurov 1, Zetterström 6:3, Jablonski 13:1, **Pedersen 15**, Szymko, did not ride, Forsberg 2, Sperz 1.

RYBNIK (H)
Thursday, May 1
Won 29-20
Chrzanowski 3:1, **Kroner 6**, Jablonski 5, Zetterström 3:2, Pedersen 7:1, Sperz 5, Karpov 0, Szymko, did not ride.

OSTROW (A)
Sunday, May 4
Lost 19-31
Chrzanowski 6, Kroner 2:1, Jablonski 6 (4), Zetterström 2, *rider replacement for Pedersen*, Szymko 1, Sperz 0, Karpov 2.

RAWICZ (H)
Sunday, May 11
Won 65-25
Chrzanowski 10:2, **Gafurov 12:3**, **Zetterström 10:2**, Kroner 8, **Jablonski 15**, Szymko 2, Sperz 3:2, Auty 5.

POZNAN (A)
Sunday, June 1
Drew 45-45
Chrzanowski 13:1, Gafurov 1, Jablonski 6:1, Zetterström 10:1, Pedersen 12, Szymko, did not ride, Sperz 0, Karpov 3.

TRACK FILE

Track: Olympic Stadium, ul. Zawodnikow 1, 890-729 Gdansk, Poland.
Telephone: 0048 058 3051225.
Website: www.lotosgdansk.pl
Track Length: 349 metres.
Track Record: 63.2 secs,Lars Gunnestad, June 24, 2001.

SQUAD
Tomasz Chrzanowski, Krzysztof Jablonski, Kamil Poplawski, Damian Sperz, Cyprian Szymko.
Foreign: Josh Auty, Billy Forsberg, Renat Gafurov, Andrey Karpov, Andrey Kobrin, Tobias Kroner, Bjarne Pedersen, Magnus Zetterström.

POZNAN (H)
Sunday, June 8
Won 53-38
Chrzanowski 11, Kroner 9:3, Zetterström 7:2, Jablonski 6, **Pedersen 11:1**, Szymko 0, Sperz 6, Forsberg 3:1.
Aggregate: Won 98-83.

RAWICZ (A)
Sunday, June 22
Won 53-37
Chrzanowski 11:1, Kroner 1, Zettterström 9, Jablonski 7:2, **Pedersen 18**, Szymko, did not ride, Sperz 0, Forsberg 7:2.
Aggregate: Won 118-62.

OSTROW (H)
Sunday, July 6
Won 48-42
Chrzanowski 6:2, Gafurov 7:1, Zetterström 11:1, Jablonski 9:2, Pedersen 10, Szymko, did not ride, Sperz 2:2, Forsberg 3.
Aggregate: Lost 67-73.

RYBNIK (A)
Sunday, July 20
Lost 40-50
Chrzanowski 2:1, Gafurov 10, Zetterström 9, Jablonski 2:2, Pedersen 11, Szymko, did not ride, Sperz 1, Forsberg 5:3.
Aggregate: Lost 69-70.

GRUDZIADZ (H)
Sunday, July 27
Won 55-35
Zetterström 12:2, Gjedde 6:1, Gafurov 5:1, Kroner 12:1, **Pedersen 15**, Szymko, did not ride, Forsberg 4:1, Sperz 1.
Aggregate: Won 107-73.

BYDGOSZCZ (H)
Sunday, August 3
Won 47-43
Zetterström 13, Gjedde 6:2, Kroner 4, Gafurov 6, Pedersen 10, Sperz 2, Forsberg 6:1, Szymko, did not ride.
Aggregate: Lost 89-91.

DAUGAVPILS (A)
Sunday, August 10
Won 46-44
Zertterström 10, Jablonski 7, Gafurov 8, Chrzanowski 6:2, Pedersen 13:1, Szymko, did not ride, Sperz 0, Karpov 2.
Aggregate: Won 99-83.

Play offs

BYDGOSZCZ (H)
Sunday, August 31
Lost 39-52
Zetterström 11, Jablonski 2:1, Gafurov 8:1, Chrzanowski 3:1, Pedersen 11, Sperz 2:1, Forsberg 2 (2), Szymko, did not ride.

POZNAN (A)
Sunday, September 7
Lost 42-48
Pedersen 13, Gjedde 2:1, Gafurov 3:2, Kroner 9, Zetterström 10, Sperz 0, Forsberg 5, Szymko, did not ride.

OSTROW (A)
Thursday, September 11
Won 48-43
Zetterström 11:1, Jablonski 7:3, Chrzanowski 10:1, Gafurov 3, Pedersen 10, Szymko, did not ride, Sperz 0, Forsberg 7:2.

POZNAN (H)
Sunday, September 21
Won 66-26
Zetterström 12, Jablonski 6:2, Chrzanowski 12:2, Gafurov 11:3, **Pedersen 15**, Sperz 4, Karpov 6:3, Kobrin 0.
Aggregate: Won 108-74.

OSTROW (H)
Sunday, September 28
Won 60-33
Zetterström 5:2, Jablonski 13:1, Chrzanowski 12:1, Gafurov 11:3, Pedersen 13:1, Szymko, did not ride, Karpov 5:1, Sperz 1:1.
Aggregate: Won 108-76.

BYDGOSZCZ (A)
Sunday, October 5
Lost 36-56
Zetterström 6:1, Jablonski 8, Chrzanowski 12:1 (4), Karpov 3, Pedersen 5:1, Kobrin, did not ride, Szymko 0, Forsberg 2:1.
Aggregate: Lost 75-108.

EKSTRALIGA PROMOTION PLAY-OFF

RZESZOW (H)
Sunday, October 12
Won 54-37
Zetterström 13, Jablonski 7:1, Chrzanowski 4:1, Gafurov 13, Pedersen 12:2, Forsberg 5:1, Kobrin 0.

RZESZOW (A)
Sunday, October 19
Lost 45-47
Zetterström 10:1, Jablonski 1:1, Chrzanowski 8, Gafurov 11:1, Pedersen 11:2 (4), Forsberg 4:1, Kobrin 0.
Aggregate: Won 99-84.

GDANSK were promoted to the 2009 Ekstrliga.

FIRST LEAGUE

	M	*W*	*D*	*L*	*BP*	*Pts*
Bydgoszcz	20	16	0	4	10	42
GDANSK	**20**	**13**	**1**	**6**	**6**	**33**
Ostrow	20	13	0	7	7	26
Poznan	20	8	1	11	4	21
Daugavpils	20	11	0	9	4	26
Rybnik	20	9	0	11	6	24
Grudziadz	20	8	0	12	3	19
Rawicz	20	1	0	19	0	2

● *Magnus Zetterström was Gdansk's only everpresent throughout the 2008 league and play-off campaign.*

Challenges

TORUN (H)
Saturday, March 15
Won 40-38
Chrzanowski 6, K. Jablonski 5:1, Zetterström 5, Gafurov 6:2, Pedersen 2, Sperz 0, Forsberg 7, Kroner 3:1, Karpov 3:2, Szymko 3.

Rider	*M*	*R*	*Pts*	*BP*	*TPts*	*Ave*	*F*	*P*	*TR*	*TPts*
Bjarne PEDERSEN	18	90	215	6	221	9.82	4	1	0	0
Tomasz CHRZANOWSKI	**17**	**75**	**154**	**16**	**170**	**9.07**	**0**	**0**	**1**	**2**
Magnus ZETTERSTRÖM	20	91	176	18	194	8.53	1	1	0	0
Krzysztof JABLONSKI	17	75	125	17	142	7.57	1	0	1	2
Tobias KRONER	**8**	**31**	**51**	**5**	**56**	**7.23**	**0**	**0**	**0**	**0**
Joshua AUTY	1	3	5	0	5	6.67	0	0	0	0
Renat GAFUROV	**15**	**70**	**92**	**18**	**110**	**6.29**	**0**	**1**	**0**	**0**
Charlie GJEDDE	3	14	14	45	18	5.14	0	0	0	0
Billy FORSBERG	**12**	**54**	**52**	**12**	**64**	**4.74**	**0**	**0**	**1**	**1**
Andrey KARPOV	8	29	28	5	33	4.55	0	0	0	0
Damian SPERZ	**19**	**35**	**23**	**6**	**29**	**3.31**	**0**	**0**	**0**	**0**
Cyprian SZYMKO	8	5	3	0	3	2.40	0	0	0	0
Andrey KOBRIN	**1**	**1**	**0**	**0**	**0**	**0.00**	**0**	**0**	**0**	**0**

Statistics do not include the Ekstraliga play-off matches against Rzeszow.

Challenges

TORUN (A)
Sunday, March 16
Lost 25-67
Chrzanowski 11, K. Jablonski 0, Zetterström 8, Gafurov 2, no rider at number five, Szymko 2, Sperz 2.

GNIEZNO (A)
Monday, March 24
Won 49-41
Karpov 13, Szymko 3:2, Kobrin 1, Gafurov 12:1, Jablonski 11, Sperz 8:2, Karol Polak [G] 1.

TORUN (A)
Thursday, March 27
Drew 39-39
K. Jablonski 9, Sperz 3:1, Gafurov 10, Karpov 4:1, Chrzanowski 9, Szymko 4:1, Lukasz Lipinski [G] 0.

GRUDZIADZ (H)
Sunday, March 30
Won 40-38
Zetterström 12, Sperz 3:1, Jablonski 11, Szymko 1, Gafurov 10, Poplawski 1, Kobrin 2.

CZESTOCHOWA (A)
Friday, April 11
Lost 18-60
Zetterström 3, Kroner 2, Jablonski 0, Gafurov 3, Chrzanowski 8, C. Szymko 0, Karpov 2.

GDANSK 2007 (H)
Sunday, September 14
Lost 40-51
Chrzanowski 7:2 (2), Forsberg 5:1, Jablonski 7:2, Gafurov 7, Pedersen 8:1, Sperz 6:1, M. Szymko 0, Poplawski, did not ride).
GDANSK 2007: Greg Hancock 11, Henrik Gustafsson 1, Robert Kosciecha 11:1, Dawid Cieslewicz 5, **Nicki Pedersen 15**, Miroslaw Jablonski 6:1, C. Szymko 1, Andrey Kobrin 1.
Lord Mayor Cup: N. Pedersen, Gafurov, Hancock, B. Pedersen.

Individual

POLISH CHAMPIONSHIP
Quarter Final
Thursday, June 5
Czerwinski 14, Chrzanowski 12, K. Jablonski 11, Knapp 11, Drabik 10, Miedzinski 10, Jagus 10, Okoniewski 8, Mroczka 6, Kosciuch 6, Kajoch 6, Jamrozy 5, Swist 4, Idziorek 3, Sperz 2, Dym 2, Szymko 0.

BRONZE HELMET
FINAL
Friday, September 26
Mroczka 13, Janowski 12, Szewczykowski 11, Sperz 11, Fleger 10, Dudek 9, Lopaczewski 8, K. Gomolski 7, Lampart 6, Musielak 6, Pyszny 5, Miturski 5, Piekarski 5, Celmer 4, Piaszczynski 3, Szostek 2, Kowalczyk 0, Lampkowski 0.

HN NOWAK GMBH CUP
Sunday, October 26
1 PAIR A 19+3 (Jablonski 13:1+3, Kobrin 6:1), 2 PAIR B 19+N (Kamil Brzozowski 13+N, M. Szymko 6:3), 3 PAIR F 13+3 (Piotr Swist 13+3), 4 PAIR D 13+2: Dawid Cieslewicz 13+2), 5 PAIR E 10 (C. Szymko 9, Slawomir Dabrowski 1:1), 6 PAIR C (Gafurov 3, Poplawski 6).

Josh Auty

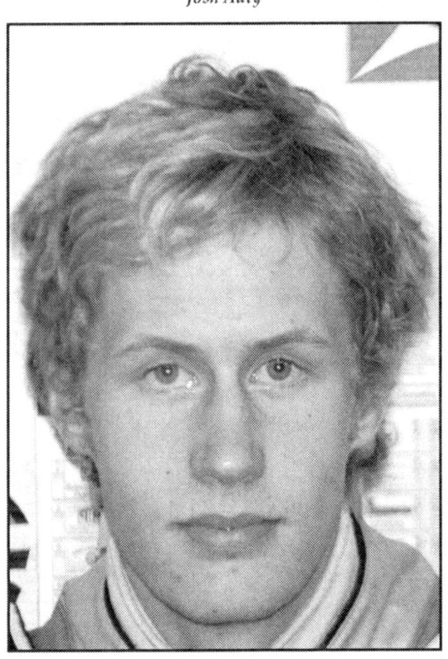
Billy Forsberg

Polish First League

GRUDZIADZ

2008 RESULTS

First League

Final position..Seventh

POZNAN (H)
Sunday, April 6
Won 46-44
Puszakowski 9, Stange 1, Allen 3, Smolinski 9, Staszek 8, Mroczka, did not ride, Risager 7:2, Brzozowski 9:3.

RAWICZ (A)
Sunday, April 13
Won 47-43
Puszakowski 7:1, Klingberg 7, Allen 8:2, Smolinski 11:1, Staszek 6:1, Mroczka 4:1, Brzozowski 1, Risager 3.

GDANSK (H)
Sunday, April 20
Lost 38-52
Puszakowski 9:2, Klingberg 9, Smolinski 0, Allen 7, Staszek 1, Risager 5:1, Brzozowski 6:1, Mroczka 1.

BYDGOSZCZ (A)
Thursday, May 1
Lost 34-59
Allen 3, Staszek 3, Smolinski 3, Stange 6, Puszakowski 9:1, Risager 4:1, Mroczka 0, Brzozowski 6 (6).

RYBNIK (A)
Sunday, May 4
Lost 34-58
Rider replacement for Kowalski, Staszek 1, Klingberg 7, Risager 7:1, Puszakowski 11:1 (4), Mroczka 0, Brzozowski 8.

OSTROW (H)
Sunday, May 11
Won 47-45
Puszakowski 10:1, *rider replacement for Kowalski*, Klingberg 2:1, Andersson 9, **Staszek 18**, Mroczka 1, Brzozowski 7:2, Pedersen, did not ride.

DAUGAVPILS (H)
Sunday, June 8
Won 62-28
Puszakowski 14:1, Andersson 6:1, Allen 9:2, Klingberg 9:2, **Staszek 14:1**, Kaczorowski, did not ride, Mroczka 2:1, Brzozowski 8:1.

TRACK FILE

Track: ul. Hallera 4, 86-300 Grudziadz, Poland.

Telephone: 0048 056 4644442.

Website: www.gtz.grudziadz.net

Track Length: 379 metres.

Track Record: 66.18 secs, Krzysztof Buczkowski, July 13, 2006.

SQUAD
Pawel Kaczorowski, Jacek Krzyzaniak, Mariusz Puszakowski, Pawel Staszek, Kamil Brzozowski, Mateusz Jurga, Rafal Kowalski, Artur Mroczka, Wojciech Zurawski.
Foreign: Oliver Allen, Eric Andersson, Niklas Klingberg, Tommy Pedersen, Robert Pettersson, Morten Risager, Martin Smolinski, Thomas Stange.

DAUGVAPILS (A)
Friday, June 13
Lost 40-52
Puszakowski 8, Andersson 5:3, Allen 11 (6), Stange 1, Staszek 11, Mroczka 3, Brzozowski 1.
Aggregate: Won 102-80.

OSTROW (A)
Sunday, June 22
Lost 40-50
Puszakowski 1, Andersson 3:1, Allen 15, Smolinski 6:1, Staszek 6, Kaczorowski, did not ride, Mroczka 6, Brzozowski 3:1.
Aggregate: Lost 87-95.

RYBNIK (H)
Sunday, July 6
Lost 41-48
Andersson 8:3, *rider replacement for Puszakowski*, Allen 1, Klingberg 9:1, Staszek 12, Mroczka 3:1, Brzozowski 6:1, Risager 2.
Aggregate: Lost 75-106.

BYDGOSZCZ (H)
Sunday, July 20
Lost 35-55
Allen 6:1, Klingberg 4, Puszakowski 8, Andersson 1, Staszek 0, Risager 9:1, Mroczka 7, Brzozowski 0.
Aggregate: Lost 69-114.

GDANSKI (A)
Sunday, July 27
Lost 35-55
Allen 5, Stange 2:1, Smolinski 10, Howe 2:1, Puszakowski 5, Risager 8:1, Mroczka 3:2, Brzozowski 0.
Aggregate: Lost 73-107.

RAWICZ (H)
Sunday, August 3
Won 51-42
Krzyzaniak 3:1, Risager 12:1, Allen 6:1, Howe 6:1, Smolinski 8, Kaczorowski, did not ride, Mroczka 5:2, Brzozowski 11:1.
Aggregate: Won 98-85.

POZNAN (A)
Sunday, August 10
Lost 36-56
Puszakowski 8, Staszek 1, Allen 11 (4), Howe 5:2, Smolinski 1, Kaczorowski, did not ride, Brzozowski 2, Risager 8:1.
Aggregate: Lost 82-100.

Play offs

DAUGAVPILS (H)
Sunday, August 24
Lost 42-50
Klingberg 11, Risager 0, Allen 10:1, Howe 0, Puszakowski 13:1 (4), Kaczorowski, did not ride, Mroczka 3:1, Brzozowski 5:2.

RAWICZ (A)
Sunday, August 31
Won 52-41
Allen 10:1, Staszek 1, Klingberg 5:1, Smolinski 12:1, Puszakowski 10, Brzozowski 5:1, Mroczka 3:2, Risager 6:1.

RYBNIK (A)
Sunday, September 7
Lost 31-61
Rider replacement for Allen, Risager 5, Klingberg 8, Smolinski 0, Puszakowski 3:1, Kaczorowski, did not ride, Mroczka 11:1 (4), Brozozowski 4.

RYBNIK (H)
Sunday, September 21
Won 46-44
Allen 6:1, Klingberg 10:1, Puszakowski 6:1, Andersson 9:1, Staszek 3, Kaczorowski, did not ride, Pedersen 2:1, Brzozowski 10:1.
Aggregate: Lost 77-105.

DAUGVAPILS (A)
Sunday, September 28
Lost 30-60
Puszakowski 5:1, Zurawski 0, Allen 4 (R), Andersson 4:1, Staszek 0, Mroczka 7, Brzozowski 10.
Aggregate: Lost 72-110.

RAWICZ (H)
Sunday, October 5
Won 60-30
Puszakowski 8, Andersson 4:1, Allen 5, Stange 6:1, Klingberg 10:1, Kaczorowski 1, Brzozowski 12:1, **Mroczka 14:1**.
Aggregate: Won 112-71.

DIVISION ONE PLAY-OFF
MISKOLC (H) and MISKOLC (A) – Miskolc withdrew.

FIRST LEAGUE

	M	W	D	L	BP	Pts
Bydgoszcz	20	16	0	4	10	42
Gdansk	20	13	1	6	6	33
Ostrow	20	13	0	7	7	26
Poznan	20	8	1	11	4	21
Daugavpils	20	11	0	9	4	26
Rybnik	20	9	0	11	6	24
GRUDZIADZ	**20**	**8**	**0**	**12**	**3**	**19**
Rawicz	20	1	0	19	0	2

Challenges

GDANSK (A)
Sunday, March 30
Lost 38-40
Puszakowski 6:1, Risager 7:1, Krzyzaniak 1, Andersson 4, Staszek 7, Mroczka 2, Jurga 2:1, Brzozowski 7, Schultz 2.

Pairs

LORD MAYOR CUP PAIRS
Sunday, September 14
1 GRUDZIADZ 19 (Brzozowski 7:1, Artur Mroczka 12), 2 GRUDZIADZ 16 (Puszakowski 10:1, Staszek 6), 3 RAWICZ 14 (Knapp 11, Jamrozy 3), 4 BYDGOSZCZ/ POZNAN 14 (J. Gollob 10, Suchecki 4), 5 BYDGOSZCZ-OPOLE 14 (Jedrzejewski 9, Pawliczel 5:1), 6 BYDGOSZCZ-GRUDZIADZ 11 (Buczkowski 10, Zurawski 1).
Pawel Staszek 15-year Benefit: Staszek, Brzozowski, Puszakowski, Mroczka.
Robert Dados Memorial: Knapp, J. Gollob, Puszakowski, Mroczka, did not ride.
■ ***For Polish Under 21 Pairs Championship semi final see main section.***

Rider	M	R	Pts	BP	TPts	Ave	F	P	TR	TPts
Oliver ALLEN	17	76	120	11	131	6.89	0	0	2	5
Niklas KLINGBERG	**12**	**58**	**91**	**7**	**98**	**6.76**	**0**	**0**	**0**	**0**
Mariusz PUSZAKOWSKI	18	94	144	12	156	6.64	0	1	2	4
Morten RISAGER	**13**	**55**	**76**	**10**	**86**	**6.25**	**0**	**0**	**0**	**0**
Kamil BRZOZOWSKI	20	81	114	15	129	6.37	0	0	1	3
Pawel STASZEK	**15**	**57**	**85**	**2**	**87**	**6.11**	**1**	**1**	**0**	**0**
Eric ANDERSSON	9	41	49	12	61	5.95	0	0	0	0
Martin SMOLINSKI	**10**	**43**	**60**	**3**	**63**	**5.86**	**0**	**0**	**0**	**0**
Artur MROCZKA	17	59	73	12	85	5.76	0	1	1	2
Jacek KRZYZANIAK	**1**	**3**	**3**	**1**	**4**	**5.33**	**0**	**0**	**0**	**0**
David HOWE	4	13	13	4	17	5.23	0	0	0	0
Thomas STANGE	**5**	**14**	**16**	**2**	**18**	**5.14**	**0**	**0**	**0**	**0**
Tommy PEDERSEN	1	3	2	1	3	4.00	0	0	0	0
Pawel KACZOROWSKI	**1**	**3**	**1**	**0**	**1**	**1.33**	**0**	**0**	**0**	**0**
Wojciech ZURAWSKI	1	1	0	0	0	0.00	0	0	0	0

Polish First League

OSTROW

2008 RESULTS

First League

Final position...Third

RAWICZ (H)
Sunday, April 6
Won 70-21
Dryml 12:1, **Nermark 9:3**, **Kylmåkorpi 14:1**, Ruud 5, **Harris 14:1**, Idziorek, did not ride, Piaszczynski 4:2, **Gomolski 12:3**.

POZNAN (A)
Sunday, April 13
Won 66-25
Dryml 14, Korneliussen 5:2, **Kylmåkorpi 15**, King 7:3, **Harris 13:2**, Idziorek, did not ride, Piaszczynski 3, Gomolski 9:3.

BYDGODZCZ (H)
Sunday, April 20
Won 46-43
Dryml 10:1, King 3:1, Kylmåkorpi 8:2, Nermark 13, Harris 8:1, Idziorek, did not ride, Piaszczynski 0, Gomolski 4.

■ Bydgoszcz unsuccessfully protested Nermark's engine after the meeting.

DAUGAVPILS (A)
Thursday, May 1
Won 49-43
Dryml 6, Miskowiak 4:1, Kylmåkorpi 10, Korneliussen 8:1, Harris 13, Sroka, did not ride, Piaszczynski 0, Gomolski 8:2.

GDANSK (H)
Sunday, May 4
Won 31-19
Dryml 4, Korneliussen 2:1, **Kylmåkorpi 5:1**, Nermark 4, **Harris 9**, Sroka, did not ride, Piaszczynski 2, Gomolski 5.

GRUDZIADZ (A)
Sunday, May 11
Lost 45-47
Dryml 17 (6), Korneliussen 1, Kylmåkorpi 5, Nermark 2, Harris 4:1, Sroka, did not ride, Roynon 3:1, Gomolski 13:3.

RYBNIK (H)
Sunday, June 1
Won 54-37
Dryml 6:1, Miskowiak 10:1, Kylmåkorpi 9:1, Ruud 10:1, Harris 8:3, Idziorek 0, Sroka, did not ride, Gomolski 11:1.

TRACK FILE

Track: ul. Paderewskiego 2-6, 63-400 Ostrow Wlkp., Poland.
Telephone: 0048 062 7387097.
Website: www.km.osw.pl
Track Length: 372 metres.
Track Record: 63.40 secs, Chris Harris, April 20, 2008.

SQUAD
Zbigniew Czerwinski, Lukasz Jankowski, Robert Miskowiak, Rafal Szombierski, Adrian Gomolski, Mateusz Gorzelanczyk, Emil Idziorek, Michal Kryjom, Maciej Piaszczynski, Karol Sroka, Piotr Szostak.
Foreign: Robin Aspegren, Lukas Dryml, Chris Harris, Daniel King, Mads Korneliussen, Igor Kononov, Joonas Kylmåkorpi, Kyle Legault, Daniel Nermark, Adam Roynon, David Ruud.

RYBNIK (A)
Sunday, June 8
Won 48-42
Dryml 8:1, Miskowiak 3, Kylmåkorpi 6:2, Ruud 9:1, Harris 8:2, Idziorek, did not ride, Piaszczynski 0, Gomolski 14.
Aggregate: Won 102-79.

GRUDZIADZ (H)
Sunday, June 22
Won 50-40
Miskowiak 10:1, *rider replacement for Kylmåkorpi*, Nermark 10:3, Ruud 13:2, Korneliussen 2:2, Piaszczynski 0, Idziorek 1, Gomolski 14.
Aggregate: Won 95-87.

GDANSK (A)
Sunday, July 6
Lost 42-48
King 7, Kylmåkorpi 9:1, Ruud 3:1, Nermark 12, Miskowiak 1, Idziorek, did not ride, Piaszczynski 0, Gomolski 10.
Aggregate: Won 73-67.

DAUGVAPILS (H)
Sunday, July 20
Won 62-28
King 11:2, Kylmåkorpi 7, Nermark 7:2, Ruud 13:1, Korneliussen 8:2, Idziorek 3, Piaszczynski 0, Gomolski 13:1.
Aggregate: Won 111-71.

BYDGOSZCZ (A)
Sunday, July 27
Lost 36-56
Harris 11:2 (4), Ruud 4:1, King 2:1, Kymåkorpi 8:1, Miskowiak 0, Piaszczynski, did not ride, Idziorek 0, Gomolski 11.
Aggregate: Lost 82-99.

Ostrow started the season with a seven point deduction due to bribery charge relating to the 2007 season.

POZNAN (H)
Sunday, August 3
Won 54-39
Harris 11:3, Ruud 9:1, King 11, Kylmåkorpi 9:3, Idziorek 1:1, Sroka, did not ride, Piaszczynski 2, Gomolski 11.
Aggregate: Won 120-64.

RAWICZ (A)
Sunday, August 10
Won 65-26
Harris 5:2, **Ruud 14:1**, King 7:3, Miskowiak 13, **Dryml 13:2**, Piaszczynski, did not ride, Idziorek 0, Gomolski 13:1.
Aggregate: Won 135-47.

Play offs

POZNAN (A)
Sunday, August 31
Won 47-42
Dryml 5:1, King 8, Harris 13, Ruud 8:2, Korneliussen 1, Piaszczynski 0, Kononov 0, Gomolski 12.

BYDGOSZCZ (H)
Sunday, September 7
Lost 42-47
Dryml 10, King 3, Harris 11:3, Ruud 10, Nermark 5, Piaszczynski 0, Kononov 3:1, Gomolski 0.

GDANSK (H)
Thursday, September 11
Lost 43-48
Ruud 13:1, Nermark 0, Dryml 5:1, Miskowiak 8, Harris 14 (2), Idziorek, did not ride, Kononov 2, Piaszczynski 1.

BYDGOSZCZ (A)
Sunday, September 21
Lost 34-57
Szostak 2, *rider replacement for Gomolski*, Miskowiak 15, Sroka 0, Ruud 13 (2), Piaszczynski 1, Idziorek 3.
Aggregate: Lost 76-104.

GDANSK (A)
Sunday, September 28
Lost 33-60
Rider replacement for Gomolski, Sroka 0, Miskowiak 12:1, Szostak 0, Ruud 13 (6), Piaszczynski 5, Idziorek 3.
Aggregate: Lost 76-108.

POZNAN (H)
Sunday, October 5
Won 52-40
Miskowiak 10:1, Korneliussen 5:1, King 12:1, Harris 9:1, Ruud 13, Piaszczynski 2, Idziorek 1:1, Sroka, did not ride.
Aggregate: Won 99-82.

FIRST LEAGUE

	M	W	D	L	BP	Pts
Bydgoszcz	20	16	0	4	10	42
Gdansk	20	13	1	6	6	33
OSTROW	**20**	**13**	**0**	**7**	**7**	**26**
Poznan	20	8	1	11	4	21
Daugavpils	20	11	0	9	4	26
Rybnik	20	9	0	11	6	24
Grudziadz	20	8	0	12	3	19
Rawicz	20	1	0	19	0	2

Challenges

LESZNO (H)
Saturday, March 15
Lost 43-47
Dryml 8, Idziorek 0, Czerwinski 8:2, Rafal Szombierski 6:1, Miskowiak 9:1, Piaszczynski 3:1, Gomolski 9:1, Sroka, did not ride.

LESZNO (A)
Monday, March 17
Lost 28-50
Dryml 5, Idziorek 2, Sroka 0, Szombierski 3:1, Miskowiak 6:1, Piasszczynski 5:2, Gomolski 7.

TARNOW (H)
Friday, March 28
Won 53-37
Dryml 6, Ruud 4:1, Miskowiak 5:1, Legault 3, Czerwinski 3, Piaszczynski 7:1, **Gomolski 8:1**, Roynon 3:1, Aspegren 1, Idziorek 2:1, Kus 3:1, **Korneliussen 8:1**.

Ostrow's seven point starting penalty effectively wiped out their season's bonus point tally. Had they not started the season under such a handicap they would actually have finished runners-up and faced Rzeszow in the promotion play-offs.

For Individual meetings see page 441

Rider	M	R	Pts	BP	TPts	Ave	F	P	TR	TPts
Adrian GOMOLSKI	16	76	160	14	174	9.16	0	1	0	0
Chris HARRIS	**15**	**75**	**151**	**21**	**172**	**9.17**	**1**	**2**	**2**	**3**
Joonas KYLMÅKORPI	12	56	105	12	117	8.36	1	2	0	0
Lukas DRYML	**12**	**56**	**110**	**8**	**118**	**8.43**	**0**	**1**	**1**	**3**
David RUUD	15	78	150	12	162	8.31	0	1	2	4
Daniel NERMARK	**9**	**35**	**62**	**8**	**70**	**8.00**	**0**	**1**	**0**	**0**
Daniel KING	10	46	71	11	82	7.13	0	0	0	0
Robert MISKOWIAK	**11**	**54**	**86**	**4**	**90**	**6.67**	**0**	**0**	**0**	**0**
Mads KORNELIUSSEN	8	27	32	9	41	6.07	0	0	0	0
Adam ROYNON	**1**	**3**	**3**	**1**	**4**	**5.33**	**0**	**0**	**0**	**0**
Maciej PIASZCZYNSKI	18	32	20	2	22	2.75	0	0	0	0
Emil IDZIOREK	**10**	**25**	**12**	**2**	**14**	**2.24**	**0**	**0**	**0**	**0**
Igor KONONOV	3	11	5	1	6	2.18	0	0	0	0
Piotr SZOSTAK	**2**	**6**	**2**	**0**	**2**	**1.33**	**0**	**0**	**0**	**0**
Karol SROKA	2	6	0	0	0	0.00	0	0	0	0

Polish First League

POZNAN

TRACK FILE

Track: Olympic Stadium, ul. Warminska 1, 60-622 Poznan, Poland.
Telephone: 0048 061 8436396.
Website: www.pszpoznan.pl
Track Length: 397 metres.
Track Record: 66.27 secs, Adam Skornicki, August 10, 2008.

SQUAD
Piotr Dziatkowiak, Lukasz Jankowski, Grzegorz Klopot, Norbert Kosciuch, Alan Marcinkowski, Daniel Pytel, Adam Skornicki, Zbigniew Suchecki, Rafal Trojanowski.
Foreign: Anders Andersen, Kauko Nieminen.

2008 RESULTS

First League

Final position ....Fourth

GRUDZIADZ (A)
Sunday, April 6
Lost 44-46
Kosciuch 13:2, *rider replacement for Skornicki*, Jankowski 5, Trojanowski 9:1, Suchecki 3, Andersen 0, Dziatkowiak, did not ride, Pytel 14:1.

OSTROW (H)
Sunday, April 13
Lost 25-66
Kosciuch 6, Klopot 5:1, Jankowski 4, Suchecki 0, Trojanowski 8 (2), Andersen 0, Dziatkowiak 1, Pytel 1:1.

DAUGVAPILS (H)
Sunday, April 20
Won 60-29
Kosciuch 13:2, Klopot 5, Skornicki 9, Jankowski 11:3, Trojanowski 8:1, Andersen 1, Dziatkowiak, did not ride, Pytel 13.

RAWICZ (A)
Thursday, May 1
Won 50-40
Kosciuch 10:1, Marcinkowski 8:1, *rider replacement for Jankowski*, Trojanowski 10:2, Skornicki 14:1, Dziatkowiak, did not ride, Andersen 0, Pytel 8.

BYDGOSZCZ (H)
Sunday, May 4
Lost 44-46
Trojanowski 15:1, *rider replacement for Jankowski*, Kosciuch 13:2, Marcinkowski 3, Scornicki 11:1, Andersen, did not ride, Dziatkowiak 0, Pytel 2.

RYBNIK (A)
Sunday, May 11
Won 46-44
Skornicki 17, *rider replacement for Jankowski*, Kosciuch 13:2, Klopot 4:3, Trojanowski 9:1, Dziatkowiak 0, Andersen, did not ride, Pytel 3.

GDANSK (H)
Sunday, June 1
Drew 45-45
Kosciuch 3:1, Jankowski 9:1, Skornicki 9, Klopot 9, Trojanowski 11, Dziatkowiak 1:1, Pytel 3.

GDANSK (A)
Sunday, June 8
Lost 38-53
Skornicki 10:2, Klopot 1, Kosciuch 7 (2), Jankowski 7:1, Trojanowski 12, Dziatkowiak 1, Pytel 0.
Aggregate: Lost 83-98.

RYBNIK (H)
Sunday, June 22
Won 47-44
Skornicki 12, Nieminen 2, Kosciuch 11, Klopot 1, Trojanowski 8:1, no rider at six, Dziatkowiak 3, Pytel 10:4.
Aggregate: Won 93-88.

BYDGOSZCZ (A)
Sunday, July 6
Lost 35-58
Skornicki 16 (6), Klopot 2, Kosciuch 8:1, no rider at four, Trojanowski 2, Dzioatkowiak 1, no rider at seven, Pytel 6.
Aggregate: Lost 79-104.

RAWICZ (H)
Sunday, July 20
Won 66-23
Skornicki 11:2, Klopot 8:1, Kosciuch 12:1, Suchecki 11:1, Trojanowski 10:1, Dziatkowiak 5:1, Pytel 9:1.
Aggregate: Won 116-63.

DAUGAVPILS (A)
Sunday, July 27
Lost 34-58
Kosciuch 12:2, Klopot 4, Trojanowski 2, Suchecki 3, Skornicki 9 (4), Dziatkowiak 0, Pytel 4.
Aggregate: Won 94-87.

OSTROW (A)
Sunday, August 3
Lost 39-54
Rider replacement for Kosciuch, Klopot 0, Trojanowski 6, Suchecki 2:1, Skornicki 14:1, Dziatkowiak 2, Pytel 15:2 (6).
Aggregate: Lost 64-120.

GRUDZIADZ (H)
Sunday, August 10
Won 56-36
Skornicki 13:2, Klopot 7, Kosciuch 6, Suchecki 9:1, **Trojanowski 13:2**, Dziatkowiak 0, Pytel 8:1.
Aggregate: Won 100-82.

Play offs

BYDGOSZCZ (A)
Sunday, August 24
Lost 28-65
Skornicki 12:1 (6), Klopot 2:1, Kosciuch 2:1, Suchecki 5, *rider replacement for Trojanowski*, Dziatkowiak 0, Pytel 7.

OSTROW (H)
Sunday, August 31
Lost 42-47
Skornicki 9:2, Marcinkowski 8:2, Kosciuch 8, Suchecki 4:1, Trojanowski 1:1, Dziatkowiak 2, Pytel 10:1.

GDANSK (H)
Sunday, September 7
Won 48-42
Skornicki 10:3, Marcinkowski 5, Kosciuch 9:1, Suchecki 2, Trojanowski 12, Dziatkowiak 4:1, Pytel 6:1.

GDANSK (A)
Sunday, September 21
Lost 26-66
Skornicki 10 (4), Marcinkowski 2, Kosciuch 5, Suchecki 1:1, Trojanowski 6, no rider at six, Dziatkowiak 1, Andersen 1.
Aggregate: Lost 74-108.

BYDGOSZCZ (H)
Sunday, September 28
Won 51-38
Skornicki 12, Marcinkowski 2:2, Kosciuch 10:2, Suchecki 11:1, Trojanowski 9, Dziatkowiak 0, Pytel 7:1, Andersen, did not ride.
Aggregate: Lost 79-103.

OSTROW (A)
Sunday, October 5
Lost 40-52
Skornicki 12, Marcinkowski 0, Kosciuch 9:1 (4), Suchecki 6, Trojanowski 4:2, Dziatkowiak 0, Pytel 9:1.
Aggregate: Lost 82-99.

FIRST LEAGUE

	M	*W*	*D*	*L*	*BP*	*Pts*
Bydgoszcz	20	16	0	4	10	42
Gdansk	20	13	1	6	6	33
Ostrow	20	13	0	7	7	26
POZNAN	**20**	**8**	**1**	**11**	**4**	**21**
Daugavpils	20	11	0	9	4	26
Rybnik	20	9	0	11	6	24
Grudziadz	20	8	0	12	3	19
Rawicz	20	1	0	19	0	2

Challenges

GNIEZNO (H)
Friday, March 28
Won 58-32
Kosciuch 11:3, Marcinkowski 7:1, Trojanowski 11, Andersen 6:2, Suchecki 8:1, Dziatkowiak 7, Pytel 8.

RAWICZ (A)
Sunday, March 30
Drew 48-48
Kosciuch 10:1, Marcinkowski 9:2, Trojanowski 9, Klopot 5:1, Suchecki 7, Pytel 3:1, Andersen 5.

GNIEZNO (A)
Friday, April 4
Won 51-39
Kosciuch 8:1, Marcinkowski 4, Trojanowski 9, Klopot 6:2, Suchecki 8:1, Dziatkowiak 3:1, Pytel 4:1, Andersen, did not ride, Jankowski 9.

Individual

2009 GRAND PRIX QUALIFIER
Polish Semi Final
Thursday, April 10
Walasek 15, Dobrucki 13, Michal Szczepaniak 11, Gapinski 11, Jeleniewski 11, K. Kasprzak 10, Swiderski 9, Kolodziej 5, Slabon 5, K. Jablonski 5, Klecha 5, Okoniewski 4, Marcinkowski 3, Trojanowski 3, Pytel 3, Mateusz Szczepaniak 1, Klopot 0, Szombierski 0.

POLISH UNDER 21 CHAMPIONSHIP
Semi Final
Thursday, July 10
Pawlaszczyk 13, Zengota 13, Brzozowski 12, Kajoch 11, Janowski 10, Mitko 10, Szewczykowski 9, Mroczka 8, Pytel 7, Sperz 7, Celmer 5, Lampkowski 5, Musielak 4, Kajzer 3, Piekarski 2, Mikorski 1, Dziatkowiak 0, Baniak 0.

Continued on page 447

Rider	*M*	*R*	*Pts*	*BP*	*TPts*	*Ave*	*F*	*P*	*TR*	*TPts*
Adam SKORNICKI	18	100	210	15	225	9.00	0	1	4	10
Norbert KOSCIUCH	**19**	**102**	**170**	**20**	**190**	**7.45**	**0**	**1**	**2**	**3**
Rafal TROJANOWSKI	19	96	155	13	168	7.00	0	1	1	1
Lukasz JANKOWSKI	**5**	**25**	**36**	**5**	**41**	**6.56**	**0**	**0**	**0**	**0**
Daniel PYTEL	19	100	135	14	149	5.96	0	0	1	3
Zbigniew SUCHECKI	**12**	**53**	**57**	**6**	**63**	**4.75**	**0**	**0**	**0**	**0**
Grzegorz KLOPOT	12	49	48	7	55	4.49	0	0	0	0
Alan MARCINKOWSKI	**7**	**32**	**28**	**5**	**33**	**4.13**	**0**	**0**	**0**	**0**
Piotr DZIATKOWIAK	17	31	21	3	24	3.10	0	0	0	0
Kauko NIEMINEN	**1**	**5**	**2**	**0**	**2**	**1.60**	**0**	**0**	**0**	**0**
Anders ANDERSEN	5	8	2	0	2	1.00	0	0	0	0

2008 RESULTS

First League

Final position..Eighth

OSTROW (A)
Sunday, April 6
Lost 21-70
Kolenko 10 (2), Dym 0, Jamrozy 1, Vlasov 3, Knapp 4, Kajzer 2:1, Pudel 1.

GRUDZIADZ (H)
Sunday, April 13
Lost 43-47
Doyle 8, Dym 2, Zieja 0, Jamrozy 15, Knapp 6:2, Kajzer 11, Pudel 1, Ratajszczak, did not ride.

RYBNIK (A)
Sunday, April 20
Lost 32-60
Jamrozy 12 (4), Vlasov 0, Nowaczyk 1, Knapp 10:1, Doyle 1, Kajzer 5, Ratajszczak 3.

POZNAN (H)
Thursday, May 1
Lost 40-50
Dym 14, Doyle 2:1, Knapp 1, Gustafsson 2, Jamrozy 10, Ratajszczak, did not ride, Jakobsen 1, Kajzer 10:1.

DAUGAVPILS (A)
Sunday, May 4
Lost 32-60
Knapp 10, *rider replacement for Kolenko*, Dym 8, no rider at four, Jamrozy 10 (4), Kajzer 2, Ratajszczak 2.

GDANSK (A)
Sunday, May 11
Lost 25-65
Jamrozy 3, Nowaczyk 3 (R), Knapp 6, Zieja 0, Dym 7, Kajzer 6, Pudel 0.

BYDGOSZCZ (H)
Sunday, June 1
Lost 41-49
Rider replacement for Kolenko, Knapp 6, Jamrozy 6:2, Nowaczyk 8:2, Dym 9, Ratajszczak, did not ride, Pudel 0, Kajzer 12.

Rawicz's only victory of the season came in the play-offs when they beat Rybnik in their final home match. It ended a seasonal run of 18 straight defeats.

TRACK FILE

Track: Florian Kapala Stadium, ul. Spokopjna 1, 63-900 Rawicz, Poland.
Telephone: 0048 065 5453526.
Website: No official website.
Track Length: 330 metres.
Track Record: 61.78 secs, Piotr Swiderski, May 23, 2004.

SQUAD
Piotr Dym, Ronnie Jamrozy, Marcel Kajzer, Grzegorz Knapp, Rafal Krygiel, Marcin Nowaczyk, Pawel Ratajszczak, Andrzej Zieja.
Foreign: Jason Doyle, Jordan Frampton, Henrik Gustafsson, Klaus Jakobsen, Jernej Kolenko, Mark Lemon, Nicola Martinec, Erik Pudel, Andrew Tully, Semen Vlasov, Casper Wortmann.

BYDGOSZCZ (A)
Sunday, June 8
Lost 17-73
Jamrozy 4, no rider at two, Nowaczyk 1, Knapp 4, Dym 6, Kajzer 2, Ratajszczak 0.
Aggregate: Lost 58-122.

GDANSK (H)
Sunday, June 22
Lost 37-53
Jamrozy 7, Doyle 9:1 (FX), Nowaczyk 3:1, Knapp 1, Dym 3, Ratajszczak, did not ride, Tully 4:1, Kajzer 10.
Aggregate: Lost 62-118.

DAUGAVPILS (H)
Sunday, July 6
Lost 42-48
Dym 7:1, Jamrozy 10:2, Doyle 4, Frampton 2, Lemon 8:1, Ratajszczak, did not ride, Pudel 1, Kajzer 10:2.
Aggregate: Lost 74-108.

POZNAN (A)
Sunday, July 20
Lost 23-66
Jamrozy 5:1, Nowaczyk 4, Lemon 4, Knapp 6, Dym 1, Ratajszczak, did not ride, Tully 0, Kajzer 3.
Aggregate: Lost 63-116.

RYBNIK (H)
Sunday, July 27
Lost 28-63
Dym 7:1, Nowaczyk 2, Knapp 7:1, Vlasov 1, Jamrozy 8 (2), Ratajszczak 0, Tully 1, Kajzer 2.
Aggregate: Lost 60-123.

GRUDZIADZ (A)
Sunday, August 3
Lost 42-51
Vlasov 3, Knapp 9, Jamrozy 13, Nowaczyk 14:3 (6), Dym 1, no rider at six, Ratajszczak 0, Pudel 2.
Aggregate: Lost 85-98.

OSTROW (H)
Sunday, August 10
Lost 26-65
Jamrozy 6, no rider at two, Knapp 4:1, Jamrozy 4:1, Nowaczyk 8 (2), Ratajszczak 0, Pudel 2:1, Kajzer 2.
Aggregate: Lost 47-135.

Play offs

RYBNIK (A)
Sunday, August 24
Lost 35-54
Knapp 11, no rider at two, Nowaczyk 4, Dym 1, Jamrozy 11:1, no rider at six, Ratajszczak 0, Kajzer 8:2.

GRUDZIADZ (H)
Sunday, August 31
Lost 41-52
Nowaczyk 3, Knapp 7:1, Jamrozy 15 (6), Doyle 9:1, Dym 3, no rider at six, Ratajszczak 0, Kajzer 4.

DAUGAVPILS (H)
Sunday, September 7
Lost 41-49
Dym 11:1, Jamrozy 8:1, Doyle 12:1, Knapp 4:3, Nowaczyk 3:1, Ratajszczak, did not ride, Pudel 1, Kajzer 2.

DAUGAVPILS (A)
Sunday, September 21
Lost 29-61
Dym 2, Jamrozy 9:1, Nowaczyk 3, no rider at four, Knapp 7, no rider at six, Ratajszczak 0, Kajzer 8.
Aggregate: Lost 70-110.

RYBNIK (H)
Sunday, September 28
Won 48-44
Jamrozy 10, Nowaczyk 5:2, Doyle 9:2, Knapp 10:1, Dym 5, Ratajszczak, did not ride, Pudel 2, Kajzer 7.
Aggregate: Lost 83-98.

GRUDZIADZ (A)
Sunday, October 5
Lost 30-60
Knapp 8, Dym 5:3, Nowaczyk 8, no rider at four, Jamrozy 8:1, no rider at six, Ratajszczak 0, Kajzer 1.
Aggregate: Lost 71-112.

FIRST LEAGUE

	M	W	D	L	BP	Pts
Bydgoszcz	20	16	0	4	10	42
Gdansk	20	13	1	6	6	33
Ostrow	20	13	0	7	7	26
Poznan	20	8	1	11	4	21
Daugavpils	20	11	0	9	4	26
Rybnik	20	9	0	11	6	24
Grudziadz	20	8	0	12	3	19
RAWICZ	**20**	**1**	**0**	**19**	**0**	**2**

Challenges

POZNAN (H)
Sunday, March 30
Drew 48-48
Zieja 5:1, Jakobsen 1, Knapp 7:1, Pudel 0, Jamrozy 6, Kajzer 5:1, Ratajszczak 2, Nowaczyk 6, Vlasov 9:1, Dym 7:1.

CZESTOCHOWA (H)
Monday, March 31
Drew 48-48
Dym 12:1, Vlasov 10:3, Jamrozy 7, Nowaczyk 8:2, Knapp 7, Jakobsen 2, Kajzer 2, Ratajszczak, did not ride.

BALAKOVO (Russia) (A)
Thursday, April 3
Lost 44-46
Nowaczyk 6, Vlasov 7, Zieja 4, Dym 10, Jamrozy 10, Kajzer 4, Andrey Kudriashov [G] 3.

Individual

EUROPEAN UNDER 19 CHAMPIONSHIP
POLISH FINAL
Wednesday, April 9
Kajzer 15, Mroczka 13, Janowski 12, Lopaczewski 10, Miturski 9, Zmarzlik 8, Szewczykowski 8, Szymura 8, Fleger 7, Piaszczynski 7, Piekarski 7, Idziorek 4, Gwozdz 4, S.Kielbasa 3, Kowalczyk 2, Lampart 2, Mitorski 1, Korbel 0.

Continued on page 451

Rawicz were relegated to the 2009 Second League after finishing bottom of the table with only one win all season.

Rider	M	R	Pts	BP	TPts	Ave	F	P	TR	TPts
Ronnie JAMROZY	20	102	171	9	180	7.06	0	0	4	8
Jernej KOLENKO	**1**	**6**	**10**	**0**	**10**	**6.67**	**0**	**0**	**1**	**1**
Jason DOYLE	8	42	54	6	60	5.71	0	0	1	0
Grzegorz KNAPP	**19**	**94**	**121**	**8**	**129**	**5.49**	**0**	**0**	**0**	**0**
Mark LEMON	2	10	12	1	13	5.20	0	0	0	0
Piotr DYM	**19**	**85**	**96**	**5**	**101**	**4.75**	**0**	**0**	**0**	**0**
Marcel KAJZER	19	95	106	6	112	4.72	0	0	0	0
Marcin NOWACZYK	**15**	**70**	**71**	**9**	**80**	**4.57**	**0**	**0**	**3**	**4**
Henrik GUSTAFSSON	1	3	2	0	2	2.67	0	0	0	0
Andrew TULLY	**3**	**11**	**5**	**1**	**6**	**2.18**	**0**	**0**	**0**	**0**
Semen VLASOV	4	13	7	0	7	2.15	0	0	0	0
Jordan FRAMPTON	**1**	**4**	**2**	**0**	**2**	**2.00**	**0**	**0**	**0**	**0**
Klaus JAKOBSEN	1	2	1	0	1	2.00	0	0	0	0
Erik PUDEL	**9**	**26**	**10**	**1**	**11**	**1.83**	**0**	**0**	**0**	**0**
Pawel RATAJSZCZAK	11	32	5	0	5	0.63	0	0	0	0
Andrzej ZIEJA	**2**	**4**	**0**	**0**	**0**	**0.00**	**0**	**0**	**0**	**0**

Polish
First
League

RYBNIK

2008 RESULTS

First League

Final position .... Sixth

BYDGOSZCZ (H)
Sunday, April 6
Lost 38-55
Aldén 0, Chromik 3, Kuciapa 8:1, Gizatullin 4, Swiderski 15:1 (6), Pawlaszczyk 8, Mitko 0, Szymura 0.

DAUGAVPILS (A)
Sunday, April 13
Lost 37-56
Kuciapa 8, Aldén 2, Gizatullin 10:1, Chromik 0, Swiderski 16 (6), Szymura 0, Mitko 0, Pawlaszczyk 1.

RAWICZ (H)
Sunday, April 20
Won 60-32
Baran 7, Kuciapa 12:1, Gizatullin 6, Aldén 5:1, **Swiderski 13:2**, Pyszny 6:1, Mitko 2:1, Pawlaszczyk 9.

GDANSK (A)
Thurday, May 1
Lost 20-29
Kuciapa 4, Chromik 0, Baran 0, Gizatullin 8 (2), Swiderski 4, Pyszny 0, Mitko 2:1, Pawlaszczyk 2.

GRUDZIADZ (H)
Sunday, May 4
Won 58-34
Kuciapa 13:1, Chromik 7:1, Baran 5, Gizatullin 12, **Swiderski 14:1**, Pyszny 0, Mitko 2:1, Pawlaszczyk 5.

POZNAN (H)
Sunday, May 11
Lost 44-46
Kuciapa 2:2, Baran 6, Chromik 10:1, Gizatullin 7, Swiderski 10, Pyszny, did not ride, Mitko 1, Pawlaszczyk 8:1.

OSTROW (A)
Sunday, June 1
Lost 37-54
Baran 7, Lindbäck 0, Gizatullin 7 (2), Chromik 2:2, Swiderski 16, Szymura 0, Mitko 1, Pawlaszczyk 4.

OSTROW (H)
Sunday, June 8
Lost 42-48
Lindbäck 3, Kuciapa 5:1, Baran 0, Gizatullin 4:1, Swiderski 11:2, Szymura, did not ride, Mitko 4:1, Pawlaszczyk 15:1.
Aggregate: Lost 79-102.

POZNAN (A)
Sunday, June 22
Lost 44-47
Gizatullin 3, Lindbäck 8:1, Chromik 8:1, Kuciapa 10:2 (2), Swiderski 12:1, Pyszny 0, Mitko 0, Pawlaszczyk 3:1.
Aggregate: Lost 88-93.

GRUDZIADZ (A)
Sunday, July 6
Won 48-41
Swiderski 12, Gizatullin 0, Chromik 2:1, Kuciapa 14, Lindbäck 11:1, Pyszny, did not ride, Mitko 1:1, Pawlaszczyk 8:2.
Aggregate: Won 106-75.

GDANSK (H)
Sunday, July 20
Won 50-40
Lindbäck 6, Gizatullin 10:1, Kuciapa 10:1, Chromik 2, **Swiderski 15**, Pyszny, did not ride, Mitko 2:1, Pawlaszczyk 5:1.
Aggregate: Won 70-69.

RAWICZ (A)
Sunday, July 27
Won 63-28
Lindbäck 13, Gizatullin 5:2, Kuciapa 11, Chromik 8:3, Swiderski 13:1, Pyszny 1, Mitko 3:1, Pawlaszczyk 9:1.
Aggregate: Won 123-60.

DAUGAVPILS (H)
Sunday, August 3
Won 58-32
Lindbäck 10:2, Gizatullin 13, Kuciapa 9, Chromik 4, Szymura, did not ride, Pyszny 0, Mitko 9:1, **Pawlaszczyk 13:2**.
Aggregate: Won 95-88.

TRACK FILE

Track: ul. Gliwicka 72, 44-200 Rybnik, Poland.

Telephone: 0048 032 4228880.

Website: www.rkm.rybnik.pl

Track Length: 357 metres.

Track Record: 63.33 secs, Mikael Max, April 15, 2007.

SQUAD
Karol Baran, Roman Chromik, Mateusz Chochlinski, Kamil Fleger, Mariusz Konsek, Piotr Korbel, Maciej Kuciapa, Michal Mitko, Pawel Paliga, Patryk Pawlaszczyk, Slawomir Pyszny, Piotr Swiderski, Bartosz Szymura, Tomasz Wolniewicz.
Foreign: Sebastian Aldén, Denis Gizatullin, Antonio Lindbäck, Henrik Moller.

BYDGOSZCZ (A)
Sunday, August 3
Lost 37-56
Swiderski, did not ride, Gizatullin 4:1, Kuciapa 8, Chromik 1, Lindbäck 21 (6), Pyszny, did not ride, Mitko 3, Pawlaszczyk 0.
Aggregate: Lost 75-111.

Play offs

RAWICZ (H)
Sunday, August 24
Won 54-35
Kuciapa 11:1, Chromik 1, Pawlaszczyk 9:1, Chochlinski 0, Swiderski 14, Pyszny 5:1, Mitko 13:1, Paliga 1.

DAUGAVPILS (H)
Sunday, August 31
Won 54-36
no rider at one, Mitko 8:2, Kuciapa 11:2, Gizatullin 6:1, **Swiderski 15**, Paliga 0, Pyszny 3:1, Pawlaszczyk 11.

GRUDZIADZ (H)
Sunday, September 7
Won 61-31
Chromik 8:2, **Lindbäck 14:1**, Kuciapa 13:1, Gizatullin 6:3, Paliga 0, Pyszny 4, Mitko 9, Pawlaszczyk 7:2.

GRUDZIADZ (A)
Sunday, September 21
Lost 44-46
Kuciapa 9, Chromik 3, Pawlaszczyk 5, Gizatullin 7, **Swiderski 18**, Pyszny 2, Paliga 0.
Aggregate: Won 105-77.

RAWICZ (A)
Sunday, September 28
Lost 44-48
Kuciapa 8:1, Pyszny 4:1, Paliga 0, Chromik 5:1, Swiderski 17:1 (4), no rider at six, Mitko 3:1, Pawlaszczyk 7.
Aggregate: Won 98-83.

DAUGAPILS (A)
Sunday, October 5
Lost 33-60
Rider replacement for Pawlaszczyk, Wolniewicz 0, Chromik 10:1, Paliga 0, Kuciapa 14 (6), Pyszny 3, no rider at seven, Mitko 6:1.
Aggregate: Lost 87-96.

FIRST LEAGUE

	M	W	D	L	BP	Pts
Bydgoszcz	20	16	0	4	10	42
Gdansk	20	13	1	6	6	33
Ostrow	20	13	0	7	7	26
Poznan	20	8	1	11	4	21
Daugavpils	20	11	0	9	4	26
RYBNIK	**20**	**9**	**0**	**11**	**6**	**24**
Grudziadz	20	8	0	12	3	19
Rawicz	20	1	0	19	0	2

Challenges

CZESTOCHOWA (A)
Wednesday, March 19
Lost 8-28
Kuciapa 3, Szymura 0, Chromik 1, Mitko 1, Swiderski 2, Pawlaszczyk 1, Korbel 0, Pyszny 0.
■ Meeting abandoned because of snow after Nicki Pedersen fell in heat seven.

RZESZOW (H)
Monday, March 31
Won 50-39
Kuciapa 12, Aldén 7:1, Gizatullin 10, Chromik 2:2, Swiderski 11, Mitko 2:1, Pawlaszczyk 5:1, Henrik Moller [G] 1:1.

Individual

POLISH UNDER 21 CHAMPIONSHIP FINAL
Tuesday, August 19
Janowski 13, Pytel 13, Zengota 12, Pawlicki 11, A. Gomolski 10, Pawlaszczyk 10, R. Kasprzak 9, Mroczka 8, Mateusz Szczepaniak 7, Szewczykowski 6, Mitko 6, Jedrzejewski 5, Lampart 4, Szostak 3, Miturski 1, Lopaczewski 0, Brzozowski 0, Kajoch 0.

LUKASZ ROMANEK MEMORIAL
Tuesday, September 23
Hancock 15, Dobrucki 13, Ulamek 12, T. Gollob 10, Holta 10, Okoniewski 9, Miedzinski 8, Drabik 8, Mateusz Szczepaniak 7, Swiderski 7, Gapinski 7, Lindbäck 4, Zabik 3, Protasiewicz 3, Sitera 3, Chromik [R] 1, Cieslar 0.

■ *The 2001 European Under 19 Champion, Lukasz Romanek (b21.8.1983, Knurow, Poland), committed suicide on June 2, 2006, at the age of 22.*

Rider	M	R	Pts	BP	TPts	Ave	F	P	TR	TPts
Piotr SWIDERSKI	16	84	215	10	225	10.71	3	2	3	8
Antonio LINDBÄCK	**9**	**45**	**86**	**5**	**91**	**8.09**	**0**	**1**	**1**	**3**
Maciej KUCIAPA	19	97	180	14	194	8.00	0	0	2	4
Patryk PAWLASZCZYK	**19**	**78**	**129**	**12**	**141**	**7.23**	**0**	**1**	**0**	**0**
Denis GIZATULLIN	17	75	112	11	123	6.56	0	0	2	2
Michal MITKO	**19**	**59**	**69**	**13**	**82**	**5.47**	**0**	**0**	**0**	**0**
Roman CHROMIK	17	68	74	13	87	5.12	0	0	0	0
Karol BARAN	**6**	**22**	**25**	**0**	**25**	**4.55**	**0**	**0**	**0**	**0**
Slawomir PYSZNY	14	33	28	5	33	4.00	0	0	0	0
Sebastien ALDÉN	**3**	**10**	**7**	**1**	**8**	**3.20**	**0**	**0**	**0**	**0**
Pawel PALIGA	6	9	1	0	1	0.44	0	0	0	0
BARTOSZ SZYMURA	**3**	**3**	**0**	**0**	**0**	**0.00**	**0**	**0**	**0**	**0**
Tomasz WOLNIEWICZ	1	3	0	0	0	0.00	0	0	0	0
Mateusz CHOCHINSKI	**1**	**1**	**0**	**0**	**0**	**0.00**	**0**	**0**	**0**	**0**

OSTROW (continued from page 434)

Individual

POLISH UNDER 21 CHAMPIONSHIP
Semi Final
Wednesday, April 23
Mateusz Szczepaniak 15, Piaszczynski 13, Kajoch 12, R. Kasprzak 11, Dabrowski 11, Mitko 9, Pawlaszczyk 9, Janowski 8, Pyszny 8, Miturski 6, Zielinski 6, Idzoriek 4, Lampart 3, Kajzer 3, S. Kielbasa 1, Kowalczyk 1, Paliga 0.
■ *Meeting switched from Rybnik due to inclement weather.*

BRONZE HELMET
Semi Final
Tuesday, September 9
Miturski 13, Lampart 12, Celmer 12, Janowski 10, K. Gomolski 10, Lopaczewski 8, Szostek 8, Piaszczynski 7, Lampkowski 7, Pieniazek 7, Mitorski 6, Idziorek 6, M. Szymko 6, Szostak 3, Machnik 2, Sroka 2, Zmarzlik 1, S. Szymko 0.

LORD MAYOR CUP
Sunday, March 30
N. Pedersen 15, P. Karlsson 12, Ulamek 11, Kylmåkorpi 10, Ruud 9, A. Gomolski 8, D. King 8, Harris 8, Miskowiak 6, Piaszczynski 5, L. Dryml 5, Czerwinski 4, Roynon 4, Legault 3, Aspegren 1.
Rif Saitgareev Memorial (*top four scorers*): Nicki Pedersen, Sebastian Ulamek, Peter Karlsson, Joonas Kylmåkorpi.

COAT OF ARMS CHAIN
Sunday, September 14
Hampel 14, Holta 10, Adams 10, Skornicki 10, Holder 9, Harris 9, Crump 8, Balinski 8, Nicholls 8, F.Lindgren 8, E.Sajfutdinov 7, Zabik 5, Protasiewicz 5, Czerwinski 4, K.Kasprzak 3, A.Dryml 2, Liberski 0.
Miroslaw Borowicz Memorial: Emil Idziorek 8, Marcin Liberski 7, Cebine Randrup 2, Stefanie Jensen 1.

RIF SAITGAREEV MEMORIAL
Sunday, October 19
Michal Szczepaniak 14, Miskowiak 14, Ruud 13, Kus 13, J. Wright 11, Pawlaszczyk 11, Mitko 9, Hansen 7, Bach 6, Gregoric 5, R. Henderson 5, Aspegren 4, D. Henderson 4, J. Andersson 3, Eklöf 3, Idziorek 1.

2009 SQUADS

GNIEZNO
Dawid **CIESLEWICZ**, *Krzysztof* **JABLONSKI**, *Miroslaw* **JABLONSKI**, *Krzysztof* **NOWACKI**, *Piotr* **PALUCH**, *Mariusz* **PUSZAKOWSKI**, *Krzysztof* **SLABON**.
Foreign: *Jason* **DOYLE**, *Manuel* **HAUZINGER**, *Andrey* **KARPOV**, *Morten* **RISAGER**, *Claus* **VISSING**.
UNDER 21
Maciej **FAJFER**, *Kacper* **GOMOLSKI**, *Marcel* **KAJZER**, *Arkadiusz* **STUROMSKI**, *Tomasz* **WISNIEWSKI**.
Foreign: *Christian* **AGÖ**, *Robin* **BERGQVIST**, *Linus* **EKLÖF**, *Simon* **NIELSEN**, *Filip* **SITERA**.

GRUDZIADZ
Sebastian **BANAS**, *Kamil* **BRZOZOWSKI**, *Gregorz* **KNAPP**, *Pawel* **STASZEK**.
Foreign: *Oliver* **ALLEN**, *Eric* **ANDERSSON**, *Niklas* **KLINGBERG**, *Matej* **FERJAN**, *Rory* **SCHLEIN**.
UNDER 21
Maciej **BRZEZINSKI**, *Pawel* **KJACZOROWSKI**, *Artur* **MROCZKA**, *Marcin* **PODLASZEWSKI**.
Foreign: *Joe* **HAINES**, *Tommy* **PEDERSEN**, *Kevin* **WÖLBERT**.

OSTROW
Sebastian **BRUCHEISER**, *Adrian* **GOMOLSKI**, *Bartosz* **KWIATKOWSKI**, *Robert* **MISKOWIAK**, *Karol* **ZABIK**.
Foreign: *Chris* **HARRIS**, *Daniel* **KING**, *Mads* **KORNELIUSSEN**, *Mark* **LORAM**, *Travis* **McGOWAN**, *Daniel* **NERMARK**, *Ulrich* **ØSTERGAARD**, *Richard* **SPEISER**, *Simon* **STEAD**.
UNDER 21
Mateusz **GORZELANCZYK**, *Emil* **IDZIOREK**, *Michal* **KRJOM**, *Roger* **LEWANDOWSKI**, *Patryk* **PAWLASZCZYK**, *Karol* **SROKA**, *Piotr* **SZOSTAK**.
Foreign: *Frank* **FACHER**, *Lars Daniel* **GUNNESTAD**, *Josh* **GRAJCZONEK**, *Nanna* **JØRGENSEN**, *Nicolai* **KLINDT**.

POZNAN
Pawel **HLIB**, *Lukasz* **JANKOWSKI**, *Grzegorz* **KLOPOT**, *Norbert* **KOSCIUCH**, *Daniel* **PYTEL**, *Zbigniew* **SUCHECKI**, *Rafal* **TROJANOWSKI**.
UNDER 21
Adam **KAJOCH**, *Grzegorz* **STROZYK**.
Foreign: *Anders* **ANDERSEN**.

RYBNIK
Zbigniew **CZERWINSKI**, *Wojciech* **DRUZNIAK**, *Ronnie* **JAMROZY**, *Adam* **PAWLICZEK**, *Marcin* **REMPALA**, *Lukasz* **SZMID**, *Mariusz* **WEGRZYK**.
Foreign: *Denis* **GIZATULLIN**, *Ricky* **KLING**, *Kyle* **LEGAULT**.
UNDER 21
Mateusz **CHOCHLINSKI**, *Kamil* **FLEGER**, *Rafal* **FLEGER**, *Piotr* **KORBEL**, *Michal* **MITKO**, *Lukasz* **PIECHA**, *Slawomir* **PYSZNY**, *Bartosz* **SZYMURA**, *Tomasz* **WOLNIEWICZ**.

RZESZOW
Maciej **KUCIAPA**, *Marcin* **LES**, *Pawel* **MIESIAC**, *Krzysztof* **SZYSZKA**.
Foreign: *Ales* **DRYML**, *Lukas* **DRYML**, *Charlie* **GJEDDE**, *Mikael* **MAX**, *Cameron* **WOODWARD**.
UNDER 21
Dawid **LAMPART**, *Mateusz* **SZOSTEK**.
Foreign: *Adam* **ROYNON**.

TARNOW
Janusz **KOLODZIEJ**, *Sebastian* **ULAMEK**, *Piotr* **SWIDERSKI**.
Foreign: *Steve* **BOXALL**, *Kevin* **DOOLAN**, *Peter* **LJUNG**, *Jesper B.* **MONBERG**, *Bjarne* **PEDERSEN**, *James* **WRIGHT**.
UNDER 21
Szymon **KIELBASA**, *Tadeusz* **KOSTRO**.
Foreign: *Tobias* **BUSCH**, *Patrick* **HOUGAARD**, *Peter Juul* **LARSEN**.

For **DAUGAVPILS** *2009 squad see* **LATVIA**.

SECOND LEAGUE REGULAR SEASON STANDINGS

	M	W	D	L	PtsF	PtsA	BP	Pts
1 MISKOLC (Hungary)	10	8	0	2	488	410	4	20
2 GNIEZNO	10	7	0	3	492	363	4	18
3 RIVNE (Ukraine)	10	6	0	4	467	432	2	14
4 LODZ	10	3	0	7	402	438	3	9
5 OPOLE	10	3	0	7	429	480	1	7
6 KROSNO	10	3	0	7	374	529	0	6

SECOND LEAGUE FINAL TABLE (after top four play-offs)

	M	W	D	L	PtsF	PtsA	BP	Pts
1 GNIEZNO	16	12	1	3	815	537	7	32
2 MISKOLC (Hungary)	16	10	0	6	757	687	6	26
3 ROVNO (Ukraine)	16	9	0	7	668	721	3	21
4 LODZ	16	4	1	11	647	736	3	12

PLAY OFFS...PLAY-OFFS...PLAY-OFFS...PLAY-OFFS...PLAY-OFFS...PLAY OFFS...PLAY OFFS...

Miskolc 34 Gniezno 58
Gniezno 58 Miskolc 34
Aggregate: Miskolc 68 Gniezno 116.

Miskolc 65 Rivne 25
Rivne 48 Miskolc 42
Aggregate: Miskolc 107 Rivne 73.

Miskolc 57 Lodz 34
Lodz 54 Miskolc 37
Aggregate: Miskolc 94 Lodz 88.

Gniezno 40 Rivne 0
Rivne 31 Gniezno 60
Aggregate: Gniezno 100 Rivne 31.

Gniezno 62 Lodz 30
Lodz 45 Gniezno 45
Aggregate: Gniezno 107 Lodz 75.

Rivne 52 Lodz 38
Lodz 44 Rivne 45
Aggregate: Rivne 97 Lodz 82.

PROMOTION PLAY-OFF

Miskolc 0 Grudziadz 40
Grudziadz 40 Miskolc 0
Aggregate: Miskolc 0 Grudziadz 80

MISKOLC opted not to compete in the promotion play-off because of the financial implications and will continue to race in the 2009 Second League.

GRUDZIADZ retain their place in the First League.

■ For full details of Miskolc see HUNGARY.
■ For full details of Rivne see UKRAINE.

GNIEZNO won promotion to the 2009 First League even though they only finished second in the regular season standings.

Beaten for top spot by Hungarian club Miskolc they came through with an end of season burst that saw them win five of their play-off matches – the top four sides met each other home and away in a round robin series.

Their only dropped point came in a 45-45 draw at Lodz who sneaked into the play-offs despite winning only three of their 10 league matches.

Four of their riders averaged over nine points a match throughout the season with import Claus Vissing a prolific scorer in his weekend jaunts.

Miskolc's decision not to go for promotion – they withdrew from a decider against First League strugglers Grudziadz – means only Rawicz drop down for the new season.

Miskolc, Krosno, Lodz, Opole and Ukrainian side Rivne are back for another season at the lowest level of professional racing while Lublin return to league activity after a year out and have put together a powerful side.

Roll of Honour

1957 .... GNIEZNO
1957 .... KRAKOW
1958 .... TARNOW
1959 .... KRAKOW
2000 .... RAWICZ
2001 .... TARNOW
2002 .... LUBLIN
2003 .... GRUDZIADZ
2004 .... OPOLE
2005 .... GNIEZNO
2006 .... GDANSK
2007 .... RAWICZ
2008 .... GNIEZNO

In 1957 two separate Third Division competitions were staged but there was no play-off between the divisional champions.

Five teams will compete in the 2009 Polish Amateur League – Bydgoszcz, Czestochowa, Leszno, Lublin and Pila.

Polish Second League

GNIEZNO

TRACK FILE

Track: ul. Wrzesinska 24, 62-200 Gniezno, Poland.

Telephone: 0048 061 4258820.

Website: www.startgniezno.pl

Track Length: 348 metres.

Track Record: 62.64 secs, Krzystof Cegielski, July 21, 2002.

SQUAD

Dawid Cieslewicz, Tomasz Cieslewicz, Maciej Fajfer, Mateusz Gorzelanczyk, Miroslaw Jablonski, Lukasz Linette, Lukasz Loman, Slawomir Musielak, Piotr Paluch, Krzysztof Stojanowski.

Foreign: Linus Eklöf, Roberto Haupt, Manuel Hauzinger, Krister Jacobsen, Kim Jansson, Simon Nielsen, Jörg Tebbe, Claus Vissing, Kevin Wölbert.

2008 RESULTS

Second League

Final position.................... Champions (Second)

KROSNO (H)
Sunday, April 13
Won 62-25
Paluch 10:2, Jacobsen 8:2, **Jablonski 10:2**, Wölbert 7, D. Ciewslewicz 12, Fajfer 5, **Eklöf 10:2.**

OPOLE (A)
Sunday, April 20
Won 48-42
Paluch 11, Eklöf 3:1, Jablonski 13, Vissing 5:3, D. Ciewslewicz 12:1, Fajfer 3, Jacobsen 1, Gorzelanczyk, did not ride.

LODZ (A)
Sunday, May 4
Won 52-39
Paluch 13, Jansson 5:1, Jablonski 4, Wölbert 10:1, D. Cieslewicz 14, Fajfer 1, Eklöf 5:1.

RIVNE (H)
Sunday, May 11
Won 49-44
Paluch 13:1, Linette 5:1, Jablonski 9, Nielsen 2:1, D. Ceiwsleicz 12:2, Fajfer 0, Wölbert 8:1.

MISKOLC (A)
Sunday, June 1
Won 49-44
Paluch 9:2, Jacobsen 7, Wölbert 5:2, Jablonski 13, D. Cieslewicz 9, Musielak 4, Eklöf 2:1.

MISKOLC (H)
Sunday, June 15
Lost 41-49
Paluch 8:1 (F), T. Cieslewicz 6:3, Jablonski 9:1, Vissing 4:1. D. Cieslewicz 8, Kozdras, did not ride, Jacobsen 6:2, Musielak 0.
Aggregate: Lost 90-93.

RIVNE (A)
Tuesday, July 22
Lost 44-46
Paluch 11:1, Jacobsen 0, Jablonski 14, T. Cieslewicz 3, D. Cieslewicz 7:1, Musielak 8, Wölbert 1:1, Fajfer, did not ride.
Aggregate: Won 93-90.

OPOLE (H)
Sunday, July 27
Won 63-28
Jablonski 12:1, Wölbert 7:3, D. Cieslewicz 5:1, T. Cieslewicz 8, **Paluch 15**, Fajfer 0, Musielak 8:3, Eklöf 8:1.
Aggregate: Won 111-70.

LODZ (H)
Friday, August 1
Won 40-0 (awarded)
Aggregate: 92-39.

KROSNO (A)
Sunday, August 3
Lost 44-46
Jablonski 13, Wölbert 9:2, Paluch 11:1, Loman 0, D. Cieslewicz 0, Fajfer 1, Musielak 3, Eklöf 7:1.
Aggregate: Won 106-71.

Play offs

RIVNE (A)
Sunday, August 24
Won 60-31
Jablonski 12, Stojanowski 5:3, **Paluch 14:1**, Wölbert 2, **D. Ciewslewicz 14:1**, Musielak 4:1, Eklöf 9:1, Fajfer, did not ride.

MISKOLC (H)
Sunday, August 31
Won 58-34
Jablonski 9:1, Stojanowski 6:2, **Paluch 13:2**, **Vissing 13:2**, D. Cieslewicz 13:1, Musielak 0, Eklöf 4:1, Fajfer, did not ride.

LODZ (A)
Sunday, September 7
Drew 45-45
Jablonski 9, Stojanowski 7:2, Paluch 7:1, Vissing 9:1, D. Cieslewicz 2, Musielak 4:1, Eklöf 7:1, Fajfer, did not ride.

LODZ (H)
Saturday, September 27
Won 62-30
Paluch 14, Wölbert 5:2, Vissing 10:3, D. Cieslewicz 13, Jablonski 12:1, Musielak 5:2, Eklöf 3:2, Fajfer, did not ride.
Aggregate: Won 107-75.

RIVNE (H)
Sunday, September 28
Won 40-0 (awarded).
Aggregate: Won 100-31.

MISKOLC (A)
Sunday, October 5
Won 58-34
Paluch 12:1, Stojanowski 9:3, Vissing 13:1, D. Cieslewicz 0, Jablonski 14, Musielak 5:1, Eklöf 4:2, Fajfer 1.
Aggregate: Won 116-68.

SECOND LEAGUE (after play-offs)

	M	*W*	*D*	*L*	*BP*	*Pts*
GNIEZNO	**16**	**12**	**1**	**3**	**7**	**32**
Miskolc	16	10	0	6	6	26
Rivne	16	9	0	7	3	21
Lodz	16	4	1	11	3	12

SECOND LEAGUE (regular season)

	M	*W*	*D*	*L*	*BP*	*Pts*
Miskolc	10	8	0	2	4	20
GNIEZNO	**10**	**7**	**0**	**3**	**4**	**18**
Rivne	10	6	0	4	2	14
Lodz	10	3	0	7	3	9
Opole	10	3	0	7	1	7
Krosno	10	3	0	7	0	6

Challenges

GDANSK (H)
Monday, March 24
Lost 41-49
D. Cieslewicz 5, Berqvist 2:1, Paluch 6:1, Eklöf 6, Loman 9, Fajfer 1:1, Jacobsen 4, Christian Agö 3, Schepin 2, Miroslaw Jablonski, did not ride, T. Cieslewicz 3.

DAUGAVPILS (A)
Tuesday, March 25
Lost 46-74
T. Cieslewicz 6:1, Eklöf 6, Loman 3, Christian Agö 1:1, Vissing 6:1, Artem Schepin 2, Karol Polak [G] 0, Robin Bergqvist 2, Jacobsen 5, M. Jablonski 6, Linette 2:1, Fajfer 1, D. Cieslewicz 6.

POZNAN (A)
Friday, March 28
Lost 32-58.
Paluch 12, Jablonski 5, Loman 4, Linette 2, Cieslewicz 8:1, Fajfer 0, Schepin 1.

POZNAN (H)
Friday, April 4
Lost 39-51
Paluch 13, Jansson 2:1, Jabłonski 6, Bergqvist 0, Wölbert 8:1, Fajfer 0, Jacobsen 5, Nielsen 1, D. Cieslewicz 4, T. Cieslewicz 0,Linette 0, Karol Polak, did not ride.

Individual

POLISH CHAMPIONSHIP
Quarter Final, Thursday, June 5
Hampel 14, Kosciecha 13, Skornicki 12, A. Gomolski 10, Slabon 10, D. Cieslewicz 8, Chromik 7, Pytel 7, Staszek 7, R. Kasprzak 6, Jankowski 6, Hlib 6, Puszakowski 5, Klopot 5, M. Jablonski 3, Kajzer 1.

BOLESAW CHOBRY CROWN
Sunday, June 29
Dobrucki 13+3, Okoniewski 14+2, Ulamek 1+12, K. Jablonski 12+0, Mieszinski 10, Kosciuch 8, Zabik 8, Hlib 7, Drabik 7, Paluch 7, Jeleniewski 6, Kosciecha 4, D. Cieslewicz 4, J. Rempala 3, Stachyra 3, M. Jablonski 2, Loman [R], Musielak [R], did not ride.

BRONZE HELMET
Semi Final, Tuesday, September 9
R. Fleger 12, Musielak 12, Mroczka 11, Piekarski 10, Pyszny 10, Dudek 10, Szewczykowski 10, Sperz 9, Pawlicki 9, L. Cyran 7, S. Kielbasa 5, Kowalczyk 4, Kajzer 4, Kostro 4, Wisniewski 3, K. Cieslar 0, Fajfer 0, Paliga 0.

Rider	*M*	*R*	*Pts*	*BP*	*TPts*	*Ave*	*F*	*P*	*TR*	*TPts*
Piotr PALUCH	14	71	161	13	174	9.80	1	3	1	0
Claus VISSING	**6**	**28**	**54**	**11**	**65**	**9.29**	**0**	**1**	**0**	**0**
Miroslaw JABLONSKI	14	69	153	6	159	9.22	0	1	0	0
Dawid CIESLEWICZ	**13**	**57**	**121**	**7**	**128**	**8.98**	**0**	**1**	**0**	**0**
Krzysztof STOJANOWSKI	4	18	27	10	37	8.22	0	0	0	0
Linus EKLÖF	**11**	**42**	**62**	**14**	**76**	**7.24**	**0**	**1**	**0**	**0**
Kevin WÖLBERT	9	38	54	12	66	6.95	0	0	0	0
Tomasz CIESLEWICZ	**3**	**12**	**17**	**3**	**20**	**6.67**	**0**	**0**	**0**	**0**
Kim JANSSON	1	4	5	1	6	6.00	0	0	0	0
Lukasz LINETTE	**1**	**4**	**5**	**1**	**6**	**6.00**	**0**	**0**	**0**	**0**
Krister JACOBSEN	5	18	22	4	26	5.78	0	0	0	0
Slawomir MUSIELAK	**10**	**37**	**41**	**7**	**48**	**5.19**	**0**	**0**	**0**	**0**
Simon NIELSEN	1	4	2	1	3	3.00	0	0	0	0
Maciej FAJFER	**9**	**17**	**11**	**0**	**11**	**2.59**	**0**	**0**	**0**	**0**
Lukasz LOMAN	1	2	0	0	0	0.00	0	0	0	0

Polish Second League

KROSNO

2008 RESULTS

Second League

Final position.. Sixth

GNIEZNO (A)
Sunday, April 13
Lost 25-62
Lukaszewicz 2, Kasprowiak 4, Druchniak 5:1, Jaros 5, Wolff 3:1, Szyszka 3:1, Machnik 0, Vandirek 3.

MISKOLC (H)
Sunday, April 20
Lost 39-51
Lukaszewicz 7:1, Santej 5:1, Druchniak 3:2, Jaros 8, Wolff 9:1, Szyszka 3, Vandirek 4, Machnik 0.

OPOLE (H)
Thursday, May 1
Won 48-45
Lukaszewicz 1:1, Kasprowiak 7, Jaros 11:1, Druchniak 9:1, Wolff 13, Szyszka 4, Vandirek 3, Machnik, did not ride.

LODZ (H)
Sunday, May 11
Won 45-44
Jaros 9, Kasprowiak 10:1, Santej 2, Druchniak 8:1, Wolff 12:1, Szyszka 0, Hadek 4:2, Machnik, did not ride.

RIVNE (A)
Sunday, June 1
Lost 36-56
Kasprowiak 7:1, Gregoric 5:1, Druchniak 2, Lukaszewicz 8, Jaros 11 (4), no rider at six, Duh 2, Machnik 1.

TRACK FILE

Track: ul. Legionow 6, 38-400 Krosno, Poland.

Telephone: 0048 013 436-34-63.

Website: www.ksmkrosno.pl

Track Length: 398 metres.

Track Record: 70.1 secs, Martin Vaculik, September 2, 2007.

SQUAD
Rafal Chinski, Wojciech Druchniak, Grzegorz Dzik, Bartosz Kasprowiak, Tomasz Lukaszewicz, Piotr Machnik, Grzegorz Szyszka, Tomasz Zywertowski.
Foreign: Matija Duh, Maks Gregoric, Michael Hadek, Jan Jaros, Martin Malek, Izak Santej, Adam Vandirek, Richard Wolff.

RIVNE (H)
Sunday, June 8
Lost 40-50
Jaros 5:1 (2), Lukaszewicz 5, Kasprowiak 9:1, Druchniak 5:1, Wolff 8, Szyszka 4, Hadek 2, Machnik 2.
Aggregate: Lost 76-106.

LODZ (A)
Sunday, June 22
Lost 38-52
Jaros 15, Gregoric 2, Kasprowiak 5:2, Druchniak 7, Wolff 5, Szyszka 3, Hadek 1:1, Machnik, did not ride.
Aggregate: Lost 83-96.

OPOLE (A)
Sunday, July 20
Lost 32-60
Kasprowiak 2, Wolff 3, Lukaszewicz 5:1, Malek 7:1, Jaros 10 (4), Szyszka 1, Machnik 0, Hadek 4.
Aggregate: Lost 80-105.

GNIEZNO (H)
Sunday, August 3
Won 46-44
Wolff 7:1, Kasprowiak 10:2, Lukaszewicz 9, Malek 6:1, Jaros 4, Szyszka 3:1. Hadek 7, Machnik 0.
Aggregate: Lost 71-106.

Rider	*M*	*R*	*Pts*	*BP*	*TPts*	*Ave*	*F*	*P*	*TR*	*TPts*
Richard WOLFF	8	35	60	4	64	7.31	0	0	0	0
Jan JAROS	**9**	**45**	**78**	**2**	**80**	**7.11**	**0**	**0**	**3**	**5**
Bartosz KASPROWIAK	9	44	61	8	69	6.27	0	0	0	0
Wojciech DRUCHNIAK	**7**	**32**	**39**	**6**	**45**	**5.63**	**0**	**0**	**0**	**0**
Martin MALEK	3	13	16	2	18	5.54	0	0	0	0
Tomasz LUKASZEWICZ	**8**	**35**	**42**	**3**	**45**	**5.14**	**0**	**0**	**0**	**0**
Adam VANDIREK	3	8	10	0	10	5.00	0	0	0	0
Izak SANTEJ	**3**	**11**	**12**	**1**	**13**	**4.73**	**0**	**0**	**0**	**0**
Michael HADEK	5	20	18	3	21	4.20	0	0	0	0
Grzegorz SZYSZKA	**8**	**25**	**21**	**2**	**23**	**3.68**	**0**	**0**	**0**	**0**
Maks GREGORIC	3	13	10	1	11	3.38	0	0	0	0
Matija DUH	**2**	**8**	**4**	**0**	**4**	**2.00**	**0**	**0**	**0**	**0**
Piotr MACHNIK	7	12	3	0	3	1.00	0	0	0	0

MISKOLC (A)
Sunday, August 10
Lost 25-65
Kasprowiak 7:1, Santej 5, Gregoric 3, Malek 3, Lukaszewicz 5, no rider at six, Duh 2, Machnik 0.
Aggregate: Lost 64-116.

SECOND LEAGUE (regular season)

	M	*W*	*D*	*L*	*BP*	*Pts*
Miskolc	10	8	0	2	4	20
Gniezno	10	7	0	3	4	18
Rivne	10	6	0	4	2	14
Lodz	10	3	0	7	3	9
Opole	10	3	0	7	1	7
KROSNO	**10**	**3**	**0**	**7**	**0**	**6**

Did not qualify for the play-offs.

Individual

POLISH CHAMPIONSHIP
Quarter Final
Thursday, June 5
Protasiewicz 14, Gapinski 13, Stachyra 12, Povazhny 11, J. Rempala 11, Kuciapa 11, Trojanowski 9, Burza 8, Miesiac 8, Piaszczynski 6, Lukaszewicz 6, Kasprowiak 3, Druchniak 3, Machnik 1, Les 1, M. Rempala 1, Miturski 1, K. Baran 0, Szyszka 0.

PRESIDENT'S CUP
Sunday, July 13
Ferjan 15, Ulamek 13, Stachyra 11, Kuciapa 11, Drabik 10, Lampart 9, Jaros 9, Vaculik 8, Wright 8, Trojanowski 7, Lukaszewicz 7, Druchniak 4, Szyszka 3, Kasprowiak 2, Sørensen 2, Machnik 1.

SECOND LEAGUE 2009 FIXTURES

Sunday, April 5
Krosno: free date
Lublin v Lodz
Miskolc v Opole
Pila v Rawicz
Monday, April 13
Lodz v Miskolc
Opole v Pila
Rawicz v Krosno
Lublin: free date
Sunday, April 19
Krosno v Opole
Lublin v Miskolc
Pila v Lodz
Rawicz: free date
Sunday, May 3
Miskolc v Pila
Lodz v Krosno
Opole: free date
Rawicz v Lublin
Sunday, May 10
Krosno v Miskolc
Lublin v Pila
Rawicz v Opole
Lodz: free date
Sunday, May 31
Lodz v Rawicz
Miskolc: free date
Opole v Lublin
Pila v Krosno
Thursday, June 11
Lublin v Krosno
Opole v Lodz
Rawicz v Miskolc
Pila: free date
Sunday, June 14
Krosno v Lublin
Lodz v Opole
Miskolc v Rawicz
Pila: free date
Sunday, June 21
Krosno v Pila
Lublin v Opole
Rawicz v Lodz
Miskolc: free date
Sunday, June 28
Lodz: free date
Miskolc v Krosno
Opole v Rawicz
Pila v Lublin
Sunday, July 5
Krosno v Lodz
Lublin v Rawicz
Pila v Miskolc
Opole: free date
Sunday, July 19
Lodz v Pila
Miskolc v Lublin
Opole v Krosno
Rawicz: free date
Sunday, July 26
Krosno v Rawicz
Lublin: free date
Miskolc v Lodz
Pila v Opole
Sunday, August 2
Lodz v Lublin
Opole v Miskolc
Rawicz v Pila
Krosno: free date

PLAY-OFFS (subject to change after Rivne's withdrawal)

Quarter Finals
Sunday, August 9: 6-1; 5-2; 4-3.
Sunday, August 16: 1-6; 2-5; 3-4.

Semi Finals
Sunday, August 30
Sunday, September 6

Championship play-off (1-4 placings)
Sunday, September 13
Sunday, September 27

TRivne (Ukraine) and Miskolc (Hungary) originalluy entered the Second League but Rivne were refused a licence because they oculd not meet financial requirements. Miskolc's 2009 squad is listed in the Hungary section on page 379.

Polish Second League

LODZ

2008 RESULTS

Second League

Final position .... Fourth

RIVNE (H)
Sunday, April 20
Won 59-23
Burza 8, Bager 2, Simota 11:2, **Schultz 15**, Eriksson 11:3, Liberski 9, Brucheiser 3.

MISKOLC (A)
Thursday, May 1
Lost 44-45
Schultz 7:3, Sajfutdinov 10, Mikolajczak 12, R. Gatiyatov 0, Simota 0, Liberski 6:2, Brucheiser 0, Dilger 9:1.

GNIEZNO (H)
Sunday, May 4
Lost 39-52
Burza 8:1, Mikolajczak 0, Sajfutdinov 0, Fijalkowski 5 (2), Eriksson 13, Liberski 9:1, Brucheiser 0, Dilger 4.

KROSNO (A)
Sunday, May 11
Lost 44-45
Burza 13, Sajfutdinov 2, Mikolajczak 9:1, R. Gatiyatov 1, Eriksson 11, Liberski 4:2, Brucheiser 3, Dilger 1:1.

OPOLE (H)
Sunday, June 1
Lost 44-45
Schultz 3, Bager 6, Burza 13, Mikolajczak 5, Eriksson 15:2, Liberski 0, Brucheiser 0, Dilger 2.

OPOLE (A)
Sunday, June 8
Won 46-43
Eriksson 6:2, Kramer 15, Kröger 5, Bager 3, Burza 9:2, Dilger 6, Liberski 2.
Aggregate: Won 90-88.

KROSNO (H)
Sunday, June 22
Won 52-38
Kramer 0, Mikolajczak 12:2, Eriksson 10:3, Schultz 10:1, Burza 14, Konsek 0, Liberski 6:1.
Aggregate: Won 96-83.

TRACK FILE

Track: I. Dziewiarska 14, 92-311 Lodz, Poland.

Telephone: 0048 042 6723508.

Website: www.orzel.lodz.pl

Track Length: 382 metres.

Track Record: 66.02 secs, Mathias Schultz, April 20, 2008.

SQUAD
Pawel Baran, Sebastian Brucheiser, Stanislaw Burza, Dariusz Fijalkowski, Mariusz Konsek, Marcin Liberski, Robert Mikolajczak.
Foreign: René Bach, Henning Bager, Max Dilger, Freddie Eriksson, Timur Garufullin, Marat Gatiyatov, Ruslan Gatiyatov, Magnus Karlsson, Stephan Katt, Emil Kramer, Matthias Kröger, Joakim Kugelmann, Denis Sajfutdinov, Mathias Schultz, Zdenek Simota, Simon Walker.

MISKOLC (H)
Sunday, July 20
Lost 44-46
Mikolajczak 7:1, Katt 1, Karlsson 3:1, Schultz 13:1, Eriksson 14:1, Liberski 3, Bach 3, Konsek, did not ride.
Aggregate: Lost 88-91.

RIVNE (A)
Sunday, July 27
Lost 30-61
M. Gatiyatov 8, *rider replacement for Burza*, Mikolajczak 2, Schultz 3:1, Sajfutdinov 10 (4), Liberski 7, no rider at seven.
Aggregate: Won 89-84.

GNIEZNO (A)
Friday, August 1
Lost 0-40 (awarded)
Aggregate: Won 79-52.

Play offs

MISKOLC (A)
Sunday, August 24
Lost 34-57
Mikolajczak 3, R. Gaityatov 6, Eriksson 12 (4), no rider at four, Burza 2, Konsek, did not ride, Liberski 9:1, Dilger 2:1.
■ *Result amended from 34-58 as Norbert Magosi ruled ineligible for Heat 14.*

RIVNE (H)
Sunday, August 31
Lost 44-45
Eriksson 10:1, Schultz 8, R. Gatiyatov 11, Mikoljaczak 3:1, Bager 2:1, Konsek 0, Liberski 9:1, Bach 1

GNIEZNO (H)
Sunday, September 7
Drew 45-45
Eriksson 16:2, Kramer 9:1, R. Gatiyatov 10, Mikolajczak 2:1, Schultz 6, Konsek 0, Liberski 2.

Rider	M	R	Pts	BP	TPts	Ave	F	P	TR	TPts
Freddie ERIKSSON	12	66	144	15	159	9.64	0	2	2	4
Zdenek SIMOTA	**2**	**6**	**11**	**2**	**13**	**8.67**	**0**	**0**	**0**	**0**
Stanislaw BURZA	7	33	67	3	70	8.48	0	0	0	0
Mathias SCHULTZ	**10**	**48**	**82**	**5**	**87**	**7.25**	**1**	**0**	**0**	**0**
Pawel BARAN	1	4	6	1	7	7.00	0	0	0	0
Dariusz FIJALKOWSKI	**1**	**3**	**5**	**0**	**5**	**6.67**	**0**	**0**	**0**	**0**
Emil KRAMER	5	21	28	1	29	5.52	0	0	0	0
Robert MIKOLAJCZAK	**11**	**48**	**59**	**7**	**66**	**5.50**	**0**	**0**	**0**	**0**
Ruslan GATIYATOV	7	34	59	7	66	5.50	0	0	0	0
Marcin LIBERSKI	**15**	**67**	**82**	**9**	**91**	**5.43**	**0**	**0**	**0**	**0**
Marat GATIYATOV	3	15	18	2	20	5.33	0	0	0	0
Denis SAJFUTDINOV	**4**	**17**	**22**	**0**	**22**	**5.18**	**0**	**0**	**1**	**2**
Matthias KRÖGER	1	4	5	0	5	5.00	0	0	0	0
Henning BAGER	**6**	**22**	**24**	**3**	**27**	**4.91**	**0**	**0**	**0**	**0**
Max DILGER	6	25	24	3	27	4.32	0	0	0	0
Magnus KARLSSON	**1**	**4**	**3**	**1**	**4**	**4.00**	**0**	**0**	**0**	**0**
Sebastian BRUCHEISER	5	10	6	2	8	3.20	0	0	0	0
René BACH	**2**	**5**	**4**	**0**	**4**	**3.20**	**0**	**0**	**0**	**0**
Mariusz KONSEK	6	15	7	2	9	2.40	0	0	0	0
Stephan KATT	**1**	**2**	**1**	**0**	**1**	**2.00**	**0**	**0**	**0**	**0**

GNIEZNO (A)
Saturday, September 27
Lost 30-62
Eriksson 12 (4), Kramer 3, R. Gatiyatov 4:1, Bager 3, Schultz 5, Konsek 0, Liberski 3.
Aggregate: Lost 75-107.

MISKOLC (H)
Sunday, September 28
Won 54-37
Eriksson 14:1, Kramer 1, R. Gatiyatov 9, Bager 8:2, Schultz 12, Konsek 5:1, Liberski 5:1.
Aggregate: Lost 84-94.

RIVNE (A)
Friday, October 10
Lost 38-52
M. Gatiyatov 9:2, *rider replacement for Burza*, R. Gatiyatov 9:2, Baran 6:1, Mikolajczak 4:1, Liberski 8, Konsek 2:1.
Aggregate: Lost 82-97.

SECOND LEAGUE (after play-offs)

	M	W	D	L	BP	Pts
Gniezno	16	12	1	3	7	32
Miskolc	16	10	0	6	6	26
Rivne	16	9	0	7	3	21
LODZ	**16**	**4**	**1**	**11**	**3**	**12**

SECOND LEAGUE (regular season)

	M	W	D	L	BP	Pts
Miskolc	10	8	0	2	4	20
Gniezno	10	7	0	3	4	18
Rivne	10	6	0	4	2	14
LODZ	**10**	**3**	**0**	**7**	**3**	**9**
Opole	10	3	0	7	1	7
Krosno	10	3	0	7	0	6

Stanislaw Burza

Polish Second League

OPOLE

TRACK FILE

Track: I. Wschodnia 2, 45233 Opole, Poland.
Telephone: 0048 077 4539600.
Website: www.KolejarzOpole.pl
Track Length: 321 metres.
Track Record: 60.4 secs, Adam Czechowicz, May 16, 2004.

2008 RESULTS

Second League

Final position...................... Fiftth

RIVNE (H)
Sunday, April 6
Won 51-42
Tomicek 9:1, Pawliczek 8:1, Czechowicz 12:1, Hautamäki 7, Lyngsø 11:1, Kildemand 3, Fleger 1:1, Chudy, did not ride.

MISKOLC (A)
Sunday, April 13
Lost 37-53
Lyngsø 6, Pawliczek 4, Tomicek 12:1, Rembas 0, Czechowicz 12:2 (4), no rider at six, Fleger 3, Larsson 0.

GNIEZNO (H)
Sunday, April 20
Lost 42-48
Lyngsø 8, Wallner 1:1, Czechowicz 10:2, Hautamäki 7:2, Tomicek 9, Fleger 3:1, Dabrowski, did not ride, Kildemand 4:1.

KROSNO (A)
Thursday, May 1
Lost 45-48
Pawliczek 5, Flis 3, Rembas 12 (6), Lyngsø 7:2, Czechowicz 6:2, Fleger 2, Dabrowski 10, Hansen 0.

SQUAD
Pawel Chudy, Adam Czechowicz, Slawomir Dabrowski, Rafal Fleger, Robert Flis, Lukasz Kasperek, Adam Pawliczek, Piotr Rembas, Marcin Sekula, Tomasz Szmid.
Foreign: Juha Hautämaki, Brian Lyngsø, Lars Hansen, Peter Kildemand, Niklas Larsson, Lee Smethills, Tomas Schmidt, Lubos Tomicek, Friedrich [Fritz] Wallner.

LODZ (A)
Sunday, June 1
Won 45-44
Czechowicz 3, Rembas 7:1, Lyngsø 9, Pawliczek 10:2, Sekula 9, no rider at six, Fleger 4, Dabrowski 3.

LODZ (H)
Sunday, June 8
Lost 43-46
Pawliczek 8:2, Czechowicz 10, Rembas 7:1, Lyngsø 7:2, Tomicek 6, no rider at six, Fleger 4, Dabrowski 1.
Aggregate: Lost 88-90.

KROSNO (H)
Sunday, July 20
Won 60-32
Rembas 6, Schmidt 5:1, Sekula 12:1, Wallner 7:2, **Czechowicz 11:1**, Chudy, did not ride, Dabrowski 8:2, **Fleger 11:1**.
Aggregate: Won 105-80.

GNIEZNO (A)
Sunday, July 27
Lost 28-63
Pawliczek 1, Rembas 2, Sekula 6:1 (2), Wallner 8,

Rider	M	R	Pts	BP	TPts	Ave	F	P	TR	TPts
Robert FLIS	1	1	3	0	3	12.00	0	0	0	0
Adam CZECHOWICZ	**10**	**43**	**79**	**11**	**90**	**8.37**	**0**	**1**	**2**	**5**
Marcin SEKULA	5	24	42	4	46	7.67	0	0	1	1
Brian LYNGSØ	**7**	**35**	**56**	**7**	**63**	**7.20**	**0**	**0**	**0**	**0**
Juha HAUTAMÄKI	2	9	14	2	16	7.11	0	0	0	0
Lubos TOMICEK	**5**	**23**	**37**	**2**	**39**	**6.78**	**0**	**0**	**0**	**0**
Friedrich WALLNER	4	18	26	4	30	6.67	0	0	0	0
Tomasz SCHMIDT	**2**	**9**	**13**	**1**	**14**	**6.22**	**0**	**0**	**0**	**0**
Adam PAWLICZEK	6	27	36	5	41	6.07	0	0	0	0
Piotr REMBAS	**7**	**31**	**42**	**4**	**46**	**5.94**	**0**	**0**	**1**	**3**
Rafal FLEGER	10	35	40	4	44	5.03	0	1	0	0
Slawomir DABROWSKI	**7**	**30**	**34**	**3**	**37**	**4.93**	**0**	**0**	**0**	**0**
Peter KILDEMAND	2	7	7	1	8	4.57	0	0	0	0
Pawel CHUDY	**1**	**1**	**0**	**0**	**0**	**0.00**	**0**	**0**	**0**	**0**
Lars HANSEN	1	2	0	0	0	0.00	0	0	0	0
Lukasz KASPEREK	**1**	**3**	**0**	**0**	**0**	**0.00**	**0**	**0**	**0**	**0**
Niklas LARSSON	1	4	3	0	0	0.00	0	0	0	0

Czechowicz 1, Chudy, did not ride, Dabrowski 1, Fleger 9.

Aggregate: Lost 70-111.

MISKOLC (H)
Sunday, August 3
Lost 43-47
Lyngsø 8:2, Sekula 11:2, Czechowicz 6:2, Wallner 10:1, Tomicek 1, Dabrowski 4, Fleger 3:1.

Aggregate: Lost 80-100.

RIVNE (A)
Sunday, August 10
Lost 35-57
Schmidt 8, Kasperek 0, Rembas 7:2, Czechowicz 9 (6), Sekula 4, Dabrowski 7, Chudy 0, Fleger 0.

Aggregate: Lost 86-99.

SECOND LEAGUE (regular season)

	M	W	D	L	BP	Pts
Miskolc	10	8	0	2	4	20
Gniezno	10	7	0	3	4	18
Rivne	10	6	0	4	2	14
Lodz	10	3	0	7	3	9
OPOLE	**10**	**3**	**0**	**7**	**1**	**7**
Krosno	10	3	0	7	0	6

OPOLE did not qualify for the play-offs.

Challenges

BALAKAVO [Russia] (H)
Thursday, April 10
Lost 37-52
Rembas 11:1, Pawliczek 10, Schmidt 5:3, Fleger 5, Sekula 2, Czechowicz 2, Chudy 2, Kasperek 0.
Balakavo: Nigmatzyanov 12, Vodiakov 10, Kosolapkin 9, Povazhny 7:2, Kuzin 7:1, Filinov 4:2, Gatiatov 2:1, Kudrashov 1, Nosov 0.

Individual

POLISH CHAMPIONSHIP
Quarter Final
Thursday, June 5
Ulamek 13, Zengota 11, Jedrzejak 11, Michal Szczepaniak 11, Swiderski 10, Miskowiak 10, Czechowicz 9, Buczkowski 7, Pawliczek 6, Zabik 6, Mateusz Szczepaniak 6, Jedrzejewski 5, Piszcz 5, Mitko 4, Rembas 4, Pawlaszczyk 2.

SILVER HELMET
Semi Final
Thursday, August 21
A. Gomolski 15, Lampart 12, Jedrzejewski 12, Pawlicki 11, Fleger 10, Musielak 9, Pytel 9, S.Kielbasa 8, Zengota 8, R. Kasprzak 7, Dudek 6, Idziorek 3, Baniak 3, Kajzer 2, Dabrowski 2, Fajfer 0.

GERARD STACH MEMORIAL
Sunday, May 11
Miskowiak 15, Czerwinski 14, Pawliczek 12, Czechowicz 12, Rembas 9, Wallner 9, Dabrowski 8, Szombierski 8, Smethills 8, M. Sekula 7, Schmidt 5, Kasperek 4, Lars Hansen 3, Fleger 2, Kowalczyk 2, Pluska 1.

JERZY SZCZAKIEL INVITATIONAL
Saturday, September 13
Michal Szczepaniak 14+3, Karpov 12+2, Kuciapa 12+R, Hlib 11+X, Klecha 11, Jamrozy 11, M. Jablonski 8, Fleger 8, Dabrowski 6, Smethills 6, Szmidt 6, Baran 6, Lukaszewicz 5.

2009 SQUADS

KROSNO
Roman **CHROMIK**, *Bartosz* **KASPROWIAK**, *Tomasz* **LUKASZEWICZ**.
Foreign: *Josef* **FRANC**, *Kenneth* **HANSEN**, *Krister* **JACOBSEN**, *Brian* **LYNGSØ**, *Martin* **MALEK**, *Lenar* **NIGMATZYANOV**, *Runa* **SOLA**, *Richard* **WOLFF**.
UNDER 21
Mateusz **KOWALCZYK**, *Piotr* **MACHNIK**.
Foreign: *Aleksander* **CONDA**, *Michael* **HADEK**, *Claes* **NEDERMARK**.

LODZ
Stanislaw **BURZA**, *Mariusz* **FRANKOW**, *Marcin* **LIBERSKI**, *Krzysztof* **STOJANOWSKI**.
Foreign: *Freddie* **ERIKSSON**, *Marat* **GATYATOV**, *Ruslan* **GATYATOV**, *Henrik* **GUSTAFSSON**, *Simon* **GUSTAFSSON**, *Emil* **KRAMER**, *Matthias* **KRÖGER**, *Denis* **SAJFUTDINOV**, *Mathias* **SCHULTZ**, *Zdenek* **SIMOTA**.
UNDER 21
Mariusz **KONSEK**, *Pawel* **PALIGA**.
Foreign: *Matija* **DUH**.

LUBLIN
Karol **BARAN**, *Pawel* **BARAN**, *Jacek* **REMPALA**, *Tomasz* **REMPALA**.
Foreign: *Lee* **COMPLIN**, *Kiril* **FILINOV**, *Richard* **HALL**, *David* **HOWE**, *William* **LAWSON**, *Andreas* **MESSING**, *Hynek* **STICHAUER**, *Lubos* **TOMICEK**.
UNDER 21
Rafal **KLIMEK**, *Maciej* **MICHALUK**, *Karol* **POLAK**.
Foreign: *Teemu* **LAHTI**, *Simon* **LAMBERT**, *Jonas* **MESSING**.

OPOLE
Adam **CZECHOWICZ**, *Robert* **FLIS**, *Lukasz* **KASPEREK**, *Piotr* **REMBAS**, *Marcin* **SEKULA**.
Foreign: *Stephan* **KATT**, *Robert* **KSIEZAK**, *Pavel* **ONDRASIK**, *Tomasz* **SCHMIDT**, *Friedrich [Fritz]* **WALLNER**.
UNDER 21
Pawel **CHUDY**, *Marcin* **KOJ**, *Lukasz* **SUSSMAN**.
Foreign: *Max* **DILGER**, *Jan* **HOLUB**.

PILA
Tomasz **CIESLEWICZ**, *Lukasz* **LINETTE**, *Krzysztof* **PECYNA**, *Piotr* **SWIST**, *Wojciech* **ZURAWSKI**.
Foreign: *Henning* **BAGER**, *Mathias* **BARTZ**, *Benji* **COMPTON**, *Cory* **GATHERCOLE**, *Jan* **GRAVERSEN**, *Roberto* **HAUPT**, *Aleksey* **KHARCHENKO**, *Steffen* **MELL**, *Kauko* **NIEMINEN**.
UNDER 21
Cyprian **SZYMKO**, *Marcel* **SZYMKO**.
Foreign: *René* **BACH**, *Nicki* **BARRETT**, *Robert*

Did not compete in League racing in 2008

LUBLIN

AFTER a year out of league racing, Lublin return to competitive action in 2009 under a total new management system.

Zbigniew Wojciechowski has taken over as President of the newly-formed Motor Club Speedway Lublin and they have declared their intention is to train young riders.

They will also work alongside the Amateur Speedway Club which ran meetings throughout 2008.

TRACK FILE

Track: Aleje Zygmuntowskie 5, 20101 Lublin, Poland.
Telephone: 0048 081 532 94 62 .
Website: www.tzlublin.com
Track Length: 388 metres.
Track Record: 66.19 secs, Tomasz Chrzanowski, July 22, 2007.

Individual

ROBERT DADOS MEMORIAL
Sunday, October 19
Daniel Jeleniewski 15+3, Jacek Rempala 11+3+2, Norbert Kosciuch 11+2+1, Adam Skornicki 13+0, Slawomir Drabik 11+R, Pawel Staszek 11+E, Pawel Miesiac 8, Grzegorz Knapp 7, Rafal Trojanowski 6, Kamil Zielinski 6, Marcin Rempala 5, Andrey Karpov 4, Rafal Klimek 4, Szymon Kielbasa 3, Tomasz Rempala 2, Maciej Michaluk 2.

RAWICZ *(continued from page 438)*

LORD MAYOR CUP
Sunday, August 17
Ulamek 15, Okoniewski 12, Jedrzejak 11, Skornicki 11, Kajzer 10, Miskowiak 10, Ferjan 9, Dym 8, Mi.Szczepaniak 8, Janowski 7, Nowaczyk 6, Suchecki 5, Kosciuch 3, Jamrozy 3, Klecha 2, Drabik 0.
■ ***For European Under 19 Team Final see EUROPE.***

HENDERSON, Peter KILDEMAND, Viatcheslav KOZACHUK.

RAWICZ
Piotr DYM, Piotr DZIATKOWIAK, Maciej JADER, Krystian KLECHA, Marcin KOZDRAS, Lukasz LOMAN, Robert MIKOLAJCZEK, Marcin NOWACZYK, Andrzej ZIEJA.
Foreign: *Sebastian ALDÉN, Voktor GOLUBOVSKY, Robert PETTERSSON, Ronny WEIS.*
UNDER 21
Foreign: *Maks GREGORIC, Stanislav OGORODNIK, Erik*

Did not compete in League racing in 2008

PILA

PILA are the second famous team to make a league comeback in 2009.

Their heady days of being Ekstraliga champions (as recently as 1999) are long gone but they return to the Second League and have made a major signing in veteran Piotr Swist.

Probably their biggest foreign signing is exciting Danish teenager René Bach.

TRACK FILE

Track: ul. Bydgoska 80, 64-920 Pila, Poland.
Telephone: 0048 0603 250059.
Website: www.poloniapila.isp.net.pl
Track Length: 349 metres.
Track Record: 61.18 secs, Hans Nielsen, April 24, 1999.

Individual

LORD MAYOR CUP
September 14
Daniel Jeleniewski 14, Dawid Stachyra 13+3, Robert Miskowiak 13+2, Krystian Klecha 11, Andrej Karpov 10, Aleksander Kharchenko 10, Marcin Nowaczyk 9, Robert Mikolajczak 9, Damian Celmer 7, Piotr Dziatkowiak 7, Grzegorz Strozyk 3, Michal Rajkowski 3, Kamil Cieslar 3, Maciej Jader 2, Mariusz Frankow 2, Marcel Kajzer 2, Pawel Ratajszczak [R] 0.

POZNAN *(continued from page 436)*

ADAM SKORNICKI TESTIMONIAL
Saturday, May 17
BLUES 28+3 (Miedzinski 9, Chrzanowski 7, Batchelor 7, Kosciuch 5+3), **WHITES 28+2** (Crump 11+2, Dobrucki 8, Okoniewski 8, Pytel 1), **REDS 22** (Adams 10, Watt 7, Skornicki 4, Screen 1), **YELLOWS 19** (Walasek 8, Drabik 7, Puszakowski 3, Dziatkowiak [TR] 1, Zabik 0).

THE PIAST SHALE
Sunday, October 12
Swiderski 14, Suchecki 14, Pytel 14, Trojanowski 11, Kosciuch 10, Skornicki 9, Paluch 8, Klecha 8, Puszakowski 6, Musielak 6, Dudek 5, Dziatkowiak 5, Piaszczynski 5, Kajzer 2, Zmarzlik 2, Loman 1.

PUDEL, Matic VOLDRIH, Simon WALKER, Casper WORTMANN.

For MISKOLC's 2009 squad see Hungary (page 379).

ROMANIA

ROMANIAN CHAMPIONSHIP

VETERAN Alexandru Toma, who has been Romania's top rider for nearly 10 years missed out on his opportunity to win a fifth national title.

Toma, 40, crashed out in the second round of the championship and that cost him any chance of a hat-trick of titles.

Bulgarian Milan Manev seized his opportunity and was unbeaten in two of the four rounds and dropped only five points in the other two.

Teenager Andrian Gheorge, 19, looks a potential champion although the lack of riders and regular track action will continue to hold back Romania's hopes of making any real impact although their riders are now beginning to spread their wings a little and several competed outside their own country in 2008.

Because of the lack of availability of the country's only track at Bahia, the championship was run over a weekend – with two meetings on the Saturday and another two on the Sunday.

Each rider had three rides with accumulated points from all four meetings counting towards the championship.

FINAL STANDINGS
1 Milan MANEV 31, 2 Fanica POPA 29, 3 Andrian GHEORGE 22, 4 Alexandru TOMA 21, 5 Marian GHEORGE 18, 6 Marian COJACARU 16, 7 Mihaj DEJMAR 11, 8 Stefan POPA 8, 9 Florian BARABASU 4.

Round 1
Braila, Saturday, September 6
Fanica Popa 7, Milan Manev 6, Marian Gheorge 6, Alexandru Toma 6, Andrian Gheorge 5, Mihaj Dejmar 5, Marian Cojacura 2, Stefan Popa 2, Florin Barabasu 1.

Round 2
Braila, Saturday, September 6
Milan Manev 9, Fanica Popa 8, Andrian Gheorge 7, Marian Gheorge 5, Marian Cojacuru 5, Mihaj Dejmar 3, Stefan Popa 2, Florin Barabasu 2, Alexandru Toma 0.

Round 3
Braila, Sunday, September 7
Milan Manev 9, Fanica Popa 8, Alexandru Toma 7, Marian Cojacaru 6, Andrian Gheorge 4, Marian Gheorge 2, Mihaj Dejmar 2, Stefan Popa 2, Florin Bartabasu 0.

Round 4
Braila, Sunday, September 7
Alexandru Toma 8, Milan Manev 7, Fanica Popa 6, Andrian Gheorge 6, Marian Gheorge 5, Marian Cojacaru 3, Stefan Popa 2, Mihaj Dejmar 1, Florin Barabasu 1.

Roll of Honour

1962	Gheorghe VOICULESCU
1983	Pavel IONEL
1984	Nicolae PURAVET
1985	Pavel IONEL
1986	Dan GASPAR
1987	Ilie Sorin GHIBU
1988	Ilie Sorin GHIBU
1989	Marius SOAITA
1990	Ilie Sorin GHIBU
1991	Ilie Sorin GHIBU
1992	Marius SOAITA
1993	Mircea AGRISAN
1994	Mircea AGRISAN
1995	Mircea AGRISAN
1996	Mircea AGRISAN
1997	Mircea AGRISAN
1998	Mircea AGRISAN
1999	Mircea AGRISAN
2000	Ilie Sorin GHIBU
2001	Mircea AGRISAN
2002	Alexandru TOMA
2003	Alexandru TOMA
2004	Mircea AGRISAN
2005	Mircea AGRISAN
2006	Alexandru TOMA
2007	Alexandru TOMA
2008	Milan MANEV (Bulgaria)

ROMANIAN UNDER 21 CHAMPIONSHIP

PREDICTABLY Andrian Gheorge, who had ridden so well in the senior championship, dominated the Under 21 Championship which was run over the same weekend as the senior title.

Three rounds – two on the Saturday and one the following day – were staged with riders having two races each, Gheorge winning all six.

FINAL STANDINGS
1 Andrian GHEORGE 18, 2 Daniel MARIN 8, 3 Florin BARABASU 7, 4 Alin CIOCLEI 2, 5 Marin OLARU 0, 6 Valentin POPA 0.

Round 1
Braila, Saturday, September 6
Andrian Gheorge 6, Daniel Marin 3, Florin Barabasu 2, Alin Cioclei 1, Marin Olaru 0, Valentin Popa 0.

Round 2
Braila, Saturday, September 6
Andrian Gheorge 6, Florin Barabasu 3, Daniel Marin 3, Alin Cioclei 1, Marin Olaru 0, Valentin Popa 0.

Round 3
Braila, Sunday, September 7
Andrian Gheorge 6, Daniel Marin 2, Florin Barabasu 2, Alin Cioclei 0, Marin Olaru 0, Valentin Popa 0.

Roll of Honour

1983	Marian GHEORGE
1984	Ilie Sorin GHIBU
1985	Mircea AGRISAN
1986	Mircea AGRISAN
1987	Mircea AGRISAN
1988	Mircea AGRISAN
1989	Mircea AGRISAN
1990	Stefan STELIAN
1991	Fanica POPA
1992	Fanica POPA
1993	Fanica POPA

2004 .... Mihaj DEJMAR
2005 .... Mihaj DEJMAR
2006 .... Mihaj DEJMAR
2007 .... Mihaj DEJMAR
2008 .... Andrian GHEORGE

Individual

ROMANIA CUP

Braila, Saturday, May 10

Alexandru Toma 12, Fanica Popa 11, Milan Manev 9, Stefan Popa 8.

GHEORGE VOICULESCO & EUGENE BOTEZATU MEMORIAL

Braila, Saturday, September 20

Tomasz Lukaszewicz 14, Kiril Cukanov 14, Vladimir Dubinin 13, Ronny Weis 10, Milan Manev 10, Alexandru Toma 0, Attila Molnar 8, Attila Lorincz 8, Piotr Machnik 8, Marian Gheorghe 7, Andrian Gheorghe 7, Sergey Borisenko 4, Fanica Popa 4, Rastislav Bandzi 2, Stefan Popa 1, Florian Barabasu 1, Daniel Marin, did not ride.

Meeting run in conjunction with the MACEC Cup round.

Roll of Honour

1991 .... Marius SOAITA
2004 .... Sebastian KOWALIK (Poland)
2005 .... Alexandru TOMA
2007 .... Alexandru TOMA
2008 .... Tomasz LUKASZEWICZ (Poland)

MACEC Cup

ALEXANDRU Toma maintained his reputation in the MACEC Cup, successfully retaining his title

He benefited from riding in all four rounds but still posted decent performances, finishing in the top six in Poland, the Ukraine, Hungary and at his home track at Braila.

Five other Romanians took part in the Braila round but only Fanicva Popa raced elsewhere, failing to score at Lviv.

Final Standings

	1	*2*	*3*	*4*	*Tot*
1 ALEXANDRU TOMA	**10**	**9**	**11**	**10**	**40**
2 Kiril CUKANOV	–	14	12	12	38
3 Tomasz LUKASZEWICZ	–	14	14	7	35
4 Milan MANEV	6	10	7	6	29
5 Vladimir DUBININ	–	13	13	–	26
6 Attila MOLNAR	7	8	10	–	25
7 Attila LORINCZ	7	8	6	–	21
8 Piotr MACHNIK	–	8	5	5	18
9 Sergey BORISENKO	6	4	5	1	16
10 Maciej MICHALUK	9	–	–	7	16
11 Tomasz PISZCZ	15	–	–	–	15
11 Zoltan ADORJAN	–	–	–	15	15
13 Jaroslav POLIUCHOVIC	–	–	14	–	14
13 Dino KOVACIC	–	–	–	14	14
15 Grzegorz KNAPP	13	–	–	–	13
16 Dawid STACHYRA	12	–	–	–	12
16 Rafal KLIMEK	12	–	–	–	12
18 Sebastian TRUMINSKI	10	–	–	–	10
18 Ronny WEIS	–	10	–	–	10
18 Nikola PIGAC	–	–	–	10	10
21 Rastislav BANDZI	4	2	–	3	9
22 Vladimir TEJGAL	4	–	4	–	8
23 Mikhail ONESHKO	–	–	8	–	8
23 Sandor FEKETE	–	–	–	8	8
23 Roland BENKO	–	–	–	8	8
26 Marian GHEORGHE	*–*	*7*	*–*	*–*	*7*
26 Andrian GHEORGHE	*–*	*7*	*–*	*–*	*7*
26 Zsolt BENCZE	–	–	–	7	7
29 Petr FEDIK	2	–	–	3	5
30 Stanislav OGORODNIK	–	–	5	–	5
31 Fanica POPA	*–*	*4*	*0*	*–*	*4*
32 Lubos DORICA	2	–	–	–	2
33 Alexander GAJKOVSKY	–	–	2	–	2
33 Zsolt NAGY	–	–	–	2	2
35 Patrik Kotta KIS	1	–	–	–	1
35 Stefan POPA	*–*	*1*	*–*	*–*	*1*
35 Florian BARABASU	*–*	*1*	*–*	*–*	*1*
35 Mate SZEGEDI	–	–	–	1	1

Round 1

Lublin, Poland, Saturday, July 26

Tomasz Piszcz 15, Grzegorz Knapp 13, Dawid Stachyra 12, Rafal Klimek 12, Sebastian Truminski 10, Alexandru Toma 10, Maciej Michaluk 9, Attila Molnar 7, Attila Lorincz 7, Sergey Borisenko 6, Milan Manev 6, Rastislav Bandzi 4, Valdimir Tejgal 4, Petr Fedik 2, Lubos Dorica 2, Patrik Kotta Kis 1, Fanica Popa, did not ride.

Round 2

Braila, Romania, Saturday, September 20

Tomasz Lukaszewicz 14, Kiril Cukanov 14, Vladimir Dubinin 13, Ronny Weis 10, Milan Manev 10, Alexandru Toma 0, Attila Molnar 8, Attil Lorincz 8, Piotr Machnik 8, Marian Gheorghe 7, Andrian Gheorghe 7, Sergey Borisenko 4, Fanica Popa 4, Rastislav Bandzi 2, Stefan Popa 1, Florian Barabasu 1, Daniel Marin, did not ride.

Round 3

Lviv, Ukraine, Sunday, September 28

Tomasz Lukaszewicz 14+3, Jaroslav Poliuchovic 14+2, Vladimir Dubinin 13, Kiril Cukanov 12, Alexandru Toma 11, Attila Molnar 10, Michail Oneshko 8, Milan Manev 7, Attila Lorincz 6, Sergey Borisenko 5, Piotr Machnik 5, Stanislaw Ogorodnik 5, Vladimir Tejgal 4, Aleksandr Gajkovsky 2, Fanica Popa 0.

Round 4

Debrecen, Hungary, Saturday, October 25

Zoltan Adorjan 15, Dino Kovacic 14, Kiril Cukanov 12, Alexandru Toma 10, Nikola Pigac 10, Sandor Fekete 8, Roland Benko 8, Tomasz Lukaszewski 7, Maciej Michaluk 7, Zsolt Bencze 7, Milan Manev 6, Piotr Machnik 5, Rastislav Bandzi 3, Petr Fedik 3, Zsolt Nagy [R] 2, Mate Szegedi 1, Sergey Borisenko 1, Sandor Konya [R] 0.

Roll of Honour

2004 .... Pawel BARAN (Poland)
2005 .... Daniel JELENIEWSKI (Poland)
2006 .... Andrey KARPOV (Ukraine)
2007 .... Alexandru TOMA (Romania)
2008 .... Alexandru TOMA (Romania)

2009 FIXTURES

ROMANIAN CHAMPIONSHIP

Round 1: Saturday, April 18, Braila.
Round 2: Saturday, May 16, Braila.
Round 3: Saturday, September 5, Braila.
Round 4: Saturday, September 12, Braila.

INDIVIDUAL

Romanian Cup, Saturday, April 11, Braila.
Eugene Botezatu & Gheorge Voiculescu Memorial, Saturday, September 19, Braila.

RUSSIA

RUSSIAN CHAMPIONSHIP

FINAL

Oktyabrsky, Saturday, August 16

EMIL Sajfutdinov's bid to complete a unique double was spiked by Eastbourne winter target Denis Gizatullin who successfully retained his title.

Sajfutdinov had completed the first leg of his attempt by winning the Under 21 crown in Togliatti.

But he was beaten four times, including a second place race-off against Grigori Laguta who was unbeaten save for an expensive puncture when he came up against eventual winner Gizatullin, who actually finished third in Heat 9.

	1	2	3	4	5	Tot	RO
1 Denis GIZATULLIN	**3**	**3**	**1**	**3**	**3**	**13**	
2 Grigori LAGUTA	3	3	R	3	3	12	3
3 Emil SAJFUTDINOV	3	2	3	2	2	12	2
4 Renat GAFUROV	2	1	2	3	3	11	
5 Denis SAJFUTDINOV	1	3	2	2	2	10	
6 Roman POVAZHNY	2	3	0	1	2	8	
7 Daniil IVANOV	0	2	3	1	1	7	
8 Sergey DARKIN	3	2	0	1	1	7	
9 Sergey KUZIN	0	0	3	3	F	6	
10 Ilya BONDARENKO	1	1	0	2	2	6	
11 Artem VODYAKOV	0	1	F	2	3	6	
12 Marat GATIYATOV	1	1	3	0	FX	5	
13 Aleksey GUZAJEV	2	1	2	F	FX	5	
14 Aleksey KHARCHENKO	1	0	1	2	1	5	
15 Viktor GOLUBOVSKY	2	0	1	1	0	4	
16 Roman IVANOV [R]	2					2	
17 Roman KANTIUKOV [R]	1					1	
18 Evgeny GOMOZOV	0	0	N2	0	0	0	

Semi Final

Balakovo, Friday, June 6

1 Grigori Laguta 14, 2 Marat Gatiyatov 12, 3 Daniil Ivanov 12, 4 Viktor Golubovsky 10, 5 Ilya Bondarenko 10, 6 Sergey Kuzin 9, 7 Aleksey Guzajev 8+3, 8 Roman Ivanov 8+2, 9 Lenar Nigmatzyanov 8+1, 10 Kiril Filinov 8+FX, 11 Andrey Kudriashov [R] 6, 12 Vasily Panhay 4, 13 Vyacheslav Kazachuk 3, 14 Alexander Kazionny 3, 15 Aleksey Izotov 2, 16 Radik Tibeev 1, 17 Oleg Kurguskin 1, 18 Mikhail Skatchkov [R] 0.

Semi Final

Salavat, Tuesday, June 17

1 Renat Gafurov 15, 2 Denis Sajfutdinov 12, 3 Sergey Darkin 12, 4 Artem Vodyakov 11, 5 Roman Povazhny 10, 6 Aleksey Kharchenko 10, 7 Evgeny Gomozov 9, 8 Eduard Shaikhullin 8, 9 Roman Kantyukov 6, 10 Denis Nosov 5, 11 Ruslan Gatiyatov 5, 12 Artem Schepin 5, 13 Igor Kononov 3, 14 Nikita Parfyonov 3, 15 Albert Tibeev 3, 16 Yuri Soloviev 2, 17 Timur Garifullin [R] 1, 18 Nikita Lazarev [R] 0.

Roll of Honour

1960 .... Igor PLECHANOV
1961 .... Igor PLECHANOV
1962 .... Igor PLECHANOV
1963 .... Yuri CZEKRANOV
1964 .... Lev KRAJEV
1965 .... Farid SZAJNUROV
1966 .... Farid SZAJNUROV
1967 .... Vladimir KORNEV
1968 .... Vladimir KORNEV
1969 .... Yuri DUBININ
1970 .... Nikolai AKESNOV
1971 .... Valeri GORDEEV
1972 .... Vladimir GORDEEV
1973 .... Nikolai KORNEV
1974 .... Viktor NIKIPIETOV
1975 .... Mikhail STAROSTIN
1976 .... Vladimir GORDEEV
1977 .... Valeri GORDEEV
1978 .... Sergey DENISOV
1979 .... Aleksandr MIKLASZEVSKY
1980 .... Aleksandr MIKLASZEVSKY
1981 .... Mikhail STAROSTIN
1982 .... Viktor KUZNETSOV
1983 .... Rif SAITGAREEV
1984 .... Rif SAITGAREEV
1985 .... Mikhail STAROSTIN
1986 .... Mikhail STAROSTIN
1987 .... Mikhail STAROSTIN
1988 .... Rif SAITGAREEV
1989 .... Rinat MARDANSCHIN
1990 .... Mikhail STAROSTIN
1991 .... Mikhail STAROSTIN
1992 .... Sergey KUZIN
1993 .... Sergey KUZIN
1994 .... Oleg KURGUSKIN
1995 .... Rif SAITGAREEV
1996 .... Rinat MARDANSCHIN
1997 .... Rinat MARDANSCHIN
1998 .... Rinat MARDANSCHIN
1999 .... Oleg KURGUSKIN
2000 .... Sergey DARKIN
2001 .... Roman POVAZHNY
2002 .... Sergey DARKIN
2003 .... Oleg KURGUSKIN
2004 .... Oleg KURGUSKIN
2005 .... Evgeny GOMOZOV
2006 .... Renat GAFUROV
2007 .... Denis GIZATULLIN
2008 .... Denis GIZATULLIN

RUSSIAN UNDER 21 CHAMPIONSHIP

FINAL

Togliatti, Thursday, August 14

EMIL SAJFUTDINOV hardly needed home track advantage to win his second Russian Under 21 title in four seasons.

The World Junior Champion first won the crown when he was only only 14 but missed out in both 2006 and 2007.

This time around he made no mistake with a 15 point maximum although he had been beaten byArtem Laguta – Grigori's younger brother – in the Vladivostok semi final earlier in the year.

The draw brought the three favourites together in Heat 19 and the finishing order in that race determined 1-2-3 on the rostrum.

Denis Alexeev and Vasily Panhay were both injured and taken to hospital during an ultra-competitive meeting.

	1	2	3	4	5	Tot	RO
1 Emil SAJFUTDINOV	**3**	**3**	**3**	**3**	**3**	**15**	
2 Artem LAGUTA	3	3	3	3	2	14	
3 Artem VODYAKOV	3	3	2	3	1	12	3
4 Igor KONONOV	3	2	3	2	2	12	2
5 Alexander KOSOLAPKIN	FX	3	2	2	3	10	
6 Artem SCHEPIN	1	2	2	1	3	9	
7 Sergey KARACHINTSEV	2	2	1	2	2	9	
8 Vyacheslav KAZACHUK	2	1	1	3	FX	7	
9 Mikhail KREMER [R]	0	3	FX	FX	3	6	
10 Aleksey IZOTOV	2	1	0	1	2	6	
11 Mikhail SKATCHKOV	0	2	1	1	1	5	
12 Denis NOSOV	0	1	FX	2	0	3	
13 Nikita PARFYONOV	FX	0	2	0	1	3	
14 Andrey KUDRIASHOV	1	FX	FX	1	1	3	
15 Vasily PANHAY	2					2	
16 Sergey SYGRYSHEV	FX	1	0	0	FX	2	
17 Denis ALEXEEV	FX					0	
18 Valeri SAVELIEV [R]	0	0	0	0		0	

Semi Final

Vladivostok, Sunday, June 29

1 Artem Laguta 15, 2 Emil Sajfutdinov 14, 3 Vasily Panhay 13, 4 Vyacheslav Kazachuk 12, 5 Mikhail Skatchkov 10, 6 Sergey Sygryshev 9, 7 Aleksey Izotov 9, 8 Sergey Karachintsev 8+3, 9 Mikhail Kremer 8+X, 10 Vladimir Ryazantsev 6, 11 Roman Zakharov 4, 11 Evgeny Sidorin 4, 12 Denis Tsyganov 2, 13 Alexander Maksakov 1, 14 Nikita Kuranov 1, 14 Alexander Marinyuk 1, 16 Vyacheslav Tyulkin 0.

Semi Final

Oktyabrsky, Wednesday, July 9

1 Artem Vodyakov 15, 2 Alexander Kosolapkin 14, 3 Igor Kononov 12, 4 Denis Nosov 10, 5 Andrey Kudriashov 10, 6 Denis Alekseev 9, 7 Nikita Parfyonov 9, 8 Artem Schepin 9, 9 Timur Garifullin 7, 10 Valeri Saveliev 5, 11 Alexander Kochetov 5, 12 Vitaly Belousov 5, 13 Vladimir Borudulin 4, 14 Renat Nigmatullin 4, 15 Dmitri Tikhonov 2, 16 Vyacheslav Shunevich 1.

Roll of Honour

1987 .... Konstantin SVINKIN
1988 .... Andrey VOLOKOV
1989 .... Alexander BIELSKI
1990 .... Not staged
1991 .... Sergey KUZIN
1992 .... Oleg KIPTIEV
1993 .... Oleg KIPTIEV
1994 .... Sergey EROSHIN
1995 .... Eduard SHAIKHULLIN
1996 .... Vladimir DUBININ
1997 .... Roman POVAZHNY
1998 .... Andrey GANTSEV
1999 .... Konstantin KORNEV
2000 .... Semen VLASOV
2001 .... Renat GAFUROV
2002 .... Denis GIZATULLIN
2003 .... Renat GAFUROV
2004 .... Denis GIZATULLIN
2005 .... Emil SAJFUTDINOV
2006 .... Aleksey KHARCHENKO
2007 .... Daniil IVANOV
2008 .... Emil SAJFUTDINOV

RUSSIAN UNDER 19 CHAMPIONSHIP

FINAL

Balakovo, Tuesday, August 26

IN the absence of Emil Sajfutdinov, favourite Artem Laguta took the Russian Under 19 Championship Final after having to settle for the silver medal 12 months earlier.

Artem Laguta 14, Vyacheslav Kazachuk 13, Artem Vodyakov 12+3, Andrey Kudriashov 12+2, Sergey Sygryshev 10, Evgeny Sidorin 10, Sergey Karachintsev 9, Valeri Saveliev 8, Fedor Poptsov 6, Evgeny Schepin 5, Nikita Parfyonov 5, Denis Inyushev 5, Dmitri Tikhonov 2, Alexander Kochenov 2, Mikhail Kremer 2, Vitaly Belousov 2, Yuri Soloviev [R] 2.

Roll of Honour

2007 .... Artem VODYAKOV
2008 .... Artem LAGUTA

RUSSIAN PAIRS CHAMPIONSHIP

FINAL

Balakovo, Saturday, August 30

1 SK TURBINA, BALAKOVO 28 (Denis Gizatullin [R] 16, Roman Povazhny 12,Sergey Kuzin, did not ride), **2 SALAVAT 26** (Renat Gafurov 17, Viktor Golubovsky [R] 5, Radik Tibeev 4), **3 TOGLIATTI 22** (Denis Sajfutdinov 10, Daniil Ivanov [R] 7, Roman Ivanov 5), **4 VLADIVOSTOK 20** (Aleksey Kharchenko 14, Maksim Karachintsev 6, Mikhail Skatchkov [R], did not ride), **5 STMK TURBINA, BALAKOVO 14** (Aleksey Guzajev [r] 10, Roman Zakharov 4, Alexander Maksakov, did not ride), **6 NEVA St. PETERSBURG 10** (Maksim Lobzenko 5, Aleksey Poptsov 5, Denis Tsyganov [R] 0), **7 JUNIOR OKTYABRSKY 3** (Yuri Soloviev 2, Nikita Parfyonov 1, Ruslan Sattarov [R] 0).

RUSSIAN UNDER 21 PAIRS

FINAL

Salavat, Thursday, October 2

1 SK TURBINA BALAKOVO 24 (Artem Vodyakov [R] 13, Alexander Kosolapkin 11, Andrey Kudriashov, dfid not ride), **2 SALAVAT 21** (Igor Kononov [R] 14, Artem Schepin 7, Valery Saveliev, did not ride), **3 TOGLIATTI 16** (Evgeny Sidorin 11, Sergey Karachintsev, 5, Alexander Antipin [R], did not ride), **4 KAMIENSK URALS 13** (Vitaly Belousov [R] 8, Dmitri Tickonov 5, Evgeny Taushkanov, did not ride), **5 STMK TURBINA BALAKOVO 11** (Aleksey Izotov [R] 8, Roman Zakharov 3, Alexander Maksakov 0), **6 JUNIOR OKTYABRSKY 5** (Yuri Soloviev 2, Ruslan Sattarov 2, Ruslan Mardanschin [R] 1).

2008 RUSSIAN LEAGUE FINAL TABLE

		M	W	D	L	PtsF	PtsA	MPts
1	TOGLIATTI	8	6	0	2	387	332	12
2	VLADIVOSTOK	8	5	1	2	381.5	337.5	11
3	BALAKOVO	8	4	0	4	375	343	8
4	CHERVONOGRAD	8	3	1	4	328	391	7
5	SALAVAT	8	1	0	7	324.5	392.5	2

For **Chervonograd** details see UKRAINE

Russian League

BALAKOVO

2008 RESULTS

Final position..Third

VLADIVOSTOK (H)
Thursday, May 29
Won 47-43
Protasiewicz 7:1, Kudriashov 1:1, Gizatullin 12:2, Gatiyatov, did not ride, Povazhny 6, Kosolapkin 1:1, Vodyakov 7:1, Walasek 13.

SALAVAT (H)
Thursday, June 26
Won 57-33
Karlsson 12, Kudriashov 0, Gizatullin 12:3, Kuzin 1:1, Povazhny 10, Kosolapkin 5, Vodyakov 10, Walasek 7.

TOGLIATTI (H)
Thursday, July 24
Lost 40-50
Nicholls 11, Kudriashov 4:3, Gizatullin 9, Gatiyatov 0, Kuzin 1:1, Kosolapkin 1:1, Vodyakov 8:2, Jonsson 6.

CHERVONOGRAD (H)
Thursday, July 31
Won 60-29
Gizatullin 14:1, Kudriashov 1, Filinov 4:1, Gatiyatov 4, Protasiewicz 11, Kosolapkin 2:1, Vodyakov 10:1, **Walasek 14:1**.

VLADIVOSTOK (A)
Thursday, August 7
Lost 37-53
Gizatullin 8, Kudriashov 0, Povazhny 8:1, Filinov 1, Karlsson 10, Kosolapkin 2:1, Vodyakov 8:2, Walasek 0.

SQUAD
Konstantin Belov, Ruslan Biktimirov,Vladimir Borodulin, Kiril Filinov, Maksim Gafurov, Marat Gatiyatov, Denis Gizatullin, Maksim Kalimullin, Aleksandr Kosolapkin, Andrey Kudriashov, Sergey Kuzin, Lenar Nigmatzyanov, Denis Nosov, Roman Povazhny, Artem Vodyakov.
Foreign: Andreas Jonsson, Peter Karlsson, Scott Nicholls, Piotr Protasiewicz, Lee Richardson, Grzegorz Walasek.

TOGLIATTI (A)
Tuesday, September 9
Lost 41-49
Gizatullin 7, Kosolapkin 3:2, Povazhny 7:3, Filinov, did not ride, Karlsson 11, Kudriashov 0, Vodyakov 7, Walasek 6.

SALAVAT (A)
Friday, September 26
Won 51-38
Gizatullin 8:1, Kudriashov 2, Povazhny 6:2, Gatiyatov, did not ride, Karlsson 12, Kosolapkin 2:1, Vodyakov 10:1, Protasiewicz 11.

CHERVONOGRAD (A)
Thursday, October 9
Lost 42-48
Povazhny 12:1, Kudriashov 3:1, Filinov 2, Gatiyatov 3:1, Kuzin 6:1, Kosolapkin 9:1, Vodyakov 5:1, Gizatullin 2.

RUSSIAN LEAGUE

	M	*W*	*D*	*L*	*Pts*
Togliatti	8	6	0	2	12
Vladivostok	8	5	1	2	11
BALAKOVO	**8**	**4**	**0**	**4**	**8**
Chervonograd	8	3	1	4	7
Salavat	8	2	1	0	2

2009 Squad

Konstantin BELOV, Vladimir BORODULIN, Denis GIZATULLIN, Maksim KALIMULLIN, Andrey KUDRIASHOV, Sergey KUZIN, Denis NOSOV, Roman POVAZHNY, Emil SAJFUTDINOV, Denis SAJFUTDINOV.

Rider	*M*	*R*	*Pts*	*BP*	*TPts*	*Ave*	*F*	*P*
Peter KARLSSON	4	18	45	0	45	10.00	2	0
Piotr PROTASIEWICZ	**3**	**13**	**29**	**1**	**30**	**9.23**	**0**	**0**
Denis GIZATULLIN	8	37	72	7	79	8.54	0	2
Grzegorz WALASEK	**5**	**20**	**40**	**1**	**41**	**8.20**	**0**	**1**
Roman POVAZHNY	6	30	49	7	56	7.47	0	0
Scott NICHOLLS	**1**	**6**	**11**	**0**	**11**	**7.33**	**0**	**0**
Artem VODYAKOV	8	41	65	7	72	7.02	0	0
Alexander KOSOLAPKIN	**8**	**25**	**25**	**8**	**33**	**5.28**	**0**	**0**
Sergey KUZIN	3	9	8	3	11	4.89	0	0
Andreas JONSSON	**1**	**5**	**6**	**0**	**6**	**4.80**	**0**	**0**
Marat GATIYATOV	3	7	7	1	8	4.57	0	0
Andrey KUDRIASHOV	**8**	**19**	**11**	**5**	**16**	**3.37**	**0**	**0**
Kiril FILINOV	3	10	7	1	8	3.20	0	0

Track: 413840, Saratov Region, g.Balakovo Boulevard, ul.Parhomenko 8, Russia.
Website: www.turbina.net

Russian League

SALAVAT

2008 RESULTS

Final position..Fifth

CHERVONOGRAD (A)
Thursday, April 24
Lost 37-53
Darkin 11, Lazarev 0, Vlasov 3:1, R. Tibeev 4:1, Shaikhullin 4, A. Schepin 2:1, Kononov 5, Gafurov 8.

TOGLIATTI (A)
Thursday, June 5
Lost 36-53
Gollob 8:1, A. Schepin 0, Darkin 12:1, Shaikhullin 0, R. Tibeev 1, Alexeev 0, Kononov 4:1, Gafurov 11:1.

BALAKOVO (A)
Thursday, June 26
Lost 33-57
Darkin 12, A. Schepin 0, Vlasov 0, Golubovsky 5:1, Kantyukov 0, Alexeev 2, Kononov 6:1, Gafurov 8:1.

VLADIVOSTOK (A)
Thursday, July 31
Lost 42-47
Darkin 6, Alexeev 0, Jedrzejak 12, Golobovsky, did not ride, Miedzinski 9, A. Schepin 1, Kononov 8:3, Gafurov 6.

VLADIVOSTOK (H)
Thursday, August 28
Lost 42.5-47.5
Darkin 2, A. Schepin 2:1, Golubovsky 7:1, Vlasov 3:1, Gafurov 12, Saveliev 0.5, Kononov 12, Jedrzejak 4.

SQUAD
Denis Alexeev, Sergey Darkin, Sergey Eroshin, Renat Gafurov, Igor Glavinsky, Viktor Golubovsky, Mikhail Ivanov, Roman Kantyukov, Roman Kashirin, Igor Kononov, Nikita Lazarev, Valery Saveljev, Artem Schepin, Eduard Shaikhullin, Evgeny Schepin, Albert Tibeev, Radik Tibeev, Gatiyatov Tsiganov, Semen Vlasov.
Foreign: Tomasz Gollob, Tomasz Jedrzejak, Jacek Krzyzaniak, Adrian Miedzinski.

CHERVONOGRAD (H)
Friday, September 19
Won 62-28
Darkin 10:2, A. Schepin 4:1, Golobovsky 9, **Vlasov 11:1**, **Gafurov 15**, Saveliev 0, **Kononov 10:2**, Kantyukov 3:1.

BALAKOVO (H)
Friday, September 26
Lost 38-51
Darkin 5:1, A. Schepin 0, Vlasov 12:1, Golubovsky 5:2, Gafurov 10, Lazarev 1, Kononov 5:1, R. Tibeev, did not ride.

TOGLIATTI (H)
Wednesday, October 1
Lost 34-56
Gafurov 10, Kononov 1:1, Vlasov 11, Darkin 1, Golubovsky 5, Lazarev 1, A. Schepin 2:1, R. Tibeev 3:1.

RUSSIAN LEAGUE

	M	W	D	L	Pts
Togliatti	8	6	0	2	12
Vladivostok	8	5	1	2	11
Balakovo	8	4	0	4	8
Chervonograd	8	3	1	4	7
SALAVAT	**8**	**2**	**1**	**0**	**2**

2009 Squad

Denis **ALEXEEV**, Igor **GLAVINSKY**, Viktor **GOLUBOVSKY**, Mikhail **IVANOV**, Roman **KASHIRIN**, Valeri **SAVELIEV**, Artem **SCHEPIN**, Evgeny **SCHEPIN**, Radik **TIBEEV**, Alexander **TSIGANOV**, Nikita **LAZAREV**.

Rider	M	R	Pts	BP	TPts	Ave	F	P
Renat GAFUROV	8	40	80	2	82	8.20	1	0
Sergey DARKIN	**8**	**34**	**59**	**4**	**53**	**7.41**	**0**	**1**
Adrian MIEDZINSKI	1	5	9	0	9	7.20	0	0
Tomasz JEDRZEJAK	**2**	**9**	**16**	**0**	**16**	**7.11**	**0**	**0**
Semen VLASOV	6	25	40	4	44	7.04	0	1
Igor KONONOV	**8**	**38**	**51**	**9**	**60**	**6.32**	**0**	**1**
Viktor GOLUBOVSKY	5	23	31	4	35	6.09	0	0
Tomasz GOLLOB	**1**	**6**	**8**	**1**	**9**	**6.00**	**0**	**0**
Radik TIBEEV	3	8	8	2	10	5.00	0	0
Roman KANTYUKOV	**2**	**4**	**3**	**1**	**4**	**4.00**	**0**	**0**
Eduard SHAIKHULLIN	2	5	4	0	4	3.20	0	0
Artem SCHEPIN	**8**	**25**	**11**	**4**	**15**	**2.40**	**0**	**0**
Nikita LAZAREV	3	5	2	0	2	1.60	0	0
Denis ALEXEEV	**3**	**8**	**2**	**0**	**2**	**1.00**	**0**	**0**
Valeri SAVELIEV	2	4	0.5	0	0.5	0.50	0	0

Track: 453250, Republic of Bashkortostan, g.Salavat, ul.Parhomenko, 8, Russia.
E-mail: motosalavat@mail.ru

Russian League

TOGLIATTI

2008 RESULTS

Final position .... Champions

CHERVONOGRAD (A)
Thursday, April 17
Lost 39-51
D.Ivanov 3:1, Bestchastnyh 2:1, Gomozov 2, Bondarenko 6, R. Ivanov 8:1, Sidorin 0, E. Sajfutdinov 17, Kurguskin 1:1.

SALAVAT (H)
Thursday, June 5
Won 53-36
Sullivan 9:1, Bestchastnyh 2:1, D. Ivanov 3, Bondarenko 6:2, R. Ivanov 6, Sidorin 2:1, **E. Sajfutdinov 13:2, Pedersen 12**.

VLADIVOSTOK (A)
Thursday, June 26
Lost 43-47
Sullivan 11, Karachintsev 2:1, Bondarenko 1, D. Ivanov 7:1, R. Ivanov 7, Sidorin 1, E. Sajfutdinov 12, D. Sajfutdinov 2:1.

BALAKOVO (A)
July 24
Won 50-40
Sullivan 14, Karachintsev 1, D. Ivanov 4, R. Ivanov 4:1, Bondarenko, did not ride, Sidorin 1, E. Sajfutdinov 11:2, **Pedersen 15**.

CHERVONOGRAD (H)
July 30
Won 46-44
D. Ivanov 7:1, Karachintsev 2:1, Bondarenko 7, D. Sajfutdinov, did not ride, R. Ivanov 9:1, Sidorin 1, **E. Sajfutdinov 15**, Gomozov 5:1.

TRACK FILE

Track: 445020, Samara, Togliatti, ul. Rodiny, 40, Russia.
Telephone: 8 8482 638856.
Website: www.megalada.ru
Track Length: 353 metres.

SQUAD
Oleg Bestchastnyh, Ilya Bondarenko, Evgeny Gomozov, Daniil Ivanov, Roman Ivanov, Sergey Karachintsev, Oleg Kurguskin, Denis Sajfutdinov, Emil Sajfutdinov, Mikhail Zelepukin, Evgeny Sidorin.
Foreign: Leigh Adams, Nicki Pedersen, Ryan Sullivan.

VLADIVOSTOK (H)
August 21
Won 51-39
Sullivan 11, Karachintsev 0, R. Ivanov 3:2, D. Ivanov 6:1, D. Sajfutdinov 2, Sidorin 2, **E. Sajfutdinov 13:2, Pedersen 14:1**.

BALAKOVO (H)
September 9
Won 49-41
Sullivan 12:1, Sidorin 0, D. Sajfutdinov 2:2, D. Ivanov 0, R. Ivanov 7, Karachintsev 1, E.Sajfutdinov 14, Adams 13.

SALAVAT (A)
October 1
Won 56-34
R. Ivanov 2, Karachintsev 0, D. Sajfutdinov 4:1, **Sullivan 15**, Bondarenko 3, Sidorin 3:1, **E. Sajfutdinov 15, Adams 14:1**.

RUSSIAN LEAGUE

	M	W	D	L	Pts
TOGLIATTI	**8**	**6**	**0**	**2**	**12**
Vladivostok	8	5	1	2	11
Balakovo	8	4	0	4	8
Chervonograd	8	3	1	4	7
Salavat	8	2	1	0	2

For 2009 squad see page 456

Rider	M	R	Pts	BP	TPts	Ave	F	P
Nicki PEDERSEN	3	14	41	1	42	12.00	2	1
Emil SAJFUTDINOV	**8**	**41**	**110**	**6**	**116**	**11.32**	**2**	**2**
Leigh ADAMS	2	10	27	1	28	11.20	0	1
Ryan SULLIVAN	**6**	**30**	**72**	**2**	**74**	**9.87**	**1**	**0**
Roman IVANOV	8	34	46	5	51	6.00	0	0
Daniil IVANOV	**7**	**26**	**30**	**4**	**34**	**5.23**	**0**	**0**
Ilya BONDARENKO	5	20	23	2	25	5.00	0	0
Denis SAJFUTDINOV	**4**	**12**	**10**	**4**	**14**	**4.67**	**0**	**0**
Evgeny GOMOZOV	2	7	7	1	8	4.57	0	0
Oleg KURGUSKIN	**1**	**2**	**1**	**1**	**2**	**4.00**	**0**	**0**
Oleg BESTCHASTNYH	2	6	4	2	6	4.00	0	0
Evgeny SIDORIN	**8**	**22**	**10**	**2**	**12**	**2.18**	**0**	**0**
Sergey KARACHINTSEV	6	16	6	2	8	2.00	0	0

Nicki Pedersen was unbeaten in his three Russian League matches for Mega Lada Togliatti.

He claimed two full scores at home to Salavat and away at Balakovo.

He also got a paid maximum against Vladivostok.

Curiously he rode as reserve in all three outings.

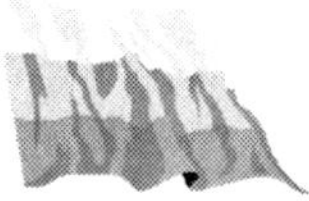

Russian League

VLADIVOSTOK

2008 RESULTS

Final position..Second

BALAKOVO (A)
Thurday, May 29
Lost 43-47
Kharchenko 5:1, Panhay 0, Puszakowski 2, Kazionny, did not ride, Jagus 14, Skatchko 0, A. Laguta 11, G. Laguta 11.

TOGLIATTI (H)
Thursday, June 26
Won 47-43
G. Laguta 14:1, Panhay 2, Kazionny, did not ride, Miesiac 6:1, Kharchenko 5:1, Kazachuk 0, A. Laguta 9, Jagus 11:1.

CHERVONOGRAD (H)
Thursday, July 24
Won 60-30
G. Laguta 15, A. Laguta 3, Skatchkov 1, Puszakowski 10:3, Kharchenkio 9:2, Panhay 5:1, Kazachuk 8:1, **Jagus 9**.

SALAVAT (H)
Thursday, July 31
Won 47-42
Kharchenko 1:1, A. Laguta 11, Karachintsev 4, Miesiac 7:1, Puszakowski 4:1, Panhay 1:1, Kazachuk 2, **G. Laguta 17:1**.

BALAKOVO (H)
Thursday, August 7
Won 53-37
Karachintsev 7:2, Panhay 1, Puszakowski 6:1, Jagus 10:1, Kharchenko 3, Kazachuk 0, A. Laguta 12:1, **G. Laguta 14:1**.

TRACK FILE

Track: 690001, Vladivostock, ul.Federal, 40, Russia.
Website: www.vostok1962.ru

SQUAD
Sergey Filyushin, Nikolai Kaminsky, Maksim Karachintsev, Vyacheslav Kazachuk, Alexander Kazionny, Aleksey Kharchenko, Mikhail Kremer, Nikita Kuranov, Artem Laguta, Grigori Laguta, Alexander Marinyuk, Mikhail Skatchkov, Vasily Panhay, Vladimir Ryazantsev, Igor Stolyarov.
Foreign: Wieslaw Jagus, Pawel Miesiac, Mariusz Puszakowski.

TOGLIATTI (A)
Thursday, August 21
Lost 39-51
Jagus 3, Panhay 2:1, Kharchenko 3, Karachintsev 5:2, Puszakowski 8, Kazachuk 1:1, A. Laguta 5:1, G. Laguta 12:1.

SALAVAT (A)
Thursday, August 28
Won 47.5-42.5
Jagus 15, Skatchkov 0, Karachintsev 0, Kharchenko 4:1, Richardson 13:1, Kazachuk 0.5, A. Laguta 4:1, G. Laguta 11:2.

CHERVONOGRAD (A)
Thursday, September 4
Drew 45-45
Kharchenko 8:1, Skatchkov 1:1, Puszakowski 8, Karachintsev 1:1, Kremer, did not ride, Kazachuyk 2:1, A. Laguta 11:1, G. Laguta 14:1.

RUSSIAN LEAGUE

	M	W	D	L	Pts
Togliatti	8	6	0	2	12
VLADIVOSTOK	**8**	**5**	**1**	**2**	**11**
Balakovo	8	4	0	4	8
Chervonograd	8	3	1	4	7
Salavat	8	2	1	0	2

2009 Squad

Renat **GAFUROV**, Ruslan **GATIYATOV**, Nikolai **KAMINSKY**, Maksim **KARACHINTSEV**, Vyacheslav **KAZACHUK**, Alexander **KAZIONNY**, Aleksey **KHARCHENKO**, Mikhail **KREMER**, Artem **LAGUTA**, Grigori **LAGUTA**, Vasily **PANHAY**, Vladimir **RYAZANTSEV**, Mikhail **SKATCHKOV**.

Rider	*M*	*R*	*Pts*	*BP*	*TPts*	*Ave*	*F*	*P*
Lee RICHARDSON	1	5	13	1	14	11.20	0	0
Grigori LAGUTA	**8**	**44**	**108**	**7**	**115**	**10.45**	**1**	**3**
Wieslaw JAGUS	6	27	62	2	64	9.48	2	0
Artem LAGUTA	**8**	**36**	**66**	**4**	**70**	**7.78**	**0**	**0**
Mariusz PUSZAKOWSKI	6	26	38	5	43	6.62	0	0
Maksim KARACHINTSEV	**5**	**14**	**17**	**5**	**22**	**6.29**	**0**	**0**
Aleksey KHARCHENKO	8	30	38	7	45	6.00	0	0
Pawel MIESIAC	**2**	**10**	**13**	**2**	**15**	**6.00**	**0**	**0**
Vyacheslav KAZACHUK	7	21	16.5	3	19.5	3.71	0	0
Vasily PANHAY	**6**	**18**	**11**	**3**	**14**	**3.11**	**0**	**0**
Mikhail SKATCHKOV	4	9	2	1	3	1.33	0	0

Lee Richardson was one of only two British riders to race in the Russian League.
The other was his Great Britain skipper Scott Nicholls who had one outing for Balakavo.

2009 FIXTURES

RUSSIAN LEAGUE

AFTER a couple of years of big money and big stars, the Russian League was in danger of collapsing completely during the winter with clubs going bankrupt.

At one stage it looked unlikely there would be a domestic league with only Balakovo, Togliatti and Vladivostok declaring themselves as definite starters.

However, after the three clubs agreed to bar all non-Russian riders from the competition, Salavat agreed to continue.

Teams will face each other twice home and away within a 14 meeting programme.

Wednesday, May 6: Balakovo v Salavat
Thursday, May 21: Balakovo v Vladivostok
Thursday, May 28: Togliatti v Vladivostok.
Thursday, June 18: Togliatti v Balakovo
Thursday, June 25: Vladivostok v Togliatti
Wednesday July 1: Salavat v Balakovo.
Thursday, July 2: Vladivostok v Togliatti.
Thursday, July 9: Togliatti v Salavat
Thursday, July 23: Balakovo v Togliatti
Thursday, July 23: Vladivostok v Salavat
Wednesday, July 29: Togliatti v Balakovo
Thursday, July 30: Vladivostok v Salavat
Thursday, August 6: Vladivostok v Balakovo
Tuesday, August 11: Vladivostok v Balakovo
Thursday, August 13: Salavat v Togliatti
Thursday, August 20: Balakovo v Togliatti
Thursday, August 20: Salavat v Vladivostok
Saturday, August 22: Salavat v Vladivostok
Thursday, August 27: Togliatti v Vladivostok
Thursday, September 3: Balakovo v Vladivostok
Thursday, September 3: Togliatti v Salavat
Thursday, September 17: Salavat v Balakovo
Thursday, September 24: Salavat v Togliatti
Saturday, October 3: Balakovo v Salavat

RUSSIAN CHAMPIONSHIP

Semi Final 1: Friday, May 15, Balakovo
Semi Final 2: Sunday, May 24, Togliatti
FINAL: Tuesday, September 8, Balakovo

RUSSIAN PAIRS CHAMPIONSHIP

FINAL: Tuesday, May 19, Balakovo

RUSSIAN UNDER 21 CHAMPIONSHIP

Quarter Final: Wednesday, June 24, Balakovo
Semi Final 1: Thursday, June 25, Balakovo
Semi Final 2: Tuesday, June 30, Vladivostok
FINAL: Saturday, September 1, Togliatti

RUSSIAN UNDER 21 PAIRS CHAMPIONSHIP

FINAL: Friday, June 12, Czerkiesk

RUSSIAN UNDER 21 TEAM CHAMPIONSHIP

GROUP A
Round 1: Saturday, May 30, Togliatti
Round 2: Monday, June 1, Balakovo
Round 3: Saturday, June 27, Vladivostok
Round 4: Saturday, August 8, Vladivostok

GROUP B
Round 1: Saturday, July 4, Balakovo
Round 2: Thursday, August 6, Salavat
Round 3: Sunday, August 9, Kamiensk Uralski

FINAL: Wednesday, September 9, Togliatti

RUSSIAN UNDER 19 CHAMPIONSHIP

FINAL: Saturday, September 12, Balakovo

2009 Togliatti Squad

Oleg **BESTCHASTNYH**, Ilya **BONDARENKO**, Sergey **DARKIN**, Evgeny **GOMOZOV**, Daniil **IVANOV**, Roman **IVANOV**, Sergey **KARACHINTSEV**, Evgeny **SIDORIN**, Sergey **SYGRYSHEV**.

OTHER TRACKS

OKTYABRSKY
Track: 452606, Republic of Bashjkortostan, g.Oktyabrsky, ul.Devonskaya, 12a, Russia.
Website: www.lukoil-speedway.ru

NOVOSIBIRSK
Track: 630048, Novosibirsk, ul,Tulskaya, 205, Russia.
Website: www.rostonso.ru

SLOVAKIA

SLOVAKIAN GOLDEN HELMET

Zarnovica, Sunday, August 24

1 Martin Vaculik 12+4+5, 2 Pawel Hlib 16+3+4, 3 Maks Gregoric 14+X+4+3, 4 Martin Malek 14+3+2, 5 Izak Santej 13+1+5+1, 6 Martin Gavenda 12+4+N, 7 Guglielmo Franchetti 8+2+3, 8 Jaroslav Petrak 9+2+2, 9 Tomas Suchanek 9+N+1, 10 Jan Holub III 8+1+0, 11 Pawel Baran 8, 12 Vladimir Visvader 7, 13 Kamil Cieslar 7, 14 Alessandro Milanese 5, 15 Manuel Novotny 5, 16 Jaromir Otruba 4, 17 Matija Duh 3, 18 Milan Manev 3, 19 Lubomir Durica 1, 20 Manuel Hauzinger 0.

■ *The top 10 scorers from the qualifying rounds went through to two five-rider semi finals and the top two from each semi final to the six rider Grand Final. Riders who finished third, fourth and fifth in each semi final went into a six rider Preliminary Final from which the top two went into the Grand Final.*

TRACK FILE

Track: AMK Zarnovica
Website: www.speedway.sk
Track Length: 400 metres.
Track Record: 70.42 secs, Rafal Szombierski, August 26, 2001.
Slovakia's top modern rider is the teenage 2007 Czech Republic champion Martin Vaculik.

SLOVENIA

SLOVENIAN CHAMPIONSHIP

The Slovenian Championship is part of the tri-national competition also involving riders from Croatia and Slovenia. The highest scoring Slovenian rider is the national champion. For full details of the rounds see Austria.

Matej Zagar was in seventh heaven as he kept hold of his Slovenian crown – to make it seven wins in a row.

He was totally untroubled, finishing well in front of closest challengers Izak Santej and Denis Stojs.

Final standings

1 Matej Zagar 152, 2 Izak Santej 131, 3 Denis Stojs 123, 4 Maks Gregoric 120, 5 Aleksander Conda 115, 6 Matija Duh 106, 7 Jernej Kolenko 100, 8 Matic Voldrih 95, 9 Aljosa Remih 48, 10 Ales Kraljic 25, 11 Dalibor Bot 15, 12 Ladislav Vida 14.

Round 1

Krsko, Sunday, March 30, 1 Matej Zagar 13+3, 2 Jernej Kolenko 13+2, 3 Izak Santej 12+3, 4 Jurica Pavlic 12+2, 5 Maks Gregoric 11, 6 Manuel Hauzinger 11, 7 Denis Stojs 7, 8 Matija Duh 7, 9 Nikola Martinec 6, 10 Manuel Novotny 6, 11 Ivan Vargek 5, 12 Heinrich Schatzer 4, 13 Aleksander Conda 3, 14 Dino Kovacic [R] 3, 15 Matic Voldrih 3, 15 Fritz Wallner 2, 17 Nikola Pigan 2.

Group B: Kreso Petkovic 12, Dino Kovacic 11, Renato Cvetko 10, Simon Lukas 9, Josef Fasching 7, Andrej Kezman 6, Daniel Gappmaier 6, Aljosa Remih 5, Christopher Fink 4, Johannes Fiala 2, Martin Fiala 2, Ales Kraljic 0.

Round 4

Ljubljana, Sunday, September 21

1 Matej Zagar 15, 2 Maks Gregoric 14, 3 Jurica Pavlic 13, 4 Izak Santej 12, 5 Denis Stojs 9, 6 Dino Kovacic 9, 7 Matic Voldrih 9, 8 Aleksander Conda 7, 9 Nikola Pigac 7, 10 Matija Duh 5, 11 Renato Cvetko 5, 12 Ivan Vargek 5, 13 Manuel Novotny 4, 14 Manuel Hauzinger 2, 15 Christian Pellikan 2, 16 Lukas Simon 1, 17 Christopher Fink 0.

Group B: Ales Kraljic 9, Marko Vlah 8, Dalibor Bot 7, Ladislav Vida 6, Daniel Gappmaier 5, Jasmin Ilijas 5, Josef Fasching 5, Christian Pellikan 2.

Roll of Honour

1992 .... Gregor PINTAR
1993 .... Kreso OMERZEL
1994 .... Gerhard LEKSE
1995 .... Gregor PINTAR
1996 .... Gregor PINTAR
1997 .... Matej FERJAN
1998 .... Matej FERJAN
1999 .... Matej FERJAN
2000 .... Matej FERJAN
2001 .... Matej FERJAN
2002 .... Matej ZAGAR
2003 .... Matej ZAGAR
2004 .... Matej ZAGAR
2005 .... Matej ZAGAR
2006 .... Matej ZAGAR
2007 .... Matej ZAGAR
2008 .... Matej ZAGAR

Slovenia was part of the Socialist Federal Republic of Yugoslavia beforer declaring indpendence in 1991. For details of Yugoslavian Champions see ***Croatia****.*

SLOVENIAN U21 CHAMPIONSHIP

Final standings

1 Aleksander Conda 107, 2 Matic Voldrih 98, 3 Matija Duh 68, 4 Aljosa Remih 52, 5 Dalibor Bot 34, 6 Ladislav Vida 31.

Round 3

Lendava, Slovenia, Saturday June 14

Matija Duh 15, Nikola Pigac 14, Aleksander Conda 13, Matic Voldrih 12, Roland Kovacs 11, Dino Kovacic 9, Renato Cvetko 8, Lukas Simon 7, Dalibor Bot 6, Aljosa Remih [R] 5, Zsolt Nagy 5, Hans Peter Kulterer 4, Kreso Petkovic 3, Ladislav Vida 3, Andrej Kezman 3, Daniel Grappmaier 1, Tamas Szilagyi 0.

Round 6

Krsko, Slovenia, Saturday, October 18

Aleksander Conda 11, Nikola Pigac 10+3, Dino Kovacic 10+2, Matic Voldrih 9, Aljosa Remih 7, Roland Kovacs 6, Renato Cvetko 6, Zsolt Nagy 5, Attila Lorincz 5, Ladislav Vida 4, Dalibor Bot 4, Jasmin Ilijas 1.

■ *For full round-by-round details see* ***AUSTRIA****.*

Roll of Honour

2007 .... Matija DUH
2008 .... Aleksander CONDA

AUSTRIA-CROATIA-HUNGARY-SLOVENIA TEAM CHAMPIONSHIP

FINAL STANDINGS

	M	Pts
1 SLOVENIA	**3**	**136+0**
2 HUNGARY	3	132+3
3 AUSTRIA	3	93
4 CROATIA	3	60

Round 1
Lendava, Slovenia, Saturday, May 3
1 SLOVENIA 55 (**Matej Zagar 15**, Izak Santej 12, Maks Gregoric 10, Aleksander Conda 9, Denis Stojs 9), **2 HUNGARY 56** (Matej Ferjan 14, Laszlo Szatmari 12, Jozsef Tabaka 12, Robert Nagy 10, Sandor Tihanyi 8), **3 AUSTRIA 16** (Matih Duh [G] 8, Fritz Wallner 7, Manuel Novotny 1, Daniel Gappmaier 0), 4 **CROATIA 15** (Dino Kovacic 4, Ivan Vargek 3, Nikola Pigac 3, Renato Cvetko 3, Nikola Martinec 2).

For full details of all rounds see AUSTRIA.

SLOVENIA AVERAGES

Rider	M	R	Pts	Ave	FM
Matej ZAGAR	1	5	15	12.00	1
Izak SANTEJ	**1**	**5**	**12**	**9.60**	**0**
Aleksander CONDA	3	14	31	8.86	0
Maks GREGORIC	**3**	**16**	**31**	**7.75**	**0**
Matija DUH	1	5	9	7.20	0
Ales KRALIJIC	**2**	**10**	**17**	**6.80**	**0**
Denis STOJS	3	14	18	5.14	0
Matic VOLDRIH	**1**	**4**	**3**	**3.00**	**0**

Individual

Ljubljana, Sunday, September 21
Matej Zagar 15, Maks Gregoric 14, Jurica Pavlic 13, Izak Santej 12, Denis Stojs 9, Dino Kovacic 9, Matic Voldrih 9, Aleksander Conda 7, Nikola Pigac 7, Matija Duh 5, Renato Cvetko 5, Ivan Vargek 5, Manuel Novotny 4, Manuel Hauzinger 2, Christian Pellikan [R] 3, Lukas Simon 1, Christopher Fink 0, Josef Fasching [R], did not ride.

Group B: Ales Kralijik 9, Marko Vlah 8, Dalibor Bot 7, Ladislav Vida 6, Daniel Grappmaier 5, Jasmin Ilijas 5, Josef Fasching 5, Christian Pellikan 2.

GOLDEN HELMET
Lendava, Sunday, August 24
Matej Zagar 14, Sebastian Ulamek 10+3+3, Mads Korneliussen 10+2+2, Matej Kus 10+1+3+N, Denis Gizatullin 10+3+FX, Josef Franc 10+R+1, Ales Dryml[2] 10+R+R, Daniil Ivanov 9, Mikael Max 9, Martin Smolinski 7, Adrian Miedzinski 6, Ulrich Østergaard 6, Sergey Darkin 5, Filip Sitera 2, Sandor Tihanyi 2, Mattia Carpanese 0.

2009 FIXTURES

CROATIA-SLOVENIA CHAMPIONSHIP
Round 1: Sunday, April 19, Gorican, Croatia.
Round 2: Saturday, August 15, Gorican, Croatia.
Round 3: Saturday, September 5, Lendava, Slovenia.
Round 4: Saturday, October 10, Krsko, Slovenia.

SOUTH AFRICA

SOUTH AFRICAN CHAMPIONSHIP

FINAL STANDINGS
1 Klondyke MAGILL 26, 2 Neil PETTIT 25, 3 Deon SWART 24, 4 Bobby DEVINE 16, 5 Bradley ZEEMAN 10, 6 Brendan COUGHLAN 10, 7 Derrick HILLIAR 8, 8 Mike RUSSELL 3, 9 Robert ALDWORTH 3.
Under 21 Champion: *Chad Durieux*

Round 1
Walkerville, Monday, March 3
Deon Swart 12, Brendan Coughlan 10, Derrick Hilliar 8, Kondyke Magill 7, Bobby Devine 5, Nei Pettit 5, Mike Russell 0.
Round 2
Walkerville, Sunday, August 24
Deon Swart 12, Neil Pettit 11, Klondyke Magill 7, Bradley Zeeman 4, Bobby Devine 4, Derrick Hilliar 1, Mike Russell 0.
Round 3
Walkerville, Sunday, October 19
Klondyke Magill 12, Neil Pettit 9, Bobby Devine 7, Bradley Zeeman 6, Mike Russell 3, Robert Aldworth 3.

Roll of Honour
2005 .... Byron BEKKER
2006 .... Brendan COUGHLAN
2007 .... Brendan COUGHLAN
2008 .... Klondyke MAGILL

GOLDEN HELMET,
Walkerville, Sunday, November 30
Neil Pettit 9, Bobby Devine 8, Mike Russell 8, Klondyke Magill 7, Derrick Hilliar 6, Byron Bekker 6, Robert Aldworth 2.
Silver Sash (Under 21): Ashley Brill 12, James McTaggart 5, Chad Durieux 3, Damien Devine 2, Justin Aldworth 2.

DUDLEIGH & ANDY LONG MEMORIAL
Walkerville, Saturday, January 24, 2009
Neil Pettit 9+3, Mike Russell 7+2, Derrick Hilliar 7+1, Bobby Devine 11+0, Byron Bekker 6, Deon Prinsloo 4, Klondyke Magill 4, Robert Aldworth 0.
Under 21: Ashley Brill 10, Justin Aldworth 7, Chad Durieux 6.

BOET STRYDOM & IAN KYLE BEST PAIRS
Walkerville, Sunday, January 25, 2009
1 KTS PROPERTIES 17 (†Deon Prinsloo 5:3, Bobby Devine 9), 2 ASSURED FREIGHT 13 (†Byron Bekker 10:1, Damien Devine 2), 3 DOT ENGINEERING 11 (†Neil Pettit 4, Chad Durieux 7), 4 TRAUMA MED 10 (†Klondyke Magill 0, Mike Russell 10). *†Handicapped. Bonus points count in final totals.*

2009 SOTH AFRICAN CHAMPIONSHIP

Round 1: Sunday, April 19, Walkerville.
Round 2: Sunday, July 26, Walkerville.
Round 3: Sunday, December 13 , Walkerville.

SWEDEN

SWEDISH CHAMPIONSHIP

FINAL

Avesta, Saturday, August 9

EVERYTHING comes to he who waits – and for Magnus Zetteström it has been a long wait!

Zorro finally landed his first Swedish title, some some 14 years after finishing 16th on his competition debut in 1994!

Rain saw the meeting result decided after it had been called off after 18 races.

The last two heats were discounted, leaving Zetterström as the clear leader, having won three of his first four races altohugh he had been behind Antonio Lindbäck in the completed but ignored Heat 17.

Jonas Davidsson, who tied on nine points with Thomas H. Jonasson, was declared runner-up on the basis of his two race wins.

	1	2	3	4	5	Tot	RO
1 MAGNUS ZETTERSTRÖM	**3**	**3**	**1**	**3**		**10**	
2 Jonas DAVIDSSON	1	3	2	3		9	
3 Tomas H. JONASSON	2	2	3	2		9	
4 Mikael MAX	2	3	3	0		8	
5 Peter KARLSSON	2	1	2	3		8	
5 Sebastian ALDÉN	1	2	2	3		8	
7 Billy FORSBERG	3	1	3	0		7	
8 Andreas JONSSON	3	3	1			7	
9 Fredrik LINDGREN	1	2	3	1		7	
10 Peter LJUNG	0	2	2	2		6	
11 Freddie ERIKSSON	2	1	0	2		5	
12 Antonio LINDBÄCK	3	0	1	0		4	
13 Niklas KLINGBERG	1	0	0	2		3	
14 Magnus KARLSSON	0	0	1	1		2	
15 Simon GUSTAFSSON	0	0	0	1		1	
16 David RUUD	0	1	0	0		1	
17 Linus EKLÖF [R]	1					1	
18 Daniel DAVIDSSON [R]	did not ride						

Qualifying Round

Eskilstuna, Wednesday, June 25

1 Magnus Zetterström 14, 2 Antonio Lindbäck 13, 3 Thomas H. Jonassson 11, 4 Billy Forsberg 10, 5 5 Niklas Klingberg 10, 6 Freddie Eriksson 9, 7 Sebastian Aldén 8, 8 Simon Gustafsson 8, 9 Magnus Karlsson 7+3, 10 Linus Eklöf 7+2, 11 Daniel Davidsson 5, 12 Ludvig Lindgren 5, 13 Ricky Kling 4, 14 Stefan Dannö 4, 15 Eric Andersson 3, 16 Robert Eriksson 2, Linus Sundström [R], Kim Nilsson [R], did not ride.

Qualifying race: Ludvig Lindgren, Magnus Karlsson, Linus Sundström, Kim Nilsson.

Roll of Honour

1936 .... Torsten SJÖBERG
1937 .... Torsten SJÖBERG
1938 .... Torsten SJÖBERG
1949 .... Olle NYGREN
1950 .... Helge BRINKEBACK
1951 .... Helge BRINKEBACK
1952 .... Göte OLSSON
1953 .... Göran NORLÉN
1955 .... Rune SÖRMANDER
1956 .... Ove FUNDIN
1957 .... Ove FUNDIN
1958 .... Rune SÖRMANDER
1959 .... Rune SÖRMANDER
1960 .... Ove FUNDIN
1961 .... Björn KNUTSSON
1962 .... Ove FUNDIN
1963 .... Björn KNUTSSON
1964 .... Ove FUNDIN
1965 .... Göte NORDIN
1966 .... Ove FUNDIN
1967 .... Ove FUNDIN
1968 .... Leif ENECRONA
1969 .... Ove FUNDIN
1970 .... Ove FUNDIN
1971 .... Gote NORDIN
1972 .... Anders MICHANEK
1973 .... Tommy JOHANSSON
1974 .... Tommy JANSSON
1975 .... Anders MICHANEK
1976 .... Anders MICHANEK
1977 .... Bernt PERSSON
1978 .... Anders MICHANEK
1979 .... Jan ANDERSSON
1980 .... Jan ANDERSSON
1981 .... Jan ANDERSSON
1982 .... Anders MICHANEK
1983 .... Tommy NILSSON
1984 .... Jan ANDERSSON
1985 .... Erik STENLUND
1986 .... Per JONSSON
1987 .... Per JONSSON
1988 .... Per JONSSON
1989 .... Peter KARLSSON
1990 .... Tony RICKARDSSON
1991 .... Peter KARLSSON
1992 .... John COOK (USA)
1993 .... Per JONSSON
1994 .... Tony RICKARDSSON
1995 .... Henrik GUSTAFSSON
1996 .... Jimmy NILSEN
1997 .... Tony RICKARDSSON

1998 .... Tony RICKARDSSON
1999 .... Tony RICKARDSSON
2000 .... Henrik GUSTAFSSON
2001 .... Tony RICKARDSSON
2002 .... Niklas KLINGBERG
2003 .... Stefan DANNÖ
2004 .... Tony RICKARDSSON
2005 .... Tony RICKARDSSON
2006 .... Andreas JONSSON
2006 .... Niklas KLINGBERG
2007 .... Andreas JONSSON
2008 .... Magnus ZETTERSTRÖM

SWEDISH UNDER 21 CHAMPIONSHIP

FINAL

Avesta, Friday, September 26

RICKY Kling had to wait nearly a month to be crowned Swedish Under 21 Champion for the first time.

The weather-hit competition was called off three times – including a four-heat cancellation – before the rain finally relented and Kling took advantage of the sudden death final to deny Simon Gustafsson completing what would have been a family double, his father Henrik having been junior champion four times.

	1	2	3	4	5	Tot	SF	F
1 Ricky KLING	**3**	**2**	**2**	**2**	**3**	**12**		**3**
2 Simon GUSTAFSSON	2	3	3	3	2	13		2
3 Ludvig LINDGREN	0	3	1	2	2	8	3	1
4 Kim NILSSON	2	0	3	3	3	11		0
5 Linus EKLÖF	3	3	2	1	1	10	2	
6 Linus SUNDSTRÖM	1	2	3	2	3	11	1	
7 Billy FORSBERG	1	3	1	3	3	11	FX	
8 Robin ASPEGREN	3	1	1	1	2	8		
9 Dennis ANDERSSON	2	2	2	2	0	8		
10 Andreas MESSING	3	0	3	0		6		
11 Anton ROSÉN	1	2	0	1	1	5		
12 Robert HENDERSON	0	0	1	3	0	4		
13 Robert PETTERSSON	1	1	2	0	0	4		
14 Christian AGÖ [R]	2	0	1	1		4		
15 Anders MELLGREN	0	1	0	0	2	3		
16 Henrik KARLSSON	0	1	0	0	1	2		
17 Christian ISOMETTÄ	0	0				0		
18 David ROHLÉN [R]	0	0				0		

FINAL

Avesta, Monday, September 8

Tomas Jonasson 3, Simon Gustafsson 3, Robert Pettersson 3, Billy Forsberg 3, Anton Rosén 2, Linus Sundström 2, Kim Nilsson 2, Andreas Messing 2, Robin Aspegren 1, Ricky Kling 1, Ludvig Lindgren 1, Anders Mellgren 1, Christian Isomettä 0, Linus Eklöf 0, Dennis Andersson 0, Robert Hendersson 0. Henrik Karlsson [R], Chistian Agö [R], did not ride.

Meeting abandoned after four heats, rain.

Qualifying Round

Nyköping, Saturday, June 28

Linus Sundström 15, Robert Henderson 11, Anders Mellgren 11, Jonas Messing 10, Dennis Andersson 10, Robert Pettersson 8, Christian Isomettä 8, Anton Rosén 8, Robin Aspegren 7, Henrik Karlsson 6+3, Linus Jansson 6+2, Christian Agö 5, David Rohlén 5, Jonas Andersson 4, Robin Törnqvist 3, Robin Bergqvist 3, Anton Göthberg [R], did not ride.

Roll of Honour

1959 .... Sören SJÖSTEN
1960 .... Williard THOMSON
1961 .... Williard THOMSON
1962 .... Sten KARLSSON
1963 .... Bengt EDERLÖV
1964 .... Karl ANDERSSON
1965 .... Terje HENRIKSSON
1966 .... Egon STENGARN
1967 .... Christer LÖFQVIST
1968 .... Hans JOHANSSON
1969 .... Karl Erik CLAESSON
1970 .... Tommy JANSSON
1971 .... Lars Inge HULTBERG
1972 .... Tomas PETTERSSON
1973 .... Sven Erik ANDERSSON
1974 .... Jan ANDERSSON
1975 .... Bo JANSSON
1976 .... Tommy KARLSSON
1977 .... Peter JOHANSSON
1978 .... Lennart BENGTSSON
1979 .... Lars ROSBERG
1980 .... Pierre BRANNEFORS
1981 .... Anders KLING
1982 .... Magnus JONSSON
1983 .... Ove ØSTERBERG
1984 .... Jimmy NILSEN
1985 .... Mikael BLIXT
1986 .... Henrik GUSTAFSSON
1987 .... Henrik GUSTAFSSON
1988 .... Henrik GUSTAFSSON
1989 .... Henrik GUSTAFSSON
1990 .... Joakim KARLSSON
1991 .... Jörgen HULTGREN
1992 .... Mikael MAX (ne KARLSSON)
1993 .... Niklas KLINGBERG
1994 .... Daniel ANDERSSON
1995 .... Robert ERIKSSON
1996 .... Emil LINDQVIST
1997 .... Peter I. KARLSSON
1998 .... Andreas JONSSON
1999 .... Joonas KYLMÅKORPI
2000 .... Andreas JONSSON
2001 .... David RUUD
2002 .... Freddie ERIKSSON
2003 .... Fredrik LINDGREN
2004 .... Fredrik LINDGREN
2005 .... Jonas DAVIDSSON
2006 .... Antonio LINDBÄCK
2007 .... Robert PETTERSSON
2008 .... Ricky KLING

WORLD CHAMPIONSHIP

EDINBURGH'S Thomas H. Jonasson headed the Swedish contingent in the 2008 World Under 21 Championship.

The qualifiers came from a one off meeting at Nyköping with the meeting also serving as a conduit for the European Under 19 Championships.

Qualifying Round
Nyköping, Saturday, May 3
Thomas H. Jonasson 15, Simon Gustafsson 13, Kim Nilsson 13, Robin Törnqvist 11, Linus Eklöf 10, Ludvig Lindgren 9, Niklas Karlsson 9, Ricky Kling 7, Jonas Messing 6, Linus Sundström 6, Dennis Andersson 5, Robin Bergqvist 5, Robert Henderson 4, Robert Pettersson 4, Jonas Andersson 3, Tommie Lundgren 0.

Individual

STOCKHOLM EXCLUSIVE CARS CUP
Stockholm, Tuesday, April 22
Joonas Kylmåkorpi 13+3, Jesper B. Monberg 13+2, Freddie Eriksson 12+1, Pawel Hlib 15+0, Martin Smolinski 11, Greg Hancock 10, Jonas Messing 8, Robert Pettersson 8, Kim Nilsson 7, Leif Karlsson 6, Jens Oskarsson 4, Peter Wall 4, Dennis Dahlborg 4, Joakim Martensson 2, Tommie Lundgren 2, Linus Jansson 1.

CHRISTER KARLSSON MEMORIAL
Västervik, Tuesday, April 22
Bjarne Pedersen 15+3, Billy Forsberg 12+2, James Wright 11+1, Tomasz Chrzanowski 12+0, Mads Korneliussen 11, Tai Woffinden 10, Robert Johansson 9, Stefan Ekberg 8, Emil Lindqvist 8, Eric Andersson 8, Peter Juul Larsen 4, Jonas Andersson 4, Tommy Allen 3, Dennis Fagerkrantz 3, Sebastian Carlsson 2.

INDIARNERNA CLUB CHAMPIONSHIP
Kumla, Tuesday, April 22
Adrian Miedzinski 14+3, Stefan Dannö 14+2, Henrik Gustafsson 11+3, Matej Ferjan 11+2, Kaj Laukkanen 10, Edward Kennett 9, Simon Gustafsson 8, Mikael Max 7, Christian Hefenbrock 7, Robert Eriksson 7, David Rohlén 5, Leon Madsen 5, Linus Sundström 4, Magnus Zetterström 3, Andreas Westlund 2, Andreas Lekander 2, Niklas Eriksson [R] 1.

KENNY OLSSON MEMORIAL
Norrköping, Thursday, April 24
Antonio Lindbäck 12+❒+3, Eric Andersson 8+3+2, Joe Screen 11+❒+1, Robert Johansson 11+❒+0, Stefan Ekberg 8+2, Ricky Kling 10+1, Andreas Lekander 10+0, Peter Juul Larsen 6, Sebastian Carlsson 6, Robert Henderson 5, Benny Johansson 5, Viktor Bergström 5, Kalle Lindgren 4, Dennis Fagerkrantz 4, Andreas Bewergström 3, Robert Eriksson 3, Daniel Henderson 3, Tommy Allen 0, Mikael Sjöqvist 0.

STIG AHS MINNE
Karlstad, Sunday, April 27
Kim Jansson 13+3, Viktor Bergström 13+2, Linus Sundström 13+1, Rene Lehtinen 13+0, Daniel Pytel 10, Teemu Lahti 8, Dennis Andersson 8, David Rohlén 8, Lennart Persson 7, Tobias Ingesson 7, Niclas Sonne 5, Jeremia Thelaus 5, Magnus Persson 3, Dennis Fagerkrantz 3, Christian Ingesson 2.

SOUTH REGION JUNIOR CHAMPIONSHIP
Målilla, Saturday, July 26
Christian Isomettä 11, Robert Pettersson 10+3, Olof Nilsson 10+1, Christian Agö 9,Robin Aspegren 9, Pontus Sundström 6, Albin Näreby 4, Marcus Åström 4, Kim Johansson 3, Kalle Fleetwood-Carlsson 3, Christopher Éberg 1, Mikael Berntsson 1.

ROBIN JOHANSSON BENEFIT
Eskilstuna, Saturday, August 30
Robin Aspegren 9+3+3, Ludvig Lindgren 11+❒+2, Robin Bergqvist 11+❒+1, Andreas Messing 13+❒+0, Jeremia Thelaus 11+2, Anders Mellgren 9+1, Jonas Andersson 9+0, David Rohlén 7, Robert Henderson 7, Robert Pettersson 7, Robin Törnqvist 7, Daniel Henderson 4, Henrik Karlssoin 3, Christian Ingesson 1, Rasmus Eklöf 1.

KIM JANSSON BENEFIT (KARLSTAD OPEN)
Karlstad, Wednesday, September 17
Rune Holta 12+3, Antonio Lindbäck 14+2, Peter Karlsson 14+1, Sebastian Aldén 12+0, Mikael Max 10, ***Kim Jansson 10***, Robert Eriksson 10, Peter Ljung 9, Jeremia Thelaus 5, David Rohlén 4, Viktor Bergström 4, Eric Andersson 4. Niklas Klingberg 4, Anders Mellgren 3, Robin Törnqvist 2, Stefan Dannö 2.
Kim Jansson was included in the programme and five other riders took his heats, scoring as follows: Niklas Klingberg 3, Peter Ljung 3, Rune Holta 1, Sebastian Aldén 1, Peter Kalrsson 2.

VARGARNA RIDERS' CHAMPIONSHIP
Norrköping, Friday, October 3
Antonio Lindbäck 12+❒+3, Eric Andersson 12+❒+2, Kim Nilsson 10+❒+1, Robert Johansson 8+3+0, Robert Pettersson 8+2, Robert Henderson 8+1, Jonas Andersson 9+0, Andreas Bergström 7, Fredrik Johansson 7, Kalle Katajisto 6, Marcus Andersson 6, Mikael Max 5, Niko Siltaniemi 5, Daniel Henderson 4, Christian Agö 4, Dennis Fagerkrantz 3, Sebastian Carlsson 3, Dennis Dahlborg 1, Jari Mäkinen 1.

SWEDISH 80cc CHAMPIONSHIP

FINAL
Avesta, Saturday, August 9
Victor Palovaara 13, Jacob Thorssell 11+3, David Nielsen [R] 11+2, Alexander Søderholm 11+1, Joel Larsson 11+FX, Dennis Hallberg 9, Matias Thörnblom 9, Jonathan Armendariz 8, Thimm P. Norberg 8, Fredrik Engman 7, Johannes Fredh 7, Jonas Enghdahl 5, Eric Åshede 4, Adrian Bergqvist 4, Joel Andersson 2, Tobias Nilsson 0, Oliuver Berntzon 0, Tobias Bäck [R], did not ride.

Roll of Honour (1975-2008)

1975	Magnus JOHNSSON
1976	Jan-Erik OTTOSSON
1977	Pierre BRANNEFORS
1978	Peder MESSING
1979	Per PEDERSEN
1980	Kenneth NYSTRÖM
1981	Per JONSSON
1982	Per JONSSON
1983	Henrik GUSTAFSSON
1984	Patrik PALOVAARA
1985	Henrik GUSTAFSSON
1986	Andreas BRUCE
1987	Andreas BRUCE
1988	Marcus ANDERSSON
1989	Robert ERIKSSON

Continued of page 541

ELITESERIEN STANDINGS

	M	W	D	L	PtsF	PtsA	BP	Pts
1 LEJONEN	18	13	0	5	935	793	9	35
2 DACKARNA	18	12	0	6	916	810	7	31
3 ELIT VETLANDA	18	11	0	7	922	805	6	30
4 PIRATERNA	18	11	0	7	878	846	5	27
5 ROSPIGGARNA	18	10	1	7	858	868	5	26
6 INDIANERNA	18	7	1	10	859	866	4	19
7 VÄSTERVIK	18	7	0	11	869	858	3	17
8 HAMMARBY	18	7	0	11	825	901	2	16
9 SMEDERNA	18	6	0	12	793	934	1	13
10 MASARNAAVESTA	18	5	0	13	776	950	1	11

LEJONEN became the 18th different club to be crowned Swedish ElitSerien champions when they beat Elit Vetlanda in the play-off final.

The Gislaved outfit hadn't even figured in the top-flight medal shake-up since their third place in 1981 – one of only four occasions in which they had been in the first three.

PLAY-OFFS

Quaifying Rounds
INDIANERNA 47 **LEJONEN 48**
LEJONEN 58 INDIANERNA 38
LEJONEN win 106-85 on aggregate.

DACKARNA 63 ROSPIGGARNA 33
ROSPIGGARNA 44 **DACKARNA 52**
DACKARNA win 115-77 on aggregate.

PIRATERNA 49 **ELIT VETLANDA 47**
ELIT VETLANDA 57 PIRATERNA 39
ELIT VETLANDA win 104-88 on aggregate.

Semi Finals
PIRATERNA 48 **LEJONEN 48**
LEJONEN 66 PIRATERNA 30
LEJONEN win 114-78 on aggregate.

DACKARNA 50 **ELIT VETLANDA 46**
ELIT VETLANDA 50 DACKARNA 46
ELIT VETLANDA win with 5-1 in deciding race after 96-96 draw on aggregate.

FINAL
ELIT VETLANDA 40 **LEJONEN 56**
LEJONEN 57 ELIT VETLANDA 39
LEJONEN win 113-79 on aggregate.

LEJONEN are the 2008 ElitSerien champions.

Roll of Honour

1948 ...... *FILBYTERNA*
1949 ...... *VARGARNA*
1950 ...... FILBYTERNA
1951 ...... VARGARNA
1952 ...... GETINGARNA
1953 ...... VARGARNA
1954 ...... VARGARNA
1955 ...... MONARKERNA
1956 ...... MONARKERNA
1957 ...... DACKARNA
1958 ...... DACKARNA
1959 ...... DACKARNA
1960 ...... VARGARNA
1961 ...... VARGARNA
1962 ...... *DACKARNA*
1963 ...... GETINGARNA
1964 ...... GETINGARNA
1965 ...... GETINGARNA
1966 ...... GETINGARNA
1967 ...... GETINGARNA
1968 ...... KAPARNA
1969 ...... GETINGARNA
1970 ...... KAPARNA
1971 ...... BYSARNA
1972 ...... BYSARNA
1973 ...... SMEDERNA
1974 ...... GETINGARNA
1975 ...... BYSARNA
1976 ...... NJUDUNGARNA
1977 ...... SMEDERNA
1978 ...... GETINGARNA
1979 ...... GETINGARNA
1980 ...... GETINGARNA
1981 ...... GETINGARNA
1982 ...... GETINGARNA
1983 ...... GETINGARNA
1984 ...... KAPARNA
1985 ...... GETINGARNA
1986 ...... VETLANDA
1987 ...... VETLANDA
1988 ...... BYSARNA
1989 ...... STOCKHOLM UNITED
1990 ...... INDIANERNA
1991 ...... INDIANERNA
1992 ...... ÖRNARNA
1993 ...... ÖRNARNA
1994 ...... ÖRNARNA
1995 ...... ROSPIGGARNA
1996 ...... ÖRNARNA
1997 ...... ROSPIGGARNA
1998 ...... VALSARNA
1999 ...... VALSARNA
2000 ...... MASARNA
2001 ...... ROSPIGGARNA
2002 ...... ROSPIGGARNA
2003 ...... KAPARNA
2004 ...... ELIT VETLANDA
2005 ...... VÄSTERVIK
2006 ...... ELIT VETLANDA
2007 ...... DACKARNA
2008 ...... LEJONEN

■ *Seasons 1948, 1949 and 1962 were not given official status by SVEMO.*

■ *Getingarna raced as Stockholm United (1988-1990), Elit Vetlanda as Njudungarna (1967-1985), Vetlanda (1986-2002) and VMS Elit (2003-2006); Dackarna raced as Svelux (1996-2001) and Luxo Stars (2002-2006); MasarnaAvesta raced as Masarna (1999-2006).*

■ *The Elitserien was launched in 1982, prior to that the top league was known as Division One.*

Champions!

2009 FIXTURES

Tuesday, April 28
Indianerna v Rospiggarna
Piraterna v Lejonen
Vargarna v Ikaros Smederna
Elit Vetlanda v Västervik

Tuesday, May 5
Lejonen v Indianerna
Dackarna v Piraterna
Ikaros Smederna v Elit Vetlanda
Vargarna v Rospiggarna

Tuesday, May 12
Indianerna v Dackarna
Rospiggarna v Lejonen
Ikaros Smederna v Västervik
Elit Vetlanda v Piraterna

Tuesday, May 19
Lejonen v Ikaros Smederna
Vargarna v Dackarna
Västervik v Indianerna
Elit Vetlanda v Rospiggarna

Tuesday, May 26
Lejonen v Elit Vetlanda
Dackarna v Västervik
Ikaros Smederna v Indianerna
Piraterna v Vargarna

Tuesday, June 2
Indianerna v Piraterna
Dackarna v Lejonen
Ikaros Smederna v Rospiggarna
Vargarna v Västervik

Tuesday, June 9
Piraterna v Ikaros Smederna
Vargarna v Indianerna
Västervik v Rospiggarna
Elit Vetlanda v Dackarna

Tuesday, June 16
Rospiggarna v Piraterna
Ikaros Smederna v Dackarna
Västervik v Lejonen
Elit Vetlanda v Vargarna

Tuesday, June 23
Indianerna v Elit Vetlanda
Dackarna v Rospiggarna
Piraterna v Västervik
Vargarna v Lejonen

Tuesday, June 30
Lejonen v Piraterna
Rospiggarna v Indianerna
Ikaros Smederna v Vargarna
Västervik v Elit Vetlanda

Tuesday, July 7
Indianerna v Lejonen
Rospiggarna v Vargarna
Piraterna v Dackarna
Elit Vetlanda v Ikaros Smederna

Tuesday, July 21
Lejonen v Rospiggarna
Dackarna v Indianerna
Piraterna v Elit Vetlanda
Västervik v Ikaros Smederna

Tuesday, July 28
Indianerna v Västervik
Rospiggarna v Elit Vetlanda
Dackarna v Vargarna
Ikaros Smederna v Lejonen

Tuesday,August 4
Indianerna v Ikaros Smederna
Vargarna v Piraterna
Västervik v Dackarna
Elit Vetlanda v Lejonen

Tuesday, August 11
Lejonen v Dackarna
Rospiggarna v Ikaros Smederna
Piraterna v Indianerna
Västervik v Vargarna

Tuesday, August 18
Indianerna v Vargarna
Rospiggarna v Västervik
Dackarna v Elit Vetlanda
Ikaros Smederna v Piraterna

Tuesday, August 25
Lejonen v Västervik
Dackarna v Ikaros Smederna
Piraterna v Rospiggarna
Vargarna v Elit Vetlanda

Tuesday, September 1
Lejonen v Vargarna
Rospiggarna v Dackarna
Västervik v Piraterna
Elit Vetlanda v Indianerna

■ *Subject to alteration.*

ElitSerien

DACKARNA

2008 RESULTS

Final position..Second

INDIANERNA (H)
Tuesday, April 29
Won 62-34
Andersen 12:2, P. Karlsson 12:2, **F. Lindgren 15**, Dryml 9:2, Jonsson 7, L.Lindgren 6, Bergström 1:1, Agö, did not ride.

SMEDERNA (A)
Tuesday, May 6
Won 55-41
F. Lindgren 8:2, Dryml 3, Andersen 8:2, P. Karlsson 14, Jonsson 11:1, Bergström 4:1, L. Lindgren 7:2, Agö, did not ride.

LEJONEN (A)
Tuesday, May 13
Lost 44-52
F. Lindgren 10:1, Batchelor 0, Andersen 10:1, P. Karlsson 10:2, Jonsson 11:1, L.Lindgren 2, Isomettä, did not ride, Agö 1.

ROSPIGGARNA (H)
Tuesday, May 20
Won 56-40
P. Karlsson 11:4, Andersen 13:1, **F. Lindgren 14:1**, Aldén 1, Jonsson 14, L. Lindgren 2, Bergström 1, Agö 0.

ELIT VETLANDA (A)
Tuesday, May 27
Lost 41-55
F. Lindgren 7:1, Dryml 0, Andersen 9:1, P. Karlsson 11:2, Jonsson 10, Bergström 1, L. Lindgren 3, Isomettä, did not ride.

VÄSTERVIK (H)
Tuesday, June 3
Won 51-45
P. Karlsson 5:1, Andersen 13, Jonsson 8:3, Dryml 9:3, F. Lindgren 12:1, L. Lindgren 3, Bergström 1, Isomettä 0.

PIRATERNA (A)
Tuesday, June 10
Lost 42-53
Jonsson 14, Dryml 4:2, Andersen 7, P. Karlsson 7, F. Lindgren 4, Bergström 2, L. Lindgren 4, Isomettä, did not ride.

TRACK FILE

Track: G&B Arena, Box 18, 5780 82 Målilla, Sweden.
Telephone: 0046 0495 21248.
Website: www.dackarna.nu
Track Length: 305 metres.
Track Record: 55.9 secs, Hans Andersen, August 1, 2006 & Nicki Pedersen, July 22, 2008.

SQUAD
Christian Agö, Sebastian Aldén, Andreas Bergström, Kim Ingmarsson, Christian Isometta, Andreas Jonsson, Mikael Karlsson, Peter Karlsson, Emil Kramer, Fredrik Lindgren, Ludvig Lindgren, Niklas Klingberg, Pontus Sundström.
Foreign: Hans Andersen, Troy Batchelor, Lukas Dryml, Kenneth Hansen, Nicolai Klindt, Tomas Topinka, Claus Vissing, Grzegorz Zengota.

HAMMARBY (H)
Tuesday, June 17
Won 57-39
Andersen 12:2, Dryml 5:1, P. Karlsson 12:1, Klingberg 6:1, **Jonsson 14:1**, L. Lindgren 2, Klindt 6:1, Isomettä, did not ride.

MASARNAAVESTA (H)
Tuesday, June 24
Won 60-36
Andersen 13:1, Dryml 4:1, P. Karlsson 14, Klingberg 6:3, Jonsson 13, L. Lindgren 5:1, Klindt 5, Isomettä, did not ride.

INDIANERNA (A)
Tuesday, July 1
Lost 39-57
P. Karlsson 5:2, F. Lindgren 9, Andersen 5, L. Lindgren 0, Jonsson 13:1, Klindt 0, Vissing 6, Isomettä 1:1.
Aggregate: Won 101-91.

SMEDERNA (H)
Tuesday, July 8
Won 55-41
Andersen 13:1, Batchelor 10, F. Lindgren 13:1, Klingberg 3:1, P. Karlsson 8:1, L. Lindgren 7, Vissing 1:1, Isomettä, did not ride.
Aggregate: Won 110-82.

LEJONEN (H)
Tuesday, July 22
Lost 43-53
Andersen 10:1, P. Karlsson 7:4, F. Lindgren 9, Vissing 1, Jonsson 8, L. Lindgren 3:1, Klindt 5, Isomettä, did not ride.
Aggregate: Lost 87-105.

ROSPIGGARNA (A)
Tuesday, July 29
Won 50-46
Andersen 11:1, Batchelor 4, F. Lindgren 8, P. Karlsson 10, Jonsson 10:1, Agö, did not ride, L.

Lindgren 7:2, Isomettä 0.
Aggregate: Won 1016-86.

ROSPIGGARNA (A)
Tuesday, July 29
Won 50-46
Andersen 11:1, Batchelor 4, F. Lindgren 8, P. Karlsson 10, Jonsson 10:1, Agö, did not ride, L. Lindgren 7:2, Isomettä 0.
Aggregate: Won 1016-86.

ELIT VETLANDA (H)
Tuesday, August 5
Won 51-45
F. Lindgren 9:2, P. Karlsson 10:2, Andersen 11, Dryml 8:2, Jonsson 8:2, L. Lindgren 3, Klindt 2:1, Isomettä, did not ride.
Aggregate: Lost 92-100.

VÄSTERVIK (A)
Tuesday, August 12
Lost 47-49
Andersen 14, Dryml 1:1, F. Lindgren 12:1, P. Karlsson 11:3, *rider replacement for Jonsson*, L. Lindgren 1:1, Klindt 8, Isomettä, did not ride.
Aggregate: Won 98-94.

PIRATERNA (H)
Tuesday, August 19
Won 55-41
F. Lindgren 10:3, P. Karlsson 6:1, **Andersen 15**, Dryml 7:3, Jonsson 11:1, Vissing 1, L. Lindgren 5, Isomettä 0.
Aggregate: Won 97-94.

HAMMARBY (A)
Tuesday, August 26
Won 56-40
Andersen 13:1, Dryml 1, F. Lindgren 9:1, **P. Karlsson 13:2**, **Jonsson 15**, Klindt 1, L. Lindgren 4, Isomettä, did not ride.
Aggregate: Won 113-79.

MASARNAAVESTA (A)
Tuesday, September 2
Won 52-43
Klingberg 2:1, Zengota 9:1, F. Lindgren 11:2, P. Karlsson 13:1, Jonsson 7, L. Lindgren 7:2, Isomettä 3.
Aggregate: Won 112-79.

PLAY-OFFS

Qualifying Round, first leg
ROSPIGGARNA (H)
Tuesday, September 9
Won 63-33
F. Lindgren 9, P. Karlsson 8:1, Andersen 11:2, Zengota 8:2, Jonsson 12:1, L. Lindgren 7, Klindt 6:2, Isomettä 2:1.

Qualifying Round, second leg
ROSPIGGARNA (A)
Tuesday, September 16
Won 52-44
Andersen 12, Zengota 3:1, F. Lindgren 11:1, P. Karlsson 9:2, Jonsson 9:1, Klindt 5:2, L. Lindgren 3.
Aggregate: Won 115-77.

Semi final, first leg
ELIT VETLANDA (H)
Tuesday, September 23
Won 50-46
F. Lindgren 6:4, P. Karlsson 9:1, Andersen 11:1, Dryml 1, Jonsson 10, L. Lindgren 2:1, Klindt 11, Isomettä, did not ride.

Semi final, second leg
ELIT VETLANDA (A)
Wednesday, September 24
Lost 46-50
Andersen 10+1, Zengota 0, F. Lindgren 6:1, P. Karlsson 9, Jonsson 10:2+0, L. Lindgren 2, Klindt 9:2, Isomettä, did not ride.
Aggregate: Lost in deciding heat after 96-96 draw.

ELITSERIEN

	M	W	D	L	PtsF	PtsA	Pts
Lejonen	18	13	0	5	935	793	35
DACKARNA	**18**	**12**	**0**	**6**	**916**	**810**	**31**
Elit Vetlanda	18	11	0	7	922	805	30
Piraterna	18	11	0	7	878	846	27
Rospiggarna	18	10	1	7	858	868	26
Indianerna	18	7	1	10	859	866	19
Västervik	18	7	0	11	869	858	17
Hammarby	18	7	0	11	825	901	16
Smederna	18	6	0	12	793	934	13
MasarnaAvesta	18	5	0	13	776	950	11

2008 PARTNER CLUB

ÖRNARNA (AllSvenskan)

2009 PARTNER CLUB

HULTSFREDS GYMNASIUM (Division One)

For 2009 squad see page 490

Rider	M	R	Pts	BP	TPts	Ave	F	P
Hans ANDERSEN	21	109	234	17	251	9.21	1	1
Peter KARLSSON	**22**	**111**	**214**	**32**	**246**	**8.86**	**0**	**1**
Andreas JONSSON	20	104	215	14	229	8.81	1	1
Fredrik LINDGREN	**20**	**101**	**192**	**22**	**214**	**8.48**	**1**	**1**
Grzegorz ZENGOTA	4	16	20	4	24	6.00	0	0
Nicolai KLINDT	**11**	**50**	**58**	**8**	**66**	**5.28**	**0**	**0**
Lukas DRYML	12	51	52	15	67	5.25	0	0
Niklas KLINGBERG	**4**	**18**	**17**	**6**	**23**	**5.11**	**0**	**0**
Troy BATCHELOR	3	11	14	0	14	5.09	0	0
Ludvig LINDGREN	**22**	**88**	**85**	**10**	**95**	**4.32**	**0**	**0**
Andreas BERGSTRÖM	6	16	10	2	12	3.00	0	0
Claus VISSING	**4**	**15**	**9**	**1**	**10**	**2.67**	**0**	**0**
Christian ISOMETTÄ	6	10	5	1	6	2.40	0	0
Christian AGÖ	**2**	**3**	**1**	**0**	**1**	**1.33**	**0**	**0**
Sebastian ALDEN	1	4	1	0	1	1.00	0	0

Number eight appearances: Christian ISOMETTÄ (10), Christian AGÖ (3).

ElitSerien

ELIT VETLANDA

2008 RESULTS

Final position..............................SEcond (Third)

MASARNAAVESTA (A)
Tuesday, April 29
Lost 46-50
Hampel 9:1, Zabik 0, Richardson 10, P. Ljung 8:1, Holta 11:1, Törnqvist 1, Jonasson 7:1, Aspegren, did not ride.

PIRATERNA (H)
Tuesday, May 6
Won 54-42
Richardson 13:2, P. Ljung 7:3, Hampel 11:2, Skornicki 3, Holta 12, Jonasson 6:2, Törnqvist 2, Mellgren, did not ride.

SMEDERNA (H)
Tuesday, May 13
Won 53-43
Zabik 3:1, P. Ljung 10:1, Hampel 11, Skornicki 4:1, Holta 13, Jonasson 7:1, Risager 5:1, Törnqvist, did not ride.

LEJONEN (A)
Tuesday, May 20
Lost 40-56
Crump 4:1, Jonasson 3:1, Hampel 10, P. Ljung 6, Holta 11, Mellgren, did not ride, Risager 6, Aspegren 0.

DACKARNA (H)
Tuesday, May 27
Won 55-41
Crump 14:1, Zabik 6:1, P. Ljung 10, Skornicki 2:1, Holta 10:2, Jonasson 4:2, Davidsson 9, Aspegren, did not ride.

HAMMARBY (A)
Tuesday, June 3
Lost 44-51
Crump 14:2, Skornicki 0, Hampel 13:1, P. Ljung 6, Holta 7, Aspegren, did not ride, Risager 3, Mellgren 1:1.

ROSPIGGARNA (H)
Tuesday, June 10
Won 52-44
Richardson 10:1, P. Ljung 7:2, Hampel 10:1, Zabik 4, Holta 9:1, Jonasson 12:2, Törnqvist 0, Aspegren, did not ride.

VÄSTERVIK (A)
Tuesday, June 17
Lost 40-56
Hampel 9, Jonasson 2:1, Richardson 11, P. Ljung 2:1, Holta 9:1, Davidsson 6, Dryml 1, Aspegren, did not ride.

INDIANERNA (A)
Tuesday, June 24
Lost 42-54
Hampel 13, Jonasson 5:2, P. Ljung 3, Richardson 9:1, Holta 7, Risager 3:1, Davidsson 2, Aspegren, did not ride.

TRACK FILE

Track: Vetlanda Motorstadion, Box 187, 574 22 Vetlanda, Sweden.
Telephone: 0046 0383 761271.
Website: www.elitvetlanda.se
Track Length: 361 metres.
Track Record: 62.4 secs, Jason Crump, May 8, 2007.

SQUAD
Robin Aspegren, Mikael Åstrand, Marcus Åström, Mikael Axelsson, Robin Bergkvist, Kim Bergström, Daniel Davidsson, Kalle Fleetwood-Carlsson, Thomas H. Jonasson, Peter Ljung, Thomas Ljung, Patrick Malmfeldt, Anders Mellgren, Robin Rundby, Robin Törnqvist.
Foreign: Jason Crump, Ales Dryml, Jaroslaw Hampel, Rune Holta, Lee Richardson, Morten Risager, Adam Skornicki, Karol Zabik.

MASARNAAVESTA (H)
Tuesday, July 1
Won 60-36
Crump 13, P. Ljung 6:2, Richardson 11:1, Jonasson 5:1, Hampel 10:2, Dryml 10:2, Davidsson 3, Aspegren 2:1.
Aggregate: Won 106-86.

PIRATERNA (A)
Tuesday, July 8
Lost 47-49
Crump 11:1, P. Ljung 6, Hampel 5:1, Richardson 9:2, Holta 11, Bergkvist, did not ride, Aspegren 1:1, Mellgren 4.
Aggregate: Won 101-91.

SMEDERNA (A)
Tuesday, July 22
Won 51-45
Richardson 9:2, Jonasson 7:2, Hampel 10, P. Ljung 10, Holta 7, Risager 5:2, Dryml 3:1, Aspegren, did not ride.
Aggregate: Won 104-88.

LEJONEN (H)
Tuesday, July 29
Won 51-45
Richardson 8:1, P. Ljung 8:3, Hampel 6, Jonasson 10:1, Holta 12:1, Dryml 7:1, Davidsson 0, Aspegren 0.
Aggregate: Lost 91-101.

DACKARNA (A)
Tuesday, August 5
Lost 45-51
Richardson 8, P. Ljung 3, Hampel 12, Jonsson 8:1, Holta 4, Risager 3, Dryml 7:1, Aspegren, did not ride
Aggregate: Won 100-92.

HAMMARBY (H)
Tuesday, August 12
Won 66-30
Richardson 12, P. Ljung 10:4, Hampel 12:1, Jonasson 4:1, Crump 14, Dryml 9:1, Risager 5:3, Aspegren, did not rider.
Aggregate: Won 110-81.

ROSPIGGARNA (A)
Tuesday, August 19
Won 57-39
Hampel 11:1, Jonasson 3, Richardson 8:3, P. Ljung 10:2, Crump 13, Törnqvist, did not ride, Zabik 10, Aspegren 2:1.
Aggregate: Won 109-83.

VÄSTERVIK (H)
Tuesday, August 26
Won 59-37
Richardson 7:2, P. Ljung 11, Hampel 11, Jonasson 4:3, Crump 13, Dryml 6:3, Risager 7:1, Aspegren, did not ride.
Aggregate: Won 99-93.

INDIANERNA (H)
Tuesday, September 2
Won 60-36
Dryml 5:1, Richardson 13:1, Hampel 11:1, Jonasson 11:3, Crump 13:1, Risager 6, Davidsson 1:1, Aspegren 0.
Aggregate: Won 102-90.
PLAY-OFFS

Qualifying Round, first leg
PIRATERNA (A)
Tuesday, September 9
Lost 47-49
Holta 9:1, Zabik 5:2, Richardson 12:2, Jonasson 1, Crump 16, Mellgren, did not ride, Dryml 3, Aspegren 1.

Qualifying Round, second leg
PIRATERNA (H)
Tuesday, September 16
Won 57-39
Holta 14:1, Richardson 11:1, Hampel 11, Zabik 4:1, Crump 12:2, Törnqvist, did not ride, Mellgren 1, Aspegren 4:1.
Aggregate: Won 104-88.

Semi Final, first leg
DACKARNA (A)
Tuesday, September 23
Lost 46-50
Holta 7, Zabik 0, Hampel 10:1, Richardson 13:2, Crump 11, Törnqvist 1, Mellgren, did not ride, Aspegren 4.

Semi Final, second leg
DACKARNA (H)
Wednesday, September 24
Won 50-46
Holta 9:1, Richardson 9:2, Hampel 12+3 P. Ljung 2, Crump

ELIT VETLANDA 2008: Lee Richardson, Peter Ljung, Morten Risager, Jason Crump, Jaroslaw Hampel, Ales Dryml, Robin Aspegren and Thomas H. Jonassson

14+2:1, Aspegren 4, Mellgren, did not ride, Bergkvist 0.
Aggregate: Won in deciding heat after 96-96 draw.

FINAL, first leg
LEJONEN (H)
Tuesday, September 30
Lost 40-56
Holta 7:1, Dryml 4:1, Hampel 14, P. Ljung 1:1, Crump 10, Risager 4, Törnqvist, did not ride, Aspegren 0.

FINAL, second leg
LEJONEN (A)
Tuesday, October 1
Lost 39-57
Holta 7:1, Zabik 8, Hampel 13, Dryml 3, Crump 6:1, Törnqvist, did not ride, Risager 2, Aspegren 0.
Aggregate: Lost 79-113.

ELITSERIEN

	M	*W*	*D*	*L*	*PtsF*	*PtsA*	*Pts*
Lejonen	18	13	0	5	935	793	35
Dackarna	18	12	0	6	916	810	31
ELIT VETLANDA	**18**	**11**	**0**	**7**	**922**	**805**	**30**
Piraterna	18	11	0	7	878	846	27
Rospiggarna	18	10	1	7	858	868	26
Indianerna	18	7	1	10	859	866	19
Västervik	18	7	0	11	869	858	17
Hammarby	18	7	0	11	825	901	16
Smederna	18	6	0	12	793	934	13
MasarnaAvesta	18	5	0	13	776	950	11

Rider	*M*	*R*	*Pts*	*BP*	*TPts*	*Ave*	*F*	*P*
Jason CRUMP	15	75	180	9	189	10.08	0	1
Lee RICHARDSON	**18**	**94**	**183**	**21**	**204**	**8.68**	**0**	**1**
Jaroslaw HAMPEL	22	117	237	11	248	8.48	0	0
Rune HOLTA	**19**	**98**	**176**	**13**	**189**	**7.71**	**0**	**1**
Peter LJUNG	19	89	126	21	147	6.61	0	0
Thomas H. JONASSON	**17**	**78**	**99**	**24**	**123**	**6.31**	**0**	**0**
Ales DRYML	11	49	58	11	69	5.63	0	0
Morten RISAGER	**11**	**43**	**49**	**8**	**57**	**5.30**	**0**	**0**
Karol ZABIK	9	39	40	5	45	4.62	0	0
Daniel DAVIDSSON	**6**	**20**	**21**	**1**	**22**	**4.40**	**0**	**0**
Adam SKORNICKI	4	13	9	2	11	3.38	0	0
Anders MELLGREN	**6**	**9**	**6**	**1**	**7**	**3.11**	**0**	**0**
Robin ASPEGREN	12	32	18	4	22	2.75	0	0
Robin TÖRNQVIST	**7**	**12**	**4**	**0**	**4**	**1.33**	**0**	**0**
Robin BERGKVIST	1	3	0	0	0	0.00	0	0

Number eight appearances: Robin ASPEGREN (9), Anders MELLGREN (1) and Robin TÖRNQVIST (1).

For 2009 squad see page 490

ElitSerien

HAMMARBY

TRACK FILE

Track: Gubbången IP, Box 6040, 122 06, Enskede, Sweden.
Telephone: 0046 08 6428205.
Website: www.bajenspeedway.se
Track Length: 387 metres.
Track Record: 65.1 secs, Tomasz Gapinski, October 25, 2007.

2008 RESULTS

Final position...Eighth

PIRATERNA (A)
Tuesday, April 29
Won 51-45
Dobrucki 11, Gapinski 3:1, Monberg 6, Zagar 9:1, Nicholls 8:1, Kylmåkorpi 10:2, Nilsson 4:1.

LEJONEN (H)
Tuesday, May 6
Won 54-42
Kylmåkorpi 7:2, Gapinski 10:1, Nicholls 7:3, Monberg 8:1, Zagar 11, Hlib 11:1, Nilsson 0.

MASARNAAVESTA (A)
Tuesday, May 13
Won 52-44
Monberg 4:1, Gapinski 9:1, Nicholls 10:1, Smolinski 7, Zagar 10, Nilsson 2, Kylmåkorpi 10.

VÄSTERVIK (H)
Tuesday, May 20
Won 52-44
Dobrucki 6:1, Gapinski 5:1, Nicholls 12, Kylmåkorpi 7, Zagar 11:1, Hlib 7:1, Nilsson 4.

ROSPIGGARNA (A)
Tuesday, May 27
Lost 46-50
Monberg 2:1, Nicholls 10:1, Smolinski 9, Dobrucki 9, Zagar 3:2, Nilsson 4, Kylmåkorpi 9.

ELIT VETLANDA (H)
Tuesday, June 3
Won 51-44
Dobrucki 4:2, Gapinski 8:1, Zagar 10, Smolinski 6:2, Nicholls 9, Kylmåkorpi 11:2, Nilsson 3.

INDIANERNA (A)
Tuesday, June 10
Lost 44-52
Gapinski 1, Dobrucki 6, Smolinski 4:1, Nicholls 12:1, Zagar 9:1, Nilsson 5, Kylmåkorpi 7:2.

DACKARNA (A)
Tuesday, June 17
Lost 39-57
Dobrucki 6, Hlib 2, Nicholls 8, Smolinski 4:3, Zagar 7:1, Eriksson 10:1, Nilsson 2:1.

SQUAD
Freddie Eriksson, Adrian Gheorghe, Kim Nilsson.
Foreign: Rafal Dobrucki, Renat Gafurov, Tomasz Gapinski, Denis Gizatullin, Pawel Hlib, Krzysztof Jablonski, Joonas Kylmåkopri, Jesper B. Monberg, Scott Nicholls, Adam Shields, Martin Smolinski, Piotr Swist, Matej Zagar.

SMEDERNA (H)
Tuesday, June 24
Lost 47-49
Zagar 11, Smolinski 7:1, Nicholls 11, Gizatullin 3:2, Dobrucki 11:2, Eriksson 3:2, Nilsson 1.

PIRATERNA (H)
Tuesday, July 1
Losty 46-50
Zagar 6:1, Smolinski 0, Kylmåkorpi 7, Nicholls 4:1, Dobrucki 14, Nilsson 9, Gizatullin 6:3.
Aggregate: Won 97-95.

LEJONEN (A)
Tuesday, July 8
Lost 41-55
Hlib 1, Kylmåkorpi 7, Zagar 9, Gafurov 7:2, Nicholls 12, Nilsson 0, Gizatullin 5:2.
Aggregate: Lost 95-97.

MASARNAAVESTA (H)
Tuesday, July 22
Won 51-45
Rider replacement for Dobrucki, Kylmåkorpi 9, Nicholls 12:2, Smolinski 10, Zagar 10:2, Nilsson 1, Gafurov 9:1.
Aggregate: Won 103-89.

VÄSTERVIK (A)
Tuesday, July 29
Lost 40-56
Nicholls 6:2, Kylmåkorpi 7:1, Zagar 9, Smolinski 5:2, Dobrucki 4, Hlib 7:1, Nilsson 2.
Aggregate: Lost 92-100.

ROSPIGGARNA (H)
Tuesday, August 5
Lost 44-51
Rider replacement for Dobrucki, Gapinski 11, Hlib 10:2, Smolinski 6:2, Zagar 11, Nilsson 3, Swist 3.
Aggregate: Lost 90-101.

ELIT VETLANDA (A)
Tuesday, August 12
Lost 30-66
Rider replacement for Nicholls, Gafurov 5, Smolinski 4, Gapinski 4, Dobrucki 13, Hlib 3, Nilsson 1.
Aggregate: Lost 81-110.

INDIANERNA (H)
Tuesday, August 19
Won 50-46
Dobrucki 8, Gapinski 15, *rider replacement for Nicholls*, Smolinski 9:3, Zagar 5:1, Nilsson 5:1, Eriksson 8:2.
Aggregate: Lost 94-98.

DACKARNA (H)
Tuesday, August 26
Lost 40-56
Rider replacement for Dobrucki, Gapinski 5, Gafurov 5:1, Smolinski 7:1, Zagar 13, Nilsson 4:1, Eriksson 6:3.
Aggregate: Lost 79-113.

SMEDERNA (A)
Tuesday, September 2
Lost 47-49
Nicholls 7, *rider replacement for Dobrucki*, Gapinski 7:3, Gafurov 15, Zagar 8:1, Smolinski 5, Nilsson 5:1.
Aggregate: Lost 94-98.

ELITSERIEN

	M	*W*	*D*	*L*	*PtsF*	*PtsA*	*Pts*
Lejonen	18	13	0	5	935	793	35
Dackarna	18	12	0	6	916	810	31
Elit Vetlanda	18	11	0	7	922	805	30
Piraterna	18	11	0	7	878	846	27
Rospiggarna	18	10	1	7	858	868	26
Indianerna	18	7	1	10	859	866	19
Västervik	18	7	0	11	869	858	17
HAMMARBY	**18**	**7**	**0**	**11**	**825**	**901**	**16**
Smederna	18	6	0	12	793	934	13
MasarnaAvesta	18	5	0	13	776	950	11

Matej Zagar, Joonas Kylmåkorpi, Scott Nicholls, front: Kim Nilsson, Tomasz Gapinski, Rafal Dobrucki

2009 Squad

Alexander **EDBERG**.
Foreign: Tero **AARNIO**, Kamil **BRZOZOWSKI**, Andrian **GHEORGE**, Denis **GIZATULLIN**, Pawel **HLIB**, Andrey **KARPOV**, Dawid **LAMPART**, Pawel **MIESIAC**, Morten **RISAGER**, Martin **SMOLINSKI**, Matej **ZAGAR**.
● *Relegated to AllSvenskan League for 2009.*

Rider	*M*	*R*	*Pts*	*BP*	*TPts*	*Ave*	*F*	*P*
Scott NICHOLLS	14	73	128	12	140	7.67	0	0
Matej ZAGAR	**17**	**93**	**152**	**11**	**163**	**7.01**	**0**	**0**
Rafal DOBRUCKI	11	56	92	5	97	6.93	0	0
Freddie ERIKSSON	**4**	**21**	**27**	**8**	**35**	**6.67**	**0**	**0**
Tomasz GAPINSKI	11	53	78	8	86	6.49	0	0
Joonas KYLMÅKORPI	**11**	**62**	**91**	**9**	**100**	**6.45**	**0**	**0**
Renat GAFUROV	5	28	41	4	45	6.43	0	0
Martin SMOLINSKI	**14**	**66**	**83**	**15**	**98**	**5.94**	**0**	**0**
Denis GIZATULLIN	3	15	14	7	21	5.60	0	0
Pawel HLIB	**7**	**34**	**41**	**5**	**46**	**5.41**	**0**	**0**
Jesper B. MONBERG	4	17	20	3	23	5.41	0	0
Kim NILSSON	**18**	**55**	**55**	**5**	**60**	**4.36**	**0**	**0**
Piotr SWIST	1	4	3	0	3	3.00	0	0

Number eight appearances: None.

2008 PARTNER CLUB

GRIPARNA
(AllSvenskan)

2009 PARTNER CLUBS

INDIANERNA
(ElitSerien)
ELDARNA
(Division One)

ElitSerien

INDIANERNA

2008 RESULTS

Final position..Sixth

DACKARNA (A)
Tuesday, April 29
Lost 34-62
Miedzinski 6, Zetterström 5:1, Ferjan 0, Kennett 5, Protasiewicz 11:1, H. Gustafsson 3, S. Gustafsson 4:1, Rohlén, did not ride.

ROSPIGGARNA (H)
Tuesday, May 6
Lost 47-49
Ferjan 9:1, Zetterström 9:1, Miedzinski 5, Kennett 0, Protasiewicz 12:1, S. Gustafsson 7, H. Gustafasson 5:2, Rohlén, did not ride.

VÄSTERVIK (A)
Tuesday, May 13
Lost 39-56
Ferjan 5:1, Zetterström 6:1, Miedzinski 11:1, Laukkanen 1, Protasiewicz 5:2, H. Gustafsson 8, S. Gustafsson 3:2.

PIRATERNA (H)
Tuesday, May 20
Won 50-45
Miedzinski 9:1, Kennett 2:1, Zetterström 4, Ferjan 9:1, Protasiewicz 13, S. Gustafsson 5:1, H. Gustafsson 8:2, Rohlén, did not ride.

MASARNAAVESTA (A)
Tuesday, May 27
Lost 38-58
Ferjan 8, Zetterström 5:2, Miedzinski 8:1, H. Gustafsson 2, Protasiewicz 13, S. Gustafsson 2, Hefenbrock 0.

SMEDERNA (A)
Tuesday, June 3
Lost 42-53
Miedzinski 12:3,H. Gustafsson 1:1, Zetterström 11, Ferjan 3, *rider replacement for Protasiewicz,* Hefenbrock 14:1, S. Gustafsson 1.

HAMMARBY (H)
Tuesday, June 10
Won 52-44
Miedzinski 11:2, H. Gustafsson 8:1, Zetterström 11, Ferjan 4, Protasiewicz 9:2, S. Gustafsson 6, Hefenbrock 3:2, Eriksson, did not ride.

TRACK FILE

Track: Kumla Motorstadion, Kungsleden 50, 692 92, Kumla, Sweden.

Telephone: 0046 058213690.

Website: www.indianerna.nu

Track Length: 375 metres.

Track Record: 63.3, Nicki Pedersen, July 20, 2004

SQUAD
Niklas Eriksson, Freddy Godlund, Henrik Gustafsson, Simon Gustafsson, Pontus Nilsson, David Rohlén, Magnus Zetterström.
Foreign: Matej Ferjan, Christian Hefenbrock, Krzysztof Jablonski, Leon Madsen, Adrian Miedzinski, Jesper B. Monberg, Piotr Protasiewicz.

LEJONEN (A)
Tuesday, June 17
Lost 38-58
Zetterström 5, Ferjan 6, Miedzinski 6:3, Monberg 9:1, Protasiewicz 9, S. Gustafsson 0, H. Gustafsson 3.

ELIT VETLANDA (H)
Tuesday, June 24
Won 54-42
Miedzinski 4:2, Monberg 7:1, Ferjan 10:2, Zetterström 9:2, Protasiewicz 11, S. Gustafsson 5:1, H. Gustafsson 8, Gudlund, did not ride.

DACKARNA (H)
Tuesday, July 1
Won 57-39
Monberg 2:1, Miedzinski 12:1, Ferjan11:1, Zetterström 7:2, Protasiewicz 11, S. Gustafsson 6:2, H. Gustafsson 8:2, Rohlén, did not ride.
Aggregate: Lost 91-101.

ROSPIGGARNA (A)
Tuesday, August 8
Drew 48-48
Miedzinski 9, Zetterström 6:1, Ferjan 9:2, Monberg 4, Protasiewicz 12, S. Gustafsson 3:1, H. Gustafsson 5:1.
Aggregate: Lost 95-97.

VÄSTERVIK (H)
Tuesday, July 22
Won 60-36
Miedzinski 9:1, Zetterström 9:1, Ferjan 10, Monberg 6:2, Protasiewicz 14, H. Gustafsson 5, S. Gustafsson 7:5, Godlund, did not ride.
Aggregate: Won 99-92.

PIRATERNA (A)
Tuesday, July 29
Lost 41-55
Monberg 2:1, Zetterström 5, Ferjan 8:1, Miedzinski 8, Protasiewicz 13, S. Gustafsson 1:1, H. Gustafsson 4:1.
Aggregate: Lost 91-100.

MASARNAAVESTA (H)
Tuesday, August 5
Won 61-35
Rider replacement for Miedzinski, Ferjan 12, Zetterström 14:3, Monberg 9:2, Protasiewicz 11:1, S. Gustafsson 7:1, Jablonski 8:3, Rohlén 0.
Aggregate: Won 99-93.

SMEDERNA (H)
Tuesday, August 12
Won 69-27
Miedzinski 5:1, Ferjan 12:1, **Monberg 14:1**, H. Gustafsson 9:4, **Zetterström 15**, S. Gustafsson 8:2, Jablonski 6:1, Godlund, did not ride.
Aggregate: Won 111-80.

HAMMARBY (A)
Tuesday, August 19
Lost 46-50
Monberg 11:1, Miedzinski 6, Ferjan 2, Zetterström 9, Protasiewicz 15, S. Gustafsson 2, Jablonski 1.
Aggregate: Won 98-94.

LEJONEN (H)
Tuesday, August 26
Lost 47-49
Ferjan 9:1, Zetterström 10:1, Miedzinski 12:1, Monberg 4:1, Protasiewicz 2, H. Gustafsson 3:1, S. Gustafsson 7:1, Godlund, did not ride.
Aggregate: Lost 85-107.

ELIT VETLANDA (A)
Tuesday, September 2
Lost 36-60
Zetterström 2:1, Miedzinski 5, Ferjan 7, Monberg 5, Protasiewicz 10:1, H. Gustafsson 5, S. Gustafsson 2:2.
Aggregate: Lost 90-102.

Play offs

Qualifying Round, first leg
LEJONEN (H)
Tuesday, September 9
Lost 47-48
Miedzinski 8:1, Ferjan 6:1, Zetterström 8:1, Monberg 7:2, Protasiewicz 9:1, H. Gustafsson 6, S. Gustafsson 3:2, Rohlén, did not ride.

Qualifying Round, second leg
LEJONEN (A)
Tuesday, September 16
Lost 38-58
Zetterström 2:1, Monberg 10, Miedzinski 1, Ferjan 7:1, Protasiewicz 8:1, S. Gustafsson 4, H. Gustafsson 6:1.
Agrgregate: Lost 85-106.

ELITSERIEN

	M	W	D	L	PtsF	PtsA	Pts
Lejonen	18	13	0	5	935	793	35
Dackarna	18	12	0	6	916	810	31
Elit Vetlanda	18	11	0	7	922	805	30
Piraterna	18	11	0	7	878	846	27
Rospiggarna	18	10	1	7	858	868	26
INDIANERNA	**18**	**7**	**1**	**10**	**859**	**866**	**19**
Västervik	18	7	0	11	869	858	17
Hammarby	18	7	0	11	825	901	16
Smederna	18	6	0	12	793	934	13
MasarnaAvesta	18	5	0	13	776	950	11

See page 488 for team photograph

2009 Squad
Simon GUSTAFSSON.
Foreign: Matej **FERJAN**, Renat **GAFUROV**, Christian **HEFENBROCK**, Rune **HOLTA**, Joonas **KYLMÅKORPI**, Leon **MADSEN**, Jesper B. **MONBERG**, Piotr **PROTASIEWICZ**, Grzegorz **WALASEK**.

2008 PARTNER CLUB
VIKINGARNA (Division One)

2009 PARTNER CLUBS
HAMMARBY (AllSvenskan)
INDIANERNA UNGDOM (Division One)

Rider	*M*	*R*	*Pts*	*BP*	*TPts*	*Ave*	*F*	*P*
Piotr PROTASIEWICZ	18	95	188	10	198	8.34	0	0
Adrian MIEDZINSKI	**19**	**95**	**147**	**18**	**165**	**6.95**	**0**	**0**
Krzysztof JABLONSKI	3	11	15	4	19	6.91	0	0
Magnus ZETTERSTRÖM	**20**	**99**	**152**	**18**	**170**	**6.87**	**1**	**0**
Matej FERJAN	20	99	147	13	160	6.46	0	0
Jesper B. MONBERG	**13**	**65**	**90**	**13**	**103**	**6.34**	**0**	**1**
Henrik GUSTAFSSON	18	74	91	16	107	5.78	0	0
Christian HEFENBROCK	**3**	**14**	**17**	**3**	**20**	**5.71**	**0**	**0**
Simon GUSTAFSSON	20	76	83	22	105	5.53	0	0
Edward KENNETT	**3**	**11**	**7**	**1**	**8**	**2.91**	**0**	**0**
Kaj LAUKKANEN	1	2	1	0	1	2.00	0	0
David ROHLEN	**1**	**1**	**0**	**0**	**0**	**0.00**	**0**	**0**

Number eight appearances: David ROHLEN (5), Freddy GODLUND (4), Niklas ERIKSSON (1)..

ElitSerien

LEJONEN

2008 RESULTS

Final position..........................Champions (First)

SMEDERNA (H)
Tuesday, April 29
Won 59-37
Holder 9:2, **Jedrzejak 12:3**, Ulamek 4, Sqwiderski 4, Pedersen 14, Klking 5:2, Ruud 11:2, Almqvist, did not ride.

HAMMARBY (A)
Tuesday, May 6
Lost 42-54
Ruud 2, Jedrzejak 5, Pedersen 16, Swiderski 4, Ulamek 7:1, Kling 4:2, Wegrzyk 4:1, Almqvist, did not ride.

DACKARNA (H)
Tuesday, May 13
Won 52-44
Pedersen 14, Ulamek 5:1, Jedrzejak 9:1, Wegrzyk 3, Swiderski 8, Kling 4:2, Ruud 9:1, A. Göthberg, did not ride.

ELIT VETLANDA (H)
Tuesday, May 20
Won 56-40
Pedersen 13, Ruud 7, Jedrzejak 7:1, Ulamek 8:1, Swiderski 6:2, Kling 3:2, Wegrzyk 12, A. Göthberg, did not ride.

VÄSTERVIK (A)
Tuesday, May 27
Won 50-46
Jedrzejak 11, Wegrzyk 0, Pedersen 11, Ruud 9:1, Ulamek 7:2, Kling 3, Jeleniewski 9:3, A. Göthberg, did not ride.

PIRATERNA (H)
Tuesday, June 3
Won 54-42
Pedersen 15, Ulamek 3:1, Jedrzejak 10:1, Holder 6, Swiderski 8, Kling 6:1, Ruud 6:2, A. Göthberg, did not ride.

MASARNAAVESTA (A)
Tuesday, May 10
Won 53-43
Jedrzejak 4, Holder 9:1, **Pedersen 14:1**, Swiderski 7:2, Ulamek 6, Kling 8:1, Ruud 5.

TRACK FILE

Track: Axelent Arena, Box 17, 332 21 Gislaved, Sweden.
Telephone: 0046 037114275.
Website: www.lejonen.se
Track Length: 380 metres.
Track Record: 65.2, Nicki Pedersen, October 1, 2008. *Nicki Pedersen recorded time of 63.7 secs in the abandoned match on August 19, 2008.*

SQUAD
Kim Almqvist, Michael Berntsson, Anton Göthberg, Viktor Göthberg, Tobias Johansson, Ricky Kling, Christoph Öberg, Robert Pettersson, David Ruud.
Foreign: Chris Holder, Daniel Jeleniewski, Tomasz Jedrzejak, Maciej Kuciapa, Henrik Moller, Piotr Paluch, Nicki Pedersen, Mariusz Staszewski, Piotr Swiderski, Sebastian Ulamek, Marius Wegrzyk.

INDIANERNA (H)
Tuesday, June 17
Won 58-38
Pedersen 8:1, Ulamek 6:2, Jedrzejak 10:1, Ruud 9:2, Swiderski 9:1, Kling 6:2, Wegrzyk 10:1, Pettersson, did not ride.

ROSPIGGARNA (A)
Tuesday, June 24
Lost 46-50
Jedrzejak 6, Ruud 2:2, Pedersen 11, Swiderski 7, Ulamek 11:2, Kling 7:1, Jeleniewski 2:1, Pettersson, did not ride.

SMEDERNA (A)
Tuesday, July 1
Lost 46-50
Pedersen 17, Swiderski 4:1, Ruud 9, Jedrzejak 8:1, Ulamek 3:1, Jeleniewski 2, Kling 3, Pettersson 0.
Aggregate: Won 105-87.

HAMMARBUY (H)
Tuesday, July 8
Won 55-41
Holder 10:1, Ulamek 10, Jedrzejak 2, Ruud 9:1, Swiderski 12, Kling 7:1, Wegrzyk 5:2, Pettersson, did not ride.
Aggregate: Won 97-95.

DACKARNA (A)
Tuesday, July 22
Won 53-43
Pedersen 15, Ulamek 9:1, Ruud 4, Jedrzejak 2:1, Swiderski 11:1, Almqvist, did not ride, Kling 11, Pettersson 1.
Aggregate: 105-87.

ELiT VETLANDA (A)
Tuesday, July 289
Lost 45-51
Pedersen 14, Ulamek 0, Holder 4:2, Jedrzejak 8, Swiderski 4:1, Kling 5, Ruud 10:1, Pettersson, did not ride.
Aggregate: 101-91.

VÄSTERVIK (H)
Tuesday, August 5
Won 52-44
Pedersen 14, Ulamek 10:2, Jedrzejak 8, Holder 3, Ruud 8, Kling 5, Jeleniewski 4:1, Pettersson, did not ride.
Aggregate: Won 102-90.

PIRATERNA (A)
Tuesday, August 12
Lost 45-51
Pedersen 18, Kuciapa 0, Ruud 7, Jedrzejak 7:2, Ulamek 10:1, Jeleniewski 3:1, Öberg, did not ride, Pettersson 0.
Aggregate: Won 99-93.

MASARNAAVESTA (H)
Tuesday, August 19
Won 62-34
Holder 7:1, Ulamek 11:3, Ruud 9:2, Kling 9, Swiderski 10:3, Kuciapa 7:1, Wegrzyk 9, Pettersson 0.
Aggregate: Won 115-77.

INDIANERNA (A)
Tuesday, August 26
Won 49-47
Holder 9, Jedrzejak 10:3, Pedersen 9:1, Ruud 3, Swiderski 7:2, Kling 4, Ulamek 7:1, Pettersson, did not ride.
Aggregate: Won 107-85.

ROPSPIGGARNA (H)
Tuesday, September 2
Won 58-38
Pedersen 10, Jedrzejak 5:1, Holder 10:1, Ruud 9:3, Swiderski 8:1, Ulamek 6:4, Kling 9:1, Pettersson 1.
Aggregate: Won 104-88.

Play offs

Qualifying Round, first leg
INDIANERNA (A)
Tuesday, September 9
Won 48-47
Holder 5, Jedrzejak 6, **Pedersen 15**, Ruud 8:1, Swiderski 2, Kling 3:2, Ulamek 9:1, Pettersson, dnr.

Qualifying Round, second leg
INDIANERNA (H)
Tuesday, September 16
Won 58-38
Pedersen 11:1, Jedrzejak 10:1, Ruud 5:1, Holder 12:1, Swiderski 4, Kling 4:2, Ulamek 12:2, Zymek, did not ride.
Aggregate: Won 106-85.

Semi Final, first leg
PIRATERNA (A)
Tuesday, September 23
Drew 48-48
Pedersen 15, Swiderski 2, Ruud 3, Jedrzejak 7, Holder 10:1, Kling 0, Ulamek 11:2, Pettersson, did not ride.

Semi Final, second leg
PIRATERNA (H)
Wednesday, September 24
Won 66-30
Pedersen 12, Jedrzejak 6:1, **Ruud 14:1**, Holder 8:2, Swiderski 12, Kling 3:1, Ulamek 11:2, Pettersson, did not ride.
Aggregate: Won 114-78.

FINAL, first leg
ELIT VETLANDA (A)
Tuesday, September 30
Won 56-40
Pedersen 13, Swiderski 6:3, Ruud 11, Jedrzejak 2:1, Holder 10:2, Kling 6:2, Ulamek 8:1, Pettersson, did not ride.

FINAL, second leg
ELIT VETLANDA (H)
Tuesday, October 1
Won 47-39
Pedersen 11, Jedrzejak 11:1, Ruud 1, Holder 9:1, Swiderski 10:1, Kling 7:3, Ulamek 8:3, Pettersson, did not ride.
Aggregate: Won 103-79.

ELITSERIEN

	M	*W*	*D*	*L*	*PtsF*	*PtsA*	*Pts*
LEJONEN	**18**	**13**	**0**	**5**	**935**	**793**	**35**
Dackarna	18	12	0	6	916	810	31
Elit Vetlanda	18	11	0	7	922	805	30
Piraterna	18	11	0	7	878	846	27
Rospiggarna	18	10	1	7	858	868	26
Indianerna	18	7	1	10	859	866	19
Västervik	18	7	0	11	869	858	17
Hammarby	18	7	0	11	825	901	16
Smederna	18	6	0	12	793	934	13
MasarnaAvesta	18	5	0	13	776	950	11

See page 489 for team photograph

2008 PARTNER CLUB

GNISTORNA
(Division One)

2009 PARTNER CLUB

ÖRNARNA
(AllSvenskan)

For 2009 squad see page 490

Rider	*M*	*R*	*Pts*	*BP*	*TPts*	*Ave*	*F*	*P*
Nicki PEDERSEN	22	108	290	4	294	10.89	5	2
Chris HOLDER	**15**	**71**	**121**	**15**	**136**	**7.66**	**0**	**0**
Sebastian ULAMEK	24	114	182	34	216	7.58	0	1
Piotr SWIDERSKI	**21**	**96**	**145**	**18**	**163**	**6.79**	**0**	**0**
Tomasz JEDRZEJAK	23	109	166	19	185	6.79	1	0
David RUUD	**24**	**112**	**170**	**20**	**190**	**6.79**	**0**	**1**
Mariusz WEGRZYK	7	30	43	4	47	6.27	0	0
Ricky KLING	**23**	**98**	**122**	**24**	**146**	**5.96**	**0**	**0**
Maciej KUCIAPA	2	6	7	1	8	5.33	0	0
Daniel JELENIEWSKI	**5**	**20**	**20**	**6**	**26**	**5.20**	**0**	**0**
Robert PETTERSSON	5	8	2	0	2	1.00	0	0

Number eight appearances: Robert PETTERSSON (11), Anton GÖTHBERG (4), Kim ALMQVIST (2), Robin ZYMEK (1)..

ElitSerien

MASARNAAVESTA

TRACK FILE

Track: Arena Avesta, Box 6, 774 21 Avesta, Sweden.
Telephone: 0046 022650360.
Website: www.masarnaavesta.nu
Track Length: 315 metres.
Track Record: 57.0 secs, Leigh Adams, August 1, 2006.

2008 RESULTS

Final position ....Tenth

ELIT VETLANDA (H)
Tuesday, April 29
Won 50-46
Bjerre 6:1, Sajfutdinov 9:1, Watt 5:1, Stead 6:1, Adams 14, Allen 9:2, D. Andersson, did not ride, Rosén 1.

VÄSTERVIK (A)
Tuesday, May 6
Lost 35-61
Bjerre 8, Stead 3:1, Watt 1, Miesiac 1, Sajfutdinov 12, Rosén, did not ride, Janniro 10:1, D. Andersson 0.

HAMMARBY (H)
Tuesday, May 13
Lost 44-52
Bjerre 4:2, Sajfutdinov 10, Watt 6, Janniro 4, Adams 12, Stead 8:1, D. Andersson, did not ride, Rosén 0.

SMEDERNA (A)
Tuesday, May 20
Won 50-46
Watt 9:2, Stead 1, Adams 14, Bjerre 10:1, Sajfutdinov 11:1, Rosén, did not ride, Janniro 5:1, D. Andersson 0.

INDIANERNA (H)
Tuesday, May 27
Won 58-38
Adams 16:1, *rider replacement for Bjerre,* Watt 5, Janniro 8:2, Sajfutdinov 11, Stead 11:2, D. Andersson, did not ride, Rosén 7:2.

ROSPIGGARNA (A)
Tuesday, June 3
Lost 36-60
Stead 7, *rider replacement for Bjerre,* Johnston 2, Miesiac 3:3, Watt 12:1, Rosén, did not ride, Janniro 11, D. Andersson 1:1.

LEJONEN (H)
Tuesday, June 10
Lost 43-53
Adams 12:1, *rider replacement for Bjerre,* Sajfutdinov 9:1, Janniro 5:2, Watt 8, Stead 9, Rosén 0, D. Andersson, did not ride.

PIRATERNA (H)
Tuesday, June 17
Lost 43-53
Adams 13:1, Stead 5:1, Bjerre 10:1, Allen 3:1, Watt 4:1, Aldén 7:1, Rosén, did not ride, D. Andersson 1.

SQUAD
Sebastian Aldén, Dennis Andersson, Fredrik Andersson, Pontus Aspgren, Andreas Bergström, Mikael Berntsson, Anton Rosén.
Foreign: Leigh Adams, Oliver Allen, Kenneth Bjerre, Billy Janniro, Steve Johnston, Pawel Miesiac, Emil Sajfutdinov, Simon Stead, Davey Watt.

DACKARNA (A),
Tuesday, June 24
Lost 36-60
Watt 12, Miesiac 3, Stead 4, Johnston 6:3, Bjerre 6, D. Andersson, did not ride, Aldén 4:2, Rosén 1.

ELIT VETLANDA (A)
Tuesday, July 1
Lost 36-60
Watt 11, Miesiac 3, Stead 5, Johnston 4:1, Bjerre 7, Rosén, did not ride, Aldén 4:1, D. Andersson 2:1.
Aggregate: Lost 86-106.

VÄSTERVIK (H)
Tuesday, July 8
Won 49-47
Adams 18, Johnston 4:2, Watt 7:1, Stead 4:1, Bjerre 8, Aldén 8, D. Andersson, did not ride, Rosén 0.
Aggregate: Lost 84-108.

HAMMARBY (A)
Tuesday, July 22
Lost 45-51
Watt 7, Johnston 1, Bjerre 12:2, Stead 6:1, Adams 14:2, Rosén, did not ride, Bergström 3:1, D. Andersson 2.
Aggregate: Lost 89-103.

SMEDERNA (H)
Tuesday, July 29
Won 53-43
Bjerre 5, Janniro 5:2, Watt 6, Stead 9:1, **Adams 15,** Johnston 11:1, Rosén 0, D. Andersson 2.
Aggregate: Won 103-89

INDIANERNA (A)
Tuesday, August 5
Lost 35-61
Watt 3, Stead 6, Adams 14, Allen 2, Bjerre 6, D. Andersson 3, F. Andersson, did not ride, Rosén 1:1.
Aggregate: Lost 93-99.

ROSPIGGARNA (H)
Tuesday, August 12
Lost 47-49
Bjerre 8:1, Janniro 4:2, Stead 7, Johnston 3:1, Adams 13:1, Aldén 9:1, D. Andersson, did not ride, Rosén 3.
Aggregate: Lost 83-109.

LEJONEN (A)
Tuesday, August 19
Lost 34-62
Watt 11:1, D. Andersson 0, Miesiac 2, Aldén 6, Bjerre 10, F. Andersson 1:1, Aspgren 4.
Aggregate: Lost 77-115.

PIRATERNA (A)
Tuesday, August 26
Lost 39-56
Sajfutdinov 5, Miesiac 1:1, Bjerre 7, Johnston 0, Watt 15, Rosén 0, Aldén 11:1.
Aggregate: Lost 82-109.

DACKARNA (H)
Tuesday, September 2
Lost 43-52
Bjerre 2, Watt 5:1, Sajfutdinov 9, Aldén 8:1, Adams 10, Miesiac 5:1, Aspgren 2, D. Andersson 2:1.
Aggregate: Lost 79-112.

ELITSERIEN

	M	W	D	L	PtsF	PtsA	Pts
Lejonen	18	13	0	5	935	793	35
Dackarna	18	12	0	6	916	810	31
Elit Vetlanda	18	11	0	7	922	805	30
Piraterna	18	11	0	7	878	846	27
Rospiggarna	18	10	1	7	858	868	26
Indianerna	18	7	1	10	859	866	19
Västervik	18	7	0	11	869	858	17
Hammarby	18	7	0	11	825	901	16
Smederna	18	6	0	12	793	934	13
MASARNAAVESTA	**18**	**5**	**0**	**13**	**776**	**950**	**11**

After finishing bottom of the Elit League in 2008, MasarnaAvesta were relegated but withdrew from the AllSvenskan League during the winter.

Division One champions Team Dalakraft, who operate from the same track, accepted promotion.

2009 Squad

Erik **ANDERSSON**, Fredrik **ANDERSSON**, Niklas **ASPGREN**, Pontus **ASPGREN**, Andreas **BERGSTRÖM**, Billy **FORSBERG**, Anton **ROSÉN**, Alexander **SÖDERHOLM**, Andreas **WESTLUND**.
Foreign: Jason **DOYLE**, Teemu **LAHTI**.
See Team Dalakraft (page 520).

Kenneth Bjerre

Simon Stead

Rider	M	R	Pts	BP	TPts	Ave	F	P
Leigh ADAMS	12	66	165	6	171	10.36	2	0
Emil SAJFUTDINOV	**8**	**44**	**76**	**3**	**79**	**7.18**	**0**	**0**
Davey WATT	17	85	127	8	135	6.35	0	0
Kenneth BJERRE	**15**	**79**	**109**	**8**	**117**	**5.92**	**0**	**0**
Sebastian ALDÉN	8	44	57	7	64	5.82	0	0
Billy JANNIRO	**8**	**43**	**52**	**10**	**62**	**5.77**	**0**	**0**
Simon STEAD	15	76	91	9	100	5.26	0	0
Oliver ALLEN	**3**	**14**	**14**	**3**	**17**	**4.86**	**0**	**0**
Steve JOHNSTON	8	33	31	8	39	4.73	0	0
Pontus ASPGREN	**2**	**6**	**6**	**0**	**6**	**4.00**	**0**	**0**
Andreas BERGSTRÖM	1	4	3	1	4	4.00	0	0
Pawel MIESIAC	**7**	**30**	**18**	**5**	**23**	**3.07**	**0**	**0**
Fredrik ANDERSSON	1	3	1	1	2	2.67	0	0
Anton ROSÉN	**10**	**26**	**13**	**3**	**16**	**2.46**	**0**	**0**
Dennis ANDERSSON	10	28	13	3	16	2.29	0	0

Number eight appearances: Dennis ANDERSSON (1).

2008 PARTNER CLUB

TEAM DALAKRAFT (Division One)

2009 PARTNER CLUBS

VÄSTERVIK (Elite Serien)

GASARNA (Division One)

ElitSerien

PIRATERNA

2008 RESULTS

Final position ....Fourth

HAMMARBY (H)
Tuesday, April 29
Lost 45-51
Walasek 8:3, Kosciecha 9:1, Balinski 2:1, Max 1, Sullivan 15, Nermark 10, Sundström 0, T. Ingesson, did not ride.

ELIT VETLANDA (A)
Tuesday, May 6
Lost 42-54
Kosciecha 8, Balinskli 7:3, Walasek 5:1, Max 0, Sullivan 9:1, Sunndström 1, Nermark 12, C. Ingesson, did not ride.

ROSPIGGARNA (H)
Tuesday, May 13
Lost 47-48
Walasek 9, Max 3, Kosciecha 8:1, Balinski 9:1, Sullivan 8, Sundström 2:1, Nermark 8:1, C. Ingesson, did not ride.

INDIANERNA (A)
Tuesday, May 20
Lost 45-50
Kosciecha 6:1, Balinski 5:1, Walasek 9, Nermark 8:1, Sullivan 11:1, Sundström 1, Dannö 5, T. Ingesson, did not ride.

SMEDERNA (H)
Tuesday, May 27
Won 52-44
Walasek 10, Nermark 7:1, Kosciecha 7:2, Balinski 10, Sullivan 5:1, Max 11:2, Sundström 2:1, T. Ingesson, did not ride.

2009 Squad

Jonas **DAVIDSSON**, Daniel **NERMARK**, Antonio **LINDBÄCK**.
Foreign: Damian **BALINSKI**, Rafal **DOBRUCKI**, Robert **KOSCIECHA**, Chris **NEATH**, Rafal **OKONIEWSKI**, Emil **SAJFUTDINOV**.

TRACK FILE

Track: Lastparrtner Arena, Box 4009, 591 04 Motala, Sweden.
Telephone: 0046 0141209990.
Website: www.piraterna.com
Track Length: 300 metres.
Track Record: 56.3 secs, Peter Karlsson, May 23, 2006.

SQUAD
Tomas Bäck, Viktor Bergström, Stefan Danno, Christian Ingesson, Tobias Ingesson, Mikael Max, Daniel Nermark, Totte Nilsson, Rickard Nyberg, Lennart Persson, Tobias Planberg, Linus Sundström,Sebastian Williams.
Foreign: Damian Balinski, Kamil Brzozowski, Robert Kosciecha, Rafal Okoniewski, Zbigniew Suchecki, Ryan Sullivan, Michal Szczepaniak, Grzegorz Walasek.

LEJONEN (A)
Tuesday, June 3
Lost 42-54
Balinski 0, Kosciecha 12:1, Walasek 3:1, Sullivan 11:2, Nermark 9:1, Sundström 0, Max 7:2, C. Ingesson, did not ride.

DACKARNA (H)
Tuesday, June 10
Won 53-42
Walasek 10:1, Sullivan 11:1, Kosciecha 7:1, Balinski 10:1, Nermark 2:1, Sundström 2:1, Max 11:1, T. Ingesson, did not ride.

MASARNAVESTA (A)
Tuesday, June 17
Won 53-43
Balinski 12:1, Kosciecha 5:1, Nermark 8:4, Walasek 11:1, Sullivan 9, Max 6, Sundström 2:1, Planberg, did not ride.

VÄSTERVIK (H)
Tuesday, June 24
Won 49-47
Walasek 7, Sullivan 7:1, Kosciecha 5:1, Balinski 10:1, Nermark 7, Sundström 4, Max 9:2, Bäck, did not ride.

HAMMARBY (A)
Tuesday, July 1
Won 50-46
Kosciecha 12:1, Balinski 7:2, Nermark 2:1, Walasek 11, Sullivan 11:1, Max 7, Sundström 0.

Aggregate: Lost 95-97.

See page 495 for team photograph

ELIT VETLANDA (H)
Tuesday, July 8
Won 49-47
Walasek 9:1, Sullivan 5, Kosciecha 10, Balinski 8, Nermark 7:3, Sundström 2:1, Szczepaniak 8:1.
Aggregate: Lost 91-101.

ROSPIGGARNA (A)
Tuesday, July 22
Won 50-46
Kosciecha 6:4, Balinski 8, Nermark 4, Walasek 12, Sullivan 6, Okoniewski 13:2, Sundström 1.
Aggregate: Won 97-94.

INDIANERNA (H)
Tuesday, July 29
Won 55-41
Walasek 8:2, Max 6:1, Kosciecha 7:3, Balinski 9:1, Sullivan 14, Sundström 4:1, Okoniewski 7:1.
Aggregate: Won 100-91.

SMEDERNA (A)
Tuesday, August 5
Lost 47-49
Kosciecha 11:2, Balinski 12:2, Walasek 8, Max 2:1, Sullivan 5:1, Okoniewski 7:1, Sundström 2.
Aggregate: Won 99-93.

LEJONEN (H)
Tuesday, August 12
Won 51-45
Walasek 8:1, Max 7, Kosciecha 7:3, Balinski 7, Sullivan 11:1, Sundström 5:2, Okoniewski 6.
Aggregate: Lost 93-99.

DACKARNA (A)
Tuesday, August 19
Lost 41-55
Kosciecha 6:1, Balinski 6:2, Walasek 7, Okoniewski 7, Sullivan 2, Max 9, Sundström 4:2.
Aggregate: Lost 94-97.

MASARNAAVESTA (H)
Tuesday, August 26
Won 56-39
Walasek 7:1, Okoniewski 10:2, Kosciecha 9:1, Balinski 7:3, Sullivan 9, Sundström 8:1, Max 6:2.
Aggregate: Won 109-82.

VÄSTERVIK (A)
Tuesday, September 2
Won 51-45
Kosciecha 9:2, Balinski 7, Walasek 6, Okoniewski 7:1, Sullivan 12, Max 7, Sundström 3:2.
Aggregate: Won 100-92.

Play offs

Qualifying Round, first leg
ELIT VETLANDA (H)
Tuesday, September 9
Won 49-47
Walasek 6, Nermark 8:3, Kosceicha 6, Balinski 5, Sullivan 8:1, Sundström 5:1, Max 11:1.

Qualifying Round, second leg
ELIT VETLANDA (A)
Tuesday, September 16
Lost 39-57
Balinski 4, Kosciecha 4:1, Walasek 11, Max 3:1, Sullivan 7:1, Szczepaniak 5:1, Sundström 5:1.
Aggregate: Lost 88-104.

■ ***PIRATERNA qualify for semi final as best losers.***

Semi Final, first leg
LEJONEN (H)
Tuesday, September 23
Drew 48-48
Walasek 5, Okoniewski 9:3, Kosciecha 10:2, Balinski 7:1, Sullivan 8, Sundström 2:1, Max 7.

Semi Final, second leg
LEJONEN (A)
Wednesday, September 24
Lost 30-66
Walasek 4, Okoniewski 7, Kosciecha 2:1, Balinski 1, Sullivan 7, Max 6:1, Sundström 3:1.
Aggregate: Lost 78-114.

ELITSERIEN

	M	*W*	*D*	*L*	*PtsF*	*PtsA*	*Pts*
Lejonen	18	13	0	5	935	793	35
Dackarna	18	12	0	6	916	810	31
Elit Vetlanda	18	11	0	7	922	805	30
PIRATERNA	**18**	**11**	**0**	**7**	**878**	**846**	**27**
Rospiggarna	18	10	1	7	858	868	26
Indianerna	18	7	1	10	859	866	19
Västervik	18	7	0	11	869	858	17
Hammarby	18	7	0	11	825	901	16
Smederna	18	6	0	12	793	934	13
MasarnaAvesta	18	5	0	13	776	950	11

Rider	*M*	*R*	*Pts*	*BP*	*TPts*	*Ave*	*F*	*P*
Ryan SULLIVAN	22	110	191	12	203	7.38	0	0
Rafal OKONIEWSKI	**9**	**46**	**73**	**10**	**83**	**7.22**	**0**	**0**
Robert KOSCIECHA	22	110	166	30	196	7.13	0	0
Grzegorz WALASEK	**22**	**106**	**174**	**12**	**186**	**7.02**	**0**	**0**
Damian BALINSKI	22	102	153	20	173	6.78	0	0
Michal SZCZEPANIAK	**2**	**9**	**13**	**2**	**15**	**6.67**	**0**	**0**
Daniel NERMARK	13	65	92	16	108	6.65	0	0
Mikael MAX	**19**	**90**	**119**	**14**	**133**	**5.91**	**0**	**0**
Linus SUNDSTRÖM	22	62	58	17	75	4.84	0	0
Stefan DANNÖ	**1**	**6**	**5**	**0**	**5**	**3.33**	**0**	**0**

Number eight non-riding appearances: Christian INGESSON (7), Tomas BÄCK (1), Tobias PLANBERG (1).

2008 PARTNER CLUB

SOLKATTERNA
(AllSvenskan)

2009 PARTNER CLUBS

SOLKATTERNA
(AllSvenskan)
CROSSBONE PIRATES
(Division One)

ElitSerien

ROSPIGGARNA

2008 RESULTS

Final position..Fifth

VÄSTERVIK (H)
Tuesday, April 29
Won 51-45
Hancock 11:1, Gjedde 7:2, Kolodziej 12:1, Tomicek 9:2, Shields 3, McGowan 5:1, Oskarsson, did not ride, J. Messing 4.

INDIANERNA (A)
Tuesday, May 6
Won 49-47
Hancock 16:1, Gjedde 6:4, Kolodziej 8, Tomicek 1, Shields 11, McGowan 6, Westlund, did not ride, J. Messing 1:1.

PIRATERNA (A)
Tuesday, May 13
Won 48-47
Hancock 14, Szczepaniak 5:1, Kolodziej 11:1, Slabon 3, Gjedde 8, McGowan 4, A. Messing, did not ride, J. Messing 3.

DACKARNA (A)
Tuesday, May 20
Lost 40-56
Hancock 5, Szczepaniak 3:2, Kolodziej 7:1, Gjedde 6, A. Messing 1:1, McGowan 8:1, Slabon 10:1, J. Messing, did not ride.

HAMMARBY (H)
Tuesday, May 27
Won 50-46
Hancock 13:2, Gjedde 7:2, Kolodziej 10, Tomicek 3, Shields 11:1, McGowan 4, A. Messing 2:1, J. Messing, did not ride.

MASARNAVESTA (H)
Tuesday, June 3
Won 60-36
Hancock 13, Gjedde 10:2, Kolodziej 6:1, Slabon 11:2, Shields 13:1, McGowan 5, A. Messing 1:1, J. Messing 1.

ELIT VETLANDA (A)
Tuesday, June 10
Lost 44-52
Hancock 13:1, Gjedde 4:1, Kolodziej 12:1, Tomicek 1, Shields 7, Slabon 3:2, A. Messing 2, J. Messing 2.

SMEDERNA (A)
Tuesday, June 17
Lost 43-53
Hancock 15, Gjedde 1, Kolodziej 11:2, Slabon 5:1, Shields 6, McGowan 2, A. Messing 2, J. Messing 1.

LEJONEN (H)
Tuesday, June 24
Won 50-46
Hancock 13, Gjedde 8:1, Kolodziej 10:1, Slabon 3:3, Shields 10, McGowan 5:1, A. Messing 0, J. Messing 1.

VÄSTERVIK (A)
Tuesday, July 1
Won 49-47
Hancock 10, McGowan 1, Kolodziej 2, Slabon 9, Shields 13, J. Messing 5:2, A. Messing 9:2.
Aggregate: Won 100-92.

INDIANERNA (H)
Tuesday, July 8
Drew 48-48
Hancock 12, Gjedde 9:1, Kolodziej 4:1, Slabon 8:1, Shields 7:1, McGowan 2, A. Messing 3:1, J. Messing 3.
Aggregate: Won 97-95.

PIRATERNA (H)
Tuesday, July 22
Lost 46-50
Hancock 14, Gjedde 6:1, Kolodziej 4:1, Slabon 7, Shields 10:1, J. Messing 2, A. Messing 3:1, R. Messing, did not ride.
Aggregate: Lost 94-97.

DACKARNA (H)
Tuesday, July 29
Lost 46-50
Hancock 13:2, Gjedde 5, Kolodziej 8:2, Szczepaniak 0, Shields 5, J. Messing 3:1, Slabon 12:1, A. Messing 0.
Aggregate: Lost 86-106.

HAMMARBY (A)
Tuesday, August 5
Won 51-44
Hancock 15, Gjedde 3, Kolodziej 14:1, Slabon 6:1, *rider replacement for Shields*, Tomicek 7,

TRACK FILE

Track: Orionparken, Tulkavägen 7, 763 34 Hallstavik, Sweden.
Telephone: 0046 017522775.
Website: www.rospiggarna.nu
Track Length: 289 metres.
Track Record: 55.0 secs, Joonas Kylmåkorpi, June 8, 2004.

SQUAD
Harald Andersson, Stefan Brolin, Robin Burestad, Fredrik Gustavsson, David Hillborg, Linus Jansson, Niklas Larsson, Andreas Messing, Jonas Messing, Robin Messing, Jens Oskarsson, Peter Wall, Andreas Westlund.
Foreign: Charlie Gjedde, Greg Hancock, Janusz Kolodziej, Travis McGowan, Adam Shields, Krzysztof Slabon, Mateus Szczepaniak, Lubos Tomicek.

A. Messing 6:1.
Aggregate: Won 101-90.

MASARNAAVESTA (A)
Tuesday, August 12
Won 49-47
Hancock 13:1, Gjedde 0, Kolodziej 6:2, Slabon 11:1, Shields 11, Tomicek 5:1. A. Messing 3.
Aggregate: Won 109-83.

ELIT VETLANDA (H)
Tuesday, August 19
Lost 39-57
Hancock 17, Tomicek 3:1, Kolodziej 2, Slabon 5:1, Shelds 6, McGowan 3:2, A. Messing 3.
Aggregate: Lost 83-109.

SMEDERNA (H)
Tuesday, August 26
Won 57-39
Hancock 18, Gjedde 11:2, Kolodziej 12:1, Slabon 3:1, *rider replacement for Shields*, Tomicek 3:1, A. Messing 10:2.
Aggregate: Won 100-92.

LEJONEN (A)
Tuesday, September 2
Lost 38-58
Hancock 20:1, Gjedde 2, Kolodziej 10, Slabon 3, *rider replacement for Shields*, Oskarsson 0, A. Messing 3.
Aggregate: Lost 88-104.

Play offs

Qualifying Round, first leg
DACKARNA (A)
Tuesday, September 9
Lost 33-63
Hancock 17, Gjedde 4, Kolodziej 7, McGowan 3, *rider replacement for Shields*, Oskarsson 1, Hillborg 1.

Qualifying Round, second leg
DACKARNA (H)
Tuesdaym, September 16
Lost 44-52
Hancock 18:1, Gjedde 4:1, Kolodziej 2, Slabon 9, *rider replacement for Shields*, McGowan 7:1, A. Messing 4,Oskarsson, did not ride
Aggregate: Lost 77-115.

ELITSERIEN

	M	*W*	*D*	*L*	*PtsF*	*PtsA*	*Pts*
Lejonen	18	13	0	5	935	793	35
Dackarna	18	12	0	6	916	810	31
Elit Vetlanda	18	11	0	7	922	805	30
Piraterna	18	11	0	7	878	846	27
ROSPIGGARNA	**18**	**10**	**1**	**7**	**858**	**868**	**26**
Indianerna	18	7	1	10	859	866	19
Västervik	18	7	0	11	869	858	17
Hammarby	18	7	0	11	825	901	16
Smederna	18	6	0	12	793	934	13
MasarnaAvesta	18	5	0	13	776	950	11

2009 Squad

Henrik **GUSTAFSSON**, Jonas **MESSING**.
Foreign: Charlie **GJEDDE**, Greg **HANCOCK**, Maciej **JANOWSKI**, Janusz **KOLODZIEJ**, Krzysztof **SLABON**, Ryan **SULLIVAN**, Lubos **TOMICEK**.

Andreas Messing, Jonas Messing, Adam Shields, Krzysztof Slabon, Janusz Kolodziej, Travis McGowan, Greg Hancock

Rider	*M*	*R*	*Pts*	*BP*	*TPts*	*Ave*	*F*	*P*
Greg HANCOCK	20	116	280	10	290	10.00	1	1
Adam SHIELDS	**13**	**63**	**113**	**4**	**117**	**7.43**	**0**	**0**
Janusz KOLODZIEJ	20	106	158	16	174	6.57	0	0
Krzysztof SLABON	**16**	**77**	**108**	**15**	**123**	**6.39**	**0**	**0**
Charlie GJEDDE	18	86	101	17	118	5.49	0	0
Lubos TOMICEK	**8**	**32**	**32**	**5**	**37**	**4.63**	**0**	**0**
Jonas MESSING	11	26	26	4	30	4.62	0	0
Travis McGOWAN	**13**	**54**	**55**	**6**	**61**	**4.52**	**0**	**0**
Andreas MESSING	16	62	52	10	62	4.00	0	0
Mateusz SZCZEPANIAK	**3**	**11**	**8**	**3**	**11**	**4.00**	**0**	**0**
David HILLBORG	1	4	1	0	1	1.00	0	0
Jens OSKARSSON	**2**	**6**	**1**	**0**	**1**	**0.67**	**0**	**0**

Number eight appearances: Jonas MESSING (2), Robin MESSING (1), Jens OSKARSSON (1).

2008 PARTNER CLUB

STJÄRNORNA
(Division One)

2009 PARTNER CLUBS

GETINGARNA
(AllSvenskan)

STJÄRNORNA
(Division One)

SMEDERNA

2008 RESULTS

Final position..Ninth

LEJONEN (A)
Tuesday, April 29
Lost 37-59
Kasprzak 8:1, Jansson 3:1, Davidsson 11, Schlein 1, Jagus 10:2, Miskowiak 3, Eklöf 1, R. Henderson 0.

DACKARNA (H)
Tuesday, May 6
Lost 41-55
Kasprzak 6:1, Buczkowski 8:1, Davidsson 5, Schlein 3, Jagus 14, Jansson 3, Karlsson 0, R. Henderson 2:1.

ELIT VETLANDA (A)
Tuesday, May 13
Lost 43-53
Jagus 12:1, Schlein 2:2, Kasprzak 12, Buczkowski 6, Davidsson 4, Eklöf 2, Miskowiak 5:1, R. Henderson, did not ride.

MASARNAAVESTA (H)
Tuesday, May 20
Lost 46-50
Jagus 12, Buczkowski 1, Kasprzak 8, Schlein 2:1, Davidsson 8:1, Miskowiak 9:1, Eklöf 6:2, R. Henderson, did not ride.

PIRATERNA (A)
Tuesday, May 27
Lost 44-52
Jagus 12:3, Schlein 2, Kasprzak 13, Buczkowski 1, Davidsson 12:1, Eklöf 3, Miskowiak 1:1, R. Henderson, did not ride.

INDIANERNA (H)
Tuesday, June 3
Won 53-42
Jagus 10:3, Miskowiak 9:1, Kasprzak 13:1, Buczkowski 5, Davidsson 10, Eklöf 4, Klindt 2:1, R. Henderson 0.

VÄSTERVIK (A)
Tuesday, June 10
Lost 44-52
Jagus 11, Schlein 2, Kasprzak 11:1, Buczkowski 4, Davidsson 9:1, Eklöf 1, Miskowiak 6:1, R. Henderson, did not ride.

ROSPIGGARNA (H)
Tuesday, June 17
Won 53-43
Jagus 12, Buczkowski 5:2, Kasprzak 11:1, Vaculik 4:3, Davidsson 9:2, Miskowiak 10, Eklöf 2, R. Henderson 0.

HAMMARBY (A)
Tuesday, June 24
Won 49-47
Jagus 11:2, Buczkowski 7:1, Kasprzak 4, Vaculik 3:1, Davidsson 9, Miskowiak 10:3, Eklöf 5:1, R. Henderson, did not ride.

LEJONEN (H)
Tuesday, July 1
Won 50-46
Jagus 12, Buczkowski 3:2, Kasprzak 9:1, Vaculik 4:2, Davidsson 8, Eklöf 5, Miskowiak 9, R. Henderson, did not ride.
Aggregate: Lost 87-105.

DACKARNA (A)
Tuesday, July 8
Lost 41-55
Buczkowski 6, King 10:1, Kasprzak 8, Vaculik 1:1, Davidsson 5:1, Schlein 10, Eklöf 1:1.
Aggregate: Lost 82-110.

ELIT VETLANDA (H)
Tuesday, July 22
Lost 45-51
Jagus 10:2, King 3, Kasprzak 9, Vaculik 0, Davidsson 15, Karlsson, did not ride, Schlein 8:1, R. Henderson 0.
Aggregate: 88-104.

MASARNAAVESTA (A)
Tuesday, July 29
Lost 43-53
Jagus 9:1, King 9:1, Kasprzak 5, Miskowiak 0, Davidsson 9:2, Schlein 10:1, D. Henderson, did not ride, Karlsson 1.
Aggregate: Lost 89-103.

PIRATERNA (H)
Tuesday, August 5
Won 49-47
Davidsson 9, Miskowiak 7, Jagus 10, King 9:2, Kasprzak 5, Buczkowski 8, Eklöf 1, Karlsson, did not ride.
Aggregate: Lost 93-99.

TRACK FILE

Track: Ikarossstadion, Box 63, 631 02 Eskilstuna, Sweden.
Telephone: 0046 016140584
Website: www.ikarossmederna.nu
Track Length: 335 metres.
Track Record: 58.3 secs, Nicki Pedersen, May 31, 2005.

SQUAD
Jesper Brolin, Henrik Karlsson, Jonas Davidsson, Linus Eklöf, Daniel Henderson, Robert Henderson, Kim Jansson
Foreign: Krzysztof Buczkowski, Krzysztof Kasprzak, Daniel King, Wieslaw Jagus, Marcin Jedrzejewski, Nicolai Klindt, Robert Mioskowiak, Rory Schlein, Martin Vaculik.

INDIANERNA (A)
Tuesday, August 12
Lost 27-69
King 10:1, *rider replacement for Davidsson,* Schlein 7, Miskowiak 1, Buczkowski 6, Jedrzejewski 1, Eklöf 2, Karlsson 0.
Aggregate: Lost 80-111.

VÄSTERVIK (H)
Tuesday, August 19
Lost 40-56
Davidsson 0, Miskowiak 7, Jagus 15:1, King 7:1, Kasprzak 5, Buczkowski 5, Eklöf 1, Karlsson 0.
Aggregate: Lost 84-108.

ROSPIGGARNA (A)
Tuesday, August 26
Lost 39-57
King 9, Schlein 1, Jagus 11, Miskowiak 1, Kasprzak 9:2, Buczkowski 6, Eklöf 2:2, Karlsson, did not ride.
Aggregate: Lost 92-100.

HAMMARBY (H)
Tuesday, September 2
Won 49-47
King 7, Miskowiak 7, Kasprzak 9:2, Buczkowski 9:2, Jagus 11, Schlein 4, Eklöf 2:2, D. Henderson, did not ride.
Aggregate: Won 98-94.

ELITSERIEN

	M	W	D	L	PtsF	PtsA	Pts
Lejonen	18	13	0	5	935	793	35
Dackarna	18	12	0	6	916	810	31
Elit Vetlanda	18	11	0	7	922	805	30
Piraterna	18	11	0	7	878	846	27
Rospiggarna	18	10	1	7	858	868	26
Indianerna	18	7	1	10	859	866	19
Västervik	18	7	0	11	869	858	17
Hammarby	18	7	0	11	825	901	16
SMEDERNA	**18**	**6**	**0**	**12**	**793**	**934**	**13**
MasarnaAvesta	18	5	0	13	776	950	11

Robert Miskowiak, Wieslaw Jagus, Krzysztof Buczkowski, Krzysztof Kasprzak, Nicolai Klindt, Rory Schlein, Linus Eklöf, Kim Jansson, Jonas Davidsson

Rider	M	R	Pts	BP	TPts	Ave	F	P
Wieslaw JAGUS	16	86	182	15	197	9.16	0	0
Krzysztof KASPRZAK	**17**	**88**	**145**	**10**	**155**	**7.05**	**0**	**0**
Jonas DAVIDSSON	15	76	123	8	131	6.89	0	0
Daniel KING	**8**	**43**	**64**	**6**	**70**	**6.51**	**0**	**0**
Robert MISKOWIAK	15	65	85	8	93	5.72	0	0
Kim JANSSON	**2**	**5**	**6**	**1**	**7**	**5.60**	**0**	**0**
Krzysztof BUCZKOWSKI	15	71	80	8	88	4.96	0	0
Martin VACULIK	**5**	**17**	**12**	**7**	**19**	**4.47**	**0**	**0**
Rory SCHLEIN	12	55	52	5	57	4.15	0	0
Nicolai KLINDT	**1**	**3**	**2**	**1**	**3**	**4.00**	**0**	**0**
Linus EKLÖF	15	50	38	8	46	3.68	0	0
Marcin JEDRZEJEWSKI	**1**	**3**	**1**	**0**	**1**	**1.33**	**0**	**0**
Robert HENDERSON	5	9	2	1	3	1.33	0	0
Henrik KARLSSON	**4**	**5**	**1**	**0**	**1**	**0.80**	**0**	**0**

Number eight appearances: Robert HENDERSON (7), Henrik KARLSSON (2), Daniel HENDERSON (2).

2008 PARTNER CLUB

TEAM BIKAB (Division One)

2009 PARTNER CLUB

TEAM BIKAB (Division One)

For 2009 squad see page 490

ElitSerien

VÄSTERVIK

2008 RESULTS

Final position..Seventh

ROSPIGGARNA (A)
Tuesday, April 29
Lost 45-51
Pedersen 11:1, Harris 0, Iversen 10:1, Chrzanowski 6:2, Gollob 13:1, J. Andersson 2, Forsberg 3:1.

MASARNAAVESTA (H)
Tuesday, May 6
Won 61-35
Gollob 15:2, *rider replacement for Pedersen*, Iversen 15:2, Chrzanowski 10:3, Harris 7:2, Korneliussen 12:1, J. Andersson 2:1. K. Johansson, did not ride.

INDIANERNA (H)
Tuesday, May 13
Won 56-39
Gollob 12, Korneliussen 5:1, **Iversen 13:2**, Chrzanowski 6, Harris 10:1, Laguta 9:2, J. Andersson 1, K. Johansson, did not ride.

HAMMARBY (A)
Tuesday, May 20
Lost 44-52
Harris 7, Korneliussen 0, Iversen 6:1, Chrzanowski 11, Gollob 10:1, J. Andersson 0, Laguta 10:2.

LEJONEN (H)
Tuesday, May 27
Lost 46-50
Pedersen 8:1, Harris 6:1, Chrzanowski 5, Laguta 6, Gollob 12, Korneliussen 8:2, J. Andersson 1, K. Johansson, did not ride.

DACKARNA (A)
Tuesday, June 3
Lost 45-51
Gollob 8:1, Laguta 8:1, Chrzanowski 5, Harris 4, Pedersen 9, Ekberg 5:2, Forsberg 6:1, J. Andersson, did not ride.

SMEDERNA (H)
Tuesday, June 10
Won 52-44
Harris 7:2, Pedersen 14, Chrzanowski 4:2, Laguta 10, Gollob 5:1, Forsberg 8, Ekberg 4:2, J. Andersson, did not ride.

ELIT VETLANDA (H)
Tuesday, June 17
Won 56-40
Laguta 9:1, Pedersen 11:2, Iversen 5:1, Harris 11:2, Gollob 7, Forsberg 9:3, Ekberg 3, J. Andersson 1.

TRACK FILE

Track: Sparbanken Arena, Box 88, 593 22 Västervik, Sweden.
Telephone: 0046 0490 36691.
Website: www.wmsk.se
Track Length: 296 metres.
Track Record: 55.2 secs, Bjarne Pedersen, September 28, 2005.

SQUAD
Eric Andersson, Jonas Andersson, Stefan Ekberg, Billy Forsberg, Jörgen Hültgren, Kim Johansson, Robert Johansson, Anders Ljung.
Foreign: Tomasz Chrzanowski, Tomasz Gollob, Chis Harris, Niels-Kristian Iversen, Mads Korneliussen, Grigori Laguta, Bjarne Pedersen, James Wright.

PIRATERNA (A)
Tuesday, June 24
Lost 47-49
Pedersen 12:1, Laguta 8:2, Harris 6:1, Forsberg 0, Gollob 15:1, E. Andersson 2, Korneliussen 4:1, J. Andersson, did not ride.

ROSPIGGARNA (H)
Tuesday, July 1
Lost 47-49
Chrzanowski 4:1, Pedersen 13, Iversen 8, Laguta 0, Gollob 13:1, Forsberg 9:1, J. Andersson 0, K. Johansson, did not ride.
Aggregate: Lost 92-100.

MASARNAAVESTA (A)
Tuesday, July 8
Lost 47-49
Iversen 10, Chrzanowski 1, Harris 11, Wright 3:1, Pedersen 9:1, Forsberg 4, Korneliussen 9:1, J. Andersson, did not ride.
Aggregate: Won 108-84.

INDIANERNA (A)
Tuesday, July 22
Lost 36-60
Pedersen 13, Laguta 7, Iversen 1, Wright 1, Gollob 9, J. Andersson 0, Korneliussen 5:1.
Aggregate: Lost 92-99.

HAMMARBY (H)
Tuesday, July 29
Won 56-40
Laguta 4:1, Pedersen 10:1, Iversen 10, Harris 8:2, Gollob 14, Forsberg 9:1, Ekberg 1:1, J. Andersson, did not ride.
Aggregate: Won 100-92.

LEJONEN (A)
Tuesday, August 5
Lost 44-52
Pedersen 8:2, Laguta 6:1, Iversen 0, Harris 9:1, Gollob 11:1, Ekberg 1:1, Forsberg 9, J. Andersson, did not ride.
Aggregate: Lost 90-102.

DACKARNA (H)
Tueasday, August 12
Won 49-47
Chrzanowski 1, Pedersen 9:1, Iversen 8:1, Harris 5:2, **Gollob 15**, Forsberg 10, J. Andersson 1:1.
Aggregate: Lost 94-98.

SMEDERNA (A)
Tuesday, August 19
Won 56-40
Pedersen 5:2, Laguta 12, Iversen 11:2, Harris 6:3, Gollob 11, Ekberg 1, Forsberg 10:1, J. Andersson, did not ride.
Aggregate: Won 108-84.

ELIT VETLANDA (A)
Tuesday, August 26
Lost 37-59
Pedersen 10, Laguta 5:2, Iversen 6, Harris 5, Gollob 9, Ekberg 0, Forsberg 2, J. Andersson, did not ride.
Aggregate: Lost 93-99.

PIRATERNA (H)
Tuesday, September 2
Lost 45-51
Forsberg 4, Pedersen 12:2, Chrzanowski 0, Harris 7, Gollob 13:1, R. Johansson 3, Wright 6:1, J. Andersson, did not ride.
Aggregate: Lost 92-100.

ELITSERIEN

	M	W	D	L	PtsF	PtsA	Pts
Lejonen	18	13	0	5	935	793	35
Dackarna	18	12	0	6	916	810	31
Elit Vetlanda	18	11	0	7	922	805	30
Piraterna	18	11	0	7	878	846	27
Rospiggarna	18	10	1	7	858	868	26
Indianerna	18	7	1	10	859	866	19
VÄSTERVIK	**18**	**7**	**0**	**11**	**869**	**858**	**17**
Hammarby	18	7	0	11	825	901	16
Smederna	18	6	0	12	793	934	13
MasarnaAvesta	18	5	0	13	776	950	11

For 2009 squad see page 490

Tomasz Gollob, Billy Forsberg, Joan Andersson, Tomasz Chrzanowski, team manager Pekka Helgesson. Front: Mads Korneliussen, Chris Harris, coach Marvyn Cox, Niels-Kristian Iversen

Rider	M	R	Pts	BP	TPts	Ave	F	P
Tomasz GOLLOB	17	90	192	10	202	8.98	0	0
Bjarne PEDERSEN	**15**	**80**	**154**	**14**	**168**	**8.40**	**0**	**0**
Niels-Kristian IVERSEN	13	63	103	10	113	7.17	0	1
Chris HARRIS	**16**	**75**	**109**	**16**	**125**	**6.67**	**0**	**0**
Grigori LAGUTA	13	66	94	12	106	6.42	0	0
Billy FORSBERG	**13**	**61**	**83**	**8**	**91**	**5.97**	**0**	**0**
Mads KORNELIUSSEN	7	37	43	7	50	5.41	0	0
Tomasz CHRZANOWSKI	**11**	**52**	**53**	**8**	**61**	**4.69**	**0**	**0**
Stefan EKBERG	7	18	15	6	21	4.67	0	0
James WRIGHT	**3**	**11**	**10**	**2**	**12**	**4.36**	**0**	**0**
Robert JOHANSSON	1	4	3	0	3	3.00	0	0
Eric ANDERSSON	**1**	**3**	**2**	**0**	**2**	**2.67**	**0**	**0**
Jonas ANDERSSON	**9**	**19**	**8**	**2**	**10**	**2.11**	**0**	**0**

Number eight appearances: Jonas ANDERSSON (9), Kim JOHANSSON (4)..

2008 PARTNER CLUB
VARGARNA (AllSvenskan)

2009 PARTNER CLUB
MASARNA (AllSvenskan)

Photo: Roger Hultgren

DACKARNA 2008:
Back: team manager Daniel Nelson, Andreas Jonsson, Fredrik Lindgren, Peter Karlsson, Lukas Dryml, team manager Morgan Andersson. Front: Ludvig Lindgren, Nicolai Klindt, Grzegorz Zengota and Hans Andersen

INDIARNERNA 2008:
Magnus Zetterström, team manager Daniel Andersson, Piotr Protasiewicz, Adrian Miedzinski, Simon Gustafsson, Edward Kennett, Matej Ferjan, David Rohlén, Henrik Gustafsson, team manager Ove Österberg

LEJONEN 2008:
Robert Pettersson, David Ruud, Tomasz Jedrzejak, Sebastian Ulamek, Nicki Pedersen, Daniel Jeleniewski, Maciej Kuciapa

PIRATERNA 2008:
Linus Sundström, Ryan Sullivan, Mikael Max, Stefan Dannö, Grzegorz Walasek
Front: Daniel Nermark, Robert Kosiecha, Damian Balinski

2009 ELITE LEAGUE Squads

DACKARNA
Andreas **JONSSON**, Peter **KARLSSON**, Fredrik **LINDGREN**, Ludvig **LINDGREN**.
Foreign: Hans **ANDERSEN**, Kenneth **BJERRE**, Nicolai **KLINDT**, Rory **SCHLEIN**, Claus **VISSING**, Grzegorz **ZENGOTA**.

ELIT VETLANDA
Mikael **ASTRAND**, Mikael **AXELSSON**, Ted **HAGANSBO**, Thomas H. **JONASSON**, Peter **LJUNG**, Thomas **LJUNG**, Anders **MELLGREN**, Patrik **MALMFELT**.
Foreign: Jason **CRUMP**, Adrian **GOMOLSKI**, Jaroslaw **HAMPEL**, Patrick **HOUGAARD**, Jurica **PAVLIC**, Lee **RICHARDSON**, Karol **ZABIK**.

LEJONEN
Dennis **ANDERSSON**, Johannes **FREDH**, Robert **PETTERSSON**, David **RUUD**.
Foreign: Leigh **ADAMS**, Chris **HOLDER**, Tomasz **JEDRZEJAK**, Daniel **JELENIEWSKI**, Nicki **PEDERSEN**, Piotr **SWIDERSKI**, Sebastian **ULAMEK**, Davey **WATT**.

SMEDERNA
Linus **EKLÖF**, Henrik **KARLSSON**, Mikael **MAX**, Magnus **ZETTERSTRÖM**.
Foreign: Troy **BATCHELOR**, Krzysztof **BUCZKOWSKI**, Wieslaw **JAGUS**, Krzysztof **KASPRZAK**, Daniel **KING**, Robert **MISKOWIAK**, Martin **VACULIK**.

VÄSTERVIK
Billy **FORSBERG**.
Foreign: Kevin **DOOLAN**, Tomasz **GOLLOB**, Chris **HARRIS**, Niels-Kristian **IVERSEN**, Tomasz **GAPINSKI**, Artem **LAGUTA**, Grigori **LAGUTA**, Przemyslaw-**PAWLICKI**,

● *Other Elite League 2009 squads are listed on their respective review pages.*

ALLSVENSKAN LEAGUE STANDINGS

	M	W	D	L	PtsF	PtsA	Pts
1 GRIPARNA	12	7	0	5	604	546	14
2 ÖRNARNA	12	7	0	5	592	557	14
3 VARGARNA	12	7	0	5	580	570	14
4 VALSARNA	12	6	1	5	580	571	13
5 SOLKATTERNA	12	2	1	9	519	631	5

PLAY-OFFS

Semi Finals
GRIPARNA 51 **VALSARNA 45**
VALSARNA 55 GRIPARNA 41
VALSARNA win 100-92 on aggregate.

VARGARNA 62 ÖRNARNA 34
ÖRNARNA 44 **VARGARNA 52**
VARGARNA win 114-78

FINAL
VARGARNA 51 VALSARNA 45
VALSARNA 47 **VARGARNA 49**
VARGARNA win 100-92 on aggregate.

KAPARNA'S demise left the AllSvenskan League looking a sorry affair – reduced to just five clubs.

And that left a somewhat curious fixture list in which teams met two of their rivals four times (twice home and away) and the other two only twice.

Perhaps that also explained why only one point separated regular season table-toppers Griparna and fourth-placed Valsarna!

Only Solkatterna, who won only two matches all year, missed out on the play-offs which saw league leaders Griparna dumped out in the first round by Valsarna who went on to lose the Final against Norrköping's Vargarna.

It was sweet revenge for the Wolves who had lost out to the Rollers in the previous year's play-offs!

Vargarna's victory saw them return to the ElitSerien after two years in the AllSvenskan and leaves Nyköping's Griparna still seeking their first league title.

Roll of Honour

1950 A ....PIRATERNA
1950 B ....SAXARNA
1950 C ....VETLANDA
1951 E ....VIKINGARNA
1951 W ....KAPARNA
1952 ....MONARKERNA
1953 ....VIKINGARNA
1958 ....ÖRNARNA
1959 ....FOLKARE
1960 ....FILBYTERNA
1961 N ....FOLKARE
1961 S ....KAPARNA
1962 ....GETINGARNA
1963 ....ÖRNARNA
1964 ....VARGARNA
1965 ....GAMARNA
1966 ....NJUDUNGARNA
1967 ....INDIANERNA
1968 ....LEJONEN
1969 ....ÖRNARNA
1970 ....BYSARNA
1971 E ....DACKARNA
1971 W ....SMEDERNA
1972 E ....DACKARNA
1972 W ....INDIANERNA
1973 E ....KAPARNA
1973 W ....INDIANERNA
1974 A ....LEJONEN
1974 B ....MASARNA
1975 ....NJUDUNGARNA
1976 ....ÖRNARNA
1977 ....SKEPPARNA
1978 ....LEJONEN
1979 ....SKEPPARNA
1980 N ....PIRATERNA

1980 S .... KAPARNA
1981 N .... SOLKATTERNA
1981 S .... VARGARNA
1982 N .... SOLKATTERNA
1982 S .... KAPARNA
1983 N .... GAMARNA
1983 S .... VARGARNA
1984 .... SOLKATTERNA
1985 .... BYSARNA
1986 .... DACKARNA
1987 .... GAMARNA
1988 .... ROSPIGGARNA
1989 .... SMEDERNA
1990 .... SKEPPARNA
1991 .... DACKARNA
1992 .... SMEDERNA
1993 .... VALSARNA
1994 .... ROSPIGGARNA
1995 .... DACKARNA
1996 A .... VARGARNA
1996 B .... GETINGARNA
1997 A .... KAPARNA
1997 B .... NÄSSJO
1998 .... MASARNA
1999 .... FILBYTERNA
2000 .... BYSARNA
2001 .... ÖRNARNA
2002 .... VETLANDA
2003 .... PIRATERNA
2004 .... ÖRNARNA
2005 .... BAJEN
2006 .... KAPARNA
2007 .... LEJONEN
2008 .... VARGARNA

2009 ALLSVENSKAN LEAGUE

SEVEN teams will take part in the 2009 AllSvenskan League and while it is a long way from the eight sides that were involved as recently as 2007 at least it's a major improvement on last year.

Hammarby withdrew from the ElitSerien during the winter after annoucing a loss of around a quarter of a million pounds (3 million Swedish kronor) in 2008 alone.

TRACK FILE

Track: Gubbängens IP, Tobaksvägen 41, 123 57, Farsta, Sweden.
Telephone: 0046 0860488202.
Website: www.getingarna.com
Track Length: 387 metres.
Track Record: 65.1 secs, Tomasz Gapinski, October 25, 2007.

2009 SQUAD

Robin **BURESTAD**, Freddie **ERIKSSON**, Henrik **GUSTAFSSON**, Joakim **MÅRTENSSON**, Andreas **MESSING**, Jonas **MESSING**.
Foreign: James **HOLDER**, Timo **LAHTI**, Kalle **KATAJISTO**, Peter **KILDEMAND**, Niko **SILTANIEMI**, Adrian **SZEWCZYKOWKSKI**, Craig **WATSON**.

They have been joined in the second tier by the returning Getingarna – they did not race in a league last year – and when relegated MasarnaAvesta closed down, Team Dalakraft accepted an invitation to join after an unbeaten 2008 Division One campaign.

At one time it looked as if they would use the name Gasarna but, in the end, have opted to be called Masarna, at least keeping that name alive.

Griparna, Örnarna, Solkatterna and Valsarna are back for another season but the odd numbers means that one club will sit out fixtures every week!

2009 FIXTURES

Thursday, April 30
Hammarby v Masarna
Solkatterna v Valsarna
Griparna v Örnarna
Thursday, May 7
Masarna v Solkatterna
Örnarna v Hammarby
Getingarna v Griparna
Thursday, May 14
Valsarna v Masarna
Hammarby v Getingarna
Solkatterna v Örnarna
Thursday, May 21
Örnarna v Masarna
Getingarna v Solkatterna
Griparna v Valsarna
Thursday, May 28
Masarna v Getingarna
Valsarna v Örnarna
Hammarby v Griparna
Thursday, June 4
Solkatterna v Hammarby
Getingarna v Valsarna
Griparna v Masarna
Thursday, June 11
Hammarby v Valsarna
Örnarna v Getingarna
Griparna v Solkatterna
Thursday, June 25
Masarna v Hammarby
Valsarna v Solkatterna
Örnarna v Griparna
Thursday, July 2
Hammarby v Örnarna
Solkatterna v Masarna
Griparna v Getingarna
Thursday, July 9
Masarna v Valsarna
Örnarna v Solkatterna
Getingarna v Hammarby
Thursday, July 23
Masarna v Örnarna
Thursday, July 30
Örnarna v Valsarna
Getingarna v Masarna
Griparna v Hammarby
Thursday, August 6
Masarna v Griparna
Valsarna v Getingarna
Hammarby v Solkatterna
Thursday, August 13
Valsarna v Hammarby
Solkatterna v Griparna
Getingarna v Örnarna
Thursday, August 23
Valsarna v Griparna
Wednesday, September 23
Solkatterna v Getingarna

AllSvenskan League

GRIPARNA

2008 RESULTS

Final position.......................... Joint Third (First)

VARGARNA (A)
Thursday, May 1
Won 54-42
Nieminen 7, Jablonski 3, **Eriksson 13:2**, Hougaard 9, Lekander 6:1, Nilsson 12, Hautamäki 4:2, Pettersson 0.

ÖRNARNA (H)
Thursday, May 8
Won 51-45
Lekander 2:2, Hougaard 10:1, Nieminen 14, Hautamäki 9:5, Puszakowski 5, Nilsson 11, Pettersson 0.

SOLKATTERNA (H)
Thursday, May 22
Won 51-45
Puszakowski 5:2, Hautamäki 11:1, Sitera 9:2, Jablonski 6, Nilsson 9, Lekander 11:3, Dahlborg 0.

VALSARNA (A)
Thursday, May 29
Lost 47-49
Nieminen 15, Hautamäki 5, *rider replacement for Sitera*, Jablonski 8:2, Eriksson 10:1, Dahlborg 0, Lekander 9.

VARGARNA (H)
Thursday, June 5
Lost 45-51
Hougaard 4, Lekander 4:1, Nieminen 8:2, Hautamäki 0, Eriksson 14, Nilsson 10, Kristiansen 5:2.

ÖRNARNA (A)
Thursday, June 26
Lost 46-50
Nieminen 12, Nilsson 6:3, Hougaard 5:1, Jablonski 5, Eriksson 5:2, Lekander 5:1, Hautamäki 8.

VARGARNA (H)
Thursday, July 3
Won 57-39
Eriksson 10:3, Lekander 10, Hansen 8:3, Nilsson 5, Nieminen 11, Hautamäki 13:1, Dahlborg 0.

ÖRNARNA (A)
Thursday, July 10
Lost 42-53
Nilsson 6:2, Lekander 5:1, Eriksson 10:2, Hautamäki 5, Nieminen 12:1, Kristiansen 4, Dahlborg 0.

TRACK FILE

Track: Nyköpings Motorstadion, Fockstigen 21m 613 35 Oxelösund, Sweden.
Telephone: 0046 0155214591.
Website: www.griparna.nu
Track Length: 294 metres.
Track Record: 58.3 secs, Peter Ljung, August 7, 2008.

SQUAD
Mats Boström, Dennis Dahlborg, Alexander Edberg, Freddie Eriksson, Adrian Gheorge, Andreas Lekander, Kim Nilsson, Robert Pettersson.
Foreign: Kenneth Hansen, Juha Hautamäki, Patrick Hougaard, Miroslaw Jablonski, Jesper Kristiansen[1], Kauko Nieminen, Maciej Piaszczynski, Mariusz Puszakowski, Filip Sitera.

SOLKATTERNA (A)
Thursday, July 31
Won 56-40
Hansen 7:1, Nilsson 11, Nieminen 11:1, Hougaard 9:3, Eriksson 12:1, Dahlborg 1, Lekander 5.

VALSARNA (H)
Thursday, August 7
Won 57-39
Nieminen 10:1, Hautamäki 9:3, Nilsson 7:1, Hansen 12:2, Sitera 8, Lekander 11:1, Dahlborg 0.

VARGARNA (A)
Thursday, August 14
Lost 44-52
Nieminen 11, Hougaard 4:1, Hansen 5:1, Puszakowski 6, Eriksson 7:1, Dahlborg 0, Lekander 11:2.

ÖRNARNA (H)
Thursday, August 28
Won 54-41
Hansen 4:1, Hautamäki 12:1, **Hougaard 13:2**, Jablonski 6:1, Eriksson 10, Lekander 8:1, Dahlborg 1.

ALL SVENSKAN

	M	*W*	*D*	*L*	*PtsF*	*PtsA*	*Pts*
GRIPARNA	**12**	**7**	**0**	**5**	**604**	**546**	**14**
Örnarna	12	7	0	5	592	557	14
Vargarna	12	7	0	5	580	570	14
Valsarna	12	6	1	5	580	571	13
Solkatterna	12	2	1	9	519	631	5

■ Even though they finished top of the AllSvenskan League during the regular season, the Griffins were knocked out in the semi final of the play-offs, losing to Valsarna.

They had actually got the better of their two previous meetings with their conquerors, losing by only two points at Hagfors and having a comfortable 18 points win in the return.

Play offs

Semi Final, first leg
VALSARNA (H)
Thursday, September 4
Won 51-45
Nieminen 11:1, Hautamäki 5:1, Nilsson 4:2, Hougaard 8:1, Eriksson 9:1, Lekander 4:1, Jablonski 10:1, Dalhborg, did not ride.

Semi Final, second leg
VALSARNA (A)
Friday, September 5
Lost 41-55
Hougaard 13:2, Hautamäki 1, Eriksson 8, Nilsson 6, Hansen 5, Lekander 2:1, Jablonski 6, Dahlborg, did not ride.

Aggregate: Lost 92-100.

2009 Squad

Marcus **ANDERSSON**, Mats **BOSTRÖM**, Dennis **DAHLBORG**, Andreas **LEKANDER**, Kim **NILSSON**.
Foreign: Oliver **ALLEN**, Henning **BAGER**, Kenneth **HANSEN**, Juha **HAUTAMÄKI**, Miroslaw **JABLONSKI**, Simon **NIELSEN**, Filip **SITERA**.

Griparna were one of the few teams to actually record a small profit in 2008.

The club plan to erect a new clubhouse at the track in 2009 and also want to improve the lighting and install an air fence.

They are also confident that their new look side will reach the play off final after last year's last-gasp disappointment.

Rider	M	R	Pts	BP	TPts	Ave	F	P
Kauko NIEMINEN	11	59	122	6	128	8.68	0	0
Freddie ERIKSSON	**11**	**59**	**108**	**13**	**121**	**8.20**	**0**	**1**
Filip SITERA	2	10	17	2	19	7.60	0	0
Patrick HOUGAARD	**9**	**45**	**75**	**10**	**85**	**7.56**	**0**	**1**
Juha HAUTAMÄKI	12	53	82	14	96	7.25	0	0
Kenneth HANSEN	**6**	**28**	**41**	**8**	**49**	**7.00**	**0**	**0**
Kim NILSSON	11	55	87	8	95	6.91	0	0
Andreas LEKANDER	**14**	**64**	**93**	**14**	**107**	**6.69**	**0**	**0**
Mariusz PUSZAKOWSKI	3	12	16	2	18	6.00	0	0
Miroslaw JABLONSKI	**7**	**33**	**44**	**5**	**49**	**5.94**	**0**	**0**
Jesper KRISTIANSEN	2	8	9	2	11	5.50	0	0
Dennis DAHLBORG	**8**	**19**	**2**	**0**	**2**	**0.42**	**0**	**0**
Robert PETTERSSON	2	4	0	0	0	0.00	0	0

Number eight appearances: Dennis DAHLBORG (2).

2008 PARTNER CLUB

HAMMARBY
(ElitSerien)

2009 PARTNER CLUBS

VARGARNA
(ElitSerien)
FILBYTERNA
(Division One)

Kauko Nieminen

Filip Sitera

AllSvenskan League

ÖRNARNA

2008 RESULTS

Final position........................Joint third (Second)

VALSARNA (H)
Thursday, May 1
Won 50-46
Aldén 9:2, Kramer 12, Howe 4:3, Olsson 6, Klingberg 13, Mäkinen 2, Agö 4:1.

GRIPARNA (A)
Thursday, May 8
Lost 45-51
Bergström 2, Kosciuch 4, Olsson 2, Jamrozy 7, Klingberg 14, Lindgren 12:1, Agö 4:2.

SOLKATTERNA (A)
Thursday, May 15
Won 54-41
Howe 12, Kramer 2, Jamrozy 11, L. Lindgren 6:1, Klingberg 9:1, Agö 9:1, Isomettä 5:2.

VARGARNA (H)
Thursday, May 22
Lost 45-51
Olsson 5, Kramer 8:1, Kosciuch 14, Jamrozy 1:1, Klingberg 9, Isomettä 5, Agö 3:1.

VARGARNA (A)
Thursday, June 12
Lost 45-51
Kramer 4:2, Kosciuch 10:3, Howe 9, Lindgren 1:1, Klingberg 15, Agö 1, Olsson 5.

GRIPARNA (H)
Thursday, June 26
Won 50-46
Klingberg 12:1, Lindgren 4:1, Jamrozy 13:1, Kramer 3:1, Kosciuch 14, Olsson 2, Agö 2:1.

VALSARNA (A)
Thursday, July 3
Won 56-40
Kramer 9, **Kosciuch 12:3**, Jamrozy 9, Howe 9:1, Klingberg 12:1, Agö 1, Isomettä 4.

GRIPARNA (H)
Thursday, July 10
Won 53-42
Olsson 5:1, Kramer 3, **Jamrozy 14:1**, Lindgren 7:1, Klingberg 12, Isomettä 7:1, Agö 3:1, Nilsson 2.

TRACK FILE

Track: CanVac Arena, Vallby 6, 542 92 Mariestad, Sweden.
Telephone: 0046 050120230.
Website: www.ornarna.nu
Track Length: 295 metres.
Track Record: 56.0 secs, Tony Rickardsson, July 28, 1998.

SQUAD
Christian Agö, Sebastian Aldén, Andreas Bergström, Joakim Engstrand, Niklas Eriksson, Kim Hansson, Oskar Hedfors, Kim Ingmarsson, Christian Isomettä, Mikael Karlsson, Emil Kramer, Ludvig Lindgren, Olof Nilsson, Tomas Olsson, Mikael Renner, Daniel Sjögren, Pontus Sundström.
Foreign: David Howe, Ronnie Jamrozy, Norbert Kosciuch, Piotr Paluch.

SOLKATTERNA (H)
Thursday, July 24
Won 64-32
Kosciuch 14, Olsson 2:2, Klingberg 14, Howe 7:3, Jamrozy 12:1, Agö 6:2, Isomettä 7, Nilsson 2:1.

VARGARNA (A)
Thursday, July 31
Lost 40-56
Kosciuch 7:1, Paluch 8:1, Klingberg 9, Howe 8:2, Olsson 4:1, Nilsson 1, Agö 3.

VARGARNA (H)
Thursday, August 21
Won 49-47
Kosciuch 11:1, Paluch 9:1, Jamrozy 9:1, Lindgren 4:1, Klingborg 8, Agö 4, Isomettä 4, Nilsson, did not ride.

GRIPARNA (A)
Thursday, August 28
Lost 41-54
Klingberg 11:1, Olsson 0, Paluch 8:2, Jamrozy 8:2, Kosciuch 7, Nilsson 3:1, Agö 4:1.

ALL SVENSKAN

	M	W	D	L	PtsF	PtsA	Pts
Griparna	12	7	0	5	604	546	14
ÖRNARNA	**12**	**7**	**0**	**5**	**592**	**557**	**14**
Vargarna	12	7	0	5	580	570	14
Valsarna	12	6	1	5	580	571	13
Solkatterna	12	2	1	9	519	631	5

2009 Squad

Christian AGÖ, Niklas ERIKSSON, Anton GÖTHBERG, Oskar HEDFORS, Ricky KLING, Emil KRAMER.
Foreign: David HOWE, Ronnie JAMROZY, Norbert KOSCIUCH, Piotr PALUCH, Mariusz WEGRZYK, Kevin WÖLBERT.

Play offs

Semi Final, first leg
VARGARNA (A)
Thursday, September 4
Lost 34-62
Kosciuch 3, Jamrozy 6:2, Klingberg 12, Kramer 4:1, Paluch 6:1, Nilsson 0, Agö 3.

Semi Final, second leg
VARGARNA (H)
Friday, September 5
Lost 44-52
Paluch 6:1, Kramer 8:2, Jamrozy 12, Isomettä 0, Klingberg 13, Agö 5:1, Nilsson 0.
Aggregate: Lost 78-114.

Did you know?

Örnarna are one of the clubs actively involved in SVEMO Children's Committee developed plan.

Parents and young riders under the age of 12 are put through a series of training skills which see them awarded diplomas at bronze helmet, silver helmet and gold helmet level.

At least one month must elapse between the silver and bronze and only when a youngster reaches gold helmet level by passing a theoretical exam do they qualify for a competition licence. Successful students usually feature on the Örnarna website.

Rider	*M*	*R*	*Pts*	*BP*	*TPts*	*Ave*	*F*	*P*
Niklas KLINGBERG	14	74	163	4	167	9.03	0	0
Sebastian ALDÉN	**1**	**5**	**9**	**2**	**11**	**8.80**	**0**	**0**
Norbert KOSCIUCH	10	50	96	8	104	8.32	0	1
David HOWE	**6**	**29**	**49**	**9**	**58**	**8.00**	**0**	**0**
Ronnie JAMROZY	11	56	102	9	111	7.93	0	1
Piotr PALUCH	**5**	**26**	**37**	**6**	**43**	**6.62**	**0**	**0**
Ludvig LINDGREN	6	26	34	6	40	6.15	0	0
Emil KRAMER	**9**	**42**	**53**	**7**	**60**	**5.71**	**0**	**0**
Christian ISOMETTÄ	7	27	32	3	35	5.19	0	0
Christian AGÖ	**14**	**58**	**52**	**11**	**63**	**4.34**	**0**	**0**
Tomas OLSSON	9	36	31	4	35	3.89	0	0
Olof NILSSON	**7**	**13**	**8**	**2**	**10**	**3.08**	**0**	**0**
Andreas BERGSTRÖM	1	3	2	0	0	2.67	0	0
Jari MÄKINEN	**1**	**3**	**2**	**0**	**2**	**2.67**	**0**	**0**

Number eight appearances: None.

2008 PARTNER CLUBS

DACKARNA
(ElitSerien)

TEAM CANVAC
(Division One)

2009 PARTNER CLUBS

LEJONEN
(ElitSerien)

GNISTORNA
(Division One)

David Howe

Ludvig Lindgren

AllSvenskan League

SOLKATTERNA

2008 RESULTS

Final position..Fifth

VALSARNA (H)
Thursday, May 8
Won 55-41
Max 9:1, Bergström 10, Dannö 9:1, Sundström 5:1, **Nermark 15**, Lehtinen 6:1, Persson 1:1, Thelaus, did not ride.

ÖRNARNA (H)
Thursday, May 15
Lost 41-54
Max 9, Bergström 2, Dannö 9, Sundström 6:2, Nermark 13, Kjellberg 1, Persson 1.

GRIPARNA (A)
Thursday, May 22
Lost 45-51
Graversen 0, Bergström 0, Dannö 5:2, Pytel 12:1, **Max 18**, Kjellberg 5:1, Lehtinen 5:1.

VARGARNA (A)
Thursday, May 29
Lost 44-51
Pytel 3:1, Dannö 7:1, Nermark 13:1, Vissing 7:1, Max 7, Kjellberg 4, Thelaus 3.

VALSARNA (H)
Thursday, June 5
Drew 48-48
Max 13:1, Sundström 8:1, Dannö 7, Bergström 0, Nermark 12, Kjellberg 0, Lehtinen 7:2, Thelaus 1:1.

VALSARNA (A)
Thursday, June 26
Lost 36-60
Dannö 0, Sundström 6, Nermark 14, Graversen 3:1, Max 8:1, Persson 0, Thelaus 5.

VALSARNA (H)
Thursday, July 10
Lost 45-51
Max 8:1, Sundström 5:3, Bergström 2:2, Dannö 6, Nermark 13, Lehtinen 6, Thelaus 5:1.

ÖRNARNA (A)
Thursday, July 24
Lost 32-64
Max 11, Sundström 5:1, Dannö 4, Graversen 4, Moller 2, Thelaus 5:2, Kjellberg 1.

TRACK FILE

Track: Kalvholmens Motorstadion, Kalvholmsgatan, Kalvholmens Ind omr, Karlstad, Sweden.
Telephone: 0046 054185500.
Website: www.solkatterna.com
Track Length: 297 metres.
Track Record: 56.3 secs, Tony Rickardsson, September 8, 2004.

SQUAD
Viktor Bergström, Stefan Dannö, Dan Kjellberg, Mikael Max, Daniel Nermark, Magnus Persson, Simon Rudin, Linus Sundström, Jeremia Thelaus.
Foreign: Jan Graversen, Manuel Hauzinger, Adam Kajoch,Rene Lehtinen, Henrik Moller, Daniel Pytel, Claus Vissing.

GRIPARNA (H)
Thursday, July 31
Lost 40-56
Pytel 6:1, Moller 2:1, Max 12, Sundström 5:1, Kajoch 2, Thelaus 8:1, Lehtinen 3, Kjellberg 2.

VARGARNA (H)
Thursday, August 7
Won 49-47
Dannö 7:1, *rider replacement for Nermark*, Sundström 11:1, Bergström 8:2, Max 16, Thelaus 7:2, Kjellberg 0.

VALSARNA (A)
Thursday, August 14
Lost 38-58
Bergström 9:1, *rider replacement for Nermark*, Dannö 9:1, Moller 4, Graversen 2, Persson 1, Thelaus 13:1.

VALSARNA (A)
Thursday, August 28
Lost 46-50
Nermark 11:1, Bergström 3:1, Dannö 4, Sundström 5:1, Max 11, Persson 0, Thelaus 12:3.

ALL SVENSKAN

	M	W	D	L	PtsF	PtsA	Pts
Griparna	12	7	0	5	604	546	14
Örnarna	12	7	0	5	592	557	14
Vargarna	12	7	0	5	580	570	14
Valsarna	12	6	1	5	580	571	13
SOLKATTERNA	**12**	**2**	**1**	**9**	**519**	**631**	**5**

2009 Squad

Viktor **BERGSTRÖM**, Oliver **BERNTZON**, Magnus **KARLSSON**, Dan **KJELLBERG**, Thimm Persson **NORBERG**, Magnus **PERSSON**, Linus **SUNDSTRÖM**.
Foreign: Jan **GRAVERSEN**, Manuel **HAUZINGER**, Michael **JESPEN**, Peter **JUUL** Larsen, Daniel **PYTEL**.

Rider	M	R	Pts	BP	TPts	Ave	F	P
Daniel NERMARK	7	38	91	2	93	9.79	1	0
Mikael MAX	**11**	**58**	**122**	**4**	**126**	**8.69**	**1**	**0**
Claus VISSING	1	5	7	1	8	6.40	0	0
Jeremia THELAUS	**9**	**45**	**59**	**11**	**70**	**6.22**	**0**	**0**
Daniel PYTEL	3	16	21	3	24	6.00	0	0
Linus SUNDSTRÖM	**9**	**46**	**56**	**11**	**67**	**5.83**	**0**	**0**
Stefan DANNÖ	11	54	67	6	73	5.41	0	0
Rene LEHTINEN	**5**	**24**	**27**	**4**	**31**	**5.17**	**0**	**0**
Viktor BERGSTRÖM	8	35	34	6	40	4.57	0	0
Dan KJELLBERG	**7**	**17**	**13**	**1**	**14**	**3.29**	**0**	**0**
Henrik MOLLER	3	12	8	1	9	3.00	0	0
Jan GRAVERSEN	**4**	**17**	**9**	**1**	**10**	**2.35**	**0**	**0**
Adam KAJOCH	1	4	2	0	2	2.00	0	0
Magnus PERSSON	**5**	**12**	**3**	**1**	**4**	**1.33**	**0**	**0**

Number eight non-riding appearances: Jeremia THELAUS (1).

2008 PARTNER CLUBS

PIRATERNA
(ElitSerien)

CROSSBONE PIRATES
(Division One)

2009 PARTNER CLUBS

PIRATERNA
(ElitSerien)

CROSSBONE PIRATES
(Division One)

Solkatterna's Linus Sundström in action during a visit to England last season – riding in the colours of defunct Bristol Bulldogs at Swindon

AllSvenskan League

VALSARNA

TRACK FILE

Track: Tallhnults Motorstadion

Uddeholmsväghen 10, 683 30 Hagfors, Sweden.

Telephone: 0046 056312605 / 0046 056312123.

Website: www.valsarna.nu

Track Length: 290 metres.

Track Record: 53.8 secs, Mikael Max, May 9, 2000.

2008 RESULTS

Final position......................Runners-up (Fourth)

SQUAD

Robin Aspegren, Gustaf Bjur, Daniel Davidsson, Robert Eriksson, Robin Hollgren, Magnus Karlsson, Peter Ljung, Thomas Ljung, Anders Mellgren, Mattias Persson, Robin Rundby, Robin Törnqvist

Foreign: Henning Bager, Adrian Gomolski, Christian Henry, Krister Jacobsen, Cameron Woodward.

ÖRNARNA (A)
Thursday, May 1
Lost 46-50
Eriksson 9, Törnqvist 1:1, Karlsson 6:1, Davidsson 7, P. Ljung 14, Bergkvist 3:2, Persson, did not ride, Mellgren 6.

SOLKATTERNA (A)
Thursday, May 8
Lost 41-55
Eriksson 12:2, Davidsson 9, Karlsson 4:1, Jacobsen 6, *rider replacement for P. Ljung*, Bergkvist 2, Mellgren 8:3.

VARGARNA (A)
Thursday, May 15
Lost 45-50
Eriksson 9, Davidsson 6:2, Bager 7:1, Törnqvist 3:1, Jonasson 10:1, Jacobsen 7, Mellgren 3:1.

GRIPARNA (H)
Thursday, May 29
Won 49-47
Eriksson 8, Törnqvist 3:1, Woodward 10:1, Karlsson 6:2, P. Ljung 14:1, Bergkvist 4:1, Mellgren 4:2, Persson, did not ride.

SOLKATTERNA (A)
Thursday, Jubne 5
Drew 48-48
Davidsson 10:1, Jacobsen 4:2, Woodward 6:1, Eriksson 8:2, P. Ljung 11, Bergkvist 1:1, Mellgren 8:2, Persson, did not ride.

SOLKATTERNA (H)
Thursday, June 26
Won 60-36
Davidsson 9, Karlsson 6:1, Jonasson 9:3, Eriksson 10:2, P. Ljung 14, Persson 2, Mellgren 10.

ÖRNARNA (H)
Thursday, July 3
Lost 40-56
Davidsson 8, T. Ljung 3:1, Aspegren 0, Eriksson 14, Woodward 4:1, Bergkvist 6:1, Mellgren 5:2, Persson, did not ride.

SOLKATTERNA (A)
Thursday, July 10
Won 51-45
Davidsson 9:2, Eriksson 8:2, Jonasson 11, Jacobsen 4, P. Ljung 14, Mellgren 3, Bergkvist 2, Persson, did not ride.

VARGARNA (H)
Thurdsday, July 24
Won 53-43
Davidsson 9:1, Törnqvist 3:1, Jonasson 10:2, Eriksson 7:2, **P. Ljung 15**, Bergkvist 3:1, Mellgren 6, Persson, did not ride.

GRIPARNA (A)
Thursday, August 7
Lost 39-57
Woodward 7, Törnqvist 0, Eriksson 10, Karlsson 3, P. Ljung 10, Bergkvist 3, Mellgren 6:1, Persson, did not ride.

SOLKATTERNA (H)
Thursday, August 14
Won 58-38
Davidsson 14, Mellgren 4, Eriksson 8:1, Karlsson 10:2, Woodward 9:2, Persson 1, Törnqvist 12.

SOLKATTERNA (H)
Thursday, August 28
Won 50-46
Davidsson 11, Mellgren 4:1, Woodward 8, Eriksson 11:1, P. Ljung 9, Törnqvist 3:1, Bergkvist 4:1.

ALL SVENSKAN

	M	W	D	L	PtsF	PtsA	Pts
Griparna	12	7	0	5	604	546	14
Örnarna	12	7	0	5	592	557	14
Vargarna	12	7	0	5	580	570	14
VALSARNA	**12**	**6**	**1**	**5**	**580**	**571**	**13**
Solkatterna	12	2	1	9	519	631	5

Play offs

Semi Final, first leg
GRIPARNA (A)
Thursday, September 4
Lost 45-51
Davidsson 13, Mellgren 0, Eriksson 4:1, Gomolski 11:2, Jonasson 11, Bergkvist 1, Aspegren 5, Persson, did not ride.

Semi Final, second leg
GRIPARNA (H)
Friday, September 5
Won 55-41
Davidsson 10:2, Gomolski 13:1, Woodward 1, Eriksson 12, Jonasson 9:2, Mellgren 10:1, Bergkvist 0, Persson, did not ride.
Aggregate: Won 100-92.

FINAL, first leg
VARGARNA (A)
Thursday, September 11
Lost 45-51
Davidsson 7, Mellgren 3:1, Bager 11, Eriksson 9:1, Jonasson 7, Törnqvist 0, Jacobsen 7:3, Bergkvist 1.

FINAL, second leg
VARGARNA (H)
Friday, September 12
Lost 47-49
Davidsson 9, Eriksson 10:1, Mellgren 0, Karlsson 10:1, Bager 9:1, Aspegren 4:1, Törnqvist 5:2, Bergkvist 0.
Aggregate: Lost 92-100.

2009 Squad

Sebastien **ALDÉN**, Andreas **ANDERSSON**, Robin **ASPEGREN**, Daniel **DAVIDSSON**, Robert **ERIKSSON**, Alexander **LILJEQVIST**, Mattias **PERSSON**, Jeremia **THELAUS**, Robin **TÖRNQVIST**, Per **WESTER**.
Foreign: Kauko **NIEMINEN**, Krister **JACOBSEN**, Cameron **WOODWARD**.

Had Thomas H. Jonasson (above) been fit for the end-of-season play-offs he could well have helped the Hagfors outfit reclaim their ElitSerien place after six successful seasons in the AllSvenskan League.

With Peter Ljung and Adrian Gomolski also missing from both legs of the play-off Final against Vargarna, the Rollers were beaten in both legs and had to be content with the silver medal.

Their current status is in marked contrast to the glory days at the turn of the century.

ElitSerien champions in 1998 and 1999, they were runners-up in 2000 before being relegated in 2003 when they won only three of their 18 matches.

Since then they have failed to make it back into the top-flight, going down in the play-off final in each of the last three seasons.

Rider	M	R	Pts	BP	TPts	Ave	F	P
Peter LJUNG	8	40	101	1	102	10.20	1	0
Adrian GOMOLSKI	**2**	**11**	**24**	**3**	**27**	**9.82**	**0**	**0**
Thomas H. JONASSON	7	33	67	8	75	9.09	0	0
Robert ERIKSSON	**16**	**81**	**149**	**15**	**164**	**8.10**	**0**	**0**
Daniel DAVIDSSON	14	71	131	8	139	7.83	0	0
Henning BAGER	**3**	**15**	**27**	**2**	**29**	**7.73**	**0**	**0**
Magnus KARLSSON	7	34	45	8	53	6.24	0	0
Cameron WOODWARD	**7**	**34**	**45**	**5**	**50**	**5.88**	**0**	**0**
Krister JACOBSEN	5	24	28	5	33	5.50	0	0
Anders MELLGREN	**16**	**70**	**80**	**15**	**95**	**5.43**	**0**	**0**
Robin TÖRNQVIST	9	34	30	7	37	4.35	0	0
Thomas LJUNG	**1**	**4**	**3**	**1**	**4**	**4.00**	**0**	**0**
Robin ASPEGREN	3	11	9	1	10	3.64	0	0
Robin BERGKVIST	**13**	**44**	**30**	**6**	**36**	**3.27**	**0**	**0**
Mattias PERSSON	3	6	3	0	3	2.00	0	0

Number eight appearances: Mattias PERSSON (8).

AllSvenskan League

VARGARNA

2008 RESULTS

Final position........................Champions (Third)

GRIPARNA (H)
Thursday, May 1
Lost 42-54
Forsberg 2, R. Johansson 11:1, E. Andersson 8:2, Ekberg 8, Screen 8:2, Carlsson 0, Juul 5, J. Andersson 0.

VALSARNA (H)
Thursday, May 15
Won 50-45
Lindbäck 9, Lindqvist 6:2, R. Johansson 10, Ekberg 4:1, **Screen 15**, Söderström, did not ride, Fagerkrantz 3, Carlsson 3:1.

ÖRNARNA (A)
Thursday, May 22
Won 51-45
R. Johansson 8:2, Ekberg 4:1, Lindbäck 12:1, E. Andersson 10:1, Doolan 10:1, Fagerkrantz 0, Carlsson 0, J. Andersson 7.

SOLKATTERNA (H)
Thursday, May 29
Won 51-44
Lindbäck 9:1, E. Andersson 11, Doolan 11:2, F. Johansson 2:1, Screen 11, J. Andersson 4:1, Fagerkrantz 1, Carlsson 2.

GRIPARNA (A)
Thursday, June 5
Won 51-45
E.Andersson 7:1, Lindqvist 4:1, Doolan 9:1, Ekberg 9:2, Screen 14, J. Andersson 1, Juul 7:1, Carlsson, did not ride.

ÖRNARNA (H)
Thursday, June 12
Won 51-45
R. Johansson 2:1, Woffinden 12, Lindbäck 12:1, Juul 4:2, Screen 10, J. Andersson 5, Fagerkrantz, did not ride, Carlsson 6:3.

GRIPARNA (A)
Thursday, July 3
Lost 39-57
Doolan 6, Juul 4:2, Lindbäck 10, E. Andersson 5:2, Lawson 6, J. Andersson 4, Lindgren 4:2, Fagerkrantz, did not ride.

TRACK FILE

Track: Norrköpings Motorstadion, Kråkvilan, 605 92 Norrköping, Sweden.
Telephone: 0046 011182801.
Website: www.vargarna.nu
Track Length: 279 metres.
Track Record: 57.0 secs, Tony Rickardsson, June 30, 1998.

SQUAD
Eric Andersson, Jonas Andersson, Marcus Andersson, Sebastian Carlsson, Stefan Ekberg, Dennis Fagerkrantz, Billy Forsberg, Oscar Fyhrman, Robert Henderson, Fredrik Johansson, Robert Johansson, Antonio Lindbäck, Kalle Lindgren, Emil Lindqvist, Joakim Söderström.
Foreign: Steve Boxall, Kevin Doolan, Peter Juul Larsen, William Lawson, Joe Screen, Tai Woffinden.

VALSARNA (A)
Thursday, July 24
Lost 43-53
Screen 9:1, Juul 1:1, Lindbäck 12, R. Johansson 7:1, Woffinden 7:1, Carlsson 3, J. Andersson 4, Fagerkrantz, did not ride.

ÖRNARNA (H)
Thursday, July 31
Won 56-40
Screen 9:1, Woffinden 12:1, Doolan 6:1, R. Henderson 2, Lindbäck 13:1, J. Andersson 8:1, Carlsson 6:2, Fagerkrantz, did not ride.

SOLKATTERNA (A)
Thursday, August 7
Lost 47-49
R. Johansson 6:1, Ekberg 7:1, Doolan 9:1, E. Andersson 1, Lindbäck 13, J. Andersson 3:1, Juul 7:1, Carlsson 1.

GRIPARNA (H)
Thursday, August 14
Won 52-44
Screen 10, R. Johansson 8:2, Woffinden 13:1, R. Henderson 0, Lindbäck 14, Carlsson 4, Lindgren 3:2, Fagerkrantz, did not ride.

ÖRNARNA (A)
Thursday, August 21
Lost 47-49
Screen 9:2, Juul 0, Woffinden 8, R. Johansson 6, Lindbäck 16, Carlsson 1, J. Andersson 7:1, Fagerkrantz, did not ride.

ALL SVENSKAN

	M	W	D	L	PtsF	PtsA	Pts
Griparna	12	7	0	5	604	546	14
Örnarna	12	7	0	5	592	557	14
VARGARNA	**12**	**7**	**0**	**5**	**580**	**570**	**14**
Valsarna	12	6	1	5	580	571	13
Solkatterna	12	2	1	9	519	631	5

Play offs

Semi Final, first leg
ÖRNARNA (H)
Thursday, September 4
Won 62-34
Doolan 9:2, R. Johansson 12:2, Screen 12, J. Andersson 1:1, **Lindbäck 15**, Juul 5:2, R. Henderson 8:1, Carlsson, did not ride.

Semi Final, second leg
ÖRNARNA (A)
Friday, September 5
Won 52-44
R. Johansson 6, J. Andersson 2:1, Forsberg 10:2, Doolan 8:1, Lindbäck 14, Carlsson 5:2, R. Henderson 7, Fagerkrantz 0.
Aggregate: Won 114-78.

FINAL, first leg
VALSARNA (H)
Thursday, September 11
Won 51-45
Doolan 12, R. Johansson 7:2, Screen 12, J. Andersson 1:1, Lindbäck 9, Juul 5:2, R. Henderson 5:1, Carlsson, did not ride.

Semi Final, second leg
VALSARNA (A)
Friday, September 12
Won 49-47
Forsberg 9, J. Andersson 2:1, Screen 7:2, R. Johansson 9:2, **Lindbäck 15**, Juul 5, R. Henderson 2, Carlsson 0.
Aggregate: Won 100-92.

Antonio Lindbäck made a stunning comeback to regular league racing with Vargarna, riding in all but two of their 16 official matches.
Both his full maximums came in the play-offs as he helped the Wolves win promotion to the top-flight.

VARGARNA is probably the most famous club name in Sweden – the Scandinavian equivalent of Belle Vue Aces.

The first ever team meeting was staged at Norrköping under the inspirational leadership of Arne Bergström who launched speedway in Sweden.

The team name Wolves was taken from a local textile factory and in the first season of (unofficial) league racing, in 1948, they finished third but discovered one of the country's brightest young stars in Olle Nygren who actually won the unofficial Swedish Championship that year.

In 1950, the Wolves won the first of five league titles in the space of 11 years with sensational 17-year-old Dan Forsberg finishing eighth in the Swedish Final, won by team-mate Henge Brinkeback.

In Dan Forsberg became the first Swedish rider to qualify for a World Final, finishing fifth at Wembley.

Other former Vargarna riders include ex-World Champion Björn Knutsson, Sören Sjösten, Torbjörn Harrysson, Hasse Holmkvist and Per Olof Söderman.

They dropped out of the top-flight for the first time at the end of the 1980 campaign and since then they have struggled to recapture their former glories despite having, at one time or another, riders of the calibre of Erik Gundersen, Jimmy Nilsen and Jason Crump in their ranks.

In 2009 they have a chance to re-establish themselves as a major force.

2009 Squad

Jonas **ANDERSSON**, Niklas **KLINGBERG**.
Foreign: Edward **KENNETT**, Matej **KUS**, Adrian **MIEDZINSKI**, Scott **NICHOLLS**, Adam **SHIELDS**, Joe **SCREEN**, Adam **SKORNICKI**, Tai **WOFFINDEN**.
● *Vargarna won promotion to the 2009 ElitSerien.*

Rider	M	R	Pts	BP	TPts	Ave	F	P
Antonio LINDBÄCK	14	72	173	4	177	9.83	2	0
Joe SCREEN	**12**	**59**	**126**	**8**	**134**	**9.08**	**1**	**0**
Tai WOFFINDEN	5	27	52	7	59	8.74	0	0
Kevin DOOLAN	**9**	**46**	**80**	**9**	**89**	**7.74**	**0**	**0**
Billy FORSBERG	3	12	21	2	23	7.67	0	0
Robert JOHANSSON	**12**	**61**	**92**	**14**	**106**	**6.95**	**0**	**0**
Eric ANDERSSON	6	29	42	6	48	6.62	0	0
Emil LINDQVIST	**2**	**8**	**10**	**3**	**13**	**6.50**	**0**	**0**
Stefan EKBERG	5	24	32	5	37	6.17	0	0
William LAWSON	**1**	**4**	**6**	**0**	**6**	**6.00**	**0**	**0**
Peter JUUL Larsen	10	42	43	11	54	5.14	0	0
Sebastian CARLSSON	**12**	**34**	**31**	**8**	**39**	**4.59**	**0**	**0**
Jonas ANDERSSON	14	50	49	8	57	4.56	0	0
Kalle LINDGREN	**2**	**10**	**7**	**4**	**11**	**4.40**	**0**	**0**
Robert HENDERSON	6	24	24	2	26	4.33	0	0
Fredrik JOHANSSON	**1**	**4**	**2**	**1**	**3**	**0.0**	**0**	**0**
Dennis FAGERKRANTZ	3	6	4	0	4	2.67	0	0
Joakim SÖDERSTRÖM	1	0	0	0	0	n.a.	0	0

Number eight appearances: Dennis FAGERKRANTZ (5), Sebastian CARLSSON (3).

2008 PARTNER CLUBS

VÄSTERVIK (ElitSerien)

FILBYTERNA (Division One)

2009 PARTNER CLUB

GRIPARNA (AllSvenskan)

DIVISON ONE STANDINGS

	M	W	D	L	PtsF	PtsA	Pts
1 TEAM DALAKRAFT	18	18	0	0	1084	616	36
2 TEAM BIKAB	18	13	0	5	956	736	26
3 NJUDUNGARNA	18	13	0	5	924	800	26
4 FILBYTERNA	18	11	0	7	958	730	22
5 STJÄRNORNA	18	9	0	9	897	776	18
6 CROSSBONE PIRATES	18	7	0	11	783	924	14
7 VIKINGARNA	18	7	0	11	755	922	14
8 GNISTORNA	18	6	0	12	786	903	12
9 TEAM CANVAC	18	3	1	14	733	988	7
10 ELDARNA	18	2	1	15	612	1093	5

TEAM Dalakraft began their league season with a 24 points win away against Njudungarna.

And that was a taste of what was to come for the Avesta club who had dropped down at the beginning of the year after six successive seasons in the AllSvenskan League.

Even though they dispensed with foreign riders, they were still far too strong for all the opposition and went through the entire summer without dropping a point!

Their success was total vindication for the decision to step down and also the general insistence at this level of using only their own home-grown talent.

While the name may have disappeared in 2009, the spirit will live on as they will now race as Masarna and have returned to the AllSvenskan.

The title race was a foregone conclusion almost from that first victory in Vetlanda but there was an interesting fight for second spot between Team Bikab and Njudungarna, deciding eventually on race points.

The division allowed a fairly free hand in terms of age and experience with ex-World Finalist Henrik Gustafsson actually having one unbeaten outing for Vikingarna as he winds down his career.

But generally it was a playground for the young and ambitious, giving vital experience to many of the Swedish prospects without outside contracts elsewhere in Europe.

The 2009 season will follow a similar pattern with an absence of non-Swedish riders.

Team Dalakraft (Avesta), Njudungarna (Vetlanda), Vikingarna (Örebro) and Team Canvac (Mariestad) have gone but they have been replaced by Masarna (Avesta), Team Hagfors, Indianerna Ungdom (Kumla) and Hultsfreds Gymnasium (Mälilla).

Roll of Honour

1963 N .... FILBYTERNA
1963 S .... DACKARNA
1964 A .... TAXARNA
1964 B .... KAPARNA
1965 A .... LEJONEN
1965 B .... KAPARNA
1966 .... INDIANERNA
1967 E .... BYSARNA
1967 W .... SMEDERNA
1968 E .... SKEPPARNA
1968 W .... FILBYTERNA
1969 E .... BYSARNA
1969 W .... ELDARNA
1970 E .... FILBYTERNA
1970 W .... VIKINGARNA
1971 .... VALSARNA
1972 .... GAMARNA
1973 .... PIRATERNA
1974 .... JAMTARNA
1975 N .... GAMARNA
1975 S .... PIRATERNA
1976 N .... ELDARNA
1976 S .... SOLKATTERNA
1977 W .... VIKINGARNA
1977 N .... GAMARNA
1977 S .... BRASSARNA
1978 N .... PILARNA
1978 S .... FILBYTERNA
1979 E .... ELDARNA
1979 W .... SOLKATTERNA
1980 .... PILARNA
1981 .... BRASSARNA
1982 NE .... LINDARNA
1982 SW .... BRASSARNA
1983 N .... ELDARNA
1983 S .... FILBYTERNA
1984 N .... VIKINGARNA
1984 S .... LEJONEN
1985 N .... TUNA REBELS
1985 S .... PIRATERNA
1986 N .... VALSARNA
1986 S .... SKEPPARNA
1987 N .... GRIPARNA
1987 S .... BRASSARNA
1988 N .... SOLKATTERNA
1988 S .... FILBYTERNA
1989 N .... VALSARNA
1989 S .... KAPARNA
1990 N .... MASARNA
1990 S .... KORPARNA
1991 .... KAPARNA
1992 E .... STOCKHOLM
1992 W .... ZAAGS
1993 A .... KORPARNA
1993 B .... HUSARERNA
1994 A .... TEAM VIKING
1994 B .... NJUDUNGARNA
1995 A .... KARLSTAD
1995 B .... NJUDUNGARNA
1998 .... TEAM VIKING
1999 .... PIRATERNA
2000 .... LEJONEN
2001 .... GASARNA
2002 .... ELDARNA
2003 .... ELDARNA
2004 .... SKEPPARNA
2005 .... TEAM BIKAB
2006 .... SOLKATTERNA
2007 .... TEAM KUMLA PROMOTION
2008 .... TEAM DALAKRAFT

2009 DIVISION ONE FIXTURES

Monday, May 4
Gnistorna v Gasarna

Wednesday, May 6
Indianerna Ungdom v Hultsfreds Gymnasium
Filbyterna v Stjärnorna
Eldarna v Team Hagfors

Saturday, May 9
Crossbone Pirates v Team Bikab

Wednesday, May 13
Gasarna v Filbyterna
Team Hagfors v Indianerna Ungdom
Stjärnorna v Crossbone Pirates
Team Bikab v Eldarna

Saturday, May 16
Hultsfreds Gymnasium v Gnistorna

Wednesday, May 20
Team Hagfors v Hulstfreds Gymnasium
Indianerna Ungdom v Team Bikab
Filbyterna v Gnistorna
Eldarna v Stjärnorna

Sunday, May 24
Crossbone Pirates v Gasarna

Wednesday, May 27
Gasarna v Eldarna
Stjärnorna v Indianerna Ungdom
Gnistorna v Crossbone Pirates
Team Bikab v Team Hagfors

Sunday, May 31
Hultsfreds Gymnasium v Filbyterna

Wednesday, June 3
Team Hagfors v Stjärnorna
Indianerna Ungdom v Gasarna
Team Bikab v Hultsfreds Gymnasium
Crossbone Pirates v Filbyterna
Eldarna v Gnistorna

Wednesday, June 17
Gasarna v Team Hagfors
Filbyterna v Eldarna
Stjärnorna v Team Bikab
Gnistorna v Indianerna Ungdom
Hultsfreds Gymnasium v Crossbone Pirates

Wednesday, June 24
Team Hagfors v Gnistorna
Indianerna Ungdom v Filbyterna
Stjärnorna v Hultsfreds Gymnasium
Team Bikab v Gasarna
Eldarna v Crossbone Pirates

Wednesday, July 1
Gasarna v Stjärnorna
Filbyterna v Team Hagfors
Gnistorna v Team Bikab
Crossbone Pirates v Indianerna Ungdom

Sunday, July 5
Hultsfreds Gymnasium v Eldarna

Wednesday, July 8
Gasarna v Hultsfreds Gymnasium
Team Hagfors v Crossbone Pirates
Indianerna Ungdom v Eldarna
Stjärnorna v Gnistorna
Team Bikab v Filbyterna

Wednesday, July 22
Gasarna v Gnistorna
Team Hagfors v Eldarna
Stjärnorna v Filbyterna
Hultsfreds Gymnasium v Indianerna Ungdom
Team Bikab v Crossbone Pirates

Wednesday, July 29
Indianerna Ungdom v Team Hagfors
Filbyterna v Gasarna
Gnistorna v Hultsfreds Gymnasium
Eldarna v Team Bikab

Saturday, August 1
Crossbone Pirates v Stjärnorna

Wednesday, August 5
Gasarna v Crossbone Pirates
Stjärnorna v Eldarna
Gnistorna v Filbyterna
Team Bikab v Indianerna Ungdom

Saturday, August 8
Hultsfreds Gymnasium v Team Hagfors

Sunday, August 9
Crossbone Pirates v Gnistorna

Wednesday, August 12
Team Hagfors v Team Bikab
Indianerna Ungdom v Stjärnorna
Filbyterna v Hultsfreds Gymnasium
Eldarna v Gasarna

Wednesday, August 19
Gasarna v Indianerna Ungdom
Filbyterna v Crossbone Pirates
Stjärnornar v Team Hagfors
Gnistorna v Eldarna

Sunday, August 23
Hultsfreds Gymnasium v Team Bikab

Wednesday, August 26
Team Hagfors v Gasarna
Indianerna Ungdom v Gnistorna
Team Bikab v Stjärnorna
Eldarna v Filbyterna

Saturday, August 29
Crossbone Pirates v Hultsfreds Gymnasium

Wednesday, September 2
Gasarna v Team Bikab
Filbyterna v Indianerna Ungdom
Gnistorna v Team Hagfors

Saturday, September 5
Crossbone Pirates v Eldarna

Sunday, September 6
Hultsfreds Gymnasium v Stjärnorna

Wednesday, September 9
Team Hagfors v Filbyterna
Indianerna Ungdom v Crossbone Pirates
Stjärnorna v Gasarna
Team Bikab v Gnistorna
Eldarna v Hultsfreds Gymnasium

Wednesday, September 16
Filbyterna v Team Bikab
Gnistorna v Stjärnornar
Eldarna v Indianerna Ungdom

Saturday, September 19
Crossbone Pirates v Team Hagfors

The following clubs are competing in the 2009 Swedish First Division: Crossbone Pirates (Motala), Eldarna (Huddinge), Filbyterna (Linköping), Gasarna (Avesta), Gnistorna (Malmö), Hultsfreds Gymnasium (Målilla), Indianerna Ungdom (Kumla), Stjärnorna (Hallstavik), Team Bikab (Eskilstuna) and Team Hagfors (Hagfors).

Division One

CROSSBONE PIRATES

2008 RESULTS

Final position..Sixth

VIKINGARNA (H)
Wednesday, April 30
Won 51-43
Sundström 12:3, **Max 15**, C. Ingesson 10:1, L. Persson 5:1, T. Ingesson 8:1, Planberg 0, Bäck 1.

TEAM BIKAB (H)
Wednesday, May 7
Lost 39-57
Sundström 11, Thelaus 0, C. Ingesson 5:1, **Max 15**, T. Ingesson 5, Bäck 1, Planbberg 2.

TEAM DALAKRAFT (H)
Wednesday, May 14
Lost 38-58
Sundström 13, M. Persson 2, C. Ingesson 6, L. Persson 3:1, T. Ingesson 7:1, Planberg 5, Bäck 2.

ELDARNA (A)
Wednesday, May 21
Won 53-40
Sundström 15, **Thelaus 11:4**, C. Ingesson 0, Persson 7, T. Ingesson 9, Bäck 1, Planberg 10:2.

STJÄRNORNA (H)
Wednesday, May 28
Won 50-44
Sundström 14, Thelaus 9:1, C. Ingesson 9, Persson 0, T. Ingesson 9, Planberg 7:2, Bäck 2:1.

NJUDUNGARNA (A)
Wednesday, June 4
Lost 36-60
Sundström 14, Thelaus 4:1, C. Ingesson 2, M. Persson 2, T. Ingesson 4, Planberg 6:1, Bäck 4:1.

TEAM CANVAC (H)
Wednesday, June 11
Lost 38-57
C. Ingesson 7, T. Ingesson 4, Kjellberg 7:1, Thelaus 4:1, Sundström 8, Planberg 6:1, Bäck 2.

Brothers Christian and Tobias Ingesson were both everpresents for Crossbone Pirates in their 18 league matches – the only other rider not to miss a meeting was reserve Tomas Bäck.

TRACK FILE

Track: Motorstadion Motala, Box 4009, 591 04 Motala, Sweden.
Telephone: 0046 14120999.
Website: www.piraterna.com
Track Length: 300 metres.
Track Record: 56.3 secs, Peter Karlsson, May 23, 2006.

SQUAD
Tomas Bäck, Christian Ingesson, Tobias Ingesson, Dan Kjellberg, Mikael Max, Totte Nilsson, Rickard Nyberg, Lennart Persson, Magnus Persson, Tobias Planberg, Simon Rudin, Linus Sundström, Jeremia Thelaus, Sebastian Williams.

GNISTORNA (A)
Wednesday, June 18
Lost 32-63
Planberg 2:1, C. Ingesson 7, Thelaus 7:1, Kjellberg 7, T. Ingesson 4, Bäck 5, no rider at 7.

FILBYTERNA (H)
Wednesday, July 2
Lost 38-54
Planberg 4, Thelaus 11, C. Ingesson 9:1, Bäck 0, T. Ingesson 8, Nyberg 6, no rider at 7.

VIKINGARNA (A)
Wednesday, July 9
Won 51-44
Thelaus 12:2, Kjellberg 9:1, Sundström 14, C. Ingesson 8:1, T. Ingesson 6, Bäck 2, Planberg 0.

TEAM BIKAB (A)
Wednesday, July 16
Lost 38-57
Sundström 15, Thelaus 7, C. Ingesson 2:1, Kjellberg 5, T. Ingesson 5, Bäck 0, Planberg 4:1.

TEAM DALAKRAFT (A)
Wednesday, July 23
Lost 24-68
Sundström 9:1, Thelaus 6, C. Ingesson 3, Bäck 1, T. Ingesson 5, no riders at 6 or 7.

ELDARNA (H)
Wednesday, July 30
Won 71-25
Sundström 15, **C. Ingesson 12:3**, **Thelaus 14:1**, Kjellberg 5:2, **T. Ingesson 13:2**, Bäck 10:1, Nilsson 2.

STJÄRNORNA (A)
Wednesday, August 6
Lost 38-57
Thelaus 16, C. Ingesson 0, T. Ingesson 4, Planberg 3, Kjellberg 5, Bäck 7:1, Nilsson 3:2.

NJUDUNGARNA (H)
Wednesday, August 13
Lost 33-63
Planberg 3:1, Kjellberg 6, Thelaus 14, C. Ingesson 1, T. Ingesson 5, Bäck 4, no rider at 7.

TEAM CANVAC (A)
Wednesday, August 20
Won 52-43
Sundström 12, C. Ingesson 3, Planberg 7, T. Ingesson 6:2, Thelaus 14, Bäck 10, Nilsson 0.

GNISTORNA (H)
Wednesday, August 27
Won 64-32
Sundström 11:1, C. Ingesson 8:2, Thelaus 13:1, T. Ingesson 4:2, **Max 15**, Bäck 3:1, Planberg 10:1.

FILBYTERNA (A)
Wednesday, September 3
Lost 37-59
Sundström 13, C. Ingesson 1, **Thelaus 14:1**, T. Ingesson 0, Kjellberg 4, Bäck 1, Planberg 4.

DIVISION ONE

	M	W	D	L	PtsF	PtsA	Pts
Team Dalakraft	18	18	0	0	1084	616	36
Team Bikab	18	13	0	5	956	736	26
Njudungarna	18	13	0	5	924	800	26
Filyterna	18	11	0	7	958	730	22
Stjärnorna	18	9	0	9	897	776	18
CROSSBONE PTS	**18**	**7**	**0**	**11**	**783**	**924**	**14**
Vikingarna	18	7	0	11	755	922	14
Gnistorna	18	6	0	12	786	903	12
Team Canvac	18	3	1	14	733	988	7
Eldarna	18	2	1	15	612	1093	5

2009 Squad

Tobias **BÄCK**, Tomas **BÄCK**, Christian **INGESSON**, Tobias **INGESSON**, Joachim **LINDQUIST**, Totte **NILSSON**, Rickard **NYBERG**, Lennart **PERSSON**.
Will also have availability of Piraterna and Solkatterna riders.

MAX-imum effect

Former Grand Prix star Mikael Max rode in three matches for the Motala club and didn't drop a point.
He scored maximums at home to Gnistorna, Team Bikab and Vikingarna, taking five rides in each meeting.
He was the only rider to be unbeaten by an opponent in Division One.

Rider	M	R	Pts	BP	TPts	Ave	F	P
Mikael MAX	3	15	45	0	45	12.00	3	0
Linus SUNDSTRÖM	**14**	**67**	**176**	**5**	**181**	**10.81**	**3**	**2**
Jeremia THELAUS	16	76	156	13	169	8.89	0	3
Rickard NYBERG	**1**	**4**	**6**	**0**	**6**	**6.00**	**0**	**0**
Lennart PERSSON	3	12	15	2	17	5.67	0	0
Tobias INGESSON	**18**	**87**	**106**	**8**	**114**	**5.24**	**0**	**1**
Christian INGESSON	18	79	93	10	103	5.22	0	1
Dan KJELLBERG	**8**	**40**	**48**	**4**	**52**	**5.20**	**0**	**0**
Totte NILSSON	3	6	5	1	6	4.00	0	0
Tomas BÄCK	**18**	**87**	**56**	**5**	**61**	**2.80**	**0**	**0**
Magnus PERSSON	2	7	4	0	4	2.29	0	0

2008 PARTNER CLUB

PIRATERNA
(ElitSerien)

2009 PARTNER CLUB

PIRATERNA
(ElitSerien)
SOLKATTERNA
(AllSvenskan)

Division One

ELDARNA

2008 RESULTS

Final position ....**Tenth**

STJÄRNORNA (A)
Wednesday, April 30
Lost 22-74
Dahlborg 0, Mårtensson 4:1, Åström 4, Edenhall 2, T. Lundgren 8, Nyström 4, Hård 0.

NJUDUNGARNA (H)
Wednesday, May 7
Lost 43-52
Mårtensson 11, Edenhall 6:3, Lekander 15, P. Lundgren 0, Nyström 6:1, Hård 2:1, Brolin 3:1.

TEAM CANVAC (A)
Wednesday, May 14
Drew 48-48
Dahlborg 4, Mårtensson 8, Åström 5, Edenhall 9, T. Lundgren 7, Nyström 10, Hård 5.

CROSSBONE PIRATES (H)
Wednesday, May 21
Lost 40-53
Edenhall 9, Mårtensson 7:1, Åström 5:1, Dahlborg 8:1, T. Lundgren 2, Hård 5:1, Nyström 4:1.

FILBYTERNA (A)
Wednesday, May 28
Lost 25-71
Edenhall 0, Mårtensson 4, Åström 3, Dahlborg 6, T. Lundgren 3, Nyström 5:2, Hård 4:1.

VIKINGARNA (H)
Wednesday, June 4
Lost 46-49
Edenhall 5:1, Mårtensson 7:2, Åström 2, Dahlborg 9:1, T. Lundgren 9, Hård 3:1, Nyström 11:2.

TEAM BIKAB (A)
Wednesday, June 11
Lost 28-67
Lekander 3, Mårtensson 1:1, Nyström 4, Dahlborg 9, T. Lundgren 5, Hård 0, Edenhall 6.

TEAM DALAKRAFT (H)
Wednesday, June 18
Lost 38-57
Lekander 13, Mårtensson 4, Edenhall 2:2, Dahlborg 8, T. Lundgren 5:1, Brolin 0, Nyström 6:1.

Three of Eldarna's five points came against Team Canvac via an away draw and home win.

TRACK FILE

Track: Huddinge Motorstadion, c/o Conny Hyll, Fnyskväg 8, 135 49 Tyresö, Sweden.

Telephone: 0046 705 194268.

Website: www.eldarna.nu

Track Length: 311 metres.

Track Record: Not known.

SQUAD
Magnus Åhnström, Stefan Åström, Dan Berglund, Mats Boström, Stefan Brolin, Dennis Dahlborg, Alexander Edberg, Viktor Edenhall, Mikael Eriksson, Andrian Gheorge, Marian Gheorge, Mattias Hård, Jimmy Hyll, Tommy Jonsson, Andreas Lekander, Pelle Lundgren, Tommie Lundgren, Joakim Mårtensson, Joel Nyström, Benny Olsson.

GNISTORNA (H)
Saturday, July 5
Won 42-39
Lekander 11, Mårtensson 5:1, Dahlborg 4:2, Nyström 5:1, T. Lundgren 5, Hård 1:1, Edenhall 11:2.

STJÄRNORNA (H)
Wednesday, July 9
Lost 24-72
Nyström 1, Dahlborg 5, Mårtensson 6, Edenhall 3, T. Lundgren 7, Hård 1, Brolin 1.

NJUDUNGARNA (A)
Friday, July 18
Lost 22-74
Dahlborg 3, Hård 0, Mårtensson 7:1, Edenhall 4, Nyström 5, Brolin 0, Heyman 3:1.

TEAM CANVAC (H)
Wednesday, July 23
Won 54-41
Dahlborg 9:1, Nyström 12, Mårtensson 7:2, Edenhall 8:1, Hård 4, P. Lundgren 5:2, Brolin 9:2.

CROSSBONE PIRATES (A)
Wednesday, July 30
Lost 25-71
Nyström 5, Brolin 1:1, Mårtensson 6, Edenhall 5:1, Dahlborg 3, P. Lundgren 5, Hyll 0.

FILBYTERNA (H)
Wednesday, August 6
Lost 24-72
Nyström 2:1, T. Lundgren 5, Mårtensson 6, Edenhall 3:2, Dahlborg 6, P. Lundgren 0, Brolin 2.

VIKINGARNA (A)
Wednesday, August 13
Lost 44-52
Mårtensson 9:1, Edenhall 5:2, Nyström 7, T. Lundgren 2, Dahlborg 8:1, Hård 7:3, Brolin 6:1.

Did you know?

In their biggest defeat of the season – 17-79 against Team Dalakraft – Eldarna were on the receiving end of 15 5-1s and a 4-2 in Heat 7 when Tommi Lundgren saved the whitwash by finishing ahead of opposition number one Niklas Aspgren.
Stjärnorna (home and away) and Filbyterna also broke through the 70-point barrier against the Flames.

TEAM DALAKRAFT (A)
Wednesday, August 27
Lost 17-79
Mårtensson 1, Edenhall 3, Nyström 3, T. Lundgren 4, Dahlborg 4, Hård 1, Brolin 1.

GNISTORNA (A)
Saturday, September 6
Lost 41-55
Mårtensson 10, Edenhall 3:2, T. Lundgren 8:1, Brolin 3:1, Dahlborg 8, Hård 6:1, P. Lundgren 3.

TEAM BIKAB (H)
Sunday, September 14
Lost 29-67
Mårtensson 5, Edenhall 2, T. Lundgren 10:1, Hård 2:1, Dahlborg 6, P. Lundgren 1:1, Brolin 3.

DIVISION ONE

	M	W	D	L	PtsF	PtsA	Pts
Team Dalakraft	18	18	0	0	1084	616	36
Team Bikab	18	13	0	5	956	736	26
Njudungarna	18	13	0	5	924	800	26
Filyterna	18	11	0	7	958	730	22
Stjärnorna	18	9	0	9	897	776	18
Crossbone Pirates	18	7	0	11	783	924	14
Vikingarna	18	7	0	11	755	922	14
Gnistorna	18	6	0	12	786	903	12
Team Canvac	18	3	1	14	733	988	7
ELDARNA	**18**	**2**	**1**	**15**	**612**	**1093**	**5**

Did you know?

In nine home matches Eldarna attracted only 442 supporters to their Huddinge track (15 kilometres south of Stockholm) – an average of 49 – despite a population of over 86,000.
Their highest recorded attendance was 75 for the visit of Vikingarna and on three separate occasions they recorded crowds of just 35!

ELDARNA reached a new agreement with the city fathers to remain at their southern Stockholm Huddinge venue in 2008 but their off track problems were also reflected in performances as they finished bottom of Division One.

Their clear lack of top end scoring – apart from when Andreas Lekander was in their line-up – saw them win only two matches all season and their battle to survive was hardly helped by the poorest crowds in Sweden at this level.

But to their credit not only did they complete a full season but they were also among the first clubs to declare they would once again be competing in the third tier in 2009.

They will be hoping that some of the riders given extensive opportunities last summer will show marked improvement for the experience.

But, sadly, they appear to lack a big hitter although it will be interesting to see how Romania's top young prospect Andrian Gheorge copes with racing at this level for his first full-time season.

2009 Squad

Harald **ANDERSSON**, Lars **ÅSTRÖM**, Alexander **EDBERG**, Viktor **EDENHALL**, Mikael **ERIKSSON**, Andreas **HÅRD**, Mattias **HÅRD**, Michael **HEYMAN**, Jimmy **HYLL**, Tommy **JONSSON**, Pelle **LUNDGREN**, Tommie **LUNDGREN**, Joel **NYSTRÖM**, Benny **OLSSON**.
Foreign: Adrian **GHEORGE**.

Rider	M	R	Pts	BP	TPts	Ave	F	P
Andreas LEKANDER	4	17	42	0	42	9.88	0	0
Joakim MÅRTENSSON	**18**	**89**	**108**	**10**	**118**	**5.30**	**0**	**0**
Dennis DAHLBORG	17	83	100	6	106	5.11	0	0
Tommie LUNDGREN	**14**	**65**	**80**	**3**	**83**	**5.11**	**0**	**0**
Joel NYSTRÖM	16	80	90	9	99	4.95	0	0
Viktor EDENHALL	**18**	**87**	**86**	**16**	**102**	**4.69**	**0**	**0**
Pelle LUNDGREN	6	19	14	4	18	3.79	0	0
Stefan BROLIN	**10**	**37**	**29**	**6**	**35**	**3.78**	**0**	**0**
Lars ÅSTRÖM	5	22	19	1	20	3.64	0	0
Michael HEYMAN	**1**	**5**	**3**	**1**	**4**	**3.20**	**0**	**0**
Mattias HÅRD	15	64	41	10	51	3.19	0	0
Jimmy HYLL	**1**	**4**	**0**	**0**	**0**	**0.00**	**0**	**0**

Division One

FILBYTERNA

TRACK FILE

Track: Linköpings Motorstadion, 585 92 Linköping, Sweden.

Telephone: 0046 013362690.

Website: www.lms.se/speedway

Track Length: 335 metres.

Track Record: Not known.

2008 RESULTS

Final position ....Fourth

GNISTORNA (H)
Wednesday, April 30
Won 60-35
B. Johansson 14, Östergren 10:4, Lindgren 7, Carlsson 9:2, F. Johansson 11, Fagerkrantz 9:2, Eilersén 0.

VIKINGARNA (A)
Wednesday, May 7
Won 58-38
B. Johansson 12, Östergren 2:1, Lindvqivst 11:2, Lindgren 10:2, F. Johansson 8:1, Carlsson 10, Fagerkrantz 5:2.

TEAM BIKAB (H)
Wednesday, May 14
Won 52-44
B. Johansson 6, Östergren 3:2, Lindqvist 8:2, Lindgren 8:1, Johansson 12, Carlsson 9:2, Fagerkrantz 6:1.

TEAM DALAKRAFT (A)
Wednesday, May 21
Lost 42-53
B. Johansson 10, Östergren 0, Lindqvist 11, Söderström 0, F. Johansson 6:1, Carlsson 9:2, Fagerkrantz 6:1.

ELDARNA (H)
Wednesday, May 28
Won 71-25
Lindqvist 13:2, Östergren 11:2, **Lindgren 13:2**, **Carlsson 13:2**, **B. Johansson 11:1**, Fagerkrantz 9:1, Eilersén 1.

STJÄRNORNA (A)
Wednesday, June 4
Won 60-35
F. Johansson 14:1, Östergren 5:1, B. Johansson 8:1, **Lindgren 9**, Söderström 2:2, **Carlsson 16:2**, Fagerkrantz 6:1.

NJUDUNGARNA (H)
Wednesday, June 11
Lost 45-50
F. Johansson 10:1, Östergren 4:3, Lindgren 7:1, Carlsson 7, B. Johansson 10:1, Söderström 2, Fagerkrantz 5.

SQUAD
Harald Andersson, Marcus Andersson, Sebastian Carlsson, David Eilersén, Dennis Fagerkrantz, Oscar Fyhrman, Robert Henderson, Benny Johansson, Fredrik Johansson, Patrick Johansson, Kalle Lindgren, Emil Lindqvist, Sören Östergren, Joakim Söderström, Patrick Sohlberg, Michael Sjöqvist, Niklas Woxler.

TEAM CANVAC (A)
Wednesday, June 18
Won 51-43
F. Johansson 14:1, Söderström 2:1, Lindgren 10, Fagerkrantz 9:3, B. Johansson 12, Sohlberg 4:1, no rider at 7.

CROSSBONE PIRATES (A)
Wednesday, July 2
Won 54-38
F. Johansson 12:1, Östergren 5, Lindgren 12:2, Fagerkrantz 7:1, B. Johansson 12, Söderström 0, H. Andersson 6:1.

GNISTORNA (A)
Wednesday, July 9
Lost 41-55
F. Johansson 10:1, Östergren 5:3, Lindgren 8:1, Fagerkrantz 5, B. Johansson 9, Söderström 1, M. Andersson 3:2.

VIKINGARNA (H)
Wednesday, July 16
Lost 45-51
F. Johansson 10:1, Woxler 0, Östergren 8:1, Fagerkrantz 3, B. Johansson 17, M. Andersson 5:1, H. Andersson 2:1.

TEAM DALAKRAFT (H)
Wednesday, July 30
Lost 40-56
F. Johansson 4, Lindgren 5:1, Henderson 9, Östergren 1, B. Johansson 10, Carlsson 6:1, Fagerkrantz 2, M. Andersson 3.

ELDARNA (A)
Wednesday, August 6
Won 72-24
F. Johansson 7, **Carlsson 9:3**, Henderson 11:1, **Lindgren 13:2**, **B. Johansson 15**, **M. Andersson 9:3**, Fagerkrantz 8:2.

STJÄRNORNA (H)
Wednesday, August 13
Won 72-24
F. Johansson 11:4, **Carlsson 11:1**, **Henderson 11:1**, Lindgren 8:2, **B. Johansson 15**, Östergren 7:1, Fagerkrantz 5:1, M. Andersson 4.

TEAM BIKAB (A)
Saturday, August 16
Lost 31-35
F. Johansson 2, Östergren 4, Henderson 4, Carlsson 4, Lindgren 8, M. Andersson 7:1, H. Andersson 2.

NJUDUNGARNA (A)
Wednesday, August 20
Lost 31-65
F. Johansson 10:1, Carlsson 4:1, Östergren 2, Fagerkrantz 2, B. Johansson 7:1, Sjöquist 1:1, M. Andersson 5.

TEAM CANVAC (H)
Wednesday, August 27
Won 74-22
F. Johansson 13:2, **Carlsson 10:2**, Östergren 8:4, Lindgren 13:1, **B. Johansson 15**, M. Andersson 7:3, Fagerkrantz 8.

CROSSBONE PIRATES (H)
Wednesday, September 3
Won 59-37
F. Johansson 6:1, Carlsson 7:2, Henderson 8:2, Lindgren 9:2, B. Johansson 11, Östergren 8:2, Fagerkrantz 10:1, M. Andersson [no 8].

DIVISION ONE

	M	W	D	L	PtsF	PtsA	Pts
Team Dalakraft	18	18	0	0	1084	616	36
Team Bikab	18	13	0	5	956	736	26
Njudungarna	18	13	0	5	924	800	26
FILYTERNA	**18**	**11**	**0**	**7**	**958**	**730**	**22**
Stjärnorna	18	9	0	9	897	776	18
Crossbone Pirates	18	7	0	11	783	924	14
Vikingarna	18	7	0	11	755	922	14
Gnistorna	18	6	0	12	786	903	12
Team Canvac	18	3	1	14	733	988	7
Eldarna	18	2	1	15	612	1093	5

2009 Squad

Andreas **BERGLUND**, Sebastian **CARLSSON**, Dennis **FAGERKRANTZ**, André **HERTZBERG**, Benny **JOHANSSON**, Fredrik **JOHANSSON**, Patrik **JOHANSSON**, Kalle **LINDGREN**, Tobias **PLANBERG**, Michael **SJÖQUIST**, Martina **WASSBERGER**.

MARTINA Wassberger is on course to create her own slice of history – by becoming the first girl to hold down a regular team place in the Swedish League.

The 17-year-old teenager from Rimforsa has been named in Filbyterna's 2009 squad and will be hoping to make the historic breakthrough.

She rode in 80cc for Indianerna and Västervik last season after being tempted to try the sport when she saw it on TV.

She is also hoping to be accepted at the Hultsfreds Speedway School to further her ambition to establish herself in Swedish racing.

Rider	M	R	Pts	BP	TPts	Ave	F	P
Emil LINDQVIST	4	20	43	6	49	9.80	0	1
Benny JOHANSSON	**17**	**86**	**194**	**4**	**198**	**9.21**	**3**	**1**
Kalle LINDGREN	15	70	140	17	157	8.97	0	2
Robert HENDERSON	**5**	**21**	**43**	**4**	**47**	**8.95**	**0**	**1**
Sebastian CARLSSON	14	66	124	20	144	8.73	0	5
Fredrik JOHANSSON	**17**	**81**	**160**	**16**	**176**	**8.69**	**0**	**4**
Marcus ANDERSSON	8	32	43	10	53	6.63	0	1
Dennis FAGERKRANTZ	**17**	**74**	**105**	**16**	**121**	**6.54**	**0**	**0**
Sören ÖSTERGREN	16	67	83	24	107	6.39	0	0
Patrick SOHLBERG	**1**	**4**	**4**	**0**	**4**	**4.00**	**0**	**0**
Harald ANDERSSON	3	134	10	2	12	3.69	0	0
Joakim SÖDERSTRÖM	**5**	**14**	**7**	**3**	**10**	**2.86**	**0**	**0**
Michael SJÖQUIST	1	3	1	1	2	2.67	0	0
David EILERSÉN	**2**	**8**	**1**	**0**	**1**	**0.50**	**0**	**0**
Niklas WOXLER	1	2	0	0	0	0.00	0	0

Number eight appearances: Marcus ANDERSSON (1).

Harald ANDERSSON (see also Stjärnorna); Robert HENDERSON (see also Team Bikab); Emil Lindqvist (see also Stjärnorna).

2008 PARTNER CLUB

None

2009 PARTNER CLUB

GRIPARNA
(AllSvenskan)

Division One

GNISTORNA

2008 RESULTS

Final position...Eighth

FILBYTERNA (A)
Wednesday, April 30
Lost 35-60
Almqvist 3, S. Näreby 1, A. Näreby 3:1, J. Nilsson 4, M. Nilsson 13, Öberg 4:3, Blomgren 7.

STJÄRNORNA (H)
Saturday, May 10 (raced at Gislaved)
Won 51-45
M. Nilsson 10:1, Blomgren 9, Almqvist 7, J. Nilsson 0, **Kling 14:1**, A. Näreby 1:1, Öberg 0, A. Göthberg 10:1.

VIKINGARNA (A)
Wednesday, May 14
Lost 43-53
A. Göthberg 9:1, Almqvist 5:1, Öberg 2, S. Näreby 6, Blomgren 7:1, A. Näreby 5:2, Zymek 9:1.

NJUDUNGARNA (H)
Wednesday, May 21
Won 59-36
Ruud 15, Blomgren 5, M. Nilsson 13, Almqvist 4:3, Kling 10:1, A. Göthberg 12:2, Zymek 0.

TEAM BIKAB (A)
Wednesday, May 28
Lost 28-67
Blomgren 3, Almqvist 3, A. Göthberg 7, S. Näreby 3, Kling 9, A. Näreby 3, no rider at 7.

TEAM BIKAB (H)
Wednesday, June 4
Won 59-37
Kling 11:1, Almqvist 10:1. A. Göthberg 10:1, Blomgren 4, M, Nilsson 14, Krantz 7, Zymek 3:1.

TEAM DALAKRAFT (A)
Wednesday, June 11
Lost 32-46
A. Göthberg 8, Blomgren 2:1, M .Nilsson 5:1, Almqvist 5, Kling 9, Öberg 1:1, A. Näreby 2.

CROSSBONE PIRATES (H)
Wednesday, June 18
Won 63-32
A. Göthberg 8, Almqvist 7:1, **Pettersson 14:1**, Berntsson 8:2, **M. Nilsson 15**, Krantz 4:1, Blomgren 7, Zymek 0.

TRACK FILE

Track: Malmö Motorstadion, Elisedalsvägen, 21377 Malmö, Sweden.
Telephone: 0046 040499645.
Website: www.gnistorna.se
Track Length: 347 metres.
Track Record: Not known.

SQUAD
Kim Almqvist, Michael Berntsson, Peter Blomgren, Anton Göthberg, Viktor Göthberg, Tobias Johansson, Ricky Kling, Tony Krantz, Albin Näreby, Sven Näreby, Jonas Nilsson, Mattias Nilsson, Jonathan Normén, Christopher Öberg, Patrik Olsson, Per Pedersen, Robert Pettersson, David Ruud, Robin Zymek.

ELDARNA (A)
Saturday, July 5
Lost 39-42
A. Göthberg 9, Almqvist 1, Pettersson 9:1, Berntsson 1, M .Nilsson 10, Öberg 1, Blomgren 8:1.

FILBYTERNA (H)
Wednesday, July 9
Won 55-41
A. Göthberg 10:1, Almqivst 2, Pettersson 14, Berntsson 2, M. Nilsson 13:1, S. Näreby 6, Blomgren 8:2, A. Näreby [no. 8].

STJÄRNORNA (A)
Saturday, July 19
Lost 26-69
A. Göthberg 2, Blomgren 4, Pettersson 11, S. Näreby 1, Almqvist 4, A. Näreby 0, Öberg 4:1.

VIKINGARNA (H)
Wednesday, July 23
Lost 45-50
M. Nilsson 12, Almqvist 4, Pettersson 13:1, Blomgren 3, Berntsson 6, S. Näreby 4:1, Öberg 3.

NJUDUNGARNA (A)
Friday, August 1
Lost 41-55
Kling 8:1, Pettersson 5:2, M. Nilsson 14, Berntsson 6:1, Almqvist 4, A. Näreby 1:1, Blomgren 3, Öberg [no. 8] 0.

TEAM BIKAB (H)
Wednesday, August 6
Lost 46-50
Pettersson 11, A. Näreby 2, Berntsson 8:2, Blomgren 2, M. Nilsson 16:1, J. Nilsson 6:1, Öberg 1.

TEAM CANVAC (A)
Wednesday, August 13
Lost 45-51
J. Nilsson 5:2, Pettersson 4:1, M. Nilsson 11, Blomgren 6, Berntsson 8, Öberg 4:2, A. Näreby 7:1.

TEAM DALAKRAFT (H)
Wednesday, August 20
Lost 32-64
M. Nilsson 10, Blomgren 0, Pettersson 9:1, Kling 8:3, Berntsson 2, Öberg 1, A. Näreby 2.

CROSSBONE PIRATES (A)
Wednesday, August 27
Lost 32-64
M. Nilsson 6, Berntsson 4:1, J. Nilsson 1:1, Blomgren 7, Pettersson 9:1, Öberg 2, A. Näreby 3:1.

ELDARNA (H)
Saturday, September 6
Won 55-41
M. Nilsson 14:1, Blomgren 7:1, Berntsson 9, A. Näreby 1, Pettersson 11:1, J. Nilsson 11:2, Öberg 2.

DIVISION ONE

	M	W	D	L	PtsF	PtsA	Pts
Team Dalakraft	18	18	0	0	1084	616	36
Team Bikab	18	13	0	5	956	736	26
Njudungarna	18	13	0	5	924	800	26
Filyterna	18	11	0	7	958	730	22
Stjärnorna	18	9	0	9	897	776	18
Crossbone Pirates	18	7	0	11	783	924	14
Vikingarna	18	7	0	11	755	922	14
GNISTORNA	**18**	**6**	**0**	**12**	**786**	**903**	**12**
Team Canvac	18	3	1	14	733	988	7
Eldarna	18	2	1	15	612	1093	5

2009 Squad

Marcus ÅSTRÖM, Joel BLOMSTRAND, Michael BERNTSSON, Tony KRANTZ, Albin NÄREBY, Jonas NILSSON, Mattias NILSSON, Christopher ÖBERG, Robin ZYMEK.

MALMÖ is certainly one of the oldest clubs in Sweden, having been formed in 1924, long before speedway was known in Europe.

And it is also the most Southerly-based of the tracks and has a far warmer climate than others, allowing a long season for training.

Originally they used the city centre football stadium, home of the first World Final outside England, but since 1974 they have had their own stadium on the outskirts where they are able to run both 500cc and 80cc racing.

They also have a thriving veterans' section which stages events where competitors have included 75-year-old Göran Nilsson.

Ricky Kling

Rider	M	R	Pts	BP	TPts	Ave	F	P
David RUUD	1	5	15	0	15	12.00	1	0
Mattias NILSSON	**15**	**74**	**176**	**4**	**180**	**9.73**	**1**	**1**
Ricky KLING	7	33	69	7	76	9.21	0	1
Robert PETTERSSON	**11**	**56**	**110**	**9**	**119**	**8.50**	**0**	**1**
Anton GÖTHBERG	10	47	85	6	91	7.74	0	0
Tony KRANTZ	**2**	**8**	**11**	**1**	**12**	**6.00**	**0**	**0**
Michael BERNTSSON	10	44	54	6	60	5.45	0	0
Peter BLOMGREN	**18**	**75**	**92**	**6**	**98**	**5.23**	**0**	**0**
Jonas NILSSON	6	26	27	6	33	5.08	0	0
Kim ALMQVIST	**13**	**56**	**59**	**6**	**65**	**4.64**	**0**	**0**
Robin ZYMEK	4	14	12	2	14	4.00	0	0
Sven NÄREBY	**6**	**26**	**21**	**2**	**23**	**3.54**	**0**	**0**
Albin NÄREBY	12	47	30	7	37	3.15	0	0
Christopher ÖBERG	**13**	**53**	**25**	**7**	**32**	**2.42**	**0**	**0**

Number eight non-riding appearances: Albin NÄREBY (1).

Michael BERNTSSON (see also Team Dalakraft).

Did not compete in League racing

INDIANERNA UNGDOM

2009 PARTNER CLUBS
INDIANERNA (EliteSerien)

INDIANERNA are investing in the project in the hope of continuing their impressive record of discovering and encouraging fresh-faced talent.

Guiding the youngsters will be experienced 38-year-old Göran Flood who is a more than steady scorer at this level, having got 144 points in 17 matches for Vikingarna in 2008.

His guidance will be vital to the progress of the younger riders now that Indianerna legend Henrik Gustafsson has moved on to Rospiggarna.

But with his heart in the Indians it will be a major surprise if Henka, who made his debut for the club two decades ago, isn't around at every home meeting to dispense his own brand of advice!

For Track File see INDIANERNA.

2009 Squad

Daniel **AHLIN**, Emil **ARONSSON**, Tomas **ARONSSON**, Daniel **AXLING**, Alexander **CLAESSON**, Dennis **EKSTRAND**, Niklas **ERIKSSON**, Göran **FLOOD**, Freddy **GODLUND**, Sonny **HOLM**, Marcus **JOHANSSON**, Pontus **NILSSON**, Ove **OSTERBERG**, Mikael **RENNER**, Christer **ROHLÉN**, David **ROHLÉN**.

Division One

NJUDUNGARNA

2008 RESULTS

Final position..Third

SQUAD
Robin Aspegren, Mikael Åstrand, Marcus Åström, Mikael Axelsson, Kim Bergström, Robin Bergkvist, Gustaf Bjur, Kalle Fleetwood-Karlsson, Robin Hollgren, Thomas H. Jonasson, Niklas Larsson, Peter Ljung, Thomas Ljung, Patrik Malmfelt, Anders Mellgren, Mattias Persson, Robin Rundby.

TEAM DALAKRAFT (H)
Friday, May 2
Lost 36-60
T. Ljung 15, Malmfelt 0, Åström 6, Axelsson 1:1, Aspegren 8:2, Fleetwood-Karlsson 6, Åstrand 0.

ELDARNA (A)
Wednesday, May 7
Won 52-43
T. Ljung 9:1, Malmfelt 4:1, Larsson 14, Åström 1:1, Aspegren 9, Fleetwood-Karlsson 9, Axelsson 6:2.

STJÄRNORNA (H)
Sunday, May 11
Won 52-44
T. Ljung 13:1, Malmfelt 5:1, Larsson 8, Åström 2, Aspegren 11:2, Axelsson 1:1, Mellgren 12:2.

NJUDUNGARNA

Rider	*M*	*R*	*Pts*	*BP*	*TPts*	*Ave*	*F*	*P*
Peter LJUNG	1	5	15	0	15	12.00	1	0
Robin ASPEGREN	**18**	**92**	**197**	**12**	**209**	**9.09**	**3**	**1**
Anders MELLGREN	8	44	92	7	99	9.00	0	0
Niklas LARSSON	**12**	**59**	**120**	**11**	**131**	**8.88**	**0**	**1**
Thomas LJUNG	18	87	158	20	178	8.18	0	1
Robin BERGKVIST	**9**	**45**	**84**	**8**	**92**	**8.18**	**0**	**0**
K. FLEETWOOD-KARLSSON	13	58	72	12	84	5.79	0	0
Marcus ÅSTRÖM	**15**	**60**	**67**	**11**	**78**	**5.20**	**0**	**0**
Patrik MALMFELT	14	57	63	8	71	4.98	0	1
Mikael AXELSSON	**15**	**63**	**56**	**16**	**72**	**4.57**	**0**	**0**
Mikael ÅSTRAND	1	3	0	0	0	0.00	0	0
Did not ride: Marcus ÅSTRÖM (1).								
Niklas LARSSON (see also Stjärnorna).								

TRACK FILE

Track: Vetlanda Motorstadion, Box 187, 57422 Vetlanda, Sweden.
Telephone: 0046 0383761271.
Website: www.elitvetlanda.se
Track Length: 361 metres.
Track Record: 62.4 secs, Jason Crump, May 8, 2007.

GRIPARNA (A)
Wednesday, May 21
Lost 36-59
T. Ljung 8:1, Malmfelt 0, Bergkvist 14, Åström 3, Aspegren 4, Fleetwood-Karlsson 4, Axelsson 3:1.

TEAM CANVAC (A)
Wednesday, May 28
Won 49-47
T. Ljung 9, Malmfelt 2:2, Larsson 7:1, Åström 3:1, Aspegren 8:1, Fleetwood-Karlsson 7:3, Mellgren 13:3.

CROSSBONE PIRATES (H)
Wednesday, June 4
Won 60-36
T. Ljung 12:2, Åström 10:3, Larsson 12:1, Bergkvist 8:1, Aspegren 10:1, Fleetwood-Karlsson 4, Axelsson 4:1.

FILBYTERNA (A)
Wednesday, June 11
Won 50-45
Axelsson 2:1, Åström 6, Bergkvist 6, Aspegren 14, T. Ljung 3:1, Fleetwood-Karlsson 2, Mellgren 17.

VIKINGARNA (H)
Wednesday, June 18
Won 66-30
T. Ljung 11:1, Axelsson 3:1, Bergkvist 7:2, Åström 11:1, **Aspegren 15**, Fleetwood-Karlsson 6:2, Malmfelt 13.

TEAM BIKAB (A)
Wednesday, July 2
Lost 41-54
Bergkvist 4:1, Larsson 6:1, T., Ljung 8:1, Åström 0, Aspegren 11, Mellgren 12, Malmfelt 0.

TEAM DALAKRAFT (A)
Wednesday, July 9
Lost 27-69
T. Ljung 1:1, Åström, did not ride, Larsson 6:1, Mellgren 7, Aspegren 10, Axelsson 3, Fleetwood-Karlsson 0.

ELDARNA (H)
Friday, July 18
Won 74-22
T. Ljung 9:3, **Malmfelt 14:1**, Åström 10:3, **Larsson 11:1**, **Aspegren 12**, Fleetwood-Karlsson 11:2, Axelsson 7:2.

STJÄRNORNA (A)
Wednesday, July 23
Lost 36-60
T. Ljung 11:1, Malmfelt 0, Åström 0, Bergkvist 13:1, Aspegren 9, Axelsson 3, no rider at 7.

Did you know?

Patrik Malmfelt, who scored a paid maximum at home to Eldarna, was 40 on March 9 but didn't take up racing until he was 30. He's also gone through most of his career with his name mispelt – there's no d between the l and t of his surname!

GNISTORNA (H)
Friday, August 1
Won 55-41
T. Ljung 9, Mellgren 10:1, Larsson 12, Åström 1, Aspegren 9:2, Axelsson 2:1, Malmfelt 12:2.

TEAM CANVAC (H)
Wednesday, August 6
Won 56-40
T. Ljung 11, Malmfelt 4, Bergkvist 11:1, Åström 2:1, **Aspegren 15**, Fleetwood-Karlsson 8, Axelsson 5:2.

CROSSBONE PIRATES (A)
Wednesday, August 13
Won 63-33
T. Ljung 9:4, Mellgren 8, Larsson 12:2, Bergkvist 10:1, Aspegren 13:1, Fleetwood-Karlsson 6:1, Axelsson 5:1.

FILBYTERNA (H)
Wednesday, August 20
Won 65-31
T. Ljung 5:2, **P. Ljung 15**, Larsson 11:2, Bergkvist 11:1, **Aspegren 13:2**, Åström 7, Malmfelt 3.

VIKINGARNA (A)
Wednesday, August 27
Won 53-43
T. Ljung 5, Malmfelt 0, Larsson 10, Mellgren 13:1, Aspegren 12:1, Fleetwood-Karlsson 7:2, Axelsson 6:1.

TEAM BIKAB (H)
Friday, September 5
Won 53-43
Aspegren 14, Åström 5:1, T. Ljung 10:1, Fleetwood-Karlsson 2:2, Larsson 11:2, Axelsson 5:1, Malmfelt 6:1.

DIVISION ONE

	M	W	D	L	PtsF	PtsA	Pts
Team Dalakraft	18	18	0	0	1084	616	36
Team Bikab	18	13	0	5	956	736	26
NJUDUNGARNA	**18**	**13**	**0**	**5**	**924**	**800**	**26**
Filyterna	18	11	0	7	958	730	22
Stjärnorna	18	9	0	9	897	776	18
Crossbone Pirates	18	7	0	11	783	924	14
Vikingarna	18	7	0	11	755	922	14
Gnistorna	18	6	0	12	786	903	12
Team Canvac	18	3	1	14	733	988	7
Eldarna	18	2	1	15	612	1093	5

2009 Squad

Not running a second team in 2009.

Division One

STJÄRNORNA

2008 RESULTS

Final position .... Fifth

ELDARNA (H)
Wednesday, April 30
Won 74-22
Oskarsson 13:2, **Larsson 10:5**, Westlund 10:1, Burestad 6:2, **Jansson 13:2**, Wall 7:1, **J. Messing 15**.

GNISTORNA (A)
Saturday, May 10 (raced at Gislaved)
Lost 45-51
Oskarsson 8, Larsson 5:3, Westlund 3:1, Burestad 3, Jansson 8, Wall, did not ride, Andersson 3:3, J. Messing 15.

NJUDUNGARNA (A)
Sunday, May 11
Lost 44-52
Wall 7:2, Larsson 3, Westlund 2:1, Burestad 7, Jansson 7, **J. Messing 15**, Andersson 3:2.

TEAM CANVAC (H)
Wednesday, May 21
Won 69-25
Oskarsson 9:2, Larsson 12:1, Jansson 5:3, Westlund 12:1, Hillborg, did not ride, Burestad 6:1, **Wall 11:4**, **J. Messing 14:1**.

CROSSBONE PIRATES (A)
Wednesday, May 28
Lost 44-50
Oskarsson 8:2, Larsson 10:1, Westlund 0, Wall 0, Hillborg 6:1, J. Messing 17, Andersson 3.
▼ *Partners Westlund and Wall crashed out in Heat 3 and neither was able to take any further part.*

FILBYTERNA (H)
Wednesday, June 4 (at Gävle)
Lost 35-60
Oskarsson 8:2, Larsson 8:1, Hillborg 7, Burestad 0, Jansson 7:2, Wall 2:1. R. Messing 3:1.

VIKINGARNA (A)
Wednesday, June 11
Won 28-26
Oskarsson 2:1, Larsson 5, J. Messing 4:1, Jansson 7:1, Hillborg 3, Burestad 4, Wall 3.
● *Meeting abandoned after nine races, result to stand.*

Niklas Larsson finished behind his partner in all five races in Stjärnorna's opening league match of the season, a big win over strugglers Eldarna.

TRACK FILE

Track: Orionparken, Tulkavägen 7, 76334 Hallstavik, Sweden.
Telephone: 0046 017522775.
Website: www.rospiggarna.nu
Track Length: 289 metres.
Track Record: *Not available.*

SQUAD
Harald Andersson, Stefan Brolin, Robin Burestad, Fredrik Gustavsson, David Hillborg, Linus Jansson, Niklas Larsson, Emil Lindqvist, Andreas Messing, Jonas Messing, Robin Messing, Jens Oskarsson, Peter Wall, Andreas Westlund.

TEAM BIKAB (H)
Wednesday, June 18
Won 49-47
Oskarsson 5:3, Larsson 4:1, Jansson 4:1, Westlund 6:1, Lindqvist 10, Hillborg 5:3, **J. Messing 15**, R. Messing 0.

TEAM DALAKRAFT (A)
Wednesday, July 2
Lost 36-56
J. Messing 11, Larsson 0, Oskarsson 3, Jansson 2:2, Lindqvist 10:1, Hillborg 8, Westlund 2:2.

ELDARNA (A)
Wednesday, July 9
Won 72-24
J. Messing 14:1, Westlund 8:2, Oskarsson 8:1, Jansson 7:1, **Hillborg 13:2**, Wall 13:1, R. Messing 9:3.

GNISTORNA (H)
Saturday, July 19
Won 69-26
J. Messing 13:1, Oskarsson 11, **Lindqvist 13:2**, Jansson 6:1, Hillborg 3, Wall 5:2, **Larsson 12:3**, R. Messing 6:1.

NJUDUNGARNA (H)
Wednesday, July 23
Won 60-36
J. Messing 14, Larsson 3:1, Lindqvist 12, Westlund 10:2, Jansson 6, Wall 6:1, Burestad 9:2.

TEAM CANVAC (A)
Wednesday, July 30
Lost 38-58
Lindqvist 6, Westlund 3:2, Hllborg 5, Larsson 1:1, J. Messing 7:1, Burestad 11, Wall 5:3.

CROSSBONE PIRATES (H)
Wednesday, August 6
Won 57-38
J. Messing 12, Oskarsson 8:2, Lindqvist 10, Westlund 7:4, Hillborg 9:1, R. Messing 4:1, Burestad 7:1.

Rider	M	R	Pts	BP	TPts	Ave	F	P
Jonas MESSING	13	64	166	5	171	10.69	3	2
Emil LINDQVIST	**9**	**42**	**90**	**5**	**95**	**9.05**	**0**	**1**
Andreas MESSING	1	5	11	0	11	8.80	0	0
Peter WALL	**12**	**50**	**71**	**17**	**88**	**7.04**	**0**	**1**
David HILLBORG	13	57	88	10	98	6.88	0	1
Jens OSKARSSON	**15**	**67**	**99**	**16**	**115**	**6.87**	**0**	**1**
Andreas WESTLUND	14	60	85	17	102	6.80	1	0
Linus JANSSON	**13**	**58**	**84**	**14**	**98**	**6.76**	**0**	**1**
Niklas LARSSON	16	73	101	22	123	6.74	0	2
Robin BURESTAD	**11**	**47**	**64**	**9**	**73**	**6.21**	**0**	**0**
Robin MESSING	8	27	29	8	37	5.48	0	0
Harald ANDERSSON	**3**	**14**	**9**	**5**	**14**	**4.00**	**0**	**0**

Did not ride: David HILLBORG (1), Peter WALL (1).

Harald ANDERSSON (see also Filbyterna); Niklas LARSSON (see also Njudungarna); Emil LINDQVIST (see also Filbyterna).

2008 PARTNER CLUB

ROSPIGGARNA (ElitSerien)

2009 PARTNER CLUBS

ROSPIGGARNA (ElitSerien)

GETINGARNA (AllSvenskan)

FILBYTERNA (A)
Wednesday, August 13
Lost 24-72
Westlund 6, Larsson 0, Oskarsson 3, Wall 1, Hillborg 5, R. Messing 4:2, Burestad 5.

VIKINGARNA (H)
Wednesday, August 20 (raced at Gävle)
Won 67-27
Oskarsson 7, Wall 9:2, Lindqvist 8:2, **Westlund 15**, Hillborg 10:1, R. Messing 3:2, Larsson 15:1.

TEAM BIKAB (A)
Wednesday, August 27
Lost 40-56
Lindqvist 13, Westlund 1:1, Hillborg 6, Oskarsson 6:1, Jansson 8, Wall 2, Larsson 4:1.

TEAM DALAKRAFT (H)
Wednesday, September 3
Lost 46-50
Hillborg 8, Jansson 4:1, Lindqvist 8, Oskarsson 0, A. Messing 11, Burestad 6:3, Larsson 9:3, R. Messing 0.

DIVISION ONE

	M	W	D	L	PtsF	PtsA	Pts
Team Dalakraft	18	18	0	0	1084	616	36
Team Bikab	18	13	0	5	956	736	26
Njudungarna	18	13	0	5	924	800	26
Filyterna	18	11	0	7	958	730	22
STJÄRNORNA	**18**	**9**	**0**	**9**	**897**	**776**	**18**
Crossbone Pirates	18	7	0	11	783	924	14
Vikingarna	18	7	0	11	755	922	14
Gnistorna	18	6	0	12	786	903	12
Team Canvac	18	3	1	14	733	988	7
Eldarna	18	2	1	15	612	1093	5

Reserve Peter Wall and number eight Jonas Messing took 10 rides between them at home to Team Canvac – and were both unbeaten by an opponent!

2009 Squad

David **HILLBORG**, Linus **JANSSON**, Niklas **LARSSON**, Emil **LINDQVIST**, Robin **MESSING**, Thomas **MESSING**, Tobias **MESSING**, Jens **OSKARSSON**, Peter **WALL**.

AFTER agreeing to stage two of their 2008 Division One matches at Gävle (they replaced that club at late notice) Stjärnorna plan to race all their home matches at their Hallstavik circuit in 2009.

They overcame that partcicular handicap – their only home defeat came at their adopted, temporary home – to finish a respectable midtable with Jonas Messing a prolific scorer everywhere.

Old head Emil Lindqvist provided sufficient back-up to Messing and the Stars never had a discernible weak link in their regular squad, usually scoring fairly solidly down the order, including that astonishing match against Team Canvac when the two reserves picked up 25 points between them!

At least seven of the 2008 squad – including Lindqvist – are back again with the addition of yet two more Messings, Thomas and Tobias, which suggests they could improve on their past performances.

Did you know?

Stjärnorna raced Division One matches on successive nights – a rarity in Swedish speedway. They travelled to Gislaved to face Gnistorna on Saturday, May 10 and the following afternoon took on Njudungarna, 73 miles (118 kilometres) away at their Vetlanda raceway.

Division One

TEAM BIKAB

2008 RESULTS

Final position..Second

TEAM CANVAC (A)
Wednesday, April 30
Won 53-43
Gallon 12, Karlsson 5:2, **R. Henderson 15**, Edberg 3, L. Eklöf 10, D. Henderson 5:1, R. Eklöf 3.

CROSSBONE PIRATES (A)
Wednesday, May 7
Won 57-39
Gallon 13, Karlsson 6:3, R. Henderson 8, Edberg 3:1, L. Eklöf 8, D. Henderson 13.1, Hertzberg 6:3, R. Eklöf 0.

FILBYTERNA (A)
Wednesday, May 14
Lost 44-52
R. Henderson 13:1, D. Henderson 2, Karlsson 8:1, Edberg 2, L. Eklöf 16, Hertzberg 2, R. Eklöf 1.

VIKINGARNA (H)
Wednesday, May 21
Won 58-37
Gallon 7:2, Karlsson 10:1, R. Henderson 11:1, J. Jansson 8:1, Edberg 7:1, D. Henderson 8:1, Hertzberg 6:3, R. Eklöf 1:1.

GNISTORNA (H)
Wednesday, May 28
Won 67-28
Gallon 13:1, **Karlsson 13:2**, R. Henderson 12:2, Edberg 6:2, J. Jansson 10:1, D. Henderson 9:2, Hertzberg 2:1. Eklöf 2:1.

TEAM DALAKRAFT (A)
Wednesday, June 4
Lost 44-52
Gallon 8:1, J. Jansson 0, R. Henderson 6:2, Karlsson 8:1, L. Eklöf 12, D. Henderson 8:1, Hertzberg 0, R. Eklöf 2:1.

ELDARNA (H)
Wednesday, June 11
Won 67-28
Gallon 10, Edberg 10:3, Karlsson 11:1, D. Henderson 9:2, **R. Henderson 15**, Hertzberg 6:1, R. Eklöf 6.

Despite only having six riders and going into four heats with only one rider Team Bikab won 55-40 at Vikingarna.

TRACK FILE

Track: Eskilstuna Motorstadion, Box 63, 63102 Eskilstuna, Sweden.
Telephone: 0046 016140584.
Website: www.smederna.nu
Track Length: 335 metres.
Track Record: 58.3 secs, Nicki Pedersen, May 31, 2005.

SQUAD
Jesper Brolin, Alexander Edberg, Linus Eklöf, Rasmus Eklöf, Torbjörn Eriksson, Nicklas Gallon, Daniel Henderson, Robert Henderson, Andre Hertzberg, Kim Jansson, Jimmy Jansson, Henrik Karlsson, David Strömberg.

Linus Eklöf was unbeaten in five starts in the away match against Stjärnorna – and for the home side Jonas Messing recorded a 15 point maximum.

STJÄRNORNA (A)
Wednesday, June 18
Lost 47-49
L. Eklöf 13:2, D. Henderson 2:1, Karlsson 10, Edberg 2:1, R. Henderson 15, Hertzberg 3, R. Eklöf 2.

NJUDUNGARNA (H)
Wednesday, July 2
Won 54-41
Gallon 11:1, Karlsson 5, L. Eklöf 11:2, D. Henderson 4, R. Henderson 12:1, R. Eklöf 4:4, Edberg 7:1.

TEAM CANVAC (H)
Wednesday, July 9
Won 63-33
Gallon 13, D. Henderson 6:2, L. Eklöf 13:1, Karlsson 4:2, R. Henderson 13:1, R. Eklöf 4:2, Edberg 10:2.

CROSSBONE PIRATES (H)
Wednesday, July 16
Won 57-38
Gallon 10:1, D. Henderson 5, L. Eklöf 8:2, Karlsson 12:1, R. Henderson 11, R. Eklöf 2:1, Edberg 9:1.

VIKINGARNA (A)
Wednesday, July 30
Won 55-40
D. Henderson 11, J. Jansson 2, Karlsson 12, Edberg 8:2, K. Jansson 12:1, R. Eklöf 10:1, no rider at 7.

GNISTORNA (A)
Wednesday, August 6
Won 50-46
L. Eklöf 14, J. Jansson 0, Karlsson 7:2, D. Henderson 3, K. Jansson 11:1, R. Eklöf 5:2, Edberg 10:1.

TEAM DALAKRAFT (H)
Wednesday, August 13
Lost 39-57
L. Eklöf 10:1, Edberg 3:2, Karlsson 4:1, Gallon, did not ride, K. Jansson 10:2, Hertzberg 1, D. Henderson 11:1.

FILBYTERNA (H)
Saturday, August 16
Won 35-31
L. Eklöf 8:1, J. Jansson 1, Karlsson 3, D. Henderson 3, K. Jansson 8, Hertzberg 4, Edberg 8:1.
● *Match abandoned after 11 races, result to stand.*

STJÄRNORNA (H)
Wednesday, August 27
Won 56-40
L. Eklöf 13:1 J. Jansson 6:3, Karlsson 3:1, Edberg 10:1, D. Henderson 13, R. Eklöf 6:2, Hertzberg 5:1.

NJUDUNGARNA (A)
Friday, September 5
Lost 43-53
L. Eklöf 15, J. Jansson 3:2, Karlsson 8:2, Edberg 5, D. Henderson 8, Hertzberg 4:1, R. Eklöf 0.

ELDARNA (A)
Sunday, September 14
Won 67-29
L. Eklöf 15, Edberg 7:3, D. Henderson 11, J. Jansson 8:2, Karlsson 13:2, R. Eklöf 8:1, Hertzberg 5.

DIVISION ONE

	M	W	D	L	PtsF	PtsA	Pts
Team Dalakraft	18	18	0	0	1084	616	36
TEAM BIKAB	**18**	**13**	**0**	**5**	**956**	**736**	**26**
Njudungarna	18	13	0	5	924	800	26
Filyterna	18	11	0	7	958	730	22
Stjärnorna	18	9	0	9	897	776	18
Crossbone Pirates	18	7	0	11	783	924	14
Vikingarna	18	7	0	11	755	922	14
Gnistorna	18	6	0	12	786	903	12
Team Canvac	18	3	1	14	733	988	7
Eldarna	18	2	1	15	612	1093	5

2009 Squad

Robin **BERGQVIST**, Linus **EKLÖF**, Rasmus **EKLÖF**, Nicklas **GALLON**, Daniel **HENDERSON**, Robert **HENDERSON**, Jimmy **JANSSON**.

Kim Jansson was paralysed after crashing during Team Bikab's Division One match against Filbyterna on Saturday, August 16. As a mark of respect, the scheduled match four days later against Eldarna was postponed until the following month.

Rider	*M*	*R*	*Pts*	*BP*	*TPts*	*Ave*	*F*	*P*
Robert HENDERSON	11	56	131	8	139	9.93	2	0
Nicklas GALLON	**9**	**42**	**97**	**6**	**103**	**9.81**	**0**	**0**
Linus EKLÖF	14	72	166	10	176	9.78	1	2
Kim JANSSON	**4**	**19**	**41**	**4**	**45**	**9.47**	**0**	**0**
Henrik KARLSSON	18	85	142	22	164	7.72	0	2
Alexander EDBERG	**17**	**77**	**110**	**22**	**132**	**6.86**	**0**	**0**
Jimmy JANSSON	8	28	38	9	47	6.71	0	0
Daniel HENDERSON	**18**	**88**	**131**	**12**	**143**	**6.50**	**0**	**0**
Rasmus EKLÖF	16	58	56	16	72	4.97	0	0
Andre HERTZBERG	**12**	**47**	**44**	**10**	**54**	**4.60**	**0**	**0**

Did not ride: Nicklas GALLON (1).

Robert HENDERSON (see also Filbyterna).

2008 PARTNER CLUBS

SMEDERNA (ElitSerien)

TEAM BIKAB B (Division Two)

2000 PARTNER CLUB

SMEDERNA (ElitSerien)

Division One

TEAM CANVAC

2008 RESULTS

Final position..Ninth

TEAM BIKAB (H)
Wednesday, April 30
Lost 43-53
Agö 9:2, Lindgren 12:1, Isometta 7, Sundström 1, Nilsson 6:1, Hansson 5:2, Renner 3.

TEAM DALAKRAFT (A)
Wednesday, May 7
Lost 34-62
Olsson 11, Isomettä 6:2, Nilsson 4, Sundström 3, Agö 7, Renner 3:1, no rider at 7.

ELDARNA (H)
Wednesday, May 14
Drew 48-48
Agö 15, Linder 8, Hansson 1:1, Sundström 8:1, **Isomettä 13:2**, Renner 2, Eriksson 1.

STJÄRNORNA (A)
Wednesday, May 21
Lost 25-69
Agö 11, Linder 2, Hansson 0, Sundström 5, Renner 4, Eriksson 3, no rider at 7.

NJUDUNGARNA (H)
Wednesday, May 28
Lost 47-49
Agö 15, Isomettä 11:2, Olsson 12, Sundström 0, Nilsson 6, Eriksson 2, Renner 1.

GNISTORNA (A)
Wednesday, June 4
Lost 37-59
Agö 8:1, Sundström 2:1, Isomettä 11, Hansson 1:1, Nilsson 8, Eriksson 5, Renner 2:2.

CROSSBONE PIRATES (A)
Wednesday, June 11
Won 57-38
Klingberg 12:2, Isomettä 9, **Olsson 12:3**, Nilsson 11:1, Agö 2, Sundström 8, Hansson 3:1.

FILBYTERNA (H)
Wednesday, June 18
Lost 43-51
Olsson 12, Hansson 6:1, Nilsson 5, Eriksson 2, Agö 7:1, Renner 5:1, Hedfors 6:2.

TRACK FILE

Track: CanVac Arena, Vallby 6, 54292 Mariestad, Sweden.
Telephone: 0046 050120230.
Website: www.ornarna.nu
Track Length: 295 metres.
Track Record: 56.0 secs, Tony Rickardsson, July 28, 1998.

SQUAD
Christian Agö, Joakim Engstrand, Niklas Eriksson, Kim Hansson, Oscar Hedfors, Christian Isomettä, Kim Ingmarsson, Mikael Karlsson, Niklas Klingberg, Emil Kramer, Martin Linder, Ludvig Lindgren, Olof Nilsson, Tomas Olsson, Mikael Renner, Daniel Sjögren, Pontus Sundström.

VIKINGARNA (A)
Wednesday, July 2
Lost 35-61
Nilsson 3, Sundström 4, Agö 10, Hansson 1, **Olsson 15**, Eriksson 1, Hedfors 1.

TEAM BIKAB (A)
Wednesday, July 9
Lost 33-63
Lindgren 11:1, Isomettä 2:2, Nilsson 7, Agö 4, Sundström 2, Hansson 7, Hedfors 0.

TEAM DALAKRAFT (H)
Wednesday, July 16
Lost 37-59
Olsson 10:1, Agö 10, Isomettä 8:1, Nilsson 2, Hansson 2, Hedfors 1:1, Renner 4.

ELDARNA (A)
Wednesday, July 23
Lost 41-54
Agö 17, Sundström 6:1, Nilsson 7, Renner 2, Hansson 5, Eriksson 1, Hedfors 3.

STJÄRNORNA (H)
Wednesday, July 30
Won 58-38
Olsson 14:1, Nilsson 5, **Lindgren 15**, Isomettä 7:3, **Agö 14:1**, Hansson 1, Sundström 2.

NJUDUNGARNA (A)
Wednesday, August 6
Lost 40-56
Isomettä 14, Sundström 3:2, Nilsson 7, Hansson 4, Agö 10, Eriksson 1, Hedfors 1.

GNISTORNA (H)
Wednesday, August 13
Won 51-45
Olsson 12, Nilsson 8:2, Agö 13, Hansson 1,

Isomettä 13:1, Hedfors 0, Eriksson 4.

CROSSBONE PIRATES (H)
Wednesday, August 20
Lost 43-52
Sundström 1, Nilsson 12, Renner 0, Isomettä 11:1, Agö 13:1, Hedfors 4, Eriksson 2:2.

FILBYTERNA (A)
Wednesday, August 27
Lost 22-74
Sundström 5, Renner 1, Agö 8, Nilsson 5, Hansson 0, Eriksson 3, Hedsfors 0.

VIKINGARNA (H)
Wednesday, September 3
Lost 39-57
Isomettä 9:2, Agö 9, Sundström 3:1, Nilsson 7, Hansson 2:1, Hedfors 5:1, Eriksson 4:1.

DIVISION ONE

	M	W	D	L	PtsF	PtsA	Pts
Team Dalakraft	18	18	0	0	1084	616	36
Team Bikab	18	13	0	5	956	736	26
Njudungarna	18	13	0	5	924	800	26
Filyterna	18	11	0	7	958	730	22
Stjärnorna	18	9	0	9	897	776	18
Crossbone Pirates	18	7	0	11	783	924	14
Vikingarna	18	7	0	11	755	922	14
Gnistorna	18	6	0	12	786	903	12
TEAM CANVAC	**18**	**3**	**1**	**14**	**733**	**988**	**7**
Eldarna	18	2	1	15	612	1093	5

2009 Squad

Not running a second team in 2009.

Did not compete in League racing

HULTSFREDS GYMNASIUM

2009 PARTNER CLUBS
DACKARNA (EliteSerien)

FORMER rider Anders Kling will coach the new Hultsfreds Gymnasium team in their baptism year in Division One.

The Målilla Motor Club decided to run a second team to provide riders from their 80cc side with a natural progression all the way through to the ElitSerien.

The team name comes from the Training School run in conjunction with a local school in nearby Hultsfreds.

TRACK FILE

Track: G&B Arena, Box 18, 5780 82 Målilla, Sweden.
Track Length: 305 metres.
Track Record: 55.9 secs, Hans Andersen, August 1, 2006 & Nicki Pedersen, July 22, 2008.
See DACKARNA.

2009 Squad

Eric **ASHEDE**, Jonas **EINARSSON**, Kalle **FLEETWOOD-KARLSSON**, Tim **GUDMUNDSSON**, Kim **INGMARSSON**, Christian **ISOMETTÄ**, Anders **KLING**, Joel **LARSSON**, Mikael **KARLSSON**, Niklas **LARSSON**, Olof **NILSSON**, Robin **RUNDBY**, Pontus **SUNDSTRÖM**.

Rider	M	R	Pts	BP	TPts	Ave	F	P
Niklas KLINGBERG	1	5	12	2	14	11.20	0	0
Tomas OLSSON	**8**	**38**	**98**	**5**	**103**	**10.84**	**2**	**2**
Ludvig LINDGREN	3	15	38	2	40	10.67	1	0
Christian AGÖ	**18**	**90**	**182**	**7**	**189**	**8.40**	**2**	**1**
Christian ISOMETTÄ	13	66	121	16	137	8.30	0	1
Olof NILSSON	**16**	**74**	**103**	**4**	**107**	**5.78**	**0**	**0**
Martin LINDER	2	10	10	0	10	4.00	0	0
Pontus SUNDSTRÖM	**15**	**70**	**53**	**6**	**59**	**3.37**	**0**	**0**
Kim HANSSON	15	63	39	7	46	2.92	0	0
Niklas ERIKSSON	**12**	**50**	**29**	**3**	**32**	**2.56**	**0**	**0**
Mikael RENNER	11	50	27	3	30	2.40	0	0
Oskar HEDFORS	**10**	**42**	**21**	**4**	**25**	**2.38**	**0**	**0**

Niklas ERIKSSON (see also Vikingarna).

2008 PARTNER CLUB

ÖRNARNA (ElitSerien)

Division One

TEAM DALAKRAFT

2008 RESULTS

Final position..........................Champions (First)

NJUDUNGARNA (A)
Friday, May 2
Won 60-36
N. Aspgren 15, Hagansbo 8:4, Berntsson 3:1, P. Aspgren 10:1, D. Andersson 12, Rundby 5:2, Karlsson 7:1.

TEAM CANVAC (H)
Wednesday, May 7
Won 62-34
N. Aspgren 15, Rundby 0, Rosén 13:1, F. Andersson 4:2, D. Andersson 11:2, Hagansbo 10, P. Aspgren 9:2.

CROSSBONE PIRATES (A)
Wednesday, May 14
Won 58-38
N. Aspgren 15, Hagansbo 5:1, D. Andersson 6, F. Andersson 8:1, Rosén 11, P. Aspgren 11:2, Rundby 2.

FILBYTERNA (H)
Wednesday, May 21
Won 53-42
N. Aspgren 12:2, Berntsson 3:1, D. Andersson 12:1, P. Aspgren 7:1, Rosén 11:1, Hagansbo 5, Karlsson 3.
▼ *Niklas Aspgren's unbeaten run came to an end in Heat 16 when he and partner Anton Rosén were beaten by Emil Lindqvist after 18 successive race wins and a paid win in Heat 14.*

VIKINGARNA (A)
Wednesday, May 28
Won 64-32
N. Aspgren 15, Berntsson 1, Rosén 13, P. Aspgren 6:2, **D. Andersson 14:1, Hagansbo 13:2**, Rundby 2.

TEAM BIKAB (H)
Wednesday, June 4
Won 52-44
N. Aspgren 14:1, Björk, did not ride, D. Andersson 9, P. Aspgren 4:2, Rosén 11, Hagansbo 8, Karlsson 6:1.

2009 Squad

*Running in Division One as **Gasarna** and will use riders on the books of AllSvenskan League Masarna.*

TRACK FILE

Track: Arena Avesta, Box 6, 774 21 Avesta Sweden.
Telephone: 0046 0226 503 60.
Website: www.masarnaavesta.nu
Track Length: 315 metres.
Track Record: 57.0 secs, Leigh Adams, August 1, 2006.

SQUAD
Sebastian Aldén, Niklas Aspgren, Pontus Aspgren, Daniel Andersson, Dennis Andersson, Fredrik Andersson, Andreas Bergström, Michael Berntsson, Patrik Björk, Ted Hagansbo, Henrik Johansson, Leif Karlsson, Johan Liljegren, Anton Rosén, Robin Rundby.

GNISTORNA (H)
Wednesday, June 11
Won 46-32
N. Aspgren 7:1, Rosén 10:1, Björk, did not ride, Hagansbo 5, D. Andersson 7:1, P. Aspgren 11:2, Karlsson 6:4.
● *Meeting abandoned after 13 heats, result to stand.*

ELDARNA (A)
Wednesday, June 18
Won 57-38
N. Aspgren 12, D. Andersson 11:2, Rosén 5, P. Aspgren 3:1, Bergström 13, Hagansbo 11:3, Rundby 2.

STJÄRNORNA (H)
Wednesday, July 2
Won 56-36
N. Aspgren 12:2, Rosén 11:1, D. Andersson 14, Hagansbo 4:2, Aldén 8, P. Aspgren 4, Rundby 3.

NJUDUNGARNA (H)
Wednesday, July 9
Won 69-27
N. Aspgren 7:2, **D. Andersson 15**, Bergström 6:1, Rosén 12:2, **Aldén 11:1**, P. Aspgren 7:4, Hagansbo 11:1.

TEAM CANVAC (A)
Wednesday, July 16
Won 59-37
N. Aspgren 12:1, Rosén 9:2, D. Andersson 10:1, F. Andersson 0, Bergström 11:2, Hagansbo 7:3, Karlsson 10:1.

CROSSBONE PIRATES (H)
Wednesday, July 23
Won 68-24
N. Aspgren 12:1, **D. Andersson 15,** Rosén 12:1, F. Andersson 2:1, Bergström 11:2, Hagansbo 8:1, Karlsson 8:4, Rundby 0.

Team Dalakraft went through the entire campaign without dropping a point to record a 100% record of 18 wins in 18 matches. In their final match Stjärnorna led all the way through until a 5-1 in Heat 15.

FILBYTERNA (A)
Wednesday, July 30
Won 56-40
N. Aspgren 13, Rosén 6:4, Bergström 8:1, F. Andersson 3:1, D. Andersson 11:2, Hagansbo 10:1, P. Aspgren 5:3, Rundby 0.

VIKINGARNA (H)
Wednesday, August 6
Won 74-22
N. Aspgren 15, F. Andersson 3:1, **Aldén 12:3, Rosén 13:2**, D. Andersson 11:1, Hagansbo 10:3, P. Aspgren 10:2.

TEAM BIKAB (A)
Wednesday, August 13
Won 57-39
N. Aspgren 14:1, F. Andersson, did not ride, **Aldén 13:2**, Rosén 9, Bergström 6:1, Hagansbo 9, P. Aspgren 6:4.

GNISTORNA (A)
Wednesday, August 20
Won 64-32
N. Aspgren 11:1, D. Andersson 5:2, **Aldén 12**, Rosén 11:1, Bergström 6:1, Hagansbo 10:3, P. Aspgren 9:2.

ELDARNA (H)
Wednesday, August 27
Won 79-17
N. Aspgren 8:2, **Rosén 12, Aldén 10:5, Hagansbo 13:2, D. Andersson 15, F. Andersson 8:4, P. Aspgren 13:2.**
▲ *Niklas Aspgren finished third in Heat 7 (beaten by Tommie Lundgren) to wreck chances of a 16 Heat whitewash.*

STJÄRNORNA (A)
Wednesday, September 3
Won 50-46
N. Aspgren 11, F. Andersson 1:1, P. Aspgren 6:2, **Rosén 13:2**, D. Andersson 17, Karlsson 2, no rider at 7.
▲ *Victory meant Team Dalakraft had completed a 100% league record – but they had to survive a mighty scare to make it!*

DIVISION ONE

	M	W	D	L	PtsF	PtsA	Pts
TEAM DALAKRAFT	**18**	**18**	**0**	**0**	**1084**	**616**	**36**
Team Bikab	18	13	0	5	956	736	26
Njudungarna	18	13	0	5	924	800	26
Filyterna	18	11	0	7	958	730	22
Stjärnorna	18	9	0	9	897	776	18
Crossbone Pirates	18	7	0	11	783	924	14
Vikingarna	18	7	0	11	755	922	14
Gnistorna	18	6	0	12	786	903	12
Team Canvac	18	3	1	14	733	988	7
Eldarna	18	2	1	15	612	1093	5

Sebastian Aldén made six appearances for Team Dalakraft and dropped only four points to opponents – and all of those were in the one match, at home to Stjärnorna on Wednesday, July 2, when he scored eight points from four starts, including a tapes touching exclusion. The only rider to actually finish in front of him was Jonas Messing in Heat 12.

Rider	M	R	Pts	BP	TPts	Ave	F	P
Sebastian ALDÉN	6	27	66	11	77	11.41	1	4
Niklas ASPGREN	**18**	**86**	**220**	**14**	**234**	**10.88**	**5**	**2**
Dennis ANDERSSON	17	83	195	13	208	10.02	3	1
Anton ROSÈN	**17**	**80**	**182**	**18**	**200**	**10.00**	**1**	**2**
Andreas BERGSTRÖM	7	32	61	8	69	8.63	0	0
Ted HAGANSBO	**17**	**88**	**147**	**26**	**173**	**7.86**	**0**	**2**
Pontus ASPGREN	16	80	121	32	153	7.65	0	1
Fredrik ANDERSSON	**8**	**22**	**29**	**11**	**40**	**7.27**	**0**	**1**
Leif KARLSSON	7	33	42	7	49	5.94	0	0
Michael BERNTSSON	**3**	**12**	**7**	**1**	**8**	**2.67**	**0**	**0**
Robin RUNDBY	8	25	14	2	16	2.56	0	0

Did not ride: Fredrik ANDERSSON (1), Patrik BJÖRK (2).
Michael BERNTSSON (see also Gnistorna).

2008 PARTNER CLUB
MASARNAAVESTA (ElitSerien)

2009 PARTNER CLUB
MASARNA (AllSvenskan)

Division One

VIKINGARNA

2008 RESULTS

Final position..Seventh

CROSSBONE PIRATES (A)
Wednesday, April 30
Lost 43-51
Flood 10:1, Johansson 0, Eriksson 8, Ahlin 3, Rohlén 8, Claesson 5:3, Godlund 9:1.

FILBYTERNA (H)
Wednesday, May 7
Lost 38-58
Flood 5, Erikssson 3, Aronsson 4:1, Rohlén 7:1, H. **Gustafsson 15**, Johansson 0, Godlund 4.

GNISTORNA (H)
Wednesday, May 14
Won 53-43
Flood 8:2, Eriksson 9:3, Godlund 10, Ahlin 7:2, **Rohlén 15,** Janehult 4, Johansson 0.

TEAM BIKAB (A)
Wednesday, May 21
Lost 37-58
Flood 11:3, Janehult 0, Eriksson 3, Godlund 8, Rohlén 14, Jansson 0, Johansson 1.

TEAM DALAKRAFT (H)
Wednesday, May 28
Lost 32-64
Flood 8:1, Godlund 3:1, Eriksson 6, Ahlin 4:2, Rohlén 6, Janehult 5:1, Johansson 0.

ELDARNA (A)
Wednesday, June 4
Won 49-46
Flood 12, Janehult 2, **Eriksson 15**, Godlund 2:1, Rohlén 14, Jansson 1, Holm 3.

STJÄRNORNA (H)
Wednesday, June 11
Lost 26-28
Flood 6, Ahlin 4:1, Eriksson 3:2, Godlund 4, Rohlén 5, Claesson 3, Johansson 1.
● *Meeting abandoned after nine heats, result to stand.*

NJUDUNGARNA (A)
Wednesday, June 18
Lost 30-66
Flood 7, Godlund 1:1, Aronsson 5:2, Eriksson 3, Rohlén 11, Janehult 1, Claesson 2.

TRACK FILE

Track: Örebro Motostadion, Västra Vintergatan 112, 70344 Örebro, Sweden.

Telephone: 0046 019241001.

Website: www.vikingarna.se

Track Length: 289 metres.

Track Record: *Not available.*

SQUAD
Kenneth Adolfsson, Daniel Ahlin, Tomas Aronsson, Mickael Berntsson, Alexander Claesson, Dennis Ekstrand, Niklas Eriksson, Göran Flood, Freddy Godlund, Henrik Gustafsson, Simon Gustafsson, Anders Gustavsson, Sonny Holm, David Janehult, Rickard Jansson, Marcus Johansson, Tomas Karlsson, Pontus Nilsson, Patrik Olsson, David Rohlén, Magnus Zetterström.

TEAM CANVAC (H)
Wednesday, July 2
Won 61-35
Flood 8:1, Ahlin 6:4, Eriksson 10:2, Aronsson 7:2, Rohlén 11, Godlund 11:3, Claesson 8:3.

CROSSBONE PIRATES (H)
Wednesday, July 9
Lost 44-51
Flood 9:1, Godlund 4, Eriksson 6, Ahlin 4, Rohlén 8, Janehult 5:1, Claesson 8:2.

FILBYTERNA (A)
Wednesday, July 16
Won 51-45
Flood 9:2, Eriksson 7, Aronsson 5:2, Godlund 6:2, Rohlén 12, Janehult 1, Claesson 11:1.

GNISTORNA (A)
Wednesday, July 23
Won 50-45
Flood 9, Eriksson 7:3, Aronsson 9:2, Godlund 4:3, Rohlén 12, Johansson 0, Claesson 9.

TEAM BIKAB (H)
Wednesday, July 30
Lost 40-55
Claesson 8, Eriksson 6:1, Aronsson 7, Godlund 2:2, Rohlén 10, Johansson 4:1, Ekstrand 3:1.

TEAM DALAKRAFT (A)
Wednesday, August 6
Lost 22-74
Flood 5:1, Godlund 1, Eriksson 4, Ekstrand 1, Rohlén 8, Janehult 1, Johansson 2:1.

ELDARNA (H)
Wednesday, August 13
Won 52-44
Flood 6, Godlund 11:2, Eriksson 13:1, Claesson 3:1,

2009 Squad

Not competing in 2009 league racing.

Rohlén 15, Ekstrand 1, Johansson 3.

STJÄRNORNA (A)
Wednesday, August 20
Lost 27-67
Flood 7, Godlund 3:1, Eriksson 4, Ekstrand 1, Rohlén 9, Johansson 3, no rider at 7.

NJUDUNGARNA (H)
Wednesday, August 27
Lost 43-53
Flood 2, Godlund 8:2, Eriksson 10, Claesson 7:1, Rohlén 14:1, Johansson 0, Ekstrand 2.

TEAM CANVAC (A)
Wednesday, September 3
Won 57-39
Flood 8:2, Godlund 9:2, Eriksson 8:1, Claesson 8:2, **Rohlén 15**, Ekstrand 9:2, no rider at 7.

DIVISION ONE

	M	W	D	L	PtsF	PtsA	Pts
Team Dalakraft	18	18	0	0	1084	616	36
Team Bikab	18	13	0	5	956	736	26
Njudungarna	18	13	0	5	924	800	26
Filyterna	18	11	0	7	958	730	22
Stjärnorna	18	9	0	9	897	776	18
Crossbone Pirates	18	7	0	11	783	924	14
VIKINGARNA	**18**	**7**	**0**	**11**	**755**	**922**	**14**
Gnistorna	18	6	0	12	786	903	12
Team Canvac	18	3	1	14	733	988	7
Eldarna	18	2	1	15	612	1093	5

Did you know?

Vikingarna won seven of their 18 Division One matches but actually had a better away record with only three of those victories coming at their own Örebro track!
They were victorious against Eldarna, Filbyterna, Gnistorna and Team Canvac.

Rider	M	R	Pts	BP	TPts	Ave	F	P
Henrik GUSTAFSSON	1	5	15	0	15	12.00	1	0
David ROHLÉN	**18**	**92**	**194**	**2**	**196**	**8.52**	**2**	**0**
Tomas ARONSSON	6	26	37	9	46	7.08	0	0
Göran FLOOD	**17**	**84**	**130**	**14**	**144**	**6.86**	**1**	**0**
Alexander CLAESSON	11	50	72	13	85	6.80	0	0
Niklas ERIKSSON	**18**	**91**	**125**	**13**	**138**	**6.07**	**1**	**0**
Daniel AHLIN	6	26	28	9	37	5.69	0	0
Freddy GODLUND	**18**	**86**	**100**	**21**	**121**	**5.63**	**0**	**0**
David JANEHULT	8	25	19	2	21	3.36	0	0
Dennis EKSTRAND	**6**	**24**	**17**	**3**	**20**	**3.33**	**0**	**0**
Sonny HOLM	1	5	3	0	3	2.40	0	0
Marcus JOHANSSON	**12**	**33**	**14**	**2**	**16**	**1.94**	**0**	**0**
Rickard JANSSON	2	6	1	0	1	0.67	0	0

Niklas ERIKSSON (see also Team Canvac).

Division Two

TEAM HAGFORS

2009 PARTNER CLUBS
ELIT VETLANDA (EliteSerien)
VALSARNA (AllSvenskan)

AFTER their successful 2008 campaign in which they went through the entire Division Two season without being beaten, Valsarna's second team have moved up to Division One.

They will clearly call on the bulk of Valsarna's AllSvenskan side as they compete at a higher level.

Their stand-out star in a record breaking season was 17-year-old local discovery Anders Mellgren who was unbeaten by an opponent in all seven matches.

An accomplished ice hockey and bandy player – he was good enough at the latter to win representative honours – he was the 2007 FIM 80cc Youth Gold Trophy winner and has been named in ElitSerien Elit Vetlanda's 2009 squad.

He's expected to concentrate on his top-flight career but Hagfors fans will be hoping to see him again.

For Track File see VALSARNA.

2009 Squad

Sebastian **ALDÉN**, Andreas **ANDERSSON**, Robin **ASPEGREN**, Daniel **DAVIDSSON**, Robert **ERIKSSON**, Patrick **JARNSTAM**, Alexander **LILJEQVIST**, Mattias **PERSSON**, Jeremia **THELAUS**, Robin **TÖRNQVIST**, Per **WESTER**.

2008 PARTNER CLUB

INDIANERNA B
(Division Two)

DIVISION TWO STANDINGS

	M	1	2	3	4	5	RPts	Pts
1 TEAM HAGFORS	10	10	0	0	0	0	341	40
2 TEAM BIKAB	10	0	6	3	1	0	272+2	25
3 STOCKHOLM ROCKETS	10	0	3	4	1	1	212+5	18
4 LOTSARNA	10	2	1	1	4	2	231+2	17
5 INDIANERNA	10	0	2	2	3	3	204	13
6 JÄMTARNA	10	0	0	2	3	5	152	7

[Scoring: 4-3-2-1-0].

2008 RESULTS

Östersund, Saturday, May 31
1 TEAM HAGFORS 42+3 (**Anders Mellgren 17:4+3**, Mattias Persson 9:1, Dan Kjellberg 16:1), **2 TEAM BIKAB 42+2** (Henrik Karlsson 17+2, Daniel Henderson 16:3, Rasmus Eklöf 9:3), **3 JÄMTARNA 22** (Lars Dannö 9, Mattias Gudmundsson 9:1, Sonny Gudmundsson 2:1, Tim Gudmundsson 2), **4 LOTSARNA 14** (David Adiels 3:1, Kim Johansson 9, Mats Andersson 2). **STOCKHOLM ROCKETS** did not compete.
▼ *Dan Kjellberg broke Fredrik Lindgren's 2005 track record in Heat 1.*

Eskilstuna, Saturday, June 7
1 TEAM HAGFORS 36 (**Anders Mellgren 10:2**, **Robin Törnqvist 10:2**, Mattias Persson 4:2, **Robin Bergqvist 12**), **2 INDIANERNA 28** (Alexander Edberg 15, Sonny Holm 10:1, Marcus Johansson 3:2), **3 TEAM BIKAB 26** (Daniel Henderson 13:1, Rasmus Eklöf 2:1, Andre Hertzberg 11:2), **4 LOTSARNA 20** (David Adiels 8:1, Kim Johansson 1, Sven Näreby 6:1, Albin Näreby 5:1), **5 JÄMTARNA 9** (Lars Dannö 3, Mattias Gudmundsson 3, Per Lindgren 2, Sonny Gudmundsson 1).

Huddinge, Saturday, June 14
1 LOTSARNA 37 (Kim Johansson 11:3, **Robin Bergkvist 18**, Niklas Larsson 8:2), **2 INDIANERNA 29** (David Rohlen 13:2, Freddy Godlund 10:1, Alexander Claesson 6:3), **3 TEAM BIKAB 26** (Daniel Henderson 17, Andre Hertzberg 5, Peter Wall 4:2), **4 JÄMTARNA 16** (Mattias Gudmundsson 6, Lars Dannö 5, Tim Gudmundsson 3, Sonny Gudmundsson 2:2), **5 STOCKHOLM ROCKETS 12** (Tommie Lundgren 5, Stefan Brolin 5, Jimmy Hyll 2:1).

Kumla, Saturday, July 5
1 TEAM HAGFORS 40 (Robin Bergqvist 14, **Anders Mellgren 12:3**, **Mattias Persson 8:4**, **Robert Eriksson 6**), **2 LOTSARNA 28** (Kim Johansson 10:3, David Adiels 8:3, Niklas Larsson 10), **3 STOCKHOLM ROCKETS 25** (Linus Jansson 14:2, David Hillborg 10, Peter Wall 1), **4 JÄMTARNA 16** (Mattias Gudmundsson 6, Lars Dannö 5:1, Tim Gudmundsson 4, Sonny Gudmundsson 1), **5 INDIANERNA 11** (David Janehult 6, Marcus Johansson 4, Emil Aronsson 1:1, Dennis Ekstrand 0).

Hagfors, Sunday, July 6
1 TEAM HAGFORS 33 (**Anders Mellgren 17:1**, Robin Bergqvist 13:2, Mattias Persson 3:1), **2 TEAM BIKAB 29** (Henrik Karlsson 16, Alexander Edberg 11:3, Rasmus Eklöf 2:1), **3 STOCKHOLM ROCKETS 25** (Linus Jansson
Västervik, Saturday, September 13
6, David Hillborg 6, Peter Wall 6:3, Niklas Larsson 7), **4 INDIANERNA 21** (Freddy Godlund 6:1, Marcus Johansson 2, Jeremia Thelaus 13), **5 JÄMTARNA 12** (Lars Dannö 6, Mattias Gudmundsson 4, Tim Gudmundsson 1:1, Sonny Gudmundsson 1:1).

Västervik, Saturday, July 12
1 TEAM HAGFORS 31 (Jeremiah Thelaus 11:2, Robin Bergqvist 13:1, Mattias Persson 7:2), **2 STOCKHOLM ROCKETS 28** (Jens Oskarsson 5:3, David Hillborg 12:1, Peter Wall 11:1), **3 INDIANERNA 22** (**David Rohlén 18**, Marcus Johansson 0, Dennis Ekstrand 4), **4 TEAM BIKAB 20** (Henrik Karlsson 10, Rasmus Eklöf 7:1, Stefan Wallin 3:1), **5 LOTSARNA 19** (Kim Johansson 11, Niklas Larsson 7:1, Mats Andersson 1).

Hagfors, Saturday, July 26
1 TEAM HAGFORS 28 (**Robin Törnqvist 9**, Robin Bergqvist 9:2, Mattias Persson 2:1, **Anders Mellgren 8:1**), **2 TEAM BIKAB 21** (Daniel Henderson 7, (Henrik Karlsson 9, Alexander Edberg 5:3), **3 LOTSARNA 20** (Niklas Larsson 6, Peter Wall 6:1, Jens Oskarsson 8:1), **4 INDIANERNA 14** (Jeremiah Thelaus 10, Dennis Ekstrand 2:1, Mikael Renner 2), **5 JÄMTARNA 13** (Mattias Gudmundsson 7, Lars Dannö 4, Tim Gudmundsson 2:2).
● *Meeting abandoned after Heat 17 following crash involving Daniel Henderson. Result to stand.*

Östersund, Saturday, August 2
1 TEAM HAGFORS 32 (**Robin Törnqvist 16:2**, Robin Bergqvist 14:1, Sonny Gudmundsson 2), **2 TEAM BIKAB 23** (Alexander Edberg 8, Rasmus Eklöf 6:3, David Hillborg 9:1), **3 JÄMTARNA 22** (Mattias Gudmundsson 12, Lars Dannö 6, Tim Gudmundsson 4:2), **4 STOCKHOLM ROCKETS 21** (Linus Jansson 8, Robin Burestad 7, Peter Wall 6:1), **5 INDIANERNA 20** (Freddy Godlund 13, Marcus Johansson 3:2, Dennis Ekstrand 4:1).

Eskilstuna, Saturday, August 23
1 TEAM HAGFORS 32 (Robin Bergqvist 9, Anders Mellgren 11:1, Robin Törnqvist 8:1, Mattias Persson 4:1), **2 TEAM BIKAB 31** (Daniel Henderson 7:1, Henrik Karlsson 9:2, Alexander Edberg 11:1, Rasmus Eklöf 4), **3 STOCKHOLM ROCKETS 25** (Linus Jansson 9:3, David Hillborg 10, Peter Wall 6), **4 LOTSARNA 22** (Niklas Larsson 7:2, Kim Johansson 7:2, Jens Oskarsson 8), **5 JÄMTARNA 10** (Mattias Gudmundsson 1, Lars Dannö 1, Sonny Gudmundsson 3, Tim Gudmundsson 5:1).

1 LOTSARNA 31 (Robin Bergkvist 18, Niklas Larsson 9:1, Kim Johansson 4:2, David Eilersen, did not ride), **2 STOCKHOLM ROCKETS 30** (David Hillborg 13:2, Jens Oskarsson 6:2, Peter Wall 11), **3 TEAM BIKAB 29** (Alexander Edberg 10:2, Linus Eklöf 16, Rasmus Eklöf 3:1), **4 INDIANERNA 19** (Alexander Claesson 12, Dennis Ekstrand 5:1, Marcus Johansson 2:2), **5 JÄMTARNA 11** (Mattias Gudmundsson 3, Tim Gudmundsson 5, Sonny Gudmundsson 3).

Kumla, Saturday, September 20

1 TEAM HAGFORS 33 (Robin Bergqvist 13:2, Robin Törnqvist 16:1, Mattias Persson 4:1), **2 TEAM BIKAB 25** (Alexander Edberg 17, Andre Hertzberg 7, Rasmus Eklöf 1), **3 STOCKHOLM ROCKETS 22+3** (David Hillborg 8:1+3, Andreas Westlund 5, Robin Burestad 9), **4 LOTSARNA 22+2** (Niklas Larsson 9:1+2, Kim Johansson 4:1, Jens Oskarsson 9), **5 INDIANERNA 18** (Alexander Claesson 6, Freddy Godlund 7, Dennis Ekstrand 1, Marcus Johansson 4).

Huddinge, Sunday, September 21

1 TEAM HAGFORS 34 (Anders Mellgren 14:1, Robin Bergqvist 15:2, Andre Hertzberg 5:2), **2 STOCKHOLM ROCKETS 24** (David Hillborg 7:1, Andreas Westlund 14:1, Robin Burestad 3), **3 INDIANERNA 22** David Rohlén 16, Dennis Ekstrand 1:1, Mikael Renner 5), **4 JÄMTARNA 21** (Robin Messing 5:2, Jimmy Hyll 3:2, Jens Oskarsson 13), **5 LOTSARNA 18** (Niklas Larsson 13, Kim Johansson 5:2).

Roll of Honour

1999	PIRATERNA
2001 N	KAVALJERERNA
2001 S	DUNUNGARNA
2002 E	SJÖRÖVARNA
2002 W	TEAM HAGFORS
2002 S	DUNUNGARNA
2003 A	FILBYTERNA
2003 S	GISLAVED
2003 E	STJÄRNORNA
2003 W	FALKARNA
2004 N	ELDARNA
2004 S	DACKARNA
2004 E	HUSARERNA
2004 W	TEAM HAGFORS
2005 S	GISLAVED
2005 E	ILVARNA
2005 W	FALKARNA
2006 N	TEAM BIKAB
2006 S	GISLAVED
2007 N	AVESTA
2007 S	NJUDUNGARNA
2008	TEAM HAGFORS

2008 TEAMS

The Division Two league programme was run over 12 rounds with five teams per round.

Stockholm Rockets did not contest the first round and were accordingly placed fifth in the meeting.

Kaparna's second side Gastarna were going to compete in the League, racing their home meeting at Kumla, but withdrew when the parent club hit financial problems.

Team Hagfors replaced them and went on to win all 10 rounds.

TEAM BIKAB B
For Track Data see Smederna, Division One.
Partner club: *Vikingarna (Division One).*

TEAM HAGFORS
For Track Data see Valsarna, AllSvenskan League.
Partner clubs: *Team Bikab (Elitserien), Valsarna (AllSvenskan League).*

INDIANERNA II
For Track Data see Indianerna, Elitserien.
Partner club: *Vikingarna (Division One).*

LOTSARNA (Gothenburg Speedway Klubb)
Address: c/o Lars Angbom, Hagensväg 8, 443 74 Sjövik, Sweden.
Tel: 0046 0706 330044.
Website: www.goteborgspeedwayklubb.se
Partner club: *Nässjo.*
● *Lotsarna was a new team run by Gothenburg Speedway Klubb (formed in 2007) which had no connection with the other club in the city who have raced for many years as Kaparna. They did not have a home track and raced both their rounds at Västervik.*

JÄMTARNA (Jämtlands MK)
Track: Östersunds Motorstadion (Lukashov), Skolgatan 39, 83145 Östersund, Sweden.
Tel: 0046 06333121.
Website: www.jmk.nu
Track Length: 325 metres.
Track Record: 65.2 secs, Dan Kjellberg, May 31, 2008.
Partner club: *None.*

STOCKHOLM ROCKETS
For Track Data see Eldarna, Division One.
Partner club: *Eldarna (Division One).*

OTHER CLUBS

BOHUSLÄNS SPEEDWAY KLUBB
Korparna
Track: New stadium planned.
Tel: 0046 0521256122.
Website: www.korparna.nu

GOTLANDS MF:S SPEEDWAY KLUBB
Bysarna
Track: Gotlands Motorstadion, Box 1035, 62121 Visby, Sweden.
Tel: 0046 0498216780.
Website: www.bysarna.com
Track Length: 297 metres.

LINDE MOTORSPORTKLUBB
Lindarna
Track: Motorbanan Hagalund, Box 80, 71122 Lindesberg, Sweden.
Tel: 0046 058115258.
Website: www.lindarnaspeedway.com
Track Length: 304 metres.
● *Staged training sessions and several veterans' meetings in 2008.*

NÄSSJÖ SPEEDWAYKLUBB
Nässjö
Track: Motorstadion, Skogsvallen, 57141 Nässjö, Sweden.
Tel: 0046 038074765.
Website: www.nassjospeedway.se
Track Length: 290 metres.
● *Staged meetings on their 80cc track and originally expected to host two of Lotsarna's Divisiuon Two matches.*

SMK GÄVLE
Gävle
Track: Gävle Motorstadion, Box 1066, 81821 Valbo, Sweden.
Tel: 0046 026643540.
Website: www.smkgavle.nu
Track Length: 285 metres.
● *Staged two of Stjärnorna's Division One matches in 2008.*

FINAL DIVISION TWO AVERAGES

Rider	Team	M	R	Pts	BP	TPts	Ave	F	P
Anders MELLGREN	Team Hagfors	7	35	92	13	105	12.00	0	7
Robert ERIKSSON	**Team Hagfors**	**1**	**2**	**6**	**0**	**6**	**12.00**	**1**	**0**
Robin TÖRNQVIST	Team Hagfors	5	23	59	6	65	11.30	1	2
David ROHLÉN	**Indianerna**	**3**	**18**	**47**	**2**	**49**	**10.89**	**1**	**0**
Linus EKLÖF	Team Bikab	1	6	16	0	16	10.67	0	0
Robin BERGQVIST	**Team Hagfors**	**9**	**46**	**112**	**10**	**122**	**10.61**	**1**	**1**
Daniel HENDERSON	Team Bikab	5	27	60	5	65	9.63	0	0
Henrik KARLSSON	**Team Bikab**	**5**	**28**	**63**	**2**	**65**	**9.29**	**0**	**0**
Alexander EDBERG	Team Bikab	6	33	62	9	71	8.61	0	0
Alexander CLAESSON	**Indianerna**	**3**	**14**	**24**	**3**	**27**	**7.71**	**0**	**0**
Sonny HOLM	Indianerna	1	6	10	1	11	7.33	0	0
Freddy GODLUND	**Indianerna**	**4**	**22**	**36**	**2**	**38**	**6.91**	**0**	**0**
Mattias PERSSON	Team Hagfors	8	36	41	13	54	6.00	0	1
Mattias GUDMUNDSSON	**Jämtarna**	**9**	**40**	**51**	**1**	**52**	**5.20**	**0**	**0**
Tommi LUNDGREN	Stockholm Rockets	1	4	5	0	5	5.00	0	0
David JANEHULT	**Indianerna**	**1**	**5**	**6**	**0**	**6**	**4.80**	**0**	**0**
Rasmus EKLÖF	Team Bikab	8	38	34	10	44	4.63	0	0
Lars DANNÖ	**Jämtarna**	**8**	**36**	**39**	**1**	**40**	**4.44**	**0**	**0**
Stefan WALLIN	Team Bikab	1	4	3	1	4	4.00	0	0
Tim GUDMUNDSSON	**Jämtarna**	**8**	**35**	**26**	**5**	**31**	**3.54**	**0**	**0**
Stefan BROLIN	Stockholm Rockets	1	6	5	0	5	3.33	0	0
Dennis EKSTRAND	**Indianerna**	**7**	**29**	**17**	**4**	**21**	**2.90**	**0**	**0**
Marcus JOHANSSON	Indianerna	7	34	18	6	24	2.82	0	0
Andre HERTZBERG	**Team Bikab**	**3**	**21**	**23**	**2**	**25**	**2.76**	**0**	**0**
Sonny GUDMUNDSSON	Jämtarna	7	29	13	4	17	2.34	0	0
Jimmy HYLL	**Stockholm Rockets**	**1**	**6**	**2**	**1**	**3**	**2.00**	**0**	**0**
Per LINDGREN	Jämtarna	1	4	2	0	2	2.00	0	0
Emil ARONSSON	**Indianerna**	**1**	**4**	**1**	**1**	**2**	**2.00**	**0**	**0**
Guests									
Robin BERGQVIST	**Lotsarna**	**2**	**12**	**36**	**0**	**36**	**12.00**	**2**	**0**
Dan KJELLBERG	Team Hagfors	1	6	16	1	17	11.33	0	0
Alexander EDBERG	**Indianerna**	**1**	**6**	**15**	**0**	**15**	**10.00**	**0**	**0**
David HILLBORG	Team Bikab	1	4	9	1	10	10.00	0	0
Linus JANSSON	**Stockholm Rockets**	**4**	**18**	**37**	**5**	**42**	**9.33**	**0**	**0**
Jens OSKARSSON	Jämtarna	1	6	13	0	13	8.67	0	0
Jeremia THELAUS	**Team Hagfors**	**1**	**6**	**11**	**2**	**13**	**8.67**	**0**	**0**
David HILLBORG	Stockholm Rockets	7	39	69	5	74	7.59	0	0
Niklas LARSSON	**Stockholm Rockets**	**1**	**5**	**9**	**0**	**9**	**7.30**	**0**	**0**
Niklas LARSSON	Lotsarna	8	43	71	7	78	7.26	0	0
Sven NÅREBY	**Lotsarna**	**1**	**4**	**6**	**1**	**7**	**7.00**	**0**	**0**
Peter WALL	Lotsarna	1	4	6	1	7	7.00	0	0
Andreas WESTLUND	**Stockholm Rockets**	**2**	**12**	**19**	**1**	**20**	**6.67**	**0**	**0**
Jens OSKARSSON	Lotsarna	3	16	25	1	26	6.50	0	0
Peter WALL	**Stockholm Rockets**	**6**	**29**	**41**	**5**	**46**	**6.34**	**0**	**0**
Robin BURESTAD	Stockholm Rockets	3	12	19	0	19	6.33	0	0
Kim JOHANSSON	**Lotsarna**	**9**	**49**	**62**	**13**	**75**	**6.12**	**0**	**0**
Albin NÅREBY	Lotsarna	1	4	5	1	6	6.00	0	0
Peter WALL	**Team Bikab**	**1**	**4**	**4**	**2**	**6**	**6.00**	**0**	**0**
Jens OSKARSSON	Stockholm Rockets	2	11	11	5	16	5.82	0	0
Andre HERTZBERG	**Team Hagfors**	**1**	**5**	**5**	**2**	**7**	**5.60**	**0**	**0**
Robin MESSING	Jämtarna	1	5	5	2	7	5.60	0	0
Jimmy HYLL	**Jämtarna**	**1**	**5**	**3**	**2**	**5**	**4.00**	**0**	**0**
Mikael RENNER	Indianerna	2	9	7	0	7	3.11	0	0
Sonny GUDMUNDSSON	**Team Hagfors**	**1**	**4**	**2**	**0**	**2**	**2.00**	**0**	**0**
Guests (combined average)									
David HILLBORG		**8**	**43**	**78**	**6**	**84**	**7.81**	**0**	**0**
Niklas LARSSON		9	48	80	7	87	7.25	0	0
Jens OSKARSSON		**6**	**33**	**49**	**6**	**55**	**6.67**	**0**	**0**
Peter WALL		8	37	51	8	59	6.38	0	0

■ *Statistics include race-off rides and points to determine final round placings.*

UKRAINE

UKRAINE CHAMPIONSHIP

FINAL

Chervonograd, Saturday, May 17

	1	2	3	4	5	Tot	RO
1 Aleksandr LOKTAYEV	**3**	**2**	**2**	**3**	**3**	**13**	
2 Aleksandr BORODAJ	3	3	2	2	2	12	
3 Jaroslav POLIUCHOVIC	3	3	3	2	F	11	3
4 Andrey SINKOVSKY	2	3	3	3	FX	11	F
5 Oleg MIENCZUK	E	2	3	3	3	11	N
6 Vladimir TEJGAL	2	3	2	0	3	10	
7 Vladimir TROFIMOV	3	1	2	1	3	10	
8 Michail ONESHKO	1	1	3	1	1	7	
9 Vladimir KOLODY (jun)	0	2	1	2	2	7	
10 Stanislav OGORODNIK	2	2	0	2	1	7	
11 Petr FEDYK	2	1	3	R		6	
12 Vladimir OMELIAN	1	1	FX	1	2	5	
13 Sergey BORISENKO	1	1	1	1	R	4	
14 Pavel MOSKOVCZENKO	1	0	FX	0	2	3	
15 Pavel KOTOVCZENKO	0	1	0	F		1	
16 Aleksandr GAJKOVSKY	F	0	0	1	F	1	
17 Nikolai MIRONOV	0	0				0	
17 Oleg DOSAJEV	0					0	
17 Andrey KRIUCZKOV	FX					0	

Roll of Honour

1961 .... Viktor TROFIMOV
1962 .... Boris SAVOJSKI
1963 .... Afansi KOWALCZUK
1964 .... Viktor TROFIMOV
1965 .... Viktor TROFIMOV
1966 .... Viktor TROFIMOV
1967 .... Sergey LYATOSINSKI
1968 .... A. RAJEWSKI
1969 .... Viktor TROFIMOV
1970 .... Grigori KHLINOVSKI
1971 .... O. MISZUROV
1972 .... Oleg DZIADYK
1973 .... Boris KOPYLOV
1974 .... Anatoli MIRONOV
1975 .... Anatoli MIRONOV
1976 .... Vladimir ROZANCZUK
1977 .... Anatoli MIRONOV
1978 .... Anatolj FROLOV
1979 .... Grigori KHLINOVSKI
1980 .... Anatoli FROLOV
1981 .... Anatoli MIRONOV
1982 .... Vladimir TROFIMOV
1983 .... Aleksandr KLIMANTOV
1984 .... Viktor KUZNETSOV
1985 .... Viktor KUZNETSOV
1986 .... Anatoli ZABCZIK
1987 .... Aleksandr KOSTENKO
1988 .... Igor ZWIERIEV
1989 .... Vladimir TROFIMOV
1990 .... Flur KALIMULIN
1991 .... Vladimir KOLODY (sen)
1992 .... Vladimir TROFIMOV
1993 .... Igor MARKO
1994 .... Vladimir KOLODY (sen)
1995 .... Vladimir KOLODY (sen)
1996 .... Igor MARKO
1997 .... Aleksandr LYATOSINSKI
1998 .... Aleksandr LYATOSINSKI
2000 .... Aleksandr LYATOSINSKI
2001 .... Igor MARKO
2002 .... Aleksandr LYATOSINSKI
2003 .... Aleksandr LYATOSINSKI
2004 .... Vladimir LYATOSINSKI
2005 .... Andrey KARPOV
2006 .... Igor MARKO
2007 .... Jaroslav POLIUCHOVIC
2008 .... Aleksandr LOKTAYEV

UKRAINE UNDER 21 CHAMPIONSHIP

FINAL

Rivne, Saturday, May 24

	1	2	3	4	Tot	RO
1 KIRIL CUKANOV	**3**	**3**	**3**	**3**	**12**	
2 Stanislav OGORODNIK	2	3	3	3	11	
3 Maciej MICHALUK	2	2	2	3	9	
4 Vladimir KOLODY (jun)	FX	2	3	3	8	
5 Vladimir OMELIAN	3	F	3	2	8	
6 Michail ONESHKO	1	3	2	2	8	
7 Sergey BORISENKO	2	2	1	1	6	
8 Evgeni MITROFANOV	2	FX	0	2	4	
9 Andrey MUDRAK	0	2	1	0	3	
10 Aleksandr GAJKOVSKY	1	1	N	1	3	
11 Vladimir TEJGAL	FX				0	

Roll of Honour

1986 .... Aleksandr KRISZTAL
1987 .... Konstantin SVINKIN
1990 .... Ruzil VALIYEV
1991 .... Igor GLAVINSKI
1994 .... Petr VELESYK
1995 .... Petr VELESYK
1996 .... Petr VELESYK
2001 .... Sergey SENKO
2002 .... Sergey SENKO
2003 .... Sergey SENKO
2004 .... Sergey SENKO
2005 .... Sergey SENKO
2006 .... Andrey KARPOV
2007 .... Jaroslav POLIUCHOVIC
2008 .... Kiril CUKANOV

Plans for a 2009 Ukraine League were announced towards the end of 2008 and four teams will compete in the inaugural championship, including two independent clubs based at the Rivne track.

In 2008, Rivne competed in the Polish League and Chervonograd raced in the Russian League but both will have teams in the new league – the second time in six years that the authorities have tried to launch an internal league competition.

Two teams from Rivne (Cascade and Equal Trofimov SK) will take part along with SK Lviv and Shahkter Chervonograd while Cascade Rivne were refused a licence to compete in the Polish Second League.

Russian League

CHERVONOGRAD

2008 RESULTS

Final position ....Fourth

TOGLIATTI (H)
Thursday, April 17
Won 51-39
Chrzanowski 9, Tejgal 0, Gatiyatov 7:3, Dubinin 7, Borodaj 3, Kobrin 1:1, Karpov 12:1, **Zetterström 12**.

SALAVAT (H)
Thursday, April 24
Won 53-37
Chrzanowski 8:2, Tejgal 1, Gatiyatov 9:1, Dubinin 8:1, Borodaj 0, Kobrin 2:1, Karpov 14, Zetterström 11.

VLADIVOSTOK (A)
Thursday, July 24
Lost 30-60
Jablonski 8, Izotov 1:1, Dubinin 6, Gatiyatov 4:1, Borodaj 1:1, Cukanov 2, Karpov 2, Chrzanowski 6:1.

TOGLIATTI (A)
Wednesday, July 30
Lost 44-46
Jablonski 7:1, Izotov 1, Dubinin 7:1. Gatiyatov 7, Borodaj 0, Cukanov 0, Karpov 13, Chrzanowski 9.

BALAKOVO (A)
Thursday, July 31
Lost 29-60
Jablonski 7, Cukanov 0, Dubinin 1, Gatiyatov 2:1, Borodaj 2:1, Izotov 1:1, Karpov 7, Chrzanowski 9.

Magnus Zetterström was an everpresent in Chervonograd's four Russian League home matches.

TRACK FILE

Website: www.speedway.chervonograd.com

SQUAD
Sergey Borisenko, Aleksandra Borodaj, Kiril Cukanov, Vladimir Dubinin, Alexander Gajkovsky, Ruslan Gatiyatov, Aleksey Guzajev, Aleksey Izotov, Andrey Karpov, Andrey Kobrin, Vladimir Kolody, Stanislav Ogorodnik, Jaroslav Poliuchovic, Vladimir Tejgal, Vladimir Trofimov,
Foreign: Tomasz Chrzanowski, Matej Ferjan, Krzysztof Jablonski, Magnus Zetterström.

VLADIVOSTOK (H)
Thursday, September 4
Drew 45-45
Ferjan 11:1, Izotov 0, Gatiyatov 4:1, Dubinin 3, Borodaj, did not ride, Cukanov 2:1, Karpov 12, Zetterström 13:1.

SALAVAT (A)
Friday, September 19
Lost 28-62
Guzajev 0, Izotov 1, Dubinin 3:1, Gatiyatov 9, Borodaj 0, Cukanov 4:3, Tejgal 1:1, Karpov 10.

BALAKOVO (H)
Thursday, October 9
Won 48-42
Jablonski 12, Izotov 2:1, Dubinin 5:2, Paluchovich 1, Gatiyatov 7:1, Cukanov 3, Karpov 8, Zetterström 10:3.

RUSSIAN LEAGUE

	M	W	D	L	Pts
Togliatti	8	6	0	2	12
Vladivostok	8	5	1	2	11
Balakovo	8	4	0	4	8
CHERVONOGRAD	**8**	**3**	**1**	**4**	**7**
Salavat	8	2	1	0	2

Rider	M	R	Pts	BP	TPts	Ave	F	P
Magnus ZETTERSTRÖM	4	18	46	4	50	11.11	1	0
Matej FERJAN	**1**	**5**	**11**	**1**	**12**	**9.60**	**0**	**0**
Andrey KARPOV	8	41	78	1	79	7.71	0	0
Tomasz CHRZANOWSKI	**5**	**23**	**41**	**3**	**44**	**7.65**	**0**	**0**
Krzysztof JABLONSKI	4	20	34	1	35	7.00	0	0
Ruslan GATIYATOV	**8**	**39**	**49**	**8**	**57**	**6.00**	**0**	**0**
Vladimir DUBININ	8	33	40	4	44	5.33	0	0
Aleksandr BORODAJ	**6**	**9**	**6**	**2**	**8**	**3.56**	**0**	**0**
Kiril CUKANOV	6	18	11	4	15	3.33	0	0
Andrey KOBRIN	**2**	**6**	**3**	**2**	**5**	**3.33**	**0**	**0**
Aleksey IZOTOV	6	16	6	3	9	2.25	0	0
Jaroslav POLIUCHOVIC	**1**	**2**	**1**	**0**	**1**	**2.00**	**0**	**0**
Aleksey GUZAJEV	1	3	0	0	0	0.00	0	0
Vladimir TEJGAL	**3**	**8**	**2**	**1**	**3**	**1.50**	**0**	**0**

Individual

IGOR MARKO MEMORIAL TROPHY

Tuesday, October 14 1 Andrey Karpov 13+3, 2 Grzegorz Zengota 12+2, 3 Ilya Bondarenko 10+1, 4 Mariusz Puszakowski 9+3+0, 5 Kjastas Puodzhuks 9+2, 6 Piotr Dym 9+1, 7 Matej Kus 8, 8 Vladimir Dubinin 8, 9 Ruslan Gatiyatov 8, 10 Pawel Miesiac 7, 11 Pawel Staszek 6, 12 Ronnie Jamrozy 6, 13 Jaroslaw Paluchowicz 5, 14 Aleskey Izotov 4, 15 Andrey Kobrin 3, 16 Marat Gatiyatov 3.

Polish Second League

RIVNE

2008 RESULTS

Polish Second League

Final position..Third

OPOLE (A)
Sunday, April 6
Lost 42-51
Frankow 17 (6), no rider at two, Kolody [sen] 1, Filinov 8:1, Nigmatzyanov 6, Kolody [jun], did not ride, Kus 7:2, Michaluk 3.

LODZ (A)
Sunday, April 20
Lost 23-59
Frankow 1:1, Kolody [sen], did not ride, Guzajev 5, Stachowiak 0, Kolody [jun] 0, Kus 16:1 (4), Michaluk 1.

■ *Kosolapkin scored seven points but they were deducted from the final result after his machine was taken from the pits without the referee's permission.*

MISKOLC (H)
Sunday, May 4
Won 48-38
Frankow 11, Kolody [sen] 5, Filinov 0, Nigmatzyanov 10, Ivanov 10:2, Kolody [jun] 1, Kus 11:2, Michaluk, did not ride.

GNIEZNO (A)
Sunday, May 11
Lost 44-49
Frankow 11:1, Les 0, Kharchenko 4:2, Guzajev 6:1, Ivanov 4:1, Michaluk 1, Kus 18 (6).

KROSNO (H)
Sunday, June 1
Won 56-36
Frankow 11, Kolody [sen] 4, Czerwinski 12, Guzajev 7:1, Kosolapkin 10, Kolody [jun] 2:1, Kus 10:2, Michaluk, did not ride.

KROSNO (A)
Sunday, June 8
Won 50-40
Frankow 12, Kosolapkin 1, Nigmatzyanov 8:1, Bondarenko 10:2, Czerwinski 6, Michaluk 1, Kus 12.
Aggregate: Won 106-76.

Rivne is also sometimes referred to as Rovno and either name is correct.

● *For details of their proposed 2009 Polish Second League squad see page 543.*

TRACK FILE

Track: u. Kurchatov 3, Rivne, Ukraine.

Website: www.speedway-radiorivne.com.ua

SQUAD
Kiril Cukanov, Vladimir Kolody (sen), Vladimir Kolody (jun), Alexander Kosolapkin, Vladimir Omelian.
Foreign: Ilya Bondarenko, Zbigniew Czerwinski, Mariusz Frankow, Kiril Filinov, Alexey Guzajev, Roman Ivanov, Aleksey Kharchenko, Matej Kus, Marcin Les, Maciej Michaluk, Lenar Nigmatzyanov, Damian Stachowiak, Rafal Szombierski.

GNIEZNO (H)
Tuesday, July 22
Won 46-44
Frankow 9:1, Kolody [jun] 5, Czerwinski 13, Bondarenko 3, Szombierski 4, Omelian 0, Kus 12.
Aggregate: Lost 90-93.

LODZ (H)
Sunday, July 27
Won 61-30
Frankow 8:3, Filinov 7:1, **Czerwinski 14:1**, Nigmatzyanov 6:1, **Szombierski 12:3**, Kus 12, Omelian 2.
Aggregate: Lost 84-89.

MISKOLC (A)
Thursday, July 31
Lost 40-50
Frankow 7:1, Guzajev 0, Czerwinski 12 (0), Nigmatzyanov 6, Szombierski 2, Kolody [jun] 0, Kus 13.
Aggregate: Drew 88-88.

OPOLE (H)
Sunday, August 10
Won 57-35
Frankow 12, **Kolody [sen] 11:4**, Czerwinski 9, Guzajev 1, Szombierski 7:1, Omelian, did not ride, **Kus 15**, Cukanov 2.
Aggregate: Won 99-86.

Play-offs

GNIEZNO (H)
Sunday, August 24
Lost 31-60
Frankow 10 (4), Nigmatzyanov 2:1, Czerwinski 0, Filinov 8, Ivanov 9, Cukanov 2, Kolody [jun] 0.

LODZ (A)
Sunday, August 31
Won 45-44
Frankow 11, Nigmatzyanov 1, Filinov 11:1, Szombierski 5:1, Czerwinski 12, Michaluk 1:1, Kosolapkin 4.

MISKOLC (A)
Sunday, September 7
Lost 25-65
Frankow 10, Kharchenko 6, Czerwinski 7, Szombierski 1, *rider replacement for Kus*, Michaluk 0, Cukanov 1.

Rider	M	R	Pts	BP	TPts	Ave	F	P	TR	TPts
Matej KUS	11	59	140	8	148	10.03	1	1	2	5
Mariusz FRANKOW	**15**	**74**	**155**	**10**	**165**	**8.92**	**0**	**1**	**2**	**5**
Zbigniew CZERWINSKI	1	53	113	3	116	8.75	0	3	1	0
Vladimir KOLODY [sen]	**4**	**15**	**21**	**5**	**26**	**6.93**	**0**	**1**	**0**	**0**
Roman IVANOV	4	21	33	3	36	6.86	0	0	0	0
Kiril FILINOV	**6**	**28**	**43**	**4**	**47**	**6.71**	**0**	**0**	**0**	**0**
Ilya BONDARENKO	3	15	20	3	23	6.13	0	0	0	0
Rafal SZOMBIERSKI	**6**	**27**	**31**	**6**	**37**	**5.48**	**0**	**1**	**0**	**0**
Aleksey KHARCHENKO	3	14	16	2	18	5.14	0	0	0	0
Lenar NIGMATZYANOV	**7**	**34**	**39**	**3**	**42**	**4.94**	**0**	**0**	**0**	**0**
Aleksey GUZAYEV	5	20	18	3	21	4.20	0	0	0	0
Aleksandr KOSOLAPKIN	**4**	**15**	**15**	**0**	**15**	**4.00**	**0**	**0**	**0**	**0**
Vladimir KOLODY [jun]	7	18	9	1	10	2.22	0	0	0	0
Maciej MICHALUK	**6**	**18**	**7**	**1**	**8**	**1.78**	**0**	**0**	**0**	**0**
Kiril CUKANOV	5	18	6	0	6	1.33	0	0	0	0
Vladimir OMELIAN	**4**	**8**	**2**	**0**	**2**	**1.00**	**0**	**0**	**0**	**0**
Damian STACHOWIAK	1	3	0	0	0	0.00	0	0	0	0
Marcin LES	**1**	**4**	**0**	**0**	**0**	**0.00**	**0**	**0**	**0**	**0**

MISKOLC (H)
Thursday, September 25
Won 48-42
Frankow 11:2, **Czerwinski 14:1**, Kharchenko 5:1, Bondarenko 7:1, Ivanov 10, Cukanov 1.
Aggregate: Lost 73-107.

GNIEZNO (A)
Sunday, September 28
Lost 0-40 (awarded).
Aggregate: Lost 31-100.

LODZ (H)
Thursday, October 9
Won 52-38
Frankow 14:1, Omelian 0, Filinov 9:1, no rider at four, **Czerwinski 14:1**, Cukanov 0, **Kus 14:1**, Kolody [jun] 1.
Aggregate: Won 97-82.

SECOND LEAGUE (after play-offs)

	M	W	D	L	BP	Pts
Gniezno	16	12	1	3	7	32
Miskolc	16	10	0	6	6	26
RIVNE	**16**	**9**	**0**	**7**	**3**	**21**
Lodz	16	4	1	11	3	12

SECOND LEAGUE (regular season)

	M	W	D	L	BP	Pts
Miskolc	10	8	0	2	4	20
Gniezno	10	7	0	3	4	18
RIVNE	**10**	**6**	**0**	**4**	**2**	**14**
Lodz	10	3	0	7	3	9
Opole	10	3	0	7	1	7
Krosno	10	3	0	7	0	6

Individual

IGOR MARKO MEMORIAL TROPHY
Sunday, October 12
1 Pawel Miesiac 10+3+3, Matej Kus 13+3+2, Ilya Bondarenko 10+2+1, Jacek Rempala 13+2+0, Andrey Korolev 12+1, Kjastas Puodzhuks 12+1, Ruslan Gatiyatov 9+0, Ronnie Jamrozy 9+0, Vyacheslav Girutsky 9, Piotr Dym 6, Tomasz Piszcz 6, Vladimir Kolody [sen] 5, Tomasz Rempala 3, Marat Gatiyatov 2, Mikhail Oneshko [R] 1.

2009 FIXTURES

UKRAINE OPEN CHAMPIONSHIP
FINAL: Friday, September 11-Saturday, September 12, Rivne.

UKRAINE UNDER 21 OPEN CHAMPIONSHIP
FINAL: Friday, May 8, Chervonograd.

UKRAINE PAIRS CHAMPIONSHIP
FINAL: Saturday, August 29, Lviv.

UKRAINE LEAGUE
Wednesday, April 8: Chervonograd v SKT Rivne.
Wednesday, April 29: SKT Rivne v Cascade Rivne.
Wednesday, May 6: Cascade Rivne v Lviv.
Wednesday, May 20: Cascade Rivne v Chervonograd.
Thursday, May 28: Lviv v SKT Rivne.
Saturday, June 20: Lviv v Chervonograd.
Wednesday, June 24: SKT Rivne v Lviv.
Saturday, July 11: Chervonograd v Cascade Lviv.
Friday, August 7: Chervonograd v Lviv.
Wednesday, August 19: Cascade Rivne v SKT Rivne.
Saturday, August 22: SKT Rivne v Chervonograd.
Wednesday, September 16: Final.
Saturday, September 19: Final.
Saturday, October 3: Final.
Saturday, October 10: Final.

INDIVIDUAL
Chervonograd Cup, Sunday, August 30.
MACEC Cup, Round 4, Saturday, September 26, Lviv.

UKRAINE CUP
Chernomorsk, Saturday, November 1
The first meeting at a new track – built by former rider Oleg Dosaev – opened with a 2,000 crowd.
Vladimir Kolody [sen] 15, Kiril Cukanov 13, Vladimir Omelian 12, Vladimir Tejgal 11, Mikhail Oneshko 10, Andrey Kobrin 10, Vladimir Kolody [jun] 10, Piotr Fedyk 8, Shevchuk 7, Nikolai Mironov 6, Pawel Moskovchenko 6, Aleksandr Gajkovsky 5, A Zhadan 3, Igor Borisenko 2, V Aliev 0, Andrey Kruchkov 0.
■ *The 2009 staging will be on Saturday, October 24*

USA

AMA AMERICAN CHAMPIONSHIP

BILLY Janniro was crowned AMA national champion for the first time in his career – after completely dominating the series.

He punctured in his opening race in the third and final round in Northern California and was beaten by Kenny Ingalls in his final qualifying round at Auburn.

But they were the only times he didn't take the chequered flag in his 18 title races as he finished a whopping 20 points ahead of his nearest challenger, veteran Bart Bast.

Of the younger brigade, Bryan Yarrow, who had such a torrid time at Coventry in 2004, picked up the bronze medal while teenager Ricky Wells was fifth to underline his reputation as the brightest of the currect crop of young Yanks.

Mike Faria, who turned 51 at the beginning of the season, finished just outside the top three and the even older Bobby Schwartz (52 in August) provided further evidence of the longevity of some of America's top racers!

FINAL STANDINGS

	1	2	3	Tot
1 Billy JANNIRO	**21**	**21**	**20**	**62**
2 Bart BAST	10	18	14	42
3 Bryan YARROW	3	16	19	38
4 Mike FARIA	14	12	12	38
5 Ricky WELLS	16	9	10	35
6 Charlie VENEGAS	12	14	9	35
7 Kenny INGALLS	5	4	16	25
8 Tommy HEDDEN	4	8	11	23
9 Jim FISHBACK	11	11	0	22
10 Nate PERKINS	6	6	8	20
11 Buck BLAIR	9	10	–	19
12 Billy HAMILL	18	–	–	18
13 Bobby SCHWARTZ	8	1	–	9
14 JJ MARTYNESE	0	3	5	8
15 Shawn McCONNELL	7	–	–	7
15 JT MABRY	0	0	7	7
15 Ben ESSARY	–	7	0	7
18 Greg HOOTEN	–	0	6	6
19 Eddie CASTRO	–	2	4	6
20 Tim GOMEZ	0	5	0	5
21 Ivan SEVERT	–	0	3	3
22 Travis HENDERSON	2	–	–	2
22 Devin DEFREECE	–	0	2	2
24 Bryce STARKS	–	0	1	1
24 Neil FACCHINI	1	–	–	1
26 Alex MARCUCCI	–	0	–	0

Point scoring throughout series: 1 – 20; 2 – 18; 3 – 16; 4 – 14; 5 – 12; 6 – 11; 7– 10; 8 – 9, 9 – 8; 10 7; 11 – 6; 12 – 5; 13 – 4; 14 – 3; 15 – 2; 16 – 1. The rider finishing top of the qualifying heats was awarded an extra point.

ROUND 1

Costa Mesa, California, Friday, June 7

BILLY Janniro got off to the perfect start in his title bid – going through the card to record six straight wins.

Even though he had only arrived in California on the morning of the meeting – after a flight from Britain – he showed no signs of tiredness. Making the start, he led the position deciding final from the tapes while Mike Faria was passed by both Billy Hamill and Under 21 Champion Ricky Wells.

	1	2	3	4	5	Tot	RO	F
1 Billy JANNIRO	**3**	**3**	**3**	**3**	**3**	**15**		**3**
2 Billy HAMILL	3	2	3	3	R	11		2
3 Ricky WELLS	3	3	2	2	2	12		1
4 Mike FARIA	3	1	3	3	2	12		0
5 Charlie VENEGAS	E	2	3	2	1	8	4	3
6 Jimmy FISHBACK	1	3	0	1	3	8	2	2
7 Bart BAST	2	0	2	3	1	8	1	1
8 Buck BLAIR	2	2	1	1	2	8	3	0
9 Bobby SCHWARTZ	1	1	2	2	1	7		3
10 Shawn McCONNELL	2	1	1	1	3	8	0	2
11 Nate PERKINS	2	0	2	FX	3	7		1
12 Kenny INGALLS	1	3	1	1	0	6		0
13 Tommy HEDDEN	0	0	1	2	2	5		3
14 Bryan YARROW	0	2	0	0	1	3		2
15 Travis HENDERSON	0	1	0	0	0	1		1
16 Neil FACCHINI	FX	0	R	R	0	0		0
17 Dale FACCHINI [R]	1					1		
18 Tim GOMEZ [R]	0					0		

Elimination Series

Heat 1: Shawn McConnell, Dale Facchini, Travis Henderson, J.J. Martynese.

Heat 2: Neil Facchini, Tim Gomez, Mike Bloom. JT Mabry [E].

Heat 3: Tim Gomez, Travis Henderson, Dale Facchini, Mike Bloom.

Heat 4: Shawn McConnell, Travis Henderson, Neil Facchini, Tim Gomez.

ROUND 2

Auburn, California, Friday, July 25

CHARLIE Venegas' hopes of preventing Billy Janniro from building up a virtually unassailable lead ended when he nudged the tapes in the first running of the A Final.

He argued his case with the meeting steward but his plea to be re-instated fell on deaf ears leaving BJ a fairly comfortable tapers-to-flag victory to secure the maximum 21 points to extend his lead to 14.

Billy Hamill, who would surely have put Janniro under pressure after his first round second place, withdrew through injury.

	1	*2*	*3*	*4*	*5*	*Tot*	*RO F*
1 Billy JANNIRO	**3**	**3**	**3**	**3**	**3**	**15**	**3**
2 Bart BAST	2	3	2	2	3	12	2
3 Bryan YARROW	3	1	3	2	2	11	1
4 Charlie VENEGAS	0	3	3	3	2	11	E
5 Mike FARIA	1	2	2	3	1	9	3
6 Jimmy FISHBACK	3	2	F	0	3	8	2
7 Buck BLAIR	3	2	2	0	3	10	1
8 Ricky WELLS	0	0	3	3	1	7	0
9 Tommy HEDDON	E	2	1	1	2	6	3
10 Ben ESSARY	2	1	1	2	0	6	2
11 Nate PERKINS	1	3	0	2	0	6	1
12 Tim GOMEZ	1	1	1	1	1	5	0
13 Kenny INGALLS	2	0	2	1	0	5	3
14 J.J. MARTYNESE	2	1	E	1	1	5	2
15 Eddie CASTRO	0	E	1	0	0	1	1
16 Bobby SCHWARTZ	1	0	0	0	2	3	0
17 Alex MARCUCCI [R]	0	0				0	
17 Bryce STARKS [R]	0					0	

Elimination Series

Heat 1: J.J. Martynese, Bryce Starks, Devin Defreece, Jon Stasiefski [F].

Heat 2: Alex Marcucci, JT Mabry, Ben Essary, Greg Hooton [F].

Heat 3: Ben Essary, Bryce Starks, JT Mabry, Devin Defreece [FX].

Heat 4: J.J. Martynese, Ben Essary, Alex Marcucci, Bryce Starks.

ROUND 3

Auburn, California, Friday, September 20

NOT even an opening outing puncture could prevent Billy Janniro from chalking up his third round win to seal the title.

He could have afforded an off night such was his lead going into the final round but he wasn't content with coasting to victory as he made it three out of three.

	1	*2*	*3*	*4*	*5*	*Tot*	*RO F*
1 Billy JANNIRO	**R**	**3**	**3**	**3**	**2**	**11**	**3**
2 Bryan YARROW	3	2	3	1	3	12	2
3 Kenny INGALLS	1	2	3	3	3	12	1
4 Bart BAST	3	3	2	0	3	11	0
5 Mike FARIA	2	3	1	2	2	10	3
6 Tommy HEDDEN	3	3	2	2	1	11	2
7 Ricky WELLS	F	2	2	2	2	8	1
8 Charlie VENEGAS	3	1	0	3	3	10	0
9 Nate PERKINS	1	0	3	3	0	7	3
10 JT MABRY	2	1	1	1	1	6	2
11 Greg HOOTEN	2	1	1	0	0	4	1
12 J.J. MARTYNESE	2	2	0	1	1	6	0
13 Eddie CASTRO [R]	2	2				4	3
14 Ivan SEVERT	1	0	0	0	1	2	2
15 Devin DEFREECE	0	0	0	0	0	0	1
16 Bryce STARKS	0	0	2	1	0	3	0
17 Tim GOMEZ	1	1	0			2	
18 Ben ESSARY [R]	0					0	

Elimination Series

Owing to the withdrawals of Buck Blair, Jim Fishback, Billy Hamill, Shawn McConnell and Bobby Schwartz, of the eight competitors in the pre-event eliminators only one did not qualify for the meeting.

Qualifiers: Greg Hooten, Bryce Starks, JT Mabry, Ivan Severt, Devin Defreece, Ben Essary [R] and Eddie Castro [R].

Heat 1: Shawn McConnell, Dale Facchini, Travis Henderson, JJ Martynese.

Heat 2: Neil Facchini, Tim Gomez, Mike Bloom, JT Mabry [E].

Heat 3: Tim Gomez, Travis Henderson, Dale Facchini, Mike Bloom.

Heat 4: Shawn McConnell, Travis Henderson, Neil Facchini, Tim Gomez.

Roll of Honour

1925 .... Sprouts ELDER
1927 .... Art PECHAR
1930 .... Miny WALN
1931 .... Miny WALN
1932 .... Miny WALN
1933 .... Ray GRANT
1934 .... Cordy MILNE
1935 .... Cordy MILNE
1936 .... Jack MILNE
1937 .... Benny KAUFMAN
1946 .... Wilbur LAMOUREAUX
1947 .... Cordy MILNE
1948 .... Cordy MILNE
1968 .... Rick WOODS
1969 .... Steve BAST
1970 .... Rick WOODS
1971 .... Mike BAST
1972 .... Rick WOODS
1973 .... Mike BAST
1974 .... Steve BAST
1975 .... Mike BAST
1976 .... Mike BAST
1977 .... Mike BAST
1978 .... Mike BAST
1979 .... Mike BAST
1980 .... Bruce PENHALL
1981 .... Bruce PENHALL
1982 .... Shawn MORAN
1983 .... Kelly MORAN
1984 .... Kelly MORAN
1985 .... Alan CHRISTIAN
1986 .... Bobby SCHWARTZ
1987 .... Brad OXLEY
1988 .... Steve LUCERO
1989 .... Bobby SCHWARTZ
1990 .... Mike FARIA
1991 .... Mike FARIA
1992 .... Chris MANCHESTER
1993 .... Sam ERMOLENKO

1994 .... Sam ERMOLENKO
1995 .... Greg HANCOCK
1996 .... Steve LUCERO
1997 .... Mike FARIA
1998 .... Greg HANCOCK
1999 .... Billy HAMILL
2000 .... Greg HANCOCK
2001 .... Billy HAMILL
2002 .... Billy HAMILL
2003 .... Greg HANCOCK
2004 .... Greg HANCOCK
2005 .... Greg HANCOCK
2006 .... Greg HANCOCK
2007 .... Billy HAMILL
2008 .... Billy JANNIRO

SRA AMERICAN CHAMPIONSHIP

BILLY Janniro made it a Stars and Stripes double – adding the Speedway Riders' Association national title to his AMA crown.

In the penultimate meeting of Costa Mesa's busy summer season, Janniro was outstanding yet again, making light of his Transatlantic commuting.

And again he totally dominated the opposition, winning his four qualifying races and then making it five wins in a row to regain the championship he had first won in 2004.

Seventeen-year-old Ricky Wells, who dropped his only points to BJ – losing to him in the qualifiers and again in the final – made sure of the silver medal, chasing all the way to flag.

Some of the contenders came through a somewhat torturous and complex format, racing four qualifying races and then a semi final and a Last Chance repechage, the last three heats all embracing five-man races.

FINAL

Costa Mesa, California, Friday, October 4

	1	2	3	4	Tot	RO	SF	LC	F
1 Billy JANNIRO	**3**	**3**	**3**	**3**	**12**		❑	❑	**4**
2 Ricky WELLS	3	2	3	3	11	3	❑	❑	3
3 Chris MANCHESTER	3	3	3	2	11	2	❑	❑	2
4 Charlie VENEGAS	3	3	2	3	11	1	❑	3	1
5 Bobby SCHWARTZ	2	2	2	2	8		❑	4	0
6 Shawn McCONNELL	3	1	0	3	7		4	2	
7 Shaun HARMATIUK	2	2	2	2	8		❑	1	
8 Jimmy FISHBACK	2	3	0	3	8		❑	0	
9 Nate PERKINS	1	2	1	1	5		3		
10 Bryan YARROW	0	3	1	2	6		2		
11 Mike FARIA	2	1	3	0	6		1		
12 Neil FACCHINI	2	1	R	2	5		0		
13 Mike BLOOM	0	0	3	1	4				
14 Russell GREEN	1	1	2	0	4				
15 Tommy HEDDEN	1	1	1	1	4				
16 Jason RAMIREZ	1	2	F	0	3				
17 J.T. MABRY	0	0	2	1	3				
18 Mikey BUMAN	0	0	0	1	1				
18 Brad SAUER	1	0	0	0	1				
18 Robbie SAUER	0	0	1	0	1				
21 Doug GRAYSON [R]	did not ride								

Roll of Honour

1997 .... Mike FARIA
1998 .... Bart BAST
1999 .... Brad OXLEY
2000 .... Charlie VENEGAS
2001 .... Chris MANCHESTER
2002 .... Billy HAMILL
2003 .... Scott BRANT
2004 .... Billy JANNIRO
2005 .... Chris MANCHESTER
2006 .... Charlie VENEGAS
2007 .... Billy HAMILL
2008 .... Billy JANNIRO

US OPEN CHAMPIONSHIP

FINAL

Owego, New York, Sunday, July 27

PHIL Collins showed glimpses of his old form – overcoming a string of poor starts to thrill the crowd at Owego.

But it was evergreen Shawn McConnell who kept his nerve when it really mattered, overcoming the challenge of Shaun Harmatiuk in a series of Grand Finals to win his third US Open Championships.

1 Shawn McCONNELL, 2 Shaun HARMATIUK, 3 Casey DONHOLT, 4 Aaron HESMER, 5 Phil COLLINS, 6 Mikey BUMAN, 7 Lenny McBRIDE, 8 Adam MITTL, 9 Gene BONSIGNOR, 10 Tuff McBRIDE, 11 Warren DIEM, 12 Jesse DIEM, 13 Dave CLARK, 14 Brian HOLLENBECK, 15 Josh CARR, 16 Jerry HARMAN, 17 Keith HAWKINS, 18 Corey BROOKS, 19 Jeff OROSZ, 20 Russ CORNELL.

Roll of Honour

1977 .... Bobby SCHWARTZ
1978 .... Norman ROBINSON
1979 .... Michael BAST
1980 .... Gene WOODS
1981 .... Gene WOODS
1982 .... Rick MILLER
1983 .... John COOK
1984 .... Gene WOODS
1985 .... Bruce NELSON
1986 .... Warren DIEM
1987 .... Tom BURGE
1988 .... Warren DIEM
1989 .... Warren DIEM
1990 .... Warren DIEM
1991 .... Warren DIEM
1992 .... Warren DIEM
1998 .... Chris MANCHESTER
1999 .... Jimmy SISEMORE
2000 .... Josh LARSEN
2001 .... Jimmy SISEMORE
2002 .... Cam RAFFERTY
2003 .... Bobby SCHWARTZ
2004 .... Tommy SEPHTON
2005 .... Shawn McCONNELL
2006 .... Charles ERMOLENKO
2007 .... Shawn McCONNELL
2008 .... Shawn McCONNELL

Ricky Wells became the latest American to try his hand in Britain – joining Elite League Coventry for the 2009 season. It was originally hoped he could double up – with Premier League Stoke his likely lower league destination – but the new British Speedway Promoters' Association regulation prevented him from doing so because he was on an assessed average. His debut was delayed because of work permit problems.

AMERICAN UNDER 21 FINAL

FINAL

Auburn, California, Friday, August 29

RICKY Wells booked his spot in the 2009 World Under 21 Championship as he successfully retained his national title.

The New Zealand born racer was unbeaten in his five rides, edging out Kenny Ingalls for top spot.

Alex Marcucci, who rode in the 2008 world rounds, completed the rostrum party in front of the smallest crowd of the season at the Northern California track.

Completing a full programme of racing as the 20-heat Youth Championships, won by Brad Pappalardo after a three-rider run-off for first place.

Pappalardo, 15, certainly has the pedigree to go a lot further – he's the nephew of former World Champion and Grand Prix star Greg Hancock.

	1	2	3	4	5	Tot	RO F
1 Ricky WELLS	**3**	**3**	**3**	**3**	**3**	**15**	
2 Kenny INGALLS	3	3	2	3	3	14	
3 Alex MARCUCCI	2	2	3	3	2	12	
4 Jason RAMIREZ	0	3	3	2	1	9	
5 J.T. MABRY	1	3	3	1	1	9	
6 Tim GOMEZ	2	2	0	2	3	9	
7 Bryce STARKS	3	1	0	1	3	8	
8 Russell GREEN	3	2	2	1	0	8	
9 Casey DONHOLT	2	1	1	2	2	8	
10 Ben ESSARY	1	0	1	3	2	7	
11 Ricky FELICIO	2	2	2	0	1	7	
12 Travis HENDERSON	1	1	0	2	2	6	
13 Jay RICKETTS	0	0	0	1	1	2	
14 Tom FEHRMAN	0	1	1	0	0	2	
15 Tori HUBBERT	0	0	1	0	0	1	
16 John RANDOLF	0	1	0	0	0	1	

Roll of Honour

2003 .... Eric CARILLO
2004 .... Justin BOYLE
2005 .... Skyler GREYSON
2006 .... Dale FACCHINI
2007 .... Ricky WELLS
2008 .... Ricky WELLS

USA Youth Championship

1 Brad Pappalardo 13+3, 2 Cody Cicarelli 13+2, 3 Gino Manzares 13+1, 4 Austin Novratil 12, 5 Thomas Reich 11, 6 Tyler Warren 9, 7 Tanner Kane 8, 8 Joey Holt 8, 9 River McDougall 7, 10 Ricky Reimer 6, 11 Amber Felicio 6, 12 Kendra Warren 5, 13 Jameson Dilkey 4, 14 Desi Fehrman 3, 15 Sam Ramirez 0.

AMA AMERICAN LONG TRACK CHAMPIONSHIP

FINAL

Stark County Fairgrounds, Canton, Ohio
Saturday, May 24

JEFF Orosz retained his AMA national Long Track Championship – winning all four races on the way to victory.

The 38-year-old Canadian, whose father Jim raced in the seventies, added a second American title to the Canadian Speedway crown he had won in 1997.

But the meeting, on the half-mile limestone Ohio track, was marred by a crash which saw Brian Dailly, Gary Hesmer and Dan Crawford forced to pull out, Dailly after he had won his opening race.

The event – part of a two-day bike festival – attracted a mixture of riders, including 70-year-old flat track legend Ronnie Rall who had won five AMA national titles on the half mile, short track and TT circuits, in the sixties and seventies.

Farmer and father of seven Rall, whose son Chad took second place, was inducted into the American Motorcyclist Association's Hall of Fame in 2001.

1 Jeff OROSZ, 2 Chad RALL, 3 Rob DIXON, 4 Chris THOMAS, 6 Daniel WEICHT, 6 Steve GLASGOW, 7 Ronny RALL, 8 Dave WEICHT, 9 Michael CALLEN, 10 Marc MONRO, 11 Peter PEDERSEN, 12 Doug HORNER, 13 Chris HATHAWAY, 14 Jon MASSIE, 15 Tim MURRAY, 16 Phil MOSQUERA, 17 Kevin SEXTON.

Roll of Honour

2007 .... Jeff OROSZ
2008 .... Jeff OROSZ

OHIO LONG TRACK CHAMPIONSHIP

Fulton County Fairgrounds, Wauseon, Ohio
Friday, July 18

1 Chad Rall, 2 Chris Thomas, 3 Daniel Weicht, 4 Chris Hathaway, 5 Michael Callon, 6 John Debats, 7 David Weicht, 8 Marc Monroe, 9 Jon Massie, 10 Kevin Sexton, 11 Doug Horner, 12 Ronnie Rall.

Roll of Honour

2007 .... John DEBATS
2008 .... Chad RALL

California State Championship

Industry Hills, Wednesday, September 17

CHARLIE Venegas won his third California State title to join Bast brothers Mike and Steve, Bobby Schwartz, Steve Lucero and Mike Faria as multi-champions.

He overcame what could have been a disastrous fourth race when he finished behind Shawn McConnell and Ricky Wells.

The exciting teenager Wells needed to win his final race to force a run-off but was beaten by Mike Faria, recovering from a sluggish start to the meeting to win his last two heats.

Veteran Bobby Schwartz, who won the first of his two titles way back in 1984, finished one point off the podium.

	1	2	3	4	5	Tot	RO F
1 Charlie VENEGAS	**3**	**3**	**3**	**1**	**3**	**13**	
2 Ricky WELLS	2	3	3	2	2	12	
3 Shawn McCONNELL	2	2	1	3	3	11	
4 Tommy HEDDEN	3	3	1	0	3	10	
5 Bobby SCHWARTZ	1	3	2	3	1	10	
6 Mike FARIA	1	1	2	3	3	10	
7 Shaun HARMATIUK	2	2	3	2	1	10	
8 Jimmy FISHBACK	3	2	2	1	2	10	
9 Eddie CASTRO	E	2	2	3	2	9	
10 Neil FACCHINI	1	1	3	2	0	7	
11 Russell GREEN	3	1	0	1	1	6	
12 Dale FACCHINI	2	0	0	2	2	6	
13 Robbie SAUER	1	0	0	1	R	2	
13 John MARQUEZ	F	1	1	0	0	2	
13 Brad SAUER	0	0	1	0	1	2	
16 Jason RAMIREZ	0					0	
17 Tim GOMEZ [R]	F					0	
18 John DeFRIES [R]			did not ride				

Roll of Honour

1968 ....Sonny NUTTER
1969 ....Steve BAST
1970 ....Steve BAST
1971 ....Steve BAST
1972 ....Steve BAST
1973 ....Mike BAST
1974 ....Steve BAST
1975 ....Steve BAST
1976 ....Mike BAST
1977 ....Mike BAST
1978 ....Mike BAST
1979 ....Mike BAST
1980 ....Alan CHRISTIAN
1981 ....Bruce PENHALL
1982 ....Lance KING
1983 ....Mike BAST
1984 ....Bobby SCHWARTZ
1985 ....Steve LUCERO
1986 ....Bobby OTT
1987 ....Mike FARIA
1988 ....Sam ERMOLENKO
1989 ....Steve LUCERO
1990 ....Mike FARIA
1991 ....Bobby SCHWARTZ
1992 ....Mike FARIA
1993 ....Chris MANCHESTER
1994 ....Mike FARIA
1995 ....Steve LUCERO
1996 ....Steve LUCERO
1997 ....Charlie VENEGAS
2006 ....Josh LARSEN
2007 ....Charlie VENEGAS
2008 ....Charlie VENEGAS

Mid America Championship

PHOTO: **Kurt BAUER**

CHICAGO-BASED Polish rider Wieslaw Oskiewicz grabbed the Mid American Championship at Indianapolis – by a single point after 13 rounds.

The former Grudziadz and Warsaw rider was in second place going into the final round but finished ahead of long-time leader Paul Huggins to snatch his first title.

Thirty-one-year-old Oskiewicz – who picked up a bronze medal in the 1998 Junior Team Championship – rode regularly in his native Poland from his debut for Grudziadz in 1995 until his final match for Warsaw in 2002 and then emigated to America.

Oskiewicz rode in 10 of the 13 rounds and actually won nine – missing out to Huggins in the final round on October 18 when he only needed to finish second to his rival to claim the championship.

FINAL STANDINGS

1 Wieslaw OSKIEWICZ 217, 2 PAUL HUGGINS 216, 3 Joe GARRISON 186, 4 BJ FESSELMEYER 185, 5 Jim TERCHILA 150, 6 Ricky LEAK 150, 7 Preston DORFMEYER 144, 8 Dan WEICHT 118, 9 Barry BENKERT (jun) 93, 10 Chris HATHAWAY 86, 11 Dave WEICHT 83, 12 Todd EADS 62, 13 Gabor KUSCERA 40, 14 Cory EADS 26, 15 Eddie KELLEY 10, 16 Morgan HENDRICK 8, 17 Brad AMBURGEY 7.

Championship raced over 13 rounds at the Marion County Fairgrounds track in Indianapolis with the best 12 scores to count .

Roll of Honour

2001 ....Greg COMSTOCK
2002 ....Eddie KELLEY
2003 ....Keith CHRISCO
2004 ....Joe GARRISON
2005 ....Joe GARRISON
2006 ....Todd EADS
2008 ....Wieslaw OSKIEWICZ

New York State Championship

FINAL STANDINGS

1 Gene BONSIGNORE 191, 1 Adam MITTL 191, 3 Mike BURMAN 116, 4 Tuff McBRIDE 115, 5 Casey DONHOLT 97, 6 Josh CARR 78, 7 Jason BONSIGNORE 62, 7 Aaron HESMER 62, 9 Lenny McBRIDE 53, 10 Dave OAKDEN 48, 11 Jerry HARMAN 43, 12 Dave CLARK 40, 13 Corey BROOKES 38, 14 Dee HOLDEN 27, 15 Keith HAWKINS 7, 16 Stefan LAESSING 2, 18 Russ CORNELL 1.

Round 1
Batavia, Friday, June 27
1 Gene Bonsignore, 2 Jason Bonsignore, 3 Mark Bradley, 4 Goody Goodman.

Round 2
Owego, Saturday, June 28
Qualifying: Adam Mittl 12, Casey Donholt 11, Gene Bonsignore 7, Tuff McBride 7, Lenny McBride 7, Keith Hawkins 7, Mikey Buman 5, Jerry Harman 5, Corey Brookes 4, Dave Clark 4, Stefan Laessing 2, Russ Cornell 1.
Semi Final 1: Buman, Harman, L. McBride, Clark.
Semi Final 2: T. McBride, Bonsignore, Brookes, Hawkins.
Final: Mittl, T. McBride, Buman, L. McBride, Donholt, Bonsignore.

Round 3
Henrietta, Friday, July 11
1 Adam Mittl, 2 Aaron Hesmer, 3 Mikey Buman, 4 Tuff McBride, 5 Gene Bonsignore, 6 Casey Donholt.

Individual

NEW YEAR'S CLASSIC
Victorville, Saturday, February 2
1 Billy Janniro, 2 Chris Kerr, 3 Ricky Wells, 4 Buck Blair.

CHAMPIONS CUP
Victorville, Saturday, March 1
1 Ricky Wells, 2 Buck Blair, 3 Michael Hull, 4 Shawn McConnell.

HIGH DESERT PAIRS CHAMPIONSHIP
Victorville, Saturday, April 5
1 Ricky Wells & Greg Ayers, 2 Michael Hull & Dale Facchini, 3 Robbie Sauer & John Marquez, 4 Russell Green & Billy Lyons.
Division Three: Jeff Remington 5, Tony DeAlmeida 8 = 13, Jonni Jade 6, John Weller 6 = 12, Rick Huspek 5, Jeff Shaffer 4 = 9.
Division Two: Bryan Buffington 5, Russell Green 10 = 15, Max Eddy 4, Rohn Zellner 7 = 11, Brad Moreau 1, Steve Dziadus 3 = 4.

FRIENDS OF SPEEDWAY SPRING CLASSIC
Perris, Sunday, April 13
Ricky Wells 12+□+3, Nate Perkins 11+□+2, Jason Ramirez 9+4+1, J.T. Mabry 9+□+0, Brad Sauer 8+3, John Marquez 4+2, Russell Green 4+N, Donnie Robinson 4+N, Robbie Sauer 3, Allen Doss 3, Philip Harmatiuk 1.

STALLONE'S CYCLES SPRING CLASSIC
Victorville, Saturday, April 19
Tim Gomez 9+□+3, Michael Hull 6+□+2, Robbie Sauer 8+2+1, Buck Blair 10+□+R, John Marquez 4+1, Russell Green 8+0.

HIGH DESERT SPRING FESTIVAL
Ridgecrest, Saturday, April 26
Billy Hamill 9+3+3, Buck Blair 7+3+2, Ricky Wells 6+2+1, Tim Gomez 4+2+0, Dale Facchini 7+1, Neil Facchini 3+3+1, Tommy Hedden 6+0, Robbie Sauer 4+0, J.T. Mabry 3+2, Brad Sauer 3+1, John Marquez 2, Nate Perkins 0.

SPRING CLASSIC
Costa Mesa, Friday, May 10
Mike Faria 10+4+4, Bobby Schwartz 12+3+3, Shawn McConnell 11+2+3+2, Jimmy Fishback 9+4+1, Buck Blair 10+3+0, J.T. Mabry 7+2+1+2, Greg Ayers 7+2+1+1, Neil Facchini 7+4+2+0, Billy Hamill 12+FN, Dale Facchini 8+N^2, Travis Henderson 7+E, Mike Bloom 5, John Marquez 3, Russell Green 3, Doug Greyson 3, Billy Lyons 2, Marvin Sonnier 2, John Stunkard 1, Denny Scopellite 0, Vince Giamformaggio 0.
All races with five riders.

ELIMINAPOLIS 500
Victorville, Friday, May 24
Ricky Wells 6+2+3, Buck Blair 9+3+2, Dale Facchini 7+3+1, Shawn McConnell 5+2+0, Neil Facchini 6+1, Robbie Sauer 4+1, Jason Ramirez 7+0, Tim Gomez 4+0, Billy Lyons 2, Tony Bienert 2, Russell Green 1, Donnie Robinson [R] 1, Allen Doss 0.

Batavia, New York State, Friday, July 25
Shaun Harmatiuk 12+□+4, Shawn McConnell 10+□+3, Phil Collins 9+□+2, Casey Donholt 9+□+1, Mikey Burman 8+3+0, Aaron Hesmer 8+2, Adam Mittl 9+1, Gene Bonsignore 6+0, Lenny McBride 5+3, Tuff McBride 6+2, Jesse Diem 3+1, Josh Carr 4+0, Katalin Davis 2+3, Dee Holden 1+2, Mark Bradley 1+1, Warren Diem 3+N.

NORM ROBINSON CUP
Batavia, August 10
1 Gene Bonsignore, 2 Adam Mittl, 3 Jason Bonsignore, 4 Mike Robinson, 5 Jon Stasiefski.

KING OF SPEEDWAY
Overall Standings
1 Shawn McConnell 84, 2 Tommy Hedden 75+3, 3 Adam Mittl 75+2, 4 Aaron Hesmer 69, 5 Bart Bast 64, 6 Mikey Buman 63, 7 Tuff McBride 62, 8 Lenny McBride 58, 9 Gene Bonsignore 51, 10 Corey Brookes 50, 11 Josh Carr 45, 12 Dave Clark 41, 13 Shawn Engel 30, 14 Keith Hawkins 28, 15 Andy Crawford 26, 16 Jeff Garlinghouse 24, 17 Russ Cornell 24, 18 Katalin Davis 17, 19 Alex Heath 13, 20 Stefan Laessing 9.

Round 1
Batavia, Friday, August 29
Mikey Buman 26, Shawn McConnell 25, Tommy Hedden 24, Adam Mittl 23, Lenny McBride 22, Aaron Hesmer 21, Tuff McBride 20, Bart Bast 19, Josh Carr 18, Gene Bonsignore 17, Corey Brookes 16, Jeff Garlinghouse 15, Shawn Engel 14, Mike Hammond 13, Andy Crawford 12, Katalin Davis 11.

Round 2

Action Park, Green, Saturday, August 30

Shawn McConnell 20, Tommy Hedden 19, Aaron Hesmer 18, Adam Mittl 17, Bart Bast 16, Mikey Burman 15, Tuff McBride 14, Dave Clark 13, Senior Steve 12, Keith Hawkins 11, Corey Brookes 10, Josh Carr 9, Gene Bonsignor 8, Lenny McBride 7, Andy Crawford 6, Katalin Davis 5, Russ Cornell 4, Jeff Garlinghouse 3.

Round 3

Champion, Owego, Sunday, August 31

Shawn McConnell 39, Adam Mittl 35, Tommy Hedden 32, Aaron Hesmer 30, Lenny McBride 29, Bart Bast 29, Tuff McBride 28, Dave Clark 28, Gene Bonsignore 26, Corey Brookes 24, Mikey Buman 22, Russ Cornell 20, Josh Carr 18, Keith Hawkins 17, Shawn Engel 16, Alex Heath 13, Stefan Laessing 9, Andy Crawford 8, Jeff Garlinghouse 6, Katalin Davis 1.

Top five riders contested a four-leg Grand Final

AUBURN TRACK CHAMPIONSHIP

Auburn, Friday, September 5

Charlie Venegas 15, Bart Bast 13, Ricky Wells 12, Mike Faria 11, Kenny Ingalls 11, Bryan Yarrow 11, Tommy Hedden 9, J.T. Mabry 8, Chad Felicio 8, Alex Marcucci 6, Ben Essary 5, J.J. Martynese 4, Jim Lewis 2, Devin Defreece 2, Shawn Eldridge 2, Kell Kerrigan 1.

JOHN MATHERSON CUP

Costa Mesa, Saturday, September 6

Shawn McConnell 12+□+4, Mike Faria 12+□+3, Bobby Schwartz 11+3+2, Ricky Wells 12+□+1, Jimmy Fishback 10+□+0, Neil Facchini 7+2, Brad Sauer 8+1, Jason Ramirez 8+0, Robbie Sauer 7, Greg Ayers 7, Doug Greyson 7, Russell Green 5, Mike Bloom 4, John Stunkard 3, Eloy Medellin 2, Allen Doss 2, Marvin Sonnier 2, John Marquez 1.

WARREN RUSSELL CUP

Costa Mesa, Saturday, September 13

Bobby Schwartz 11+3+□+4, Ricky Wells 11+3+□+3, Shawn McConnell 1 +4+□+2, Mike Faria 9+4+□+1, Jimmy Fishback 8+2+3+0, Dale Facchini 6+2+1+2, Russell Green 6+3+2+1, Robbie Sauer 8+1+0, Neil Facchini 6+4+0, Brad Sauer 8+0, Jason Ramirez 6+1, Tim Gomez 6+0, Mike Bloom 4, John Stunkard 4, Greg Ayers 4, Doug Greyson 4, Bobby Krips 3, John Marquez 3, Eloy Medellin 2, Allen Doss 1.

JACK MILNE CUP

Costa Mesa, Saturday, September 27

Bobby Schwartz 10+4+□+4, Shawn McConnell 9+2+3+3, Jimmy Fishback 9+3+□+2, Shaun Harmatiuk 10+3+□+1, Ricky Wells 9+4+□+0, Nate Perkins 7+2+2, Tommy Hedden 7+1+1, Charlie Venegas 8+1+0, Mike Faria 9+0, Brad Sauer 6+0, Mike Bloom 6, Russell Green 6, Robbie Sauer 5, J.T. Mabry 5, Greg Ayers 4, Jason Ramirez 3, John Marquez 2, Doug Greyson 2, John Stunkard 2, Tuff McBride 1.

AMATEUR NATIONAL CHAMPIONSHIP

Perris, Sunday, October 5

Division One: Russell Green 10+4, Jason Ramirez 11+3, Greg Ayers 8+2, Mikey Buman 5+1, Mike Bloom 4+N, Phil Bast 1.

Division Two: Philip Harmatiuk 11+□+4, Dylan Black 7+4+3, Tyson Burmeister 9+5+2, Allen Doss 11+□+1. Brian Pappalardo 11+□+R, Donnie Robinson 9+3, Steve Bowen 8+2, Eloy Medellin 7+1, Billy Braden 7+0, Rick Fehrman 6, Vince Giamformaggio 6, Kim Stevens 5, Rudy Laurer 5, Rohn Zellner 5, Mark Lane 3, Steve Dziadus 2, Damon Barry 1, Eddie Martinez 1, Rick Fritch 1.

Division Three: Ryan Brant 10+□+4, Michael Novratil 12+□+3, Tim McGrath 9+3+2, Billy Vaughn 9+2+1, Miike Schultz 10+□+0, Bubba Vazzana 9+1, Ralph Chudy 7, Tony DeAlmeida 6, Mike Boyle 5, Jeff Shaffer 5, Rick Huspek 3, Samantha Ramirez 2, Jeff Remington 2.

FALL CLASSIC

Costa Mesa, Saturday, October 22

Charlie Venegas 8+3+4, Ricky Wells 10+4+3, Shaun Harmatiuk 8+4+2, Jason Ramirez 10+3+1, Bobby Schwartz 10+1+3+0, Buck Blair 10+2+2, Brad Sauer 7+2+1, Russell Green 7+1+0, Neil Facchini 8+0, Greg Ayers 7+0, Mike Bloom 6, John Stunkard 6, John Marquez 5, Doug Greyson 4, Robert Christian 4, Philip Harmatiuk 3, Tyson Burmeister 3, Eloy Medellin 2, Justin Boyle 1, Rick Farron 1.

DESERT EMPIRE FAIR CHAMPIONSHIP

Ridgecrest, Friday, October 17

Charlie Venegas 12+3, Buck Blair 11+2, Jason Ramirez 7+1, Neil Facchini 7+0, Shaun Harmatiuk 3+3, Russell Green 4+2, Jon Stasiefski 1+1, Marvin Sonnier 2+0.

NEW YEAR CLASSIC

Perris, Sunday, January 25, 2009

Kenny Ingalls 8+3, Jason Ramirez 6+2, J.T. Mabry 4+1, Shaun Harmatiuk 8+0, Mike Bloom 3, Jaimie Pickard 3, Greg Ayers 6, Tyson Burmeister 2, Bryce Starks 0, Russell Green 0.

SEASON OPENER

Victorville, Monday, March 9, 2009

Billy Janniro 9+3+3, Eddie Castro 8+2+2, Tyson Burmeister 6+2+1, Buck Blair 7+3+0, Nate Perkins 6+1, Neil Facchini 4+1, Russell Green 4+N, Jason Ramirez 3+3+F, Bryce Starks 3+2, Billy Lyons 3+1.

Team events

CIVIL WAR CHALLENGE

Auburn, Friday, July 18

NORTH 76 (Bart Bast 17+8, Chad Felicio 5, Mike Faria 10, Tommy Hedden 9+4, Kenny Ingalls 12+4, Greg Hooten 6+1)

SOUTH 65 (Charlie Venegas 16 (6)+2, Scott Brant 7, Nate Perkins 10+3, Eddie Castro 5+2, Bryan Yarrow 13+6, Jon Stasiefski 1).

[Scoring: 3-2-1-0 in first 16 heats then 4-3-2-1 and 8-6-4-2 in top-scorers races]. Charlie Venegas rode as a tactical rider, scoring double points in one race.

Victorville, Saturday, March 1
VICTORVILLE VIKINGS 42 (Buck Blair 10:1, *rider replacement*, Shawn McConnell 8:1, Billy Lyons 8:1, Michael Hull 9:1, Rohn Zellner 2:1, Rudy Laurer 5)
LOS ANGELES ACES 36 (**Ricky Wells 15**, Marvin Sonnier 0, *rider replacement*, John Marquez 4, Greg Ayers 8, Allen Doss 5:2, Bryan Buffington 4:1, Donnie Robinson 0).

Perris, Sunday, April 20
VICTORVILLE VIKINGS 50 (**Billy Janniro 15**, Mike Bloom 6:1, Tim Gomez 5:1, Jason Ramirez 11, Jimmy Fishback 7, Russell Green 4:1, Jim Painter 2) **LOS ANGELES ACES 39** (Ricky Wells 10:2, Greg Ayers 7, Michael Hull 11, Travis Henderson 1, Dale Facchini 2, Austin Novratil 3, John Marquez 5:1).

International

THE now traditional late season international was again staged at Northern California track Auburn.

Three Poles, a Czech, a German and comeback racer Phil Collins provided the Rest of the World opposition.

Auburn, Friday, October 24
UNITED STATES OF AMERICA 56
Bart Bast 10:2, Tommy Hedden 10:2, Mike Faria 8, Charlie Venegas 11:2, Kenny Ingalls 5:1, Ricky Wells 12:1, Bobby Hedden 0.
REST OF THE WORLD 52
Mariusz Puszakowski 2:2, Lubos Tomicek 11, Maciej Janowski 13:1, Janusz Kolodziej 10:1, Phil Collins 0, Martin Smolinski 14, Bobby Hedden [R] 2.

TEAM CHAMPIONSHIP

A TEAM championship involving four tracks was run in the final weeks of the American season.

The four-team tournament was run over 28 heats with eight riders per team and the conventional points scoring.

American Champion Billy Janniro rode in the second round, after returning home from England.

	RPts	Pts
1 PERRIS Eagles	82	10
2 VICTORVILLE Vikings	62	8
3 RIDGECREST Aces	52	6
4 INDUSTRY HILLS Heathens	37	0

[Match points: 6-4-2-0].

Round 1
Perris, Sunday, November 2
1 PERRIS EAGLES 50 (Ricky Wells 11, Greg Ayers 9, Mike Bloom 6, Joey Holt 5, Rick Fehrman 4, Ryan Tovatt 3, Bubba Vazzana 6, Brad Pappalardo 6), **2 RIDGECREST ACES 29** (Buck Blair 8, John Marquez 6, Tyson Burmeister 4, Steve Dziadus 3, Mark Lane 4, Jonni Jade 1, Tony DeAlmeida 1, Paul Thornton 2), **3 VICTORVILLE VIKINGS 28** (Neil Facchini 6, Russell Green 7, Jon Stasiefski 4, Rohn Zellner 3, Austin Novratil 3, Mike Novratil 1, Tim McGrath 2, Drew Coates 2), **4 INDUSTRY HILLS HEATHENS 25** (Jason Ramirez 11, Allen Doss 0, *rider replacement*, Kelly Sorensen 3, Brad Moreau 3, Giro Manzares 3, Mike Schultz 3, Rick Huspek 2).

Round 2
Victorville, Saturday, November 8
VICTORVILLE VIKINGS 33 (Shawn McConnell 6, Dale Facchini 1, Neil Facchini 4, Austin Novratil 6, Rohn Zellner 6, Tim McGrath 5, Drew Coates 5), **2 PERRIS EAGLES 32** (**Billy Janniro 9**, **Ricky Wells 9**, Charlie Venegas 7, Joey Holt 2, Rick Fehrman 2, Michelle Fehrman 0, Bubba Vazzana 3), 3 **RIDGECREST ACES 22** (Buck Blair 7, John Marquez 2, Tyson Burmeister 3, Steve Dziadus 2, Billy Lyons 4, Tony DeAlmeida 1, Jonni Jade 3), **4 INDUSTRY HILLS HEATHENS 15** (Jason Ramirez 2, Russell Green 1, Tony Bienert 3, Steve Bowen 1, Brad Moreau 1, Mike Schultz 3, Mike Novratil 4).

TRACKS

ACTION PARK
Address: Airport Road, Route 12N, Greene, New York State.
Tel: 001 607 6568885/585 7239746.
Formerly known as River Valley Speedway, was originally built in the 60s as an asphalt oval and road course for go-karts, and cars.

In 1982, tenant Joe Morello built a speedway track over the oval and ran successfully for eight years before a divorce forced him to close.

The track was dug up and re-opened for autocross and go karts before Jason Bonsignore became the owner in 2001.

AUBURN
Address: Gold Country Fairgrounds, Recreation Drive, Auburn, California 95603.
Tel: 001 530 87872236.
Website: www.fastfridays.com
Organised a 20-meeting schedule for 2008 including two rounds of the AMA National Championship and an end of season USA v Rest of the World international.

They have 21 Friday night events lined up for 2009, running from May 8 to October 9.

BATAVIA SPEEDWAY
Address: The Polarwave Snow Park, 3500 Harloff Road, Batavia, New York 14020.
Tel: 001 585 3450638/585 7239746.
Website: www.bataviamotorspeedway.com

CHAMPION SPEEDWAY
Address: 344 East River Drive, Owego, New York 13827.
Tel: 001 607 6877819.
Champion Speedway began in 1975 and boomed for a 10-year period but went through a traumatic period where it closed twice over the next decade due to ownership and promoter changes, and legal problems.Resurrected by Jason Bonsignore in 1997,

staging 13 meetings in 2008, including the US Open Championship Final.

COSTA MESA SPEEDWAY
Address: Orange County Fair and Event Center, 88 Fair Drive, Costa Mesa, California 92626.
Tel: 001 949 4929933.
Website: www.costamesaspeedway.net

The longest surviving track in America, having originally been opened on Friday, June 13, 1968, by Harry Oxley whose family are still running weekly meetings, some 40-odd years later.

They have a provisional 2009 fixture list of 18 meetings opening on Saturday, May 2, running through until October 10 including two meetings in three nights during the Orange County Fair (July 10-12).

GOLDEN GATE SPEEDWAY
Address: Solano County Fairgrounds, 900 Fairgrounds Drive, Vallejo, California 94589.
Tel: 001 949 4929933.

Promoted by rider Charlie Venegas, the temporary track – which was in the car park of the Fairgrounds – opened on July 26, 2008, and had seven scheduled meetings on its condensed calendar.

INDUSTRY HILLS SPEEDWAY
Address: The Grand Industry Hills Expo Center, 16200 Temple Ave City of Industry, California 91744.
Tel: 001 949 6400455.
Website: www.industryexpocenter.com/industryspeedway

Promoted by rider Charlie Venegas, the track opened on July 26, 2008, and had seven scheduled meetings on its condensed calendar.

It has now been taken over by Jeff Immediato and his partner, two-times World Champion Bruce Penhall who have a lease with the Expo Center until 2014.

They are planning a full programe of weekly Wednesday night meeting at the indoor arena.

MID AMERICA SPEEDWAY
Address: Marion County Fairgrounds, 7300 East Troy Avenue, Indianapolis 46239.
Tel: 001 607 6877819.
Website : www.midamspeedway.com

Bikes returned to Indy after a one-year hiatus. Replacing the old tight bullring on the west side of town were the big, wide-open turns at the Marion County Fairgrounds on the east side of Indianapolis.

Eleven meetings were staged from the end of May until the middle of October and another five were postponed because of rain.

A minimum of eight events are scheduled for 2009.

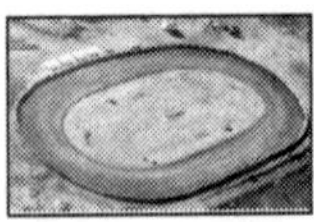

PERRIS RACEWAY
Address: 1205 Burton Road, Perris, California 92570.
Tel: 001 310 3099418.

Promoted by Steve Evans, they were the first track to open in 2009, staging the New Year Classic at the end of January.

Also hosted the two-day Gumball Rally in February and plan further meets on March 15, April 12, October 4 and November 2.

Had eight Sunday dates on their 2008 calendar, racing on a track also used regularly by the Southern California Flat Track Association.

RED BLUFF SPEEDWAY
Address: Tehama District Fairgrounds, 650 Antelope Boulevard, Red Bluff, California 96080.
Tel: 001 530 526-0609.

Scott and Sherry Johnston staged first meeting on May 17, 2008, but the track was very rough and in the opening meeting first and second place went to former moto-cross riders.

Staged a second meeting a fortnight later but do not appear to have held further meetings.

RIDGECREST SPEEDWAY
Address: Desert Empire Fairgrounds, 520 South Richmond Road, Ridgecrest, California 93555.
Tel: 001 760 3758000.

Wolverhampton fan Steve Evans opened the track and has five meetings scheduled for 2009 – May 15, July 4, August 1, September 11 and October 24.

VENTURA SPEEDWAY
Address: Ventura Raceway, 10, West Harbor Boulevard, Ventura, California, 93001.
Tel: 001 805 6487223.
Wesbite: www.venturaraceway.com

Held only two meetings in 2008 and do not appear to be running in 2009.

VICTORVILLE SPEEDWAY
Address: San Bernardino County Fairgrounds, Victorville, California.
Tel: 001 310 3099418.

Another track run by Steve Evans with around nine scheduled meetings in 2009, including the Spring Classic on April 4 and the Eliminapolis on May 23.

Other speedway dates are: March 14, April 18, July 11 (provisional), July 18, July 25, August 8, September 5, October 17 and November 14.

The 2008 Industry Hills season was marred by a serious accident in the sidecar events on the programme on Wednesday, August 6. Uncle and nephew Scott and Sean Driggers went straight into the five-foot, wooden retaining wall, the impact moving the wall and temporarily trapping the riders. On-site emergency medical personnel began attending to the Driggers and were joined by the City of Industry and the Los Angeles County Fire Department. Scott, 48, was initially on life support at the Los Angeles County-University of Southern California Medical Centre with internal injuries as well as a broken thigh. He had previously suffered a heart attack burt recovered sufficiently to compete regularly.

CZECH REPUBLIC tracks

Continued from page 332

AK BREZOLUPY
Tel: 00420 728 063844.
Website: www.brezolupy.cz/autoklub
Track Length: 410 metres.
Track Record: 67.2 secs, Robert Nagy, May 11, 1999.

CHABAROVICE
Track Length: 339 metres.
Tracak Record: 65.6 secs, Bohumil Brhel, May 12, 1988.

AK DIVISOV
Website: www.speedwaydivisov.cz
Track Length: 322 metres.
Track Record: 64.46 secs, Antonin Kasper.

KOPRIVNICE
Track Length: 450 metres.
Track Record: 76.09 secs, Vaclav Verner, July 29, 1985.

SPEEDWAY KLUB MSENO V ACR
Boleslavská 398,
277 35 Mseno, Czech Republic
Tel: 00420 315 693910.
Website: www.pdkmseno.net
Traqck Length: 354 metres.
Track Record: 64 secs, Antonin Kasper.

PK PLZEN www.pkplzen.com
Track Length: 400 metres.
Track Record: 66.1 secs, Antonin Kasper, April 22, 1994.

PSK OLYMP PRAHA (PRAGUE)
Tel: 00420 233358487 [tickets].
Website: www.speedway-prague.cz
Track Length: 353 metres.
Track Record: 62.4 secs, Greg Hancock, May 17, 1997.

ZP PARDUBICE
tř. 17.listopadu 203, 53021 Pardubice,
Czech Republic.
Tel: 00420 466 303 628.
Website: www.zlataprilba.cz
Track Length: 391.5 metres.
Track Record: 67.15 secs, Lukas Dryml, September 11, 2002.

AK SLANY
Speedway Stadium,
Netovická 1509, 27401 Slany,Czech Republic.
Tel: 00420 312 522 519.
Website: www.speedwayslany.wbs.cz
Track Length: 382 metres.
Track Record: 68.07 secs, Marian Jirout, August 28, 2001.

AK SVITAVY
Hálkova 7, 568 02 Svitavy, Czech Republic.
Tel: 00420 606103476.
Website: www.speedway.wz.cz
Track Length: 386 metres.
Track Record: 68.4 secs, Marian Jirout, June 26, 1994.

CZECH REPUBLIC PAIRS CHAMPIONSHIP

From page 322

CZECHOSLOVAKIA

Roll of Honour

1977	Red Star PRAGUE
1978	CSAD PLZEN
1979	Red Star PRAGUE
1980	Red Star PRAGUE
1986	Red Star PRAGUE
1987	Red Star PRAGUE
1988	Red Star PRAGUE
1989	Red Star PRAGUE
1990	Red Star PRAGUE
1991	PSK OLYMP PRAGUE

FINLAND

Continued from page 363

The 2009 Finnish Extraliiga will be run on an eight-round four team basis with Haukat-Royals (SsMK, Lahti-Forssa), Jokerit (KauhjMK, Kauhajoki), Keittiopiste (KMMK, Kuusankoski) and Kotkat (Seinäjoki) following the withdrawal of 2008 contestants Paholaiset (PMK, Pori).

The Kaupunki Cup will also be held again, over six rounds, with six teams: Pori, Seinäjoki, Haapajärvi, Kauhajoki and two from Lahti.

2009 SQUADS

JOKERIT: Markku Autio, Kalle Katajisto, Joni Keskinen, Niko Siltaniemi.
HAUKAT ROYALS: Jani Eerikäinen, Aarni Heikkilä, Joni Kitala, Janne Nyman, Tomi Reima.
KEITTIÖPISTE: Tero Aarnio, Teemu Lahti, Timo Lahti, Aleksey Poptsov, Fedor Poptsov, Toni Stenberg.
KOTKAT: Juha Hautamäki, Kaj Laukkanen, Rene Lehtinen, Appe Mustonen.

2009 FIXTURES

EXTRALIIGA
Round 1: Saturday, May 30, Seinäjoki.
Round 2: Sunday, May 31, Lahti.
Round 3: Saturday, June 13, Kuusankoski.
Round 4: Sunday, June 14, Kauhajoki.
Round 5: Saturday, July 11, Seinäjoki.
Round 6: Sunday, July 12, Lahti.
Round 7: Saturday, August 7, Kuusankoski.
Round 8: Sunday, August 8, Kauhajoki.
Reserved dates: Tuesday, June 23; Tuesday, June 30; Sunday, August 23.

KAUPUNKI CUP
Round 1: Sunday, May 10, Pori.
Round 2: Sunday, May 17, Seinäjoki.
Round 3: Sunday, July 5, Haapajärvi.
Round 4: Saturday, July 18, Lahti.
Round 5: Saturday, September 5, Kauhajoki.
Round 6: Sunday, September 6, Lahti.

FINNISH CHAMPIONSHIP
FINAL 1: Saturday, June 27, Seinäjoki.
FINAL 2: Saturday, August 1, Pori.

FINNISH UNDER 21 CHAMPIONSHIP
FINAL: Saturday, July 25, Haapajärvi.

GERMANY

Continued from page 373

The first ever two-team Bundesliga match ended in a tight home win for Diedenbergen Rockets as they took the match points against Brokstedt.

The Vikings were managed by Sabrina Harms, who gave Mads Korneliussen a tactical joker ride in Heat 14 as he became the first rider to score double points in the competition.

Sunday, March 22
DIEDENBERGEN 46 (Thomas Stange 7:2, Christian Hefenbrock 15:1, Grzegorz Zengota 14:1, René Deddens 4, Frank Facher 6), **BROKSTEDT 41** (Mads Korneliussen 20 (6), Mathias Kröger 11:1, Leon Madsen 6, Stephan Katt 1, Sönke Petersen 3).

GREAT BRITAIN

Continued from page 393

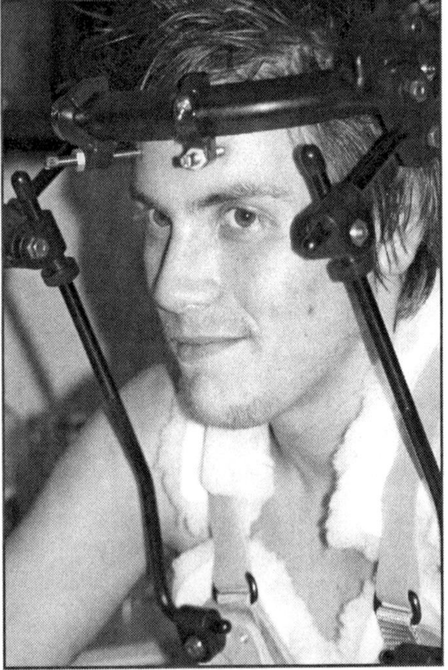

■ **ADAM Roynon** was the first major casualty of the new season when he suffered head and neck injuries while at the Great Britain training camp.

New GB boss Rob Lyon had called up the 20-year-old Roynon for the two day practice and talk-in at King's Lynn's Norfolk Arena.

Roynon crashed around lunchtime on the second day (Friday, March 6) while riding on his own when his front wheel worked loose.

He was taken to King's Lynn's Queen Elizabeth Hospital where scans revealed a blood clot close to his brain and a broken bone at the top of his neck.

He was immediately transferred to Addenbrooke's Hospital, Cambridge, and spent several days in the Critical Care Unit on a ventilator.

Thankfully he made swift progress and was released to return to his Barrow-in-Furness home on Tuesday, March 17, with his neck in a brace.

He is hoping to have the halo removed by June and plans to get back into action as quickly as possible.

Roynon, who hasn't raced competitively since breaking his leg at Rye House on June 2, 2008, had been signed by his parent club Coventry to share a doubling up reserve spot in the Elite League and by Premier League Workington.

Roynon was forced to withdraw from the British Under 21 Championship (see draw) and was replaced by both the Bees and Comets in their starting line-ups.

■ Unlucky **Craig Watson** shattered his leg in a crash in Newport's re-opening under new owners Steve and Nicky Mallett.

Watson, back in the Wasps colours, came down in Heat 13 of the Prince of Wales Trophy on Sunday, March 15, after winning his first three rides.

He had surgery the following morning and the initial verdict by doctors was that he would be out for the season.

Newport moved to fill the gap by signing former Queensway Meadows favourite Paul Fry.

■ Poole's **Jason Doyle** crashed in the following heat and suffered further damage to his suspect shoulder.

He returned home to Australia for an operation but hopes to be back at Wimborne Road mid-summer.

■ Fellow Australian **Kozza Smith** was also an early season victim, crashing on his debut for Elite League Ipswich in their early season challenge against Lakeside on Thursday, March 19.

The King's Lynn rider, named as one of the Witches' doubling up reserves, suffered four broken ribs, a fractured shoulder, a broken arm and a punctured lung.

In the same meeting Witches' skipper **Leigh Lanham** broke his little finger and suffered other hand injuries.

He had surgery at Ipswich Hospital and was told he would be out for a month.

■ Poole's early season woes continued when winter signing **Kyle Legault** was forced to withdraw after three rides on his debut for the Pirates in the first leg of the Elite Shield at Eastbourne on Sunday, March 22.

He aggravated the leg injury which had marred his 2008 campaign and was ruled out long term by the Dorset club.

BRITISH UNDER 21 CHAMPIONSHIP
Semi Final 1: Friday, April 10, Plymouth
Harland Cook, Gary Cottham, Jamie Courtney, Richard Franklin, Nicki Glanz, Daniel Halsey, Kyle Hughes, Jaimie Pickard, Scott Meakins, Kye Norton, Scott Richardson, Charlie Saunders, Robert Smith, Danny Stoneman, Paul Starke, Charles Wright.
Semi Final 2: Tuesday, April 14, Isle of Wight
Aaron Baseby, Mark Baseby, Matthew Bates, Michael Bovis, Andrew Braithwaite, Jerran Hart, Ben Hopwood, Brendan Johnson, Adam Lowe, Kyle Newman, Oliver

Rayson, John Resch, Lee Strudwick, Ben Taylor, Tim Webster, Adam Wrathall.

FINAL, Lakeside, Friday, April 24
Seeded qualifiers: Josh Auty, Ben Barker, Lewis Bridger, Joe Haines, Simon Lambert, Robert Mear, Lee Smart, Tai Woffinden.

AFTER the success of their star-studded 60th Anniversary Celebration opening meeting of the season, Swindon announced they would be launching the Bob Kilby Memorial Meeting on similar lines at the beginning of each new season.

The first will be on Sunday, March 21, 2010.

Robins' co-owner and promoter Gary Patchett said: "We had wanted to honour Bob in the very best way possible and with a meeting of the ultimate quality.

"The Anniversary Celebration showed us that the public and riders alike have the appetite for a meeting of this stature at the start of the season."

ITALY

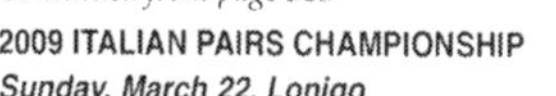

Continued from page 383

2009 ITALIAN PAIRS CHAMPIONSHIP
Sunday, March 22, Lonigo
1 MC La FAVORITA di SAREGO 28 (Mattia Carpanese 17, Massimo Zambon 4, Massimo Mora 7), **2 MC OLIMPIA de TERENZANO 24** (Andrea Maida 17, Mattia Tadiello 7), **3 ASM ABATO de BADIA CALAVENA 22** (Marco Gregnanin 15, Mattia Cavicchioli 7), **4 MC LONIGO 22** (Guglielmo Franchetti 13, Alessandro Milanese 9), **5 MC TITANO RACING 14** (Simone Tadiello 8, Alessandro Novello 6), **6 MC CIALTRONI del NORD EST 9** (Andrea Baroni 4, Jonatha Seren 5), **7 MC PASTORELLI-BERGANTINO 6** (Stefano Mazzall 3, Federico Stevanini 3).

RUSSIA

Continued from page 460

There was major confusion over the future of the 2009 Russian League when doubts were cast at the end of March about whether Togliatti and Balakovo would be competing.

As on April 1, it was agreed that the league would commence as planned at the beginning of May but there must still be question marks over whether or not this happens.

Information given on the 2009 Russian League in this book was as accurate at the time of going to the printers but events could well have been overtaken by the time you are reading this.

One possible solution (looking from afar) is to combine the Russian and Ukraine Leagues or to have Rivne, who were refused a licence to race in the Polish Second League, join the other clubs in the Russian League.

SWEDEN

Continued from page 465

80cc ROLL OF HONOUR

1990 .... Daniel ANDERSSON
1991 .... Peter I KARLSSON
1992 .... Benny OLSSON
1993 .... Peter I KARLSSON
1994 .... Andreas BERGSTRÖM
1995 .... Andreas JONSSON
1996 .... Freddie ERIKSSON
1997 .... Jonas DAVIDSSON
1998 .... Mattias NILSSON
1999 .... Fredrik LINDGREN
2001 .... Andreas MESSING
2002 .... Ricky KLING
2003 .... Simon GUSTAFSSON
2004 .... Simon GUSTAFSSON
2005 .... Jonas MESSING
2006 .... Anders MELLGREN
2007 .... Anders MELLGREN
2008 .... Victor PALOVAARA

UKRAINE

Continued from page 531

Squads for the 2009 Ukraine League are listed below. Teams can only track two foreign riders in a match.

CASCADE RIVNE
Alexander **BORODAJ**, Anatoli **CHABCZIK**, Vladimir **KOLODY** [jun], Paul **KONDRATIUK**, Vladimir **KOLODY** [sen], Vitaly **LYSAK**, Mikhail **ONESHKO**, Vitaly **OMELIAN**, Vladimir **OMELIAN**.
Foreign: Ilya **BONDARENKO**, Roman **IVANOV**.

SPEEDWAY CLUB TROFIMOV, RIVNE
Aleksandr **DIKAL**, Vladimir **KONOPLASTY**, Stanislav **OGORODNIK**, Jaroslav **POLIUCHOVIC**, Yuri **SIROVATKO**, Vladimir **TROFIMOV**, Sergiy **YUZENCHUK**.
Foreign: Andrej **KOROLEV**, Vyachetslav **GIRUTSKY**.

SKA LVIV
Igor **BORISENKO**, Sergey **BORISENKO**, Kiril **CUKANOV**, Vladimir **DUBININ**, Aleksandr **GAJKOVSKY**, Taras **FEDORENKO**, Andrey **SINKOVSKY**.
Foreign: Daniil **IVANOV**, Semen **VLASOV**.

SHAKTER CHERVONOGRAD
Andrey **KARPOV**, Andrey **KOBRIN**, Nikolai **MIRONOV**, Alexander **LOKTAYEV**, Vladimir **TEJGAL**.
Foreign: Ruslan **GATIATOV**, Kjastas **POUDZHUKS**.

2009 Rivne Squad

This squad that was originally named to compete in the Polish Second League in 2009 was:
Igor **BORISENKO**, Alexander **BORODAJ**, Vladimir **KOLODY** [sen].
Foreign: Ilya **BONDARENKO**, Daniil **IVANOV**, Roman **IVANOV**, Jan **JAROS**, Igor **KONONOV**, Kamil **ZIELINSKI**.

There is not necessarily a universally accepted translation of many of the symbols used in the Cyrillic alphabet (there are more than 40 compared with the 26 of the English language) and we have, therefore, tried to adopt what we believe is the closest true translation for riders from countries that use that alphabet in everyday life. We accept other sources will vary.

Printed in the United Kingdom by
Lightning Source UK Ltd., Milton Keynes
140738UK00001B/309/P

9 780948 882371